H A N D B O O K OF
PSYCHOTHERAPY AND
BEHAVIOR CHANGE

HANDBOOK OF
PSYCHOTHERAPY AND
BEHAVIOR CHANGE

Third edition

Editors

SOL L. GARFIELD
Department of Psychology
Washington University

ALLEN E. BERGIN
Department of Psychology
Brigham Young University

JOHN WILEY & SONS

NEW YORK   CHICHESTER   BRISBANE   TORONTO   SINGAPORE

Library of Congress Cataloging in Publication Data:

Handbook of psychotherapy and behavior change.

   Includes bibliographies and indexes.
   1. Psychotherapy.   2. Psychotherapy—Research.
I. Garfield, Sol L. (Sol Louis), 1918–
II. Bergin, Allen E., 1934–   [DNLM: 1. Behavior
Therapy.   2. Psychotherapy. WM 420 H2323]
RC480.H286   1986   616.89'14   86-7817
ISBN 0-471-79995-5

Printed in the United States of America

10 9 8 7 6 5 4 3 2 1

CONTRIBUTORS

THOMAS M. ACHENBACH, Ph.D.
Professor and Director
Center for Children, Youth, and Families
Department of Psychiatry
University of Vermont
Burlington, Vermont

THOMAS G. ARIZMENDI, Ph.D.
Private Practice
San Francisco, California

AARON T. BECK, M.D.
University Professor of Psychiatry
University of Pennsylvania
Philadelphia, Pennsylvania

RICHARD L. BEDNAR, Ph.D.
Professor and Director of
Comprehensive Clinic
Brigham Young University
Provo, Utah

ALLEN E. BERGIN, Ph.D.
Professor of Psychology
Brigham Young University
Provo, Utah

LARRY E. BEUTLER, Ph.D.
Professor and Chief of Clinical Psychology
University of Arizona Health Sciences Center
Tucson, Arizona

SHARON S. BREHM, Ph.D.
Professor of Psychology
University of Kansas
Lawrence, Kansas

JAMES BUTCHER, Ph.D.
Professor of Psychology
University of Minnesota
Minneapolis, Minnesota

MARJORIE A. CRAGO, Ph.D.
Research Assistant
Department of Psychiatry
University of Arizona Health Sciences Center
Tucson, Arizona

PAUL M. G. EMMELKAMP, Ph.D.
Senior Lecturer in Clinical Psychology
Department of Clinical Psychology
Academic Hospital
Groningen
The Netherlands

ROBERT D. FELNER, Ph.D.
Professor of Psychology
University of Illinois
Champaign, Illinois

SOL L. GARFIELD, Ph.D.
Professor of Psychology
Washington University
St. Louis, Missouri

CONTRIBUTORS

ALAN S. GURMAN, Ph.D.
Professor of Psychiatry
University of Wisconsin Medical School
Madison, Wisconsin

STEVEN D. HOLLON, Ph.D.
Associate Professor of Psychology
Vanderbilt University
Nashville, Tennessee

KENNETH I. HOWARD, Ph.D.
Professor and Head of Clinical Psychology
Northwestern University
Evanston, Illinois

THEODORE J. KAUL, Ph.D.
Associate Professor of Psychology
Ohio State University
Columbus, Ohio

ALAN E. KAZDIN, Ph.D.
Professor of Psychiatry and Psychology
University of Pittsburgh School of Medicine
Pittsburgh, Pennsylvania

DAVID P. KNISKERN, Psy.D.
Associate Professor of Clinical Psychology
University of Cincinnati College of Medicine
Cincinnati, Ohio

GERALD L. KLERMAN, M.D.
Professor of Psychiatry
Cornell University Medical School
New York, New York

MARY P. KOSS, Ph.D.
Professor of Psychology
Kent State University
Kent, Ohio

MICHAEL J. LAMBERT, Ph.D.
Professor of Psychology
Brigham Young University
Provo, Utah

RAYMOND P. LORION, Ph.D.
Professor and Director of Clinical Psychology
University of Maryland
College Park, Maryland

RUTH G. MATARAZZO, Ph.D.
Professor of Medical Psychology
School of Medicine
Oregon Health Sciences University
Portland, Oregon

ROGER A. MYERS, Ph.D.
Professor of Psychology and Education
Teachers College
Columbia University
New York, NY

THOMAS H. OLLENDICK, Ph.D.
Professor and Director of Clinical Training
Virginia Polytechnic Institute and State University
Blacksburg, Virginia

DAVID E. ORLINSKY, Ph.D.
Professor of Behavioral Sciences
University of Chicago
Chicago, Illinois

WILLIAM M. PINSOF, Ph.D.
Assistant Professor of Psychiatry and Behavioral
  Sciences
Northwestern University Medical School
Chicago, Illinois

DAVID R. PATTERSON, Ph.D.
Harbor View Medical Center
Seattle, Washington

OVIDE F. POMERLEAU, Ph.D.
Professor of Psychology in Psychiatry
Director of Behavioral Medicine Program
University of Michigan School of Medicine
Ann Arbor, Michigan

JUDITH RODIN, Ph.D.
Philip R. Allen Professor of Psychology
Professor of Medicine and Psychiatry
Yale University
New Haven, Connecticut

DAVID A. SHAPIRO, Ph.D.
MRC/ESRC Social and Applied Psychology Unit
University of Sheffield
Sheffield, England

TIMOTHY W. SMITH, Ph.D.
Assistant Professor of Psychology
University of Utah
Salt Lake City, Utah

*This book is
affectionately dedicated
to
Amy and Marian*

PREFACE

We are pleased once again to publish a new edition of our *Handbook*. The response to the previous two editions has been most gratifying. The *Handbook* has become a standard reference throughout the world, wherever psychotherapy is an important subject, and it has served as a textbook for numerous graduate programs in the United States. We could not have asked for a better reception and we are grateful for it. At the same time, we wish to thank publicly all of the past and present contributing authors, advisory editors, and consultants who have made this collaborative venture successful. It appears that there has been wide acceptance of an empirical and eclectic approach to this subject, which has not always been the case.

Those who are familiar with the previous editions will note a number of changes in the present edition. First, the size of the book has been reduced by approximately 100 pages. This was purposely done in an attempt to keep the cost down and make it more readily obtainable by students. However, this was not our only reason. Psychotherapy is a dynamic and changing field and there is considerable variability in research and development among the different special areas. Thus, decisions were made to omit chapters in areas where relatively little new empirical research was produced since the publication of the last edition. We also attempted to combine closely related chapters. At the same time, we did add new chapters representing areas of more recent investigation and development.

The decision to omit some of the chapters that appeared in the previous editions was not an easy one. This was particularly true of the previous chapters, "Research on Psychotherapy with Children" and "Quantitative Research on Psychoanalytic Therapy." After much consultation and perusal of the published literature in these areas, we decided there was insufficient *new* material to warrant complete chapters in this edition of the *Handbook*. We feel it is unfortunate that so little research has been conducted in these important areas, but that clearly was our perception of the situation. Most of the newer research on therapy with children has been done by behaviorally oriented therapists, and that work is included in the present edition. Also, clinical work with children has been carried out increasingly in a family context, and research in this area is included in the chapter on marital and family therapy. Advances and research in psychodynamic therapy have been evident primarily in the briefer forms of therapy, and these findings are presented in a number of the chapters in the present volume, particularly in Chapter 14. Chapters 5 through 8 also include many references to research in dynamic therapies, and these chapters have become omnibus accounts of research on the verbal, exploratory, and expressive therapies in general. Thus, it was our view that although the two chapters referred to here do not appear in the present edition, the important new material in the respective areas is covered in other chapters. Nevertheless, we do know that some individuals will be disappointed with our decision.

We have also omitted the previous chapter on "Psychobiological Foundations of Psychotherapy and Behavior Change" and in its place have substituted a new chapter on "Developmental Perspectives on Psychotherapy and Behavior Change." A developmental perspective seemed like a desirable emphasis with more direct relevance to psychotherapy. Originally, we wanted the chapter to cover the life span, because there is currently a considerable interest in work with the aged. However, this turned out to be unfeasible. This, in some ways, was unfortunate since research on psychotherapy with this population was not adequate for an entire chapter.

We also felt that biological factors could be covered in part by the chapter on drugs and psychotherapy, and by adding a new chapter on what appears to be a very rapidly developing and important area, namely, behavioral medicine and health psychology. In addition, in response to a number of requests, we have included a chapter that appeared in the first edition, but not in the second edition. This is the chapter on educational and vocational counseling. The *Handbook* apparently has been used by a number of graduate counseling programs and we did respond

to their requests to include this chapter again. Some other chapters were essentially combined. Thus, the four previous chapters on behavioral therapies have been condensed into two, and the two chapters on cognition and cognitive therapies have been combined into one. The chapter on placebo effects has also been omitted but the chapter in the previous edition still remains as a significant resource for the student.

We do not expect that everyone will agree with our decisions concerning the present selection of the chapters in the current *Handbook*, but most should respond favorably to the chapters included because 16 of the 19 current ones are revised versions of those from the previous edition. As in the previous editions, the emphasis in the present volume is on a critical appraisal of existing empirical research findings with an evenhanded or eclectic attitude toward divergent orientations in the area of psychotherapy and behavior change along with their implication for research and practice.

A number of interesting developments have taken place since the appearance of the previous edition. Among them are an increased sophistication in the design of research on psychotherapy, the introduction of specific training manuals that allow for a greater specification and monitoring of the operations of specific therapies, and the application of more objective and quantitative procedures such as a meta-analysis for conducting reviews of research studies. Although the proliferation of therapeutic approaches has seemingly not abated, a greater interest has also been evident in rapprochement and integration among a number of well-known psychotherapists, as well as a greater willingness to consider potential therapeutic variables common to most forms of psychotherapy. The integration of cognitive and behavioral approaches is one example of this. There has also been a continuation of the controversy over the general effectiveness of psychotherapy with an apparent greater demand for evidence of efficacy. Clearly, the field has not been dormant in the past decade and discussions of these and other matters will be found in many chapters of the current edition.

As with the previous editions, the editors have found the preparation of the present volume a very demanding, but stimulating and rewarding experience. We find it necessary to immerse ourselves in an incredibly complex and broad effort to be aware of important issues and studies throughout the field, and then to negotiate with each author the best possible summary and interpretation of developments in his or her special area. We have once again been fortunate in securing the collaboration of knowledgeable experts who have performed admirably. We wish to express our gratitude to our contributing authors, our consulting editors, and the outside reviewers, all of whom helped immeasurably to make this edition of the *Handbook* a product worthy of our best efforts. We sincerely hope that the *Handbook* will continue to be of value to students, researchers, and practitioners in the area of psychotherapy and behavior change.

Sol L. Garfield
Allen E. Bergin

ACKNOWLEDGMENTS

We are grateful to all of those who assisted the editors and contributors in completing this third edition of the *Handbook*. We specifically acknowledge the help of individuals whom we called upon to review specific chapters for us. They are: Arthur Auerbach, Ann Garner, Neil Jacobson, Donald Kiesler, Michael J. Lambert, John Livesly, Morris Parloff, Jeanne Phillips, John Rush, and M. Duncan Stanton. We also want to express our gratitude and appreciation to Marie McDonnell for her efforts in our behalf and to Ann and David Olszewski, who prepared the subject and author indexes.

We also gratefully acknowledge the grant received by one of us (SLG) from the Graduate School of Arts and Sciences of Washington University to help prepare the indexes for this volume.

And we are grateful to the following editors, publishers, and publications for granting us permission to reproduce previously published materials:

American Psychological Association

Association for Advancement of Behavior Therapy

Little, Brown & Co.

Pergamon Press

Plenum Press

Sage Publications

Society for the Experimental Analysis of Behavior, Inc.

S.L.G.
A.E.B.

CONTENTS

PART I

HISTORICAL, METHODOLOGICAL, AND CONCEPTUAL FOUNDATIONS

1

INTRODUCTION AND HISTORICAL OVERVIEW

SOL L. GARFIELD

Washington University

ALLEN E. BERGIN

Brigham Young University

Psychotherapy clearly has been a dynamic and rapidly developing field. It is also apparent that it is much more recognized and accepted by the public at large today than it was 20 or 30 years ago. Articles about psychotherapy appear frequently in the popular press and many radio and television programs feature psychotherapists. Public interest in psychotherapy has also been stimulated by new developments in marital therapy, family therapy, and sexual therapy, among others. This increased awareness of psychotherapy as a procedure for helping individuals with psychological disorders, however, has had differential effects. On the one hand, it has led to a greater acceptance of psychotherapy as a treatment modality for mental disorders. On the other hand, as psychotherapy has come more fully into the public spotlight, critical questions have been raised concerning its effectiveness. In general, a more critical stance on the part of several groups has been evident and the need for more definitive research findings emphasized. Before we examine these more recent developments, however, let us take a brief look at some of the important events that occurred in the past.

HISTORICAL BACKGROUND

Although the roots of psychotherapy can be traced back to antiquity, we usually think of it as having taken on its modern form in the latter part of the nineteenth century. Although there were others, Sigmund Freud was the most significant figure, and his creation, psychoanalysis, was the first distinctively recognized form of psychotherapy. In our opinion, it has also been the most influential, and it clearly dominated psychotherapeutic thought through about the 1960s.

There were certain features of psychoanalysis that tended to distinguish it from other forms of psychotherapy. First of all, it gradually became a long-term therapy. This was due theoretically to the view that repressed unconscious conflicts were the source of the patient's difficulties and that these had to be brought to the patient's awareness if improvement was to occur. Considerable time was required to overcome the defenses and resistances of the patient with reference to this "uncovering" process. The therapist's role was somewhat passive, but interpretations were given to the patient's free associations and aspects of the therapeutic relationship. The frequency of therapy ranged from three to five days per week. There were thus certain prerequisites for the "good patient." Generally, the patient had to be motivated to endure the long, demanding process, be intelligent, and also have sufficient financial resources to pay for this expensive treatment.

For many years psychoanalysis was considered the most intensive form of psychotherapy and superior to other forms of treatment. Psychoanalytic training in the United States was conducted at institutes approved by the American Psychoanalytic Association and limited to physicians. At first, very few other centers offered much in the way of therapeutic training, either in psychiatric residencies or in graduate programs in clinical psychology. Thus, analysts were highly regarded and their training eagerly sought by psychiatrists. However, since these training resources were limited, other independent institutes gradually were established and were usually multidisciplinary in nature. Most of these espoused a psychoanalytic or related orientation, and the type of therapy was generally referred to as psychoanalytically oriented or "psychodynamic," and not classical psychoanalysis. Therapy was somewhat briefer and less frequent and the patient usually sat in a chair instead of reclining on a couch. The theoretical orientation, however, was psychoanalytic or neo-Freudian and emphasized unconscious conflicts, which had to be recovered and overcome, as the sources of difficulty.

Gradually, psychodynamic therapy and classical psychoanalysis began to decline in popularity and relative importance. There was probably no single cause for this, but instead several interrelated developments, some of which will be discussed in greater detail later in this chapter. One possible factor was the development of clinical and counseling psychology programs after the Second World War. Al-though psychoanalytic theory was embraced by large numbers of clinical psychologists, there were other competing influences. Psychology departments had a more critical stance than psychoanalytic institutes toward theories and therapies that provided little research evidence in support of their views. Carl Rogers' (1942, 1951) client-centered therapy, which was quite different, and also research oriented, attracted a number of both clinical and counseling psychologists. Another significant influence was the gradual rise of behavioral therapy in the late 1950s and early 1960s. This was an approach that in many respects was diametrically opposed to the theories and procedures of psychoanalysis. Although it was not as popular as the psychodynamic therapies, it constituted a challenge in terms of its research emphasis and relative brevity of treatment.

Besides the competition these developments provided for psychoanalysis, there were other influences of a somewhat different sort. One was the report of the Joint Commission on Mental Illness and Health, appointed by the United States Congress. The commission conducted a comprehensive study of mental illness and treatment that took five years and issued a multivolume report including a summary report, *Action for Mental Health* (Joint Commission on Mental Illness and Health, 1961).

Among the problems noted in the commission's report was the fact that long-term therapy, particularly psychoanalysis, was provided mainly to individuals in the middle and upper social classes. The report was specific and critical in this regard: "In sum, then, psychoanalysis is adapted neither to the treatment of the psychoses, nor to mass application of any kind. It is principally effective for a limited number of carefully selected patients who are not totally incapacitated by their illness and do not require hospitalization" (Joint Commission of Mental Illness and Health, 1961, p. 80).

The period of the 1960s was one with many changes. It also marked the beginning of what has been called the community mental health movement. This movement, fostered by federal legislation and financial funding, followed the Joint Commission's report. Several of the emphases of this movement did have an impact on the field of psychotherapy. These included an emphasis on the availability of community services for the underprivileged, the desirability of briefer therapies, the availability of therapy in times of emergency, and an emphasis on crisis intervention. Thus, again, these were forces that were opposite to the major emphases and practices of psychoanalysis.

Most of the decisions made about psychotherapy during this earlier period were based on perceived social needs, personal opinions, and the styles of the time or what has been termed the *zeitgeist*. Very little research was conducted, and it played an essentially minor role in decisions about psychotherapy. Some questions were raised in the 1940s about the efficacy of psychoanalysis by some well-known analysts (Obendorf, 1943; Obendorf, Greenacre, & Kubie, 1948). Nevertheless, no apparent research efforts appeared to follow these discussions; however, a critical review of existing research reports by the British psychologist Hans Eysenck, in 1952, appeared to have a very different impact.

Very briefly, on the basis of 24 studies, Eysenck concluded that there was no evidence to support the efficacy of psychotherapy, particularly psychoanalysis. This rather startling conclusion was challenged by several individuals, and although the controversy has by no means been conclusively settled to date (Garfield, 1983b), a large amount of research has appeared since that time and will be reviewed in Chapter 5. In general, the results have been relatively favorable for psychotherapy. There has been evident also an increasing emphasis on the importance of research in answering questions about the efficacy of psychotherapy, although as is apparent in the following paragraph, it has not influenced all of psychotherapy.

During this period also a large number of new forms of psychotherapy gradually made their appearance on the therapeutic scene. In fact, we were able to identify over 60 different forms of psychotherapy in the early 1960s. Unfortunately, most of these psychotherapies were introduced and publicized without any empirical evidence of therapeutic efficacy. Nevertheless, this did not appear to retard the steady accumulation of diverse forms of psychotherapy, and it has continued until the present time. This continued proliferation of the psychotherapy "cafeteria" constitutes a problem since most of the psychotherapies have neither a clear conceptual nor empirical basis to support their claims. Instead, they appear to lend support and credence to those individuals and groups who have manifested critical attitudes toward psychotherapy in general.

THE PRACTITIONERS OF PSYCHOTHERAPY

During the time of Freud and for some time thereafter, practically all practitioners of psychotherapy were physicians. Mental illness had been viewed historically as resulting from some type of organic brain involvement, and thus appeared to be the province of the psychiatrist. Although Freud, himself, took a different view and accepted "lay analysts," psychoanalysts in the United States consistently held to the view that only physicians could be accepted into the analytic institutes. In addition, there were relatively few positions open for clinical psychologists, and their major function was to administer psychological tests.

After the Second World War, however, the situation changed drastically as clinical and counseling psychology programs were instituted, government support was available for graduate training, and jobs became plentiful (Garfield, 1983a). Within a relatively short time, psychologists became involved in psychotherapy and it became their primary clinical activity (Kelly, 1961). Although there were conflicts between the two national professional organizations representing psychologists and psychiatrists, which is not surprising, the intensity of conflict has greatly diminished and is not a serious issue at the present time. Members of the two professions work together in clinical settings, in professional organizations devoted to psychotherapy, and in scholarly and research organizations.

Although psychiatrists and clinical psychologists perhaps have been the most influential people in psychotherapy, the field is by no means exclusively theirs. Counseling psychologists, school psychologists, social workers, psychiatric nurses, pastoral counselors, and a number of other professional groups participate in some type of psychotherapy or counseling; indeed, these groups account for the largest portion of therapy hours conducted annually. Thus, it is evident that psychotherapy does not constitute a distinctive profession but rather is an activity that is performed by members of many different professions. Furthermore, there are some individuals referred to as paraprofessionals who also function in a psychotherapeutic role. Several factors contributed to this development, and we can allude to them briefly here.

In the immediate postwar period there was a shortage of mental health personnel, and various programs were instituted to help rectify this situation. Apart from federal support for programs to train psychiatrists, psychologists, and psychiatric social workers and nurses, other more innovative programs were also instituted. One of the most successful experimental programs was one developed by Margaret Rioch and her colleagues (Rioch, 1967; Rioch, Elkes, & Flint, 1965) to train middle-aged college-educated women in a two-year half-time program. In brief, these women became excellent therapists, but only a relatively small number of programs were modeled after this one. In some other settings, nonprofessionals were trained to provide a variety of professional activities, including psychotherapy, under the supervision of professionals. In inner-city store-front centers and walk-in clinics, so-called indigenous nonprofessionals functioned in a variety of ways.

The use of "nonprofessionals" has not been universally accepted and, as might be expected, has sometimes been viewed as a threat to the established programs of professional training and practice. At the same time, a number of studies have been reported that have attempted to compare the performance of professional and nonprofessional counselors and therapists. Two recent reviews of this literature have concluded that the paraprofessionals have performed at least as well as the professionals with whom they were compared (Durlak, 1979; Hattie, Sharpley, & Rogers, 1984). The first review was criticized by Nietzel and Fisher (1981) and a rebuttal published by Durlak (1981). This lack of agreement is not unusual in the area of psychotherapy, and the issue is certainly far from settled. (See Chapter 5 for a more extensive discussion of this matter.)

All of these results suggest that no one group of therapists, professional or otherwise, has a monopoly on securing positive results and that we are still not sure as to the actual therapeutic variables that are responsible for positive change. Attempts to set up ideal training programs for psychotherapists and to develop a separate profession of psychotherapy have not been successful (Holt, 1971). The separate professions involved have been reluctant to give up their professional identities. As a result, today there are many different professional groups as well as nonprofessional groups providing a variety of psychotherapeutic and counseling activities in a number of different settings.

BEHAVIORAL, COGNITIVE, AND BRIEF THERAPIES

During the past 20 years or so, other developments of importance also have occurred in the field of psychotherapy. One such development was the rise of the behavioral therapies. These therapies, in their inception, differed noticeably from the psychodynamic and client-centered therapies mentioned earlier. Behavior therapy had its theoretical base in learning theory derived from the psychological laboratory. In contrast to psychodynamic therapy, behavior therapy does not view the individual's problems as manifestations of repressed unconscious conflicts. Rather, the problem behavior is deemed to be learned behavior, that is, the result of some conditioning process. Furthermore, it is postulated that what has been learned can be modified or "unlearned." The treatment thus is direct, and the therapist leads and guides the treatment.

Behavior therapy posed a distinct challenge to the prevailing emphases in psychotherapy, but it has now become a significant influence in the field. Its main emphases and contribution have been a clear focus on the patient's complaints, devising specific treatments for specific problems, relatively brief periods of treatment, and systematic appraisals of outcome. The latter aspect has been a particular feature of value to a field that often lacked rigorous evaluative studies. In fact some have said that the research-oriented emphasis is the single feature that unites and exemplifies the behavior therapies. Many new journals have been established and give testimony to this aspect of behavior therapy.

Although behavior therapists have emphasized their linkage with theories of learning and have attempted to focus primarily on behavior while avoiding inferential constructs, there have been some changes or moderation evident in their views recently. The largest or most noticeable change pertains to the importance of cognitions in therapy. As Emmelkamp (1986) mentions in his chapter in this volume:

While in the early days behavior therapy was defined as the application of "established laws of learning," or was viewed to be based on "modern learning theories," more recently behavior therapy has become broader in its conceptualization. The claim that established behavior therapy procedures (e.g., aversion therapies and systematic desensitization) are exclusively based on learning paradigms seems nowadays no longer tenable. The experimental literature does not support such a claim; rather it shows that additional factors such as cognitive processes (e.g., expectancy) play an important role (Emmelkamp, 1982; Emmelkamp and Walta, 1978).

Somewhat independently, several different forms of therapy were also developed that tended to emphasize cognitions. Ellis (1958) developed a therapy that he first called rational therapy. Later he gave it the name of Rational Emotive Therapy (1962). The main premise of this therapeutic approach is that an individual's difficulties are due to faulty expectations and irrational thoughts. If clients can be taught to modify their thinking and to think rationally, their problems can be overcome.

Another well-known and more recently developed form of cognitive therapy is that of A. T. Beck (1976; Beck, Rush, Shaw, Emery, 1979). "This new approach—cognitive therapy—suggests that the individual's problems are derived largely from certain distortions of reality based on erroneous premises and assumptions" (Beck, 1976, p. 3). The task of the therapist is thus to aid the patient in understanding his or her distortions and to learn more realistic ways of coping with reality. Although the basic premises are very similar to those of Ellis, there are some differences in the way the two therapies are actually applied or used with patients. Beck and his co-workers have published a detailed manual for their form of therapy (Beck et al., 1979), and this approach has been evaluated more systematically than that of Ellis.

Although cognitive therapies such as Beck's and Ellis' were not derived from either behavior therapy or academic cognitive psychology, they have included a number of behavioral procedures. The latter fact at first received little formal recognition in the descriptions of the two therapies. There is now, however, a greater recognition and acceptance of the fact that behavioral approaches use and incorporate cognitive components and vice versa. Thus, there has been some blurring between these two orientations or emphases in psychotherapy, and increasingly we see references to cognitive-behavioral therapies (Kendall & Hollon, 1979). To the extent that this development represents a broadening of therapeutic outlook and procedures, it would appear to be a desirable one and one consistent with another recent trend to be mentioned shortly. The fact is that in humans, cognitions and behaviors *both* are involved in the process of adjustment to one's environment. Consequently, this recognition and integration of two important aspects of the human condition is in accord with actual reality. In addition, retaining the behavior therapists' emphasis on research evaluation and appraisal is also a positive feature.

RAPPROACHMENT, INTEGRATION, AND ECLECTICISM

Another trend that has become apparent in recent years is a trend for a more eclectic orientation among psychotherapists and, also, a subsidiary and related trend for some type of integration advocated by psychotherapists coming from different therapeutic backgrounds and orientations. Both of these overlapping trends are worthy of mention here.

The Eclectic Trend
Since the publication of the second edition of this *Handbook* in 1978, a decisive shift in opinion has quietly occurred; and it has created an irreversible change in professional attitudes about psychotherapy and behavior change. The new view is that the long-term dominance of the major theories is over and that an eclectic position has taken precedence. None of the traditional theories of change has succeeded in convincing the professional public that it deserves singular precedence; consequently, practitioners and researchers are exploring ways of synthesizing diverse elements into flexible multifaceted orientations. The blossoming of this perspective has occurred over the past 10 years, but it has a long history. Eminent American historical figures, such as psychologist-philosopher William James (1842–1910) and psychiatrist Adolf Meyer (1886–1950) construed human beings from what might be con-

sidered an eclectic frame of reference. Despite such distinguished early precedents, eclecticism did not become prominent but was overwhelmed by the emergence of distinctive schools of thought, such as psychoanalysis and behaviorism. It was not until mid-century that electic themes emerged in psychotherapy. The creative efforts of Dollard and Miller (1950), though they had a behavioristic flavor, were clearly multidimensional. Frederick Thorne (1950) was an early, but lonely, voice asserting that psychotherapy, like medicine, deals with a complex set of phenomena requiring diverse conceptualizations and techniques of intervention; and he explicitly used the term "eclectic" to describe his position. The situation has gradually changed, however, and eclectics appear to constitute a dominant group within American psychotherapy.

In a large survey of members of the Division of Clinical Psychology of the American Psychological Association, Kelly (1961) reported that 40 percent identified themselves as eclectics in terms of theoretical preference. This was just under the 41 percent of the sample that identified themselves as favoring one of the psychodynamic orientations. In an attempted replication in the next decade with a comparable sample, Garfield and Kurtz (1976) reported that the relative position of these two orientations had been reversed. Almost 55 percent of the sample said they favored an eclectic orientation in their clinical work, whereas all of those with a dynamic orientation constituted 19 percent of the sample. There have been several other smaller surveys that need not be referenced here that have shown a similar pattern of results. Eclecticism, therefore, seems to be a particularly popular orientation for clinical psychologists.

The true significance or meaningfulness of this trend is difficult to fully evaluate. The fact that two psychotherapists are eclectics, for example, does not mean that they perform their therapeutic functions in exactly the same way. This was clearly illustrated in a study of a sample of 154 eclectic clinical psychologists (Garfield & Kurtz, 1977). These eclectic psychologists indicated 32 different combinations of theoretical orientations as indicative of their particular eclectic views. The most frequent of these combinations are listed in Table 1.1.

As can be noted in Table 1.1, there is, not only an interesting variety of theoretical combinations, but

TABLE 1.1   Combinations of Theoretical Orientations Selected by Five or More Respondents

Orientation	n
Psychoanalytic & learning theory	21
Neo-Freudian & learning theory	16
Neo-Freudian & Rogerian	9
Learning theory & humanistic	8
Rogerian & learning theory	8
Psychoanalytic & Rogerian	7
Sullivanian & learning theory	7
Learning theory & rational-emotive	7
Psychoanalytic & neo-Freudian	6
Rogerian & humanistic	5
Sullivanian & humanistic	5
Psychoanalytic & humanistic	5

Source: From "A Study of Eclectic Views" by S. L. Garfield and R. Kurtz, *Journal of Consulting and Clinical Psychology*, 1977, 45, 78–83. Copyright © 1977 by the American Psychological Association. Reprinted by permission.

also combinations of views that appear to be diametrically opposed to each other theoretically. Thus, psychoanalytic and learning theory are combined by 21 subjects and the latter is also combined with neo-Freudian, Rogerian, humanistic, Sullivanian, and rational-emotive orientations. These results do indicate that there is no single or precise theoretical definition of an eclectic orientation. Individual eclectics apparently work out different approaches and procedures that they believe make the most sense therapeutically.

The essence of the eclectic approach is the lack of strict allegiance to any single theoretical system. Therapists are not constrained by adherence to one approach or one set of procedures. They can select and use whatever procedures or methods they think will work best with specific patients. What individual therapists may actually do in working with individual patients thus may vary significantly. Consequently, it is exceedingly difficult to characterize an eclectic approach in terms of either theory or procedures. The fact that a large number of psychotherapists have chosen an eclectic approach, however, is a finding of some significance. We believe it indicates a certain dissatisfaction with following or limiting oneself to a particular orientation of psychotherapy. At the same time, because eclecticism does not represent any systematic view, no real research on the nature of this "approach" has been done, nor is it really possible. Some more organized attempts at integrating an eclectic orientation are necessary if systematic findings are to be obtained, and such a beginning has recently been made, as discussed below.

In the 1970s, some rather novel reports were published that detailed attempts of several psychotherapists to bring psychoanalytic and behavioral procedures together (Birk & Brinkley-Birk, 1974; Marmor, 1971, 1973; Wachtel, 1977). This attempt to consider some synthesis of these two quite different approaches came, surprisingly, primarily from psychoanalytically oriented therapists. Marmor (1971), a psychoanalytically oriented therapist, discussed the need for both dynamically oriented therapists and behaviorists to become more aware of the overlap and similarities between the two forms of psychotherapy. He also emphasized the need for greater flexibility so that the most appropriate procedures would be selected for the individual patient.

Jerome Frank (1971, 1973), an outstanding psychotherapy researcher, was influential in calling attention to nonspecific or common factors among the psychotherapies as being of importance. One of the present writers also emphasized the importance of common factors as therapeutic variables that played a role in positive outcome among the different therapies (Garfield, 1974) and based his own eclectic approach largely on such potential factors (Garfield, 1980). These include such variables as the therapeutic relationship, opportunities for emotional release, explanations and interpretations, support, reassurance, advice, suggestion, facing anxiety-provoking stimuli (exposure), and the like.

The behavioral psychologist Marvin Goldfried (1980, 1982) has also been a leader in writing about integration in psychotherapy and in helping to form an organization of therapists dedicated to exploring this goal. A new organization has been formed called the Society for the Exploration of Psychotherapy Integration (SEPI), and its Newsletter is edited jointly by Goldfried and Paul Wachtel. What impact this new organization and movement will have on future developments in psychotherapy remains to be seen. It is, however, an interesting and potentially important aspect of the current psychotherapy scene. One feature of this development is the apparent recognition on the part of behavior therapists of the importance of the relationship between therapist and client in psychotherapy (Goldfried & Davidson, 1976; Wilson & Evans, 1977). Another interesting aspect is that this movement for integration has tended to feature some integration or combination of apparently very different orientations, as indicated earlier.

Other recent advocates of the same philosophy include, among numerous others, Lazarus (1967, 1976, 1981), Goldstein and Stein (1976), Norcross (1986), Prochaska (1984), and Beutler (1983). The gathering within SEPI of prominent individuals representing divergent therapeutic traditions also has been an ecumenical phenomenon of historical significance.

The present Handbook has, of course, been eclectic in orientation from the time the first edition (Bergin & Garfield, 1971) was conceived in 1967. Empirical findings on all approaches were welcomed and each was highlighted within its own research domain. Being open to divergent approaches was important, but emphasizing empirical tests of efficacy has been an equally vital feature of the Handbook and of the modern eclectic trend. Without an unyielding link to empirical research, eclecticism could deteriorate into another inflexible school dominated by the opinions of its leaders. We were therefore pleased to note that in a national survey (Smith, 1982) this book, as well as Lazarus' trend-setting position (1976), was considered most representative of the current zeitgeist in the field.

Our commitment to these developments is longstanding (Bergin, 1970; Garfield, 1974, 1980), but we realize, as Goldfried has aptly pointed out (1980), that a systematic eclecticism has not been achieved and presents a future conceptual task of formidable proportions. One of the barriers to quick forward momentum has been the fact that viable ideas from different schools of thought (e.g., behaviorism, psychoanalysis, cognition, phenomenology, humanism) appear to be contradictory. While there is growing respect across schools for the diverse observations that have been made, there is considerable frustration in trying to meld together seemingly incompatible concepts and styles of intervention.

Although we cannot review here the details of attempts to work out this problem, the dilemma may be more apparent than real. Our theoretical efforts may be addressed too strictly toward a kind of comprehensive integration that is not reasonable or feasible. A comprehensive conception of how the body works does not demand that every system or organ of the body operate according to the same principles. Thus, our view of how the circulatory system works is quite different from our view of the nervous system. The forces and actions of the human heart operate according to the principles of fluid mechanics, whereas the principles of electrochemistry apply to the transmission of nerve impulses through the neuron; yet these two quite different processes occur in the same human body and are coordinated harmoniously despite their apparently disparate functions.

Similarly, human personality may operate in accordance with a complex interaction of seemingly disparate processes that act together, though each differently and in its own sphere. Thus, it is conceivable that the same individual may suffer at one time from a repressed conflict, a conditioned response, an incongruent self-image, and irrational cognitions; and that each of these dysfunctions may operate in semi-independent systems of psychic action that are amenable to rather different interventions, each of which is compatible with the "system" to which it is being applied. Diagnosis and therapy might then become concerned with the locus of the disorder or with which portion or portions of the multisystem psyche is involved. Systems theory may or may not be applicable to such individual psychological processes; but the systems approach, as shown in Gurman, Kniskern, and Pinsof's chapter in this volume on marriage and family therapy (Chapter 13), has proved its viability. It is a possible tool in the quest for a systematic eclecticism.

The Eclectic Trend and Specific Therapies

A war of words and tumult of opinions used to prevail in this field, but that has given way to respectful exchanges. While some older advocates of the supremacy of specific therapies continue in entrenched positions, recent generations have moved to higher ground. What has happened to the specific therapies and arguments about their relative effectiveness?

It could be said that psychoanalysis once dominated the field, that client-centered therapy opened a new alternative challenge to that domination, and

that behavior therapy completed the task of displacing the old tradition. In a sense, behavior therapy won a major battle, but it did not win the war.

Behavior therapists and researchers essentially proved their point. They showed that change could be targeted on specific symptoms, that taking action is an essential part of change, that intervention can be brief and move rapidly even in difficult cases, that resolution of transference and making the unconscious conscious are not essential to improvement in many cases, and that extended training in psychoanalysis and personal analysis are not necessarily relevant to therapeutic success. They also showed superior results with several difficult problems, including ones with which psychotherapists previously had no success at all. At the same time, it was shown that extinction, counterconditioning, and reinforcement theory all had to be stretched beyond recognition to account for change phenomena in human subjects. Consequently, many behavioral methods are widely used by practitioners who have no allegiance to any classical behavior theories.

This trend away from strict behaviorism, as noted earlier, opened the way for a resurgence and refinement of cognitive therapies. Generally, behavior therapists have adopted and incorporated cognitive ideas and methods into their approaches. Indeed, it was the frustration in applying behavioral theories experienced by leading behavior modifiers that resulted in many of the most important cognitive innovations (e.g., Bandura, 1969, 1982).

It is also of interest that some behavior therapists have now incorporated modified versions of psychoanalytic terms into their approaches—for instance, the use of "automatic thoughts" in cognitive behavior therapy as an alias for unconscious processes.

It must be said that while psychoanalysis lost a major battle, its power and presence continue, as in the foregoing example, but also in numerous other forms in many therapies, including group and family techniques. It is likely that viable aspects of that tradition have been incorporated into the therapy mainstream and will remain there, while psychoanalysis in its purer forms is clearly slowly disappearing from the scene. It is doubtful that any truly superior therapist functions without having benefited from some psychoanalytic influences, such as skill in reading hidden meanings in communications, the ability to form a therapeutic alliance with the patient, and the capacity to construe dynamic links between early familial experiences and current interpersonal styles. Indeed, it may be reasonable to assert that persons unskilled in basic psychodynamics are less likely to be completely skilled with any other methods, for all interactions are probably tinged to an extent by the processes described and defined by psychoanalysis.

Although elements of the traditional therapies are thus being extracted and synthesized into broader orientations, new techniques continue to proliferate (Corsini, 1981), ranging from specific behavioral/cognitive methods like biofeedback to complicated family (Gurman et al., this volume, Chapter 13) and community (Lorion & Felner, this volume, Chapter 17) techniques and to extreme procedures having little connection with a scholarly research base. Many of these remain untested and uncriticized (Bergin, 1982). The multiplying of methods is one result of the disinhibiting effects of eclecticism, and it is affected by weak public and legal regulation of practice, not to mention the benefits accruing (at least temporarily) to those who lead out with another innovation. It is something of a professional scandal that the good impulses attending a more open situation in the field often deteriorate into therapeutic irresponsibility and commercialism. Our field is thus in a chaotic state similar to that of medicine prior to the Flexner report at the turn of the century, which ultimately led to better standardization and regulation of practice. While our eclectic view has always favored innovation, we also side with Flexner's conservative trend favoring rigor in training, high standards of practice, and a scientific underpinning to all applied work. Professional ethics suggest that the Flexner standards are right and that the unstandardized proliferation of new methods without objective clinical evaluation is not in the public interest.

THE TRAINING OF PSYCHOTHERAPISTS

Because there is no single accepted profession of psychotherapy and many different groups offer such services, the training of psychotherapists also shows great diversity. Psychiatrists are trained in medical schools and then in residencies in psychiatry. Psychiatric social workers are trained in schools of social work and in practica or field placements in clinical settings. Counseling psychologists have been trained primarily in university departments of psychology and education. Clinical psychologists in the United States undoubtedly show the greatest variation in training programs and training sites. Since the mid-1940s, for a period of about 25 years, there was one model of the clinical psychologist—the scientist-practitioner (American Psychological Association, 1947). Since 1968, however, a number of different types of training programs have made their appearance. These include Doctor of Psychology (Psy.D.) programs offered in university settings, in independent professional schools of psychology, and in medical schools. The Ph.D. programs in clinical psychology are also offered in these very same settings, so it is difficult to draw conclusions from the type of degree or the type of training setting.

Consequently, psychotherapists and counselors receive their initial and basic training in diverse settings with different disciplinary and value emphases. They also may be exposed to different therapeutic approaches and emphases. Generally, the criteria for successful completion of the different training programs are not based primarily on competence in psychotherapy. Rather, they include a variety of criteria that derive from the setting and the discipline. Many of these are academic or intellectual criteria that do not necessarily bear a direct relationship to skills in psychotherapeutic activities. Furthermore, in the training offered in psychotherapy the usual criterion of successful performance is the supervisor's evaluation rather than the client or patient's improvement. Studies that evaluate therapists' attributes or performance, interestingly, rarely rely on therapy outcome as the primary criterion (Garfield, 1977; Garfield & Bergin, 1971).

Thus, would-be psychotherapists graduate from a variety of programs with different values, orientations, disciplinary identifications, and amounts and types of therapeutic training. This, however, by no means describes the training "opportunities" available in diverse types of psychotherapy. There are a number of different postdoctoral training programs, psychoanalytic institutes, and the like that offer training over a period of a year or more in specific types of psychotherapy. In addition, there are numerous brief institutes, usually for a few days or a weekend. The latter may offer specific certificates and credit for continuing professional education. In a recent issue of the APA *Monitor*, we were able to identify at least 50 such programs listed for the month of August 1984 (C. E. Calendar, 1984). These workshops and institutes covered a wide range of topics.

It is very difficult to evaluate the adequacy of the different and diverse types of training programs. Most graduate training programs are usually evaluated for certification by an agency of a particular profession and the criteria are based on broader professional goals than that of competency in psychotherapy. At this stage of development, it is also impossible to state which type of training program turns out the most competent psychotherapists. In the various brief institutes mentioned previously, no measures of performance are taken as far as we know.

What may be said at present is that the training of psychotherapists may be influenced by the recent development of training manuals for specific forms of therapy (Beck et al., 1979; Klerman, Rounsaville, Chevron, Neu, & Weissman, 1984; Strupp & Binder, 1984). To the extent that these training manuals focus on specific therapeutic procedures over the course of therapy, they conceivably may make the learning, teaching, and supervision of psychotherapy more operationally explicit. This may be a positive development. On the other hand, to the extent that it again emphasizes specific theoretical orientations and procedures, it is not in line with the developments described previously for integration and eclecticism in psychotherapy. We shall have to await the judgment of time.

THE TREND TOWARD BRIEFER THERAPIES

The length of time or number of sessions required for psychotherapy has been a matter of conjecture without any clear research evidence to support any particular view. Although Freud expressed concern about the length of psychoanalysis, the latter apparently has increased in length since his death. The average number of sessions mentioned in one report was 835 hours (Voth & Orth, 1973), and a common estimate appears to be between 4 and 6 years. Quite clearly, such therapy is beyond the reach of most people, even though it has been viewed by its adherents as the most intensive form of psychotherapy. Its efficacy, however, has not been adequately demonstrated, and on the basis of many reports, it is obvious that most of the psychotherapy provided to the public at large is relatively brief (See Chapter 6), is as effective as psychoanalysis, and is less expensive.

The trend toward brief psychotherapy has become increasingly clear in recent years (Budman & Gurman, 1983; also see Chapter 14). Apart from the brief duration of treatment noted in statistical reports of the average number of clinic visits made by patients and the impetus from the community mental health movement for emergency and crisis-oriented therapies, there was also a definite movement to develop brief therapies. As is true with the longer forms of psychotherapy, there are also many different forms of brief psychotherapy that range from psychodynamic varieties to cognitive and behavioral ones. The goals of these briefer therapies tend to be more specific and circumscribed theoretically and the role of the therapist more active than is true of the longer term therapies. These briefer therapies also seem to be more in line with the desires and expectations of most people who seek psychotherapeutic help.

There are several other aspects of brief therapy that are also of some significance. It is obvious that briefer treatments are less expensive of both time and money for the patient. This also has very evident implications for both governmental agencies and companies that provide health insurance. Both groups have been understandably reluctant to provide insurance payments for treatments that require long periods of time and large expenditures of funds. This, of course, is particularly true if in addition the efficacy of such long-term treatments has not been clearly established. Thus, from the standpoint of potential patients, as well as of governmental agencies and insurance companies, usually referred to as third-party payers, brief therapy has many attractions over the more traditional type of long-term psychotherapy. For such reasons, also, therapists themselves have begun to think more realistically about brief forms of therapy. Even psychodynamically oriented therapists recognize that long-term psychotherapy is not required realistically for many people (Strupp, 1978).

There is also another reason that we can expect that the emphasis on brief psychotherapy will continue and even become stronger. Psychotherapy research is a relatively complicated process, as will become evident in the next chapter. Even moderate sized studies require a period of several years to collect the proper sample of carefully defined patients, who then receive a specific kind(s) of psychotherapy. This is the case when the therapy is relatively brief, that is, 20 sessions or less.

Research on long-term psychotherapy, on the other hand, would require many years for completion. The best known study of this type, conducted at the Menninger Clinic in Topeka, took 18 years from the time the study began until the final report was published (Kernberg et al., 1972). During this period of time a total of only 42 patients were treated and evaluated. It is apparent, therefore, that research on psychotherapy that requires many years for its completion is going to be a more arduous, expensive, and time-consuming activity. This may explain in part why there has been so little systematic research on long-term therapy. Most of the research on the efficacy of psychotherapy has been conducted on the briefer forms of psychotherapy, and this would appear to hold true for future research as well.

One of the recent trends in psychotherapy, mentioned earlier, has been the development of training manuals for specific forms of psychotherapy. These manuals serve at least two important functions. On the one hand, they provided a detailed manual for training individuals in the particular type of psychotherapy and in defining operationally that specific type of therapy. On the other hand, they facilitate research because the therapy is more clearly defined, individuals can be trained to the therapy's specification, and the therapy can be monitored more accurately. Increasingly, such manuals will be required for research on psychotherapy and, at present, all such manuals have been developed for brief forms of psychotherapy. Ordinarily, this might not be seen as a matter of importance in the field of psychotherapy, since most practitioners have not been overly concerned with issues of research. However, in recent years, the situation regarding psychotherapy has changed greatly, and concerns

about the efficacy of psychotherapy have been voiced in a number of quarters. We now turn our attention to such issues.

EFFICACY AND ACCOUNTABILITY

Another important aspect of psychotherapy that has received increasing attention in the past few years is the whole issue of the efficacy of psychotherapy. Although an apparent interest in this problem was evident in the research studies conducted on psychotherapy outcome over the past 30 years or so, this seemingly was limited to a small number of clinical researchers. The majority of psychotherapists showed relatively little interest or concern in such matters, and the same apparently was true of the consumers of psychotherapy. As mentioned earlier, the new and sometimes exotic or bizarre forms of therapy appeared on the therapeutic scene with amazing frequency, and usually with no evidence of effectiveness. Whereas something over 60 therapies were identified in the early 1960s (Garfield, 1982), by 1980 mention was made of around 250 different types of psychotherapy (Herink, 1980). Such an astonishing number of diverse psychotherapies, all claiming to be effective treatments, began to arouse suspicion and concern among a number of individuals and groups. In the absence of adequate research findings, how was one to select an appropriate therapy and to differentiate an effective from an ineffective treatment? Questions such as these called for answers and emphasized the issues related to demonstrating efficacy.

Although, as indicated earlier, the amount of research conducted on psychotherapy has increased since Eysenck's critical article in 1952, and although the quality of the research has also increased, the results reported have not been seen as sufficiently definitive by a number of individuals, especially insurance executives and political leaders, who were increasingly called upon to pay for psychotherapy. This issue will be discussed in greater detail in several other chapters of this *Handbook*. However, a few aspects can be mentioned here.

One aspect, with clear implications for the cost of therapeutic services, is that of length of psychotherapy, and we have already commented upon this matter. Essentially, little evidence has been presented to support the efficiacy of long-term psycho-therapy over brief psychotherapy. This has raised some doubts about the efficacy and necessity of long-term therapy, with clear implications for cost accounting.

Another aspect is the frequently reported finding that of the psychotherapies evaluated in comparative studies, the outcome results have been comparable (Garfield, 1981). The comparability of results for supposedly very different treatments has also made some people question the worth of the entire enterprise, and to believe that such therapy is basically superficial (Klein & Rabkin, 1984).

Still another concern is the fact that psychotherapeutic treatment is often nonspecific or overly general. That is, there were very few specialized forms of psychotherapy that had been devised for helping with specific types of mental or behavioral disorders. Most psychotherapies appeared to be what one of us has termed "universal therapies" (Garfield, 1980).

Finally, not all of the research findings on the effectiveness of psychotherapy tended to agree. Some, usually a majority, were positive, but there were also reports that found no particular effectiveness for psychotherapy. Furthermore, the percentage of clients helped in the different studies showed a wide range (Bergin, 1971). The conflicting findings in the research literature as well as the continuing controversy over the effectiveness of psychotherapy between critics and defenders of psychotherapy has also tended to lessen confidence in these methods of treatment.

The controversy has also gone beyond the boundaries of those who are primarily involved in the practice and research investigation of psychotherapy. A number of semipopular or nontechnical publications written for the more general public have also appeared. Tennov (1975) published a book entitled *Psychotherapy: The Hazardous Cure.* As you might imagine, the book is not very complimentary regarding the efficacy of psychotherapy. Gross (1978), a popular writer, also wrote an extremely critical book about psychotherapy. Even Zilbergeld (1983), a practicing psychotherapist, wrote a critical book entitled *The Shrinking of America. Myths of Psychological Change.* In addition to these critical accounts, there have been demands from funding sources and legislators for

demonstrations that psychotherapy is an effective treatment for personality and behavior disorders. An article in *Science* magazine, "Psychotherapy Works, But for Whom?", also referred to the criticism of psychotherapy emanating from Congress (Marshall, 1980).

Overlapping the above criticisms were some concerns at the National Institute of Mental Health about limitations in existing research on psychotherapy. As a result, it was planned to organize a study of psychotherapy that would not suffer from most of the limitations of existing research. Toward this end, a collaborative study of two well-known forms of psychotherapy of depression and an accepted pharmacotherapy was to be conducted in three large medical centers. This study, described briefly in the next chapter, contains a number of significant improvements in research design and includes a large, carefully selected sample of patients. As this is being written, the necessary data are being collected and at least the posttreatment data will have been secured. It is expected that this study will have a significant effect on the issue of efficacy as well as on research designs in psychotherapy.

It is clear, therefore, that the issue of the efficacy of psychotherapy has become an important one for all parties concerned with the psychological treatment of mentally and emotionally disturbed individuals. Furthermore, as research interest and research methodology have increased, both positive and perhaps negative effects are potentially possible. As the collaborative study indicates, we are now asking more specific questions about specific psychotherapies with specified forms of disturbance. The question being asked is not, "Does psychotherapy work?" Rather, it is, "How effective are Cognitive-Behavior Therapy and Interpersonal Therapy, as defined by specific therapy manuals, and delivered by therapists trained to meet certain criteria with carefully diagnosed cases of unipolar depression?" The question is thus more highly specified and the research design and methodology much more extensive and sophisticated.

On the positive side, such research may indicate a new and higher standard for future research investigations. On the negative side, such a research project is a very expensive undertaking and evaluates only two of the many forms of psychotherapy that are available today. To conduct such studies for a large number of psychotherapies would require many years and huge sums of money, particularly if we were to evaluate them for each of the numerous forms of psychopathology. As one astute observer of this problem has noted: "Consider the consequences: A systematic approach to dealing with a matrix of 250 psychosocial therapies and 150 classes of disorders would require approximately 4.7 million separate comparisons. Clearly, some simplification of the task is required" (Parloff, 1982, p. 723).

It is obvious that an attempt to evaluate all the diverse forms of psychotherapy is not a feasible project and that it will not be undertaken in the foreseeable future. In fact, if such a project were to be initiated, it would still leave some issues unresolved. For example, what kinds of patients with what kinds of problems would respond best to what kind of therapy administered by what kind of therapist? Apart from type of therapy and type of disorder, there are also potential client and therapist variables that conceivably could play a role in the outcome. As was mentioned earlier, research on psychotherapy is a complex matter and securing definitive answers is not a simple process. Nevertheless, some progress has been made, and we have some answers currently that were not available 30 years ago. Hopefully, as our research knowledge increases, the issue of efficacy will be somewhat less of an issue in the future.

ETHICS AND VALUES

Ethics

There has been a recent surge of interest in ethics and values in the mental health disciplines, which is manifested by an array of publications (cf. Bergin, 1985) and a number of new emphases in professional ethics (Carroll, Schneider, & Wesley, 1985; Rosenbaum, 1982; Steininger, Newell, & Garcia, 1984; Thompson, 1983). This has become a focus of vital concern to practitioners, educators, administrators, researchers, and social activists, and the trend has had an impact upon research, especially in a new emphasis upon informed consent and protection from harm for participants in empirical studies (Stricker, 1982). While there is continuing concern that the use of no-treatment or placebo control groups may be unfair or harmful to clients,

thus far this has not significantly affected research in psychotherapy. However, there is a growing disillusionment with the value of such control groups (cf. Chapter 5, this volume) and an increasing emphasis on comparing one treatment with another, which reduces the need for untreated controls. This development is one possible alternative in response to ethical concerns about withholding treatment, an issue that was raised early in the history of controlled therapy outcome studies (Rogers & Dymond, 1954).

The protection of subjects' rights and welfare has generally been a positive development. It has made researchers much more sensitive and responsible about their work. The use of elaborate consent forms and Human Subjects Review Committees has effectively changed previous abuses of participants' welfare. Although taking this to extremes can inhibit creative inquiry and slow down progress unnecessarily, such developments have generally had a positive effect on research.

Other standards for the conduct of research studies have always been very clear and generally well conformed with. These pertain to complete objectivity and honesty in recording, tabulating, analyzing, and reporting results of studies. Professional ethics are very specific on these points, and any violation of them should be promptly confessed or reported, for without such basic integrity, no science can exist for very long. It is imperative that we avoid the slightest breach in such principles, let alone the fraudulent practices noted in some fields that have been exposed in recent years, which has included fraudulent tampering with data or even the reporting of nonexistent data!

Thus far, psychotherapy research has not been tainted by such revelations. There is a related ethical standard that is, however, not adhered to rigidly enough in our field, and that concerns the *interpretation* of one's own or other hypotheses or theories. There have been, perhaps, too many instances of setting up double standards for interpreting findings: a *severe* standard for evaluating the validity of data contradicting one's position and a *flexible* standard for evaluating results that support one's views. Given the difficulties of doing precise research in this field and the ambiguities attending measurements of outcome, it is possible to stretch one's interpretive criteria so greatly as to keep one's prejudices intact almost regardless of the weight of contrary evidence.

All of us are subject to such temptations and the rationalizations that accompany our decisions and actions; but it seems that a reasonable degree of humility would assist progress toward increased knowledge a great deal. An unfortunate episode in the history of this field has been a tendency to insist on one's correctness despite weak support or contrary evidence. This was especially evident during the long debate between the merits of psychodynamic and behavioral therapy. Proponents of the validity or superiority of each approach held to rigid positions and engaged in strident claims and acrimonious debates. The resulting reviews of studies comparing these methods were therefore often quite divergent, the reviews of the famous study by Sloane, Staples, Cristol, Yorkston, and Whipple (1975) being a specific case in point (Garfield, 1983b).

We can recall comparing our evaluations of studies with the assessments of other reviewers and sometimes wondering whether we had read the same studies. Although reviewers sometimes make mistakes in reviewing studies, they are generally willing to correct such miscues; but it is quite a different matter to cling to a biased interpretation for the sake of defending one's prior position. The motives for such behavior soon become all too apparent, and the defensive reviewer loses credibility while trying to win debating points. As Strupp (1979) has so aptly put it, the point of this kind of research is to discover the mechanisms of change and not to engage in scientifically futile "horse races."

From an ethical point of view, we have to recognize that having prejudices is not necessarily unethical; rather, it is when the prejudice grossly distorts the interpretation of data that one may become systematically unfair, and thus dishonest, in reporting or evaluating. An ingenious corrective for this tendency is the invention of meta-analysis by Gene Glass (Glass, McGaw, & Smith, 1981). Although meta-analysis can be used in the service of personal distortions of evidence, its procedures are public and exacting; consequently, the specific points of biasing can be identified and other reviewers can reliably repeat the review process with a precision and objectivity not heretofore possible. Meta-analytic procedures thus provide a powerful means for exposing deliberately distorted reviewing practices, and is thus a tool that can serve ethical reporting.

Values

Despite the foregoing developments, the research community still largely operates on the assumption that values and science are separate domains. A particular example of this is the content of the present *Handbook*. Thousands of studies are reported here that examine change processes concerning the most intimate and profound aspects of people's lives, yet the reports are antiseptic and technical, as though the grist of human experience can be condensed into numerical indexes having little to do with how life is lived in its social context, or how it should be lived.

Recent progress in developing new and more effective techniques of psychotherapy has obscured the fact that subjective value decisions underlie the choice of techniques, the goals of change, and the assessment of what is a "good" outcome. It is important, in our quest for behavioral technology, to remember that we are effecting changes not in mechanical objects but in human beings. Therapeutic changes therefore affect the way in which people view themselves and life, and the changes thus influence the family and society as well. Accomplishing an understanding of these issues is not difficult when the individual, the professional therapist, and the family or community have agreed-upon goals. Difficult problems arise when there are different views from these sources as to what is desirable (Strupp & Hadley, 1977).

Outcome evaluations often ignore the societal impact of individual behavior in favor of strictly clinical criteria; but as Strupp and Hadley (1977) showed, the ideals that guide the setting of standards of outcome should have, in addition to an individual or symptom basis, a societal reference base. By examining the treatment of individual symptoms in different problem areas, one can observe the role of value decisions in assessing treatment outcomes and their social consequences (Bergin, 1983). For example, it is widely assumed today that many anxiety and depressive symptoms can be overcome by assertiveness, since many persons suffering from these problems are inhibited, feel inadequate, and have no mastery of effective social skills. This procedure has many merits, but it, too, is often applied with more emphasis upon immediate relief for the client than upon the situation and other persons involved. It is possible to feel a new sense of power, independence, and freedom as a result of becoming appropriately assertive.

Assertive methods are appropriately designed to aid people in overcoming extremely dependent and exploitive situations. Wise therapists attempt to help clients achieve a balanced style of self-expressiveness that lies between humiliating passivity and intimidating aggression, but this is always a difficult challenge. For example, in the case of a woman who was bullied by her mother-in-law, self-assertive responses were rewarded by the therapist (Wolpe, 1973, p. 88):

Mrs A: Suppose my husband starts up with me. "You shouldn't talk like that to my mother. You are not cementing relationships; you are putting them farther apart." How do I handle that situation?
Therapist: You have to say, "If your mother makes unjust remarks I have to tell her and I will tell her. If your mother makes reasonable criticisms, I will be very interested in what she has to say. But she is always at me, and she has gotten into the habit of it because I have been allowing her to say whatever she likes. I am not going to have it anymore."

The problem here is that the deficient client behavior has become the therapeutic *target*, similar to the symptom focus in sexual therapies. This excerpt does not reveal how the mother-in-law responds, nor the consequences to the husband or the marital relationship. There is an implication in this work that clients are to be trained in gaining "emotional victories" (Wolpe, 1973, pp. 89–90) without adequate reference to learning other skills of patience, understanding, and love toward the abusive person. Does a "soft answer turn away wrath"? Would deeper understanding of the mother-in-law's conflicts, needs, and motives be helpful? Would examination of the dynamic social system permit an approach that would soften everyone's mode of interacting in this case, thus ensuring a long-term, rewarding familial network as opposed to "liberating" the wife, providing her with the tools of emotional combat, and counting her "cured" when she tops the distribution on assertiveness scores? Do therapists so ally themselves with their client and focus so much upon relieving his or her symptomatic distress that they ignore or harm other persons in the process? Are they rewarded too much for acting like doctors treat-

ing bacteria and not enough for the less dramatic and more difficult role of life counselor and social facilitator?

Such questions reveal how pervasively psychotherapy techniques and outcome measurements are infected by value choices and how often these values emphasize individualism, immediate consequences, and self-focus.

Values and Comparisons of Techniques

It should now be clear that judgments regarding the effectiveness of different techniques will vary a great deal, depending upon the social and value perspective being used. Judged solely in immediate and sensual terms, one of the new sex therapies that focuses on physical reactions rather than relationships would appear to be the superior therapy in terms of magnitude of change on a sexuality change index. Those who argue that marital disloyalty can be therapeutic have such a narrow view. But judging in terms of broader relationship satisfaction and life impact, relationship therapy that strengthens mutual commitment and self-sacrifice would appear to be superior, because the consequences are likely to be beneficial in social and moral terms. A good assessment strategy would be to evaluate both dimensions (e.g., LoPiccolo, Heiman, Hogan, & Roberts, 1985), since many sex therapy studies lack a moral dimension.

Similarly, many other techniques, such as desensitization for phobias, exposure for compulsions, and biofeedback for headaches, often ignore contexts and relationships and the concepts by which people guide their lives. These latter need to be considered in treatment and its evaluation; otherwise the consequences of overly individualized and technologized therapies could be socially negative. It is already clear that the former hope for a behavioral technology cannot be achieved by conceiving change in terms of automatic mechanisms, with clients as objects and therapists as technicians. What we *have* learned is that techniques can be powerful aids to a multidimensional therapy that takes into account the fabric of social life and keeps the technologies subservient to the social consequences that count most, rather than allowing the technologies and associated outcome studies to subvert such values.

Ultimately, the welfare of the individual will be enhanced more by such an orientation than by a simple devotion to technical methods for obtaining self-focused improvements that may reinforce narcissism (Lasch, 1978; Vitz, 1977).

If we restrict ourselves to standard outcome criteria, such as inventory scales or behavioral indices, we might observe immediate positive results from most of the major therapies in terms of symptom relief; but we would have fulfilled a clinically pragmatic value and not necessarily a moral one that assesses the individual's *lifestyle* and the ultimate consequences of that lifestyle for the person and the social system (Bergin, 1985).

Perhaps correlated with the recent upsurge of interest in ethics and values has been a renewed interest in religion as a factor in therapeutic process and outcome. This new literature spans the spectrum from conceptual and practitioner issues (Bergin, 1980a, 1980b, Ellis, 1980; Lovinger, 1984; Miller & Jackson, 1985; Spero, 1985; Walls, 1980) to rigorous empirical ones (Bergin, 1983; Spilka, Hood, & Gorsuch, 1985). An NIMH bibliography also covers pertinent literature (Summerlin, 1980).

EQUAL OUTCOMES AND COMMON FACTORS

Many techniques reported on in this book show positive effects; but it is a somewhat startling experience to read accounts of dozens of studies comparing different treatments that found no differences in therapeutic outcomes. For instance, the chapter on cognitive therapies describes numerous comparisons of diverse cognitive interventions, very few of which show any significant differences. The same can be said of behavioral methods and of comparisons between them and other techniques, as well as various child therapy methods. Similarly, group and individual strategies do not differ in efficacy, nor do many marital and family approaches. The data on professionals versus preprofessionals also reveal only a few differences. A new study on different modes of sex therapy likewise revealed equal outcomes across methods (LoPiccolo et al., 1985).

Aside from many evidences that a number of approaches are shown to "work," this equal outcomes phenomenon may be the most frequent and striking theme in the book. One might, therefore, be inclined to say that more evidence is provided throughout these chapters to support Jerome Frank's

long-held view that "common factors" are the main therapeutic ingredients of psychotherapy techniques than for any other theory (see Frank, 1973, and Frank, 1978, which includes a 206-item bibliography of his writings).

This is not to say that all results show this or that no differences exist; but, rather, that the majority of results to date support such a view. If this trend is further confirmed by a failure to obtain significant differences across techniques in the current NIMH collaborative study on depression, which is the largest and most precise comparative study of psychotherapy ever undertaken, then a major effort will have to be put into defining, measuring, and enhancing the therapeutically active factors that are common to the different approaches.

Consideration of these matters is taken up in several places in this volume, particularly Chapters 5, 7, and 8, as well as in other recent publications (Gelso & Carter, 1985; Stiles, Shapiro, & Elliott, in press).

OVERVIEW OF THE BOOK

The preceding pages have described some of the important developments in psychotherapy that have taken place in the past as well as trends that appear to be occurring currently. In what is to follow in the rest of the book, the emphasis will be placed on current developments in major areas of psychotherapy. This, of course, is partially dependent on the relative development in different areas of psychotherapy. As indicated in the Preface, some areas, such as cognitive behavioral therapy, have been quite active in research and development. Others, however, such as psychoanalysis and traditional forms of psychotherapy with children, have appeared to be relatively dormant. This is particularly the case with reference to the state of research in these latter areas. Since the emphasis on empirical research is a basic feature of this *Handbook*, chapters on these topics are not included, and readers are therefore referred to the previous editions for pertinent reviews.

In line with the increased emphasis recently on the importance of research in psychotherapy, each of the chapters to follow will present a survey and evaluation of empirical research in a specific area.

Although we have of necessity been selective in our choice of topics, all major areas that have a reasonably adequate body of research have been included.

The first part of the *Handbook* emphasizes methodological and conceptual foundations of psychotherapy and consists of a chapter on research designs, one on social psychological approaches to psychotherapy and behavioral change, and one on developmental perspectives. There is a reasonably clear rationale for each of these chapters. Knowledge of research methodology is absolutely essential for evaluating the existing research in any field and it is exceedingly true for the field of psychotherapy and behavior change. As the reader progresses through the remaining pages of this book, he or she will find frequent references to the limitations in much of the existing research and the concurrent need for more definitive and clinically relevant research. The awareness of adequate research design and methodology is thus of great importance even for practicing clinicians who do no research themselves.

Because psychotherapy in great part involves social perception, social interaction, and even processes such as social influence and persuasion, some knowledge of social psychological processes appears desirable. Consequently, a survey of material derived from social psychology with potential implications for the psychotherapeutic process is included. A similar reason exists for evaluating developmental perspectives on psychotherapy and behavior change. Both a social and a developmental perspective appear to enrich the individual's understanding and appraisal of the psychotherapeutic interaction. The chapters in the first section, therefore, provide an introduction, a foundation, and a perspective for the rest of the book.

The following part, consisting of four chapters, provides an evaluation of process and outcome in psychotherapy and behavior change. As already indicated, the evaluation of therapeutic outcome has been and remains a major concern. Thus it appears early in the *Handbook* and provides a frame of reference for all the remaining chapters, each of which in some fashion reflects the general interest in evaluation. The following two chapters deal with the available research on the principal participants in psychotherapy, the client or patient, and the therapist. Some of the findings reported will

be surprising to readers who have had relatively little experience with psychotherapy. At the same time, it will become apparent that surprising or not, psychotherapists need to be knowledgeable about such findings.

The final chapter in this part reviews the available data on the relation of processes during the therapeutic sessions to outcome. In many respects, this is also a matter of critical importance. Although it is essential to first evaluate the effectiveness of psychotherapy and to secure some indications of efficacy, we also need to understand how psychotherapy works. What therapeutic procedures or processes appear to be significant in producing positive change in the client?

Many individuals, particularly those interested in psychodynamic forms of psychotherapy, have been interested in studying the process of psychotherapy. However, in the past, most of them seemingly had no particular interest in relating process to outcome. They were interested in process per se. To the present editors, this appears to be a limited type of appraisal unless the processes of psychotherapy hypothesized to influence change can be related directly to outcome. Such an emphasis is provided in this chapter in the *Handbook*.

Parts III and IV, which follow the above section, are devoted to specific types of psychotherapy. The first group of chapters deals with developments in the behavioral and cognitive therapies. As mentioned earlier, these therapies have exerted considerable influence on the field of psychotherapy, particularly with reference to the empirical appraisal of their work. A recent development, behavioral medicine and health psychology, which aims to apply behavioral procedures and psychological principles to the general area of health, constitutes one of these chapters.

The above part is followed by two chapters dealing with child and family therapies. The first focuses on behavior therapy with children and adolescents and illustrates the many diverse approaches and programs developed by behaviorally oriented therapists for working with a variety of children's problems. Unfortunately, there has been so little new published research on other varieties of psychotherapy with children that no such additional chapter appears in the present volume. Children's problems, however, have been increasingly viewed as involving the families of the children, and family therapy has become increasingly popular. The chapter on maritial and family therapy discusses and evaluates the developments in this area.

The following, and next to last, part consists of five chapters on what are considered special topics. One chapter deals with the research on brief psychotherapy. Although sometimes considered a special form of psychotherapy, there are actually many different forms of brief therapy, which together constitute the modal form of psychotherapy today. At the same time, the different types of brief therapy appear also to have certain basic features that are quite similar. The existing research on brief forms of therapy is carefully appraised in this chapter.

There is also a chapter that evaluates the research on group and related therapies. Various types of experiential groups became very popular a few years ago, and although their popularity appears to have diminished, various types of group therapy continue to be used in a number of settings. Educational and vocational counseling is the topic of the chapter that follows and is of particular interest to psychologists and counselors who work in educational settings. Although such counseling is generally seen as somewhat specialized, there is a gray area between counseling and psychotherapy. Furthermore, such matters as career choices are sometimes areas of conflict and crisis.

The remaining two chapters in this part also deal with special topics, but differ from the preceding chapters. One chapter presents and evaluates the research on intervention with the disadvantaged. This reflects an important and more recent concern for those who in earlier periods tended to be neglected by mental health workers. Such individuals present special problems and needs as compared with the more typical middle-class psychotherapy patient, who has tended to be the focus in the past.

The last chapter in this part is devoted to an appraisal of research on drugs and psychotherapy. A major emphasis in this chapter is the evaluation of studies that have attempted to compare the relative effectiveness of drugs and psychotherapy on patients with various forms of psychopathology. In addition to comparative studies, some research has also focused on the potential values of combining drugs and psychotherapy.

Finally, the last part consists of just one chapter on the training of psychotherapists. The material reviewed in that chapter also may be somewhat surprising to many readers. Despite the fact that the proper training of psychotherapists and counselors is considered to be important, comparatively little systematic research of a meaningful nature has been conducted on this matter. What research has been carefully done has centered more around interviewing skills than on the actual skills of conducting "real" psychotherapy. There are some interesting indications, however, that this situation is beginning to change.

The reader now has been presented with a brief overview of psychotherapy and its major developments as well as a preview of the chapters that follow. It is our hope that the latter will give the reader a sound basis for evaluating the current empirical status of psychotherapy and help him or her to appraise developments that take place in the future.

REFERENCES

Bandura, A. (1969). *Principles of behavior modification.* New York: Holt, Rinehart, & Winston.

Bandura, A. (1982). Self-efficacy mechanism in human agency. *American Psychologist, 37,* 122–147.

Beck, A. T. (1976) *Cognitive therapy and the emotional disorders.* New York: International Universities Press.

Beck, A. T., Rush, A. J., Shaw, B. F., & Emery, G. (1979) *Cognitive therapy of depression: A treatment manual.* New York: Guilford.

Bergin, A. E. (1970). Cognitive therapy and behavior therapy: Foci for a multidimensional approach to treatment. *Behavior Therapy, 1,* 546–549.

Bergin, A. E. (1971). The evaluation of therapeutic outcomes. In A. E. Bergin & S. L. Garfield (Eds.), *Handbook of psychotherapy and behavior change.* New York, Wiley.

Bergin, A. E. (1980a). Psychotherapy and religious values. *Journal of Consulting and Clinical Psychology, 48,* 95–105.

Bergin, A. E. (1980b). Religious and humanistic values: A reply to Ellis and Walls. *Journal of Consulting and Clinical Psychology, 48,* 642–645.

Bergin, A. E. (1982). Sixty-four therapies—but who will evaluate them? *Contemporary Psychology, 27,* 685–686.

Bergin, A. E. (1983a). Religiosity and mental health: A critical reevaluation and meta-analysis. *Professional Psychology, 14,* 170–184.

Bergin, A. E. (1983b). Values and evaluating therapeutic change. In J. Helm & A. E. Bergin (Eds.), *Therapeutic behavior modification* (pp. 9–14). Berlin, East Germany: VEB Deutscher Verlag der Wissenschaften.

Bergin, A. E. (1985). Proposed values for guiding and

evaluating counseling and psychotherapy. *Counseling and Values, 29,* 99–116.

Bergin, A. E., & Garfield, S. L. (Eds.). (1971). *Handbook of psychotherapy and behavior change.* New York: Wiley.

Beutler, L. E. (1983). *Eclectic psychotherapy: A systematic approach.* New York: Pergamon.

Birk, L., & Brinkley-Birk, A. (1974) Psychoanalysis and behavior therapy. *The American Journal of Psychiatry, 131,* 499–510.

Budman, S. H., & Gurman, A. S. (1983) The practice of brief therapy. *Professional Psychology; Research and Practice, 14;* 277–292.

Calendar, C. E., (1984, July). *A.P.A. Monitor,* p. 25.

Carroll, M. A., Schneider, H. G., & Wesley, G. R. (1985). *Ethics in the practice of psychology.* Englewood Cliffs, NJ: Prentice-Hall.

Corsini, R. J. (Ed.). (1981). *Handbook of innovative psychotherapies.* New York: Wiley.

Dollard, J., & Miller, N. E. (1950). *Personality and psychotherapy: An analysis in terms of learning, thinking, and culture.* New York: McGraw-Hill.

Durlak, J. A. (1979). Comparative effectiveness of paraprofessional and professional helpers. *Psychological Bulletin, 86,* 80–92.

Durlak, J. A. (1981). Evaluating comparative studies of paraprofessional and professional helpers: A reply to Nietzel and Fisher. *Psychological Bulletin, 89,* 566–569.

Ellis, A. (1958). Rational psychotherapy. *The Journal of General Psychology, 59,* 35–49.

Ellis, A. (1962). *Reason and emotion in psychotherapy.* New York: Stuart.

Ellis, A. (1980). Psychotherapy and atheistic values: A response to A. E. Bergin's "Psychotherapy and religious values." *Journal of Consulting and Clinical Psychology, 48,* 635–639.

Emmelkamp, P. M. G. (1986). Behavior therapy with adults. In S. L. Garfield & A. E. Bergin (Eds.), *Handbook of psychotherapy and behavior change (3rd ed.).* New York: Wiley.

Eysenck, H. J. (1952). The effects of psychotherapy: An evaluation. *Journal of Consulting Psychology, 16,* 319–324.

Frank, J. D. (1971). Therapeutic factors in psychotherapy. *American Journal of Psychotherapy, 25,* 350–361.

Frank, J. D. (1973). *Persuasion and healing (2nd ed.).* Baltimore: Johns Hopkins University Press.

Frank, J. D. (1978). *Psychotherapy and the human predicament: A psychosocial approach.* New York: Schocken Books.

Garfield, S. L. (1974). *Clinical psychology. The study of personality and behavior.* Chicago: Aldine.

Garfield, S. L. (1977). Research on the training of professional psychotherapists. In A. Gurman & A. Razin (Eds.), *Effective psychotherapy: A handbook of research.* New York: Pergamon.

Garfield, S. L. (1980). *Psychotherapy. An eclectic approach.* New York: Wiley.

Garfield, S. L. (1981). Psychotherapy: A forty-year appraisal. *American Psychologist, 36,* 174–183.

Garfield, S. L. (1982). Eclecticism and integration in psychotherapy. *Behavior Therapy, 13,* 610–623.

Garfield, S. L. (1983a). *Clinical psychology. The study of personality and behavior (2nd ed.).* Hawthorne, NY: Aldine.

Garfield, S. L. (1983b). The effectiveness of psychotherapy: The perennial controversy. *Professional Psychology, 14,* 35–43.

Garfield, S. L., & Bergin, A. E. (1971). Therapeutic conditions and outcome. *Journal of Abnormal Psychology, 77,* 108–114.

Garfield, S. L., & Bergin, A. E. (Eds.). (1978). *Handbook of psychotherapy and behavior change (2nd ed.).* New York: Wiley.

Garfield, S. L., & Kurtz, R. (1976). Clinical psychologists in the 1970's. *American Psychologist, 31,* 1–9.

Garfield, S. L., & Kurtz, R. (1977). A study of eclectic views. *Journal of Consulting and Clinical Psychology, 45,* 78–83.

Gelso, C. J., & Carter, J. A. (1985). The relationship in counseling and psychotherapy: Components, consequences and theoretical antecedents. *The Counseling Psychologist, 13,* 155–243.

Glass, G. V., McGaw, B., & Smith, M. L. (1981). *Meta-analysis in social research.* Beverly Hills: Sage.

Goldfried, M. R. (1980). Toward the delineation of therapeutic change principles. *American Psychologist, 35,* 991–999.

Goldfried, M. R. (Ed.). (1982). *Converging themes in the practice of psychotherapy.* New York: Springer.

Goldfried, M. R., & Davison, G. C. (1976). *Clinical behavior therapy.* New York: Holt, Rinehart & Winston.

Goldstein, A. P., & Stein, N. (eds.). (1976). *Prescriptive psychotherapies.* New York: Pergamon.

Gross, M. L. (1978). *The psychological society: A critical analysis of psychiatry, psychotherapy, psychoanalysis, and the psychological revolution.* New York: Random House.

Hattie, J. A., Sharpley, C. F., & Rogers, H. J. (1984). Comparative effectiveness of professional and paraprofessional helpers. *Psychological Bulletin, 95,* 534–541.

Herink, R. (Ed.). (1980). *The psychotherapy handbook. The A to Z guide to more than 250 different therapies in use today.* New York: New American Library.

Holt, R. R. (Ed.). (1971). *New horizon for psychotherapy.* New York: International Universities Press.

Joint Commission on Mental Illness and Health. (1961). *Action for mental health.* New York: Basic Books.

Kelley, E. L. (1961). Clinical Psychology—1960. Report of survey findings. *Newsletter, Division of Clinical Psychology,* Winter, 1–11.

Kendall, P. C., & Hollon, S. D. (1979). *Cognitive-behavioral interventions. Theory, research, and procedures.* New York: Academic Press.

Kernberg, O. P., Burstein, E. D., Coyne, L., Appelbaum, A., Horwitz, L., & Voth, H. (1972). Psychotherapy and psychoanalysis: Final report of the Menninger Foundation's Psychotherapy Research Project, *Bulletin of the Menninger Clinic, 36,* (Nos. 1/2), 1–276.

Klein, D. F., & Rabkin, J. G. (1984). Specificity and strategy in psychotherapy research and practice. In J. B. W. Williams & R. L. Spitzer (Eds.), *Psychotherapy research. Where are we and where should we go?* (pp. 306–329) New York: Guildford.

Klerman, G. L., Rounsaville, B., Chevron, E., Neu, C., & Weissman, M. M. (1984). *Interpersonal psychotherapy of depression (IPT).* New York: Basic Books.

Lasch, C. (1978). *The culture of narcissism.* New York: Norton.

Lazarus, A. A. (1967). In support of technical eclecticism. *Psychological Reports, 21,* 415–416.

Lazarus, A. A. (1976). *Multimodal behavior therapy*. New York: Springer.

Lazarus, A. A. (1981). *The practice of multimodal therapy*. New York: McGraw-Hill.

LoPiccolo, J., Heiman, J. R., Hogan, D. R., & Roberts, C. W. (1985). Effectiveness of single therapists versus cotherapy teams in sex therapy. *Journal of Consulting and Clinical Psychology, 53*, 287–294.

Lovinger, R. J. (1984). *Working with religious issues in therapy*. New York: Jason Aronson.

Marmor, J. (1971). Dynamic psychotherapy and behavior therapy. Are they irreconcilable? *Archives of General Psychiatry, 24*, 22–28.

Marmor, J. (1973). The future of psychoanalytic therapy. *The American Journal of Psychiatry, 130*, 1197–1202.

Marshall, E. (1980). Psychotherapy works, but for whom? *Science, 207*, 506–508.

Miller, W. R., & Jackson, K. A. (1985). *Practical psychology for pastors*. Englewood Cliffs, NJ: Prentice-Hall.

Nietzel, N. T., & Fisher, S. G. (1981). Effectiveness of professional and paraprofessional helpers: A comment on Durlak. *Psychological Bulletin, 89*, 555–565.

Norcross, J. C. (Ed.). (In press). *Handbook of eclectic psychotherapy*. New York: Brunner/Mazel.

Oberndorf, C. P. (1943). Results of psychoanalytic therapy. *International Journal of Psychoanalysis, 24*, 107–114.

Oberndorf, C. P., Greenacre, P., & Kubie, L. (1948). Symposium on the evaluation of therapeutic results. *International Journal of Psychoanalysis, 29*, 7–33.

Parloff, M. B. (1982). Psychotherapy research evidence and reimbursement decisions: Bambi meets Godzilla. *American Journal of Psychiatry, 139*, 718–727.

Prochaska, J. O. (1984). *Systems of psychotherapy: A transtheoretical analysis* (2nd ed.). Homewood. IL: Irwin.

Rioch, M. J. (1967). Pilot projects in training mental health counselors. In E. L. Cowen, E. A. Gardner, & M. Zax (Eds.), *Emergent approaches to mental health problems* (pp. 110–127). New York: Appleton-Century-Crofts.

Rioch, M. J., Elkes, C., & Flint, A. A. (1965), *National Institute of Mental Health project in training mental health counselors*. Washington, DC: U.S. Department of H.E.W. Public Health Service Publication No. 1254.

Rogers, C. R. (1942). *Counseling and psychotherapy*. Boston: Houghton Mifflin.

Rogers, C. R. (1951). *Client-centered therapy*. Boston: Houghton Mifflin.

Rogers, C. R., & Dymond, R. F. (Eds.). (1954). *Psychotherapy and personality change*. Chicago: University of Chicago Press.

Rosenbaum, M. (Ed.). (1982). *Ethics and values in psychotherapy: A guidebook*. New York: Free Press.

Sloane, R. B., Staples, F. R., Cristol, A. H., Yorkston, N.J., & Whipple, K. (1975). *Psychotherapy versus behavior therapy*. Cambridge: Harvard University Press.

Smith, D. (1982). Trends in counseling and psychotherapy. *American Psychologist, 37*, 802–809.

Spero, M. H. (Ed.). (1985). *Psychotherapy of the religious patient*. Springfield, IL: Charles C. Thomas.

Spilka, B., Hood, R. W., & Gorsuch, R. L. (1985). *The psychology of religion: An empirical approach*. Englewood Cliffs, N.J.: Prentice-Hall.

Steininger, M., Newell, J. D., & Garcia, L. T. (1984). *Ethical issues in psychology*. Homewood, IL: Dorsey.

Stiles, W. B., Shapiro, D. A., & Elliott, R. (In press). Are all psychotherapies equivalent? *American Psychologist*.

Stricker, G. (1982). Ethical issues in psychotherapy research. In M. Rosenbaum (Ed.), *Ethics and values in psychotherapy: A guidebook* (pp. 402–424). New York: Free Press.

Strupp, H. H. (1978). Psychotherapy research and practice: An overview. In S. L. Garfield & A. E. Bergin (Eds.). *Handbook of psychotherapy and behavior change (2nd ed.)*, (pp. 3–22). New York: Wiley.

Strupp, H. H. (1979). Psychotherapy: Assessing methods. *Science, 207*, 590.

Strupp, H. H., & Binder, J. L. (1984). *Psychotherapy in new key. A guide to time-limited dynamic psychotherapy*. New York: Basic Books.

Strupp, H. H., & Hadley, S. M. (1977). A tripartite model of mental health and therapeutic outcomes, *American Psychologist, 32*, 187–196.

Summerlin, F. A. (1980). *Religion and mental health: A bibliography*. Rockville, MD: National institute of Mental Health.

Tennov, D. (1975). *Psychotherapy: The hazardous cure*. New York: Abelard-Schuman (T. Y. Crowell).

Thompson, A. (1983). *Ethical concerns in psychotherapy and their legal ramifications*. New York: University Press of America.

Thorne, F. C. (1950). *Principles of personality counseling: An eclectic view*. Brandon, VT: Journal of Clinical Psychology.

Vitz, P. (1977). *Psychology as religion: The cult of self-worship*. Grand Rapids, MI: Eerdmans.

Voth, H. M., & Orth, M. H. (1973). *Psychotherapy and the role of the environment*. New York: Behavioral Press.

Wachtel, P. L. (1977). *Psychoanalysis and behavior therapy: Toward an integration*. New York: Basic Books.

Walls, G. B. (1980). Values and psychotherapy: A comment on "Psychotherapy and religious values." *Journal of Consulting and Clinical Psychology, 48*, 640–641.

Wilson, G. T., & Evans, I. M. (1977). The therapist-client relationship in behavior therapy. In A. S. Gurman & A. M. Razin (Eds.), *Effective psychotherapy. A handbook of research*. New York: Pergamon Press.

Wolpe, J. (1973). *The practice of behavior therapy*. New York: Pergamon.

Zilbergeld, B. (1983). *The shrinking of America. Myths of psychological change*. Boston: Little, Brown.

2

THE EVALUATION OF PSYCHOTHERAPY: RESEARCH DESIGN AND METHODOLOGY

ALAN E. KAZDIN

Western Psychiatric Institute and Clinic
University of Pittsburgh School of Medicine

INTRODUCTION

Psychotherapy holds great interest not only for professionals who are involved in its investigation and application but for others as well. Professional interest is evident in the continued evaluation of alternative treatment techniques, elaboration of their possible theoretical bases, and integration of alternative conceptual views and treatment approaches (see Garfield, 1980; Goldfried, 1982; Harvey & Parks, 1982). Apart from many substantive issues, methodological advances have also helped to sustain interest in psychotherapy research (e.g., Hersen, Michelson, & Bellack, 1984; Kazdin, 1980). As an example, the application of meta-analysis to the evaluation of psychotherapy (e.g., Smith, Glass, & Miller, 1980) has fostered renewed attention to basic

Completion of this chapter was supported by a Research Scientist Development Award (MH00353) and a grant (MH35408) from the National Institute of Mental Health.

questions about how treatment should be evaluated and the criteria for high-quality research.

Professional interest no doubt has been influenced by increased public scrutiny of psychotherapy. Proposals in the United States to include psychotherapy as part of a national health-care program and to underwrite the costs of psychotherapy have focused public, professional, and legislative attention on the efficacy, costs, and benefits of therapy (Garfield, 1981; Kiesler, 1980; Parloff, 1979). Professionals have attempted to identify the current status of psychotherapy research and the next steps that are needed to address critical questions (e.g., Hadley, 1984; Williams & Spitzer, 1984).

The questions of psychotherapy outcome are multiple. They have been integrated into a single, "ultimate question," expressed as: "*What* treatment, by *whom*, is most effective for *this* individual with *that* specific problem, under *which* set of circumstances?" (Paul, 1967b, p.111). The question has been widely cited and occasionally elaborated to specify further the conditions under which treatment produces change (Parloff, Wolfe, Hadley, & Waskow, 1978; Paul, 1969; Wilson & Rachman, 1983).

Developments within clinical psychology, psychiatry, and other mental health–related fields have helped to ensure that answers—or at least simple answers—to the above question are increasingly out of reach. To begin with, the number of therapy techniques has proliferated. Although at any given time it is difficult to pinpoint the precise number of techniques in use, surveys have revealed tremendous growth. In the early 1960s, approximately 60 different types of psychotherapy were identified (Garfield, 1982). By the mid-1970s, over 130 techniques were delineated (NIMH, 1975). By the late 1970s, growth continued to encompass over 250 techniques (Herink, 1980). A more recent count has placed the number of existing techniques well over 400 (Karasu, personal communication, March 1, 1985). The sheer number of techniques makes addressing the question about what techniques are to be applied to what problem a formidable task.

The effects of therapy of course need to be evaluated in relation to specific clinical problems. The maladaptive behaviors, target complaints, and dysfunctions now recognized as clinical problems have also proliferated. Consider, for example, the classification of clinical disorders over the last 35 years. Changes in the *Diagnostic and Statistical Manual of Mental Disorders* (*DSM*) illustrate the proliferation of recognized disorders. In the first edition (APA, 1952), slightly over 100 diagnostic categories were recognized; in the second edition (APA, 1968), this increased to over 180. In the third and most recent edition (APA, 1980), over 260 diagnostic categories were included. A linear extrapolation of this rate of growth would suggest that approximately 340 disorders will be delineated for the next edition (Sprock & Blashfield, 1983). As an illustration, the *DSM* conveys the proliferation of clinical disorders as finer distinctions are made in psychopathology. To evaluate therapy techniques in relation to clinical problems becomes increasingly difficult as the number of recognized problems increases.

Finally, the methods of assessing therapy outcome have also proliferated (see Lambert, Christensen, & DeJulio, 1983). Increased recognition of the diverse perspectives of evaluating treatment effects, multiple outcome criteria, and the multifaceted nature of clinical problems has increased the range of dependent measures appropriate for treatment evaluation. Also, specific areas of clinical assessment (e.g., cognitive assessment) have emerged with an expanding array of measurement tools (e.g., Kendall & Hollon, 1981; Merluzzi, Glass, & Genest, 1981). The further development and proliferation of assessment techniques increases the potential diversity of answers that can be reached about alternative treatments.

In short, the growth and complexity of the field have made the ultimate question to psychotherapy quite difficult to answer. Yet the complexity of the question about the effects of psychotherapy techniques on clinical problems does not make the situation hopeless. There are ways to address portions of the question in individual studies as part of a programmatic and broad-based research plan. The purpose of the present chapter is to elaborate alternative strategies that address the questions of treatment research and the assessment and design issues they raise. The chapter discusses different levels of analysis to evaluate therapy including a single-case and between-group research, as well as meta-analysis, different types of research such as laboratory analogues and clinical trials, and requirements of research that will optimize the conclusions that can be drawn about treatment.[1]

TREATMENT EVALUATION STRATEGIES

At the level of the individual investigation, questions about the effects of therapy can be evaluated through several different strategies (Kazdin, 1980). The individual strategies, illustrated below, convey how the questions of efficacy are addressed and the progression in the complexity of questions.

---

[1]There are several methodological issues pertinent to the evaluation of psychotherapy that are not addressed in the present chapter. With occasional exceptions, issues detailed in discussions of research design in previous editions of this *Handbook* will not be duplicated. For example, illustrations of naturalistic (correlational) and experimental studies and their integration, carefully detailed in the first edition (Kiesler, 1971), will not be duplicated here. Similarly, the discussion of alternative control groups and their characteristics, developed in the second edition (Gottman & Markman, 1978), will not be discussed.

Treatment Package Strategy

This strategy evaluates the effects of a particular treatment as that treatment ordinarily is used. The notion of a "package" emphasizes that treatment is examined in toto. The technique may be multifaceted and include several components, each of which may exert influence in its own right. Yet the question of initial concern is whether treatment introduced as a package produces therapeutic change. To rule out the influence of change as a function of historical events, maturation, spontaneous remission of the dysfunction, repeated testing, and other threats to internal validity, a no-treatment or waiting-list control condition is usually included in the design.

For example, Gordon et al. (1980) evaluated the effectiveness of a multifaceted psychosocial intervention with cancer patients (ages 18 to 75). The purpose of treatment was to ameliorate medical, psychological, and interpersonal problems associated with cancer including physical discomfort, emotional and affective reactions, psychiatric impairment, quality of life, and other domains. Patients ($n = 358$) with different types of cancer were assigned to either treatment or control conditions. Assignments were made in waves lasting six months to a year in part to avoid making simultaneous assignments of patients in the same hospital room to different groups. Patients assigned to the psychosocial intervention received special contact with a counselor during and after hospitalization. The intervention entailed educating the patient regarding how to live effectively with the disease, counseling the patient with regard to reactions and feelings, and providing supplementary resources that included consultations with other health care agents and professionals, as needed. Although counselors for the project represented different mental health disciplines, each patient was seen by a single counselor throughout the treatment. Contact with the patient was made daily in the hospital and posthospitalization as needed. Patients in the control group received routine medical treatment and hospital care but did not participate in the program.

Although the results varied in part as a function of cancer site (breast, lung, melanoma), the overall effects demonstrated greater improvements for treatment than for control subjects. Specifically, patients who received the psychosocial treatment showed greater reduction in negative affect, more realistic outlook on life, greater involvement in activities, and higher rate of return to work than did control patients. Moreover, the benefits were evident up to six months posthospitalization.

The investigation demonstrated the effectiveness of a multifaceted treatment involving multiple contacts, inpatient and outpatient components, referral to outside agencies and other mental health professionals, as needed, and so on. Many questions that might be raised about these ingredients and their impact on and contribution to therapeutic change extend beyond the treatment package strategy.

The treatment package strategy raises the most basic question about treatment, namely, does it work? Although the question of the treatment package strategy is stated generally, the treatment is evaluated in relation to a specific clinical problem and population. Thus, one can evaluate whether a particular treatment "works," given a narrow focus, rather than making assumptions that the treatment will affect heterogeneous groups of patients and problems in a uniform fashion (Kiesler, 1971). In clinical work, the strategy has immediate significance because of the priority accorded the alteration of a particular clinical problem. Once the technique has been shown to be effective for a particular problem, a variety of other research questions can be raised to understand how the technique works, how it can be improved, and its relative effectiveness when compared to various alternatives.

Dismantling Treatment Strategy

This dismantling strategy consists of analyzing the components of a given treatment package (Lang, 1969). After a particular package has been shown to produce therapeutic change, research that begins to analyze the basis for change assumes importance. To dismantle treatment, individual components are eliminated or isolated from the treatment. In a dismantling investigation, some subjects may receive the entire package, and others may receive the package minus one or more components. Dismantling strategies may determine the necessary and sufficient components for therapeutic change.

Dismantling research can serve multiple purposes. First, the strategy points to the specific ingredients or combinations of ingredients that are responsible for change. Hence, clinical practice can be improved by emphasizing those aspects that are more important to outcome than others. Second, the approach often has important theoretical implications. When crucial ingredients are identified, the investigator may be in a position to comment on the reasons *why* treatment produces change. The theoretical uses of dismantling treatment research are important, because they may suggest changes for the technique or new techniques that may prove to be even more effective.

As an example, Jacobson (1984) conducted a dismantling study to evaluate behavioral marital therapy for married couples currently living together. The treatment consists of two major components referred to as behavior exchange and communication problem-solving skills training. The components themselves are multifaceted but differ in their focus on identifying and altering behaviors at home (behavior exchange) or in identifying problems and applying strategies to anticipate future conflict situations (problem-solving skills). Clients were assigned to receive one of three treatment variations and received both components (the package), behavior exchange alone, or problem-solving skills training alone.

At the end of 12 to 16 treatment sessions, the alternative treatments showed significant improvements relative to waiting-list controls. The groups did not differ from each other on marital satisfaction and presenting problems but showed a few differences on positive and negative exchange behaviors. The group with the most consistent changes was the behavior exchange condition. Immediately after treatment, however, the components generally were no less effective than the overall package. At a six-month follow-up, important differences among treatments emerged. The full package and problem-solving groups maintained their gains and improved in some areas, whereas the behavior exchange group deteriorated. The results suggest that the problem-solving component makes a special contribution in helping to sustain the gains achieved in treatment.

The dismantling strategy requires that the treatment package consist of a delimited and reasonably well specified set of treatment components. Dismantling research can be completed only if the ingredients are carefully specified as part of the treatment. Dismantling research is greatly facilitated by having a tentative theoretical basis for explaining

the technique. The theory specifies the crucial interpretation of the mechanisms of treatment and directs the investigator to a particular set of components that warrant investigation. The results of the investigation ultimately may reflect on the specific theoretical proposition from which the research was derived.

Constructive Treatment Strategy

The constructive treatment strategy refers to developing a treatment package by adding components that may enhance outcome. In this sense, the constructive approach is the opposite of the dismantling strategy. Constructive treatment research begins with a treatment that may consist of one or a few ingredients or a larger package and adds various ingredients to determine whether the effects can be enhanced. The strategy asks the question, "What can be added to treatment to make it more effective?" As constructive research continues, theoretically a given technique may grow to encompass more and more procedures. Actually, in constructive research some ingredients are likely to enhance treatment and others will not. Those that improve outcome are retained, and added and those that do not are cast aside.

As an example, Weissman et al. (1979) evaluated whether the combination of interpersonal psychotherapy and medication (amitriptyline) combined was superior to either treatment given alone when administered to depressed adults (ages 18 to 65). Depressed patients were assigned either to individual psychotherapy that focused on the factors related to the personal and social context of depression, to medication, to both treatments combined, or to a nonscheduled-treatment control. In the control condition, patients could phone or visit a therapist for general supportive therapy as needed. Treatments were administered over a 16-week period. The results indicated that psychotherapy and medication administered separately were more effective in reducing symptoms than the nonscheduled-control treatment condition. The combined treatment was more effective than the other two treatments in reducing symptoms and delaying the symptoms when they recurred.

As with the dismantling strategy, the constructive approach may have implications for the theoretical basis of therapy or the nature of the clinical problem. Also, selected procedures may be identified through clinical work that suggests the limits of a singular approach on diverse facets of a problem. For example, for the treatment of depression, some evidence suggests that the combination of medication and psychotherapy may be especially useful because they each alter different aspects of the dysfunction (Klerman & Schechter, 1982). Thus, constructing a combined intervention has often produced broader therapeutic change than the individual components, although there are exceptions (e.g., Murphy, Simons, Wetzel, & Lustman, 1984). In the general case, however, more treatments (added to a package) may not necessarily produce better outcome. A constructive strategy is the means of addressing the question empirically.

Parametric Treatment Strategy
The parametric treatment strategy refers to altering specific aspects of a treatment to determine how to maximize therapeutic change. Dimensions or parameters are altered to find the optimal manner of administering the treatment. The approach resembles dismantling and constructive evaluation strategies because variations of a particular treatment are evaluated. However, components of treatment are not withdrawn (dismantling approach) or added (constructive approach). Rather, variables within the existing treatment are altered to find the optimal variation. Essentially, parametric research focuses on refining a particular technique. In parametric research, variations often are made along quantitative dimensions by presenting more or less of a given portion of treatment. Different groups might receive the same general treatment but differ in quantitative variations of a particular dimension associated with that treatment.

For example, parametric studies have been conducted with flooding as a treatment of agoraphobia (Stern & Marks, 1973) and obsessive-compulsive disorder (Rabavilas, Boulougouris, & Stefanis, 1976). Flooding requires confronting the patient with stimuli that promote anxiety or arousal until the adverse reaction is reduced and eliminated. An important parameter is the duration of exposure to the anxiety-provoking stimuli. The above investigations have demonstrated that longer periods of exposure are more effective than shorter ones and that exposure conducted in actual situations is more effective

than when conducted through imagery. These findings indicate two dimensions that can be manipulated within flooding to enhance treatment effects.

Most techniques include several dimensions that are unspecified in practice or research. A particular treatment can be conducted in many different ways and still qualify as that technique. For example, modeling generally consists of observing others engage in responses that are to be developed in the client. However, the general procedure leaves unspecified many important variables such as who the model is, how the model performs, how many models are presented, and so on (Rosenthal & Bandura, 1978). These variables all influence the effectiveness of the procedure, as investigated in parametric research.

Parametric treatment research is extremely important because it attempts to develop a particular technique. Relatively little parametric work exists. This is unfortunate because techniques often are proposed as effective and tested against other procedures before basic research has been conducted to explore parametric variations that maximize therapeutic change. Parametric research can have important implications for the theoretical basis of treatment in addition to developing more effective variations. The parametric variations that influence outcome may suggest the mechanisms responsible for therapeutic change. Also, and as noted with other strategies, understanding the mechanisms of change may lead to eventual improvements in treatment.

Comparative Treatment Strategy
In this strategy two or more different treatments are compared. The question addressed by this strategy is which treatment is better (or best) among various alternatives for a particular clinical problem. This strategy is extremely familiar to researchers because of the very wide interest that comparative studies hold. The interest derives from the specific treatments that are compared. Often the treatments are based on opposing conceptual approaches. Hence, the investigations of alternative techniques often are viewed as critical and even definitive tests of the constituent techniques.

Major comparative treatment studies have been completed in the last several years. For example, Paul and Lentz (1977) compared social learning and milieu therapies with routine hospital care for chronic psychiatric patients. In the social learning program, patients received tokens (colored plastic chips exchangeable for a variety of other rewards) for engaging in adaptive behaviors on the ward such as attending activities, going to group meetings and therapy sessions, and engaging in self-care behaviors (showering, grooming) and social interaction. Patients in the milieu condition participated in a therapeutic community, a way of structuring the ward to foster group interaction and responsibility. Expectations were made by staff for milieu patients to take responsibility for their behavior and to participate in group decision making and problem solving. Other patients received routine hospital care that excluded each of the above active interventions. Patients in both social learning and milieu programs improved more than routine care patients. Yet the social learning program was consistently more effective on measures of performance in the hospital, discharge of patients, and adjustment to the community from 1½ to 5 years after termination of the program.

In another landmark comparative study, Rush, Beck, Kovacs, and Hollon (1977) evaluated the relative effectiveness of pharmacotherapy and cognitive therapy for depressed outpatients. Pharmacotherapy patients received imipramine, a frequently used medication for clinical depression. Cognitive therapy patients received individual therapy designed to identify and alter maladaptive cognitions (attributions, interpretations, and beliefs) that fostered depression. Both treatments were conducted over a 12-week period. Although both treatments produced significant improvements in depressive symptoms, over the course of a one-year follow-up cognitive therapy tended to be superior (Kovacs, Rush, Beck, & Hollon, 1981).

In a final illustration, Sloane, Staples, Cristol, Yorkston, and Whipple (1975) compared behavior therapy and psychotherapy for outpatients with neurotic and personality disorders. Behavior therapy consisted of several procedures including systematic desensitization, relaxation, assertion training, and other techniques, as needed, as long as they focused directly on the client's behavioral problems. Psychotherapy consisted of such interventions as interpreting or reflecting memories, encouraging reports of dreams, and similar types of intrapsychic-oriented procedures. Other subjects

were placed in a waiting-list control group. For measures of target symptoms and general areas of functioning, behavior therapy and psychotherapy were no different from each other in effectiveness but both were superior to waiting-list controls. This latter group also improved over the four-month intervention in which other groups were treated.

The above comparative studies and others like them have attracted wide attention in part because they place into the empirical arena the many conflicting and hyperbolic claims made for the superiority of one technique over another. Yet comparative research introduces a number of special research problems that make it one of the more complex treatment evaluation strategies (Kazdin, 1980). When opposing techniques are compared, special difficulties often arise in keeping the techniques distinct, in holding constant variables associated with treatment administration (e.g., amount of treatment, spacing of treatment), utilizing therapists who can conduct both (or all) of the treatments, and ensuring the integrity of the individual treatments. In many comparative studies, questions can be raised about whether one treatment, usually the one to which the investigator may be less committed, received fair representation.

For example, in the Rush et al. (1977) study, concerns were voiced that the type, dose, and duration of the medication regimen to which cognitive therapy was compared were inappropriate or less than optimal (Becker & Schuckit, 1978). Similarly, complaints by proponents of behavior therapy have been levied at the Sloane et al. (1975) study, stating that the treatments were not adequately tested (Kazdin & Wilson, 1978b). Skepticism about whether each treatment within a comparative study is fairly tested has been bolstered by results of meta-analyses. Evidence suggests that the treatments to which investigators show allegiance yield greater therapeutic change (larger effect sizes) than those to which they are opposed or neutral (Smith et al., 1980). These results could suggest that treatments favored by investigators are more faithfully or enthusiastically rendered than comparison conditions. Whatever the reason for the difference, the results of individual comparative studies are more likely to stir controversy than to resolve the primary question of the relative efficacy of alternative treatments to anyone's satisfaction.

The comparative treatment strategy has obvious

value. In the long run, comparisons are essential to determine which technique should be applied to a given problem. Yet the importance of comparative research and the wide interest it attracts may lead to premature comparisons. Techniques often are compared long before they are well investigated or well understood. Hence, the versions that are compared may not provide the optimal treatment, and conclusions that are drawn may not be very meaningful or definitive.

The major contribution of comparative studies often is interim comparisons of the treatments (processes) rather than posttreatment effects (outcomes). Evaluation of the individual treatments may reveal important similarities and differences in how the treatments are executed that are significant in their own right. For example, in the Sloane et al. (1975) study, it was instructive to see that behavior therapists and psychotherapists were similar on such characteristics as warmth and positive regard and to see further that behavior therapists showed significantly higher levels of accurate empathy and interpersonal contact. The generality of the conclusions can be seriously questioned given the small number of psychotherapists ($n = 3$) and behavior therapists ($n = 3$). Nevertheless, the findings suggest that many of the differences in discussions about alternative therapies may be blurred in the actual practice of the treatments. Also, the findings provide information on the oft-cited characterization of behavior therapists as relatively cold, mechanical, and devoid of interpersonal attributes considered to be central to the treatment process, that is, the therapist resembles "a social reinforcement machine" (Krasner, 1962).

Within the Sloane et al. study, important differences emerged in how treatment was conducted, showing that behavior therapists were more directive than psychotherapists. Also, within the sessions, psychotherapists talked less than their patients, whereas the reverse was true of behavior therapists. These findings suggest some of the concrete ways in which alternative approaches manifest their differences and the many ways in which alternative approaches overlap. Only a comparative study that applied identical assessment strategies to processes of treatment could reveal such differences and similarities. Thus, comparative studies often are important for their contribution in characterizing alternative approaches empirically.

Process Research Strategy

The strategies outlined to this point reflect several outcome questions. The process of therapeutic change occasionally is not conceived as a strategy relevant to outcome research. Traditionally, process research has addressed questions about transactions between therapists and clients, the type of interactions, and their interim effects on client or therapist behavior (see Orlinksy & Howard, 1978). For example, process research may examine the perceptions of the clients and therapists over the course of treatment. Although such process factors may eventually be related to outcome, typically they have been studied independently of treatment efficacy.

Although processes of therapy can obviously be studied without regard to outcome, they can provide critical information regarding therapeutic change (Kiesler, 1973; Orlinsky & Howard, 1978; Rosen & Proctor, 1981). To begin with, measures during the course of treatment and within individual treatment sessions may be of clinical significance in their own right. The measures may reflect emotional, affective, or cognitive states (e.g., anxiety, pessimism), concrete behaviors (e.g., tics), or other symptoms (e.g., headache, elevated blood pressure). The fact that these measures are obtained during the treatment sessions does not in any way gainsay their clinical importance.

Second, processes within the session not directly related to symptoms may predict outcome. The processes identify antecedents to therapeutic change and may shed light on the treatment and/or the dysfunction to which it is applied. For example, research on psychotherapy processes has suggested that the attribute of "patient involvement" in the sessions predicts improvement at the end of treatment (Gomes-Schwartz, 1978; O'Malley, Suh, & Strupp, 1983). Patient involvement suggests a possible mechanism through which treatment achieves its effects. Further research is, of course, needed to examine the patient, therapist, and technique variables that may account for such a relationship; however, the process variable reflects an important antecedent to therapeutic change.

Third, and related to the above, the study of processes and outcomes together is a critical step in generating or evaluating theory about the basis of particular treatment techniques. Tests of the theoretical bases of alternative treatments are difficult to conduct in outcome research. The leap from theory about treatment to effects produced in outcome studies is rather large because many alternative interpretations invariably can account for the pattern of results. Process measures are essential to identify critical links between intervention and outcome and to operationalize constructs that are posited as important in theory (Rosen & Proctor, 1981). For example, in rational-emotive psychotherapy, intervention effects are considered to result from changes in irrational beliefs that patients bring to treatment. Smith (1983) demonstrated that outpatients assigned to rational-emotive therapy decreased in irrational beliefs and that the degree of change was related to symptom improvement. This finding is a valuable beginning to support the theoretical notions about the technique. Further work can relate similar irrational beliefs at different points in treatment to subsequent outcome and examine whether belief changes result from the attention they explicitly receive in treatment or occur in other treatment or control conditions even if they are not discussed.

Given the above points, it should be clear that process studies are not ancillary to or independent of outcome research. The study of therapy processes can impinge on each of the different treatment evaluation strategies. For example, the study of processes can help reveal the impact of different components of treatment (e.g., as in dismantling, constructive, and parametric strategies) or delineate unique characteristics of alternative treatments (e.g., as in comparative studies). To address the theoretical questions about alternative techniques and their impact on therapeutic change requires the simultaneous examination of process and outcome (Kiesler, 1971).

Client and Therapist Variation Strategy

Previous strategies emphasize the technique as a major source of treatment variance. Obviously, the effectiveness of alternative treatments is likely to vary as a function of characteristics of the clients and therapists. The client and therapist variation strategy examines whether alternative attributes of the clients or therapists contribute to outcome.

The usual way in which the strategy is implemented is to select clients, (or therapists) according to a particular subject variable such as age, gender, socioeconomic standing, marital status, education, severity of the disorder, level of anxiety or introver-

sion, and so on (Garfield, 1978). Therapist variables have been studied in a similar fashion by looking at such characteristics as therapist training, years of experience, age, interest, empathy, warmth, and so on (Barrett & Wright, 1984).

An illustration of the impact of therapist characteristics on outcome was reported in a study that evaluated treatment for families of juvenile delinquents (Alexander, Barton, Schiavo, & Parsons, 1976). Adolescents (ages 13 to 16) and their families were seen in treatment that was designed to alter family communication patterns and interaction. Treatment focused on modeling, prompting, and reinforcement of clear communication and clear presentation of demands and on generating alternative solutions to problems. Therapist characteristics were rated prior to treatment and included several dimensions such as affective behavior, humor, warmth, directiveness, self-confidence, self-disclosure, blaming, and clarity of communications. Given the intercorrelation patterns, two larger dimensions were generated to describe the therapists and were referred to as relationship (affective behavior, warmth, and humor) and structuring (directiveness and self-confidence) dimensions. The results indicated that treatment outcome, as defined by recidivism among the adolescents, changes in family communication, and continuing in treatment were predicted by relationship and structuring dimensions of the therapist. Indeed, approximately 60 percent of the outcome variance was accounted for by these therapist dimensions.

When clients and therapists are classified according to a particular variable, the main question addressed is whether treatment is more or less effective with certain kinds of participants. The question is directed to the generality of treatment effects by looking at the types of clients to whom treatment can be extended. Examination of the generality of treatment effects in this fashion greatly increases the information about treatment and addresses sophisticated questions about outcome. The question of which treatment or treatment variation produces greater effects is a very global one. Research among diverse techniques and clinical problems suggests that treatments are differentially effective as a function of other variables related to clients and therapists (e.g., Monroe, Bellack, Hersen, & Himmelhoch, 1983; Steinmetz, Lewinsohn, & Antonuccio, 1983). Outcome research can profit greatly from increasing the degree of specificity in delineating the characteristics of persons who receive and who provide treatment and integrating these characteristics into a theoretical framework about the processes leading to therapeutic change.

Combined Strategies

The alternative strategies identify questions about treatment and some of the variables with which treatment interacts. The delineation of specific strategies has didactic value by isolating questions about treatment effects. Moreover, investigators frequently follow one of the strategies very closely. Yet the individual strategies can be readily combined. Their combinations warrant brief comment because they reflect the movement toward greater specificity in the question asked of therapy.

A combined strategy might be delineated as a client–therapist–technique strategy that recognizes that the effects of a given technique may well depend upon characteristics of client, therapist, and treatment. The variables that are altered to evaluate the technique may embrace any of the strategies noted above. Client, therapist, and techniques are not the only domains of variables that are combined. However, their emphasis is important for different reasons. Kiesler (1966) has noted that uniformity myths implicit in psychotherapy research result from a failure to distinguish among types of clients, therapists, and techniques. The combined strategy addresses the assumptions about uniformity by testing interactions among client, therapist, and technique variables (Kiesler, 1971; Paul, 1969). Factorial designs can evaluate increasingly specific questions about what techniques work for whom and under what circumstances.

General Comments

The delineation of specific evaluation strategies isolates different types of questions that are essential to address in understanding fully how a particular technique operates and how it can be applied so as to maximize its efficacy. The strategies focus on different types of studies and domains of variables. Although emphasis was placed on client, therapist, and technique domains, there are a number of other variables that do not fit into these categories. Variations of the methods by which clients select treatments or therapists, instructional sets, and whether or how clients pay for treatment, for example, can be fit into the above categories and strate-

gies but address another domain that might be more aptly denoted as contextual variables. Thus, the above delineation of strategies is not necessarily exhaustive in the context of what can be studied in or about psychotherapy.

The different strategies reflect a logical progression in the type of questions that are addressed about treatment. The progression can be seen in the specificity of the questions and the type of control and comparison conditions they require. The treatment package strategy, as an initial approach, addresses a rather gross question about the effects of a treatment with a particular problem and population. Once the technique has been shown to predict change, more analytic and synthetic questions become important as reflected by dismantling, parametric, constructive, and possibly process studies.

A high degree of operationalization is needed to investigate dismantling, constructive, and parametric questions. In each case, specific components or ingredients of therapy have to be sufficiently well specified to be withdrawn, added, or varied in an overall treatment package. In relatively few therapy techniques are the critical procedures specified to permit careful analytic investigation for dismantling, constructive, or parametric research.

Comparative research probably warrants attention after prior work has been conducted that not only indicates the efficacy of individual techniques but also shows how the techniques should be administered to increase their efficacy, that is, based on information about the parametric variations, applications to specify types of clients or therapists, and so on. Obviously, comparative research can be and frequently is conducted before very much is known about the constituent techniques.

The progression of research can also be discerned by examining the different types of control or comparison groups (see Gottman & Markman, 1978). Basic questions about treatment packages require use of no-treatment and waiting-list control groups to rule out influences associated with history, maturation, repeated testing, and others. Alternatively, attempts to evaluate the bases of treatment or why it produces the effects it does may utilize so-called attention-placebo conditions or a form of therapist–patient contact that is designed to exclude putatively crucial treatment ingredients. As treatment evaluation progresses, active treatments varying in specific parameters of components may be used as the comparison conditions. And, of course, in comparative research alternative treatments serve as the comparison groups.

Although it is easy to identify logical progressions of therapy research in terms of the complexity of questions that are addressed or the type of control group that is employed, the actual emergence of research does not necessarily follow this pattern (see Agras & Berkowitz, 1980). The reasons are manifold but in part include the significance of certain types of demonstrations whenever they occur in the evolution of research. For example, even though outcome research on psychoanalysis and systematic desensitization are at quite different stages, a solid treatment package study on either approach for the treatment of virtually any problem in a well defined and clearly delineated clinical population would be an important and timely contribution. The sophistication of the clinical-research question is not the only determinant of the contribution of the study. The individual merit of the study and its relevance to theory or clinical work also play important roles in determining the progression of research.

CONDITIONS OF RESEARCH

The evaluation strategies identify the major types of questions that research can address. The experimental conditions in which these questions are investigated can vary widely. The conditions are often delineated by the extent to which they resemble treatment of patients in clinical settings. Analogue research and clinical trials, two points on a continuum of resemblance of research conditions to clinical practice, have been utilized heavily in treatment outcome studies and raise central issues for the evaluation of psychotherapy.

Analogue Research
Characteristics
Conducting outcome research raises a host of problems that can impede careful experimentation. To begin with, it is often difficult to obtain a sufficient number of clients with the same or similar clinical problem. Similarity among the clients is important so that the same sorts of measures can be used. Even if enough clients with similar problems can be

found, there often are restraints in assigning clients to conditions. Random assignment, dictated by sound methodology, often cannot be permitted because of the client's preferences for treatment and administrative restrictions for assigning persons to groups (e.g., inpatient treatment). Difficulties also arise in obtaining therapists who are willing to participate in an outcome study and who can administer alternative treatments or treatment variations.

Ethical issues can also impede clinical research. Many of the important questions of therapy require control groups that withhold specific aspects of treatment. Assigning clients to "control" conditions that have a low probability of producing change would be an obvious violation of the professional commitment to treatment. Also, the possible or relative ineffectiveness of various treatment or control conditions can lead to high levels of attrition, which can greatly interfere with research.

The research problems highlighted here suggest that clinical settings may not be the place to address all or perhaps even most of the questions entailed by therapy. To overcome many of the obstacles, research has been conducted in situations and under circumstances *analogous* to those of the clinic. Research that evaluates treatment under conditions that only resemble or approximate the clinical situation has been referred to as *analogue research*.

Different types of analogue research have been employed to evaluate therapeutic processes and behavior change. Analogue research can vary widely in the degree of resemblance to the clinical situation to which the investigator may wish to generalize. Animal (infrahuman) analogues have been used to study behavior change processes that appear to be relevant for therapy (Adams & Hughes, 1976). Alternatively, contrived laboratory arrangements with human subjects provide analogues of specific phenomena or processes that occur in therapy (Heller, 1971).

In contemporary treatment research, analogue studies refer primarily to investigations of treatment procedures in the context of highly controlled laboratory conditions. Analogue studies have several characteristics (Borkovec & Rachman, 1979; Kazdin, 1978). First, the target problem usually departs from the typical problems seen in inpatient or outpatient treatment. The problems (e.g., fears, social skills deficits) usually are less severe and more circumscribed than those problems patients ordinarily bring to treatment. The problems in analogue research and clinical treatment may differ along quantitative and qualitative dimensions.

Second, the persons who receive treatment in analogue research usually differ from persons seen in clinical settings. Typically, college students and volunteers serve as subjects. They are recruited quite differently from the procedures that bring clinical patients to treatment. In analogue research, subjects are actively solicited; course credit or money often are offered as incentives for participation. The resulting sample is likely to vary in subject and demographic variables from persons usually seen in clinics.

Third, the motivations and expectancies of persons seen in analogue research are likely to vary from those who ordinarily seek treatment. In clinical settings, persons usually seek treatment for relief from a particular problem that may have reached a crisis point. Patients are likely to expect to benefit from the results and to hope for improvements before and during treatment (Frank, 1973). In contrast, subjects in analogue research may not be interested in treatment or in "cures" for their problems. The expectancies of persons who receive the intervention may be quite different in analogue and clinical research.

Fourth, graduate or undergraduate students usually serve as therapists in analogue research and differ considerably in subject and demographic variables and clinical experience from professional clinicians. The differences may also extend to the credibility of the therapist as a provider of treatment and to the expectations for improvement that therapists generate in their clients.

Fifth, the manner of delivering treatment in analogue research varies greatly from treatment in clinical settings. In analogue research, treatments often are standardized, so that all persons in a particular treatment condition or group receive the identical treatment with little or no individualization. Many features of treatment, such as duration or number of sessions, and statements that can be made by the therapist, usually allowed to vary in clinical settings, are often meticulously controlled in analogue research. Treatment may be administered in a relatively pure form in analogue research, because it is applied to a circumscribed problem. Because clinical patients usually bring complex problems to treatment, techniques are often combined and included as part of a multifaceted intervention.

Advantages and Limitations

Analogue research has as its major advantage the capacity to surmount many of the methodological, practical, and ethical issues associated with conducting research in clinical settings. The limited experimental control allowed in many clinical settings restricts the type of questions that can be asked in clinical outcome studies. The priority of analogue research is the experimental question rather than treatment delivery. Thus, conditions in analogue research can be arranged in ways that usually would not be feasible in clinical settings. Because of obstacles in clinical research, and often the lack of availability of clinical populations to researchers, circumscribed features of the therapy process and behavior change are often examined in analogue studies. Analogue research provides opportunities to evaluate mechanisms of therapeutic change and to dismantle treatment by looking at basic elements and their contribution to outcome. The ability to control multiple conditions of the experiment and, consequently, to minimize variability in the data, permits analogue research to address questions that would otherwise be difficult to study.

Analogue research, however, bears potential costs as well as benefits. The obvious concern with analogue research is the extent to which the results can be generalized to the clinical setting. Since analogue studies depart in varying degrees from the clinical situation, perhaps the applicability and generality of the results depart commensurately. Generality of results from analogue studies to clinical situations probably is a complex function of the several variables, including the treatment technique, the clinical problem, and characteristics of the patients and the therapist (Kazdin, 1978). Thus, the fact that treatment research is conducted under well-controlled analogue conditions does not automatically delimit the results.

Clinical Trials

Characteristics

Clinical trials refer generally to outcome investigations conducted in clinical settings. Because the research is conducted in a clinical setting, methodological compromises and sacrifices often have to be made to meet practical, administrative, and, of course, ethical demands (Kraemer, 1981). For example, withholding treatment, as practiced for no-treatment or waiting-list control conditions, is especially difficult with a clearly identified clinical problem for a patient in distress. Yet the obstacles can be overcome in varying degrees to address the important questions of extending research to clinical settings.

In relation to analogue research, the characteristics of clinical trials usually are easily discerned. Instead of students or volunteers, patients who actively seek treatment are included in clinical studies; instead of graduate students, professional therapists and clinicians provide treatment; instead of treatment of relatively mild, subclinical, and circumscribed problems, relatively severe or multifaceted clinical disorders are treated. In short, in a clinical trial, treatment is tested under many of the conditions where it would ordinarily be applied.

Actually, clinical trials are not qualitatively different from analogue research. On a variety of dimensions related to the resemblance of research to the clinical situation, analogue research and clinical trials represent end points. However, resemblance to the clinical situation is a matter of degree on each dimension. Table 2.1 illustrates several dimensions and different points on the continuum of degree of resemblance to the clinical situation. As shown in the table, an investigation with conditions listed under analogue research or clinical trials, respectively, departs considerably from or very closely resembles the usual conditions of clinical settings. Once the extreme points are identified, it is clear that research can in varying degrees fall somewhere between these extremes.

Much of contemporary research probably falls between the categories of clear analogue research or clinical trials. For example, in the extreme case, analogue studies have focused on college students with subclinical problems (e.g., Paul, 1966). In contrast, clinical trials have focused on patients who have come for treatment at a clinic under the usual conditions for obtaining treatment (e.g., Paul & Lentz, 1977; Sloane et al., 1975). A considerable amount of contemporary research utilizes subjects who fall intermediate in terms of how they are recruited. Through the use of newspaper, television, and radio advertisements, researchers frequently solicit volunteers from the community setting who are interested in receiving treatment. The stringency of the screening criteria that are invoked further determines the extent to which the study will resemble conditions of clinical practice. If stringent criteria are invoked to identify persons with clear dysfunctions, then, of course, the severity of the problems that are studied may be very close to what is seen in clinical work. If lenient criteria or no criteria are invoked, the investigation may constitute only a nugatory step above the usual analogue population.

Even if subjects are recruited because of the clinical severity of their problems, they may differ slightly from persons with similar problems who ordinarily seek treatment (cf. Berrier, Galassi, & Mullinix, 1981; Galassi, Berrier, & Mullinix, 1982). Perhaps volunteers have not sought treatment previously because they did not perceive their dysfunction as sufficiently debilitating or because other aspects of their lives (e.g., work, marital adjustment, social network) were quite satisfactory. The advertisements for free treatment may have provided a sufficient impetus to try treatment that would otherwise have not been sought. A clinical population with the "same" presenting problem might differ from a volunteer population in a variety of background or contextual dimensions that make the need for treatment more pressing. The differences between volunteers solicited for treatment and clients with similar problems and the relevance of these differences for generality of the conclusions that are reached with volunteer populations have not been fully addressed in research.

Consider as a concrete example, variations of an investigation that is designed to identify effective treatments for obesity. An analogue variation of the study might include college students who are 5 to 10 percent overweight and who do not fall within the usual range of obesity. A clinical trial might be conducted at a treatment facility and include a more extreme group of persons who are say, 20 percent or greater in their overweight. A study falling intermediate might seek volunteers from the community who are interested in losing weight. Suppose only those persons who meet stringent standards (e.g., 20 percent or more overweight) are included in the investigation. Thus, the presenting problem is of equal severity to that seen in clinic settings. The fact

TABLE 2.1   Selected Dimensions Along Which Investigations May Vary in Their Degree of Resemblance to the Clinical Situation

Dimension	Resemblance to the Clinical Situation		
	Relatively Little Resemblance (Analogue Research)	Moderate Resemblance	Identity with or Relatively High Resemblance (Clinical Trials)
Target problem	Nonproblem behavior, laboratory task performance, mild problem at subclinical levels	Similar to that seen in the clinic but probably less severe or more circumscribed	Problem seen in the clinic, intense or disabling
Population	Infrahuman subjects, nonclinical group such as college students chosen primarily because of their accessibility	Volunteers screened for problem and interest in treatment	Clients in outpatient clinic
Manner of recruitment	Captive subjects who receive special incentives (e.g., course credit) for participating	Persons recruited especially for available treatment	Clients who have sought treatment without solicitations from the clinic
Therapists	Nontherapists, nonprofessionals, students, automated presentation of major aspects of treatment (audio or videotapes)	Therapists in training with some previous clinical experience	Professional therapists
Selection of treatment	Client assigned to treatment with no choice of specific therapist or condition	Client given choice over some alternatives in an experiment	Client chooses therapist and specific treatment
Client set	Expect an experimental arrangement with a nontreatment focus	Expect "experimental" treatment with unclear effects	Expect a veridical treatment and improvement
Setting of treatment	Laboratory; academic, psychology department	University clinic devised for treatment delivery with established clientele	Professional treatment facility with primary function of delivering treatment
Variation of treatment	Standardized, abbreviated, or narrowly focused version of treatment	Variation that permits some individualization and flexibility in content and/or duration	Treatment tailored to the individual or determined on the basis of the client's problems

that in one case (clinical trials) subjects were not solicited to come to a treatment setting and in the other case they were may not be relevant in terms of generality of the results to the clinical situation.

Treatments shown to be effective in reducing weight might not depend on how these subjects were recruited.

On the other hand, it is possible that volunteers

recruited for research differ in important ways from persons who seek and perhaps repeatedly have sought treatment. Volunteers may be more (or less) responsive to an intervention because of fewer previous formal treatment trials, have special motivation to adhere to treatment demands, have less dysfunction in other areas of their lives, have stronger support systems (e.g., spouses, children) that can sustain gains produced with treatment, and so on. The existence of such differences and their plausibility in influencing generality of the results obtained with volunteers to clinical samples are a matter of surmise. The general point, however, is that even when volunteers and clinical samples share the same presenting problems, generality may still be an open question because of other differences between the samples.

Clinical trials can vary markedly along a variety of dimensions and in their resemblance to the clinical situation where treatment is ordinarily practiced. In clinical trials, as in analogue research, many features of treatment delivery may be altered to permit evaluation of the intervention. The research exigencies may make the situation slightly different from the clinical situation. Thus, in some clinical trials, the most severely disturbed or impaired patients may be excluded. For example, depressed patients whose dysfunctions are severe may be intentionally excluded from the protocol and placed under immediate care because treatments with known efficacy exist. Similarly, screening criteria of patients for clinical trials often select patients who have circumscribed or well-delineated dysfunctions rather than diffuse and multiple disorders. In any case, patients included in clinical trials are not always the same as those seen in routine treatment.

Advantages and Limitations

Clinical trials are conducted under varying conditions that closely resemble clinical settings, but the conditions are not necessarily identical. There is general agreement that clinical trials represent something of a final achievement or end point in outcome research in terms of the evolution of evaluation strategies (Parloff, 1979). Positive leads from case studies, uncontrolled trials, and analogue studies can culminate in a clinical demonstration. Once a controlled clinical trial attests to the efficacy of treatment, the research process has achieved a major accomplishment. The evidence is considered to attest to the effectiveness of treatment when applied clinically.

Even though clinical trials test treatments under clinic conditions, generality of the results to clinical settings may still be a relevant concern. Clinical trials often introduce special features into the situation to meet the demands of research that depart from most clinical applications of treatment (Agras & Berkowitz, 1980; Emmelkamp, 1979). The degree of experimental control, the careful application of treatment, and monitoring of treatment administration are some of the features that characterize research rather than clinical applications of treatment. The differences in rigor and care in administering treatment may be quite relevant to the outcome. Whether the effects of treatment applied in clinical practice achieve the effects demonstrated in research is an open question.

General Comments

An obviously central issue is the extent to which the results of analogue research can be generalized to the clinical setting. Many important considerations must be borne in mind in even raising this question. Since both analogue and clinical studies depart from the clinical situation, an overriding generality issue is the extent to which findings obtained in research generalize to clinical work. The extent to which variation on particular characteristics in analogue and clinical studies affects generality of results raises questions that can be settled only empirically. There are few data on the individual dimensions and how they affect outcome. Recent meta-analyses of psychotherapy effects have, however, yielded evidence on selected issues. For example, effect sizes have been shown to be greater for treatments applied to college students and volunteers than for patients who solicit treatment (Smith et al., 1980). This would suggest that conclusions about the magnitude of treatment effects obtained with college student volunteers who often are unselected for a particular dysfunction could overestimate the effects obtained with patient samples. Dimensions that may affect generality of results from analogue research to clinical trials and from research to practice need further study.

Analogue research and clinical trials represent complementary types of research. Analogue research is especially well suited to analyze facets of treatment and to evaluate the underlying mechanisms responsible for change, the parameters that influence treatment efficacy, and similar questions requiring careful experimental control. Clinical trials are especially well suited for examining the effectiveness of alternative techniques under conditions that approximate routine clinical care. The complexities and priorities of the treatment settings make evaluation of subtle questions about particular treatments difficult. Hence theory testing, dissection of treatment, and evaluation of subtle treatment parameters that may influence outcome are usually reserved for analogue research. The selection of analogue or clinical research needs to be dictated by the questions that are addressed and the conclusions the investigator ultimately wishes to draw.

EVALUATION IN CLINICAL PRACTICE

Research on treatment and its effect typically has been conducted in the context of between-group experimental designs, following the strategies outlined earlier. In the last several years, there has been increased recognition of the need for research strategies that can evaluate treatment with the single case, that is, the individual client who is seen in treatment. Single-case research designs serve several different functions. First, the absence of a clear research methodology at the level of the individual client helps to foster and sustain the frequently lamented hiatus between clinical research and practice. Persons who conduct research rarely also engage in clinical practice, and vice versa (Garfield & Kurtz, 1976). Treatment research often is conducted in academic departments and university clinics, where the conditions of treatment administration and the types of clients depart considerably from those found in clinical treatment services (Kazdin, 1978; Raush, 1974). Consequently, treatment investigations often have little bearing on the questions and concerns of practitioners (Fishman, 1981).

Researchers and clinicians alike have repeatedly acknowledged the basic irrelevance of clinical research to clinical practice (Bergin & Strupp, 1972; Hayes, 1981). Part of the problem is that clinical investigations are invariably conducted with groups of persons in order to meet the demands of traditional experimental design and statistical evaluation. But investigation of groups and conclusions

about average patient performance can misrepresent the effects of treatments on individuals. Hence, researchers have suggested that experimentation at the level of the individual case can provide insights into therapeutic change (Barlow, 1981; Bergin & Strupp, 1972).

A second and related benefit of single-case designs pertains directly to treatment evaluation. Single-case designs can address several important questions of outcome research with individual clients. The most basic question is whether a particular treatment is responsible for change. This question can be addressed by any one of several single-case designs. In addition, certain designs allow comparison of alternative treatments or combinations of treatments for a given client. In treating individual clients, the clinician does not have the luxury enjoyed by researchers of applying a standardized treatment in a predetermined fashion independent of its effects on the client. Rather, the clinician must try to produce change and make decisions about modifying treatments in light of the client's progress. Single-case designs permit changes to be made in the course of ongoing treatment and evaluation of progress.

The full gamut of outcome questions for treatment research is not always of interest to the practicing clinician. Some questions address theoretical issues about treatment and the mechanisms through which change is produced. Although these questions are important, it may not be appropriate to examine them at the level of the individual patient who is in need of treatment. The practicing clinician is, however, interested in basic outcome questions, such as whether treatment produces change, whether one treatment works better than another, and whether a combination of alternative treatments is superior to the constituent treatments alone. All of these questions are amenable to single-case research.

A third benefit of single-case research and intensive study of the individual case is related to the emergence of research on the organization of personality and behavior. Personality research characteristically has focused on the assessment of groups of persons, although several proposals to investigate the individual have been advanced and pursued in varying degrees (Allport, 1962; Kelly, 1955). More recent work has underscored the importance of focusing on the individual for assessment in clinical work. The organization of behavior and personality includes idiosyncratic components that sometimes can be revealed and investigated only at the level of the individual (e.g., Pervin, 1977; Wahler, 1975). Identification of idiosyncratic patterns of behavior does not gainsay the significance of more general patterns of responses among subjects. However, the assessment of individual subjects and evaluation of their idiosyncratic patterns of organizing response repertoires may be particularly relevant for understanding clinical problems and evaluating the broad effects that interventions are likely to have across behaviors and settings and over time (Kazdin, 1982b).

Although intensive study of the individual client in clinical work can provide important information, the yield depends on how the evaluation is conducted. In delineating the different strategies to study the single case, it is useful to distinguish three types of strategies mentioned by Campbell and Stanley (1966). They included pre-experimental research, quasi-experiments, and true experiments. The strategies differ in the extent to which they rule out threats to internal validity in experimentation and hence make implausible rival interpretations of the results.

In *pre-experimental* demonstrations "causal interpretations" cannot be drawn regarding the impact of a particular intervention. The uncontrolled case study qualifies as pre-experimental. In *quasi-experiments* the impact of threats to internal validity can often be minimized. Yet critical features of the demonstrations (e.g., assignment of subjects to conditions) often cannot be arranged in such a way as to rule out threats to internal validity with a high degree of confidence. Whether such threats are ruled out is a matter of degree. The distinguishing characteristic is that central features that minimize the impact of threats to internal validity (e.g., random assignment of subjects to conditions) cannot be invoked. Often quasi-experiments can be designed in such a way as to maximize the scientific yield and approach the level of confidence achieved with true experiments. *True experiments* are those demonstrations in which the most stringent methodological desiderata can be applied and control over the intervention and assignment of subjects is maximized.

Case Study

The case study, or the intensive study of the individual, has played a central role in clinical psychology.

Indeed, understanding of the individual is considered to be a distinguishing characteristic of clinical psychology (Korchin, 1976; Watson, 1951). The intensive study of the individual client has contributed to knowledge in several areas of clinical work. Modern psychiatric diagnosis began with the careful analyses and accumulation of individual cases (Kraepelin, 1883). Also, information about disorders that are relatively rare (e.g., multiple personality) has come primarily from careful, in-depth descriptions of individual cases (e.g., Thigpen & Cleckley, 1957). Perhaps the greatest impact of the case study has been in the area of treatment. The history of many psychotherapy techniques or conceptual models on which they are based can be traced to the influence of one or a few cases (e.g., Little Hans, Anna O., Little Albert, Peter).

The case study can serve several valuable functions such as casting doubt on general theories, generating hypotheses about treatment and clinical dysfunction, evaluating rare phenomena, providing opportunities for new applications of existing treatments, and others (Kazdin, 1980; Lazarus & Davison, 1971). Despite its recognized heuristic value, the case study usually is considered to be inadequate as a basis for drawing scientifically valid inferences. Uncontrolled case studies characteristically rely on anecdotal information such as clinical impressions, judgments, and inferences. They lack the experimental control procedures that are required to draw firm conclusions. For example, treatment for a particular case may be associated with therapeutic change. However, the basis of change cannot be determined from an uncontrolled case study. Even if treatment were responsible for change, several alternative interpretations of the case might be proposed. These alternative interpretations of course refer to threats to internal validity, which may be mistaken for treatment effects (Campbell & Stanley, 1966).

Alternative proposals have been advanced to study individuals in a way that would permit valid inferences to be drawn about therapeutic change (Chassan, 1979; Shapiro & Ravenette, 1959). Single-case research designs have emerged as a unique methodology within the last several years and permit experimental evaluation of alternative treatments with individual subjects. It is useful to first outline true single-case experiments because they are more familiar than quasi-experimental arrangements involving the single case. Also, characteristics that can be used to rule out threats to internal validity in quasi-experiments are related to essential features of single-case experiments.

True Experimental Designs

Single-case experiments permit inferences to be drawn about intervention effects by utilizing the patient as his or her own control. The impact of treatment is examined in relation to changes in the patient's dysfunction over time. There are several characteristic requirements to determine whether therapeutic change has occurred and whether the intervention rather than extraneous factors accounts for change.

Characteristics

A major requirement of single-case experiments is specification of the goals of treatment or those symptoms and areas of functioning that are to be altered. Operationally, this means that measures need to be selected that would be expected to reflect progress in treatment. There are no inherent limitations regarding the facets of the patient's symptoms that are assessed. Measures of cognition, affect, behavior, psychophysiology, or personality dimensions can be used. Yet the clinician needs to identify prior to applying treatment what sorts of changes will be used to evaluate progress.

Second, single-case designs require the use of repeated observations of performance over time. The measures selected to evaluate progress in treatment are administered on several occasions, usually before the treatment is applied and continuously over the course of treatment. Ideally, assessment is conducted on a daily basis or at least on multiple occasions each week. Continuous assessment allows the clinician to examine the pattern and stability of performance before treatment is initiated and to compare performance under different conditions (e.g., treatment and no-treatment or alternative treatment conditions).

Third, single-case experiments require the delineation of different phases or periods in which alternative conditions (baseline, treatment) are in effect. Typically, the designs begin with a period of assessment referred to as the baseline (pretreatment) phase. Baseline data are obtained on several occasions before treatment is initiated. Baseline data describe the existing level of the problem and hence serve a descriptive function. The data also serve as a basis for predicting the likely level of performance in

the immediate future if treatment is not provided. This predictive function is critical to the logic of single-case designs. Data from the treatment phase are compared with the level of performance predicted from baseline. Essentially, the projected level of baseline serves as a criterion to evaluate whether treatment has led to change. Presumably, if treatment is effective, performance during the treatment phase will differ from the projected level of baseline. The use of multiple phases where projections of performance are tested against actual behavior once conditions (phases) are changed provide the basis for drawing causal relations between interventions and behavior change.

Fourth, it is important that the data be relatively stable because performance across phases is used to predict how the patient will respond in the immediate future. A stable rate of performance means the absence of a trend and relatively little variability. A trend in baseline data is problematic only if it is in a therapeutic direction, that is, reflecting an improvement. Unless the onset of treatment is associated with a sharp acceleration in this trend, it might be difficult to discern whether improvements were associated with treatment. Similarly, if variability in the data is relatively large, it is difficult to predict a stable level of performance in the future. Obtaining stable performance data during baseline and treatment phases usually is not a problem. When these problems do arise, statistical techniques can be used to clarify the data (Kazdin, 1982a).

There are other characteristics that have been associated with single-case designs but are not defining characteristics. For example, most designs use one or a few subjects, although the number of subjects per se is not a central feature. Outside of the context of psychotherapy studies, the designs have been used to evaluate interventions involving thousands or even more than a million subjects as in large-scale community and city-wide applications (McSweeney, 1978; Schnelle et al., 1978). Single-case designs have been used to evaluate intervention effects on overt behavior. The methodology is not restricted to overt behavior but only requires continuous assessment over time. Finally, data generated in single-case research typically have been evaluated through visual inspection rather than inferential statistics. Part of the reliance on visual inspection results from interest in identifying strong intervention effects that produce clear and clinically significant changes (Baer, 1977). Yet statistical techniques are available and can often be applied to data from single-case designs (Kazdin, 1984).

Illustration

There are several different single-case designs that vary in how baseline and intervention conditions are arranged and presented to the subject(s).[2] The designs are true experiments because the scheduling and presentation of the intervention are arranged in such a way as to rule out or make highly implausible the impact of extraneous factors. For example, in a multiple-baseline design, the intervention is introduced sequentially across different behaviors, clients, or settings. Essentially, two or more baselines are assessed (e.g., symptom areas or performance across different situations). The effect of treatment is demonstrated if changes are associated with the application of treatment to the specific symptoms or situation as treatment is extended in a sequential fashion.

For example, Kandel, Ayllon, and Rosenbaum (1977) treated a severely withdrawn boy (diagnosed as autistic) enrolled in a school for children with speech, hearing, and emotional disorders. At school, the child spent his free time alone, often talking to himself. Treatment was designed to increase social interaction with his peers. Treatment was introduced into two free-play periods at school. Treatment consisted of first having a trainer model or demonstrate appropriate social interaction for the child. Two other children were included and were encouraged to play with the boy. Rewards (candy) were given to the two children for their help with training. To demonstrate that the intervention was responsible for change, it was introduced to the two free-play periods at school at different points in time (on the playground and in the courtyard at juice time). As shown in Figure 2.1, social interaction increased in each of the situations when treatment was introduced. The increases in interaction in each situation only when training was introduced strongly suggest that training was responsible for change. Follow-up evaluation, conducted three weeks later when the program was no longer in effect, showed that the changes were maintained. A nine-month follow-up (upper portion of Figure 2.1) was obtained after the child had been attending a regular school where

[2]Specific experimental designs are discussed and illustrated in several sources (Barlow & Hersen, 1984; Kazdin, 1982a; Kratochwill, 1978).

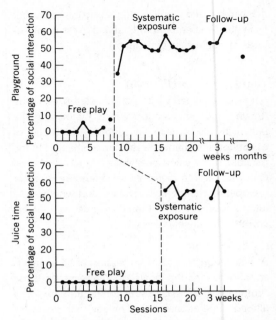

Figure 2.1 Social interaction at school in two separate free-play situations: on the playground and in the courtyard. The intervention was introduced to each situation at different points in time to meet the requirements of a multiple-baseline design across situations (reprinted with permission from *Journal of Behavior Therapy and Experimental Psychiatry, 8,* 75–81, H.J. Kandel, T. Ayllon, & M.S. Rosenbaum, Flooding or systematic exposure in the treatment of extreme social withdrawal in children, Copyright © 1977, Pergamon Press, Ltd.).

free time was observed. The high levels of social interaction were maintained at the regular school.

Single-case experimental designs have been applied successfully and often dramatically in case reports in which the effects of treatment have been carefully documented with complex clinical problems. The designs, however, often impose special requirements (e.g., withdrawing or withholding treatment at different points in the design) that are not always feasible in clinical situations. Consequently, some authors have suggested that the designs have not really been applied as widely as they should (Barlow, 1980) and perhaps often cannot be applied because of the ethical, methodological, and practical obstacles inherent in clinical settings (Kazdin & Wilson, 1978b). In the clinical situation, single-case experimental designs are to be encouraged when opportunities exist. When such designs are not feasible, quasi-experimental arrangements represent viable alternatives that greatly enhance the yield over traditional uncontrolled case studies.

Quasi-experiments

Single-case experiments, as highlighted in the previous section, provide the strongest basis for drawing inferences about intervention effects with the single case. When these designs are not feasible, several features of experimentation can be incorporated into the case study to help rule out threats to internal validity. The result is an increase in the strength of the inferences that can be drawn about the effects of the intervention.

Characteristics

It is assumed that essential features of single-case experiments cannot be implemented in the situation for which quasi-experiments are an appropriate alternative. The essential features involve implementing and withdrawing alternative conditions (baseline, treatment), withholding treatment for its sequential introduction (across separate baselines), and other variations pertaining to the intervention and its application. Yet some features of single-case methodology can be adopted to strengthen the basis for drawing valid references (Kazdin, 1981).

First, the type of data that are gathered is central to drawing inferences about treatment effects. Objective quantitative assessment information is critical. In uncontrolled case studies, anecdotal information and narrative accounts of client improvement are provided. Quantitative data (e.g., self-report inventories, ratings by others, observations of overt behavior) are essential to document that change has occurred in treatment. The data provide a precondition for beginning to identify the basis of change. Without quantitative information even a rigorously designed experiment might be uninterpretable. The quantitative information in quasi-experiments by itself is insufficient to identify the basis for therapeutic effects, when such changes occur. Additional characteristics address the threats to internal validity more directly.

Second, the number of assessment occasions and how they are distributed over the course of treatment can aid in drawing inferences about the case. Assessment of treatment outcome in group research is usually conducted on a one- or two-shot basis (e.g., posttreatment only or pre- and posttreatment). If assessment is conducted on a continuous basis, the inferences that can be drawn about treatment are strengthened. Specifically continuous assessment on two or more occasions before treatment has begun and then again during or after treatment can rule out a number of threats to internal validity (e.g., testing, instrumentation, statistical regression) associated with one- or two-shot assessment occasions. Data from continous assessment prior to treatment can also serve as a basis for making predictions about likely performance in the future, as discussed with single-case experiments. The effects of treatment can be judged by the extent to which departures in the data are evident from previously projected performance.

Third, past and future projections of performance, if available, can be utilized to help rule out threats to internal validity. Projections of performance may derive from continuous assessment, which might show that the problem is stable or even becoming worse without intervening. Additional information to make such projections may be derived from understanding the course of a particular clinical problem. For example, for some problems (e.g., obesity, social withdrawal), a stable, extended history is important from the standpoint of drawing inferences when change occurs. If change occurs following the implementation of treatment, the plausibility that treatment induced the change is greatly increased. On the other hand, changes occurring with acute or episodic problems may be less easily interpreted because improvement is more likely to be coincident with treatment.

Projections of the future course of the problem are also relevant to drawing inferences about treatment. Research may suggest that the clinical problem is likely to improve, worsen, or remain the same. These alternative prognoses may be important when drawing inferences about treatment. In general, the plausibility that the changes are a result of treatment partially depends on the extent to which changes in client performance depart from the expected and predicted pattern.

Fourth, the type of effects that are evident when treatment is implemented also has implications for drawing inferences about treatment effects. The immediacy and magnitude of changes are the two most salient dimensions. Usually, the more immediate the changes after the onset of treatment and the greater the magnitude of changes, the more likely that treatment was responsible for change. Alternatively, gradual or delayed changes make it more difficult to attribute the effects to an intervention. With many, if not most, clinical problems (e.g., schizophrenia, antisocial personality), immediate and large changes may not be evident with existing techniques. Yet there are problems areas (e.g., agoraphobia, social withdrawal) where selected techniques may begin to show improvement relatively early in the treatment course.

Fifth, the number and heterogeneity of subjects included in the demonstration obviously strengthens the inferences that can be drawn about treatment. The more cases that show changes associated with treatment, the less likely that an extraneous event was responsible for change. An extraneous event that covaries with treatment and leads to therapeutic changes is an unlikely rival hypothesis because the event must be common to all cases. Also, if change is demonstrated across several clients who differ in subject and demographic characteristics and the time that they are treated, the inferences that can be drawn are much stronger than if this diversity does not exist. As the diversity and heterogeneity of the clients and the conditions of treatment increase, it becomes increasingly plausible that the common experience shared by the clients (i.e., treatment) accounts for the changes.

The above dimensions when applied to clinical cases greatly increase the strength of inferences that can be drawn relative to uncontrolled cases. Depending upon how the different dimensions are addressed within a particular demonstration, it is quite possible that the inferences closely approximate those that could be obtained from single-case experimental designs. Not all of the dimensions are under control of the clinician (e.g., immediacy and strength of treatment effects). On the other hand, critical features upon which conclusions depend, such as the use of objective measures and their implementation on a number of occasions, can be controlled by clinicians and greatly enhance the strength of the demonstration. Indeed, these assessment characteristics are the core features of single-case experiments. The assessment strategies are usually quite compatible with the demands of clinical work because they do not require some of the special and problematic arrangements associated with treatment implementation.

Illustration

The use of resources within clinical applications to construct a quasi-experimental demonstration are unfortunately infrequent (see Kazdin, 1982a). As a recent example, Dollinger (1983) reported a case of a 15-year-old girl who was referred for treatment because of repeated blackouts. Most of the blackouts lasted for a few seconds but some continued for several minutes. Their frequency had ranged from 9 to 78 per day, with an estimated average of approximately 10 per day at the beginning of treatment. Within the context of family therapy to deal with multiple parent–child and sibling issues, a behavioral contingency was implemented to focus specifically on blackouts. The girl monitored the frequency of her blackouts and earned extra time in practicing her driving (in preparation for her driving test) if the frequency of her blackouts showed a systematic reduction. A changing criterion was set so that the reward would be earned only if there was a reduction of one blackout per day in relation to the level set for the previous week. The number of blackouts, plotted in Figure 2.2, showed a steady decline over the course of the reward contingency. Follow-up contact three years later indicated that the patient remained symptom free.

The demonstration does not meet criteria of a true experiment in showing that treatment rather than extraneous factors (e.g., history, maturation) led to change. Yet features of single-case methodology were adopted. First, the use of quantitative information (estimated or actual frequencies), the assessment on multiple occasions before and during treatment, stability of the problem given its extended history and lack of response to previous (self-monitoring) efforts, the likely continuation without intervention, and the systematic changes in level of blackouts in response to changes within the study all contributed to the inferences that can be drawn. The treatment itself was complex and multifaceted; the reward contingency alone may not have produced change without family therapy conducted concurrently. Nevertheless, the conclusions that can be drawn about the change and the factors that led to it are vastly improved in this report over what would be available from a traditional uncontrolled case study.

General Comments

There has been an increased recognition of the need to reduce the hiatus between research and

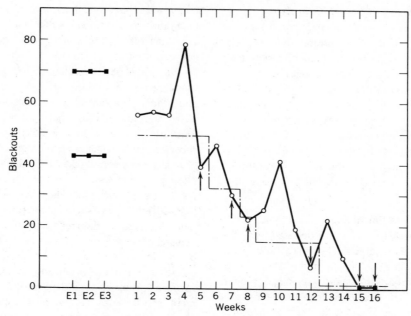

Figure 2.2   Number of blackouts per week. The broken lines indicate the reward criterion and the arrows signify that the reduction in blackouts from the previous week met the reward criterion in effect at that time. Solid squares shown in estimated (E) weeks (E1 to E3) reflect the client's estimated blackout frequency for a 6- to 10-day period before beginning self-monitoring (Dollinger, S.J. (1983). A case report of Dissociative Neurosis (Depersonalization Disorder) in an adolescent treated with family therapy and behavior modification. *Journal of Consulting and Clinical Psychology*, 51, 479–484. Copyright © 1983 by the American Psychological Association. Reprinted/Adapted by permission of the author).

practice and between researchers and practitioners. The reasons are manifold but include the relative lack of impact of research on practice (and vice versa), and the increased focus on professional accountability. Single-case designs, broadly conceived, provide tools that may help to integrate evaluation into clinical work with the single case. Single-case experimental designs first began to be widely used in applied research in the late 1960s and early 1970s (Baer, Wolf, & Risley, 1968). There was an implicit view that the designs could be readily integrated into clinical practice. Over the years, the compatibility of true experimental designs with clinical work has been questioned (Kazdin & Wilson, 1978b). As a result, increased efforts have been made to introduce evaluation into clinical practice when true experiments are not viable. Recommendations have been made to utilize variations of single-case designs that might be more suitable for clinical work or only selected components of

these designs (Barlow, Hayes, & Nelson, 1984; Bloom & Fischer, 1982; Kazdin, 1981) and assessment strategies that will facilitate evaluation (Nelson, 1981; Thyer & Curtis, 1983). The adaptation of designs for clinical work is a positive move that could greatly improve the knowledge base that emerges from applications of treatment and the hypotheses for subsequent large-scale investigation.

ASSESSMENT AND DESIGN ISSUES

The focus on alternative strategies of research, as reflected in the foregoing discussions, convey ways of approaching the overriding questions of treatment efficacy and the multiple conditions under which treatments produce change. Progress in addressing the ultimate questions of psychotherapy depend very much on how investigations are conducted in general. Selected issues are addressed that relate to the quality of evidence that is provided about treatment.

Delineation of the Client/Patient Sample

The need to describe basic characteristics of the sample that is included in the treatment study is obvious. The need stems from the interest in relating client characteristics to therapeutic change. Typically, rudimentary subject and demographic information regarding age, gender, socioeconomic status, marital status, and other basic descriptors are included. This is not invariably the case, and occasionally only broad descriptors such as "outpatients," "introductory college students," or "disturbed children" are provided with little or no further description.

Evaluation of Clinical Status

A more pervasive issue is the delineation of the clinical status of the sample. The clinical status of the client refers to the dysfunction and related characteristics that serve as the basis for seeking or providing treatment. The need exists to delineate the sample in sufficient detail and with objective measures so that comparisons can be made with other samples across clinic or research settings. The information that is required extends beyond the narrative accounts that the sample is disturbed or that clients have difficulty in their social, work, or other areas of function.

One way of delineating the clinical dysfunction of the sample is through the use of a standardized system of diagnosis such as the *DSM-III* (APA, 1980). The advantage of such a system is that it presents a widely used means of delineating severity, breadth, and chronicity of dysfunction. If patients in a study meet the criteria for a particular diagnosis, this conveys relevant descriptive information.[3] Although persons who meet criteria for a particular (Axis I) diagnosis are likely to be heterogeneous, the fact that they meet diagnostic criteria provides useful information in communicating clinically relevant characteristics of the sample. The utility of the information derives in part from the fact that a specific threshold of impairment or dysfunc-

tion needs to be passed in terms of target behaviors, their duration, and impact for the criteria to be met. There are other alternative systems that might be adopted such as the Research Diagnostic Criteria (Spitzer, Endicott, & Robins, 1978), International Classification of Diseases (ICD-9; WHO, 1979), and others. The diagnostic systems need not be based on traditional (Kraepelinian) models of dysfunction. Several different multivariate models of classification and alternative diagnostic systems have been developed (Blashfield, 1984), although these are not in widespread use clinically.

The use of psychiatric diagnoses, as reflected in *DSM-III*, is frequently avoided intentionally in treatment studies rather than reflecting an oversight. The reasons entail serious concerns about the putative or actual model(s) that psychiatric diagnosis reflect, the deleterious effects of labeling, continued, even if reduced, problems regarding reliability of assessment, the absence of treatment implications for most psychiatric diagnoses, and many others (see Kazdin, 1983; Matarazzo, 1983). These concerns cannot be dismissed. Yet diagnosis and assessment of "psychiatric" dysfunction provides a standardized way of describing client impairment. Since the *DSM-III* is widely used in clinical work and since it is closely related to the international system of classification of dysfunction (WHO, 1979), there are some communicative benefits to its use.[4]

The use of psychiatric diagnosis is by no means the only alternative to describe the level, type, and severity of clinical dysfunction. Standardized assessment methods where there is an extensive normative and comparative data base might provide similar and even greater benefits in terms of

---

[3]As the reader is well aware, *DSM-III* diagnoses encompass five axes or dimensions. These include: Clinical Syndromes (Axis I), Personality Disorders and Specific Developmental Disorders (Axis II), Physical Disorders and Conditions (Axis III), Severity of Psychosocial Stressors (Axis IV), and Highest Level of Adaptive Functioning (Axis V). The present discussion considers primarily Axis I diagnosis of clinical dysfunction.

[4]To obtain a diagnosis, several assessment devices are available. Alternative interview measures are most frequently used. Prominent among these for adults include the Schedule for Affective Disorders and Schizophrenia (Endicott & Spitzer, 1978) and the Diagnostic Interview Schedule (Robins, Helzer, Croughan, & Ratcliff, 1981), to mention two. Similar measures have been developed for children such as the Schedule for Affective Disorders and Schizophrenia for School-Age Children (Chamber, Puig-Antich, & Tabrizi, 1978) and Diagnostic Interview for Children and Adolescents (Herjanic, 1980), although these are less well developed and evaluated than the measures for adults. The alternative instruments are designed to cover a wide array of symptoms and target complaints, and such domains as severity, breadth, and duration of dysfunction so that a diagnosis can be reached.

communicating about the population. For example, description of alternative symptom profiles on the Minnesota Multiphasic Personality Inventory (MMPI) would offer information that could describe broad characteristics of patient samples and be used to make comparisons across studies. Obviously, an extremely wide range of measures to describe clinical problems is available. The benefits of the use of diagnostic systems such as *DSM-III* or profiles from such measures as the MMPI is that their already frequent use facilitates integration of research findings.

Apart from detailing the severity, breadth, and other characteristics of the complaints that serve as the basis of treatment, additional areas of dysfunction may be important to describe as well. It is critical to note, for example, the extent to which the problems have impact on daily functioning. In many treatment studies, nonstandardized procedures and narrative accounts are provided. For example, readers are told that if the subjects were diagnosed they would probably meet criteria for schizophrenia or conduct disorder or that subjects experienced a particular problem (e.g., phobias) and that the problems really interfered with their daily lives. Such descriptions are well intended but are unnecessarily imprecise. If treatment effectively alters performance, there will still be the problem of noting for whom the techniques worked.

Recruitment and Subject Selection

Critical information about the subjects pertain to the manner in which they were obtained. Clients may be selected from self-referred clinic cases, from consecutive hospital admissions, through newspaper advertisements, from college student volunteers, or from captive student subject pools. The path of entry into the protocol and the number of persons who have entered through different paths should be described. The means of recruitment of subjects provides basic information that will facilitate interpretation and replication of the findings and permit evaluation of alternative rival hypotheses or failures to replicate. The manner of subject recruitment has been a particularly sensitive issue in the outcome literature because of the concern over analogue studies, as discussed earlier.

Related to recruitment are the screening criteria that may be invoked for inclusion of the subjects.

The inclusion and exclusion criteria may relate to the assessment of clinical status, as mentioned before. The precise measures and criterion points on the measures for inclusion obviously need to be elaborated fully. Also, additional subject and demographic variables and, if not obvious, how these were assessed should be described. Where there is initial screening, it is important to specify the number of persons initially recruited or available for the project and the portion that was ultimately retained by invoking screening criteria. Often in therapy studies the criteria for subject inclusion, the portion of those selected from those available, and bases for exclusion are not reported.

An important issue related to subject selection is attrition or loss of subjects. Attrition is a self-selection phenomenon and needs to be elaborated within the study. Several points need to be specified including the number of persons who dropped out, when in the study they dropped out, and differences in attrition as a function of any experimental condition (e.g., subject type, therapist, treatment group). In addition, there should be an explicit, even if arbitrary, criterion for deciding when someone has "dropped out," if special problems emerge over the course of treatment such as inconsistent attendance to sessions or completion of some but not all of the sessions. The criteria for excluding such subjects from posttreatment and follow-up assessment and from data analyses need to be clearly described.

When in the study the subjects drop out may be as important in interpreting the results as how many do so. Subjects may drop out during some facet of pretreatment assessment and before assignment has been made to experimental conditions. Alternatively, subjects may drop out after one or a few sessions. Different interpretations of the data derive from the different periods of leaving the study. Obviously, if attrition varies between groups after clients have been assigned to and have participated in their treatment (e.g., Rush et al., 1977; Weissman et al., 1979), this may reflect an important dependent measure about the effects (or side effects) of treatment.

General Comments

These issues reflect requirements within individual research studies. The information about subjects, their characteristics, and how they were obtained are fundamental to address major outcome questions. If the effects of treatment depend very much on the characteristics noted previously, interpretation of the outcome literature for many treatment techniques will be difficult. Relatively little attention has been given to basic clinical descriptions of the treated populations. The consequence is considerable ambiguity in noting for which clients a particular technique works and for what level of severity of dysfunction.

Delineation and Specification of Treatment

A critical requirement of outcome research is delineation of the treatment. This includes a description of what treatment is, why it is used, and how it is expected to alter the problem to which it is applied. Beyond the general rationale and description, additional features that are essential to specify, to the extent possible, are the concrete procedures that therapists and clients follow and the criteria to evaluate whether treatment was executed appropriately.

Conceptual Delineation

A precondition of specification of treatment is to identify the conceptual basis of the treatment and the connections between treatment techniques and the specific dysfunction that is to be treated. Treatment can be conceptualized at varying levels of abstraction, as defined by the number of intervening variables and the extent to which they are removed from the concrete operations of treatment. To help establish the reasons why therapeutic change was achieved, it eventually will be important to operationalize these variables and to show the correspondence between change on these measures and measures of treatment outcome. However, the purpose of the initial conceptualization of treatment is to specify those features that will affect the clinical problem. Conceptual connections between treatment and the clinical problem help to identify those components that define the treatment and that need to be optimized. At the conceptual level, the components refer to the mechanisms through which therapeutic effects are achieved. At the concrete level, the components refer to specific procedures that need to be implemented or characteristics of the behaviors of patient, therapist, or their interactions.

Specific Ingredients and Procedures

The conceptual connections between treatment and amelioration of the clinical problem underlie the identification of the procedures used in therapy. To the extent possible, the procedures need to be described in a format that can be followed by those who administer treatment. The concrete specification of treatment procedures is not only important to determine what in fact has been done in the study at hand, but also to make possible replication of treatment in subsequent investigations and applications.

The development of a treatment manual is essential. A manual is defined here broadly to include primarily written materials that are designed to guide the therapist in the goals of treatment, the procedures, techniques, topics, themes, therapeutic maneuvers, and other behaviors and activities that are to transpire over the course of treatment. Such manuals may vary considerably in their degree of specificity and the nature of the materials (e.g., written, audio, audiovisual) used to convey treatment. Obviously, some treatments are more readily specified and codified in manual form than others. Generally, those treatments that focus on concrete and prescriptive procedures are more readily specified than those that focus on emerging processes. Thus, relaxation training, systematic desensitization, and behavioral rehearsal are more easily specified in manual form than experiential or psychodynamic therapy. However, treatment manuals have been increasingly used for nonbehavioral therapies including supportive−expressive−psychoanalytically oriented therapy, short-term psychodynamic therapy, interpersonal psychotherapy, and cognitive therapy (see Luborsky & DeRubeis, 1984).

The manuals vary greatly on the extent to which they specify concrete procedures. At the highest level of specification, the manuals may be able to identify specific tasks and activities for therapist and patient on a session-by-session or stage-by-stage basis. At the other extreme, where the technique focuses on processes, only more general guidelines and statements may be possible. The manual may identify themes of the sessions, possible progressions of such themes, the facilitative types of responses that therapists make or the conditions that are provided to establish a particular climate.

Among the possibly less tangible influences, the therapeutic relationship, perhaps more than any other characteristic of treatment, has been accorded a significant role in the therapeutic change process (see Waterhouse & Strupp, 1984). The relationship cannot be reduced to technical procedures codified in a treatment manual. On the other hand, one need not take the extreme view that the patient–therapist relationship is unique, unspecifiable, and beyond the boundaries of operationalization and investigation. If relationship factors are considered to be important, it is essential that the characteristics be specified to the extent possible and that criteria to determine whether these characteristics were evident be defined through specific measurement strategies.

Studies have frequently identified relationship factors that relate to outcome. For example, Waterhouse and Strupp (1984) suggest that patient skills in relating comfortably to the therapist, patient feelings of being accepted, understood, and liked by the therapist, and a relationship characterized by warmth and mutual respect enhance outcome. Considerable work has been done on identifying the correlates of successful outcomes in terms of therapeutic processes and relationship factors. Much more work is needed to identify those characteristics that can be translated into guidelines so that relationship factors that do influence outcome can be actively promoted.

Alternative treatments and alternative components within a given treatment vary in the extent to which they lend themselves to codification in treatment manuals. However, the diverse features of treatment, such as technique, relationship, nonspecific and other "categories" of influence, can be specified to some degree. Treatments need to be specified so that the procedures, broadly defined, can be trained and so that their "correct" or optimal execution can be ascertained.

Treatment Integrity

Conceptual and procedural delineation of treatment occurs before the treatment is implemented. Once treatment begins, it is essential to ensure that it is carried out as intended. The extent to which treatment has been carried out as intended is referred to as treatment integrity (Quay, 1977; Yeaton & Sechrest, 1981). The integrity of treatment can be evaluated in a definitive sense only after treatment has been completed.

Unfortunately, treatment integrity has been a largely neglected issue in outcome research. Yet interpretation of outcome effects depends completely on the strength of the evidence that the procedures were actually carried out as intended.

Conclusions drawn about differences or the absence of differences between treatment and control groups assume that the treatment was implemented correctly.

Treatment can depart from the intended procedures in a number of different ways. It is possible that the treatment sessions really were not held, that they were held less often or for shorter periods than intended, that specific procedures within the sessions were not carried out or were carried out inconsistently, and so on. Depending upon the technique, execution of treatment may require that certain procedures be followed, that certain conditions be provided by the therapist, or that certain reciprocal behaviors and affect emerge between patient and therapist, to mention a few.

There are several steps required to ensure treatment integrity beyond the specification of treatment. First, therapists need to be trained to carry out the techniques. The exact training procedures that are employed and the criteria for deciding when therapists are considered to be trained need to be specified. Ideally, the criteria would include demonstrated proficiency. In the absence of agreed-upon criteria for what that would mean, training is usually defined by duration of training, completion of practice cases, or therapist "experience." In any case, the methods used, if any, to develop skills in execution of treatment need to be stated explicitly in any report of treatment.

Second, when treatment has begun, the procedures used to ensure integrity need to be described. These procedures may include supervising treatment sessions, listening to or viewing tapes of selected sessions, meeting regularly with therapists to review procedures or to provide feedback, and so on. Without supervision and feedback, therapists may drift from the specified processes central to treatment.

Third, whether or not there is any supervision of therapists during the course of treatment, it is essential to assess the extent to which the procedures are carried out correctly. Assessment requires ways of coding therapist and/or patient behavior and identifying ways in which adherence to and departures from the treatment manual are evident. A sample of the treatment sessions may be recorded and/or transcribed and evaluated in a way that permits a quantitative estimate of treatment integrity. In addition, more basic information may also be needed regarding completion of treatment sessions, assessment of their duration, spacing, and frequency. These dimensions address the more fundamental issue that the sessions were held and usually can be assessed from summary reports completed by the therapists themselves or obtained from clinical records.

Fourth, the information obtained from assessment of treatment integrity can be used in different ways. If the information can be transcribed and interpreted immediately, it can be used as the basis for providing feedback to therapists to ensure that integrity is sustained. More likely, the data may need to be evaluated at the end of the study.[5]

It is essential to identify the criteria that will define whether treatment was carried out adequately. Obviously, these criteria should be identified in advance and independently of the effects of treatment. Some departures from prescribed treatment are likely to occur. The departures vary as a function of characteristics of the technique, clinical population and problem, and therapists. And some departures will be regarded as more significant than others. The issue is whether the treatment was carried out within some acceptable range of variation. Conceivably, the "acceptable range" eventually could be defined empirically and therapist performance and therapy conditions outside of this range would, for selected problems, clients, and other conditions, fail to produce therapeutic change. However, the range of practices that would be counted as acceptable within a given study is a matter of judgment. The only reasonable requirement for research is that the judgments be based on explicit criteria.

General Comments

Assessment of treatment integrity goes beyond relating treatment processes to therapeutic outcome. The purpose is to identify what constitutes the ingre-

[5]An excellent illustration of the specification of treatment and the evaluation and monitoring of treatment integrity is the NIMH Collaborative Study (see Waskow, 1984) which compares the effects of cognitive therapy, interpersonal psychotherapy, imipramine, and placebo (pill) treatments for nonbipolar and nonpsychotic depressed patients. Treatments were specified in manual form, training and supervision were conducted by experts in the individual techniques, competence criteria were identified before therapists could treat cases for the study itself, and treatment integrity will be assessed at the end of treatment.

dients of therapy and to demonstrate that these ingredients were included. Referring to the "ingredients" does not trivialize the variables that influence change nor make light of the difficulty of their investigation. Assessment of integrity is naturally facilitated when concrete tasks can be observed and when specific behaviors such as verbalizations of the therapist or patient can be coded. However, for more general and mutlifaceted influences such as the therapeutic relationship, assessment devices are available (e.g., Hartley & Strupp, 1982; Luborsky, 1984; Marziali, Marmor, & Krupnick, 1981). The measures need to be used to help define the central ingredients, to identify whether criteria have been met on important relationship factors, and to establish what can be done in treatment to help attain such criteria.

Treatment integrity needs to be distinguished from the *differentiation* of one treatment from another. In outcome studies where two or more different treatments are compared, assessment of treatment sessions (e.g., from transcripts) is often completed to see whether treatments differ from one another. This differentiation is important in and of itself. Obviously if the treatments do not differ from each other on critical measures during their execution, the absence of differences at outcome and the distinction between the treatments on conceptual grounds are open to question. However, differentiation of alternative treatments is different from treatment integrity. Integrity refers to whether treatment was conducted as intended. Treatments in a comparative study may be differentiated from each other (e.g., in types of statements made, types of conditions provided by the therapist) and not have high integrity. Integrity refers to a comparison of treatment as it actually was with how it should have been conducted; differentiation refers to identifying differences in how two or more treatments were conducted. The distinction has important implications for conclusions about therapy outcome.

For example, Luborsky, Woody, McLellan, O'Brien, and Rosenzweig (1982) evaluated independent clinical judges' ratings of alternative treatments (drug counseling, psychoanalytically oriented therapy, and cognitive-behavior therapy). The treatments were evaluated on specific and global criteria. Each treatment was rated as fitting the characteristics of its own manual more than characteristics of the other treatment manuals. This finding demonstrates differentiation of treatments. Yet these data by themselves would not establish the extent to which any treatment was carried out as intended (integrity). Several studies have compared characteristics of alternative techniques and the specific processes with which they are associated (e.g., Brunink & Schroeder, 1979; DeRubeis, Hollon, Evans, & Bemis, 1982; Sloane et al., 1975). These studies have made important advances in elaborating similarities and differences among treatments. Also, since such research identifies components that are common among alternative treatment, the findings may have major implications for eventually defining what effective treatments need to include.

Specific and Nonspecific Treatment Factors

The specification of treatment and the evaluation of treatment integrity raise issues about the critical ingredients in therapy. The assumption is that there are a number of readily specifiable ingredients in therapy. Their specification, identification, and verification are essential for understanding the mechanisms through which therapeutic change is produced.

The issue of the mechanisms of therapeutic change and the specification of treatment ingredients raises a central question for treatment evaluation. That question in its most general form asks whether therapeutic change results from the characteristics unique to the specific treatment that is applied or to more general factors that are included in that treatment but perhaps all other treatments as well. For example, as a more specific case in point, are the effects of desensitization due to those unique treatment characteristics proposed as central within the treatment (e.g., hierarchy construction, relaxation training) or due to the potential benefits resulting from talking about one's problems with an interested professional, attending treatment sessions, believing that therapeutic change is going to occur, and so on. Perhaps client expectancies for change are induced by participation in treatment and change occurs as a result.[6]

[6]The question is formulated here as either/or, that is, therapeutic change may be due either to treatment-unique characteristics or to more general transtechnique characteristics. This formulation is provided merely to introduce the issue. It is quite possible, if not likely, that the combination of treatment-specific and so-called nonspecific factors operate simultaneously in an additive or multiplicative fashion.

Placebo Effects

Major impetus for investigation of the role of client expectancies for change in the context of psychotherapy has derived from placebo effects in medication research. In medical treatment, placebos consist of interventions that are known to be pharmacologically inert in relation to the specific problem to which they are applied (Shapiro & Morris, 1978). For example, in clinical trials of medications, placebo controls are frequently used in which patients receive an inert substance that looks like the active medication but in fact includes no biochemical agents that could promote therapeutic change. Although the impact of various chemical agents has been carefully demonstrated for many different medical and behavioral dysfunctions, there is little doubt that placebos can produce reliable change as well. Thus, the evaluation of new medications typically requires examining whether the proposed medication produces change beyond the increments obtained with a placebo.

Issues embedded in the notion and evaluation of placebo effects have been transferred to psychotherapy for different reasons. First, the notion of placebo effects emphasizes the critical nature of client expectancies and the potent influences of administering treatment. Second, placebos (inert medications) have been used to provide relief from psychological symptoms (Frank, 1978). Thus it is clear that patient beliefs about the procedures they receive may affect their psychological dysfunction. This has raised the question of whether psychotherapeutic change occurs *because of* placebo effects (Rosenthal & Frank, 1956).

The notion of placebos when transferred to psychotherapy is problematic, if not altogether inappropriate. The defining characteristic of placebos is that the basic intervention is known to be inert in relation to the specific problem to which it is applied. In the context of psychotherapy, there is no analogous procedure that can be said to be inert. Psychotherapy, broadly conceived, is fundamentally an interpersonal experience that encompasses perceptions, cognitions, and attributions. Beliefs or expectancies brought to treatment by the client or generated in the client by the procedures themselves are not inert in the sense that this term is used in reference to placebos. It is meaningful to evaluate the role of client beliefs in therapy and the impact of such beliefs on outcome; however, this is different from placebo effects per se.

Nonspecific Factors

In psychotherapy research, the question analogous to placebo effects has been reframed as the evaluation of nonspecific factors in treatment. These factors refer to features of therapy that are common to most techniques such as having the patient come to sessions at a treatment setting, providing a statement about the problem and how treatment will effect its amelioration, engaging in some prescribed tasks or activities that are promoted as therapeutic, and others. These factors occasionally have been referred to as *nonspecific* because they are common to virtually all therapies. The presence of such factors raises a question for the evaluation of treatments; namely, to what extent does a given treatment produce therapeutic changes over and above the changes that would result from the presence of these nonspecific factors alone?

To address this general question, researchers have devised various control conditions in which clients are provided with therapist contact and engage in a variety of procedures that are considered, on a priori grounds, not to be therapeutic. The purpose of course is to assess whether a specific form of treatment (e.g., psychodynamically oriented psychotherapy, systematic desensitization) produces effects over and above those achieved with any form of contact with another person that is presented as therapy. Paul (1966) conducted a seminal investigation of systematic desensitization and devised an "attention-placebo" control group that received a "fast-acting tranquilizer" (actually a placebo) and engaged in a task (identifying noxious sounds), both of which were embedded in a rationale that explained how the procedures would alter anxiety. On a variety of outcome measures, the procedure produced reliable changes, some of which were sustained up to a two-year follow-up (Paul, 1967a).

Apart from the substantive contributions of the Paul study, the methodological impact of the attention-placebo condition was major. Studies began to evaluate alternative treatments in relation to control conditions that followed the letter or spirit of the attention-placebo group used by Paul. The idea was to expose clients to procedures (e.g., tachistoscopic presentation of allegedly relevant stimuli, false bio-

feedback) that were couched in credible rationales that would induce them to anticipate therapeutic change (see Lick & Bootzin, 1975). Novel procedures emerged such as providing counterdemand instructions that would convey to clients that therapeutic change would or would not begin until a particular point in treatment, if at all (Steinmark & Borkovec, 1974; Suedfeld, 1984). All such procedures are designed to control for client expectancies for change that are promoted by participation in treatment. By design, the procedures were considered to fall outside the realm of what most professionals would ascribe to "activity therapy" because the conditions do not rely on many of the rationales of contemporary treatment approaches (e.g., psychodynamic, behavioral, nondirective).

Reconsideration of Nonspecifics

In the 20 years since Paul's study was conducted, different problems began to become evident with conditions that were designed to provide credible but "inert" control conditions. For one, it became clear that control conditions generally were less credible to clients and generated lower expectancies for therapeutic change than did the treatments to which they were often compared (Kazdin & Wilcoxon, 1976). When control conditions do generate high levels of credibility that equal the credibility of treatment conditions, treatment and "placebo" control conditions rarely differ in outcome. Second, and perhaps more important, the entire notion of nonspecific factors of therapy has been reconsidered. If any change occurs with attention-placebo control conditions, this says something about a veridical behavior change process. The procedure by its very nature is not inert. Third, and related, the procedures that would be regarded as active or veridical treatments or attention-placebo control conditions are a matter of dispute. A placebo control group in one study might be considered as the active experimental treatment condition in another study (Shapiro, 1984).

Other influences contributed to the reconsideration of nonspecific factors, including the proliferation of the number of different techniques (Herink, 1980), mounting evidence that in practice putatively competing treatments overlap considerably (Klein, Dittman, Parloff, & Gill, 1969; Sloane et al., 1975), and individual studies as well as large-scale evaluations suggesting that different treatments produce similar outcomes (Luborsky, Singer, & Luborsky, 1975; Sloane et al., 1975; Smith & Glass, 1977). Factors common to a variety of different techniques provide a plausible and parsimonious explanation of the effects of diverse techniques.

"Nonspecific factors" suggests that there are some unspecified, if not mysterious, ingredients that may influence change but may not be central to the procedure. Yet there are conceptual problems with this rendition of nonspecific factors. Many of those features that are common among different treatments are not necessarily incidental accoutrements but rather very central components (Wilkins, 1979). Alternative positions have been advanced to suggest that the crucial ingredients of therapy are embodied by different techniques in fundamentally similar ways, although the techniques may differ in details.

For example, Frank (1961, 1973, 1982) has suggested that therapies produce their effects because they provide: (1) an emotionally charged and confiding relationship; (2) a setting in which patients' expectancies for help and confidence in the therapist's role as a healer are strengthened; (3) a rationale or conceptual scheme that plausibly explains the symptoms and prescribes a procedure for their resolution; and (4) a set of procedures in which both patient and therapist engage that they believe to be the means of restoring the patient. Frank believes that the rationale to explain the patient's problems (the myth) and the procedures in which therapist and patient engage (the ritual) provide new learning experiences, evoke expectancies for help, provide opportunities for rehearsal and practice, and strengthen the therapeutic relationship. Other interpretations of psychotherapy have been advanced such as self-efficacy theory (Bandura, 1977) and integrationism (Goldfried, 1982). These too suggest that the features common among alternative treatments are responsible for producing therapeutic change.

Apart from theoretical excursions, fine-grained analyses of what actually is done in alternative treatments suggest that there are factors that are common to many different techniques. For example, as noted earlier, Luborsky et al. (1982) evaluated samples of quite different treatments including drug counseling, supportive-psychodynamically oriented therapy, and cognitive-behavioral therapy. As expected, various therapist behaviors, such as the type

of statements and the focus of the sessions, differed among the techniques. Interestingly, however, the attribute "giving support," which was supposed to be especially characteristic of supportive-psychodynamically oriented therapy, was indistinguishable among the treatments. Other studies have shown that such characteristics as therapist empathy and the use of interpretive and clarifying statements are similar among such seemingly diverse techniques as Gestalt therapy, psychodynamically oriented psychotherapy, and behavior therapy (Brunink & Schroeder, 1979; Sloane et al., 1975). These results do not imply that technique-specific characteristics are not found. Yet the fact that broad commonalities exist in patient–therapist interactions, relationship factors, and client expectancies serve to recast the matter of specific and nonspecific effects.

Current Status and Research Implications
The conceptualization of specific and nonspecific factors and the evaluation of therapy outcome have evolved considerably. Attempts to rule out through various control procedures the multiple factors referred to as nonspecific are problematic for different reasons. First, the notion of nonspecific factors raises its own type of uniformity myth, viz, that there is a homogeneous set of variables common to different treatments that are similar in their effects across patients, techniques, and therapists. So-called nonspecific factors constitute a large class of specifiable variables, most if not all of which can be studied empirically. Whether they contribute to therapeutic change is a matter for research.

Second, attempts to rule out through control procedures many "nonspecific" factors may represent a misinterpretation of what psychotherapy is and how it works. Some nonspecific factors such as the patient–therapist relationship and support from the therapist may be the core ingredients of therapy (cf. Strupp & Hadley, 1979). It is meaningful to evaluate their impact as variables in the treatment process, but they are not artifacts to be cast aside casually in control conditions. Control groups that provide an opportunity for clients to discuss superficial issues casually with a professional do not necessarily control for such core factors as the relationship or therapist support unless these factors are equal in intensity and scope to the treatment group. The dilemma has been that such a control group with demonstrated similarities on such variables would probably produce considerable therapeutic change. Control groups to date that attempt to rule out en masse large sets of unidentified nonspecific factors may merely provide highly diluted variations of these factors.

From the standpoint of the evaluation of psychotherapy, where does the above discussion leave the inclusion of control groups? The answer very much depends upon the question of interest to the investigator. There remain situations where interpretation of the results of an outcome investigation depends upon a comparison group that has received some contact with a therapist. For example, a recent study demonstrated that cognitive-behavioral and psychodynamic group therapy were essentially equally effective in the treatment of depression in a geriatric population (Steuer et al., 1984). No control group was included in the design. From the results, it is possible to state that both treatments worked and were equally effective. It is also possible to pose that meeting depressed persons in a group and chatting about "life" or "current events" would have produced similar improvements (leaving aside the matter of improvements without any intervening treatment). The theoretically current and intricate procedures, highly trained and well supervised professionals, and other accoutrements of treatment may have been superfluous. The absence of any control group to rule out some of these factors makes it difficult to draw inferences about treatment. When two (or more) different treatments are compared and they produce similar results, the absence of control conditions raises interpretive problems.

In treatment research in general, there is an obvious role for conditions that help to identify specific ingredients in therapy. However, the traditional "attention-placebo" control group may be inadequate. Such groups attempt to lump together all sorts of nonspecific factors and may provide highly diluted versions of variables that are veridical parts of treatment, for example, the therapeutic relationship. Instead of testing the role of nonspecifics, the study compares different treatments. One of the treatments probably has a more plausible rationale, is more believable to therapist and client alike, and includes more "therapeutic ingredients" or selected ingredients at a higher level (e.g., relationship factors, support). The other treatment is probably

markedly weaker in one or more of these characteristics. These treatments have been labeled as treatment and control conditions but the latter may be a misnomer because of the ambiguity in what is being controlled, the adequacy with which such factors are equalized or controlled across groups, and whether "controlling" for some of the factors is meaningful.

Although the conceptualization of nonspecific factors and their control in outcome research has evolved, further changes are needed in the delineation of these factors and their integration with other variables in contemporary therapy research (see Critelli & Newmann, 1984; Kirsch, 1978; Wilkins, 1979). Typically, the variables of interest in therapy research have fallen into broad domains of technique, patient, and therapist variables (and their combinations). Ignoring important conceptual distinctions for the moment, two broad types of variables can be sorted, viz., those that produce or contribute to therapeutic change and those that do not. Identifying what variables fall into these classes is a task for research. Referring to a large set of variables as nonspecific treatment factors has thwarted their careful analysis and empirical evaluation as veridical components of treatment and their integration into theoretical frameworks of alternative approaches.

Comparison or control groups are still required to help identify critical variables in therapy. Greater specificity is needed, however, in identifying exactly those variables a particular group is designed to control. Also, the extent to which groups differ or are similar on particular variables needs to be assessed directly. The specific variables that are controlled can be dictated by the question implicit in alternative treatment evaluation strategies, noted above, and/or theoretical views about the critical components of a particular treatment.

Assessment of Psychotherapy Outcomes

The assessment of treatment outcome raises central issues for the evaluation of psychotherapy. Over the years assessment of psychotherapy outcome has come into its own as an area of theory and research. The emergence of behavioral assessment illustrates the attention accorded the area as reflected in a large number of books (e.g., Haynes & Wilson, 1979; Hersen & Bellack, 1981; Mash & Terdal,

1981) and two separate journals.[7] Although the increased attention to therapy outcome assessment is illustrated by behavioral assessment, the attention extends beyond singular approaches or orientations (see Lambert et al., 1983). The full gamut of assessment issues that are relevant to psychotherapy research cannot be addressed here. The comments to follow focus on salient issues that influence conclusions reached about the multiple questions of therapy outcome.

Criteria for Evaluating Outcome

Over the last decade, the assessment of psychotherapy outcome has become increasingly multifaceted. Outcome studies have increased in the number and types of measures and the sources of information to evaluate treatment (Lambert, 1983). The diversity and multiplicity of assessment procedures reflect an increased recognition of the complexity of outcome criteria. Strupp and Hadley (1977) have directed attention to the different perspectives that are relevant for evaluating treatment outcome. The perspectives refer to different interested parties in defining mental health and include: society (significant persons in the patient's life), the patient, and mental health professionals. The perspectives reflect different standards and values and ultimately of course are assessed through different measurement strategies. Conclusions about the effects of therapy may depend heavily upon the perspective that is assessed. Discrepancies among perspectives might be expected.

From a different vantage point, Kazdin and Wilson (1978a) suggested that treatment can be evaluated from different classes of variables including patient-related changes (e.g., importance of the changes made in treatment, proportion of patients who improve, breadth and durability of changes), efficiency and cost-related variables (e.g., brevity of treatment, professional attention required, cost to the patient, cost-effectiveness), and consumer variables (e.g., acceptability of the procedures and the treatment focus to prospective patients). The different classes of variables and the many measures within each class may not necessarily correlate posi-

tively. Consequently, conclusions reached about treatment may vary greatly as a function of the precise measure.

The multifaceted nature of assessment has also stemmed from consideration of the nature of clinical problems and the manner in which they can be evaluated. Recommendations have been made for using multiple channels of assessment involving self-report, overt behavior, psychophysiological processes, cognitive assessment, and other modalities, to the extent that a particular clinical problem has manifestations or correlates in these areas (e.g., Hersen & Bellack, 1981). Thus, problems such as depression, phobias, headache, and sexual dysfunction are typically assessed with a number of different strategies that reflect specific but alternative facets of the problems.

The complex and multifaceted nature of therapy outcome can be traced to additional influences as well. As has long been recognized, different therapeutic approaches address different facets of clinical dysfunction and rely on different constructs. For example, psychodynamic therapy may be appropriately evaluated on psychodynamic criteria, rather than symptomatic or behavioral criteria (Malan, 1976). Also, within a given approach there has been increased recognition of the situational specificity of performance. Self-report or direct measures of overt behavior cannot be assumed to reflect pervasive performance characteristics that transcend a variety of situations. Although it is clear that there are continuities in many areas of performance, it is also clear that the correlations from one measure to another or from performances across settings are not invariably high. The implications for outcome assessment are clear. Measures need to sample different types of constructs (e.g., characteristics, behaviors, symptoms) across different situations.

The different perspectives, types of variables, and modalities of assessment mentioned above do not exhaust the types of measures relevant to the evaluation of psychotherapy (see Lambert et al., 1983). Those that were mentioned are not mutually exclusive. The point in mentioning them is to convey the complexity of therapy outcome assessment and the large number of variables that are considered to be appropriate. The diversity of potential measures raises obvious problems. To begin with, from the

---

[7]The two journals are *Behavioral Assessment* (Pergamon Press) and *Journal of Psychopathology and Behavioral Assessment* (Plenum Publishing Corporation).

seemingly infinite measurement options, the results from separate outcome studies are not likely to be comparable, even if many other features of the studies (e.g., techniques, therapists, and patients) were relatively similar. The absence of comparability of results from different studies raises a problem regarding the accumulation of knowledge.

To redress this problem, recommendations have emerged from the National Institute of Mental Health for researchers to use a core battery of assessment devices in their outcome research (Waskow & Parloff, 1975). The measures entail many of the different perspectives, criteria, and modalities noted here. Thus, the perspectives of patient, others in the patient's life, therapist, and independent clinician were included. Also, different modalities such as paper-and-pencil measures, ratings of overt behavior, and psychophysiological measures were recommended.[8] The idea of a core assessment battery is very attractive for different reasons. Nevertheless, several problems or objections have emerged such as disputes about the adequacy of individual instruments, their relevance to different sorts of clinical problems (Beutler & Crago, 1983; Kolotkin & Johnson, 1983), and whether a single core battery is feasible given the different types of conceptual approaches to treatment and the different types of changes they seek (Lambert, 1979).

Not all variables included in a standard or core assessment battery are likely to be relevant to each patient. Moreover, some problem areas of individual patients in a particular investigation are likely to be ignored by a standard battery. Consequently, there has been a movement toward individualization of assessment of treatment outcome, as reflected in the use of Goal Attainment Scaling (Kiresuk & Sherman, 1968) and the Problem-Oriented Record (Klonoff & Cox, 1975). Other measures have focused on alternative ways of measuring individual presenting problems (target

complaints) and their severity (Mintz & Kiesler, 1982). These and related measurement strategies focus on individual goals of treatment and permit, in varying degrees, quantification of the extent to which these goals are approached or met.

Individualized measures raise special assessment issues of their own. For example, because the measures are individualized, their anticipated relation to other standardized measures is not straightforward. Thus, large-scale validation efforts to help identify what is being measured by comparing individualized with more standardized assessments are relatively rare (Mintz & Kiesler, 1982). The adequacy of individualized measures and agreement on what they assess require greater empirical attention. Nevertheless, individualized assessment provides a way of quantifying the unique characteristics of individual patient's problems. Use of such measures is by no means incompatible with a core assessment battery.

Over a decade has passed since the formal recommendation to use a core assessment battery without its widespread adoption. As a compromise to a single all-encompassing core battery, Lambert (1979) has suggested the use of several specific core batteries that are more treatment or problem specific. Such batteries might be limited in number and designated by problem area (e.g., anxiety disorders). Although multiple cores would resolve some problems (e.g., attempting to represent diverse problems with a single battery where many measures may not be relevant), it would clearly exacerbate others (e.g., disputes about the specific measures that should be used). Yet abandonment of the goal to which core assessment battery was devoted has its own unfortunate consequences.

Follow-up Assessment

Assessment immediately after treatment is referred to as posttreatment assessment; any point beyond that ranging from weeks to years, typically is referred to as follow-up assessment. Follow-up information is obvious important in evaluating therapy techniques. Although the importance of follow-up data is widely accepted, follow-up assessment in outcome studies remains infrequent. Also, follow-up information, when obtained, is in relatively close temporal proximity to posttreatment. One survey of alternative therapy techniques showed an average

---

[8]The core battery included the specific devices, by category: (1.) Patient or client measures-Hopkins Symptom Checklist, Target Complaints, and the Minnesota Multiphasic Personality Inventory; (2.) Therapist Measures—Target Complaints; (3.) Independent Evaluator Measures—Psychiatric Status Schedule; (4.) Significant Other Category—Katz Adjustment Scales, Personal Adjustment, and Role Skills Scales.

(median) follow-up duration of four weeks after treatment (Agras & Berkowitz, 1980).

Follow-up assessment is beset with problems that make the paucity of follow-up studies understandable. Patient attrition is the major problem and tends to be a direct function of the duration of posttreatment−follow-up interval. The loss of subjects raises a host of questions such as whether the conclusions drawn from the remaining sample are the same as those that would have been reached with the full sample, whether, after loss of subjects, there is sufficient power to detect group differences, whether the effects of different treatment and control conditions have been diluted by intervening experiences (e.g., other treatments) and so on.

The reason for mentioning follow-up assessment here is its implications for drawing conclusions about the efficacy of treatment. The familiar issue raised in the absence of follow-up assessment is whether the treatment gains are maintained. This issue is obviously important because of the possibility that differences between treatment (and control) groups at posttreatment assessment may not be maintained at follow-up. In fact, it has long been recognized that techniques that may differ in effectiveness immediately after treatment may not differ at follow-up. For example, Staudt and Zubin (1957) found that several somatotherapies (including psychosurgery, insulin, Matrazol, electroconvulsive shock) led to greater posttreatment improvements than custodial care for the treatment of schizophrenics, but after two to three years of follow-up, the treatments were no more effective than routine care.

The failure of treatment effects to be maintained is not the central issue to be raised here. There is a larger issue of which maintenance is only a part, namely, that conclusions about the effectiveness of alternative treatments may differ as a function of the point in time that assessment is completed. The attenuation of treatment effects over time is not the most dramatic instance in which conclusions based on posttreatment results may be misleading. There are now several investigations that point to entirely different conclusions about the effects of treatments at posttreatment and follow-up. For example, Kingsley and Wilson (1977) found that individual behavior therapy was more effective in reducing weight of obese individuals at posttreatment assess-

ment when compared to a social pressure (group-based) treatment. Yet at a one-year follow-up, the social pressure treatment was superior. Similarly, Jacobson (1984) found that behavioral marital therapy, behavioral exchange, and problem-solving skills training were equally effective at posttreatment in improving marital satisfaction and reducing presenting problems; at follow-up six months later, however, behavior exchange subjects declined in performance, whereas the other two groups either maintained or improved on the measures.

The above outcome investigations, and many others that could be cited (e.g., Deffenbacher & Shelton, 1978; Heinicke, 1969; Patterson, Levene, & Breger, 1977), go beyond illustrating the issue of maintenance of changes in psychotherapy. They point clearly to the impact of drawing conclusions about the effect of treatment at a single point in time. It is quite possible that the conclusions about the effects or relative efficacy of alternative treatments that are drawn at posttreatment are diametrically opposed to those that would be reached at follow-up. The possibility for more intricate relationships exist as well because conclusions might vary at different follow-up durations and among alternative measures. The implications go beyond the methodological issues here. It is quite possible that different treatments may need to be aimed at shorter term as opposed to longer term outcomes, that different treatments need to be sequenced at different points over time to achieve initial impact on the problem and to sustain or enhance gains later, and so on. These questions, beyond the scope of the present discussion, revert back to the central issue. The questions about the effects of treatment are not simply addressed without adding a qualifier about the point in time at which assessment has been conducted.

General Comments

The assessment issues discussed here point to the difficulties in drawing conclusions about the effects of psychotherapy. The effects may vary considerably by (interact with) perspective, measure, assessment modality, the point in time at which assessment is conducted, and other dimensions of assessment. The indefinite number of assessment methods and timing options can in principle generate an equal number of different conclusions about treatment. These issues need to be recognized at the level of individual investigations when they are designed and their results are discussed. Also, at the level of identifying answers to the broad questions of psychotherapy outcome, the inherent difficulties and possible indeterminacies also need to be acknowledged.

META-ANALYSIS

The alternative design and evaluation strategies and the various issues they raise have been discussed in the context of individual outcome investigations. The empirical evaluation of psychotherapy has taken a new turn in the last decade with the emergence of meta-analysis and its application to the complex questions of the effects of psychotherapy and the variables that influence outcome.

Meta-analysis refers to a set of quantitative procedures that can be used to evaluate a body of literature. The essential feature is to provide an "analysis of analyses" (Smith et al., 1980, p. 80). The method has been proposed as an alternative to traditional narrative and qualitative evaluation (i.e., a review of the literature) where the reviewer synthesizes multiple studies and derives conclusions about alternative techniques and the variables of which their effectiveness is a function. A striking feature of qualitative reviews has been the varied conclusions that are drawn from the same literature (see Smith et al., 1980). Part of the problem is that there are no established rules for evaluating, combining, or weighting alternative studies based on their merit or strength of effects or for even drawing conclusions about the effects of a given treatment when the data from different studies are not in perfect agreement. Meta-analysis is designed to improve upon the information that can be culled from a body of research both in terms of how that information is obtained and the range of questions that can be addressed.

The most common way of evaluating the literature through meta-analysis is to compute *effect size*, which provides a common metric across a variety of investigations. Effect size constitutes the dependent measure for the analysis. Typically, effect size is calculated as the difference between means of an experimental and control group divided by the standard deviation (of the control group or the pooled sample from both groups). Within meta-analysis, characteristics of the investigations become the independent variables. These characteristics may encompass virtually all variables that distinguish studies including the types of subjects, the different interventions to which they were exposed, the type of dependent measures, the settings in which the interventions were applied, and others.

The initial and now familiar analyses of Smith and Glass (1977; Smith et al., 1980) looked at the effects of psychotherapy in general. The initial investigation began by evaluating 375 controlled studies drawn from journal articles, books, and dissertations. For each study, an effect size was calculated separately for each dependent variable. More than 850 different effect sizes were used as the basis for conducting the meta-analysis. The original study was expanded by Smith et al. (1980) and encompassed 475 studies and over 1760 different effect sizes. From these seminal meta-analyses, several conclusions were drawn. Two of the more general conclusions have exerted considerable impact (and generated considerable controversy). These conclusions are that alternative psychotherapies tend to produce greater effect sizes than no-treatment control conditions and that different treatments, based on alternative models or approaches (e.g., psychodynamic, behavioral) tend to produce similar degrees of therapeutic change.

Since these original studies, several replications using portions of the original data base, alone or supplemented with additional outcome studies have appeared (e.g, Andrews & Harvey, 1981; Landman & Dawes, 1982; Prioleau, Murdock, & Brody, 1983; Shapiro & Shapiro, 1982; Steinbrueck, Maxwell & Howard, 1983). These studies have addressed a variety of questions about psychotherapy including the effects of treatment relative to no-treatment and placebo-control conditions, the impact of alternative treatments, and many others. Other meta-analyses have appeared that focus more narrowly on specific types of techniques, patient populations, or clinical disorders such as the effectiveness of alternatives to psychiatric hospitalization (Straw, 1983), variations of cognitive therapies (Dush, Hirt, & Schroeder, 1983; Miller & Berman, 1983), and alternative treatments for headache (Blanchard, Andrasik, Ahles, Teders, & O'Keefe, 1980).

Benefits and Limitations

The emergence of meta-analysis has generated two sorts of literature: (1) Direct meta-analyses of alternative bodies of research and (2) evaluations and critiques of direct meta-analyses (sort of a qualitative "meta" meta-analyses). One or both of these literatures are reflected in various books (e.g., Glass, McGaw, & Smith, 1981; Light, 1983; Smith et al., 1980), journal issues with special series, critiques, and commentaries (e.g., Garfield, 1983; Michelson, 1985; Prioleau et al., 1983), and evaluative review papers (e.g., Cook & Leviton, 1980; Green & Hall, 1984; Wortman, 1983). In these sources, the advantages and limitations of meta-analysis have been quite thoroughly discussed. Many of the debates have focused on the conclusions reached from meta-analyses of psychotherapy and how these converge or fail to converge with qualitative evaluations of the evidence or with what generally is accepted. The purpose here is not to duplicate evaluation of the substantive conclusions of previous meta-analyses but rather to highlight major characteristics of the procedures as a research methodology for treatment evaluation.

Objective and Quantitative Analyses

Meta-analysis is designed to provide a more objective means of evaluating the literature and drawing conclusions than provided by traditional narrative reviews. The analysis requires several judgments for which there is no appeal to a priori or uniformly accepted rules. Thus, there is indeed subjectivity in meta-analysis in deciding what studies to include, how each study is to be evaluated, and others (Cook & Leviton, 1980; Strube & Hartmann, 1983). What is unique to meta-analysis is that the decisions, rules, and judgments need to be made explicit. Thus, if there are discrepancies among meta-analyses, these can be more readily traced to differences in what literature was used, how it was treated statistically, and so on.

New Research Possibilities

Meta-analysis can be used to ask questions about the impact of a broad range of variables. To convey the contribution of meta-analysis, it is useful to distinguish two very general types of variables. The first type consists of those variables that can be readily addressed within the context of a single therapy study (within-study variables). Typically, these variables reflect substantive questions about treatment such as the effectiveness of alternative treatments, the parameters of treatment, and characteristics of therapists and clients that influence treatment and others, as discussed earlier. Substantive questions that are addressed in individual studies can be addressed in meta-analysis by combining a large number of studies. The combination of multiple studies greatly increases the strength and generality of conclusions because of the inherent limits of any single study in terms of a restricted range of subjects, measures and other conditions. Also, by combining studies, a wider range of variations across a given variable can be studied (e.g., duration of treatment). Moreover, the impact of a given variable on effect size can be quantified across studies.

The second type of variable refers to those types of questions that are not readily addressed within a given study but require evaluation across several different studies (between-study variables). General examples would include evaluation of various characteristics associated with assessment and experimental design such as the impact of random assignment, reactive measures, the internal validity of the study, and other variables that either are not or cannot be examined within a given study. Methodological characteristics, but other features as well, can be evaluated empirically by coding studies on such variables and evaluating the impact of these characteristics on effect size.

For example, Smith et al. (1980) reported that there was no correlation between effect size and the overall rated internal validity of the study ($r = .03$). The absence of correlation suggests that relatively poorly designed studies do not lead to different conclusions about treatment efficacy than better controlled studies. This conclusion is subject to several alternative interpretations (see Wortman, 1983). However, if it is validated in subsequent studies, the implications would be tremendous. Similarly, effect size was correlated with reactivity of assessment ($r = .18$); dependent measures that are more reactive in the study (e.g., patient-completed measures) show greater treatment effects than less reactive measures (e.g., psychophysiological assessment). Quality of design and reactivity of assessment as possible mediators of effect size are readily studied by meta-analysis.

There are many between-study research questions in the therapy literature that entail assumptions about the impact of alternative variables on treatment outcome. An obviously important one that has been bandied about for sometime has been the use of college students who are recruited for "treatment," as opposed to "real patients," in terms of the conclusions reached about the efficacy of therapy. Obviously, a comparison of treatments among college students and patients could be conducted in a single investigation, although this is difficult to accomplish and well beyond the resources accessible to most investigators. Meta-analysis can readily address this matter by examining effect sizes across studies that differ in subject populations. As noted earlier, results of such an analysis suggest that effect sizes are larger for recruited populations of students than for patient samples (Smith et al., 1980).

Similarly, implicit in the evaluation of many individual studies is the view that the investigator's commitment to a particular therapeutic school may have impact on the results of the study. It is instructive then to see that meta-analysis in fact shows greater effect sizes when the technique is one to which the investigator is likely to show an allegiance than another to which he or she is indifferent or is opposed conceptually (Smith et al., 1980). The data on effect sizes for the issue of analogue populations and possible experimenter bias are subject to a large number of alternative interpretations. The critical point here, however, is to note that research on broad issues can be addressed by meta-analysis.

Informative Value

Meta-analyses have been beneficial in pointing to diverse characteristics of a body of research. When these characteristics constitute deficiencies in the literature, meta-analysis makes them salient and may help contribute toward improved research. The informative value or feedback function of meta-analysis can be readily seen in the analyses of psychotherapy research. To begin with, meta-analysis has clearly pointed to the inadequacies of individual studies in their reporting of information. For example, Shapiro and Shapiro (1983) noted that means and standard deviations were presented in only 60 percent of the sources they included in their meta-analysis. Moreover, they noted missing information on a variety of characteristics among studies, including statements about the experience of the thera-

pists (in approximately 37 percent of the studies), subject attrition (approximately 19 percent of the studies), number of therapists (approximately 26 percent of the studies), and the extent to which persons who gathered data were "blind" (45 percent of the studies). The documentation of gaps in information suggests that standards of reporting adhered to by authors, reviewers, and editors are inadequate (Fiske, 1983). The problem goes beyond obtaining the needed data for meta-analysis but suggests a level of imprecision that obscures interpretation of individual studies.

A related feature of meta-analysis has been that it sensitizes researchers to the notion of effect size in general and to consideration of the impact of treatment. The message is by no means new and frequently arises in discussions of clinical versus statistical significance. Meta-analysis has contributed by addressing the question of impact directly, by reemphasizing the focus and by translating the results of outcome studies into summary statistics that reflect the impact of treatment. Recommendations have been made for incorporating effect size estimates routinely into research (e.g., Rosenthal, 1983); this would greatly improve the yield from individual studies.

Sources of Controversy

Meta-analysis has engendered considerable criticism and controversy. To begin, the objectivity of the procedure has been questioned because of the many decisions that need to be reached in coding individual investigations along multiple dimensions (e.g., type of therapy, quality of design). There is no objective basis for making many of these decisions, and controversy naturally has resulted. However, some of the decisions (e.g., grouping of different techniques or approaches) occasionally have been reviewed as flagrant misrepresentations of the field (Rachman & Wilson, 1980). Also, the objectivity of the meta-analysis and the improvement it provides over qualitative reviews have been challenged by noting that conclusions drawn from meta-analyses of the same or overlapping literature (e.g., Andrews & Harvey, 1981; Shapiro & Shapiro, 1982; Smith et al., 1980) are often quite discrepant (Wilson & Rachman, 1983).

Another issue pertains to use of individual investigations as "subjects" to evaluate within- and between-study variables. Dramatic conclusions have been reached about important substantive and methodological characteristics of outcome studies. For example, in one meta-analysis evaluating studies in which treatment was compared with a "placebo" (nonspecific treatment) condition, no significant relationship was found between effect size and sample size, duration of therapy, use of "real" patients rather than volunteer subjects, and reactivity of assessment (Prioleau et al., 1983). The absence of significant differences does not mean that the variables made no difference. The meta-analysis was based on a small sample ($n = 32$ studies), each of which was counted as having one effect size (mean effect size across all measures within a study). The ability of this meta-analysis to detect significant differences can be questioned.

A related concern pertains to the confound of variables within studies. There are inherent biases within the data because certain sorts of studies are likely to vary systematically on a number of characteristics (Mintz, 1983). For example, studies of the behavior therapies tend to be completed with a narrower range of populations and clinical problems than studies of many psychotherapies. Attempts have been made to correct statistically for the impact of one sort of variable (e.g., treatment technique) on another (e.g., clinical problem). The fact is, however, that experimentally, a particular variable of interest to the meta-analysis is not balanced equally or crossed with other variables of interest. Statistical corrections can go only so far in separating the impact of confounds. A large number of other concerns have been raised about meta-analysis, such as the failure of specific analyses to include large sets of studies that would materially alter the conclusions about treatment efficacy, the unclear relevance of the results of meta-analyses for clinical work, and others (see Kazdin, 1985; Rachman & Wilson, 1980; Strube & Hartmann, 1982, 1983; Wilson & Rachman, 1983).

Meta-Analysis in Context

In its brief history, meta-analysis has already had profound impact on the evaluation of treatment. Although meta-analysis can be evaluated on its own, it is important to place the methodology in the context of other design approaches that are used to evaluate psychotherapy. There are different levels of analysis of psychotherapy effects that reflect the extent to which a study generates conclusions about the effects of treatment on the individual patient.

At the first level is single-case research designs, which consist of evaluation of treatments at the level of the individual patient. The effectiveness of a given treatment or alternative treatments is evaluated on one or a few patients. Conclusions drawn about treatment reflect directly the performance of individuals included in the study. Of course, there are several inherent issues raised by experimentation and evaluation at the level of the single case such as the extent to which performance on a particular measure or set of measures in a given situation reflects behavior in everyday life, whether the results can be generalized to other individuals not included in the demonstration, and so on (see Barlow & Hersen, 1984; Kazdin, 1982a). From the standpoint of the evaluation strategy, however, single-case designs demonstrate changes directly on the behavior of individual clients.

At the second level is between-group research in which alternative treatment and/or control conditions are compared. Between-group studies are somewhat removed from the performance of individuals. This is not an inherent feature of the designs, since individuals typically are the focus of the conditions administered to experimental and control groups. However, in between-group studies treatment effects usually are evaluated by comparing average (mean) performance of the groups and of one group over time (pre-post changes). Mean performance reflects how the group has responded and in this sense constitutes information that is a step removed from individual performance. While the mean performance represents everyone in the group in general, it fails to represent anyone in particular. Thus, the mean has no necessary referent in demonstrating the clinical impact of treatment on the behavior of individual subjects. To the extent that the individual data are not scrutinized, the results of between-group research do not directly characterize the behavior of individuals.

At the third level is meta-analysis. Instead of the client or group, the individual investigations become the "subjects." Meta-analysis examines dependent variables in general by calculating effect sizes. Several different measures may be combined (self-report, overt behavior, psychophysiological measures). The effect size obviously has no representation in performance of individuals included in the original studies. Nor do the effect sizes necessarily reflect any individual study since the mean of a new variable (effect size) is examined so that general conclusions can be made about treatment. There is a tremendous leap from the performance of individuals and groups to the general results of studies whose diverse characteristics and measures are combined. One can question whether, by being so far removed from the original clinical source and datum, the study of effect size yields critical information about treatments that are applicable clinically. Yet as a method of evaluating the literature, meta-analysis makes a unique contribution.

In qualitative reviews, large and consistent effects are needed across studies for conclusions to be drawn about a given body of literature. Only large and consistent effects that overcome nuances and idiosyncracies of subject judgments can be detected. If the literature that is to be reviewed includes a large number of studies and there is not a consistent pattern in the results, the effects of specific variables are more difficult to discern through qualitative analyses. Large effects may be evident and clear within individual studies. Yet between-study effects and methods by which they are achieved vary considerably. Thus, the conclusions that can be reached are often quite tentative. The tentativeness may stem from the conflicting pattern of findings and/or from the incapacity of judgment to weigh the different studies in some systematic way to draw firmer conclusions. The use of statistical procedures is likely to identify and to bring veridical effects into a much sharper focus (Green & Hall, 1984).

To suggest that meta-analysis can clarify relationships and produce firmer conclusions than qualitative reviews of the literature is a matter of dispute. There are some data that can be brought to bear on the question. There are instances in the literature where a qualitative review has suggested few or no reliable effects but where meta-analysis of the same literature has shown otherwise (Eagly, 1978; Eagly & Carli, 1981). Also, in a laboratory analogue study, the superiority of statistical methods of integrating studies has been demonstrated (Cooper & Rosenthal, 1980). Subjects were given seven studies that in fact supported conclusions of a veridical effect for a particular variable. The effects were much more consistently detected by subjects who evaluated the studies statistically than through narrative or qualitative review. In general, the findings suggest that meta-analysis is more likely to be able to detect reliable effects of variables than narrative reviews.

Apart from the analysis of overall effects of variables within a particular literature, the unique contribution of meta-analysis is the evaluation of between-study factors. As noted earlier, such variables as quality of the experimental design, follow-up duration, allegiance of the experimenter to the major treatment condition, and the like are readily evaluated in meta-analysis. Such variables typically are not addressed in qualitative reviews and conclusions about their effects, in any case, are extremely difficult to reach in a reliable fashion.

As the number of studies in a body of literature increases, the clarity and definitiveness of conclusions drawn from qualitative reviews are likely to decline. A large number of studies is not only likely to be associated with increased diversity of the findings, but also greater heterogeneity in the range of designs, assessment methods, and procedures that have been used. From the standpoint of the reviewer, these other variables serve as noise and increase the tentativeness of what can be detected and concluded. Meta-analysis is not burdened by a larger literature in quite the same way. Although there are practical problems of a large literature (e.g., coding all of the studies for all of the variables of interest, computing effect sizes), the conclusions are strengthened rather than weakened by inclusion of a large number of studies. Indeed, meta-analysis depends on a large literature in part to separate independent variables from each other (statistically). Thus, as a method of reviewing a body of literature and making claims about the impact of within- and between-studies variables, meta-analysis provides a unique evaluation strategy.

Basic if not Hidden Issues
There are fundamental issues in psychotherapy research that have important implications for any conclusions that are reached about the efficacy of alternative treatments. Not all of the questions can be reduced to empirical hypotheses that themselves

are addressed in a simple fashion by meta-analysis. Rather, they reflect basic issues and assumptions about psychotherapy and how its effects should be evaluated. Consider a few of the issues briefly.

First, criteria that need to be invoked to define a "high quality" or well-controlled outcome study are not agreed upon. The criteria that should be invoked in the general case have been carefully identified (e.g., Fiske et al., 1970). Invoking methodological criteria in reviews of the literature—whether qualitative or quantitative reviews (e.g., Luborsky et al., 1975; Smith & Glass, 1977)—is a matter of some debate (Kazdin & Wilson, 1978b; Rachman & Wilson, 1980). The tremendous discrepancies that occur in evaluating the quality of research can be shown concretely in how individual studies are viewed.

For example, the outcome study by Sloane and his colleagues (1975) that compared psychotherapy and behavior therapy has been cited as one of the best if not the best outcome study to be completed (e.g., Bergin & Lambert, 1978; Marmor, 1975; Smith et al., 1980; Strupp, Hadley, & Gomes-Schwartz, 1977). The same study has been frequently cited as one of (but not) the worst studies from the standpoint of design and interpretability (Bandura, 1978; Rachman & Wilson, 1980). If such discrepancies occasionally arise in evaluating a single study, multiple studies entered into a meta-analysis no doubt are likely to magnify the problem and make quite debatable any conclusions that are reached. In short, there are important qualitative decisions that need to be made before entering a study into an analysis. The decisions reflect fundamental issues about how research is to be viewed and evaluated.

A common rejoinder to the above objection has been that meta-analysis can address alternative methodological issues empirically by coding studies on selected variables and evaluating them on effect size (Glass & Kliegl, 1983; Glass et al., 1981). For many important variables, this may not be entirely true. For example, a central characteristic that defines the adequacy of treatment is the extent to which treatment has been carried out as intended, that is, treatment integrity, as discussed earlier. Without assurances that treatment has been carried out in a particular fashion, even a large number of studies might be difficult to interpret (cf. Sechrest,

White, & Brown, 1979). Attempts have been made to estimate from the original articles the extent to which treatment was faithfully executed (e.g., Shapiro & Shapiro, 1983), but the information is not really retrievable from most original articles. The variable cannot be carefully analyzed because the integrity assessment procedures are rarely carried out in outcome research. An estimate of the impact of variations of integrity in different therapy techniques is currently unavailable. This, of course, is not the fault of, nor brought on by, meta-analysis. In studies for which the integrity of treatment is unknown, the conclusions or discrepancies in the literature need to be considered as tentative. As with other underlying issues in psychotherapy research, it is important to keep this in mind when evaluating qualitative or quantitative reviews.

A second issue pertains to the broad topic of outcome assessment. Multiple assessment questions such as how to measure treatment outcome, what measures or criteria should be used, how they should be weighted in drawing conclusions, the extent to which various measures correlate with actual behavior or adjustment outside of the treatment context, and many others are yet to be resolved (see Lambert et al., 1983). Ambiguities about outcome assessment have critical implications for drawing conclusions about the effects of treatment. The fact that meta-analysis combines effect sizes across studies or across measures within a study is not necessarily problematic within the goals of this methodology. Yet combining measures skips over many fundamental issues. It is always important to keep in mind that results of meta-analysis do not address fundamental assessment considerations upon which the interpretation of treatment effects very much depends.

Third, the complexity of outcome questions and findings are not fully addressed by meta-analysis. There is still some interest among researchers in addressing manageable portions of the "ultimate question" of what treatment, by whom, and so on. It is not clear that the question has been addressed adequately in the meta-analyses conducted to date. Indeed, the analyses typically collapse across variables in the quest to reach general conclusions. But such conclusions are of unclear value or meaning.

There is a similar point that can be examined on a smaller scale. Subtleties of findings in individual research reports often are neglected in meta-analysis. Thus, interaction effects involving characteristics of patients with treatment or parametric variations of treatment that affect outcome typically are difficult to evaluate. Broad classes of variables and their combinations can be studied (see Shapiro & Shapiro, 1982). Yet for any specific interaction effects, there usually is no extensive literature to which meta-analysis can be applied. There is a limit to what findings can be integrated and analyzed in a meta-analysis. Interpretations of outcome research need to take such interactions into account whether or not multiple studies are available for their inclusion in meta-analysis.

Meta-analysis has provided an important breakthrough for evaluating research. As with any other methodological technique, there are places where crucial decisions need to be made. These decisions themselves are open for debate and reflect fundamental issues that are far from resolved. Naturally, the results of any meta-analysis will be accepted as valid only to the extent that initial decisions and assumptions are acceptable. The quantification of outcome effects provided by meta-analysis usually yields much more information than does the traditional narrative review. Yet many of the basic questions about research studies and what is to be counted need to be evaluated carefully and qualitatively.

CONCLUSIONS

Advances in psychotherapy have been slow, a fact often attributed to the inherent complexity and multiplicity of the clinical problems to which treatments are directed. Recent progress has stemmed in part from recognition of the complexity of the topic and the underlying conceptual and methodological issues treatment evaluation raises. A flurry of outcome research alone will not begin to address the many questions of psychotherapy. Advances in conceptualization of treatment and evaluation methodology are essential for accelerated progress. Theoretical advances help generate hypotheses about what features of the complex treatment processes need to be scrutinized and how they may relate to process and outcome. In an important sense, theory helps to focus attention and to bring order and meaning to what otherwise is difficult to view in a coherent fashion.

The present chapter has addressed various design and methodological issues to help examine propositions about treatment. The treatment evaluation strategies elaborated earlier codify many of the different ways in which the complex questions of psychotherapy can be empirically divided and conquered. The elaborate questions facing psychotherapy cannot be addressed at the global level at which they are usually posed. But systematic evaluation of treatments as they progress through the different strategies can yield answers.

Large-scale studies in laboratory and clinical settings as well as tests of treatment at the level of individual cases are complementary and need to be encouraged. Comprehensive summary evaluations of treatments to evaluate the questions of psychotherapy such as meta-analyses need to be promoted as well to further cull information from available research and to direct attention to the kinds of deficits that need to be redressed in individual studies. Any individual level of analysis suffers serious limitations and can be readily criticized. It is precisely because no single type of study or level of analysis is flawless that methodological pluralism needs to be fostered.

There have been important methodological advances in therapy research. Increased attention to the codification of treatments in manual form and assessment of treatment integrity are two that have direct implications for the quality of treatment investigations. Advances occasionally have emerged from controversy that in years past may have remained at the level of armchair theorizing. For example, controversies over meta-analyses have not merely sparked rebuttals but "new and improved" meta-analyses to confront criticisms directly. There are increasingly shared objectives and views about psychotherapy research. The explicit movement toward integrationism reflects an important development (Goldfried, 1982). Apart from its ultimate contribution to research and practice, its reflects a renewed appreciation of the commonalities of alternative approaches. In addition, there may be greater consensus now than ever before that the effects of therapy reduce to empirical questions for all approaches. Further progress is likely to result from some of the overriding areas of agreement about the need to search for conceptual underpinnings of treatment and to improve the methods used to evaluate outcome.

REFERENCES

Adams, H. E., & Hughes, H. H. (1976). Animal analogues of behavioral treatment procedures: A critical evaluation. In M. Hersen, R. M. Eisler, & P. M. Miller (Eds.), *Progress in behavior modification* (Vol. 3, pp. 207–239). New York: Academic Press.

Agras, W. S., & Berkowitz, R. (1980). Clinical research in behavior therapy: Halfway there? *Behavior Therapy, 11,* 472–487.

Alexander, J. F., Barton, C., Schiavo, R. S., & Parsons, B. V. (1976). Systems-behavioral intervention with families of delinquents: Therapist characteristics, family behavior, and outcome. *Journal of Consulting and Clinical Psychology, 44,* 656–664.

Allport, G. W. (1962). The general and the unique in psychological science. *Journal of Personality, 30,* 405–422.

American Psychiatric Association. (1952). *Diagnostic and statistical manual of mental disorders.* Washington, DC: Author.

American Psychiatric Association. (1968). *Diagnostic and statistical manual of mental disorders* (2nd ed.). Washington, DC: Author.

American Psychiatric Association. (1980). *Diagnostic and statistical manual of mental disorders* (3rd ed.). Washington, DC: Author.

Andrews, G., & Harvey, R. (1981). Does psychotherapy benefit neurotic patients? *Archives of General Psychiatry, 38,* 1203–1208.

Baer, D. M. (1977). "Perhaps it would be better not to know everything." *Journal of Applied Behavior Analysis, 10,* 167–172.

Baer, D. M., Wolf, M. M., & Risley, T. R. (1968). Some current dimensions of applied behavior analysis. *Journal of Applied Behavior Analysis, 1,* 91–97.

Bandura, A. (1977). Self-efficacy: Toward a unifying theory of behavioral change. *Psychological Review, 84,* 191–215.

Bandura, A. (1978). On paradigms and recycled ideologies. *Cognitive Therapy and Research, 2,* 79–103.

Barlow, D. H. (1980). Behavior therapy: The next decade. *Behavior Therapy, 11,* 315–328.

Barlow, D. H. (1981). On the relation of clinical research to clinical practice: Current issues, new directions. *Journal of Consulting and Clinical Psychology, 49,* 147–155.

Barlow, D. H., Hayes, S. C., & Nelson, R. O. (1984). *The scientist-professional: Research and accountability and research settings.* New York: Pergamon.

Barlow, D. H., & Hersen, M. (1984). *Single-case experimental designs: Strategies for studying behavior change* (2nd ed.). New York: Pergamon.

Barrett, C. L., & Wright, J. H. (1984). Therapist variables. In M. Hersen, L. Michelson, & A. S. Bellack (Eds.), *Issues in psychotherapy research* (pp. 361–391). New York: Plenum.

Becker, J., & Schuckit, M. A. (1978). The comparative efficacy of cognitive therapy and pharmacotherapy in the treatment of depressions. *Cognitive Therapy and Research, 2,* 193–197.

Bergin, A. E., & Lambert, M. J. (1978). The evaluation of therapeutic outcomes. In S. L. Garfield & A. E. Bergin (Eds.), *Handbook of psychotherapy and behavior change: An empirical analysis* (2nd ed., pp. 139–189). New York: Wiley.

Bergin, A. E., & Strupp, H. H. (Eds.). (1972). *Changing frontiers in the science of psychotherapy.* Chicago: Aldine-Atherton.

Berrier, G. D., Galassi, J. P., & Mullinix, S. D. (1981). A comparison of matched clinical and analogue subjects on variables pertinent to the treatment of assertion deficits. *Journal of Consulting and Clinical Psychology, 49,* 940–981.

Beutler, L. E., & Crago, M. (1983). Self-report measures of psychotherapy outcome. In M. J. Lambert, E. R. Christensen, & S. S. DeJulio (Eds.), *The assessment of psychotherapy outcome* (pp. 453–497). New York: Wiley.

Blanchard, E. B., Andrasik, R., Ahles, T. A., Teders, S. J., & O'Keefe, D. (1980). Migraine and tension headache: A meta-analytic review. *Behavior Therapy, 11,* 613–631.

Blashfield, R. K. (1984). *The classification of psychopathology: Neo-Kraepelinian and quantitative approaches.* New York: Plenum.

Bloom, M., & Fischer, J. (1982). *Evaluating practice: Guidelines for the accountable professional.* Englewood Cliffs, NJ: Prentice-Hall.

Borkovec, T., & Rachman, S. (1979). The utility of analogue research. *Behavior Research and Therapy, 17,* 253–261.

Brunink, S., & Schroeder, H. (1979). Verbal therapeutic behavior of expert psychoanalytically oriented, Gestalt, and behavior therapists. *Journal of Consulting and Clinical Psychology, 47,* 567–574.

Campbell, D. T., & Stanley, J. C. (1966). *Experimental and quasi-experimental designs for research and teaching.* Chicago: Rand McNally.

Chambers, W., Puig-Antich, J., & Tabrizi, M. A. (1978, October). *The ongoing development of the Kiddie-SADS (Schedule for Affective Disorders and Schizophrenia for School-age Children).* Paper presented at the American Academy of Child Psychiatry, San Diego.

Chassan, J. B. (1979). *Research design in clinical psychology and psychiatry* (2nd ed.). New York: Irvington.

Cook, T. D., & Leviton, L. C. (1980). Reviewing the literature: A comparison of traditional methods with meta-analysis. *Journal of Personality, 48,* 449–472.

Cooper, H. M., & Rosenthal, R. (1980). Statistical versus traditional procedures for summarizing research findings. *Psychological Bulletin, 87,* 442–449.

Critelli, J. W., & Neuman, K. F. (1984). The placebo: Conceptual analysis of a construct in transition. *American Psychologist, 39,* 32–39.

Deffenbacher, J. L., & Shelton, J. L. (1978). Comparison of anxiety management training and desensitization in reducing test and other anxieties. *Journal of Counseling Psychology, 25,* 277–282.

DeRubeis, R. J., Hollon, S. E., Evans, M. D., & Bemis, K. M. (1982). Can psychotherapies for depression be discriminated? A systematic investigation of cognitive therapy and interpersonal therapy. *Journal of*

Consulting and Clinical Psychology, 50, 744−756.

Dollinger, S. J. (1983). A case report of dissociative neurosis (Depersonalization Disorder) in an adolescent treated with family therapy and behavior modification. *Journal of Consulting and Clinical Psychology, 51,* 479−484.

Dush, D. M., Hirt, M. L., & Schroeder, H. (1983). Self-statement modification with adults: A meta-analysis. *Psychological Bulletin, 94,* 408−422.

Eagly, A. H. (1978). Sex differences in influenceability. *Psychological Bulletin, 85,* 86−116.

Eagly, A. H., & Carli, L. L. (1981). Sex of researchers and sex-typical communications as determinants of sex differences in influenceability: A meta-analysis of social influence studies. *Psychological Bulletin, 90,* 1−20.

Emmelkamp, P. M. G. (1979). The behavioral study of clinical phobias. In M. Hersen, R. M. Eisler, & P. M. Miller (Eds.), *Progress in behavior modification* (Vol. 8, pp. 55−125). New York: Academic Press.

Endicott, J., & Spitzer, R. L. (1978). A diagnostic interview: The Schedule of Affective Disorders and Schizophrenia. *Archives of General Psychiatry, 35,* 837−844.

Fishman, S. T. (1981). Narrowing the generalization gap in clinical research. *Behavioral Assessment, 3,* 243−248.

Fiske, D. W. (1983). The meta-analytic revolution in outcome research. *Journal of Consulting and Clinical Psychology, 51,* 65−70.

Fiske, D. W., Hunt, H. F., Luborsky, L., Orne, M. T., Parloff, M. B., Reiser, M. F., & Tuma, A. H. (1970). Planning of research on effectiveness of psychotherapy. *Archives of General Psychiatry, 22,* 22−32.

Frank, J. D. (1961). *Persuasion and healing.* Baltimore, MD: Johns Hopkins University Press.

Frank, J. D. (1973). *Persuasion and healing: A comparative study of psychotherapy* (2nd ed.). Baltimore, MD: Johns Hopkins University Press.

Frank, J. D. (1978). Expectations and therapeutic outcome—The placebo effect and the role induction interview. In J. D. Frank, R. Hoehn-Saric, S. D. Imber, B. L. Liberman, & A. R. Stone (Eds.), *Effective ingredients of successful psychotherapy* (pp. 1−34). New York: Brunner/ Mazel.

Frank, J. D. (1982). Therapeutic components shared by all psychotherapies. In J. H. Harvey & M. M. Parks (Eds.), *Psychotherapy research and behavior change (Vol. 1): The Master Lecture Series* (pp. 5−37). Washington, DC: American Psychological Association.

Galassi, J. P., Berrier, G. D., & Mullinix, S. D. (1982). The appropriateness of using statistically-selected college students as analogues to adult clinical subjects: A preliminary comparison on measures of psychological adjustment. *The Behavior Therapist, 5,* 179−180.

Garfield, S. L. (1978). Research on client variables in psychotherapy. In S. L. Garfield & A. E. Bergin (Eds.), *Handbook of psychotherapy and behavior change: An empirical analysis* (2nd ed., pp. 191−232). New York: Wiley.

Garfield, S. L. (1980). *Psychotherapy: An eclectic approach.* New York: Wiley.

Garfield, S. L. (1981). Psychotherapy: A 40-year appraisal. *American Psychologist, 36,* 174−183.

Garfield, S. L. (1982). Eclecticism and integration in psychotherapy. *Behavior Therapy, 13,* 610−623.

Garfield, S. L. (1983). Meta-analysis and psychotherapy: Introduction to special section. *Journal of Consulting and Clinical Psychology, 51,* 3.

Garfield, S. L., & Kurtz, R. (1976). Clinical psychologists in the 1970s. *American Psychologist, 31,* 1−9.

Glass, G. V., & Kliegl, R. M. (1983). An apology for research integration in the study of psychotherapy. *Journal of Consulting and Clinical Psychology, 51,* 28−41.

Glass, G. V., McGaw, B., & Smith, M. L. (1981). *Meta-analysis in social research.* Beverly Hills: Sage.

Goldfried, M. R. (Ed.). (1982). *Converging themes in psychotherapy: Trends in psychodynamic, humanistic and behavioral practice.* New York: Springer.

Gomes-Schwartz, B. (1978). Effective ingredients in psychotherapy: Prediction of outcome from process variables. *Journal of Consulting and Clinical Psychology, 47,* 310−316.

Gordon, W. A., Freidenbergs, I., Diller, L., Hibbard, M., Wolf, C., Levine, L., Lipkins, R., Ezrachi, O., & Lucido, D. (1980). Efficacy of psychosocial intervention with cancer patients. *Journal of Consulting and Clinical Psychology, 48,* 743−759.

Gottman, J. M., & Markman, H. J. (1978). Experimental designs in psychotherapy research. In S. L. Garfield & A. E. Bergin (Eds.), *Handbook of psychotherapy and behavior change: An empirical analysis* (2nd ed., pp. 23−62). New York: Wiley.

Green, B. F., & Hall, J. A. (1984). Quantitative methods for literature reviews. *Annual Review of Psychology, 35,* 37−53.

Hadley, S. W. (1984). Preface to special issue: Progress and prospects in psychotherapy research. *Clinical Psychology Review, 4,* 1−3.

Hartley, D., & Strupp, H. H. (1982). The therapeutic alliance: Its relationship to outcome in brief psychotherapy. In J. Masling (Ed.), *Empirical studies in psychoanalytic techniques.* New Jersey: Psychoanalytic Press.

Harvey, J. H., & Parks, M. M. (Eds.). (1982). *Psychotherapy research and behavior change.* Washington, DC: American Psychological Association.

Hayes, S. C. (1981). Single-case experimental design and empirical clinical practice. *Journal of Consulting and Clinical Psychology, 49,* 193−211.

Haynes, S. N., & Wilson, C. C. (1979). *Behavioral assessment: Recent advances in concepts, methods and outcome.* San Francisco: Jossey-Bass.

Heinicke, C. M. (1969). Frequency of psychotherapeutic sessions as a factor affecting outcome: Analysis of clinical ratings and test results. *Journal of Abnormal Psychology, 74,* 553−560.

Heller, K. (1971). Laboratory interview research as an analogue to treatment. In A. E. Bergin & S. L. Garfield (Eds.), *Handbook of psychotherapy and behavior change: An empirical analysis* (pp. 126−153). New York: Wiley.

Herink, R. (Ed.). (1980). *The psychotherapy handbook.* New York: New American Library.

Herjanic, B. (1980). *Washington University Diagnostic Interview for Children and Adolescents* (DICA). St. Louis: Washington University School of Medicine.

Hersen, M., & Bellack, A. S. (Eds.). (1981). *Behavioral*

assessment: A practical handbook (2nd ed.) New York: Pergamon.

Hersen, M., Michelson, L., & Bellack, A. S. (Eds.). (1984). *Issues in psychotherapy research.* New York: Plenum.

Jacobson, N. S. (1984). A component analysis of behavioral marital therapy: The relative effectivness of behavior exchange and communication/problem-solving training. *Journal of Consulting and Clinical Psychology, 52,* 295–305.

Kandel, H. J., Ayllon, T., & Rosenbaum, M. S. (1977). Flooding or systematic exposure in the treatment of extreme social withdrawal in children. *Journal of Behavior Therapy and Experimental Psychiatry, 8,* 75–81.

Kazdin, A. E. (1978). Evaluating the generality of findings in analogue therapy research. *Journal of Consulting and Clinical Psychology, 46,* 673–686.

Kazdin, A. E. (1980). *Research design in clinical psychology.* New York: Harper & Row.

Kazdin, A. E. (1981). Drawing valid inferences from case studies. *Journal of Consulting and Clinical Psychology, 41,* 183–192.

Kazdin, A. E. (1982a). *Single-case research designs: Methods for clinical and applied settings.* New York: Oxford University Press.

Kazdin, A. E. (1982b). Symptom substitution, generalization, and response covariation: Implications for psychotherapy outcome. *Psychological Bulletin, 91,* 349–365.

Kazdin, A. E. (1983). Psychiatric diagnosis, dimensions of dysfunction and child behavior therapy. *Behavior Therapy, 14,* 73–99.

Kazdin, A. E. (1984). Statistical analyses for single-case experimental designs. In D. H. Barlow & M. Hersen (Eds.), *Single-case experimental designs: Strategies for studying behavior change* (2nd ed., pp. 285–324). New York: Pergamon.

Kazdin, A. E. (1985). The role of meta-analysis in the evaluation of psychotherapy. *Clinical Psychology Review, 5,* 49–61.

Kazdin, A. E., & Wilcoxon, L. A. (1976). Systematic desensitization and nonspecific treatment effects: A methodological evaluation. *Psychological Bulletin, 83,* 729–758.

Kazdin, A. E., & Wilson, G. T. (1978a). Criteria for evaluating psychotherapy. *Archives of General Psychiatry, 35,* 407–416.

Kazdin, A. E., & Wilson, G. T. (1978b). *Evaluation of behavior therapy: Issues, evidence, and research strategies.* Cambridge, MA: Ballinger.

Kelly, G. A. (1955). *The psychology of personal constructs.* New York: Norton.

Kendall, P. C., & Hollon, S. D. (Eds.). (1981). *Assessment strategies for cognitive-behavioral interventions.* New York: Academic Press.

Kiesler, C. A. (1980). Mental health policy as a field of inquiry for psychology. *American Psychologist, 35,* 1066–1080.

Kiesler, D. J. (1966). Some myths of psychotherapy research and the search for a paradigm. *Psychological Bulletin, 65,* 110–136.

Kiesler, D. J. (1971). Experimental designs in psychotherapy research. In A. E. Bergin, & S. L. Garfield (Eds.), *Handbook of psychotherapy and behavior change: An empirical analysis* (pp. 36–74). New York: Wiley.

Kiesler, D. J. (1973). *The process of psychotherapy.* Chicago: Aldine.

Kingsley, R. G., & Wilson, G. T. (1977). Behavior therapy for obesity: A comparative investigtion of long-term efficacy. *Journal of Consulting and Clinical Psychology, 45,* 288–298.

Kiresuk, T. J., & Sherman, R. E. (1968). Goal attainment scaling: A general method for evaluating comprehensive community mental health programs. *Community Mental Health Journal, 4,* 443–453.

Kirsch, I. (1978). The placebo effect and the cognitive-behavioral revolution. *Cognitive Therapy and Research, 2,* 255–264.

Klein, M. H., Dittmann, A. T., Parloff, M. B., & Gill, M. M. (1969). Behavior therapy: Observations and reflections. *Journal of Consulting and Clinical Psychology, 33,* 259–266.

Klerman, G. L., & Schechter, G. (1982). Drugs and psychotherapy. In E. S. Paykel (Ed.), *Handbook of affective disorders* (pp. 329–337). New York: Guilford.

Klonoff, H., & Cox, B. A. (1975). Problem-oriented approach to analysis of treatment outcome. *American Journal of Psychiatry, 132,* 836–841.

Kolotkin, R. L., & Johnson, M. (1983). Crisis intervention and measurement of treatment outcome. In M. J. Lambert, E. R. Christensen, & S. S. DeJulio (Eds.), *The assessment of psychotherapy outcome* (pp. 132–159). New York: Wiley.

Korchin, S. J. (1976). *Modern clinical psychology.* New York: Basic Books.

Kovacs, M., Rush, A. J., Beck, A. T., & Hollon, S. D. (1981). Depressed outpatients treatment with cognitive therapy or pharmacotherapy. *Archives of General Psychiatry, 38,* 33–39.

Kraemer, H. D. (1981). Coping strategies in psychiatric clinical research. *Journal of Consulting and Clinical Psychology, 49,* 309–319.

Kraepelin, E. (1883). *Compedium der psychiatrie.* Leipzig: Abel.

Krasner, L. (1962). The therapist as a social reinforcement machine. In H. H. Strupp & L. Luborsky (Eds.), *Research in psychotherapy* (Vol. II, pp. 61–94). Washington, DC: American Psychological Association.

Kratochwill, T. R. (Ed.). (1978). *Single-subject research: Strategies for evaluating change.* New York: Academic Press.

Lambert, M. J. (1979). *The effects of psychotherapy* (Vol. 1). Montreal, Quebec: Eden.

Lambert, M. J. (1983). Introduction to assessment of psychotherapy outcome: Historical perspective and current issues. In M. J. Lambert, E. R. Christensen, & S. S. DeJulio (Eds.), *The assessment of psychotherapy outcome* (pp. 3–32). New York: Wiley.

Lambert, M. J., Christensen, E. R., & DeJulio, S. S. (Eds.). (1983). *The assessment of psychotherapy outcome.* New York: Wiley.

Landman, J. T., & Dawes, R. M. (1982). Psychotherapy outcome: Smith and Glass' conclusions stand up under scrutiny. *American Psychologist, 37,* 504–516.

Lang, P. J. (1969). The mechanics of desensitization and the laboratory study of fear. In C. M. Franks (Ed.),

Behavior therapy: Appraisal and status (pp. 160–191). New York: McGraw-Hill.

Lazarus, A. A., & Davidson, G. C. (1971). Clinical innovation in research and practice. In A. E. Bergin & S. L. Garfield (Eds.), *Handbook of psychotherapy and behavior change: An empirical analysis* (pp. 196–213). New York: Wiley.

Lick, J., & Bootzin, R. (1975). Expectancy factors in the treatment of fear: Methodological and theoretical issues. *Psychological Bulletin, 82,* 917–931.

Light, R. J. (Ed.). (1983). *Evaluation studies: Review annual* (Vol. 2). Beverly Hills: Sage.

Luborsky, L. (1984). *Principles of psychoanalytic psychotherapy: A manual for supportive expressive treatment.* New York: Basic Books.

Luborsky, L., & DeRubeis, R. J. (1984). The use of psychotherapy treatment manuals: A small revolution in psychotherapy research style. *Clinical Psychology Review, 4,* 5–14.

Luborsky, L., Singer, B., & Luborsky, L. (1975). Comparative studies of psychotherapies: Is is true that "everyone has won and all must have prizes"? *Archives of General Psychiatry, 32,* 995–1008.

Luborsky, L., Woody, G. E., McLellan, A. T., O'Brien, C.P., & Rosenzweig, J. (1982). Can independent judges recognize different psychotherapies? An experience with manual-guided therapies. *Journal of Consulting and Clinical Psychology, 50,* 49–62.

Malan, D. H. (1976). *Toward the validation of dynamic psychotherapy: A replication.* New York: Plenum.

Marmor, J. (1975). Foreword. In R. B. Sloane, F. R. Staples, & A. H. Cristol, N. J. Yorkston, & K. Whipple, *Psychotherapy versus behavior therapy* (pp. xv–xviii). Cambridge, MA: Harvard University Press.

Marziali, E., Marmor, C., & Krupnick. J. (1981). Therapeutic alliance scales: Development and relationship to psychotherapy outcome. *American Journal of Psychiatry, 138,* 361–364.

Mash, E. J., & Terdal, L. G. (Eds.). (1981). *Behavioral assessment of childhood disorders.* New York: Guilford.

Matarazzo, J. D. (1983). The reliability of psychiatric and psychological diagnosis. *Clinical Psychology Review, 3,* 103–145.

McSweeny, A. J. (1978). Effects of response cost on the behavior of a million persons. Charging for directory assistance in Cincinnati. *Journal of Applied Behavior Analysis, 11,* 47–51.

Merluzzi, T. V., Glass, C. R., & Genest, M. (Eds.). (1981). *Cognitive assessment.* New York: Guilford.

Michelson, L. (1985). Editorial: Introduction and commentary. *Clinical Psychology Review, 5,* 1–2.

Miller, R. C., & Berman, J. S. (1983). The efficacy of cognitive behavior therapies: A quantitative review of the research evidence. *Psychological Bulletin, 94,* 39–53.

Mintz, J. (1983). Integrating research evidence: A commentary on meta-analysis. *Journal of Consulting and Clinical Psychology, 51,* 71–75.

Mintz, J., & Kiesler, D. J. (1982). Individualized measures of psychotherapy outcome. In P. C. Kendall & J. N. Butcher (Eds.), *Handbook of research methods in clinical psychology* (pp. 491–534). New York: Wiley.

Monroe, S. M., Bellack, A. S., Hersen, M., & Himmel-hoch, J. M. (1983). Life events, symptom course, and treatment outcome in unipolar depressed women. *Journal of Consulting and Clinical Psychology, 51,* 604–615.

Murphy, G. E., Simons, A. D., Wetzel, R. D., & Lustman, P. J. (1984). Cognitive therapy and pharmacotherapy: Singly and together in the treatment of depression. *Archives of General Psychiatry, 41,* 33–41.

National Institute of Mental Health. (1975). *Research in the service of mental health.* Report of the Research Task Force. Rockville, MD: Department of Health Education and Welfare.

Nelson, R. O. (1981). Realistic dependent measures for clinical use. *Journal of Consulting and Clinical Psychology, 49,* 168–182.

O'Malley, S. S., Suh, C. S., & Strupp, H. H. (1983). The Vanderbilt Psychotherapy Process Scale: A report on the scale development and a process outcome study. *Journal of Consulting and Clinical Psychology, 51,* 581–586.

Orlinsky, D. E., & Howard, K. I. (1978). The relation of process to outcome in psychotherapy. In S. L. Garfield & A. E. Bergin (Eds.), *Handbook of psychotherapy and behavior change: An empirical analysis* (2nd ed., pp. 283–329). New York: Wiley.

Parloff, M. B. (1979). Can psychotherapy research guide the policymaker?: A little knowledge may be a dangerous thing. *American Psychologist, 34,* 296–306.

Parloff, M. B., Wolfe, B., Hadley, S., & Waskow, I. E. (1978). *Assessment of psychosocial treatment of mental disorders: Current status and prospects.* Report by NIMH Working Group, Advisory Committee on Mental Health, Institute of Medicine, National Academy of Sciences.

Patterson, V., Levene, H., & Breger, L. (1977). A one-year follow-up of two forms of brief psychotherapy. *American Journal of Psychotherapy. 31,* 76–82.

Paul, G. L. (1966). *Insight versus densensitization in psychotherapy: An experiment in anxiety reduction.* Stanford, CA: Stanford University Press.

Paul, G. L. (1967a). Insight vs. densensitization in psychotherapy two years after termination. *Journal of Consulting Psychology, 31,* 333–348.

Paul, G. L. (1967b). Outcome research in psychotherapy. *Journal of Consulting Psychology, 31,* 109–118.

Paul, G. L. (1969). Behavior modification research: Design and tactics. In C. M. Franks (Ed.), *Behavior therapy: Appraisal and status* (pp. 29–62). New York: McGraw-Hill.

Paul, G. L., & Lentz, R. J. (1977). *Psychosocial treatment of chronic mental patients; Milieu versus social-learning program.* Cambridge, MA: Harvard University Press.

Pervin, L. (1977). The representative design of person-situation research. In D. Magnusson & N. S. Endler (Eds.), *Personality at the crossroads: Current issues in interactional psychology* (pp. 371–384). Hillsdale, NJ: Erlbaum.

Prioleau, L., Murdock, M., & Brody, N. (1983). An analysis of psychotherapy versus placebo studies. *The Behavioral and Brain Sciences, 6,* 275–310.

Quay, H. C. (1977). The three faces of evaluation: What can be expected to work. *Criminal Justice and Behavior, 4,* 341–354.

Rabavilas, A. D., Boulougouris, J. C., & Stefanis, C. (1976). Duration of flooding sessions in the treatment of obsessive-compulsive patients. *Behaviour Research and Therapy, 14,* 349–355.

Rachman, S. J., & Wilson, G. T. (1980). *The effects of psychotherapy.* New York: Pergamon.

Raush, H. L. (1974). Research, practice and accountability. *American Psychologist, 29,* 678–681.

Robins, L. N., Helzer, J. E., Croughan, J., & Ratcliff, K. S. (1981). National Institute of Mental Health Diagnostic Interview Schedule: Its history, characteristics, and validity. *Archives of General Psychiatry, 38,* 381–389.

Rosen, A., & Proctor, E. K. (1981). Distinctions between treatment outcomes and their implications for treatment evaluation. *Journal of Consulting and Clinical Psychology, 49,* 418–425.

Rosenthal, D., & Frank, J. D. (1956). Psychotherapy and the placebo effect. *Psychological Bulletin, 55,* 294–302.

Rosenthal, R. (1983). Assessing the statistical and social importance of the effects of psychotherapy. *Journal of Consulting and Clinical Psychology, 51,* 4–13.

Rosenthal, T. L., & Bandura, A. (1978). Psychological modeling: Theory and practice. In S. L. Garfield & A. Bergin (Eds.), *Handbook of psychotherapy and behavior change* (2nd ed., pp. 621–658). New York: Wiley.

Rush, A. J., Beck, A. T., Kovacs, M., & Hollon, S. (1977). Comparative efficacy of cognitive therapy and pharmacotherapy in the treatment of depressed outpatients. *Cognitive Therapy and Research, 1,* 17–38.

Schnelle, J. F., Kirchner, R. E., Macrae, J. W., McNees, M. P., Eck, R. H., Snodgrass, S., Casey, J. D., & Uselton, P. H. (1978). Police evaluation research: An experimental and cost-benefit analysis of a helicopter patrol in a high crime area. *Journal of Applied Behavior Analysis, 11,* 11–21.

Sechrest, L., White, S. O., & Brown, E. D. (Eds.). (1979). *The rehabilitation of criminal offenders: Problems and prospects.* Washington, DC: National Academy of Sciences.

Shapiro, A. K. (1984). Opening comments: "What works with what?" Psychotherapy efficacy for specific disorders—An overview of the research. In J. B. W. Williams & R. L. Spitzer (Eds.), *Psychotherapy research: Where are we and where should we go?* (pp. 106–107). New York: Guilford.

Shapiro, A. K., & Morris, L. A. (1978). The placebo effect in medical and psychological therapies. In S. L. Garfield & A. E. Bergin (Eds.), *Handbook of psychotherapy and behavior change: An empirical analysis* (2nd ed., pp. 369–410). New York: Wiley.

Shapiro, D. A., & Shapiro, D. (1982). Meta-analysis of comparative therapy outcome studies: A replication and refinement. *Psychological Bulletin, 92,* 581–604.

Shapiro, D. A., & Shapiro, D. (1983). Comparative therapy outcome research: Methodological implications of meta-analysis. *Journal of Consulting and Clinical Psychology, 51,* 42–53.

Shapiro, M. B., & Ravenette, T. (1959). A preliminary experiment of paranoid delusions. *Journal of Mental Science, 105,* 295–312.

Sloane, R. B., Staples, F. R., Cristol, A. H., Yorkson, N.J., & Whipple, K. (1975). *Psychotherapy versus behavior therapy.* Cambridge, MA: Harvard University Press.

Smith, M. L., & Glass, G. V. (1977). Meta-analysis of psychotherapy outcome studies. *American Psychologist, 32,* 752–760.

Smith, M. L., Glass, G. V., & Miller, T. I. (1980). *The benefits of psychotherapy.* Baltimore, MD: Johns Hopkins University Press.

Smith, T. W. (1983). Change in irrational beliefs and the outcome of rational-emotive psychotherapy. *Journal of Consulting and Clinical Psychology, 51,* 156–157.

Spitzer, R. L., Endicott, J., & Robins, E. (1978). Research diagnostic criteria: Rationale and reliability. *Archives of General Psychiatry, 35,* 773–382.

Sprock, J., & Blashfield, R. K. (1983). Classification and nosology. In M. Hersen, A. E. Kazdin, & A. S. Bellack (Eds.), *The clinical psychology handbook* (pp. 289–307). New York: Pergamon.

Staudt, V. M., & Zubin, J. (1957). A biometric evaluation of the somatotherapies in schizophrenia. *Psychological Bulletin, 54,* 171–196.

Steinbrueck, S. M., Maxwell, S. R., & Howard, G. S. (1983). A meta-analysis of psychotherapy and drug therapy in the treatment of unipolar depression with adults. *Journal of Consulting and Clinical Psychology, 51,* 856–863.

Steinmark, S. W., & Borkovec, T. D. (1974). Active and placebo treatment effects on moderate insomnia under counterdemand and positive demand instructions. *Journal of Abnormal Psychology, 83,* 157–163.

Steinmetz, J. L., Lewinsohn, P. M., & Antonuccio, D. O. (1983). Prediction of individual outcome in a group intervention for depression. *Journal of Consulting and Clinical Psychology, 51,* 331–337.

Stern, R., & Marks, I. M. (1973). Brief and prolonged flooding. *Archives of General Psychiatry, 28,* 270–276.

Steuer, J. L., Mintz, J., Hammen, C. L., Hill, M. A., Jarvik, L. F., McCarley, T., Motoike, P., & Rosen, R. (1984). Cognitive-behavioral and psychodynamic group psychotherapy in treatment of geriatric depression. *Journal of Consulting and Clinical Psychology, 52,* 180–189.

Straw, R. B. (1983). Deinstitutionalization in mental health: A meta-analysis. In R. J. Light (Ed.), *Evaluation studies: Review annual* (Vol. 8., pp. 253–278). Beverly Hills: Sage.

Strube, M. J., & Hartmann, D. P. (1982). A critical appraisal of meta-analysis. *British Journal of Clinical Psychology, 21,* 129–139.

Strube, M. J., & Hartmann, D. P. (1983). Meta-analysis: Techniques, applications, and functions. *Journal of Consulting and Clinical Psychology, 51,* 14–27.

Strupp, H. H., & Hadley, S. W. (1977). A tripartite model of mental health and therapeutic outcomes. *American Psychologist, 32,* 187–196.

Strupp, H. H. & Hadley, S. W., (1979). Specific vs nonspecific factors in psychotherapy. *Archives of General Psychiatry, 36,* 1125–1137.

Strupp, H. H., Hadley, S. W., & Gomes-Schwartz, B. (1977). *Psychotherapy for better or worse: An analy-*

sis of the problem of negative effects. New York: Jason Aronson.

Suedfeld, P. (1984). The subtractive expectancy placebo procedure: A measure of non-specific factors in behavioral interventions. *Behaviour Research and Therapy, 22,* 159–164.

Thigpen, C. H., & Cleckley, H. M. (1957). *Three faces of Eve.* New York: McGraw-Hill.

Thyer, B. A., & Curtis, G. C. (1983). The repeated pretest-posttest single-subject experiment: A new design for empirical clinical practice. *Journal of Behavior Therapy and Experimental Psychiatry, 14,* 311–315.

Wahler, R. G. (1975). Some structural aspects of deviant child behavior. *Journal of Applied Behavior Analysis, 8,* 27–42.

Waskow, I. E. (1984). Specification of the technique variable in the NIMH Treatment of Depression Collaborative Program. In J. B. W. Williams & R. L. Spitzer (Eds.), *Psychotherapy research: Where are we and where should we go?* (pp. 150–159). New York: Guilford.

Waskow, I. E., & Parloff, M. B. (1975). *Psychotherapy change measures.* Washington, DC: DHEW.

Waterhouse, G. J., & Strupp, H. H. (1984). The patient–therapist relationship: Research from the psychodynamic perspective. *Clinical Psychology Review, 4,* 77–92.

Watson, R. I. (1951). *The clinical method in psychology.* New York: Harper.

Weissman, M. M., Prusoff, B. A., Dimascio, A., Neu, C., Goklaney, M., & Klerman, G. L. (1979). The efficacy of drugs and psychotherapy in the treatment of acute depressive episodes. *American Journal of Psychiatry, 136,* 555–558.

Wilkins, W. (1979). Heterogeneous referents, indiscriminate language, and complementary research purposes. *Journal of Consulting and Clinical Psychology, 47,* 856–859.

Williams, J. B. W., & Spitzer, R. L. (Eds.). (1984). *Psychotherapy research: Where are we and where should we go?* New York: Guilford.

Wilson, G. T., & Rachman, S. J. (1983). Meta-analysis of psychotherapy outcome: Limitations and liabilities. *Journal of Consulting and Clinical Psychology, 51,* 54–64.

Wortman, P. M. (1983). Meta-analysis: A validity perspective. *Annual Review of Psychology, 34,* 223–260.

World Health Organization. (1979). *International classification of diseases, injuries, and causes of death* (9th ed.). Geneva: Author.

Yeaton, W. H., Sechrest, L. (1981). Critical dimensions in the choice of successful treatments: Strength, integrity, and effectiveness. *Journal of Consulting and Clinical Psychology, 49,* 156–167.

3

SOCIAL PSYCHOLOGICAL APPROACHES TO PSYCHOTHERAPY AND BEHAVIOR CHANGE

SHARON S. BREHM
University of Kansas

TIMOTHY W. SMITH
University of Utah

Much of the history of psychotherapeutic endeavors in the twentieth century can be summarized in terms of a recurring tension between individually centered approaches to psychological difficulties and more social psychological approaches. The early years, devoted to establishing psychotherapy as a distinctive and viable treatment, were characterized by an assortment of "schools," most of which could be classified as emphasizing either more biologically based, intrapsychic processes (Freud, Jung) or more culturally influenced, interpersonal processes (Adler, Fromm, Horney, Sullivan). Similarly, the major paradigm debate of the 1960s between psychodynamic and behavioristic proponents threw into stark contrast the role of internal forces (such as motivation and cognition) against the determinism

We are grateful to Carol Ford, Frances Haemmerlie, Frederick Rhodewalt, C. R. Snyder, and Gifford Weary for their comments on an earlier version of this chapter.

of external reinforcement contingencies, often implemented through social interactions. Both individual and social perspectives continue in the mainstream of current clinical interest as reflected in, for example, intensive efforts to develop sophisticated, state-of-the-art biochemical models of psychological disorder, and, on the other hand, the increasing attention being paid by systems theorists and marital and family therapists to the importance of existing social networks. Thus, although we practice an inherently social discipline whenever we attempt to treat psychological problems through psychological means, the history of psychotherapy and behavior change suggests a marked ambivalence about just how much "socialness" should be included in our views of our clients and our understanding of our treatment techniques.

One indicator of this ambivalence is found in the erratic course of the relationship between the two subdisciplines of clinical and social psychology. Initially, the two seemed comfortably wedded, as they shared the same American Psychological Association journal (the *Journal of Abnormal and Social Psychology*) for 44 years. By 1965, however, what had been the integrative gleam in the eyes of Morton Prince and Floyd Allport in the 1920s had become a troublesome union of little convenience to either constituency. There were too many manuscripts to be processed, too few truly integrative papers, and too much disparity between the interests of clinicians and those of social psychologists (Hill & Weary, 1983). In response to these difficulties, *JASP* split into its two present-day descendants: the *Journal of Abnormal Psychology* and the *Journal of Personality and Social Psychology*.

With all the benefit of retrospective wisdom, this dissolution can now be seen as the product of the end of an era. During the early sixties, clinical psychologists appeared, for the most part, to be sharply divided from their colleagues in social psychology. One group practiced psychotherapy; the other group conducted basic, theoretical research. One group read case studies; the other would consider results only from methodologically rigorous experiments. One group cared about the "real world"; the other seemed content to study college sophomores. What could not be imagined then was how radically things would change.

For no sooner had the practical scientists been divorced from the "pure" researchers in terms of their joint APA journal, than both moved into new roles. The advent of behavioral approaches to the treatment of psychological problems enormously increased clinicians' concerns and sophistication about methodological rigor and empirical validation. The "crisis" in social psychology encouraged a whole generation of social psychologists to reclaim the "birthright" (Hendrick, 1983) left to them by Kurt Lewin and (re)create the field of applied social psychology. Moreover, throughout the entire 17 years when clinical and social did not share a common American journal, there were always some persistent advocates of remarriage (in order of publication: Frank 1961/1973; Heller, 1963; Goldstein, Heller, & Sechrest, 1966; Carson, 1969; Goldstein, 1971; Brehm, 1976; Sheras & Worchel, 1979; Strong & Claiborn, 1982; Weary & Mirels, 1982). By 1983, professional interests had come

full circle, and there was sufficient cross-subdiscipline communication to support the creation of a new journalistic merger, the *Journal of Social and Clinical Psychology*.

As a leading sourcebook for both practitioners and researchers, the *Handbook of Psychotherapy and Behavior Change* has made a vital contribution to sustaining an integrative approach through its chapters by Goldstein and Simonson (1971) and Strong (1978) in the two previous editions. Indeed, these chapters can be compared with the present one to provide an overview of how the social-clinical integration has itself changed and developed in response to concurrent changes in each separate field. Goldstein and Simonson, for example, devoted the greater part of their chapter to examining how the social psychological literature on enhancing interpersonal attraction might be applied in a psychotherapeutic setting. Such a focus reflected then current interests in both social psychology (e.g., interpersonal attitudes and evaluations) and clinical/counseling psychology (e.g., credibility and prestige of the therapist as an important factor in promoting therapeutic improvement).

Seven years later, Strong's chapter placed relatively little emphasis on the role of therapist attractiveness, giving far more attention to the social and cognitive variables that promote a client's sense of effective self-control. This orientation fit extremely well into the psychological *zeitgeist* of the moment, when the effects of feelings of control (or the lack thereof) preoccupied both clinical/counseling and social psychologists—as they considered, for example, Seligman's (1975) theory of learned helplessness as a model of depression and Bandura's (1977) theory of self-efficacy as a model of behavior change.

The present chapter is also a child of its time. Here, we have left aside the issue of therapist attractiveness, not because it is unimportant but because we would have little to add to existing reviews (e.g., Corrigan, Dell, Lewis, & Schmidt, 1980). Recent work on learned helplessness and self-control will be addressed, but neither constitutes our primary topic or orientation. Instead, this chapter, like so much of present-day clinical/counseling and social psychology, will display a decidedly cognitive bent. With all its advantages *and* disadvantages, the cognitive revolution has come to rest in the heart of modern psychology. More psychologists today spend more time thinking about how other people think than ever before. One result of this revolution is that it has opened wide the door to integrative efforts: *within* the clinical area, it gets harder and harder to tell the difference among different therapeutic approaches since so many of them now emphasize cognitive components; *between* clinical/counseling and social psychologists, both seem increasingly to share similar interests in cognitive processes. It is our hope that since the dialogue has become easier to conduct, this chapter can serve to increase its breadth as well as its impact.

A SOCIAL PSYCHOLOGICAL PERSPECTIVE

Though most previous examinations of the connections between clinical/counseling and social psychology have concentrated on only a selected aspect of the larger therapeutic arena, their cumulative contribution has been to sketch out a whole range of potentially fruitful integrations. In this chapter, we describe such a range in terms of three major components. First, there is the social psychology of the therapist—a person who is embedded in his or her own social milieu, and who is subject to at least some of the same factors that influence the judgments of nonprofessionals. Second, we consider the social psychology of the client—embedded in his or her existing social network; affected in his or her thoughts, feelings, and behavior by a variety of social psychological processes. Finally, there is the social psychology of therapeutic interventions: the use by the therapist of social psychological principles to help develop and maintain more adaptive functioning on the part of the client.

This range of application may well be the unique benefit to be derived from a social psychological approach to psychotherapy and behavior change. As therapists have become more eclectic in their theoretical orientations and more willing to adopt various clinical perspectives regardless of the "brand name" under which they were first created, it would be regressive—and foolhardy—to argue that any one set of principles holds the magic key to our understanding of maladaptive behavior or our ability to facilitate therapeutic change. It would, however, be equally shortsighted to fail to appreciate that when our focus is on the *interpersonal* treatment of what are to a significant extent *interpersonal* problems in living, the massive research effort in social psychology over the last three decades offers a particularly valuable resource for the clinical enterprise.

THE THERAPIST: THE SOCIAL PSYCHOLOGY OF CLINICAL SERVICES

The Social Milieu of the Therapist

Perhaps nowhere has the ambivalence among clinicians toward taking a social psychological approach been greater than when it comes to considering the social milieu of the therapist. While psychodynamic theorists have been sensitive to the effects of the therapist's history of psychosocial development on his or her functioning as a therapist, extraordinarily little attention has been paid by any model of therapeutic intervention to how a therapist's present, ongoing social situation (both personal and professional) might influence his or her clinical effectiveness. We seem to view therapists as socially impermeable agents who, though they can effect change in others through interpersonal means, are themselves impervious to social influence.

It is, of course, obvious that therapists do not exist in a social vacuum. Indeed, they are, by profession, highly social individuals: having a personal social life with family and friends; a professional social life with peers; and a clinical social life with their clients. Furthermore, as Maslach (1978, 1982) has noted in regard to all workers in human service industries, the social life one has with clients is inherently stressful. Interactions with clients are defined by a disproportionate emphasis (relative to other kinds of social interactions) on negative and distressing information, and by role-restricted behavior such that the human services worker provides help to the client but not vice versa. In addition, there may be a relatively low probability of success for one's efforts with at least some clients, success or failure may at times be difficult to determine, and direct positive feedback from the client may be relatively rare. Thus, therapists spend much of their lives hearing more about other people's problems than their successes, give help without receiving it in return, and often are beset by high risk of failure in or extreme ambiguity about their job performance.

Maslach has suggested that these characteristics of social interaction with clients render human services workers especially vulnerable to "burnout." According to Maslach and Jackson (1981), burnout is a syndrome consisting of the three components of emotional exhaustion, a depersonalized and negative attitude toward clients, and a lowered sense of personal accomplishment in the job. Burnout (or, at least, one or more of the components of the syndrome) has been linked by Maslach's research (see Maslach & Jackson, 1981, for a review) to negative mood states, job dissatisfaction, difficulties with family and friends, insomnia, and use of alcohol and other drugs. Higher levels of reported burnout have been found in the context of working with an increased number of clients, spending a greater proportion of time providing direct client care, and perceiving less direct feedback from the job itself regarding effectiveness of performance.

Maslach and Jackson (1982) suggest that there are two major ways to cope with burnout. First, one can get away from other people: take a vacation; shift to more paperwork and less people-work. They note, however, the negative consequences that can ensue when the coping strategy of social avoidance extends to family and friends. Second, one can turn to other people, especially one's professional peers, for increased assistance and support: responsibility can be shared; mechanisms can be instituted that facilitate obtaining more positive feedback. The importance of one's co-workers has also been emphasized by Fine (1982), whose research indicates that working in what one perceives as an unresponsive organization may promote negative attitudes toward one's clients. Moreover, mental health workers themselves report that receiving social support from their colleagues is one of the most widely used and most effective ways of reducing the psychological discomfort they experience as a consequence of their jobs (Shinn, Rosario, Mørch, & Chestnut, 1984).

Thus, the literature on burnout points to the need to recognize the inherently stressful aspects of providing assistance to clients, as well as the possibility of counteracting this stresss by increasing the social support available from peers. Unfortunately, as will be described in more detail in a later section, trying to understand exactly what "social support" is has

proven unexpectedly difficult. One source of this difficulty involves trying to separate the stress-relieving from the stress-inducing aspects of social interaction. For example, while each of the peer-related ways to provide social support noted previously may be beneficial, each could also have undesirable effects. Sharing responsibility with others may be welcomed on some occasions, but it also requires devoting time and energy to achieving greater coordination and cooperation. Mechanisms that are intended to increase positive feedback from peers may also increase negative comments. Working in a more responsive organization offers the benefit of being able to influence policies and procedures, but it can also add substantially to a person's workload, directly by requiring more administrative work and/or indirectly by increasing the person's concerns about what policies and procedures should be.

Presently, we know far too little about social support—what it is, how it operates—to think of it as a panacea for therapists (or, as we describe later, for clients). More generally, it is still too early to draw any firm conclusions about what type of strategies will assist therapists to cope with the stresses of their profession. Creating such strategies will depend on our developing a much better understanding of the social psychology of the therapist's social network.

Beliefs about Psychological Disorders

The delivery of mental health services occurs within the context of beliefs about the nature of psychological problems. Clinicians, their clients, and the general public all maintain beliefs about the causes of mental and behavioral disorders and how such problems should be treated. While often poorly articulated and rarely examined closely, these beliefs influence several aspects of mental health services. For example, beliefs about psychological disorders held by the public may influence responses to identified patients. Beliefs about their own problems may affect clients' use of services and, subsequently, the outcome of interventions. Clinicians' beliefs channel the initial assessment process and may also bear directly on the effectiveness of their treatments. Moreover, this network of beliefs is closely interconnected; the beliefs of the public and clients are malleable, and the beliefs held and espoused by mental health professionals can have a pronounced effect on the rest of the community (see Farina & Fisher, 1982, for a review).

Although beliefs about mental health may vary on many dimensions, a continuum anchored by the medical/illness model on the one hand and the behavioral/social-learning model on the other appears to be a central focus. This dimension not only reflects a lively, current debate in psychology and psychiatry, but also the research reviewed here suggests that it influences many aspects of mental health services as well.

Healthy subjects holding beliefs reflecting the traditional medical model have been shown to view psychiatric patients as more disturbed and difficult than subjects holding beliefs consistent with a social learning perspective (Golding, Becker, Sherman, & Rappaport, 1975). In a study asking healthy subjects to make judgments about an individual who was responsible for an automobile accident, Ommundsen and Ekland (1978) found that psychiatric patients described as having an illness were evaluated more harshly than were psychiatric patients described as having interpersonal and social problems. More generally, Farina and his colleagues (Farina, Fisher, Getter, & Fisher, 1978; Fisher & Farina, 1979) have demonstrated that descriptions of mental disturbance as an illness rather than as a result of social learning factors affect several important attitudes of healthy subjects. Individuals provided with an illness perspective, compared to those given a social learning frame of reference, saw patients as less able to help themselves, reported that they themselves would be less likely to use the services of a counseling center if they were to develop problems (see also Colson, 1970), felt that it would be less valuable for them to try to identify causes and solutions for their own emotional problems, and felt that the cure of such problems was out of an individual's control.

Beliefs held by clients seem to be similarly important. In an early simulation study of the effects of client beliefs (Rothaus, Hanson, Cleveland, & Johnson, 1963), hospitalized psychiatric patients were judged by independent employment interviewers as less likely to be given jobs when they presented themselves (in accordance with experimental instructions) as suffering from an illness than when they

followed experimental instructions to present themselves as suffering from social problems. Moreover, Morrison et al. (1977) found that among a sample of psychiatric outpatients, believing that their condition reflected an illness was positively correlated with felt dependency on the mental health system. It is also of considerable interest to note that clients' beliefs may be influenced by the type of treatment they receive. Research by Whitman and Duffey (1961) indicated that the initiation of drug treatment for psychiatric problems resulted in a shift among those receiving medication toward a more organic-based view of their condition.

Though the ways that clinicians' judgments are affected by specific information processing variables are described in the next section of this chapter, the small number of studies on the effects of clinicians' more general beliefs are relevant for the present topic. Cohen and Struening (1964) found that staff beliefs in the illness versus social-learning basis of psychiatric problems were related to the length of time patients remained in the community after discharge from hospitalization. Independent of the level of severity of the disturbance, patients treated previously by an illness-oriented staff remained in the community without rehospitalization for a shorter period of time than did patients treated by a social-learning-oriented staff. Clinician beliefs in the psychodynamic versus behavioral basis of problems may also be related to aspects of patient care. Langer and Abelson (1974) found that psychodynamic clinicians rated a videotaped patient as more maladjusted than did behaviorally oriented clinicians. Further, description of the interviewee as a patient, rather than as a job applicant, resulted in increased ratings of severity of maladjustment by the analytic clinicians; the same description did not influence the ratings of the behavioral clinicians.

In a reanalysis of the data from the Langer and Abelson study, Snyder (1977) noted a parallel pattern in the clinicians' attributions concerning the locus of the problem. When the interviewee was described as a psychiatric patient, psychoanalytic clinicians made more attributions to internal sources (such as the patient's personality characteristics) for the interviewee's difficulties than did the behavioral clinicians. Though not assessed by Abelson and Langer or by Snyder, it seems likely that clinicians' expectations regarding the rate and degree of a patient's response to intervention would be related to their evaluations of severity and beliefs about etiology of the problem.

Despite the limited research in this area, the studies described above suggest that beliefs about psychological disturbance can either facilitate or undermine effective care at several different loci—the public's response to identified patients and utilization of services when in need; the client's response to and dependency on treatment; and the clinician's evaluation of the client's behavior. Farina and Fisher (1982) note that these loci may interact to form a vicious cycle exacerbating clients' problems and working against the development of more adaptive behaviors in their daily lives. Consider, for example, the possible effects when clients confronting personal and interpersonal problems are prescribed medication by a mental health professional. Such a treatment response may itself increase the likelihood that clients will view themselves as suffering from an illness, and, thereby, lower their perceived ability to cope in the absence of medication (see section, The Therapy: Attribution Therapy Revisited: The Therapeutic Utilization of Causal Attributions). To the extent that the larger community shares this "illness orientation," such beliefs and self-evaluations on the part of clients may be reinforced and sustained by public opinion. In the long run, the client may become more vulnerable to feelings of inadequacy and may fail to develop adequate coping skills, which may, in turn, increase the likelihood that his or her (now) chronic difficulties will be seen by clinicians and significant others as a manifestation of an irremediable "illness."

Such a possible scenario should not be mistaken as a condemnation of psychopharmacology; the utility of such treatment in many cases cannot be denied. Instead, the present analysis seeks to highlight the often subtle, frequently multidirectional influences within the belief network of clinician−client−public, and to direct our attention to the potential impact these beliefs may have on treatment outcome.

The Clinical Judgment Process

Clinical services begin with a series of judgments. Is this person psychotic? Should this person be hospitalized? Would this person respond well to psycho-

therapy? Though cloaked in the respectable garments of supposed scientific objectivity, these are, in fact, interpersonal judgments. As such, they are subject to at least some of the same limitations and biases that characterize everyday social cognition. Meehl (1960) voiced an early concern about the cognitive activity of the clinician, suggesting that it should be given close, empirical scrutiny. The call to study clinical judgment directly was then greatly amplified by the publication of Rosenhan's (1973) "On being sane in insane places." Rosenhan's exposé of the relative ease with which imposters can mislead diagnosticians provoked considerable controversy (Davis, 1976; Millon, 1975; Spitzer, 1975), but it was never denied that the processes of assessment and diagnosis were in need of critical study.

Consistent with a professional and societal concern for social justice, many studies have addressed the possibility of biased evaluations of women, minorities, and the poor in mental health settings (see Abramowitz & Dokecki, 1977; Smith, 1980; Whitley, 1979; Wills, 1978, for reviews). Typically, these studies have been concerned with *static* biases toward groups of clients. More recently, current models of the active *process* of social cognition have been applied to the arena of clinical judgment and evaluation. Cantor (1982), in particular, has made a strong and compelling argument that the process of clinical judgment is not immune to the limitations of social judgment revealed in recent social psychological research, but is, rather, just a special case.

Much of the current interest in the cognitive activity of the clinician was anticipated by Chapman and Chapman's (1967) work on illusory correlation. Troubled by the continued clinical use of assessment devices found to be lacking in validity (e.g., the Draw a Person Test), the Chapmans sought to determine why clinicians did not abandon such procedures. Two landmark studies (Chapman & Chapman, 1967, 1969) indicated that clinicians and naive subjects acting as clinicians shared the same predilection to "discover" a correlation between test responses and thematically consistent psychological traits (e.g., large eyes on the DAP and paranoia, large shoulders and concerns over masculinity) in spite of the absence of a true, statistical relationship. Thus, the co-occurrence of logically related events was consistently overestimated, if not completely manufactured. Chapman and Chapman speculated that this tendency to "see" the validity of questionable tests in going over clinical protocols was the basis for the continued use of invalid procedures.

Subsequent research has replicated the illusory correlation phenomenon and found it to be robust and difficult to eliminate or even attenuate with training (Golding & Rorer, 1972; Kurtz & Garfield, 1978; Mowery, Doherty, & Keeley, 1979; Starr & Katkin, 1969; Waller & Keeley, 1978). Further, illusory correlations appear to increase as a direct function of the information processing demands of the task (Lueger & Petzel, 1979), suggesting that large amounts of clinical data per case or a large number of cases may magnify the bias. Such illusions are, of course, common in everyday human judgments (Kahneman & Tversky, 1973; Nisbett & Ross, 1980; Ross, 1977). That they are also present in the process of clinical evaluations is disturbing; that they are resistant to attempts at modification raises critical concerns regarding training and practice in clinical assessment.

Another important area of the clinical judgment process concerns the effects of the clinician's expectations about the client. Recent social psychological research has documented in some detail the way in which expectations influence ongoing social interaction so as to elicit expectancy confirmation in both the mind of the judge and the behavior of the target of the judge's expectations (e.g., Snyder & Swann, 1978a, 1978b; Snyder, Tanke, & Berscheid, 1977; see Darley & Fazio, 1980, for a review). Moreover, this research suggests that a bias in the manner in which individuals gather information and test interpersonal hypotheses may underlie much of the expectancy-confirming outcome. The question of whether or not the same confirmatory biases guide the hypothesis testing of clinicians has received only limited attention to date. While some evidence indicates that counselors do not employ biased strategies (Strohmer & Newman, 1983), other findings suggest that they not only occur, but are *positively* correlated with clinical experience (Hirsch & Stone, 1983). Regardless of the prevalence of biased questioning on the part of clinical interviewers, it does seem clear that, if present, such questioning will have marked effects on the overt behavior of the client during the interview (Bandura, Lipsher, & Miller, 1960).

The sequence in which information is obtained may also lend itself to expectancy confirmation. "Anchoring errors" (Tversky & Kahneman, 1974) refer to those judgments about new information that are biased by information previously received. Such errors can occur during the clinical judgment process when significant pathognomonic information is provided early as opposed to late in a sequence of case materials. In their study of clinical anchoring errors, Friedlander and Stockman (1983) asked experienced clinicians to make judgments about the degree of psychopathology evident in a transcript of five psychotherapy sessions. Some of the clinicians received transcripts that included pathognomonic information (i.e, a history of anorexia nervosa) in the first therapy session; others read transcripts in which this same information was contained in the fourth session. When all the clinicians had completed the entire five-session transcript, those who had been provided with pathognomonic information early in the sequence of case materials judged the client as being more impaired and less likely to improve than did those clinicians who had read this information later in the series. It seems likely that the clinicians receiving the pathognomonic information early interpreted subsequent information as consistent with the apparent pathology, thereby "confirming" their expectation and increasing the amount of pathology they perceived. Interestingly, this kind of anchoring error was *not* found when clinicians were replaced by naive subjects (Friedlander & Phillips, 1984).

Expectancy confirmation can occur at the level of recall as well as during the elicitation and processing of information. When asked to recall previously presented material about a target person, material consistent with expectations is most likely to be recalled; factual material inconsistent with expectancy has a much lower likelihood of being remembered (Rothbart, Evans, & Fulero, 1979; Snyder & Cantor, 1979; Snyder & Uranowitz, 1978). Similar biases have been demonstrated in the processing of clinical information by counselors (Casas, Brady, & Ponterotto, 1983; Wampold, Casas, & Atkinson, 1981). Such confirmatory biases may, in part, explain instances where clinicians are overconfident in their judgments. Though the relationship between the amount of clinical information examined and the accuracy of judgments by clinicians quickly becomes asymptotic, clinicians' subjective confidence in their judgments continues to increase monotonically with additional case history information, resulting in an unwarranted level of confidence (Oskamp, 1965).

In addition to sharing the "discovery" of illusory correlations and the effects of confirmatory biases, clinicians and untrained consumers of social information may be similar in the types of social categories they employ (Cantor, 1982). The social categories used by clinicians, one would suppose, should closely resemble the categories of psychiatric nosology. The categorization system described in *DSM-III,* for example, consists of a set of nonoverlapping syndromes, each defined by a set of specific criteria. In contrast, the category systems employed in everyday social cognition lack specific defining criteria and are overlapping (Cantor & Mischel, 1979); these categories are based on prototypes and loose boundaries rather than exact inclusion–exclusion rules. Research by Cantor and her associates (Cantor, Smith, French, & Mezzich, 1980) suggests that the social category systems actually used by clinicians to describe patients resemble the loose categories of the prototype system to a far greater extent than they do the more precise, formal nosological system. The prototype system may also provide a better explanation for diagnostic disagreements than that implied by formal diagnostics. In the Cantor et al. study, clinicians disagreed on the diagnosis of cases where the correct category prototype had a number of features in common with another, incorrect prototype. While not answering the obvious question of what type of system is more valid, it does appear that models based on more general processes of social cognition can accurately describe the diagnostic behavior of clinicians.

Clinical judgments, of course, typically go considerably further than simply assigning clients to one from among a set of diagnostic categories. Most clinicians have a vital interest in understanding the causes of their clients' behavior, both the symptomatic concerns that brought the client into therapy and the client's responses to therapeutic procedures. Here, too, basic processes of social cognition may play a major role.

Perhaps the best documented similarity between causal attributions made by clinicians and those made by the lay public involves the "actor–observer difference" (Jones & Nisbett, 1971/1972). Despite some conflicting results (as highlighted in the review by Monson & Snyder, 1977), the essential actor–observer difference appears to be a reasonably robust phenomenon (Watson, 1982). Across a variety of settings, individuals are likely to assign causality for their own behavior to external, situational factors, but assign causality for the behavior of others to internal, dispositional factors. Thus, the actor–observer difference would predict that clinicians, in their role of observing and explaining their clients' behavior, would tend to emphasize dispositional etiologies such as personality rather than situational influences.

In general, the results of several studies indicate that clinicians do display such an emphasis on attributing the difficulties of their clients to internal, dispositional factors (Batson, 1975; Harari & Hosey, 1981; Snyder, 1977). Moreover, this tendency increases as the observed behavior of the target person becomes more deviant (Harari & Hosey, 1981); is (as noted previously) more pronounced among psychodynamic than behavioral clinicians (Snyder, 1977); and is more likely among professional than nonprofessional helpers (Batson, 1975). The tendency to make dispositional versus situational attributions for client complaints is also related to the type of referral clients are likely to receive (Batson, 1975). Clinicians attributing a client's difficulties to dispositional factors are likely to make referrals to agencies that attempt to change people (e.g., mental health agencies), whereas clinicians attributing the client's problems to the situation are likely to make referrals to agencies that attempt to alter the individual's living situation (e.g., agencies providing financial and vocational counseling).

Some suggestive evidence from a role-play study by Snyder, Shenkel, and Schmidt (1976) raises the possibility that clinicians' attributions may differ from those made by their clients. In this study, college students in the role of "counselor" attributed clients' complaints to personality factors, while college students in the role of "client" attributed those same complaints to aspects of their situation. Taken as a whole, the research on clinicians' attributional tendencies suggests that causal attributions made by mental health professionals may not differ a great deal from those made by nonprofessional observers, and that these attributions are meaningfully related to important aspects of mental health services. What is far more difficult to determine is whether the therapist's dispositional *bias* reflects the reality of the causal processes impinging on the client or is, in fact, a fundamental attribution *error* (Harvey & McGlynn, 1982; Harvey, Town, & Yarkin, 1981; Reeder, 1982; Ross, 1977).

At some point in time, at least some aspects of clinical judgments will be communicated to the client. A wealth of research by Snyder and his colleagues suggests that clients are not likely to be discriminating consumers of such feedback. In general, they are likely to accept interpretations and evaluations of their behavior (Snyder, Shenkel, & Lowery, 1977). However, clients also display a number of preferential biases: viewing positive feedback as more accurate than negative feedback (Snyder & Cowles, 1979); believing feedback based on personality tests to be more accurate than that based on intelligence tests (Snyder & Cowles, 1979); perceiving clinicians who provide positive feedback as more skilled than those who provide negative feedback (Snyder & Shenkel, 1976). Although perhaps reflecting an unwarranted faith in clinical evaluation (particularly in the more socially acceptable aspects of it), client acceptance of feedback can be used constructively. As demonstrated by Halperin and Snyder (1979), clients given clinical evaluations describing them as likely to profit from therapy achieved more behavioral and self-reported gains during treatment than clients not given such evaluations. The more immediate danger, then, may lie on the clinician's side of the fence: should client acceptance of feedback be accepted by the clinician as an index of clinical accuracy, the clinician may find himself or herself led down the primrose path of the client's social-evaluative biases.

It should be clear from the discussion throughout this section that clinical judgments differ from more routine social judgments in content but not necessarily in the process by which they occur. The same cognitive shortcuts that allow laypeople to cope with an otherwise overwhelming amount of data from their social world operate within the mental health system. The social cognition of the clinician includes sources of bias and inaccuracy; the flawed products that sometimes are generated by these biases and inaccuracies may be accepted as valid by clients;

and such acceptance could act to make the clinician even more certain of his or her original, faulty conclusions. Given the vulnerability of the therapeutic interaction to these kinds of self-fulfilling prophecies, the need for further research into clinical judgment processes seems clear and pressing (Arkes, 1981).

THE CLIENT: SOCIAL PSYCHOLOGICAL DETERMINANTS OF ADJUSTMENT

Social Support: The Client and His or Her Existing Social Network

It is probably inevitable in the building of any new profession that claims for the unique benefits it offers are exaggerated, and the possibility of deriving similar benefits from informal, nonexpert associations derogated. Only when the profession becomes securely established can it afford to be more tolerant of and even ally itself with sources of benefit that lie outside professional boundaries. Thus, lawyers have only recently become more accepting of do-it-yourself handling of routine legal matters; physicians more curious about the actual effects of folk medicine and healing; clinicians and counselors more interested in understanding and promoting the ways that existing, informal relationships provide social support for ongoing healthy adjustment.

It may also be inevitable that once professionals acknowledge possible benefits to be gleaned from nonprofessional sources, they may tend to exaggerate them. This seems to be the case in the area of social support. During the mid-1970s, there was an upsurge of interest in and confidence about the positive effects that social support was believed to have on both psychological well-being and physical health (Caplan & Killilea, 1976; Cassel, 1974, 1976; Cobb, 1976, 1979; Lynch, 1977; Vaillant, 1977). It was as though professionals had discovered a "magic bullet" (Cohen & Syme, 1985) that was going to cure psychological disorder without a therapist, prevent physical debilitation without a physician, and protect individuals from the harmful consequences of stress without having to change either their behavior or the broader social and economic structure of the society.

Since these early days of great enthusiasm, there has been a tremendous outpouring of research on social support and, increasingly, recognition that the issue is far more complex than had been anticipated. This section provides a brief overview of some of the major conceptual issues raised by recent critiques (Cohen & McKay, 1984; Gore, 1981; Heller, 1979; Monroe, 1983; Thoits, 1982; Wallston, Alagna, DeVellis, & DeVellis, 1983) as well as a description of current trends in research and theory on social support.

Conceptual and Methodological Problems

Correlation is not causation. Perhaps the single, most problematic aspect of much of the previous work on social supports is its attempt to deduce an etiological implication from purely associational results. Thus, while Leavy's (1983) review details the consistent finding that there is "a relationship between a lack of support and serious psychological disorder" (p. 9), he is careful to note that we have no compelling evidence on how this relationship might come about. Lack of social support could increase the likelihood of a person's developing psychological difficulties; but exhibiting deviant and/or distressing behavior could reduce a person's access to social support from others; or some third variable (such as socioeconomic status) could contribute to both psychological disorder and low levels of available social support (Morgan, 1976).

Not all social relationships are equally beneficial. The earliest and most simplistic way of defining social support emphasized sheer quantity of social relations, regardless of the quality of these relationships or the needs of the individual involved. It rapidly became apparent that this quantitative approach was inadequate and that, instead, the specific *source of social support* (Berkman & Syme, 1979; LaRocco, House, & French, 1980), *the type of stress* the individual is under (Morrow, Hoagland, & Carnrike, 1981), and *the type of socially supportive action* the individual receives (Andrews, Tennant, Hewson, & Vaillant, 1978)—and, sometimes, all three (Bankoff, 1983)—must be taken into account.

Not all social relationships are beneficial. Throughout the social support literature, there are various examples of what might be called "negative social support"—that is, instances in which the presence of apparent support in the person's social environment is associated with harmful effects on adjustment. Consider, for example:

- In research by Schaefer, Coyne, and Lazarus (1981), the number of social support sources was *positively* correlated with depression.
- Middle-and upper-level business executives at *greatest* risk for physical illness were characterized by higher job stress, lower scores on the personality dimension of "hardiness," and *higher* levels of perceived support from their families (Kobasa & Puccetti, 1983).

Though causation can no more be determined from these negative associations than from the more typical positive correlation between social support and adjustment, at least one possible causal connection would be consistent with both common sense and clinical outcome research. Just as we now realize that there can be deterioration effects for some clients with some therapists, so does any social relationship have the potential to do more harm than good (Rook, 1984). Sandler and Barrera (1984) have suggested that one might expect especially negative effects from relationships that are both supportive *and* upsetting to the individual. Presumably the support in such cases acts to increase the person's dependency on a relationship that is, in other respects, distressing.

When is social support not a life event? One widely adopted view of the relationship between social support and adjustment is in terms of the "buffer model." This model (first explicitly described by Cassel, 1974) holds that social support has its most (or, perhaps, only) beneficial effect when the individual is under stress; social support is thus seen as a buffer against what would otherwise be the harmful consequences of stressful experience. Recent reviews have pointed to the inconsistent empirical confirmation for this model (Cohen & McKay, 1984; Leavy, 1983), and the possibility that much of the relevant research may suffer from serious methodological flaws (Gore, 1981; Monroe, 1983; Thoits, 1982). The major issues that make the model problematic center around the relationship between life events and social support.

As several investigators (Heller, 1979; Schaefer et al. 1981; Thoits, 1982) have pointed out, when negative life events involve social loss, the stress of life events becomes directly confounded with social support. Thus, comparisons between people who are high in life events change and low in social support versus those who are high in life events change and high in social support may, in fact, be comparing people who have suffered a social loss versus those who have not. If so, the former group may have experienced more stress than the latter, contrary to the assumption made by many researchers that the two groups are equated for stress and differ only in terms of social support. Not only does such a confound stack the deck in favor of the buffer model (Thoits, 1982), it obscures the vital point that to have lost a significant person in one's life is not necessarily the same as never having had such a person (Heller, 1979; Slater & Depue, 1981).

We also have to ask whether the *presence* of social support should more simply be considered as a subset of *positive* life events. If so, other—nonsocial—positive outcomes could presumably be equally beneficial to the individual. Research by the Sarasons and their colleagues (Sarason, Levine, Basham, & Sarason, 1983; Sarason & Sarason, 1982) has found a positive relationship between social support and positive life events. Moreover, in some studies, positive life events have been shown to have a similar (Cohen & Hoberman, 1983) or even more reliable (Holahan & Moos, 1981) effect than social support on various measures of physical and psychological well-being.

Perhaps the most striking evidence of the importance of general good fortune comes from an experiment by Reich and Zautra (1981). These investigators used prescribed positive events (i.e., instructing subjects to engage in activities they enjoyed but had not done for awhile) as a treatment technique. For subjects who had reported many previous negative life events, those who were told to engage in a greater number of positive activities indicated less psychiatric distress after engagement than those instructed to engage in fewer such activities. This difference did not occur for subjects reporting few negative life events. Thus, in one of the rare experimental, prospective demonstrations of a buffer effect, the buffer was not amount of social support, but number of pleasurable activities. One must wonder, then, whether there is anything special

about social support, or would a variety of social and nonsocial positive life events do just as well?

Though most recent reviews of the social support literature are critical of both existing conceptual and methodological shortcomings, the eventual goal is a constructive one. Research on social support offers the potential for increasing scientific understanding of social relationships and developing effective interventions to improve the welfare of individuals. From a historical perspective, we can now see that it took the pioneers of contemporary interest in social support (Caplan, Cassel, Cobb) to broaden our view of therapeutic encounters to include informal as well as formal, professionally sanctioned interactions. Perhaps, then, current criticism will serve to wean us away from hopes for a "magic bullet" to the more complicated but still crucial reality of day-to-day social interaction. Indeed, there is every indication that newly developing perspectives on social support are more sophisticated conceptually as well as more consistent with recent trends in clinical/counseling psychology.

Current Trends in the Study of Social Support
Social support as a psychological variable. Recent research has seen an increasing emphasis on the psychological nature of the social support process. Though early studies took a quantitative—more is better—approach, later work has been concerned with the quality of relationships. The focus of attention has also shifted from an enumeration of the assistance or support that one has received in the past to an assessment of the social benefits that people perceive as available to them in the future. A number of writers (e.g., Andrews et al., 1978; Cohen & Hoberman, 1983; Heller & Swindle, 1983; Procidano & Heller, 1983; Sarason et al., 1983; Sarason & Sarason, 1982; Schulz & Decker, 1982; Stokes & Wilson, 1984) have indicated their belief that the perceived availability of help from others is at least as important as previous help received. Finally, the role of tangible, instrumental assistance is being reassessed, with the recognition that it may be the individual's interpretation of this assistance that is the province of psychological interest and investigation (e.g., Cohen & McKay, 1984; House, 1981). Thus, there seems an increasing inclination toward "psychologizing" social support and paying

more heed to people's perceptions, expectations, and interpretations of their social relations.

Specificity versus generality. As investigators have become discouraged with nonspecific models of social support, they have begun to develop more specific, structural approaches such as network analysis (Gottlieb, 1981; Hirsch, 1980, 1981; Phillips & Fischer, 1981; Wellman, 1981; Wilcox, 1981a). In network analysis, the relationships among the *providers* of social support are examined in terms of such variables as density (amount of interrelationship among network members) and overlap (amount of interrelationship among members of networks defined as separate on a criterion variable). The multidimensionality (different types of activities engaged in) of the relationships between the target individual and network members is also frequently considered. One of the goals of network analysis is to discover the specific types of networks that are most beneficial for individuals in specific types of (usually stressful) situations.

There may, however, be a general component as well. In a number of discussions of the process of social support (Gottlieb, 1983; Heller & Swindle, 1983; Moss, 1973; Wilcox, 1981b; Wortman & Dunkel-Schetter, 1979), it has been suggested that an individual's self-esteem may play a crucial, mediating role between receiving social support and benefiting psychologically and/or physiologically. Recent research has begun to indicate some of the possible connections that may exist among these three factors. First, diverse measures of social support have been found to have significant associations with measures of self-esteem (e.g., Hirsch, 1980; LaRocco & Jones, 1978; Sarason et al., 1983). Second, in a study by Cohen and Hoberman (1983) on social support and life-change stress, "self-esteem support" (the measure of which closely resembles traditional self-esteem scales) was found to be one of the most reliable buffers against depression and physical symptomatology.

Third, and perhaps most important, a longitudinal study by Pearlin and his associates (Pearlin, Menaghan, Lieberman, & Mullan, 1981) explicitly examined self-esteem as a mediator between the stress of job disruption and the psychological consequence of depression. These investigators found no direct effects of currently existing levels of social support on changes in depression during the four-year period covered in their study. However, high levels of social support in the face of job disruption during this time period were associated with positive changes in self-esteem and feelings of mastery, which, in turn, were associated with reduced depression over the course of the study. Although it is regrettable that Pearlin et al. measured social support only during the second of their two waves of interviews and, thus, could not ascertain the relationship between *changes* in social support and *changes* in mastery and self-esteem, their results provide the most compelling evidence to date that social support may act *indirectly* on the person's adjustment status through its effects on feelings about the self.

Thus, the "new look" in social support has begun to focus on people's interpretations of social events and on the impact of these interpretations on their feelings of mastery and self-esteem. Social support researchers are also beginning to provide a more refined and detailed map of the connections between specific types of social networks and specific types of benefit. Both approaches offer great potential for clinical intervention. For example, social support may be there for a client, but not be perceived, or be misinterpreted so that self-esteem is not enhanced. Therapeutic work on these issues seems well within the scope of the more cognitive orientation in clinical/counseling psychology described throughout this chapter. In addition, enhanced self-esteem as a product of the therapeutic relationship may open up more possibilities for clients to establish socially supportive relationships in their existing social environments. Finally, should we be able to develop more precise network–benefit maps, the therapist may be able to serve as a guide to assist the client in discovering more beneficial social territories.

Social Cognition Processes

Attributions and Depression

The study of attributional processes in maladaptive behavior has been one of the most active areas in the interface between social and clinical psychology, with a major focus on reformulated, attributional models of the relationship between learned helplessness and depression (Abramson, Seligman,

& Teasdale, 1978; Miller & Norman, 1979; Peterson & Seligman, 1984). Though the earlier version of this relationship (Seligman, 1975) had stimulated a massive research effort with animal as well as normal and clinical human subject populations, it fell under sharp criticism in the late 1970s (e.g., Buchwald, Coyne, & Cole, 1978; Costello, 1978). Attributional models were then developed in order to deal with limitations in the earlier perspective that had become apparent to both its proponents and its critics. What has not perhaps been fully appreciated is the conceptual complexity involved in this effort to find new, more cognitive clothes for the older theory.

Basing our interpretation on the most recent published version of the reformulated model (Peterson & Seligman, 1984), we gather that there have been four major changes from the old to the new. First, the description of the sufficient prerequisite psychological condition for the production of learned helplessness has been drastically modified. In Seligman's original framework this prerequisite condition was described as the perception that personal responses and event outcomes were noncontingent; the reformulated model defines this condition as consisting of the expectation that "no action will control outcomes in the future" (Peterson & Seligman, 1984, p. 349). Though the reasons for this modification are seldom addressed, it was presumably necessary in order to accommodate the new role of attributional processes. In the original theory, the organism was depicted as bewildered, without any understanding of why painful events were occurring. The essence of the reformulated model, on the other hand, is that the organism does understand why, but that it is this explanation that is itself pernicious.

The second major change from the original to the reformulated model of learned helplessness involves the inclusion of attributional mediators to account for when the experience of a specific, negative, uncontrollable (i.e., unavoidable) outcome will engender the expectation of uncontrollability in the future. The original model did not specify mediating conditions between specific experience and the perception of noncontingency; indeed, it seemed to assume that if the experimenter knew there was, in fact, noncontingency, the subject would so perceive it. The reformulated model proposes that our expectations of future uncontrollability reflect our explanations for current uncontrollability. If we posit a cause that should endure across time (stability) and should be applicable across settings (global), then failure in the present should create generalized expectations for failure in the future. (It might be noted that the earlier learned helplessness theory explicitly postulated that noncontingent positive outcomes as well as noncontingent negative ones should lead to a state of helplessness and, thereby, performance deficits. The reformulated model restricts itself to negative outcomes.)

A third theoretical development embodied in the reformulated model concerns how an individual's causal explanations of failure affect depressive symptomatology. As we understand the reformulated model, most of the deficits manifested in the depressive state (i.e., motivational, cognitive, emotional) are presumed to flow relatively automatically from expecting future uncontrollability as a function of having attributed current failure to stable, global causes. This sequence, however, is not regarded as sufficient to produce the low level of self-regard that is usually seen as a hallmark symptom of depression. The reformulated model must, therefore, add on another attributional mediator: ascribing failure to personal, internal causes. It is this internal attribution (independent, it appears, of its stability or globality) that results in decreased self-esteem.

Finally, the reformulated model of learned helplessness goes beyond the original paradigm that involved an event and the generalization of its effects to subsequent behavior. The model has enlarged its purview to include individual differences among people in the way they typically account for negative events in their lives. Thus, those individuals who typically draw upon global, stable, and internal explanations for the undesirable things that happen to them are said to be vulnerable in the face of adversity to becoming depressed. The propensity to make these kinds of attributions for negative outcomes is labeled the "depressive attributional style."

Like its nonattributional predecessor, the reformulated attributional model has been subjected to considerable empirical investigation. Also like its predecessor, it has evoked criticism and controversy (e.g., Coyne & Gotlib, 1983; Krantz & Rude, 1984). The present chapter does not attempt an exhaustive review of the numerous studies examining various aspects of the reformulated model. Its more limited objective is to focus on two central questions: (1) Do depressives display the depressive attributional style? and (2) What evidence currently exists to indicate that this style is a causal agent in the development of depression?

Several studies have found that subclinical depressives, in contrast to nondepressives, tend to attribute *actual failure on laboratory tasks* to internal factors. However, they also attribute successes internally, a finding that is inconsistent with the reformulated model (Kuiper, 1978; Rizley, 1978). Moreover, depressed and nondepressed psychiatric patients do not appear to differ in their attributions regarding laboratory tasks (Miller, Klee, & Norman, 1982). In terms of *imagined failure on hypothetical events*, both subclinical and clinical adult depressives have been found to make internal, stable, global attributions (Eaves & Rush, 1984; Janoff-Bulman, 1979; Peterson, Schwartz, & Seligman, 1981; Raps et al. 1982; Seligman, Abramson, Semmel, & von Baeger, 1979), as have depressed children (from both normal—Kaslow, Rehm, & Siegel, 1984; Leon, Kendall & Garber, 1980; Seligman et al., 1984—and clinical—Kaslow, Rehm, Pollack, & Siegel, Note 1—populations). However, some studies using hypothetical events have been unable to demonstrate the expected difference between depressed and nondepressed psychiatric patients (Hamilton & Abramson, 1983; Miller et al., 1982), while others have found depressed and nondepressed subjects to differ in terms of stability and globality but not internality (Blaney, Behar, & Head, 1980; Sweeney, Shaeffer, & Golin, 1982).

When we turn to attributions for *recent negative life events*, the empirical evidence continues to be inconsistent. In some studies, depressives have tended to attribute their most stressful, recent negative life event to internal factors (Gong-Guy & Hammen, 1980; Miller et al., 1982). Other investigators, however, have failed to find an association between depression and internal attributions for recent negative events (Coyne, Aldwin, & Lazarus, 1981; Hammen & Cochran, 1981; Hammen & deMayo, 1982; Hammen, Krantz, & Cochran, 1981). Still others have provided mixed support: depression has correlated with stable and global attributions but not internal ones (Barthé & Ham-

men, 1981; Firth & Brewin, 1982); and with internal but also controllable factors (Harvey, 1981). Quite unexpectedly, depression was found to be associated with external attributions for recent unemployment (Feather & Davenport, 1981). Similarly conflicting results prevail concerning the persistence of the depressive attributional style after depression remits (Eaves & Rush, 1984; Hamilton & Abramson, 1983). Thus, the present empirical data base regarding the existence of a consistent depressive attributional style is both confusing and, at times, contradictory.

A second, crucial set of studies addresses the issue of whether or not the depressive attributional style *predicts* the development of depression. Again, the results are inconsistent. Studies of depression arising after childbirth (Cutrona, 1983; O'Hara, Rehm, & Campbell, 1982), after poor performance on classroom examinations (Metalsky et al., 1982), and simply over time (Golin, Sweeney, & Shaeffer, 1981; Seligman et al., 1984) have provided some, though not uniform, support. Other studies employing a very similar methodology have failed to find the expected, prospective relationship between attributional style and depression (Manly, McMahon, Bradley, & Davidson, 1982; Peterson et al., 1981), and instead suggest that attributional style is a concomitant of depression (see also Lewinson, Steinmetz, Larson, & Franklin, 1981). The possibility that the depressive attributional style may act to maintain, even if it does not elicit, depression has been argued by some investigators (Eaves & Rush, 1984), though some research indicates that chronicity may be predicted only by some of the specific aspects of the overall style (Firth & Brewin, 1982).

Even this brief review of the research on two limited, though crucial, issues addressed by the reformulated, attributional model of learned helplessness is sufficient to document that, at least in the area of depression, reformulation has not cured the empirical difficulties encountered by Seligman's original proposal. The conflicting results that have been obtained are certainly suggestive that attributional processes play some sort of role in depression. But whether that role is best characterized as that of a causal agent, a concomitant, or a maintenance factor cannot be presently determined.

Nor is it clear what specific class of attributions

might be of greatest significance in any of these roles. It is, for example, particularly troublesome that so many of the conflicting findings involve the effects of internal attributions. As noted in our earlier description of the conceptual evolution from Seligman's original theoretical framework to the current attributional model, internal attributions are explicitly posited as necessary for decreased self-esteem, and most learned helplessness theorists seem to accept that such decrements in self-regard are a cardinal feature of the depressive state. Thus, the model appears most vulnerable to disconfirmation where it makes its most specific statement in regard to clinical depression. An additional problem that we would emphasize involves the size of the effects that have been obtained by studies that confirm the model's predictions. Typically, these correlations between depression and attributional style have ranged from .25 to .35, suggesting that whatever the role that attributional style may play in regard to depression, it is of minor consequence. In light of these difficulties, it may well be that the study of the relationship between attributional processes and depression would profit from the development of new conceptual frameworks—frameworks less tied to the learned helplessness perspective and more responsive to both the properties of clinical phenomena (Depue & Monroe, 1978) and the full range of existing research findings.

Attributions in Anxiety, Family Process, and Mental Retardation

Depression is not the only psychological disorder that has been examined from the point of view of attribution theory. Attributions associated with other clinical problem areas have been the focus of several studies. For example, shy males have been found to differ from their non-shy counterparts by attributing social failures, but not social successes, to their own abilities (Girodo, Dotzenroth, & Stein, 1981). Similarly, test-anxious students were characterized by a greater tendency, compared to non-anxious students, to emphasize characterological rather than behavioral or external explanations for poor performance on classroom exams (Arkin, Kolditz, & Kolditz, 1983).

Attributional analyses of disturbed family relationships have also been offered. Recent research has indicated that distressed marital couples differ from non-distressed couples by making more global attributions for the negative responses of their spouses and by viewing the causes of positive spouse behaviors as less controllable (Fincham & O'Leary, 1983). Similarly, distressed couples appear more likely than non-distressed couples to attribute their spouses' negative behaviors to internal factors, but less likely to make internal attributions for positive spousal behavior (Fichten, 1984; Jacobson, McDonald, Follette, & Berley, 1985). Attributional processes may also be involved in child abuse. Abusing mothers have been found to make internal, stable atttributions for the negative behavior of their own, but not other's children. Further, these abusing mothers tended to make external, unstable attributions for the positive behavior of their own children. Nonabusing mothers did not demonstrate these comparative biases (Larrance & Twentyman, 1983).

Another area where attributional factors have been examined involves the lack of behavioral persistence demonstrated by mentally retarded children following failure or frustration. Weisz (1981) found attributional differences in adult judgments of equivalent task failures produced by a "six year old child" versus a "nine year old retarded child with a mental age of six years." Failure by the six year old was attributed to lack of effort, while the same level of performance in the case of the retarded child was attributed to insufficient ability. In commenting on his results, Weisz noted how the attributional bias of adults toward retarded children may lead to their providing less encouragement to such children, thus making them particularly vulnerable to deficits in behavioral persistence.

The research reviewed in this section is at a much earlier stage of development than the investigation of the possible relationship between attributional processes and depression. It is always possible that the positive and reasonably consistent results of these preliminary studies may be followed by some of the empirical inconsistency so troublesome for our understanding of depression. It is also possible, however, that causal attributions may have clearer and/or stronger effects in these newer areas of inquiry. Perhaps especially promising are those efforts (Fincham & O'Leary, 1983; Jacobson et al., 1985; Larrance & Twentyman, 1983; Weisz, 1981) that concentrate on the way attributive processes guide social judgments. In reference to this research, one might recall that much of the initial work in social psychology on attribution theory (Heider, 1958; Jones & Davis, 1965) was concerned with the attributions that observers make about others. Bem's (1967, 1972) theory of self-perception then opened the way for a consideration of internal attributive processes. Clinical research on the role of causal attributions now appears to be moving back to the earlier, more social perspective.

Self-perception

Information processing. The self-concept has a rich history in psychology (Cooley, 1902; James, 1890; Mead, 1934; Rogers, 1951) and, in recent years, has received renewed attention in social psychology (e.g., Rosenberg & Kaplan, 1982; Wegner & Vallacher, 1980). One facet of this renewed interest has involved the use of paradigms developed by experimental psychologists. Based on these information-processing paradigms where recall and recognition rates are the primary dependent measures, recent studies have demonstrated that the self-concept (or self-schema) facilitates and organizes the encoding and recall of self-relevant information (Kuiper & Rogers, 1979; Markus, 1977; Rogers, Kuiper, & Kirker, 1977). Thus the way we regard ourselves has direct implications for the way we will interpret and remember incoming information from the environment.

An information-processing approach to the self-concept has clear utility for the study of clinically relevant behavior. Beck (1967), for example, has emphasized the role of a negative view of self as a major factor contributing to depression, and the relationship among depression, negative self-schema, and information processing has been extensively explored by subsequent research. In general, the results of these studies have supported the hypothesis that depressives differ from nondepressives in their increased recall of negative information when the stimuli presented are potentially self-relevant (e.g., Derry & Kuiper, 1981). The few instances of discrepant results (e.g., Davis, 1979) seem to be plausibly accounted for by methodological artifacts (cf. Kihlstrom & Nasby, 1981; Kuiper & Derry, 1982). Further, the enhanced processing of negative self-relevant information by depressives is

not eliminated by a recent success experience, contrary to what is observed in nondepressed subjects (Ingram, Smith, & Brehm, 1983). In terms of more enduring depressive episodes, some data indicate that the enhanced processing of negative, self-relevant information may increase with the chronicity of depression (Davis & Unruh, 1981).

This consistent pattern of enhanced recall of negative self-relevant information among depressed individuals lends strong support to Beck's original emphasis on the importance of cognitive factors, especially cognitions about the self, in depressive disorders. It is critical to note, however, that none of the available information-processing studies can document a causal link between selectively attending to negative information about the self and becoming depressed. As with the relationship between attributions and depression, there are multiple potential causal connections. A particular information-processing strategy may make an individual more susceptible to becoming depressed; depressed mood may itself make particular strategies more probable (cf. Clark & Teasdale, 1982); both the mood and information-processing orientation may arise as concomitants from some other psychological and/or physiological factors. Regardless of exact etiological sequence, however, it is likely that the tendency of depressives to focus on negative information about the self contributes to the maintenance of the depressed state. Developing therapeutic interventions that break into this self-confirmatory cycle, where negative regard for the self is confirmed by selectively attending to and recalling negative information about oneself, has become a major focus for clinical work with depressed clients (Beck, Rush, Shaw, & Emery, 1979).

Information-processing models may also be relevant for our understanding of psychological difficulties other than depression. For example, Smith, Ingram, and Brehm (1983) investigated the reaction of socially anxious persons to social-evaluative threats. High and low socially anxious subjects participated in either a high-stress, socially evaluative interaction or one that was low in stress and socially innocuous. High socially anxious subjects in the evaluative situation differed from the other three groups in demonstrating enhanced processing of information concerning potential evaluations of them by others also present in the stressful situation.

Thus, the results from this study were consistent with clinical models (e.g., Ellis, 1962) that suggest that the socially anxious individual is preoccupied with concerns about negative evaluations by others, especially during times of interpersonal stress. Though no causal implications can be derived from these findings, they do offer some support for believing that treatments of social anxiety focusing on covert rumination (e.g., Meichenbaum, 1977) and concerns about the opinion of others (e.g., Kanter & Goldfried, 1979) are addressing a critical aspect of this problem.

Objective self-awareness. Recent social psychological theory has also highlighted the relevance of attentional processes in relation to the self. Objective self-awareness theory (Duval & Wicklund, 1972; Wicklund, 1975) details the effects of attention focused inwardly on the self as opposed to outwardly toward the environment. When an individual is attending primarily to self, he or she is more aware of discrepancies between actual performance and personal standards for desired performance (Duval & Wicklund, 1972; Wicklund, 1975), experiences existing affective states more intensely (Scheier & Carver, 1977; Scheier, Carver, & Gibbons, 1981), is more likely to attribute his or her own behavior to internal causes (Duval, Wicklund, 1972; Duval, Duval, & Neely, 1979), and generates more accurate self-reports (Pryor et al., 1977).

Parallels between these effects of self-focused attention and empirical findings in the study of cognitive factors in depression led Smith and Greenberg (1981) to speculate that depressives would be characterized by a greater level of self-focused attention than nondepressives. Subsequent research has documented this association (Ingram & Smith, 1984; Smith & Greenberg, 1981). Moreover, experimental manipulations of self-focused attention have been found to result in increased dysphoric affect in depressed patients (Gibbons et al., 1985). Thus, increased attention to the self during depressive episodes may contribute to the affective as well as cognitive features characterizing depressed persons. This possible relationship between depression and self-focused attention has led to the inclusion of attentional processes in recent cognitive-behavioral models of depression (Lewinsohn, Hoberman, Teri, & Hautzinger, 1985).

Objective self-awareness has also been cited as a factor contributing to alcohol abuse (Hull, 1981). Briefly, this model asserts that ingestion of alcohol interferes with the self-relevant information processing fundamental to the state of objective self-awareness. By reducing self-awareness, alcohol consumption can reduce negative self-evaluation following failure (i.e., reduce the salience of discrepancies between performance and standards). Such reductions in negative self-evaluation then become a potent reinforcer for alcohol consumption. Though not without limitations (Wilson, 1983), this model has been supported by the results of several recent studies.

Ingestion of alcohol has been found to reduce self-focused attention, even when subjects do not expect to consume alcohol (Hull, Levenson, Young, & Sher, 1983, experiments 1 and 2), and to reduce the processing of self-relevant information (Hull et al., 1983, experiment 3). Further, individuals with dispositionally high levels of self-focused attention have been found to drink more following failure than following success; success versus failure, however, had no effect on the drinking behavior of individuals characterized by low levels of self-focused attention (Hull & Young, 1983). Finally, relapse among treated alcoholics with dispositionally high levels of self-focused attention increased as a direct function of a greater proportion of failures versus successes in life events; the valence of life events did not have a similar effect on the relapse rates of alcoholics who were low in dispositional self-focused attention (Hull & Young, 1983). Such findings would seem to suggest that assisting clients to develop alternative, nonabusive methods of reducing self-focused attention would be a useful addition to the repertoire of targets included in cognitive-behavioral interventions for problem drinking (e.g., Marlatt, 1979).

The work reviewed throughout this section on self-perception reflects particularly integrative efforts on the part of present-day researchers, as the study of self has become a common enterprise among clinical, experimental, and social psychologists. Not surprisingly, there remain a number of difficulties in coordinating such a complex set of perspectives. The concept of the self differs widely among specific investigators; research tends to become segmented by nonoverlapping dependent measures (e.g., recall versus emotional state). Gradually, however, we are accumulating an extensive and detailed data base from which we can derive an understanding of self-relevant processes that will encompass both the psychology of everyday life and those variations that contribute to psychological distress.

Self-handicapping and Psychological Symptoms Clinical and counseling psychologists have long assumed that clients often *use* their symptoms and complaints to explain away other problems. Adler (1929), for example, argues that patients employ their symptoms as "safeguards":

> *The patient selects certain symptoms and develops them until they impress him as real obstacles. Behind his barricade of symptoms the patient feels hidden and secure. To the question, "What are you making of your talents?" he answers, "This thing stops me; I cannot go ahead," and points to his self-erected barricade. (p. 13)*

The analysis of the behavior of psychiatric patients in terms of impression management (Braginsky, Braginsky, & Ring, 1969; Goffman, 1959) elaborated this notion of the functional utility of symptoms. For example, patients' degree of behavioral disturbance appears to vary as a function of their goals regarding hospitalization; those patients wanting discharge can suppress their symptoms in interview and experimental situations, while those desiring to remain hospitalized can dramatize their disturbance (Braginsky & Braginsky, 1967; Fontana & Klein, 1968).

More recent examinations of the strategic use of symptoms have been based on attribution theory. Jones and Berglas (1978; Berglas & Jones, 1978) introduced the term "self-handicapping" in this context. In self-handicapping, the individual finds or creates impediments that might reduce responsibility for failure and enhance responsibility for success. Such a strategy takes advantage of the discounting and augmentation principles of attribution theory (Kelley, 1971/1972). When there is failure, the influence of an individual's ability is discounted in favor of another viable explanation—the handicap. In the event of success, the attribution of the outcome to ability is augmented since success occurred despite the inhibiting handicap. Thus, Berglas and Jones

(1978) found that male (but not female) subjects facing the threat of failure chose a performance-inhibiting drug over a performance-facilitating one. Drug choice, in this instance, reflected the adoption of a self-handicap. Moreover, Jones and Berglas (1978) have argued that self-handicapping may underlie clinical problems such as underachievement and alcohol abuse. Some support for their perspective on alcohol abuse comes from a study by Tucker, Vuchinich, and Sobell (1981), who found that preexposure to noncontingent success on intelligence test items combined with the anticipation of future evaluation of performance resulted in increased alcohol consumption. These results, however, do not allow us to distinguish between the use of alcohol as a relatively direct way to reduce existing anxiety (or to reduce dissonance arousal; see Steele, Southwick, & Critchlow, 1981) versus the use of alcohol to provide an excuse in the event of future failure.

In their expanded version of the self-handicapping concept, Snyder and Smith (1982) propose that self-handicapping involves the adoption of behaviors or characteristics that though superficially constituting a problem or weakness actually aid the individual in (1) controlling attributions about success and failure (i.e., discounting failure and augmenting success), (2) avoiding evaluative settings altogether, or (3) maintaining environments that maximize self-esteem. Subsequent studies have indicated that reports of symptoms do appear to reflect, at least in part, self-handicapping. For example, Smith, Snyder, and Handelsman (1982) found that test-anxious subjects in an evaluative setting reported more symptoms of test anxiety when anxiety could serve as an excuse for poor performance than when anxiety was precluded as an explanation. Nonanxious subjects did not demonstrate a strategic use of symptoms. This general pattern has been replicated in reports of physical symptoms by hypochondriacal individuals (Smith, Snyder, & Perkins, 1983), of anxiety by shy males (but not females; Snyder, Smith, Augelli, & Ingram, 1985), and of stressful life events (DeGree & Snyder, 1985). As is apparent from the detailed examination of excuses in all their guises offered by Snyder and his colleagues (Snyder, Higgins, & Stucky, 1983), the self-handicapping concept offers an empirically based account of a rich clinical tradition—the strategic use of symptomatic behaviors.

Person Perception

The perception of other people is a traditional topic within social psychology that has recently been studied within a clinical framework. The basic question addressed in this research concerns whether various clinical groups form distinctive perceptions of other people, perceptions that may then contribute to the dysfunctional behavior of the perceivers. To date, a number of studies suggest that particular ways of viewing others may characterize a variety of psychological problems. For example, Nasby, Hayden, and De Paulo (1980) found that aggressive, as opposed to nonaggressive, institutionalized boys tended to attribute more hostility toward individuals depicted in photographs. Similarly, Smith and Brehm (1981) demonstrated that subjects who scored high on the hard-driving-competitiveness dimension of the Type A coronary-prone behavior pattern viewed a target person as more competitive when they expected to engage in a potentially competitive interaction with that person than when they expected someone else to interact with the target. Subjects scoring low on the hard-driving-competitiveness dimension displayed the opposite pattern of person perception: they believed the target individual was *less* competitive when he was presented as a potential opponent. In a study of person-perception and depression, Hoehn-Hyde, Schlottman, and Rush (1982) found that depressed subjects evaluated people viewed in videotaped social interactions more negatively than did nondepressed subjects, though this difference occurred only when subjects were asked to imagine that the interactions they observed were directed toward them.

These results may have some relevance for the continuing debate over the psychodynamic concept of defensive projection (Holmes, 1981; Sherwood, 1981, 1982). No matter what their origin, however, the kinds of person-perception processes evidenced in the studies described here may well serve to channel social interactions so as to elicit confirming behavior from the observed target. Aggressive boys may, because they perceive hostility in others, act more aggressively toward others and elicit increased aggression in response. Type A's expect and thus may elicit competitiveness; depressives expect and thus may elicit negative social interactions with others. Regardless, then, of the accuracy of the way we view others (Coyne, 1982), our perceptions of per-

sons act as a set of expectations that can engender social responses that maintain both the expectations and maladaptive behavior (see also previous discussion of expectancy-confirmation processes in section, The Therapist: The Clinical Judgment Process).

How Social Is Social Cognition?

In terms of conceptual development, the study of social cognition appears to be retracing the steps involved in the study of individual differences in personality characteristics. Each began with research that paid little attention to the social, interactional milieu in which persons are embedded. Thus, the multitudinous empirical investigations of the predictive utility of individual difference variables for a wide range of behavioral responses can be regarded as a conceptual parallel to theoretical frameworks proposing a direct causal connection between certain cognitions at Time 1 and certain behaviors at Time 2. Neither approach examined in any detail the ongoing, mutual impact between external, situational factors and internal processes of personality and cognition.

Personality researchers, however, soon realized that such a socially isolated view of personality was inadequate and that the interactive fit between personality characteristics and specific (often social) situations would yield considerably more predictive power (see Endler & Magnusson, 1976; Magnusson & Endler, 1977, for reviews). Similarly, researchers in social cognition have begun to borrow heavily from cognitive social-learning theories (e.g., Bandura 1978; Mischel, 1973) and to emphasize the reciprocal relationships among cognition, behavior, and situations. The resulting cognitive-social approach to personality processes (Cantor & Kihlstrom, 1981, 1982) makes salient the dynamic interaction between the person and the situation: Cognitive and motivational factors influence individuals' choices of which situation to enter; once entered, situations affect behavior through the individual's cognitive appraisal of situational properties; behavior by the individual can, in turn, modify the situation.

Throughout the present consideration of social cognition, we have alluded to this broader perspective (see also Carson, 1982). We have, for example, noted how certain perceptions of others may affect the perceiver's behavior and, thereby, the behavioral response of the perceived. Attributional processes may also have an impact on social interactions. Certain causal attributions (for one's own or another's behavior) may make certain behaviors more likely which, in turn, may elicit responses from others that maintain the initial behavior—even if the original attributional analysis is forgotten or no longer applies. Self-handicapping may also generate its own maintenance if the adoption of an impediment from the fear of having failure reflect on one's ability results, in fact, in increased likelihood of failing. On the other hand, not all of life is a self-confirming prophecy. Social judgments can be disconfirmed (Swann & Ely, 1984) and causal attributions can change, eliciting a new cognitive appraisal of others and/or the self and evoking a different set of behaviors. Success can be experienced in spite of a person's inclination to self-handicap and may reduce this inclination in the future.

In short, neither the person nor the situation is a closed system; they have an active, ongoing effect on each other. As research on social cognition becomes more sensitive to this kind of interactional complexity, it offers the intriguing possibility of bringing rigorous, experimental methodology into contact with more traditional interactive perspectives in both social (e.g., Lewin, 1935) and clinical (Anchin & Kiesler, 1982; Carson, 1969; Sullivan, 1953; Wachtel, 1977) psychology.

THE THERAPY: SOCIAL PSYCHOLOGICAL PROCESSES IN THERAPEUTIC ENDEAVORS

Client Choice and Personal Control

Over the past decade, there have been a number of studies suggesting that maximizing clients' choices during therapy can have a beneficial effect on therapeutic outcome. Such studies can also be viewed as part of the larger, continuing fascination that the issue of self-control has had for psychologists—academicians and practitioners alike. After briefly reviewing the empirical literature on the effects of client choice, we turn to some recent concerns that have been raised in the context of this larger perspective.

Choosing to Continue Treatment or Not

Though many therapists and counselors are firmly convinced that successful therapeutic outcomes are substantially more difficult to achieve with nonvoluntary client populations, the results of applied (and, therefore, necessarily correlational) research on this issue have not provided support for this belief (Bastien & Adelman, 1984; Goldenberg, Smith, & Town, 1980; Gove & Fain, 1977; Spensley, Edwards, & White, 1980). The importance of choosing to continue in treatment was evident, however, in experimental work by Cooper (1980), who in two analogue studies with college students found that having made an explicit choice to continue in the treatment study led to increased approach behavior for snake-fearing subjects and increased assertiveness for subjects initially low in assertion.

A subsequent attempt by Axsom and Cooper (1981) to demonstrate the effectiveness of client choice to continue treatment was less successful, though the overweight women in their study who *perceived* themselves to have had greater choice for continuing in a treatment program requiring a great deal of effort on their part had lost more weight at follow-up assessments than women who had participated in a less effortful treatment regime or those who perceived themselves as having had less choice about continuing in the high effort treatment. Bastien and Adelman (1984) also report a positive correlation between adolescent clients' perceptions of choosing to remain in a private social rehabilitation facility and treatment progress. Thus, while the specific determinants of perceived choice to receive treatment are far from clear and may not parallel official status as voluntary or nonvoluntary, there is some support for the inference that once perceived, a personal choice to remain in treatment has a beneficial effect on treatment effectiveness.

Choosing the Type of Treatment

Considerably more research has focused on potential treatment benefits to be derived from having clients choose the type of treatment they receive. Several analogue investigations have indicated that subjects who receive their chosen or preferred intervention procedure benefit more than do those who never choose or state a preference (Devine & Fernald, 1973; Gordon, 1976; Liem, 1975) or those who receive a treatment different from the one they chose or preferred (Devine & Fernald, 1973; Kanfer & Grimm, 1978). A school setting was employed by

Champlin and Karoly (1975) in their investigation of the effects of choice upon treatment success. These researchers administered four sessions of study skills training to eight students having difficulty in an introductory psychology course. Subjects in the "negotiated-contract" group were allowed to select the problem areas they wished to concentrate on and the study schedule they wished to follow. Subjects in the "imposed-contract" condition agreed to contract terms that were "yoked" to those of students in the negotiated group. Subjects' self-recorded data indicated that those in the negotiated-contract condition improved more in terms of total study time than did those in the imposed-contract group. Other researchers have also found that choice often acts to enhance learning (Savage, Perlmeuter, & Monty, 1979) and academic performance (Brigham, 1979).

Two research teams have examined the influence of choice on the adjustment status of retirement home residents. Langer and Rodin (1976) found that residents who received experimental manipulations emphasizing self-responsibility and describing the many choices available to them in their daily lives increased more in alertness, happiness, sociability, and participation in activities than did residents who received manipulations stressing the staff's responsibility in caring for them. In an 18-month follow-up investigation (Rodin & Langer, 1977), nurses' ratings still indicated greater sociability, self-initiation, and active interest in the environment on the part of the "responsibility-induced" subjects; these subjects also demonstrated better general health and a lower mortality rate than did control-group residents.

In a study by Schulz (1976), retirement-home subjects who either controlled or were able to predict the timing and duration of visits from undergraduate students scored higher on indices of health status, psychological status, and activity level than did subjects who received random visits or no visits at all. However, follow-up data collected at intervals of 24, 30, and 42 months (Schulz & Hanusa, 1978) indicated that intervention effects were not maintained, with subjects in the control and predict groups declining on measures of health and psychological status once the visits stopped. These follow-up data strongly suggest that perceiving oneself as being able to predict and/or control important life

events is not always beneficial to the individual, especially when, in fact, the events are externally controlled and may result in an undesired outcome. We will return to this issue later in this section.

Though the results of these studies are consistent with the notion that an individual's therapeutic success may be enhanced (at least for a while) by the opportunity to select the treatment techniques that he or she receives, most of these investigations have employed brief one-session analogue programs, nonclinical populations, and/or self-report measures of outcomes. A recent study by Mendonca and Brehm (1983) addressed these methodological concerns by utilizing a treatment program of longer duration, more clinically relevant subjects, and an objective measure of treatment outcome.

Subjects in this research were 15 boys and girls whose parents responded to advertisements of a treatment program for overweight children; they ranged in age from 9 to 15 years and were from 28 to 74 percent over the ideal body weight for their height and sex. Those children who were randomly assigned to the choice condition were given written information describing three supposed weight control programs currently offered at the clinic and allowed to make their choice of program without parental advice. Once a firm decision had been made, subjects were told that the name of the program they had chosen was the "Take Control Program." They also received "choice reminders" mailed to them at their homes throughout the duration of the program. These reminders consisted of a weekly quiz on information presented at the preceding treatment session that was entitled "Questions for Clients Who Chose the Take Control Program." Children in the no-choice condition read over the same information presented to the choice subjects but were informed that only one program was available at the present time; their quizzes were entitled "Questions for Clients in the Take Control Program." Divided into four treatment groups (two consisting of children in the choice condition and two of those in the no-choice condition), all subjects received the same eight-week behavioral weight loss program conducted by an advanced-level graduate student (Mendonca), who was unaware of subjects' experimental condition.

Results at the end of the treatment program as well as at follow-up four weeks later indicated that children in the choice condition lost more weight than children in the no-choice condition. A similar trend was obtained at a six-month follow-up, but this difference was not statistically significant and the follow-up data were flawed by severe attrition of subjects in the choice condition. Despite the lack of clear follow-up data, however, the short-term findings can be considered impressive. A relatively small difference in how treatment programs were presented to subjects in their initial intake session, bolstered only by a small difference in the label on weekly quizzes, made a significant difference in the weight loss obtained by obese children and young adolescents over a three-month period. While replication with this and other clinically relevant populations is obviously required, these results stand as the strongest evidence to date that treatment benefits can be enhanced by providing clients with their choice of treatment program.

But Is Having Choice Always Beneficial?
The notion that increasing client choice may have positive effects on therapeutic outcome was developed in concert with the common assumption that enhancing perceptions of personal control is, in general, beneficial. Increasing personal control has been viewed as an intrinsic motive for mastery (White, 1959), a ubiquitous nonspecific factor in therapy (Bandura, 1977, 1983; Kanfer, 1977; Kanfer & Hagerman, 1981), and a crucial aspect of dealing adequately with stress (Glass & Singer, 1972; Seligman, 1975). With the rare exception of a few unusually perspicacious investigators who pointed out some possible drawbacks to having personal control (e.g., Averill, 1973; Houston, 1972), the overwhelming consensus of North American psychology has been that having control is "good for you."

Recent research and theory, however, have begun to take a more critical look at this prescription. For example, reviews by Matthews, Scheier, Brunson, and Carducci (1980) and Miller (1981) on the effects of predictability (which, though different from controllability, often overlaps with it) have both made a strong argument for a more situation-specific assessment of what facilitates adequate coping. In some situations, they note, continued arousal and vigilance will be dysfunctional, while distraction and emotional blunting will be more beneficial to

the individual (see, e.g., Langer, Janis, & Wolfer, 1975). Matthews et al. propose that many of the supposedly positive effects of predictability in dealing with stress come about because predictability can lead to clearly demarcated periods of decreased attention and vigilance. In her review, Miller takes this line of reasoning one step further by noting that where the stressor is uncontrollable by the individual and persists over time, predictability can *interfere* with distraction and make adjustment more difficult (see also Averill, 1973). Abbott, Schoen, and Badia (1984) also focus on the chronicity of the stressor in their review of the animal literature; they conclude that for long-term stressors, unpredictable shock enhances adaptation and reduces physiological stress relative to shock delivered predictably. Thus, these papers all indicate that rather than assuming that there is some necessary linkage between predictability and reduced stress, one needs to assess whether continued engagement with the stressor will be beneficial and, if not, how *disengagement* can be facilitated.

The assumption that there is any necessary linkage between personal control and reduced stress has also begun to be questioned. In their careful examination of this issue, Rodin, Rennert, and Solomon (1980) report research indicating that choice is not always preferred over not having a choice, and that choice itself can lead to decreased self-esteem. Similarly, Burger, Brown, and Allen (1983) have demonstrated some negative effects of choice on self-esteem and mood. What both sets of authors emphasize is the way that choice, by increasing responsibility for the outcome obtained, can make us more anxious when we lack confidence that our choice will result in a desirable outcome. When we choose what we will do, we know we will have fewer excuses available if we fail (Phares, 1979; Snyder et al., 1983).

Recent reviews (Folkman, 1984; Miller, 1980; Thompson, 1981) on the effects of personal control on coping with objective (usually physical) stressors agree that control is less than universally beneficial. Though people usually prefer having control over an *anticipated stressor* (i.e., having the ability to regulate its occurrence, intensity, and/or duration) and such control usually reduces stress during the anticipatory period itself, there are exceptions to even these general principles. Miller (1980), for example, demonstrated that personal control over an anticipated stressor was preferred only if the person felt competent to excercise it. Moreover, research by Wright (1984) points out that the positive effects of having control during the anticipatory period depend on specific characteristics of the control activity. In Wright's study, subjects who did not have to make an effort to figure out what they needed to do in order to avoid receiving electric shock (low response uncertainty) and who believed that the control activity would be easy to perform successfully (low effortfulness of control activity) experienced less physiological arousal and subjective distress than those who were confronted with making a difficult decision about what to do or those who believed that the control activity was a difficult task. It should be noted, however, that none of the personal control groups in this study manifested significantly less arousal or distress than those subjects who were informed that they had no control over whether or not they would be shocked.

The evidence that having control reduces the negative impact of the stressor when it is received is extremely inconsistent, and again, it appears that characteristics of the control activity may play a crucial role. The person who engages in control tactics designed to ward off a stressor must allocate time and energy to this endeavor and take on responsibility for its outcome. It is not, therefore, surprising that a number of investigators have found that exercising control over aversive stimulation during actual contact with that stimulation can be more taxing physiologically than not trying to control it (e.g., Light & Obrist, 1980; Smith, Houston, & Stucky, 1985; Solomon, Holmes, & McCaul, 1980).

Taken as a whole, this recent work cautions against confusing the benefits of a general belief in controllability with the specific effects of particular control endeavors. In facing many of life's difficulties, there is probably something to be said for a general belief in controllability (Taylor, 1983; Taylor, Lichtman, & Wood, 1984; Warren & McEachren, 1983). People seem to sustain such a belief, even when it is illusory (Langer, 1975; Langer & Roth, 1975; Lefcourt, 1973; Wortman, 1975), and the absence of such illusions may be maladaptive (Abramson & Alloy, 1980).

But the probable benefits of a general belief in controllability should not be overgeneralized to mean that enhancing perceptions of self-control will be beneficial for all individuals in all situations. The specific effects of such perceptions appear to depend on the desirable level of motivation and the probable outcome of the person's efforts. In the therapeutic setting, when therapists and counselors want their clients to try hard to change specific behaviors, thoughts, and feelings and when they believe that such efforts are likely to be successful, increasing perceptions of self-control and personal responsibility (through, for example, making more explicit the client's choice for continuing therapy and/or increasing the client's choice about treatment programs) is likely to have beneficial effects.

There will be occasions during therapy, however, when enhanced perceptions of self-control are not desirable. For instance, continued high levels of motivation to exert personal control are sometimes debilitating: someone else may be able to do it—and do it better—for the client; some realities may not be modifiable, and distraction and endurance may be more functional than continued efforts to control; some realities may be modifiable but at too high a price. Furthermore, a chosen outcome may be perceived by the client as a failure. Though as both dissonance theory (Brehm & Cohen, 1962; Wicklund & Brehm, 1976) and self-perception theory (Bem, 1972) would tell us, choosing something increases the probability that we will regard it positively, choice cannot act as a guarantee of perceived success. When a client fails on a chosen endeavor, the resulting blow to self-esteem could be far more harmful to the therapeutic program than any increment in self-control experienced while making the choice.

The use of choice and the enhancement of perceived self-control in therapeutic settings require, then, a fine-grained analysis of the client and his or her situation. Maximizing perceptions of personal control should be therapeutically desirable when the goal is motivated striving toward what will likely be positive experiences; such efforts can be crucial during therapy as well as in order to maintain benefits after its conclusion (see section, The Therapy: Attribution Therapy Revisited: The Therapeutic Utilization of Causal Attributions). However, when the therapeutic goal is different (e.g., to learn to endure rather than attempt to change; to try something out even though one's initial attempts are likely to fail), increasing choice and perceptions of personal control and responsibility may well be distinctly *non-therapeutic*.

Paradoxical Interventions and Psychological Reactance

The history of paradoxical interventions is both long and, from a theoretical perspective, remarkably fragmented. According to Mozdzierz, Macchitelli, and Lisiecki (1976), Alfred Adler was the first psychotherapist to use paradox as part of his efforts to avoid therapeutic power struggles and enhance therapeutic cooperation. Paradox appears again in the writing of learning theorist Knight Dunlap (1932, 1942), who advocated "negative practice" (prescribing the symptom) for dysfunctional motor patterns such as stammering. Dunlap's ideas were later reformulated into Hullian terms, called "massed practice," and used in the treatment of tics (Yates, 1958), examination anxiety (Malleson, 1959), and the Gilles de la Tourette syndrome (tics and compulsive swearing; Clark, 1966).

During the 1950s and 1960s, paradoxical techniques were described as useful for schizophrenic individuals (Lindner, 1954; Rosen, 1953) and the families of schizophrenics (the Palo Alto group: Watzlawick, Beavin, & Jackson, 1967). Haley (1963, 1973) and Frankl (1960, 1966) advocated paradoxical interventions for a wide range of psychological difficulties. More recently, the family therapy techniques developed by Selvini Palazzoli, Boscolo, Cecchin, and Prata (1978) have stimulated renewed interest in the therapeutic utility of paradox.

In addition to these more or less explicitly paradoxical approaches, a variety of other therapies have been seen as involving, at least in part, paradoxical principles: Raskin and Klein (1976) view implosive therapy as paradoxical (Stampfl & Levis, 1967); Weeks and L'Abate (1982) point out the paradoxical elements in stimulus satiation (e.g., Ayllon, 1963) and provocative therapy (Farrelly & Brandsma, 1974); Ascher (1979) notes that some aspects of the Masters and Johnson (1970) treatment of sexual dysfunction (e.g., forbidding intercourse) can be construed as paradoxical.

Thus far, the clinical use of paradoxical techniques has far outstripped their empirical validation. Much of the research literature consists of uncontrolled studies of single cases (e.g., excessive blushing: Lamontagne, 1978; "fused identity": Fish, 1972; insomnia: Relinger, Bornstein, & Mungas, 1978; obsessional ruminations about flatulence: Milan & Kolko, 1982) or multiple cases (e.g., phobias and obsessive-compulsive disorders: Gerz, 1966; obsessive thought patterns: Solyom, Garza-Perez, Ledwidge, & Solyom, 1972; insomnia: Ascher & Efran, 1978; Relinger & Bornstein, 1979; urinary retention: Ascher, 1979; school performance: Kolko & Milan, 1983). Most of the controlled studies available (Ascher, Bowers, & Schotte, 1985, provide a detailed review and critique) have examined the effects of a single paradoxical technique (prescribing the symptom) on a limited number of behavioral problems (for example, agoraphobia: Ascher, 1981; insomnia: Ascher & Turner, 1979, 1980; Turner & Ascher, 1979; procrastination: Lopez & Wambach, 1982; Wright & Strong, 1982). Controlled outcome studies on other types of paradoxical techniques are still rare. Strong and his colleagues (Beck & Strong, 1982; Feldman, Strong, & Danser, 1982) have investigated the effects of reframing (i.e., making a positive interpretation of existing symptomatic behavior) in short-term counseling with mildly and moderately depressed college students, while Wagner, Weeks, and L'Abate (1980) explored the use of "paradoxical letters" in an enrichment program with nondistressed couples.

Summarizing the results of these published, controlled studies (as well as those from some unpublished studies conducted under his supervision), Strong (1984) draws three conclusions about the empirically demonstrated effectiveness of paradoxical techniques. First, such techniques produce more benefit than no treatment at all. Second, they appear to be superior to the effects of attention-placebo control conditions. Third, it is not clear, however, that they are superior to alternative, standard behavioral approaches. In addition, Strong takes note of the present lack of understanding about the psychological processes through which paradoxical techniques contribute to therapeutic improvement.

The profusion of paradoxical techniques in the absence of a commonly accepted theoretical framework has also been emphasized by other investigators as one of the major difficulties in using such techniques clinically. Dell (1981), for example, cites "the lack of a comprehensive theory that explains

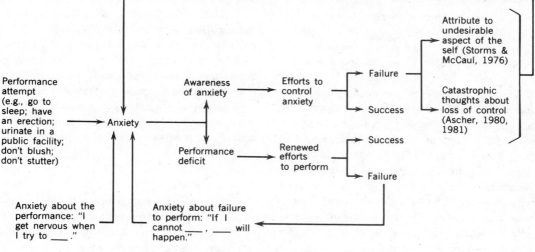

Figure 3.1   The vicious cycle of performance anxiety.

the role of paradox in human problems" (p. 37), and Watzlawick (in his comments on Dell's paper) decries the "increasingly glib and incorrect use of 'paradoxical' for any intervention that somehow contradicts common sense and established theoretical dogma" (p. 45).

Though it would be far beyond the purpose of this chapter, and the capabilities of its authors, to propose a comprehensive theory of paradox, it does seem possible to us to establish a modicum of clarity in what are currently very muddy waters. First, we suggest that the essence of therapeutic paradox may be quite simple: the client expects the therapist to advocate healthy psychological functioning ("the good") and oppose unhealthy functioning ("the bad"). Paradoxical techniques disconfirm these expectancies, by advocating and/or failing to oppose "the bad," and sometimes opposing "the good." While far more elaborate philosophical and psychological models of therapeutic paradox can be developed (e.g., see paper, comments, and rejoinder in Dell, 1981), such complexities may not be especially helpful at this stage of conceptual development.

Second, we propose that our understanding of how paradoxical techniques have their effects can be greatly enhanced by using two existing frameworks: the classification of paradoxical techniques as either compliance-based or defiance-based (Tennen, Rohrbaugh, Press, & White, 1981) and the

theory of psychological reactance (Brehm, 1966; Brehm & Brehm, 1981). Finally, we believe that in spite of the numerous, and different, listings of types of paradoxical interventions (e.g., Bogdan, 1982; Fisher, Anderson, & Jones, 1981; Haley, 1973; Weeks & L'Abate, 1982), the major and unique aspects of paradox as a therapeutic technique are fully displayed in two specific intervention strategies: prescribing the symptom and joining the resistance.

"Advocating The Bad": Prescribing the Symptom
Compliance-based.   From Dunlap to Frankl to recent researchers such as Ascher as well as Relinger and Bornstein, one of the most common uses of symptom-prescription has been in the treatment of disorders that are, at least in part, maintained by the anxiety generated by unsuccessful attempts to control anxiety. In these cases of what Watzlawick, Weakland, and Fisch (1974) characterized as "when the solution becomes the problem" (p. 31) and Ascher (1980) called the "circular performance anxiety process" (p. 280), the client's attempt to perform generates performance anxiety that interferes with the desired performance. Moreover, the state of being anxious becomes itself a focus of attention, leading to anxiety-control efforts, which, if they fail, increase the client's anxiety even more. Figure 3.1 provides an illustration of the feedback loops involved in this vicious circle.

Symptom prescription cuts directly into this escalating anxiety by directing the client to engage in all the preliminary behaviors necessary for the performance goal, but then to engage in the undesirable behavior (blushing, stuttering, staying awake, not having an erection, not urinating). Thus, three sources of anxiety are short-circuited: anxiety about the desired performance itself, anxiety about failure to perform, and anxiety triggered by failed attempts to control the anxiety created by performance efforts. This is not to say that the client will be rendered anxiety-free by complying with symptom prescriptions, but the remaining anxiety (associated with, for example, the setting in which performance usually takes place) may well become more amenable to standard techniques (e.g., systematic desensitization) for reducing anxiety.

Defiance-based. Defiance-based symptom-prescription stands in vivid contrast to the compliance-based technique described above. In compliance-based interventions the therapeutic intention is for the client to try to continue to engage in symptomatic (i.e., undesirable) behavior; in defiance-based interventions, the therapeutic intention is for the client to rebel against the prescription and try to not perform the symptom. It is crucial to realize that these two therapeutic goals are incompatible. If, for example, the therapist tells an insomniac to try staying awake and the client rebels by trying to go to sleep, his or her anxiety about being too anxious to do what he or she wishes should only increase. Defiance-based symptom-prescriptions are, then, inappropriate for symptoms that are maintained through the anxiety involved in efforts to control them and are appropriate only when the therapist can ensure that the client will rebel.

It is in assisting the therapist to influence the level of client rebellion that the theory of psychological reactance may be most helpful (Brehm, 1976; Brehm & Brehm, 1981; Seltzer, 1983; Tennen et al., 1981). Reactance theory holds that every individual has a set of established behavioral expectations or "freedoms," behaviors in which he or she expects to be free to engage. When a freedom is threatened or eliminated, the person should experience psychological reactance and be motivated to reestablish that specific free behavior. There are two major ways to increase the magnitude of reactance

arousal. First, one can increase the importance and/or number of the freedoms being threatened. Although clients probably do not see symptoms as behavioral freedoms—usually believing that they have no choice about whether or not to engage in them—they do have other specific, behavioral freedoms that can be threatened by the prescription of a symptom. Thus, according to this model of defiance-based paradoxical effects, client rebellion against the symptom prescription should be enhanced by:

1. Increasing the importance of the free behaviors threatened by engaging in the symptom: "Next week, do not go to the ballgame, but stay home and spend the time thinking about all the ways your mother-in-law makes it impossible for you and your wife to get along together."
2. Increasing the number of free behaviors threatened by engaging in the symptom: "You say you've been having severe crying episodes about once a week; it would help if you had them more often. You need to cry at least three times a week."
3. Increasing the implied threat to future free behaviors: "I think you're right. You're never going to get over this; you'll have this problem the rest of your life."

The second way to increase reactance arousal and, therefore, to increase the likelihood that clients will rebel against complying with the therapist's prescription of symptomatic behavior is to increase the magnitude of the threat. The therapist who wants rebellion can telegraph clearly his or her intent to persuade the client ("You must do exactly what I tell you"), increase the sources of pressure on the client to comply ("I will be pleased when you do more of this, and, in addition, I'll remit some of your payment for therapy"), and in general, convey a forceful yet not overwhelming directive to obey. Obviously, ensuring that such directives elicit rebellion rather than compliance will require careful tailoring to fit the individual client (Beutler, 1979).

It should be noted that these basic tenets of reactance theory have multiple therapeutic uses. Just as reactance arousal can be increased by increasing the importance and/or numbers of the freedoms threatened and the magnitude of the threat, so too can reactance be reduced (and compliance made more likely) by decreasing the importance and/or numbers of the freedoms threatened and the magnitude of the threat. Moreover, the same reactance analysis can be made for paradoxical interventions involving "opposing the good"—telling the client to inhibit desirable behaviors.

"Not Opposing the Bad": Joining the Resistance
The reactance theory framework is also useful in considering how "joining the resistance" can bring about therapeutic change. As Adler emphasized, there are some resistance behaviors that are maintained primarily by the negative response they elicit from the therapist:

I know that if I allow it, [the client] will no longer want to do it. I know that if I hinder him, he will start a war. I always agree. (1956, p. 347)

This kind of resistance by the client can be considered as reactance-maintained: on his or her own, the client is not highly motivated to engage in such behaviors, but if they are opposed by the therapist, reactance is aroused and the client becomes determined to continue them. In such cases, it should be sufficient for the therapist merely not to oppose the undesirable, resisting behaviors. A stronger and more dramatically paradoxical response would be to urge the client to engage in them, thereby "prescribing the resistance."

Although we believe that reactance theory is extremely pertinent to all paradoxical strategies (providing guidelines for how to provoke client opposition as well as how to avoid it), we do not mean to indicate that reactance (the presence or absence of it) is all there is to paradox. Scheduling the symptom may, in addition to threatening important behavioral freedoms, provide the client with a greater sense of control over symptomatic behaviors as he or she determines when they will take place. Reframing and relabeling techniques may, in addition to failing to provide the expected reactance-arousing opposition, increase self-esteem by unexpectedly pointing out "the good" in what the client(s) thought was "bad." Furthermore, there may be some general effects of paradoxical strategies, such as decreased anxiety resulting from the therapist's appearing not to view the symptom as so dangerous

or the destabilization of entrenched systems brought about by "stupefying" (Selvini Palazzoli in Dell, 1981) communications from the therapist. We do believe, however, that reactance motivation lies at the heart of paradoxical strategies and that an understanding of the theory should benefit the therapeutic practice.

Problems with Paradox: Paradox and Self-control
There seems general agreement that the use of paradoxical techniques carries with it the possibility of distinct therapeutic risks: clients may terminate therapy (Fisher et al., 1981) or the therapeutic relationship may be damaged (Brehm & Smith, 1982; Jacobson & Margolin, 1979; Weeks & L'Abate, 1982) if paradox is used in the absence of a strong commitment to therapy. It is also possible that paradoxical interventions may sometimes trade short-term gains for more long-term progress.

Our concern here rests on the relationship between paradoxical techniques and the client's perception of his or her coping abilities. In their description of the therapeutic double-bind, the Palo Alto group (e.g., Watzlawick et al., 1967) seems to suggest a positive connection between symptom prescription by the therapist and enhanced feelings of self-control for the client. If clients comply when symptoms are prescribed, "they cannot fail to realize that somehow they have control over [them]" (p. 248). If the client resists, "he can only do so by *not* behaving symptomatically" (p. 241)—which, one gathers, involves the perception of having the self-control necessary to prevent the symptom's recurrence. We wonder, though, if either proposition must necessarily hold true. Indeed, the first assumption seems clearly invalid: if a person skins her knee, and you tell her to keep bleeding, we doubt she will feel increased self-control if she does. Nor is it clear that symptom reduction as an effect of paradoxical interventions is necessarily accompanied by increased feelings of self-control.

In his description of Milton Erickson's therapeutic endeavors, Haley (1973) emphasizes that paradoxical techniques work by creating symptom reduction without the client's knowing how or why it came about. While such mysterious change has the benefit of preventing the client from attributing change to direct influence by the therapist (see Strong, 1982), it may also have the perhaps undesirable effect of preventing attributions to the self. Recent research has been unable to find any evidence that paradoxical techniques that reduce symptoms also enhance clients' perceptions of self-control (Feldman et al., 1982). Indeed, subjects in directed self-control counseling reported experiencing more self-control than did subjects in a symptom-prescription condition (Lopez & Wambach, 1982), while the open-ended responses of subjects in the Wright and Strong (1982) study suggested to these researchers that clients in paradoxical therapy may attribute change "to factors over which they have no personal control" (p. 101). Thus, if clients' attributions of therapeutic change to their own efforts and capabilities are critical in maintaining therapeutic gains (see section, The Therapy: Attribution Therapy Revisited: The Therapeutic Utilization of Causal Attribution), the beneficial confusion of paradox may need to be augmented by explicit efforts to facilitate clients' taking both the responsibility and the credit for their improvement.

Self-Confrontation in Therapy

Videotape and audiotape feedback are often used in therapy as a primary or adjunct technique to enhance therapeutic gains. In reviewing the research relevant to such self-confrontation techniques, Gur and Sackeim (1978) suggested that since these techniques are designed to increase attention to the self, the social psychological theory of objective self-awareness (Duval & Wicklund, 1972; Wicklund, 1975) may provide a conceptual and empirical framework for understanding the effects of this clinical practice. Strong (1978) envisioned an even broader role for objective self-awareness in therapeutic endeavors, viewing it as a nonspecific, beneficial factor in psychotherapy.

Contrary to Strong's optimistic notions about objective self-awareness (see also Sanborn, Pyke, & Sanborn, 1975) and more in line with Gur and Sackeim's reservations about the efficacy of self-confrontation during therapy, recent research examining the direct effects of increased attention to the self on clinical populations suggests the need for therapeutic caution. Gibbons et al. (1985) exposed psychiatric patients to a standard self-focusing stimulus—a mirror—while they filled out several questionnaires. Their results indicated that increased self-focus increased negative affect among general psychiatric patients (Study I) and depressed patients

(Study II); accuracy of self-reports was increased for these two patient groups as well as for a sample of patients receiving treatment for alcoholism (Study I). Increased self-focus had no effect, however, on any group's assumption of responsibility for either their problems or their treatment. Thus, this research found very little evidence of positive gain produced by enhanced attention to the self, and the increased negative mood for some groups points to the potential for iatrogenic damage.

It is possible, however, that variations in the application of self-confrontation techniques could prevent such undesirable effects. Steenbarger and Aderman (1979) demonstrated that self-focused attention produced negative affect and reduced self-esteem among normal subjects only for those who had been led to believe that there was little they could do to improve their behavior. For subjects who had been told there were specific ways they could improve their performance, self-focused attention did not produce negative effects on mood and self-regard. Unfortunately, even if we assume that psychotherapy resembles the latter condition more than the former one, the research by Steenbarger and Aderman indicates only a method by which to guard against harm; it does not imply any positive therapeutic effect.

Thus, we would agree with Gur and Sackeim as well as Strong in their idea that the study of objective self-awareness may well have implications for clinical practice. At this point, however, it appears that these implications may provide more of a cautionary tale than setting us on the road to therapeutic success through the use of self-confrontation.

Attribution Therapy Revisited

"Misattribution Therapy"

Experimental social psychologists have long been interested in developing therapeutic interventions based on attribution theory. In several early studies, having subjects misattribute their arousal to an external source such as a pill or a noise was effective in reducing fear of electric shock (Nisbett & Schachter, 1966; Ross, Rodin, & Zimbardo, 1969), decreasing insomnia (Storms & Nisbett, 1970), and making it easier for smokers to stop smoking for a short period (Barefoot & Girodo, 1972). Providing false feedback about the degree as well as the source of arousal increased approach behavior toward feared objects (Valins & Ray, 1967). While these initial results were most encouraging, subsequent studies with more clinically relevant populations often failed to replicate (failures to replicate the results of Storms and Nisbett include studies by Bootzin, Herman, & Nicassio, 1976; Kellog & Baron, 1975; Lowery, Denney, & Storms, 1979; Singerman, Borkovec, & Baron, 1976; failures to replicate Valins and Ray include studies by Gaupp, Stern, & Galbraith, 1972; Kent, Wilson, & Nelson, 1972; Rosen, Rosen, & Reid, 1972; Sushinsky & Bootzin, 1970) or provided plausible alternative explanations (as in Calvert-Boyanowsky & Leventhal's, 1975, explanation of the Ross et al. results in terms of accurate expectations about subsequent arousal rather than misattribution of the source of that arousal).

Indeed, as pointed out by Brehm (1976), the whole notion of a "misattribution therapy" appears to have rested on a serious misreading of Schachter's two-factor theory of emotion (Schachter, 1964; Schachter & Singer, 1962) from which it derived and the earliest empirical data (Nisbett & Schachter, 1966) on which it was based. Schachter views emotion as dependent on both physiological arousal and an emotional label for the arousal. When the cause of the arousal is ambiguous, it is possible for a false label to be adopted and for a "false" emotion to be experienced. Thus, in order to substitute one attribution of arousal for another, the initial cause must be unclear. Moreover, the arousal itself must be relatively mild since intense states of arousal would usually be correlated with known causes or, if unexplained, would be experienced as irremediably aversive (Marshall & Zimbardo, 1979; Maslach, 1979; Schachter & Singer, 1979).

This critical role of the intensity of arousal was demonstrated in Nisbett and Schachter's seminal study. In their experiment, only those subjects who were led to be mildly fearful of the upcoming electric shock found the shock less painful when their symptoms of fear were attributed to a pill they had taken. Subjects led to be highly fearful of shock did not show any reduction in perceived pain of the shock as a function of having their arousal attributed to a pill. Following this line of reasoning, Conger, Conger, and Brehm (1976) were able to replicate the Valins and Ray false-feedback effect on snake-avoidance for those subjects who were initially only mildly afraid of snakes; high-fear subjects showed

no reduction of snake-avoidance due to false-feedback about their state of arousal.

Bandura's (1969) early admonition thus appears to be accurate: "It is doubtful that strong fears and inhibitions can be eliminated through either mislabeling internal reactions or attributing them to erroneous factors" (p. 448). Strong emotional states of the sort that bring people into therapy are usually firmly (even if erroneously) attached to known, familiar causes. Though there may be specific, relatively mild clinical problems (see Brodt & Zimbardo, 1981, versus Slivken & Buss, 1984, for differing conclusions on this issue) and/or some individuals with specific personality characteristics (see Brockner & Swap, 1983) that can benefit from misattribution therapy, the current general consensus is that "the data do not seem to justify enthusiasm concerning the therapeutic usefulness of misattribution treatment" (Reisenzein, 1983, p. 256; see also Fincham, 1983; Kopel & Arkowitz, 1975; Ross & Olson, 1981).

The Therapeutic Utilization of Causal Attributions

A more recent approach to the role of attributional processes in therapy views attributions as useful for maximizing gains derived from existing intervention techniques (Kopel & Arkowitz, 1975) and perhaps crucial in maintaining therapeutic gains already achieved (Brehm & McAllister, 1980; Davison, Tsujimoto, & Glaros, 1973; Sonne & Janoff, 1982). This approach suggests that therapies will be effective and therapeutic progress maintained to the extent that clients attribute their improvement to internal, personal factors and minimize attributions to external factors such as drugs or the therapist.

Haemmerlie and Montgomery (1982, 1984; see also Haemmerlie, 1983) provide a cogent example of the use of attributional processes to facilitate therapeutic outcomes. Basing their work on Bem's (1972) theory of self-perception, these researchers suggested that socially anxious individuals base their low view of themselves as well as their low rates of social interaction on initial observations of their limited social activity: "I don't date much, so I must be socially inadequate, so I shouldn't try to date anyone." If, then, socially anxious individuals were exposed to positive social outcomes that could not be attributed to idiosyncratic behavior by the other person or to situational constraints, the same self-perception process should result in inferences of social competence and increased willingness to attempt social interactions. In the studies investigating this hypothesis, it was found that, as expected, having socially anxious individuals engage in a series of social interactions with different members of the opposite sex—all of which interactions had positive outcomes (as arranged by the experimenters without the subjects' knowledge)—resulted in decreases in self-report, behavioral, and physiological indices of social anxiety. By providing the subject with multiple successful interactions with different individuals, the experimenters presumably were able to force the subject into making an internal, self-competent attribution. It should be noted, however, that none of these studies offered any direct evidence for the causal mediation of attributions.

Marital therapy is another clinical intervention where the role of attribution processes is receiving a good deal of attention (Epstein, 1982; Harvey & Galvin, 1984; Hurvitz, 1970; Wright & Fichten, 1976). In addition to examining the patterns of attributions made by distressed spouses (see section, The Client: Social Cognition Processes: Attributions in Anxiety, Family Process, and Mental Retardation), marital therapists have become concerned that a therapist's overt direction of behavior by spouses toward one another may lead to their discounting (Kelley, 1971/1972) of positive behavior: "You're just doing that because Dr. Jones told you to." Tangible rewards and punishments could have the same effect, and, indeed, Jacobson (in press) states that in order to avoid such discounting he has eliminated contingency contracting from his version of behavioral marital therapy. Clients are still asked to make public, written commitments to behavioral change within the marriage, but no rewarding or punishing consequences for change or the lack of it are specified.

Attribution therapy has also been suggested as a way to prevent the harmful effects of going through a stressful experience. According to Wilson and Linville (1982), college students often attribute their difficulties during the first year of college to personal inadequacies rather than to the common, situationally induced stress of adjusting to a new environment. In order to prevent such attributions to self, Wilson and Linville exposed a group of college freshmen to information that indicated that difficulties in the first year occurred for most students and

that, in general, performance in school and personal adjustment improved over time. By the end of their second year in college, fewer students who had been exposed to this information had dropped out of school than among a control group; for those who remained in school, the information-treated group had a higher GPA than those who had not received information. Though these results (as well as those from a more recent paper by Wilson & Linville, 1985) are intriguing in their suggestion that a relatively brief, inexpensive preventive intervention can assist students during the stress of adjusting to college, various inconsistencies in the data from the original study (Block & Lanning, 1984), the possibility that the effect is limited to males, and the rather modest size of the effect itself indicate the need for further research on this technique.

Perhaps some of the most interesting clinical implications to be derived from attribution theory concern the way in which specific causal attributions for change during therapy may affect the long-term maintenance of these changes. This issue of the "robustness" of therapeutic gains—that is, the likelihood that improvement during therapy will generalize beyond the confines of the therapeutic interaction and will be maintained once therapy is terminated—has become a major focus of clinical interest and research (see, for example, volumes by Goldstein & Kanfer, 1979; Karoly & Steffen, 1980). As Stokes and Baer (1977) pointed out, transfer and durability of therapeutic change cannot be assumed to occur, but must be explicitly programed into treatment procedures. An attributional analysis may offer one source of ideas about how to accomplish this.

The relevance of causal attributions for maintenance of behavior change was first suggested in an early laboratory study by Davison and Valins (1969). Subjects in this experiment received a series of electric shocks and set individual thresholds for pain and tolerance. Then, all subjects ingested a pill (which was, in fact, a placebo) and continued with a second series of shocks. During the second series, shock intensity was reduced while the number of shocks was increased, so that subjects thought they were receiving more total shock, although, in fact, they received exactly the same total amount as in the first series. All subjects at this point believed that the "drug" had affected their tolerance for shock. After this, one-half of the subjects were told that the drug was a placebo; the other half were not disabused of their belief that the drug was real. In a third series of shocks, it was found that subjects who knew the drug was a placebo tolerated more shock and found it less painful than those subjects who believed in the efficacy of the supposed drug. Davison and Valins suggested that subjects who were informed that the drug was a placebo were able to attribute their perceived greater capacity to cope with the second series of shocks to their own ability to endure pain, and this belief in self-endurance enabled them to tolerate more shock more easily in the third series. Subjects who continued to believe that the drug was real could not make a self-attribution, should have seen enhanced tolerance for shock as drug-dependent, and, when the drug was not administered, were not able to tolerate high levels of shock on their own.

Though attributing treatment effects to oneself rather than to a drug may not have a differential impact on the initial elicitation of behavior change (Wilson & Thomas, 1973) and the drawback of drug-attributions for continued improvement may be strongest among subjects having an internal locus of control (Chambliss & Murray, 1979), research with clinically relevant populations has provided some support for the general notion that self-attributions can enhance the maintenance of treatment gains. Working with clients who participated in a nonaversive program to stop smoking, Colletti and his associates (Colletti & Kopel, 1979; Colletti & Stern, 1980) found that long-term maintenance of abstinence was positively correlated with assigning a greater degree of responsibility for behavior change to change in personal attitudes. Maintenance of weight loss achieved in weight-control programs also appears to be enhanced by interventions that maximize attributions of change to clients' own efforts and abilities. Jeffrey (1974), for example, compared the effects of a weight loss program emphasizing self-control with one emphasizing environmental control over eating behavior. Though both treatments were equally effective at the end of the treatment period, the self-control group had lost more weight by the end of a six-week follow-up.

In their replication and extension of Jeffrey's work, Sonne and Janoff (1979) provided a detailed examination of the role of attributions to the self. These investigators exposed clients seeking weight reduction to either a self-control or environmental-control program. Like Jeffrey, they found the two programs to be equally effective at the end of treatment, but the self-control program to be superior at a six-week follow-up. The greater effectiveness of the self-control program in fostering the maintenance of weight lost during treatment was even more apparent at a second follow-up at 11 weeks posttreatment. Most important, Sonne and Janoff also obtained self-reports from clients about their attributions of responsibility for, control over, and contribution to the weight loss they hoped to achieve (pretreatment) and the weight loss they had actually obtained (posttreatment). As would be expected, the self-control and environmental-control groups did not differ in their expectations for responsibility/control/contribution prior to treatment. At posttreatment, however, self-control clients attributed more of their obtained weight loss to their own personal responsibility/control/contribution than did environmental-control clients.

Sonne and Janoff then explored the relationship of the posttreatment attributions to weight status at follow-up. At the first follow-up, these attributions did not significantly correlate with weight status (i.e., continued loss, maintenance, or gain). By the second follow-up, however, there was a significant correlation. Indeed, a multiple regression analysis revealed that two of the attributions (control over and contribution to) accounted for 22 percent of the variance of weight status at the 11-week follow-up. Finally, Sonne and Janoff reported that amount of weight lost during treatment was not significantly correlated with weight status at either the first or second follow-up.

These data suggest a rather dramatic *and delayed* effect of causal attributions to the self on the course of therapeutically induced weight loss. The differential effectiveness of the two programs became apparent only some time after treatment had terminated. The major role of self-attributions showed up only after an even longer period of time. Thus, it was only almost three months after treatment had ended that all the pieces fell into place: the self-control program was superior in preventing regression to pretreatment weight levels, attributions to the self predicted follow-up weight status, and initial weight loss during the program itself was not predictive. In our concluding comments on the role of attributions in therapy, we will return to the issues raised by this kind of timing of effects.

Thus far, we have considered the way in which attributing positive therapeutic change to one's own efforts and capacities may increase the long-term maintenance of these changes. It may also be the case, however, that making self-attributions for one's undesirable behaviors can interfere with maintenance. In discussing cognitive processes involved in alcoholism, both Marlatt (1978) and Wilson (1978) describe how the attribution of a relapse to negative characteristics of the self can create perceptions of loss of control, increase anxiety, and, thereby, make extended drinking more likely. Polivy (1976) and Mahoney and Mahoney (1976) have alluded to a similar sequence that may affect individuals who are trying to maintain dieting behavior. This perspective suggests that clinical use of the attributional link to improved maintenance may need to be twofold: (1) assisting the client to make a positive self-attribution for positive change experienced in therapy, *and* (2) preparing the client to be able to avoid making a negative self-attribution for relapses that occur after therapy is over.

Besides their possible role in enhancing therapeutic effectiveness and maintenance, attributions for psychological distress may also have an impact on the early orientation of clients toward therapy. Snyder and Ingram (1983) demonstrated that attributional manipulations can be useful in increasing help-seeking for psychological problems; providing highly test-anxious subjects with consensus information (i.e., telling them that test anxiety is a common problem) increased these subjects' stated intentions to seek therapeutic assistance in dealing with their anxiety. Snyder and Ingram interpreted these findings to indicate that consensus information led to increased causal attributions to remediable situational factors rather than to more intractable personal characteristics, though subjects' attributions were not themselves directly assessed. Once therapy has begun, the results of a study by Hoffman and Teglasi (1982) suggest, stressing internal, *changeable* factors as the source of psychological difficulties can increase clients' positive expectations about and motivation for treatment. Forsyth and Forsyth (1982) point out, however, that this positive effect may be most pronounced for (or even restricted to) clients who initially display an internal locus of control.

Attributions and Therapy: Concluding Remarks
From one perspective, the shift in the application of attribution theory to clinical practice is obvious and straightforward. Early suggestions for clinical application involved the use of "misattribution" with the therapist proposing causal sources that he or she believed were inaccurate. More recent applications involve proposing causal sources that are, to some extent at least, veridical. The perspective from which one can so easily distinguish between these two approaches is, however, that of the therapist or of an outside observer of the therapeutic interaction. From the client's point of view, it is not so obvious that a shift has occurred. If a client believes in a certain causal attribution that the therapist disputes, it may not matter awfully much whether the therapist views the "therapeutic attribution" as true or false.

This is not to say that changes in the client's attributions cannot be accomplished by explicit efforts by the therapist to alter "the perceived plausibility of alternative causes" (Fincham, 1983, p. 196). The research by Sonne and Janoff (1979) offers compelling evidence that different therapeutic approaches will enhance different types of attributions for change. As Peterson (1982) has noted, however, such differential enhancement may not be easy, especially among clients who are committed to an alternative causal analysis. Research on the ways that people process information and draw conclusions relevant to that information has made it abundantly clear that distortion, bias, and sheer disregard of "the facts" are part of the human condition (Nisbett & Ross, 1980; Ross, 1977). As therapists we may know that a certain attribution is both therapeutically desirable and veridical, but still fail to convince our clients to adopt it.

In other words, while a change in cognitive structure may be the therapeutic goal, a cognitive approach in therapy (presenting information; offering logical reasoning) may not allow us to achieve it. It is at this juncture of opening up the client's cognitive construction of the world so that information and reason can have the desired effect that *interpersonal* (e.g., the therapist's credibility with the client; the therapist's ability to empathize with the client and, thereby, tailor the presentation of information to the client's existing views) and *motivational* (e.g., the use of dissonance- and reactance-inducing procedures [Brehm, 1976]; the enhancement of commitment to change through increasing client choice; the strategic inclusion of appropriate paradoxical procedures) variables may be crucial.

We also want to comment here on the difficult choice that therapists may face in deciding whether to strive for short-term or long-term gains. The difficulty arises because the two may not be the same. Brehm and McAllister (1980) make the general point that immediate, dramatic behavior change is best generated by coercive therapeutic techniques—making symptomatic behavior extremely costly for the client and nonsymptomatic/healthy behavior extremely rewarding. However, as reviewed by Brehm and McAllister, the thrust of the social psychological literature over the past 30 years strongly suggests that behavior change that is coerced will not endure.

This disjunction between immediate and long-term effects is relevant to our consideration of the role of attributions in therapy. As described previously, Sonne and Janoff (1979) found a difference between their two treatments in attributions but not in weight loss immediately after treatment, and the predictive effect of attributions on behavior was observed only some time after treatment was over. On the other hand, Chaney and Bugental (1982) found that providing a self-control treatment to hyperactive male children produced the expected shift in attributions (i.e., an increase in internal attributions for academic performance), but no behavioral differences at the end of a six-month follow-up. Their comparative treatment—involving contingent social reinforcement—failed to affect attributions, but did produce behavior change.

Thus, the therapist is confronted with a difficult dilemma. He or she may decide to forgo immediate, dramatic behavior change in hopes of fostering more lasting improvement. Determining whether this hope is justified, however, is exceedingly complex. Sometimes, as in Sonne and Janoff's study, a cognitive change at the end of therapy will translate into a behavioral advantage at a later time. On other occasions, as in Chaney and Bugental's work, a cognitive change may not have any impact on behavior, either at the end of treatment or later. (One could, of course, argue that had Chaney and Bugental conducted a longer follow-up, an effect of cognition on behavior would have been demonstrated.

Our position is that six months is a quite sufficient period of observation, and if no behavioral changes have appeared by then, later improvement is unlikely.)

We can offer no simple way out of this dilemma. The relationship between cognition and behavior is not easily understood; nor is the relationship between immediate change (cognitive or behavioral) and later development. The best general statement that can be made at this point is that *within* a given therapeutic procedure, it appears that efforts to maximize the attributions for therapeutic success to the client's own efforts and capabilities should promote maintenance of these successes. This does not mean, however, that solely attending to causal attributions offers a sufficient therapeutic approach (Kopel, 1982), nor that self-control therapies are necessarily the treatment of choice for all psychological difficulties (see section, The Client: Client Choice and Personal Control: But Is Having Choice Always Beneficial?). Beyond this premise and this hedge, we, like everyone else, have to await further research for clarification and guidance.

CONCLUSION

It was our intention in the present chapter to survey the most active areas of current research bearing on the integration of social and clinical psychology. While it is fair to say that progress in this integrative endeavor has been encouraging, it is also clear that no definitive integration—no single overriding social-clinical orientation—has emerged. Nor is one likely to be generated in the foreseeable future. In its modern incarnation (since approximately the mid-1950s), social psychology has been resolute in its preference for small, circumscribed models and theories, and determined in its rejection of any kind of Unified Field Theory of human behavior. This perspective has proved both a boon and a hindrance in promoting recognition of the relevance of social psychological inquiry to clinical practice. On the positive side, the rigorous adoption of conceptions limited in scope has facilitated empirical investigations of the kind of complex psychological functioning of interest to clinicians. On the negative side, the lack of theoretical integration within social psychology makes it impossible for social psychology to offer anyone the royal road to anything. By its very nature, social psychology can provide only relatively specific information that might have relatively specific uses within the clinical arena; it cannot give the clinician a general, unified framework with which to meet many of the unforeseen complications that arise in clinical work. It is possible, however, that the present state of our knowledge about psychological processes precludes valid universal theories from any bailiwick, and we hope that it is apparent from the material reviewed in this chapter that even "pockets" of integration can be extremely useful. In our concluding remarks, we would like to address three general issues that may well affect both the extent and utility of the social-clinical integration in the future.

An important place to start is to underscore the need for full awareness of the conceptual climate in both clinical and social psychology today. The cognitivism that pervades both has been a valuable stimulus to theory and research, but we are most likely to end up with enduring increments in knowledge if we place this cognitive emphasis within careful limits. There are, for instance, a number of crucial conceptual issues that must be considered. As Wilson, Hull, and Johnson (1981) point out, cognitive models in social psychology have been a good deal more successful in predicting behavioral effects than they have been in obtaining self-report evidence that the cognitive mediators posited by the model did, in fact, produce the behavior. This marked disjunction between overt behavior and self-reports of internal states can be accounted for in at least two ways. First, it may be that the problem lies in our difficulty in gaining access to and reporting on what we are thinking and feeling (Nisbett & Wilson, 1977). Alternatively, the models may be heuristically useful, but invalid. The presumed cognitive mediators may allow for the prediction of the subject's behavior, but actually exist only in the mind of the researcher.

In trying to determine whether cognitions act as causes, it will not be sufficient to demonstrate that a certain set of conditions produces both the predicted cognition and the predicted behavior. The two may be created independently of one another. Or, perhaps more interestingly, the cognition may occur in response to the behavior and be a reaction that is especially likely to be elicited by curious researchers but has itself no causal role (Covington

& Omelich, 1979). Thus, Coyne's (1982) criticism that current models assuming cognitions as causal in the etiology of maladaptive behavior are both conceptually simplistic and empirically unsubstantiated is likely to hold until investigators routinely assess presumed cognitive mediators (Kopel, 1982) *and* can document *at least* that changes in the cognition parallel changes in the behavior.

Unfortunately, such parallel changes may be statistically significant but relatively trivial in the amount of behavioral variance they account for unless we develop more cogent, higher order interaction models of the *reciprocal* relationships among person variables (cognition, behavior, emotion, and motivation), and between the person and the situation. We realize that any one model, if it is to have the precision necessary for empirical investigation, cannot capture all of these relationships. We are, however, convinced (see section, The Client: Social Cognition Processes: How Social Is Social Cognition?) that the study of cognition in relative isolation from other aspects of the person and from situational variation is unlikely to uncover reliable phenomena even in the laboratory, much less inform us about psychological processes that could survive the translation into the shifting sands of the real world.

In urging the placing of limits on the cognitive revolution, our primary concern here is with the potential for therapeutic error that too ready an embrace of cognitivism may bring with it. Consider, for example, the scenario in which a client comes into therapy complaining of being disliked by other people and having few, if any, satisfying relationships. In the world of cognitive research (see Swann & Read, 1981), it would be possible to analyze this presenting complaint in terms of an existing conception of the self: the client expects to be disliked; in order to confirm this expectation, he or she behaves in ways that tend to generate dislike from others; and, in retrospect, the client selectively recalls being disliked. The implication of this analysis is that by changing the client's view of self all else will follow; motivation, behavior, and memory will also change. There is, however, another equally plausible account of the same problem in living. It could be that the client tries to create rewarding interactions for others but fails because he or she lacks the necessary social skills and, therefore, that the remembrance of a dismal social past is accurate. From this perspective, the treatment of choice would be direct training in social skills. Finally, there is the possibility that both self-regard and behavioral performance could and should be addressed in therapy: inadequate skills may make it difficult for the client to elicit others' positive reactions; low self-regard may make it difficult for the client to perceive positive reactions when they do occur. The moral of this example is simply that if therapeutic interventions are to be generated in response to presumed etiology, the clinician is obligated to examine carefully a variety of contenders for the causal role.

Moreover, as we noted earlier (see section, The Therapy: Attribution Therapy Revisited: Concluding Remarks), even if we are correct in designating cognitions as major etiological factors, changes in other person-variables should not be overlooked as a therapeutic entry point. Even explicitly cognitive therapies (e.g., Beck et al., 1979) often preface cognitive change techniques with prescriptions for changed activities. In addition, the effectiveness of behavioral methods for altering presumably cognitively mediated problems has been suggested in theory (Bandura, 1977) and may be reflected empirically in Haemmerlie and Montgomery's (1982, 1984) work described earlier (see section, The Therapy: Attribution Theory Revisited: The Therapeutic Utilization of Causal Attributions). Social psychologists themselves have a long tradition of emphasizing the effects of behavior on attitudes (e.g., Festinger's, 1957, theory of cognitive dissonance; see Brehm & Cohen, 1962, and Wicklund & Brehm, 1976), and there is reasonable evidence (Fazio & Zanna, 1981) that the relationship between prior attitudes and subsequent behavior is strengthened when the attitudes stem from direct experience rather than being based on more abstract principles and/or the opinions of others.

Beyond the need to develop more sophisticated, interactional models involving cognitive processes and to ensure that these models are useful in furthering more effective treatment interventions, a second general issue for the social-clinical integration of the future involves research methodology. Social and clinical psychologists have historically differed quite dramatically in their approach to research—in terms of subject populations, attention paid to various threats to internal and external valid-

ity, characteristics of appropriate control groups, and so on. Indeed, comparison of model experiments in these two subdisciplines (e.g., a one-hour experiment with college sophomores versus a three-month treatment outcome study with psychiatric outpatients) might suggest that methodological integrations are not feasible. It has been our contention (Brehm & Smith, 1982), however, that a range of research methodologies does exist that will allow us to build the data base for meaningful integration. Examples of this range of research strategies, along the continuum defined by traditional social versus clinical research, include basic laboratory research; use of populations experiencing minor clinical problems (e.g., text anxiety); work with precursor clinical populations (e.g., young people exhibiting the Type A behavior pattern; anhedonic college students); inclusion of clinical populations in laboratory experiments; outcome studies examining the effect of social psychological variables on standard treatment approaches; evaluations of treatments based primarily on social psychological variables. We believe that increased recognition of this available range may serve to move us beyond quarrelsome debate about which single research strategy is better than another and toward a more productive consideration of each one's limited but useful contribution.

A third and final point we wish to make about the social-clinical integration involves the two levels of utility we see for the role of social psychology in contributing to clinical endeavors. In this chapter we have focused on how the application of social psychological theory and research might improve the delivery of clinical services, increase our understanding of the origin and maintenance of maladaptive behavior, and aid in creating more useful treatment interventions. A related benefit that has received implicit acknowledgment throughout this chapter is the cross-fertilization between social psychology and traditional clinical theory. The analysis of Adler's model of the strategic use of symptoms in terms of attribution theory; the translation of paradox into the language of reactance theory; the parallels between the interpersonal perspective in personality and psychotherapy on the one hand and emerging cognitive-social approaches to personality on the other—these all indicate how clinical theories can nurture social psychological concepts, and how social psychology can revitalize our appreciation of these theories. As the dialogue between social and clinical psychology continues, we learn that no one has a lock on truth, but discover that we can open more doors when we share our separate keys.

REFERENCE NOTES

1. Kaslow, N.J., Rehm, L.P., Pollack, S.L., & Siegel, A.W. Attributional style and self-control behavior in depressed and nondepressed children and their parents. Manuscript submitted for publication.

REFERENCES

Abbott, B.B., Schoen, L.S., & Badia, P. (1984). Predictable and unpredictable shock: Behavioral measures of aversion and physiological measures of stress. *Psychological Bulletin, 96*, 45−71.

Abramowitz, C.V., & Dokecki, P.R. (1977). The politics of clinical judgment: Early empirical returns. *Psychological Bulletin, 84*, 460−476.

Abramson, L.Y., & Alloy, L.B. (1980). Judgment of contingency: Errors and their implications. In A. Baum & J.E. Singer (Eds.), *Advances in environmental psychology. Vol 2: Applications of personal control.* Hillsdale, NJ: Erlbaum.

Abramson, L., Seligman, M., & Teasdale, J. (1978). Learned helplessness in humans: Critique and reformulation. *Journal of Abnormal Psychology, 87*, 49−74.

Adler, A. (1929). *Problems of neuroses: A book of case histories.* London: Kegan Paul, Trench, Truebner.

Adler, A. (1956). *The individual psychology of Alfred Adler* (H.L. Ansbacher & R.R. Ansbacher, Ed. & Trans.). New York: Harper & Row.

Anchin, J.C., & Kiesler, D.J. (Eds.). (1982). *Handbook of interpersonal psychotherapy.* New York: Pergamon.

Andrews, G., Tannant, C., Hewson, D.M., & Vaillant, G.E. (1978). Life event stress, social support, coping style, and risk of psychological impairment. *Journal of Nervous and Mental Disease, 166*, 307−316.

Arkes, H.R. (1981). Impediments to accurate clinical judgment and possible ways to minimize their impact. *Journal of Consulting and Clinical Psychology, 49*, 323−330.

Arkin, R.M., Kolditz, R.A., & Kolditz, K.K. (1983). Attributions of the test-anxious student: Self-assessments in the classroom. *Personality and Social Psychology Bulletin, 9*, 271−280.

Ascher, L.M. (1979). Paradoxical intervention in the treatment of urinary retention. *Behaviour Research and Therapy, 17*, 267−270.

Ascher, L.M. (1980). Paradoxical intention. In A. Goldstein & E.B. Foa (Eds.), *Handbook of behavioral interventions.* New York: Wiley.

Ascher, L.M. (1981). Employing paradoxical intention in the treatment of agoraphobia. *Behaviour Research and Therapy, 19*, 533−542.

Ascher, L.M., & Efran, J.S. (1978). Use of paradoxical intention in a behavioral program for sleep onset insomnia. *Journal of Consulting and Clinical Psychology, 46*, 547−550.

Ascher, L., & Turner, R. (1979). Paradoxical intention and insomnia: An experimental investigation. *Behaviour Research and Therapy, 17*, 408−411.

Ascher, L., & Turner, R. (1980). A comparison of two methods for the administration of paradoxical intention. *Behaviour Research and Therapy, 18*, 121−126.

Ascher, L.M., Bowers, M.R., & Schotte, D.E. (1985). A review of data from controlled case studies and experiments evaluating the clinical efficacy of paradoxical intention. In G.R. Weeks (Ed.), *Promoting change through paradoxical therapy.* Homewood, IL: Dow Jones-Irwin.

Averill, J.R. (1973). Personal control over aversive stimuli and its relationship to stress. *Psychological Bulletin, 80*, 286−303.

Axsom, D., & Cooper, J. (1981). Reducing weight by reducing dissonance: The role of effort justification in inducing weight loss. In E. Aronson (Ed.), *Readings about the social animal* (3rd ed.). San Francisco: Freeman.

Ayllon, T. (1963). Intensive treatment of psychotic behavior by stimulus satiation and food reinforcement. *Behaviour Research and Therapy, 1*, 53−62.

Bandura, A. (1969). *Principles of behavior modification.* New York: Holt, Rinehart & Winston.

Bandura, A. (1977). Self-efficacy: Toward a unifying theory of behavioral change. *Psychological Review, 84*, 191−215.

Bandura, A. (1978). The self-system in reciprocal determinism. *American Psychologist, 33*, 344−358.

Bandura, A. (1983). Self-efficacy determinants of anticipated fears and calamities. *Journal of Personality and Social Psychology, 45*, 464−469.

Bandura, A., Lipsher, D.H., & Miller, P.E. (1960). Psychotherapists' approach-avoidance reactions to patients' expressions of hostility. *Journal of Consulting Psychology, 24*, 1−8.

Bankoff, E.A. (1983). Social support and adaptation to widowhood. *Journal of Marriage and the Family, 45*, 815−826.

Barefoot, J.C., & Girodo, M. (1972). The misattribution of smoking cessation symptoms. *Canadian Journal of Behavioral Sciences, 4*, 358−363.

Barthé, D.G., & Hammen, C.L. (1981). A naturalistic extension of the attributional model of depression. *Personality and Social Psychology Bulletin, 7*, 53−58.

Bastien, R.T., & Adelman, H.S. (1984). Noncompulsory versus legally mandated placement, perceived choice, and response to treatment among adolescents. *Journal of Consulting and Clinical Psychology, 52*, 171−179.

Batson, C.D. (1975). Attribution as a mediator of bias in helping. *Journal of Personality and Social Psychology, 32*, 455−466.

Beck, A.T. (1967). *Depression: Causes and treatment.* Philadelphia: Univ. of Pennsylvania Press.

Beck, A.T., Rush, A.J., Shaw, B.F., & Emery, G. (1979). *Cognitive therapy of depression.* New York: Guilford.

Beck, J.T., & Strong, S.R. (1982). Stimulating therapeutic change with interpretations: A comparison of positive and negative connotation. *Journal of Counseling Psychology, 29*, 551–559.

Bem, D.J. (1967). Self-perception: An alternative interpretation of cognitive dissonance phenomena. *Psychological Review, 74*, 183–200.

Bem, D.J. (1972). Self-perception theory. In L. Berkowitz (Ed.), *Advances in experimental social psychology* (Vol. 6). New York: Academic Press.

Berglas, S., & Jones, E.E. (1978). Drug choice as a self-handicapping strategy in response to noncontingent success. *Journal of Personality and Social Psychology, 36*, 405–417.

Berkman, L., & Syme, S. (1979). Social networks, host resistance, and mortality: A nine year followup study of Alameda County residents. *American Journal of Epidemiology, 109*, 186–204.

Beutler, L.E. (1979). Toward specific psychological therapies for specific conditions. *Journal of Consulting and Clinical Psychology, 47*, 882–897.

Blaney, P.H., Behar, V., & Head, R. (1980). Two measures of depressive cognitions: Their association with depression and with each other. *Journal of Abnormal Psychology, 89*, 678–682.

Block, J., & Lanning, K. (1984). Attribution therapy requestioned: A secondary analysis of the Wilson-Linville Study. *Journal of Personality and Social Psychology, 46*, 705–708.

Bogdan, J.L. (1982). Paradoxical communication as interpersonal influence. *Family Process, 21*, 443–452.

Bootzin, R.R., Herman, C.P., & Nicassio, P. (1976). The power of suggestion: Another examination of misattribution and insomnia. *Journal of Personality and Social Psychology, 34*, 673–679.

Braginsky, B., & Braginsky, D. (1967). Schizophrenic patients in the psychiatric interview: An experimental study of their effectiveness at manipulation. *Journal of Consulting Psychology, 31*, 546–551.

Braginsky, B.M., Braginsky, D.D., & Ring, K. (1969). *Methods of madness: The mental hospital as a last resort.* New York: Holt, Rinehart & Winston.

Brehm, J.W. (1966). *A theory of psychological reactance.* New York: Academic Press.

Brehm, J.W., & Cohen, A.R. (1962). *Explorations in cognitive dissonance.* New York: Academic Press.

Brehm, S.S. (1976). *The application of social psychology to clinical practice.* Washington, DC: Hemisphere.

Brehm, S.S., & Brehm, J.W. (1981). *Psychological reactance: A theory of freedom and control.* New York: Academic Press.

Brehm, S.S., & McAllister, D.A. (1980). A social psychological perspective on the maintenance of therapeutic change. In P. Karoly & J.T. Steffen (Eds.), *Improving the long-term effects of psychotherapy: Models of durable outcome.* New York: Gardner.

Brehm, S.S., & Smith, T.W. (1982). The application of social psychology to clinical practice: A range of possibilities. In G. Weary & H.L. Mirels (Eds.), *Integrations of clinical and social psychology.* New York: Oxford University Press.

Brigham, T.A. (1979). Some effects of choice on academic performance. In L.C. Perlmeuter & R.A. Monty (Eds.), *Choice and perceived control.* Hillsdale, NJ: Erlbaum.

Brockner, J., & Swap, W.C. (1983). Resolving the relationships between placebos, misattribution and insomnia: An individual-differences perspective. *Journal of Personality and Social Psychology, 45*, 32–42.

Brodt, S.E., & Zimbardo, P.G. (1981). Modifying shyness-related and social behavior through symptom misattribution. *Journal of Personality and Social Psychology, 41*, 437–449.

Buchwald, A.M., Coyne, J.C., & Cole, C.S. (1978). A critical evaluation of the learned helplessness model of depression. *Journal of Abnormal Psychology, 87*, 180–193.

Burger, J.M., Brown, R., & Allen, C.K. (1983). Negative reactions to personal control. *Journal of Social and Clinical Psychology, 1*, 322–342.

Calvert-Boyanowsky, J., & Leventhal, H. (1975). The role of information in attenuating behavioral responses to stress: A reinterpretation of the misattribution phenomenon. *Journal of Personality and Social Psychology, 32*, 214–221.

Cantor, N. (1982). "Everyday" versus normative models of clinical and social judgment. In G. Weary & H.L. Mirels (Eds.), *Integrations of social and clinical psychology.* New York: Oxford University Press.

Cantor, N., & Kihlstrom, J.F. (Eds.). (1981). *Personality, cognition, and social interaction.* Hillsdale, NJ: Erlbaum.

Cantor, N., & Kihlstrom, J.F. (1982). Cognitive and social processes in personality. In G.T. Wilson & C. Franks (Eds.), *Contemporary behavior therapy: Conceptual and empirical foundations.* New York: Guilford.

Cantor, N., & Mischel, W. (1979). Prototypes in person perception. In L. Berkowitz (Ed.), *Advances in experimental social psychology* (Vol. 12). New York: Academic Press.

Cantor, N., Smith, E., French, R., & Mezzich, J. (1980). Psychiatric diagnosis as prototype categorization. *Journal of Abnormal Psychology, 89*, 181–193.

Caplan, G., & Killilea, M. (1976). *Support systems and mutual help.* New York: Grune & Stratton.

Carson, R.C. (1969). *Interaction concepts of personality.* Chicago: Aldine.

Carson, R.C. (1982). Self-fulfilling prophecy, maladaptive behavior, and psychotherapy. In J.C. Anchin & D.J. Kiesler (Eds.), *Handbook of interpersonal psychotherapy.* New York: Pergamon.

Casas, J.M., Brady, S., & Ponterotto, J.G. (1983). Sexual preference biases in counseling: An information processing approach. *Journal of Counseling Psychology, 30*, 139–145.

Cassel, J. (1974). Psychosocial processes and "stress": Theoretical formation. *International Journal of Health Sciences, 6*, 471–482.

Cassel, J. (1976). The contribution of the social environment to host resistance. *American Journal of Epidemiology, 104*, 107–123.

Chambliss, C., & Murray, E.J. (1979). Cognitive procedures for smoking reduction: Symptom attribution versus efficacy attribution. *Cognitive Therapy and Research, 3*, 91–95.

Champlin, S.M., & Karoly, P. (1975). Role of contract negotiation in self-management of study time. *Psychological Reports, 37*, 724–726.

Chaney, L.A., & Bugental, D.B. (1982). An attributional

approach to hyperactive behavior. In C. Antaki & C. Brewer (Eds.), *Attributions and psychological change*. London: Academic Press.

Chapman, L.J., & Chapman, J.P. (1967). Genesis of popular erroneous psychodiagnostic observations. *Journal of Abnormal Psychology, 72*, 193–204.

Chapman, L.J., & Chapman, J.P. (1969). Illusory correlation as an obstacle to the use of valid psychodiagnostic signs. *Journal of Abnormal Psychology, 74*, 271–280.

Clark, D. (1966). Behavior therapy of Gilles de la Tourette syndrome. *British Journal of Psychiatry, 112*, 771–778.

Clark, D.M., & Teasdale, J.D. (1982). Diurnal variation in clinical depression and accessibility of memories of positive and negative experiences. *Journal of Abnormal Psychology, 91*, 87–95.

Cobb, S. (1976). Social support as a moderator of life-stress. *Psychosomatic Medicine, 38*, 300–314.

Cobb, S. (1979). Social support and health through the life course. In M. White Riley (Ed.), *Aging from birth to death: Interdisciplinary perspectives*. Boulder, CO: Westview Press.

Cohen, J., & Struening, E.L. (1964). Opinions about mental illness: Hospital social atmosphere profiles and their relevance to effectiveness. *Journal of Consulting Psychology, 28*, 292–298.

Cohen, S., & Hoberman, H.M. (1983). Positive events and social supports as buffers of life change stress. *Journal of Applied Social Psychology, 13*, 99–125.

Cohen, S., & McKay, G. (1984). Social support, stress and the buffering hypothesis: A theoretical analysis. In A. Baum, J.E. Singer, & S.E. Taylor (Eds.), *Handbook of psychology and health* (Vol. 4). Hillsdale, NJ: Erlbaum.

Cohen, S., & Syme, S.L. (1985). Issues in the study and application of social support. In S. Cohen & S.L. Syme (Eds.), *Social support and health*. Orlando, FL: Academic Press.

Colletti, G., & Kopel, S.A. (1979). Maintaining behavior change: An investigation of three maintenance strategies and the relationship of self-attribution to the long-term reduction of cigarette smoking. *Journal of Consulting and Clinical Psychology, 47*, 614–617.

Colletti, G., & Stern, L. (1980). Two-year follow-up of a nonaversive treatment for cigarette smoking. *Journal of Consulting and Clinical Psychology, 48*, 292–293.

Colson, L.E. (1970). Effects of different explanations of disordered behavior on treatment referrals. *Journal of Consulting and Clinical Psychology, 34*, 432–435.

Conger, J.D., Conger, A.J., & Brehm, S.S. (1976). Fear level as a moderator of false feedback effects in snake phobics. *Journal of Consulting and Clinical Psychology, 44*, 135–141.

Cooley, C.H. (1902). *Human nature and the social order*. New York: Charles Scribner's Sons.

Cooper, J. (1980). Reducing fears and increasing assertiveness: The role of dissonance reduction. *Journal of Experimental Social Psychology, 16*, 199–213.

Corrigan, J.B., Dell, D.M., Lewis, K.N., & Schmidt, L.D. (1980). Counseling as a social influence process: A review. *Journal of Counseling Psychology, 27*, 395–441.

Costello, C.G. (1978). A critical review of Seligman's labo-

ratory experiments on learned helplessness and depression in humans. *Journal of Abnormal Psychology, 87*, 21–31.

Covington, M.V., & Omelich, C.L. (1979). Are causal attributions causal? A path analysis of the cognitive model of achievement motivation. *Journal of Personality and Social Psychology, 37*, 1487–1504.

Coyne, J.C. (1982). A critique of cognitions as causal entities with particular reference to depression. *Cognitive Therapy and Research, 6*, 3–13.

Coyne, J.C., Aldwin, C., & Lazarus, R.S. (1981). Depression and coping in stressful episodes. *Journal of Abnormal Psychology, 90*, 439–447.

Coyne, J.C., & Gotlib, I.H. (1983). The role of cognition in depression: A critical appraisal. *Psychological Bulletin, 94*, 472–505.

Cutrona, C.E. (1983). Causal attributions and perinatal depression. *Journal of Abnormal Psychology, 92*, 161–172.

Darley, J.M., & Fazio, R.H. (1980). Expectancy confirmation processes arising in the social interaction sequence. *American Psychologist, 35*, 867–881.

Davis, D.A. (1976). On being *detectably* sane in insane places: Base rates and psychodiagnosis. *Journal of Abnormal Psychology, 85*, 416–422.

Davis, H. (1979). Self-reference and the encoding of personal information in depression. *Cognitive Therapy and Research, 3*, 97–110.

Davis, H., & Unruh, W.R. (1981). The development of the self-schema in adult depression. *Journal of Abnormal Psychology, 90*, 125–133.

Davison, G.C., Tsujimoto, R., & Glaros, A. (1973). Attribution and the maintenance of behavior change in falling asleep. *Journal of Abnormal Psychology, 82*, 124–133.

Davison, G.C., & Valins, S. (1969). Maintenance of self-attributed and drug-attributed behavior change. *Journal of Personality and Social Psychology, 11*, 25–33.

DeGree, C.E., & Snyder, C.R. (1985). Adler's psychology (of use) today: Personal history of traumatic life events on a self-handicapping strategy. *Journal of Personality and Social Psychology, 48*, 1512–1519.

Dell, P.F. (1981). Some irreverent thoughts on paradox. *Family Process, 20*, 37–51 (including Comments and Rejoinder).

Depue, R.A., & Monroe, S.M. (1978). Learned helplessness in the perspective of the depressive disorders: Conceptual and definitional issues. *Journal of Abnormal Psychology, 87*, 3–20.

Derry, P.A., & Kuiper, N.A. (1981). Schematic processing and self-reference in clinical depression. *Journal of Abnormal Psychology, 90*, 286–297.

Devine, D.A., & Fernald, P.S. (1973). Outcome effects of receiving a preferred, randomly assigned, or nonpreferred therapy. *Journal of Consulting and Clinical Psychology, 41*, 104–107.

Dunlap, K. (1932). *Habits: Their making and unmaking*. New York: Liveright.

Dunlap, K. (1942). The teaching of negative practice. *American Journal of Psychology, 55*, 270–273.

Duval, S., Duval, V.H., & Neely, R. (1979). Self-focus, felt responsibility, and helping behavior. *Journal of Personality and Social Psychology, 37*, 1769–1778.

Duval, S., & Wicklund, R.A. (1972). *A theory of objective self-awareness*. New York: Academic Press.

Eaves, G., & Rush, A.J. (1984). Cognitive patterns in

symptomatic and remitted unipolar major depression. *Journal of Abnormal Psychology, 93,* 31–40.

Ellis, A. (1962). *Reason and emotion in psychotherapy.* New York: Lyle Stuart.

Endler, N.S., & Magnusson, D. (1976). Toward an interactional psychology of personality. *Psychological Bulletin, 83,* 56–74.

Epstein, N. (1982). Cognitive therapy with couples. *The American Journal of Family Therapy, 10,* 5–16.

Farina, A., & Fisher, J.D. (1982). Beliefs about mental disorders: Findings and implications. In G. Weary & H.L. Mirels (Eds.), *Integrations of social and clinical psychology.* New York: Oxford University Press.

Farina, A., Fisher, J.D., Getter, H., & Fischer, E.H. (1978). Some consequences of changing people's views regarding the nature of mental illness. *Journal of Abnormal Psychology, 87,* 272–279.

Farrelly, F., & Brandsma, J. (1974). *Provocative therapy.* Fort Collins, CO: Shields Publishing.

Fazio, R.H., & Zanna, M.P. (1981). Direct experience and attitude-behavior consistency. In L. Berkowitz (Ed.), *Advances in experimental social psychology* (Vol. 14). New York: Academic Press.

Feather, N.T., & Davenport, P.R. (1981). Unemployment and depressive affect: A motivational and attributional analysis. *Journal of Personality and Social Psychology, 41,* 422–436.

Feldman, D.R., Strong, S.R., & Danser, D.B. (1982). A comparison of paradoxical and nonparadoxical interpretations and directives. *Journal of Counseling Psychology, 29,* 572–579.

Festinger, L. (1957). *A theory of cognitive dissonance.* Evanston, IL: Row, Peterson.

Fichten, C.S. (1984). See it from my point of view: Videotape and attribution in happy and distressed couples. *Journal of Social and Clinical Psychology, 2,* 125–142.

Fincham, F.D. (1983). Clinical applications of attribution theory: Problems and prospects. In M. Hewstone (Ed.), *Attribution theory: Social and functional extensions.* Oxford: Basil Blackwell Publishers.

Fincham, F.D., & O'Leary, K.D. (1983). Causal inferences for spouse behavior in maritally distressed and nondistressed couples. *Journal of Social and Clinical Psychology, 1,* 42–57.

Fine, M. (1982). When nonvictims derogate: Powerlessness in the helping professions. *Personality and Social Psychology Bulletin, 8,* 637–643.

Firth, J., & Brewin, C. (1982). Attributions and recovery from depression: A preliminary study using cross-lagged correlation analysis. *British Journal of Clinical Psychology, 21,* 229–230.

Fish, J.M. (1972). Dissolution of a fused identity in 1 therapeutic session: Case study. *Journal of Consulting and Clinical Psychology, 41,* 462–465.

Fisher, J.D., & Farina, A. (1979). Consequences of beliefs about the nature of mental disorders. *Journal of Abnormal Psychology, 88,* 320–327.

Fisher, L., Anderson, A., & Jones, J.E. (1981). Types of paradoxical intervention and indications/contraindications for use in clinical practice. *Family Process, 20,* 25–35.

Folkman, S. (1984). Personal control and stress and coping processes: A theoretical analysis. *Journal of Personality and Social Psychology, 46,* 839–852.

Fontana, A.F., & Klein, E.B. (1968). Self-presentation and the schizophrenic "deficit." *Journal of Consulting and Clinical Psychology, 32,* 250–256.

Forsyth, N.L., & Forsyth, D.R. (1982). Internality, controllability, and the effectiveness of attributional interpretations in counseling. *Journal of Counseling Psychology, 29,* 140–150.

Frank, J.D. (1961/1973). *Persuasion and healing: A comparative study of psychotherapy* (rev. ed.). Baltimore: The Johns Hopkins University Press.

Frankl, V.E. (1960). Paradoxical intervention: A logotherapeutic technique. *American Journal of Psychotherapy, 14,* 520–535.

Frankl, V.E. (1966). Logotherapy and existential analysis—a review. *American Journal of Psychotherapy, 20,* 252–260.

Friedlander, M.L., & Phillips, S.D. (1984). Preventing anchoring errors in clinical judgment. *Journal of Consulting and Clinical Psychology, 52,* 366–371.

Friedlander, M.L., & Stockman, S.J. (1983). Anchoring and publicity effects in clinical judgment. *Journal of Clinical Psychology, 39,* 637–643.

Gaupp, L.A., Stern, R.M., & Galbraith, G.C. (1972). False heart-rate feedback and reciprocal inhibition by aversive relief in the treatment of some avoidance behavior. *Behavior Therapy, 3,* 7–20.

Gerz, H.O. (1966). Experience with the logotherapeutic technique of paradoxical intention in the treatment of phobic and obsessive-compulsive patients. *American Journal of Psychiatry, 123,* 548–553.

Gibbons, F.X., Smith, T.W., Ingram, R.E., Pearce, K., Brehm, S.S., & Schroeder, D.J. (1985). Self-awareness and self-confrontation: Effects of self-focused attention on members of a clinical population. *Journal of Personality and Social Psychology, 48,* 662–675.

Girodo, M., Dotzenroth, S.E., & Stein, S.J. (1981). Causal attribution bias in shy males: Implications for self-esteem and self-confidence. *Cognitive Therapy and Research, 5,* 325–338.

Glass, D.C., & Singer, J.E. (1972). *Urban stress.* New York: Academic Press.

Goffman, E. (1959). *The presentation of self in everyday life.* New York: Doubleday.

Goldenberg, E.E., Smith, T.E., & Towne, B.D. (1980). Comparing treatment patterns of involuntary and voluntary patients. *Psychiatric Forum, 6,* 31–35.

Golding, S.G., & Rorer, L. (1972). Illusory correlation and subjective judgment. *Journal of Abnormal Psychology, 80,* 249–260.

Golding, S.L., Becker, E., Sherman, S., & Rappaport, J. (1975). The behavioral expectations scale: Assessment of expectations for interaction with the mentally ill. *Journal of Consulting and Clinical Psychology, 43,* 109.

Goldstein, A.P. (1971). *Psychotherapeutic interaction.* New York: Pergamon.

Goldstein, A.P., Heller, K., & Sechrest, L.B. (1966). *Psychotherapy and the psychology of behavior change.* New York: Wiley.

Goldstein, A.P., & Kanfer, F.H. (Eds.). (1979). *Maximizing treatment gains: Transfer enhancement in psychotherapy.* New York: Academic Press.

Goldstein, A.P., & Simonson, N.R. (1971). Social psychological approaches to psychotherapy research. In

A.E. Bergin & S.L. Garfield (Eds.), *Handbook of psychotherapy and behavior change: An empirical analysis*. New York: Wiley.

Golin, S., Sweeney, P.D., & Shaeffer, D.E. (1981). The causality of causal attributions in depression: A cross-lagged panel correlational analysis. *Journal of Abnormal Psychology, 90,* 14–22.

Gong-Guy, E., & Hammen, C. (1980). Causal perceptions of stressful events in depressed and nondepressed outpatients. *Journal of Abnormal Psychology, 89,* 662– 669.

Gordon, R.M. (1976). Effects of volunteering and responsibility on perceived value and effectiveness of a clinical treatment. *Journal of Consulting and Clinical Psychology, 44,* 799–801.

Gore, S. (1981). Stress-buffering functions of social supports: An appraisal and clarification of research methods. In B.S. Dohrenwend & B.P. Dohrenwend (Eds.), *Stressful life events and their contexts*. New York: Prodist.

Gottlieb, B.H. (1981). Preventative interventions involving social networks and social supports. In B.H. Gottlieb (Ed.), *Social networks and social support*. Beverly Hills: Sage.

Gottlieb, B.H. (1982). Social support as a focus for integrative research in psychology. *American Psychologist, 38,* 278–287.

Gove, W.R., & Fain, T. (1977). A comparison of voluntary and committed psychiatric patients. *Archives of General Psychiatry, 34,* 669–676.

Gur, R.C., & Sackeim, H.A. (1978). Self-confrontation and psychotherapy: A reply to Sanborn, Pyke, and Sanborn. *Psychotherapy: Theory, Research and Practice, 15,* 258–265.

Haemmerlie, F.M. (1983). Heterosexual anxiety in college females: A biased interaction treatment. *Behavior Modification, 7,* 611–623.

Haemmerlie, F.M., & Montgomery, R.L. (1982). Self-perception theory and unobtrusively biased interactions: A treatment for heterosocial anxiety. *Journal of Counseling Psychology, 29,* 362–370.

Haemmerlie, F.M., & Montgomery, R.L. (1984). Purposefully biased interventions: Reducing heterosocial anxiety through self-perception theory. *Journal of Personality and Social Psychology, 47,* 900–908.

Haley, J. (1963). *Strategies of psychotherapy*. New York: Grune & Stratton.

Haley, J. (1973). *Uncommon therapy: The psychiatric techniques of Milton H. Erickson, M.D.* New York: Norton.

Halperin, K.M., & Snyder, C.R. (1979). Effects of enhanced psychological test feedback on treatment outcome: Therapeutic implications of the Barnum Effect. *Journal of Consulting and Clinical Psychology, 47,* 140–146.

Hamilton, E.W., & Abramson, L.Y. (1983). Cognitive patterns and major depressive disorder: A longitudinal study in a hospital setting. *Journal of Abnormal Psychology, 92,* 173–184.

Hammen, C.L., & Cochran, S.D. (1981). Cognitive correlates of life stress and depression in college students. *Journal of Abnormal Psychology, 90,* 23–27.

Hammen, C., & de Mayo, R. (1982). Cognitive correlates of teacher stress and depressive symptoms: Implications for attributional models of depression. *Journal of Abnormal Psychology, 91,* 96–101.

Hammen, C., Krantz, S., & Cochran, S. (1981). Relationships between depression and causal attributions about stressful life events. *Cognitive Therapy and Research, 5,* 351–358.

Harari, O., & Hosey, K.R. (1981). Attributional biases among clinicians and nonclinicians. *Journal of Clinical Psychology, 37,* 445–450.

Harvey, D. (1981). Depression and attributional style: Interpretations of important personal events. *Journal of Abnormal Psychology, 90,* 134–142.

Harvey, J.H., & Galvin, K.S. (1984). Clinical implications of attribution theory and research. *Clinical Psychology Review, 4,* 15–34.

Harvey, J.H., & McGlynn, R.P. (1982). Matching words to phenomena: The case of the fundamental attribution error. *Journal of Personality and Social Psychology, 43,* 345–346.

Harvey, J.H., Town, J.P., & Yarkin, K.L. (1981). How fundamental is "The fundamental attribution error"? *Journal of Personality and Social Psychology, 40,* 346–349.

Heider, F. (1958). *The psychology of interpersonal relations*. New York: Wiley.

Heller, K. (1963). Experimental analogues of psychotherapy: The clinical relevance of laboratory findings of social influence. *Journal of Nervous and Mental Disease, 137,* 420–426.

Heller, K. (1979). The effects of social support: Prevention and treatment implications. In A.P. Goldstein & F.H. Kanfer (Eds.), *Maximizing treatment gains: Transfer enhancement in psychotherapy*. New York: Academic Press.

Heller, K., & Swindle, R.W. (1983). Social networks, perceived social support, and coping with stress. In R.D. Felner, L.A. Jason, J.N. Moritsuga, & S.S. Farber (Eds.), *Preventative psychology: Theory, research and practice*. New York: Pergamon.

Hendrick, C. (1983). Clinical social psychology: A birthright reclaimed. *Journal of Social and Clinical Psychology, 1,* 66–78.

Hill, M.G., & Weary, G. (1983). Perspectives on the *Journal of Abnormal and Social Psychology:* How it began and how it was transformed. *Journal of Social and Clinical Psychology, 1,* 4–14.

Hirsch, B.J. (1980). Natural support systems and coping with major life changes. *American Journal of Community Psychology, 8,* 159–172.

Hirsch, B.J. (1981). Social networks and the coping process: Creating personal communities. In B.H. Gottlieb (Ed.), *Social networks and social support*. Beverly Hills: Sage.

Hirsch, P.A., & Stone, G.L. (1983). Cognitive strategies and the client conceptualization process. *Journal of Counseling Psychology, 30,* 566–572.

Hoehn-Hyde, D., Schlottmann, R.S., & Rush, A.J. (1982). Perception of social interactions in depressed psychiatric patients. *Journal of Consulting and Clinical Psychology, 50,* 209–219.

Hoffman, M.A., & Teglasi, H. (1982). The role of causal attributions in counseling shy subjects. *Journal of Counseling Psychology, 29,* 132–139.

Holahan, C.J., & Moos, R.H. (1981). Social support and psychological distress: A longitudinal analysis. *Journal of Abnormal Psychology, 90,* 365–370.

Holmes, D.S. (1981). Existence of clinical projection and the stress-reducing function of attributive projection: A reply to Sherwood. *Psychological Bulletin, 90,* 460–466.

House, J.S. (1981). *Work stress and social support.* Reading, MA: Addison-Wesley.

Houston, B.K. (1972). Control over stress, locus of control, and response to stress. *Journal of Personality and Social Psychology, 21,* 249–255.

Hull, J.G. (1981). A self-awareness model of the causes and effects of alcohol consumption. *Journal of Abnormal Psychology, 90,* 586–600.

Hull, J.G., Levenson, R.L., Young, R.D., & Sher, K.J. (1983). Self-awareness reducing effects of alcohol consumption. *Journal of Personality and Social Psychology, 44,* 461–473.

Hull, J.G., & Young, R.D. (1983). Self-consciousness, self-esteem, and success-failure as determinants of alcohol consumption in male social drinkers. *Journal of Personality and Social Psychology, 44,* 1097–1109.

Hull, J.G., & Young, R.D. (1983). The self-awareness reducing effects of alcohol consumption: Evidence and implications. In J. Suls & A.G. Greenwald (Eds.), *Psychological perspectives on the self* (Vol. 2). Hillsdale, NJ: Erlbaum.

Hurvitz, N. (1970). Interaction hypotheses in marriage counseling. *Family Coordinator, 19,* 64–75.

Ingram, R.E., & Smith, T.W. (1984). Depression and internal versus external focus of attention. *Cognitive Therapy and Research, 8,* 139–152.

Ingram, R.E., Smith, T.W., & Brehm, S.S. (1983). Depression and information processing: Self-schemata and the encoding of self-referent information. *Journal of Personality and Social Psychology, 45,* 412–420.

Jacobson, N.S. (In press). Expanding the range and applicability of behavioral marital therapy. *The Behavior Therapist.*

Jacobson, N.S., McDonald, D.W., Follette, W.C., & Berley, R.A. (1985). Attributional processes in distressed and nondistressed married couples. *Cognitive Therapy and Research, 9,* 35–50.

Jacobson, N.S., & Margolin, G. (1979). *Marital therapy: Strategies based on social learning and behavior exchange principles.* New York: Brunner/Mazel.

James, W. (1890). *Principles of psychology.* New York: Holt.

Janoff-Bulman, R. (1979). Characterological versus behavioral self-blame: Inquiries into depression and rape. *Journal of Personality and Social Psychology, 37,* 1798–1809.

Jeffrey, D.B. (1974). A comparison of the effects of external-control and self-control on the modification and maintenance of weight. *Journal of Abnormal Psychology, 83,* 404–410.

Jones, E.E., & Berglas, S. (1978). Control of attributions about the self through self-handicapping strategies: The appeal of alcohol and the role of underachievement. *Personality and Social Psychology Bulletin, 4,* 200–206.

Jones, E.E., & Davis, K.E. (1965). From acts to dispositions: The attribution process in person perception. In L. Berkowitz (Ed.), *Advances in experimental social psychology* (Vol. 2). New York: Academic Press.

Jones, E.E., & Nisbett, R.E. (1971/1972). The actor and the observer: Divergent perceptions of the causes of behavior. In E.E. Jones, D.E. Kanouse, H.H. Kelley, R.E. Nisbett, S. Valins, & B. Weiner (Eds.), *Attribution: Perceiving the causes of behavior.* Morristown, NJ: General Learning Press.

Kahneman, D., & Tversky, A. (1973). On the psychology of prediction. *Psychological Review, 80,* 237–256.

Kanfer, F.H. (1977). The many faces of self-control, or behavior modification changes its focus. In R.B. Stuart (Ed.), *Behavioral self-management: Strategies, techniques, and outcomes.* New York: Brunner/Mazel.

Kanfer, F.H., & Grimm, L.G. (1978). Freedom of choice and behavior change. *Journal of Consulting and Clinical Psychology, 46,* 873–878.

Kanfer, F.H., & Hagerman, S. (1981). The role of self-regulation. In L.P. Rehm (Ed.), *Behavior therapy for depression: Present status and further directions.* New York: Academic Press.

Kanter, N., & Goldfried, M. (1979). Relative effectiveness of rational restructuring and self-control desensitization in the reduction of interpersonal anxiety. *Behavior Therapy, 10,* 472–490.

Karoly, P., & Steffen, J.J. (Eds.). (1980). *Improving the long-term effects of psychotherapy: Models of durable outcome.* New York: Gardner.

Kaslow, N.J., Rehm, L.P., & Siegel, A.W. (1984). Social-cognitive and cognitive correlates of depression in children. *Journal of Abnormal Child Psychology, 12,* 605–620.

Kelley, H.H. (1971/1972). Attribution in social interaction. In E.E. Jones, D.E. Kanouse, H.H. Kelley, R.E. Nisbett, S. Valins, & B. Weiner (Eds.), *Attribution: Perceiving the causes of behavior.* Morristown, NJ: General Learning Press.

Kellog, R., & Baron, R.S. (1975). Attribution theory, insomnia, and the reverse placebo effect: A reversal of Storms and Nisbett's findings. *Journal of Personality and Social Psychology, 32,* 231–236.

Kent, R.N., Wilson, G.T., & Nelson, R. (1972). Effect of false heart-rate feedback on avoidance behavior: An investigation of "cognitive desensitization." *Behavior Therapy, 3,* 1–6.

Kihlstrom, J.F., & Nasby, W. (1981). Cognitive tasks in clinical assessment: An exercise in applied psychology. In P.C. Kendall & S.D. Hollon (Eds.), *Assessment strategies for cognitive-behavioral interventions.* New York: Academic Press.

Kobasa, S.C.O., & Puccetti, M.C. (1983). Personality and social resources in stress resistance. *Journal of Personality and Social Psychology, 45,* 839–850.

Kolko, D.J., & Milan, M.A. (1983). Reframing and paradoxical instruction to overcome "resistance" in the treatment of delinquent youths: A multiple baseline analysis. *Journal of Consulting and Clinical Psychology, 51,* 655–660.

Kopel, S.A. (1982). Commentary: Social psychological processes in the development of maladaptive behaviors. In G. Weary & H.L. Mirels (Eds.), *Integrations of clinical and social psychology.* New York: Oxford University Press.

Kopel, S., & Arkowitz, H. (1975). The role of attribution and self-perception in behavior change: Implications for behavior therapy. *Genetic Psychology Monographs, 92,* 175–212.

Krantz, S.E., & Rude, S. (1984). Depressive attributions: Selection of different causes or assignment of dimensional meanings? *Journal of Personality and Social Psychology, 47,* 193–203.

Kuiper, N.A. (1978). Depression and causal attributions for success and failure. *Journal of Personality and Social Psychology, 36,* 236–246.

Kuiper, N.A., & Derry, P.A. (1982). Depressed and nondepressed content self-reference in mild depressives. *Journal of Personality, 50,* 67–80.

Kuiper, N.A., & Rogers, T.B. (1979). Encoding of personal information: Self-other differences. *Journal of Personality and Social Psychology, 37,* 499–514.

Kurtz, R.M., & Garfield, S.L. (1978). Illusory correlations: A further exploration of Chapman's paradigm. *Journal of Consulting and Clinical Psychology, 40,* 1009–1015.

Lamontagne, Y. (1978). Treatment of erythrophobia by paradoxical intention. *Journal of Nervous and Mental Disease, 166,* 304–306.

Langer, E.J. (1975). The illusion of control. *Journal of Personality and Social Psychology, 32,* 311–328.

Langer, E.J., & Abelson, R.P. (1974). A patient by any other name . . . : Clinician group difference in labeling bias. *Journal of Consulting and Clinical Psychology, 42,* 4–9.

Langer, E.J., Janis, I.L., & Wolfer, J.A. (1975). Reduction of psychological stress in surgical patients. *Journal of Experimental Social Psychology, 11,* 155–165.

Langer, E.J., & Rodin, J. (1976). The effects of choice and enhanced personal responsibility for the aged: A field experiment in an institutional setting. *Journal of Personality and Social Psychology, 34,* 191–198.

Langer, E.J., & Roth, J. (1975). Heads I win, tails it's chance: The illusion of control as a function of the sequences of outcomes in a purely chance task. *Journal of Personality and Social Psychology, 32,* 951–955.

LaRocco, J.M., House, J.S., & French, J.R.P., Jr., (1980). Social support, occupational stress, and health. *Journal of Health and Human Behavior, 21,* 202–218.

LaRocco, J.M., & Jones, A.P. (1978). Co-worker and leader support as moderators of stress-strain relationships in work situations. *Journal of Applied Psychology, 63,* 629–634.

Larrance, D.T., & Twentyman, C.T. (1983). Maternal attributions and child abuse. *Journal of Abnormal Psychology, 92,* 449–457.

Leavy, R.L. (1983). Social support and psychological disorder: A review. *Journal of Community Psychology, 11,* 3–21.

Lefcourt, H.M. (1973). The function of the illusion of control and freedom. *American Psychologist, 28,* 417–425.

Leon, G.R., Kendall, P.C., & Garber, J. (1980). Depression in children: Parent, teacher, and clinical perspectives. *Journal of Abnormal Child Psychology, 8,* 221–235.

Lewin, K. (1935). *A dynamic theory of personality: Selected papers.* New York: McGraw-Hill.

Lewinsohn, P.M., Hoberman, H., Teri, L., & Hautzinger, M. (1985). An integrative theory of depression. In S. Reiss & R. Bootzin (Eds.), *Theoretical issues in behavior therapy.* New York: Academic Press.

Lewinsohn, P.M., Steinmetz, J.L., Larson, D.W., & Franklin, J. (1981). Depression-related cognitions: Antecedent or consequences? *Journal of Abnormal Psychology, 90,* 213–219.

Liem, G.R. (1975). Performance and satisfaction as affected by personal control over salient decisions. *Journal of Personality and Social Psychology, 31,* 232–240.

Light, K.C., & Obrist, P.A. (1980). Cardiovascular response to stress: Effects of opportunity to avoid, shock experience, and performance feedback. *Psychophysiology, 17,* 243–252.

Lindner, R. (1954). *The fifty minute hour.* Toronto: Clarke, Irwin.

Lopez, F.G., & Wambach, C. (1982). Effects of paradoxical and self-control directives in counseling. *Journal of Counseling Psychology, 29,* 115–124.

Lowery, C.R., Denney, D.R., & Storms, M.D. (1979). Insomnia: A comparison of the effects of pill attribution and nonpejorative self-attribution. *Cognitive Therapy and Research, 3,* 161–164.

Lueger, R.J., & Petzel, T.P. (1979). Illusory correlation in clinical judgment: Effect of amount of information to be processed. *Journal of Consulting and Clinical Psychology, 47,* 1120–1121.

Lynch, J.J. (1977). *The broken heart: The medical consequences of loneliness.* New York: Basic Books.

Magnusson, D., & Endler, N.S. (Eds.). (1977). *Personality at the crossroads: Current issues in interactional psychology.* Hillsdale, NJ: Erlbaum.

Mahoney, K., & Mahoney, M.J. (1976). Cognitive factors in weight reduction. In J.D. Krumboltz & G.E. Thoresen (Eds.), *Counseling methods.* New York: Holt, Rinehart & Winston.

Malleson, N. (1959). Panic and phobia. *Lancet, 1,* 225–227.

Manly, P.C., McMahon, R.J., Bradley, C.F., & Davidson, P.O. (1982). Depressive attributional style and depression following childbirth. *Journal of Abnormal Psychology, 91,* 245–254.

Markus, H. (1977). Self-schemas and processing information about the self. *Journal of Personality and Social Psychology, 35,* 63–78.

Marlatt, G.A. (1978). Craving for alcohol, loss of control, and relapse: A cognitive-behavioral analysis. In P.E. Nathan, G.A. Marlatt, & T. Løberg (Eds.), *Alcoholism: New directions in behavioral research and treatment.* New York: Plenum.

Marlatt, G.A. (1979). Alcohol use and problem drinking: A cognitive-behavioral analysis. In P.C. Kendall & S.D. Hollon (Eds.), *Cognitive-behavioral interventions: Theory, research, and procedures.* New York: Academic Press.

Marshall, G.D., & Zimbardo, P.G. (1979). Affective consequences of inadequately explained psychological arousal. *Journal of Personality and Social Psychology, 37,* 970–988.

Maslach, C. (1978). The client role in staff burn-out. *Journal of Social Issues, 34,* 11–124.

Maslach, C. (1979). Negative emotional biasing of unexplained arousal. *Journal of Personality and Social Psychology, 37,* 953–969.

Maslach, C. (1982). *Burnout—The cost of caring*. Englewood Cliffs, NJ: Prentice-Hall.

Maslach, C., & Jackson, S.E. (1981). The measurement of experienced burnout. *Journal of Occupational Behavior, 2,* 99–113.

Maslach, C., & Jackson, S.E. (1982). Burnout in health professions: A social psychological analysis. In G.S. Sanders & J. Suls (Eds.), *Social psychology of health and illness*. Hillsdale, NJ: Erlbaum.

Masters, W.H., & Johnson, V. (1970). *Human sexual inadequacy*. Boston: Little, Brown.

Matthews, K.A., Scheier, M.F., Brunson, B.I., & Carducci, B. (1980). Attention, unpredictability, and reports of physical symptoms: Eliminating the benefits of predictability. *Journal of Personality and Social Psychology, 38,* 525–537.

Mead, G.H., (1934). *Mind, self, and society*. Chicago: University of Chicago Press.

Meehl, P.E. (1960). The cognitive activity of the clinician. *American Psychologist, 15,* 19–27.

Meichenbaum, D. (1977). *Cognitive-behavior modification*. New York: Plenum.

Mendonca, P.J., & Brehm, S.S. (1983). Effects of choice on behavioral treatment of overweight children. *Journal of Social and Clinical Psychology, 1,* 343–358.

Metalsky, G.I., Abramson, L.Y., Seligman, M.E.P., Semmel, A., & Peterson, C. (1982). Attributional styles and life events in the classroom: Vulnerability and invulnerability to depressive mood reactions. *Journal of Personality and Social Psychology, 43,* 612–617.

Milan, M.A., & Kolko, D.J. (1982). Paradoxical intention in the treatment of obsessional flatulence ruminations. *Journal of Behavior Therapy and Experimental Psychiatry, 13,* 167–172.

Miller, I.W., Klee, S.H., & Norman, W.H. (1982). Depressed and nondepressed inpatients' cognitions of hypothetical events, experimental tasks, and stressful life events. *Journal of Abnormal Psychology, 91,* 78–81.

Miller, I.W., & Norman, W.H. (1979). Learned helplessness in humans: A review and attribution theory model. *Psychological Bulletin, 86,* 93–118.

Miller, S.M. (1980). Why having control reduces stress: If I can stop the roller coaster, I don't want to get off. In J. Garber & M.E.P. Seligman (Eds.), *Human helplessness: Theory and application*. New York: Academic Press.

Miller, S.M. (1981). Predictability and human stress: Toward a clarification of evidence and theory. In L. Berkowitz (Ed.), *Advances in experimental social psychology* (Vol. 14). New York: Academic Press.

Millon, T. (1975). Reflections on Rosenhan's "On being sane in insane places." *Journal of Abnormal Psychology, 84,* 456–461.

Mischel, W. (1973). Toward a cognitive social learning reconceptualization of personality. *Psychological Review, 80,* 252–283.

Monroe, S.S. (1983). Social support and disorder: Toward an untangling of cause and effect. *American Journal of Community Psychology, 11,* 81–97.

Monson, T.C., & Snyder, M. (1977). Actors, observers, and the attribution process: Toward a reconstruction. *Journal of Experimental Social Psychology, 13,* 89–111.

Morgan, L.A. (1976). A reexamination of widowhood and morale. *Journal of Gerontology, 31,* 687–695.

Morrison, J.K., Bushell, J.D., Hanson, G.D., Fentiman, J.R., & Holdridge-Crane, S. (1977). Relationship between psychiatric patients' attitudes toward mental illness and attitudes of dependence. *Psychological Reports, 41,* 1194.

Morrow, G.R., Hoagland, A., & Carnrike, L.M., Jr. (1981). Social support and parental adjustment to pediatric cancer. *Journal of Consulting and Clinical Psychology, 49,* 763–765.

Moss, G.E. (1973). *Illness, immunity and social interaction*. New York: Wiley.

Mowery, J.D., Doherty, M.E., & Keeley, S.M. (1979). The influence of negation and task complexity on illusory correlation. *Journal of Abnormal Psychology, 88,* 334–337.

Mozdzierz, G., Macchitelli, F., & Lisiecki, J. (1976). The paradox in psychotherapy: An Adlerian perspective. *Journal of Individual Psychology, 32,* 169–184.

Nasby, W., Hayden, B., & De Paulo, B.M. (1980). Attributional bias among aggressive boys to interpret unambiguous social stimuli as displays of hostility. *Journal of Abnormal Psychology, 89,* 459–468.

Nisbett, R.E., & Ross, L. (1980). *Human inference: Strategies and shortcomings of social judgment*. Englewood Cliffs, NJ: Prentice-Hall.

Nisbett, R.E., & Schachter, S. (1966). Cognitive manipulation of pain. *Journal of Experimental Social Psychology, 2,* 227–236.

Nisbett, R.E., & Wilson, T.D. (1977). Telling more than we know: Verbal reports on mental processes. *Psychological Review, 84,* 231–259.

O'Hara, M.W., Rehm, L.P., & Campbell, S.B. (1982). Predicting depressive symptomatology: Cognitive-behavioral models and postpartum depression. *Journal of Abnormal Psychology, 91,* 457–461.

Ommundsen, R., & Ekeland, T.J. (1978). Psychiatric labeling and social perception. *Scandinavian Journal of Psychology, 19,* 193–197.

Oskamp, S. (1965). Overconfidence in case-study judgments. *Journal of Consulting Psychology, 29,* 261–265.

Pearlin, L.I., Menaghan, E.G., Lieberman, M.A., & Mullan, J.T. (1981). The stress process. *Journal of Health and Social Behavior, 22,* 337–356.

Peterson, C. (1982). Learned helplessness and attributional interventions in depression. In C. Antaki & C. Brewer (Eds.), *Attributions and psychological change*. London: Academic Press.

Peterson, C., Schwartz, S.M., & Seligman, M.E.P. (1981). Self-blame and depressive symptoms. *Journal of Personality and Social Psychology, 41,* 253–259.

Peterson, C., & Seligman, M.E.P. (1984). Causal explanations as a risk factor for depression: Theory and evidence. *Psychological Review, 91,* 347–374.

Phares, E.J. (1979). Defensiveness and perceived control. In L.C. Perlmeuter & R.A. Monty (Eds.), *Choice and perceived control*. Hillsdale, NJ: Erlbaum.

Phillips, S.L., & Fischer, C.S. (1981). Measuring social support networks in general populations. In B.S. Dohrenwend & B.P. Dohrenwend (Eds.), *Stressful life events and their context*. New York: Prodist.

Polivy, J. (1976). Perception of calories and regulation of intake in restrained and unrestrained subjects. *Addictive Behaviors, 1,* 237–244.

Procidano, M.E., & Heller, K. (1983). Measures of perceived social support from friends and from family: Three validation studies. *American Journal of Community Psychology, 11,* 1−24.

Pryor, J.B., Gibbons, F.X., Wicklund, R.A., Fazio, R.H., & Hood, R. (1977). Self-focused attention and self-report validity. *Journal of Personality, 45,* 513−527.

Raps, C.S., Peterson, C., Reinhard, K.E., Abramson, L.Y., & Seligman, M.E.P. (1982). Attributional style among depressed patients. *Journal of Abnormal Psychology, 91,* 102−108.

Raskin, D.E., & Klein, Z.E. (1976). Losing a symptom through keeping it: A review of paradoxical treatment techniques and rationale. *Archives of General Psychiatry, 33,* 548−555.

Reeder, G.A. (1982). Let's give the fundamental attribution error another chance. *Journal of Personality and Social Psychology, 43,* 341−344.

Reich, J.W., & Zautra, A. (1981). Life events and personal causation: Some relationships with satisfaction and distress. *Journal of Personality and Social Psychology, 41,* 1002−1012.

Reisenzein, R. (1981). The Schachter theory of emotion: Two decades later. *Psychological Bulletin, 94,* 239−264.

Relinger, H., & Bornstein, P.H. (1979). Treatment of sleep onset insomnia by paradoxical instruction: A multiple baseline design. *Behavior Modification, 3,* 203−222.

Relinger, H., Bornstein, P.H., & Mungas, D.M. (1978). Treatment of insomnia by paradoxical intervention: A time series analysis. *Behavior Therapy, 9,* 955−959.

Rizley, R. (1978). Depression and distortion in the attribution of causality. *Journal of Abnormal Psychology, 87,* 32−48.

Rodin, J., & Langer, E.J. (1977). Long-term effects of a control-relevant intervention with the institutionalized aged. *Journal of Personality and Social Psychology, 33,* 897−902.

Rodin, J., Rennert, K., & Solomon, S.L. (1980). Intrinsic motivation for control: Fact or fiction. In A. Baum & J.E. Singer (Eds.), *Advances in environmental psychology. Vol. 2: Application of personal control.* Hillsdale, NJ: Erlbaum.

Rogers, C.R. (1951). *Client centered therapy.* Boston: Houghton Mifflin.

Rogers, T.B., Kuiper, N.A., & Kirker, W.S. (1977). Self-reference and the encoding of personal information. *Journal of Personality and Social Psychology, 35,* 677−688.

Rook, K.S. (1984). The negative side of social interaction: Impact on psychological well-being. *Journal of Personality and Social Psychology, 46,* 1097−1108.

Rosen, G.M., Rosen, E., & Reid, J.D. (1972). Cognitive desensitization and avoidance behavior: A reevaluation. *Journal of Abnormal Psychology, 80,* 176−182.

Rosen, J. (1953). *Direct psychoanalysis.* New York: Grune & Stratton.

Rosenberg, M., & Kaplan, H.B. (Eds.). (1982). *Social psychology of the self-concept.* Arlington Heights, IL: Harlan Davidson.

Rosenhan, D.L. (1973). On being sane in insane places. *Science, 179,* 250−258.

Ross, L. (1977). The intuitive psychologist and his shortcomings: Distortions with attribution process. In L. Berkowitz (Ed.), *Advances in experimental social psychology* (Vol. 10). New York: Academic Press.

Ross, L., Rodin, J., & Zimbardo, P.G. (1969). Toward an attribution therapy: The reduction of fear through induced cognitive-emotional misattribution. *Journal of Personality and Social Psychology, 12,* 279−288.

Ross, M., & Olson, J.M. (1981). An expectancy-attribution model of the effects of placebos. *Psychological Review, 88,* 408−437.

Rothaus, P., Hanson, P.G., Cleveland, S.E., & Johnson, D.L. (1963). Describing psychiatric hopsitalization: A dilemma. *American Psychologist, 18,* 85−89.

Rothbart, M., Evans, M., & Fulero, S. (1979). Recall for confirming events: Memory processes and the maintenance of social stereotypes. *Journal of Experimental Social Psychology, 15,* 343−355.

Sanborn, D.E., Pyke, H.F., & Sanborn, L.J. (1975). Videotape playback and psychotherapy: A review. *Psychotherapy: Theory, Research and Practice, 12,* 179−186.

Sandler, I.N., & Barrera, M., Jr. (1984). Toward a multimethod approach to assessing the effects of social support. *American Journal of Community Psychology, 12,* 37−52.

Sarason, I.G., Levine, H.M., Basham, R.B., & Sarason, B.R. (1983). Assessing social support: The social support questionnaire. *Journal of Personality and Social Psychology, 44,* 127−139.

Sarason, I.G., & Sarason, B.R. (1982). Concomitants of social support: Attitudes, personality characteristics, and life experiences. *Journal of Personality, 50,* 331−344.

Savage, R.E., Perlmeuter, L.C., & Monty, R.A. (1979). Effect of reduction in the amount of choice and perception of control on learning. In L.C. Perlmeuter & R.A. Monty (Eds.), *Choice and perceived control.* Hillsdale, NJ: Erlbaum.

Schachter, S. (1964). The interaction of cognitive and physiological determinants of emotional state. In L. Berkowitz (Ed.), *Advances in experimental social psychology* (Vol. 1). New York: Academic Press.

Schachter, S., & Singer, J. (1962). Cognitive, social, and physiological determinants of emotional state. *Psychological Review, 69,* 379−399.

Schachter, S., & Singer, J.E. (1979). Comments on the Maslach and Marshall-Zimbardo experiments. *Journal of Personality and Social Psychology, 37,* 989−995.

Schaefer, C., Coyne, J.C., & Lazarus, R.S. (1981). The health-related functions of social support. *Journal of Behavioral Medicine, 4,* 381−406.

Scheier, M.F., & Carver, C.S. (1977). Self-focused attention and the experience of emotion: Attraction, repulsion, elation, and depression. *Journal of Personality and Social Psychology, 35,* 625−636.

Scheier, M.F., Carver, C.S., & Gibbons, F.X. (1981). Self-focused attention and reactions to fear. *Journal of Research in Personality 15,* 1−15.

Schulz, R. (1976). Effects of control and predictability on the physical and psychological well-being of the institutionalized aged. *Journal of Personality and Social Psychology, 33,* 563−573.

Schulz, R., & Decker, S. (1982). Social support, adjustment, and the elderly spinal cord injured: A social psychological analysis. In G. Weary & H.L. Mirels (Eds.), *Integrations of clinical and social psychology.* New York: Oxford University Press.

Schulz, R., & Hanusa, B.H. (1978). Long-term effects of control and predictability-enhancing interventions: Findings and ethical issues. *Journal of Personality and Social Psychology, 36,* 1194–1201.

Seligman, M.E.P. (1975). *Helplessness: On depression, development, and death.* San Francisco: Freeman.

Seligman, M.E.P., Abramson, L.Y., Semmel, A., & von Baeger, L. (1979). Depressive attributional style. *Journal of Abnormal Psychology, 88,* 242–247.

Seligman, M.E.P., Peterson, C., Kaslow, N.J., Tannenbaum, R.L., Alloy, L.B., & Abramson, L.Y. (1984). Attributional style and depressive symptoms among children. *Journal of Abnormal Psychology, 93,* 235–238.

Seltzer, L.F. (1983). Influencing the "shape" of resistance: An experimental exploration of paradoxical directives and psychological reactance. *Basic and Applied Social Psychology, 4,* 47–71.

Selvini Palazzoli, M.S., Boscolo, L., Cecchin, G., & Prata, G. (1978). *Paradox and counterparadox.* New York: Jason Aronson.

Sheras, P.L., & Worchel, S. (1979). *Clinical psychology: A social psychological approach.* New York: Van Nostrand.

Sherwood, G.G. (1981). Self-serving biases in person perception: A reexamination of projection as a mechanism of defense. *Psychological Bulletin, 90,* 445–459.

Sherwood, G.G. (1982). Consciousness and stress reduction in defensive projection: A reply to Holmes. *Psychological Bulletin, 91,* 372–375.

Shinn, M., Rosario, M., Mørch, H., & Chestnut, D.E. (1984). Coping with job stress and burnout in the human services. *Journal of Personality and Social Psychology, 46,* 864–876.

Singerman, K., Borkovec, T., & Baron, R.S. (1976). Misattribution and placebo effects on speech anxiety. *Behavior Therapy, 7,* 306–313.

Slater, J., & Depue, R.A. (1981). The contribution of environmental events and social support to serious suicide attempts in primary depressive disorder. *Journal of Abnormal Psychology, 90,* 275–285.

Slivken, K.E., & Buss, A. (1984). Misattribution and speech anxiety. *Journal of Personality and Social Psychology, 47,* 396–402.

Smith, M.L. (1980). Sex bias in counseling and psychotherapy. *Psychological Bulletin, 87,* 392–407.

Smith, T.W., & Brehm, S.S. (1981). Person perception and the Type A Coronary-Prone behavior pattern. *Journal of Personality and Social Psychology, 40,* 1137–1149.

Smith, T.W., & Greenberg, J. (1981). Depression and self-focused attention. *Motivation and Emotion, 5,* 323–331.

Smith, T.W., Houston, B.K., & Stucky, R.J. (1985). Effects of threat of shock and control over shock on finger pulse volume, pulse rate, and systolic blood pressure. *Biological Psychology, 20,* 31–38.

Smith, T.W., Ingram, R.E., & Brehm, S.S. (1983). Social anxiety, anxious self-preoccupation, and recall of self-relevant information. *Journal of Personality and Social Psychology, 44,* 1276–1283.

Smith, T.W., Snyder, C.R., & Handelsman, M.M. (1982). On the self-serving function of an academic wooden leg: Test anxiety as a self-handicapping strategy. *Journal of Personality and Social Psychology, 42,* 314–321.

Smith, T.W., Snyder, C.R., & Perkins, S.C. (1983). The self-serving function of hypochondriacal complaints: Physical symptoms as self-handicapping strategies. *Journal of Personality and Social Psychology, 44,* 787–797.

Snyder, C.R. (1977). "A patient by any other name" revisited: Maladjustment or attributional locus of problem? *Journal of Consulting and Clinical Psychology, 45,* 101–103.

Snyder, C.R., & Cowles, C. (1979). Impact of positive and negative feedback based on personality and intellectual assessment. *Journal of Consulting and Clinical Psychology, 47,* 207–209.

Snyder, C.R., Higgins, R.L., & Stucky, R.J. (1983). *Excuses: Masquerades in search of grace.* New York: Wiley.

Snyder, C.R., & Ingram, R.E. (1983). "Company motivates the miserable": The impact of consensus information on help seeking for psychological problems. *Journal of Personality and Social Psychology, 45,* 1118–1127.

Snyder, C.R., & Shenkel, R.J. (1976). Effects of "favorability," modality, and relevance upon acceptance of general personality interpretations prior to and after receiving diagnostic feedback. *Journal of Consulting and Clinical Psychology, 44,* 34–41.

Snyder, C.R., Shenkel, R.J., & Lowery, C.R. (1977). Acceptance of personality interpretations: The "Barnum effect" and beyond. *Journal of Consulting and Clinical Psychology, 45,* 104–114.

Snyder, C.R., Shenkel, R.J., & Schmidt, A. (1976). Effects of role perspective and client psychiatric history on locus of problem. *Journal of Consulting and Clinical Psychology, 44,* 467–472.

Snyder, C.R., & Smith, T.W. (1982). Symptoms as self-handicapping strategies: The virtues of old wine in a new bottle. In G. Weary & H.L. Mirels (Eds.), *Integrations of clinical and social psychology.* New York: Oxford University Press.

Snyder, C.R., Smith, T.W., Augelli, R.W., & Ingram, R.E. (1985). On the self-serving function of social anxiety: Shyness as a self-handicapping strategy. *Journal of Personality and Social Psychology, 48,* 970–980.

Snyder, M., & Cantor, N. (1979). Testing hypotheses about other people: The use of historical knowledge. *Journal of Experimental Social Psychology, 15,* 330–342.

Snyder, M., & Swann, W.B., Jr. (1978a). Behavioral confirmation in social interaction: From social perception to social reality. *Journal of Experimental Social Psychology, 14,* 148–162.

Snyder, M., & Swann, W.B., Jr. (1978b). Hypothesis-testing processes in social interaction. *Journal of Personality and Social Psychology, 36,* 1202–1212.

Snyder, M., Tanke, E.D., & Berscheid, E. (1977). Social perception and interpersonal behavior: On the self-fulfilling nature of social stereotypes. *Journal of Personality and Social Psychology, 35,* 656–666.

Snyder, M., & Uranowitz, W.W. (1978). Reconstructing the part: Some cognitive consequences of person perception. *Journal of Personality and Social Psychology, 36,* 941–980.

Solomon, S., Holmes, D.S., & McCaul, K.D. (1980). Behavior control over aversive events: Does control that requires effort reduce anxiety and physiological arousal? *Journal of Personality and Social Psychology, 39,* 729–736.

Solyom, L., Garza-Perez, J., Ledwidge, B.L., & Solyom, C. (1972). Paradoxical intention in the treatment of obsessive thoughts: A pilot study. *Comparative Psychiatry, 3,* 291–297.

Sonne, J., & Janoff, D. (1979). The effect of treatment attributions on the maintenance of weight reduction: A replication and extension. *Cognitive Therapy and Research, 3,* 389–397.

Sonne, J.L., & Janoff, D.S. (1982). Attributions and the maintenance of behavior change. In C. Antaki & C. Brewer (Eds.), *Attributions and psychological change.* London: Academic Press.

Spensley, J., Edwards, D.W., & White, E. (1980). Patient satisfaction and involuntary treatment. *American Journal of Orthopsychiatry, 50,* 725–727.

Spitzer, R.L. (1975). On pseudoscience in science, logic in remission, and psychiatric diagnosis: A critique of Rosenhan's "On being sane in insane places." *Journal of Abnormal Psychology, 84,* 442–452.

Stampfl, T.G., & Levis, D.J. (1967). Essentials of implosive therapy: A learning theory-based psychodynamic behavioral therapy. *Journal of Abnormal Psychology, 72,* 496–503.

Starr, J.G., & Katkin, E. (1969). The clinician as an abberant actuary: Illusory correlation and the Incomplete Sentences Blank. *Journal of Abnormal Psychology, 74,* 670–675.

Steele, C.M., Southwick, L.L., & Critchlow, B. (1981). Dissonance and alcohol: Drinking your troubles away. *Journal of Personality and Social Psychology, 41,* 831–846.

Steenbarger, B., & Aderman, D. (1979). Objective self-awareness as a nonaversive state: Effect of anticipating discrepancy reduction. *Journal of Personality, 47,* 330–339.

Stokes, J.P., & Wilson, D.G. (1984). The inventory of socially supportive behaviors: Dimensionality, prediction, and gender differences. *American Journal of Community Psychology, 12,* 53–69.

Stokes, T.F., & Baer, D.M. (1977). An implicit technology of generalization. *Journal of Applied Behavior Analysis, 10,* 349–367.

Storms, M.D., & McCaul, K.D. (1976). Attribution processes and emotional exacerbation of dysfunctional behavior. In J.H. Harvey, W.J. Ickes, & R.F. Kidd (Eds.), *New directions in attribution research* (Vol. 1). Hillsdale, NJ: Erlbaum.

Storms, M.D., & Nisbett, R.E. (1970). Insomnia and the attribution process. *Journal of Personality and Social Psychology, 16,* 319–328.

Strohmer, D.E., & Newman, L.J. (1983). Counselor hypothesis-testing strategies. *Journal of Counseling Psychology, 30,* 557–565.

Strong, S.R. (1978). Social psychological approach to psychotherapy research. In S.L. Garfield & A.E. Bergin (Eds.), *Handbook of psychotherapy and behavior change: An empirical analysis* (2nd ed.). New York: Wiley.

Strong, S.R. (1982). Emerging integration of clinical and social psychology: A clinician's perspective. In G. Weary & H.L. Mirels (Eds.), *Integrations of clinical and social psychology.* New York: Oxford University Press.

Strong, S.R. (1984). Experimental studies in explicitly paradoxical interventions: Results and implications. *Journal of Behavior Therapy and Experimental Psychiatry, 15,* 189–194.

Strong, S.R., & Claiborn, C.D. (1982). *Change through interaction: Social psychological processes of counseling and psychotherapy.* New York: Wiley.

Sullivan, H.S. (1953). *The interpersonal theory of psychiatry.* New York: Norton.

Sushinsky, L.S., & Bootzin, R.R. (1970). Cognitive desensitization as a model of systematic desensitization. *Behaviour Research and Therapy, 8,* 29–34.

Swann, W.B., Jr., & Ely, R.J. (1984). A battle of wills: Self-verification versus behavioral confirmation. *Journal of Personality and Social Psychology, 46,* 1287–1302.

Swann, W.B., Jr., & Read, S.J. (1981). Self-verification processes: How we sustain our self-conceptions. *Journal of Experimental Social Psychology, 17,* 351–372.

Sweeney, P.D., Shaeffer, D., & Golin, S. (1982). Attributions about self and others in depression. *Personality and Social Psychology Bulletin, 8,* 37–42.

Taylor, S.E. (1983). Adjustment to threatening events: A theory of cognitive adaptation. *American Psychologist, 38,* 1161–1173.

Taylor, S.E., Lichtman, R.R., & Wood, J.V. (1984). Attributions, beliefs about control, and adjustment to breast cancer. *Journal of Personality and Social Psychology, 46,* 489–502.

Tennen, H., Rohrbaugh, M., Press, S., & White, M.D. (1981). Reactance theory and therapeutic paradox: A compliance-defiance model. *Psychotherapy: Theory, Research and Practice, 18,* 14–22.

Thoits, P.A. (1982). Conceptual, methodological, and theoretical problems in studying social support as a buffer against life stress. *Journal of Health and Social Behavior, 23,* 145–159.

Thompson, S.C. (1981). Will it hurt less if I can control it? A complex answer to a simple question. *Psychological Bulletin, 90,* 89–101.

Tucker, J.A., Vuchinich, R.E., & Sobell, M.B. (1981). Alcohol consumption as a self-handicapping strategy. *Journal of Abnormal Psychology, 90,* 220–230.

Turner, R., & Ascher, M. (1979). Controlled comparison of progressive relaxation, stimulus control, and paradoxical intervention therapies for insomnia. *Journal of Consulting and Clinical Psychology, 47,* 500–508.

Tversky, A., & Kahneman, D. (1974). Judgment under uncertainty: Heuristics and biases. *Science, 185,* 1124–1131.

Vaillant, G.E. (1977). *Adaptation to life.* Boston: Little, Brown.

Valins, S., & Ray, A. (1967). Effects of cognitive desensitization on avoidance behavior. *Journal of Personality and Social Psychology, 7,* 345–350.

Wachtel, P.L. (1977). *Psychoanalysis and behavior therapy.* New York: Basic Books.

Wagner, V., Weeks, G., & L'Abate, L., (1980). Enrichment and written enhancement messages with couples. *American Journal of Family Therapy, 8,* 36–44.

Waller, R.W., & Keeley, S.M. (1978). Effects of explanation and information feedback on the illusory correlation phenomenon. *Journal of Consulting and Clinical Psychology, 46,* 342–343.

Wallston, B.S., Alagna, S.W., DeVellis, B., Mc., & DeVellis, R.F. (1983). Social support and physical health. *Health Psychology, 4,* 367–391.

Wampold, B.E., Casas, J.M., & Atkinson, D.R. (1981). Ethnic bias in counseling: An information processing approach. *Journal of Counseling Psychology, 28,* 498–503.

Warren, L.W., & McEachren, L. (1983). Psychosocial correlates of depressive symptomatology in adult women. *Journal of Abnormal Psychology, 92,* 151–160.

Watson, D. (1982). The actor and the observer: How are their perceptions of causality different? *Psychological Bulletin, 92,* 682–700.

Watzlawick, P., Beavin, J.H., & Jackson, D.D. (1967). *Pragmatics of human communication.* New York: Norton.

Watzlawick, P., Weakland, J.H., & Fisch, R. (1974). *Change: Principles of problem formation and problem resolution.* New York: Norton.

Weary, G., & Mirels, H.L. (Eds.). (1982). *Integrations of clinical and social psychology.* New York: Oxford University Press.

Weeks, G.R., & L'Abate, L. (1982). *Paradoxical psychotherapy.* New York: Brunner/Mazel.

Wegner, D.M., & Vallacher, R.R. (Eds.). (1980). *The self in social psychology.* New York: Oxford University Press.

Weisz, J.R. (1981). Effects of the "mentally retarded" label on adult judgments about child failure. *Journal of Abnormal Psychology, 90,* 371–374.

Wellman, B. (1981). Applying network analysis to the study of support. In B.H. Gottlieb (Ed.), *Social networks and social support.* Beverly Hills: Sage.

White, R.W. (1959). Motivation reconsidered: The concept of competence. *Psychological Review, 66,* 297–333.

Whitley, B.E. (1979). Sex roles and psychotherapy: A current appraisal. *Psychological Bulletin, 86,* 1309–1321.

Whitman, J.R., & Duffey, R.F. (1961). The relationship between type of therapy received and a patient's perception of his illness. *Journal of Nervous and Mental Disease, 113,* 288–292.

Wicklund, R.A. (1975). Objective self-awareness. In L. Berkowitz (Ed.), *Advances in experimental social psychology* (Vol. 8). New York: Academic Press.

Wicklund, R.A., & Brehm, J.W. (1976). *Perspectives on cognitive dissonance.* Hillsdale, NJ: Erlbaum.

Wilcox, B.L. (1981a). Social support in adjusting to marital disruption: A network analysis. In B.H. Gottlieb (Ed.), *Social networks and social support.* Beverly Hills: Sage.

Wilcox, B.L. (1981b). Social support, life stress, and psychological adjustment: A test of the buffering hypothesis. *American Journal of Community Psychology, 9,* 371–386.

Wills, T.A. (1978). Perceptions of clients by professional helpers. *Psychological Bulletin, 85,* 968–1000.

Wilson, G.T. (1978). Booze, beliefs, and behavior: Cognitive processes in alcohol use and abuse. In P.E. Nathan, G.A. Marlatt, & T. Løberg (Eds.), *Alcoholism: New directions in behavioral research and treatment.* New York: Plenum.

Wilson, G.T. (1983). Self-awareness, self-regulation, and alcohol consumption: An analysis of J. Hull's model. *Journal of Abnormal Psychology, 92,* 505–513.

Wilson, G.T., & Thomas, M.G.W. (1973). Self- versus drug-produced relaxation and the effects of instructional set in standardized systematic desensitization. *Behaviour Research and Therapy, 11,* 278–288.

Wilson, T.D., Hull, J.G., & Johnson, J. (1981). Awareness and self-perception: Verbal reports on internal states. *Journal of Personality and Social Psychology, 40,* 53–71.

Wilson, T.D., & Linville, P.W. (1982). Improving the academic performance of college freshmen: Attribution therapy revisited. *Journal of Personality and Social Psychology, 42,* 367–376.

Wilson, T.D., & Linville, P.W. (1985). Improving the performance of college freshmen with attributional techniques. *Journal of Personality and Social Psychology, 49,* 287–293.

Wortman, C.B. (1975). Some determinants of perceived control. *Journal of Personality and Social Psychology, 31,* 282–294.

Wortman, C.B., & Dunkel-Schetter, C.D. (1979). Interpersonal relations and cancer: A theoretical analysis. *Journal of Social Issues, 35,* 120–155.

Wright, J., & Fichten, C. (1976). Denial of responsibility, videotape feedback and attribution theory: Relevance for behavioral marital therapy. *Canadian Psychology Review, 17,* 219–230.

Wright, R.A. (1984). Motivation, anxiety, and the difficulty of avoidant control. *Journal of Personality and Social Psychology, 46,* 1376–1404.

Wright, R.M., & Strong, S.R. (1982). Stimulating therapeutic change with directives: An explorative study. *Journal of Counseling Psychology, 29,* 199–202.

Yates, J. (1958). The application of learning theory to the treatment of tics. *Journal of Abnormal and Social Psychology, 56,* 175–182.

4

THE DEVELOPMENTAL STUDY OF PSYCHOPATHOLOGY: IMPLICATIONS FOR PSYCHOTHERAPY AND BEHAVIOR CHANGE

THOMAS M. ACHENBACH

University of Vermont

Most theories of psychopathology and its treatment assume developmental antecedents for adult disorders. Freud, for example, constructed a vast theory of psychosexual development to explain what he observed in adult neurotics. Supporting his developmental inferences largely with adult recollections of childhood and case histories such as that of Little Hans (Freud, 1909), he did not study or treat children directly. Nevertheless, he had a profound impact on views of child development, in terms of both theory about how children develop and prescriptions for how they should be raised.

The father of American behaviorism, John B. Watson (1919), saw adult deviance as a direct outgrowth of childhood learning histories. Like Freud, Watson supported his inferences with illustrative examples of childhood phenomena, but did little to test the developmental antecedents of adult pathol-

ogy. Later efforts to combine psychodynamic and learning theories also emphasized the developmental origins of pathology, but did not test these origins in children (Dollard & Miller, 1950; Mahl, 1971; Wachtel, 1977). Family systems theorists likewise imply that childhood experiences within the family establish patterns that explain later problems (see Goldenberg & Goldenberg, 1980). In the organic sphere, genetic and other theories imply that certain developmental sequences culminate in overt disorders such as schizophrenia (Gottesman & Shields, 1982).

Despite widespread emphasis on developmental antecedents, the study of psychopathology has been largely separate from the study of development. Rather than focusing directly on the course of development, the study of psychopathology often starts with adult disorders and then extrapolates backward to hypothesized antecedents in childhood. Although there is a great deal of developmental research on normal children, it is just beginning to be applied to psychopathology (see Achenbach, 1982; Cicchetti, 1984; Rutter & Garmezy, 1983).

Developmental factors are especially relevant to psychotherapy and behavior change during the period of rapid growth from birth to maturity. Consider, for example, a newborn baby. Now think of a 2-year-old toddler, a 4-year-old preschooler, an 8-year-old second grader, a 14-year-old eighth grader, and an 18-year-old graduating from high school. The differences are enormous. Some of the differences, such as physical size, might be viewed as quantitative. Yet most of the differences in cognition, behavior, social relations, and biological maturation are much more than quantitative. Many of the most crucial differences involve major changes in the *organization* of thought, behavior, and social relationships, as well as the emergence of wholly new functions and abilities.

Developmental periods and processes have obvious implications for clinical interventions with children and adolescents, but may also be important for interventions with adults. To highlight developmental variables, I will focus first on theoretical issues in the study of development. I will then outline major developmental periods, characteristic disorders from birth to maturity, and problems in defining disorders. Thereafter, I will consider the developmental implications of different types of interventions and the evaluation of their results.

THEORETICAL ISSUES IN THE STUDY OF DEVELOPMENT

It would be gratifying to present a unified theory of development with which to explain the origins and course of all psychopathology. From such a theory, we could derive prescriptions for specific therapies to be applied to each disorder. Psychodynamic and learning theory have both aspired to provide such all-encompassing explanations. Unfortunately, as research has become more sophisticated, questions about both development and psychopathology have become far too complex and diverse to be answered by any single theory. The inability of grand theories to integrate data from these often disparate realms argues not for abandoning theory, but for basing theoretical constructs more directly on empirical data.

Just as we no longer expect anything like a humoral theory to explain *all* physical illnesses, we should not expect a single theory to explain all of development and its aberrations. Instead, specialized paradigms and constructs are needed to deal with specific aspects of development and specific aberrations. Although we also need to forge links between specialized approaches whenever possible, excessive reliance on sweeping theoretical assumptions risks premature closure on important questions that need to be addressed empirically. The following sections deal with some theoretical issues arising in developmental research.

Concepts of Development

Considerable effort has been devoted to defining concepts of "development" from a variety of perspectives (e.g., Harris, 1957; Stevenson, 1966). Some concepts of development are specific to a particular theory, such as that of Gesell (1954) or Piaget (1983), whereas others are generic to a broad topic of study, such as the development of perception or object relations. In either case, however, it is probably futile to attempt an authoritative definition of development, just as it would be futile to attempt an authoritative definition of "learning" that would be accepted by all students of that topic.

Besides providing an umbrella label for workers whose interests overlap enough to share journals, meetings, and organizations, broad concepts of development have a heuristic value in the generation of ideas. Whether one prefers to think of major changes in behavior in terms of "development" or "learning," concepts of this sort help to generate testable hypotheses. Once the hypotheses are actually tested, the data and conclusions typically concern more molecular variables and processes than the higher order heuristic concepts. Although empirical underpinnings at the molecular level are essential, higher order concepts of development spawn research strategies and guidelines for integrating molecular findings. Such concepts of development highlight the following factors:

1. The massive, multidimensional *changes* that are so evident when we compare children of different ages.

2. The major *reorganizations* of functioning associated with the observable changes.
3. The *processes* underlying developmental changes.
4. The major *transitions, continuities, and discontinuities* occurring over the course of development.
5. The *sequences* of adaptational tasks and challenges that humans face as they grow.
6. *Normative* expectations for functioning at each level of development.

These factors are handled differently by the different developmental paradigms that we shall now consider.

Developmental Paradigms

Thomas Kuhn's (1970) analysis of the history of science in terms of conceptual paradigms offers a handy way to compare and contrast approaches to the study of development. A *paradigm* is a schematic model for representing phenomena and the relations among them. Whereas theories are devised to provide specific explanations, paradigms are more general systems of terms and concepts shared by workers who do not necessarily agree on particular theoretical explanations. Multiple theories may stem from the same general paradigm but differ in their hypothetical constructs and ways of explaining phenomena encompassed by the paradigm. When S-R behaviorism dominated American psychology from the 1930s through the 1950s, for example, several learning theories flourished within the general S-R paradigm. Despite their differences, they shared basic assumptions about the subject matter of psychology (observable behavior); the primary variables (stimuli and responses); the mechanism of behavioral change (learning); and the eventual application of the same principles to all behavior, no matter how complex.

Because of the diversity of variables and perspectives relevant to the study of development, it is worth considering several paradigms that deal with development in different ways.

The S-R Paradigm

Although some might regard the S-R paradigm as the antithesis of "developmental" paradigms, it has inspired a great deal of theory about behavioral changes occurring between birth and maturity. It is important, however, to distinguish between the *theoretical* and *methodological* aspects of the S-R paradigm. Dating from Aristotle, the earliest and purest form of the theoretical view was that the child begins life as a *tabula rasa* on which sensory impressions write their messages. Development, then, is merely the accumulation of these sensory impressions. The basic process hypothesized to account for development was *association*—the formation of associative bonds between sensory impressions that were phenomenologically similar, occurred together in time, were especially vivid, and so on. Adult thinking could thus be explained by the accumulation and associative bonding of experiences occurring since birth.

In contrast to the theoretical aspect of the S-R paradigm, its *methodological* aspect originated with Pavlov, Bekhterev, and Thorndike, who controlled animal behavior through conditioning without recourse to unobservable thought processes. By extrapolating animal conditioning principles to human behavior, John B. Watson (1913) popularized the *methodological* behaviorism that eventually set standards for most psychological research, even research generated by theories contradicting S-R *explanations* of behavioral change.

Under the dominance of the S-R paradigm from the 1930s through the 1950s, American psychology concentrated on physically defined stimuli and responses. However, methodological behaviorism—focusing on the measurable activity of the organism—has been assimilated by other approaches that differ markedly from theoretical behaviorism, such as information-processing and computer-simulation paradigms for human cognition, nativist theories of language development, and behavior genetics. As illustrated by Ollendick (this volume), many therapeutic approaches also use S-R methods to change behavior, even though they do not necessarily *explain* disorders in terms of theoretical behaviorism.

In short, behavioral methods are shared to some degree by nearly all developmental paradigms, but there are major disagreements with classical behavioral theories that *explained* development solely in terms of associative processes. Despite their implications for development, the classical S-R theories of Watson, Thorndike, Hull, and Skinner generated relatively little research on the actual changes occurring between birth and maturity (see Stevenson,

1983). Social learning theorists such as Bandura (1977) have extended behavioral theory to many variables beyond observable stimuli, responses, and reinforcers, but, in doing so, have given up the basic explanatory principles, objectivity, and parsimony claimed by classical S-R theories. Contemporary applications of associationist concepts to behavioral development have become increasingly linked to the study of organic and cognitive aspects of development and constructs derived from other paradigms, such as those discussed next.

The Organismic-Developmental Paradigm

This paradigm encompasses several approaches that rely on organic growth as a model for psychological development. Accordingly, development is viewed not as the acquisition of specific responses but as changes in the *structuring* of cognition and behavior. This structuring reflects the emergence of new abilities, analogous to advances in organic functioning brought about by physical maturation. Like physical maturation, major advances in psychological functioning are assumed to occur in a uniform sequence, with advanced levels depending on the prior emergence of less advanced levels. Although environmental inputs are needed to actualize each successive advance, the effect of the environment depends on the organism's existing level of development. As a consequence, manipulations of environmental stimuli are thought unlikely to bring about advanced developmental levels unless the organism has reached the appropriate preliminary level.

Whereas the S-R paradigm is a product of empiricist-associationist epistemology, the organismic-developmental paradigm is largely a product of nativist-structuralist epistemology. A basic tenet of this view is that inborn characteristics of our minds structure all of our experience. Exponents of nativist-structuralist views have ranged from Plato through Kant and the Gestalt psychologists. Darwin's (1859) theory of evolution was another important forerunner of the organismic-developmental theorists, who view the development of individuals *(ontogeny)* as reflecting principles of adaptation like those governing the evolutionary development of species *(phylogeny)*.

Organismic-developmental theorists often allude to "stages" or "periods" of development. For some developmentalists, such as Gesell (1954), "stages" are defined largely in terms of behavior that is char-

acteristic of a particular age. Calling developmental psychology "the embryology of behavior," Gesell carefully documented infant and child behavior at successive ages, much as the differentiation of embryos is documented. On the basis of his observations, he assembled standardized stimulus situations for eliciting behavior and then constructed age norms for responses to these situations. His infant tests and their successors, such as the Bayley Scales (1969), have functioned like IQ tests for children in the first years of life. Probably because infants are incapable of the symbolic reasoning that is so central to later tests of ability, infant test scores do not predict later IQs very well in most populations (see Achenbach, 1982; Kopp, 1983). The infant tests may provide a good index of current problems, however, and the high heritabilities found for infant test scores indicate that they tap aspects of early behavioral development having a large biological component (Matheny, Dolan, & Wilson, 1976).

Somewhat analogous to Gesell's embryological view of early behavioral development, Heinz Werner (1957) analyzed a broad range of perceptual-cognitive phenomena in terms of progressive differentiation and hierarchic integration. An example is the dimension of field independence versus field dependence, which is correlated both with developmental level and certain personality characteristics (Weisz, O'Neill, & O'Neill, 1975; Witkin & Goodenough, 1980).

Piaget's Organismic-Developmental Theory

Unlike Gesell and Werner, Piaget (1983) portrayed development in terms of inferred psychological structures. Although Piaget's theory is often summarized in terms of stages and periods, he stressed that these represent artificial segmentations of a continuous process. Piaget's purpose in studying development was to answer the epistemological question of how knowledge is created. He began by documenting children's responses to various problem situations. Struck by the qualitative differences in responses by children of different ages, Piaget gradually constructed a theory of the processes and sequences through which knowledge is created. Although Piaget's theory is far from completely validated, it is worth highlighting as the most comprehensive guide to aspects of adaptive development that are often slighted in the study of psychopathology and its treatment.

At birth, babies are equipped with reflexive behaviors such as sucking and startle reflexes. They are also equipped with two general modes of adaptation that Piaget called *accommodation*—the tendency to alter one's behavior in response to environmental realities—and *assimilation*—the tendency to construe or modify environmental stimuli for one's own purposes. Most adaptive functioning involves an interplay between accommodation and assimilation. Extreme forms of accommodation are exemplified in normal imitative behavior and in abnormal excesses of conformity. By contrast, extreme forms of assimilation are exemplified in normal fantasy play and in the abnormalities of psychotic thinking.

The Sensory-motor Period. The adaptive techniques typically developed by a species are jointly determined by the genetically transmitted growth plans of the species and the major environmental contingencies encountered. The interplay between heredity and environment is evident in many ways during the first 18 months of life, which Piaget called the *sensory-motor period*. Adaptive development begins with the progressive modification of genetically determined behavior as babies adapt their reflexes to environmental realities. The sucking reflex, for example, becomes coordinated with looking, grasping, and other behaviors, while it also becomes more differentiated and discriminating as to what is sucked. The progressive refinement of reflexive behaviors in response to environmental contingencies is compatible with S-R views of development. Piaget, however, was most interested in behaviors that are harder to explain in S-R terms, such as babies' systematic exploration of their environments, using their eyes and mouth at first and then their hands.

This rudimentary epistemic activity involves patterns called *circular reactions*. These occur when the baby accidentally discovers an interesting sight or sound and then repeatedly tries to recreate it. For example, as my two-month-old daughter flailed about in an infant seat one afternoon, her hand went up in front of her face. Her eyes fixated on the hand, and she drew it toward her face. She then repeated this sequence seven times, her interest manifested in the convergence of her eyes each time on the approaching hand. Piaget's term "circu-

lar reaction" aptly describes the circular pattern that her hand followed as it was repeatedly raised, brought toward her eyes, lowered, and thrust out before being raised again.

The first circular reactions focus on the infant's own body *(primary circular reactions)*. They then progress to the repetition of accidentally discovered effects involving other objects *(secondary circular reactions)*, such as shaking a rattle to repeat the noise. Later, there is more deliberate experimentation, such as banging objects together to see what will happen *(tertiary circular reactions)*. Although the observed behavior is quite elementary, Piaget viewed it as prototypical of human adaptive development in three important ways:

1. It exemplifies a biologically determined tendency to seek *knowledge* of the environment.
2. It demonstrates organized *patterns* of behavior composed of a series of actions that are not readily explicable in terms of molecular stimuli, responses, and reinforcers.
3. It illustrates a *developmental sequence* whereby organized patterns or "schemes" progress from simple to more complex levels.

The Transition to Mental Representation. Toward the age of 18 months, new phenomena emerge that Piaget interpreted as reflecting a new ability to think in terms of mental representations. Although some representations may consist of pictorial images, they are not merely copies of perceptual input. Instead, representations are constructed and manipulated by organized mental activities analogous to the sensory-motor activities evident earlier. The child may thus engage in mental trial-and-error by imagining new sequences of events.

The advent of mental representation heralds a crucial difference between Piaget's theory and most other theories. This is Piaget's (1977) distinction between the *figurative* and *operative* aspects of thought. The *figurative* aspect encompasses mental signifiers, such as images, symbols, and words that stand for specific stimuli. These signifiers are somewhat analogous to subvocal labels hypothesized by S-R theorists who postulate strings of covert mediating responses between observable stimuli and responses (e.g., Kendler & Guenther, 1980). They are also analogous to the mental symbols of psychoanalytic theory.

Although most theories allow for mental contents analogous to Piaget's figurative aspect of thought, they do not have a clear counterpart of what Piaget called the *operative* aspect of thought. This refers to organized mental *activities* that operate on the figurative contents of thought, just as overt actions operate on physical stimuli. Once mental representation emerges around the age of 18 months, it becomes a powerful factor in children's lives, enabling them to assimilate a great deal of information through being told by others, as well as through direct observation. Yet children's reality testing remains limited until the operative aspect of thought becomes more logical in later years. As a result, toddlers and preschoolers may be unduly terrified by imaginary creatures but not sufficiently cautious about real dangers. Their imaginative powers, however, may help them cope with the problems they create for themselves, as illustrated by one two-year-old's solution to monsters under his bed. His parents noticed that he had stopped complaining of monsters after he began taking a big toy frog to bed with him. Yet he seemed to dislike the frog, since, after demanding it be put in his bed, he abruptly pushed it toward his feet. When his parents finally asked why he wanted the frog so much and then pushed it away, he explained: "Dat fwoggie so ugly . . . it keep da monsters fwom comin' up da wall by me bed!" His cure for monsters was a product of the same cognitive system that spawned them in the first place!

The Concrete Operational Period.   Between the ages of five and seven, children begin to show more logical forms of thought. Piaget demonstrated this transition through hundreds of experiments, the best known of which concern *conservation* of quantitative attributes. As an example, a child is shown two identical glasses filled with equal amounts of water. After the child agrees that the glasses contain equal amounts, the contents of one glass are poured into a tall, thin graduated cylinder. When asked to compare the quantities now, young children generally reply that the cylinder has more water than the glass, because it is higher. They thus seem to think that the actual quantity is altered by a superficial change in the appearance of the water, even though they see that no water is added or subtracted. By about the age of seven, however, children not only recognize that the quantity is conserved despite its

changed appearance but also give logical reasons why it must be conserved. For example, "It rises higher but it's narrower"; or "Nothing's been added or taken away"; or "If you poured it back into the first glass, it would be the same as before."

According to Piaget, children's new understanding of quantitative relations reflects an important advance in the operative aspect of thought. Instead of being analogues of overt physical activities, mental activities after about the age of seven embody a *system* of interrelated logical operations. Although children are not consciously aware of this system, their ability to use logic distinguishes them sharply from younger children, whose thinking seems dominated by appearances and subjective associations.

Just as mental images can frighten the toddler, however, the logic of the school-aged child can spawn problems of its own. In particular, children may become critical of the flaws and inconsistencies detected in what they hear from parents and teachers. The loss of faith in parents' omniscience may foster disappointment, defiance, and a sense of superiority expressed in argument, criticism, and what Elkind (1979) calls *cognitive conceit*. Yet the logic of this period is concrete and rigid, causing the child to insist on yes-or-no, black-or-white answers.

The Formal Operational Period.   By about the age of 11 or 12, children seem increasingly aware of more abstract formal logic involving relations among multiple possibilities rather than single concrete properties. Piaget provided numerous experimental demonstrations of the onset of reasoning in terms of multiple possibilities, as applied to practical problems. However, these reasoning powers are also evident in adolescents' preoccupation with moral issues, philosophical questions, and social values. Whereas concrete operational children detect specific flaws in adult logic, formal operational adolescents may question the whole system of values and reality represented by their parents and society. The newfound ability to think relativistically in terms of multiple possibilities may be a source of uncertainty about one's personal identity, as well as contributing to other aspects of adolescent distress and rebellion. Fourteen-year-old Charles exemplifies adolescent conflicts between the intricacies of formal operational thought, previously unquestioned religious faith, and the emergence of normal sexual urges:

Brought to a mental health clinic at the urging of his parish priest, Father Riley, Charles had been making ever longer and more elaborate confessions, repeatedly returning to the confessional to correct his earlier confessions. He also spent hours after confession trying to explain to Father Riley the "escape hatches" he detected in the confessional procedure.

When interviewed, Charles reported that his problems had started when he realized that the normal confessional did not cover sinful intentions that had been held back in previous confessions. This raised problems of grammatical tense in confessing sins. The many possible permutations of tense, intention, category of behavior, category of sin, and degree of sinfulness could leave escape hatches for sins which could not be properly confessed. The possible permutations were so numerous that Charles envisioned them stretching out in front of him to infinity. Looking at obscene pictures and getting erections were the sins that concerned him the most. (Achenbach, 1982, p. 63)

Like earlier developmental advances, adolescents' reasoning abilities bring not only potential problems but also new adaptive possibilities, such as the capacity to appreciate literary and dramatic depictions of life's problems. The ability to consider alternatives to the world they see may also inspire a quest for ideals incomprehensible at younger ages.

Causes of Development. A mass of research by Piaget and others supports many of the developmental changes he outlined. This does not necessarily mean that every aspect of a child's functioning can be attributed to a "stage" of cognitive development or that various facets of cognitive functioning are linked together as tightly as Piaget's theoretical models sometimes imply. Instead, the outline of major changes and the descriptions of the interplay between organic and environmental characteristics offer guidelines for understanding development between birth and maturity, as well as cognitive aspects of adaptive functioning throughout the life span.

Major questions remain, however, about the causes of development, its aberrations, and its upper limits (Commons, Richards, & Armon, 1984).

Piaget proposed that there were four major contributors to cognitive development:

1. *Biological maturation*, determined largely by genetically transmitted growth plans.
2. *Experience* gained through interaction with the physical world.
3. *Social transmission of information* via language, modeling, and teaching.
4. *Equilibration*.

The first three contributors have counterparts in nearly all views of development. But the fourth contributor—*equilibration*—is based on Piaget's view that cognitive development cannot be explained solely as a product of genetic programming and environmental contingencies. Instead, the child progressively *constructs* new concepts and epistemic procedures from a combination of genetically determined capabilities and specific experiences with the real world. The intensive exploration and experimentation evident in most young children is symptomatic of the struggle for more powerful concepts. This is the essence of the equilibration process, which Piaget (1977) regards as the key to cognitive development, but which has not been fully explained by his theory or other approaches.

Although they do not use his terminology, information-processing and artificial intelligence researchers face problems like those raised by Piaget. Until recently, they have focused on either what Piaget called the figurative aspect or the operative aspect of cognition. Some theorists have attempted to explain everything in terms of symbolic representations, that is, the "data base" of cognition. Others have attempted to explain everything in terms of rule-governed procedures (see Siegler, 1983).

In one of the most ambitious efforts to formulate a conceptual framework for higher mental processes, John Anderson (1983) has postulated both a data base corresponding to the system's "declarative knowledge" and rules for operating on the data, corresponding to the system's "procedural knowledge." Despite the sophistication of Anderson's system, however, it is restricted to mature adult cognition, with no provision for the major changes that must occur between birth and the attainment of the adult system. Although information-processing and artificial intelligence approaches dominate the study of cognition, they have largely ignored the issue of development. As Siegler (1983) put it: "Those of us who have adopted the information processing approach have evaded, avoided, and hidden from this issue. We are not alone in this nonconfrontational policy—adherents of other approaches have not done any better—but this is no excuse. The lack of success in identifying mechanisms of development has hindered theoretical progress" (p. 193).

Until we have better bridges between the computerized precision of research on adult cognition and the fascinating phenomena of cognitive development, Piaget's approach is our richest guide to cognitive phenomena relevant to the developmental study of psychopathology.

The Psychodynamic Paradigm

In his effort to construct a general model of psychological functioning, Freud evolved two distinct theories of developmental change. One was his theory of *psychosexual development,* which postulated a sequence in the distribution of *libidinal* (sexual) energy to the *oral zone* in infancy, followed by the *anal zone* from about 1-1/2 to 3 years of age, and the *phallic zone* from about 3 to 5 years. These were followed by the libidinal quiescence of the latency period and the reactivation of genitally focused libido at puberty. Freud seems to have thought that libidinal phases are biologically predetermined and that elements common to all human cultures make certain conflicts inevitable during each phase. The precise form, intensity, and outcome of the conflicts, however, are affected by environmental variables. Although all boys face an oedipal conflict during the phallic phase, for example, an event such as the loss of the father would alter the form of the conflict, the resulting character structure, and the potential for future neurosis.

Freud's other developmental theory concerned *motivation and learning.* It included many aspects of nineteenth-century associationist theory, whereby ideas could become mentally associated through contiguity of sensory impressions, similarities, vividness, and so on. It also included a drive-reduction model like that of twentieth-century learning theories. Behaviors that discharged tensions arising from the "instinctual drives" of sex and aggression would be learned and repeated. Furthermore, drive states could elicit complexes of thoughts previously associated with similar drive states.

For Freud, drive reduction and associative mechanisms helped to explain the development of cognitive processes, as well as the id—ego—superego personality structure. He hypothesized, for example, that the infant in a state of intense hunger—a component of the libidinal drive—hallucinates objects, such as the breast or bottle, that were previously associated with reduction of the drive state. These hallucinations provide temporary gratification until the infant's needs are met. Freud believed that such hallucinations constitute the first defensive efforts to circumvent direct conflicts between instinctual impulses and environmental realities. By this means, the ego eventually becomes differentiated as the seat of cognition. Through an analogous defensive process, the superego becomes differentiated during the oedipal conflict via *identification with the aggressor* (same sex parent), and remains as the seat of the conscience and ego ideal. Unlike Piaget, who saw cognitive development as a process of adaptation through the construction of knowledge, Freud viewed cognitive development as a by-product of the defensive struggle between id impulses and environmental reality.

Psychoanalytic Ego Psychology. One of the founders of psychoanalytic ego psychology, Heinz Hartmann (1939), proposed that there are innate determinants of ego functions such as thinking, language, perception, and learning. Because he thought these functions could develop and operate independently of conflict, he referred to them as the *conflict-free sphere of the ego.*

Hartmann agreed with Freud that some ego functions arise as defensive reactions to conflict, but he hypothesized that they could then function independently of the conflicts that spawned them. A child might defend against jealousy of a new sibling by being very loving *(reaction formation),* for example, but then continue to be loving because of the rewards it earns. Because of the many ego functions that were either initially or eventually autonomous from conflict, Hartmann (1950) advocated studying the ego in its own right, using developmental research methods other than those of psychoanalysis. Other psychodynamic ego theorists, such as David Rapaport (1967) and Robert White (1963), also emphasized positive adaptive functions that operate independently of id drives and conflicts.

Anna Freud (1946, 1965) expanded the role of defense mechanisms in ego development and proposed a *developmental profile* for assessing children's functioning according to analytic developmental theory. This entails a summary of inferences about the child's drive development (libidinal and aggressive); ego and superego development; regressions and fixation points; conflicts; and general characteristics, such as frustration tolerance and sublimation potential. The inferences are intended to culminate in diagnostic categorizations such as the following:

1. In spite of current behavior disturbance, personality growth is within the wide range of "normality."
2. Symptoms are of a transitory nature and can be classed as by-products of developmental strain.
3. There is a permanent drive regression to fixation points, which leads to neurotic conflicts.
4. There is drive regression plus ego and superego regressions, which lead to infantilisms, borderline psychotic, delinquent, or psychotic disturbances.
5. There are primary organic deficiencies or early deprivations, which distort development and produce retarded, defective, and nontypical personalities.
6. There are destructive processes at work of organic, toxic, or psychic origin that have caused or are about to cause a disruption of mental growth. (Adapted from A. Freud, 1965, p. 147.)

Although the developmental profile is often used as a model of psychoanalytic assessment (e.g., Yorke, 1980), reliability and validity data have not been published. Furthermore, many of the theoretical constructs, such as instinctual drives, fixations, and cathexes, are being deemphasized in analytic theory (Rosenblatt & Thickstun, 1977).

Erik Erikson's Version of the Psychodynamic Paradigm

Whereas Freud defined early development in terms of oral, anal, and phallic libidinal phases, Erikson (1963, 1980) interprets development much more broadly in terms of *psychosocial* functioning. Although he acknowledges the initial importance of the oral zone, he focuses on the child's overall *mode* of *incorporative* activity, which centers in not just the mouth but all the sense organs. Because incorporation is so crucial to the infant, Erikson considers the chief *modality* of *social interaction* with other people to be *getting*—learning how to get others to provide what is needed and to receive what they provide. If all goes well, this pattern of interaction with others will be learned and form a building block for further development. Similarly, the anal and genital zones are involved in subsequent modes of action and modalities of social interaction, but the general modes and modalities concern much broader aspects of social functioning than implied by libido theory.

Erikson views developmental conflicts largely in terms of the social aspects of the ego. During each major developmental stage, he hypothesizes a dominant conflict whose resolution shapes subsequent conflicts and their resolutions. During the initial oral-sensory stage, for example, the main conflict is over the development of a sense of *trust versus mistrust,* followed by conflicts over the development of *autonomy verus shame and doubt,* and then *initiative versus guilt.* Erikson's theory of stages and conflicts extends through adulthood, culminating with the conflict of *ego integrity versus despair* when death must be faced in old age.

Several studies using interviews, questionnaires, and projective techniques have found evidence for the conflicts hypothesized by Erikson. The negative aspects of certain conflicts seem to remain prominent for long periods, however, while concern with other conflicts rises and falls (e.g., Ciaccio, 1971; Vaillant & Milofsky, 1980; Waterman, Geary, & Waterman, 1974). Erikson's theory thus offers a useful source of concepts for research on personality development continuing through the life cycle, although it does not provide *explanations* for either normal or abnormal development.

To summarize the status of psychodynamic approaches, classical Freudian theory made ambitious claims about the developmental origins of psychopathology and normal personality. It has been a rich source of clinical concepts and has inspired considerable research. The developmental aspects have seldom been directly tested, however, and the few empirical comparisons of Freudian developmental theory with others, such as Piaget's, have not supported Freud's views (e.g., Gouin-Décarie, 1965). Obstacles arise from difficulties in operationalizing Freud's developmental concepts and analytic theorists' failure to seek an empirical basis for their theory.

Anna Freud's extension of analytic theory to the assessment and treatment of children has been widely hailed in the psychodynamic literature, but has not been adequately tested. The psychoanalytic ego psychologists stressed the positive aspects of normal adaptive development and the common ground between psychoanalysis and developmental psychology, although they did not support their views with empirical research. Erik Erikson's extension of the psychodynamic paradigm has had a major impact on views of psychosocial development and has inspired research supporting some of the developmental conflicts he hypothesized. It has not provided testable explanations for normal or abnormal development, however. Another offshoot of the psychodynamic paradigm, the object relations school of psychoanalysis, has given rise to quite a different thrust in developmental theory, as is discussed next.

The Ethological Paradigm

Ethology is rooted in Darwin's (1872) application of evolutionary theory to the survival value of behavior. A systematic science of ethology emerged in the 1930s when Lorenz and Tinbergen not only made careful observations of animal behavior in its natural environment but also did laboratory and field experiments to test the effects of various stimuli on behavior assumed to be genetically determined.

From observations and experimental manipulations, ethologists attempt to identify the most basic organized behavioral sequences that characterize a species. Designated as *fixed action patterns* (FAPs), these sequences are thought to be triggered by environmental stimuli called *sign stimuli* or *releasers*. FAPs constitute basic building blocks of development somewhat analogous to behavioral responses in the S-R paradigm and schemes in Piaget's theory. Rather than being a product of the individual's history, however, FAPs are assumed to be genetically organized adaptive units that function—or at one time functioned—to enhance survival.

Although FAPs are preprogrammed behaviors,

Lorenz (1965) hypothesized that the ability to learn from experience is also a product of evolutionary selection. As such, it is constrained by other aspects of a species' inheritance. Some forms of learning may therefore be limited to a particular range of behavioral possibilities occurring only at a particular developmental stage. Birds, for example, "learn" to use locally available materials to build nests using genetically determined construction techniques.

Infant Attachment Behavior. Applications of ethology to human development have included broad popularizations (e.g., Morris, 1967), detailed studies of infants' facial expressions (e.g., Oster, 1978), and observational studies of children in groups (e.g., McGrew, 1972). The most ambitious applications with implications for psychopathology, however, stem from John Bowlby's (1977, 1980) theory of *attachment*. Bowlby was originally a psychoanalyst of the *object relations* school, which disagreed with the ego-analytic view that an infant's attachment to its mother is learned through the mother's repeated association with reduction of instinctual drives. Instead, object relations analysts hold that instinctual drives are innately focused toward human objects (Fairbairn, 1952). They thus downplay the role of learning in psychoanalytic developmental theory by expanding the scope of instinctual drive theory beyond sex and aggression.

Bowlby (1980), however, has dispensed entirely with instinctual drive theory. According to his ethologically oriented theory, attachment behavior involves an innately determined control system whereby separation from the attachment figure causes anxiety. This triggers crying, searching, following, and clinging to restore contact with the attachment figure. Because proximity-maintaining behaviors are essential for the survival of many species, Bowlby hypothesizes that they are a product of natural selection. In humans, failure to develop a secure sense of attachment may explain later psychopathology.

In Bowlby's terms, "attachment" refers not only to proximity-maintaining behaviors but also to a hypothetical construct inferred from attachment behaviors directed toward a particular person. Ainsworth, Blehar, Waters, and Wall (1978) have used the pattern of behaviors displayed by a child upon reunion with the parent to construct a classification of children as *securely attached, avoidant* (child avoids and ignores the parent), or *ambivalent* (child both seeks and resists proximity).

Using Ainsworth's system, Sroufe, Fox, and Pancake (1983) found that children classified as securely attached at 12 and 18 months of age were less dependent at ages 4 to 5 years than were children whose attachment was initially classified as avoidant or ambivalent. Furthermore, boys classified as securely attached at age 1 year have been reported to show fewer behavioral problems at age 6 than boys classified as avoidant or ambivalent at age 1 (Lewis, Feiring, McGuffog, & Jaskir, 1984). This study showed no significant relation between attachment and later behavior problems among girls, however, and other factors—such as life-stress and demographic variables—affected the predictive power of attachment found for boys. Although correlational data of this sort do not necessarily prove a causal role for attachment, they do suggest that insecure attachment may be an early indicator of long-term problems, at least for some boys. Identification of links between operationally defined phenotypes across developmental periods is a much needed step in developmental research on psychopathology, as discussed in the following sections.

SOME CURRENT TRENDS IN DEVELOPMENTAL RESEARCH

The four paradigms just discussed encompass broad aspects of psychological development and functioning. They have indeed been major sources of ideas and research. Like many areas of psychology, however, the study of development is becoming increasingly specialized. Although the major paradigms continue to contribute, research is increasingly devoted to more circumscribed topic areas that engender their own miniature theories, specialized methodology, and literature for the cognoscenti. It is impossible here to cover all developmental topics of potential relevance to psychopathology, but I will summarize three topics whose proponents have been especially concerned with implications for maladaptive development. These are temperament, social cognition, and children at risk.

The Study of Temperament

Temperament is an old concept that is enjoying new acclaim largely as a result of a longitudinal study of children's behavior disorders. Initiated by Thomas, Chess, and Birch (1968) in the 1950s, the study began with ratings of babies on nine dimensions: activity level, rhythmicity (regularity) of biological functions, approach to new stimuli, adaptability to new situations, threshold of responsiveness, intensity of reactions, positive versus negative mood, distractibility, and attention-span persistence. These were conceptualized as aspects of temperament, defined by Thomas et al. as the basic behavioral *style* of the child. Although this style was thought susceptible to developmental changes and environmental influences, it was assumed to be determined mostly by biological factors.

Of the 136 children in the study, 42 showed some sort of behavioral disturbance between the ages of 2 and 9. It was found that certain early temperamental patterns were overrepresented among children who developed behavior disorders. The rate of behavior disorders was especially high (71%) among children who initially showed what was called the *difficult child pattern*. This was characterized by irregularity in biological functions, withdrawal from new stimuli, slow adaptation to environmental changes, frequent negative moods, and highly intense reactions. Although parental behavior did not seem to *cause* this pattern, differences in parents' reactions did seem to affect the development of behavior disorders, as exemplified by two children who initially showed similar patterns:

> *Both youngsters, one a girl and the other a boy, showed similar irregular sleep patterns, constipation and painful evacuations at times, slow acceptance of new foods, prolonged adjustment periods to new routines, and frequent and loud periods of crying. . . . Parental attitudes and practices, however, differed greatly. The girl's father was usually angry with her. In speaking of her, he gave the impression of disliking the youngster and was punitive and spent little or no recreational time with her. The mother was more concerned for the child, more understanding, and more permissive, but quite inconsistent. . . . The boy's parents on the other hand, were unusually tolerant and consistent. The child's lengthy ad-*

*justment periods were accepted calmly; his stri-
dent altercations with his younger siblings were
dealt with good-humoredly. The parents waited
out his negative moods without getting angry.
They tended to be very permissive, but set safety
limits and consistently pointed out the needs and
rights of his peers at play.*

*By the age of five and a half years . . . the boy's
initial difficulties in nursery school had disappeared, he was a constructive member of his
class, had a group of friends with whom he exchanged visits, and functioned smoothly in most
areas of daily living. The girl, on the other hand,
had developed a number of symptoms of increasing severity. These included explosive anger,
negativism, fear of the dark, encopresis, thumb-
sucking, insatiable demands for toys and sweets,
poor peer relationships, and protective lying.
(Thomas et al., 1968, pp. 82–83)*

The apparent explanatory power of early temperamental patterns makes them popular with pediatricians and others who advise parents about behavior
problems of early childhood. Nevertheless, temperamental patterns often show marked changes during infancy (Kronstadt, Oberklaid, Ferb, & Swartz,
1979). It may therefore be wrong to label children
as intrinsically "difficult," "slow to warm up," or
"easy." Furthermore, the dimensions used by
Thomas et al. were not rigorously derived by analyses of large samples (Thomas & Chess, 1977), and
other approaches to the study of temperament have
derived different dimensions (see Campos et al.,
1983). Despite the lack of definitive phenotypic
measures of temperament, however, there is considerable evidence for genetic influence on at least
some variables considered to represent temperament (Buss & Plomin, 1984; Scarr & Kidd, 1983).
This does not necessarily mean that these variables
are immutable from birth onward, because the nature of their expression and degree of genetic influence may vary greatly from one age to another. A
firm understanding of their developmental course,
however, requires good phenotypic measures that
can be linked from one developmental period to
another, a key issue in the developmental study of
psychopathology, to which we shall return.

The Study of Social Cognition

Earlier, we considered the Piagetian and information-processing approaches to cognition. As devel-

opmental research has shifted increasingly to social
and emotional functioning, efforts have been made
to extend the study of thinking into these areas as
well. One approach, originating with Piaget (1932),
has been to study moral judgments as a facet of
cognitive development. Although other factors may
also affect moral judgment, qualitative changes in
verbal responses to moral dilemmas follow a cognitive developmental sequence like that manifest in
judgments of physical phenomena (e.g., Kohlberg,
1978). Furthermore, the understanding of psychological concepts depends on the development of
certain cognitive operations. The concept of *projection* as a defense mechanism, for example, does not
seem to be understood by children lacking formal
operational abilities (Chandler, Paget, & Koch,
1978). This suggests that even interventions oriented
toward social and emotional functioning must take
account of children's cognitive development.

Interpersonal Cognitive Problem-solving Skills
Aside from the application of Piaget's cognitive model
to social and emotional content, much current research on social cognitive development concerns
interpersonal problem solving. Spivack and Shure
(1982), for example, have hypothesized a set of
general skills needed for successful interpersonal
relations. These skills involve consideration of the
consequences of social acts, generation of alternative solutions, and means–ends thinking—that is,
mental representations of steps needed to solve
problems. The lack of such skills is hypothesized to
lead to maladaptive responses, such as immediate
surging ahead or withdrawal in response to stress,
defensive thinking that hinders appropriate cognitive strategies, and exaggeration of obstacles to
solutions.

Spivack and Shure (1982) assess the hypothesized skills via tests and interviews that present
hypothetical social situations. Scores on several
measures of skills have correlated significantly with
social adjustment and prosocial behavior in the
classroom. Training of missing skills has also been
shown to improve performance on the skills measures and, in some cases, subsequent social adjustment in school. These methods may thus be adapt-
able to therapeutic interventions.

Social Information Processing
Taking a different approach to social cognition,
Dodge (1986) has questioned the role of the gen-

eral cognitive skills stressed by Spivack and Shure. He argues that the *content* of solutions may be more important than the number of solutions generated. Aggressive children, for example, may not generate fewer problem solutions than nonaggressive children, but their solutions are more antagonistic. To link social cognition more closely to specific behaviors, Dodge analyzes the processing of social information into five computer-like operations:

Step 1.   Encoding social cues in the environment.
Step 2.   Mentally representing and interpreting the cues.
Step 3.   Searching for possible behavioral responses.
Step 4.   Deciding on an optimal response.
Step 5.   Enacting the chosen response.

In applying his social-information processing model to deviant behavior, Dodge has experimentally studied differences in the way various groups of children handle each step. During the encoding process (Step 1), for example, he found that aggressive boys sought fewer cues before judging other people's behavior than nonaggressive boys did. During the interpretation process (Step 2), aggressive boys interpreted ambiguous cues as indicating hostility more than nonaggressive boys did. In linking social information processing to actual social behavior, Dodge has shown that measures of the five hypothesized steps collectively correlate with successful entry to a group of peers, responses to provocations, and teachers' ratings of aggression.

Information-processing deficiencies are not restricted to aggressive children, however, as Dodge, Murphy, and Buchsbaum (1984) found similar misinterpretations of ambiguous cues by nonaggressive children who are neglected by peers. The same study indicated major developmental changes in children's ability to identify signs of hostile and prosocial intentions. Because children identify hostile intentions at earlier ages than prosocial intentions, developmental lags in social cognition could account for the persistence of maladaptive behaviors such as aggression by some children and fearfulness or withdrawal by others. A major task is thus to determine what combination of developmental lags and other variables lead to different maladaptive patterns, such as aggression versus withdrawal.

Developmental Research on Children at Risk

Research on temperament and social cognitive development starts with childhood phenomena and traces their implications for maladaptive development. A contrasting strategy is to start with particular disorders and then to trace back to their developmental antecedents. Antecedents of major adult disorders have often been inferred from studies of people who already manifest a disorder, their recollections of childhood, and other retrospective data vulnerable to distortion as a consequence of the disorder itself. A vast literature on the hypothesized antecedents of schizophrenia, for example, is based on the study of people diagnosed as schizophrenic. Yet it is difficult to untangle the antecedents from consequences that may include alienation from other people, disruption of occupational functioning, hospitalization, chemotherapy, and psychotherapy.

As an alternative to seeking antecedents in people who already manifest a disorder, Sarnoff Mednick proposed longitudinal research on children who are statistically at high risk for developing certain disorders (Mednick, Griffith, & Mednick, 1981). By comparing the developmental course of children at risk who eventually manifest schizophrenia, at-risk children who do not manifest it, and control children who are not at high risk, Mednick hopes to pinpoint the etiology of schizophrenia. He is doing this via a longitudinal study of Danish children who have schizophrenic mothers and a demographically similar group whose immediate families are free of schizophrenia. Denmark was chosen because it has centralized case registers of mental disorders and other means for tracking people over long periods, major assets in longitudinal high-risk studies.

When the study began in the 1960s, the children ranged in age from 9 to 15. At the first 5-year follow-up, approximately 10 percent—the percent expected to become schizophrenic—indeed showed significant psychopathology thought to be symptomatic of schizophrenia. Birth records showed a much higher rate of perinatal abnormalities in this group than in the nondisturbed at-risk children and the group who were not thought to be at risk (Mednick & Schulsinger, 1972). A study of adult monozygotic twins discordant for schizophrenia also reported more perinatal problems among the schizophrenic than the nonschizophrenic co-twins (Pollin, Stabenau, Mosher, & Tupin, 1966). Together, these findings suggested that perinatal organic damage further increases the risk of schizophrenia in individuals who may be genetically vulnerable to schizophrenia.

Later follow-ups of both samples cast doubt on these conclusions, however, because the diagnostic pictures of many subjects changed with further development. Among the initially nonschizophrenic co-twins, for example, several later showed symptoms of schizophrenia (Belmaker, Pollin, Wyatt, & Cohen, 1974). In Mednick's study, a second follow-up five years after the first showed that subjects initially thought to be schizophrenic no longer seemed to be, whereas other subjects now showed symptoms of schizophrenia. Instead of perinatal problems as a common antecedent, it appeared that there were major sex differences in antecedents for the schizophrenic-like symptoms now evident. Among males, psychophysiological lability was a statistically significant antecedent, whereas among females, early onset of schizophrenia in their mothers was a significant antecedent (Mednick et al., 1978). Furthermore, among the psychophysiologically labile boys, those who later became schizophrenic had experienced more paternal absences and more institutional care, especially in infancy and the elementary school years (Walker et al., 1981). Teacher ratings also showed different associations with later diagnoses of schizophrenia in males and females: boys who were later diagnosed schizophrenic had been rated by teachers as behaving inappropriately and presenting disciplinary problems. By contrast, girls later diagnosed schizophrenic had been rated as poorly controlled, anhedonic, withdrawn, and isolated (John, Mednick, & Schulsinger, 1982).

Longitudinal studies have thus revealed unexpected complexities in schizophrenia, especially because the diagnostic picture now looks so much less stable than was previously assumed. Long-term studies of severe adult schizophrenics have also revealed unexpected diversity in course and outcome for what had been thought of as a progressively deteriorating condition (e.g., Ciompi & Müller, 1976; Harding, 1984; Tsuang, Woolson, & Fleming, 1979). In addition, research comparing children at risk for affective disorders with those at risk for schizophrenia has shown that both groups have similar attention deficits (Harvey, Winters, Weintraub, & Neale, 1981).

The high-risk and longitudinal findings indicate that developmental research may cast doubt on assumptions entrenched by generations of nondevelopmental research on adult, as well as child, psychopathology. These findings also underline the need for a much clearer picture of various forms of psychopathology over successive developmental periods. In the next section, I will briefly outline disorders characterizing major periods of child and adolescent development. I will then address ways in which developmental research can be brought more firmly to bear on clinical problems.

DEVELOPMENTAL PERIODS FROM BIRTH TO MATURITY

Most theories of development imply a series of stages, levels, or periods. Although it is recognized that these are artificial segmentations of processes that are actually continuous, certain ages are typically characterized by multiple interdependent changes that invite segmentation. It should be remembered, however, that the ages used to mark each segment are merely approximations that do not imply complete uniformity across all children nor abrupt changes within individual children.

I will take the first 2 years as the initial developmental period—*infancy*—which ends when marked advances in mobility, cognition, and language transform children's relations with the world around them. The next period—the *preschool period*—typically ends around the age of 5 in Western countries with the start of formal schooling. Transitions at this point include changes that Piaget interpreted as the onset of concrete operational thought, S-R theorists have interpreted as advances in verbal mediation, and Freud interpreted as the latency period. This is followed by the *elementary school period*, which ends around the age of 11, when *adolescence* is heralded by the biological changes of puberty, the onset of formal operational thought, and concomitant advances in social and educational status. As a final demarcation point, I will use the age of 20, when most people have to face the world as adults. After their early 20s, most adults reach plateaus in biological, cognitive, social-emotional, and educational development, making subsequent development less dramatic than in the period from birth to maturity.

Infancy: Birth to Two Years

Recent research reveals that human infants are much more competent with respect to perceptual and adaptive organization than was previously assumed (e.g., Banks & Salapatek, 1983; Olson & Sherman, 1983). Their survival under fantastically diverse childrearing conditions attests to their adaptability. Yet, more than most species, human babies must communicate their needs to others. According to the developmental theorists reviewed earlier, healthy development requires a secure attachment to caretakers (Bowlby, 1980), a sense of "basic trust" (Erikson, 1963), and concepts of permanent objects (Piaget, 1983). Aside from these common elements, however, there are large individual differences in the needs, abilities, temperaments, and communicative styles of babies and their parents.

The myriad possibilities for mismatches between parents and their children makes a certain amount of frustration almost inevitable. Most early frustrations arise from mismatches between babies' biorhythms and their parents' abilities to recognize and meet their needs. Common sources of problems include eating, especially vomiting and painful digestion (colic); defecation, especially constipation, painful bowel movements, and diarrhea; sleeping, especially failure to go to sleep or remain asleep at night; and excess crying. Even when temporary, such problems can make parents feel overwhelmed, guilty, or angry, sometimes to the point of child abuse. Although early problems of biological functioning and mismatches between parents and child may be outgrown, these problems can establish conflictual attitudes and patterns that shape subsequent behavioral development, as illustrated earlier in the contrasting vignettes of "difficult" children from the Thomas et al. (1968) longitudinal study. Later interventions may have to contend with long-established family patterns of this sort before the child can be helped directly.

As children become more mobile and independent, conflicts increasingly arise from parents' efforts at socialization through control of dangerous and destructive behavior, aggression, feeding, bedtimes, and toileting. A survey of infant behavior problems, for example, showed that temper tantrums and stubbornness were reported for about 30 percent of children between 6 and 11 months of age, rising steadily to about 60 percent by 18 to 23 months (Heinstein, 1969). Toilet training problems also became common by 18 to 23 months, when they were reported for 55 percent of boys and 51 percent of girls.

Characteristic Syndromes

Besides the common problems of infancy, several distinctive syndromes become evident during this period. Some organic syndromes are manifest in a combination of physical abnormalities and mental retardation, such as Down syndrome (mongolism), phenylketonuria (PKU), and galactosemia. Others may involve organic predispositions but are currently diagnosable only in terms of behavioral abnormalities. Some cases of the "difficult child" pattern may be of this nature, as well as certain unexplained lags in social, cognitive, and motor development.

The most publicized and studied syndrome of this period is *early infantile autism*, although its prevalence is probably less than 1 in 1000 children (Werry, 1979). When Leo Kanner (1943) proposed the syndrome, he emphasized that it (1) differed from childhood schizophrenia and (2) probably involved an "innate inability to form the usual, biologically provided affective contact with people" (p. 250). Nevertheless, others soon used "infantile autism" synonymously with "schizophrenia," "childhood psychosis," and "atypical personality," which they attributed to environmental factors, especially parental psychodynamics (e.g., Bettelheim, 1967; Rank, 1949; Wolman, 1970). Supported mainly by psychodynamic interpretations of individual cases, these views blamed parents for causing their child's autism (e.g., Kysar, 1968). An increasing body of empirical research, however, shows no evidence that parental attitudes or childrearing practices cause autism, although the stress of having an autistic child may be responsible for certain parental characteristics (see Achenbach, 1982). Research on organic factors has not pinpointed any specific etiology (see Cohen & Shaywitz, 1982), but there is certainly no justification for blaming autism on parents.

Certain other syndromes of infancy may be instigated primarily by environmental factors, although biological factors and developmental level affect the child's response to the environment. Babies who lose their primary attachment figure between about six and eight months of age, for example, may become apathetic and withdrawn, a syndrome known as *anaclitic depression*. Loss of an attachment figure at earlier or later ages may not have this effect, and single separations of up to about a week do not seem to have long-term consequences (Quinton & Rutter, 1976).

Failure to thrive and *psychosocial growth retardation* involve apathy and behavioral retardation, plus stunting of physical growth despite adequate nutrition. Previously reported among orphans raised in impersonal institutions (Provence & Lipton, 1962), these conditions are also seen in home-reared children who are seriously neglected, abused, or understimulated. Improved environments can restore normal physical growth, but follow-up research shows continuing behavioral problems after such children return home (Elmer, Gregg, & Ellison, 1969). Findings of this sort underline the fact that a disorder occurring at one developmental period may have a variety of long-term implications, such as the following:

1. It may be symptomatic of enduring vulnerabilities that will continue to place the individual at risk in subsequent developmental periods.
2. It may directly disrupt adaptive development.
3. If adverse environmental conditions continue, they may cause new problems later.
4. Some types of problems may stimulate the development of new adaptive techniques especially suited to that particular child in its particular environment.

Although it is often assumed that the chronological priority of events during infancy magnifies their effects on later development, research has not necessarily supported this assumption (Clarke & Clarke, 1976). Just as certain physical illnesses are much more severe when contracted by adults than by children, certain events may have a much greater impact at later developmental periods than in infancy. Because every period is likely to be important in its own way, developmental research is needed to determine what characteristics and disorders are of greatest importance at each period and how disorders at one period relate to those at other periods.

The Preschool Period: Ages Two to Five

Major advances in motility, cognition, self-care, and play markedly expand the child's world and social relations during this period. From mismatches between babies' biorhythms and their parents' ability to recognize and meet their needs, the friction points shift increasingly to social relations, including development of skills in communicating and getting along with others, and the growth of independence, including conflicts between (1) the need for independence in mastering developmental tasks and (2) risks that exceed children's ability to avoid harm. As illustrated earlier, preschoolers' newfound capacity for mental imagery, not yet inhibited by logic, becomes a source of both imagined dangers and delightful adaptive possibilities.

The central role of language in social relations gives speech abnormalities a special significance during this period. Although the first word usually emerges between about 12 and 18 months, and two-word combinations emerge between about 15 and 28 months, there are wide variations in the development of verbal communication. Some speech abnormalities may be early signs of emotional or cognitive problems. Most, however, are merely temporary maturational lags or difficulties in articulating certain sounds. It is not until the age of 5, for example, that 75 percent of children master the *j, fl, rp,* and *shr* sounds; other sounds are not mastered until the age of 7 or 8 (Templin, 1957). Stuttering occasionally emerges and subsides during the preschool period, although it sometimes remains a lifelong affliction. Even when speech problems are temporary, however, frustration over being misunderstood or ridiculed for "baby talk" may be met with *elective mutism,* withdrawal, or aggression.

In Heinstein's (1969) survey of behavioral problems, contrary and stubborn behaviors were the most common problems, reported for about 60 percent of children between the ages of 2 and 5. After reaching a high of 60 percent between the ages of 18 and 23 months, reports of temper tantrums declined through age 5, when they were reported to be problems for 41 percent of boys and 27 percent of girls. Toilet training problems declined more steeply, from 50 percent at age 2, to 11 percent at age 3, and 5 percent at age 5. Problems of disobedience, resistance to bedtime, wanting too much attention, and easily hurt feelings were reported for 30 to 50 percent of preschoolers. In another study, significant fears were reported for 67 percent of 3-year-old girls, dropping to 36 percent by age 5 (MacFarlane, Allen, & Honzik, 1954). For boys, the figure remained at about 45 percent throughout the preschool period.

Characteristic Syndromes

Although infantile autism (by definition) typically begins in infancy, some cases are not diagnosed until the child fails to speak at the expected age or shows abnormalities of speech, such as *echolalia,* a mechanical "echoing" of other people's speech. Not only is autism marked by deviant speech development during the preschool period, but persisting communication deficits are among the strongest predictors of poor outcomes among autistic children (Lotter, 1974).

Aside from autism, severe abnormalities of speech development may be caused by a variety of organic problems, including hearing loss and defective neural functioning, resulting in partial impairment *(dysphasia)* or a total lack of speech *(aphasia)*. When accompanied by general lags in other adaptive functions and cognition, slow speech development may be one of the clearest signs of mental retardation. When social and emotional abnormalities are evident without cognitive retardation, severe speech problems may be symptoms of emotional disturbance, abuse, or neglect.

During the early preschool period, help for troublesome behavior is sought mainly from pediatricians and child development clinics. Problems of speech, motor development, fears, and socialization are often construed as reflecting developmental stages that will pass. Many problems of great concern to parents—such as temper tantrums, negativism, and struggles over toileting—are, in fact, transient, with little long-term significance. By the age of 4 or 5, however, behavior problems start to crystallize into syndromes that remain evident during succeeding developmental periods. Multivariate analyses of behavior problems reported for 4- to 5-year-olds, for example, show syndromes of depression, withdrawal, somatic complaints, sex problems, hyperactivity, and aggression similar to those found for 6- to 11-year-olds (Achenbach & Edelbrock, 1983). Although these syndromes do not necessarily persist in the same form over the course of a child's development, there is evidence that some deviant personality orientations are remarkably persistent. A follow-up of boys who had severe gender-identity problems in early childhood, for example, showed that all were homosexual as adults (Money & Russo, 1979). Because children are seldom referred to mental health services before the age of about 6, however, less evidence is available

on disorders of clinical magnitude during the preschool period than during the elementary school period, when referrals rise rapidly.

The Elementary School Period: Ages 6 to 11

The school years bring new opportunities for achievement and social contacts, but also for failure and conflict. The cognitive advances described by Piaget in terms of concrete operational logic are manifest not only in academic tasks, but also in competitive play governed by complex rules, ranging from sports such as baseball to lengthy board games such as Monopoly. Similar abilities underlie children's emergent interests in hobby collections, money-making enterprises, and the formation of neighborhood clubs.

School poses the greatest challenges for most children in terms of both social and academic adaptation. Despite children's differences in maturation, motivation, adaptive style, and home environments, they are expected to conform to the school's routines, standards of conduct, and age-graded instructional programs. Failure to master the complex skills of reading, writing, and arithmetic on schedule can engender feelings of inferiority and fear of intellectual challenges.

The new sources of stress and conflict bring a sharp rise in mental health referrals, many of which are precipitated by school problems. This is especially true for elementary school boys, who are referred for special educational and mental health services at two to four times the rate of girls, with a peak at ages 8 and 9 years (Mumpower, 1970; Rosen, 1979). A survey of behavior problems reported for 6- to 11-year-olds showed the biggest difference between clinically referred and nonreferred boys in *poor school work* (70% versus 15%), followed by *disobedient at school* (72% versus 19%), *doesn't get along with other children* (66% versus 16%), and *feels worthless or inferior* (66% versus 16%; Achenbach & Edelbrock, 1981). Among girls, the biggest differences were for *unhappy, sad, or depressed* (76% versus 10%) and *doesn't get along with other children* (66% versus 13%), followed by *poor school work* (57% versus 6%), *can't concentrate* (72% versus 29%), and *feels worthless or inferior* (62% versus 14%).

Characteristic Syndromes

Throughout the 1970s, hyperactivity (or "hyperkinesis") was the most publicized disorder of the elementary school period. Originally thought to reflect brain damage, hyperactivity has been used by some as a virtual synonym for "MBD" (minimal brain damage or dysfunction; e.g., Ochroch, 1981). Research on brain-damaged children, however, has shown that they are not necessarily hyperactive and that hyperactive children are not necessarily brain-damaged (Brown et al., 1981; Shaffer, McNamara, & Pincus, 1974). Claims that neurotransmitter abnormalities (Wender & Wender, 1978) and food sensitivities (Feingold, 1976) cause hyperactivity have not been supported by research, either.

Reflecting a change in views of hyperactivity, *DSM-III* replaced the *DSM-II* diagnostic category of Hyperkinetic Reaction with a category entitled *Attention Deficit Disorder,* divided into subtypes with and without hyperactivity. Attentional problems are certainly as important in these disorders as overactivity, but there is no firm evidence that they are rooted in specific attentional deficits. Diagnoses of hyperactivity and attention deficit disorders, in fact, often encompass children who have major problems in other areas. Loney and Milich (1982), for example, found that some boys treated for hyperactivity were deviant mainly in aggression, some in hyperactivity, some in both, and some in neither area. Follow-ups of these boys showed that, despite treatment, initial hyperactivity scores predicted poor school achievement in adolescence, while initial aggression scores predicted delinquent behavior in adolescence.

The lack of specificity in the initial definition of disorders and in their sequelae reflects a pervasive problem in the study of childhood disorders, especially during the elementary school years. Many problems of concern to parents and teachers involve behavior that is not intrinsically pathognomonic but that is seen in most children at some time. Referral for mental health services is often the culmination of long-standing problem behavior that interferes with social relations and the acquisition of age-appropriate skills, or is especially irksome to adults. Existing diagnostic categories often focus on only a portion of the child's adaptational difficulties. A major task for the developmental study of psychopathology is, therefore, to take better account of quantitative and situational variations in problem behavior than categorical nosologies do.

Besides behavioral problems that interfere with mastery of age-appropriate skills, learning problems that are not just by-products of behavioral problems assume great significance during this period. Although school failure may result from lack of motivation, emotional problems, and general cognitive retardation, learning disabilities may also explain school failure. Teachers are in an especially good position to detect learning problems, although detailed diagnostic evaluations are needed to tease apart all the potential contributing factors. A proper assessment should include systematic reports and ratings by parents as well as teachers, direct observations of the child in school, the child's own report of the problems, and well-differentiated psychometric assessment of achievement and abilities. Comprehensive assessments of this sort often reveal problems in multiple areas that may either help to explain the learning problems or may be by-products of the learning problems.

Where learning problems are confined to a particular skill—such as reading, writing, or arithmetic—and ability measures reveal corresponding deficits, there may indeed be a specific learning disability. Specific disabilities in reading (called *developmental dyslexia*) are the most studied. In children of normal IQ, at least some specific reading disabilities are probably genetically based, but family pedigree studies suggest that there are several types of disability involving different genetic factors (Finucci et al., 1976).

Some reading disabilities may merely involve slight lags in the maturation of perceptual-motor functions necessary for the initial acquisition of reading skills. To identify such perceptual-motor lags in first graders, Hagin, Silver, and Kreeger (1976) developed the SEARCH battery of tests, including visual matching, auditory discrimination, rote sequencing, verbal expression, and auditory-graphic ability. In a controlled study, first graders identified as being at risk by the SEARCH battery were assigned to one of three conditions: (1) six months of tutoring in a program (called TEACH) designed to train the perceptual functions found weakest on the SEARCH tests; (2) traditional tutoring in reading and math; (3) a no-treatment control condition (Arnold et al., 1977).

On cognitive and achievement measures, the TEACH group improved more than the other two groups, whose outcomes did not differ from each other. A one-year follow-up showed continued advancement by the TEACH group, while the other two groups worsened in several areas, including cognitive functioning and behavior problems. Training immature perceptual-motor functions thus seems to have overcome reading problems significantly better than either direct tutoring of reading or maturation alone. Yet all three groups showed significant improvements of similar magnitude on the SEARCH battery itself. This underlines the developmental nature of the problems tapped by the SEARCH battery and the fact that the consequences of such problems may continue long after the initial problems are outgrown. As Arnold et al. put it,

> . . . the "wait and see" attitude toward first-grade perceptual problems is not entirely without foundation; they do tend to improve "by themselves." What this attitude ignores, though, is the academic, behavioral, and emotional sequelae of frustration/failure, with destructive effects on self-esteem, learning attitude, achievement, behavior, and even measurable IQ. The data presented demonstrate that for the children identified as vulnerable, the spontaneous improvement in perceptual skills is not accompanied by an equally spontaneous improvement in behavior, reading achievement, or IQ scores. On the contrary, without some kind of intervention there tends to be deterioration in all three of these areas, sometimes reaching statistical significance, despite the significant improvement in perceptual skills! (p. 1292)

Some specific learning disabilities may be due to enduring cognitive or perceptual deficits rather than temporary developmental lags. The SEARCH and TEACH research suggests, however, that temporary developmental lags cause mismatches with age-graded expectations. Long after the developmental lags are overcome, the effects of an initial mismatch may continue in stunted educational development, inferiority feelings, fear of intellectual challenges, and resulting behavior problems. In light of the evidence for a complex interplay of maturational, experiential, and situational variables in learning problems, even relatively circumscribed disorders such as "specific developmental dyslexia" are being increasingly viewed in multidimensional terms (Goldberg, Schiffman, & Bender, 1983).

Besides anxieties associated with school achievement, children often fear school attendance per se. Most children experience at least some anxiety when starting school, changing schools, and returning to school after illness or holidays. When the fear reaches panic proportions, however, it is known as *school phobia*. During the elementary school years, school phobias may reflect fear of separation from parents more than fear of school itself. If the child is quickly returned to school, parents are firm about school attendance, and there is no major psychopathology in the family, school phobias of the elementary school period may be readily overcome (Kennedy, 1965; Miller, Barrett, & Hampe, 1974). In later years, however, new school phobias emerge that are associated with more severe psychopathology of the adolescent period, to which we now turn.

Adolescence: Ages 12 to 20

Pubertal changes are the most conspicuous markers of the transition from the elementary school years to adolescence. According to psychodynamic theory, the upsurge of the sex drive at puberty shatters the latency period, reactivates earlier psychosexual conflicts, and unleashes the *Sturm und Drang* of adolescence. There is also evidence for more subtle effects of sex hormones on emotional and cognitive functioning (Ehrhardt & Meyer-Bahlburg, 1981; Peterson & Wittig, 1979). In Erikson's (1980) theory of psychosocial development, the massive bodily changes help to trigger conflicts that he has exquisitely portrayed in terms of *identity versus identity confusion* (previously called "role confusion"). Not only the social-emotional by-products of puberty but also the long lag between physical maturity and adult social status are thought to make adolescence inherently stressful in Western countries. The onset of formal operational cognition can also fuel adolescent alienation and rebellion, because it applies a harsh new logic of multiple possibilities to previously unquestioned values and assumptions.

There is no doubt that puberty, the need to forge new identities, and cognitive changes confront adolescents with major challenges. Changes in voice and body shape, body hair, acne, and growth spurts also require radical adjustments of childhood self-images. The wide variation in the timing of adolescent physical changes—from about the age of 10 to 17—can disrupt long-standing friendships, as those who mature especially early or late suddenly find themselves out of phase with their age-mates. Acute sensitivity to peer opinion may spur efforts to win acceptance through extreme styles of dress and behavior.

Despite the stress and turmoil ascribed to adolescence, longitudinal studies show that many adolescents do not suffer severe turmoil and that adolescent developmental conflicts are not necessarily a source of psychopathology (Offer & Offer, 1975; Rutter, Graham, Chadwick & Yule, 1976). In early adolescence, many referrals reflect long-standing problems rather than completely new disorders (Rutter et al., 1976). Between the ages of 12 and 16, for example, *poor school work* continues to be the problem showing the greatest difference between referred and nonreferred boys (78% versus 19%), while *unhappy, sad, or depressed* continues to show the greatest difference between referred and nonreferred girls (77% versus 12%; Achenbach & Edelbrock, 1981). Mental health referrals rise, however, especially for girls, whose rate is substantially higher than at younger ages, yet still lower than that for boys (Rosen, 1979).

Although delinquent behaviors become increasingly associated with referrals for both sexes, certain delinquent behaviors are now reported more often for referred girls than boys. These include *lying or cheating, runs away from home, truancy,* and *uses alcohol or drugs* (Achenbach & Edelbrock, 1981). Not only delinquent behavior, but criminal activities, suicidal behavior, unwed pregnancy, and "dropping out" raise concerns well beyond the purview of the mental health and educational agencies that are the main sources of help for younger children.

Characteristic Syndromes

Delinquent and antisocial behaviors are the most publicized problems of adolescence, but they occur in diverse forms and combinations. Many normal adolescents commit sporadic delinquencies without adopting delinquent values or lifestyles. Among adolescents living in high crime areas or multiproblem families, delinquency may reflect a lack of rewarding alternatives, rather than psychopathology. For other adolescents, however, delinquent and antisocial behavior may reflect alienation from others, thought disorders, or lack of self-control (Lewis & Balla, 1976).

Considerable research supports a distinction between "socialized delinquent," "unsocialized aggressive," and "neurotic" or "disturbed" delinquent syndromes (see Achenbach, 1982). Yet it is also important to view antisocial and delinquent behaviors in relation to a broad spectrum of other behavioral problems and competencies. Cluster analyses of multidimensional behavior profiles, for example, have revealed one group of aggressive adolescent boys who also have many immature and hyperactive behaviors, while another group is exceptionally uncommunicative (Edelbrock & Achenbach, 1980). A focus on only their aggressive behavior might lead both groups to be called "unsocialized" or "acting out" aggressives. Yet this would ignore important behavioral differences that might signify differences in etiology, type of help needed, or prognosis.

Depression is another problem thought to be especially characteristic of adolescence. Psychiatric nosologies have long recognized depressive and bipolar (manic-depressive) disorders in adults and late adolescents, but despite early reports of such disorders in children (e.g., Kasanin & Kaufman, 1929), the psychoanalytic theory dominant from the 1930s through the 1960s denied that true depressive disorders could occur before personality structure was fully crystalized in late adolescence.

A resurgence of interest in adult depression and the apparent efficacy of antidepressant drugs, however, has sparked a new search for depression in children. In the absence of empirical criteria for childhood depression, assumptions about the biological basis for adult depressive disorders have been extrapolated to children, and "depressive illness" has been inferred from such diverse "symptoms" as abdominal pain, headaches, fears, temper tantrums, aggression, and changes in school performance (Frommer, 1967; Weinberg et al., 1973). The quest for childhood depression was broadened still further by the construct of *masked depression,* inferred from aggressive, hyperactive, and other problem behaviors used defensively "to ward off the unbearable feelings of despair" (Cytryn & McKnew, 1979, p. 327). Masked depression has since been repudiated as a construct (Cytryn, McKnew, & Bunney, 1980; Kashani et al., 1981), but there is continuing confusion about child and adolescent depression.

A major source of confusion is the failure to distinguish clearly between depression as an *affect,* as a *syndrome* of co-occurring features, and as a *disorder.* For adult depression, the apparent success of antidepressant drugs has reinforced the medical model of a circumscribed disease entity, which was then extrapolated downward to adolescents and children. There has been, however, a tendency to equate signs and interview reports of unhappiness or depressed affect with depressive disorders, even when there is little other evidence for such disorders.

Depressed affect is unquestionably an important concomitant of many childhood disorders. In fact, across the age range from 4 to 16, parent and teacher ratings of children on the item *unhappy, sad, or depressed* were found to discriminate more strongly between clinically referred and nonreferred children than any of 117 other problem items (Achenbach & Edelbrock, 1981, 1986). As Figure 4.1 indicates, the item showed an especially great difference between referred and nonreferred 12- and 13-year-old girls (86% versus 13%). There are multiple reasons, however, why depressed affect is so strong a sign that all is not well: In some cases, it may be a response to rejection occurring when others are irked by a child's problem behavior; in other cases, it may reflect children's own awareness of their maladaptive behavior; in still others, it may be one of several responses to life stress; and in at least some, it may indeed be a symptom of a depressive disorder per se.

Moving now from depression as an affect to depression as a syndrome, multivariate studies of parents' ratings have identifed a clear-cut syndrome of problems including *unhappy, sad, or depressed, complains of loneliness, fears he/she might think or do something bad, feels or complains that no one loves him/her, feels too guilty,* and *feels worthless or inferior* (Achenbach & Edelbrock, 1983). This syndrome is quite similar for both sexes at ages 4 to 5 and 6 to 11. In adolescents, however, depressive problems do not co-occur so consistently to form a syndrome. Instead, they co-occur with several other groups of problems indicative of anxiety, withdrawal, and obsessiveness. This suggests that affects and problem behaviors that indeed form a syndrome during the early years become more generalized and less discriminating of a particular disorder in adolescence.

There is longitudinal evidence that preadolescents whose primary disorder is depression continue having depressive episodes in adolescence (Kovacs et al., 1984). This suggests the existence of depressive disorders during childhood and adolescence that resemble long-term adult depressive disorders. The question of what constitutes a depressive disorder in adolescence is complicated by the rise of other serious problems, however, such as suicidal behavior, anorexia, and thought disorders.

According to parents' reports on clinically referred children, suicidal talk occurs among up to 24 percent of 14- and 15-year-old girls and suicide attempts among up to 19 percent of 16-year-old girls (Achenbach & Edelbrock, 1981). Completed suicides rise from less than 1 per 100,000 in the general population of 10- to 14-year-olds, to over 7 per 100,000 at ages 15 to 19, and over 16 per 100,000 at ages 20 to 24 (National Center for Health Statistics, 1977; *New York Times,* 1984). Thus, about 170 10- to 14-year-olds, 1600 15- to 19-year-olds, and 3200 20- to 24-year-olds kill themselves annually in the United States. The high accident and homicide rates among adolescents may also reflect suicidal behavior (Holinger, 1979). Although females make more suicidal attempts than males, three to five times as many males actually complete suicide (Shaffer & Fisher, 1981).

Even though suicidal behavior may seem to reflect depression, multivariate analyses show that it is not consistently associated with any particular syndrome in adolescence (Achenbach & Edelbrock, 1983). Clinical impressions also suggest that it has a variety of determinants, including thought disorders, interpersonal conflicts, developmental crises, and the breakup of love affairs, rather than necessarily being a sign of depression.

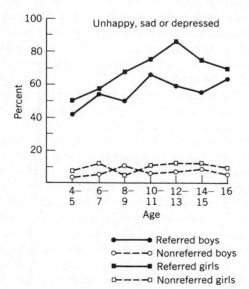

Figure 4.1   Percent of clinically referred and nonreferred children whom parents reported to be unhappy, sad, or depressed. (From Achenbach and Edelbrock, 1981, p. 32.)

Anorexia nervosa is another potentially fatal problem of adolescence that may be viewed as a sign of depression but probably has multiple causes and meanings. Rare before the age of 10 and peaking in adolescence, it is much more common in females than males (Halmi, 1974). "Anorexia" is actually a misnomer, because many anorectics do not lose their appetites. In fact, many go on eating binges *(bulimia)* and then purge themselves by vomiting or taking laxatives. Instead of loss of appetite, fear of becoming fat and insensitivity to their own emaciation are common among anorectics. In adolescent girls, anorexia may be used to ward off sexual development and menstruation, both of which are inhibited by weight loss. However, a manipulative personality style and family dynamics may also contribute when the adolescent's eating habits become enmeshed in family power struggles (Minuchin, Rosman, & Baker, 1978; Van Buskirk, 1977).

Besides the foregoing disorders, adolescence brings an increase in feelings of depersonalization and alienation. These are experienced by many adolescents, but may sometimes be accompanied by schizophreniform symptoms such as poor reality testing, flattening of affect, withdrawal, hallucinations, or delusions. Although "childhood schizophrenia" was once a general wastebasket term for most severe childhood disorders including autism, such disorders have little in common with adult schizophrenia. Incidence rates suggest that most of these severe disorders emerge either before the age of 2-1/2 or after the age of 12 (Rutter, 1974). Those emerging before the age of 2-1/2 mainly resemble infantile autism, whereas those emerging after the age of 12 are more similar to adult schizophrenia.

As discussed earlier, research on children having schizophrenic parents shows that the emergence of schizophrenic-like psychopathology in adolescence does not necessarily signify a continuing schizophrenic disorder (Mednick et al., 1978). It is not merely that temporary adolescent phenomena deceive the diagnosticians, but that what has been viewed as a unitary and chronic disease is much more variable over the life cycle than was previously recognized (Ciompi & Müller, 1976; Harding, 1984; Tsuang et al., 1979). Despite the ominous and de-

bilitating nature of schizophreniform problems in adolescence, we therefore need more precise documentation of the developmental course of such problems in adulthood as well as in adolescence.

Summary of Developmental Periods

The developmental study of psychopathology highlights the multifaceted changes that occur from birth to maturity and the need to understand the nature and course of psychopathology in relation to these changes. To summarize our overview of development and psychopathology, Table 4.1 outlines the major developmental periods in terms of Freud's, Erikson's, and Piaget's theories, the achievements expected during each period, common behavior problems, and characteristic disorders.

To view relations between development and disorders from another perspective, Figure 4.2 shows referral rates to three types of agencies for ages 2 through 16 in Aberdeen, Scotland (Baldwin, Robertson, & Satin, 1971). The specific rates may differ in other localities, but these data are of particular value because virtually all Aberdeen children were served by the same agencies and could be tracked by means of a centralized case register. From Figure 4.2 we can therefore see the overall rate of referral, as well as referrals to each type of agency. The *guidance* group consisted of referrals for help with major educational problems; the *probation* group consisted of first offenders referred to juvenile court; and the *psychiatry* group consisted of referrals for emotional and behavioral problems, excluding the mentally retarded.

It should be noted that the scale on the vertical axis of Figure 4.2 ranges from 0 to 30 per thousand population in intervals of 5 for boys, but from 0 to 12 per thousand in intervals of 2 for girls. The higher referral rates for boys are found in most localities, especially when the total referral rates across all services are considered. The peak of guidance referrals during the elementary school period shows that most problems of that period concern school, whereas the rise of probation cases during the later years shows that the juvenile court becomes increasingly involved in handling deviant behavior. Referrals for girls to each service were lower than for boys until girls' psychiatric referrals approached those for boys in adolescence.

TABLE 4.1   A Developmental Overview

Approximate Age	Cognitive Period	Psychosexual Phase	Psychosocial Conflict	Normal Achievements	Common Behavior Problems[a]	Clinical Disorders
0–2	Sensory-Motor	Oral	Basic Trust vs. Mistrust	Eating, digestion, sleeping, social responsiveness, attachment, motility, sensory-motor organization	Stubbornness, temper, toileting	Organically based dysfunctions, anaclitic depression, autism, failure to thrive
2–5	Pre-Operational	Anal	Autonomy vs. Shame and Doubt	Language, toileting, self-care skills, safety rules, self-control, peer relationships	Argues, brags, demands attention, disobedient, jealous, fears,[c] prefers older children, over-active, resists bedtime, shows off, shy,[c] stubborn talks too much, temper, whines	Speech and hearing problems, phobias, unsocialized behavior
		Phallic-Oedipal	Initiative vs. Guilt			
6–11	Concrete Operational	Latency	Industry vs. Inferiority	Academic skills, school rules, rule-governed games, hobbies, monetary exchange, simple responsibilities	Argues, brags,[b] can't concentrate,[b] self-conscious, shows off, talks too much[c]	Hyperactivity, learning problems, school phobia, aggression, withdrawal
12–20	Formal Operational	Genital	Identity vs. Role Confusion	Relations with opposite sex, vocational preparation, personal identity, separation from family, adult responsibilities	Argues, brags[b]	Anorexia, delinquency, suicide attempts, drug and alcohol abuse, schizophrenia, depression

Source: T.M. Achenbach, *Developmental Psychopathology*, 2nd ed. (New York: Wiley, 1982), p. 67.
[a]Problems reported for at least 45% of children in nonclinical samples.
[b]Indicates problem reported for ≥45% of boys only.
[c]Indicates ≥45% of girls only.

PROBLEMS IN DEFINING DISORDERS

As we have considered successive periods of development, we have repeatedly faced problems in defining and discriminating between disorders. Most referrals of children for mental health services are prompted by the concerns of parents, teachers, pediatricians, and other adults about behavior that impedes the child's development or infringes on other people. Both the referral process and the nature of children's problems contrast sharply with the nosological and service models for adult psychopathology in the following ways:

1. Because children seldom have realistic conceptions of mental health problems or services, they seldom seek help for themselves.
2. When brought for services, children do not readily assume the role of patient and cannot be relied on for the anamnestic data typically provided by adult patients.
3. Whereas adult disorders often involve either declines from attained levels of functioning or the onset of pathognomonic symptoms, childhood disorders typically involve a failure to develop expected behaviors and/or quantitative or situational deviance in behavior that most children show in some degree.

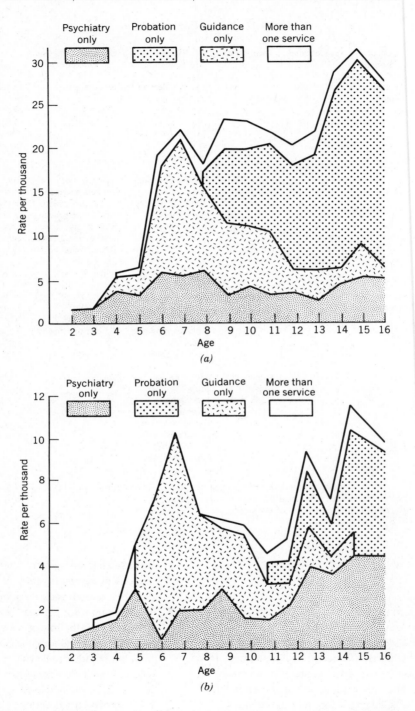

Figure 4.2 Annual rate of referrals for psychiatric, probation, and educational guidance services in Aberdeen, Scotland. (a) Annual rate of referrals per 1000 boys. (b) Annual rate of referrals per 1000 girls. Note different increments on vertical axis for boys and girls. (Reprinted, by permission, from J.A. Baldwin, N.C. Robertson, and D.G. Satin, *The incidence of reported deviant behavior in children*. International Psychiatry Clinics, 1971, pp. 3, 161–175, copyright © by Little, Brown & Co.)

4. Unlike adults, who reach plateaus in cognitive, educational, social, and biological development, children continually undergo major changes in multiple spheres of functioning.
5. To judge whether a child's condition is truly pathological, we need to know whether it impedes subsequent development.
6. To help children, we need to be able to facilitate continued development rather than returning them to a premorbid level of functioning, which is an appropriate goal of adult treatment.

These contrasts have important implications for how we conceptualize disorders, as discussed next.

Kraepelinian Nosology

Current concepts of adult disorders originated with nineteenth-century efforts to apply medical models to psychopathology. The success of research in identifying organic causes for physical illnesses fostered the assumption that mental disorders are brain diseases (Griesinger, 1845). Accordingly, it became important to identify syndromes as a first step toward uncovering specific organic etiologies. From a hodgepodge of syndromes proposed by different workers, Emil Kraepelin (1883) assembled a taxonomy that has continued to shape views of mental disorders for over a century.

Reflecting the nineteenth-century medical view of mental disorders, Kraepelin sought to provide descriptions of syndromes that could then be categorized within a general nosology. Each category was assumed to represent a distinctive disease entity for which a specific organic etiology would ultimately be found. The prototype of this approach was *general paresis,* which had been identified as a distinct syndrome through progressively better descriptions of symptoms from 1798 through the 1840s. These descriptions converged on a definition of the syndrome as a combination of mental symptoms, such as irrationality and memory loss, with physical symptoms of motor impairment, usually ending in death.

Once paresis was consistently described, research could focus on a reasonably well-defined class of patients presumed to share the same underlying disease. After autopsy studies from the 1840s through the 1870s revealed inflammation in the brains of most people who died of paresis, the pos-

sible causes were narrowed down to syphilitic infection, which was confirmed by the end of the nineteenth century. Thereafter, the Wassermann test was developed to detect syphilis clinically, and specific therapies were devised, culminating eventually with penicillin.

The powerful example of paresis inspired hopes that all mental disorders would eventually yield to a process of descriptive categorization that would facilitate the discovery of specific organic etiologies. Indeed, by the 1899 edition of Kraepelin's nosology, categories had been established for several major adult disorders that still appear in current nosologies, such as manic-depressive conditions and *dementia praecox* (renamed *schizophrenia* by Bleuler in 1911). The severity of deviance and the distinctive symptoms characterizing these disorders conformed nicely to the model established by general paresis. By 1915, however, Kraepelin's nosology also included disorders viewed as psychological in origin, as well as personality disorders thought to border between illness and eccentricity.

The Diagnostic and Statistical Manual of Mental Disorders (DSM)

Later American nosologies are direct descendants of Kraepelin's system. They avow a descriptive approach to disorders of unknown etiology and retain many of Kraepelin's categories. Although the 1952 and 1968 editions of the *DSM* defined neurotic disorders largely in terms of psychodynamic inferences, even these disorders were presented as discrete categorical entities. In returning more fully to the Kraepelinian ideal of descriptive diagnosis, the *DSM-III* (American Psychiatric Association, 1980) has dispensed with psychodynamic inferences. A major innovation of *DSM-III* is the provision of explicit decision rules for each diagnostic category. For some of the major adult categories, such as schizophrenia and bipolar disorders, the decision rules are based on previously developed research diagnostic criteria (RDC). Many of the adult categories and all the child categories, however, lack any basis in previous RDC. In fact, many of the child categories have little history at all.

The *DSM-I* (American Psychiatric Association, 1952) offered only two categories of childhood disorders: Adjustment Reaction and Schizophrenic Reaction, Childhood Type. The *DSM-II* (American

Psychiatric Association, 1968) added several child and adolescent disorders, but Adjustment Reaction continued to be the most common diagnosis (American Academy of Child Psychiatry, 1983). In adding numerous new categories of child and adolescent disorders, *DSM-III* relied largely on a process of committee negotiation, rather than empirical research. This has also been true of other efforts to formulate Kraepelinian nosologies of childhood disorders (Group for the Advancement of Psychiatry, 1966; Rutter, Shaffer, & Shepherd, 1975).

The lack of a research basis for most categories of childhood disorders raises questions about how well the categories fit the actual disorders. Interjudge reliabilities have been mediocre for most *DSM* childhood diagnoses (see Achenbach, 1985). Two studies have obtained lower reliabilities for *DSM-III* than *DSM-II* diagnoses of children (Mattison, Cantwell, Russell, & Will, 1979; Mezzich & Mezzich, 1979). The *DSM-III* field trials also showed a decline in reliabilities from an early draft of the childhood disorders to the final draft (American Psychiatric Association, 1980, Appendix F). The highest reliabilities have been found for diagnosis of major disorders in inpatients, but these represent only a small proportion of children referred for mental health services (Strober, Green, & Carlson, 1981; Werry, Methven, Fitzpatrick, & Dixon, 1983). Reliabilities are generally poorest for the large majority of childhood disorders that involve quantitative or situational deviations in behavior that most children show at some time.

Multivariate Approaches to the Identification of Disorders

Owing to the neglect of childhood disorders in the prevailing nosologies and the weakness of the categories that were included, child clinical researchers have turned to more empirical methods for identifying and defining disorders. These have mainly involved factor analysis of ratings by parents, teachers, and mental health workers. Such data include inferential items, as well as descriptions of behavior. The instruments vary in many ways, including the number and specificity of items, types of response scales, conditions under which the children are seen, and time periods covered by the ratings. The subject samples and methods of analysis also vary widely. Nevertheless, among studies meeting certain minimal methodological standards, there has been con-

siderable convergence in the identification of a few relatively global, broad-band syndromes and more numerous narrow-band syndromes. Table 4.2 summarizes syndromes found in at least two multivariate studies that have met the minimal methodological criteria. The names given the syndromes are intended to summarize their descriptive content rather than representing diagnostic inferences.

Relations between Nosological and Multivariate Approaches

Some of the empirically derived syndromes have counterparts in contemporary categorical nosologies. The syndrome designated as Hyperactive in Table 4.2, for example, corresponds roughly to *DSM-III*'s Attention Deficit Disorder with Hyperactivity. Similarly, *DSM-III* has counterparts to the syndromes designated as Aggressive, Delinquent, Depressed, Obsessive-compulsive, Schizoid, and Somatic Complaints. There are some important differences, however, having potential implications for conceptions of psychopathology and its treatment across the life span. These differences can be summarized as follows:

1. Contemporary psychiatric nosologies are derived from clinical concepts of disorders negotiated by committees (e.g., Spitzer & Cantwell, 1980). In the multivariate approach, by contrast, syndromes are derived statistically from covariation among attributes assessed in samples of individuals.

2. The criterial attributes for nosological categories are typically assessed as present versus absent, whereas the criterial attributes for multivariate syndromes are scored in terms of gradations.

3. If the criterial attributes of a nosological category are judged to be present, it is concluded that a particular disorder is present. Otherwise, the disorder is absent. In the multivariate approach, by contrast, each syndrome is indexed quantitatively as a function of scores on criterial attributes. Rather than being categorized as *having* versus *not having* each syndrome, individuals are thus assessed in terms of the *degree to which* they manifest the attributes of each syndrome.

4. Although multiple descriptors are often used

TABLE 4.2   Number of Studies in which Syndromes have been Identified in Multivariate Analyses

Syndrome	Case Histories	Mental Health Workers	Teachers	Parents	Total
Broad Band					
Overcontrolled	2	1	6	6	15
Undercontrolled	3	3	6	7	19
Pathological detachment	3	—	1	—	4
Learning problems	—	—	1	1	2
Narrow Band					
Academic disability	—	1	—	3	4
Aggressive	3	4	2	8	17
Anxious	1	2	2	2	7
Delinquent	3	1	1	7	12
Depressed	2	1	1	5	9
Hyperactive	3	2	2	7	14
Immature	—	1	1	3	5
Obsessive-compulsive	1	—	1	2	4
Schizoid	3	4	—	5	12
Sexual problems	1	2	—	3	6
Sleep problems	—	—	—	3	3
Social withdrawal	1	1	2	5	9
Somatic complaints	1	—	—	7	8
Uncommunicative	—	1	—	2	3

Source: T.M. Achenbach, *Developmental Psychopathology,* 2nd ed. (New York: Wiley, 1982). p. 556, plus subsequent findings summarized by Achenbach, 1985.

to define nosological categories, there is seldom a specific data base for the number of descriptors, the degree of association among them, and the cutoff point for judging the presence versus absence of the disorder. The multiple descriptors defining multivariate syndromes, by contrast, are selected on the basis of their mutual covariation in samples of cases. Furthermore, the distribution of syndrome scores (e.g., sum of scores on all descriptors) can be compared in different criterion groups (e.g., normal versus referred individuals) to find the most discriminating cutting points.

5. The criteria for nosological categories imply deviance from "normal" functioning, but they provide no measurement operations for assessing normal baselines or deviations from them. The quantification of multivariate syndromes, however, provides a metric that can be calibrated on normative samples to provide a baseline from which to assess the deviance of individuals.

6. When individuals meet criteria for more than one nosological category, they must either get multiple diagnoses or one category must preempt the others, often with no empirical basis for choosing which categories should have priority. When syndromes are viewed quantitatively, however, there is no need for multiple diagnoses or for assigning priorities among categories that may reflect important characteristics of the individual. Instead, an individual's scores on all the multivariate syndromes relevant to his or her age and sex can be preserved in a profile format.

7. Nosological categories are usually defined by one or two dimensions of descriptors, whereas profiles of multivariate syndromes can be used to construct multidimensional "types." By cluster analyzing profiles, for example, we can identify groups of individuals who have similar patterns across multiple syndromes, rather than basing categories on each syndrome taken in isolation.

The long dominant nosological approach conforms to the prevailing medical system, of which mental health services are often considered a part. It may therefore seem to be the "natural" format for diagnostic concepts. It is important, however, to distinguish between (1) the functional value of nosological categories for conceptualizing certain types of information, and (2) preferences for such categories that merely reflect habits of thought.

Nosological categories are most useful for physical illnesses having a clear-cut symptom syndrome, a specific known etiology, and a well-documented course. Examples range from measles to tuberculosis and syphilis. Even though people vary in the severity and patterning of their physical responses to these diseases, the specificity of the etiological agents and the comprehensive understanding of them justify thinking in categorical, *present* versus *absent* terms. Certain less completely understood physical illnesses, such as cancer, also invite nosological categorization, because tumors and other forms of cancer can usually be diagnosed as present versus absent. Our lack of etiological knowledge, however, makes it harder to draw clear categorical boundaries between types of cancer. For other physical problems, such as broken bones, classification is descriptive with little reference to the specific event that caused the problem, even though such events are usually known. Still other physical disorders, such as hypertension, may be defined largely as quantitative deviations from age and sex norms. Although a specific etiology may sometimes be known, most cases can be identified and treated without knowledge of the specific etiology.

Despite the utility of categorical concepts, medical conditions do not all fit into neat categories. Not only do some disorders consist of quantitative deviations from a normative level (e.g., hypertension), but in many cases, quantitative diagnostic measures—such as blood pressure—and descriptive procedures—such as X-rays—are required to define disorders.

Current nosological categories for childhood behavior disorders are not based on knowledge of etiology or course. Nor are there physical symptoms to mark a condition as an illness or to define boundaries between disorders. Instead, mental health services are typically sought for behavior that violates expectations for the child's age. To determine whether the child's behavior is truly deviant, we need comparisons with normative data for children of the same age, sex, and, possibly, socioeconomic status. To determine whether a child's deviance corresponds to patterns recognizable in other children, multivariate analyses of large samples can identify prevailing patterns, although exceptionally rare syndromes, such as infantile autism, may not be identifiable in this way. To determine the need for intervention, longitudinal studies are required to assess the typical outcome of particular disorders under conditions of intervention and nonintervention.

Classical Versus Prototype Views of Taxonomy
Both the nature of childhood disorders and the level of our knowledge about them argue for quantitative, normative-epidemiological, and longitudinal appraisals. Because it may nevertheless remain necessary to mesh quantitatively based concepts with categorical systems, it is instructive to consider recent research on the psychology of categorical thinking. This research highlights a distinction between the *classical* view of categorization and the *prototype* view.

The Classical View of Categories
According to the classical view, "a category is defined by a small set of singly necessary and jointly sufficient features" (Cantor, Smith, French, & Mezzich, 1980, p. 182). For a case to be a member of a category, it must have all the defining features of the category. Conversely, any case that has all the defining features is ipso facto a member of the category. This view of categories has two important implications for concepts of psychopathology:

1. Because the defining features of each category determine a disorder's membership on a yes-or-no basis, the boundaries of each category should be distinct, with few or no borderline cases.
2. The cases placed in a category should be homogeneous with respect to the defining features of the category.

Our incomplete understanding of most disorders and the plethora of potentially relevant variables make it hard to construct categorical taxonomies.

Yet research on people's use of intuitively obvious categories—such as animals, plants, clothing, and games—shows that members of even these categories do not all share a single set of defining features. Instead, there is considerable variety among cases assigned to a category, and there are many borderline and uncertain cases.

Even with a familiar category such as furniture, Rosch and Mervis (1975) found that no single defining feature characterized all the items that people assigned to the category. Items judged to be most typical of a category (e.g., table, chair), however, shared certain features lacked by less typical items (e.g., lamp, rug). [The items considered to be most typical are categorized the most accurately, quickly, and reliably (Smith, 1978).] This suggests that certain features of categories are more strongly associated with the categories than are other features, and that items having many of these central features are "purer" instances of the categories than are items having fewer central features.

The Prototype View

The prototype view is based on findings of how people actually use categories thought to be of the classical type. Instead of identifying category members on the basis of necessary and sufficient defining features, people seem to think of categories in terms of groups of correlated features. Although some features may be *necessary* for category membership (e.g., birds must have feathers and wings), they may not be sufficient. Other features may be neither necessary nor sufficient but correlated with category membership (e.g., many but not all birds fly and sing). An especially clear exemplar of a category is called a *prototype*.

According to the prototype view, a case's category membership can be determined by computing the overlap between the case's features and the list of prototype features. If a case has features of more than one category, it can be assigned to the category with which its features correspond most closely. This is exactly the procedure for classifying individuals according to syndromes derived from factor analyses and cluster analyses. Each syndrome consists of a list of features found to be statistically intercorrelated. An individual's category membership (syndrome) can be determined by computing the number of prototypic features that the individual

manifests. Individuals who manifest features of more than one syndrome can be judged to have the syndrome for which they have the most features.

Besides simple sums of features, more sensitive indices of protoypicality can be computed by using gradations in the initial assessment of features and summing these graded scores. Features can also be differentially weighted by using factor scores—that is, by multiplying feature scores by their factor loadings and summing their products. Profile patterns derived from cluster analyses of individuals can be used as a more comprehensive basis for prototype classification, and an individual's correspondence to profile types can be determined by computing an intraclass correlation between the individual's profile and each of the prototype profiles (see Achenbach & Edelbrock, 1983, for examples).

The need for quantitative, prototype approaches to taxonomy is especially evident in child psychopathology, because of the lack of well-validated categories, the quantitative and situational variations in most problems, and the centrality of developmental norms in judging deviance. The growing application of these approaches to the developmental study of psychopathology, however, may stimulate revision of entrenched nosological assumptions about adult disorders as well (see Achenbach, 1985, for detailed illustrations).

IMPLICATIONS FOR INTERVENTIONS

The developmental study of psychopathology has many implications for psychotherapy and behavior change. The most obvious involve the search for the developmental roots of later psychopathology and the hope that etiological discoveries will improve prevention and treatment. It is indeed likely that a comprehensive understanding of many disorders, both child and adult, will require thorough developmental studies. As discussed earlier, longitudinal research on children at risk for schizophrenia and on adult schizophrenics has already cast doubt on long-held asumptions about the course of the disorder (e.g., Harding, 1984; Mednick et al., 1981).

Research on the developmental origins of psychopathology is difficult, slow, and costly. The cadre of scientists having the commitment, expertise, and support to do such research is small and scattered.

Although developmental psychopathology is now clearly emerging as a distinct field (Achenbach, 1982; Cicchetti, 1984; Rutter & Garmezy, 1983), it cannot overnight solve the long-standing epigenetic puzzles of major mental disorders. Nevertheless, the developmental study of psychopathology promises to shed light on a broad range of disorders, as illustrated in the following sections.

Implications of Developmental Levels

We have considered development from birth to maturity in terms of several theoretical perspectives and in terms of age periods marked by a variety of biological, cognitive, social, and educational transitions. Although "stage" and "level" constructs abound in developmental theory, we need not adhere literally to these constructs to see their implications for psychotherapy and behavior change. For most purposes, chronological age provides a rough index of children's level of functioning, but adjustments must be made for mentally retarded children and others whose development is otherwise out of step with that of their age-mates.

Massive age differences in biological maturation, competencies, types of problems, characteristic syndromes, family relations, and developmental tasks make it impossible for any single therapeutic approach to be equally applicable at all ages. In the past, adherents of a particular therapeutic orientation—such as psychodynamic, behavioral, family systems, or psychopharmacological—tended to view all problems in terms of their favorite therapy. As each approach grows more differentiated, however, it is becoming clear that none has all the answers. Although a few controlled outcome studies show short-term efficacy for stimulant drugs in reducing hyperactivity and for various behavioral techniques in reducing some specific problem behaviors, long-term follow-ups do not show enduring benefits (e.g., Gittelman, 1982; Rutter & Garmezy, 1983). Furthermore, comparisons of different treatment modalities show that interactions between client characteristics (e.g., age, SES) and type of treatment often outweigh the main effects of treatment per se (Love & Kaswan, 1974; Miller, Barrett, Hampe, & Noble, 1972; Sloane et al., 1976). It thus appears that the efficacious components of various therapies need to be carefully culled and matched to the problems, developmental levels, and clients for which they are most appropriate. It is also necessary to include assessments of outcome across more situations and longer time periods than has been typical.

Cognitive Developmental Levels

Children's cognitive limitations constrain the feasibility of particular therapies. Despite a large literature on interpretive psychotherapy with preschool and elementary school children, for example, there is little reason to believe that such children are cognitively capable of understanding the interpretive process. As Harter (1983) points out, preschoolers lack the understanding of causal inference needed to grasp interpretations of free association or play sequences. It is also unlikely that preschoolers can grasp the multiple perspectives on behavior that are often invoked in interpretive therapy.

Cognitive constraints are less severe when children attain concrete operational logic during the elementary school period. The cognitive abilities of this period, however, are attuned to the logical ordering of concrete, observable phenomena, rather than introspective analysis of psychological processes. The attainment of formal operational logic in adolescence brings the ability to understand psychological concepts, such as defense mechanisms, that could not be clearly grasped earlier (Chandler, Paget, & Koch, 1978). Yet the type of therapeutic alliance needed for interpretive therapy may be difficult to establish with many adolescents, because they resist the intrusion of adult authority figures.

As an alternative to interpretive therapies, Harter (1983) has outlined approaches that take better account of children's cognitive levels. These approaches are based on a hypothesized developmental sequence in children's ability to think about emotions. During the preoperational period, for example, children seem able to think about only one emotion in response to a particular situation. They thus think of themselves as feeling "all mad" or "all happy," even when ambivalence or a mixture of emotions would be expected. This restriction to one emotion at a time parallels their inability to coordinate two or more perceptual dimensions in Piaget's tests of conservation, discussed earlier.

At the next level, corresponding to Piaget's concrete operational period, children can think about the co-occurrence of two emotions, but only *sequentially*, rather than simultaneously. They later become able to recognize two or more emotions occurring together in response to a single situation. Even after dual emotions are recognized, however, it remains hard to recognize simultaneous positive and negative feelings toward the same object, that is, ambivalence.

To help troubled children recognize multiple feelings, Harter draws a circle, which she then subdivides to represent the child's different feelings. The multidimensionality of emotions can also be illustrated with cartoon figures whose contrasting thoughts are represented in bifurcated balloons over their heads and with dolls whose rotating heads have different expressions on different sides. Concrete repesentations of different emotions may facilitate the recognition of complex and multiple emotions, as well as encouraging better differentiation of the self-concept. Rather than allowing incompetence in one domain to stigmatize a child's entire self-image, for example, smart and dumb or good and bad aspects can be assigned to different areas of the same self-representation.

Besides levels in awareness of the multidimensionality of one's own emotions, there are also levels in the ability to recognize emotional complexity in other people, such as parents, and in the possibilities for hiding, denying, and repressing emotions. Selman (1980), for example, has proposed that children move from an inability to think in terms of hidden emotions, to an awareness that feelings can be hidden, to a recognition that thoughts and feelings can be forced out of consciousness. In adolescence, they may ultimately arrive at a concept of the unconscious as an explanatory construct.

These developmental changes argue for very different therapeutic approaches with children of different ages. Instead of insight-oriented probes aimed at getting the child to infer underlying reasons for behavior, it may be more fruitful to encourage young children merely to recognize the *consequences* of specific behavior, rather than its motives or other determinants. Among adolescents, on the other hand, a penchant for looking below the surface for hidden explanations may be a powerful therapeutic lever, if the therapist can win the status of ally rather than intruder.

Harter's (1983) analysis of developmental aspects of therapy highlights

> . . . the importance of recognizing how the individual's very theory of mind, motives, emotions,

and self changes with developmental level, which in turn has implications for therapeutic intervention. The most general implication is that we identify the particular developmental level at which the child is operating, in the sphere that is most critical to our choice of treatment strategies. Interpretations or interventions may then begin at that level, or may encourage the child to psychologically reach for the next level if that seems appropriate. (pp. 116–117)

Other Developmental Levels

Constructs of cognitive levels generally imply a sequence of relatively discrete information-processing systems, analogous to a series of progressively more powerful computer programs. In the psychodynamic tradition, Freud's theory of psychosexual development and Erikson's theory of psychosocial development imply somewhat analogous sequences of personality development. It now seems unlikely that Freud's theory could be correct about libidinal phases, the development of an id-ego-superego personality structure, or the development of secondary process thinking. Erikson's outline of psychosocial conflicts, however, is a useful guide to issues relevant to children, adolescents, and adults of successive ages, although none of them is necessarily inevitable or universal. The conflict that Erikson (1980) calls *identity versus identity confusion* (previously called "role confusion"), for example, may not be experienced by adolescents who have no choice about their occupational or social roles.

Interventions must also take account of biological maturation, changing relations with family members, and educational levels. On the biological front, growth in size, physical abilities, and coordination offer opportunities for helping children master sports and other skills that can promote feelings of competence. In females, the hormonal changes of puberty that establish the menstrual cycle also introduce a periodicity into girls' emotions. In adolescent males, testosterone levels are associated with aggressive responses to provocation (Olweus, Mattson, Schalling, & Löw, 1980). Biologically based emotional changes of this sort need to be recognized in tailoring interventions to children and adolescents. Drug responses also vary greatly with biological maturation. Many psychoactive drugs used with adults are either hazardous or ineffective for children (Campbell, Cohen, & Perry, 1983). Some, such as stimulants and antidepressants, have been regarded as showing opposite or "paradoxical" effects on children and adults, although this may be largely a function of differences in sensitivity to particular dose levels or in the behavioral responses assessed (Solanto, 1984).

Changes in relations to parents have major implications for therapeutic interventions. The massive dependence of infants and preschoolers dictates family involvement in most interventions. Even where residential treatment is used to treat severe disorders, gains are often lost if family members are not taught to maintain a therapeutic regimen when the child returns home (Rutter & Garmezy, 1983). Behavioral methods usually require extensive cooperation by family members, although parent training and clear-cut behavioral programming can potentially enhance parents' feelings of competence in dealing with their children's problems more than most other approaches do. By adolescence, however, it is increasingly necessary to deal directly with the identified patient as an individual in his or her own right. This does not preclude family approaches, but they may need to focus more on reciprocal contracting among family members than on behavioral manipulations by parents or on the alteration of subtle family dynamics. It has been found, for example, that behavioral family therapy emphasizing contingency contracting is significantly more effective with adolescent delinquents than are psychodynamic and nondirective family therapies (Klein, Barton, & Alexander, 1980).

Children's educational progress normally follows a series of levels having different implications for interventions. At the preschool and elementary school levels, for example, one teacher usually has major responsibility for the child. This offers opportunities to obtain comprehensive information on the child's school functioning from one source and to coordinate school interventions with those occurring elsewhere. Yet if the teacher contributes to the child's problems or is difficult to work with, this can doom school interventions until the child moves to another class. At the junior and senior high school levels, a broader picture of children's functioning may be obtained from standardized ratings by teachers seeing them in different classes. The short time spent in each classroom, however, usually makes it harder to obtain in-depth pictures from teachers and to arrange intensive interventions.

Implications of Developmental Concepts of Disorders

As discussed earlier, both the referral process and the nature of children's problems argue for concepts of disorders differing from those of Kraepelinian nosology. The differences involve the crucial role of people other than the child in determining that help is needed; the importance of developmental lags and quantitative or situational deviance; the developmental changes children continually undergo; the need to judge pathology in terms of developmental outcomes; and the priority that facilitating development should have over returning children to premorbid levels of functioning.

Multivariate research has yielded syndromes scorable from standardized ratings by parents, teachers, and mental health workers (Table 4.2). Some of the multivariate syndromes resemble nosological categories based on clinicians' concepts of disorders. Unlike classical categories defined in terms of necessary and sufficient criteria, however, the multivariate syndromes consist of groups of features that tend to co-occur, as shown by their covariation in large samples of cases. Syndromes defined by intercorrelated features correspond to the *prototype* concept of categories. According to this concept, all members of a category need not possess identical defining features. Instead, their correspondence to a category can be assessed *quantitatively* in terms of the degree to which they manifest the category's defining features. Those having the most features of the prototype are the purest exemplars of the category.

The quantification implicit in the prototype concept can capture the developmental aspects of disorders far better than classical nosological categories do. As outlined earlier, syndrome scores can be computed not only by counting the number of a syndrome's features manifested by a child, but by summing the scores obtained when each feature is assessed quantitatively (e.g., on rating scales) and, if desired, by summing weighted feature scores. Syndromes derived separately for children of different age levels can reflect developmental differences in the prevalence and patterning of syndromes. By standardizing syndrome scores on normative samples grouped by age (and other important variables, such as sex), a child's standing on each syndrome can be compared with that of peers.

Because children often display different problems

and competencies in different settings, syndromes and their standard scores can be derived separately from data provided by different informants, such as parents, teachers, trained observers, and children themselves. In the clinical assessment of individual children, multidimensional syndrome scores derived from standardized ratings by each type of informant can be compared to pinpoint the behaviors and situations in which the child's greatest deficits and assets are seen. Multidimensional and multisituational assessment of this sort can provide a much better basis for planning the treatment of most child and adolescent disorders than can assessment limited to nosological categories (Achenbach, 1985, provides detailed illustrations).

If quantified multidimensional and multisituational assessment is initially used to guide treatment planning, it can be repeated periodically to determine whether the intended changes are occurring. Rather than restricting reevaluation to a circumscribed target problem, the continued use of multidimensional-multisituational assessment enables the therapist to see whether desirable changes are occurring in all areas. Otherwise, favorable reports about a few target problems may mask a lack of improvement or worsening in behaviors or situations that are not periodically reassessed.

Outcome and follow-up evaluations should continue to use the same multidimensional-multisituational assessment procedures, so that quantitative changes in each area can be identified in a uniform fashion from the initial baseline assessment to each subsequent reassessment. If the assessment scores are standardized on normative samples appropriate for each age at which a child is assessed, the fact that the child grows older from baseline to follow-up will not distort the comparisons with age-mates. Besides assessing quantitative changes in the child's reported problems and competencies, norm-based scores also indicate whether or not the child reaches the normal range. While therapists are naturally gratified by reductions in reported problems, it is equally important to determine whether these reductions leave the child still deviant or within the normal range.

CONCLUSION

The developmental study of psychopathology has multiple implications for psychotherapy and behav-ior change. The multifaceted nature of development is highlighted by the differing emphases of the S-R, organismic-developmental, psychodynamic, and ethological paradigms. Current developmental research, however, focuses more on circumscribed topic areas than on general theoretical explanations for major aspects of development. Examples having particular relevance to psychopathology include developmental research on temperament, social cognition, and children at risk for mental disorders.

The rapid changes occurring on many fronts make a developmental approach to psychopathology especially necessary from birth to maturity. We considered the course of normal development and its aberrations in terms of four periods marked by major transitions in the biological, cognitive, socio-emotional, and educational spheres: infancy (ages 0–2); the preschool period (ages 2–5); the elementary school period (ages 6–11); and adolescence (ages 12–20). Although not rigidly separated from one another, these periods reflect major differences in developmental tasks, competencies, stresses, and adaptational problems. Many of the problems for which mental health services are sought involve either lags in the development of expected behavior or exaggerations of behavior that most children show in some degree.

The lack of appropriate nosological categories for most child and adolescent disorders has stimulated efforts to identify syndromes through multivariate analyses of checklists for scoring children's problems as seen by parents, teachers, and mental health workers. Although some of the empirically derived syndromes resemble those embodied in nosological categories, they differ from classical nosological categories in being quantified. The quantitative nature of multivariate syndromes corresponds to the *prototype* concept of categories. By using norm-based standard scores for each syndrome, casting all the syndromes for a particular age within a profile format, and constructing separate profiles of syndromes scored from different informants, it is possible to obtain a multidimensional-multisituational view of disorders that is potentially more powerful and comprehensive than any categorical view, prototypic or otherwise.

A developmentally normed, multidimensional-multisituational approach to assessment and taxonomy can help in targeting interventions on specific deficits occurring in specific life situations, while also providing means for periodic reevaluations across multiple dimensions of problems and competencies. By using this approach to assessment and taxonomy to improve the matching of interventions to the client's developmental level, we can advance the prevention and treatment of many child and adolescent disorders. This approach may also aid in understanding and preventing adult disorders that originate in childhood and may be applicable to the assessment and treatment of at least some disorders in adulthood.

REFERENCES

Achenbach, T.M. (1982). *Developmental psychopathology* (2nd ed.). New York: Wiley.

Achenbach, T.M. (1985). *Assessment and taxonomy of child and adolescent psychopathology*. Beverly Hills: Sage.

Achenbach, T.M., & Edelbrock, C.S. (1981). Behavioral problems and competencies reported by parents of normal and disturbed children aged four to sixteen. *Monographs of the Society for Research in Child Development, 46*, Serial No. 188.

Achenbach, T.M., & Edelbrock, C.S. (1983). *Manual for the Child Behavior Checklist and Revised Child Behavior Profile*. Burlington, VT: Dept. of Psychiatry, University of Vermont.

Achenbach, T.M., & Edelbrook, C.S. (1986). *Manual for the Teacher's Report Form and Teacher Version of the Child Behavior Profile*. Burlington, VT: Dept. of Psychiatry, University of Vermont.

Ainsworth, M., Blehar, M., Waters, E., & Wall, S. (1978). *Patterns of attachment*. Hillsdale, NJ: Erlbaum.

American Academy of Child Psychiatry (1983). *Child psychiatry: A plan for the coming decades*. Washington, DC: Author.

American Psychiatric Association (1st ed., 1952; 2nd ed., 1968; 3rd ed., 1980). *Diagnostic and statistical manual of mental disorders*. Washington, DC: Author.

Anderson, J. R. (1983). *The architecture of cognition*. Cambridge, MA: Harvard University Press.

Arnold, L.E., Barnebey, N., McManus, J., Smeltzer, D.J., Conrad, A., Winer, G., & Desgranges, L. (1977). Prevention by specific perceptual remediation for vulnerable first-graders. *Archives of General Psychiatry, 34*, 1279–1294.

Baldwin, J.A., Robertson, N.C., & Satin, D.G. (1971). The incidence of reported, deviant behavior in children. *International Psychiatry Clinics, 8*, 161–175.

Bandura, A. (1977). *Social learning theory*. Englewood Cliffs, NJ: Prentice-Hall.

Banks, M.S., & Salapatek, P. (1983). Infant visual perception. In P.H. Mussen (Ed.), *Handbook of child psychology. Vol. II. Infancy and developmental psychobiology* (4th ed., M.M. Haith & J.J. Campos, Vol. Eds.). New York: Wiley.

Bayley, N. (1969). *Bayley Scales of Infant Development*. New York: Psychological Corporation.

Belmaker, R., Pollin, W., Wyatt, R.J., & Cohen, S. (1974). A follow-up of monozygotic twins discordant for schizophrenia. *Archives of General Psychiatry, 30*, 219–222.

Bettelheim, B. (1967). *The empty fortress*. New York: Free Press.

Bleuler, E. (1911). *Dementia praecox or the group of schizophrenias* (trans.). New York: International Universities Press, 1950.

Bowlby, J. (1977). The making and breaking of affectional bonds. 1. Aetiology and psychopathology in the light of attachment theory. *British Journal of Psychiatry, 130*, 201–210.

Bowlby, J. (1980). *Attachment and loss. Vol. III. Loss, sadness and depression*. New York: Basic Books.

Brown, G., Chadwick, O., Shaffer, D., Rutter, M., & Traub, M. (1981). A prospective study of children with head injuries. III. Psychiatric sequelae. *Psychological Medicine, 11*, 63–78.

Buss, A.H., & Plomin, R. (1984). *Temperament: Early developing personality traits*. Hillsdale, NJ: Erlbaum.

Campbell, M., Cohen, I.L., & Perry, R. (1983). Psychopharmacological treatment. In T.H. Ollendick & M. Hersen (Eds.), *Handbook of child psychopathology*. New York: Plenum.

Campos, J.J., Barrett, K.C., Lamb, M., Goldsmith, H.H., & Stenberg, C. (1983). Socioemotional development. In P.H. Mussen (Ed.), *Handbook of child psychology. Vol. II. Infancy and developmental psychobiology*. (4th ed., M.M. Haith & J.J. Campos, Vol. Eds.). New York: Wiley.

Cantor, N., Smith, E., French, R., & Mezzich, J. (1980). Psychiatric diagnosis as prototype categorization. *Journal of Abnormal Psychology, 89*, 181–193.

Chandler, M.J., Paget, K.F., & Koch, D.A. (1978). The child's demystification of psychological defense mechanisms: A structural and developmental analysis. *Developmental Psychology, 14*, 197–205.

Ciaccio, N.V. (1971). A test of Erikson's theory of ego epigenesis. *Developmental Psychology, 4*, 306–311.

Cicchetti, D. (1984). Special issue: Developmental psychopathology. *Child Development, 55*, 1–316.

Ciompi, L., & Müller, C. (1976). Lebensweg und Alter Schizophrenen. *Eine Katamnestic Lonzeitstudies bis ins Senum*. Berlin: Springer-Verlag.

Clarke, A.M., & Clarke, A.D.B. (1976). *Early experience: Myth and evidence*. New York: Free Press.

Cohen, D.J., & Shaywitz, B.A. (1982). Preface to the special issue on neurobiological research in autism. *Journal of Autism and Developmental Disorders, 12*, 103–107.

Commons, M.L., Richards, F.A., & Armon, C. (Eds.). (1984). *Beyond formal operations*. New York: Praeger.

Cytryn, L., & McKnew, D.H. (1979). In J. Noshpitz (Ed.), *Basic handbook of child psychiatry* (Vol. 2). New York: Basic Books.

Cytryn, L., McKnew, D.H., & Bunney, W. (1980). Diagnosis of depression in children: Reassessment. *American Journal of Psychiatry, 137*, 22–25.

Darwin, C.R. (1859). *Origin of species*. London: J. Murray.

Darwin, C.R. (1872). *The expression of the emotions in man and animals*. London: J. Murray.

Dodge, K.A. (1986). A social information processing model of social competence in children. In M. Perlmutter (Ed), *Minnesota Symposium on Child Psychology*. Hillsdale, NJ: Erlbaum.

Dodge, K.A., Murphy, R.R., & Buchsbaum, K. (1984). The assessment of intention-cue detection skills in children: Implications for developmental psychopathology. *Child Development, 55,* 163–173.

Dollard, J., & Miller, N. (1950). *Personality and psychotherapy.* New York: McGraw-Hill.

Edelbrock, C., & Achenbach, T.M. (1980). A typology of Child Behavior Profile patterns: Distribution and correlates for disturbed children aged 6 to 16. *Journal of Abnormal Child Psychology, 8,* 441–470.

Ehrhardt, A.A., & Meyer-Bahlburg, H.F.L. (1981). Effects of prenatal sex hormones on gender-related behavior. *Science, 211,* 1312–1318.

Elkind, D. (1979). *The child and society: Essays in applied child development.* New York: Oxford University Press.

Elmer, E., Gregg, G.S., & Ellison, P. (1969). Late results of the "failure to thrive" syndrome. *Clinical Pediatrics, 8,* 584–589.

Erikson, E.H. (1963). *Childhood in society* (2nd ed.). New York: Norton.

Erikson, E.H. (1980). Elements of a psychoanalytic theory of psychosocial development. In S.I. Greenspan & G.H. Pollock (Eds.), *The course of life: Psychoanalytic contributions toward understanding personality development. Vol I. Infancy and early childhood.* Adelphi, MD: NIMH Mental Health Study Center.

Fairbairn, W.R.D. (1952). *Psycho-analytic studies of the personality.* London: Tavistock.

Feingold, B.F. (1976). Hyperkinesis and learning disabilities linked to the ingestion of artificial food colors and flavors. *Journal of Learning Disabilities, 9,* 551–559.

Finucci, J.M., Guthrie, J.T., Childs, A.L., Abbey, H., & Childs, B. (1976). The genetics of specific reading disability. *Annals of Human Genetics, 40,* 1–23.

Freud, A. (1946). *The ego and the mechanisms of defense* (translated by Cecil Baines). New York: International Universities Press.

Freud, A. (1965). *Normality and pathology in childhood.* New York: International Universities Press.

Freud, S. (1909). Analysis of a phobia in a five-year-old boy. In *Standard edition of the complete psychological works of Sigmund Freud* (Vol. 7). London: Hogarth Press, 1953.

Frommer, E.A. (1967). Treatment of childhood depression with antidepressant drugs. *British Medical Journal, 1,* 729–732.

Gesell, A. (1954). The autogenesis of behavior. In L. Carmichael (Ed.), *Manual of child psychology.* New York: Wiley.

Gittelman, R. (1982). Prospective follow-up study of hyperactive children. Presented at American Academy of Child Psychiatry, Washington, DC.

Goldberg, H.K., Schiffman, G.B., & Bender, M. (1983). *Dyslexia. Interdisciplinary approaches to reading disabilities.* New York: Grune & Stratton.

Goldenberg, I., & Goldenberg, H. (1980). *Family therapy: An overview.* Monterey, CA: Brookes/Cole.

Gottesman, I.I., & Shields, J. (1982). *Schizophrenia. The epigenetic puzzle.* New York: Cambridge University Press.

Gouin-Décarie, T. (1965). *Intelligence and affectivity in early childhood.* New York: International Universities Press.

Griesinger, W. (1845). *Die Pathologie und Therapie der psychischen Krankheiten* (translated as *Mental pathology and therapeutics* by C.L. Robertson & J. Rutherford). London: New Sydenham Society, 1867.

Group for the Advancement of Psychiatry. (1966). Psychopathological disorders in childhood: Theoretical considerations and a proposed classification. *GAP Report No. 62.*

Hagin, R.A., Silver, A.A., & Kreeger, H. (1976). *TEACH: A preventive approach for potential learning disability.* New York: Walker Educational Book Corp.

Halmi, K. (1974). Anorexia nervosa: Demographic and clinical features in 94 cases. *Psychosomatic Medicine, 36,* 18–25.

Harding, C.M. (1984). Long-term outcome functioning of subjects rediagnosed as meeting the DSM-III criteria for schizophrenia. Unpublished Ph.D. dissertation, University of Vermont, Dept of Psychology.

Harris, D.B. (Ed.). (1957). *The concept of development.* Minneapolis: University of Minnesota Press.

Harter, S. (1983). Cognitive-developmental considerations in the conduct of play therapy. In C.E. Schaefer & K.J. O'Connor (Eds.), *Handbook of play therapy.* New York: Wiley.

Hartmann, H. (1939). *Ego psychology and the problem of adaptation.* New York: International Universities Press.

Hartmann, H. (1950). Psychoanalysis and developmental psychology. *Psychoanalytic Study of the Child, 5,* 7–17.

Harvey, P., Winters, K., Weintraub, S., & Neale, J.M. (1981). Distractibility in children vulnerable to psychopathology. *Journal of Abnormal Psychology, 90,* 298–304.

Heinstein, M. (1969). *Behavior problems of young children in California.* Berkeley: California Department of Public Health.

Holinger, P.C. (1979). Violent deaths among the young: Recent trends in suicide, homicide, and accidents. *American Journal of Psychiatry, 136,* 1144–1147.

John, R.S., Mednick, S.A., & Schulsinger, F. (1982). Teacher reports as a predictor of schizophrenia and borderline schizophrenia: A Bayesian decision analysis. *Journal of Abnormal Psychology, 91,* 399–413.

Kanner, L. (1943). Autistic disturbances of affective contact. *Nervous Child, 2,* 217–250.

Kasanin, J., & Kaufman, M.R. (1929). A study of the functional psychoses in childhood. *American Journal of Psychiatry, 9,* 307–384.

Kashani, J.M., Husain, A., Shekim, W.O., Hodges, K.K., Cytryn, L., & McKnew, D.H. (1981). Current perspectives on childhood depression: An overview. *American Journal of Psychiatry, 138,* 143–153.

Kendler, H.H., & Guenther, K. (1980). Developmental changes in classificatory behavior. *Child Development, 51,* 339–348.

Kennedy, W.A. (1965). School phobia: Rapid treatment of 50 cases. *Journal of Abnormal Psychology, 70,* 285–289.

Klein, N.C., Barton, C., & Alexander, J.F. (1980). Intervention and evaluation in family settings. In R.H. Price & P.E. Polister (Eds.), *Evaluation and action in the social environment.* New York: Academic Press.

Kohlberg, L. (1978). The cognitive developmental approach to behavior disorders: A study of the development of moral reasoning in delinquents. In G. Serban (Ed.), *Cognitive defects in the development of mental illness.* New York: Brunner/Mazel.

Kopp, C.B. (1983). Risk factors in development. In P.H. Mussen (Ed.), *Handbook of child psychology. Vol. II. Infancy and developmental psychobiology.* (4th ed., M.M. Haith & J.J. Campos, Vol. Eds.). New York: Wiley.

Kovacs, M., Feinberg, T.L., Crouse-Novak, M., Paulauskas, S.L., Pollock, M., & Finkelstein, R. (1984). Depressive disorders in childhood. II. A longitudinal study of the risk of a subsequent major depression. *Archives of General Psychiatry, 41,* 643–649.

Kraepelin, E. (1st ed., 1883). *Psychiatrie.* Leipzig: Abel (8th ed., Leipzig: Barth), 1915.

Kronstadt, D., Oberklaid, F., Ferb, T.E., & Swartz, J.P. (1979). Infant behavior and maternal adaptations in the first six months of life. *American Journal of Orthopsychiatry, 49,* 454–464.

Kuhn, T.S. (1970). *The structure of scientific revolutions* (2nd ed.) Chicago: University of Chicago Press.

Kysar, J.E. (1968). The two camps in child psychiatry: A report from a psychiatrist father of an autistic and retarded child. *American Journal of Psychiatry, 125,* 103–109.

Lewis, D.O., & Balla, D.A. (1976). *Delinquency and psychopathology.* New York: Grune & Stratton.

Lewis, M., Feiring, C., McGuffog, C., & Jaskir, J. (1984). Predicting psychopathology in six-year-olds from early social relations. *Child Development, 55,* 123–136.

Loney, J., & Milich, R. (1982). Hyperactivity, inattention, and aggression in clinical practice. In M. Wolraich & D.K. Routh (Eds.), *Advances in behavioral pediatrics* (Vol. 2). Greenwich, CT: JAI Press.

Lorenz, K.Z. (1965). *Evolution and modification of behavior.* Chicago: Univ. of Chicago Press.

Lotter, V. (1974). Factors related to outcome in autistic children. *Journal of Autism and Childhood Schizophrenia, 4,* 263–277.

Love, L.R., & Kaswan, J.W. (1974). *Troubled children: Their families, schools, and treatments.* New York: Wiley.

MacFarlane, J.W., Allen, L., & Honzik, M.P. (1954). *A developmental study of the behavior problems of normal children between twenty-one months and fourteen years.* Berkeley: University of California Press.

Mahl, G. (1971). *Psychological conflict and defense.* New York: Harcourt Brace Jovanovich.

Matheny, A.P., Dolan, A.B., & Wilson, R.S. (1976). Twins: Within-pair similarity on Bayley's Infant Behavior Record. *Journal of Genetic Psychology, 128,* 263–270.

Mattison, R., Cantwell, D.P., Russell, A.T., & Will, L. (1979). A comparison of DSM-II and DSM-III in the diagnosis of childhood psychiatric disorders. *Archives of General Psychiatry, 36,* 1217–1222.

McGrew, W.C. (1972). *An ethological study of children's behavior.* New York: Academic Press.

Mednick, S.A., Griffith, J.J., & Mednick, B.R. (1981). Problems with traditional strategies in mental health research. In F. Schulsinger, S.A. Mednick, & J. Knop (Eds.), *Longitudinal research. Methods and uses in behavioral science.* Boston: Nijhoff.

Mednick, S.A., & Schulsinger, F. (1972). *Studies of children at high risk for schizophrenia.* Unpublished manuscript, New School for Social Research, New York.

Mednick, S.A., Schulsinger, F., Teasdale, T.W., Schulsinger, H., Venables, P.H., & Rock, D.R. (1978). Schizophrenia in high-risk children: Sex differences in predisposing factors. In G. Serban (Ed.), *Cognitive defects in the development of mental illness.* New York: Brunner/Mazel.

Mezzich, A.C., & Mezzich, J.E. (1979). Diagnostic reliability of childhood and adolescent behavior disorders. Presented at American Psychological Association, New York.

Miller, L.C., Barrett, C.L., Hampe, E., & Noble, H. (1972). Factor structure of childhood fears. *Journal of Consulting and Clinical Psychology, 39,* 264–268.

Miller, L.C., Barrett, C.L., & Hampe, E. (1974). Phobias of childhood in a prescientific era. In A. Davids (Ed.), *Child personality and psychopathology* (Vol. I). New York: Wiley.

Minuchin, S., Rosman, B.L., & Baker, L. (1978). *Psychosomatic families. Anorexia nervosa in context.* Cambridge, MA: Harvard University Press.

Money, J., & Russo, A.J. (1979). Homosexual outcome of discordant gender identity/role in childhood: Longitudinal follow-up. *Journal of Pediatric Psychology, 4,* 29–41.

Morris, D. (1967). *The naked ape.* London: Jonathan Cape.

Mumpower, D.L. (1970). Sex ratios found in various types of referred exceptional children. *Exceptional Children, 36,* 61–62.

National Center for Health Statistics. (1977). Table 292. Deaths from suicide by 5-year age groups. Hyattsville, MD: Health Resources Administration.

New York Times (March 4, 1984). The haunting specter of teen-age suicide. P. 8E.

Ochroch, R. (Ed.). (1981). *The diagnosis and treatment of minimal brain dysfunction in children. A clinical approach.* New York: Human Sciences Press.

Offer, D., & Offer, J.B. (1975). *From teenage to young manhood.* New York: Basic Books.

Olson, G.M., & Sherman, T. (1983). Attention, learning, and memory in infants. In P.H. Mussen (Ed.), *Handbook of child psychology. Vol. II. Infancy and developmental psychobiology.* (4th ed. M.M. Haith & J.J. Campos, Vol. Eds.). New York: Wiley.

Olweus, D., Mattson, A., Schalling, D., & Löw, H. (1980). Testosterone, aggression, physical, and personality dimensions in normal adolescent males. *Psychosomatic Medicine, 42,* 253–269.

Oster, H. (1978). Facial expression and affect development. In M. Lewis & L.A. Rosenblum (Eds.), *The development of affect.* New York: Plenum.

Peterson, A.C., & Wittig, M.A. (1979). Differential cognitive development in adolescent girls. In M. Sugar (Ed.), *Female adolescent development.* New York: Brunner/Mazel.

Piaget, J. (1932). *The moral judgment of the child.* New York: Harcourt.

Piaget, J. (1977). The role of action in the development of thinking. In W.F. Overton & J.M. Gallagher (Eds.), *Knowledge and development* (Vol. I). New York: Plenum.

Piaget, J. (1983). Piaget's theory. In P.H. Mussen (Ed.),

Handbook of child psychology. Vol. I. History, theory, and methods. (4th ed., W. Kessen, Vol. Ed.). New York: Wiley.

Pollin, W., Stabenau, J.R., Mosher, L., & Tupin, J. (1966). Life history differences in identical twins discordant for schizophrenia. American Journal of Orthopsychiatry, 36, 492–509.

Provence, S., & Lipton, R.C. (1962). Infants in institutions. New York: International Universities Press.

Quinton, D., & Rutter, M. (1976). Early hospital admissions and later disturbances of behavior: An attempted replication of Douglas' findings. Developmental Medicine and Child Neurology, 18, 447–459.

Rank, B. (1949). Adaptation of the psychoanalytic technique for the treatment of young children with atypical development. American Journal of Orthopsychiatry, 19, 130–139.

Rapaport, D. (1967). Merton Gill (Ed.), Collected papers of David Rapaport. New York: Basic Books.

Rosch, E., & Mervis, C.G. (1975). Family resemblances: Studies in the internal structure of categories. Cognitive Psychology, 7, 573–605.

Rosen, B.M. (1979). An overview of the mental health delivery system in the United States and services to children. In I.N. Berlin & L.A. Stone (Eds.), Basic handbook of child psychiatry (Vol. 4). New York: Basic Books.

Rosenblatt, A.D., & Thickstun, J.F. (1977). Modern psychoanalytic concepts in a general psychology. Psychological Issues, 11, Monographs 42/43.

Rutter, M. (1974). The development of infantile autism. Psychological Medicine, 4, 147–163.

Rutter, M., & Garmezy, N. (1983). Developmental psychopathology. In P.H. Mussen (Ed.), Handbook of child psychology (4th ed., Vol. IV). New York: Wiley.

Rutter, M., Graham, P., Chadwick, O.F.D., & Yule, W. (1976). Adolescent turmoil: Fact or fiction? Journal of Child Psychology and Psychiatry, 17, 35–56.

Rutter, M., Shaffer, D., & Shepherd, M. (1975). A multiaxial classification of child psychiatric disorders: An evaluation of a proposal. Geneva: World Health Organization.

Scarr, S., & Kidd, K.K. (1983). Developmental behavior genetics. In P.H. Mussen (Ed.), Handbook of child psychology. Vol. II. Infancy and developmental psychobiology (4th ed., M.M. Haith & J.J. Campos, Vol. Eds.). New York: Wiley.

Selman, R. (1980). Interpersonal understanding. New York: Academic Press.

Shaffer, D., & Fisher, P. (1981). Suicide in children and young adolescents. In C.F. Wells & I.R. Stuart (Eds.), Self-destructive behavior in children and adolescents. New York: Van Nostrand Rheinhold.

Shaffer, D., McNamara, N., & Pincus, J.H. (1974). Controlled observations on patterns of activity, attention, and impulsivity in brain-damaged and psychiatrically disturbed boys. Journal of Psychological Medicine, 4, 4–18.

Siegler, R.S. (1983). Information processing approaches to development. In P.H. Mussen (Ed.), Handbook of child psychology Vol. I. History, theory, and methods. (4th ed., W. Kessen, Vol. Ed.). New York: Wiley.

Sloan, R.B., Staples, F.R., Cristol, A.H., Yorkston, N.J., & Whipple, K. (1976). Patient characteristics and outcome in psychotherapy and behavior therapy. Journal of Consulting and Clinical Psychology, 44, 330–339.

Smith, E.E. (1978). Theories of semantic memory. In W.K. Estes (Ed.), Handbook of learning and cognitive processes (Vol. 5). Hillsdale, NJ: Erlbaum.

Solanto, M.V. (1984). Neuropharmacological basis of stimulant drug action in attention deficit disorder with hyperactivity: A review and synthesis. Psychological Bulletin, 95, 387–409.

Spitzer, R.L., & Cantwell, D.P. (1980). The DSM-III classification of the psychiatric disorders of infancy, childhood, and adolescence. Journal of the American Academy of Child Psychiatry, 19, 356–370.

Spivack, G., & Shure, M.B. (1982). The cognition of social adjustment: Interpersonal cognitive problem-solving thinking. In B.B. Lahey & A.E. Kazdin (Eds.), Advances in clinical child psychology (Vol. 5). New York: Plenum.

Sroufe, L.A., Fox, N.E., & Pancake, V.R. (1983). Attachment and dependency in developmental perspective. Child Development, 54, 1615–1627.

Stevenson, H.W. (Ed.). (1966). Concept of development. Monographs of the Society for Research in Child Development, 31, Serial No. 107.

Stevenson, H.W. (1983). How children learn—The quest for a theory. In P.H. Mussen (Ed.), Handbook of child psychology. Vol. I. History, theory, and methods (4th ed., W. Kessen, Vol. Ed.). New York: Wiley.

Strober, M., Green, J., & Carlson, G. (1981). The reliability of psychiatric diagnosis in hospitalized adolescents. Archives of General Psychiatry, 38, 141–145.

Templin, M.C. (1957). Certain language skills in children. Their development and interrelationships. Minneapolis: University of Minnesota Press.

Thomas, A., Chess, S., & Birch, H.G. (1968). Temperament and behavior disorders in children. New York: New York University Press.

Thomas, A., & Chess, S. (1977). Temperament and development. New York: Brunner/Mazel.

Tsuang, M.T., Woolson, R.F., & Fleming, J.A. (1979). Long-term outcome of major psychoses. I. Schizophrenia and affective disorders compared with psychiatrically symptom-free surgical conditions. Archives of General Psychiatry, 36, 1295–1301.

Vaillant, G.E., & Milofsky, E. (1980). Natural history of male psychological health: IX. Empirical evidence for Erikson's model of the life cycle. American Journal of Psychiatry, 137, 1348–1359.

Van Buskirk, S.S. (1977). A two-phase perspective on the treatment of anorexia nervosa. Psychological Bulletin, 84, 529–538.

Wachtel, P.L. (1977). Psychoanalysis and behavior theory: Toward an integration. New York: Basic Books.

Walker, E., Hoppes, E., Mednick, S., Emory, E., & Schulsinger, F. (1981). Environmental factors related to schizophrenia in psychophysiologically labile high-risk males. Journal of Abnormal Psychology, 49, 313–320.

Waterman, A.S., Geary, P.S., & Waterman, C.K. (1974). Longitudinal study of changes in ego identity status from the freshman to the senior year of college. Developmental Psychology, 10, 387–392.

Watson, J.B. (1913). Psychology as the behaviorist views it. Psychological Review, 20, 158–177.

Watson, J.B. (1919). *Psychology from the standpoint of a behaviorist.* Philadelphia: Lippincott.

Weinberg, W.A., Rutman, J., Sullivan, L., Penick, E.C., & Dietz, S.G. (1973). Depression in children referred to an educational diagnostic center: Diagnosis and treatment. *Journal of Pediatrics, 83,* 1065–1072.

Weisz, J.R., O'Neill, P., & O'Neill, P.C. (1975). Field dependence-independence on the Children's Embedded Figure Tests: Cognitive style or cognitive level? *Developmental Psychology, 11,* 539–540.

Werner, H. (1957). The concept of development from a comparative and organismic point of view. In D.B. Harris (Ed.), *The concept of development.* Minneapolis: University of Minnesota Press.

Wender, P., & Wender, E. (1978). *The hyperactive child and the learning disabled child. A handbook for parents.* New York: Cramm.

Werry, J.S. (1979). The childhood psychoses. In H.C.

Quay & J.S. Werry (Eds.), *Psychopathological disorders of childhood* (2nd ed.). New York: Wiley.

Werry, J.S., Methven, R.J., Fitzpatrick, J., & Dixon, H. (1983). The interrater reliability of DSM-III in children. *Journal of Abnormal Child Psychology, 11,* 341–354.

White, R.W. (1963). Ego and reality in psychoanalytic theory. *Psychological Issues, 3* (Monogr. 11).

Witkin, H.A., & Goodenough, D.R. (1980). Cognitive styles: Essence and origins. *Psychological Issues,* No. 51.

Wolman, B.B. (1970). *Children without childhood.* New York: Grune & Stratton.

Yorke, C. (1980). The contribution of the Diagnostic Profile and the assessment of developmental lines to child psychiatry. *Psychiatric Clinics of North America, 3,* 593–603.

EVALUATION OF PROCESS AND OUTCOME IN PSYCHOTHERAPY AND BEHAVIOR CHANGE

PART II

EVALUATION OF PROCESS
AND OUTCOME IN
PSYCHOTHERAPY AND
BEHAVIOR CHANGE

5

THE EFFECTIVENESS
OF PSYCHOTHERAPY

MICHAEL J. LAMBERT
Brigham Young University

DAVID A. SHAPIRO
University of Sheffield

ALLEN E. BERGIN
Brigham Young University

In this chapter we review the status of empirical evidence on the efficacy of psychotherapy, mainly with adult outpatients. We also discuss related issues, such as (1) change without treatment, (2) negative effects, (3) comparative outcomes across techniques, (4) causal factors in outcome, and (5) techniques for measuring change. As in the previous editions of the *Handbook*, we consider here mainly the practice of individual therapies such as the many variations of psychoanalytically oriented psychotherapy, various humanistic and relationship therapies, as well as eclectic mixtures of these and similar types of interventions. Cognitive and behavioral therapies are considered briefly where essential to the issues at hand; but full accounts of these approaches are reserved for other chapters.

Research on therapy outcome from the 1930s through the mid-1970s was summarized in the two previous editions of this chapter (Bergin, 1971; Bergin & Lambert, 1978). Our review of this literature and the related controversies is well documented in these earlier editions. Research and reviews since those editions have confirmed our original conclusion—that psychotherapies, in general, have positive effects—but added considerable information and raised numerous other issues. The interested reader is invited to review earlier editions of this chapter in order to gain an appreciation of the historical context of the current chapter, the nature and quality of prior research, and the controversies that have attended analyses of therapeutic outcomes.

Before introducing specific studies and results, however, it is important to note that significant changes have occurred in recent years that alter the complexion of our review by comparison with previous editions in that the field is maturing in many respects (Williams & Spitzer, 1984)

As noted in Chapter 1, there is a major trend toward eclecticism or integration of diverse techniques and concepts into a broad, comprehensive, and pragmatic approach to treatment that avoids strong allegiances to narrow theories or schools of thought. While there are some exceptions to this trend—there continue to exist rigid adherents to specific orientations—the field as a whole has moved to a new position of cooperative endeavor. Smith's survey (1982) of the counseling and clinical divisions of the American Psychological Association is but one of many documentations of this phenomenon. A startling 98 percent of his 415 respondents identified some form of eclectic system as representing the future trend in counseling and psychotherapy.

The present chapter, like the book as a whole, has always been eclectic in the sense of being open to evidence, positive or negative, concerning any and all approaches. The current status of the evidence, as we see it, requires that this view be emphasized even more in this edition.

For such reasons, in this third edition of the chapter we have tried to highlight somewhat more the positive contributions of diverse approaches rather than restricting ourselves solely to comments on traditional verbal therapies. Readers of the previous editions may have noted that we briefly expressed positive evaluations of behavioral, cognitive, and other methods in the context of our main focus on self-exploratory techniques. We did this because the other methods were the main topic of other chapters. However, in the context of a growing eclecticism, we will discuss more on these topics in this chapter.

It is difficult to provide a review that is perceived as evenhanded by a variety of therapeutic orientations, but that is our goal: Advocates of different positions have tended to set up a double standard of judgment regarding data in the literature by which evidence favorable to their therapy is interpreted flexibly despite a variety of defects, while contrary data are either ignored or treated to a methodological hatchet job that makes the original findings unrecognizable. We have tried to avoid taking sides and we believe the vast majority of research-oriented therapists have moved beyond defensive posturing

as the field has matured. There is no question that advocates of diverse orientations have made important and lasting contributions to the field, and the growing acceptance of this fact has caused attitudes to become much more flexible in assessing the meaning of outcome data.

Given these orienting remarks, we now turn to the business of specifically assessing the results of studies concerning verbal, self-exploratory therapies and comparing them with other methods, such as cognitive and behavioral approaches.

THE GENERAL EFFECT OF PSYCHOTHERAPY

Early reviews of outcome studies were limited in part by an insufficiency of controlled trials in which patients were assigned at random to a treatment or no-treatment control group. The present summary has, however, benefited from the growing number of controlled studies that have appeared in the literature. Many new treatments and variations on the old ones have evolved during the past 15 years so that improvements in research methodology have gone hand in hand with changes in the phenomenon under investigation. There is now little doubt, however, that psychological treatments are, overall and in general, beneficial, although it remains equally true that not everyone benefits to a satisfactory degree. The evidence for this conclusion is demonstrated in part by quantitative surveys of the literature that have used the technique of *meta-analysis* to summarize large collections of empirical data.

Psychotherapy outcome research is but one of several domains of the social and behavioral sciences with a history of controversy and dispute concerning the interpretation of the evidence at hand (e.g., Bergin & Lambert, 1978; Rachman & Wilson, 1980). To meet the need for efficient and maximally objective integrative summaries of such data sets, the technique, or family of techniques, known as meta-analysis was developed (cf. *Clinical Psychology Review*, Michelson, 1985; Asay, Lambert, Christensen, & Beutler, unpublished manuscript; Glass, McGaw, & Smith, 1981; Garfield, 1983b; Rosenthal, 1980; Shapiro & Shapiro, 1982b; Strube & Hartmann, 1982, 1983).

Meta-analysis applies the methods and principles of empirical research to the process of reviewing literature. It begins with a systematic search of the literature to locate studies meeting predefined inclusion criteria. The findings of individual studies are then quantified on some common metric (such as an effect size expressing differences between group means in standard deviation units, or a statistical probability level). Salient features of each study (such as the nature of the client population, type of treatment, and methodological strengths and weaknesses of the study) are recorded systematically, and statistical techniques are then used to arrive at summary statements of the size or statistical significance of the effects cumulated across studies addressing a common question. Further statistical analyses are used to identify quantitative relationships between study features and the results obtained (see Kazdin, Chapter 2 in this volume, for a more complete review of meta-analysis as a method).

Early applications of meta-analysis to psychotherapy outcomes (Smith & Glass, 1977; Smith, Glass, & Miller, 1980) addressed the overall question of the extent of benefit associated with psychotherapy as evidenced in the literature as a whole, compared the outcomes of different treatments, and examined the impact of methodological features of studies upon the reported effectiveness of treatment. For example, Smith et al. (1980) found an average effect size of 0.85 standard deviation units over 475 studies comparing treated and untreated groups. This indicates that, at the end of treatment, the average treated person is better off than 80 percent of the untreated sample.

Subsequent meta-analytic reviews, including both critical replications using the same data base as Smith et al. (1980) (Andrews & Harvey, 1981; Landman & Dawes, 1982) and independent analyses of new samples of studies, have yielded comparable effects (Shapiro & Shapiro, 1982a). A listing of meta-analytic summaries of outcome research is presented in Table 5.1. These studies provide data that are *far more complex* than can be conveyed from this table but provide the reader with a general picture of the results of meta-analysis. They represent summary figures on thousands of patients and hundreds of therapists from across the Western world. They represent data from mildly disturbed persons with specific limited symptoms as well as severely impaired patients whose disorders are both

personally intolerable and socially dysfunctional. The data average changes in these patients across diverse and comprehensive measures of improvement that include a variety of perspectives of importance to patients, patients' families, and society in general.

As can be seen from Table 5.1, the average effect associated with psychological treatment approaches one standard deviation unit. For the sake of comprehensiveness and to display general trends across techniques, meta-analyses of behavioral and cognitive therapies are included there. By the standards developed by Cohen (1977) for the quantitative evaluation of empirical relations in behavioral science, the effects shown are large. The results of meta-analysis suggest that the assignment to treatment versus control conditions accounts for some 10 percent of the variation in outcome among individuals assessed in a typical study. Smith et al. (1980) illustrated the clinical meaning of this effect size by contrasting effect sizes derived from therapy outcome studies to those achieved in other situations. For example, in elementary schools the effects of nine months of instruction in reading is about 0.67 standard deviation units. The increment in mathematics achievement resulting from the use of computer-based instruction is 0.40 standard deviation units.

The effect sizes produced in psychotherapy can also be compared to those that are derived from the use of psychoactive medication. For example, Andrews found that treatments of agoraphobics involving graded exposure produced a median effect size of 1.30 while antidepressant medication produced an average effect size of 1.10 (Quality Assurance Project, 1983). With depression the effect sizes produced for antidepressants ranged from 0.81 to 0.40 depending upon the type of antidepressant and patient population. Thus, the effect sizes produced through the application of psychotherapies are typically as large as or larger than those produced by a variety of methods typically employed during medical and educational interventions.

While the aforementioned data provide one way of examining the effects of therapy and the strength of psychosocial treatments on symptoms and adjustments, effect sizes are an abstraction. There is a need to move from the abstraction of an effect size back to the clinical significance of changes summa-

TABLE 5.1   Meta-analytic Reviews that Bear on the Question of the General
Effects of Therapy

	Patient Diagnosis	Number of Studies	Effect Size
Smith, Glass, & Miller (1980)	Mixed	475	0.85
Andrews & Harvey (1981)	Neurotic	81	0.72
Landman & Dawes (1982)	Mixed	42	0.90
Prioleau, Murdock, & Brody (1983)	Mixed	32	0.42[a]
Shapiro & Shapiro (1982a)	Mixed	143	1.03
Nicholson & Berman (1983)	Neurotic	47[b]	0.70
Blanchard et al. (1980)	Headache	35	% improvement[c]
Quality Assurance Project (1982)	Agoraphobia	25	1.20[d]
Quality Assurance Project (1983)	Depression	200	0.65
Steinbrueck, Maxwell, & Howard (1983)	Depression	56	1.22
Dush, Hirt, & Schroeder (1983)	Anxiety/ Depression	69	0.74
Miller & Berman (1983)	Depression/ Anxiety	38	0.83
Wampler (1982)	Marital communication	20	0.43
Asay, Lambert, Christensen, & Beutler (unpublished)	Mixed mental health	9[e]	0.82

[a] Psychotherapy vs. placebo.
[b] Number of comparisons.
[c] Percentage improved 40–80% in psychological treatments and 20–40% in placebo controls.
[d] Based on pre–post gains rather than control group.
[e] Number of mental health centers studied.

rized in the effect size statistic. Rosenthal (1983) recognized the need for making effect sizes more intuitively appealing and suggested that an effect size could be re-expressed as a comparison of the percent of cases considered improved versus the percent of cases considered unimproved. The expression of the 10 percent figure mentioned by Smith et al. (1980) and noted above, when transformed into percentage of persons improved, can be illustrated in the following table (Table 5.2), adapted from Rosenthal (1983). This shows that the proportion of variance accounted for is equivalent to increasing the success rate from 34 percent to 66 percent.

Another method of converting effect size data into more clinically meaningful statistics was reported by Asay et al. (unpublished) in their study of community mental health center clients. In this study the average effect size for the 2405 clients (seen at nine different locations and exposed to a wide variety of treatments) was 0.92. When one sets a cutoff score of 0.50 standard deviation units as the defining point for considering people improved, then 66 percent of the cases would be considered improved, 26 percent unchanged, and 8 percent worse. Thus, the effect size can be used to estimate improvement rates.

It is important to reiterate that the changes occurring in patients as a result of therapy are not trivial nor just cold statistics but rather substantial. A considerable number of people who might be classified as "cases" before treatment would be considered sufficiently enough improved that they would no longer be so classified following treatment. Although the exact proportion who are improved is subject to considerable interpretation (Jacobson, Follette, & Revenstorf, 1984a), these kinds of change are present whether the goals of treatment are narrowly

TABLE 5.2 The Binomial Effect Size Display for a Correlation between Assignment to Treatment and Therapeutic Outcome of 0.32.[a]

| | Treatment Outcome | | |
Condition	Percent Improved	Percent Not Improved	Sum
Treatment	66	34	100
Control	34	66	100
Sum	100	100	200

[a]That is, when 10% of the variance is accounted for.
Source: Adapted from Rosenthal (1983).

defined and specific (e.g., symptoms of anxiety, depressed affect, sleep disturbance, grade point average) or are more global in nature (social adjustment, work adjustment, marital adjustment, etc.; Shapiro & Shapiro, 1983).

Research on psychotherapy outcome suggests that patients with a variety of problems are helped by many methods that have been put to the empirical test. The results of psychotherapy outcome research by no means suggest, however, that every participant gains from treatment to a clinically meaningful extent; results are also compatible with the suggestion, discussed elsewhere in this chapter, that some clients may deteriorate during therapy.

The use of meta-analysis in psychotherapy outcome research has provoked controversy, despite its claims to objectivity. It is unfortunate that critics of the method sometimes confuse the procedures used with particular meta-analytic reviews. This error has led them to reject not only specific reviews but the method itself. Another objection to meta-analysis has to do with the inclusion of studies of varying quality within a single analysis that disregards the fact that some of these studies are seriously deficient methodologically. Detailed consideration of such issues is beyond our present scope; but Kazdin (Chapter 2, this volume) provides a more complete analysis of these issues.

We may note, however, that the inclusion of studies of varying quality permits the meta-analyst to study systematically the impact of methodological features upon the results obtained. For example, the apparent effects of psychotherapies are indeed inflated when highly reactive outcome measures are

used (i.e., measures that are susceptible to distortion by participants responding in accordance with demands or expectations that they record treatment benefits). On the other hand, available evidence suggests that psychotherapy outcome studies whose designs are marred by noncomparability between treated and control groups tend to yield weaker, rather then stronger, effects of treatment (Shapiro, 1985). In sum, the overall finding that psychological treatments are in general effective cannot be "explained away" by reference to methodological weaknesses in the data reviewed or in the reviewing method. A large number of controlled studies reveal a positive therapeutic effect when compared with no treatment; and very few reviewers disagree with this basic overall observation. Much of this chapter, and much of the rest of this book, is therefore devoted to analyzing other specific questions that take us beyond the issue of whether an average positive change occurs in treated cases. (see Parloff, London, & Wolfe, 1986, for a similar viewpoint).

Positive Change in Untreated Cases
If treatments for psychological disorders are to be considered effective, then they should produce improvements in patients that exceed those improvements made in the absence of formal treatment. To what extent do rates of success in psychological treatments capitalize on the effects of extratherapeutic events or homeostatic mechanisms? Are there reliable "baseline" figures that represent improvement in neurotic patients who go untreated? It was these kinds of questions concerning spontaneous remission raised by Eysenck (1952) more than three decades ago that touched off the early controversy over the value of psychotherapy. He attempted to show that two-thirds of the people with a neurotic disorder improve over a two-year period whether they receive psychotherapy or not.

Unfortunately, most early studies of psychotherapy did not use a research design that randomly assigned clients to either a therapy or a no-treatment control group. This research problem made it difficult to make reasonable comparisons between treated and untreated patients. Subsequent reviews of the same literature and additional studies indicated that the actual rates of improvement in the absence of formal therapy were much lower than Eysenck's original estimate; however, improved research designs and analytical methods have made reliance on spontaneous remission estimates unneccesary. The curious reader may wish to see our analysis of the data on improvement in untreated cases (Bergin, 1971; Bergin & Lambert, 1978; Lambert, 1976), which suggests that rather than two-thirds, the average spontaneous improvement rate is close to 40 percent. This figure, of course, obscures a wide variation in spontaneous change rates that seem to vary as a function of diagnosis, type of outcome measure, and so on. In any case, there does not presently exist a truly reliable single spontaneous remission figure or set of figures. Our earlier tabulations are still available in the previous editions of this chapter, but there has been little to add to them that changes the overall picture or the ambiguity involved in trying to establish a baseline figure.

Some new data relevant to this matter have been published on improvement rates in treated groups over time that show a rate of change that is above and beyond any spontaneous remission estimates that have been previously hypothesized. Howard, Kopta, Krause, and Orlinsky (1986) reported a meta-analysis on 2431 patients from published research covering a 30-year period. Their analysis showed a stable pattern across studies reflecting the relationship of amount of therapy and improvement. An illustration of their results displaying the dose-response relationship is reproduced in Figure 5.1.

Their analysis of these data indicates that by the eighth session approximately 50 percent of patients are measureably improved and that 75 percent of patients have shown measurable improvement by the end of six months of once-weekly psychotherapy (26 sessions), thus indicating a substantial therapeutic effect and one that occurs in a relatively short period of time. These authors also estimate that 15 percent of patients will show measurable improvement before attending their first session, presumably a result of the relief that follows the scheduling of therapy. Conceivably, these rapid changers are the least disturbed patients.

Do the Effects of Therapies Exceed Those Resulting from Placebo Controls?

It has been adequately demonstrated that a variety of psychotherapies have effects that are greater than those of spontaneous remission and of a variety of no-treatment controls. This is no small achievement,

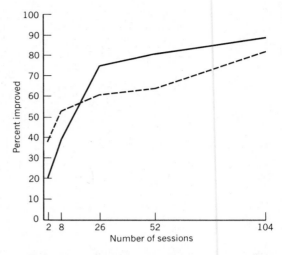

Figure 5.1 Relation of number of sessions of psychotherapy and percent of patients improved: objective ratings at termination (solid line); subjective ratings during therapy (broken line). (Reproduced with permission from H. I. Howard, S. M. Kopta, M.S. Krause, & D. E. Orlinsky, 1986. The dose-effect relationship in psychotherapy. *American Psychologist*)

but public and academic pressure do not allow for basking in this benign condition, for psychotherapy's effect in relation to placebo controls remains controversial.

The idea of placebo controls was borrowed from medicine, where the effects of an active chemical agent were contrasted with a pharmacologically inert substance. This contrast makes good sense in medicine, allowing attributions of success to pharmacological agents rather than psychological agents. It makes less sense, however, when extended to psychotherapy research where the effects of treatments and placebos depend upon psychological mechanisms.

In psychological treatments, the placebo construct has taken on a variety of meanings. For example, Rosenthal and Frank (1956) defined a placebo as therapeutically inert from the standpoint of the *theory* of the therapy studied. As Critelli and Neumann (1984) have pointed out, a problem with this definition is that "virtually every currently established psychotherapy would be considered inert, and therefore a placebo, from the viewpoint of other established theories of cure" (p. 33), making this definition of placebo highly questionable.

In addition, placebos have also been labeled as "nonspecific" factors. This conceptualization, however, raises serious questions about the definition of "nonspecific." For example, once a "nonspecific" is labeled does it then fall outside the domain of a placebo effect?

We favor the term "common factors" as the most useful substitute for the term "placebo" in studies of the psychosocial therapies. Common factors are those dimensions of the treatment setting (therapist, therapy, client) that are not specific to a particular technique. Those factors that are common to most therapies (such as expectation for improvement, persuasion, warmth and attention, understanding, encouragement, etc.) should not be viewed as theoretically *inert* nor as *trivial*; indeed they are central to psychological treatments and play an active role in patient improvement (cf. Critelli & Neumann, 1984; Paul, in press; Wilkins, 1984; Kazdin, Chapter 2, this volume, for a further discussion of this issue).

Common factors also play a central role in evaluating psychotherapies. The most effective therapies should be recommended for patients whether their effects are the result of common factors or unique techniques. Psychotherapy research is often designed to find effects that are incremental to common factors. And in interpreting this research, it is important to keep in mind that failure to find incremental effects (effects beyond those attributable to common factors) for a specific therapy is not a finding that argues against the efficacy of psychotherapy. It is rather a finding that suggests that the technique's additive effectiveness beyond the effects of common factors has not been demonstrated. *This is a critical point because research that is aimed at discovering the incremental effects of therapy has been misinterpreted as suggesting that therapies are ineffective* (e.g., Prioleau, Murdock, & Brody, 1983; Shepherd, 1984).

The most controversial article on this subject was published by Prioleau et al. (1983), who reanalyzed data from Smith et al. (1980). This analysis suggested that formal psychotherapy was not more effective than "placebo therapies" designed to emphasize attention and support; but the validity of the conclusions of this review were seriously questioned in the majority of commentaries accompanying the article. It did not appear to be a serious study of "placebo" effects but rather a misinterpretation of a finding already reported in the literature (Bloch & Lambert, 1985).

As expected, patients in so-called placebo control groups typically show greater improvement than patients who are assigned to a wait-list or no-treatment control group. For example, Smith et al. (1980) estimated the size of effect for so-called placebo therapies to be 0.56 (p. 90). In the partial reanalysis of subsets of the Smith et al. data, Andrews and Harvey (1981) and Landman and Dawes (1982) found similar effect sizes (0.55 and 0.58 respectively). This research clearly shows that a variety of methods used as placebo treatments that emphasize the usual common factors (relaxation, discussion, attention, warmth, etc.) yield substantial effect sizes, but smaller ones than formal psychotherapy.

The results of several other meta-analytic reviews suggest similar findings. The Quality Assurance Project (1983) suggested that placebo effects with depressed patients (measured from pretest to posttest rather than in relation to no-treatment controls) were 1.07 (p. 135) in contrast to the psychotherapies, which achieved an effect size of 1.72. The estimate of improvement in headaches by Blanchard et al. (1980), who studied the effects of relaxation, biofeedback, and autogenic training, showed the average improvement to be 35.3 percent for psychological placebos and 34.8 percent for medication placebos, in contrast to an average improvement rate of 60 percent for psychological treatments. Miller and Berman (1983) in their study of cognitive and behavior therapies found only a small difference (effect size, E.S. = 0.12) between wait-list controls and placebo controls with the results favoring the placebo treatment.

Summary

Psychotherapy outcome research shows that some control patients improve with the passage of time, that a variety of "placebo" control procedures produce gains that exceed those in no-treatment controls, and that psychotherapies produce gains that exceed those obtained through the use of "placebo" controls. Psychotherapists are more than placebologists. As noted earlier, however, an important aspect of all therapies is the hope they engender in patients with low morale and dysfunctional symptoms. That many psychological methods offer common factors such as attention, respect, reassurance, support, modeling, and encouragement of risk taking and mastery efforts is not to suggest that the gains made during treatment are superficial and temporary. Indeed there is considerable evidence that the effects of even brief intervention can be enduring—a point we consider next.

Are Patients Who Improve in Therapy Able to Maintain Their Gains?

Several issues are important when one considers the long-term effects of therapies. While research has focused primarily upon the immediate post-treatment status of patients who have participated in therapy, there is considerable interest in the long-term effects of treatment. What kinds of changes persist? At what level? What factors influence the likelihood of maintenance and relapse? How can we maximize the likelihood that the resolution of current and past problems will also increase the patient's ability to cope with future events?

Although there is no reason to believe that a single course of psychotherapy should inoculate a person forever from psychological disturbance and the development of symptoms, many patients who undergo therapy achieve healthy adjustment for long periods of time. This is true despite the fact that they have had a long history of recurrent problems. At the same time there is clear evidence that a portion of patients who are improved do relapse and continue to seek help from a variety of mental health providers including their former therapist. In fact, several problems such as addictions, alcohol abuse, smoking, obesity, and depression are so likely to recur that they are not considered properly studied without data collection one year after treatment.

Nicholson and Berman (1983) used meta-analytic techniques to answer the question: Is follow-up necessary in evaluating psychotherapy? In their review of research in this area they were primarily concerned with whether follow-up evaluations provided different evidence and conclusions than posttreatment evaluations. The review excluded psychotics, organic disorders, antisocial personality disorders, and addictive problems such as obesity, smoking, and alcoholism. They included 67 studies (21 percent of which evaluated a verbal therapy) of a broad range of neurotic disorders that were self-referred rather than recruited and that involved both post-

testing and follow-up data. The analysis was approached in several ways: (1) Does posttreatment status correlate with follow-up status? (2) Were treatment differences apparent at the posttesting still apparent at follow-up? (3) Are any changes at follow-up testing due to deterioration or improvements in treated groups?

The results of this meta-analytic review are complicated by the divergence in the studies that were examined; but, in general, the findings suggest that treatment gains are maintained. Posttherapy status correlated with follow-up status; differences between treatments apparent at the end of therapy were virtually the same at follow-up. This finding held up whether the comparison was with no-treatment controls or another therapy. And the level of outcome was typically unchanged during the follow-up period. These findings held across a variety of treatment methods (mostly behavioral), patient populations, and sources for assessing outcome. The mean length of follow-up assessment was over eight months, but varied from one month to several years. The correlation between posttreatment and follow-up results were unrelated to the length of follow-up. The authors conclude:

> Past reviews have revealed that psychotherapy produces considerable initial improvement, and our findings indicate that for a broad range of disorders this improvement stands the test of time. Thus, our evidence should be heartening both to practitioners, who are increasingly being asked to defend the efficacy of treatment, and to researchers, who have long struggled with the costs of follow-up designs. (Nicholson & Berman, 1983; p. 275)

The review of Nicholson and Berman (1983) is especially important because it stands in marked contrast to past reviews both in its conclusions and in its methodological sophistication. For example, Smith et al. (1980) as well as Shapiro and Shapiro (1982a), using meta-analysis, and Goldstein, Lopez, & Greenleaf (1979), using traditional reviewing methods, all found that differences between treated groups and controls were smaller at follow-up than at the end of therapy. Their posttreatment and follow-up results, however, were not based on the same patients or studies. In contrast, Landman and

Dawes (1982), who, with a subset of Smith et al.'s data, examined only studies that had both posttreatment and follow-up assessment, reported results consistent with Nicholson and Berman (1983). Andrews and Harvey (1981) also found improvement to be stable over time. They concluded that improvement following treatment is stable for many months and then slowly declines at a rate of 0.2 effect size units per annum.

These reviews looked at a broad spectrum of problems and at a full range of therapies (especially behavior therapy). But as they point out, rather than a moratorium on follow-up studies, greater selection in their use is recommended. For example, depressions are known for their tendency to both remit and relapse following treatment. Continuing use of follow-up studies of depression outcome is recommended and, indeed, the development of therapies that substantially reduce relapse rates in depression would be a significant breakthrough.

Some research has been done on the strategies that are most likely to result in maintenance of change (Goldstein & Kanfer, 1979; Karoly & Steffen, 1980). Imber, Pilkonis, Harway, Klein, and Rubinsky (1982) have suggested some possibilities for future research. They suggest that the likelihood of maintenance will be increased if patients see change and maintenance as a result of their own efforts and if they are helped to anticipate future life crises and their reactions to them.

Borrowing methods from behavioral, cognitive, and dynamic therapies such as "booster sessions" and "tapering off," Imber et al. propose a four-session follow-up format spread out over a 16-week period that focuses on future stresses, attributional style, and patient strengths. As yet, no definitive research has been done on this procedure, but it appears to encompass a number of important dimensions identified through past research as important in maintenance.

A major factor in maintaining treatment gains seems to be the degree to which patients (as well as therapists) recognize that changes are partially the result of effective patient effort. For example, in a series of studies reported by the Johns Hopkins Psychotherapy Research Unit, patients who attributed their improvement to medication (actually a placebo) were *not* able to maintain improvement, while those who understood improvement to be a result of their own efforts did maintain their gain

(Frank, 1976; Liberman, 1978). This is also consistent with maintenance of change in psychosomatic problems such as headache. Rather than long-term improvements resulting from a single course of treatment with biofeedback, those who are able to maintain treatment gains continue to use relaxation techniques (Lambert, 1982) or cognitive coping strategies (Holdroyd & Andarasik, 1982) or exposure (Mathews, Teasdale, & Munby, 1977) after therapy has been terminated. There may be no "magic pill" or simple insight that brings about ultimate recovery—recovery is more likely to result from continued efforts on the part of the patient.

While we have reason to be optimistic about the lasting effects of therapy for many people, more research needs to be done on this topic. And clinicians would do well to continue to focus specific attention on helping clients maintain the gains that they achieve while in treatment.

COMPARISONS AND CAUSATIVE FACTORS IN TREATMENT OUTCOMES: THE ROLE OF COMMON FACTORS AND SPECIFIC THERAPY INTERVENTIONS

In the following section we review research that further clarifies the factors associated with improvement during psychotherapy. This research, to a large extent, employs research designs that are aimed at discovering the effects of specific therapeutic factors by contrasting an established treatment with a new treatment, an effective treatment with one or more of its component factors, or an effective treatment with a different effective treatment on a group of patients with special characteristics.

First, we explore evidence that deals with the differential effectiveness of different schools of therapy. Afterwards we return to the possibility that factors common across therapies may account for many of the therapeutic gains that are apparent in treatment groups.

Does the "Dodo Bird Verdict" Still Hold?
Historically, there has been a clear difference of approach and philosophy between "schools" of therapy associated with psychodynamic and humanistic theories, on the one hand (sometimes collectively labeled "verbal" therapies), and with behavioral

and cognitive theories and associated experimental-psychological research, on the other. This divergence is reflected in the structure of training programs producing psychotherapists, and in the types of materials emphasized in the training of these therapists (clinical case studies, theoretical writings, personal experience in the client role vs. scientific principles, experimental data, treatment technology).

Of course, it cannot be assumed that such global and philosophical divisions between treatment approaches are faithfully or functionally represented in the actual procedures implemented in the delivery of their respective therapies. There is a growing body of evidence, however, that the use of "manuals" to specify treatment techniques characteristic of the different schools results in objectively discriminable therapist behaviors (Luborsky & DeRubeis, 1984). How this relates to treatment in everyday routine clinical practice is an open question, however.

Several past reviews have analyzed studies comparing the psychotherapies (e.g., Bergin & Lambert, 1978; Bergin & Suinn, 1975; Beutler, 1979; Goldstein & Stein, 1976; Kellner, 1975; Lambert & Bergin, 1973; Meltzoff & Kornreich, 1970; Rachman & Wilson, 1980). The conclusion of most, but not all, of these reviews is similar to that drawn by Luborsky, Singer, and Luborsky (1975), who suggested a verdict similar to that of the Dodo bird in *Alice in Wonderland*: "Everyone has won and all must have prizes."

These reviews used traditional scholarly methods of reaching conclusions without reference to the newer meta-analytic procedures. Meta-analytic methods have now been extensively applied to large groups of comparative studies, however, resulting in largely the same conclusion. For example, Smith et al. (1980) concluded that differences between therapies were slight or nonexistent.

This finding was reached, however, only after the relatively large effect sizes reported for the behavior therapies were reduced because they were based upon dependent measures that were judged to be reactive to experimental demand characteristics. This adjustment has both fair and unfair aspects, a dilemma to which we shall return shortly.

Data from several additional recent meta-analytical reviews also bear on this issue: Shapiro and Shapiro (1982a), Nicholson and Berman (1983),

Dush, Hirt, and Schroeder (1983), Miller and Berman (1983), Quality Assurance Project (1983). These meta-analytic data tend to yield a small but consistent advantage for cognitive and behavioral methods over traditional verbal and relationship-oriented therapies. The strength of this conclusion, however, is limited by the shortcomings of data aggregation techniques and the nature of past research. There are reasons, therefore, to believe in both the theory of equal effects of therapies and the notion of superior effects of cognitive and behavior therapies. We will attempt to explain this as we further evaluate meta-analyses and specific exemplary studies.

For instance, a problem in most of the comparisons in many meta-analytic reviews is that they are cross-study comparisons in which behavior therapy in one study is compared with verbal therapy from another study. In this situation many variables besides treatment modality also differ across studies. Comparisons like this, of which there are many in the Smith et al. report, cannot be as conclusive as comparisons in which the compared treatments are offered *within* a given study. These studies are much more likely to hold numerous variables constant while comparing one type of therapy with another.

To examine this issue more carefully, let us consider Shapiro and Shapiro's (1982b) extensive meta-analysis, which focused exculsively upon studies comparing two or more active treatments with control conditions. In consequence, their data contained more replicated comparisons between treatment methods than found in the Smith et al. (1980) review and permitted more definitive statements concerning the comparative efficacy of treatments. Based on an examination of 143 studies, Shapiro and Shapiro (1982b) found that cognitive and various behavioral treatments yielded more favorable outcomes (1.00 and 1.06 E.S., respectively) than the other treatments with which they were compared, while dynamic and humanistic therapies tended to yield inferior outcomes (E.S. 0.40).

As in the Smith et al. study, however, these authors also attributed the larger effect sizes to strong biases in the behavioral and cognitive literature toward analogue studies, mild cases, and highly reactive criteria. They stated that the treatments and cases studied were unrepresentative of clinical practice but very representative of the simple experiments on these techniques that are frequently conducted in university settings. These criticisms have validity but they can be overdone in a way that does not do justice to cognitive and behavioral interventions. When verbal therapies were applied to presumably clinical populations, they did not fare as well as cognitive and behavioral methods that had large effect sizes across different symptoms and levels of severity.

Another issue of interest to practitioners and researchers is the relative effectiveness of cognitive versus behavioral methods. The Shapiro and Shapiro report showed a significantly larger effect size for cognitive therapy over systematic desensitization. This conclusion, however, has been challenged by yet another meta-analysis. Miller and Berman (1983) compared cognitive behavior therapy with various therapies, mainly behavioral. The procedures followed were quite similar to those of Smith et al. (1980) except that the *study* rather than the individual measure of effect was used as the unit of analysis, and cognitive behavior therapies that differed in their emphasis upon behavioral techniques were accorded their own effect sizes within an analysis contrasting such treatments.

In comparisons with untreated groups, cognitive behavior therapies secured a mean effect size of 0.83 posttreatment (38 studies) and 0.63 at follow-up (18 studies). Comparisons with other therapies yielded a differential effect size of 0.21 at the end of treatment (36 studies) and 0.24 at follow-up (26 studies). Comparison with desensitization, the most frequent alternate treatment, yielded a nonsignificant effect size difference of 0.21 posttreatment (13 studies) and 0.23 at follow-up (9 studies).

A subsequent analysis (Berman, Miller, & Massman, 1985) using a larger sample of studies showed no difference between cognitive and desensitization therapies (E.S. difference 0.06). It also revealed that the larger effect sizes for cognitive therapy occurred in studies conducted by investigators having an allegiance to that method. Finally, the combination of desensitization with a cognitive method did not increase effects beyond that obtainable by either treatment alone. These results suggest that there may be important common factors in these two modes of treatment that account for the equal outcomes, and that the common factor problem is not limited to comparisons with verbal expressive therapies.

A similar Dodo bird verdict was reported by Dush et al. (1983) in their review of 69 studies of a form of cognitive therapy involving self-statement modification. The "typical" treatment comprised some five sessions over four weeks and included at least three treatment features alongside self-statement modification, of which cognitive restructuring (33 studies) and modeling (32 studies) were the most widespread. The findings of this meta-analysis included a mean effect size for self-statement modification of 0.74 over 93 comparisons with untreated groups, and 0.52 over 54 comparisons with placebo groups. Other treatments obtained a mean effect size of 0.49 in comparison with untreated groups, and 0.44 in comparison with placebo groups.

Comparisons between self-statement modification and other treatments yielded no clear differences. Although systematic desensitization came off almost half a standard deviation worse than self-statement modification when contrasted with no-treatment controls, this difference vanished from comparisons that included placebo controls. Studies involving relaxation training yielded weak results for both relaxation and self-statement modification. Contrasts with "other" cognitive therapies and "other" behavioral therapies (admittedly a pair of vague terms including diverse methods) yielded essentially similar effects for self-statement modification and the alternate, active treatment.

The foregoing meta-analyses reveal a mixed picture. There is a strong trend toward no differences between techniques in amount of change produced, which is counterbalanced by indications that, under some circumstances, cognitive and behavioral methods are superior even though they do not differ in efficacy among themselves. An examination of selected exemplary studies allows us to further explore this matter. Research carried out with the intent of contrasting two or more bona fide treatments shows surprisingly small differences between the outcomes for patients who undergo a treatment that is fully intended to be therapeutic. Several studies illustrate this point.

Illustrative Comparative Studies
Among the most substantial studies comparing verbal and behavioral methods, the work of Sloane, Staples, Cristol, Yorkston, and Whipple (1975) established a standard of methodological sophistica-

tion that few subsequent studies have surpassed. Ninety predominantly neurotic outpatients were assigned at random to short-term analytically oriented psychotherapy, behavior therapy, or a minimal-treatment wait-list group. The therapists were experienced and respected exponents of their respective approaches, who assented to a list of stipulated definitions of the techniques to be used. An independent assessment of therapist activities was based upon a single recorded session from each case. Four months after commencing treatment, all three groups had improved significantly on target symptoms, but the treated groups had improved significantly more than the wait-list group. There were no differences between behavior therapy and psychotherapy on any of the target symptoms as rated by an independent assessor, kept as blind as possible to the assignment of patients to treatments. Ratings of global improvement and of social functioning based upon a structured interview slightly favored the behavior therapy group—within-group differences were significant pre- to posttesting but between-group differences were not significant. There was some suggestion that behavior therapy was helpful with a broader range of patients. The eight-month follow-up data, albeit compromised by further treatment received by patients in all three groups, showed no overall differences among the groups on any measure. Patients seemed to maintain treatment gains over time, while wait-list (minimal treatment) patients eventually reached the improvement levels attained by the patients who had undergone either of the active therapies.

This study has several merits, including the use of experienced therapists, the recruitment of a large number of well-motivated clinic patients, random allocation to treatment or control groups, low attrition, and the inclusion of a wait-list control group. A number of criticisms of this study have been raised (Bergin & Lambert, 1978; Rachman & Wilson, 1980) and responded to (Sloane & Staples, 1984); but despite these problems it represents one of the best this area has to offer. Wolpe (1975) referred to it as "unmatched—in the history of psychotherapy" (p. xix). It provides evidence for the notion that experts using their favorite method, whether behavioral or psychodynamic, can produce substantial therapeutic change.

Of perhaps even more contemporary interest is a recently reported study that compared a form of behavior therapy to a dynamic-supportive therapy with phobics. Based on past research one might have thought such a comparison would show clear superiority for behavioral techniques with this problem.

Klein, Zitrin, Woerner, and Ross (1983) compared three treatment groups of phobics. The first group received behavior therapy, including relaxation training and imaginal desensitization, in vivo homework assignments, and assertiveness training, in a supportive therapeutic context, together with chemotherapy (imipramine); the second group received the same behavior therapy package with placebo medication; and the third group received supportive psychotherapy (a dynamically oriented, nondirective method in which the patient took the initiative in all discussions, with the therapist remaining nonjudgmental and empathic, encouraging the patient to ventilate feelings and discuss problems, anxieties, and interpersonal relationships, confrontation of feared situations only encouraged after the patient proposed it), together with imipramine. All therapists were trained and experienced in both methods and treated patients in both modalities. Assessment methods included interviews by a treatment-blind independent evaluator.

Essentially, the results showed no difference in outcomes between the groups treated with behavioral and dynamic therapies (both groups also receiving imipramine). For the simple phobic subgroup of patients, for whom imipramine was ineffective, a more powerful comparison of the psychotherapies was made possible by combining the two behavior therapy groups (one having received imipramine, the other placebo). There was still no difference between psychotherapy and behavior therapy except on the (non-blind) therapist ratings of improvement, a measure that may be subject to bias in view of the common belief that behavior therapy is superior for simple phobias.

Klein et al. (1983) offer a thoughtful commentary upon possible explanations of their findings. They note that the behavior therapy undoubtedly contained specific ingredients of structured directiveness, which, the results suggest, may not be of central importance to patient change. They note also that the degree of improvement for behavior therapy patients was respectable, with the apparently unexpected element in the findings being the comparable efficacy of supportive therapy. Perhaps, because they also practiced behavior therapy, therapists were more sympathetic to patients' self-initiated changes during supportive therapy than would be the traditional dynamic therapist. And the authors speculate whether some supposedly insightful interpretations offered in traditional dynamic therapy but absent in their supportive treatment could be deleterious. The authors reject the suggestion that the concurrent use of imipramine prevented a treatment difference on account of ceiling effects by noting that there was no drug effect for simple phobics, with whom the superiority of behavior therapy was most strongly expected, and that even mixed phobics and agoraphobics given imipramine had room for further improvement than was shown.

Among other points discussed by Klein et al. (1983), the most relevant to our discussion is the possibility that "there is nothing to explain," that is, that the supposed superiority of behavior therapy of this kind (the principal ingredient of which was systematic desensitization) has not, after all, been established in clinical populations comparable to theirs. This is congruent with its standing in the meta-analysis by Shapiro and Shapiro (1982a), where desensitization was bettered by multimodal behavioral therapies and was generally equivalent in efficacy to other behavioral treatments.

In the Sheffield Psychotherapy Project (Shapiro & Firth, in press), a cognitive/behavioral treatment (termed "Prescriptive" therapy) including relaxation and anxiety management, rational restructuring, and job-related social and problem-solving skills training was compared with a relationship-oriented treatment ("Exploratory" therapy) based on Hobson's (1985; Goldberg et al. 1984; Maguire et al. 1984) Conversational Model. Clients were professional and managerial workers who had neurotic depression or anxiety. This study used a crossover design in which each client-therapist pair spent eight consecutive weekly sessions working in one mode of treatment, followed by a further eight sessions in the other mode of treatment. Reasons for selecting this design included its powerful control of extraneous client and therapist variables and the possibilities it presents for evaluating the effects of sequential application of theoretically heterogeneous treatments, which has become a pressing research requirement with the advent and discussion of eclectic methods and theoretical integration among therapeutic approaches (Beutler, 1983; Goldfried, 1982; Wachtel, 1977).

The results suggested an advantage of Prescriptive over Exploratory therapy on a standardized psychiatric interview, the Present State Examination (PSE), the Beck Depression Inventory, and the Symptom Checklist 90. The difference between treatments was modest, however, and statistically significant in only 7 of 30 comparisons. In a context of substantial improvement during both treatments, PSE improvement during Exploratory therapy was 80 percent of that during Prescriptive therapy with an effect size difference between treatments of no more than 0.4, suggesting slight superiority of questionable clinical import for this cognitive/behavioral treatment.

In yet another comparative outcome study, Pilkonis, Imber, Lewis, and Rubinsky (1984) compared the effects of mode of treatment rather than different treatment orientations on patients who participated in individual, group, or conjoint marital psychotherapy. Sixty-four outpatients were assigned to one of these treatment modalities offered by experienced private clinicians for an average of 27 sessions. This study is probably the first simultaneous comparison of these commonly used treatment modalities. The therapists were nine (three for each modality) M.D. or Ph.D. practitioners with at least seven years of postdoctoral experience who were either dynamic or humanistic in orientation. The patients were diagnosed as neurotic or personality disordered, willing to participate in conjoint therapy if required, and living with another adult who would agree to act as an informant in the study.

The outcome of this study at termination and follow-up was based on a variety of measures tapping global and symptomatic improvement as well as dimensions that were thought to be most responsive to a particular treatment modality. Thus, a scale measuring self-awareness/self-exploration (thought to be a primary target of individual therapy), scales tapping interpersonal anxiety and control in interpersonal relations (a target of group therapy), and a scale aimed at tapping the family climate and ability to solve problems (thought to be sensitive to conjoint therapy) were given to all patients in this study.

Data regarding outcome were collected from the patient, a significant other, and the therapist.

The results of this study show little unique effect of treatment modality on patient outcome. Despite the fact that patients improved on 14 of 15 measures during the treatment period, and maintained their gains during the eight-month follow-up, effects could not be attributed to modality. There were clear indications, however, that outcome was affected by patient social class, degree of disturbance, and individual differences between the therapists.

Summary

The meta-analytic summary data and the relatively high-quality individual studies reviewed here, in sum, tend toward the conclusion that psychosocial therapies are relatively equal in efficacy. In many respects this is a fair statement.

Cognitive and behavior therapists have a point, however, in claiming that reviewers (e.g., Smith et al., 1980) have unfairly subtracted a substantial portion of their observed effects by adjusting the outcomes that are based on so-called reactive measures, that is, outcome measures that are very sensitive to change or are very similar to in-therapy processes and thus lack independence as outcome estimates. "Reactive" measures are, however, often essential in measuring behavior therapy outcomes. If the therapeutic target is a specific behavior, such as a phobia, then how else should change be measured than in terms of avoidance responses? A global adjustment rating might make outcome easier to compare with the effects of dynamic therapy, but would it be a fair estimate of the behavioral treatment? Meta-analyses summing across diverse measures like this are misleading because they average rather different effects and make them look more similar than they are. The specific benefits of behavioral methods can thus be made to look more obscure than is the case.

If reviewers granted the behavioral or cognitive approaches superiority in terms of their "reactive" measures, psychodynamic therapists could, however, justifiably counter with the argument that the outcome of verbal therapies would look much better if self-exploration-oriented therapists matched the energy, skill, criterion inventiveness, and commitment to comparative outcome research shown by adherents of behavioral and cognitive therapies.

For example, wouldn't their effect sizes be larger if they used change measures that estimated the frequency and quality of insights rather than adjustment test scores or symptom evaluations by assessors? Such a strategy would be comparable to behavioral and cognitive studies that employ an outcome measure very similar to the in-process behavior that is being reinforced. Change is certainly likely to look greater when such process and outcome similarity exists.

Another argument by traditional therapists is that most of the research has been done by behavioral and cognitive therapists, and that this "stacks the deck" in favor of "their" criteria. A related point is that Smith et al. (1980) found a mean effect size of 0.95 when studies were done by persons having an allegiance to the technique being evaluated, whereas E.S. was only 0.66 when the studies were done by unaligned investigators. Since most studies are done by persons aligned with the cognitive and behavioral therapies, their comparative effect sizes may be inflated by such a biasing factor.

Another possible perspective on the equal effects argument is that no differences are found between treatments in many major studies because the samples of cases are dominated by or have large proportions of garden variety outpatient neuroses in which anxiety, low self-esteem, demoralization, depression, and interpersonal difficulties of moderate or mild severity constitute the main problem. This was the case in a number of important comparative studies, including the one by Sloane et al. (1975). Perhaps the common ingredients in the different therapies have their main effects with such nonspecific symptoms and thus the differences that do exist between the therapies cannot be demonstrated with such cases.

The small advantage shown for behavioral and cognitive methods in many reviews might then be attributed to the fact that there are a *few* cases in omnibus samples that have specific sypmtoms that respond better to these specific interventions; but this advantage is then obscured by the larger number of cases that respond to the common therapeutic ingredients helpful to all of the cases being tested.

Certainly, the one area of clearest advantage for the specific therapies has been with specific symptoms that can be targeted by a particular procedure. When criteria are designed to estimate changes in such specified targets, these criteria tend to show substantial improvements. Thus, the literature on sexual dysfunctions, childhood behavior disorders, phobias, compulsive rituals, and a number of other problem areas appears to reveal superior outcomes for these specific therapies (cf. Behavioral and Cognitive Therapy chapters in this *Handbook* by Emmelkamp and by Hollon & Beck). While several meta-analyses do not support this view, their conclusions usually are based on averages summed across divergent cases and criteria, or on modified effect sizes thought to be overly reactive or sensitive to change.

Common Factors and Outcome

Despite the fact that clinicians emphasize the differences between their favorite therapeutic interventions and those of other therapists, the common factors are prominent ingredients in all forms of practice. In addition to warm support, reassurance, suggestion, credibility, therapist attention, expectancy for improvement, and demand for improvement, many therapies can be interpreted as exposing people to their fears or as changing people's expectations for personal effectiveness, therapeutic elements once regarded as unique to behavioral interventions. These and related factors common across therapies seem to make up a significant portion of the effective ingredients of psychotherapy.

Cross and Sheehan (1982), for example, studied common factors (secondary variables) in their analysis of short-term insight-oriented therapy and behavior therapy. They found that behavior therapists believed more in the efficacy of their treatment and perceived their clients to be more positively disposed to them than did insight-oriented therapists. Given the occurrence of such differences, they emphasize the potential error in attributing therapeutic effects solely to the traditional primary variables of treatment technique.

Among the common factors most frequently studied have been those identified by the client-centered school as "necessary and sufficient conditions" for patient personality change: accurate empathy, positive regard, nonpossessive warmth, and congruence or genuineness. Virtually all schools of therapy accept the notion that these or related therapist relationship variables are important for significant progress in psychotherapy and, in fact, fundamental in the formation of a working alliance.

Studies showing both positive and equivocal support for the hypothesized relationship have been reviewed elsewhere (cf. Gurman, 1977; Lambert, DeJulio, & Stein, 1978; Levant & Shlien, 1984; Mitchell, Bozarth, & Krauft, 1977; Parloff, Waskow, & Wolfe, 1978; Patterson, 1984; and Chapters 7 and 8 in this volume). Reviewers are virtually unanimous in their opinion that the therapist-patient relationship is critical; however, they point out that research support for this position is more ambiguous than was once the case. Studies using client-perceived ratings of the relationship factors, rather than objective raters, obtain consistently more positive results, but the larger correlations with outcome are often between client process ratings and client self-reports of outcome, which possibly inflates the correlations.

It is becoming increasingly clear that the attributes of the patient, as well as the therapist, play an important part in creating the quality of the therapeutic relationship and in the outcome of psychotherapy. Strupp (1980a, 1980b, 1980c, 1980d) reported a series of four studies, in each of which two patients were seen by one therapist in time-limited psychotherapy. In each instance, one of the therapist's patients was seen as having a successful outcome while the other was considered to be a treatment failure. These individualized reports were part of a larger study that used extensive outcome measures and an analysis of patient-therapist interactions during the process of therapy. In each instance the therapist was working with college males who were suffering from anxiety, depression, and social withdrawal. Although each therapist was seen as having good interpersonal skills, a different relationship developed with the two patients. In all reports (eight cases with four therapists) the patients who had successful outcomes appeared more willing and able to have a meaningful relationship with the therapist, whereas the patients who did not do well in therapy did not relate well to the therapist and had a tendency to keep the interaction on a more superficial level.

In Strupp's analysis, the contributions of the therapists remained relatively constant throughout therapy and the difference in outcome could be attributed to patient factors such as the nature of the patients' personality makeup, including ego organization, maturity, motivation, and ability to become productively involved in the verbal psychotherapy being offered. He adds:

> . . . given the "average expectable" atmosphere created by a person functioning in the therapeutic role, that is, a person who is basically empathic and benign, the key determinants of a particular therapeutic outcome are traceable to characteristics of the patient that have been described: if the patient is, a person who, by virtue of his past life experience is capable of human relatedness and therefore is amenable to learning, mediated within that context, the outcome, even though the individual may have suffered traumas, reverses, and other vicissitudes, is likely to be positive. . . . If, on the other hand, his early life experiences have been so destructive that human relatedness has failed to acquire a markedly positive valence, and elaborate neurotic and characterological malfunctions have created massive barriers to intimacy (and therefore to "therapeutic learning"), chances are that psychotherapy either results in failure or at best in very modest gains. (Strupp, 1980b, p. 716)

The importance of patient pretherapy interpersonal relations for in-therapy performance and outcome was also supported by Moras and Strupp (1982), although correlations were lower than expected. Similar conclusions were suggested by Luborsky, Bachrach, Graff, Pulver, and Christoph (1979) in their study of transference interpretations in psychoanalysis and psychotherapy. In their view, the experiencing of a helping relationship may be a function of the object relations repertoire that the patient brings to treatment, or of the therapist's ability to impart that experience to the patient, or some combination of the two. In considering the impact of the therapeutic relationship on outcome, these authors hypothesized that the patient's ability to experience a positive along with a negative component of helping relationships may be necessary for the patient to derive benefit from interpretations. Following this line of reasoning, the therapeutic relationship, as defined by both therapist and patient involvement, has a major impact on the acceptance of in-therapy interpretations and on the outcome of therapy itself.

Not only can one find support for the importance of relationship factors in the dynamic therapies, but, as in the Cross and Sheehan (1982) report, even some literature on behavior therapy suggests the importance of these variables. Morris and Suckerman (1974a, 1974b, 1975) and Wolowitz (1975), for example, discussed the place of therapist warmth in behavioral desensitization. This therapist-relationship variable was shown to be necessary for affecting positive change with desensitization. These studies demonstrated that even with a simple phobia and the application of a technical behavioral procedure, a therapist variable (such as warmth) may play a significant role in mediating change. Other research on this topic, however, has been more equivocal. For example, Morris and Magrath (1979) studied the effect of therapist warmth on the contact (in vivo) desensitization treatment of acrophobia without finding a relationship between therapist warmth and outcome. Thus, the findings in this area are not always consistent.

Miller, Taylor, and West (1980) investigated the comparative effectiveness of various behavioral approaches aimed at helping problem drinkers control their alcohol consumption. While the focus of the study was upon the comparative effects of focused versus broad-spectrum behavior therapy, the authors also collected data on the contribution of therapist empathy to patient outcome.

One finding—surprising to the authors and important for our discussion—was the discovery of a strong relationship between empathy and patient outcome obtained from the six- to eight-month follow-up interviews dealing with drinking behavior. Therapist rank on empathy correlated significantly ($r = .82$) with patient outcomes. These results, though as yet unreplicated and possibly inflated by the rank-order correlation, argue for the importance of therapist communicative skills even with behavioral interventions. They were also presented in a context where variations in specific techniques did not prove to have a similar powerful effect on outcome.

Another approach to understanding the contribution of the therapist to effective outcome has involved the use of behavioral or adjective checklists filled out by clients following their therapeutic contacts. Lorr (1965), for example, had 523 psychotherapy patients describe their therapist on 65 different statements. A subsequent factor analysis identified five factors—understanding, accepting, authoritarian (directive), independence-encouraging, and critical-hostile. Scores on these descriptive factors were correlated with improvement ratings, with the result that client ratings of understanding and accepting correlated most highly with client- and therapist-rated improvement.

In a more recent study, Cooley and LaJoy (1980) attempted to replicate the Lorr study. In addition, they studied the relationship between therapist ratings of themselves and outcome, as well as the relationship of discrepancies between patient and therapist, to outcome ratings. The patients were 56 adult community mental health outpatients who had been treated by one of eight therapists at the clinic.

As with the Lorr study, client ratings of therapist understanding and acceptance correlated most highly with client-rated outcome. On the other hand, when therapist ratings of therapist attributes were compared to therapist-rated patient outcome, the correlations were insignificant, suggesting that therapists did not perceive their personal attributes as a factor influencing therapeutic outcome.

Patients frequently attribute their success in treatment to personal qualities of the therapists. That these personal qualities bear a striking resemblance to each other, across studies and methodologies, is evidence that they are important in psychotherapy outcome. This notion was also emphasized by Lazarus (1971) in an uncontrolled follow-up study of 112 patients whom he had seen in therapy. These patients were asked to provide information about the effects of their treatment, the durability of improvement, and their perceptions of the therapeutic process and characteristics of the therapist. With regard to therapist characteristics, those adjectives used to describe Lazarus most often were sensitive, gentle, and honest. Patients clearly felt that the personal qualities of the therapist were more important than specific technical factors, about which there was little agreement.

In their study comparing behavioral and more traditional insight-oriented therapy, Sloane et al. (1975) reported a similar finding and elaborated upon the place of therapist variables in positive outcome. Although they failed to find a relationship between judges' ratings of therapists' behavior during the third therapy session (on empathy) and later outcome, they did find that patients tended to em-

phasize the personal qualities of their therapists as causing personality changes. These authors administered a 32-item questionnaire four months following treatment. These items included statements descriptive of both behavior therapy techniques (e.g., training in muscle relaxation) and dynamic therapy techniques (e.g., explaining the relationship of your problem to early life events). In addition, some characteristics thought to be common in all forms of therapy were included. Each item was rated on a five-point scale.

Surprisingly, perhaps, the successful patients in both therapies placed primary importance on more or less the same items. In fact, 70 percent or more of these successful patients listed the following items as "extremely important" or "very important" in causing their improvement:

1. The personality of the therapist.
2. His helping to understand problems.
3. Encouragement to gradually practice facing the things that bothered them.
4. Being able to talk to an understanding person.
5. His helping them to greater self-understanding.

None of the items regarded as "very important" by the majority of either patient group described techniques specific to one therapy (although item 3 is, in general, approached more systematically in behavior therapies). Marmor (1975), in his foreword to the Sloane et al. (1975) book, identified these factors as *relationship, insight, practice-"working through," catharsis,* and *trust.* He compared these to a previously published set of factors that he considered to be the primary common ingredients in all therapies: (1) *release of tension,* (2) *cognitive learning,* (3) *operant conditioning,* (4) *identification with the therapist,* and (5) *reality testing.* He suggested ways to construe both dynamic and behavioral intervention in these terms. While these items have not been specifically scaled and monitored, as such, in research studies, they provide further ideas for such assessments.

The foregoing suggests that, at least from the patient's point of view, effective treatment was due to factors associated with relationship variables, self-understanding, and active involvement. Although this type of data is limited by methodological problems (e.g., patients may not actually know how they are being helped), its repeated occurrence along with the related findings described in this section suggests (cf. Ryan & Gizynski, 1971; Strupp, Fox, & Lessler, 1969) that so-called common interpersonal factors are prominent ingredients of change in all therapies and that future outcome studies will have to take these themes into account more systematically.

The Comparative Effectiveness of Professional, Paraprofessional, Experienced and Inexperienced Therapists

In addition to no-treatment and wait-list control groups and in keeping with the previous description of common factors, effects of psychotherapy have been contrasted with the effects of helping efforts on the part of lay therapists, paraprofessionals, and inexperienced clinicians. The studies in this area have been aimed at sorting out the value of therapy beyond the contribution of warm and caring human encounters and wise advice. On the surface, studies that control the effects of an untrained, noncredentialed "therapist" might be ideal for illustrating the unique effects of psychotherapy. A related set of studies have examined the relationship of amount of therapist experience to outcome.

The available literature on such efforts has been reviewed and debated. Bergin and Lambert (1978), for example, suggested that more experienced clinicians obtain superior outcomes. Auerbach and Johnson (1977), on the other hand, found less support for this conclusion and suggested little difference in outcome as a function of level of experience.

Most meta-analytic reviews (e.g., Quality Assurance Project, 1982; Shapiro & Shapiro, 1983; Smith, et al., 1980) have analyzed the relationship of experience and outcome by correlating effect size data with experience level. These correlational data do not suggest a significant relationship between experience and outcome; however, experience levels were usually compared across studies rather than within studies, and comparisons often were between inexperienced and slightly experienced clinicians. Differences in outcome between highly experienced and inexperienced therapists have generally not been tested.

Durlak (1979), using traditional reviewing techniques, compared the outcomes of professionals and paraprofessionals and suggested little if any difference in outcome for the two groups. Lambert (1979), Stein (1980), and Nietzel and Fisher (1981) were all highly critical of Durlak's review. Of the 42 studies reviewed by Durlak and considered acceptable, few seemed to meet criteria necessary for comparative analysis. Nietzel and Fisher (1981), for example, suggested that only five of the studies reviewed by Durlak provided evidence on comparative effectiveness, and concluded that there is some evidence that paraprofessionals working under professional supervision could achieve outcomes equal to or better than therapists with master's degrees.

Hattie, Sharpley, and Rogers (1984) reanalyzed the studies reviewed by Durlak using meta-analytic methods. One hundred fifty-four comparisons from 39 studies indicated that clients who seek help from paraprofessionals are more likely to achieve resolutions of their problems than those who consult professionals (E.S. = .34). Despite this overall conclusion, several subcomparisons suggested that the most effective therapists were those who were currently undergoing training or had just completed it (graduate students), and that experienced paraprofessionals were superior to less experienced paraprofessionals. There was also a positive relationship between amount of training received by paraprofessionals and outcome.

A major problem with the Hattie et al. review was its reliance on a questionable data base. Rather than perform a more up-to-date review with rigorous inclusion criteria, Hattie et al. (1984) relied on the Durlak data base, which included many questionable studies and is somewhat dated. Berman and Norton (1985) replicated this meta-analysis excluding some of the poorer studies. They also excluded studies that counted social workers as paraprofessionals and reported that there was no difference in effect size for the two classes of service providers and that professionals tended to have better results in brief treatments and with patients over 21 years of age.

In contrast to the preceding reviews, Stein (1980) and Stein and Lambert (1984) were more selective in their choice of research literature. For example, studies of vocational counseling and academic advising and analogue interviews were not included in this review. In addition, reliable ratings were made of the design characteristics of each study (e.g., random assignment of patients to therapists, etc.), and greater attention was directed toward operationally defining experience and training.

Despite improvements in the selection and inclusion of studies for review, Stein and Lambert (1984) reported results similar to those of Berman and Norton (1985). In general there was no difference between the outcome of patients treated by trained and untrained persons.

Nevertheless, differences in outcome were most likely to occur when there was a large discrepancy in experience between the therapists offering treatment, and when the treatment modality involved more than simple counseling or specific behavioral techniques (e.g., psychodynamic therapy, marital therapy).

An exemplary study in this area was published by Strupp and his colleagues at Vanderbilt University (Strupp & Hadley, 1978); they contrasted the effectiveness of professionally trained expert therapists and a select group of college professors. This study examined process and outcome in therapy offered to 15 mildly neurotic college students by five analytically or experientially oriented psychotherapists compared with "therapy" offered by seven nonprofessional college professors, who were popular student advisors, to 15 clients with similar disturbances. Outcomes for the two treatment groups were also contrasted with those attained by students who were assigned to either a minimal contact wait-list control group or a so-called silent control group of students from the college population who achieved similar MMPI profiles as the treatment subjects but who had not sought help for their problems.

Change was measured by the MMPI, patients', therapists', and clinicians' ratings of changes in target complaints, self-rated overall change, and experts' ratings on clinical scales of disturbance. Comparisons of amount of change among groups revealed the following: There were no significant differences on any of the six measures based on the patient's own perspective, nor on therapist measures of change, nor on ratings of the two groups made by an independent clinical evaluation. Post hoc pairwise comparisons showed that both treated groups were significantly more improved than the control group on four of these six variables. On the remaining two variables, only the Therapist group was significantly more improved than the controls.

Although the failures of this literature generally to show unique therapeutic effectiveness for trained professionals are sobering, these studies are flawed in several respects. Many of the studies deal with types of cases that are not typical of those treated in the outcome studies reported in this chapter. Controls, criteria, and follow-up are often not rigorous; and frequently we seem to be observing improvements in the morale of schizophrenics or mildly distressed persons due to attention and support. We are not observing substantial therapeutic effects in the usual kinds of cases. This is not to downgrade the importance of the effects observed but to suggest that they have some limitations. They may not generalize to representative patient populations or less selective groups of paraprofessionals. On the other hand, the studies do suggest that common therapeutic factors are not the sole domain of formal therapy and that they may be useful in many cases or settings. Definitive studies are yet to be done on this matter.

From Common Factors and General Comparisons of Schools Toward Specific Techniques

One recent trend evident in psychotherapy and behavior change research is the tendency to move away from comparisons between major orientations toward an examination of the possible effects of specific techniques on specific disorders, in a pragmatic way, regardless of the traditions from which the methods originated (e.g., Kazdin's discussion in Chapter 2 of this volume; Beutler, 1983; Goldstein & Stein, 1976). An example of this trend, that originated in the behavioral tradition, is research on the treatment of psychophysiological disorders such as headache and insomnia. Research in this area in many ways symbolizes the status of research on "specific therapies for specific disorders." With headaches, for example, different types of headache have been thought to be responsive to specific treatments: biofeedback (hand warming) with migraine versus relaxation with tension headache. The specific treatments for these disorders involve relatively concrete interventions that can be more easily manipulated than most psychosocial interventions. They therefore represent a fertile testing ground for the effect of specific interventions on specific problems.

Research on the treatment of headache has been

reviewed by Blanchard et al. (1980). With respect to muscle tension headache, these authors conclude from a meta-analytic comparison that relaxation and EMG biofeedback are equally effective. Experiments designed to identify the critical ingredients of EMG biofeedback have found that training procedures that *increase* or hold constant the level of muscle activity are just as effective as those aimed at reducing the excessive muscle activity believed to characterize tension headache. In addition, most studies have failed to obtain a correlation between EMG changes during biofeedback sessions and symptom reduction, with some participants reporting improvement in the absence of EMG changes.

A particular problem for this field has arisen from the surprising effectiveness of hand-*cooling* (i.e., thermal biofeedback in which the participant believes that the hand temperature is rising when in fact it is falling), which was originally introduced as a credible placebo control procedure! Of course, it remains possible that self-efficacy and increased awareness of the antecedents of headache, as invoked by Blanchard and Andrasik (1982) in relation to tension headache treatment, could apply to migraine. It is clear from these authors' review that evidence for the originally presumed mechanism of thermal biofeedback, whereby biofeedback leads to decreased sympathetic activity, is patchy and unconvincing and that some common factor such as relaxation or self-efficacy is the mechanism leading to a positive outcome.

Along similar lines, research on insomnia has been characterized by elegant and determined efforts to uncover the mechanisms of change, by a combination of dismantling-type studies comparing treatments comprising different elements of the combined package under investigation, with creative use of process data, correlating indices of the presumed change mechanism with measures of outcome.

The evidence concerning the treatment of insomnia has been reviewed by Borkovec (1982). Relaxation and biofeedback are consistently effective, yeilding an average reduction of 45 percent in latency of sleep onset. Several studies have used credible placebos and/or counterdemand instructions to show that relaxation is an effective ingredient in the treatment of the subjective aspects of insomnia. The balance of the evidence favors

relaxation over placebo conditions in terms of physiologically monitored sleep data; frontalis EMG biofeedback emerges from Borkovec's (1982) review as virtually identical in its efficacy to relaxation.

Another area that has seen extensive experimental analysis of treatment effectiveness via dismantling studies is the cognitive-behavioral approach to depression. This series of studies was based on Rehm's (1977) self-control formulation of depression, whereby depressed persons are viewed as manifesting maladaptive self-monitoring, self-evaluation (including self-attribution), and self-reinforcement behavior. Encouraging results were obtained by Fuchs and Rehm (1977) and Rehm, Fuchs, Roth, Kornblith, and Romano (1979) for the treatment as a whole. When broken down into constituent components in a study by Rehm et al. (1981), however, the results did not favor the additive effects of specific procedures. Surprisingly, the self-evaluation and self-reinforcement components were found to add little or no additional efficacy to the impact of self-monitoring alone. A subsequent study by Kornblith, Rehm, O'Hara, and Lamparski (1983) included a didactic condition lacking homework assignments, in addition to the full treatment, a condition lacking only the self-reinforcement element, and an active control treatment—problem-oriented, psychodynamic group psychotherapy. All four treatments were equally effective, and the authors of this very carefully conducted and well-reported study were driven by their findings to ponder anew the commonalities among seemingly diverse treatments of depression:

Looking across cognitive and behavioral therapy procedures for treating depression generally, it is apparent that these packages have at least three important characteristics in common. First, they each present a concrete rationale. This rationale includes a vocabulary for describing and defining the problems of depression in ways that may be very new to participants. Rationales also provide a vocabulary for describing the mechanisms of change. Second, all of these therapy programs are highly structured. They provide clear plans for producing change in a logical sequence of steps. Third, all of these programs provide feedback and support so that participants can clearly see changes in their own behavior and are reinforced for these changes. . . . Research . . . needs to look more closely at characteristics of packages such as these, rather than merely at details of procedure or abstract differences in underlying theories. (Kornblith et al., 1983, p. 525)

Kornblith et al. (1983) suggest that even their group psychotherapy control condition, by virtue of the problem-oriented approach it followed, was an active, problem-seeking process aimed at the current life situation of each participant, using problem-solving techniques such as redefining the problem and listing alternatives.

Similar conclusions were reached by Zeiss, Lewinsohn, and Munoz (1979). These authors compared interpersonal skills training, a reinforcement-theory based program to increase pleasant activities and the enjoyment of potentially pleasant activites, and a cognitive approach to the modification of depressive thoughts. They found that all treatments were associated with reduction in depression, without any differential changes specific to aspects of the patient's problems targeted by the three treatments. Zeiss et al. (1979), noting the improvements also recorded by the waiting-list group, cite Frank's (1973) demoralization hypothesis as the most parsimonious explanation for the results and suggest that the impact of treatment was due to the enhancement of self-efficacy via training in self-help skills, thus increasing expectations of mastery and perception of greater positive reinforcement as a function of the patients' greater skillfulness. Thus the "nonspecific" components of therapy for depression emerge as important. On the other hand, it should be noted that the experience level of the therapists was not high (counseling psychology graduate students and M.A.'s) and there was no monitoring of the therapists' contributions to therapy; thus treatment delivery according to the design is not assured.

Common and Specific Factors and the Use of Treatment Manuals

A major limitation of past studies (most of which show no differences between treatments) may have been that they did not specify particular treatments and ensure that they were offered to patients in the prescribed manner. An important development in psychotherapy (even a "minor revolution," Luborsky & DeRubeis, 1984) is the emergence of therapy treatment manuals. These manuals, which are used

to guide practice, can be traced back to the sixties (Lang & Lazovik, 1963) but became common with some treatment approaches in the seventies. Their initial use was in group workshops that emphasized training and teaching more than therapy (i.e., assertiveness training with shy college students, or interpersonal skills training in both in- and outpatient populations, behavior therapy with overweight clients). In the 1980s there has already been an increased interest in the use of such manuals in individual psychosocial therapies, in their application to a wider variety of patient problems, and with a variety of treatment approaches. Waskow (1984), for example, identified seven different manuals describing various behavioral, cognitive, and psychodynamic approaches to treating outpatients, mainly those who are depressed (Beck, Rush, Shaw, & Emery, 1979; Bellack, Hersen, & Himmelhoch, 1981; Fuchs & Rehm, 1977; Klerman, Rounsaville, Chevron, Neu, & Weissman, 1979; Lewinsohn, Antonuccio, Steinmetz, & Teri, 1982; Luborsky, 1984; Strupp & Binder, 1984).

The major advantage of treatment manuals is that they (1) standardize (to a greater degree) the treatment being offered; (2) provide a method of training therapists to offer a standard treatment; (3) allow for the development of rating scales to judge whether a therapy is being properly offered; and (4) allow researchers another method of sorting out the common factors from the unique factors associated with specific treatment approaches.

The development and use of treatment manuals by the Depression Collaborative Study (Waskow, Parloff, Hadley, & Autry, in press) illustrates the possibilities of manuals and associated rating scales in psychotherapy research. The NIMH project (Waskow et al., in press) involves the comparison of Cognitive Therapy (CT), Interpersonal Therapy (IPT), and Clinical Management (CM) (a standardized approach to pharmacotherapy) with adult outpatient nonbipolar, nonpsychotic depression. Each of the therapies is offered in each of three different settings. The manuals have been used to guide the selection of therapists; to train therapists; to develop various rating scales to assess the effects of training; to test the degree to which the therapy offered conforms to the manual; and to measure the degree to which therapies can be discriminated. Eventually the design of the study may allow researchers to see whether a particular treatment (of those considered) is more efficacious or works best with specific types of individuals, and, most relevant to our discussion, whether a specific set of therapy techniques adds anything to the factors that are common across therapies. While the outcome data are not yet published, there are some other data dealing with the identification of therapeutic operations that are unique to a given treatment, as well as shared by treatments (DeRubeis, Hollon, Evans, & Bemis, 1982; Evans et al., 1983; Luborsky, Woody, McLellan, O'Brien, & Rosenzweig, 1982; Neu, Prusoff, & Klerman, 1978).

The identification and distillation of the most valued techniques of specific treatment approaches in a manual format, with its promise of greater specificity and differential treatment, may yet allow for a demonstration of differential psychotherapy outcome. Clearly, the challenge to sort out unique from common factors is difficult, and it has not yet been accomplished despite the enthusiasm generated by exponents of therapeutic schools. Indeed, this separation could be infeasible because common factors may activate or mediate specific ones.

In any case, the manualization of therapy has its advantages. It crystallizes the tendency toward more rapid intervention by placing greater expectancy for positive outcome in time-limited treatment and for periodic, *early* assessment of the degree to which patients respond to treatment. Thus, it moves us closer to making early judgments about the effects of treatment, the necessity of altering treatment approaches, or referring patients to alternative treatments. Finally, it provides more clear-cut guidelines for training, and the evaluation of the consequences of training in very concrete ways. As a result, training for practice can move toward more competency-based criteria, and hopefully this competency in providing treatments will have the expected payoff in patient improvement and in the identification of the relative contribution of common factors and specific techniques.

Although many of the psychotherapies that have been tested empirically have been shown to be generally effective, and we are arriving at a clearer picture of the causal factors in these positive changes, there are two additional important issues to consider: (1) How can we identify and promote larger effects? (2) What is the extent of negative effects during therapy?

THE SEARCH FOR LARGER EFFECTS

Despite the fact that faith in treatment efficacy has increased over the years due to increasing positive evidence, concerns about therapeutic potency continue and engender hope that new knowledge will enhance the amount of change experienced as a result of treatment. There are several important themes that bear on this matter.

We have argued for many years (Bergin, 1966) that average psychotherapy and behavior change outcome indices mask a great deal of variability, and that this variability represents a diversity in therapeutic potency ranging from bad to excellent. Translating average outcomes into effect sizes does not change this fact; indeed, the meta-analyses based on effect sizes have abundantly documented this point. While the average effect sizes discussed in this chapter are impressive by comparison with no treatment or by comparison with other kinds of social interventions, it is a point of some concern that an average effect size of 0.85 implies that somewhere near half of the treated samples attained effects *smaller than* 0.85, and many of these had to be near zero due to the large standard deviations of the average effect sizes reported. Indeed, Shapiro and Shapiro (1982a) reported that about 30 percent of their 1828 E.S.'s were near zero and 11 percent were negative!

While meta-analyses have been very useful, and while we have to class the Smith et al. book (1980) in particular as a significant achievement that has drastically affected our view of outcome statistics, we still have to be sobered by the average sizes of the effects and we have to look closely at the tremendous variability in the changes reported. This variability is a likely key to discovering the means of improving therapeutic effects because hidden in the variation are some very large changes that tend to get washed out by averaging the data. The following sections deal with some of these problems.

The Therapist Factor: An Untested Contaminating Variable in Comparisons of Techniques

Although an excellent chapter in this book reviews a massive number of studies on therapist characteristics in relation to outcome, these are essentially correlational data that do not address the question of differences in individual therapists' efficacy. The reason for this is that there is virtually no literature that tests the outcomes of each therapist. Such data are hidden in comparisons of techniques. If, however, we were to compare the outcomes of each therapist as we do each technique, we may find considerable variation in effectiveness. Of course, therapists are always using "techniques," so such comparisons actually analyze therapist "styles," which inevitably confound personal and technical aspects of interventions (Henry, 1985).

This idea was, of course, in part the import of the section in the first edition of this chapter, which was devoted to improvement effects versus deterioration effects. It was assumed there that some *therapists* (with their techniques), as opposed to techniques per se, obtained large positive effects while many obtained modest effects, and a few often caused people to worsen in adjustment.

Orlinsky and Howard (1980) have produced an interesting set of data on this question. Although this was a retrospective study based on case files, important hypotheses about therapist differences were generated. The outcome ratings of 143 female cases seen by 23 traditional verbal psychotherapists were listed therapist by therapist. Six of the 23 therapists were rated $\sqrt{}$ +, which means that at least 70 percent of their cases were improved, and none were rated worse. Overall, 84 percent of their cases were improved. Five of the 23 therapists, on the other hand, were x-rated, which means that 50 percent or less of their cases improved while more than 10 percent were worse. Overall, 44 percent of their 25 cases improved. The types of cases seen by the different therapists were generally similar, although the results have to be interpreted with some caution because there was neither random assignment of cases to therapists nor any attempt to equate caseloads for severity of disturbance. Further analyses showed that experienced therapists obtained better results and, rather dramatically, that the ambulatory female schizophrenics in the sample improved at an 89 percent rate with female therapists but only at a 43 percent rate with male therapists.

These findings reveal how much improvement rates may vary as a function of therapist factors and suggest how outcomes with other samples may improve when poorer therapists are dropped out, thus indicating the larger effects of the better therapists. *It is possible that outcome statistics in general are deflated by the use of practitioners who are*

conducting only a mere semblance of psychotherapy. The improvement rate for the better therapists in this study is comparable to the high rates reported during the early days of behavior therapy by Wolpe (1958, 1964) and Lazarus (1963). It is also representative of the effectiveness shown by the six therapists in the Sloane study who were preselected for their expertise in dynamic and behavioral methods. Indeed, Wolpe and Lazarus were two of the therapists. Sloane (1983) reported that there were no differences in improvement rates across the six therapists in that study.

A study bearing on this matter by Miller, Taylor, and West (1980) found that in behavior therapy with problem drinkers, therapists varied widely in effectiveness. Their success rates ranged from 100 percent to 25 percent. Surprisingly, their efficacy as behavior therapists was highly correlated with ratings of their empathy levels!

Another behavioral study, by Turner and Ascher (1982), revealed a substantial difference in efficacy between one very experienced therapist and a group of inexperienced therapists in the treatment of insomnia. This occurred despite careful training of the therapists in the exact procedures to be followed in the highly structured treatments that were used.

A significant program of inquiry into the therapist's contribution is being conducted by the University of Pennsylvania psychotherapy research group (Crits-Christoph et al., 1985; Luborsky, McClellan, Woody, O'Brien, & Auerbach, 1985). Large differences in therapist efficacy have been found even when using highly experienced therapists, treatment manuals, and a diversity of techniques. Similar findings were discovered by this group when they analyzed studies conducted at Johns Hopkins University, the University of Pittsburgh, and McGill University. Therapist differences have typically been larger than treatment differences in this set of studies.

Therapist factors may well interact with treatment techniques. An example of this was obtained in the Sheffield Psychotherapy Project (Shapiro & Firth, in press), where, it will be recalled, each client-therapist pair worked in both of two treatments. Firth and Shapiro (unpublished) found that the advantage of Prescriptive over Exploratory therapy was largely confined to one of two principal project therapists. Such an interaction effect may reflect differential skill, aptitude or attitudinal compatibility with the two techniques.

Of course, the studies cited here constitute a mere beginning, and other studies can be cited that contradict these findings. We simply do not know enough yet about the therapist factor to specify when and how it makes a difference, nor when it matters more than technique. What we do know is that there are intriguing possibilities for new discoveries here and that this issue has been ignored to a surprising degree. Researchers, influenced by mechanical models, have placed their bets more on technique factors as the powerful ones in therapeutic change. Of course, technique is still likely to be important even if reliable therapist differences are found. The differences in effectiveness between therapists not only result from personal qualities but are likely to reflect variations in technical skill as well. Thus, therapist differences may well be partly reflections of technique differences. To the extent that this is true, studies of techniques have been contaminated by heterogeneity in the purity or quality of technique being applied. Preliminary findings like those cited previously suggest that even treatment manuals have not consistently cured this problem; consequently, monitoring of individual therapist variation in skill (and personal qualities like warmth) is essential in outcome studies.

Information like the foregoing suggests that when good therapists are used, outcomes may be more homogeneous around a high average improvement rate or effect size. It may be that the outcome studies that have been meta-analyzed embrace a number of small effect sizes engendered by incompetent or even deleterious therapy. As standards of therapist selection and training continue to improve, and as well-trained therapists are included more frequently in research studies, we can expect average effect sizes to improve. It is also anticipated that the effective use of treatment manuals will help with these problems by more carefully training therapists in skills and by allowing supervisors to monitor more carefully the application of therapy.

Effect sizes are also likely to be increased by eliminating or moderating the influence of therapist maladjustment and personality problems. Beutler, Crago, & Arizmendi (Chapter 7, this volume) and Parloff, Waskow, and Wolfe in the previous edition (1978) have shown a negative correlation between the therapist's personal difficulties and client progress.

Of course, effect sizes also vary with severity of client disturbance; however, it is not clear yet how much this variation can be reduced by careful therapist selection. Evidence from the Landman and Dawes (1982) meta-analysis provides evidence that patients with severe problems (schizophrenia, depression, alcoholism, and delinquency) in 20 studies showed an average E.S. of 0.68 while those with circumscribed problems (snake phobias, test anxiety, etc.) in 22 studies showed an E.S. of 1.11. It is conceivable that therapists with appropriate styles or skills could improve the E.S. for severe cases considerably. This is a difficult and complicated problem that is discussed more fully elsewhere in this book, especially by Beutler et al. Suffice it to say here that client levels or kinds of disturbances are not absolute predictors of outcome. They may look that way when only average effects are examined, as was done by Landman and Dawes (1982); but once again, average effects appear to obscure variability in effectiveness.

In this regard Orlinsky (1985) has noted that therapists generally are not "good" or "bad" in an absolute sense; but rather, they vary in the *range* or *types* of cases they deal with effectively. The Orlinsky and Howard report showed, for instance, that therapists with poor average outcomes actually did very well with some cases. There is as yet no study that has carefully selected therapists for their known effectiveness with special patient groups; however, such individuals are known by reputation in the field. It would, therefore, be valuable to test the effects of such a selected sample of therapists against other therapists in the treatment of homogeneous groups of cases that the selected therapists are supposed to be good with. Positive results would have important implications for the practice and study of psychotherapy.

A related issue concerns the relative potency of specific techniques versus therapist personal qualities, an issue that is discussed many times in this book. It is possible that too much energy is being devoted to technique studies at the expense of examining *therapists as persons* and in interaction with techniques. Therapist-by-therapist outcomes will need to be more carefully studied, and such studies may well show not only potent therapist differences but that technique differences are inseparably bound with therapist differences. It is possible, even likely, that interactions between therapist and technique influence outcome. Some therapists recoil at the use of aversive conditioning. Others love to dazzle people with powerful insights. Until researchers respond to the incredible complexity of the change process and stop loading the dice in favor of large main effects (specific technique studies), in an imitation of clinical drug trials or experimental psychology studies, it is doubtful that the effective ingredients of optimal change will be unraveled.

Control Group Data as Moderators of Therapeutic Effects

We have stated previously (Bergin, 1971) that true no-treatment control groups are impossible to set up as contrast groups for psychotherapy efficacy studies. Distressed human beings do not sit still like rats in cages waiting for an experiment to end. They act to relieve their distress, and we documented in the previous editions of this chapter how they may seek relief from their pain. A follow-up of a previous U.S. national study on this matter by Veroff, Kulka, and Douvan (1981), spanning the period 1957 to 1976, revealed an amazing increase in resources and methods of self-help outside of the formal mental health establishment. Past studies showed that as many as 50 percent of persons seeking formal therapeutic help had also sought help from other sources (cf. Bergin, 1971). Veroff et al. found in their 1976 sample that 20 percent to 38 percent of persons who felt they were "ready for professional help" also sought informal help.

The range and substance of life-changing events occurring in so-called control subjects is rarely monitored. One study that did so (Cross, Sheehan, & Khan, 1980) showed that a surprising amount of advice- and counsel-seeking occurred in both treated and untreated groups. Even more surprising is that the treated groups engaged in this behavior more than the control group and that the behavior therapy cases did so substantially more than the insight therapy cases! If this finding holds up, it would prove the opposite of our contention that control groups deflate effect sizes by participating in quasi-therapy experiences during the control period. Even though controls *are* obtaining outside counsel, they are doing *less* of it than the treated cases. If outside support and advice has positive effects, then some of the therapeutic effect sizes in treated groups is due to

extratherapy factors, especially in behavior therapy. Of course, it may be that good therapy stimulates people to utilize outside resources more effectively, which is in itself an important therapeutic benefit.

In any event, it is evident that treated and untreated groups differ in several ways other than treatment versus no-treatment. Until such differences are eliminated or are systematically measured, correlated with outcomes, or held constant by analysis of covariance, and so on, ambiguity must continue in our interpretation of effect sizes. The true size of therapeutic effect may be larger or smaller, depending on the results of such new observations.

A related problem is introduced by the matter of so-called *placebo controls*. Over the years, we have changed our view. Originally, we thought a placebo therapy control condition would be a better test baseline for examining therapeutic effects than untreated groups. Since then, it has been shown, as discussed earlier in this chapter, that placebo therapy is not a better control comparison than untreated controls. Too many things are happening in such human experiments. Placebo groups are, in essence, therapy groups and effective ones include many of the very same ingredients as treatment groups. Consequently, placebo therapies are generally not valid criterion baselines against which to test therapy, and they tend to yield smaller effect sizes for the treated groups due to the therapeutic changes occurring in them. A better procedure would be to vary the dosage of therapeutic ingredients across several groups and observe whether effect sizes vary as dosages vary. This would avoid current problems but it is an ideal that is extremely difficult to employ in practice.

As things stand now, it appears that the various control group methods that have been designed are inadequate, that they do not provide fair tests of therapy effects, and that often effect sizes for therapy would be larger if they were not reduced in magnitude by subtracting the effect sizes of so-called control groups. A real experiment ought to be uncontaminated by control conditions that overlap with the treated conditions.

In general, we doubt that assessments of therapeutic efficacy have benefited much from trying to apply the traditional scientific model of experimental controls to psychotherapy research. It is also doubtful that human beings are "dependent" variables upon which "effects" are "caused." Indeed, progress may well have been retarded by such imitations of physical and biological research models. In this respect we even have reservations about the common usage of terms like "therapeutic effects" or "effect size" unless the terms are construed to be the results of *client* efforts as agents of their own change.

DETERIORATION, NEGATIVE EFFECTS, AND ESTIMATES OF THERAPEUTIC CHANGE

We suggested in the preceding commentary on the therapist factor in estimating outcomes that therapist variability has an effect on average estimates of change. Evidence was presented there of rather large differences in outcome rates when they were estimated therapist by therapist. In that context, negative change appeared in some cases and was associated more with some therapists than with others. To the extent that negative changes occur, they obviously subtract from overall therapeutic effect sizes. To the extent that such events can be understood and reduced, improvement effects will be larger.

Bergin (1966, 1971) proposed the term "deterioration effect" to describe the general finding that a certain portion of psychotherapy patients were worse after treatment. Such an effect was first suggested by studies in which treated groups showed an increase in variance compared with control groups on outcome measures. This implied that therapy groups included cases that were diverging from the mean change scores in both directions, positive and deterioration. Therapy effects, including negative ones, can, however, be distributed so as to show no change or even a restriction in variance at treatment termination.

Strupp, Hadley, and Gomes-Schwartz (1977) suggested the term "negative effect" to replace the "deterioration effect" as a label for therapy-induced worsening of the patient's condition. On the other hand, Mays and Franks (1980, 1985) have favored the term "negative outcome," advocating a definition that excludes causal reference to the therapist or therapy since causality is an issue that can (must) be studied separately. The use of the term "negative outcome" like the term "negative effect" also has

the advantage of being free from the biological connotations of "deterioration." We reject as unrealistic, however, the suggestion by Franks & Mays (1980; Mays & Franks, 1980, 1985) and Rachman and Wilson (1980) that there is no causal link between therapist activities and patient worsening. Indeed, it is doubtful that Mays and Franks would have devoted an entire book, with many authors, to the subject if there were no substance to the phenomenon of negative effects.

Needless to say, negative effects are difficult if not impossible to study in an experimentally controlled way. Nevertheless, research more than suggests that some patients are worse as a result of psychotherapy. This does not mean that all worsening is therapy-produced. Some cases may be on a progressive decline that no therapist effort can stop. The extent or rate of such negative change or of "spontaneous" deterioration in untreated groups has never been determined, so there is no baseline from which to judge deterioration rates observed in treated groups. The alternative is to observe negative change in experiments using treated versus control conditions and in studies of specific connections between therapy processes and patient responses.

In prior work (Bergin & Lambert, 1978; Lambert, Bergin, & Collins, 1977) evidence (based on over 50 studies) about the incidence, prevalence and magnitude of negative change was described. That process involved piecing together obscure bits of evidence, since there are few, if any, definitive studies. There has been considerable hesitation to address this issue directly, and most outcome studies did not include a category of "worse." The evidence is, however, slowly changing as studies improve. There is a paradoxical fact, though, that as precision of inquiry into this question is improving, quality of therapy is also improving. The research itself stimulates better quality control and inclusion of competent therapy in outcome studies, so study of the phenomenon may decrease its extent and its visibility.

At the time of our earlier review, we concluded that the negative effects found in therapy were sufficient to reduce estimates of the efficacy of therapy. In addition, it was concluded that the occurrence of therapy or therapist-induced worsening was widespread—occurring across a variety of treatment modalities including group and family therapies.

Further, we implied that there was a causal link between negative outcomes and therapeutic activities in interaction with patient variables. The sufficiency of the empirical evidence for establishing prevalence and causation has been critically evaluated by several writers (cf. Bergin, 1970; Bergin, 1980; Braucht, 1970; Eysenck, 1967; Franks & Mays, 1980; Lambert et al., 1977; May, 1971; Mays & Franks, 1980, 1985; Rachman & Wilson, 1980; Strupp et al., 1977).

Several recent meta-analytic reviews provide yet another source for evaluating the extent of negative effects. For example, Smith et al. (1980) in their review of over 475 psychotherapy outcomes concluded that:

> Little evidence was found for the alleged existence of the negative effects of psychotherapy. Only 9 percent of the effect-size measures were negative (where the mean for the control group was higher than the mean for the psychotherapy group). Nor was there convincing evidence in the dispersions of the treatment groups that some members became better and some worse as a result of psychotherapy. (p. 88)

Smith et al.'s conclusion is surprising. Only 9 percent negative effect sizes is a large number. We never previously observed a statistically significant average negative effect in a treated group; consequently, we assume that this 9 percent refers to instances where mean change in the control group was larger than in the treated group, yielding a negative sign in the numerator of the ratio for computing an effect size. Presumably, these negative effect sizes were not substantially different from zero, that is, no difference between experimental and control means. A difference of zero between experimentals and controls may mean that both improvement and negative change are occurring in the treated group, which averages to a change index equal to no treatment. This was found in nine studies we reported previously (Bergin & Lambert, 1978).

Shapiro and Shapiro (1982a), in their meta-analysis, reported that of 1828 effect sizes calculated, 106 or 11.3 percent were negative while about 30 percent more were null, thus indicating further the possibility of negative change.

Most meta-analytic studies did not report detailed information about increased variance in control groups and treatment groups following therapy and so offer little information on this issue. One might argue that the presence of 9 percent to 11 percent negative effect sizes does provide some added evidence for negative therapeutic effects. Few data are offered about the magnitude of these negative effects, however, and the type of dependent measure they have reference to. Thus, it is difficult to judge whether they greatly exceed negative effects expected on the basis of measurement error.

Strupp, Hadley, and Gomes-Schwartz (1977), while also noting the shortcomings in the data for establishing causality and rates of deterioration, do not question the presence and importance of negative effects. This position was also supported in their survey of eminent clinicians and researchers. In response to the question: "Is there a problem of negative effects of psychotherapy?" there was a virtually unanimous "Yes" by the 70 experts who responded to the questionnaire. The concern of these experts is supported by specific studies. For example, the Orlinsky and Howard (1980) report, described earlier, indicated a 6 percent to 7 percent rate of negative change during treatment, which was associated much more with a small subgroup of therapists. It is our view, after reviewing the empirical literature and the critiques of the evidence accumulated, that although there are many methodological shortcomings and ambiguities in the data as pointed out by the critics who have been cited, the evidence that does exist suggests that psychotherapy can and does cause harm to a portion of those it is intended to help. At this time the research literature does not suggest how pervasive and central in reducing the overall estimate of the effects of different therapies this phenomenon is. At the same time, the study of negative change has important implications for the selection of clients for treatment, the suitability of specific procedures for some clients, and the selection, training, and monitoring of therapists. We turn now to a discussion of these issues and a review of studies that further elucidate the nature of the problem.

What Causes Deterioration?

Client and technique interaction effects. Several important variables have been implicated as possible causal agents in therapy—induced negative outcomes. Despite the lack of specificity in research reports, it is apparent that certain client variables correlate with negative change. Patient diagnosis and degree of disturbance are related variables that appear to be linked to deterioration, especially when they are present and combined with therapeutic techniques that are aimed at breaking down, challenging, or undermining habitual coping strategies or defenses. Indications are that more severely disturbed (psychotic) patients, as in Fairweather et al. (1960) and Feighner, Brown, and Oliver (1973); borderline patients, as in Horwitz (1974) and Weber, Elinson, and Moss (1965); or the initially most disturbed encounter group participants, as in Lieberman, Yalom, and Miles (1973), are the most likely to experience negative outcomes. Berzins, Bednar, and Severy (1975) also found that the patients who showed a consistent pattern of negative change were typified by a disproportionate number of schizophrenics and that other client characteristics were not significantly related to this pattern.

In a widely quoted study reported by Lieberman et al. (1973), it was found that variables such as low involvement in the group, low levels of self-esteem, low positive self-concept, higher growth orientation, and greater anticipation or need for fulfilment were positively related to deterioration. Likewise, casualties were less effective at using interpersonal skills in their adaptation to the group experience.

As in the work of Lieberman et al. (1973), Kernberg (1973) reported that low quality of interpersonal relationships was a prognostically poor sign, and that this, coupled with low initial anxiety tolerance and low motivation, yielded poor outcomes in psychoanalysis and purely supportive psychotherapies but better outcomes in supportive-expressive treatments. Strupp et al. (1980a–d) obtained a similar set of findings in their analyses of improvers and nonimprovers in the Vanderbilt study. Similar conclusions were reached by Stone (1985) in an analysis of his own private practice of dynamic therapy. Of those who were worse at the end of therapy seven out of eight were either borderline or psychotic.

Therapist factors. An important examination of mechanisms through which negative effects are transmitted by therapists was described by Yalom and Lieberman (1971). The main finding was that the style of the group leaders was most predictive of negative outcomes. These leaders were impatient and authoritarian in approach, and they insisted on immediate self-disclosure, emotional expression, and attitude change. There were five leaders of this type, and all produced casualties. The one exception stated that he realized there were fragile persons in his group, so that he deviated from his usual style and "pulled his punches."

Kaplan (1982), as well as Bentley, DeJulio, Lambert, and Dinan (unpublished manuscript), replicated the Lieberman, Yalom, and Miles study. Both replications found far less evidence for negative effects. Although these studies used somewhat different methodology, the major difference seemed to be the *power* of the leaders. In both replications the group leaders (who were graduate students) were not nearly as confrontive and aggressive as those in the original study.

Information on negative consequences of therapist maladjustment, exploitiveness, and immaturity can be gathered with ease from client self-reports. Striano (1982), in a consumer report study, examined the personal experiences of 25 selected cases who had been to more than one therapist, one of whom was reported as being helpful and one of whom was said to be unhelpful or harmful. She documented through the reports of these clients a variety of "horror stories" of the type that are often shared privately among clients and professionals but are rarely published. A number of such reports are also recounted in previous editions of this chapter and in Lambert et al. (1977). Grunebaum (1985) has added to this repertoire of reports via surveys of mental health professionals who described therapy they had undergone. Ten percent of these professionals reported being harmed by therapy. Such accounts lack documentation independent of client report, so they could be laden with subjective biases to an unknown degree; however, such complaints are of social and clinical importance, and they provide reasons to continue inquiries into therapist factors in negative change.

Another study more extensively and objectively examined the process of positive and negative change conducted by two contrasting therapists. Ricks (1974) studied the adult status of a group of disturbed adolescent boys who had been seen by either of two therapists in a major child guidance clinic. Although the long-term outcomes of these two therapists were not different for less disturbed clients, there were striking differences in their therapeutic styles and outcomes with the more disturbed boys. For all cases in the sample, 55 percent were judged to have become schizophrenic in adulthood. Only 27 percent of therapist A's cases, however, had such an outcome, whereas 88 percent of therapist B's cases deteriorated to such a state. The caseloads of the two therapists were equal in degree of disturbance and other characteristics at the beginning of therapy.

In analyzing differences in therapist styles, it was found that therapist A devoted more time to those who were most disturbed while the less successful therapist B did the opposite. Therapist A also made more use of resources outside of the immediate therapy situation, was firm and direct with patients, supported movement toward autonomy, and facilitated problem solving in everyday life, all in the context of a strong therapeutic relationship.

Therapist B seemed to be frightened by severe pathology and emotionally withdrew from the more difficult cases. B frequently commented on the difficulties of cases and seemed to become depressed when confronted with a particularly unpromising one. He became caught up in the boys' depressed and hopeless feelings, and thereby reinforced the client's sense of self-rejection and futility. Careful studies like this give strong support to traditional clinical beliefs regarding the effects of therapist personality and countertransference phenomena on outcomes.

Sachs (1983) conducted one of the most careful empirical investigations specifically aimed at illuminating the process that leads to negative effects. Using data from the Vanderbilt study (Strupp & Hadley, 1978), she applied the Vanderbilt Negative Indicators Scale (VNIS) to therapist-patient interactions drawn from the first three therapy sessions. This instrument, devised for this study, contained 42 items, which were rated by two trained judges. The total scale was made up of five subscales whose items were developed through an analysis of past literature on patient deterioration (cf. Lambert et al., 1977; Strupp et al., 1977) and from an earlier version of the scale applied in this same project (Gomes-Schwartz, 1978).

The VNIS items and subscales were successfully

used to predict outcome, which was assessed with six different dependent measures (drawn from different perspectives). Negative factors in the therapeutic relationship, as measured by the VNIS, were shown to be highly associated with therapeutic outcome. Most dramatic in identifying success and failure in psychotherapy, however, was the Errors in Technique subscale ratings, which indicated that therapist competence and skill in applying verbal techniques led to positive or negative change. One error in technique that could be reliably rated, and proved all too frequent, involved the failure to *structure* or *focus* the session as operationalized by the following rating scale definition:

The session seems aimless or lacks coherence. The therapist fails to make intervention that would help to organize the content or process of the therapy session. Evidence for this item includes:

1. Therapist fails to identify focal therapeutic issues in material presented to the patient.
2. Therapist fails to integrate the material by the patient. The therapist does not identify themes or patterns in the patient's communications, reported behaviors, or manner of interaction with the therapist.
3. Therapist lets the patient ramble and/or repeatedly pursue tangents.

Additionally, several other errors seemed important, including the failure of the therapist to address patient's negative attitudes toward either the therapist or therapy, the passive acceptance of problematic aspects of the patient's behavior such as resistance or evasiveness, and the use of harmful interventions such as poorly timed or inappropriate interpretations.

Other Factors

We still know little about the natural course of negative change in the absence of treatment. The lack of such information limits our knowledge of specific effects within therapy. Thoits (1985) has suggested that patients' life events be carefully monitored during treatment experiments for negative stresses in much the same way we have advocated monitoring positive extra-therapy events. It would then be possible to more precisely partial-out treatment-related negative consequences from "spontaneous" ones.

Another consideration is therapist selection in studies. It looks evident that when therapists are carefully chosen, as in the Sloane et al. study (1975), patients rarely become worse. Negative effects then seem to virtually disappear. Empirical studies may actually be biased against showing negative effects because the therapists involved know they are being monitored, often in an academic or medical setting, which institutes powerful constraints on malpractice. In ordinary, unmonitored practice situations, however, such as in Striano's consumer report, negative therapist influences appear to be more frequent and blatant. Such variations in context and recording produce sharp variations in the extent of observed effects.

It is also worth considering whether different therapy modalities produce differential rates of negative outcome. While negative effects have been observed widely across the spectrum, including group and marriage and family therapy, there is presently no clear evidence on differential effects. It may be that dynamic treatments with seriously disturbed cases and aggressive group techniques yield more risk while nondirective therapy and behavior therapies yield less risk but, thus far, the data on these hypotheses are limited. Some behavioral methods involving aversion or environmental controls have been reported as producing negative consequences, but the data are unsystematic (cf. Bergin & Lambert, 1978). Previous fears that "flooding" (intense or prolonged exposure to anxiety-provoking stimuli) would produce harmful effects have not so far been supported (Shipley & Boudewyns, 1980).

Concluding Remarks

The controversial status of negative effects is an invitation for continued research on this topic. While research supports the existence of the phenomenon, it should be kept in mind that studying it presents unique problems not inherent in the study of positive outcomes. As has been pointed out elsewhere (Bergin, 1980), "When a research team finds deterioration, it may be difficult to publish because of possible negative reflections upon the clinic or hospital within which the researchers operate" (p. 97). Often the researchers are themselves the therapists or friends and colleagues of the therapists; and when people know they're being monitored, it is likely that they perform better.

In general, the data to date indicate that psychotherapy is indeed for better or worse. The documen-

tation of negative outcomes not only supports the idea that the therapy experience has powerful consequences, but also should influence clinicians and researchers to give earnest and immediate attention to the selection and training of therapists, as well as to the role of licensing and continuing education policies adopted for practitioners. The double-edged effects of treatment lead toward a more complex view of psychotherapy and toward ways of arranging the change process so as to enhance positive effects.

CRITERION-MEASUREMENT: ISSUES, TECHNIQUES, AND RECOMMENDATIONS

As much of the preceding discussion implies, advancements in our knowledge of how to facilitate behavior changes in those seeking treatment is dependent on our ability to assess the effects of treatment. Thus, we conclude this chapter with a discussion of measurement issues and recommendations for assessing psychotherapy outcomes. These recommendations follow our earlier review of this literature as well as the handbook on assessing outcome edited by Lambert, Christensen, and DeJulio (1983).

Although measurement and quantification are central properties of empirical science, the earliest attempts at quantifying treatment gains lacked scientific rigor. The field has gradually moved from complete reliance on therapist ratings of improvement to the use of outcome indices from a variety of viewpoints including the patient, outside observers, relatives, physiological indices, and environmental data such as employment records. The data generated from these viewpoints are always subject to the limitations inherent in the methodology relied upon; none are "objective" or most authoritative.

Attempts at evaluating psychotherapy have frequently reflected current, in-vogue theoretical positions. Thus early studies of psychotherapy applied devices that developed from Freudian dynamic psychology. Not at all uncommon was the use of projective methodologies, including the Rorschach Inkblot Test, the Thematic Apperception Test (TAT), Draw-a-Person, and sentence-completion methods. Problems with the psychometric qualities of these tests, their reliance on inference, and derivation from a theoretical position based on the unconscious all resulted in their waning use as indices of outcome. Rarely today does one hear the virtues of such tests for outcome measurement. Changes in the quality of fantasy material as produced on the TAT and other projective tests simply do not convince most researchers and observers that significant improvement has occurred in the actual lives of patients.

Projective methodology gave way to assessment devices derived from other theories. Client-centered psychology, for example, concentrated on measures of perceived-self ideal-self discrepancies based on the Q-sort technique. These and related measures of self-concept proved only slightly better than projective techniques. The disappearance of such devices as the sole index of improvement in outcome research and acceptance of the idea that the effects of psychotherapy should extend into the daily functioning of patients must be viewed as signs of progress.

These theoretically derived devices have been replaced by atheoretical measures of such factors as adequate role performance, symptomatology, and the direct observation of target behaviors fostered by behavior theory. Enthusiasm for outcome measures that tap socially relevant and syptomatically important changes is still high. There is, however, a growing disillusionment with behavioral assessment (Eifert & Klaut, 1983; Kent & Foster, 1977; Nelson, 1983).

Clearly, a review of past and current practices for assessing psychotherapy outcome indicates that the field, while not without its problems, is maturing. Assessment procedures are becoming more complex and are also relying more heavily on standardized instruments that deal with specific kinds of change. Although there are many problems with current measurement methods, they hold considerable excitement, if not promise, for the future. But despite the current interest in outcome assessment, there is a long way to go before consensus will be reached on the type of yardstick to apply to the results of psychotherapy and behavior-change techniques. One has the impression that despite improvements in assessment practices, more effort needs to be directed toward comprehensive assessments of change. Researchers are not prone to clarify the limits of their assessment practices. They do not discuss the general philosophy underlying their choice of instruments or the implications of

such choices. In the following section an attempt is made to discuss some of the important unspoken conceptual issues that have guided and should guide the selection of instruments for assessing the effects of psychotherapy.

Conclusion 1: Change Is Multidimensional
Clearly, one of the most important conclusions to be drawn from past psychotherapy outcome research is that the results of studies can be easily misunderstood and even misrepresented through failure to appreciate the multidimensionality of the change process. It has proved far too simplistic to expect clients to show consistent and integrated improvement as a result of therapy. The now necessary and, to some degree, common practice of applying multiple criterion measures in research studies (Lambert, 1983) has made it obvious that multiple measures of even simple fears do not yield unitary results. For example, in studies using multiple criterion measures we find that a specific treatment used to reduce seemingly simple fears may result in a decrease in behavioral avoidance of the feared object while not affecting the self-reported level of discomfort associated with the feared object (Mylar & Clement, 1972; Ross & Proctor, 1973; Wilson & Thomas, 1973). Likewise, a physiological indicator of fear may show no change in response to a feared object as a result of treatment, whereas improvement in subjective self-report will be marked.

For example, Glaister (1982), in a review of the effects of relaxation training, found that relaxation in contrast to control procedures (mainly exposure) had its principal impact on physiological indices of change. Indeed it was superior to other treatments in 11 of 12 comparisons while the control (exposure) conditions were superior in 28 of 38 comparisons that used verbal reports of improvement. On behavioral measures (including assessor ratings) neither exposure nor relaxation appeared superior.

Farrell, Curran, Zwick, and Monti (1983), while showing that raters can discriminate social skill deficits from anxiety level on the Simulated Social Skills Test, also found that there was poor correspondence between self-ratings and behavior ratings of these variables. This lack of convergence between measurement methods was also apparent when physiological measures were added (Monti et al., 1983). Little convergent validity was found for measurement method. It appears that often *different* measures of the same target problem disagree (e.g., self-report of sexual arousal and physiological measures; Sabalis, 1983). In addition *even similar* measures of the same behavior sometimes produce inconsistent responses (e.g., different measures of self-reported assertiveness show low intercorrelations; Furnham & Henderson, 1983; Galassi & Galassi, 1980).

One interpretation of these findings is that divergent processes are occurring in therapeutic change; that people themselves embody divergent dimensions or phenomena; and that divergent methods of criterion measurement must be used to match the divergency in human beings and in the change processes that occur within them. This conclusion is further supported by factor analytic studies that have combined a variety of outcome measures.

The main factors derived from some "older" studies that employed factor analytic data tend to be closely associated with the measurement method or the source of observation used in collecting data rather than being identified by some theoretical or conceptual variable that would be expected to cut across techniques of measurement (Cartwright, Kirtner, & Fiske, 1963; Forsyth & Fairweather, 1961; Gibson, Snyder & Ray, 1955; Nichols & Beck, 1960; Shore, Massimo, & Ricks, 1965). A recent example was reported by Pilkonis, Imber, Lewis, and Rubinsky (1984), who factor analyzed 15 scales representing a variety of traits and symptoms from the client, therapist, expert judges, and significant others. These scales were reduced to three factors that most clearly represented the *source* of data rather than the content of the scale.

The consistency of findings regarding the presence of factors associated with the source of ratings rather than the content of patient problems highlights the need to pay careful attention to the complexity of changes that follow psychological interventions. Few studies recognize or deal adequately with these complexities, although creative efforts and some progress have been made.

A study by Berzins et al. (1975) directly addressed the issue of consensus among criterion measures. The authors studied the relationship among outcome measures in 79 client–therapist dyads, using the MMPI, the Psychiatric Status Schedule, and the Current Adjustment Rating Scale. Sources of outcome measurement involved the client, therapist, and trained outside observers. Data from all three

sources and a variety of outcome measures showed generally positive outcomes for the treated group as a whole at termination. There was the usual lack of consensus between criterion measures.

Their primary thesis, however, was that problems of intersource consensus can be resolved through the application of alternatives to conventional methods of analysis. The principal components analysis showed four components: (1) changes in patients' experienced distress as reported by clients on a variety of measures; (2) changes in observable maladjustment as noted by psychometrist, client, and therapist (an instance of intersource agreement); (3) changes in impulse expression (an instance of intersource disagreement between psychometrist and therapist); and (4) changes in self-acceptance (another type of client-perceived change). The practical implications of these findings, although replication could result in changes in the groupings, is that a single criterion might suffice for measuring changes in observable maladjustment, whereas this practice would be misleading if "impulse control" were the outcome criterion. When outcome measures were partitioned into patient sources and other sources and analyzed with canonical analysis, further specification of areas of agreement between sources of outcome were identified. For example, considerable agreement between patient and psychometrist regarding changes in psychoticism were found.

The multiple assessment of outcome was also discussed in an article by Green, Gleser, Stone, and Siefert (1975). These authors compared final status scores, pretreatment to posttreatment difference scores, and direct ratings of global improvement in 50 patients seen in brief crisis-oriented psychotherapy. The Hopkins Symptom Checklist was filled out by the patient while a research psychiatrist rated the patient on the Psychiatric Evaluation Form and the Hamilton Depression Rating Scale. Ratings of global improvement were made by the patient and the therapist.

Green and colleagues concluded that the type of rating scale used has a great deal to do with the percentage of patients considered improved, more so, in fact, than improvement per se! They also suggested that outcome scores have more to do with the "finesse" of rating scales than whether ratings are "objective." Global improvement ratings by therapists and patients showed very high rates of improvement with no patients claiming to do worse. When patients had to rate their symptoms more specifically, however, as with the Hopkins Symptom Checklist, they were likely to indicate actual intensification of some symptoms and to provide more conservative data than gross estimates of change (see also, Garfield, Prager, & Bergin, 1971).

Additionally, patient and therapist global ratings correlated with final status but not initial status. This reinforces the claim that global improvement ratings primarily reflect final status rather than actual change in status. Even so, the results suggest that regardless of source, clients, therapists, and the research psychiatrist were all focusing on similar variables, that is, a decrease in symptomatology and improvement in daily functioning.

Mintz, Luborsky, and Christoph (1979) addressed the question of intersource consensus by analyzing data in two large uncontrolled studies of psychotherapy—the Penn Psychotherapy Project and the Chicago study reported by Cartwright, Kirtner, and Fiske (1963). They reported that there was substantial agreement among the viewpoints of patient, therapist, and outside raters when outcome was broadly defined as posttherapy adjustment or overall benefit. They concluded that, contrary to common opinion, consensus measures of psychotherapy outcome could be meaningfully defined. Despite this consensus, they note that "distinct viewpoints do exist" (p. 331). In fact, if one considers the effect sizes reported by Mintz et al. (1979), it is clear that the range of improvement varied, as a minimum, from 0.52 to 0.93 on pre- to post-changes. The lowest effect size came from the MMPI Hypochondriasis scale and the highest from the Inventory of Social and Psychological Functioning, an observer rating of social adjustment. In addition, although correlations between viewpoints were statistically significant, they were often low. For example, in the Chicago data ($N = 93$) correlations between viewpoints on ratings of adjustment ranged from 0.39 to 0.59.

The lack of consensus across sources of outcome evaluation, especially when each source is presumably assessing the same phenomena, has been viewed as a threat to the veracity of data. Indeed, it appears that outcome data do provide evidence about changes made by the individual as well as information about the differing value orientations and motivations of the individuals providing outcome data. This issue has been dealt with in several

ways ranging from discussion of "biasing motivations" and ways to minimize bias, to discussions of the value orientation of those involved (e.g., Strupp & Hadley, 1977). Until more is known about the interrelationships between sources of data and the differential impact of specific kinds of therapy, outcome assessment will remain a complex process and the search for the specific effects of specific techniques will be limited. In addition, the selection of outcome measures in future research will continue to be based on researchers' familiarity with scales instead of knowledge of their sensitivity to the kind of change one desires to examine.

Conclusion 2: A Meaningful Conceptual Scheme Is Needed to Systematize Outcome Measurement

If change is multidimensional and several instruments are needed to reflect this change, then what guiding principles might most profitably direct researchers in their choice of measures? To a great degree researchers are bound by practical constraints. These constraints are likely to include the needs and comfort of clients, time, and money. A theoretically sound and comprehensive list of instruments must usually give way to these practical considerations. Despite this, an ideal scheme may be presented for the purpose of giving direction to, and illuminating the limitations of, the final assessment package. Figure 5.2 presents such a scheme. It has evolved from earlier, simpler schemes that have been most typically based on dichotomies, such as the idea that outcome should represent measures of "dynamic" versus "symptomatic" improvement; "internal" versus "behavioral" changes; "source" versus "surface" traits; and the like (Bergin & Lambert, 1978).

Most categorizations of outcome measures have been based on practical grounds emphasizing the source providing the data or have been derived directly from existing psychotherapy interventions. Researchers have had difficulty in finding a unified frame of reference from which to view outcome measures, one that gives due consideration to both theoretical and methodological concerns. Shall we consider outcome from the point of view of source of data, type of rating scale, aim of assessment, type of patient problem, process producing the data, or some other point of view?

While researchers' choice of outcome measures

CONTENT	TECHNOLOGY	SOURCE
INTRAPERSONAL	EVALUATION	SELF-REPORT
	1	1
affect	2	2
1	.	.
2	.	.
.	DESCRIPTION	TRAINED OBSERVERS
.	1	1
behavior	2	2
1	.	.
2	.	.
.	OBSERVATION	RELEVANT OTHER
.	1	1
cognition	2	2
1	.	.
2	.	.
.	STATUS	THERAPIST RATING
.	1	1
INTERPERSONAL	2	2
1	.	.
2	.	.
.		INSTITUTIONAL
.		1
SOCIAL ROLE PERFORMANCE		2
1		.
2		.
.		
.		

Figure 5.2. Critical dimensions of assessment tools.

may be determined by their theory of behavior change and mutual agreement with clients over desired outcomes, we recommend attention also be given to a pragmatic view of comprehensive outcome assessment. Such a conception places due emphasis on the fact that different *sources* of ratings correlate at modest levels but seem to provide separate information that is important to consider. It also recognizes that the data can be collected by various *methods* or technologies. These can take the form of behavioral observations, psychophysiological monitoring, judgments, descriptions, and the like. Each of these methods of data collection presents a different view of the change process, and perhaps each should be represented in outcome assessment. For the sake of convergent validity, at least two different methods ought to be employed.

Finally, in addition to source and method, one must consider range of *content*. The focus of evalu-

ation could be on such varied content areas as mood, symptoms (psychopathology), self-concept, role performance, self-regulation of self-control, and physical performance. We recommend the division of content into three categories: intrapersonal, interpersonal, and social role performance. The categories reflect our interest in assessing outcomes that range from those affecting mainly the individual and the symptoms that are an indication of disturbance, to those that reflect the individual's intimate relationship with significant others, and those that emphasize the individual's relationship and contribution to society.

We have further subdivided intrapersonal content into affect, cognition, and behavior (including physiological responding). One defense for such a division is the tendency of different therapies to emphasize one or another of these aspects of people to the exclusion of others (e.g., Garfield, 1980).

Viewing therapy intervention strategies, as well as outcome, from the point of view of cognition, affect, and behavior may result in a clearer understanding of the change process and lead to greater understanding of the effects of specific interventions.

This conceptualization does not necessarily imply that the treatment should be selected to match the component (content) that is disturbed—cognitive therapy for cognitive problems, behaviorally based theories for behavioral disturbance. The behavior of clients in new situations may directly alter affect and cognitions rather than altering cognitions that serve as an intermediary. Coyne (1982) has argued along similar lines while suggesting the fallibility of attributing causality to cognition or affect.

Zajonc's (1980) view (although hardly a new idea in psychology) would be that affects precede cognitions and that cognitions and affect do not closely share the same system. This, of course, is contrary to the view of cognitive therapists. And there is some growing support for the view that thought, feelings, and behavior are not modified in the way cognitive theorists have suggested.

Master and Gershman (1983), for example, showed that physiological responses can be conditioned to irrational beliefs as well as directly (i.e., without cognition). In addition, several reports are drawing attention to the fact that changes in affect and mood disturbances, in general, may well proceed or take place without cognitive changes. Simons, Garfield, and Murphy (1984), reporting on the effects of either cognitive or pharmacological treatment on 28 depressed outpatients, studied both symptomatological and mood changes as well as changes in cognitions. They concluded that changes in cognitions were found whether they were focused on in therapy or not, and that these changes seemed to be part of the general improvement of persons rather than the precursors of change.

Likewise, Silverman, Silverman, and Eardley (1984) studied the dysfunctional thoughts of depressed persons as well as their mood and concluded that these thoughts were a symptom of their illness rather than a character trait. They suggest that cognitive therapy works because of common therapeutic factors rather than the direct modification of thinking. Still others suggest that effective therapies may work in a variety of ways. For example, cognitive therapy and drugs may not change

negative "self-talk" but detach undesirable affect from negative self-talk.

A single outcome study, using a wide variety of assessment sources and multiple "methods" of assessment, can hardly hope to adequately assess improvement in all relevant content areas. The result of this dilemma is that progress will be slow, but without systematic efforts at understanding the interrelationship of sources, methods, and content areas, progress will be even slower.

We recommend that researchers attempt to assess change with full attention to content, technology, and source. When their efforts fall short of comprehensive assessment, the inherent limitations of this methodology should be noted.

Conclusion 3: Individualized Outcome Criteria Are Desirable but Are Difficult to Use Effectively In assessing changes in groups of patients, it is common for researchers to apply a single criterion such as the MMPI or State-Trait Anxiety Scale to all patients in treatment regardless of their diagnosis. By giving all clients the same scales while considering movement in opposite directions for different clients' improvement, or by using diverse standardized measures tailored to the individual client, more precision can be brought into outcome studies. The possibility of tailoring change criteria to each individual in therapy was mentioned frequently in the 1970s, and the idea offers intriguing alternatives for resolving several recalcitrant dilemmas in measuring change.

This notion strongly supports the development of a general trend toward specific rather than global improvement indices. Thus, if a person seeks help for severe depression and shows little evidence of pathological anxiety, we would emphasize changes in depression rather than changes in anxiety level or global psychological status. Taken together, the trends to specify and individually tailor criteria offer a strong antidote to the sometimes vague and unimpressive conclusions often reported in the outcome literature.

An example of this trend that has received widespread attention and increased use is Goal Attainment Scaling (GAS) (Kiresuk & Sherman, 1968). Goal Attainment Scaling requires that a number of mental health goals be set up prior to treatment. These goals are formulated by an individual or a combination of clinicians, client, and/or a committee assigned to the task. For each goal specified, a scale with a graded series of likely outcomes, ranging from least to most favorable, is devised. These goals are formulated and specified with sufficient precision that an independent observer can determine the point at which the patient is functioning at a given time. The procedure also allows for transformation of the overall attainment of specific goals into a standard score.

In using this method for the treatment of obesity, for example, one goal could be the specification and measurement of weight loss. A second goal could be a reduction of depressive symptoms as measured by a scale from a standardized test such as the MMPI. The particular scale examined could be varied from patient to patient, and, of course, other specific types of diverse measures from additional points of view could also be added.

Woodward, Santa-Barbara, Levin, and Epstein (1978) examined the role of GAS in studying family therapy outcome. The authors used content analysis to analyze the nature of the goals that were set and the kind of goals set by therapists of different types. In their study, which focused on termination and six-month follow-up goals, 270 families were considered. This resulted in an analysis of 1005 goals. The authors, who seem to be advocates of GAS, reported that the ratings were reliable and reflected diverse changes in the families studied. They also noted that GAS correlated with other measures of outcome and thus seemed to be valid. This interesting although somewhat uncritical report is a good demonstration of the flexibility and wealth of information resulting from the use of these procedures.

More critical analyses show that GAS suffers from many of the same difficulties as other goal-setting procedures. The correlations for goals seems to be around 0.65. Goals judged either too easy or hard to obtain are often included for analysis, but most important, goal attainment is judged on a relative rather than an absolute basis so that behavior change is confounded with expectations. Further, the choice of goals and the attainment of goals are related to client as well as therapist characteristics.

Calsyn and Davidson (1978) reviewed and assessed GAS as an evaluative procedure. These authors suggest that GAS has poor reliability in that there is insuffficient agreement between raters on the applicability of predefined content categories to

particular patients. In addition, the interrater agreement for goal attainment ranged from $r = 0.51$ to 0.85, indicating variability between those making ratings (e.g., therapist, client, expert judge). In general, studies that have correlated GAS improvement ratings with other ratings of improvement such as MMPI scores, client satisfaction, and therapist improvement ratings have failed to show substantial agreement (frequently coefficients have been below 0.30). In addition, Calsyn and Davidson (1978) point out that the use of GAS also frequently eliminates the use of statistical procedures, such as covariance, that could otherwise correct for sampling errors. Because of this problem, as well as the unknown effects of low reliability, it is suggested that GAS be used in conjunction with standard scales applied to all patients. Suggestions for the use of GAS in psychotherapy research have also been made by Mintz and Kiesler (1982).

Similar procedures that have been used in the evaluation of mental health services include the Problem-Oriented System (POS) (Klonoff & Cox, 1975; Weed, 1969), the Monthly Behavioral Process Report, and Projection Line System (Lloyds, 1983). These procedures suffer from some of the same deficiencies: they are only frameworks for structuring the statement of goals and do not assure that the individualized goals that are specified will be much more than poorly defined subjective decisions by patient or clinician. This leads to problems with setting up goals, which are often not only difficult to state but are written at various levels of abstraction.

Given the above problems, the likelihood that units of change derived from individually tailored goals are unequal and therefore hardly comparable, the likelihood that different goals are differentially susceptible to psychotherapy influence, the tendency for goals to change early in therapy, and the fact that some therapies have a unitary goal or set of goals, the status of individually tailored goals is tenuous. Effective individualization of goals remains an ideal rather than a reality.

Conclusion 4: Psychotherapy Outcome Measures Should Provide Data That Are Clinically Meaningful

A common criticism of psychotherapy research is that the results of studies, as they are typically reported, obscure both the clinical relevance of the findings and the impact of treatment on specific individuals. Statistically significant improvements do not equal practically important improvements. Psychotherapy research would be improved if researchers paid more attention to specifying criteria for meaningful improvement.

Rather than returning to the use of gross rating scales of "improved," "cured," and the like, future researchers might consider the adoption of a well-defined convention for improvement. These sort of criteria are common in drug and alcohol studies in the form of abstinence rates. Other examples of such conventions can be found in the literature. For example, in the treatment of sexual dysfunctions adequate sexual performance has been defined as a ratio of orgasms to attempts at sex, or as time to orgasm following penetration (Sabalis, 1983). These criteria are based on data about the normative functioning of individuals. These sorts of data could be easily developed in the treatment of obesity, where reasonable criteria for weight by height have been developed and can be used to decide the point at which someone is clinically obese. In the same way conventions defining improvement can be developed for almost all the disorders that are commonly treated. These can be defined either with regard to the presence or absence of symptoms or in reference to scores on standard assessment tools. Standards of clinical improvement can be based on normative data and posttreatment status rather than the magnitude of change.

Jacobson et al. (1984a), for example, suggest that improvement be defined as a movement from dysfunctional to functional on whatever variable is being used to measure change. They suggest the use of data on functional and dysfunctional populations and appropriate cutoff scores based on this data base. Of course such a solution has several limitations; for example, data may not be available on dysfunctional populations, or purely functional populations; and some severely disturbed populations cannot be expected to achieve "normality." Nevertheless, they do provide standard criteria that can be applied across studies in a variety of patient populations.

They also propose a "reliable change index" as a standard method for determining whether treatment gains reliably exceed measurement error and for making similar judgments about deterioration during psychotherapy.

In an application of these criteria to behavioral marital therapy Jacobson et al. (1984b) reanalyzed the results of four outcome studies. Across the four studies 148 couples received behavioral marital therapy. The results of these reanalyses suggest that the methods proposed by Jacobson et al. (1984a) are more conservative than traditional data analysis techniques, thus reinforcing their call for standard methods for establishing improvement rates.

Although many problems exist with the methods proposed by Jacobson et al. (1984a) (including the fact that the common use of multiple outcome measures complicates conclusions about client status), they promise to make the specification of outcome more meaningful and useful to the clinician. Serious attention should be given by researchers to adopting their procedures, or similar procedures that emphasize clinical rather than statistical significance, in reporting outcome.

Summary
The history of assessing change following psychological treatments shows considerable growth, maturity, and improvement in methods and procedures. This growth is most obvious in our recognition of the complexity of the task. Multiple measures of outcome are now common (Beutler, 1983; Lambert, 1983), and emphasis on practical behavior rather than theoretical issues has increased; this is true both in verbal therapies and behavioral approaches. One can detect, however, similar cycles of unbounded optimism about new measurement strategies, followed by disillusionment and then abandonment that one sees in the psychotherapies themselves. While this cycle is clear in traditional verbal therapies, it is becoming apparent in behavior therapies as well. There is some current disillusionment with behavioral assessment based partially on the expense, time, and obtrusiveness of collecting data as well as the fact that there are surprising inconsistencies between methods and within content areas.

There is a hint that in addition to actually making advances in effective measurement we are moving in a circular motion. And clearly there is much work to be done before we will have sensitive, acceptable measures of the effects of psychotherapy.

Suggestions of Useful Techniques
The preceding discussion focused on general issues of measuring outcome. We now provide brief com-

mentaries on specific outcome criteria that appear most promising for the evaluation of psychological treatments. Even this analysis must remain at a somewhat general level because patient populations are highly diverse and therefore require measures unique to the pathology that is addressed. For a more extensive analysis of suitable outcome measures for use with homogeneous patient populations, the reader should consult Lambert et al. (1983), Waskow and Parloff (1975), or one of the following volumes on behavioral assessment: Ciminero, Calhoun, and Adams (1977a), Hersen and Bellack (1981), Kendall and Hollon (1981), Barlow (1981), or Conger and Conger (1982).

As previous conclusions and recommendations imply, we favor the use of multiple outcome measures; we also favor the use of indices from a variety of viewpoints. In addition to giving a more complete picture of the change process, assessing change from diverse viewpoints prevents systematic bias and, therefore, unwarranted conclusions. To encourage this diversity we have organized outcome measures under the headings that indicate their source: Patient Self-report, Trained Outside Observer/Expert Observer Ratings, Relevant Others Ratings, Therapist Ratings, and Institutional Ratings.

Patient Self-report

There is an abundance of measures calling on the client for an elaboration of his or her thoughts, feelings, beliefs, behaviors, and current status. Various measures are differentially subject to a host of biasing procedures (e.g., the "hello—good-bye" effect, social desirability). Methodological problems in research with self-report inventories have been identified by Gynther and Green (1982). Despite methodological concerns, self-reported change remains a central method for estimating treatment effects. Most measures reported and summarized by Buros (1978) that are relevant to behavior change have potential as outcome measures. Those that seem most promising are described below.

1. Posttherapy questionnaires/satisfaction measures. Historically, a majority of psychotherapy studies have included a measure of patient-felt improvement that taps both global estimates of therapy-induced improvement and improvements on specific targets. In addition, evaluation studies

have frequently used a measure of overall satisfaction with treatment. In general, these scales are simple and quick and have high face validity (Lebow, 1982; Strupp et al. 1969). The resulting scores often correlate with other assessments of change, therapist qualities, treatment variables, client demographics, and other important variables (Berger, 1983; Bornstein & Rychtarik, 1983; Kirchner & Hogan, 1982). It appears, however, that they are inordinately influenced by the patient's condition at treatment termination rather than actual change from pretherapy status (Garfield, 1978). Because of their lack of sensitivity to initial levels of disturbance and changes that follow, their usefulness as outcome measures has been questioned. Often their use seems to be intended to prove a treatment program is effective rather than to advance scientific interests (Garfield, 1983a) and there is some question about whose satisfaction is being assessed (Kiesler, 1983).

Beutler and Crago (1983) and Beutler (1983) have suggested a possible solution to some of these problems and a sample questionnaire format for posttherapy ratings of improvement. This format calls for the patient to rate initial levels of disturbance (on global and specific dimensions) as well as current status at treatment termination. The mean difference between these two ratings represents the amount of treatment-related change. The global and specific change scores are then combined with each other (through weighting, etc.) and possibly with other measures of change to provide an index of patient-perceived improvement. Although these ratings probably add little beyond the information obtained from the measures next reviewed, their use in program evaluation and clinical practice seems warranted.

2. Symptom checklists. Generally, checklists that have been used in psychotherapy research are of two types: (1) single symptoms/single trait—such as the Beck Depression Inventory (Beck, Ward, Mendelson, Mock, & Erbaugh, 1961) or the State-Trait Anxiety Inventory (Spielberger, Gorsuch, & Luchene, 1970) or (2) multiple checklists such as the Hopkins Symptom Checklist (Derogatis, Lipman, Rickels, Uhlenhuth, & Covi, 1974), which attempt to provide scores on a number of dimensions simultaneously. The simple symptom checklist is most appropriate when a homogeneous population is being studied, while the multiple checklist is well suited to a more general clinical population. The advantage of these devices is that they are straightforward, quickly administered (and readministered on several occasions), more rigorous and standardized than posttherapy questionnaires (e.g., satisfaction measures characteristically show 85 percent of patients satisfied while the same patients may show improvement and worsening on a variety of symptoms), and yet more sensitive to the effects of interventions than personality tests such as the MMPI.

We recommend the use of symptom checklists for assessing the effects of treatment. Most promising among the multiple checklists is the Symptom Checklist-90R (SCL-90R) (Derogatis et al., 1974). This scale, a revision of the longer Hopkins Symptom Checklist, and a predecessor to the Brief Symptom (53 items) Inventory (Derogatis & Melisaratos, 1983), is a 90-item list consisting of nine symptom dimensions and three global indices of distress. The checklist shows adequate reliability and validity data, although the use of all nine subscales is questionable. The SCL-90R is most useful as a global index of psychopathology or psychological distress (Roberts, Aronoff, Jensen, & Lambert, 1983) rather than as a measure of a more specific disturbance such as depression.

While multiple checklists may be appropriate for some studies, researchers may find it more useful to use one or more single checklists to more thoroughly assess specific symptoms. For this purpose we recommend using the Beck Depression Inventory, the Zung Self-Rating Depression Scale (Zung, 1965), and possibly the SR Inventory of Anxiousness (Endler, Hunt, & Rosenstein, 1962) or State-Trait Anxiety Inventory (Spielberger et al., 1970) in studies that deal with affective disorders or generalized anxiety disorders in general clinical populations. The advantages and disadvantages of these measures have been summarized elsewhere (Beutler & Crago, 1983; Moran & Lambert, 1983; Roberts et al., 1983), and the conclusions seem fairly consistent. These devices do a fairly good job of assessing the symptoms of disorders as defined by the *Diagnostic and Statistical Manual* (APA, 1980) or (RDC) Research Diagnostic Criteria (Feighner et al., 1972) criteria of anxiety or depression. They tap a variety of symptoms dealing with affect, cognition, physiological reactions, and behavioral manifestations such that they fairly well cover symptoms in the diagnostic categories of depression and anxiety. They are brief (e.g., Beck, 21 items; Zung, 20 items; State-Trait Anxiety Inventory, 40 items), thus lending themselves to painless readministrations. It is also important that they seem to be sensitive to the effects of psychological and chemical interventions (Edwards et al., 1984; Lambert, Hatch, Kingston, & Edwards, 1986).

It should be mentioned that in addition to these symptom measures there are a host of adequate measures of situation-specific fears such as the Fear Survey Schedule (Wolpe & Lang, 1964) and Fear Questionnaire (Watson & Marks, 1971) as well as measures of social anxiety, assertiveness, and so on. A review of these instruments is provided in Lambert et al. (1983) and in Ciminero et al. (1977a). Bellack (1983) has identified recurrent problems in the assessment of social skills. There is a fast growing body of literature on measuring social skills with single inventories (e.g., Furnham & Henderson, 1983).

3. Self-monitoring. A valuable self-report procedure used extensively by behavioral and cognitive schools is self-monitoring (Hollon & Kendall, 1981). These procedures call for the client to record in vivo cognitions, affects, or target behaviors. Most studies have focused on motor responses alone. Serious questions about the accuracy and reliability of self-monitoring have been raised (Kazdin, 1974; Mahoney, 1977). Ciminero, Nelson, and Lipinski (1977b) have suggested that the following factors can influence the accuracy of self-monitoring: valence of the phenomenon, nature of the target, reinforcement provided (or intrinsic) for monitoring, temporal schedule, nature of concurrent activities, recording device, recognition of accuracy, and training in self-monitoring. This host of methodological issues, the problems of reactivity of measurement, and the covert nature of some of the targets (cognitions, affective reactions) has resulted in some pessimism for this method. Nevertheless, self-monitoring with proper attention to methodology remains one of the most important and convincing measures of change. It has been applied effectively in the study of addictive behavior, migraine, compulsive behaviors, study behavior, classroom performance, and a host of negative habits. Its use in cognitive therapy, especially with reference to dysfunctional thoughts, is yet to be demonstrated and may prove hard to verify, but it has become popular in the last five years (Hollon & Kendall, 1981).

For example, Kendall and Hollon (1981) suggest a number of strategies for assessing self-referent speech including the use of the Self-Statement Inventory to assess the degree to which people engaged in thoughts that might be expected to hinder or help coping behavior. The Automatic Thoughts Questionnaire (Kendall & Hollon, 1981) was developed for use with depressed patients. Sutton-Simon (1981) reported 15 separate self-report scales used to measure irrational beliefs, the most widely used being the Irrational Beliefs Test (Jones, 1968). While none of these self-report scales can be recommended for general use, and their relation to changes in symptomatology is not well established, there is clearly a trend for exploration of cognitive changes with these devices.

4. Personality tests.   The use of so-called objective personality tests is still common in the assessment of psychological treatments. These tests tend to measure somewhat more enduring and broad needs, conflicts, symptoms, and trait patterns than the checklists. They also tend to be more subtle and include many more items. To a great extent they overlap the devices listed under symptom checklists in that many clearly focus on psychopathology, although they also provide data on nonpathological characteristics.

Currently, there is considerable skepticism about the value of personality assessment. This skepticism comes from various quarters including (1) the popularity of behavioral approaches and the corresponding lack of interest in standard assessment methods that lead to the assigning of people to diagnostic catetories or in elaborating on internal dynamics; (2) the humanistically derived belief that the testing and diagnostic enterprise is itself an unhelpful way of relating to persons seeking help; and (3) the belief that personality tests do not work very well and have unimpressive validity coefficients because they largely measure personality traits to the exclusion of situational variables (cf. Mischel, 1972, 1977). Although we do not believe that traditional psycholog-

ical tests should be abandoned, we are in sympathy with those who emphasize the need to assess situation-specific behaviors in addition to more global and pervasive traits.

The MMPI continues to be used with high frequency in outcome studies. Beutler and Crago (1983) found that it was used in 50 percent of the studies that employed a general personality measure, while Lambert (1983), in a survey covering five years of published research, reported that it was the most widely used instrument of this type. The common practice is for researchers to use either specialty scales such as the Taylor MAS and Welsh Scales, or a limited number of clinical scales (Pt, D, and Sc Scales) that have been shown to be sensitive to treatment. The sum of the clinical scales has also been widely used in past research (Dahlstrom & Welsh, 1960). Despite the popularity and advantages of the MMPI (not the least of which is its value as a diagnostic instrument) and our previous recommendation (Bergin & Lambert, 1978) that it be used in outcome research, several points argue against its inclusion in an outcome battery. These points hinge less on criticisms that it is outmoded than on the lack of clear meaning of its specific scales. In addition to occasional low reliability for some scales, the MMPI has a strongly nosological orientation that is not designed to assess therapeutic change. It can still be used to identify suitable patient samples and to describe patient populations, but it is too cumbersome and perhaps insensitive to serve as a measure of change. Repeated testing with the same individuals is a necessity in outcome research, yet a serious problem with the MMPI. And the limited data on outcome that are obtained, especially when one considers the increasing tendency to study homogeneous samples, argues against its use in most studies.

Suitable alternatives, however, do not exist. The most popular may be the Eysenck Personality Inventory (EPI) (Eysenck & Eysenck, 1969). Emotionality or fearfulness is measured on a Neuroticism Scale, while conditionability is measured on the dimension of extroversion-introversion. These personality dimensions are measured by 100 items that produce scores with considerable reliability. Unfortunately, these dimensions are seen as rather enduring personality traits and their usefulness as indices of outcome is not well established. Although useful as a personality measure, the EPI is less promising for assessing change than any of several measures of anxiety, such as the S-R Inventory of Anxiousness, that measure symptoms common in anxiety states rather than more enduring personality traits.

A test of contemporary interest that may be useful in assessing change in personality disorder is the Millon Clinical Multi-axial Inventory (Millon, 1977). To our knowledge it has not as yet been used in outcome research but may show promise with a wide range of patients.

For a variety of reasons discussed earlier, it is not recommended that more general measures of personality such as the TAT, Rorschach, and similar projective tests be employed as outcome measures. While they may provide suitable data for personality analysis, changes on scores derived from them do not provide convincing evidence of clinical improvement, nor have they proved to be economical, or sensitive to treatment interventions.

5. Measures of self-regulation/self-esteem. Lakey (1977), in her review of self-concept instruments, found more than 200 measures reported in the literature. Scales measuring self-esteem, self-acceptance, and self-control/regulation provide a domain uniquely suited to self-report methodology. Historically, the most widely used measure of self-concept in psychotherapy research has been the Butler-Haigh Q-sort (Dymond, 1954), from which a score representing real-self/ideal-self discrepancy is derived as well as an adjustment score. The major drawback with the Q-sort methodologies is not their psychometric properties, but the time involved in administration, which will average out to about $1\frac{1}{2}$ hours per administration. While we can recommend its continued use as a measure of self-concept, there are briefer (e.g., Interpersonal Checklist; Cooper, 1983) and possibly better measures for assessing changes in self-perception. Among these we include the Tennessee Self Concept Scale (Fitts, 1965), Personal Attribute Inventory (Kappes & Parish, 1979), and the Rosenberg Self-Esteem Scale (Rosenberg, 1965). These can be administered in under 15 minutes, thus enabling the researcher to collect additional data from subjects. Although it can be argued that none of the self-concept scales measures anything other than psychological distress, and therefore adds little to an assessment battery

that includes a distress measure, there is some evidence (Seeman, 1979; Warr, Barter, & Brownbridge, 1983) that they tap an additional dimension such as the strength of a positive self-view. Currently, we would argue for the inclusion of a separate self-concept measure when self-concept is the target of treatment, as well as when it is expected to be a likely specific secondary gain of treatment.

The currently popular trend of trying to effect changes in a person's self-control and self-regulation has not yet resulted in the development of acceptable measures of this area of common difficulty among modern clinic populations. Recently Rosenbaum (1980) reported on the development of the Self Control Schedule, a self-report questionnaire that consists of 36 items that describe the use of coping strategies, the ability to delay gratification, and the ability to perceive self-efficacy. Its value as an outcome measure is yet to be demonstrated. This dimension of patient change seems important, and measures of it have arisen mostly in the form of behavior ratings and self-monitoring devices. They include timing devices, mechanical counters, self-monitoring cards, and specific uses of videotape equipment.

Expert and Trained Observers

Despite the primary importance of the patient's report of change in therapy, observations by persons who did not participate in the process seem essential in providing a more balanced and sometimes convincing picture of change. There are a number of ways in which these data can be collected—through the use of behavior counts performed in vivo or in simulated settings, via interviews conducted by well-trained clinicians, or through observations of performance in critical situations. These methods share in common the imposition of a performance standard with the use of a person external to the therapy as a judge. The underlying assumption is that the forthcoming data will be reliable (and perhaps objective) and add to or confirm data from the client.

The reader is reminded that judges' ratings may, depending on the nature of the rating scale, suffer from biases that result from both the clients' view of the situation (e.g., desire to put best foot forward) and the raters' biases (e.g., tendency to use the middle points on a scale, leniency error, assigning patient to a category and then giving ratings consistent with that class, rating patient higher when they have trait rater doesn't have). These and similar errors are even present, although to a lesser degree, in situations where observers are simply required to count target behaviors (Nelson, 1983). Expert or trained rater judgments should not be viewed as necessarily more authoritative than patient self-report, but rather as an additional view of patient status with its own unique strengths and limitations.

1. Standardized interviews and expert ratings. Current research practice has moved away from the unacceptable procedure of relying upon clinical judgment without reference to rating scales and trait definitions. Large numbers of appropriate interview schedules for assessing social adjustment have been reviewed by Weissman (1975) and Weissman, Sholomakas, and John (1981). Several procedures have reached useful levels of development in standardizing interviews to assess global and specific areas of functioning and can be recommended for use with outpatient adults.

The first of these is the Social Adjustment Scale (SAS) (Weissman & Paykel, 1974). The SAS was derived from the Structural and Scaled Interview to Assess Maladjustment. It rates the patient's adjustment in six roles (work, social and leisure activities, extended family, relationship with spouse, parental role, and member of family unit) by asking 41 questions and rating answers on a five-point scale. The questions tap performance of roles, friction in roles, as well as felt distress in role performance. This semistructured interview can be administered by a trained research assistant in 45 to 90 minutes. The questions are suitable for a variety of adult patients, especially outpatients, with a focus on role performance over the previous $2\frac{1}{2}$ months. Preliminary data suggest that the scales have reasonable reliability and are sensitive to therapeutic interventions (Weissman & Paykel, 1974). Another characteristic that favors the SAS is its availability in a self-report version. Correlations between the interviewer and self-report forms range from 0.40 to 0.76, with a mean of 0.54. The global self-report score and interviewer score correlated 0.72 (Weissman & Bothwell, 1976).

Like its predecessor the SSIAM, the SAS seems to provide standards for adequate role performance based on middle-class values. Thus, the "reference group" may not be appropriate for some patients. Nevertheless, the SAS can be recommended as an instrument that balances the need for objectivity and reliability with the need to tap broad areas of clinically and socially meaningful functioning.

A second interview device that can be recommended is the Denver Community Mental Health Questionnaire (DCMHQ) (Ciarlo & Reihman, 1977). The goal of this interview is to assess broad-based community mental health treatment outcome. It consists of 79 items rated by a trained nonprofessional in a 45-minute interview. The questions probe into the frequency of various problems and, in contrast to the SAS, the scores are based more on these data than on the judgments of the interviewer.

The items have been clustered into 13 scales including psychological distress, interpersonal isolation from family and friends, interpersonal aggression, productivity at work and home, role performance at home, legal difficulties, public system dependence, alcohol abuse, drug abuse, and client satisfaction. The scales appear to have high reliability (median of 0.92) and to be relatively independent from each other.

A disadvantage of the DCMHQ is that it is probably most appropriate for a community mental health population. In addition, not a great deal is known about its sensitivity as an outcome measure, although the content and technology of the scales suggests it would be sensitive to changes in patients who undergo treatment.

A third expert rating that shows promise is the Global Adjustment Scale (GAS) (Endicott, Spitzer, Fleiss, & Cohen, 1976). The GAS has the advantage of producing a simple index of adjustment on a 100-point scale. A modification of the Health Sickness Rating Scale, it is less time consuming with brief definitions worded in terms of behaviorally defined scale points. Change scores are based on post- minus prescore ratings. GAS provides a reasonably reliable (range of interrater agreement 0.61–0.91) way of quantifying the degree of disturbance present in individuals who have had an intake interview. Like other global ratings, GAS provides only crude estimates of pathology, and the field needs to do a lot better.

Finally, mention should be made of the Hamilton Rating Scale for Depression (HRS) (Hamilton,

1967). Unlike the interviews previously reviewed, the HRS aims to assess a single type of difficulty, that is, the severity of clinical depression. The HRS consists of 17 items assessed in the course of a clinical interview by an expert clinician taking into account all available information (data from significant others, etc.). Based on interview material alone, the HRS has high interrater reliability (0.80–0.90). The Hamilton also seems to be highly sensitive to therapeutic interventions. Edwards et al. (1984) compared the HRS with the Beck Depression Inventory in 19 studies where both were used to assess outcome. These studies, which had 1150 patients divided into 41 treatment groups, showed the HRS effect size score to be 1.29 on the average, while change as measured with the Beck averaged 0.89. This relatively large effect size suggests that HRS scores can be expected to change following treatment. The HRS is well suited for psychotherapy outcome research with major depressive disorders (Lambert et al., 1986).

Although the interview schedules listed are important, they are not exhaustive. For a more detailed analysis of suitable rating scales the interested person is referred to Auerbach (1983), Newman (1983), and Wittenborn (1984). The value of "expert" ratings can be questioned on the grounds that, with the exception of the Hamilton, they are too global. Nevertheless, we recommend continued application and exploration of expert ratings, especially for assessing social role performance, diagnosis, and the like.

2. Behavioral counts. In addition to expert clinicians using interviews and rating scales to provide data on patients, there are a variety of behavioral counts and observational rating forms that are completed by nonprofessional observers. These procedures have been well documented, especially in the literature on therapy with children. A variety of such procedures have proved useful to researchers because of the high levels of reliability obtained and the likelihood that they will be collected in vivo and thereby prove to be socially significant. However, Kern (1984), in trying to validate Role Play Tests, found that the typical methodology was, indeed, more likely to reflect *response capability* rather than actual performance. Thus, they exaggerate the amount of improvement actually achieved by participants who undergo treatment. A review of methods is provided by Hersen and Bellack (1981), Cone and Hawkins (1977), and Ciminero et al. (1977a).

Evaluation by Relevant Others
A source of data that can prove invaluable is that which can be obtained from informants who have contact with the patient outside the consulting room. We list among these relevant others: parents, spouse, siblings, friends, teachers, employer, and other third parties who, by virtue of these relationships with the patient, can provide data that may be outside the scope of that obtained via self-report or clinical observation. These informants may be used to corroborate self-report data, as with data on the use of tobacco or alcohol, or to provide an entirely separate source of information. The importance of this data source varies as a function of the targets of treatment. For the treatment targets associated with family, marital, and sex therapies, for example, such data are mandatory. In the assessment of phobic disorders or psychophysiological reactions such data may be far less valuable, although certainly not irrelevant. In studies of alcoholism and drug dependence where patients are known to provide questionable self-report data, and no other means of verification are possible, informants can be quite useful.

There are numerous problems in collecting data from relevant others: sometimes they are not available, cooperation may be lacking, and the motivations for providing data are hard to control. Davidson and Davidson (1983) have also suggested that the ethical issues in obtaining this kind of data are sometimes prohibitive or result in highly intrusive, expensive, and cumbersome procedures. Despite these difficulties, ratings from significant others provide such an important potential data source that the psychotherapy researcher must consider devices from this area.

Measures of social adjustment. Most of the measures tapping the views of relevant others in adult psychotherapy have measured social adjustment. Among these is the Katz Adjustment Scale-Relatives Form (KAS-R) (Katz & Lyerly, 1963). The KAS-R is completed by a relative who has close contact with the patient and refers back over a period of three weeks. The KAS-R is composed of

205 items in five areas that include symptoms and social behavior and takes from 30 to 60 minutes to complete. The KAS-R has the advantage of having been used frequently and therefore considerable data are available regarding it (e.g., Hargreaves, Glick, Drues, Shewstack, & Feigenbaum, 1977). On the other hand, it is most appropriate for severely disturbed patients and does not have built-in validity scales. There is evidence that responses may vary considerably across informants—thus one is encouraged to use the pooled ratings of more than a single informant (Davidson & Davidson, 1983). A competing scale, and one that is briefer than the very lengthy KAS-R, is the Personal Adjustment and Role Skills-III (Ellsworth, 1975). This scale in its original form was used with male veterans to assess functioning after hospitalization. The PARS-III is appropriate for both males and females and can be completed as a mailed questionnaire.

Measures of sexual behavior and marital satisfaction. Another area of considerable research activity in adult assessment involves the use of ratings from spouses, who may also be participants in the therapy. The common procedure is to collect the views of both the primary patient and the spouse on measures of sexual behavior as well as global and specific areas of marital satisfaction. The Locke-Wallace Marital Adjustment Test (Locke & Wallace, 1959) is a frequently used scale that shows adequate reliability, validity, and sensitivity to numerous interventions. In addition, the Sexual Interaction Inventory (LoPiccolo & Steger, 1974) provides a measure that is specific to sexual behavior, a topic partially covered by the Locke-Wallace Scale. The interested reader is referred to Sabalis (1983) and to Jacobson, Elwood, and Dallas (1981) for a further discussion of methodological issues and potential scales in this area.

Evaluation by the Therapist
Evaluation of outcome by the therapist has dropped drastically from a position of prominence to relative obscurity in recent years (Lambert, 1983). While some would applaud this movement, there is a paradox involved. Newman (1983) pointed out that on the one hand we are willing to give the therapist sole responsibility for the provision of therapy, yet hesitate to include the therapist as a source for judging outcome. This is unfortunate, however un-

derstandable, because the therapist as a participant-observer in the process is privy to information that can be gained from no other source. While we hope the therapist will never again become the sole source of information about treatment outcome, the therapist is in a position to provide important data. There are adequate standard measures available for use by the therapist. The typical procedure involves collecting ratings of improvement based either on global improvement ratings from a review of case notes or impressions recorded on partially standardized scales such as the Level of Functioning Scale created by Carter and Newman (1980) or the Global Assessment Scale (Endicott et al., 1976). Many scales that are completed by expert judges can also be filled out by the therapist. We recommend use of one of the following scales.

The target complaints technique (Battle et al., 1966) is an individualized measure that requires the therapist to list three focal problems early in the therapy, rate their severity, and then rerate these problems at treatment termination. The procedure takes less than 15 minutes and has been shown to be reliable and sensitive to change (cf. Sloane et al., 1975). Limitations of this device include its possible susceptibility to demand characteristics, and it is considered by some to be superficial. It is similar to Goal Attainment Scaling (Kiresuk & Sherman, 1968), the Problem Oriented Record (Weed, 1969), and the Davis Goal Scaling Form (Edwards, 1974). While all these methods can tap data from a wide range of problem areas, they suffer from a variety of other limitations previously discussed under the topic of individualized outcome measures. While most critiques of therapist assessments focus on the self-serving bias that such ratings involve, there is evidence that if proper methodological procedures are employed, therapist judgments turn out to be as reliable and valid as ratings from other sources (Mintz, Auerbach, Luborsky, & Johnson, 1973; Newman, 1983). We continue to feel that the target complaints method holds promise as an outcome measure and recommend that it be used in accordance with guidelines spelled out by Mintz and Kiesler (1982).

Assessment Through Institutional Means
In addition to the preceding sources of data, a final source for outcome data is that found in the community at large. These data are obtained from re-

cords maintained primarily for the internal use of an organization or agency such as schools, law enforcement agencies, employment offices, hospitals, and the like. While not listing any specific devices we conclude that this data source, which usually exists completely independent of the study, is frequently untapped in prospective research but can provide a wealth of information about the real-life consequences of treatment. The independent nature of these data and their reliance upon complex behaviors that integrate the thoughts, feelings, and behaviors of the individual along with their interaction with the larger community make data from institutional sources quite convincing evidence that treatment effects are socially significant. The most frequently used measures of this sort are measures of recidivism. Thus, with alcoholic, drug-abusing, and correctional populations, rearrest records can be invaluable. Hospital readmission rates and medical utilization records also provide socially and personally important criteria for successful treatment of inpatients and psychophysiological disorders. For a discussion of the limitations of these data, suggestions for sound procedures, and problems in data collection, the reader is referred to Andrews (1983) and Maisto and Maisto (1983).

CONCLUSIONS

Research on psychotherapy outcomes has resulted in conlcusions that have implications for research and clinical practice.

1. Many psychotherapies that have been subjected to empirical study have been shown to have demonstrable effects on a variety of clients. These effects are not only statistically significant but clinically meaningful. Psychotherapy facilitates the remission of symptoms. It not only speeds up the natural healing process but often provides additional coping strategies and methods for dealing with future problems. Psychologists, psychiatrists, social workers, and marriage and family therapists as well as patients can be assured that a broad range of therapies, when offered by skillful, wise, and stable therapists, are likely to result in appreciable gains for the client.

2. The effects of therapy tend to be lasting. While some problems, such as addictive disorders, tend to recur, the gains many patients make in therapy endure. This is probably due to the fact that most therapists are interested in enduring changes rather than symptomatic improvements. Research suggests that therapists should expend greater *systematic* efforts at helping patients solidify the gains made in therapy and focus attention near the end of treatment on the meaning of improvement to the patient and methods of coping with future problems.

3. Not only is there clear evidence for the effectiveness of therapy, relative to untreated patients, but psychotherapy patients show gains that surpass those resulting from pseudotherapies and placebo controls. These types of control groups are aimed at discovering whether therapies add anything beyond what can be achieved through treatments that offer a supportive relationship and hope or expectancy of improvement. Again, psychotherapists are more than placebologists. Indeed, the placebo concept is not viable in psychotherapy research. Psychotherapy placebos, like medical placebos, have their effects through psychological means, which is the central medium of psychotherapeutic procedures. Future research would do well to focus more on comparative treatment studies or studies aimed at identifying therapeutic factors than on outdated notions of placebo controls.

4. Although research continues to support the efficacy of those therapies that have been rigorously tested, differences in outcome between various forms of therapy are not as pronounced as might have been expected. Behavior therapy, cognitive therapy, and eclectic mixtures of these show superior outcomes to traditional verbal therapies in several studies on specific disorders, although this is by no means the general case. When this superiority is in evidence, the results have been attributed to the bias of researchers and the selectivity in criteria of change; however, the critics can be biased and selective too. Although there is little evidence of clinically meaningful superiority of one form of psychotherapy over another with respect to moderate outpatient disorders, behavioral and cognitive methods appear to add a significant increment of efficacy with respect to a number of difficult problems (e.g., phobias and compulsions) and to provide useful methods with a number of nonneurotic problems with which traditional therapies have shown little effectiveness (e.g., childhood aggression, psychotic behavior, stuttering).

Given the growing evidence that there are probably some specific technique effects, as well as large common effects across treatments, the vast majority of therapists have become eclectic in orientation. This appears to reflect a healthy response to empirical evidence and a rejection of previous trends toward rigid allegiances to schools of treatment.

5. Interpersonal, social, and affective factors common across therapies still loom large as stimulators of patient improvement. It should come as no surprise that helping people deal with depression, inadequacy, anxiety, and inner conflicts, as well as helping them form viable relationships and meaningful directions for their lives, can be greatly facilitated in a therapeutic relationship that is characterized by trust, warmth, acceptance, and human wisdom. These relationship factors are probably crucial even in the more technical therapies that generally ignore relationship factors and emphasize the importance of technique. This is not to say that techniques are irrelevant but that their power for change is limited when compared with personal influence. Common factors that are currently popular for explaining improvement in therapy also include exposure to anxiety-provoking stimuli, the encouragement to participate in other risk-taking behavior, and making mastery efforts. Research suggests not only that clients would be wise to pick therapists on the basis of their ability to relate but that training programs should emphasize the development of the therapist as a person in parity with the acquisition of therapeutic techniques.

Recognition of the important place held by therapist relationship skills, facilitative attitudes, wisdom based on experience, and a variety of nontechnical skills in producing positive change in patients should in no way be construed as suggesting that technical proficiency has no unique contribution to make. Future research should focus not only on the important factors common across therapies but also on the specific effects of particular interventions. The current trend to provide therapy in a systematic way, as characterized by the use of treatment manuals, and further studies of the process of therapy may yet allow for more definitive conclusions regarding the contribution of technique factors.

6. Research on the effects of less experienced clinicians and paraprofessionals complements the conclusions drawn about schools of therapy and common factors. Paraprofessionals, who in many cases are selected, trained, and supervised by professional therapists, are sometimes able to be as helpful as practicing clinicians. These paraprofessionals should continue to play an important role in providing some mental health services. They are especially useful in providing social support and in offering structured treatment programs under supervision.

We hope that more empirical tests will be conducted to examine the question of whether there are especially complex disorders that yield only to sophisticated, expert interventions as opposed to the "simpler" force of an especially humane, interpersonal encounter.

7. Empirical research has been adequate to confirm the positive effect of many of the therapies so far put to the test. However, more research must be undertaken using valid and sensitive assessments. To the extent that we rely on gross, symptomatic scales, it will be difficult to answer questions of more contemporary concern. Psychometric advances are needed, both in terms of the measuring instruments we use and in terms of our conceptualizations of what it is that needs to be assessed. Intrapersonal, interpersonal, and social role performance are broad areas that need systematic investigation.

8. The development and use of meta-analytic procedures for integrating outcome research is a methodological advancement that will enable scholars and clinicians to better understand research findings. Meta-analysis, however, is not a panacea and cannot be used to create worthwhile information if based upon poorly designed studies. In addition, meta-analysis would not appear to be highly useful in between-study comparisons due to the large amount of variability across studies that cannot be controlled statistically. Thus, the work of Smith et al. (1980) illustrates the possibilty of these analytic tools, but is limited by their heavy reliance on between-study comparisons. Nevertheless, the next generation of meta-analytic reviews should provide an even more appropriate use of meta-analysis (cf. Lambert et al., in press; Miller & Berman, 1983). An important task of future meta-analytic reviews will be to translate the abstract review into clinically meaningful terms.

9. Although the foregoing broad, positive statements about psychotherapy can be made with more

confidence than ever before, it is still important to point out that average positive effects mask considerable variability in outcomes. Wide variations exist in therapist qualities and technical skills, in patient characteristics, and in interactions between patients and therapists. The therapist factor, as a contributor to this variability, is looming larger in the assessment of outcomes. Some therapists appear to be unusually effective. Nevertheless, we end this review on a cautionary note. It is apparent that not all are helped by therapy and that a portion of those whom it is intended to help are actually harmed by inept applications of treatments, negative therapist attitudes or poor combinations of treatment technique and patient problem.

Much more research needs to be conducted before the exact relationship between the process of therapy and its outcome will be known (cf. Orlinsky and Howard chapter in this volume). The public deserves treatments that are based not only on our best clinical judgment but also on systematic research conducted under controlled situations. It is our duty to be sensitive to both the positive and negative effects of therapy and to base our treatment efforts on a broad empirical foundation.

REFERENCES

American Psychiatric Association (1980). *Diagnostic and Statistic Manual of Mental Disorders (DSM-III)* (3rd ed.). Washington, DC: APA.

Andrews, D. A. (1983). Assessment of outcome in correctional samples. In M. J. Lambert, E. R. Christensen, & S. S. DeJulio (Eds.), *The assessment of psychotherapy outcome* (pp. 160–201). New York: Wiley.

Andrews, G., & Harvey, R. (1981). Does psychotherapy benefit neurotic patients? A re-analysis of the Smith, Glass & Miller data. *Archives of General Psychiatry, 38*, 1203–1508.

Asay, T. P., Lambert, M. J., Christensen, E. R., & Beutler, L. E. (Unpublished) A meta-analysis of mental health treatment outcome. Unpublished manuscript, Brigham Young University, Department of Psychology.

Auerbach, A. H. (1983). Assessment of psychotherapy outcome from the viewpoint of expert observer. In M. J. Lambert, E. R. Christensen, & S. S. DeJulio (Eds.), *The assessment of psychotherapy outcome* (pp. 537–568). New York: Wiley.

Auerbach, A. H., & Johnson, M. (1977). Research on the therapist's level of experience. In A. S. Gurman & A. M. Razin (Eds.), *Effective psychotherapy: A handbook of research* (pp. 84–102). New York: Pergamon Press.

Barlow, D. H. (Ed.). (1981). *Behavioral assessment of adult disorders*. New York: Guilford Press.

Battle, C. C., Imber, S. D., Hoehn-Saric, R., Stohe, A. R., Nash, C., & Frank, J. D. (1966). Target complaints as criterial of improvement. *American Journal of Pyschotherapy, 20*, 184–192.

Beck, A. T., Rush, A. J., Shaw, B. F., & Emery, G. (1979). *Cognitive therapy of depression*. New York: Guilford Press.

Beck, A. T., Ward, C. H., Mendelson, M., Mock, J., & Erbaugh, J. (1961). An inventory for measuring depression. *Archives of General Psychiatry, 4*, 561–571.

Bellack, A. S., Hersen, M., & Himmelhoch, J. (1981). Social skills training with pharmacotherapy and psychotherapy in the treatment of unipolar depression. *American Journal of Psychiatry, 138*, 1562–1567.

Bellack, A. S. (1983). Recurrent problems in the behavioral assessment of social skill. *Behavior Research and Therapy, 21*, 29–41.

Bentley, J. C., DeJulio, S. S., Lambert, M. J., & Dinan, W. (1975). *The effects of traditional versus confrontive leadership styles in producing casualties in encounter group participants*. Unpublished manuscript, Brigham Young University, Provo, UT.

Berger, M. (1983). Toward maximizing the utility of consumer satisfaction as an outcome. In M. J. Lambert, E. R. Christensen, & S. S. DeJulio (Eds.), *The assessment of psychotherapy outcome* (pp. 56–80). New York: Wiley.

Bergin, A. E. (1966). Some implications of psychotherapy research for theapeutic practice. *Journal of Abnormal Psychology, 71*, 235–246.

Bergin, A. E. (1970). The deterioration effect: A reply to Braucht. *Journal of Abnormal Psychology, 75*, 300–302.

Bergin, A. E. (1971). The evaluation of therapeutic outcomes. In A. E. Bergin & S. L. Garfield (Eds.), *Handbook of psychotherapy and behavior change* (pp. 217–270). New York: Wiley.

Bergin, A. E. (1980). Negative effects revisited: A reply. *Professional Psychology, 11*, 93–100.

Bergin, A. E., & Garfield, S. L. (Eds.), (1971). *Handbook of psychotherapy and behavior change*. New York: Wiley.

Bergin, A. E., & Lambert, M. J. (1978). The evaluation of therapeutic outcomes. In S. L. Garfield & A. E. Bergin (Eds.), *Handbook of psychotherapy and behavior change: An empirical analysis*. New York: Wiley.

Bergin, A. E., & Suinn, R. M. (1975). Individual psychotherapy and behavior therapy. *Annual Review of Psychology, 26*, 509–556.

Berman, J. S., Miller, R. C., & Massman, P. J. (1985). Cognitive therapy versus systematic desensitization: Is one treatment superior? *Psychological Bulletin, 97*, 451–461.

Berman, J. S., & Norton, N. C. (1985). Does professional training make a therapist more effective? *Psychological Bulletin, 98*, 401–406.

Berzins, J. I., Bednar, R. L., & Severy, L. J. (1975). The problem of intersource consensus in measuring therapeutic outcomes: New data and multivariate perspectives. *Journal of Abnormal Psychology, 84*, 10–19.

Beutler, L. E. (1979). Toward specific psychological therapies for specific conditions. *Journal of Consulting and Clinical Psychology, 47*, 882–892.

Beutler, L. E. (1983). *Eclectic psychotherapy: A systematic approach.* New York: Pergamon.

Beutler, L. E., & Crago, M. (1983). Self-report measures of psychotherapy outcome. In M. J. Lambert, E. R. Christensen, & S. S. De Julio (Eds.), *The assessment of psychotherapy outcome* (pp. 453–497). New York: Wiley.

Beutler, L. E., Crago, M., & Arizmend, T. G. (1986). Therapist variables in psychotherapy process and outcome. In S. L. Garfield & A. E. Bergin (Eds.), *Handbook of Psychotherapy and behavior change.* New York: Wiley.

Blanchard, E. B., & Andrasik, F. (1982). Psychological assessment and treatment of headache: Recent developments and emerging issues. *Journal of Consulting and Clinical Psychology, 50*, 859–879.

Blanchard, E. B., Andrasik, F., Ahler, T. A., Teders, S. J., & O'Keefe, D. O. (1980). Migraine and tension headache: A meta-analytic review. *Behavior Therapy, 11*, 613–631.

Bloch, S., & Lambert, M. J. (1985). What price psychotherapy? A rejoinder. *British Journal of Psychiatry, 146*, 96–98.

Borkovec, T. D. (1982). Insomnia. *Journal of Consulting and Clinical Psychology, 50*, 880–895.

Bornstein, P. H., & Rychtarik, R. G. (1983). Consumer satisfaction in adult behavior therapy: Procedures, problems, and future perspectives. *Behavior Therapy, 14*, 191–208.

Braucht, G. N. (1970). The deterioration effect: A reply to Bergin. *Journal of Abnormal Psychology, 75*, 293–299.

Buros, O. K. (Ed.). (1978). *The eighth mental measurements yearbook* (2 vols.). Highland Park, NJ: Gryphon Press.

Calsyn, R. J., & Davidson, W. S. (1978). Do we really want a program evaluation strategy based on individualized goals? A critique of goal attainment scaling. *Evaluation Studies: Review Annual, 1*, 700–713.

Carter, D. E., & Newman, F. L. (1980). *A client oriented system of mental health service delivery and program management: A workbook and guide* (Series FN No. 4, DHHS No. 80–307). Rockville, MD: Mental Health Service System Reports.

Cartwright, D. S., Kirtner, W. L., & Fiske, D. W. (1963). Method factors in changes associated with psychotherapy. *Journal of Abnormal and Social Psychology, 66*, 164–175.

Ciarlo, J. A., & Reihman, J. (1977). The Denver community mental health center questionnaire: Development of a multidimensional program evaluation instrument. In R. Coursey, G. Spector, S. Murrell, & B. Hunt (Eds.), *Program evaluation for mental health: Methods, strategies, and participants.* New York: Grune & Stratton.

Ciminero, A. R., Calhoun, K. A., & Adams, H. E. (1977a). *Handbook of Behavioral Assessment.* New York: Wiley.

Ciminero, A., Nelson, R. O., & Lipinski, D. (1977b). Self-monitoring procedures. In A. R. Ciminero, K. R. Calhoun, & H. E. Adams (Eds.), *Handbook of behavioral assessment.* New York: Wiley.

Clinical Psychology Review, L. Michelson (1985). Special Issue: Meta-analysis & clinical psychology, 5, Pergamon Press.

Cohen, J. (1977). *Statistical power analysis for the behavioral sciences.* New York: Academic Press.

Cone, J. D., & Hawkins, R. P. (Eds.). (1977). *Behavioral assessment: New directions in clinical psychology.* New York: Brunner/Mazel.

Conger, J. C., & Conger. A. J. (1982). Components of heterosocial competence. In J. P. Curran & P. M. Monti (Eds.), *Social skills training: A practical handbook for assessment and treatment* (pp. 313–347). New York: Guilford.

Cooley, E. F., & LaJoy, R. (1980). Therapeutic relationship and improvement as perceived by clients and therapists. *Journal of Clinical Psychology, 36*, 562–570.

Cooper, S. E. (1983). The influence of self-concept on outcomes of intensive alcoholism treatment. *Journal of Studies on Alcohol, 44*, 1087–1093.

Coyne, J. C. (1982). A critique of cognitions as causal entities with particular reference to depression. *Cognitive Therapy and Research, 6*, 3–13.

Critelli, J. W., & Neumann, K. F. (1984). The placebo: Conceptual analysis of a construct in transition. *American Psychologist, 39*, 32–39.

Crits-Christoph, P., Luborsky, L, McClellan, A. T., Woody, G., Piper, W., Liberman, B., & Imber, S. (1985, June). *Do psychotherapists vary much in their success? The answer within four outcome studies.* Paper presented at the Society for Psychotherapy Research Annual Convention, Evanston, IL.

Cross, D. G., & Sheehan, P. W. (1982). Secondary therapist variables operating in short-term insight-oriented and behavior therapy. *British Journal of Medical Psychology, 55*, 275–284.

Cross, D. G., Sheehan, P. W., & Khan, J. A. (1980). Alternative advice and counsel in psychotherapy. *Journal of Consulting and Clinical Psychology, 48*, 615–625.

Dahlstrom, W. G., & Welsh, G. S. (1960). Treatment. In W. Dahlstrom & G. Welsh (Eds.), *An MMPI handbook* (pp. 355–393). Minneapolis: University of Minnesota Press.

Davidson, C. V., & Davidson, R. H. (1983). The significant other as data source and data problem in psychotherapy outcome research. In M. J. Lambert, E. R. Christensen, & S. S. DeJulio (Eds.), *The assessment of psychotherapy outcome* (pp. 569–602). New York: Wiley.

Derogatis, L. R., Lipman, R. S., Rickels, R., Uhlenhuth, E. H., & Covi, L. (1974). The Hopkins symptom check-list (HSCL): A self-report symptom inventory. *Behavioral Science, 19*, 1–15.

Derogatis, L. R., & Melisaratos, N. (1983). The brief symptom inventory: An introductory report. *Psychological Medicine, 13*, 595–605.

DeRubeis, R. J., Hollon, S. D. Evans, M. D., & Bemis, K. M. (1982). Can psychotherapies for depression be discriminated? A systematic investigation of cognitive therapy and interpersonal therapy. *Journal of Consulting and Clinical Psychology, 50*, 744–756.

Durlak, J. A. (1979). Comparative effectiveness of paraprofessional and professional helpers. *Psychological Bulletin, 86*, 80–92.

Dush, D. M., Hirt, M. L., & Schroeder, H. (1983). Self-statement modification with adults: A meta-analysis. *Journal of Consulting and Clinical Psychology, 94,* 408–422.

Dymond, R. F. (1954). Adjustment changes over therapy from self-sorts. In C. R. Rogers & R. F. Dymond (Eds.), *Psychotherapy and personality change* (pp. 76–84). Chicago: University of Chicago Press.

Edwards, B. C., Lambert, M. J., Moran, P. W., McCully, T., Smith, K. C., & Ellingson, A. G. (1984). A meta-analytic comparison of the Beck Depression Inventory and Hamilton Rating Scale for Depression as measures of treatment outcome. *British Journal of Clinical Psychology, 23,* 93–99.

Edwards, D. W. (1974). *Davis outcome assessment system* (version 2). Unpublished manuscript, University of California at Davis, Department of Psychology.

Eifert, G. H., & Klaut, M. (1983). Inadequate presentation of behavioral measures of fear in the major journals. *Journal of Behavior Therapy and Experimental Psychiatry, 14,* 219–221.

Ellsworth, R. B. (1975). Consumer feedback in measuring the effectiveness of mental health programs. In E. L. Struening & M. Guttentag (Eds.), *Handbook of evaluation research* (Vol. 2, pp. 239–274). Beverly Hills: Sage.

Endicott, J., Spitzer, R. L., Fleiss, J. L., & Cohen, J. (1976). The Global Assessment Scale: A procedure for measuring overall severity of psychiatric disturbance. *Archives of General Psychiatry, 33,* 766–771.

Endler, N. S., Hunt, J. McV., & Rosenstein, A. J. (1962). An S-R inventory of anxiousness. *Psychological Monographs: General and Applied, 76,* 1–31.

Evans, M., Hollon, S., DeRubeis, R., Auerbach, A., Tuason, V. B., & Wiemer, M. (1983, July). *Development of a system for rating psychotherapies for depression.* Paper presented at the 14th annual meeting of the Society for Psychotherapy Research, Sheffield, England.

Eysenck, H. J. (1952). The effects of psychotherapy: An evaluation. *Journal of Consulting Psychology, 16,* 319–324.

Eysenck, H. J. (1967). The non-professional psychotherapist. *International Journal of Psychiatry, 3,* 150–153.

Eysenck, H. J., & Eysenck, S. B. G. (1969). *Personality structure and measurement.* San Diego: R. R. Knapp.

Fairweather, G., Simon, R., Gebhard, M. E., Weingarten, E., Holland, J. L., Sanders, R., Stone, G. B., & Reahl, J. E. (1960). Relative effectiveness of psychotherapeutic programs: A multicriteria comparison of four programs for three different patient groups. *Psychological Monographs: General and Applied, 74,* (5, Whole No. 492).

Farrell, A. D., Curran, J. P., Zwick, W. R., & Monti, P. M. (1983). Generalizablity and discriminant validity of anxiety and social skills ratings in two populations. *Behavioral Assessment, 6,* 1–14.

Feighner, J. P., Brown, S. L., & Oliver, J. E. (1973). Electrosleep therapy. *Journal of Nervous and Mental Disease, 157,* 121–128.

Feighner, J. P., Robins, E., Guze, S. B., Woodruff, R. A., Winokur, G., & Munoz, R. (1972). Diagnostic criteria for use in psychiatric research. *Archives of General Psychiatry, 26,* 57–63.

Firth, J. A., & Shapiro, D. A. (unpublished). Individual differences in response to Prescriptive vs. Exploratory psychotherapy. University of Sheffield: SAPU Memo 765.

Fitts, W. F. (1965). *Tennessee self-concept scale manual.* Nashville: Counselor Recordings and Tests.

Forsyth, R. P., & Fairweather, G. W. (1961). Psychotherapeutic and other hospital treatment critera: The dilemma. *Journal of Abnormal and Social Psychology, 62,* 598–604.

Frank, J. D. (1973). *Persuasion and healing* (2nd ed.). Baltimore: Johns Hopkins University Press.

Frank, J. D. (1976). Psychotherapy and the sense of mastery. In R. L. Spitzer & D. F. Klein (Eds.), *Evaluation of psychotherapies: Behavioral therapies, drug therapies and their interactions* (pp. 47–56). Baltimore: Johns Hopkins University Press.

Franks, C. M., & Mays, D. T. (1980). Negative effects revisited: A rejoinder. *Professional Psychology, 11,* 101–105.

Fuchs, C. Z., & Rehm, L. P. (1977). A self-control behavior therapy program for depression. *Journal of Consulting and Clinical Psychology, 45,* 206–215.

Furnham, A., & Henderson, M. (1983). Assessing assertiveness: A content and correlational analysis of five assertiveness inventories. *Behavioral Assessment, 6,* 79–88.

Galassi, M. D., & Galassi, J. P. (1980). Similarities and differences between two assertion measures: Factor analysis of the college self-expression scale and the Rathus assertiveness schedule. *Behavioral Assessment, 2,* 43–57.

Garfield, S. L. (1978). Research on client variables in psychotherapy. In S. L. Garfield & A. E. Bergin (Eds.), *Handbook of psychotherapy and behavior change: An empirical analysis.* New York: Wiley.

Garfield, S. L. (1980). *Psychotherapy. An eclectic approach.* New York: Wiley.

Garfield, S. L. (1983a). Does psychotherapy work? Yes, no, maybe. *The Behavioral and Brain Sciences, 6,* 592–593.

Garfield, S. L. (Ed.) (1983b). Special Section: Meta-analysis and psychotherapy. *Journal of Consulting and Clinical Psychology, 36,* 3–75.

Garfield, S. L., Prager, R. A., & Bergin, A. E. (1971). Evaluation of outcome in psychotherapy. *Journal of Consulting and Clinical Psychology, 37,* 307–313.

Gibson, R. L., Snyder, W. U., & Ray, W. S. (1955). A factor analysis of measures of change following client-centered psychotherapy. *Journal of Counseling Psychology, 2,* 83–90.

Glaister, B. (1982). Muscle relaxation training for fear reduction of patients with psychological problems: A review of controlled studies. *Behavior Research and Therapy, 20,* 493–504.

Glass, G. V., McGaw, B., & Smith, M. L. (1981). *Meta-analysis in social response.* Beverly Hills: Sage.

Goldberg, D. P., Hobson, R. F., Maguire, G. P., Margison, F. R., O'Dowd, T., Osborn, M. S., & Moss, S. (1984). The clarification and assessment of a method of psychotherapy. *British Journal of Psychiatry, 144,* 567–575.

Goldfried, M. (1982). *Converging themes in psychotherapy.* New York: Springer.

Goldstein, A. P., Kanfer, F. H. (Eds.). (1979). Maximizing treatment gains: Transfer enhancement in psychotherapy. New York: Academic Press.

Goldstein, A. P., Lopez, M., & Greenleaf D. O. (1979). Introduction. In A. P. Goldstein & F. H. Kanfer (Eds.), *Maximizing treatment gains: Transfer enhancement in psychotherapy* (pp. 1–22). New York: Academic Press.

Goldstein, A. P., & Stein, N. (1976). *Prescriptive psychotherapies.* New York: Pergamon.

Gomes-Schwartz, B. (1978). Effective ingredients in psychotherapies: Prediction of outcome from process variables. *Journal of Consulting and Clinical Psychology, 46,* 1023–1035.

Green, B. C., Gleser, G. C., Stone, W. N., & Siefert, R. F. (1975). Relationships among diverse measures of psychotherapy outcome. *Journal of Consulting and Clinical Psychiatry, 43,* 689–699.

Grunebaum, H. (1985). Helpful and harmful psychotherapy. *The Harvard Medical School Mental Health Newsletter, 1,* 5–6.

Gurman, A. S. (1977). The patient's perception of the therapeutic relationship. In A. S. Gurman & A. M. Razin (Eds.), *Effective psychotherapy: A handbook of research* (pp. 503–543). New York: Pergamon.

Gynther, M. D., & Green, S. B. (1982). Methodological problems in self report. In P. C. Kendall & J. N. Butcher (Eds.), *Handbook of research methods in clinical psychology* (pp. 355–428). New York: Wiley.

Hamilton, M. (1967). Development of a rating scale for primary depressive illness. *British Journal of Social and Clinical Psychology, 6,* 278–296.

Hargreaves, W. A., Glick, I. D., Drues, J., Shewstack, J. A., & Feigenbaum, E. (1977). Short vs. long hospitalization: A prospective controlled study. VI. Two year follow-up results for schizophrenics. *Archives of General Psychiatry, 34,* 305–311.

Hattie, J. A., Sharpley, C. F., & Rogers, H. J. (1984). Comparative effectiveness of professional and paraprofessional helpers. *Psychological Bulletin, 95,* 534–541.

Henry, W. P. (1985). The time released placebo: A reply to Critelli and Neumann. *American Psychologist, 40,* 239.

Hersen, M., & Bellack, A. S. (1981). (Eds.). *Behavioral assessment: A practical handbook* (2nd ed.). New York: Pergamon.

Hobson, R. F. (1985). *Forms of feeling: The heart of psychotherapy.* New York: Tavistock Publications.

Holdroyd, K. A., & Andrasik, F. (1982). Do the effects of cognitive therapy endure? A two-year follow-up of tension headache sufferers treated with cognitive therapy or biofeedback. *Cognitive Therapy and Research, 6,* 325–334.

Hollon, S. D., & Kendall, P. C. (1981). In vivo assessment techniques for cognitive-behavioral strategies. In P. C. Kendall & S. D. Hollon (Eds.), *Assessment strategies for cognitive-behavioral interventions* (pp. 319–356). New York: Academic Press.

Horwitz, L. (1974). *Clinical prediction in psychotherapy.* New York: Jason Aronson.

Howard, K. I., Kopta, S. M., Krause, M. S., & Orlinsky, D. E. (1986). The dose-effect relationship in psychotherapy. *American Psychologist, 41,* 159–164.

Imber, S. D., Pilkonis, P. A., Harway, N. I., Klein, R. H., &

Rubinsky, P. A. (1982). Maintenance of change in the psychotherapies. *Journal of Psychiatric Treatment and Evaluation, 4,* 1–5.

Jacobson, N. S., Elwood, R. W., & Dallas, M. (1981). Assessment of marital dysfunction. In D. H. Barlow (Ed.), *Behavioral assessment of adult disorders* (pp. 439–479). New York: Guilford.

Jacobson, N. S., Follette, W. C., Revenstorf, D. (1984a). Psychotherapy outcome research: Methods for reporting variability and evaluating clinical significance. *Behavior Therapy, 15,* 336–352.

Jacobson, N. S., Follette, W. C., Revenstorf, D., Baucom, D. H., Hahlwey, K., & Margolin, G. (1984b). Variability in outcome and clinical significance of behavioral marital therapy: A reanalysis of outcome data. *Journal of Consulting and Clinical Psychology, 52,* 497–504.

Jones, R. A. (1968). *A factored measure of Ellis' irrational belief system with personality and maladjustment correlates.* Unpublished doctoral dissertation, Texas Technological College.

Kaplan, R. E. (1982). The dynamics of injury in encounter groups: Power, splitting, and the mismanagement of resistance. *International Journal of Group Psychotherapy, 32,* 163–187.

Kappes, B. M., & Parish, T. S. (1979). The personal attribute inventory: A measure of self-concepts and personality profiles. *Educational and Psychological Measurement, 39,* 955–958.

Karoly, P., & Steffen, J. (1980). *Improving the long-term effects of psychotherapy.* New York: Gardner.

Katz, M. M., & Lyerly, S. B. (1963). Methods for measuring adjustment and social behavior in the community: 1. Rationale, description. discriminative validity and scale development. *Psychological Reports, 13,* 1503–1555.

Kazdin, A. E. (1974). Effects of covert modeling and model reinforcement in assertive behavior. *Journal of Abnormal Psychology, 83,* 240–252.

Kellner, R. (1975). Psychotherapy in psychosomatic disorders: A survey of controlled outcome studies. *Archives of General Psychiatry, 35,* 1021–1028.

Kendall, P. C., & Hollon, S. D. (1981). *Strategies for cognitive-behavioral interventions.* New York: Academic Press.

Kent, R. N., & Foster, S. L. (1977). Direct observational procedures: Methodological issues in naturalistic settings. In A. Ciminero, D. Calhoun, & H. Adams (Eds.), *Handbook for behavioral assessment.* New York: Wiley.

Kern, J. M. (1984). Relationships between obtrusive laboratory and unobtrusive naturalistic behavioral fear assessments: Treated and untreated subjects. *Behavioral Assessment, 6,* 45–60.

Kernberg, O. F. (1973). Summary and conclusion of "psychotherapy and psychoanalysis: Final report of the Menninger Foundation's Psychotherapy Research Project." *International Journal of Psychiatry, 11,* 62–77.

Kiesler, C. A. (1983). Social psychologic issues in studying consumer satisfaction with behavior therapy. *Behavior Therapy, 14,* 226–236.

Kirchner, J. H., & Hogan, R. A. (1982). Patient feedback at a community mental health center: Year three. *Professional Psychology, 13,* 431–438.

Kiresuk, T. J., & Sherman, R. E. (1968). Goal attainment scaling: A general method for evaluating comprehensive community mental health programs. *Community Mental Health Journal, 4*, 443–453.

Klein, D. F., Zitrin, C. M., Woerner, M. G., & Ross, D. C. (1983). Treatment of phobias: Behavior therapy and supportive psychotherapy: Are there any special ingredients? *Archives of General Psychiatry, 40*, 139–145.

Klerman, G. L., Rounsaville, B., Chevron, E., Neu, G., & Weissman, W. M. (1979). *Manual for short-term interpersonal psychotherapy (IPT) of depression.* Unpublished manuscript, Yale University, New Haven, CT.

Klonoff, H., & Cox, B. A. (1975). Problem-oriented approach to analysis of treatment outcome. *American Journal of Psychiatry, 132*, 836–841.

Kornblith, S. H., Rehm, L. P., O'Hara, M. W., & Lamparski, D. M. (1983). The contribution of self-reinforcement training and behavioral assignments to the efficacy of self-control therapy for depression. *Cognitive Therapy and Research, 7*, 499–528.

Lakey, J. (1977). *A multitrait-multimethod validation of measures of student school self-concept.* Unpublished doctoral dissertation, California State University at Long Beach.

Lambert, M. J. (1976). Spontaneous remission in adult neurotic disorders: A revision and summary. *Psychological Bulletin, 83*, 107–119.

Lambert, M. J. (1979). *The effects of psychotherapy* (Vol. 1). New York: Eden Press.

Lambert, M. J. (1982). *The effects of psychotherapy* (Vol. 2). New York: Human Sciences Press.

Lambert, M. J. (1983). Introduction to assessment of psychotherapy outcome: Historical perspective and current issues. In M. J. Lambert, E. R. Christensen, & S. S. DeJulio (Eds.), *The assessment of psychotherapy outcome* (pp. 3–32). New York: Wiley-Interscience.

Lambert, M. J., & Bergin, A. E. (1973). Psychotherapeutic outcomes and issues related to behavioral and humanistic approaches. *Cornell Journal of Social Relations, 8*, 47–61.

Lambert, M. J., Bergin, A. E., & Collins, J. L. (1977). Therapist-induced deterioration in psychotherapy. In A. S. Gurman & A. M. Razin (Eds.), *Effective psychotherapy: A handbook of research* (p. 452–481). New York: Pergamon.

Lambert, M. J., Christensen, E. R., & DeJulio, S. S. (1983). *The assessment of psychotherapy outcome.* New York: Wiley–Interscience.

Lambert, M. J., DeJulio, S. S., & Stein, D. M. (1978). Therapist interpersonal skills: Process, outcome, methodological considerations and recommendations for future research. *Psychological Bulletin, 85*, 467–489.

Lambert, M. J., Hatch, D. R., Kingston, M. D., & Edwards, B. C. (1986). Zung, Beck, and Hamilton rating scales as measures of treatment outcome: A meta-analytic comparison. *Journal of Consulting and Clinical Psychology, 54*, 54–59.

Landman, J. T., & Dawes, R. M. (1982). Psychotherapy outcome: Smith and Glass conclusions stand up under scrutiny. *American Psychologist, 37*, 504–516.

Lang, P. J., & Lazovik, A. D. (1963). Experimental desensitization of a phobia. *Journal of Abnormal and Social Psychology, 66*, 519–525.

Lazarus, A. A. (1963). An evaluation of behavior therapy. *Behavior Research and Therapy, 63*, 504–510.

Lazarus, A. A. (1971). *Behavior therapy and beyond.* New York: McGraw-Hill.

Lebow, J. L. (1982). Consumer satisfaction with mental health treatment. *Psychological Bulletin, 91*, 244–259.

Levant, R. F., & Shlien, J. M. (Eds.). (1984). *Client-centered therapy and the person-centered approach: New directions in theory, research and practice.* New York: Praeger.

Lewinsohn, P. M., Antonuccio, D., Steinmetz, J., & Teri, L. (1982). *The coping with depression course: A psychoeducational intervention for unipolar depression.* Eugene: University of Oregon Press.

Liberman, B. L. (1978). The maintenance and persistence of change: Long-term follow-up investigations of psychotherapy. In J. D. Frank, R. Hoehn-Saric, S. D. Imber, & B. L. Liberman, & A. R. Stone (Eds.), *Effective ingredients of successful psychotherapy.* New York: Brunnel/Mazel.

Lieberman, M. A., Yalom, I. D., & Miles, M. B. (1973). *Encounter groups: First facts.* New York: Basic Books.

Lloyds, M. E. (1983). Selecting systems to measure client outcome in human service agencies. *Behavioral Assessment, 5*, 55–70.

Locke, H. J., & Wallace, K. M. (1959). Short marital adjustment prediction tests: Their reliability and validity. *Marriage and Family Living, 21*, 251–255.

LoPiccolo, J., & Steger, J. C. (1974). The sexual interaction inventory: A new instrument for assessment of sexual dysfunction. *Archives of Sexual Behavior, 3*, 585–595.

Lorr, M. (1965). Client perceptions of therapists. *Journal of Consulting Psychology, 29*, 146–149.

Luborsky, L. (1984). *Principles of psychoanalytic psychotherapy: A manual for supportive-expressive treatment.* New York: Basic Books.

Luborsky, L., Bachrach, H., Graff, H., Pulver, S., & Christoph, P. (1979). Preconditions and consequences of transference interpretations: A clinical-quantitative investigation. *Journal of Nervous & Mental Disease, 167*, 391–401.

Luborsky, L., & DeRubeis, R. J. (1984). The use of psychotherapy treatment manuals—a small revolution in psychotherapy research style. *Clinical Psychology Review, 4*, 5–14.

Luborsky, L., McClellan, A. T., Woody, G. E., O'Brien, C. P., & Auerbach, A. (1985). Therapist success and its determinants. *Archives of General Psychiatry, 42*, 602–611.

Luborsky, L., Singer, B., & Luborsky, L. (1975). Comparative studies of psychotherapy. *Archives of General Psychiatry, 32*, 995–1008.

Luborsky, L., Woody, G., McLellan, A. T., O'Brien, C. P., & Rosenzweig, J. (1982). Can independent judges recognize different psychotherapies? *Journal of Consulting and Clinical Psychology, 50*, 49–62.

Maguire, G. P., Goldberg, D. P., Hobson, R. F., O'Dowd, T., Margison, F., & Moss, S. (1984). Evaluating the teaching of a method of psychotherapy. *British Journal of Psychiatry, 144*, 575–581.

Mahoney, M. J. (1977). Reflections on the cognitive-learning trend in psychotherapy. *American Psychologist, 32*, 5–13.

Maisto, S. A., & Maisto, C. A. (1983). Institutional measures of treatment outcome. In M. J. Lambert, E. R. Christensen, & S. S. De Julio (Eds.), *The assessment of psychotherapy outcome* (pp. 603–626). New York: Wiley.

Marmor, J. (1975). Foreword. In B. Sloane, F. Staples, A. Cristol, N. Yorkston, K. Whipple (Eds.), *Psychotherapy versus behavior therapy.* Cambridge, MA: Harvard University Press.

Master, S., & Gershman, L. (1983). Physiological responses to rational-emotive self-verbalizations. *Journal of Behavior Therapy and Experimental Psychiatry, 14,* 289–296.

Mathews, A. M., Teasdale, J., & Munby, M. (1977). A home-based treatment program for agoraphobics. *Behavior Therapy, 8,* 915–924.

May, P. R. A. (1971). For better or for worse? Psychotherapy and variance change: A critical review of the literature. *The Journal of Nervous and Mental Disease, 152,* 184–192.

Mays, D. T., & Franks, C. M. (1980). Getting worse: Psychotherapy or no treatment. The jury should still be out. *Professional Psychology, 11,* 78–92

Mays, D. T., & Franks, C. M. (1985). *Negative outcome in psychotherapy and what to do about it.* New York: Springer.

Meltzoff, J., & Kornreich, M. (1970). *Research in Psychotherapy.* New York: Atherton Press.

Miller, R. C., & Berman, J. S. (1983). The efficacy of cognitive behavior therapies: A quantitative review of the research evidence. *Psychological Bulletin, 94,* 39–53.

Miller, W. R., Taylor, C. A., & West, J. C. (1980). Focused versus broad-spectrum behavior therapy for problem drinkers. *Journal of Consulting and Clinical Psychology, 48,* 590–601.

Millon, T. (1977). *Millon clinical multi-axial inventory manual.* Minneapolis: National Computer Systems.

Mintz, J., Auerbach, A. H., Luborsky, L., & Johnson, M. (1973). Patients', therapists' and observers' view of psychotherapy: A "rashomon" experience or a reasonable consensus. *British Journal of Psychology, 46,* 83–89.

Mintz, J., & Kiesler, D. J. (1982). Individualized measures of psychotherapy outcome. In P. C. Kendall & J. N. Butcher (Eds.), *Handbook of research methods in clinical psychology* (pp. 491–534). New York: Wiley.

Mintz, J., Luborsky, L., & Christoph, P. (1979). Measuring the outcomes of psychotherapy: Findings of the Penn. Psychotherapy Project. *Journal of Consulting and Clinical Psychology, 47,* 319–334.

Mischel, W. (1972). Direct versus indirect personality assessment: Evidence and implications. *Journal of Consulting and Clinical Psychology, 38,* 319–324.

Mischel, W. (1977). On the future of personality research. *American Psychologist, 32,* 246–254.

Mitchell, K. M, Bozarth, J. D., & Krauft, C. C. (1977). A re-appraisal of the therapeutic effectiveness of accurate empathy, nonpossessive warmth, and genuineness. In A. S. Gurman & A. M. Razin (Eds.), *Effective psychotherapy: A handbook of research.* New York: Pergamon.

Moran, P. W., & Lambert, M. J. (1983). A review of current assessment tools for monitoring changes in depression. In M. J. Lambert, E. R. Christensen, & S. S. DeJulio (Eds.), *The assessment psychotherapy outcome* (pp. 263–303). New York: Wiley.

Moras, K., & Strupp, H. H. (1982). Pretherapy interpersonal relations, patient alliance, and outcome in brief therapy. *Archives of General Psychiatry, 39,* 405–409.

Morris, R. J., & Magrath, K. H. (1979). Contribution of therapist warmth to the contact desensitization treatment of acrophobia. *Journal of Consulting and Clinical Psychology, 47,* 786–788.

Morris, R. J., & Suckerman, K. R. (1974a). Therapist warmth as a factor in automated systematic desensitization. *Journal of Consulting and Clinical Psychology, 42,* 244–250.

Morris, R. J., & Suckerman, K. R. (1974b). The importance of therapeutic relationship in systematic desensitization. *Journal of Consulting and Clinical Psychology, 42,* 148.

Morris, R. J., & Suckerman, K. R. (1975). Morris and Suckerman reply. *Journal of Consulting and Clinical Psychology, 43,* 585–586.

Mylar, J. L., & Clement, P. W. (1972). Prediction and comparison of outcome in systematic desensitization and implosion. *Behavior Research and Therapy, 10,* 235–246.

Nelson, R. O. (1983). Behavioral assessment: Past, present, and future. *Behavioral Assessment, 5,* 195–206.

Neu, C., Prusoff, B., & Klerman, G. (1978). Measuring the interventions used in the short-term psychotherapy of depression. *American Journal of Orthopsychiatry, 48,* 629–636.

Newman, F. L. (1983). Therapist's evaluation of psychotherapy. In M. J. Lambert, E. R. Christensen, & S. S. DeJulio (Eds.), *The assessment of psychotherapy outcome* (pp. 498–536). New York: Wiley.

Nichols, R. C., & Beck, K. W. (1960). Factors in psychotherapy change. *Journal of Consulting Psychology, 24,* 388–399.

Nicholson, R. A., & Berman, J. S. (1983). Is follow-up necessary in evaluating psychotherapy? *Psychological Bulletin, 93,* 261–278.

Nietzel, M. T., & Fisher, S. G. (1981). Effectiveness of professional and paraprofessional helpers: A comment on Durlack. *Psychological Bulletin, 89,* 555–565.

Orlinsky, D. E. (1985). Personal communication.

Orlinsky, D. E., & Howard, K. I. (1980). Gender and psychotherapeutic outcome. In A. M. Brodsky & R. T. Hare-Mustin (Eds.), *Women and psychotherapy* (pp. 3–34). New York: Guilford.

Parloff, M. B., London, P., & Wolfe, B. (1986). Individual psychotherapy and behavior change. In M. R. Rosenzweig & L. W. Porter (Eds.), *Annual Review of Psychology.* Palo Alto, Calif.: Annual Reviews.

Parloff, M. B., Waskow, I. E., & Wolfe, B. E. (1978). Research on therapist variables in relation to process and outcome. In S. L. Garfield & A. E. Bergin (Eds.), *Handbook of psychotherapy and behavior change.* New York: Wiley.

Patterson, C. H. (1984). Empathy, warmth, and genuineness in psychotherapy: A review of reviews. *Psychotherapy, 21,* 431–438.

Paul. G. L. (In press). Can pregnancy be a placebo effect? Terminology, designs, conclusions in the study of psychosocial and pharmacological treatments of behavior disorders. In L. White, B. Tursky, & G. F. Schwartz (Eds.). *Placebo: Clinical phenomena and new insights.* New York: Guilford.

Pilkonis, P. A., Imber, S. D., Lewis, P., & Rubinsky, P. (1984). A comparative outcome study of individual, group, and conjoint psychotherapy. *Archives of General Psychiatry, 41,* 431–437.

Prioleau, L., Murdock, M., & Brody, N. (1983). An analysis of psychotherapy versus placebo studies. *The Behavioral and Brain Sciences, 6,* 275–310.

Quality Assurance Project (1982). A treatment outline for agoraphobia. *Australian and New Zealand Journal of Psychiatry, 16,* 25–33.

Quality Assurance Project (1983). A treatment outline for depressive disorders. *Australian and New Zealand Journal of Psychiatry, 17,* 129–146.

Rachman, S. J., & Wilson, G. T. (1980). *The effects of psychological therapy: Second enlarged edition.* New York: Pergamon.

Rehm, L. P. (1977). A self-control model of depression. *Behavior Therapy, 8,* 787–804.

Rehm, L. P., Fuchs, L. Z., Roth, D. M., Kornblith, S. J., & Romano, J. M. (1979). A comparison of self-control and assertion skills treatments of depression. *Behavior Therapy, 10,* 429–442.

Rehm, L. P., Kornblith, S. J., O'Hara, M. W., Lamparski, D. M., Roman, J. M., & Volkin, J. (1981). An evaluation of major components in a self-control behavior therapy program for depression. *Behavior Modification, 5,* 459–489.

Ricks, D. F. (1974). Supershrink: Methods of a therapist judged successful on the basis of adult outcomes of adolescent patients. In D. F. Ricks, M. Roff, & A. Thomas (Eds.), *Life history research in psychopathology.* Minneapolis: University of Minnesota Press.

Roberts, S., Aronoff, J. Jensen, J., & Lambert, M. J. (1983). Measurement of outcome in anxiety disorders. In M. J. Lambert, E. R. Christensen, & S. S. DeJulio (Eds.), *The assessment of psychotherapy outcome* (pp. 304–355). New York: Wiley.

Rosenbaum, M. (1980). A schedule of assessing self-control behaviors: Preliminary findings. *Behavior Therapy, 11,* 109–121.

Rosenberg, M. (1965). *Society and adolescent self-image.* Princeton: Princeton University Press.

Rosenthal, D., & Frank, J. D. (1956). Psychotherapy and the placebo effect. *Psychological Bulletin, 53,* 294–302.

Rosenthal, R. (1980). Summarizing significance levels. In R. Rosenthal (Ed.), *New directions for methodology of social and behavioral science: Quantitative assessment of research domains.* San Francisco: Jossey-Bass.

Rosenthal, R. (1983). Assessing the statistical importance of the effects of psychotherapy. *Journal of Consulting and Clinical Psychology, 51,* 4–13.

Ross, S. M., & Proctor, S. (1973). Frequency and duration of hierarchy item exposure in a systematic desensitization analogue. *Behavior Research and Therapy, 11,* 303–312.

Ryan, V., & Gizynski, M. (1971). Behavior therapy in retrospect: Patients' feelings about their behavior therapists. *Journal of Consulting and Clinical Psychology, 37,* 1–9.

Sabalis, R. F. (1983). Assessing outcome in patients with

sexual dysfunctions and sexual deviations. In M. J. Lambert, E. R. Christensen, & S. S. DeJulio (Eds.), *The assessment of psychotherapy outcome* (pp. 205–262). New York: Wiley.

Sachs, J. S. (1983). Negative factors in brief psychotherapy: An empirical assessment. *Journal of Consulting and Clinical Psychology, 51,* 557–564.

Seeman, J. (1979). Personal correspondence. George Peabody College for Teachers.

Shapiro, D. A. (1985). Recent applications of meta-analysis in clinical research. *Clinical Psychology Review, 5,* 13–34.

Shapiro, D. A., & Firth, J. A. (in press). Prescriptive vs. Exploratory psychotherapy: Outcomes of the Sheffield Psychotherapy Project. *British Journal of Psychiatry.*

Shapiro, D. A., & Shapiro, D. (1982a). Meta-analysis of comparative therapy outcome studies: A replication and refinement. *Psychological Bulletin, 92,* 581–604.

Shapiro, D. A., & Shapiro, D. (1982b). Meta-analysis of comparative therapy outcome research: A critical appraisal. *Behavior Psychotherapy, 10,* 4–25.

Shapiro, D. A., & Shapiro, D. (1983). Comparative therapy outcome research: Methodological implications of meta-analysis. *Journal of Consulting and Clinical Psychology, 51,* 42–53.

Shepherd, M. (1984). What price psychotherapy? *British Medical Journal, 288,* 809–810.

Shipley, R. H., Boudewyns, P. A. (1980). Flooding and implosive therapy: Are they harmful? *Behavior Therapy, 11,* 503–508.

Shore, M. F., Massimo, J. L., & Ricks, D. F. (1965). A factor analytic study of psychotherapeutic change in delinquent boys. *Journal of Clinical Psychology, 21,* 208–212.

Silverman, J. S., Silverman, J. A., & Eardley, D. A. (1984). Do maladaptive attitudes cause depression? *Archives of General Psychiatry, 41,* 28–30.

Simons, A. D., Garfield, S. L., & Murphy, G. E. (1984). The process of change in cognitive therapy and pharmacotherapy for depression. *Archives of General Psychiatry, 41,* 45–51.

Sloane, R. B., Staples, F. R., Cristol, A. H., Yorkston, N. J., & Whipple, K. (1975). *Psychotherapy versus behavior therapy.* Cambridge, MA: Harvard University Press.

Smith, D. (1982). Trends in counseling and psychotherapy. *American Psychologist, 37,* 802–809.

Smith, M. L., & Glass, G. V. (1977). Meta-analysis of psychotherapy outcome studies. *American Psychologist, 32,* 752–760.

Smith, M. L., Glass, G. V., & Miller, T. I. (1980). *The benefits of psychotherapy.* Baltimore: John Hopkins University Press.

Spielberger, C. D., Gorsuch, R. L., & Luchene, R. E. (1970). Manual for the State-Trait Anxiety Inventory. Palo Alto, CA: Consulting Psychologists Press.

Stein, D. M. (1980). *The comparative effectiveness of paraprofessional theapists.* M. J. Lambert (chair), Society for Psychotherapy Research, Pacific Grove, CA.

Stein, D. M., & Lambert, M. J. (1984). On the relationship between therapist experiences and psychotherapy outcome. *Clinical Psychology Review, 4,* 1–16.

Steinbrueck, S. M., Maxwell, S. E., & Howard, G. S.

(1983). A meta-analysis of psychotherapy and drug therapy in the treatment of unipolar depression with adults. *Journal of Consulting and Clinical Psychology, 51*, 856–863.

Stone, M. H. (1985). Negative outcome in borderline states. In D. T. Mays & C. M. Franks (Eds.), *Negative outcome in psychotherapy and what to do about it.* New York: Springer.

Striano, J. (1982). Client perception of "helpful" and "not helpful" psychotherapeutic experiences (*Dissertation Abstracts International,* 1982, 43, 4303B. University Microfilms No. 80-17, 382).

Strube, M. J., & Hartmann, D. P. (1982). A critical appraisal of meta-analysis. *British Journal of Clinical Psychology, 21.*

Strube, M. J., & Hartmann, D. P. (1983). Meta-analysis: Techniques, applications, and function. *Journal of Consulting and Clinical Psychology, 51*, 14–27.

Strupp, H. H. (1980a). Success and failure in time-limited psychotherapy: A systematic comparison of two cases—comparison 1. *Archives of General Psychiatry, 37*, 595–603.

Strupp, H. H. (1980b). Success and failure in time-limited psychotherapy: A systematic comparison of two cases—comparison 2. *Archives of General Psychiatry, 37*, 708–716.

Strupp, H. H. (1980c). Success and failure in time-limited psychotherapy: With special reference to the performance of a lay counselor. *Archives of General Psychiatry, 37*, 831–841.

Strupp, H. H. (1980d). Success and failure in time-limited psychotherapy: A systematic comparison of two cases—comparison 4. *Archives of General Psychiatry, 37*, 947–954.

Strupp, H. H., & Binder, J. L. (1984). *Psychotherapy in a new key: A guide to time limited-dynamic psychotherapy.* New York: Basic Books.

Strupp, H. H., Fox, R. E., & Lessler, K. J. (1969). *Patients view their psychotherapy.* Baltimore: Johns Hopkins University Press.

Strupp, H. H., & Hadley, S. W. (1977). A tripartite model of mental health and therapeutic outcomes: With special reference to negative effects in psychotherapy. *American Psychologist, 32*, 187–196.

Strupp, H. H., & Hadley, S. W. (1978). Specific versus nonspecific factors in psychotherapy: A controlled study of outcome. *Archives of General Psychiatry, 36*, 1125–1136.

Strupp, H. H., Hadley, S. W., & Gomes-Schwartz, B. (1977). *Psychotherapy for better or worse.* New York: Jason Aronson.

Sutton-Simon, K. (1981). Assessing belief systems: Concepts and strategies. In P. C. Kendall & S. D. Hollon (Eds.), *Strategies for cognitive-behavioral interventions* (pp. 59–84). New York: Academic Press.

Thoits, P. (1985). Negative outcome: The influence of factors outside therapy. In D. T. Mays & C. M. Franks (Eds.), *Above all do no harm: Negative outcome in psychotherapy and what to do about it.* New York: Springer.

Turner, R. M., & Ascher, L. M. (1982). Therapist factor in the treatment of insomnia. *Behavior Research and Therapy, 20*, 33–40.

Veroff, J., Kulka, R. A., & Douvan, E. (1981). *Mental health in America.* New York: Basic Books.

Wachtel, P. L. (1977). *Psychoanalysis and behavior therapy: Toward integration.* New York: Basic Books.

Wampler, K. S. (1982). Bringing the review of literature into the age of quantification: Meta-analysis as a strategy for integrating research findings in family studies. *Journal of Marriage and Family Therapy, 11*, 1009–1023.

Warr, P., Barter, J., & Brownbridge, G. (1983). On the independence of positive and negative affect. *Journal of Personality and Social Psychology, 44*, 644–651.

Waskow, I. E. (1984). Specification of the technique variable in the NIMH treatment of depression collaborative research program. In J. B. W. Williams & R. S. Spitzer (Eds.), *Psychotherapy research: Where are we and where should we go?* (pp. 150–159). New York: Guilford.

Waskow, I. E., & Parloff, M. B. (1975). *Psychotherapy change measures.* DHEW Publication No. (ADM) 74–120.

Waskow, I. E., Parloff, M. B., Hadley, S. W., & Autry, J. H. (In press). The NIMH treatment of depression collaborative research program: Background and research plan. *Archives of General Psychiatry.*

Watson, J. P., & Marks, I. M. (1971). Relevant and irrelevant fear in flooding: A crossover study of phobic patients. *Behavior Research and Therapy, 2*, 275–293.

Weber, J. J., Elinson, J., & Moss, L. M. (1965). The application of ego strength scales to psychoanalytic clinic records. In G. S. Goldman & D. Shapiro (Eds.), *Developments in psychoanalysis at Columbia University: Proceedings of the 20th anniversary conference.* New York: Columbia Psychoanalytic Clinic for Training and Research.

Weed, L. L. (1969). *Medical records, medical education and patient care: The problem oriented record as a basic tool.* Cleveland: Case Western Reserve University Press.

Weissman, M. M. (1975). The assessment of social adjustment: A review of techniques. *Archives of General Psychiatry, 32*, 357–365.

Weissman, M. M., & Bothwell, S. (1976). The assessment of social adjustment by patient self-report. *Archives of General Psychiatry, 33*, 1111–1115.

Weissman, M. M., & Paykel, E. S. (1974). *The depressed woman: A study of social relationships.* Chicago: University of Chicago Press.

Weissman, M. M., Sholomakas, D., & John, K. (1981). The assessment of social adjustment. *Archives of General Psychiatry, 38*, 1250–1258.

Wilkins, W. (1984). Psychotherapy: The powerful placebo. *Journal of Consulting and Clinical Psychology, 52*, 570–573.

Wilson, G. T., & Thomas, M. G. (1973). Self versus drug-produced relaxation and the effects of instructional set in standardized systematic desensitization. *Behavior Research and Therapy, 11*, 279–288.

Williams, J. B. W., & Spitzer, R. L. (Eds.). (1984). *Psychotherapy research: Where are we and where should we go?* New York: Guilford.

Wittenborn, J. R. (1984). Psychological assessment in treatment. In G. Goldstein & M. Hersen (Eds.), *Handbook of psychological assessment* (pp. 405–420). New York: Pergamon.

Wolowitz, H. M. (1975). Therapist warmth: Necessary or sufficient condition in behavioral desensitization? *Journal of Consulting and Clinical Psychology, 42*, 584.

Wolpe, J. (1958). *Psychotherapy by reciprocal inhibition.*

Stanford: Stanford University Press.

Wolpe, J. (1964). Behavior therapy in complex neurotic states. *British Journal of Psychiatry, 110,* 28–34.

Wolpe, J. (1975). Foreword. In B. Sloane, F. Staples, A. Cristol, N. Yorkston, & K. Whipple (Eds.), *Psychotherapy versus behavior therapy.* Cambridge, MA: Harvard University Press.

Wolpe, J., & Lang, P. J. (1964). A fear survey schedule for use in behavior therapy. *Behavior Research and Therapy, 2,* 27–30.

Woodward, C. A., Santa-Barbara, J., Levin, S., & Epstein, N. B. (1978). The roles of goal attainment scaling in evaluating family therapy outcome. *American Journal of Orthopsychiatry, 48,* 464–475.

Yalom, I. D., & Leiberman, M. A. (1971). A study of encounter group casualties. *Archives of General Psychiatry, 25,* 16–30.

Zajonc, R. B. (1980). Feeling and thinking: Preferences need no inferences. *American Psychologist, 35,* 151–175.

Zeiss, A. M., Lewinsohn, P. M., & Munoz, R. F. (1979). Nonspecific improvement effects in depression using interpersonal skills training, pleasant activity schedules, and cognitive training. *Journal of Consulting and Clinical Psychology, 47,* 427–439.

Zung, W. W. K. (1965). A self-rating depression scale. *Archives of General Psychiatry, 12,* 371–379.

6

RESEARCH ON CLIENT VARIABLES IN PSYCHOTHERAPY

SOL L. GARFIELD

Washington University

Whether our concern is research or practice, the client is clearly an important variable in psychotherapy and has been the focus of many research investigations and theoretical discussions. In attempting to appraise the diverse material on this topic, the author once more has devoted primary attention to the results of empirical research investigation. Clinical and theoretical discussions of psychotherapy, individual case studies, or descriptive accounts without supporting data have generally been bypassed.

In any conceptualization of the psychotherapeutic process, it is apparent that at least five main influences can be postulated: the client or patient, the therapist, the resulting interaction of these two variables, the therapeutic procedures, and the potential influence of external events on the client. Ideally, each of these variables should be studied as they interact in the actual therapeutic situation and evaluated in relation to significant criteria of therapy. Unfortunately, the study of the interaction of patient and therapist variables in relation to specific outcome criteria has been a rarity (Beutler, 1973; Kiesler, 1966; Orlinsky & Howard, 1975; Parloff,

Waskow, & Wolfe, 1978; Paul, 1967; Saltzman, Luetgert, Roth, Creaser, & Howard, 1976). This has also been true with reference to the impact of external life events on outcome in therapy, although such factors are beginning to be recognized as important in evaluating continuation and outcome in psychotherapy (Garfield, 1980; Greenberg, 1983).

A variety of studies have attempted to relate differing client attributes to selected variables. Among the client attributes have been social class variables, personality variables, diagnosis, age, sex, intelligence, and the like. These have been related to therapeutic outcome, continuation in psychotherapy, in-therapy behavior, and similar variables. To the extent that research findings are replicated on new samples, we may have findings that have potential relevance for clinical practice and theory. If research reports are weak methodologically and there are conflicting findings in the literature, however, one must be cautious in the conclusions derived from such data.

One problem in research on psychotherapy is a tendency to discuss and view psychotherapy or psychotherapeutic treatment with little specification. With well over 200 different kinds of psychotherapy in existence, one cannot speak meaningfully of psychotherapy in general (Herink, 1980), even though there may be commonalities among the psychotherapies. Although there has been a trend very recently, not only to designate the specific therapeutic approach used in research studies, but also to use a training manual to operationalize and to monitor the therapy, there are still instances where only crude designations have been used (e.g., behavioral or dynamic therapy) with little attempt to describe the actual operations of psychotherapy.

Under these circumstances, it is not surprising that research on client variables may produce conflicting or inconsistent results. Although such problems tend to limit the value or generalizability of much research, we have become more cognizant of these difficulties recently and have improved our research strategies. A careful review of past research, thus, may indicate what findings appear to have some tenability and application, and the direction future research should take. The present chapter, therefore, will focus on empirical investigations in the field of psychotherapy that attempt to study client variables in relationship to some external criterion or outcome. Representative samples of the available research data will be evaluated and an attempt made to draw some implications for practice and research.

THE SELECTION OF CLIENTS FOR PSYCHOTHERAPY

One interesting aspect of psychotherapy pertains to the potential pool of psychotherapy clients. There are individuals who voluntarily seek out psychotherapeutic treatment, individuals who are referred for psychotherapy, those who eventually are selected for psychotherapy, and those who refuse psychotherapy. This is an intriguing problem with a number of implications for practice. Several kinds of data are available to help us appraise this matter, although, admittedly, they are incomplete. Most reports tend to come from clinics and community surveys, and there is a relative dearth of information concerning clients who are seen by private practitioners. If we can hypothesize that there is a significant difference between those who go to some type of public or community clinic and those who receive

long-term psychotherapy on a private basis (Udell & Hornstra, 1975), then it is apparent that the reported findings provide only a partial picture of who gets psychotherapy.

Frank (1974a) has suggested the importance of demoralization as a possible factor that brings people to seek out personal psychotherapy. Several studies have found that those individuals who secured treatment exhibited more helplessness, social isolation, and a sense of failure or lack of worth than those who did not seek treatment (Galassi & Galassi, 1973; Kellner & Sheffield, 1973; Vaillant, 1972). In another study, a group of treated depressed patients were matched with an untreated group for degree of depression. The treated group was found to be more self-accusatory and helpless (Katz, 1971). Frank also believes that the most frequent symptoms of patients in psychotherapy, anxiety and depression, are expressions of the patients' feelings of demoralization.

Research conducted in the past has indicated that not all individuals who applied for treatment received psychotherapy. Schaffer and Myers (1954), for example, found that social class status was positively related to acceptance for treatment. This finding, with minor variations, has also been reported in two other studies (Brill & Storrow, 1960; Cole, Branch, & Allison, 1962). Somewhat comparable results were also reported by Rosenthal and Frank (1958). They examined those patients who were specifically referred for psychotherapy from the total group who were seen at the Henry Phipps Clinic. They found a significant relationship between such variables as age, race, education, income, diagnosis, and motivation, and referral for psychotherapy. Thus, in all four studies, carried out in a medical school complex, there was some relationship between social class variables and referral or acceptance for psychotherapy.

Similar findings were secured in a study of a VA Mental Hygiene Clinic (Bailey, Warshaw, & Eichler, 1959). Assignment to psychotherapy was reported to be related to high socioeconomic status, intrapsychic complaints, age, expressed desire for psychotherapy, psychological test evaluation, and previous psychotherapy. Assignment to the psychosomatic clinic, on the other hand, was related to low socioeconomic status, somatic complaints, lack of recommendation from the psychological test evaluation, and no previous psychotherapy.

Somewhat comparable findings were reported in a study of a large urban mental health center (Lubin, Hornstra, Lewis, & Bechtel, 1973). Significant associations were found between such variables as education, occupation, age, race, and diagnosis, and the type of treatment initially accorded the patient. Patients with less than 12 years of education and with lower occupational ratings were assigned disproportionately more frequently to inpatient treatment and less frequently to individual psychotherapy. The converse was true for those with some college education and higher occupational ratings. Race and age were also related to type of assignment, with blacks and those over 39 years of age being overrepresented in the inpatient service and underrepresented in individual psychotherapy. A study of a walk-in clinic also found a significant relationship between low socioeconomic status and the likelihood of receiving drugs rather than psychotherapy (Shader, 1970).

Reference can be made to another aspect of this problem. As pointed out by Hollingshead and Redlich (1958) in their classic study, different social classes received different kinds of treatment, with long-term psychoanalytic treatment given mainly to middle- and upper-class clients. It is very likely that such individuals make up the largest proportion of those in private therapy. The results of the mental health survey reported by Ryan (1969) for the city of Boston would appear to support this view. For example, of those who are judged to be emotionally disturbed, less than 10 percent will apply for treatment at one of the outpatient psychiatric clinics in Boston—and of these, less than half may be accepted for treatment. Less than 1 percent of those judged to be disturbed will be treated by psychiatrists in private practice, and these appear to be a highly selected group. About two-thirds are females, four out of five have gone to college or are in college, "and occupations are generally consistent with education, reflecting a class level in the middle and upper ranges" (Ryan, 1969, p. 15).

A study of different kinds of clinics in New York City also indicated varying admission criteria related to social-class variables (Lorenzen, 1967). These clinics had very different criteria with one, a psychoanalytic training clinic, being highly selective in terms of age, education, and relation to health professions. This particular clinic did not accept clients under 20 or over 34 years of age. Widely different acceptance rates were also noted among the clinics. Two clinics accepted about 10 to 20 percent of applicants, whereas one clinic accepted 85 percent. Obviously, the kinds of problems and generalizations derived from such diverse samples of clients would also be expected to vary widely. The length of therapy also differed among the clinics and appeared to be related to the orientation of the clinic and its selectivity. Studying many of the same clinics, Kadushin (1969) concluded that social class was the most important factor distinguishing the applicants to the various clinics. Furthermore, "the more closely affiliated a clinic is with the orthodox psychoanalytic movement, the higher the social class of its applicants will be" (Kadushin, 1969, p. 51).

It would appear that many clinics have been somewhat selective in whom they accept for treatment, that this varies for the type of clinic, that selection is frequently related to social-class criteria, and that the more expert the therapeutic staff, the more stringent are the procedures used for selection and acceptance of clients. Psychoanalytic or psychoanalytically oriented clinics that are looking for suitable candidates for their particular variants of psychotherapy use some degree of selectivity in deciding which clients are best suited for treatment, and generally these are the better educated, intelligent, verbal, and "motivated" clients. On the other hand, such selectivity poses a problem for those who are seen as less desirable candidates, or who appear less interested in psychotherapy. Because of increased attention to this and related problems in recent years, there have been some innovative attempts to provide services to lower-class individuals and to adapt therapeutic procedures accordingly. Some reference to this work will be made later in this chapter and in more detail in Chapter 17. It is also possible that with a reduction in governmental funding and an increase in third party payments, many clinics (and practitioners) might be less selective than they have been in the past.

Refusal of Therapy

There is another side to the problem of who receives psychotherapy, however, that is quite different from the one just discussed. This concerns the number of patients who refuse psychotherapeutic treatment. Not all individuals who are offered psychotherapy actually accept it—a finding that is very surprising to most graduate students. Nevertheless, this does appear to be supported by research data. For example, two reports indicated that approximately one-third of clients judged to be in need of psychotherapy, and to whom it was offered, refused such treatment (Garfield & Kurz, 1952; Rosenthal & Frank, 1958). In another investigation, 230 patients out of 603, or 38 percent, failed to return for treatment or disposition even though they were given a definite appointment (Weiss & Schaie, 1958). In a study of a sample of 2551 cases drawn from 17 community mental health facilities, it was found that 40.8 percent of the cases failed to return after the intake interview (Sue, McKinney, & Allen, 1976). A report of 2922 students seen at a university counseling center over a period of eight years indicates that almost 49 percent failed to come to the first therapy session (Phillips & Fagan, 1982). Marks (1978) also mentions that of several hundred patients who were offered behavioral treatment in his unit at the Maudsley Hospital from 1971 to 1974, 23 percent refused the treatment. Comparable results were secured by Betz and Shullman (1979), with 24 percent of clients failing to show for the first interview.

In a report of therapy for sexual difficulties, 142 couples out of 339 who had requested therapy refused it when therapy was offered to them (Fordney-Settlage, 1975). This is approximately 42 percent of the group originally requesting therapy. Everaerd (1983) makes reference to a study by Arentewicz and Schmidt (1980) in which 27 percent of couples who had registered for sex therapy did not actuallly begin therapy. It is pointed out, too, that males less readily accept such treatment than do females. Similarly, it is reported in one study that 6 of 18 men with agoraphobia refused treatment as compared with 4 of 49 women patients (Hafner, 1983).

Several studies have investigated the possible factors or variables related to this rejection of therapy. Rosenthal and Frank (1958) found a significant relationship between acceptance on the part of the client and the client's income, and between acceptance and rated level of motivation. Level of education was related to acceptance only at a suggestive level of significance ($p < .10$). Yamamoto and Goin (1966) also reported a significant correlation between lower socioeconomic status and the failure of

a client to keep his initial appointment. Thus, there is a suggestion of some relationship between socioeconomic variables and the acceptance of psychotherapy on the part of patients. In one other study in which 64 self-referred patients who failed to keep their first therapy appointment were compared with a comparable number of those who did, no differences were secured in terms of age, sex, or education (Noonan, 1973). A difference was noted between these groups of patients, however, in the way they originally presented their problems. The pretherapy dropouts tended to state their problems in a vague and evasive manner, whereas the others verbalized more specific problems.

Two reports based on two different samples of referrals to the Psychiatric Outpatient Department of Boston City Hospital also indicated a large percentage of nonattenders for the initial appointment. In one study of 267 referrals, 42 percent did not keep their appointment (Raynes & Warren, 1971a), whereas in the other, 40 percent of 738 referrals did not attend (Raynes & Warren, 1971b). In the first report, it was also found that age and race were related to attendance. Blacks and those under 40 were significantly more likely to fail to keep their appointments. No such data were reported in the second study (Raynes & Warren, 1971b), but there appeared to be a relationship between time on the waiting list and nonattendance. Although Brandt (1964; Riess & Brandt, 1965) challenged the finding that about a third of those who apply to clinics for outpatient treatment reject psychotherapy, his investigations contained methodological difficulties (e.g., incomplete samples, insufficient data), which limit his conclusions (Garfield, 1978).

Although some relationship between selected social-class variables and rejection of therapy has been secured, we still do not have a completely adequate explanation for this phenomenon. A number of possible hypotheses have been advanced including the following: inadequate motivation to undergo therapy, fear of finding out that one is seriously disturbed, a reluctance to acknowledge that one needs help in resolving personal difficulties, the possible stigma of seeing a mental health professional, and a significant change in one's life situation. The possible causes, of course, may vary with different individuals. However, research investigation in this area has been limited.

RESEARCH PERTAINING TO CONTINUATION IN PSYCHOTHERAPY

A related problem encountered in clinical practice concerns those patients who do begin psychotherapy but terminate their participation and drop out of therapy relatively early. Generally, such termination appears to be initiated by the client before there has been some mutual agreement that therapy has been completed. Such discontinuers, premature terminators, or dropouts constitute a sizable percentage of those who begin therapy, and they have been considered problems since the therapeutic process has not been completed and a considerable amount of staff time may have been devoted to such cases.

It may be worthwhile first to review briefly some representative findings on the nature of this problem. In Table 6.1 data are presented on the length of psychotherapy, expressed in terms of the number of interviews, for 560 patients seen at a VA Mental Hygiene Clinic (Garfield & Kurz, 1952). This group of patients consisted of all of those who had been offered and had accepted treatment at the clinic, and whose cases were officially closed at the time of the study. The clinic staff prided themselves as offering intensive psychodynamic therapy. Contrary to that orientation, as is apparent in the table, the median length of treatment was around 6 interviews, with approximately two-thirds of the cases receiving less than 10 interviews. By contrast, less than 9 percent of the patients came for 25 or more interviews and only 7 cases received over 50 treatment interviews.

Although the data just presented were published in the early 1950s and are the actual findings secured with the population of one clinic, they are .

TABLE 6.1 Length of Treatment

Number of Interviews	Number of Cases	Percentage of Cases
Less than 5	239	42.7
5–9	134	23.9
10–14	73	13.0
15–19	41	7.3
20–24	24	4.3
25 and over	49	8.8
Total	560	100.0

typical of the kinds of results secured from a number of other clinics over a period of many years. For example, in the more recent large-scale study of Sue et al. (1976), it can be noted that 23 percent of the cases actually starting therapy dropped out after the first session. Furthermore, 69.6 percent dropped out before the tenth session, which is quite comparable to the 66.6 percent indicated in Table 6.1. Comparable figures are reported in a recent study of psychiatrists and psychologists in private practice, with 65 and 63 percent of the patients, respectively, terminating before the tenth session (Taube, Burns, & Kessler, 1984). The respective medians were four and five sessions in this study.

Table 6.2 summarizes the findings of a representative number of investigations carried out in several types of clinics that reported such data. As can be seen there, a majority of the clinics have terminated or lost half of their therapy clients before the eighth interview! Although the median length of treatment varies from 3 to 12 interviews for the different clinics, there is a clustering around 6 interviews. It can be emphasized, also, that in those studies that excluded all the patients who were offered therapy but refused it, and included only actual therapy patients, the median number of interviews was between 5 and 8 (Berrigan & Garfield, 1981; Garfield & Kurz, 1952; Kurland, 1956; Rosenthal & Frank, 1958; Schaffer & Myers, 1954).

Similar findings have been reported in a number of other studies. Haddock and Mensh (1957) studied two university student health services and one VA Mental Hygiene Clinic. About two-thirds of the patients were seen fewer than 5 hours, and only one patient in 20 was seen for more than 20 hours. Furthermore, between a third and a half of the cases terminated treatment on their own without discussing it with the therapist. In another study of 400 clinic patients, 45 percent were seen for less than five interviews, with a majority simply discontinuing treatment (Gabby & Leavitt, 1970). More recent studies in three urban mental health centers have also revealed that 37 to 45 percent of adult outpatients terminate psychotherapy after the first or second session (Fiester & Rudestam, 1975). Another report from an inner-city mental health clinic indicates that only 57 percent of patients admitted to the clinic remained for four or more interviews (Craig & Huffine, 1976).

TABLE 6.2   Median Number of Psychotherapy Interviews for Outpatient Clinics

Clinic	Median No. Interviews	Date	Source
VA Clinic, St. Louis	5	1948	Blackman
VA Clinic, Boston	10	1949	Adler, Valenstein, & Michaels
VA Clinic, Milwaukee	6	1952	Garfield & Kurz
VA Clinic, Baltimore	4	1956	Kurland
Va Clinic, Oakland	9	1958	Sullivan, Miller, & Smelzer
VA Clinic, Chicago	3	1959	Affleck & Mednick
Psychiatric Clinics— General Hospitals, N.Y.C	6	1949	N.Y.C. Committee on Mental Hygiene
Clinics in Four States plus VA Clinic, Denver	5–7	1960	Rogers
Yale University Clinic	4	1954	Schaffer & Myers
Henry Phipps Clinic	6	1958	Rosenthal & Frank
Nebraska Psychiatric Institute	12	1959	Garfield & Affleck
Nebraska Psychiatric Institute	8	1961	Affleck & Garfield
University of Oregon Clinic	4	1964	Brown & Kosterlitz
Ohio State University Clinic	4	1970	Dodd
Private Psychology Practice—Ohio	8	1980	Koss
Washington University Psychological Service Center	8	1981	Berrigan & Garfield
Texas Tech Psychology Clinic	6	1982	Walters, Solomon, & Walden
Three Outpatient Clinics— San Francisco Bay Area	5	1984	Billings & Moos

The problem of continuation was even more apparent in a study of length of treatment in a barrio-neighborhood mental health service (Kahn & Heiman, 1978). In this setting, where the clinic population is composed largely of lower socioeconomic Mexican-Americans, *75 percent of the cases come for only one interview, 15 percent for two interviews, and only 10 percent for three or more interviews.*

Statistical reports on psychiatric clinics in several states indicate that a majority of patients have terminated treatment before the eighth interview (Gordon, 1965; Rogers, 1960). A comparable report by the National Center for Health Statistics (1966) stated that the average number of psychiatric visits was 4.7. A more recent report of outpatient statistics on over 350,000 children and youths seen in selected outpatient facilities indicated that 69 percent

had 5 visits or less and 12.5 percent had more than 10 visits (National Institute of Mental Health, 1981). Eiduson (1968), in an earlier review, concluded that "30 percent to 65 percent of all patients are dropouts in facilities representing every kind of psychiatric service."

It is interesting to note that this pattern has occurred over time in a variety of clinical settings with different types of patients or disorders, and with varied forms of therapy. For example, in the 10-year report of the Berlin Psychoanalytic Institute published in 1930, 241 cases out of 721, or 33 percent of the cases, were considered to have terminated prematurely (Bergin, 1971). The situation has not really changed, as we have already noted, and is evident also in several recent reports with diverse types of patients. In a university psychological service center, 26 percent of the 91 cases studied dropped out of treatment (Berrigan & Garfield, 1981). In a study of depressed patients in a psychiatric setting, McLean and Hackstian (1979) reported dropout rates that ranged from 5 percent for behavior therapy to 30 percent for dynamic psychotherapy and 34 percent for drug therapy. Dropouts were defined as clients "who chose to terminate treatment prematurely" (p. 823). Finally, a report on the psychological group treatment of 107 obese essential hypertensives indicated that 26 percent attended 6 or fewer sessions (Basler, Brinkmeier, Buser, Hoehn, & Mölders-Kober, 1982).

It is apparent, therefore, that contrary to many traditional expectations concerning length of therapy, *most clinic clients remain in therapy for only a few interviews*. In practically all of the clinics studied, this pattern was viewed as a problem and was not the result of a deliberately planned brief therapy, even in clinics that rely on brief therapy. Rather, in most instances, the patient failed to return for a scheduled appointment.

It can be stated with some degree of confidence, therefore, that the finding of an unplanned and premature termination from psychotherapy on the part of a large number of clients in traditional clinic settings has been a reasonably reliable one. The apparent rejection of psychotherapy by a number of those who appear to be in need of it has been a somewhat surprising and perplexing finding which, for a while, tended to be relatively ignored. After a steady output of research reports, however, the problem has received increased attention in recent years. This has been evident particularly in research on psychotherapy where the problem of dropouts can be a major concern. Although the latter problem is generally handled by securing larger sample sizes and making additional statistical analyses, overcoming the problem in the clinical situation is a different matter. Some of the attempts made to remediate this problem will be reviewed later.

A number of studies have attempted to discover correlates and predictors of premature termination, and we shall review some of this literature shortly. Before we do so, however, the reader should be alerted to some of the problems in this area of investigation. A major problem is the definition of the dropout or premature terminator. The definition that I have followed in my own research on this topic is as follows: "A dropout from psychotherapy is one who has been accepted for psychotherapy, who actually has at least one session of therapy, and who discontinues treatment on his/her own initiative by failing to come for any future arranged visits with the therapist." There is no mutual agreement between patient and therapist to terminate therapy, and therapy is viewed by the therapist as just begun, in process, or noncompleted. Individuals who never show up for their first appointment would be viewed as rejectors of therapy rather than premature terminators since therapy had not yet been instituted.

Although the above definition appears reasonable to me, it has not been followed with any consistency in the published literature. A similar problem is encountered in the operational designation of "remainers" or "continuers" in psychotherapy. In some studies, as will be illustrated shortly, arbitrary designations have been used that seriously limit the comparability of studies, particularly when potential predictors of continuation are sought. Thus, in some studies four sessions may be the dividing line between continuers and dropouts (Imber, Nash, & Stone, 1955; Vail, 1978), whereas in others 20 sessions or more may be used to designate continuers in therapy (Hiler, 1959). As a result, one must carefully scrutinize research reports in this area to ascertain operational definitions of the categories used, and generalization is hampered.

Social Class and Actuarial Variables

One group of variables that has been studied in relation to length of stay in psychotherapy concerns social class. Some investigations have used one of the popular indices of social class such as that of Hollingshead, while others have studied specific components such as education, income, occupation, and the like. Those who have used the former have generally found some relationship between length of stay and social-class index. In one study only 57.1 percent of lower-class patients stayed beyond the fourth interview, whereas 88.9 percent of middle-class patients went beyond the fourth interview (Imber et al., 1955). In another study about 12 percent of the two lower-social-class groups, classified according to the Hollingshead classification, remained for over 30 interviews as compared with 42 percent of those in the highest two social-class groups (Cole et al., 1962). Gibby, Stotsky, Hiler, and Miller (1954), using occupational status primarily as a measure of social class, also found that middle-class patients remained in therapy longer than did lower-class patients. Dodd (1970) reported that patients from the upper three social classes on the Hollingshead Index remained longer in treatment than those in the lower two classes, but the finding was not replicated on a smaller sample of 57 patients. Fiester and Rudestam (1975) also found a relationship between social-class status on the Hollingshead Index and premature termination in one clinic but not in a hospital-based community health center. In another study no significant relationship between social class and premature termination from therapy was found, but four therapy sessions were used as the criterion of early termination (Albronda, Dean, & Starkweather, 1964).

More recently, using more rigorously defined criteria, Berrigan and Garfield (1981) found a significant relationship between socioeconomic status (Hollingshead Index) and premature termination. In fact, there was a clear linear relationship between social class and continuation in psychotherapy, with increasing proportions of dropouts as social class level decreased. The range was from zero in Class I to 50 percent in Class V. It should also be mentioned that several studies have indicated significant differences between individuals in social classes IV and V (Lorion, 1978; Shubert & Miller, 1980). The largest dropout rates are noted for those in Class V.

A recent study in Great Britain also secured comparable results. Termination of attendance in outpatient clinics was significantly related to lower social class (Weighill, Hodge, & Peck, 1983). Furthermore, in this study as well as the one by Berrigan and Garfield (1981), lower-class patients missed more scheduled appointments. On the basis of the latter study in particular, missed appointments, as contrasted with canceled appointments, were related to discontinuation of therapy.

Education, which is one of the factors in the Hollingshead two-factor index and is highly correlated with social class, has also been evaluated separately. While most studies have reported a positive relationship between education and length of stay (Bailey, et al., 1959; Blackburn, Bishop, Glenn, Whalley, & Christie, 1981; Carpenter & Range, 1983; McNair et al., 1963; Rosenthal & Frank, 1958; Rosenzweig & Folman, 1974; Rubinstein & Lorr,

1956; Sue et al., 1976; Sullivan, Miller, & Smelzer, 1958), some have not (Garfield & Affleck, 1959; Pope, Geller, & Wilkinson, 1975; Simons, Levine, Lustman, & Murphy, 1984; Weissman, Geanakapolos, & Prusoff, 1973). Part of this limited lack of agreement may be due to differences in the samples used, the type of screening employed in selecting patients for psychotherapy, and other variables. Where there are more rigorous standards for acceptance into treatment, the dropout rate tends to be less and the sample biased in favor of better educated clients. Other factors may also play a role. In the study by Weissman et al. (1973), for example, 40 depressed patients received both casework and drugs. The low attrition rate and lack of difference between socioeconomic groups secured may have been influenced by the administration of medication, since it appears that the medication may facilitate treatment continuation (Craig & Huffine, 1976; Dodd, 1970). In any event, it does appear that educational level is related to continuation in psychotherapy.

Although a majority of studies indicate some relationship between socioeconomic status and length of stay in psychotherapy, there are some features of the research conducted on this problem that merit mention here. In the past, most of the studies on attrition have been based on a sample of a particular clinic's regular caseload. In other words, these clients were seen when they sought outpatient services and were not selected initially to be participants in a research study. The subject sample tends to be varied in terms of diagnosis and type of disorder, and the data are usually secured retrospectively from closed clinic case files. In more recent years, research samples have been selected more frequently in advance to meet certain set criteria. Thus, in these instances, the samples are more highly selected and generally are more similar in terms of diagnostic criteria. The type of therapy may also be more rigidly prescribed.

In light of this, it is possible that there may be variations in the results secured with regard to continuation, depending upon the type of study and sample used. For example, there have been several studies conducted with depressed patients in which different forms of therapy have been compared. Although the problem of premature termination is a serious one for such researchers, since it can reduce sample size and result in unequal groups, not all investigators report adequate data on this matter. For example, in a recent report in which seven studies were compared, two studies provided no information on dropouts, whereas different types of information were provided by the other studies (Simons et al., 1984). Furthermore, since there may be more efforts made to keep research subjects in a study than in normal clinic practice, the results on continuation conceivably may not be completely comparable.

Besides education and social class, the most frequently studied actuarial variables examined in relation to length of stay have been sex, age, and diagnosis. Although income and occupation have also been evaluated, these have frequently been combined with education in estimates of social class.

The variable of sex has been investigated in several studies with most of the results showing no significant differences between males and females in terms of premature termination (Affleck & Garfield, 1961; Berrigan & Garfield, 1981; Craig & Huffine, 1976; Frank, Gliedman, Imber, Nash, & Stone, 1957; Garfield & Affleck, 1959; Grotjahn, 1972; Heisler, Beck, Fraps, & McReynolds, 1982; Koran & Costell, 1973; Koss, 1980; Rodolfa, Rapaport, & Lee, 1983; Weighill et al., 1983). In five studies, males were found more frequently to be continuers in psychotherapy (Brown & Kosterlitz, 1964; Carpenter & Range, 1983; Cartwright, 1955; Rosenthal & Frank, 1958; Weiss & Schaie, 1958). However, in Cartwright's (1955) study, only a small proportion of the total variance in length of therapy could be attributed to the sex of the patient. On the whole, it does not appear that sex is an important predictor of continuation in psychotherapy (Garfield, 1977b), although there is a trend favoring males.

A somewhat similar generalization can be made for age of client. Age does not appear to be an important variable as far as continuation in psychotherapy is concerned (Affleck & Garfield, 1961; Berrigan & Garfield, 1981; Cartwright, 1955; Frank et al., 1957; Garfield & Affleck, 1959; Heisler et al., 1982; Rosenthal & Frank, 1958; Rubinstein & Lorr, 1956). In two studies where age was related significantly to premature termination, the actual findings were not impressive. In one, the mean difference in age was less than two years (Sullivan et al., 1958).

In the other study, because of the large number of subjects, the obtained correlation of .06 was significant at the .01 level (Sue et al., 1976).

For practical purposes, therefore, age is not a significant variable in terms of continuation in therapy, even though the age range of the patients in the reported studies varied widely. Other variables appear much more important than age as far as premature termination is concerned.

Psychiatric diagnosis has also been evaluated as a variable in terms of length of stay in outpatient psychotherapy. By and large, in spite of the effort devoted to formulating a psychiatric diagnosis for patients, such classification appears to bear no significant relationship to continuation in outpatient psychotherapy in most studies (Affleck & Garfield, 1961; Bailey, Warshaw, & Eichler, 1959; Garfield & Affleck, 1959; Lief, Lief, Warren, & Heath, 1961; Pope et al., 1975; Rosenthal & Frank, 1958). In one study, patients diagnosed as having anxiety or depressive reactions remained in treatment significantly longer than all others (Frank et al., 1957). In another study (Dodd, 1970), patients diagnosed as having either a psychotic or a psychoneurotic reaction remained in treatment longer than those with other diagnoses. This finding was not replicated with a new sample of 57 patients, however, and Sue et al. (1976) reported that patients diagnosed as psychotic were more likely to drop out of treatment than patients with other diagnoses. On the other hand, Craig and Huffine (1976) reported that patients with a psychosis or personality disorder remained longer in therapy than did patients diagnosed as having a neurosis or transient situational disorder. They also found, however, a relationship between length of stay and prescription of medication. Since psychotic patients almost always were prescribed medication, the results are questionable.

On the whole, psychiatric or clinical diagnosis as such has not been shown to be related to continuation in psychotherapy. It is possible that patients with certain diagnoses may reject psychotherapy or be excluded from it much more than others, and thus have less opportunity to drop out of therapy. Nevertheless, premature termination has been reported for all groups of patients receiving therapy for specifically targeted syndromes or disorders.

Another variable that has been investigated in relation to continuation in psychotherapy is that of race. Although race has tended to be correlated with social-class status, it has also been studied separately and with reference to client–therapist interactions.

Krebs (1971) conducted a study of all cases opened during a nine-month period in an adult outpatient service and analyzed the type of therapy assignment and number of appointments kept in terms of race and sex. It was found that a disproportionate number of black females were assigned to crisis-oriented brief therapy as compared with whites and black males. Black females also were reported to have missed a significantly larger number of appointments than white males or females, or black males. Although the black females had a higher rate of hourly employment than their white counterparts, a factor of possible importance, those that missed a majority of their appointments did not differ on this variable from the black women who kept a majority of their appointments.

Another study attempted to appraise the differential attitudes of black and white families toward treatment in a child guidance clinic (Warren, Jackson, Nugaris, & Farley, 1973). In terms of eight major categories of response, there were not significant differences between the black and white patients, and the length of therapy was not significantly longer for white patients.

In a relatively large-scale study of 17 community mental health clinics, black patients were found to attend significantly fewer sessions than whites and also to terminate therapy more frequently after the intake session (Sue, McKinney, Allen, & Hall, 1974). There was a greater tendency for black patients in another study to see their therapists only briefly (Yamamoto, James, & Palley, 1968), and similar findings were reported in an additional investigation that included a small number of nonwhites (Salzman, Shader, Scott, & Binstock, 1970). Rosenthal and Frank (1958) also reported that almost twice as many white patients as black patients remained for six therapy interviews. On the other hand, Weiss and Dlugokinski (1974) did not find race related to length of treatment for children, and at the Stanford University Mental Health Clinic, the termination rates of black students did not differ from those of other students (Gibbs, 1975).

In a study of lower-class black patients in an inner-city community mental health clinic, 43 patients who came for three sessions or less were considered dropouts and compared with 44 patients who continued after the third session (Vail, 1978). The patients were assigned randomly to therapists who were black, white, male, or female. The only significant result secured was a sex of therapist × sex of patient interaction with most of this interaction related to male therapists securing less continuation from black males. Various measures of attitudes toward whites were unrelated to continuation.

In the study by Billings and Moos (1984), patients' sociodemographic characteristics generally showed little relationship to their actual treatment experiences in the settings evaluated. Among their results was the finding that ethnic minority (nonwhite) patients did not receive less intensive treatment than whites. It is possible that the more recent studies reflect a more positive view of psychotherapy on the part of minority patients, and that this, in turn, is responded to more positively by therapists.

In another recent study, 25 Mexican-Americans, 25 Black Americans, and 24 Anglo-Americans who had previously terminated treatment in a public psychiatric outpatient clinic were interviewed (Acosta, 1980). Most of them were low-income patients and all had left therapy within six sessions without notifying their therapists or receiving their therapists' consent to terminate treatment. The patients had received psychodynamic therapy for a wide range of symptomatic problems. Seven common reasons for termination were given by all groups and rank ordered in the same way. The four with the greatest frequency were: negative attitudes toward the therapist; therapy of no benefit; environmental constraints; and self-perceived improvement. It is interesting that all groups of terminators appeared to give similar reasons for their early termination.

Some related investigations also can be mentioned. In a study of precollege counseling, three experienced black counselors and eight experienced white counselors each saw 13 black and 13 white students (Ewing, 1974). The racial similarity of client and counselor was not found to be an important factor in this situation. Cimbolic (1972) studied black clients paired with white and black counselors and did not find any significant racial preference. In a study of preferences toward Mexican-American and Anglo-American psychotherapists by Acosta and Sheehan (1976), two groups of college students selected from these ethnic classifications both indicated a clear preference for the Anglo-American professional. Although none of these studies were concerned with continuation in therapy, their findings are indirectly of interest.

Sattler (1977) also reviewed a number of studies pertaining to the possible effects of therapist—client racial similarity in psychotherapy. Most of these, like the last few studies discussed, essentially deal with interview and questionnaire data concerning attitudes toward black or white therapists or counselors, and must be viewed with caution. In 10 of 19 studies the black subjects revealed a preference for black therapists or indicated negative opinions toward white therapists. In the other 9 studies, no preference was expressed for either a white or black therapist. Most of these studies, as indicated, deal with attitudes and did not investigate premature termination.

The overall picture is thus far from conclusive. Although there appears to be a tendency for a more frequent early termination from psychotherapy by black clients than for whites, this is by no means a consistent pattern. This problem is also compounded by social-class factors that generally have not been partialed out in most investigations.

Thus, our survey of research findings on continuation in psychotherapy indicates a frequent relationship between social class and length of stay, some relationship of educational level, particularly an inverse one at the lower educational levels, and no clear relationship between length of stay and such variables as age, sex, and psychiatric diagnosis. It is possible, as mentioned earlier, that such variables as social class may be related to other variables that could influence continuation in psychotherapy. A few studies have discussed this matter and can be reviewed briefly.

In one study (Brill & Storrow, 1960), in which acceptance for psychotherapy was positively related to social-class status, an attempt was made to evaluate "Psychological Mindedness" in relation to social class. Low social class was found to be significantly related to low estimated intelligence, a tendency to view the problem as physical rather than emotional, a desire for symptomatic relief, lack of understanding of the psychotherapeutic process, and lack of desire for psychotherapy. In addition, the intake interviewer had less positive feelings for lower-class patients and saw them as less treatable by means of psychotherapy. In terms of the data already discussed, the last statement appears to have elements of a self-fulfilling prophecy. The findings, however, do suggest some interaction effect between attributes and expectations of lower-class clients and attitudes of middle-class therapists, which may play a role in length of stay in psychotherapy.

In one other study, socioeconomic level was related to therapists' ratings of patient attractiveness, ease of establishing rapport, and prognosis, each of which in turn was related to continuation in psychotherapy (Nash et al., 1965). Another study investigated the relationship between values, social class, and duration of psychotherapy, and found a relationship between the interaction of social class and the discrepancy between patient and therapist values and continuation (Pettit, Pettit, & Welkowitz, 1974).

Other studies, to which we will refer shortly, have attempted to investigate personality and other correlates of continuation in psychotherapy. Such variables as motivation, verbal ability, ability to introspect, and attitudes toward psychotherapy have been designated as being of importance in this regard. While such attributes have not always been evaluated in relation to social class, as the study by Brill and Storrow (1960) has shown, there may be some relationship between these two sets of variables.

A related aspect that has been commented upon by Hollingshead and Redlich (1958), as well as by others (Lerner & Fiske, 1973), is that therapists generally appear to prefer and be more comfortable with clients in the upper classes, that is, clients who talk their language and are more similar to them.

The relationship reported between social-class variables and continuation in psychotherapy thus may be a function of several variables acting independently or in interaction with each other. The attributes and expectation of the patient clearly contribute one source of variance to this problem, while the personality, attitudes, and skill of the therapist contribute another. These, furthermore, may act singly or in combination. We clearly need to know much more about such interactions and their potential impact. Researchers are becoming more aware of the complexities involved in trying to unravel the various phenomena of psychotherapy. As a result, univariate studies are gradually giving way to multivariate studies.

Pretherapy Training and Continuation

As a result of the findings reported above, several attempts have been made to deal with the problem of premature terminators. One type of response made previously to the problem of premature termination was that more careful screening should take place before clients are assigned for psychotherapy since premature termination from psychotherapy constitutes a waste of professional manpower. Consequently, the emphasis would be placed on accepting those clients who are viewed as being more amenable to psychotherapy and screening out the "unsuitable client." Such a view would appear to favor the more educated, intelligent, psychologically sophisticated, and less disturbed client as the preferred one for psychotherapy.

A second approach that has emerged is that of providing pretherapy training to help prepare the client for psychotherapy (Heitler, 1976), or to prepare the therapist to deal with anticipated problems. In some instances, this has called for a more active and flexible role on the part of the therapist (Baum & Felzer, 1964). Several such programs have been instituted and have reported somewhat mixed results. In one study, a "Role Induction Interview," based on the anticipatory socialization interview of Orne and Wender (1968), was developed to give the patient appropriate expectations about certain aspects of psychotherapy in the hope that this would facilitate the process and outcome of therapy (Hoehn-Saric et al., 1964). The Role Induction Interview stressed (1) a general exposition of psychotherapy; (2) the expected behavior of patient and therapist; (3) preparation for certain phenomena in therapy such as resistance; and (4) expectation for improvement within four months of treatment. The experimental group significantly exceeded the control group in this study on 6 of the 16 criterion measures used, including that of attendance at scheduled therapy sessions. The results thus suggest that attempts to prepare the patient for psychotherapy may have some impact on his attendance and progress in therapy.

Truax and co-workers (Truax & Carkhuff, 1967; Truax & Wargo, 1969) developed a 30-minute tape recording of excerpts of "good" therapy behavior, which allowed prospective clients to experience group psychotherapy prior to their own therapy. Although not applied to the problem of continuation in psychotherapy, the procedure apparently had a moderately beneficial effect on outcome. Two other studies with adult patients, however, did not secure any significant differences in premature termination as a result of therapy preparation (Sloane, Cristol, Pepernik, & Staples, 1970; Yalom, Houts, Newell, & Rand, 1967).

There have been several reports of specific attempts to prepare lower-class individuals for psychotherapy. Heitler (1973) utilized an "anticipatory socialization interview" with 48 inpatients in expressive group psychotherapy. Although no data on outcome or continuation are provided, the experimental group did exceed the control group on a number of process measures. Strupp and Bloxom (1973) developed a role-induction film for lower-class patients and compared its effectiveness with a role-induction interview and a control film with 122 patients with an average grade level of 10.8. Twelve weekly group therapy sessions were conducted. Those patients receiving the role-induction film and the induction interview showed significantly more gains on a number of attitudinal and in-therapy measures, as well as indicating higher ratings of improvement. However, there were no differences between the groups on attendance, on therapists' ratings of improvement, and on a symptom checklist.

In another study (Jacobs, Charles, Jacobs, Weinstein, & Mann, 1972), lower-class patients (Classes IV and V, Hollingshead Scale) in a walk-in clinic were assigned to one of four groups. In one, the patient was given a brief preparatory interview; in another, the resident psychiatrist was given brief instruction in working with lower-class patients; in a third, both patients and therapists were "prepared"; and the fourth was essentially a control group. Although the report is unclear, it appears that the dropout rate was not affected by the experimental treatment. More patients who were in the three preparation groups came for more than four sessions, however, and were judged to be more improved than was true for the control group.

Still another attempt at some type of pretherapy training or instruction is reported in a study of 55 "low-prognosis" clients in connection with time-limited, client-centered psychotherapy (Warren &

Rice, 1972). This training consisted of two parts and involved four half-hour sessions with someone other than the therapist. These sessions preceded the second, third, fifth, and eighth therapy sessions. The first part, labeled "stabilizing," was designed to encourage the client to discuss problems he might be having with therapy or the therapist, and lasted from 5 to 10 minutes. The remaining time was spent in "structuring," which was an attempt to train the client to participate productively in the process of client-centered therapy. The experimental group had a significantly smaller amount of attrition than the control group.

Last, mention can be made of a study by Holmes and Urie (1975) in which half of a group of 88 children were given a therapy preparation interview, while the controls were given a social history interview. The prepared children dropped out significantly less than did the control children, but outcome ratings were not affected.

Besides these innovative attempts to improve attendance and outcome in psychotherapy, some attempts have been made to modify or adapt conventional procedures in order to better meet the needs of those who tend to be viewed as poor candidates for therapy (Lorion, 1974). Goldstein (1973), for example, developed a structured learning therapy for the poor. These issues and the response to them with regard to disadvantaged groups have been examined also by Heitler (1976) and are discussed more fully in Chapter 17. We will next review research that has investigated other types of variables in relation to continuation in psychotherapy.

Psychological Test Variables and Continuation in Psychotherapy

Psychologists, not surprisingly, have investigated the value of psychological tests for predicting continuation in psychotherapy. A variety of investigations utilizing many different tests and procedures have been reported. However, research in this area is beset by many difficulties. In addition to variations in psychotherapy, there are also sample differences, varying criteria for determining dropouts from therapy, different statistical analyses and approaches to the data, different uses of the same test, and variations in therapists and therapeutic settings. Such differences, of course, complicate the problem and make replications difficult. They must be kept in mind, however, in evaluating existing research.

The Rorschach Test, because of its wide clinical use in the past, has also been applied to investigations of continuation in psychotherapy. Overall, the findings have been contradictory, and there no longer appears to be any great need to review these findings here. Those who are interested in this earlier work are referred to the review in the previous edition (Garfield, 1978). Essentially, the findings were not definitive enough to warrant use of the Rorschach or related procedures as bases for selecting patients for psychotherapy. Hardly any studies in this area have used the Rorschach in recent years.

Other tests and techniques also have been tried in relation to continuation in psychotherapy. There is relatively little to be gained, however, in a review of single studies that have not been replicated. For example, Taulbee (1958), on the basis of selected MMPI and Rorschach variables, concluded that those who continue in therapy beyond the thirteenth interview are initially less defensive and more persistent, dependent, anxious, and introspective than are those who terminate early. These results, however, were not cross-validated, and in another study no significant differences on the MMPI were found between continuers and terminators (Sullivan et al., 1958). The latter study was well-designed, used three moderately large groups of subjects, and attempted two cross-validations of the findings secured with the initial sample of subjects, an important and exemplary but rare event in clinical research. In this investigation significant differences between the Stay and Non-Stay groups were found for several MMPI scales for each of the several groups of subjects studied. These scales were different for each of the groups studied, however, and not one single scale held up for even two of the groups. The authors concluded their report by emphasizing the necessity for cross-validation in studies of this type, a conclusion that is clearly supported by much of the research reported in this area.

Generally, investigations utilizing the MMPI, or scales derived therefrom, have not reported any consistent results with regard to continuation in psychotherapy. Wirt (1967) secured significant, modest correlations between continuation and three MMPI scales for 24 female patients, but no such relationship was secured for 33 male subjects. The small sample and lack of replication obviously limit these findings, and just the opposite findings were reported recently by Walters, Solomon, and Walden (1982). In this study, the MMPI was found to have some predictive value for male outpatients, but not for females. This result was based on a cross-validation using a discriminant function based on 13 scales of the MMPI. The correct prediction for males was only 60 percent, however, slightly above chance. Males who continued in therapy tended to be less defensive while experiencing greater distress.

In the study and cross-validation by Dodd (1970), MMPI scores did not differentiate between continuers and remainers. Similarly, scores on the Barron Ego Strength Scale were not significantly different for continuers and remainers in group therapy, although the number of patients studied was small (Rosenzweig & Folman, 1974). Nacev (1980) also found no correlation between the Barron Ego Strength Scale and continuation.

Imber, Frank, Gliedman, Nash, and Stone (1956) studied the relationship of suggestibility, as measured by the sway test, to length of stay in psychotherapy. They found that 77 percent of the swayers remained for 4 or more interviews, whereas 54 percent of the nonswayers terminated before the fourth interview. It is again pertinent to point out that whereas Imber et al. define continuation in terms of 4 interviews, others have used 13 to 20 interviews. As indicated in Table 6.1, very different percentages of clinic populations are included when such diverse criteria are used. Obviously, with such variation in the criterion variable as well as in patient and therapist samples, prediction will be difficult, if not impossible!

Before concluding this section, some mention should be made of the systematic research of Lorr and his colleagues. This research used relatively large samples of subjects at many VA outpatient clinics, and several replications were performed (Lorr, Katz, & Rubinstein, 1958; Rubinstein & Lorr, 1956). In the initial study, four short tests and questionnaires, referred to as the TR battery, were found to be predictive of length of stay. The tests, increased to five in the second study, included a shortened version of the Taylor Manifest Anxiety Scale, a 20-item F. Scale, a Behavior Disturbance Scale, a 15-item Vocabulary Scale, and a brief self-rating scale. These instruments were selected on the basis of a double cross-validation on two random halves of a sample of 128 cases and were then further evaluated on two new samples of 115 cases each.

Because of the particular distribution, those who stayed less than 7 weeks were compared with those who remained more than 26 weeks. It is interesting that none of the tests based on the scoring keys derived from the original cross-validation differentiated the two new samples, although the scores were consistently in the predicted direction. This is, of course, a perennial problem in psychological research. It is of some importance, however, for findings based on the initial group studied become truly significant only when they can be applied to other comparable groups. In this investigation, with two subsamples available, further analyses were done on one sample and then applied to the other. This did produce some statistically significant results. However, the multiple correlation of .67 for these test patterns shrank to .39 when one moved from the first subsample from which they were derived to the second subsample. In general, remainers were found to be more anxious, more self-dissatisfied, more willing to explore problems, more persistent and dependable, and less likely to have a history of antisocial acts.

The above study was cross-validated on another VA sample of 282 patients with somewhat comparable results (McNair et al., 1963). The multiple R of the TR test battery was .44 as contrasted with .39 previously. Furthermore, while different criteria were used in selecting terminators in the two studies, the overall accuracy of prediction was about 15 percent higher than the sample base rates. These investigators thus replicated their findings several times, something that is rare in this area of research, and eventually came up with some stable results. Since this research is somewhat of a model for other researchers to emulate, it is disheartening to have to refer next to a study that utilized three of the TR tests and found no significant relationship between predictions and continuation in therapy (Stern, Moore, & Gross, 1975). The latter investigators took the view that previous research on termination confounded personality with social-class variables and that the prediction of termination with the TR scale was based primarily on social class. These assertions, however, were not supported by a detailed analysis of the existing research (Garfield, 1977a). It was noted, furthermore, that besides possible sample differences, patients were considered to be remainers "if they kept appointments for six consecutive sessions or if they missed only one of these sessions but had notified their therapist beforehand'' (Stern et al., 1975, p. 342). Clearly, the definition of continuation used differed considerably from that of the previous studies.

Sufficient studies have now been reviewed to give the reader some picture of this area of research. Although conflicting and unreplicated findings have been frequent, the reasons should be apparent. The studies have utilized different definitions of early termination, the samples and methods of appraisal have differed, therapeutic conditions and frequency of therapy have not been consistent, comparable information on certain variables has not been available, and a number of similar types of difficulties have been encountered. Such variations, of course, make reliable or clear-cut generalizations difficult. In contrast to the findings secured with psychological tests, social class variables appear to show a somewhat more consistent relationship to the phenomena being studied and are relatively easy to appraise.

Other psychological attributes that may or may not be related to social class have not given as consistent results, nor have they been systematically studied in relation to social class. One of the problems here is that personality variables discussed or studied in psychotherapy research are defined and measured differently in the various investigations. For example, motivation has been mentioned frequently as an important variable in psychotherapy (Garfield, 1980; Malan, 1976) and has considerable face validity. Although McNair et al. (1963) found therapists' ratings of motivation related to length of stay, however, in three other studies, ratings of motivation were not so related (Affleck & Garfield, 1961; Garfield, Affleck, & Muffley, 1963; Siegel & Fink, 1962). The problem may be related to the vagueness of the constructs used, to the inadequacy of the measuring instruments used for appraisal, or to still other factors. Reliable and clinically useful findings are still difficult to secure.

Client Expectations in Relation to Continuation in Psychotherapy

Another area of investigation has been the relationship of the clients' expectancies concerning therapy to duration of stay. Clients may have various expectations about psychotherapy, and if these are incongruent with what actually occurs, the client could become dissatisfied and withdraw from therapy.

Heine and Trosman (1960) investigated the initial expectations and attitudes of 46 patients toward psychiatric treatment. Later the total group was dichotomized in terms of those still in treatment after six weeks. The terminators tended to emphasize passive cooperation as a means of reaching their goal in treatment, and sought medicine or diagnostic information. The remainers, on the other hand, emphasized active collaboration and advice or help in changing behavior. These latter expectations were seen as being congruent with the expectations of the therapists. By contrast, the type of presenting complaint, whether somatic or emotional, or the degree of conviction that treatment would help, was unrelated to continuation.

In another study, patients who came for 12 or fewer interviews expressed some significantly different expectations of their therapists than did those who remained for 13 or more interviews (Heine, 1962). More terminators expected specific advice on their problems in the first therapy interview than did the continuers, and the latter more frequently expected a permissive attitude on the part of the therapist than did those who discontinued. In these respects, the continuers were more similar in their expectations to the therapists than were the discontinuers.

In a study of 40 lower-class patients, their expectations about therapy were secured and were then reevaluated after the first interview in terms of their perception of that interview (Overall & Aronson, 1962). The results indicated that these patients tended to expect a "medical-psychiatric" interview, with the therapist assuming an active supportive role. Furthermore, those patients whose expectations were generally least accurate in terms of therapist role were significantly less likely to return for treatment.

In a somewhat different type of study, Garfield and Wolpin (1963) evaluated the expectations of 70 patients referred for outpatient psychiatric treatment. The median level of education was 12 years, and none of the patients had had previous psychiatric treatment. In general, these patients indicated psychotherapy as the treatment of choice (88 percent), and a majority of them saw emotional factors as important in their difficulties. Despite such positive attitudes toward psychotherapy, however, over a third of them thought the therapy sessions would last 30 minutes or less, 73 percent anticipated some improvement by the fifth session, and 70 percent expected treatment to last 10 sessions or less. The latter expectations were clearly not congruent with those held by the therapists, but are not too discrepant from the median length of treatment reported by most clinics. In fact, one might even say that the clients were accurate in their expectations while the therapists were not!

Somewhat comparable findings have been reported also in a more recent study of therapy expectations (Kupst & Shulman, 1979). In comparing professional and lay expectations of psychotherapy, the largest difference was found on the following item: "If I saw a professional helper, I would expect it to take a long time before I solved my problems, maybe years." Whereas only 17 percent of the lay group agreed with this statement, 96 percent of the mental health professionals agreed.

It does appear that many professionals exhibit a bias favoring long-term psychotherapy even when the preponderance of the therapy provided is relatively short-term. For example, a descriptive report of the psychotherapy program developed by the Harvard Community Health Plan indicated that only 1 to 2 percent of patients require long-term psychotherapy (Bennet & Wisneski, 1979). In a study of clients seen in private practice, Koss (1979) also concluded that "The view that long-term psychotherapy is the treatment of choice for verbal, mild to moderately disturbed persons is questioned by the results. Long-term psychotherapy was rejected by a high proportion of clients who appeared to be appropriate candidates" (p. 211).

A study of outpatient drug treatment is also worth mentioning here (Freedman et al., 1958). In this study the doctors' notes of the initial interview were analyzed in terms of the warmth or detachment of the relationship provided by the therapist. Although those patients who dropped out of therapy did not differ from those remaining in terms of the warmth of the doctor-patient relationship, when the type of relationship was matched with the patients' expectations about treatment, a significant interaction was found. Patients who denied mental illness and encountered a warm relationship tended to drop out, whereas the reverse was true with those patients who accepted their illness and were exposed to a warm relationship. This study also illustrates the importance of examining possible interactions between patient and therapist variables as compared with reliance solely on individual variables.

Finally, reference can be made to a recent study and review that is critical of the view that lower-class individuals have treatment conceptions that are inappropriate and differ from those of other patients (Frank, Eisenthal, & Lazare, 1978). Using an 84-item questionnaire to study the requests for help of 278 walk-in-clinic clients, the investigators obtained no really marked social-class differences. Patients from Class I through IV showed no differences. Class V patients did differ on some categories, for example, requests for social interventions, administrative help, and psychological expertise, but the differences were not really pronounced. The investigators concluded that social-class differences in treatment disposition and outcome reflected the attitudes of middle-class therapists.

It does appear that patients today are somewhat more sophisticated about psychotherapy than they were in the past. They do not necessarily seek medication or a passive role. Most, however, do expect or favor relatively brief psychotherapeutic treatment. At the same time, there are individual differences among patients that influence their preferences and expectations and that interact with therapist variables.

Other Variables in Relation to Continuation to Psychotherapy

Although our focus here is on client variables or attributes, as indicated in the preceding section, how the therapist perceives and regards the client may also affect the progress of therapy. If the therapist regards the client as unmotivated, overly defensive, hostile, and difficult, it is conceivable that his or her attitudes may be communicated to the client and influence his or her participation and continuation in psychotherapy. Some studies that appear pertinent to this hypothesis can be briefly alluded to here.

In one study, therapists' ratings at the end of the second session of group therapy on three factors were related significantly to continuation in therapy (Rosenzweig & Folman, 1974). These were the therapist's estimate of his ability to empathize with the client, his positive feelings toward the client, and his judgment of the client's ability to form a therapeutic relationship. In another study, the therapists' positive feelings toward clients and their positive prognoses for treatment were related to continuation, whereas ratings of psychopathology were not so related (Shapiro, 1974). Ratings of therapeutic prognosis also were found to be related to continuation in outpatient therapy in one other investigation (Garfield & Affleck, 1961). However, an attempt to replicate this finding with a new sample failed (Affleck & Garfield, 1961). It seems prudent to regard unreplicated findings as primarily suggestive, and to withhold final judgments until the findings are replicated.

The skill or experience of the therapist and how he or she is perceived by the client may also play a role in continuation. Dodd (1970) found that medical students had a significantly higher rate of dropouts from psychotherapy with their patients than did psychiatric residents, and this finding was also cross-validated on a new sample of 57 patients. Baekeland and Lundwall (1975) also report some relationship between therapist experience and continuation in psychotherapy in their review article, and a relationship between judged therapists' level of skill and continuation has been reported by Garfield et al. (1963). It can also be noted that in a well-known study that used very experienced and nationally recognized therapists, there were no dropouts at the fourth interview, the point set for designating dropouts (Sloane, Staples, Cristol, Yorkston, & Whipple, 1975).

Some interesting findings have also been reported in a study that investigated certain aspects of the therapeutic relationship as they may pertain to both continuation and outcome in psychotherapy (Saltzman et al., 1976). The subjects in this study were 91 students who sought treatment at a university counseling center. Dropouts were defined as those who did not continue beyond the ninth interview. Both clients and therapists filled out forms pertaining to the treatment process after each of the first 10 interviews, and analyses were made of the responses to the first, third, and fifth interviews, the period during which most of the premature terminations occurred.

At the end of the first session, dropouts reported less anxiety than did the remainers. At the third and fifth sessions, dropouts were significantly lower than remainers on a number of dimensions pertaining to the relationship, such as the therapist's respect, confidence in the therapist, and involvement in therapy. In a complementary fashion, dropouts were significantly lower than remainers on items completed by the therapists that pertained to the therapist's respect for the client and his or her own involvement

in therapy. Thus, both clients' and therapists' views of the relationship early in therapy appeared to be related to continuation in therapy. Therapist experience level and gender similarity of client–therapist pairs, however, were not related to either continuation or outcome.

Because the following chapter deals primarily with the research on therapist variables in psychotherapy, we will not deal extensively with such variables here. Because the interaction of therapist and client variables are potentially of great importance, however, some mention of therapist variables is unavoidable, and we will make reference to a few additional investigations.

Feister (1977) compared therapists with high client attrition rates versus therapists with low attrition rates on demographic and initial-session therapy-process variables. The two groups did not differ in such variables as age, sex, profession, experience, or personal therapy. On the other hand, several process variables did differentiate the groups, and the author concluded that such variables have greater explanatory power for attrition than do client characteristics.

In another study, little relationship was found between continuation and therapists' sex, professional affiliation, and democratic values (Carpenter & Range, 1982). Mogul (1982), in reviewing studies dealing with the sex of the therapist in relation to duration of treatment and satisfaction with treatment, also concluded that there were "no clear, replicable results salient to decision making" (p. 1).

In a different investigation the distance traveled to the clinic in miles was also of value in predicting continuation (Fraps, McReynolds, Beck, & Heisler, 1982). The criteria of continuation used was somewhat atypical, however, and travel of 50 miles or more would not apply to most urban clinics. Nevertheless, it would appear that both situational and behavioral or interactional variables may be associated with attendance in therapy.

Two other kinds of results can be mentioned before concluding this section. In one investigation, 32 individuals who terminated after the first interview were compared with a like number who continued for additional interviews (the precise number is not given) (Duehn & Proctor, 1977). Stimulus-response congruence (whether the clinician's verbal responses acknowledge the content of the patient's preceding communication) and content congruence (the clinician's verbal statement being consistent with the patient's expectations concerning what was to be discussed) were the variables appraised. It was reported that the therapists were significantly more incongruent with defectors and that their verbal content was also significantly more irrelevant to the content expectations of the defectors.

The other interesting and somewhat serendipitous finding that seems worth mentioning here has been noted in three studies. This is that patients who are asked to complete test questionnaires prior to therapy, and who do in fact comply with this request, are more likely to continue in therapy than those who fail to complete the test. In one study, those patients completing the MMPI continued in therapy significantly more than those who failed to do so (Wirt, 1967). In the second investigation, similar findings were secured with one sample of patients, but not with another smaller sample in an attempted replication (Dodd, 1970). In a third study, those patients who failed to complete a pretherapy packet of questionnaires dropped out of group therapy significantly more than those who completed the questionnaires (Koran & Costell, 1973). Does compliance with requests to complete questionnaires indicate a more general pattern of compliance or determination, or does it reflect greater motivation to cooperate in therapy? The matter of compliance with medication schedules has also been viewed as a problem recently, and the issue is worthy of further study.

Although the material discussed thus far is representative of the research carried out, it must be mentioned again that different samples of patients and therapists, as well as different procedures and criteria for defining continuation, have been used in the various studies. In a similar manner, the meaning and definition of expectancies or expectations have also come under critical scrutiny in recent years (Bootzin & Lick, 1979; Lick & Bootzin, 1975; Wilkins, 1973, 1979). Since this latter problem has been investigated more extensively with regard to outcome in psychotherapy, we shall postpone further discussion of it until later.

In the light of what has been said, it would be of interest to know the clients' own reasons for terminating their psychotherapy. One small follow-up study of 12 individuals who dropped out of psychotherapy before the seventh interview has been reported (Garfield, 1963). Eleven of the 12 cases

were contacted by a social worker and, among other questions, were asked why they discontinued psychotherapy. Six of the terminators gave as their reason some external difficulty, such as lack of transportation, no babysitter, and inability to get away from work. Of the remaining 5, 3 were dissatisfied with the results of therapy or with the therapist, and 2 stated that they had improved. Although long-term studies with adequate samples have not been made, on the basis of this study and one other (Riess & Brandt, 1965), it appears that very few of such terminators apply for therapy elsewhere after dropping out.

Silverman and Beech (1979) raised a question about viewing dropouts as dropouts. Essentially, they questioned whether all dropouts should be viewed as failures. This is a reasonable question, but the investigation they reported does not provide an adequate answer. The sample used was small and not clearly described. Furthermore, only 25 percent of the group that had failed to return for treatment after the first interview participated in the study. The fact that 70 percent of those interviewed by phone expressed satisfaction with the service received and that 79 percent stated that the problem for which they sought help had been solved is interesting, but I'm not sure what it means. I would agree that not all dropouts automatically should be viewed as treatment failures. One may ask, however, what went on during the one therapy session that patients stated had helped solve their problems, but apparently was not perceived that way by the therapist. This phenomenon indicated a discrepancy between patients' and therapists' view of psychotherapy, and it would be very worthwhile to know about the potentially therapeutic variables that were operating that therapists appeared to miss. On the other hand, the statement in the report that 65 percent of the patients who were "expecting insight" received it during the one interview attended does leave one somewhat uncertain as to what is being appraised.

There are also a few reports where dropouts from group therapy were asked their reasons for terminating therapy. Although group therapy has some special features that distinguish it from individual psychotherapy, in the absence of other data, it is worth noting the results of these studies. Yalom (1966) was able to contact 26 of 35 dropouts and reported that there was rarely "a single cause for any patient's termination and often it was difficult to determine the major reason for the dropout" (p. 397). He grouped his responses into nine different categories, some of which dealt specifically with the group process. However, 7 patients did indicate that they had a mistaken notion of therapy. A second, smaller study of 9 of 15 dropouts also secured results that were similar to those of Yalom's in showing a diversity of reasons for termination (Koran & Costell, 1973).

In another study 29 percent of prepared patients, who indicated later that they had been adequately prepared for therapy, dropped out of group therapy after entering therapy (Lothstein, 1978). "Although the patients' reasons for dropping out focused on such factors as no longer needing treatment and scheduling problems, the therapists focused on dynamic reasons for the dropouts. All of the therapists reported that they disliked the patients who dropped out, and many of those patients were seen as hostile toward the therapist" (p. 1494). Although the manner in which information is reported in this article leaves much to be desired, the author does mention that some dropouts also felt that the therapist and other patients were unsympathetic. This type of reason is quite different from those mentioned earlier. The author concludes, however, that the dropout rate may not be preventable, and in fact is necessary for development of cohesiveness in the group. This is cleary conjectural and remains in need of verification. Variations in therapists, clients, and type of therapy, singly or in interaction, could influence the dropout rate.

We have reviewed a number of variables in relation to duration of stay in psychotherapy and have commented upon some of the difficulties and complexities evident in securing reliable and generalizable results. Many findings are not confirmed when applied to new samples, and conditions from clinic to clinic and study to study vary. As a result, findings that have not been cross-validated on new samples have to be viewed as suggestive at best. Some variables also have not been very systematically explored. For example, in several of the studies reviewed, IQ did show some positive relationship to length of stay in traditional outpatient psychotherapy (Affleck & Mednick, 1959; Auld & Eron, 1953; Gibby et al., 1954; Hiler, 1958). In most of these studies, however, the analyses of IQ data have been secondary to other analyses and were carried out on a smaller number of subjects than was used in the main study. One would also expect to find a positive correlation between IQ and indices of social class.

Of the variables studied, those pertaining to social class appear to have the most consistent supporting evidence. While this relationship does have some empirical support, the precise reasons advanced to explain this relationship must be viewed somewhat tentatively. Mutuality of expectation on the part of therapists and client is one hypothesis that seems plausible and has some supporting data. The matter of differing value systems and orientations among middle-class therapists and lower-class clients has been hypothesized as a possible explanation for the results secured (Myers & Schaffer, 1958), but systematic research on this has been limited (Lerner & Fiske, 1973).

Finally, it can be noted that premature termination and rejection of therapy occur with practically all forms of psychotherapy. The reasons for this occurrence undoubtedly vary, and one general explanation would not appear to be adequate. In some cases, the individual may terminate because his concerns about his difficulties have lessened, and the therapist apparently fails to recognize this. In other instances, however, as indicated earlier, a variety of factors may account for the termination. In this chapter we have focused on client variables. On the basis of the research reviewed, however, it does appear that investigators will have to go beyond single variables if real progress is to be made in understanding premature termination. As indicated in the beginning of the chapter, psychotherapy involves a complex interaction process. A recognition of this is becoming more clearly apparent in the research on psychotherapy process and outcome.

RESEARCH ON CLIENT VARIABLES AND OUTCOME IN PSYCHOTHERAPY

Although the problem of continuation in psychotherapy is of some importance, the most important consideration is what kind of outcome is eventually secured. Because the assumption is usually made that a certain amount of contact with a therapist must be made if progress in psychotherapy is to be attained, early termination on the part of the client frequently is viewed as a failure in psychotherapy, even though there has been little systematic research evaluating outcome in such cases. Here, as elsewhere, various beliefs concerning psychotherapy are frequently held with relatively little attempt made to secure research data to support or refute these beliefs.

The relationship of length of therapy to outcome, however, is not a central concern here. Of possibly greater importance than length of therapy per se is how therapy is structured for the client and how the therapy meets his or her expectations. In comparative reviews of brief time-limited therapy and unlimited therapy, for example, no clear differences in outcome between the two types of therapy have been secured (Butcher & Koss, 1978; Gurman & Kniskern, 1978; Luborsky, Singer, & Luborsky, 1975; Smith, Glass, & Miller, 1980).

Premature Termination and Outcome
Detailed evaluations of the outcome of early terminators have not been made. In one follow-up study of 12 terminators and 12 remainers who had been studied more intensively for another purpose, both groups stated that they were getting along quite well, and if anything, the terminators gave more favorable reports (Garfield, 1963). However, the follow-up was based on the self-reports of the clients and no pre- and posttherapy measures were used. In contrast to this report, Yalom (1966) indicated that all but perhaps 3 of 35 dropouts from group therapy showed no improvement. Still other results, as indicated previously (Silverman & Beech, 1979), were secured on the basis of a telephone inquiry. Thus, these reports do not allow for any firm conclusions.

More recently, a follow-up investigation was conducted to appraise the adjustment of patients who had dropped out of outpatient psychotherapy at four clinics of a community mental health center (Pekarik, 1983). Although 168 patients agreed to participate, only 64 provided the data for the study. They were divided into dropouts or appropriate terminators on the basis of their therapists' judgments. A dropout was defined as a client in need of further treatment; an appropriate terminator required no further treatment. A brief symptom inventory, administered by phone or by mail three months after the initial intake session, was used to evaluate adjustment. Over four-fifths of the clients had 4 or fewer visits, with the dropouts averaging 2.8 visits and the other group, 3.8 visits. Sixty-four percent of the group were considered dropouts. The author

concluded that the appropriate terminators had better outcomes than the dropouts, but this finding was mainly due to those patients who attended only one session. The rest were quite comparable. The relatively small client samples, the brevity of the therapy, as well as the criteria used seriously limit the conclusions to be drawn. It would appear that individuals leave therapy for a variety of reasons and that their outcomes are also likely to be variable.

Problems in Evaluating Outcome
Let us now proceed to discuss the research on client variables and outcome in psychotherapy. At the outset, something should be said about the difficulties inherent in outcome research, even though such matters have been discussed in other chapters of this volume. (See particularly Chapters 2 and 5.) Although the length of psychotherapy, as determined by the number of interviews, provides a reasonably clear and objective criterion for research investigation, when we turn our attention to outcome, we encounter a large number of variable and fallible criteria. Among the frequently used criteria for appraising outcome are therapists' judgments, clients' evaluations, ratings by judges, a variety of tests and questionnaires, behavioral tasks, and the like. This variety of measures poses a number of difficulties in comparing the results of potential predictor variables among different studies. Several investigations, for example, have shown rather low agreement among different outcome criteria (Cartwright, Kirtner, & Fiske, 1963; Garfield, Prager, & Bergin, 1971; Horenstein, Houston, & Holmes, 1973; Keniston, Boltax, & Almond, 1971; Sloane et al., 1975). In some of these studies, it has also been shown that clients' and therapists' ratings of outcome tend to be more positive than other measures. In addition to these problems, there have also been methodological issues concerning whether only global ratings of outcome at termination are used, or whether difference scores, in terms of pre−post measures, or other procedures to take into account initial differences between clients have been used (Fiske et al., 1970; Luborsky et al., 1975; Mintz, 1972). As a result, it is exceedingly difficult and, at times, misleading to lump together studies that have utilized different measures of outcome.

In addition to the problems encountered with outcome criteria, there are also variations in the type of therapy offered, in the training and competence of the therapists studied, and in the kinds of client samples treated. Such problems, as we have already noted, not only place limitations on the value of any specific study, but also seriously limit the drawing of reliable and valid generalizations from the existing studies. With this, then, as a caveat, let us look at some representative studies. For the sake of convenience, the types of studies will again be classified into a few broad categories.

Social-class Variables and Outcome

Although social-class variables have received considerable attention in relation to such matters as assignment to psychotherapy and premature termination, they have not been studied as frequently with regard to outcome. In the extensive review of factors influencing outcome in psychotherapy by Luborsky et al. (1971), for example, only a relatively small number of such studies were mentioned. In general, other variables have received greater attention. Consequently, our discussion of social-class variables and their relationship to outcome will be brief.

In their review of five studies dealing with social class, Luborsky et al. (1971) reported essentially no relationship betwen this variable and outcome. Two studies found no relationship (Brill & Storrow, 1960; Katz, Lorr, & Rubenstein, 1958), two found a positive relationship (McNair, Lorr, Young, Roth, & Boyd, 1964; Rosenbaum, Friedlander, & Kaplan, 1956), and in one study of 35 patients, *lower* socioeconomic status was found to be associated with positive outcome in brief psychotherapy (Gottschalk, Mayerson, & Gottlieb, 1967). The study by Rosenbaum et al. (1956) had several deficiencies that make its findings questionable. "Social strata" were defined very grossly and two of the three outcome groups had to be combined in order to obtain a significant chi square.

Lorion (1973) in a general discussion of socioeconomic status and traditional treatment approaches also concluded that "while socioeconomic status appears to be a significant correlate of acceptance for, and duration of, individual psychotherapy, it does not relate to treatment outcome" (p. 263). Thus, two previous reviews of this problem have come to quite similar conclusions. Besides those studies already mentioned, Rosenthal and Frank (1958), Cole et al. (1962), Albronda et al. (1964), and Schmidt and Hancey (1979) also did not find

any relationship between social class and outcome in their investigations.

A few studies have also examined outcome in terms of the educational status of the client, and the findings here tend to be more positive. Four studies have reported positive findings (Bloom, 1956; Hamburg et al., 1967; McNair et al., 1964; Sullivan et al., 1958), while two found no significant results (Knapp, Levin, McCarter, Wermer, & Zetzel, 1960; Rosenbaum et al., 1956). It should be noted, however, that in most of these studies therapists' ratings constituted the main criterion of outcome, in some the samples were small, and in Bloom's study, the criterion of poor outcome also included premature termination.

It is also of interest to note that whereas the importance of socioeconomic status has been discussed a number of times with reference to so-called traditional or psychodynamic psychotherapy, it is rarely mentioned in reports of behavioral therapy. This is evident in a review of individual psychotherapy and behavior therapy by Gomes-Schwartz, Hadley, and Strupp (1978). The section of the review devoted to psychotherapy has a subsection devoted to socioeconomic status, but there is no such subsection in the section devoted to behavior therapy. These reviewers state initially that lower-class patients "are less likely to be accepted for traditional insight-oriented therapy . . . and less likely to benefit from expressive psychotherapies" (Gomes-Schwartz et al., 1978, p. 439). Shortly after making this statement, however, they also state that these views have begun to be challenged and that some of the more negative results may be related to the attitudes and expectations that many therapists may have toward such patients.

Several other individuals also have discussed the matter of differential therapists' attitudes toward lower-class patients and their potential importance for continuation in psychotherapy (Jones, 1974; Lerner, 1972; Lorion, 1973, 1974). However, there have been few, if any, systematic studies that attempted to relate therapists' attitudes toward lower-class patients and outcome in psychotherapy. The existing data do not indicate any strong relationship between social class and outcome, although there is a suggestion of some relationship between education and outcome.

More recently, Jones (1982) compared four comparable groups of black and white clients who were seen by equal numbers of black and white thera-pists. All clients had to have been seen for at least eight sessions in individual dynamic therapy. Essen-tially similar results were secured for the four groups, and the investigator concluded that "Therapist–patient racial match has little influence on outcome in longer term psychotherapy" (Jones, 1982, p. 730). A possible limitation of the study is that the criteria of outcome were therapists' ratings.

Age and Outcome

It has generally been assumed that older people tend to be more rigid and fixed in their ways. Their patterns of behavior have a longer reinforcement history and supposedly their defenses and character structure are most resistant to change. We do know from more systematic studies that older subjects show some decline in mental functioning (Matar-azzo, 1972) and that they may not learn new skills as readily as younger individuals. Consequently, it could be presumed that they would be less favor-able candidates for psychotherapy in terms of their potential for change. This, apparently, was Freud's view and, in my opinion, it has been an influential view for a number of therapists. However, I do not believe that there are research data to support the view that older clients are less desirable in terms of most psychotherapeutic approaches.

There is a problem pertaining to the research on age and outcome, however, that does not exist with regard to the variable of sex. By and large, in the latter instance, all studies use the same criteria and subjects are classified into the same two categories—male and female. Age, however, is a different mat-ter. It is a continuous variable and not a dichoto-mous one. Consequently, one cannot generalize from a group of studies unless they have compara-ble samples of subjects. If one investigator has a group of patients ranging in age from 20 to 40 years, and another has a sample that ranges in age from 30 to 60 years, the "older" patients in the two samples vary. Thus, it is difficult to draw any meaningful conclusions— and this problem has limited the find-ings reported in this area.

In a tally of 11 studies made by Luborsky et al. (1971), four studies purportedly secured a positive relationship between age and outcome (favoring the younger age), two secured a negative relation-ship, and five secured no relationship. However, the reviewers included the study by Zigler and Phillips

(1961) as one of the positive studies, although it does not deal with age and psychotherapy out-come. Instead, it is an investigation of social compe-tence and hospitalization. Thus, this reduces the "positive" studies to three, and although Luborsky et al. (1971) concluded that "Older patients tend to have a slightly poorer prognosis" (p. 151), the data in support of this conclusion are weak. More de-tailed analyses of the individual studies are contained in an earlier review by the present writer (Garfield, 1978).

Although there has been an increased interest re-cently in work with the elderly, there has been rela-tively little systematic research on psychotherapy with the aged (Mintz, Steuer, & Jarvik, 1981; Stor-andt, 1983). It does seem, however, that the more negative views toward the elderly associated with long-term analytically oriented psychotherapy may have diminished greatly as the modal therapy today is distinctly brief therapy. For example, in a recent study of 412 patients who entered treatment for unipolar depression in six different treatment cen-ters, there was "little evidence of clinician bias against providing treatment to less 'desirable' pa-tients, such as those who were older or of lower social status" (Billings & Moos, 1984, p. 119). It can also be noted that Smith et al. (1980) secured an overall correlation of .00 between age and outcome in their large-scale meta-analysis of outcome in psychotherapy.

Sex and Outcome in Psychotherapy

The prevailing evidence with regard to sex and outcome also appears to indicate that there is no strong relationship. Most of the studies show no differences in outcome. It is conceivable, however, that there are possible interaction effects between the sex of the therapist and that of the client. If this is so, then focusing solely on one part of the equation may not provide meaningful answers. In any event, a few comments can be offered.

Most studies, as indicated, have reported no rela-tionship between sex and outcome (Cartwright, 1955; Gaylin, 1966; Hamburg et al., 1967; Knapp et al., 1960). Two have reported positive findings for women. In one, the positive finding is based on a small sample of 18 men and 11 women (Seeman, 1954). The other study utilized only 12 women and 15 men (Mintz, Luborsky, & Auerbach, 1971) and significant results were secured only with one of the two therapist rating scales used.

More recently, a comparison and reanalysis of two well-known studies also indicated inconclusive findings as regards sex and outcome in psychotherapy (Luborsky, Mintz, & Christoph, 1979). Although in the University of Chicago Counseling Center Project (Fiske, Cartwright, & Kirtner, 1964) there were low but significant correlations (.26, .33) between sex of client and two measures of outcome, the comparable correlations secured in the Penn psychotherapy project were not significant (Luborsky et al., 1979). In the Temple University study comparing psychotherapy and behavior therapy, the "amount of improvement shown appeared to be independent of the sex of the patient" (Sloane et al., 1975). Similar findings were also reported in a study of psychoanalytically oriented psychotherapy conducted at the Michael Reese Medical Center in Chicago (Siegel, Rootes, & Taub, 1977). An educational approach to depression based on social learning theory also found no relationship between sex and outcome (Steinmetz, Lewinsohn, & Antonuccio, 1983). The review by Gomes-Schwartz et al. (1978), although referring to only a few studies, also refers to null or conflicting results when discussing the relation of sex to outcome.

One recent study did attempt to evaluate the impact of client and therapist gender on psychotherapy process and outcome (Jones & Zoppel, 1982). Former therapy clients were interviewed about their experiences in treatment and assessments of their therapy were secured. In general, women therapists appeared to form more effective therapeutic alliances with clients of both sexes, but both male and female clients of the male therapists reported significant improvement in therapy. The authors concluded "that gender was not an overriding influence in psychotherapy" (p. 271).

On the basis of the results mentioned above, one cannot make a strong case for sex of client as a significant variable related to outcome in psychotherapy. Other factors would appear to be of greater importance. This same conclusion would also appear to hold for the other demographic variables discussed earlier.

Personality and Test Variables Related to Outcome

A number of studies carried out in the search for variables related to outcome in psychotherapy have dealt with the personality and test patterns of clients. The prognostic and personality variables investi-

gated have been quite numerous and have included the following among others: level or degree of disturbance, life situation, support systems, expectancies for improvement, type of symptoms, duration of symptoms, likability, motivation for treatment, ego strength, developmental level, ability to form therapeutic relationships, cognitive structures, and neuroticism. No attempt will be made here to review all of the individual and frequently unreplicated studies that exist in the published literature. Again, attention will be given to studies that have appeared promising or that illustrate research problems in this area.

In the late 1940s and 1950s particularly, when psychologists were identified to a large extent with psychological tests, a variety of investigations were conducted in which test findings were related to outcome in psychotherapy. In one early study, Rosenberg (1954), for example, examined the responses to the Wechsler-Bellevue Scale, the Rorschach, and a sentence completion test of 40 patients who received psychotherapy in a VA outpatient clinic. The protocols of the Rorschach and the sentence completion tests for half of each of the improved and unimproved groups of patients were then evaluated by two psychologists and rated in terms of 23 intellectual and personality variables. On seven of the variables, as well as IQ, the two groups were significantly differentiated. The two raters were then informed of the variables that had differentiated the two groups of patients and were asked to predict improvement in the remaining 20 patients. Each was able to make at least 15 correct predictions. It was concluded that the successful patient has superior intelligence, has the ability to produce associations easily, is not rigid, has a wide range of interests, is sensitive to his environment, feels deeply, exhibits a high energy level, and is free from bodily concerns. The use of clinical evaluations and predictions in this study, however, clearly limited its applicability to other situations utilizing other clinicians and other patients.

In another study, Roberts (1954) compared 11 Rorschach indices alleged to have prognostic significance for treatment with rather careful ratings of pre- and posttreatment status by three judges. None of the measures were significantly related to the outcome criteria. In a similar study, 50 patients judged to be unimproved by their therapists were compared with 59 patients judged to be "slightly improved" or "improved" (Rogers & Hammond,

1953). Ninety-nine Rorschach signs and three types of clinical judgments were used but failed to differentiate significantly between the two groups.

The problems of subject variability and failure of replication were evident also in other studies reported at this time. Whereas Harris and Christiansen (1946) found positive results with the Rorschach Prognostic Index and no relationship between improvement and intelligence test scores, Barron (1953a) secured just the opposite results with these measures. The subjects in the latter study were much higher in IQ than were the subjects in the other study. Also, most of the patients evaluated by Harris and Christiansen were hospitalized during therapy; those in Barron's study were outpatients.

Degree of Disturbance and Related Variables
Probably the most frequent client variable evaluated in relation to outcome has been some variant of degree of personality disturbance, integration, or psychopathology. Most of the studies to be reviewed in this section will make some reference to such variables.

A five-year follow-up study by Stone, Frank, Nash, and Imber (1961) utilized a self-report scale tapping five areas of symptomatology as a measure of initial disturbance and reported a significant association between greater initial disturbance and more positive outcome. Truax, Tunnell, Fine, and Wargo (1966) secured somewhat comparable results for group psychotherapy clients on four scales of the MMPI. However, Barron (1953a) found that the least "sick" patients at the beginning of therapy were most likely to get well. Somewhat similar results were secured by Kirtner and Cartwright (1958), who used clients' initial Thematic Apperception Test (TAT) protocols and an interview as a measure of initial disturbance. However, the two successful groups of clients were composed of only four clients each.

The report of the Wisconsin Project on a hospitalized group of psychotic patients also indicated a negative relationship between degree of disturbance and outcome in psychotherapy—high mental health ratings and a generally low level of manifest psychotic disturbance were positively related to outcome, as well as to ratings of therapist empathy (Rogers, Gendlin, Kiesler, & Truax, 1967). It should be noted, however, that such chronic schizophrenic patients differ quite noticeably from most outpatient samples; consequently, the degree of disturbance is also different since it includes many types of thought disorders, rather than merely increased degree of personal distress.

In contrast to these studies, the one by Katz et al. (1958) with 232 outpatients in VA clinics found no relationship between degree of disturbance and outcome. In this instance, degree of disturbance was based on four categories of diagnosis: psychoneurosis, psychosomatic disorders, character disorder, and psychosis. *Both* diagnoses and ratings of improvement were provided by the therapists. Another study of 83 patients in a VA clinic using the MMPI, however, found significant differences on a majority of the clinical scales, indicating "that those persons who are least equipped to meet life challenges are the ones who stand to gain least from psychotherapy" (Sullivan et al., 1958, p.7). Despite this conclusion, essentially null results were reported in three other, earlier studies (Cartwright & Roth, 1957; Muench, 1965; Seeman, 1954).

In a more recent study, the improved and unimproved patients were similar in initial ratings of "ego-weakness," but differed on manifest distress level as rated by nurses on the ward (Jacobs, Muller, Anderson, & Skinner, 1972). However, ratings of manifest distress level by therapists, other staff members, and patients were unrelated to outcome. Moreover, the results were confounded by the fact that the patients also received milieu therapy and medication, as well as psychotherapy.

Sloane et al. (1975) found that the less disturbed patients, as measured by the MMPI, secured more positive outcome with analytically oriented psychotherapy. On the other hand, "behavior therapy was equally successful whether the patient had a high or low degree of pathology" (p. 176). In this instance, at least, the type of therapy appeared to be an important variable. They also reported that those patients in both groups who spoke in longer utterances showed more improvement than those who spoke in shorter units.

The 18-year research project conducted at the Menninger Foundation evaluated 21 patients who had undergone psychoanalysis and 21 who received psychoanalytic psychotherapy (Kernberg et al., 1972). In this study, clinical appraisals of ego strength were found to correlate positively with a measure of global improvement ($r = .35$). However, these investigators also emphasized that the appraisals of ego strength were relative to the population studied—basically a group of patients falling within the broad categories of neurosis and "borderline" conditions.

In another study of psychoanalytically oriented therapy (Siegel et al., 1977), no differences were obtained when patients were dichotomized into two broad groupings of diagnostic categories. The latter consisted of a "severe" group made up of borderline, narcissistic characters and a few schizophrenics, and a group made up of the "milder neurotic entities" (p. 327). When the patients are viewed in terms of the focus of symptomatology or distress, however, there appeared to be a differential response to psychotherapy. Patients with a "neurotic focus" tended to secure good outcomes, whereas those whose complaints focused on a "behavioral" area, ordinarily under voluntary control, did not.

In a study of time-limited counseling, degree of client-disturbance as rated by therapists after the initial session did not correlate with therapists' ratings of outcome after treatment or with clients' ratings of outcome one month or 18 months after treatment (Gelso, Mills, & Spiegel, 1983). Although adequacy of client functioning is mentioned as one of the relatively better predictors of outcome in the Penn psychotherapy project, the basis for this is not clear, and the overall correlations reported are low (Luborsky et al., 1979).

Recently also, Steinmetz et al. (1983) reported the results of a study of 75 depressed clients who received a group psychoeducational treatment for unipolar depression. In this instance, a clear relationship was evident between degree of depression at the start of therapy and at termination. "Participants at all levels of depression severity improved markedly, but those who were initially more depressed tended to maintain their relative ranking in posttreatment" (p. 331). The pretreatment scores of the Beck Depression Inventory accounted for 27 percent of the variance in posttreatment scores and was clearly the best predictor of outcome. Although the study has not been replicated, somewhat comparable findings were reported in another study of depressed outpatients (Rounsaville, Weissman, & Prusoff, 1981).

Undoubtedly, variations in samples, procedures, and criteria of disturbance and outcome contribute to the variation in the results obtained in the different studies. Before discussing these methodological problems, however, let us continue our discussion of personality and test variables in relation to outcome.

Because *ego strength* has been mentioned frequently as a possible correlate of positive outcome in psychotherapy, various attempts have been made to measure this personality variable. Two in particular have received a moderate amount of research attention. One of these, the ES Scale, was devised by Barron and consisted of selected items from the MMPI. Barron (1953b) reported a positive relationship between the scale and outcome. However, this was followed by a number of nonpositive results (Fiske et al., 1964; Gallagher, 1954; Getter & Sundland, 1962; Gottschalk, Fox, & Bates, 1973; Newmark, Finkelstein, & Frerking, 1974; Sullivan et al., 1958; Taulbee, 1958).

More positive results have been reported with the use of another index of ego strength derived from six components of the Rorschach Test, the Rorschach Prognostic Rating Scale (RPRS) (Klopfer, Kirkner, Wisham, & Baker, 1951). Cartwright (1958) reported positive results with the RPRS and psychotherapy outcome in a study of 13 clients, and Johnson (1953) also reported similar results with 21 retardates in play therapy. Others reporting positive findings are Bloom (1956), Endicott and Endicott (1964), Kirkner, Wisham, and Giedt (1953), Mindess (1953), Newmark et al. (1974), and Sheehan, Frederick, Rosevear, and Spiegelman (1954). Studies that have secured negative findings, however, have been reported by Filmer-Bennett (1955), Fiske et al. (1964), and Lessing (1960). The Penn psychotherapy project, which used this measure among others, also failed to secure any positive findings between ego strength and outcome (Luborsky et al., 1980).

Although positive findings have been reported more frequently than negative findings, it is difficult to draw definite conclusions. The mean scores for various groups of subjects (judged to be improved or unimproved) show considerable variability, there is a noticeable overlap in scores between improved and unimproved clients, and the predictive norms provided by Klopfer et al. (1951) do not always appear applicable. The criteria for judging improvement also vary considerably among the studies just cited and, consequently, there is a question of what is actually being predicted (Garfield, 1978).

Finally, as Frank (1967) has emphasized, the use

of the RPRS in predicting outcome leads to a correct prediction in about two-thirds of the cases, which, on the basis of some reported success rates in psychotherapy, might be predicted without utilizing any measures. Here, we have the old problem of base rates, which is frequently overlooked in this area of research. An effective predictor, however, should exceed the base rates. The overall impression, therefore, is that whereas those with adequate ego strength or personality integration, as measured by the RPRS, appear to do better in psychotherapy than those with poor ego strength, prediction on this basis may not exceed the base rates for this problem. Nevertheless, if the RPRS can be shown to predict consistently at this level of accuracy, it might have value in studying the unsuccessfully predicted cases.

Other Personality Attributes

Other studies have also made reference to related or similar personality attributes in relation to psychotherapy outcome. Frank (1974b), in a review of 25 years of research, concluded "that the most important determinants of long-term improvement lie in the patient" (p. 339). He found that symptoms of anxiety and depression improved the most, whereas poorer results were secured with somatic complaints. The presence of anxiety at the initiation of therapy has also been noted as a positive prognostic sign in other studies (Kernberg et al., 1972; Luborsky et al., 1975), although inconclusive studies have also been reported. The type and severity of anxiety must also be considered, as well as the stimuli that influence it. As Frank (1974b) emphasized, "long-term prognosis largely depends on the strength of the person's coping capacities and the modifiability of the stress which leads him to seek help . . ." (p. 339). In other words, as indicated in another study also, patients who manifest anxiety in relation to their current situation or stress appear to secure better outcome (Smith, Sjöholm, & Niélzén, 1975).

Studies of behavior therapy also have dealt with correlates of behavior change or outcome. In one study of participant modeling with snake phobics, "Neither initial attitudes toward snakes, severity of phobic behavior, performance aroused fears, nor fear proness correlated with degree of behavior change" (Bandura, Jeffrey, & Wright, 1974, p. 62). However, some measures of fear reduction taken after the initiation of therapy were predictive of

subsequent behavioral change. The greater the fear decrements on the initially failed task and the less fear aroused by this task, the greater the degree of improvement.

In another study of 36 phobic patients, attempts were made to evaluate several predictor variables in relation to outcome with desensitization, flooding, and a control treatment (Mathews, Johnston, Shaw, & Gelder, 1974). Only two measures were significantly related to outcome at both termination and follow-up, and these both pertained to extroversion and traits related to it. However, severity of symptoms, high anxiety and neuroticism, low expectancy, and low rated motivation for treatment were not related to outcome. In general, "There was no evidence that by using the measures examined, patients could be individually allocated in advance to the treatment most likely to help them" (Mathews et al., 1974, p. 264). As in the previous study (Bandura et al., 1974), however, there was a greater reduction in measures of rated anxiety early in therapy by those who subsequently improved. It may be possible to predict subsequent outcome more accurately at a certain stage in therapy than at the very beginning, a hypothesis that receives some support from some studies of psychotherapy process to which we shall refer later.

Somewhat comparable results have also been reported by the preceding investigators in their research on agoraphobia and in their appraisal of research on this disorder (Mathews, Gelder, & Johnston, 1981). "Nearly all published reports of behavioral treatment have included a section on prognostic factors that describes efforts to improve patient selection. The results have been almost uniformly disappointing" (Mathews et al., 1981, p. 143). Emmelkamp and Kuipers (1979) in a four-year follow-up study of agoraphobic clients also did not secure positive findings between selected client variables and outcome. "No clear relationship was found between external control, social anxiety, depression and duration of the complaint at the beginning of treatment on the one hand and the results at follow-up on the other" (Emmelkamp & Kuipers, 1979, p. 352).

An essentially similar conclusion was reached by Rachman and Hodgson (1980) in their work on obsessions and compulsions. However, a recent report of research on behavioral treatments of obsessive-compulsives contains some positive findings

(Foa, et al., 1983). Low initial anxiety was positively related to successful outcome, whereas high levels of depression were correlated with failure. Earlier age of onset of symptoms was also related to successful outcome at follow-up.

One variable that was discussed earlier in relation to continuation and that has been emphasized by dynamically oriented therapists with regard to outcome is motivation. Although it seems quite reasonable to assume that a client without adequate motivation will not continue or do well in therapy, the empirical evidence to support this view is not very convincing. In some of the work in this area the selection of subjects is not random, motivation is not appraised in the same way in different studies, and ratings are not infrequently made by the investigators or therapists (Butcher & Koss, 1978; Keithly, Samples, & Strupp, 1980; Malan, 1963; Sifneos, 1972). One recent study conducted with a sample of 18 clients attempted to overcome these difficulties (Keithly, et al., 1980). Nevertheless, some problems remained. Although the motivation scale used was based on one devised by Sifneos (1972), the investigators had to modify the latter scale for their own situation. Furthermore, their new nine-point scale included two items on expectations and an item on "level of felt distress" among others that are not always viewed as aspects of motivation per se. In any event, the results of multiple regression analyses showed significant relationships between ratings of motivation and therapists' and clinicians' ratings of outcome (p < .05), but not with two sets of patients' rating of change. The findings thus are not completely interpretable in terms of the construct of motivation, in terms of the differences among outcome criteria, and with respect to clinical significance.

Another variable that has received some attention is that of *intelligence*. Although probably most therapists would prefer reasonably intelligent clients who also possess other virtues (Schofield, 1964), no clear-cut minimum requirement has been established for successful performance in psychotherapy. However, certain types of therapy may require more highly intelligent or selected clients than others. In psychoanalysis, where candidates apparently are rigorously screened, the majority are college graduates or better and presumably of above average or superior intelligence (Hamburg et al., 1967; Reder & Tyson, 1980; Siegel, 1962). At the other end of

the pole, behavior therapists have apparently not been concerned with this matter. It is interesting, too, that two previous reviews of research on this topic appear to reach somewhat different conclusions.

In the review by Luborsky et al. (1971), 10 of 13 studies are listed as showing a positive relationship between intelligence and outcome in psychotherapy. Although some studies merely indicate that a significant difference was obtained between improved and unimproved subjects, some list correlations ranging from .24 to .46. In the study reporting the correlation of .46 the total group of patients had a relatively high mean IQ (117), with the unimproved group alone having a mean IQ of 112 (Barron, 1953a). If one were to attempt to apply these findings, he might presumably reject over 75 percent of the population as psychotherapy candidates!

Meltzoff and Kornreich (1970), in their review, come up with a somewhat different tally. They mention seven studies as showing a positive relationship between IQ and outcome, and eight studies as indicating no relationship. One of the studies listed as positive by Luborsky et al. (1971) is listed otherwise by them since two different criteria are referred to by the different authors. Since Meltzoff and Kornreich's tally differs from that of Luborsky et al., the former reach a different conclusion and state that high intelligence is not a necessary condition for successful psychotherapy, even though it may be more important in some therapies than others.

What then might we conclude? If psychotherapy is a learning process or involves learning, as many believe, then some minimum amount of intelligence would seem to be required. As yet no precise estimate of this has been clearly agreed upon. Most psychotherapists might also agree that other aspects of the individual besides sheer intellect are also of importance, and perhaps of greater significance. If we were to take a correlation of around .30 as indicating the possible relationship of intelligence to outcome, intelligence would still account for less than 10 percent of the variance. For the time being, we should maintain a flexible posture on this matter.

Methodological Issues
Besides the studies mentioned, there are others that have reported both positive and negative findings with various scores or determinants from a variety of

evaluative techniques. There is little point in reviewing these studies. To the extent that studies have used idiosyncratic procedures, small subject samples, and questionable outcome criteria and have not been replicated, they can be passed over. It is preferable, instead, to discuss and evaluate some of the methodological problems in this area of research. This is important in appraising the generalizations and tentative conclusions drawn from previous reviews of research concerning personality variables of the client, particularly degree of disturbance, in relation to outcome in psychotherapy.

Some of the measurement problems may be illustrated by reference to a specific study (Prager & Garfield, 1972). A number of indices of client disturbance were used, as well as six measures of outcome. In general, ratings of disturbance made at the beginning of therapy by clients, therapists, and supervisors were unrelated to the six measures of outcome used. Initial disturbance as measured by the mean scale elevation of the MMPI, elevation of the neurotic triad of the MMPI, and a disturbance scale completed by the client, however, were significantly and negatively correlated with various ratings of outcome provided by clients, therapists, and supervisors at the completion of therapy. At the same time, these latter measures of initial disturbance were not significantly related to three outcome measures based on differences in scores obtained at the beginning and termination of therapy. Thus, the finding that degree of initial or felt disturbance was negatively related to outcome was true *only* for certain indices of disturbance *and* certain criteria of outcome.

Two other observations made by Prager and Garfield (1972) are worth noting here. First, those studies that found that patients with higher levels of disturbance secured more positive results than those with less disturbance generally used the same instrument to measure both initial level of disturbance and outcome. Studies that reported a negative relationship between initial level of disturbance and outcome used an independent outcome measure such as therapists' or judges' ratings. The problem of regression toward the mean could be a factor in the findings reported in the first set of studies. The second point is that initial level of disturbance is found to be inversely related to outcome primarily when global ratings of improvement, made at the termination of therapy, are used as the criteria of outcome. In these instances, the judgment of change involves the rater's *perception of change,* whereas actual difference scores require information relevant to the symptoms and feelings of the client at a particular time. It has also been reported that judgments of outcome, particularly by therapists, tend to be more favorable than other types of measures or ratings (Garfield et al., 1971; Horenstein et al., 1973).

The points illustrated above undoubtedly contribute to the discrepant findings discussed earlier concerning the relationship of the degree of adjustment or level of disturbance to outcome in psychotherapy. How outcome is evaluated is one important consideration. As Mintz (1972) has pointed out, global ratings of improvement made at the *end* of treatment tend to be very much influenced by the actual condition of the client at that time, irrespective of how the individual was at the beginning of therapy. Consequently, the person who functions at a relatively high level at the start and shows only slight change is still rated as greatly improved as compared with someone who begins at a much lower level and, while progressing more, does not function terminally at the high level of the other client. It may well be that part of this apparent confusion is due to *what* is being evaluated as well as to *how* it is being evaluated. Clients who begin therapy at a *high level of functioning* terminate therapy at higher levels than those who begin at relatively low levels. However, those patients with the *greatest symptom distress* will tend to show the greatest reduction in symptom distress.[1]

Thus, although amount of positive change resulting from therapy may appear to be a straightforward matter, it is actually more complicated. Another aspect relevant to the present discussion is the fact that in psychotherapy there has been also an implicit goal of adequate functioning at the end of therapy. Consequently, an individual who gains more than another, but whose final level of adjustment is below that of the other on some norm, may be considered less successful. For example, an individual whose IQ increased from 40 to 65 would show a greater gain than one who progressed from 110 to 120, but he would still be regarded as mentally

[1] I am indebted to Arthur Auerbach of the Department of Psychiatry of the University of Pennsylvania for his help in clarifying this issue.

retarded. If the goal were "normal" intelligence, his progress would be regarded as limited.

Another important problem concerns how personality functioning or psychopathology is defined or appraised. Severity of disturbance, for example, can be viewed in terms of clinical diagnosis ("psychosis" versus "neurosis"), intensity of discomfort or symptoms, duration of disturbance or chronicity, adjustment to current life situation, degree of impairment socially or occupationally, or in terms of scores on tests or rating scales. If a hypothetical personality construct such as ego strength, presumably reflecting personality integration and adjustment, is assessed by different techniques that show little relationship to each other, conflicting or confusing results are very likely to occur, as we have noted earlier.

Another matter that is relevant here concerns the actual predictive value of some of the positive findings reported. Actually, most of the results secured do not even obtain statistical significance. In most instances where statistically significant results are secured, the correlations tend to be low and to account for a limited portion of the variance. In one of the earlier and comprehensive attempts to evaluate whether psychotherapeutic changes were predictable, the investigators reported that their results were "distinctly unpromising" (Fiske et al., 1964). The more recent report of the findings of the Penn psychotherapy project also indicated very limited ability to predict the outcomes of psychotherapy. "The success of the predictive measures was generally insignificant, and the best of them were in the .2 to .3 range, meaning that only 5% to 10% of the outcome variance was predicted" (Luborsky, Mintz, & Christoph, 1979, p. 471).

Luborsky et al. (1971), in an earlier review, concluded that the "initially sicker patients do not improve as much with psychotherapy as the initially healthier do" (p. 149). As already indicated, one must be cautious in interpreting such generalizations. Even in this review, only 56 percent of the separate findings listed by Luborsky et al. (1975) showed a positive relationship between adequacy of adjustment and outcome in therapy. In addition, several of the methodological problems discussed previously were evident in the research evaluated by these reviewers (Garfield, 1978).

It would appear then that although some investigators have reported positive findings, most of the relationships secured have been of limited strength and have varied from one investigation to another depending on methods of appraisal, criteria, subject samples, and the like. It may well be that client variables centering on adjustment and personality may not be highly predictive of outcome despite views to the contrary. It may be that part of the difficulty is related to the fact that most of the older studies used groups of subjects with a variety of diagnoses. However, as a result of the emphasis by behavior therapists on devising treatments for specific behavioral disorders, and as a result of the new *DSM-III* classification of mental disorders, there is evident today a trend for investigators to seek prognostic variables for patients with particular disorders. This emphasis on specific treatments for specific disorders clearly has had an impact on both practice and research. It may be that more specific research of this type will provide us with better correlates and predictors of outcome in psychotherapy. For the present, however, we will have to withhold judgment.

Client Expectations and Other Variables in Relation to Outcome in Psychotherapy

Another area of investigation that has received a fair amount of interest concerns the expectancies that the client has concerning psychotherapy. In previous years, this referred mainly to the expectations that the client had prior to initiating psychotherapy. More recently, there have also been attempts to manipulate experimentally certain specified expectations.

Frank and his colleagues were among the earliest to call attention to client expectancies and their relation to symptom change (Frank, 1959; Frank, Gliedman, Imber, Stone, & Nash, 1959; Rosenthal & Frank, 1956). Among other things, they asserted that the beliefs or expectations about therapy that the patient brings to therapy may influence the results of therapy, and that the greater the distress or need for relief, the greater the expectancy or likelihood of such relief. This did receive some support from other investigators. In one study, a group of control patients showed a significant correlation between their expected and perceived improvement (Goldstein, 1960), and other studies also secured a positive relationship between expectations of improvement in patients and their judged improvement (Lennard & Bernstein, 1960; Lipkin, 1954).

Goldstein and Shipman (1961) reported a positive relationship between expectancy and perceived symptom reduction, and also between expectancy and symptom intensity after the initial psychotherapeutic interview. In this study, however, the relationship between expectancy and symptom reduction was a curvilinear one—that is, those patients with very high or very low expectations for improvement showed the smallest symptom reduction. In another study (Friedman, 1963), a direct relationship between expectancy and symptom reduction was found in 43 patients after an initial evaluation interview. The symptoms associated with anxiety and depression were the ones most affected. Goldstein (1962) also published a comprehensive account of both therapist and patient expectations.

Since these earlier writings, there has been a continuing output of studies. Because of space limitations and because there are several critical reviews available (Lick & Bootzin, 1975; Morgan, 1973; Wilkins, 1971, 1973, 1979), our discussion of the available studies will be brief.

Tollinton (1973), utilizing a variety of measures, found that initial expectations were significantly related to outcome in the early stages of treatment, but were "dissipated over time by the effects of neuroticism" (p. 256). In another study, Uhlenhuth and Duncan (1968) used symptom checklists, the MMPI, and subjects' ratings and reported that more favorable expectations were associated with improvement. Piper and Wogan (1970), however, did not find a relationship between prognostic expectations and reported improvement. Negative results were also secured in another study where attempts were made to induce a positive expectancy for improvement within a treatment period of four weeks (Imber et al., 1970).

Although many of the studies have indicated a positive association between client expectations and outcome, these investigations also have been criticized (Perotti & Hopewell, 1980; Wilkins, 1973). Among the deficiencies noted have been the fact that expectancies have been inferred rather than actually measured or appraised, and that most studies have relied on self-reports for measures of expectancies *and* of outcome. The matter of how the effects of expectancies are appraised appears to be a problem of some importance. Wilson and Thomas (1973), for example, secured significant correlations between high expectancy ratings and self-report measures of

outcome, but found no relationship between expectancy ratings and a behavioral measure of outcome.

Perhaps because of the former criticism, several studies have attempted to manipulate and measure the expectations of the client. In contrast to the studies mentioned previously, which have been characterized as studies of "expectancy traits," the more recent investigations have focused on experimentally created "expectancy states" and have tended largely to be studies of behaviorally oriented therapy.

In his review of expectancy states and their effect on outcome, Wilkins (1973) lists six studies that showed positive results, eight that did not show such effects, and one that showed both effects. Such conflicting findings would suggest that no reliable conclusions can be drawn. A number of conceptual and methodological issues are discussed by Wilkins (1973), including how the expectancy instructions are given, whether or not the therapists were blind to the experimental conditions, confounding of measures of outcome with those of expectancy, and confounding of expectancy and feedback effects. Accordingly, he concluded that there was insufficient evidence to support the construct of expectancy of therapeutic gain.

Another review of expectancy factors in the treatment of fears by Lick and Bootzin (1975) came to a somewhat different conclusion and highlighted some additional problems. One of the points made by Lick and Bootzin (1975) was that most of the subjects used in the studies of systematic desensitization (SD) they reviewed were students who manifested relatively mild fears of small animals and who became subjects in order to meet course requirements. They also emphasized the importance of the way in which expectancies are created and assessed, as well as the importance of developing creditable placebo conditions for subjects in such studies. In addition, they stated that although methodological problems in previous research "preclude firm empirical conclusions about the importance of therapeutic instruction in SD . . . , the available data do suggest that these influences are sizable" (Lick & Bootzin, 1975, p. 925).

Reviewing many of these same studies, Perotti and Hopewell (1980) also concluded that expectancy effects are important in SD, but they differentiated two kinds of expectancies. Initial expectancy, which the client has at the beginning of therapy with regard to the probable success of treatment and which has been the focus in most studies, they believe has little effect. The second type, however, which deals with beliefs the subject has during the treatment process that he is improving and is increasingly able to handle fear-provoking stimuli, is considered to be of some importance. A somewhat similar point is made by Lick and Bootzin (1975), who hypothesize that expectancy manipulation may motivate subjects to more readily test reality conditions that could increase fear extinction and provide further reinforcement for improved behavior. This appears to be a reasonable hypothesis and at least is congruent with studies that indicate better predictions of outcome after a few early therapy sessions than at pretreatment assessment (Bandura et al., 1974; Mathews et al., 1974).

The possible importance of client expectancies for research on evaluating the effectiveness of SD and psychotherapy generally was stressed in an article by Kazdin and Wilcoxin (1976). Particular emphasis was placed on the importance of creating control conditions that are as potent in creating positive client expectancies for improvement as the experimental therapy being evaluated. Thus, expectations for therapeutic success are viewed as of some significance by these authors.

Expectancy was reported to be a significant predictor of outcome in a study of 36 agoraphobics (Mathews et al., 1976). In this study expectancy was appraised by having the patients estimate prior to treatment how likely they believed they would be to achieve each of 15 phobic situations in the behavioral hierarchy. In this instance, the patients who were most confident about possible improvement were the most likely to improve. However, a simpler rating of expectations did not predict outcome. Thus, the method of securing expectations is of potential importance, and an overly gross measure may not be effective.

It appears that the degree of importance client expectations have as predictors of outcome in psychotherapy is still to be determined. In addition to the more recent distinction between expectancy traits and states, there is also the issue of what different individuals mean when they employ the general term expectancy. In some instances, it has been used to designate the expectation a client has with regard to positive outcome or the therapeutic effectiveness of a particular therapist. In other instances, some of us have discussed the expectations clients have about the procedures in psychotherapy, the role of the therapists, the length of therapy, and the like (Bent, Putnam, Kiesler, & Nowicki, 1975; Garfield & Wolpin, 1963). It would appear that future research will have to be more precise in specifying the types of expectancies under investigation, as well as considering the possible interaction of different kinds of expectancies and the interaction of expectancies with other variables. One study, for example, besides validating an expectancy manipulation on one group of subjects and then testing its effectiveness for behavioral effects with another group, also compared the effects of initial expectations concerning the helpfulness of psychotherapy, as well as those of an experimental manipulation (Lott & Murray, 1975). The results showed a positive effect for the expectancy manipulation but not for the initial expectancy. Although the measure of initial expectancy used may leave something to be desired, this type of design appears to offer more promise than more simplistic ones.

Client–Therapy Interaction

Another area of recent research has been concerned with the frame of reference of the client in relation to type of therapy and outcome. In one study, two groups of clients were exposed to different forms of therapy designated as "relatively directive" and "relatively nondirective" (Abramowitz, Abramowitz, Roback, & Jackson, 1974). The locus of control was measured by nine items from the Rotter I-E Scale (1966) and several scales were utilized to appraise outcome. Although the number of cases was small, the findings appeared to indicate that "externals" did better in the directive therapy, while "internals" did better with the nondirective therapy. In another investigation, patients were rated on the basis of their symptoms or complaints as predominantly "externalizers" or "internalizers" (Stein & Beall, 1971). In this study female externalizers showed significant negative association with various therapist ratings of change, but this was not true for male externalizers.

In a study of the differential effectiveness of muscular and cognitive relaxation as a function of locus of control, Ollendick and Murphy (1977) reported that internally controlled subjects showed a greater decrement in heart rate and subjective distress with cognitive relaxation. Externally controlled subjects, on the other hand, secured better results with muscular relaxation. In the Johns Hopkins research program, internally controlled patients secured better results than externally controlled patients when they were led to believe that their improvement was due to their own efforts and not to a placebo (Liberman, 1978). The opposite results were secured when therapeutic progress was believed to be due to a placebo. On the other hand, an examination of studies that have claimed that internals are more successful in nondirective therapy and externals in directive therapy noted a number of deficiencies in these studies (Messer & Meinster, 1980). These included deficiencies in design, statistical analysis, and outcome measures.

A somewhat related study on choice of therapy was reported. In this investigation 32 subjects with a fear of snakes viewed a videotape of four therapists who described and illustrated their particular methods of treatment (Devine & Fernald, 1973). The four treatments were SD, an encounter approach, rational-emotive therapy, and a combination of modeling and behavioral rehearsal. The subjects then rated their preferences for the various therapies and were assigned to a preferred, nonpreferred, or random therapy. Although there was no significant difference in outcome between therapies, the difference between the preference conditions was significant. Subjects receiving a preferred treatment exhibited less fear of the snakes than those receiving a nonpreferred or random therapy.

Patient Attractiveness and Outcome

There are also other client characteristics that have been studied in relation to outcome in psychotherapy. Isaacs and Haggard (1966) found that high relatability, as appraised by the TAT, was related to improvement in psychotherapy. Patient attractiveness was also found to be related to outcome in a positive manner by another group of investigators (Nash et al., 1965), although this relationship was not evident in a five-year follow-up study (Liberman, et al., 1972).

Somewhat related to the preceding papers have been several studies that have attempted to appraise the importance of patient likability for therapy process and outcome. Stoler (1963) reported that successful clients received significantly higher likability ratings based on taped therapy segments than did the less successful clients and the level

of likability remained fairly constant from early to late interviews. A subsequent study carried out with schizophrenic patients instead of neurotics secured somewhat different findings (Tomlinson & Stoler, 1967). The less successful patients were better liked than the more successful ones. Therapists' ratings of patient attractiveness were not related to two general measures of outcome in another study (Luborsky et al., 1980).

In a study of psychiatric residents, Ehrlich and Bauer (1967) found that inexperienced therapists liked their patients less than did the relatively more experienced therapists; patients who were rated either extremely anxious or nonanxious were less well liked by their therapists; and patient prognosis was positively related to patient likability. Furthermore, patients who received low ratings in terms of likability were three times more likely to be placed on multiple drug regimes than were those who received high ratings. In addition, the therapists' ratings of change were positively correlated with such ratings. A positive correlation between the therapist's liking of the client and prognostic ratings of the client also has been reported (Garfield & Affleck, 1961), but more data are needed concerning the relationship of such ratings and objective criteria of outcome.

There appears to be some indication that the likability of the client is related to outcome. Because of the variation in patients, therapists, and outcome criteria, however, the available findings are far from clear. There is an obvious problem of potential contamination when therapists provide the ratings of outcome as well as of likability.

Client—Therapist Similarity

The matter of client-therapist similarity or complementarity has received some research attention, although with rather conflicting results. Carson and Heine (1962) used the MMPI to compare therapists and clients and reported that a curvilinear relationship existed between therapist-client similarity and rated improvement. Lichtenstein (1966) and Carson and Llewellyn (1966), however, failed to replicate these findings. Lesser (1961), utilizing a Q-sort, found that similarity of self-concept between counselor and client was negatively related to therapeutic progress, whereas Levinson and Kitchener (1966), utilizing a different Q-sort, secured more positive findings. Using the FIRO-B Scale, Sapolsky (1965) also reported a positive correlation between patient and doctor compatibility and outcome. On the other hand, Mendelsohn and Geller (1965), who used still another measure of compatibility, the Myers-Briggs Type Indicator, obtained a curvilinear relationship with outcome measures. In addition, some partial support for the importance of client-therapist complementarity has been offered by Swenson (1967) for one personality dimension (dominance-submission), but not for another (love-hate).

More recently, Beutler, Jobe, and Elkins (1974) have reported that initial patient-therapist similarity and acceptability of attitudes were related more to patients' ratings of improvement than was attitude dissimilarity. On the other hand, Melnick (1972) found that greater patient indentification with the therapist during therapy was moderately related to successful outcome. In a study of group therapy patients, McLachlan (1972) found that patients and therapists matched for conceptual level improved significantly on patients' ratings of improvement, but not on staff ratings of improvement. The conceptual levels of patients and therapists separately were not related to outcome. Berzins (1977) also published a comprehensive and critical review of the area of therapist-patient matching in psychotherapy. As he pointed out, although the idea of matching patients and therapists for the best therapeutic outcome is responded to favorably by clinicians and researchers alike, "there is at present no organized body of knowledge that could serve as an effective guide for implementing matching strategies . . ." (p. 222). (See also Chapter 7.)

In-therapy Process Variables and Outcome

More recently, process aspects of psychotherapy have been investigated by dynamically oriented investigators, with particular attention devoted to what has been referred to as the helping or therapeutic alliance. Essentially, this refers to the relationship established in therapy between therapist and client. This necessarily involves the therapist as well as the client and cannot be viewed solely from the standpoint of client variables. Certain client features have been emphasized in these studies, however, and we shall attempt to evaluate them here.

In a study of process variables as potential predictors of outcome in psychotherapy, Gomes-Schwartz (1978) secured the most consistent results between a variable labeled "Patient Involvement" and outcome. This variable represented both patient partic-

ipation in therapy and manifestations of patient hostility and was measured by scales derived from the Vanderbilt Psychotherapy Process Scale. The results of this investigation, based on data from the Vanderbilt research project, were particularly interesting in that psychoanalytically oriented therapists, experiential therapists, and nontherapeutically trained college professors were evaluated and compared. All three groups of "therapists" secured comparable outcomes, and for all three, patient involvement appeared as the best predictor of outcome.

Another process study focused on negative factors in psychotherapy and used the Vanderbilt Negative Indicators Scale (VNIS) (Sachs, 1983). A subscale of four items, the "Patient Qualities" subscale, did show a statistically significant correlation with outcome when it was based on the third interview, but not on the first or second interview. Patient qualities on this scale referred to such characteristics as negative attitudes and passivity. In general, the variables tapped by the VNIS showed some relationship to outcome in psychodynamic therapy, but not to experiential therapy.

An additional study investigated pretherapy interpersonal relations, the patients' therapeutic alliance, and outcome (Moras & Strupp, 1982). Although there was a small significant correlation between pretherapy interpersonal relations and the therapeutic alliance, most correlations between interpersonal relations and outcome were low. Thus, they were not considered good predictors of outcome.

In yet another study reported on the Vanderbilt Psychotherapy Process Scale using some of the same subjects used in the previously mentioned studies, patient involvement was found to have the highest relationship to outcome of the variables studied (O'Malley, Suh, & Strupp, 1983). As noted in some of the other studies, however, this relationship was not evident in the first therapy session, but emerged clearly during the third session. This type of a trend, as mentioned earlier, was also noted in some behavioral studies, although with different variables, mainly measures of early progress.

Two additional studies using other measures of the helping alliance developed at the University of Pennsylvania can also be mentioned here. Because of the low predictive power found for most of the pretherapy variables appraised, Luborsky and his colleagues explored aspects of patient-therapist interaction and developed two methods for evaluating the helping alliance. One of these methods is a global rating method, whereas the other is based on counting specific instances in which the patient experiences the therapist as providing the help needed or "in which the patient experiences treatment as a process of working together with the therapist toward the goals of the treatment" (Luborsky, Crits-Christoph, Alexander, Margolis, & Cohen, 1983, p. 481). Both procedures when applied to the 10 most improved and 10 least improved cases in the Penn psychotherapy project showed modest to moderate correlations with some composite measures of outcome. When comparable comparisons are made with the pretreatment measures used in the Penn Study for these two extreme groups of clients, however, the two types of predictions are quite similar (Morgan, Luborsky, Crits-Christoph, Curtis, & Solomon, 1982). Analyses of extreme groups selected post hoc generally produce better results than analyses based on the total distribution of clients.

Although a number of psychodynamically oriented researchers tend to emphasize the importance of the therapeutic alliance as a significant factor in therapeutic outcome as well as a potential early predictor of outcome, the matter is by no means clear. For present purposes, I will limit my comments here to a discussion of the therapeutic alliance as a predictor of outcome in psychotherapy.

As indicated by Luborsky et al. (1983), the most frequently positive helping alliance signs "were those in which the patients felt helped" (p. 482). The one category of "feels changed" is rated positively almost twice as frequently as all other categories combined for the "more improved patients" and is rated over six times as frequently for these patients as all positive categories combined for the "less improved patients." Thus, it does appear as if the patients' subjective feeling of change may really be the essential variable. If one can view this as the patients' feeling better or seeing him- or herself as improving early in therapy, then this early state of improvement may be indicative of positive outcome at termination. This view would also be congruent with the findings mentioned earlier by Bandura et al. (1974) and Mathews et al. (1974). The construct of patient involvement might also be related to the patient's feeling of being changed positively. The latter can act as a reinforcement for greater involvement in therapy. The fact that all of these related

variables are not linked to outcome until the third interview also would appear congruent with this general hypothesis.

CONCLUSIONS

We have now come to the end of our survey of research pertaining to client variables in psychotherapy. As has been noted throughout the chapter, there are numerous conceptual and methodological problems that make research and the drawing of conclusions in this area rather difficult.

The problem of what kinds of personal attributes of clients are related to outcome in psychotherapy is clearly a complex one that does not appear readily answerable by the kinds of research data currently available. The great diversity of variables under study and the variation in methods of appraisal have seriously limited generalization of findings. This is particularly so with regard to personality variables and degree of disturbance. Among the problems here are the constructs used, measuring devices, type of therapy, sampling procedures, and outcome criteria. Each of these presents many difficulties for research, and little elaboration is required here. Although the personal qualities and expectations of the client appear to be of importance to most therapists, the more exact description of these qualities and their relationship to outcome in psychotherapy still await more definitive research. Although we can state with some degree of assurance that such patient variables as social class, age, and sex do not appear to be predictive of outcome, definitive statements based on personal qualities are more difficult to formulate.

Although the problems are complex, the present reviewer believes more comprehensive, carefully planned and conducted research efforts are required if truly adequate answers are to be provided. A host of idiosyncratic studies of poorly defined populations with vaguely described therapies and exceedingly variable outcome criteria will not produce findings of any substance.

If we are to improve the practical value of our research efforts, it will be necessary also to include at least some standard procedures that all researchers would adhere to if the results are to be in any way cumulative. For example, in terms of continuation, it would greatly facilitate comparisons if all studies reported the number of clients who actually begin therapy but voluntarily terminate before the sixth interview. Those who refuse therapy should be catalogued separately. The clients who continue beyond the fifth interview can be grouped into intervals of five interviews and the data readily presented (see Table 6.1). If some such procedure is not followed, it will be exceedingly difficult to organize and to interpret the findings from the individual studies (Reder & Tyson, 1980).

Similar procedures can be followed with measures of outcome. Although I believe that some measures of outcome should be clearly tailored to the problems of the individual client, it is important also to include some standard measures of initial client status and outcome. This latter point has been made by others (Fiske et al., 1970; Waskow & Parloff, 1975), but a suitable response is apparent only in the last few years, most notably in the area of depression where most studies are now using several of the same measures.

Despite the limitations in past research, there are indications today of a greater awareness of these limitations and of the importance of sound research. Although many clinical settings do not engage in research and have expressed little interest in research findings in the past, the situation has been changing. Research findings have had an increasing impact on psychotherapeutic activities. Among other things, increased attention has been paid to the problem of premature termination, and various attempts have been made to reduce or overcome this problem. The apparent lack of efficacy of traditional programs for the disadvantaged and other groups in our society has led to the creation of new programs for them (Goldstein, 1973; Lorion, 1978; Shore & Massimo, 1973). There have also been reports of modifications of traditional clinic procedures that have been at least partially influenced by research reports (Davids, 1975; Muench, 1965). In addition, the very basic issue of the efficacy of psychotherapy can be resolved only by recourse to adequate research data. The collaborative study of depression being carried out under the auspices of the National Institute of Mental Health is one significant indication of both an elegantly designed study and the need to answer questions by means of research (Waskow, 1984).

It does appear that future research on psychotherapy increasingly will use more clearly defined and more delineated samples of clients as well as treatments. In contrast to studies of "psychotherapy" with a mixed variety of patients, we can expect to see more frequent studies of specific forms of psychotherapy (e.g., exposure treatment) applied to rather specific categories of patients (e.g., agoraphobics, unipolar depressions).

Finally, I would like to add a few closing statements regarding the matter of client variables and outcome research. We have far too frequently been satisfied with results that were significant at the .05 level of confidence when the practical significance of the results have been very weak indeed. It is time to focus more attention on the actual amount of change secured by means of psychotherapy and to appraise it realistically (Garfield, 1981). If patients show a statistically significant change in ratings of outcome from a mean rating of 4 to a mean rating of 3.2 after therapy, or a significant change from a scaled score of 79 on an MMPI scale to a score of 70, what is the practical significance of such changes? Can the client actually function better in his life situation? In essence, how much change can we accomplish with individuals of varying levels and types of disturbance and what procedures work best with what types of clients? This is a basic issue to which we need to direct more attention if we are to appraise more adequately the effectiveness of psychotherapy.

REFERENCES

Abramowitz, C. V., Abramowitz, S. I., Roback, H. B., & Jackson, C. (1974). Differential effectiveness of directive and nondirective group therapies as a function of client internal-external control. *Journal of Consulting and Clinical Psychology, 42,* 849–853.

Acosta, F. X. (1980). Self-described reasons for premature termination of psychotherapy by Mexican-American, Black-American, and Anglo-American patients. *Psychological Reports, 47,* 435–443.

Acosta, F. X., & Sheehan, J. G. (1976). Preferences toward Mexican-American and Anglo-American psychotherapists. *Journal of Consulting and Clinical Psychology, 44,* 272–279.

Adler, M. H., Valenstein, A. F., & Michaels, J. J. (1949). A mental hygiene clinic. Its organization and operation. *Journal of Nervous & Mental Disease, 110,* 518–533.

Affleck, D. C., & Garfield, S. L. (1961). Predictive judgments of therapists and duration of stay in psychotherapy. *Journal of Clinical Psychology, 17,* 134–137.

Affleck, D. C., & Mednick, S. A. (1959). The use of the Rorschach Test in the prediction of the abrupt terminator in individual psychotherapy. *Journal of Consulting Psychology, 23,* 125–128.

Albronda, H. F., Dean, R. L., & Starkweather, J. A. (1964). Social class and psychotherapy. *Archives of General Psychiatry, 10,* 276–283.

Arentewicz, G., & Schmidt, G. (1980). *Sexuell gestorte Beziehungen.* Berlin: Springer Verlag.

Auld, F., Jr., & Eron, L. D. (1953). The use of Rorschach scores to predict whether patients will continue psychotherapy. *Journal of Consulting Psychology, 17,* 104–109.

Baekeland, F., & Lundwall, L. (1975). Dropping out of treatment: A critical review. *Psychological Bulletin, 82,* 738–783.

Bailey, M. A., Warshaw, L., & Eichler, R. M. (1959). A study of factors related to length of stay in psychotherapy. *Journal of Clinical Psychology. 15,* 442–444.

Bandura, A., Jeffrey, R. W., & Wright, C. L. (1974). Efficacy of participant modeling as a function of response induction aids. *Journal of Abnormal Psychology, 83,* 56–64.

Barron, F. (1953a). Some test correlates of response to psychotherapy. *Journal of Consulting Psychology, 17,* 235–241.

Barron, F. (1953b). An ego-strength scale which predicts response to psychotherapy. *Journal of Consulting Psychology, 17,* 327–333.

Basler, H. D., Brinkmeier, U., Buser, K., Hoehn, K. D., & Mölders-Kober, R. (1982). Psychological group treatment of essential hypertension in general practice. *British Journal of Clinical Psychology, 21,* 295–302.

Baum, O. E., & Felzer, S. B. (1964). Activity in initial interviews with lower class patients. *Archives of General Psychiatry, 10,* 345–353.

Bennett, M. J., & Wisneski, M. J. (1979). Continuous psychotherapy within an HMO. *American Journal of Psychiatry, 136,* 1283–1287.

Bent, R. J., Putnam, D. G., Kiesler, D. J., & Nowicki, S., Jr. (1975). Expectancies and characteristics of outpatient clients applying for services at a community mental health facility. *Journal of Consulting and Clinical Psychology, 43,* 280.

Bergin, A. E. (1971). The evaluation of therapeutic outcomes. In A. E. Bergin & S. L. Garfield (Eds.), *Handbook of psychotherapy and behavior change: An empirical analysis.* New York: Wiley.

Berrigan, L. P., & Garfield, S. L. (1981). Relationship of missed psychotherapy appointments to premature termination and social class. *The British Journal of Clinical Psychology, 20,* 239–242.

Berzins, J. I. (1977). Therapist–patient matching. In A. S. Gurman & A. M. Razin (Eds.), *Effective psychotherapy. A handbook of research* (pp. 222–251). Oxford: Pergamon.

Betz, N., & Shullman, S. (1979). Factors related to client return following intake. *Journal of Counseling Psychology, 26,* 542–545.

Beutler, L. E. (1973). The therapy dyad: Yet another look at diagnostic assessment. *Journal of Personality Assessment, 37,* 303–315.

Beutler, L. E., Jobe, A. M., & Elkins, D. (1974). Outcomes in group psychotherapy: Using persuasion theory to increase treatment efficiency. *Journal of Consulting and Clinical Psychology, 42,* 547–553.

Billings, A. G., & Moos, R. H. (1984). Treatment experi-

ences of adults with unipolar depression: The influence of patient and life context factors. *Journal of Consulting and Clinical Psychology, 52,* 119–131.

Blackburn, I. M., Bishop, S., Glenn, M. E., Whalley, L. J., & Christie, J. E. (1981). The efficacy of cognitive therapy in depression—A treatment trial using cognitive therapy and pharmacotherapy, each alone and in combination. *British Journal of Psychiatry, 139,* 181–189.

Blackman, N. (1948). Psychotherapy in a Veterans Administration mental hygiene clinic. *Psychiatric Quarterly, 22,* 89–102.

Bloom, B. L. (1956). Prognostic significance of the underproductive Rorschach. *Journal of Projective Techniques, 20,* 366–371.

Bootzin, R., & Lick, J. (1979). Expectancies in therapy research: Interpretive artifact or mediating mechanism? *Journal of Consulting and Clinical Psychology, 47,* 852–855.

Brandt, L. W. (1964). Rejection of psychotherapy? The discovery of unexpected numbers of psuedo-rejectors. *Archives of General Psychiatry, 10,* 310–313.

Brill, N. Q., & Storrow, H. A. (1960). Social class and psychiatric treatment. *Archives of General Psychiatry, 3,* 340–344.

Brown, J. S., & Kosterlitz, N. (1964). Selection and treatment of psychiatric outpatients. *Archives of General Psychiatry, 11,* 425–438.

Butcher, J. N., & Koss, M. P. (1978). Research on brief and crisis-oriented psychotherapies. In S. L. Garfield & A. E. Bergin (Eds.), *Handbook of psychotherapy and behavior change* (2nd ed., pp. 725–768). New York: Wiley.

Carpenter, P. J., & Range, L. M. (1982). Predicting psychotherapy duration from therapists' sex, professional affiliation, democratic values, and community mental health ideology. *Journal of Clinical Psychology, 38,* 90–91.

Carpenter, P. J., & Range, L. M. (1983). The effects of patients' fee payments source on the duration of outpatient psychotherapy. *Journal of Clinical Psychology, 39,* 304–306.

Carson, R. C., & Heine, R. W. (1962). Similarity and success in therapeutic dyads. *Journal of Consulting Psychology, 26,* 38–43.

Carson, R. C., & Llewellyn, C. E. (1966). Similarity in therapeutic dyads: A re-evaluation. *Journal of Consulting Psychology, 30,* 458.

Cartwright, D. S. (1955). Success in psychotherapy as a function of certain actuarial variables. *Journal of Consulting Psychology, 19,* 357–363.

Cartwright, D. S., Kirtner, W. L., & Fiske, D. W. (1963). *Journal of Abnormal and Social Psychology, 66,* 164–175.

Cartwright, D. S., & Roth, I. (1957). Success and satisfaction in psychotherapy. *Journal of Clinical Psychology, 13,* 20–26.

Cartwright, R. D. (1958). Predicting response to client-centered therapy with the Rorschach PR scales. *Journal of Counseling Psychology, 5,* 11–17.

Cimbolic, P. (1972). Counselor race and experience effects on black clients. *Journal of Consulting and Clinical Psychology, 39,* 328–332.

Cole, N. J., Branch, C. H., & Allison, R. B. (1962). Some

relationships between social class and the practice of dynamic psychotherapy. *American Journal of Psychiatry, 118*, 1004–1012.

Craig, T., & Huffine, C. (1976). Correlates of patient attendance in an inner-city mental health clinic. *The American Journal of Psychiatry, 133*, 61–64.

Davids, A. (1975). Therapeutic approaches to children in residential treatment. Changes from the mid-1950's to the mid-1970's. *American Psychologist, 30*, 809–814.

Devine, D. A., & Fernald, P. S. (1973). Outcome effects of receiving a preferred, randomly assigned or non-preferred therapy. *Journal of Consulting and Clinical Psychology, 41*, 104–107.

Dodd, J. A. (1970). A retrospective analysis of variables related to duration of treatment in a university psychiatric clinic. *Journal of Nervous and Mental Disease, 151*, 75–85.

Duehn, W. D., & Proctor, E. K. (1977). Initial clinical interaction and premature discontinuance in treatment. *American Journal of Orthopsychiatry, 47*, 284–290.

Ehrlich, H. J., & Bauer, M. L. (1967). Therapists' feelings toward patients and patient treatment and outcome. *Social Science and Medicine, 1*, 283–292.

Eiduson, B. T. (1968). The two classes of information in psychiatry. *Archives of General Psychiatry, 18*, 405–419.

Emmelkamp, P. M. G., & Kuipers, A. C. M. (1979). Agoraphobia: A follow-up study four years after treatment. *British Journal of Psychiatry, 134*, 352–355.

Endicott, N. A., & Endicott, J. (1964). Prediction of improvement in treated and untreated patients using the Rorschach Prognostic Rating Scale. *Journal of Consulting Psychology, 28*, 342–348.

Everaerd, W. T. A. M. (1983). Failures in treating sexual dysfunctions. In E. B. Foa & P. M. G. Emmelkamp (Eds.), *Failures in behavior therapy* (pp. 392–405). New York: Wiley.

Ewing, T. N. (1974). Racial similarity of client and counselor and client satisfaction with counseling. *Journal of Consulting Psychology, 21*, 446–469.

Fiester, A. R. (1977). Clients' perceptions of therapists with high attrition rates. *Journal of Consulting and Clinical Psychology, 45*, 954–955.

Fiester, A. R., & Rudestam, K. E. (1975). A multivariate analysis of the early dropout process. *Journal of Consulting and Clinical Psychology, 43*, 528–535.

Filmer-Bennett, G. (1955). The Rorschach as a means of predicting treatment outcome. *Journal of Consulting Psychology, 19*, 331–334.

Fiske, D. W., Cartwright, D. S., & Kirtner, W. L. (1964). Are psychotherapeutic changes predictable? *Journal of Abnormal and Social Psychology, 69*, 418–426.

Fiske, D. W., Hunt, H. F., Luborsky, L., Orne, M. T., Parloff, M. B., Reiser, M. F., & Tuma, A. H. (1970). Planning of research on effectiveness of psychotherapy. *Archives of General Psychiatry, 22*, 22–32.

Foa, E. B., Grayson, J. B., Steketee, G. S., Doppelt, H. G., Turner, R. M., & Latimer, P. R. (1983). Success and failure in the behavioral treatment of obsessive-compulsives. *Journal of Consulting and Clinical Psychology, 51*, 287–297.

Fordney-Settlage, D. S. (1975). Heterosexual dysfunction: Evaluation of treatment procedures. *Archives of Sexual Behavior, 4*, 367–387.

Frank, A., Eisenthal, S., & Lazare, A. (1978). Are there social class differences in patients' treatment conceptions? *Archives of General Psychiatry, 35*, 61–69.

Frank, G. H. (1967). A review of research with measures of ego strength derived from the MMPI and the Rorschach. *Journal of General Psychology, 77*, 183–206.

Frank, J. D. (1959). The dynamics of the psychotherapeutic relationship. *Psychiatry, 22*, 17–39.

Frank, J. D. (1974a). Psychotherapy: The restoration of morale. *American Journal of Psychiatry, 131*, 271–274.

Frank, J. D. (1974b). Therapeutic components of psychotherapy. A 25-year progress report of research. *The Journal of Nervous and Mental Disease, 159*, 325–342.

Frank, J. D., Gliedman, L. H., Imber, S. D., Nash, E. H., Jr., & Stone, A. R. (1957). Why patients leave psychotherapy. *Archives of Neurology and Psychiatry, 77*, 283–299.

Frank, J. D., Gliedman, L. H., Imber, S. D., Stone, A. R., & Nash, E. H. (1959). Patients' expectancies and relearning as factors determining improvement in psychotherapy. *American Journal of Psychiatry, 115*, 961–968.

Fraps, C. L., McReynolds, W. T., Beck, N. C., & Heisler, G. H. (1982). Predicting client attrition from psychotherapy through behavioral assessment procedures and a critical response approach. *Journal of Clinical Psychology, 38*, 759–764.

Freedman, N., Engelhardt, D. M., Hankoff, L. D., Glick, B. S., Kaye, H., Buchwald, J., & Stark, P. (1958). Dropout from outpatient psychiatric treatment. *Archives of Neurology and Psychiatry, 80*, 657–666.

Friedman, H. J. (1963). Patient-expectancy and symptom reduction. *Archives of General Psychiatry, 8*, 61–67.

Gabby, J. I., & Leavitt, A. (1970). Providing low cost psychotherapy to middle income patients. *Community Mental Health Journal, 6*, 210–214.

Galassi, J. P., & Galassi, M. D. (1973). Alienation of college students: A comparison of counseling seekers and nonseekers. *Journal of Counseling Psychology, 20*, 44–49.

Gallagher, J. J. (1954). Test indicators for therapy prognosis. *Journal of Consulting Psychology, 18*, 409–413.

Garfield, S. L. (1963). A note on patients' reasons for terminating psychotherapy. *Psychological Reports, 13*, 38.

Garfield, S. L. (1977a). A note on the confounding of personality and social class characteristics in research on premature termination. *Journal of Consulting and Clinical Psychology, 45*, 483–485.

Garfield, S. L. (1977b). Further comments on "dropping out of treatment": Reply to Baekeland and Lundwall. *Psychological Bulletin, 84*, 306–308.

Garfield, S. L. (1978). Research on client variables in psychotherapy. In S. L. Garfield & A. E. Bergin, (Eds.), *Handbook of psychotherapy and behavior change* (pp. 191–232). New York: Wiley.

Garfield, S. L. (1980). *Psychotherapy. An eclectic approach*. New York: Wiley.

Garfield, S. L. (1981). Evaluating the psychotherapies. *Behavior therapy, 12,* 295–307.

Garfield, S. L., & Affleck, D. C. (1959). An appraisal of duration of stay in outpatient psychotherapy. *Journal of Nervous and Mental Disease, 129,* 492–498.

Garfield, S. L., & Affleck, D. C. (1961). Therapists' judgments concerning patients considered for psychotherapy. *Journal of Consulting Psychology, 25,* 505–509.

Garfield, S. L., Affleck, D. C., & Muffley, R. A. (1963). A study of psychotherapy interaction and continuation in psychotherapy. *Journal of Clinical Psychology, 19,* 473–478.

Garfield, S. L., & Kurz, M. (1952). Evaluation of treatment and related procedures in 1216 cases referred to a mental hygiene clinic. *Psychiatric Quarterly, 26,* 414–424.

Garfield, S. L., Prager, R. A., & Bergin, A. E. (1971). Evaluation of outcome in psychotherapy. *Journal of Consulting and Clinical Psychology, 37,* 307–313.

Garfield, S. L., & Wolpin, M. (1963). Expectations regarding psychotherapy. *Journal of Nervous and Mental Disease, 137,* 353–362.

Gaylin, N. (1966). Psychotherapy and psychological health: A Rorschach function and structure analysis. *Journal of Consulting Psychology, 30,* 494–500.

Gelso, C. J., Mills, D. H., & Spiegel, S. B. (1983). Client and therapist factors influencing the outcomes of time-limited counseling one month and eighteen months after treatment. In C. J. Gelso & D. H. Johnson (Eds.), *Explorations in time limited counseling and psychotherapy* (pp. 87–114). New York: Teachers College Press.

Getter, H., & Sundland, D. M. (1962). The Barron ego-strength scale and psychotherapy outcome. *Journal of Consulting Psychology, 26,* 195.

Gibbs, J. T. (1975). Use of mental health services by black students at a predominantly white university: A three-year study. *American Journal of Orthopsychiatry, 45,* 430–445.

Gibby, R. B., Stotsky, B. A., Hiler, E. W., & Miller, D. R. (1954). Validation of Rorschach criteria for predicting duration of therapy. *Journal of Consulting Psychology, 18,* 185–191.

Goldstein, A. P. (1960). Patients' expectancies and non-specific therapy as a basis for (un)spontaneous remission. *Journal of Clinical Psychology, 16,* 399–403.

Goldstein, A. P. (1962). *Therapist–patient expectancies in psychotherapy.* New York: Pergamon.

Goldstein, A. P. (1973). *Structured learning therapy: Toward a psychotherapy for the poor.* New York: Academic Press.

Goldstein, A. P., & Shipman, W. G. (1961). Patient expectancies, symptom reduction and aspects of initial psychotherapeutic interview. *Journal of Clinical Psychology, 17,* 129–133.

Gomes-Schwartz, B. (1978). Effective ingredients in psychotherapy: Predictions of outcome from process variables. *Journal of Consulting and Clinical Psychology, 46,* 1023–1035.

Gomes-Schwartz, B., Hadley, S. W., & Strupp, H. H. (1978). Individual psychotherapy and behavior therapy. *Annual Review of Psychology, 29,* 435–471.

Gordon, S. (1965). Are we seeing the right patients? Child guidance intake: The sacred cow. *American Journal of Orthopsychiatry, 35,* 131–137.

Gottschalk, L. A., Fox, R. A., & Bates, D. E. (1973). A study of prediction and outcome of a mental health crisis clinic. *American Journal of Psychiatry, 130,* 1107–1111.

Gottschalk, L. A., Mayerson, P., & Gottlieb, A. A. (1967). Prediction and evaluation of outcome in an emergency brief psychotherapy clinic. *Journal of Nervous and Mental Disease, 144,* 77–96.

Greenberg, L. S. (1983). Psychotherapy process research. In C. E. Walker (Ed.), *The handbook of clinical psychology* (pp. 169–204). Homewood, IL: Dow Jones-Irwin.

Grotjahn, M. (1972). Learning from dropout patients: A clinical view of patients who discontinued group psychotherapy. *International Journal of Group Psychotherapy, 22,* 306–319.

Gurman, A. S., & Kniskern, D. P. (1978). Research on marital and family therapy: Progress, perspective and prospect. In S. L. Garfield & A. E. Bergin (Eds.), *Handbook of psychotherapy and behavior change* (2nd ed., pp. 817–902). New York: Wiley.

Haddock, J. N., & Mensh, I. N. (1957). Psychotherapeutic expectations in various clinic settings. *Psychological Reports, 3,* 109–112.

Hafner, R. J. (1983). Behavior therapy for agoraphobic men. *Behaviour Research & Therapy, 21,* 51–56.

Hamburg, D. A., Bibring, G. L., Fisher, C., Stanton, A. H., Wallerstein, R. S., Weinstock, H. I., & Haggard, E. (1967). Report of Ad Hoc Committee on central fact-gathering data of the American Psychoanalytic Association. *Journal of the American Psychoanalytic Association, 15,* 841–861.

Harris, R. E., & Christiansen, C. (1946). Prediction of response to brief psychotherapy. *Journal of Psychology, 21,* 269–284.

Heine, R. W. (Ed.). (1962). *The student physician as psychotherapist.* Chicago: University of Chicago Press.

Heine, R. W., & Trosman, H. (1960). Initial expectations of the doctor–patient interaction as a factor in continuance in psychotherapy. *Psychiatry, 23,* 275–278.

Heisler, G. H., Beck, N. C., Fraps, C., & McReynolds, W. T. (1982). Therapist ratings as predictors of therapy attendance. *Journal of Clinical Psychology, 38,* 754–758.

Heitler, J. B. (1973). Preparation of lower-class patients for expressive group psychotherapy. *Journal of Consulting and Clinical Psychology, 41,* 251–260.

Heitler, J. B. (1976). Preparatory techniques in initiating expressive psychotherapy with lower-class, unsophisticated patients. *Psychological Bulletin, 83,* 339–352.

Herink, R. (Ed.). (1980). *The psychotherapy handbook. The A to Z guide to more than 250 different therapies in use today.* New York: New American Library.

Hiler, E. W. (1958). Wechsler-Bellevue Intelligence as a predictor of continuation in psychotherapy. *Journal of Clinical Psychology, 14,* 192–194.

Hoehn-Saric, R., Frank, J. D., Imber, S. D., Nash, E. H., Stone, A. R., & Battle, C. C. (1964). Systematic preparation of patients for psychotherapy. I. Effects on therapy behavior and outcome. *Journal of Psychiatric Research, 2,* 267–281.

Hollingshead, A. B., & Redlich, F. C. (1958). *Social Class and Mental Illness.* New York: Wiley.

Holmes, D. S., & Urie, R. G. (1975). Effects of preparing children for psychotherapy. *Journal of Consulting and Clinical Psychology, 43,* 311–318.

Horenstein, D., Houston, B. K., & Holmes, D. S. (1973). Clients', therapists', and judges' evaluation of psychotherapy. *Counseling Psychology, 20,* 149–158.

Imber, S. D., Frank, J. D., Gliedman, L. H., Nash, E. H., & Stone, A. R. (1956). Suggestibility, social class, and the acceptance of psychotherapy. *Journal of Clinical Psychology, 12,* 341–344.

Imber, S. D., Nash, E. H., & Stone, A. R. (1955). Social class and duration of psychotherapy. *Journal of Clinical Psychology, 11,* 281–284.

Imber, S. D., Pande, S. K., Frank, J. D., Hoehn-Saric, R., Stone, A. R., & Wargo, D. G. (1970). Time-focused role induction. *Journal of Nervous and Mental Disease, 150,* 27–30.

Isaacs, K. S., & Haggard, E. A. (1966). Some methods used in the study of affect in psychotherapy. In L. A. Gottschalk & A. H. Auerbach (Eds.), *Methods of research in psychotherapy.* New York: Appleton-Century-Crofts.

Jacobs, D., Charles, E., Jacobs, T., Weinstein, H., & Mann, D. (1972). Preparation for treatment of the disadvantaged patient: Effects on disposition and outcome. *American Journal of Orthopsychiatry, 42,* 666–674.

Jacobs, M. A., Muller, J. J., Anderson, J., & Skinner, J. C. (1972). Therapeutic expectations, premorbid adjustment, and manifest distress level as predictors of improvement in hospitalized patients. *Journal of Consulting and Clinical Psychology, 39,* 455–461.

Johnson, E. Z. (1953). Klopfer's prognostic scale used with Raven's Progressive Matrices in play therapy prognosis. *Journal of Projective Techniques, 17,* 320–326.

Jones, E. E. (1974). Social class and psychotherapy. A critical review of research. *Psychiatry, 37,* 307–320.

Jones, E. E. (1982). Psychotherapists' impression of treatment outcome as a function of race. *Journal of Clinical Psychology, 38,* 722–731.

Jones, E. E., & Zoppel, C. L. (1982). Impact of client and therapist gender on psychotherapy process and outcome. *Journal of Consulting and Clinical Psychology, 50,* 259–272.

Kadushin, C. (1969). *Why people go to psychiatrists.* New York: Atherton.

Kahn, M. W., & Heiman, E. (1978). Factors associated with length of treatment in a barrio-neighborhood mental health service. *International Journal of Social Psychiatry, 24,* 259–262.

Katz, M. M. (1971). The classification of depression. In R. R. Fieve (Ed.), *Depression in the 1970's* (pp. 31–40). Amsterdam: Excerpta Medica.

Katz, M. M., Lorr, M., & Rubinstein, E. A. (1958). Remainer patients' attributes and their relation to subsequent improvement in psychotherapy. *Journal of Consulting Psychology, 22,* 411–413.

Kazdin, A. E., & Wilcoxon, L. A. (1976). Systematic desensitization and nonspecific treatment effects: A methodological evaluation. *Psychological Bulletin, 83,* 729–758.

Keithly, L. J., Samples, S. J., & Strupp, H. H. (1980). Patient motivation as a predictor of process and outcome in psychotherapy. *Psychotherapy and Psychosomatics, 33,* 87–97.

Kellner, R., & Sheffield, B. F. (1973). The one-week prevalence of symptoms in neurotic patients and normals. *American Journal of Psychiatry, 130,* 102–105.

Keniston, K., Boltax, S., & Almond, R. (1971). Multiple criteria of treatment outcome. *Journal of Psychiatry, 8,* 107–118.

Kernberg, O. F., Burstein, E. D., Coyne, L., Appelbaum, A., Horwitz, L., & Voth, H. (1972). Psychotherapy and psychoanalysis: Final report of the Menninger Foundation's Psychotherapy Research Project. *Bulletin of the Menninger Clinic, 36* (Nos. 1/2), 1–276.

Kiesler, D. J. (1966). Some myths of psychotherapy research and the search for a paradigm. *Psychological Bulletin, 65,* 110–136.

Kirkner, F., Wisham, W., & Giedt, H. (1953). A report on the validity of the Rorschach prognosis rating scale. *Journal of Projective Techniques, 17,* 465–470.

Kirtner, W. L., & Cartwright, D. S. (1958). Success and failure of client-centered therapy as a function of client personality variables. *Journal of Consulting Psychology, 22,* 259–264.

Klopfer, B., Kirkner, F., Wisham, W., & Baker, G. (1951). Rorschach prognostic rating scale. *Journal of Projective Techniques, 15,* 425–428.

Knapp, P. H., Levin, S., McCarter, R. H., Wermer, H., & Zetzel, E. (1960). Suitability for psychoanalysis: A review of 100 supervised analytic cases. *Psychoanalytic Quarterly, 29,* 459–477.

Koran, L., & Costell, R. (1973). Early termination from group psychotherapy. *International Journal of Group Psychotherapy, 23,* 346–359.

Koss, M. P. (1979). Length of psychotherapy for clients seen in private practice. *Journal of Consulting and Clinical Psychology, 47,* 210–212.

Koss, M. P. (1980). Descriptive characteristics and length of psychotherapy of child and adult clients seen in private psychological practice. *Psychotherapy: Theory, Research, and Practice, 17,* 268–271.

Krebs, R. L. (1971). Some effects of a white institution on black psychiatric outpatients. *American Journal of Orthopsychiatry, 41,* 589–597.

Kupst, M. J., & Schulman, J. L. (1979). Comparing professional and lay expectations of psychotherapy. *Psychotherapy: Theory, Research, and Practice, 16,* 237–243.

Kurland, S. H. (1956). Length of treatment in a mental hygiene clinic. *Psychiatric Quarterly Supplement, 30,* 83–90.

Lennard, H. L., & Bernstein, A. (1960). *The anatomy of psychotherapy: Systems of communication and expectation.* New York: Columbia University Press.

Lerner, B. (1972). *Therapy in the ghetto.* Baltimore: Johns Hopkins University Press.

Lerner, B., & Fiske, D. W. (1973). Client attributes and the eye of the beholder. *Journal of Consulting and Clinical Psychology, 40,* 272–277.

Lesser, W. M. (1961). The relationship between counseling progress and empathic understanding. *Journal of Counseling Psychology, 8,* 330–336.

Lessing, E. E. (1960). Prognostic value of the Rorschach in a child guidance clinic. *Journal of Projective Techniques, 24,* 310–321.

Levinson, R., & Kitchener, H. (1966). Treatment of delinquents: Comparison of four methods for assigning inmates to counselors. *Journal of Consulting Psychology, 30,* 364.

Liberman, B. L. (1978). The role of mastery in psychotherapy: Maintenance of improvement and prescriptive change. In J. D. Frank, R. Hoehn-Saric, S. D. Imber, B. L. Liberman, & A. R. Stone, *Effective ingredients of successful psychotherapy.* New York: Brunner/Mazel.

Liberman, B. L., Frank, J. D., Hoehn-Saric, R., Stone, A. R., Imber, S. D., & Pande, S. K. (1972). Patterns of change in treated psychoneurotic patients: A five-year follow-up investigation of the systematic preparation of patients for psychotherapy. *Journal of Consulting and Clinical Psychology, 38,* 36–41.

Lichtenstein, E. (1966). Personality similarity and therapeutic success: A failure to replicate. *Journal of Consulting Psychology, 30,* 282.

Lick, J., & Bootzin, R. (1975). Expectancy factors in the treatment of fear: Methodological and theoretical issues. *Psychological Bulletin, 82,* 917–931.

Lief, H. I., Lief, U. F., Warren, C. O., & Heath, R. G. (1961). Low dropout rate in a psychiatric clinic. *Archives of General Psychiatry, 5,* 200–211.

Lipkin, S. (1954). Clients' feelings and attitudes in relation to the outcome of client-centered therapy. *Psychological Monographs, 68* (1, Whole No. 372).

Lorenzen, I. J. (1967). Acceptance or rejection by psychiatric clinics. M. A. Essay, Columbia University.

Lorion, R. P. (1973). Socioeconomic status and traditional treatment approaches reconsidered. *Psychological Bulletin, 79,* 263–270.

Lorion, R. P. (1974). Patient and therapist variables in the treatment of low-income patients. *Psychological Bulletin, 81,* 344–354.

Lorion, R. P. (1978). Research on psychotherapy and behavior change with the disadvantaged. In S. L. Garfield & A. E. Bergin (Eds.), *Handbook of psychotherapy and behavior change* (2nd ed., pp. 903–938). New York: Wiley.

Lorr, M., Katz, M. M., & Rubinstein, E. A. (1958). The prediction of length of stay in psychotherapy. *Journal of Consulting Psychology, 22,* 321–327.

Lothstein, L. M. (1978). The group psychotherapy dropout phenomenon revisited. *American Journal of Psychiatry, 135,* 1492–1495.

Lott, D. R., & Murray, E. J. (1975). The effect of expectancy manipulation on outcome in systematic desensitization. *Psychotherapy: Theory, Research, and Practice, 12,* 28–32.

Lubin, B., Hornstra, R. K., Lewis, R. V., & Bechtel, B. S. (1973). Correlates of initial treatment assignment in a community mental health center. *Archives of General Psychiatry, 29,* 497–504.

Luborsky, L., Chandler, M., Auerbach, A. H., Cohun, J., & Bachrach, H. M. (1971). Factors influencing the outcome of psychotherapy: A review of quantitative research. *Psychological Bulletin, 75,* 145–185.

Luborsky, L., Crits-Christoph, P., Alexander, L., Margolis, M., & Cohen, M. (1983). Two helping alliance methods of predicting outcomes of psychotherapy. *Journal of Nervous and Mental Disease, 171,* 480–491.

Luborsky, L., Mintz, J., Auerbach, A., Christoph, P., Bachrach, H., Todd, T., Johnson, M., Cohen, M., & O'Brien, C. (1980). Predicting the outcome of psychotherapy. *Archives of General Psychiatry, 37,* 471–481.

Luborsky, L., Mintz, J., & Christoph, P. (1979). Are psychotherapeutic changes predictable? Comparison of a Chicago Counseling Center project with a Penn psychotherapy project. *Journal of Consulting and Clinical Psychology, 47,* 469–473.

Luborsky, L., Singer, B., & Luborsky, L. (1975). Comparative studies of psychotherapies. Is it true that "Everyone has won and all must have prizes"? *Archives of General Psychiatry, 32,* 995–1007.

Malan, D. H. (1963). *A study of brief psychotherapy.* London: Tavistock.

Malan, D. H. (1976). *The frontier of brief psychotherapy: An example of the convergence of research and clinical practice.* New York: Plenum.

Marks, I. (1978). Behavioral psychotherapy of adult neurosis. In S. L. Garfield & A. E. Bergin (Eds.), *Handbook of psychotherapy and behavior change* (2nd ed., pp. 493–547). New York: Wiley.

Matarazzo, J. D. (1972). *Wechsler's measurement and appraisal of adult intelligence* (5th and enl. ed.). Baltimore: Williams & Wilkins.

Mathews, A. M., Gelder, M. G., & Johnston, D. W. (1981). *Agoraphobia. Nature and treatment.* London: Tavistock.

Mathews, A. M., Johnston, D. W., Lancashire, M., Munby, M., Shaw, P. M., & Gelder, M. G. (1976). Imaginal flooding and exposure to real phobic situations: Treatment outcome with agoraphobic patients. *British Journal of Psychiatry, 129,* 362–371.

Mathews, A. M., Johnston, D. W., Shaw, P. M., & Gelder, M. G. (1974). Process variables and the prediction of outcome in behaviour therapy. *The British Journal of Psychiatry, 125,* 256–264.

McLachlan, J. C. (1972). Benefit from group therapy as a function of patient–therapist match on conceptual level. *Psychotherapy: Theory, Research, and Practice, 9,* 317–323.

McLean, P. D., & Hakstian, A. R. (1979). Clinical depression: Comparative efficacy of outpatient treatments. *Journal of Consulting and Clinical Psychology, 47,* 818–836.

McNair, D. M., Lorr, M., & Callahan, D. M. (1963). Patient and therapist influences on quitting psychotherapy. *Journal of Consulting Psychology, 27,* 10–17.

McNair, D. M., Lorr, J., Young, H. H., Roth, I., & Boyd, R. W. (1964). A three-year follow-up of psychotherapy patients. *Journal of Clinical Psychology, 20,* 258–264.

Melnick, B. (1972). Patient–therapist identification in relation to both patient and therapist variables and therapy outcomes. *Journal of Consulting and Clinical Psychology, 38,* 97–104.

Meltzoff, J., & Kornreich, M. (1970). *Research in psychotherapy.* New York: Atherton.

Mendelsohn, G. A., & Geller, M. H. (1965). Structure of client attitudes toward counseling and their relation to client–counselor similarity. *Journal of Consulting*

Psychology, 29, 63–72.

Messer, S. B., & Meinster, M. O. (1980). Interaction effects of internal vs. external locus of control and directive vs. non-directive therapy: Fact or fiction? *Journal of Clinical Psychology, 36,* 283–288.

Mindess, M. (1953). Predicting patient's response to psychotherapy: A preliminary study designed to investigate the validity of the Rorschach Prognostic Rating Scale. *Journal of Projective Techniques, 17,* 327–334.

Mintz, J., (1972). What is "success" in psychotherapy? *Journal of Abnormal Psychology, 80,* 11–19.

Mintz, J., Luborsky, L., & Auerbach, A. H. (1971). Dimensions of psychotherapy: A factor-analytic study of ratings of psychotherapy sessions. *Journal of Consulting and Clinical Psychology, 36,* 106–120.

Mintz, J., Luborsky, L., & Christoph, P. (1979). Measuring the outcomes of psychotherapy: Findings of the Penn psychotherapy project. *Journal of Consulting and Clinical Psychology, 47,* 319–334.

Mintz, J., Steuer, J., & Jarvik, L. (1981). Psychotherapy with depressed elderly patients: Research considerations. *Journal of Consulting and Clinical Psychology, 49,* 542–548.

Mogul, K. M. (1982). Overview: The sex of the therapist. *American Journal of Psychiatry, 139,* 1–11.

Moras, K., & Strupp, H. H. (1982). Pretherapy interpersonal relations, patients' alliance, and outcome in brief therapy. *Archives of General Psychiatry, 39,* 405–409.

Morgan, R., Luborsky, L., Crits-Christoph, P., Curtis, H., & Solomon, J. (1982). Predicting the outcomes of psychotherapy by the Penn Helping Alliance Rating Method. *Archives of General Psychiatry, 39,* 397–402.

Morgan, W. G. (1973). Nonnecessary conditions or useful procedures in desensitization: A reply to Wilkins. *Psychological Bulletin, 79,* 373–375.

Muench, G. A. (1965). An investigation of the efficacy of time-limited psychotherapy. *Journal of Counseling Psychology, 12,* 294–298.

Myers, J. K., & Schaffer, L. (1958). Social stratification and psychiatric practice: A study of an outpatient clinic. In E. G. Jaco (Ed.), *Patients, physicians and illness.* Glencoe, IL: Free Press.

Nacev, V. (1980). Dependency and ego-strength as indicators of patient attendance in psychotherapy. *Journal of Clinical Psychology, 36,* 691–695.

Nash, E. H., Hoehn-Saric, R., Battle, C. C., Stone, A. R., Imber, S. D., & Frank, J. D. (1965). Systematic preparation of patients for short-term psychotherapy. II. Relations to characteristics of patient, therapist, and the psychotherapeutic process. *Journal of Nervous and Mental Disease, 140,* 374–383.

National Center for Health Statistics. (1966). *Characteristics of patients of selected types of medical specialists and practitioners: United States July 1963–June 1964.* Washington, DC: Public Health Service Publication No. 1000, Series 10, No. 28.

National Institute of Mental Health, Series CN No. 6. (1981). *Use of psychiatric facilities by children and youth. United States 1975.* DHHS Publication No. (ADM) 81–1142. Superintendent of Documents, US Government Printing Office, Washington, DC.

Newmark, C. S., Finkelstein, M., & Frerking, R. A. (1974). Comparison of the predictive validity of two measures of psychotherapy prognosis. *Journal of Personality Assessment, 38,* 144–148.

New York City Committee on Mental Hygiene of the State Charities Aid Association. (1949). *The functioning of psychiatric clinics in New York City.* New York: Author.

Noonan, J. R. (1973). A follow-up of pretherapy drop-outs. *Journal of Community Psychology, 1,* 43–45.

Ollendick, T. H., & Murphy, M. J. (1977). Differential effectiveness of muscular and cognitive relaxation as a function of locus of control. *Journal of Behavioral Therapy and Experimental Psychiatry, 8,* 223–228.

O'Malley, S. S., Suh, C. S., & Strupp, H. H. (1983). The Vanderbilt Psychotherapy Process Scale: A report on the scale development and a process-outcome study. *Journal of Consulting and Clinical Psychology, 51,* 581–586.

Orlinsky, D. E., & Howard, K. I. (1975). *Varieties of psychotherapeutic experience.* New York: Teachers College Press.

Orne, M. T., & Wender, P. H. (1968). Anticipatory socialization for psychotherapy: Method and rationale. *American Journal of Psychiatry, 124,* 1202–1212.

Overall, B., & Aronson, H. (1962). Expectations of psychotherapy in lower socio-economic class patients. *American Journal of Orthopsychiatry, 32,* 271–272.

Parloff, M. B., Waskow, I. E., & Wolfe, B. E. (1978). Research on therapist variables in relation to process and outcome. In S. L. Garfield & A. E. Bergin (Eds.), *Handbook of psychotherapy and behavior change* (2nd ed., pp. 233–282). New York: Wiley.

Paul, G. L. (1967). Strategy of outcome research in psychotherapy. *Journal of Consulting Psychology, 31,* 109–118.

Pekarik, G. (1983). Follow-up adjustment of outpatient dropouts. *American Journal of Orthopsychiatry, 53,* 501–511.

Perotti, L. P., & Hopewell, C. A. (1980). Expectancy effects in psychotherapy and systematic desensitization: A review. *JSAS: Catalog of Selected Documents in Psychology, 10* (Ms. No. 2052).

Pettit, I., Pettit, T., & Welkowitz, J. (1974). Relationship between values, social class, and duration of psychotherapy. *Journal of Consulting and Clinical Psychology, 42,* 482–490.

Phillips, E. L., & Fagan, P. J. (1982, Aug.). *Attrition: Focus on the intake and first therapy interviews.* Paper presented at the 90th Annual Convention of the American Psychological Association, Washington, DC.

Piper, W. E., & Wogan, M. (1970). Placebo effect in psychotherapy: An extension of earlier findings. *Journal of Consulting and Clinical Psychology, 34,* 447.

Pope, K. S., Geller, J. D., & Wilkinson, L. (1975). Fee assessment and outpatient psychotherapy. *Journal of Consulting and Clinical Psychology, 43,* 835–841.

Prager, R. A., & Garfield, S. L. (1972). Client initial disturbance and outcome in psychotherapy. *Journal of Consulting and Clinical Psychology, 38,* 112–117.

Rachman, S., & Hodgson, R. (1980). *Obsessions and compulsions.* Englewood Cliffs, NJ: Prentice-Hall.

Raynes, A. E., & Warren, G. (1971a). Some distinguishing features of patients failing to attend a psychiatric clinic after referral. *American Journal of Orthopsychiatry, 41,* 581–588.

Raynes, A. E., & Warren, G. (1971b). Some characteristics of "drop-outs" at first contact with a psychiatric clinic. *Community Mental Health Journal, 7*, 144–151.

Reder, P., & Tyson, R. L. (1980). Patient dropout from psychotherapy. A review and discussion. *Bulletin of the Menninger Clinic, 44*, 229–251.

Riess, B. F., & Brandt, L. W. (1965). What happens to applicants for psychotherapy? *Community Mental Health Journal, 1*, 175–180.

Roberts, L. K. (1954). The failure of some Rorschach indices to predict the outcome of psychotherapy. *Journal of Consulting Psychology, 18*, 96–98.

Rodolfa, E. R., Rapaport, R., & Lee, V. E. (1983). Variables related to premature terminations in a university counseling service. *Journal of Counseling Psychology, 30*, 87–90.

Rogers, C. R., Gendlin, E. T., Kiesler, D. J., & Truax, C. B. (Eds.). (1967). *The therapeutic relationship and its impact.* Madison: University of Wisconsin Press.

Rogers, L. S. (1960). Drop-out rates and results of psychotherapy in government-aided mental hygiene clinics. *Journal of Clinical Psychology, 16*, 89–92.

Rogers, L. S., & Hammond, K. R. (1953). Prediction of the results of therapy by means of the Rorschach test. *Journal of Consulting Psychology, 17*, 8–15.

Rosenbaum, M., Friedlander, J., & Kaplan, S. (1956). Evaluation of results of psychotherapy. *Psychosomatic Medicine, 18*, 113–132.

Rosenberg, S. (1954). The relationship of certain personality factors to prognosis in psychotherapy. *Journal of Clinical Psychology, 10*, 341–345.

Rosenthal, D., & Frank, J. D. (1956). Psychotherapy and the placebo effect. *Psychological Bulletin, 53*, 294–302.

Rosenthal, D., & Frank, J. D. (1958). The fate of psychiatric clinic outpatients assigned to psychotherapy. *Journal of Nervous and Mental Disorders, 127*, 330–343.

Rosenzweig, S. P., & Folman, R. (1974). Patient and therapist variables affecting premature termination in group psychotherapy. *Psychotherapy: Theory, Research, and Practice, 11*, 76–79.

Rounsaville, B. J., Weissman, M. M., & Prusoff, B. A. (1981). Psychotherapy with depressed outpatients. Patient and process variables as predictors of outcome. *British Journal of Psychiatry, 138*, 67–74.

Rubinstein, E. A., & Lorr, M. (1956). A comparison of terminators and remainers in outpatient psychotherapy. *Journal of Clinical Psychology, 12*, 345–349.

Ryan, W. (Ed.). (1969). *Distress in the city: Essays on the design and administration of urban mental health services.* Cleveland: Case Western Reserve University Press.

Sachs, J. S. (1983). Negative factors in brief psychotherapy: An empirical assessment. *Journal of Consulting and Clinical Psychology, 51*, 557– 564.

Saltzman, C., Luetgert, M. J., Roth, C. H., Creaser, J., & Howard, L. (1976). Formation of a therapeutic relationship: Experiences during the initial phase of psychotherapy as predictors of treatment duration and outcome. *Journal of Consulting and Clinical Psychology, 44*, 546–555.

Salzman, C., Shader, R. I., Scott, D. A., & Binstock, W. (1970). Interviewer anger and patient dropout in walk-in clinic. *Comprehensive Psychiatry, 11*, 267–273.

Sapolsky, A. (1965). Relationship between patient-doctor compatibility, mutual perception, and outcome of treatment. *Journal of Abnormal Psychology, 70*, 70–76.

Sattler, J. M. (1977). The effects of therapist–client racial similarity. In A. S. Gurman & A. M. Razin (Eds.), *Effective psychotherapy: A handbook of research* (pp. 250–288). New York: Pergamon.

Schaffer, L., & Myers, J. K. (1954). Psychotherapy and social stratification: An empirical study of practice in a psychiatric outpatient clinic. *Psychiatry, 17*, 83–93.

Schmidt, J. P., & Hancey, R. (1979). Social class and psychiatric treatment: Application of a decision-making model to use patterns in a cost-free clinic. *Journal of Consulting and Clinical Psychology, 47*, 771–772.

Schofield, W. (1964). *Psychotherapy: The purchase of friendship.* Englewood Cliffs, NJ: Prentice-Hall.

Schubert, D. S. P., & Miller, S. I. (1980). Differences between the lower social classes. *American Journal of Orthopsychiatry, 50*, 712–717.

Seeman, J. (1954). Counselor judgments of therapeutic process and outcome. In C. Rogers & R. F. Dymond (Eds.), *Psychotherapy and personality change.* Chicago: University of Chicago Press.

Shader, R. I. (1970). The walk-in service: An experience in community care. In T. Rothman (Ed.), *Changing patterns in psychiatric care.* New York: Crown.

Shapiro, R. J. (1974). Therapist attitudes and premature termination in family and individual therapy. *The Journal of Nervous and Mental Disease, 159*, 101–107.

Sheehan, J. G., Frederick, C., Rosevear, W., & Spiegelman, M. (1954). A validity study of the Rorschach Prognostic Rating Scale. *Journal of Projective Techniques, 18*, 233–239.

Shore, M. F., & Massimo, J. L. (1973). After ten years: A follow-up study of comprehensive vocationally oriented psychotherapy. *American Journal of Orthopsychiatry, 43*, 128–132.

Siegel, N. H. (1962). Characteristics of patients in psychoanalysis. *Journal of Nervous and Mental Disease, 135*, 155–158.

Siegel, N., & Fink, M. (1962). Motivation for psychotherapy. *Comprehensive Psychiatry, 3*, 170–173.

Siegel, S. M., Rootes, M. D., & Traub, A. (1977). Symptom change and prognosis in clinic psychotherapy. *Archives of General Psychiatry, 34*, 321–331.

Sifneos, P. E. (1972). *Short-term psychotherapy and emotional crisis.* Cambridge: Harvard University Press.

Silverman, W. H., & Beech, R. P. (1979). Are dropouts, dropouts? *Journal of Community Psychology, 7*, 236–242.

Simons, A. D., Levine, J. L., Lustman, P. J., & Murphy, G. E. (1984). Patient attrition in a comparative outcome study of depression. A follow-up report. *Journal of Affective Disorders, 6*, 163–173.

Sloane, R. B., Cristol, A. H., Pepernik, M. C., & Staples, F. R. (1970). Role preparation and expectation of improvement in psychotherapy. *Journal of Nervous and Mental Disease, 150*, 18–26.

Sloane, R. B., Staples, F. R., Cristol, A. H., Yorkston, N.J.,

& Whipple, K. (1975). *Psychotherapy versus behavior therapy.* Cambridge: Harvard University Press.

Smith, G. J. W., Sjöholm, L., & Nielzén, S. (1975). Individual factors affecting the improvement of anxiety during a therapeutic period of 1½ to 2 years. *Acta Psychiatrica Scandinavica, 52,* 7–22.

Smith, M. L., Glass, G. V., & Miller, T. I. (1980). *The benefits of psychotherapy.* Baltimore: The Johns Hopkins University Press.

Stein, K. B., & Beall, L. (1971). Externalizing–internalizing symptoms and psychotherapeutic outcome. *Psychotherapy: Theory, Research, and Practice, 8,* 269–272.

Steinmetz, J. L., Lewinsohn, P. M., & Antonuccio, D. O. (1983). Prediction of individual outcome in a group intervention for depression. *Journal of Consulting and Clinical Psychology, 51,* 331–337.

Stern, S. L., Moore, S. F., & Gross, S. J. (1975). Confounding of personality and social class characteristics in research on premature termination. *Journal of Consulting and Clinical Psychology, 43,* 341–344.

Stoler, N. (1963). Client likability: A variable in the study of psychotherapy. *Journal of Consulting Psychology, 27,* 175–178.

Stone, A., Frank, J. D., Nash, E., & Imber, S. (1961). An intensive five-year follow-up study of treated psychiatric outpatients. *Journal of Nervous and Mental Disease, 133,* 410–422.

Storandt, M. (1983). *Counseling and therapy with older adults.* Boston: Little, Brown.

Strupp, H. H., & Bloxom, A. L. (1973). Preparing lower-class patients for group psychotherapy: Development and evaluation of a role-induction film. *Journal of Consulting and Clinical Psychology, 41,* 373–384.

Sue, S., McKinney, H., Allen, D., & Hall, J. (1974). Delivery of community mental health services to black and white clients. *Journal of Consulting and Clinical Psychology, 42,* 794–801.

Sue, S., McKinney, H. L., & Allen, D. B. (1976). Predictors of the duration of therapy for clients in the community mental health system. *Community Mental Health Journal, 12,* 365–375.

Sullivan, P. L., Miller, C., & Smelzer, W. (1958). Factors in length of stay and progress in psychotherapy. *Journal of Consulting Psychology, 1,* 1–9.

Swenson, C. H. (1967). Psychotherapy as a special case of dyadic interaction: Some suggestions for theory and research. *Psychotherapy: Theory, Research, and Practice, 4,* 7–13.

Taube, C. A., Burns, B. J., & Kessler, L. (1984). Patients of psychiatrists and psychologists in office-based practice: 1980. *American Psychologist, 39,* 1435–1447.

Taulbee, E. S. (1958). Relationship between certain personality variables and continuation in psychotherapy. *Journal of Consulting Psychology, 22,* 83–89.

Tollinton, H. J. (1973). Initial expectations and outcome. *British Journal of Medical Psychology, 46,* 251–257.

Tomlinson, T. M., & Stoler, N. (1967). The relationship between affective evaluation and ratings of therapy process and outcome with schizophrenics. *Psychotherapy: Theory, Research, and Practice, 4,* 14–18.

Truax, C. B., & Carkhuff, R. R. (1967). *Toward effective counseling and psychotherapy: Training and prac-*

tice. Chicago: Aldine.

Truax, C. B., Tunnell, B. T., Jr., Fine, H. L., & Wargo, D. G. (1966). *The prediction of client outcome during group psychotherapy from measures of initial status.* Unpublished manuscript, Arkansas Rehabilitation Research and Training Center, University of Arkansas.

Truax, C. B., & Wargo, D. G. (1969). Effects of vicarious therapy pre-training and alternate sessions on outcome in group psychotherapy with outpatients. *Journal of Consulting and Clinical Psychology, 33,* 440–447.

Udell, B., & Hornstra, R. K. (1975). Good patients and bad therapeutic assets and liabilities. *Archives of General Psychiatry, 32,* 1533–1537.

Uhlenhuth, E. H., & Duncan, D. B. (1968). *Subjective change in psychoneurotic outpatients with medical students. II. The kind, amount, and course of change.* Unpublished manuscript, Johns Hopkins University.

Vail, A. (1978). Factors influencing lower class black patients remaining in treatment. *Journal of Consulting and Clinical Psychology, 46,* 341.

Vaillant, G. E. (1972). Why men seek psychotherapy. I: Results of a survey of college graduates. *American Journal of Psychiatry, 129,* 645–651.

Walters, G. C., Solomon, G. S., & Walden, V. R. (1982). Use of the MMPI in predicting persistence in groups of male and female outpatients. *Journal of Clinical Psychology, 38,* 80–83.

Warren, N. C., & Rice, L. N. (1972). Structuring and stabilizing of psychotherapy for low-prognosis clients. *Journal of Consulting and Clinical Psychology, 39,* 173–181.

Warren, R. C., Jackson, A. M., Nugaris, J., & Farley, G. K. (1973). Differential attitudes of black and white patients toward treatment in a child guidance clinic. *American Journal of Orthopsychiatry, 43,* 384–393.

Waskow, I. E. (1984). Specification of the Technique Variable in the NIMH Treatment of Depression Collaborative Research Program. In B. W. Williams & R. L. Spitzer (Eds.), *Psychotherapy research. Where are we and where should we go?* (pp. 150–159). New York: Guilford.

Waskow, I. E., & Parloff, M. D. (1975). *Psychotherapy change measures.* Washington, DC: National Institute of Mental Health.

Weighill, V. E., Hodge, J., & Peck, D. F. (1983). Keeping appointments with clinical psychologists. *The British Journal of Clinical Psychology, 22,* 143–144.

Weiss, S. L., & Dlugokinski, E. L. (1974). Parental expectations of psychotherapy. *Journal of Psychology, 86,* 71–80.

Weiss, J., & Schaie, K. W. (1958). Factors in patient failure to return to clinic. *Diseases of the Nervous System, 19,* 429–430.

Weissman, M. M., Geanakapolos, E., & Prusoff, B. (1973). Social class and attrition in depressed outpatients. *Social Casework, 54,* 162–170.

Wilkins, W. (1971). Desensitization: Social and cognitive factors underlying the effectiveness of Wolpe's procedure. *Psychological Bulletin, 76,* 311–317.

Wilkins, W. (1973). Expectancy of therapeutic gain: An empirical and conceptual critique. *Journal of Consulting and Clinical Psychology, 40,* 69–77.

Wilkins, W. (1979). Expectancies in therapy research: Discriminating among heterogeneous nonspecifics. *Journal of Consulting and Clinical Psychology, 47,* 837–845.

Wilson, G. T., & Thomas, M. G. W. (1973). Self- versus drug-produced relaxation and the effects of instructional set in standardized systematic desensitization. *Behavior Research & Therapy, 11,* 279–288.

Wirt, W. M. (1967). Psychotherapeutic persistence. *Journal of Consulting Psychology, 31,* 429.

Yalom, I. D. (1966). A study of group therapy dropouts. *Archives of General Psychiatry, 14,* 393–414.

Yalom, I. D., Houts, P. S., Newell, G., & Rand, K. H. (1967). Preparation of patients for group therapy. *Archives of General Psychiatry, 17,* 416–427.

Yamamoto, J., & Goin, M. K. (1966). Social class factors relevant for psychiatric treatment. *Journal of Nervous and Mental Disease, 142,* 332–339.

Yamamoto, J., James, Q. C., & Palley, N. (1968). Cultural problems in psychiatric therapy. *Archives of General Psychiatry, 19,* 45–49.

Zigler, E. S., & Phillips, L. (1961). Social competence and outcome in psychiatric disorders. *Journal of Abnormal and Social Psychology, 63,* 264–271.

7

THERAPIST VARIABLES IN PSYCHOTHERAPY PROCESS AND OUTCOME

L. E. BEUTLER
M. CRAGO

University of Arizona

T. G. ARIZMENDI

San Francisco, CA.

Among the many contributors to psychotherapy effectiveness, the role of therapist attributes is among the most interesting and complex. Virtually every psychotherapy study addresses, either directly or indirectly, the role of therapist characteristics in affecting therapeutic change, and empirical research suggests that nontechnical aspects of the therapist's contributions are among the most influential in facilitating outcomes (e.g., Lambert & DeJulio, 1978). Clinical wisdom even suggests that by behaving sensitively, the therapist can overcome many negative and counterproductive influences that may be contributed by the patient or the environment. The following pages will:

1. Define the major dimensions on which therapists differ and through which psychotherapeutic influence is potentially affected;

2. Highlight some of the major conceptual and methodological issues that must be considered by both clinical and research scientists; and

3. Provide an overview of the status of each of the major therapist variables, relative to their role in affecting psychotherapeutic change.

A TAXONOMY OF INFLUENCES

The first task of this chapter is to define the dimensions on which therapists differ and through which therapeutic change may be realized. This task requires that we impose order upon a host of interactive and often arbitrarily defined dimensions. The nature of psychotherapy is such that it is difficult at best to separate therapist from therapy, patient, and contextual factors (e.g., Strupp, 1977). Even when one can make such a determination, many therapist variables may be so highly intercorrelated that to separate them may do an injustice to their complexity. The influence of these variables on psychotherapy outcome may change as a function of the ways in which the variables interact with one another under different conditions or at different times. Hence, a system of classifying these variables must balance the need to be sensitive to the complexity of multifaceted therapist influences against the clinical and scientific value of a conceptually clear and logical system.

An adequate taxonomy of therapist variables must distinguish between those that exist independently of and coincidentally to the treatment relationship, and those that are specifically designed to have impact on the treatment process. Such a taxonomy must also be sensitive to the fact that therapist variables differ in how directly they can be observed. That is, some observations are studied as variables in their own right while others are used to infer internal attributes of the therapist. Figure 7.1 represents these considerations as two interactive dimensions on which therapist variables are classified into four quadrants.

For convenience, one may observe that the ab-

scissa in Figure 7.1 represents the degree to which therapy characteristics have a planned effect upon the therapy relationship. Extratherapy characteristics, for example, are assumed to exert an incidental or unplanned effect while therapy-specific characteristics are those designed by the therapist's experience, dogma, and training to facilitate positive therapeutic exchanges. As such, therapy-specific characteristics are assumed to be under therapist control, whereas extratherapy characteristics represent enduring, less controllable traits.

It is somewhat more difficult to classify therapists' characteristics on the dimension represented by the ordinant in Figure 7.1. Externally observed characteristics are those that require minimal inference from the defining observations. It will become apparent in the following discussion, however, that there is no clear dividing point between such externally observed characteristics and those observations that are used to imply some indwelling or internal state of the therapist. When clearly defined external observations fail to produce a significant relationship to therapeutic process or outcome, it is conventional for researchers to resort to explanations based upon the attitudinal attributes that may be inferred from these external traits. For example, certain attitudes inherent to one's gender may be

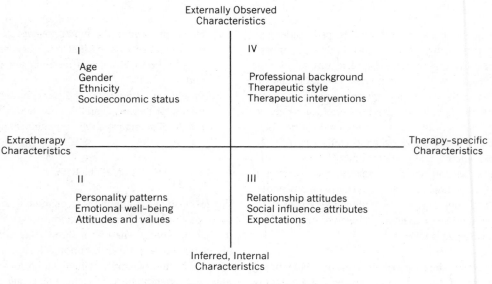

Figure 7.1   Therapist characteristics.

interpreted as mediating variables in order to explain either positive or negative findings deriving from gender-related investigations.

In quadrant I are enduring characteristics that exist or that have developed independently of the therapy relationship and that can be observed with a minimal amount of inference or extrapolation. Such externally observed, extratherapy characteristics include therapist age, gender, ethnicity, and socioeconomic status.

The second quadrant of Figure 7.1 represents those enduring, extratherapy characteristics that are also internal attributes of the therapist. These inferred constructs include various personality patterns, therapist emotional well-being, and other attitudes and values that are assumed to characterize the therapist beyond the narrow confines of therapy activities. In contrast, the third quadrant of the figure defines internal characteristics of the therapist that are assumed to be more specific to therapy-related behaviors. Attitudes toward the therapy relationship itself, social attributes of status and credibility, as well as therapist expectations about treatment process and outcome are all included in this quadrant.

The fourth quadrant presented in Figure 7.1 represents externally observed and derived character-istics of the therapist that are, nonetheless, expected to exert a specific influence upon psychotherapy. In this quadrant are characteristics of therapist behavior and background that are specifically designed to exert a therapeutic effect but whose presence can be observed without inferring an internal state. The therapist's professional background and training as well as stylistic aspects of the therapist's method of constructing interventions and the interventions themselves constitute the variables under greatest consideration.

If we remember that these dimensions represent somewhat arbitrary distinctions rather than discrete categories, it will help us understand why the influences exerted by some externally observed variables change either over the course of treatment or as a function of ongoing cultural changes. For example, therapist age and gender may exert very different effects as societal attitudes about these variables change and as the therapist's own internalized attitudes also change with maturity and experience. Hence, research findings on externally observed traits will be considered in conjunction with internal traits and attitudes whenever this is necessary in order to lend coherence to the discussion.

A CHAPTER OVERVIEW

This chapter will provide a critical overview regarding the status of each of the major therapist variables defined in the foregoing. In providing such an overview, we have elected to undertake a selective rather than an exhaustive review of the literature based on three considerations. First, we have chosen to emphasize only recent research in an effort to update the conclusions reached in prior editions of this *Handbook*. We have relied upon research accumulated since the mid-1970s except when it became apparent that an understanding of the current body of literature could not be obtained without reference to the evolution of findings over time.

Our selection of studies for review also has been governed by a judgment of relevance. This judgment has been based upon a general definition of each study's methodological adequacy. Research methods used to study psychotherapists' influence fall into essentially three categories. The first and most rigorous methodology is the true *experimental study* in which the therapist characteristic is manipulated or controlled. For example, researchers may systematically control the amount or type of information available to a patient about the therapist or the type of activities performed by the therapist. In these studies, therapists may be randomly assigned one or another quality or attribute. However, most therapist variables do not permit random assignment to therapists. For these variables, *comparison procedures* must be accepted as methodologically adequate. In these procedures, contrasting groups of therapists are studied. The best research of this type relies upon the controlled assignment of patients to therapists. Many studies, however, neither assign therapists to various characteristics nor patients to therapists of known characteristics. In this case, *naturalistic studies* are used and frequently compare therapists on several naturally occurring dimensions at once. The strength of such results is decidedly limited. In the current presentation, we have assigned the greatest relevance to experimental studies, followed in order by contrasting comparison and naturalistic investigations.

A third, related consideration that has governed our selection of studies is that of representativeness. We have given only minimal attention to the nuances of psychotherapeutic processes when these are studied independently of outcome. We have given greatest weight to studies of ongoing psychotherapy with identified clinical populations in which dependent variables are objectively defined. Experimental analogue investigations have been included in our review only when they provide the best available information about psychotherapeutic process and outcome. In selecting these latter studies we have differentiated between *subject* and *method* analogue designs. Subject analogues are those that investigate patient or therapist populations that are not representative of actual clinical samples. With few exceptions, we have elected to ignore most research of this nature. However, research investigations that employ experimental analogues of therapeutic methods or environments are presented throughout this chapter. While such method analogues have limitations, they often overcome the problem of control and random assignment that affect studies in clinical environments.

We will explore therapist variables under four major headings, representing the various quadrants presented in Figure 7.1. Each section will begin with the presentation of a summary table, which will preview the major findings for each of the variables to be considered in that section. Next, we will address each variable in turn. We will draw attention to some of the limiting features and unique problems of research in that area, describe some of the more representative or exemplary studies, and explore the current status of the literature. In this process, the reader will benefit by observing one further distinction. Some research has explored therapist variables alone in a *unidirectional* manner. This research approach contrasts with that which has explored some method of *matching* patient and therapist variables. By bearing this distinction in mind, we will be able to explore some of the methodological characteristics of each approach that facilitate or impede our understanding of the manner in which therapist variables operate.

EXTERNALLY OBSERVED, EXTRATHERAPY CHARACTERISTICS

The therapist brings to the treatment relationship a variety of relatively stable characteristics that are independent of and exist incidentally to the treatment relationship. By virtue of their stability, these characteristics are difficult to manipulate in the service of research. Hence, empirical outcome investigations of these variables are restricted to naturalistic and group comparison designs and vary in the amount of control established over the assignment of patients to therapists. The major variables given consideration in this category include the therapist's age, gender, socioeconomic background, and ethnicity. Table 7.1 provides a summary of the effects of each these variables as a function of the experimental rigor of the investigation (i.e., the type of methodological control employed). In each instance both the number of studies reviewed and the major conclusion are reported. In this and subsequent tables, we have included a combined category for reporting analogue investigations and studies that utilized process-oriented methodologies. The inclusion of this combined category of the least rigorous studies allows comparison of process and outcome research findings.

Age

Two major methodological difficulties face those who investigate the influence of therapist age. First, age is often confounded with the therapist experience level or theoretical orientation. Since experience accumulates with age and since the theoretical philosophies and offerings emphasized by training programs have changed over the course of time, these potential infuences should be considered in exploring the effects of therapist age on treatment outcome. Second, therapist age does not exert only a unidirectional effect. That is, an age difference of 15 years may exert a different effect when the therapist is the older member of the dyad than when the patient is the older member. Both *actual* and *relative* differences between patients' and the therapists' ages should be taken into consideration. Because of an awareness of this relationship in clinical settings, treatment programs are increasingly being

TABLE 7.1   External, Extratherapy Characteristics

Variable	Study Type/Quality	n	Summary of Findings[a]
A. Age			
	Comparison	1	Favors age similarity for younger patients
	Naturalistic	3	All favor age similarity
	Analogue/Process	7	Four studies favor age dissimilarity, all for mildly distressing problems; one study is n.s.; two show interactions with sex or type of problem
	Total	11	
B. Gender			
	Comparison	2	Both favor female therapists
	Naturalistic	9	Four are nonsignificant; three favor similarity; two show interaction with other variables
	Analogue/Process	8	Four favor females or gender similarity; two favor attitude dissimilarity; three are n.s.; one favors patients' preference
	Total	19	
C. Ethnicity			
	Comparison	5	Three n.s. for most outcomes; four favor similarity reducing dropout
	Naturalistic	3	Two are n.s.; one favors similarity reducing dropout
	Analogue/Process	14	Ten favor similarity enhancing relationship; four are n.s.
	Total	22	
D. SES			
	Comparison	1	Present SES similarity enhances improvement
	Naturalistic	2	Present SES similarity enhances improvement in both studies
	Analogue/Process	7	Five favor SES similarity for enhancing relationship and reducing bias; two n.s.
	Total	10	

[a]Some studies have both process and outcome relevance.

developed for the older adult (e.g., Gallagher & Thompson, 1982; Yost, Allender, Beutler, & Chaisson-Stewart, 1983) to counterbalance a more long-standing emphasis upon specialized treatment programs for the young (e.g., Jesness, 1975).

In research on therapist age, samples representing a wide range of ages among both patients and therapists ideally would be investigated, statistically or methodologically controlling for the effect of experience and theoretical orientation. However, this degree of rigor has been difficult to accomplish in most research settings. Hence, many studies have used analogue populations and situations or have employed naturalistic designs. In a well-controlled naturalistic study of 20 patients, for example, Lubor-sky, Crits-Christoph, Alexander, Margolis, and Co-hen (1983a) explored the contribution of patients' and therapists' actual age similarity to the quality of the treatment relationship. Like many studies in this area, age was considered as an ancillary variable and was inspected apart from the main objectives of the study. The findings revealed that age similarity was positively related to the development of a help-ing treatment relationship. Age similarity was also found to be significantly correlated with composite measures of treatment outcome (Morgan, Lubor-sky, Crits-Cristoph, Curtis, & Soloman, 1982). While the failure to attend to relative age differences renders this study a weak test of the influence of patient and therapist age differences, the study was strengthened both by comparing contrasting groups of improved and unimproved patients and by the wide range of ages represented by both patients and therapists.

Dembo, Ikle, and Ciarlo (1983) also studied a large group of psychiatric outpatients and their therapists. Age similarity was one of several demo-graphic variables naturalistically studied. The au-thors defined age matching as patient and therapist dyads within 10 years of age of one another, without reference to which member of the dyad was the elder. Age difference did not exert a significant effect on treatment outcome as defined by emergency room visits, psychiatric admissions, clinician ratings, and patient ratings. The only significant effect of actual age differences was the observation that pa-tients in the 18-to-30-year range whose therapists were of a similar age reported less posttreatment psychological distress and isolation than did those patients whose therapists' ages were 10 or more years different from their own.

In one of the few matching studies of both actual and relative age differences, Karasu, Stein, and Charles (1979) compared 22 patients who were from 10 to 12 years younger than their therapists, 24 who were approximately the same ages as their therapists, and 22 who were from 14 to 30 years older than their therapists. The therapists, however, presented a restricted age range, with an upper limit of 36 years. Although the findings cannot be directly generalized to older therapist groups, they nonethe-less suggest that patients and therapists of similar ages engage in more productive treatment processes than those of different ages. Therapists rated pa-tients who were younger or similar in age to them-selves as less "sick" and more treatable and judged their prognoses to be better. Therapists had a de-cided preference for treating younger patients and, in fact, when patients were older than the therapists, dropout rates increased.

An advantage in favor of patient and therapist age similarity has also been observed in some studies of relatively young patients. For example, adolescents have been found to prefer and attach most easily to age-similar counselors when discussing personal problems (Getz & Miles, 1978; Lasky & Salomone, 1977). Older therapists may be preferred, however, for discussing career as opposed to personal prob-lems (Getz & Miles, 1978), which may account for many of the analogue findings that favor age dissim-ilarity among normal students, to whom such prob-lems may be especially salient (e.g., Celotta & Bode, 1982; Martin & Thomas, 1982; Simon, 1973). While subject analogue investigations have decided limita-tions and will not be considered in depth here, they may suggest that the type of problem presented is a signficant variable in determining the influence of patient and therapist age matches on psychother-apy. Similarly, patients' sex may also alter the influence of age differences. Female patients may especially prefer therapists who are older than them-selves (e.g., Donnan & Mitchell, 1979; Simons & Helms, 1976).

To date, very little is known about either the role of therapist age or relative age similarity among patient samples of older adults. Preference surveys suggest that older adults perceive young therapists to be insufficiently wise and too immature to be maximally helpful (e.g., Donnan & Mitchell, 1979), but these preferences may be partially attenuated when the effects of therapist credibility and status are partialed out (e.g., Lasky & Salomone, 1977). These are interesting topics deserving of additional consideration in view of the perspective differences that may color relationships between young thera-pists and more elderly patients. Troll and Nowak (1976) suggest that society imbues relatively con-sistent, negative, or aversive attitudes about ad-vancing age on its citizens. Confrontation with very elderly patients may either threaten or be of no interest to younger therapists (e.g., Lewis & Johan-sen, 1982). Martin and Prosen (1976) further suggest that communication in such dyads may be impaired because young therapists are still anticipating their future while older patients, themselves, may look at the future through a spectre of impending death and find solace in the past. Finally, young therapists have not experienced some of the processes of life that are relevant to older patients, and this may both impede the development of the relationship and retard psychotherapeutic change.

In summary, it appears that as a unidirectional concept, therapist age exerts only a weak effect on treatment outcome. Among younger patients with adjustment problems, however, the therapist of a similar age may have some modest advantage in preventing dropout. This influence may become stronger when it combines with the influences of variables that accumulate with age, such as experience. Under such circumstances, age similarity may exert a modest effect on improvement, but creative research endeavors are called for that partial out the effects of skill, experience, and type of problem in order to get a clearer view of the influence of absolute and relative age differences, especially among older patients.

Sex and Gender

Sex and gender are conceptually distinct. Gender refers to one's biological identification while one's sex includes the more subjective attributes of sexual attitudes and adopted sexual roles. While studies of sexual attitudes and roles routinely hold differences in biological gender constant, studies of gender seldom assess the contribution of sexual attitudes to the outcome differences that often distinguish male and female therapists. Ideally, research methodologies would distinguish among the influences of these interrelated concepts. Investigators should also be aware that cultural changes in attitudes toward sexuality and sexual roles over the past two decades have altered the influences exerted by both sex and gender variables.

Two decades of heightened sensitivity to sexism has stimulated active research into the effects of gender (e.g., Deaux, 1984) in psychotherapy. While Parloff, Waskow, and Wolfe (1978) reported three systematic studies on the effects of therapist gender on psychotherapy process and seven on psychotherapy outcome, the number of available studies has more than doubled over the past six years.

Unfortunately, most of the research in this area continues to employ naturalistic designs in which gender is explored as a variable ancillary to more systematically investigated characteristics or treatments. This limitation is compounded by the complexity with which gender or sexuality interacts with variables such as environment (Bloom, Weigel, & Trautt, 1977), experience (Cartwright & Lerner, 1963), or type of population and problem (Bernstein & Figioli, 1983; Lee, Hallberg, Jones, & Haase, 1980; Orlinsky & Howard, 1976).

In spite of these difficulties, the best controlled research investigations available consistently suggest that therapists' gender exerts a modest effect on the selection of patients, the nature of the therapeutic process, and therapeutic change. For example, Jones and Zoppel (1982) compared therapy processes and outcomes among four groups of contrasting patient–therapist gender combinations. Careful descriptions of therapists' experience levels and reasonable post hoc matching of the groups achieved a high level of sophistication for research in this area. Female therapists saw patients of both genders as having more sexual and relationship problems than did male therapists and also rated their patients as more improved on 5 of 11 outcome measures. Male therapists, on the other hand, perceived male and female patients differently. They rated female patients as significantly less improved than male patients. Moreover, reports of the former clients generally agreed with those of their therapists. That is, similar-gender dyads were rated as more helpful than opposite-gender dyads.

In another controlled assignment study, Blase (1979) considered all possible gender pairings and evaluated a diverse group of 40 psychiatric outpatients seen over the course of 10 treatment sessions. The results indicated that patients felt more satisfied at the end of treatment after having seen a therapist of their own gender. Few other outcome benefits of gender matching were observed, however.

The benefit of gender similarity has also been suggested by some naturalistic studies (e.g., Orlinsky & Howard, 1976). For example, Kirshner, Genack, and Hauser (1978) found that among patients seeking therapy at a university health service, female patients reported greater improvement than male patients, especially if seen by female therapists. In a similar correlational study that incorporated a population of clinical outpatients and highly experienced therapists, Kaschak (1978) found that same-sex dyads, especially those with female therapists, produced more favorable estimates of change than opposite-sex dyads.

In view of the foregoing findings, it is noteworthy that most comprehensive reviews have concluded that there are few observable effects of therapist gender or patient–therapist gender matching on treatment outcome (Cavenar & Werman, 1983; Mogul, 1982; Parloff et al., 1978; Zeldow, 1978). Nonsignificant effects have been found in regard to dropout and return rates to psychotherapy (Dembo et al., 1983; Krauskopf, Baumgardner, & Mandracchia, 1981; Rodolfa, Rapaport, & Lee, 1983), rehospitalization rates (Mintz, O'Brien, & Luborsky, 1976), marital satisfaction (Ganahl, 1982), therapist estimates of prognosis (Abramowitz et al., 1976) and length of time spent in therapy (Abramowitz, Davidson, Greene, & Edwards, 1980). Collectively, these findings suggest that while similar gender matchings may exert a statistically significant effect on psychotherapy process, research methodologies must be rather rigorous and well defined in order to allow this relatively modest effect to emerge as outcome differences. In part, the contradiction between the best and the usual finding can also be attributed to the very interesting observations of Fisher and Howard (1984). Utilizing a long-term, accumulating data pool, these authors examined changes in symptoms that accrued as a joint function of patient–therapist gender and the year in which the therapy was undertaken. The results suggested that simple gender matching exerted a rather direct influence on the outcome of studies conducted during the late 1960s. In the last decade, the amount of prior therapy and the nature of the issues under discussion have come to interact with gender match in rather complex ways. In other words, as attitudes toward gender roles have changed, the effect of therapist gender may be quite different depending upon the phase of therapy being observed. As sexual attitudes have become less stereotyped, gender seems to exert an increasingly complex or interactive effect on outcome.

Pursuing further the role of the internal attributes that may be reflected in therapist and patient gender, some investigators have studied the role of matching sexual attitudes and role identities. As a general rule, and quite paradoxically, dissimilarity rather than similarity on these dimensions seems to be attractive to patients. Feldstein (1979) determined that patients both were more favorably disposed to the therapy process and judged the therapist to be more accepting when therapists held a view of sexual roles that was at odds with the traditional, normative views of one's gender mates. On the other hand, of five studies that have related various sexual attitudes directly to psychotherapy outcome, two (Andrews, 1976; Morrow, 1980) produced nonsignificant results and three (Beutler, Pollack & Jobe, 1978; Brooks, 1981; Hart, 1981) suggested that various aspects of sexual-role attitude *similarity* facilitated therapy gain. In these outcome studies, however, sexual attitudes and sexual identities are often confounded. Brooks (1981), for example, distributed questionnaires to 675 lesbians. The questionnaires asked patients to indicate the gender and sex-role identities of their therapists. Three-fourths of the patients who reported becoming worse during their treatment indicated that their therapists were heterosexual males. The nonindependence between patient self-reports and patients' own gender and gender-role identities severely limits the conclusions of such studies.

Other studies suggest that patient's and therapist's acceptance of one another's sexual attitudes is important in facilitating global improvement. Beutler et al. (1978) observed that if the two members of the dyad expressed mutual acceptance of the sexual viewpoints of one another, global improvement was enhanced. In one of the few controlled comparisons of this issue, Hart (1981) randomly assigned 48 female patients to male therapists who presented either traditional or nontraditional sexual-role attitudes. Therapists who departed from the traditional sexual attitudes of males induced more positive therapy relationships and were particularly adept at illuminating sadness and retaining a treatment focus. These findings may suggest the importance of egalitarianism and role flexibility, rather than gender attitudes per se. In support of this viewpoint, Banikiotes and Merluzzi (1981) found that college female volunteers expressed more comfort in disclosing to sexually nontraditional, egalitarian counselors of both sexes, regardless either of their own sexual role orientation or of the type of problem they presented.

Considering the foregoing findings, Berzins (1975; Berzins, Welling, & Wetter, 1978) has suggested that the flexibility with which sexual-role attitudes are held (i.e., androgyny) might be a more important concept than gender itself for understanding therapist influences. While the relevance of androgyny has been seriously questioned as applied to clinical relationships (e.g., Gilbert, 1981; Taylor & Hall, 1982; Zeldow, 1982), it still represents a promising concept for those who wish to explore possible interactions between therapist gender and sexual traditionalism in psychotherapy research.

Overall, the current findings suggest that female therapists, first, and therapists of the patient's gender, second, facilitate treatment benefit, especially if these therapists present a nonstereotypic sexual viewpoint. Treatment outcome is less consistently affected by the therapist's gender and sexual-role identities. Additional research is needed to explore the possibility that egalitarianism rather than sexual attitudes or gender roles themselves provoke change. Moreover, the relative importance of sexual attitudes may extend to those of patients as underlined by the finding of Norkus (1976) that patients who were treated by the therapists of their preferred gender tended to improve somewhat more than patients who were paired with a therapist of a nonpreferred gender.

Ethnicity

In what may be the most thorough review of the status of race effects in psychotherapy to date, Abramowitz and Murray (1983) have observed that the conclusions reached in any review of this literature may reflect the race of the reviewer. White reviewers tend to minimize the effects of ethnic differences while black reviewers emphasize findings in which differences are found (e.g., Sattler, 1977, vs. Griffith & Jones, 1978). Certainly after such a conclusion, the current Anglo writers have deciphered these findings with some degree of hesitancy.

In exploring the role of therapist ethnicity, problems arise both with adequate sampling and failure to control potentially confounding variables. With regard to the former, the assessment of treatment-related improvements has been hampered by the frequent failure to consider all possible ethnic pairs. Some studies have considered only dissimilar ethnic matches (e.g., Williams, 1974); others have in-

cluded patient groups who varied in ethnicity but therapist groups who, for the most part, represented a single ethnic background (e.g., Banks, Berenson, & Carkhuff, 1967; Costello, Baillargeon, Biever, & Bennett, 1979; Proctor & Rosen, 1981); and still other studies have included samples of ethnically diverse therapists but ethnically homogeneous patients (e.g., Gardner, 1972; Heffernon & Bruehl, 1971; Terrell & Terrell, 1984). Firm conclusions are difficult to reach based upon such restrictive sampling. It is also difficult to interpret studies in which inordinate amounts of variance in ethnicity is allowed. For example, Neimeyer and Gonzales (1983) compared "white" and "nonwhite" clients at a university counseling center. Their sample of nonwhite clients, however, included blacks, Hispanics, and Asians, each of which may respond differently in therapy.

Confounding influences also derive from the failure to control or match patient groups on the basis of type or degree of disturbance, socioeconomic status, gender, and amount of therapy received. Virtually all studies of patient and therapist ethnicity matches are subject to criticism because of some or all of these contaminating variables. Since one is unable randomly to assign ethnicity, group comparison procedures with controlled assignment represent the most rigorous investigations available. Jones (1978), for example, selected a sample of female patients and male therapists. In spite of the systematic gender confound, this study implemented a number of important controls that make it stand out among those available. The black and white comparison groups were closely matched in an effort to control for the influence of socioeconomic background, age and education; a relatively homogeneous sample of patients was used; therapists were experienced and represented similar theoretical orientations; and treatment length was constant. Jones observed that while psychotherapy processes were benefited by similar ethnic pairs, neither dropout rates nor ratings of subjective improvement by the patients and therapists distinguished the various ethnic matchings. Among the most interesting findings, Jones noted that the quality of the treatment relationship varied as a joint function of the phase of treatment and the ethnic match of the participants, underlining the weakness of studies that have utilized only a single treatment interview as a method for estimating the value of ethnic matching (e.g., Banks, 1972; Proctor & Rosen, 1981).

With few exceptions, the findings of Jones are representative of most outcome research on therapist and patient ethnicity (e.g., Barrett & Wright, 1984). Neither other comparative (e.g., Costello et al., 1979; Heffernon & Bruehl, 1971; Neimeyer & Gonzales, 1983) nor weaker, naturalistic studies (e.g., Dembo et al., 1983) have consistently found substantial differences in treatment outcome as a function of patient and therapist ethnic matches. When differences have emerged, they suggest that dropout rates (e.g., Krebs, 1971; Terrell & Terrell, 1984; Yamamoto, James, Bloombaum, & Hattem, 1967) and lack of sensitivity to ethnic issues (e.g., Turner & Armstrong, 1981) characterize ethnically dissimilar treatment dyads. Nevertheless, similar ethnic matches have been found to characterize patients' preferences and to enhance patients' participation in the early stages of treatment (Banks, 1972; Banks et al., 1967; Bryson & Cody, 1973; Carkhuff & Pierce, 1967; Ewing, 1974; Gardner, 1972; Grantham, 1973; Proctor & Rosen, 1981). Only in relatively rare instances have similar ethnic matches failed to yield significant enhancement of patients' perceptions of or attraction to the therapy relationship (e.g., Cimbolic, 1972; Young, 1973). In a representative example, Neimeyer and Gonzales (1983) utilized a pre- and posttest comparison group design to explore differences between white and nonwhite therapists and clients. While they observed few differences in outcome as a function of the therapists' ethnicity, white clients who saw white therapists attributed significantly more power to the therapy than did any of the other ethnic matches. Indeed, when such differences do occur, they usually disappear by the end of 5 to 10 treatment sessions (e.g., Heffernon & Bruehl, 1971; Jones, 1978; Neimeyer & Gonzales, 1983) and are not usually observed in outcomes or during posttherapy follow-up periods (e.g., Costello et al., 1979; Dembo et al., 1983).

Comparing analogue and clinical studies, Abramowitz and Murray (1983) concluded that the preponderance of both suggest that there may be some benefit that accrues to therapy dropout rates and treatment processes from similar ethnic matches, but very little actual difference occurs in treatment outcomes among those who remain in treatment. We see little reason to depart from this conclusion. The influence of therapists' ethnic background on treatment, however, may also be manifest in other ways not directly observed in treatment process and outcome. For example, ethnic biases may dispose white therapists to overestimate psychopathology levels (Gynther, 1972, 1979) and both to underestimate prognoses (Goldstone, 1971) among blacks and to refer them to more restrictive or different forms of treatment (Krebs, 1971; Gynther, 1979; Seligman, 1968) than they do whites. Some research suggests, however, that differences in white therapists' perception may reflect meaningful differences in the adjustment or prognoses of black and white patients (Butcher, Braswell, & Raney, 1983). It is uncertain, then, the degree to which the viewpoints of white therapists are prejudicially distorted or accurate. It may be important, therefore, both to control for ethnic variables in research (e.g., Barrett & Wright, 1984) and to seek further understanding of the role played by the therapist's attitudes toward the patient's ethnicity.

In order to respond to this latter need, Terestman, Miller, and Weber (1974) differentiated between therapists who were and were not effective at treating low socioeconomic status, minority patients and compared ratings of their psychotherapy skills. Supervisors gave "good" therapists higher marks for sensitivity and the ability to identify racial and socioeconomic class differences than "poor" therapists. In a different approach, Yamamoto et al. (1967) assessed the strength of white therapists' ethnocentric attitudes, revealing that those who maintained high levels of ethnocentrism engaged black patients for shorter treatment durations than did low ethnocentric therapists.

Collectively, the foregoing findings suggest the value of attitudinal flexibility and of being attuned to ethnic differences in promoting treatment outcome. Although ethnic similarity may exert a positive effect on premature termination, further exploration of this possibility is needed along with efforts to reveal the attitudinal characteristics of patients and therapists that may determine this effect. Research might then be productively devoted both to methods of patient–therapist assignment and to therapy preparatory methods for overcoming disruptive ethnic attitudes.

Socioeconomic Status

The role of therapist socioeconomic status (SES) has received little direct attention. A few studies have explored psychotherapy outcome as a function of the therapists's current SES status (e.g., Carkhuff & Pierce, 1967); others have given attention to the therapist's SES origins (Hill, Howard & Orlinsky, 1970; Kandel, 1966; Mitchell & Atkinson, 1983; Mitchell & Namenek, 1970); and still other studies have drawn conclusions based on sociodemographic similarities assumed to reflect some aspects of socioeconomic background or status (e.g., Holzman, 1962; Luborsky et al., 1980; Saeger, 1979). More frequently, researchers have addressed methods for working with low SES groups (see Chapter 17 in this volume; Goldstein, 1971; Schneiderman, 1965; Warren & Rice, 1972). This lack of consistency in the approach to and definition of therapist SES may reflect uncertainty about the mechanism through which SES variables exert an impact on the treatment relationship. Perhaps, as well, to the observer, therapists represent a seemingly homogeneous and unresearchable socioeconomic grouping (Heitler, 1976; Lorion, 1974). Research in this area would be well served by emphasizing a distinction between current socioeconomic *status* and *prior background.*

The most representative studies of therapist SES are naturalistic investigations in which patient and therapist SES origins or status are among numerous variables assessed retrospectively (e.g., Carkhuff & Pierce, 1967; Gardner, 1972). Many of these studies, unfortunately, are hampered by nonobjective assessments of patient–therapist SES similarity, usually based either upon the assumption of therapists' SES homogeneity (e.g., Gardner, 1972) or on assessments of the patients' SES background as derived from reports by therapists or external observers (Gottschalk, Mayerson, & Gottlieb, 1967; Kandel, 1966). The problems encountered by such studies are underlined in a series of comparison group studies by Mitchell and his colleagues. Mitchell and Namenek (1970) observed a significant tendency for therapists from low SES backgrounds to report that a high percentage of their patients were also from low SES backgrounds, relative to the reports of therapists from middle-class backgrounds. Recognizing the potential for bias in therapists' reports, Mitchell and Atkinson (1983) obtained the cooperation of 48 high and low SES therapists and

98 of their patients for a follow-up investigation. This study is one of the few available that has both included an independent definition of patient SES and distinguished between therapist status and background. Therapists were asked to identify "typical" clients in their caseloads and SES information was obtained directly from these patients and compared with therapist ratings. No relationships were observed between patient social class and therapist caseloads when patient social class was judged on the basis of data provided by the patient rather than the therapist. Neither were significant effects of therapists' current status obtained. On the strength of these findings, the authors (Mitchell & Atkinson, 1983) argue that there is no basis for the conclusion that therapist biases and distortions affect the actual selection and assignment of patients to therapists, although therapists' own SES background distorts the view they have of their patients' social status.

Current research provides only indirect inferences about the influence of therapist SES on treatment effectiveness. For example, in his report of the Penn Psychotherapy Project, Luborsky et al. (1980) analyzed several patient and therapist variables in an effort to predict improvement rates. Sociodemographic similarity failed to relate strongly to treatment outcome. On the other hand, Holzman (1962) evaluated patients and therapists along a broadly based dimension of social similarity and observed that similarity of sociodemographic views and backgrounds was associated with improvement. Previous reviews, which have concluded that the SES background of the therapist is an inconsequential factor in treatment outcome (e.g., Lorian, 1973), have usually treated psychotherapy process and outcome alike. At this point, such a conclusion is not entirely warranted, even though most of the available evidence favors SES similarity. In the absence of more outcome studies, all that can be said with confidence is that therapists who present egalitarian attitudes toward low socioeconomic status patients are likely to facilitate improvement (e.g., Howard et al., 1970; Lerner, 1972, 1973). Hence, we must accept Parloff et al.'s (1978) conclusion as still valid: Few studies are available by which the relationship between therapists' socioeconomic status or background and treatment outcome can be adequately assessed. There continues to be a need for systematic and clear research on the effects of therapist socioeconomic background and patient–therapist SES similarity on actual treatment changes.

INFERRED, INTERNAL, EXTRATHERAPY CHARACTERISTICS

The therapist characteristics explored in this section are those inferred to characterize enduring aspects of the therapists' inner experience. We have already considered some similar variables in our discussion of sexual and democratic attitudes. Attitudes as well as personality traits are constructs indirectly observed on the basis of enduring behaviors and self-reported experiences. They are assumed to characterize the therapist in lifestyle patterns both within and outside of therapy. Among the inferred traits considered to be most relevant to therapeutic effectiveness are therapist personality styles, emotional adjustment, and beliefs or value systems. Table 7.2 summarizes the data relative to these variables, following the format of Table 7.1. For simplicity and where applicable, the results of experimentally controlled and group comparison studies are reported together, since there are only very few instances of studies with true experimental methodologies and because the major conclusions are identical in all instances.

In reviewing this literature, it is interesting to note that early investigations of internal attributes relied largely upon unidirectional designs in which one or several therapist variables were correlated with therapy outcome independent of variations among patients. Such investigations made the relatively simplistic assumption that certain internal characteristics of the therapist were universally beneficial. Over the past two decades, investigators have gradually begun to explore patterns of patient and therapist interaction. Some of these more recent investigators have matched patients and therapists on the same or similar dimensions in a manner not unlike many studies that we reviewed of externally observed therapist dimensions. These *symmetrical* research designs contrast with others that have explored patient and therapist matching along different dimensions, assuming that optimal levels of compatibility require therapists to possess one trait and patients another (e.g., compatibility between therapist control and patient dependency). These

latter methodologies have been called *nonsymmetrical* (e.g., Berzins, 1977).

Personality Patterns

There are relatively few studies in current psychotherapy literature that employ the degree of methodological sophistication required to determine either the personality dimensions on which therapists might best be matched with their patients or the magnitude of influence created by those personality variables. One can choose to explore global personality concepts at the risk of being too inclusive, or relatively specific ones at the risk of overlooking more salient but unrecognized ones. The investigator is also confronted with the problem of deciding, on some a priori clinical or empirical basis the patient variables with which therapist and patient characteristics should be matched or compared. A well-conceived psychotherapy research program on therapist personality would investigate concepts that have a sound rational or theoretical basis and from which clearly defined hypotheses about the relationships of these variables to treatment process and outcome could be developed. Since such concepts are inferred, it is conceivable that selective information about the therapist could be given to patients before treatment in order to provide partial control over the attributed trait. This procedure would approximate an experimental manipulation of the therapist's personality contribution, at least in the beginning stages of therapy. Alternatively, studies employing controlled assignment of patients to therapists of contrasting personality characteristics would also provide important information about therapist influences.

The most methodologically sound comparison study available is still the Indiana Matching Project (Berzins, 1977). In this four-year study, matching dimensions were defined through factor analytic procedures, utilizing standard personality measures applied naturalistically to both therapists and patients. The initial sample of over 700 subjects was recruited from the Indiana University Student Health Clinic and was composed of student clients who received crisis-oriented, time-limited counseling. The therapists were selected for their similar philosophy and commitment to the treatment model. A variety of rationally selected and theoretically relevant patient and therapist variables were

TABLE 7.2   Inferred, Internal, Extratherapy Characteristics

Variable	Study Type/Quality	*n*	Summary of Findings[a]
A. Personality (general)			
	Comparison	1	Favors dissimilarity
	Naturalistic	7	Three favor complex relationships; two n.s.; two favor similarity
	Analogue/Process	1	Favors dissimilarity
	Total	9	
(A−B type × pt. diagnosis)			
	Comparison	5	Three n.s.; two favor match
	Naturalistic	5	Three n.s.; one partially favors match; one interacts with other variables
	Analogue/Process	3	Two favor A−B match in therapy process; one favors match for referral
	Total	13	
B. Well-being			
	Comparison	2	Both favor well-being
	Naturalistic	3	Two favor well-being; one n.s.
	Analogue/Process	5	All favor well-being and personal therapy
	Total	10	
C. Attitudes & Values (religious beliefs)			
	Experimental	2	All n.s. but favor ability to accept patients' beliefs
	Comparison	2	
	Naturalistic	1	Nonsignificant
	Analogue/Process	6	Five n.s.; one favors similarity
	Total	11	
(general attitudes)			
	Comparison	4	Two favor dissimilarity; two favor acceptance; one favors similarity
	Naturalistic	14	Five favor dissimilarity; four favor similarity; four n.s.; one complex
	Analogue/Process	7	Six favor dissimilarity for attitude change; six favor similarity for relationship enhancement
	Total	25	
(democratic attitudes)			
	Comparison	1	Favors democratic attitudes
	Naturalistic	2	One favors democratic attitudes; one n.s.
	Analogue/Process	0	
	Total	3	

[a]Some studies have both process and outcome relevance.

assessed, from which eight patient and six therapist variables were derived. Of special note, methodologically, the therapist variables were independently defined on a large, representative sample of professional therapists prior to implementation. A random assignment procedure provided data for the development of a matching algorithm, which was then cross-validated in a second sample utilizing controlled assignment procedures. The most consistent and persuasive results suggested that therapists who were most effective with dependent, submissive, inhibited, and attachment-oriented patients were those who were autonomy oriented, dominant, and individualistic in their own views and personality styles. Interestingly, the opposite relationship was also observed. That is, dependent and submissive therapists did best with autonomy-oriented and individualistic patients. Complementarity pervaded other matching dimensions as well, particularly among male patients. Indeed, the little evidence that emerged for the benefits of personality similarity were observed only in the social roles of female patients and their therapists.

In an example of a well-controlled, unidirectional study, Antonuccio, Lewinsohn, and Steinmetz (1982) investigated 106 depressed subjects as they responded to a highly controlled cognitive-behavioral therapy intervention. The prominent methodological features of this study included the selection of patients who were homogeneous on a number of dimensions and the establishment of control over the experience and training levels of the therapists by providing criterion-specific training. With these variables controlled, none of a variety of therapist personality characteristics correlated significantly with measures of treatment change even though patients' depression levels did improve from pre- to posttreatment and to follow-up.

In a naturalistic, nonsymmetrical matching investigation, Gunderson (1978) asked the therapists of 50 schizophrenic inpatients to rate their patients on 10 dimensions while two experienced clinicians rated therapist qualities. Therapists were rated for activity levels, gentleness, grandfatherliness, and various aspects of comfort, optimism, and emotional composure. Patients' qualities included passivity, hostility, psychological symptoms, and defensive styles. Raters were asked to predict the most compatible patient and therapist matches on the basis of these variables. Ratings of compatibility successfully predicted therapists' ratings of benefit in 31 of 49 patient–therapist dyads. Beneficial psychotherapy processes and outcomes were highest among therapists who were rated as comfortable, especially when their patients experienced intense affect. Dissimilarity between therapists and clients was observed in composure and anxiety levels— emotionally composed therapists did best with anxious patients.

A variety of symmetrical studies have suggested that dissimilarity between patients and therapists on dimensions of cognitive style and global personality may enhance aspects of the therapeutic relationship and outcome (e.g., Mendelsohn & Geller, 1967); however, this relationship has not been consistent enough to be entirely persuasive. On the basis of a complex factorial analysis of matching variables, for example, Dougherty (1976) concluded that no simple dimension of similarity or difference could describe effective patient–therapist combinations. Such findings led Parloff et al. (1978) to conclude that there was little evidence to demonstrate that either similarity or dissimilarity between patient and therapist personality styles was consistently associated with patient improvement. Similarly, Beutler (1981) summarized 18 outcome studies in which symmetrical comparisons of patients and therapists were made on global personality dimensions; only four of these studies suggested that initial patient and therapist similarity was related to subsequent improvement and five suggested that dissimilarity was associated with improvement. Indeed, discrepant findings frequently emerged from the same research groups (e.g., Carson & Heine, 1962, vs. Carson & Llewellyn, 1966; Mendelsohn & Geller, 1963, vs. Mendelsohn & Geller, 1967). The most frequent findings obtained a very complex or curvilinear relationship (e.g., Carson & Heine, 1962) between similarity and improvement.

Some studies have targeted more specific and narrowly defined patient and therapist dimensions than the global dimensions reviewed in the foregoing. Examples of this work are found in the large body of research on the A–B psychotherapy dimension. This originally promising line of investigation began with the observation (Whitehorn & Betz, 1960) that "A-type" therapists, who were characterized as humanistic and person oriented (Johnson, Workman, Neville, & Beutler, 1973; Razin, 1977; Stoltenberg & Dixon, 1983), were more effective in treating schizophrenic patients than were "B-type" therapists, who were characterized as authoritarian, mechanically inclined, and problem focused (Stephens, Shaffer, & Zlotowitz, 1975). This original observation was subsequently followed by the observation that B-type therapists were more effective than A-types with outpatient neurotics (McNair, Callahan, & Lorr, 1962). Several early theoretical and empirical reviews (e.g., Carson, 1967; Silverman, 1967) expressed hope that the A−B typology would integrate disparate bodies of psychotherapy research. More recent reviews, however, have consistently observed that matching on the basis of patient diagnosis and therapist A−B types produce positive effects on relationship qualities and referral patterns but inconsistent and usually inconsequential effects on outcome (e.g., Beutler, Johnson, Neville, & Workman, 1972; Beutler et al., 1973b; King & Blaney, 1977). Nonsignificant findings have been obtained in relatively large-scale studies of schizophrenic inpatients (Tuma, May, Yale, & Forsythe, 1978a), of largely neurotic outpatients (Fiester & Rudestam, 1975), and in samples that included both psychiatric inpatients and outpatients similar to those on whom the original results were obtained (e.g., Patterson & Heilbron, 1978; Young, Glick, Hargraves, Braff, & Drues, 1979).

In spite of obtaining nonsignificant effects in their general sample, Patterson and Heilbron (1978) found that among a subgroup of nonmedicated patients, compatible matches of both types produced significantly higher improvement ratings than noncompatible matches. Perhaps the advent of psychoactive medications has precipitated the demise of an effect that was of such a small magnitude that it could be observed only in quite large groups of severely distressed patients.

Unfortunately, research in this area has been plagued by the lack of a clear definition of what constitutes A and B types and a similar lack of reliability in establishing patient diagnoses. A large number of therapists can be classified as neither A nor B types, and it is possible that A−B scores reflect different aspects of personality depending upon various extraneous variables, such as sex and family background (e.g., Dent & Furse, 1978; Patterson &

Heilbron, 1978). In one of the clearer tests of the interactive hypothesis, Matthews and Burkhart (1977) obtained some support for the effectiveness of A-type therapists among schizophrenic patients, but they were unable to support the contention that outcome is improved among B-type therapists treating neurotic outpatients. Other authors have maintained that A-type therapists have the most clearly established improvement rates across patient groups and have suggested that the A−B dimension may reflect general therapist skill levels rather than a therapist type (e.g., Chartier & Weiss, 1974; Stoltenberg & Dixon, 1983). Still others have observed that those who can be classified as neither A- nor B-types may be more effective than either of their counterparts (e.g., Fiester & Rudestam, 1975).

Collectively, the influence of the therapist's personality on psychotherapy is inconclusive. The best matching studies available suggest that dissimilarity in certain interpersonal and cognitive styles may facilitate treatment process and outcome. This has not been observed to represent a consistently strong or reliable finding, however, and probably does not account for a great deal of the benefit derived from psychotherapy. It is unlikely that any single dimension of personality or personality similarity is a major facilitator or inhibitor of therapy benefit.

Efforts to look at the influence of matching patients and therapists on complex, global personality variables have not yielded much more consistent results. For example, while the most highly controlled studies on psychotherapy process suggest that matching on the A−B and patient diagnostic dimensions may have impact on the nature of the therapeutic relationship, one must conclude with Cox (1978) that there is no substantial evidence to indicate that the A−B dimension is a meaningful contributor to psychotherapy outcome. This may be an area of research that has outlived its contribution to knowledge.

Emotional Well-being

Research on the influence of therapist emotional well-being is colored by a variety of social, ethical, and moral concerns. This fact becomes apparent when one considers the probable consequence if we were to discover that therapist level of psychopathology had no significant effect on treatment. Would anyone be more likely than now to encourage the emotionally distressed to become psychotherapists?

Because there is no consistently agreed-upon definition of mental health, the influence of therapist emotional well-being has typically been addressed after the fact and indirectly through naturalistic studies of emotional "disturbance." In many of these studies, therapist disturbance levels are defined in ways that are not independent of the treatment itself (e.g., therapist disturbance is defined through analyses of therapy verbalizations). This procedure may spuriously increase the probability of obtaining significant effects. The careful investigator must also distinguish between emotional disturbance and characteristics of personality. This distinction is reflected in the difference between coping styles (a personality construct) and coping adequacy (an index of psychopathology).

If benefit accrues to psychotherapists who are well adjusted, personal psychotherapy may also enhance therapeutic effectiveness. Therapists believe that both receiving personal psychotherapy (e.g., Buckley, Karasu, & Charles, 1981; Garfield & Kurtz, 1976; Prochaska & Norcross, 1983) and conducting it (Farber, 1983) facilitate the establishment of helpful treatment roles and outcomes. However, research on this issue is contaminated by how effective the therapy may have been and how disturbed the therapist remains. Moreover, the fact that some therapists seek treatment while others do not may reflect important differences in self-confidence, faith in psychotherapy, or motivation, which may contaminate group comparisons.

These issues underline the need for creative research endeavors to control for amount and type of psychopathology, the patient population studied, and the ethical and social standards by which emotional well-being is defined. While experimental manipulation of emotional well-being is impractical and controlled assignment has seldom been attempted, there have been a few relatively well-designed naturalistic studies of this issue. For example, the study of therapist variables by Antonuccio et al. (1982), reported in the previous section, found a nonsignificant relationship between therapist neuroticism levels and either global or specific measures of patient change. Similarly, in a creative analogue effort to circumvent some of the problems produced by global concepts such as "neuroticism," Donner and Schonfield (1975) observed that student therapists

who presented high conflict levels were more prone to respond with anxiety to depressive statements from their clients than were student therapists who had low levels of conflict. Cutler (1958) also investigated moment-to-moment changes in therapists' responses as a function of whether or not the topics being addressed reflected areas of conflict for the therapists. Conflict areas that characterized two psychotherapists were defined in advance of treatment, and the therapists' responses were evaluated when these topics were discussed. When addressing issues reflective of their own conflictual areas, the therapists resorted to narcissistic and ego-oriented responses rather than patient-oriented interventions.

In other studies, therapist distress and disturbance levels have been found to be negatively related to (1) effective handling of patients' disclosures (Cutler, 1958), (2) the emotional climate of the relationship (Wogan, 1970), and (3) other aspects of therapist relationship and treatment skill (Bergin & Jasper, 1969; Bergin & Soloman, 1970; Donner & Schonfield, 1975).

One of the few outcome-focused approaches to the problem of emotional well-being was undertaken by Garfield and Bergin (1971), who observed the effectiveness of therapists who had varying elevations on selected MMPI subscales. The results suggested relatively clear differences favoring improvement in depression and defensiveness among patients whose therapists had the lowest levels of emotional disturbance. Most major reviews (e.g., Bergin, 1966; Lambert & Bergin, 1983; Parloff et al., 1978) and a preponderance of available studies support this conclusion (e.g., Bergin & Jasper, 1969; Ricks, 1974; Wogan, 1970). Most notably, Vandenbos and Karon (1971) observed that independent estimates of therapist pathogenesis were negatively related to effectiveness of treatment among schizophrenic patients, and Anchor (1977) determined that therapist personality integration was positively associated with patient willingness to remain in treatment.

The relationship between therapist personal psychotherapy and subsequent therapeutic effectiveness is less clear. In part, this lack of clarity may reflect the confounding effect of therapist emotional disturbance with the effectiveness of the treatment provided to the therapists. Moreover, most of these studies have investigated psychotherapy processes rather than outcome. Nonetheless, these findings support the general viewpoint held by psychotherapists: personal psychotherapy improves therapist self-esteem, work functioning, and ability to establish empathic and warm treatment relationships (e.g., Buckley et al., 1981; Guild, 1969). Interestingly, however, Buckley et al.'s (1981) survey of therapists revealed that at least 20 percent experienced some negative effects, which ostensibly were also a result of their personal psychotherapy experiences. Disrupted marital relationships, increased emotional withdrawal, and heightened distress were among the disturbances listed.

Peebles (1980) directly observed therapeutic transactions of student therapists who were currently in psychotherapy, comparing these to those of student therapists not receiving personal therapy. He observed that subjective distress levels were relatively higher among those in the former group. Although discomfort was not consistently reflected in the quality of treatment conducted by the therapists in this study, others (e.g., Garfield & Bergin, 1971) have found negative relationships between amount of personal therapy received by therapists and treatment effectiveness. Overall, a very mixed picture of this relationship has emerged in outcome literature as attested to by the review of Greenberg and Staller (1981). These authors found two studies that hinted at a positive relationship between personal therapy and outcome, four that indicated that there was no significant difference in effectiveness rates, and two that suggested a negative effect of personal psychotherapy on subsequent outcome. Therefore, while the best available literature suggests that the therapists' emotional well-being at least modestly facilitates both effective treatment processes and outcomes, the evidence does not consistently support the value of personal psychotherapy. Moreover, we must agree with Barrett and Wright (1984) in concluding that there has been little research in the past decade to clarify this issue.

Attitudes and Values

The importance of studying therapist attitudes and values is underlined in the observation that these beliefs influence the attitudes and belief systems of receptive patients (e.g., Beutler, 1971a, 1971b, 1979a, 1979b; Frank, 1973; Goldstein & Simonson, 1971; Goldstein, Heller & Sechrest, 1966;

Strong, 1968). In exploring the role of therapist belief systems and values in psychotherapy, a number of very salient and unique problems emerge for the psychotherapy researcher. First, since there is no consensual definition of belief, attitude, and value, operationalizing these concepts presents a significant challenge. Classically, beliefs are considered to be cognitive concepts, but attitudes and values are assumed to be reflected in feelings and behavior as well as in cognitions. Yet beliefs, behaviors, and feelings do not correspond closely, magnifying these definitional problems. Additionally, it is unlikely that all of one's beliefs or attitudes have impact on the therapy process in the same way. A theoretical or conceptual model is necessary in order to direct the researcher toward an exploration of the most promising and relevant of these concepts.

Research in this area is also confronted with the difficulty of assessing cause and effect relationships. Reviews on the topic, for example, suggest that there is a consistent and often strong relationship between convergence of patients' and therapists' belief and value systems, on one hand, and subsequent psychotherapy improvement, on the other (e.g., Beutler, 1979a, 1981). It is difficult to determine, however, whether this convergence *produces* improvement or is simply a reflection of other processes, some of which may be used to index improvement. While some efforts to predict improvement have suggested that initial patient and therapist attitudinal or value dissimilarity facilitates convergence (e.g., Beutler, 1979a, 1981), the investigator must beware of potential artifactual relationships in this process. For example, if patients and therapists are assessed on similar dimensions, attitude convergence may reflect only the amount of attitude change possible. Patients and therapists who are dissimilar have more room for movement than those who are similar. Statistical corrections for this artifact must be employed.

Finally, it is extremely difficult to conduct clinically relevant experimental studies in which therapists' attitudes are controlled. The short-term effects of therapist-expressed beliefs that occur in laboratory settings may have little relevance to the types of changes associated with improvement in psychotherapy. One is usually confined, therefore, to using the less stringent methodologies of contrasting groups or naturalistic investigations.

In an effort to address the need to specify potentially relevant attitudes and belief systems, research has begun to explore the controversial role of therapist religious and personal values (e.g., Bergin, 1980; Humphries, 1982; Henning & Tirrell, 1982). Perhaps this shift of emphasis has been spurred by the advent of cognitive therapy and its emphasis upon planned changes in belief systems. In any case, many authors are urging therapists both to attend to their own religious and attitudinal systems and to be aware of the potential value of those of their patients. Fortunately, there are also a few systematically controlled, experimental investigations of religious values in clinically relevant psychotherapy environments and populations by which we might determine whether these cautions are warranted. In one of these, Propst (1980) selected a relatively homogeneous group of depressed religious females and employed a well-defined form of cognitive therapy to explore interventions designed either to be consistent with or discrepant with the patients' religious beliefs. Patient congruent cognitive reframing emphasized religious principles while incongruent interventions were designed to represent the more usual, rational interpretations that are given to depressive distortions by cognitive therapists. Consistently better results were obtained with religiously congruent cognitive injunctions than with religiously incongruent ones, even though the therapists in this study were described as "nonreligious." In a subsequent investigation, Propst, Ostrom, and Watkins (1984) repeated the process utilizing both religious and nonreligious therapists. Subjects for this study were a closely monitored and carefully selected homogeneous sampling of religious individuals presenting major depression or neurotic depressive disturbances. Patients were randomly assigned either to a standard cognitive therapy regimen, a cognitive therapy program that employed a religious value framework, traditional pastoral care, or to a waiting-list control group. Religiously congruent cognitive therapy was again found to be most effective, whether employed by religious or nonreligious therapists. It might be concluded that the therapists' particular religious belief is not a major determiner of treatment outcome if the therapist can accept and work within the patients' religious belief systems. However, this conclusion is attenuated somewhat because the rates of therapist acceptance of and similarity to patient belief systems were not assessed in this study.

Additional research in the area of therapist attitudes, values, and religious beliefs has focused on defining areas of agreement and disagreement between the usual patient's and therapist's belief systems. While studies of this type frequently observe a relative lack of religiosity among psychotherapists vis-á-vis their patients (e.g., Bergin, 1980; Nix, 1978), these assumed differences have resulted in conclusions that have ranged from the suggestion that patients' religious beliefs are an untapped resource for the practitioner (e.g., Bergin, 1980; Henning & Tirrell, 1982), through the argument that these beliefs may be irrelevant to psychotherapy (e.g., Beit-Hallahmi, 1975), to the assertion that religious beliefs are damaging to patients (Ellis, 1962). Empirically, there appear to be more areas of patient–therapist value similarity than there are of value difference (e.g., Beutler et al., 1978) and there is little support for the point of view that either patients or therapists prefer to engage in treatment (Hill, Howard, & Orlinsky, 1970; Kandel, 1966; Lewis, 1983; Marx & Spray, 1972) or respond better to treatment (e.g., Lewis, 1983; Propst, 1980; Propst et al., 1984; Wadsworth & Checketts, 1980) with individuals who have similar religious and value backgrounds. One must be cautious about accepting a conclusion of nonsignificance, however, because of the possibility that samples of patients are universally constricted in these studies. Patients whose religious beliefs are very discrepant from those held by most psychotherapists may seek psychological assistance from religious leaders rather than from professional therapists.

Direct explorations of global belief similarity typically employ naturalistic or contrasting group designs with or without controlled patient assignment. Beutler (1971b) explored "attitudinal acceptability" between patients and therapists in an effort to devise a means by which patients and therapists could be preassigned to compatible dyads. If therapists' evaluative and religious attitudes initially fell within patients' range of acceptability, the attitudes were subsequently perceived by the patient to be more similar to his or her own than they actually were and the patient was increasingly prone to adopt the therapist's beliefs. This process was not significantly related to estimates of improvement, however. Beutler, Jobe, and Elkins (1974) later found that patients who were able to initially accept those attitudes of their therapists that were judged to represent a medium level of relevance to personal identity issues produced higher rates of improvement than patients who rejected these attitudes. This latter finding was later confirmed across a wide range of attitudes and was found to be characteristic of both individual and group therapy (Beutler, 1979b). Finally, Beutler et al. (1978) compared two methods of matching patients' and therapists' preferred belief systems prior to treatment. Utilizing a matched comparisons procedure, it was observed that estimates of improvement were more dependent on the therapists' ability to accept patients' preferred beliefs than vice versa. Patients, in contrast, felt most positively toward therapists who rejected some of their belief systems and, over the course of therapy, tended to acquire even these latter beliefs of their therapists. This finding has been partially replicated with theory-relevant psychotherapy concepts as well (e.g., Charone, 1981).

The preponderance of studies investigating the changes induced by general value differences indicate that initial patient and therapist dissimilarity of attitudes and belief systems are associated with patient beliefs converging on those of their therapist (Beutler, 1971a, 1971b; Beutler et al., 1974; Beutler, Johnson, Neville, Elkins, & Jobe, 1975; Beutler, Arizmendi, Crago, Shanfield, & Hagaman, 1983; Charone, 1981). This finding seems to hold even when statistical procedures are employed to control both for regression toward the mean and the amount of change possible (e.g. Beutler et al., 1978, 1983). However, in his review of 21 studies, Beutler (1981) found only 5 that suggested that dissimilarity in patient and therapist beliefs was associated with improvement. Twelve studies found that patient–therapist belief similarity was facilitative of treatment gain and two obtained nonsignificant results. Unfortunately, the six subject analogue studies in this series were all counted among those that favored similarity. Hence, the available evidence is inconclusive in establishing the presence of a relationship between initial belief similarity and subsequent improvement among clinical populations.

The lack of consistency observed in the foregoing probably reflects the need to explore very specific attitudes and values rather than general attitudinal similarity. In an effort to do so, Arizmendi, Beutler, Shanfield, Crago, and Hagaman (1985) undertook a microscopic analysis of the data reported by Beutler et al. (1983). In this naturalistic investigation, it was determined that improvement could be statistically described by a complex relationship of both specific value similarities and differences. Similarity of academic, intellectual, and social values combined with dissimilarity of interpersonal, sexual and attachment values to define over one-fourth of the variance in subsequent improvement estimates.

Unidirectional explorations of specific attitudes have also suggested that therapists who hold democratic attitudes are especially effective in working with low socioeconomic status patients (cf. Chapter 17). Lerner (1972), for example, demonstrated that therapists' commitment to democratic values significantly facilitated treatment gain among a group of black, lower-class individuals who were severely psychologically impaired. This finding was subsequently cross-validated among a group of 30 less impaired patients and their 14 therapists (Lerner, 1973). The only study available of the role of such attitudes in a general psychiatric population yielded nonsignificant findings (Martin & Sterne, 1976), as assessed both at the time of discharge and nine months later.

In summary, there is support for the observation that therapists and patients have different belief systems, particularly around issues of religion and morality. On the other hand, there is little evidence to suggest that patients systematically seek out psychotherapists with whom they share common belief systems. This latter conclusion must be tempered with the possibility that many religious patients seek treatment from religious rather than mental health sources. Once in treatment, however, there is apparently a decided tendency for successful therapy dyads to be associated with the patients' acquiring therapists' belief systems, both about religious and moral attitudes and about more general concepts as well. This convergence process appears to be strongly related to the amount of initial attitudinal dissimilarity that exists between patient and therapist, but such dissimilarity does not, in and of itself, predict psychotherapy improvement. Improvement may be a more complex function of initial similarities and dissimilarities of specific attitudes that are yet to be clearly defined. The studies in this area that have attempted to apply experimental manipulation or controlled assignment to contrasting groups suggest both that therapists' acceptance of patients' attitudes and values facilitates improvement and that providing treatments and interventions that are consistent with patients' values and beliefs enhances treatment outcome, even when therapists and patients do not adhere to the same belief systems.

INFERRED, THERAPY-SPECIFIC CHARACTERISTICS

Among the most productive areas of research for three decades has been that conducted on therapy-specific attitudes and internal attributes. These therapist characteristics include attitudes conveyed by the relationship, social influence attributes, and treatment expectancies. Table 7.3 previews, in summary form, the results of studies on these variables.

Collectively, the variables considered in this section are typically referred to as "nonspecific" (e.g., Frank, 1973). That is, they are thought to characterize most effective psychotherapy relationships but are not thought to be associated with specific theories or interventions. Several authors (e.g., Kazdin, 1979; Wilkins, 1979, 1984) have observed that the term *nonspecific* is both limiting and misleading. To suggest that a therapist variable is "nonspecific" often carries the connotation that it is irrelevant. The very use of the term *nonspecific* may direct research efforts away from studies of how these variables interact with and are influenced by therapists' theoretical viewpoints (cf. Cornsweet, 1983). Moreover, the designation of what variables are included under this label varies from one theory to another. Kazdin (1979) proposes that we consider these variables to represent *common* treatment factors in order to emphasize that they are not unique to specific theoretical interventions but may, nonetheless, be curative factors inherent to most therapeutic activities. Although relabeling does not eliminate the ambiguity of these attributes, it may allow us to emphasize their potential importance and generality while at the same time exploring their interface with more technical and theory-specific interventions (cf. Sweet, 1984). This emphasis may be particularly relevant in view of the belief that common variables account for a much larger percentage of therapeutic change than those derived from specific interven-

tions and theories (e.g., Frank, 1973; Lambert & DeJulio, 1978).

Relationship Attitudes

Rogers (1957; Rogers, Gendlin, Kiesler, & Truax, 1967) originally proposed that there were four "facilitative" therapist attitudes (accurate empathy, nonpossessive warmth, congruence, unconditional positive regard) that were necessary and sufficient to induce psychotherapeutic gain. The importance of such qualities have subsequently been almost universally accepted by all psychotherapies, with varying levels of emphasis. Since these attitudes are inferred qualities and are typically measured within the context of specific psychotherapy relationships, however, a number of very important issues face researchers in this area. Among the most salient of these challenges is the task of determining what portion of the attributed therapeutic attitude is a function of the therapist and what portion might best be attributed either to the patient's initiating behavior patterns or to a specific patient—therapist dyad. Gurman (1977), for example, has suggested that relationship attitudes are more a reflection of the patient than of the therapist and has seriously questioned the value of assessing such qualities by independent observers.

A related question confronting psychotherapy research in this area has to do with issues of measurement and reliability. Chinsky and Rappaport (1970), for example, have suggested that the reliability estimates of external ratings of relationship attitudes are artificially exaggerated both by statistical artifact and by rater memory. Several authors (Beutler et al., 1973a; Cicchetti & Ryan, 1976; Gurman, 1973; Mintz & Luborsky, 1971; VanderVeen, 1965) have confirmed the instability of such ratings and urge patient-based ratings as more relevant data sources.

The relationship between facilitative relationship attitudes and outcomes may also have been inflated by the tendency for many studies to utilize only therapist or only patient ratings of outcome. Certainly, some evidence exists that patient ratings of therapist understanding and acceptance correlate more highly with patient ratings of outcome than they do with the therapist outcome ratings (Cooley & Lajoy, 1980). These results may reflect both a rater bias and a halo effect that may compromise studies that rely solely on patient ratings. On the other hand, if therapist ratings are the sole index of

TABLE 7.3   Inferred, Therapy-specific Characteristics

Variable	Study Type/Quality	n	Summary of Findings[a]
A. Relationship Attitudes (facilitative conditions)			
	Comparison	2	Both favor facilitating/accepting therapists
	Naturalistic	9	Six n.s.; two favor facilitative therapist; one favors nonfacilitative therapist
	Analogue/Process	1	Favors facilitative therapist
	Total	12	
(therapeutic alliance)			
	Naturalistic	14	All favor therapeutic alliance in outcome
	Analogue/Process	0	
	Total	14	
B. Social Influence Attributes			
	Experimental	3	Two favor therapist persuasiveness/ credibility; one n.s.
	Comparison	3	All favor therapist persuasiveness/ credibility
	Naturalistic	4	All favor therapist credibility/ trustworthiness
	Analogue/Process	11	Ten favor therapist social influence in changing attitudes and facilitating relationship; one n.s.
	Total	21	
C. Expectations			
	Experimental/Role Induction	10	Nine favor patient role induction; one n.s.
	Comparison	5	Four favor positive therapist expectations; one n.s.
	Naturalistic	13	Seven favor therapist expectations, five of which favor lower dropout rates; six n.s.
	Analogue/Process	6	Four favor therapist expectations; two n.s.
	Total	34	

[a]Some studies have both process and outcome relevance.

outcome and are found to be associated with the patient's perceptions of the therapist's skill, it may only indiciate that benevolent and empathic therapists are also benevolent and empathic in their ratings of therapeutic change.

A fourth question facing researchers is the degree to which these characteristics exert the same level and type of effect across therapeutic interventions. In a naturalistic study of psychotherapists who represented a variety of theoretical orientations, for example, Mitchell, Bozarth, and Krauft (1977) found that Rogerian relationship qualities exerted a much weaker effect in non-Rogerian than in Rogerian psychotherapy. On the other hand, Sweet

(1984) concludes that these variables have impact on very specific behavioral interventions as well as relationship-oriented ones. Such findings as these raise questions about how general the influence of these variables might be and how one might best measure them in diverse therapies. The presence of an uncomfortably large number of methodological inadequacies, inconsistencies, and statistical errors in early research on facilitative skills (e.g., Lambert & DeJulio, 1977; Marshall, 1977) may lead one to question the reliability of any conclusion reached from this literature. Certainty about the role of relationship variables awaits research that can resolve three areas of continuing methodological concern: the failure to derive consistent criteria for determining what constitutes "minimal" and "optimal" levels of therapeutic skill, independent of outcome estimates themselves; the difficulty in creating or externally controlling levels of facilitative skill; and the many different and inconsistently related methods of measuring the targeted relationship attitudes (e.g., Levant & Shlien, 1984).

One method of handling some of these concerns has been to independently differentiate between therapists who have relatively high and low levels of the relevant relationship attitudes (e.g., Berenson, Mitchell, & Laney, 1968) and then to study the distinguishing qualities of these two groups. Although recent literature (e.g., Beutler & McNabb, 1981) has begun to define absolute levels of facilitative attitudes, most studies of this type have only defined these concepts relative to the restricted range that characterizes the therapist sample studied. Moreover, while such studies approximate a matched comparison procedure, they have only infrequently addressed treatment outcome. Another comparative approach (e.g., Beutler et al., 1978) is to define acceptance levels independently of and prior to actual treatment transactions.

Findings accumulating over the past decade continue to support the general conclusion (Gurman, 1977) that patients' perceptions of their therapists' relationship attitudes are more strongly related to positive outcomes than are independent observers' estimates. Contrast, for example, the positive findings based upon patients' ratings of therapist attitudes by Cooley and Lajoy (1980) and by Kolb, Beutler, Davis, Crago, and Shanfield (in press) to less favorable ones that have relied on external

observers' ratings (Altman, 1977; Bruschi, 1982; Staples & Sloane, 1976). Nonetheless, the relationship between patient ratings of therapist facilitative attitudes and treatment outcomes is far from being consistently positive (e.g., Hansen, Moore, & Carkhuff, 1968; Lesser, 1961; Lick & Heffler, 1977; Mendola, 1982).

With the awareness that therapists are not the sole contributors to the quality of the relationship, attention has turned to other ways of exploring those patient–therapist interactions that facilitate treatment outcome. Various terms have evolved to describe those relationship attitudes that seem to enhance therapeutic gain. Most of these terms reflect some form of collaborative or helping "alliance." Conceptually, the therapeutic alliance is distinct from Rogerian concepts by virtue of its emphasis on both therapist and patient contributions to effective processes. For example, Luborsky et al. (1983b) have proposed that patient and therapist language patterns belie the presence of an effective helping alliance very early in the treatment process. This alliance is indexed by verbalizations that suggest that the patient views the relationship as a collaborative or "we" centered process.

To date, investigations of the therapeutic alliance have relied on naturalistic designs, frequently supplemented with post hoc comparisons of improved and unimproved groups. By these means, a number of authors (e.g., Horowitz, Marmar, Weiss, DeWitt, & Rosenbaum, 1984; Marziali et al., 1981; Morgan, 1978; Morgan et al., 1982) have observed the close relationship between therapeutic alliance and treatment outcome. Bent, Putnam, Kiesler, and Nowicki (1976), for example, using a post hoc design, compared the process ratings of individuals who were satisfied with therapy to those who were dissatisfied. Satisfied patients were found to view their therapists as significantly warmer, more likable, more active, and more involved in the treatment process than dissatisfied patients. In a similar methodology, Caligor (1976) compared therapists who had a high number of premature terminations to those who had a relatively low number. Those in the latter group were found to be viewed by their patients as more accepting, easier to know, less uncertain, more secure and affectionate, and more able to understand the patients' problems than were those who had high termination rates. Likewise, among the numerous naturalistically occurring variables studied in the Penn Psychotherapy Project, estimates of the therapeutic collaboration or helping alliance were most consistently and significantly related to the benefits achieved by patients (Morgan, 1978).

Concomitantly with the foregoing, research increasingly is attending to the specific types of interactions that facilitate or impede the development of helpful relationships (e.g., Horowitz et al., 1984). Post hoc reports by Strupp (1980a; 1980b), for example, as well as theoretical (e.g., Tennen, Rohrbaugh, Press, & White, 1981) and naturalistic studies of treatment relationships (e.g., Horowitz et al., 1984; Kolb et al., in press), suggest that patients who are highly sensitive, suspicious, poorly motivated, and reactive against authority perform relatively poorly with therapists who are particularly empathic, involved, and accepting. Indeed, such patients may resist the viewpoints of their therapists, and if they are persuaded to adopt them, may even show retarded rates of improvement (Arizmendi et al., 1985; Beutler et al., 1983). Therapists who establish empathic relationships may be effective only if they also tend to avoid high levels of directiveness (e.g., Mintz, Luborsky, & Auerbach, 1971).

In a naturalistic study of therapy involvement, utilizing patients who initially were able to establish only unproductive therapeutic attachments to the treatment, Foreman and Marmar (1984) concluded that subsequent treatment relationships could be enhanced by therapists who directly addressed the patient's defensiveness, explored the feelings that the patient held for the therapist, confronted patient anticipations of punishment, and linked patients' problematic feelings to their general patterns of warding off uncomfortable feelings. If one can overcome the patients' interruptive defenses and enlist the patients' collaboration, patients' involvement in treatment may increase (Foreman & Marmar, 1984; O'Malley, Chong, & Strupp, 1983) and improvement may be facilitated (Gomes-Schwartz, 1978). Such findings have led Strupp (1981) to suggest that the therapist's role extends beyond being a good listener to one of enlisting involvement, systematically maintaining a concerted treatment focus, and exploring the issues of collaboration directly.

In summary, most research in the areas of the therapist relationship attitudes has been of a naturalistic and correlational design. Nonetheless, one can tentatively conclude that patients' positive perceptions of therapist facilitative attitudes has a modest tendency to enhance treatment gains. Research increasingly is attempting to determine the interactions between the patient and therapist that foster a sense of commitment and collaboration (Foreman & Marmar, 1984; Horowitz et al., 1984), with accompanying evidence that such treatment relationships are associated with beneficial treatment outcomes (Morgan, 1978; Morgan et al., 1982). Since some types of patients seem to respond poorly to therapist empathy and support, the findings that suggest that the therapist who is able to overcome such reactions and initiate patient involvement in the treatment process obtains positive treatment gains becomes even more intriguing. With such findings, it seems quite appropriate for research to turn away from simplistic conceptualizations of the therapeutic relationship as dependent solely upon therapist attitudes, as Rogers originally proposed, and to investigate interactive processes of the patient and therapist that facilitate patients' views of the therapist as supportive and helpful. The reader is referred to Chapter 8 on therapeutic processes for a more detailed analysis of research in this area.

Social Influence Attributes

In efforts to determine how one can best enlist patient involvement, a variety of therapist attributes have been extracted from social psychology literature for exploration as potential contributors to therapeutic persuasion. These "source characteristics" (Strong, 1968) include attributes of *expertness, trustworthiness,* and *attraction.* Deriving discriminative definitions of these concepts has been a major concern for psychotherapy researchers, however. Some authors, for example, include *credibility* as a source characteristic and define it as embodying both expertise, objectivity, and trustworthiness (Corrigan, 1978). Others maintain that therapist *persuasiveness* is a characteristic that subsumes all others and describes the amount of control the therapist is able to exercise over patient reinforcement (Truax, Fine, Moravec, & Millis, 1968).

In spite of the difficulty of defining these concepts, social influence attitudes are among the therapist characteristics most systematically studied in controlled experiments. Such studies manipulate the credibility, expertness, or trustworthiness of the therapist by altering or emphasizing certain types of information available to the patient before treatment begins (e.g., Bergin, 1962; McKee & Smouse, 1983). For example, the experimenter may lead the patient to believe that one therapist has greater or lesser training and experience than another in order to manipulate the expectation of credibility (e.g., Greenberg, 1969). As expected, such manipulations have been found to alter patients' ratings of therapist source characteristics (Claiborn & Schmidt, 1977; Corrigan, 1978; Hartley, 1969; McKee & Smouse, 1983; Strong & Schmidt, 1970). In spite both of the effectiveness of these experimental manipulations and of relatively strong theoretical support for the role of these influence attributes on psychotherapy process and outcome (cf. Corrigan, Dell, Lewis, & Schmidt, 1980), most actual research has employed subject and treatment analogues of fewer than three treatment sessions. The limitation of these studies is underlined by the observations (e.g., Corrigan et al., 1980; Heppner & Dixon, 1981) that the effort to create low levels of persuasive attributes for particular therapists is overshadowed early in treatment by the power assigned by the patient to the therapist role. That is, the generalized expectation of high credibility, expertness, and power that patients assign to anyone in the therapeutic role may initially outweigh the effects of any information that suggests that a particular therapist's credibility is low. Only later in treatment does the patient's view of the therapist exert more influence than the assigned role (e.g., Heppner & Dixon, 1981).

Fortunately, there have been a number of systematic studies of therapist source attributes that have included relevant clinical populations and actual psychotherapy. While such studies often sacrifice the experimental power found in the systematic manipulation of therapist attributes, they have the advantage of studying actual treatments. In a study that included relatively long-term psychotherapy and multiple estimates of outcome, Beutler et al. (1975) assessed the relationship between therapist credibility and patient improvement. In this comparison-group investigation, therapist credibility was studied in conjunction with patient and therapist attitudinal similarities. As expected, ratings of thera-

pist credibility were significantly correlated with levels of subsequent improvement. An expected interaction with levels of attitudinal similarity was not obtained, however.

Using a naturalistic design, LaCrosse (1980) followed 36 clients of a Midwestern outpatient drug-treatment program over approximately three and one-half months of treatment. These clients were asked to make initial ratings of the source attributes presented by their therapists following the first treatment session. While the therapists in this study represented relatively diverse experience and training backgrounds and while treatment duration was uncomfortably variable, the results did confirm the hypothesis that influence source characteristics are positively related to treatment influence. Therapist attractiveness, trustworthiness, and expertness collectively accounted for 35 percent of the outcome variance. Other studies (Childress & Gillis, 1977; Goldstein, 1971; Heppner & Heesacker, 1982, 1983) have also explored populations of actual clients or patients who have varied in degree and nature of psychopathology and have obtained similar results. We have been able to find only one clinical study that obtained an overall nonsignificant outcome effect as a result of therapist source attributes (Merluzzi, Merluzzi & Kaul, 1977), and even this study produced positive relationships between therapist credibility and patient outcomes in a subgroup of nonwhite therapists.

Thorough reviews available on the relative power of the separate influence attributes (e.g., Corrigan et al., 1980; Heppner & Dixon, 1981) suggest that therapist expertness is the most consistently potent of the three sources variables. The role of therapist attractiveness is somewhat more debatable, and combinations of variables as embodied in such concepts as "persuasiveness" and "credibility" show consistently positive effects that are similar in magnitude to attributed expertness. In subject and method analogue investigations, moreover, therapist expertness has been positively associated with patients' choice of therapist (Corrigan, 1978), levels of rated attraction and trustworthiness (Greenberg, 1969; McKee & Smouse, 1983), information recall (Guttman & Haase, 1972), attitudinal change (Bergin, 1962; Binderman, Fretz, Scott, & Abrams, 1972), and both self-reported and observed behavior change (Dell, 1973; Hoffman & Spencer, 1977).

While persuasive, these findings must be tempered with the observation that self-reports and therapist reports of internal change may be more susceptible to the influence of these influence attributes than are more objectively measured behavioral changes (e.g., Heppner & Dixon, 1978; Ryan & Gizynski, 1971). These points are elaborated more completely in Chapter 3 on social psychological approaches to psychotherapy.

Therapist Expectation

Therapist expectation exerts a complex influence on treatment process and outcome. Reviewers of this literature have failed to reach consistent conclusions either about the role of therapist expectations or the magnitude of their influence. On one hand, for example, Goldstein and Simonson (1971) conclude that therapists' positive expectations facilitate patient gains, and LaTorre (1977) asserts that role-induction studies confirm that congruence between patient and therapist expectations facilitates improvement. In their extensive review of literature on premature termination, moreover, Baekeland and Lundwall (1975) conclude that when patient expectations either are not confirmed or are not similar to those of the therapist, early dropout from treatment occurs.

On the other hand, Lambert and Bergin (1983) conclude that there is little support for the position that therapist expectations of the patient play a direct role in patient change. This same conclusion is reached by Duckro, Beal, and George (1979), who found that less than half of the 43 studies reviewed supported the role of congruence between patient and therapist treatment expectations in facilitating positive outcome. Both Berman (in press) and Parloff et al. (1978) have also concluded that there is only limited evidence that either therapists' expectations or congruence between patient and therapist expectations facilitate treatment change.

In part, this inconsistency can be attributed to the complex issues that face psychotherapy researchers in this area. Even before beginning to explore therapist expectations, the researcher must cope with the difficult problem of selecting the dimensions on which expectations will be assessed. Some research has explored expectations about the length of therapy, while other research has explored expectations of positive gain. Still other research has explored

expectations about how patients will behave during the treatment process.

Additionally, the researcher is confronted with the perennial problem of balancing the desirability of experimental control against the relevance of the findings. The most used experimental manipulation, for example, is to provide one of two or more groups of similarly treated patients with systematic instructions on how to perform in the patient role. While tightly controlled, such role-induction studies do not directly reflect the role of therapist expectations. The procedure is designed to bring *patient expectations* into close alliance with *therapy defined* rather than *therapist defined* objectives.

Another frequently used method is to control the amount and type of information available to the therapist about the client. This procedure is designed systematically to change therapists' perceptions and expectations. While this procedure provides for a more direct assessment of the role of therapist expectations than role-induction procedures, one is confronted with the problem of separating the effects of initial and subsequently developed expectations. Therapists seem to change their expectations in order to conform with what they observe (Heppner & Heesacker, 1983). In this process, they tend to disregard discrepant information provided in advance. For example, after manipulating therapist expectations through pretreatment information, Kumar and Pepinsky (1965) observed that when discrepancies occurred between the type of pretherapy information provided to therapists and the therapists' observations of patient behavior, *therapists believed and based treatment decisions on the observed behavior*. However, even in this process, a general tendency was observed for patients to be most interested in working with therapists who retained high expectations for them.

A third method of addressing the role of expectation is through comparison studies with controlled or matched assignment. Martin and Sterne (1975; Martin, Moore, & Sterne, 1977; Martin, Sterne, & Hunter, 1976), for example, assessed psychiatrists' and psychiatric residents' prognoses for relatively equivalent groups of patients prior to the initiation of treatment. These prognostic estimates were repeated throughout the course of treatment and patients' symptomatic changes were evaluated with pre- and posttreatment assessments. Improvement was related to the degree that therapist but not patient expectations were met. The more closely therapist pretreatment expectations conformed with information derived from the patients themselves, the closer the relationship between expectations and improvement.

Still a fourth method for investigating therapist expectations is through the use of naturalistic designs, often supplemented by post hoc comparisons of subgroups. Goldstein (1960), for example, assessed client-rated change and duration of treatment as a function of therapist outcome expectations. The author failed to find significant relationships between therapist pretreatment expectations and either treatment duration or symptomatic improvement. When patients were subsequently divided into improved and unimproved groups, however, a post hoc analysis revealed that therapist expectations of symptomatic change were higher in the group of improved patients.

A global review of the literature reveals that therapist expectations about treatment effectiveness and duration have often been significantly related to dropout rates (e.g., Garfield & Affleck, 1961; Garfield, Affleck & Muffly, 1963; Heine & Trosman, 1960) but not with complete consistency (e.g., Affleck & Garfield, 1961; Goldstein, 1960; McNeal, Johnston, & Aspromonte, 1970). Similarly, while a preponderance of studies have confirmed Martin et al.'s (1977) conclusion that various estimates of improvement and therapeutic gain are enhanced by therapist pretreatment expectations (e.g., Brucato, 1980; Goin, Yamamoto, & Silverman, 1965; Goldstein, 1960; Gulas, 1974; Martin & Sterne, 1975; Martin et al., 1976), a number of contradictory and nonsignificant findings have also been reported in this literature (e.g., Atonuccio et al., 1982; Heppner & Heesacker, 1983; June & Smith, 1983; Kreisberg, 1978; Mendelsohn, 1968; Wynne, 1982). A meta-analysis of this research by Berman (in press) revealed that less than 10 percent of the variance in outcome could be attributed to therapists' expectations.

The most consistent findings have been obtained in studies that systematically altered patient rather than the therapist expectations about treatment. For example, Yalom, Houts, Newell, and Rand (1967) provided groups of experimental subjects with a 25-minute preparatory lecture, while demographically and psychiatrically similar control subjects undertook a benign task for an equal length of time. The results indicated that experimental subjects estimated that they would require less time in treatment in order to achieve equivalent gains, compared to control subjects. There was little differential effect in dropout rates, however, and these were the only measures of outcome. Other studies of role induction tend to emphasize the positive effects of role induction (e.g., Childress & Gillis, 1977; Curran, 1976; Hoehn-Saric et al., 1964; Holliday, 1979; Jacobs, Charles, Jacobs, Weinstein, & Mann, 1972; Sloane, Cristol, Pepernik, & Staples, 1970; Strupp & Bloxum, 1973; Truax & Wargo, 1969; Warren & Rice, 1972) with a variety of outcome and effectiveness measures. Only one study we have been able to find failed to produce significant improvement differences in favor of role-inducted subjects (e.g., Jacobs, Trick, & Withersty, 1976).

In summary, patient role expectations and, to a lesser extent, therapist expectations of individual patients seem to exert an influence on therapeutic change. More specifically, when patient expectations are changed to accommodate the therapeutic role valued by the general body of psychotherapists, the probability of positive outcomes are increased. Therapists' unique expectations also apparently play a role, however, especially when they are based upon direct observations of the patient who is seeking treatment. That is, to the degree that therapist expectations reflect accurate information based on patient behavior and are flexible enough to accommodate new information throughout the course of treatment, improvement is enhanced. On the other hand, studies that induce or evaluate therapist expectations only at the beginning of treatment show inconsistent and weak effects in relating expectations to treatment gain.

Finally, both therapist expectations and patient role expectations may also influence the nature of the therapeutic process, including the selection of patients (e.g., Eells, 1964), client attraction to therapy (Heller & Goldstein, 1961), and interaction observed in treatment process (Jacobs et al., 1976). For a more intensive review of this latter literature, the reader is referred to Chapter 8 on therapeutic processes.

EXTERNALLY OBSERVED, THERAPY-SPECIFIC CHARACTERISTICS

The last category of therapist variables to be considered is that for which there is an external, noninferred referent but whose presence is designed to have a specific bearing on psychotherapy. The effects of these variables are summarized in Table 7.4 under three subclasses: therapist background, therapy style, and therapy intervention. Following the lead of Lambert and Bergin (1983), therapy *styles* are defined as the interpersonal patterns and methods by which therapists communicate, and *interventions* refer to the operations or intentional behaviors employed and guided by therapists' theories of behavior change.

Professional Background

At least three separate variables characterize the therapist's professional background: level of experience, amount of training, and type of training. Experience represents the amount of contact that therapists have had in psychotherapy. Therapist experience levels frequently are confounded with levels of training by contrasting therapists who are still in the process of being trained with fully trained therapists. Adequate control of this confound requires that levels of experience be considered independently of one's formal training. The best controlled investigations should also distinguish between *amount* (e.g., number of years) and *type* (e.g., professional discipline) of training. Unfortunately, because much research on professional background is conducted as an adjunct to investigations of other variables, such control is not often achieved.

There are also other problems confronting research on therapist professional background. Correlational studies are particularly problematic, for example, because experienced therapists tend to draw the more interesting and treatable patients, even in settings where therapists are assigned rather than chosen (e.g., Knapp, Levin, McCarter, Wermer, & Zetzel, 1960). There is also a more subtle selection process deriving from the attrition of unskilled and frustrated therapists who change professions. Because of this self-selection, groups of experienced therapists may represent a more narrowly defined range of competencies than less

experienced groups. One cannot automatically infer, therefore, that all positive effects related to therapists of differing experience levels reflect a tendency to become more effective with experience.

The researcher must also face the difficult tasks of defining what constitutes "experience" and distinguishing among various "experience levels." Studies define experience in different ways, some based on the amount of contact with patients of certain types, and others based upon the amount of longevity in the field. Moreover, some studies attempt to correlate experience levels with outcomes in constricted samples of highly experienced therapists (e.g., Sloan, Staples, Cristol, Yorkston, & Whipple, 1975), while others attempt to do so in similarly constricted groups of very inexperienced therapists (e.g., Tuma, May, Yale, & Forsythe, 1978b). When considered in such restricted ranges, the probability of obtaining significant effects is greatly reduced.

Finally, the researcher is confronted with the probability that therapists of differing experience levels come to judge the outcomes of psychotherapy in systematically different ways. Hence, research that depends on therapist ratings of therapeutic outcome may reflect the results of the different criteria used by experienced and inexperienced therapists.

In an effort to control some of these variables, Haccoun and Lavigueur (1979) defined contrasting therapist experience levels on the basis of number of prior therapy cases seen rather than by the amount of training received. Two actresses portrayed either angry or sad clients and therapists were asked to assess the client using systematic measures that reflected each therapist's own attitudes. The results suggested that experienced therapists had greater tolerance for patient expressions of anger and tended to engage in less negative stereotyping of such patients than did inexperienced therapists.

Another method of handling these difficult problems was utilized by researchers in the Vanderbilt Psychotherapy Project (Gomes-Schwartz & Schwartz, 1978; Strupp & Hadley, 1979). In this study, the effectiveness rates of therapists with equivalent amounts but different types of training were compared. One group was composed of mental health professionals and the other of college professors. Each group was randomly assigned a group of socially alienated and anxious college

TABLE 7.4 Externally Observed, Therapy-specific Characteristics

Variable	Study Type/Quality	n	Summary of Findings[a]
A. Professional Background (experience)			
	Comparison	11	Six favor experience; five n.s.
	Naturalistic	20	Fourteen n.s.; six favor experience, three with dropout rates
	Analogue/Process	4	Three favor experience; one n.s.
	Total	35	
(training/ discipline)			
	Comparison	3	Two n.s.; one favors social workers
	Naturalistic	0	
	Analogue/Process	2	One favors psychologists; one n.s.
	Total	5	
B. Intervention Style (verbal directiveness)			
	Experimental	4	Two favor matching with I-E; two n.s. with directiveness alone
	Comparison	4	Two favor matching with I-E; two n.s. with directiveness alone
	Naturalistic	8	Four favor directiveness alone; two favor nondirectiveness; two n.s.
	Analogue/Process	7	Three favor low directiveness; two favor matching with I-E; two interact with either variable
	Total	23	
(verbal activity)			
	Comparison	1	Favors high activity level
	Naturalistic	3	Two n.s.; one favors low activity
	Analogue/Process	2	Both suggest that activity level conveys therapists' attitudes
	Total	6	
(self-disclosure)			
	Comparison	0	
	Naturalistic	1	Nonsignificant
	Analogue/Process	7	All suggest self-disclosure enhances relationship
	Total	8	

TABLE 7.4 *(Continued)*

Variable	Study Type/Quality	n	Summary of Findings[a]
(nonverbal posture/ attire/decor)			
	Experimental/ Comparison	1	Favors formal attire/decor
	Naturalistic	2	Both favor forward balanced posture/ eye contact
	Analogue/Process	22	Nine favor forward posture and touch; four favor formal dress/decor; three favor complex effect of dress/decor; one favors informality; one favors no touch
	Total	25	
C. Interventions (competence)			
	Comparison	2	Both favor competence
	Naturalistic	5	Four favor competence; one n.s.
	Analogue/Process	3	All favor technical competence
	Total	10	
(technical procedures)			
	Comparison	4	Two favor affective confrontation; one favors interpretation; one n.s.
	Naturalistic	7	Four favor interpretive interventions; three n.s.
	Analogue/Process	7	All favor affective confrontation
	Total	18	
(theoretical orientations)			
	Experimental	3	Two n.s.; one favors supportive insight
	Comparison	9	Seven n.s.; two favor cognitive therapy
	Naturalistic (meta-analyses)	3	Two n.s.; one favors cognitive and behavioral therapy
	Analogue/Process	10	All suggest that differences in process distinguish schools
	Total	25	

[a]Some studies have both process and outcome relevance.

males for psychotherapy. The type of training rather than the amount of actual experience was the targeted variable, although amount of relevant experience also probably distinguished the groups. The results revealed that few differences distinguished the effectiveness rates of the therapist groups, even though there were significant differences observed in the nature of the psychotherapy processes. Mental health professionals, for example, were more likely than their academic colleagues to focus on theoretically important, therapeutic issues.

The use of statistical and methodological controls

in studying experience levels is illustrated in a study by Baum, Felzer, D'Zmura, and Shumaker (1966). These investigators compared therapists with a mean of 11 years of medical and clinical experience with those who had only one year of such experience. Comparatively, experienced therapists were found to have lower dropout rates. Because amount of psychiatric training also distinguished the groups, the authors employed a post hoc, statistical analysis to partial out these effects. When they did so, the significant relationship between experience and dropout rates disappeared.

Unlike those studies outlined above, most efforts to study the effects of therapist experience and amount of training rely upon correlational analyses in naturalistic environments. As a result of the many potential sources of contamination in such studies, major reviews on this topic have yielded contradictory conclusions. On one hand, Luborsky, Chandler, Auerbach, Cohen, and Bachrach (1971) cited 8 of 13 studies that favored a positive relationship between therapists' experience and outcome, and Baekeland and Lundwall (1975) found such a relationship in 6 out of 7 studies on psychotherapy dropout. In contrast, Auerbach and Johnson (1977) reported that only 5 out of 12 studies favored the experienced therapist, and Parloff et al. (1978) reported that only 4 out of 13 studies produced positive results. Similarly, in their meta-analysis of psychotherapeutic change factors, Smith, Glass, and Miller (1980) reported that average effect size estimates attributable to experience were of zero-order magnitude.

In an effort to clarify some of this confusion, we extracted the nonoverlapping studies cited in four prior reviews (Auerbach & Johnson, 1977; Baekeland & Lundwall, 1975; Luborsky et al., 1971; Parloff et al., 1978), excluding those that did not utilize direct measures of outcome. The result was a pool of 30 studies. Ten of these studies explored dropout rates as a function of therapist experience levels, but only 5 found evidence of a positive relationship between experience and remaining in therapy (Baum et al., 1966; Epperson, Bushway, & Warman, 1983; Kopoian, 1982; Myers & Auld, 1955; Rodolfa et al., 1983). Of 23 studies that assessed psychotherapeutic improvement or change directly, only 7 found the expected positive effects (Brown, 1970; Cartwright & Lerner, 1963; Cartwright & Vogel, 1960; Katz, Lorr & Rubinstein, 1958; Kirschner et al., 1978; Scher, 1975; Turner & Ascher, 1982) and two others found partial support of the hypothesis (Mindess, 1953; Sullivan, Miller, & Smelser, 1958).[1] Like Auerbach and Johnson (1977), we found no studies that suggested that inexperienced therapists did better than experienced ones.

Similar results were obtained in an intensive meta-analysis of 27 carefully selected studies by Stein and Lambert (1984) and of 39 studies of paraprofessionals by Hattie, Sharpley, and Rogers (1984). Few general effects of experience on outcome were obtained. By statistically controlling certain variables and comparing others, however, Stein and Lambert observed that positive effects of experience were most likely to emerge (1) when the experience levels of contrasting groups of therapists were quite distinct, (2) among difficult patients, (3) when complex and intensive treatments were investigated, and (4) when the outcome variables either were assessed early in treatment or included dropout rates. A number of studies have also suggested that the processes of psychotherapy conducted by experienced therapists is quite different from that by inexperienced therapists. Experienced therapists have been found to be more active (Grigg, 1961), to induce different levels of arousal (McCarron & Appel, 1971), and to facilitate higher session-by-session satisfaction rates (Cimbolic, 1972; Orlinsky & Howard, 1975) than their less experienced counterparts.

A number of studies have explored differences that might accrue to treatment as a function of therapist professional affiliation. Elsewhere in this volume, the effects of therapist training and professional discipline is addressed in depth. For the current purpose, it should be emphasized that few differences in outcome rates have been found among therapists of different disciplines (e.g.,

[1]Studies indicating nonsignificant dropout rates as a function of therapists' experience were Betz and Shullman (1979), Epperson (1981), Krauskopf et al. (1981), McNair et al. (1963), and Sullivan et al. (1958). Outcome studies that failed to reveal significant effects of experience were Luborsky et al. (1980), Grigg (1961), Tuma et al. (1978b), Fiske, Cartwright, and Kirtner (1964), Sloane et al. (1975), Epperson (1981), Miles, McLean, and Maurice (1976), Kopoian (1982), Mintz et al. (1976), Orlinsky and Howard (1975), Strupp and Hadley (1979), Feifel and Eells (1963), Fiske and Goodman (1965), and Lerner (1972).

McNair, Lorr, & Callahan, 1963; Mintz et al., 1976). Orlinsky and Howard (1975), however, found that among therapists representing the three major mental health professions, social workers adopted a more directive and problem-centered approach to treatment, and when difference in outcome rates did accrue, they tended to favor social workers. In contrast, Berren (personal communication) has reported that in a follow-up investigation of an earlier study (Schindler, Berren, & Beigel, 1981), utilizing samples both of former psychiatric patients and of nonpatients, psychiatrists and psychologists were rated more positively than either religious leaders or nonpsychiatric physicians. Psychiatrists were perceived to be somewhat more educated than psychologists, but were rated as less warm, less caring, and less able to listen when dealing with mental health problems other than those represented by paranoid patients and alcohol abusers. The differences between psychiatrists and psychologists were magnified among individuals who had previously received psychological treatment.

These latter findings are complemented by recent evidence that patient demographic characteristics, income, health status, and length of treatment distinguish the caseloads of psychiatrists and psychologists (Taube, Burns, & Kessler, 1984). Comparatively, the patients of psychologists are more affluent and more frequently employed than those of psychiatrists. They also received somewhat more or longer courses of therapy, had fewer medical problems, and more frequently obtained a fee discount than did patients of psychiatrists. It is unfortunate that this large-scale study did not obtain any information about effectiveness rates.

In summary, the current findings suggest that while therapist experience may facilitate treatment processes, these effects do not readily translate to assessments of outcomes. The effects of therapist experience on outcome may be most observable when treating seriously disturbed individuals with very complex or intensive treatments (e.g., Stein & Lambert, 1984), although more research on this interaction is needed. The most reliable conclusion at present is that experience exerts a complex effect that is most observable either on psychotherapy processes, early treatment gains, or dropout rates (Stein & Lambert, 1984). Likewise, one's professional discipline does not appear to be a major

variable in affecting treatment outcome, although it may influence patient perceptions of the individuals providing treatment. Further research in this area must look more specifically at some of the confounding variables we have described and attempt to isolate the effects of such potential confounding variables as therapist gender (e.g., Hill, 1975).

Therapist Style

"Therapist style" refers to those automatic and often unconscious behaviors not directly dictated by a formal theory of change. It is conventional to differentiate between verbal and nonverbal styles even though such a distinction may be unduly simplistic (e.g., Mehrabian, 1970). Communication theory, social influence theory, anthropology, and even ethnology have explored the value and role of such styles in interpersonal processes and relationships. Therefore, the salience of these variables will not be fully considered within the current context.

To gain a clearer idea of how therapist style affects psychotherapy, one must categorize not only the various means by which style is expressed, but also their methods of interaction. Hence, the distinction between verbal and nonverbal styles is valuable as one explores how they may interact in the course of psychotherapy. Mehrabian (1970) reports that listeners rely upon nonlanguage qualities of the communication in order to define speaker attitudes about the listener's person but rely upon language components in order to infer speaker attitudes toward the listener's actions. Methods of assessing these interactions remain very complex and present a significant problem for the investigator. This problem is compounded because outside observers, therapists, and patients differ widely in how they describe in-therapy behaviors (Hoyt, Xenakis, Marmar, & Horowitz, 1983; Xenakis, Hoyt, Marmar, & Horowitz, 1983). Given these differences, one is well cautioned to be wary of verbal or written reports of therapy sessions, especially those that rely solely upon therapists' process notes for assessing therapeutic transactions (cf. Malan, 1976).

Verbal Styles

Research on verbal styles must be sensitive to the observation that therapist and patient goals and verbalizations are relatively incongruent with one another in early stages of treatment and only become more consistent as treatment progresses

(Horn-George & Anchor, 1982). Hence, one might expect that verbal patterns observed in a single session or in an analogue environment are not representative of extended therapy processes. It is unfortunate, therefore, that most studies of therapist style are analogue investigations of short-term "therapist" and "client" contact.

Moreover, variations in therapist experience and training levels may modify both the verbal activity of therapists and the impact of this activity on patients. For example, highly confrontative therapeutic styles may engender high resistance and arousal when practiced by inexperienced therapists, but the same procedures may have quite a different effect when practiced by those who are experienced (e.g., McCarron & Appel, 1971). These influences should be controlled in studies of therapist styles.

The preponderance of research on therapist verbal styles has been directed to three kinds of variables: (1) therapist patterns that direct the patients' attention, action, or thought; (2) lexical characteristics of therapist language including pauses, interruptions, change of topics, and word counts; and (3) therapist self-disclosure.

Therapist directiveness.   Researchers have explored the role of therapist directiveness in a variety of ways. Hoyt (1980) explored the content of good and poor therapy sessions among a group of homogeneous patients presenting stress disorders. Through this post hoc, correlational procedure, Hoyt demonstrated that poor sessions, based upon the ratings of experts, were characterized by therapist efforts to extract factual information or to give advice.

In a similar, post hoc comparison procedure, Lieberman, Yalom, and Miles (1973) identified six leader styles from observations of group therapy processes. Managerial styles were characterized by an emphasis on directing and controlling transactions and were associated with few treatment changes being experienced by patients, either in a positive or a negative direction.

In one of the most rigorous efforts to employ and link naturalistic observations and experimental control, Patterson and Forgatch (in press) explored the effects of therapist directiveness on patient compliance. Using a sample of mothers of aggressive and delinquent adolescents, the authors first naturalisti-

cally observed patient responses that occurred immediately before and after directive and supportive therapist responses. The authors found that patients exhibited more noncompliant responses following directive/confrontative activities than following supportive ones. The authors subsequently trained therapists to vary their supportive and directive responses sequentially, on cue. These two types of responses were then administrated in an A–B–A–B design over the course of a single session. Again, patient compliance was observed to correspond negatively with the presence of directive confrontation on the part of the therapist.

Although these exemplary studies suggest some degree of consistency, the potential negative influences of therapist directiveness are apparently weak contributors to treatment outcome as evidenced by the inconsistency that exists across studies more generally. Some studies have found that low levels of directiveness are beneficial to treatment outcome (Lorr, 1965; Mintz et al., 1971); other studies suggest that moderate or high levels of directiveness may facilitate outcome (Andrews, 1976; Beutler, Dunbar, & Baer, 1980; Grigg & Goodstein, 1957; Hill et al., 1983); and still others have obtained nonsignificant or zero-order effects (Ashby, Ford, Guerney, & Guerney, 1957; Cooley & Lajoy, 1980; Goin et al., 1965; Luborsky et al., 1980).

From the foregoing, it appears that the effect of therapist directiveness is a function of its interaction with other variables. Indeed, investigations that have looked specifically at patient variables in conjunction with therapist directiveness have produced more promising results. Among one of the better, early, comparison studies in this area, Ashby et al., (1957) systematically instructed therapists to provide either reflective or directive interventions. Nonsignificant outcome effects were obtained, but post hoc analyses in which patient characteristics were considered indicated that aggressive and defensive patients became increasingly aggressive and defensive when presented with directive interventions. These patients responded more positively to reflective interventions. No such differences were noted among patients who were judged to be receptive and nondefensive.

A large number of related, nonsymmetrical matching studies on the effect of therapist directiveness on patients who differ in generalized expectations of external or internal control have also accumulated in recent years. Such studies have been successful in implementing at least a minimal amount of experimental rigor into the psychotherapy process. In reviewing these studies, Baker (1979) concluded that positive treatment effects are enhanced by directive therapists among patients with external attributions of control. While this conclusion is somewhat more positive than the one reached by Messer and Meinster (1980), it also is based upon a more complete review of the literature and maintains an important distinction between psychotherapy processes and outcome. If one excludes from these reviews both those studies conducted on nonclinical populations and those in which analogue treatments were employed, the results reveal surprising consistency. The preponderance of these clinical studies has obtained positive interactions between therapist directiveness and patient attributional style (e.g., Balch & Ross, 1975; Kaufman & Bluestone, 1974; Morey & Watkins, 1974; Rozensky & Bellack, 1976). While this is not a universal finding (e.g., Kilmann & Howell, 1974), it has been sufficiently persuasive to suggest to some (e.g., Antaki & Brewin, 1982; Forsyth & Forsyth, 1982) that therapeutic interventions should selectively encourage either controllable (internal) or uncontrollable (external) attributions, depending upon patients' attributional styles. In analogue investigations of this proposition, Forsyth and Forsyth (1982) produced evidence that led them to conclude that clients with external attributions of control may become worse when subjected to therapeutic interventions that emphasize personal control and responsibility. While these speculations are consistent with the concepts of reactance formulated and applied to psychotherapy by Brehm and Brehm (1981; Beutler, 1979c, 1983), they have stirred considerable controversy (e.g., Priddy & Stone, 1983) and are yet to be confirmed among clinical populations.

Lexical characteristics. The methodological difficulties of investigating lexical aspects of speech in a prospective research design have generally precluded the emergence of clear findings. Studies in this area have universally relied upon a correlational methodology with the result being many inconsistent findings that are probably reflective of the diversity of populations selected and the diversity of

methods utilized for analyzing speech patterns. While it can be concluded that therapist beliefs and feelings may be conveyed by language patterns (e.g., Scher, 1971) and that therapist attitudes toward patients are observable through the voice qualities they use in discussing the patient outside as well as inside of the therapy session (Rosenthal, Blanck, & Vannicelli, 1984), the relationship of lexical characteristics of speech to outcome remains controversial. Among the best correlational studies available, Scher (1975) found a nonsignificant relationship between therapist verbal activity level and improvement among counseling-center clients. Other studies (e.g., Grigg & Goodstein, 1957), utilizing similar samples, have indicated that moderately active therapists are conducive to improvement. Equally rigorous studies utilizing more disturbed, psychiatric outpatient samples of patients have suggested that low therapist activity levels are facilitative of therapeutic improvement (e.g., Staples & Sloane, 1976). One can only conclude from such diversity that undisclosed patient characteristics may play a significant role in determining the influence of therapist verbal activity. Perhaps, for example, some degree of congruence between patient and therapist verbal patterns is a key element (Tracey & Ray, 1984).

Therapist self-disclosure. Nowhere in the literature does one observe such a clear disparity between findings of analogue and clinical investigations as is true with regard to therapist self-disclosure. Judging from numerous analogue investigations, it is a virtual truism that therapist self-disclosure facilitates patient engagement in the treatment process and enhances self-inspection. Such investigations suggest a moderately strong relationship between self-disclosure and both patient subsequent self-disclosure (Davis & Skinner, 1974; Davis & Sloan, 1974; Derlega, Harris, & Chaikin, 1973; Mann & Murphy, 1975) and patient beliefs about the helpfulness of the therapy contact (Mann & Murphy, 1975; McCarthy & Betz, 1978; Murphy & Strong, 1972; Remer, Roffey, & Buckholtz, 1983). Results are much less consistent when applied either to clinical populations or to treatment outcomes (cf. reviews by Dies, 1977; Strassberg, Roback, D'Antonio, & Gabel, 1977). In one of the few available outcome studies, Alexander, Barton, Schiavo, and Parsons

(1976) explored a variety of interventions among families of adolescents with behavior disorders. In the course of this investigation, the authors gathered data on therapist qualities associated with low recidivism rates. Although originally included as a composite predictive factor, therapist self-disclosure was dropped as a variable because it failed to exert a constant effect.

In summary, literature on therapist verbal style suggests that therapist directiveness exerts a complex but generally predictive effect on treatment, dependent in part on the nature of the patient population being investigated. The effects of therapist verbal activity and disclosure levels, on the other hand, remain uncertain. Little has been added to this literature in the past decade even though clear research is needed, especially as related to therapy outcome. At present, we know more about momentary changes in therapy process than we do about the influence of these numerous stylistic variables on symptom change.

Nonverbal Styles

In recent years, a great deal of attention has been paid both to the role of noverbal communication processes in facilitating interpersonal influence (e.g., Beier & Young, 1984; Harper, Wiens, & Matarazzo, 1978) and to the ways that nonverbal behaviors enhance or retard the influences of verbal communications (e.g., Ekman, 1964; Felipe & Sommer, 1966; Harper et al., 1978; Patterson, 1982). In attempting to understand therapist nonverbal styles, two varieties of nonverbal patterns can be distinguished: (1) posture and proximics and (2) therapist attire and office decor.

Posture and proximics.   The investigator who explores the role of therapist posture and proximics in psychotherapy is faced with the joint problems of selecting what postural variables may be most relevant to the therapeutic transaction, defining a consistent way of measuring these variables, and separating causal from reactive and reciprocal influences between these variables and their assumed therapy consequences. For example, like verbal styles, postural cues may be consequences of the effective or ineffective therapy process rather than causes of it. These variables are seldom defined independently of the particular therapy relationships being studied, however. It is uncertain, therefore, whether they

reflect enduring therapist characteristics or states that are very specific to particular therapist–patient interactions. While these difficulties make the literature on postural influences difficult to decipher, several conclusions still appear to be warranted. First, many of the postural characteristics displayed by therapists transcend transactions with specific patients (Smith, 1972). Second, these patterns are influenced in relatively specific ways by attributes presented by the patient. Fairbanks, McGuire, and Harris (1982), for example, observed that psychiatry resident interviewers used body postures and behaviors during interviews that systematically enhanced the topical focus when interviewing patients with whom they were comfortable. When interviewing patients with whom they were less comfortable, however, interviewers employed behaviors that became disruptive of focus. These patterns suggest that the therapist may unintentionally utilize nonverbal cues that facilitate or impede the development of treatment relationships and that the tendency to do so may emanate from personal reactions to the interviewee.

Particular concern has been drawn to the role of physical touch. Some authors have suggested that touch may provide reassurance and may assist clients to become open to relationships (Forer, 1969; Mintz, 1969). Accordingly, many psychotherapists believe that physical touch may be beneficial to patients (Holroyd & Brodsky, 1977). In support of this contention, investigations of student volunteers suggest that physical touch may enhance subjects' perceptions of therapist expertness (Hubble, Noble, & Robinson, 1981) and facilitate patient self-exploration (Pattison, 1973). Touch, however, has also been found to be the first step in a series of interpersonal transactions that seem to increase the likelihood of sexual intercourse occurring between the therapist and the patient (Holroyd & Brodsky, 1980). Some less insidious, but still negative, effects on feelings and communication have also been observed among normal college volunteers (Tyson, 1979). Aside from the potentially negative effects of sexual contact with the patient, however, the direct effects of physical touch on treatment outcome have not been assessed.

In related research, analogue investigations of therapist posture and interpersonal distance suggest that responsive movements may have a positive impact upon subject attitudes and beliefs (Ekman,

1964), ratings of empathy (Haase & Tepper, 1972), and attachment to the interviewer (Kelly, 1972; Maurer & Tyndall, 1983; Mehrabian, 1968; Smith-Hanen, 1977). However, the actual effects of therapist posture and distance on treatment outcome have not been well documented in spite of some promising evidence. Fretz (1966), for example, found that certain movements and postures may be positively related to client satisfaction levels. Similarly, in a naturalistic study of eight categories of nonverbal behavior on treatment dropout and improvement rates, Howard et al. (1970) found that therapist facial expressions and forward balanced posture reduced premature termination in treatment. After reviewing this literature, Edinger and Patterson (1983) conclude that gaze and paralinguistic expressions facilitate attitude persuasion while eye contact, nodding, and facial expressions provide reinforcement and encouragement to what the patient is saying.

Therapist attire and office decor. Compared to the investigations of therapist posture, dress and office decor are variables more easily brought under investigator control when exploring sources of therapist influence. Hence, issues of cause and effect are, at least potentially, more easily addressed in studies of these variables relative to other aspects of nonverbal communication. In spite of the ease of investigation, current literature allows no clear statement about whether a formal or an informal environment produces the most beneficial effects in therapy. As with investigations of posture and distance, much of this difficulty can be attributed to the failure of researchers to investigate clinical populations and clinical environments. Some treatment process studies have found that beneficial attitudes toward the therapist derive from formal therapist attire or office decor (Brooks, 1974; Heppner & Pew, 1977; Kerr & Dell, 1976; Raia, 1973); others suggest that benefits accrue from an informal attire or office decor (Tessler, 1975; Widgery & Stackpole, 1972); and still others (e.g., Amira & Abramowitz, 1979) have found that positive ratings of therapists is highest in a formal office combined with informal dress. None of these studies has evaluated therapy outcome and most have involved only analogue clients and situations.

Among the few studies of actual therapy, Childress and Gillis (1977) systematically varied therapist influence power using tactics that included altering therapist attire and room decor. Improvement ratings over the course of treatment were enhanced in those environments that included formal attire and room decor. However, the authors did not separate the effects of therapist verbal and nonverbal styles in assessing relationships to outcome. Hence, the results do not provide an uncontaminated picture of how verbal and nonverbal characteristics might differentially affect treatment results.

The complex method of interaction among verbal and nonverbal variables is also underlined by other studies that suggest that therapist attire and room decor may vary with certain characteristics of the subject population. For example, Bloom et al. (1977) found that therapist credibility was rated higher when women counselors were seen in traditional and formal offices. Male credibility, on the other hand, was enhanced if counselors were seen in casually decorated offices. Finally, Widgery and Stackpole (1972) determined that highly anxious subjects preferred open, informal environments while individuals with low anxiety preferred more formal environments for counseling.

Collectively, it appears that therapist posture, touch, distance, and environment produce at least momentary changes in attitudes in both distressed and nondistressed patient groups. Even the short-term effects of dress and decor are less certain. More critically, the long-lasting effects on symptom change and comfort levels have not been clearly determined for any of these variables among clinical populations. There is a critical need for research to determine whether the many analogue findings translate into treatment interactions.

Treatment Interventions

Unlike therapeutic styles, treatment interventions reflect, to one degree or another, therapists' theories of behavior change (Lambert & Bergin, 1983). Specific interventions may range from those involving discourse and verbal exchange to those in which the therapist encourages patients to engage in theory-relevant behaviors. Not only must the nature of these activities be explored by the psychotherapy researcher, but attention must be given to the adequacy with which interventions are implemented as well. Hence, three separate classes of variables characterize research on therapist intervention. These include (1) the *competency* with which the therapist conducts the interventions, (2) the *technical procedures* themselves, and (3) the *theoretical philosophies* that direct these interventions.

Competence. At least in the current context, concepts of "competence" and "expertness" are not equivalent. *Expertness* represents a perception one holds of an internal therapist trait, usually by virtue of reputation. Such ratings are frequently applied by patients who have little knowledge of the theoretical and philosophical guidelines that dictate particular interventions. *Competence,* in contrast, refers to the adequacy or skill with which the therapist applies the procedures relative to some critical, external standard. The distinction is analogous to that drawn by Schaffer (1982) between therapist "skillfulness" and "interpersonal manner."

Unfortunately, therapist competence has not been a topic of serious investigation until recent years. Psychotherapy researchers have typically assumed that therapists do what they say they do. Additionally, they have assumed that if individuals are trained in a formal and recognized educational curriculum, competence levels are essentially equivalent. Though belated, it has recently become apparent to psychotherapy researchers, as it has been to clinicians for some time, that training programs based on time of service and exposure do not automatically produce equivalent levels of skill. Fiedler (1950) underlined this fact when he observed that experienced therapists from different theoretical schools were more similar to one another than those who differed in experience levels but were from the same theoretical school. As a result of observations like these, psychotherapy research has increasingly emphasized the importance of competency criteria against which therapists might be assessed. This emphasis has been the foundation for efforts to develop psychotherapy manuals through which therapy activities can be taught and guided. The past decade has seen a substantial tightening of theoretical concepts as writers have begun to operationalize their philosophical perspectives in order both to systematize teaching efforts and to ensure a degree of consistency in the application of therapy models. The emphasis on performance criteria has also resulted in an effort to define those therapy procedures that work against progress in various therapies. The Vanderbilt Negative Indicators Scale (Sachs, 1983), for example, has been modestly

successful in teasing out of therapy transactions the therapist behaviors related to deterioration in the patient's condition. In spite of such efforts, however, a substantial body of research has yet to accumulate on how one's competence actually influences treatment outcome.

In the literature that is available, competence is defined in one of two ways. In some studies competence has been assessed against some external standard, such as that established by a theoretical model or a panel of experts. In this method of research, criterion levels of performance are established and therapists who reliably achieve and maintain these levels are compared to those who do not. Alternatively, other research has defined competence on the basis of improvement rates. In these studies, therapists who have high improvement rates are compared to therapists who have low improvement rates. This procedure invokes a less systematic interpretation of the word *competence* and can address only therapy process differences.

As an example of the first methodology, both Luborsky, McLellan, Woody, and O'Brien (1983b) and Shaw (1983) trained therapists to criterion levels of competence in cognitive and interpersonal forms of psychotherapy. Outcome ratings and measurements were subsequently correlated with the degree to which therapists were able to maintain compliance with these levels of performance. In both of these studies, maintenance of therapist competence was shown to be a stronger contributor to improvement than was the particular therapeutic modality utilized.

Studies that have defined competence on the basis of outcome rates have provided a slightly different perspective on this problem by inspecting therapy processes themselves. Baum et al. (1966) compared the therapy behaviors of therapists who had high and low improvement rates when treating low socioeconomic status patients. Those who had high improvement rates were found to be very task-oriented in their approach, and those with low improvement rates were found to use more process- and insight-oriented comments and interventions. In a similar procedure, Terestman et al. (1974) found that those who were effective in treating low socioeconomic status patients were willing to discuss differences between their own and their patients' socioeconomic and racial assignments.

In a variation of the foregoing methodology, some

studies have assessed therapist competence through independent evaluation and then correlated these estimates with subsequent therapy process and outcome. Beutler et al. (1980), for example, independently differentiated among five therapist competence levels using supervisor ratings of clinical skill. The least competent therapists were found to be relatively insensitive to patient distress and psychopathology levels, while the more competent therapists were found to provide relatively more directive support than their counterparts. With some notable exceptions (e.g., Tuma et al., 1978b), most other correlational studies have found similar relationships between external estimates of competence and subsequent outcome (e.g., Sachs, 1983; Vaccaro, 1981) or therapy attendance rates (White & Pollard, 1982).

In summary, research on therapist competence is just beginning to evolve but, to date, suggests a rather convincing relationship with therapeutic benefit. While more research is needed in order to generalize these promising, initial findings to a broader range of treatments, many important methodological developments (e.g., treatment manuals, rating scales) promise to facilitate these efforts.

Technical procedures. Technical procedures are typically defined on the basis of their relationship to theoretical philosophies. These philosophies, in turn, are distinguished by their relative emphasis on a continuum of human experience ranging from affective sensitivity (e.g., emotive/expressive) to cognitive awareness (interpretive/educational). While technical procedures are only arbitrarily distinguished from verbal styles, their relationship to philosophical schools is captured in the difference between theoretically integrated treatment packages (schools) and discrete procedures. Technical procedures do not exist in any simple relationship to one another, and the methods of assessing them are varied. Often the same descriptive terms from two different philosophies may index quite different actual behaviors (e.g., the distinction between psychoanalytic and client-centered "insight").

Most research on the use of technical procedures has been naturalistic in design and has concentrated on comparing affective (i.e., abreactive) and cognitively (i.e., interpretive) focused procedures. Statistical procedures have also been employed to assess the interface and clustering of discrete procedures

into sensible categories. Only rarely have systematic experimental manipulations been invoked by which therapists have planfully employed one or another type of technical intervention.

Many findings have emphasized the relative effectiveness of procedures directed at patient affect compared to those with a cognitive interpretive emphasis. For example, Ehrlich, D'Augelli and Danish (1979) studied six verbal response types utilized by counselors and psychotherapists in a counseling analogue study. They found that those responses that emphasized the affective content of patient communication facilitated productive interview behavior and enhanced subsequent ratings of therapist attractiveness, expertness, and trustworthiness. Cognitively and behaviorally focused activities (i.e., advice giving, persuading), on the other hand, reduced or left these various behaviors and perceptions unaffected. Wenegrat (1976) applied a similar procedure to actual clinical interactions. She found that focusing on patient affect was more likely to enhance therapist-rated empathy levels than was a nonaffective focus.

Utilizing a contrasting comparisons procedure, Mitchell and his colleagues (Berenson et al., 1968; Berenson, Mitchell, & Moravec, 1968; Mitchell & Hall, 1971) also found that high facilitative therapists tended to confront and interpret patient affect relatively more often than low facilitative therapists. In another contrasting groups design that employed both controlled assignment and outcome assessment, Greenberg and Dompierre (1981) compared a nonemotive form of treatment to an intervention that actively confronted emotional experience. The results confirmed that therapeutic processes, patient awareness, and conflict resolution were enhanced through emotionally confrontative procedures.

Efforts to explore differences between affectively and cognitively focused responses have also suggested that affective expression on the part of the therapist may produce more improvement among marital couples than cognitively oriented interventions (Sunbury, 1981). A sex effect may be present, however, as evidenced by Mejia's (1981) demonstration that marital adjustment improved among Hispanic women in response to therapists' emotionally involving behavior, whereas Hispanic men responded better to therapist focus on verbal content and structure.

In another method of exploring this issue, Bandura, Lipsher, and Miller (1960) evaluated the moment-to-moment impact of the therapist's approach to or avoidance of the expression of anger. Comparatively, therapists who did not avoid the expression of anger promoted more realistic and goal-directed expressions of affect on the part of their clients. Indeed, evidence from many sources suggests that rousing patient affect and motivating them to confront their fears enhances both cognitive (e.g., Hoehn-Saric et al., 1974) and behavioral (e.g., Williams, Dooseman, & Kleifield, 1984) changes.

In spite of the general consistency of these findings, few directly bear on therapeutic outcome. Although a preponderance of outcome studies suggest that there is value in confronting and interpreting patient affect, this relationship has not been as consistently observed as that relating to treatment processes. For example, in their comparison of effective and ineffective groups, Lieberman et al. (1973) defined four behavioral clusters that characterized different group interventions. These clusters included caring, interpretation, and emotional stimulation. While caring and interpretation were positively associated with treatment outcome, emotional stimulation was not. A somewhat similar methodology was utilized by Mintz et al. (1971) in the investigation of psychoanalytically oriented, individual therapy. These authors found that neither emotionally tuned nor interpretive roles were strongly related to outcome.

Likewise, in her extension of the Vanderbilt Psychotherapy Project, Gomes-Schwartz (1978) found that the interpretation of the patient's particular cognitive defenses had little relationship to outcome. Subsequently, successful therapists from the same subject pool as used by Gomes-Schwartz were found to use more consistent and focused interpretations than their less effective counterparts (Sachs, 1983). In an independent replication of Gomes-Schwartz, attending to both technical interventions and global treatment packages, Beutler and Mitchell (1981) found that interpretations that focused on early childhood experiences were negatively related to outcomes. Collectively, these findings suggest that the type of cognitive or affective focus rather than their frequencies may contribute to improvement.

In a naturalistic, retrospective analysis, Malan (1976) attempted to distinguish among several varieties of interpretation that occurred in the course of successful treatment. He concluded that interpre-

tations that reflected upon the emotionally laden parent-to-therapist similarity were more closely associated with positive outcome than either therapist-to-patient or patient-to-parent interpretations. Unfortunately, both the use of case notes and nonblinded raters limited the significance of these findings. Marziali and Sullivan (1980) rerated Malan's data utilizing blind raters and provided continued support to the salience of the parent—therapist transference links. More recently, Marziali (1984) replicated Malan's findings utilizing audio recordings as a further control against therapist-reporting bias. Tentative support for the relative power of the therapist—parent transference interpretation was still obtained.

In summary, the current data suggest that psychotherapy processes and the quality of treatment relationships may be enhanced by the therapist who assumes a role that confronts patients with their feelings and actively engages patients at an emotional level. The direct teaching of cognitive content or historical interpretation seems to provide less powerful therapeutic gains in the absence of emotional arousal. Focal interpretations in the presence of emotional involvement and arousal appear to produce benefits to psychotherapy process and, to a lesser degree, to treatment outcome. However, the effectiveness of these interventions may depend on the type used and the characteristics of the patients to whom they are directed.

Theoretical orientations. On a macroscopic level, research has looked at the differential rates of effectiveness attributable to treatment procedures deriving from a variety of theoretical orientations. Not surprisingly, with over 240 different theoretical schools now in existence (e.g., Corsini, 1981), it has been extremely difficult to make direct comparisons between one therapeutic philosophy and another. Moreover, there are undoubtedly more similarities than differences among the activities of effective therapists from different schools (e.g., Fiedler, 1950). For the most part, though, therapists from different theoretical schools seem to hold different expectations (e.g., Houts, 1984) and to engage in interventions that are consistent with the philosophies expressed by those schools (e.g., Brunink & Schroeder, 1979; Cross & Sheehan, 1982; Larson, 1980; Lohmann & Mittag, 1979; Luborsky, Woody, McLellan, O'Brien, & Rosenzweig, 1982; Meara,

Pepinsky, Shannon, & Murray, 1981; Sloan et al., 1975).

In spite of the differences that characterize different therapeutic approaches, most reviewers conclude that there are few distinguishing psychotherapy outcomes among therapists from different schools (e.g., Luborsky, Singer, & Luborsky, 1975). The most extensive meta-analysis that had addressed this issue (Smith et al., 1980) yielded few significant differences in effect sizes among schools. Cognitive and behavior therapies, however, produced the two highest effect sizes and had impact on a broader range of problems than the other four classes studied. In response to criticisms that Smith et al. employed an unusually liberal definition of "psychotherapy," Shapiro and Shapiro (1982) applied a meta-analysis to a select sample of 143 studies. The results were, nonetheless, similar to those obtained earlier by Smith, Glass, and Miller. Nearly one standard deviation differentiated treated from untreated groups. Differences among treatment methods, however, accounted for only 10 percent of the variance in effect size and indicated that most of the treatment effects were produced independently of the specific theory adopted. Nonetheless, cognitive and behaviorally oriented treatments continued to produce the largest effect sizes, though modestly and nonsignificantly so.

Observing the potential power of cognitive and behavioral therapies, Miller and Berman (1983) applied a meta-analysis to 48 select studies, comparing those approaches that combined cognitive and behavioral interventions to more standard cognitive interventions. The authors found no significant differences between these two approaches, suggesting that both treatments exert a relatively consistent impact across a wide variety of problems, diagnostic categories, and types of measurement. More recently, comparative studies utilizing controlled assignment procedures confirm the conclusion that similar effects are obtained by behavioral and cognitively oriented therapy (Gallagher & Thompson, 1982; Taylor & Marshall, 1977; Wilson, Goldin, & Charbonneau-Powis, 1983). It is also noteworthy that cognitive therapy has consistently been found to exert at least an effect equal to that of antidepressant medications (Blackburn, Bishop, Glen, Whalley, & Christie, 1981; Murphy, Simons, Wetzel, & Lustman, 1984; Rush, Beck, Kovacs, & Hollon, 1977; Watkins, 1984).

The effects of cognitive therapy cannot be easily attributed to the cognitive changes induced by treatment (e.g., Simons, Garfield, & Murphy, 1984). Indeed, several studies have failed to find specific cognitive effects attributable to cognitive therapy when compared either to a behavioral or an interpersonal treatment approach (Zeiss, Lewinsohn, & Munoz, 1979). Many of these studies (e.g., Zeiss et al., 1979), however, have failed to utilize experienced therapists or have employed relatively brief treatment programs. Moreover, little attention has been paid to characteristics of patient groups, aside from their diagnostic identity.

In response to these concerns, increasing attention has been paid, in recent years, to the possibility that even though the average effects of different psychotherapies may be indistinguishable, patients with different characteristics may respond differentially to different treatment interventions. Confirmation of this point of view would lend support to the claims of most therapists that benefit is maximized if one alters therapeutic approaches to fit the unique needs of patients (e.g., Garfield & Kurtz, 1977; Norcross & Prochaska, 1983). The methodological problems in this type of investigation are overwhelming, however. One must not only define what the relevant patient dimensions are, but one must systematically control all concomitant and corollary variables at the same time that one assigns patients to different treatments on the basis of the relevant variables. If numerous variables are at work, as well they might be, effects might be masked by patients who present an undiscovered mix on several dimensions. For example, if a high score on one variable is predictive of the effectiveness of behavior therapy, pairing either treatment with individuals who are high on both variables may result in the inaccurate conclusion that the therapy exerts nondiscriminating effects.

In spite of these inordinate difficulties, the possibility of identifying some patient variables that may interact with therapy types to maximize treatment gains appears to be worthy of systematic and intensive examination. Most research on this issue has applied a correlational or post hoc methodology. Snider (1979), for example, asked therapists to describe the treatments of schizophrenic and neurotic patients. All therapists agreed that different interventions were required for the successful treatment of these two patient groups. Maintaining a specific therapeutic focus was targeted as significantly important for treating neurotics, while assuming a parental role was considered to be an important asset for working with schizophrenics. The value of such self-reports, however, cannot be totally trusted in view of the observation that even experienced therapists may require special training in order to modify their therapeutic focus to fit patient needs (Snider, 1979; Strupp, 1981).

In another post hoc effort to define relevant patient dimensions, Beutler (1979c) reviewed 52 comparative psychotherapy studies, paying particular attention to those studies in which systematic differences were found between types of psychotherapy. This effort resulted in the extrapolation of three patient dimensions that appeared to determine the effectiveness of different therapeutic procedures. In an effort to cross-validate one of these dimensions, Beutler and Mitchell (1981) differentiated between analytically oriented and experiential (e.g., emotive/abreactive) therapy on the basis of observed in-therapy behavior. Experiential therapy proved to be especially helpful for patients who relied on externalized (e.g., acting out) defenses. Specific technical procedures rather than global treatment packages, however, were more closely related to improvement.

Specific effects of psychotherapy with certain patient types were also sought in a subsequent study by the same investigators (Beutler, Frank, Scheiber, Calvert, & Gaines, 1984). In this study three distinct types of short-term group psychotherapy were provided to psychiatric inpatients. The findings suggested that supportive, process-focused interventions produced mildly positive effects among acutely disturbed patients, whereas emotionally expressive procedures actually induced deterioration among these patients and behavior therapy produced effects essentially equivalent to those obtained by the no-treatment control group.

Using naturalistic analyses of individual cases, Frances and Clarkin (1981a, 1981b) suggested that certain types of patients, including many of those with borderline disorders, should not be given regular treatment except in times of crisis. They propose that such patients may deteriorate during intensive long-term psychotherapy.

The possibility that specific psychotherapies can be tailored to fit specific patients is among the most intriguing and potentially beneficial movements in present psychotherapy research. Even though such matching of patient and technique may account for relatively little of the overall variance in treatment outcome, procedures tailored to highly specific patient dimensions offer the hope of meaningfully increasing treatment efficacy. Diagnostic groupings, however, are not sufficiently discriminatory to use effectively in this way. Systematic research is required in order to define more specific and predictive dimensions on which treatment might be matched to patients. While more promising than the usual theoretical formulations that are insensitive to variations among patients, validation of integrative treatment approaches is likely to be time consuming and expensive. Nonetheless, the proliferation of interest in this movement over the past several years (e.g., Beutler, 1983; Lazarus, 1980; Luborsky & McLellan, 1981; Prochaska, 1984) suggests that it may be an idea whose time has come.

CONCLUSIONS

Tables 7.1 through 7.4 summarize the relative influence of the major variables that have been considered in this chapter. By reference to these tables, the reader can observe that therapist gender, age, ethnicity (all in Table 7.1), general personality (Table 7.2), and verbal activity levels (Table 7.4) all exert an effect that changes as a function of the type of methodology employed. In the case of gender and general personality, significant findings are obtained among the more tightly controlled studies, with less rigorously controlled methodologies producing results that are either inconsistent or nonsignificant. This pattern suggests that these variables may exert a meaningful but relatively weak effect, which is easily masked or attenuated by other, undisclosed variables.

Although the box score approach we have used here to summarize findings does not speak directly to the *amount* of impact (e.g., effect size) exerted by a given variable, such inconsistency indirectly suggests that effect size attributable to the variable is quite small. Hence, weak methodologies prevent the emergence of significance, and well-controlled procedures are needed in order to allow these weak differences to emerge.

Inconsistency among findings does not necessarily mean that we should abandon a given area of research. In some instances, inconsistency may suggest that the concepts studied may be too broad and poorly defined to reflect meaningful changes. Consider, for example, the case in which the observed discordance is between the findings of analogue and process-focused studies, on one hand, and those that have assessed treatment outcomes on the other (e.g., therapist ethnicity, A−B type, training/discipline, theoretical orientation). Where few outcome data are available (e.g., Table 7.4—training/discipline), this discrepancy expresses the need to extend investigations to the realm of clinical effectiveness. In cases where there is an accumulation of process and outcome research, however, the same type of discrepancy suggests that the variable has little effect upon outcome and could well be discarded as a primary area of research investigation. For example, the wide differences between process and outcome findings with respect both to therapist A−B status (Table 7.2) and global theoretical orientations (Table 7.4) suggest that these two concepts have limited value for directing future research. In both of these cases, a wide variety of treatment outcomes have been explored with little indication of meaningful differences emerging.

One can easily observe that still other types of discrepancies in research findings point in yet different research directions. A reference to Table 7.1 will remind the reader that similarity in patient and therapist ethnicity seems to have quite a consistent effect upon treatment dropout rates, even though this effect is not apparent in other indices of treatment change. Given the clinical importance of dropout rates, the data argue that ethnicity may be a meaningful dimension for continued exploration. Particular attention might fruitfully be given to the means by which treatment maintenance might be enhanced in ethnically dissimilar dyads. Similarly, research attention might also be directed at understanding patient and therapy variables that may attenuate the negative influences of mismatching.

Therapist relationship attitudes (Table 7.3) are also examples of variables that exert still other types of complex effects on psychotherapy process and outcome. The effects of these variables appear to vary as a function of complex interplays among patient types, technical procedures, and therapists.

Certainly, continuing to investigate such variables within the simplistic model of unidirectional cause and effect assumptions does not appear to be warranted. More complex research models are needed that permit attention to these complexities.

Our conclusions can be summarized in the suggestion that the field would be well served by deemphasizing research on variables that have produced very discordant findings across studies of varying quality and by exploring in more creative ways those in which there is consistent or promising data and/or insufficient evidence to derive meaningful conclusions. Among the most promising therapist variables to have emerged from this review are therapist well-being, general attitude similarity, social influence attributes, expectations, intervention style, competence, SES, therapeutic alliance, and democratic attitudes. All of these variables exert an apparent and relatively consistent effect across the dimensions of methodological rigor. Some of these consistencies occur in areas where few systematic investigations have been undertaken (e.g., SES, democratic attitudes, and therapeutic alliance) and argue both for more research and cautiously optimistic conclusions. A number of other dimensions (e.g., therapists' well-being, social influence attitudes, expectation, and therapists' competence) reflect findings of relatively strong consistency within a critical accumulation of studies. The effects of these variables on treatment appears to be quite robust, meaningful, and deserving of continuing attention, both clinically and empirically.

One also observes in reviewing the tables that the consistency with which therapist characteristics have impact on change increases as one moves either from externally observed to internal characteristics or from enduring, extratherapy traits to in-therapy behaviors. Indeed, the most consistent and relatively strong effects emerge among studies of inferred, therapy-specific attributes. The more specific the variable to the treatment relationship and the more closely it reflects internal therapist experiences and attitudes, the more consistent the influence exerted by the variable. By extrapolation, consistent findings even in weak studies may reflect a relatively straightforward and/or large effect size atttributable to the therapist dimension. Considering these findings, we see little reason to depart form the conclusion of Parloff et al. (1978) that demographic variables and traits exert their effect through the mediating influences of the attitudes reflected in and characteristic of people who have these traits. The nature, formation, and influence of such attitudes in therapy-specific activities may be a more fruitful field of exploration than the simple study of extratherapy or demographic characteristics. Current research has failed to address many intriguing hypotheses about this process. For example, in our observation and in spite of the intuitively sensible hypothesis that relationship attitudes and interpersonal values may be particularly important in certain types of therapy (e.g., relationship-oriented approaches), relatively little research has been conducted on this issue. Many exciting possibilities for research in this area remain: Do the attitudes conveyed by gender, ethnicity, and so on, vary as a function of therapy type? If so, are the attitudes of equivalent importance in affecting outcome?

Finally, the current reviewers agree with Barrett and Wright (1984) in suggesting that few major advances of knowledge have accrued over the past decade. The greatest advances have been in research sophistication, methodology, and conception. The last decade is marked by the willingness of researchers to explore complex concepts and to develop new methodologies. While one observes in the foregoing review that few studies have applied systematic controls to the study of the primary variables under consideration, it is clear that recent research has exerted a considerably more creative effort to find ways of exploring therapist variables than ever before. With the awareness that unidirectional studies have produced largely weak and inconclusive results, increasing attention is being directed to understanding complex interactions between the therapist, the intervention, the patient, and the nature of outcome. The face of psychotherapy research is changing; the field is maturing; we are beginning to unravel answers to the time-worn litany of matching therapist, therapy, patient, and outcome; and new questions are emerging.

REFERENCES

Abramowitz, S. I., Davidson, C. V., Greene, L. R., & Edwards, D. W. (1980). Sex role-related countertransference revisited: A partial extension. *Journal of Nervous and Mental Disease, 168,* 309–311.

Abramowitz, S. I., & Murray, J. (1983). Race effects in psychotherapy. In J. Murray & P. R. Abramson (Eds.), *Bias in psychotherapy* (pp. 215–255). New York: Praeger.

Abramowitz, S. I., Roback, H. B., Schwartz, J. M., Yasuna, A., Abramowitz, C. V., & Gomes, B. (1976). Sex bias in psychotherapy: A failure to confirm. *American Journal of Psychiatry, 133,* 706–709.

Affleck, D. C., & Garfield, S. L. (1961). Predictive judgments of therapists and duration of stay in psychotherapy. *Journal of Clinical Psychology, 17,* 134–137.

Alexander, J. F., Barton, C., Schiavo, R. S., & Parsons, B. V. (1976). Systems-behavioral intervention with families of delinquents: Therapist characteristics, family behavior, and outcome. *Journal of Consulting and Clinical Psychology, 44,* 656–664.

Altman, B. A. (1977). Empathy, warmth and genuineness as reinforcement for patient self-exploration. *Dissertation Abstracts International, 37,* 5339B–5340B.

Amira, S., & Abramowitz, S. I. (1979). Therapeutic attraction as a function of therapist attire and office furnishings. *Journal of Consulting and Clinical Psychology, 47,* 198–200.

Anchor, K. (1977). Personality integration and successful outcome in individual psychotherapy. *Journal of Clinical Psychology, 33,* 245–246.

Andrews, S. B. (1976). The effect of sex of therapist and sex of client on termination from psychotherapy. *Dissertation Abstracts International, 36,* 4143B–4144B.

Antaki, C., & Brewin, C. (Eds.). (1982). *Attributions and psychological change.* New York: Academic Press.

Antonuccio, D. O., Lewinsohn, P. M., & Steinmetz, J. L. (1982). Identification of therapist differences in group treatment for depression. *Journal of Consulting and Clinical Psychology, 50,* 433–435.

Arizmendi, T. G., Beutler, L. E., Shanfield, S., Crago, M., & Hagaman, R. (1985). Client–therapist value similarity and psychotherapy outcome: A microscopic approach. *Psychotherapy: Theory, Research and Practice, 22,* 16–21.

Ashby, J. D., Ford, D. H., Guerney, B. G., Jr., & Guerney, L. F. (1957). Effects on clients of a reflective and a leading type of psychotherapy. *Psychological Monographs, 71,* Whole No. 453.

Auerbach, A. H., & Johnson, M. (1977). Research on the therapist's level of experience. In A. S. Gurman & A. M. Razin (Eds.), *Effective psychotherapy: A handbook of research* (pp. 84–102). New York: Pergamon.

Baekeland, F., & Lundwall, L. (1975). Dropping out of treatment: A critical review. *Psychological Bulletin, 82,* 738–783.

Baker, E. K. (1979). The relationship between locus of control and psychotherapy: A review of the literature. *Psychotherapy: Theory, Research and Practice, 16,* 351–362.

Balch, P., & Ross, A. W. (1975). Predicting success in weight reduction as a function of locus of control: A unidimensional vs. multidimensional approach. *Journal of Consulting and Clinical Psychology, 43,* 119.

Bandura, A., Lipsher, D. H., & Miller, P. E. (1960). Psychotherapists' approach-avoidance reaction to patients' expressions of hostility. *Journal of Consulting Psychology, 24,* 1–8.

Banikiotes, P. G., & Merluzzi, T. V. (1981). Impact of counselor gender and counselor sex role orientation on perceived counselor characteristics. *Journal of Counseling Psychology, 28,* 342–348.

Banks, G., Berenson, B. G., & Carkhuff, R. R. (1967). The effects of counselor race and training upon counseling process with Negro clients in initial interviews. *Journal of Clinical Psychology, 23,* 70–72.

Banks, W. M. (1972). The differential effects of race and social class in helping. *Journal of Clinical Psychology, 28,* 90–92.

Barrett, C. L., & Wright, J. H. (1984). Therapist variables. In M. Hersen, L. Michelson, & A. S. Bellack (Eds.), *Issues in psychotherapy research* (pp. 361–391). New York: Plenum.

Baum, O. E., Felzer, S. B., D'Zmura, T. L., & Shumaker, E. (1966). Psychotherapy, dropouts, and lower socioeconomic patients. *American Journal of Orthopsychiatry, 36,* 629–635.

Beier, E. G., & Young, D. (1984). *The silent language of psychotherapy: Social reinforcement of unconscious processes.* Hawthorne, NY: Aldine.

Beit-Hallahmi, B. (1975). Encountering orthodox religion in psychotherapy. *Psychotherapy: Theory, Research and Practice, 12,* 357–359.

Bent, R. J., Putnam, D. G., Kiesler, D. J., & Nowicki, S., Jr., (1976). Correlates of successful and unsuccessful psychotherapy. *Journal of Consulting and Clinical Psychology, 44,* 149.

Berenson, B. G., Mitchell, K. M., & Laney, R. C. (1968). Level of therapist functioning, types of confrontation and type of patient. *Journal of Clinical Psychology, 24,* 111–113.

Berenson, B. G., Mitchell, K. M., & Moravec, J. A. (1968). Level of therapist functioning, patient depth of self exploration and type of confrontation. *Journal of Counseling Psychology, 15,* 136–139.

Bergin, A. E. (1962). The effect of dissonant persuasive communications upon changes in self-referring attitude. *Journal of Personality, 30,* 423–438.

Bergin, A. E. (1966). Some implications of psychotherapy research for therapeutic practice. *Journal of Abnormal Psychology, 71,* 235–246.

Bergin, A. E. (1980). Psychotherapy and religious values. *Journal of Consulting and Clinical Psychology, 48,* 95–105.

Bergin, A. E., & Jasper, L. G. (1969). Correlates of empathy in psychotherapy: A replication. *Journal of Abnormal Psychology, 74,* 477–481.

Bergin, A. E., & Solomon, S. (1970). Personality and performance correlates of empathic understanding in psychotherapy. In J. T. Hart & T. M. Tomlinson (Eds.), *New directions in client-centered therapy* (pp. 223–236). Boston: Houghton Mifflin.

Berman, J. S. (In press). *Social bases of behavior.* Oxford: Oxford University Press.

Bernstein, B. L., & Figioli, S. W. (1983). Gender and credibility introduction effects on perceived counselor characteristics. *Journal of Counseling Psychology, 30,* 506–513.

Berzins, J. I. (1975, June). *Sex roles in psychotherapy: New directions for theory and research.* Paper presented at the meeting of the Society for Psychotherapy Research, Boston.

Berzins, J. I. (1977). Therapist–patient matching. In A. S. Gurman & A. M. Razin (Eds.), *Effective psychother-apy: A handbook of research* (pp. 222–251). New York: Pergamon.

Berzins, J. I., Welling, M. A., & Wetter, R. E. (1978). A new measure of psychological androgyny based on the Personality Research Form. *Journal of Consulting and Clinical Psychology, 46,* 126–138.

Betz, N.E., & Shullman, S. L. (1979). Factors related to client return rate following intake. *Journal of Counseling Psychology, 26,* 542–545.

Beutler, L. E. (1971a). Attitude similarity in marital therapy. *Journal of Consulting and Clinical Psychology, 37,* 298–301.

Beutler, L. E. (1971b). Predicting outcomes of psychotherapy: A comparison of predictions from two attitude theories. *Journal of Consulting and Clinical Psychology, 37,* 411–416.

Beutler, L.E. (1979a). Values, beliefs, religion and the persuasive influence of psychotherapy. *Psychotherapy: Theory, Research and Practice, 16,* 432–440.

Beutler, L.E. (1979b). Individual, group and family therapy modes: Patient–therapist value compatibility and treatment effectiveness. *Journal of Counseling and Psychotherapy, 2,* 43–59.

Beutler, L. E. (1979c). Toward specific psychological therapies for specific conditions. *Journal of Consulting and Clinical Psychology, 47,* 882–897.

Beutler, L. E. (1981). Covergence in counseling and psychotherapy: A current look. *Clinical Psychology Review, 1,* 79–101.

Beutler, L. E. (1983). *Eclectic psychotherapy: A systematic approach.* New York: Pergamon.

Beutler, L. E., Arizmendi, T. G., Crago, M., Shanfield, S., & Hagaman, R. (1983). The effects of value similarity and clients' persuadability on value convergence and psychotherapy improvement. *Journal of Social and Clinical Psychology, 1,* 231–245.

Beutler, L. E., Dunbar, P. W., & Baer, P. E. (1980). Individual variation among therapists' perceptions of patients, therapy process and outcome. *Psychiatry, 43,* 205–210.

Beutler, L. E., Frank, M., Scheiber, S. C., Calvert, S., & Gaines, J. (1984). Comparative effects of group psychotherapies in a short-term inpatient setting: An experience with deterioration effects. *Psychiatry, 47,* 66–76.

Beutler, L. E., Jobe, A. M., & Elkins, D. (1974). Outcomes in group psychotherapy: Using persuasion theory to increase treatment efficiency. *Journal of Consulting and Clinical Psychology, 42,* 547–553.

Beutler, L. E., Johnson, D. T., Neville, C.W., Jr., Elkins, D., & Jobe, A. M. (1975). Attitude similarity and therapist credibility as predictors of attitude change and improvement in psychotherapy. *Journal of Consulting and Clinical Psychology, 43,* 90–91.

Beutler, L. E., Johnson, D. T., Neville, C. W., Jr., & Workman, S. N. (1972). "Accurate empathy" and the A–B dichotomy. *Journal of Consulting and Clinical Psychology, 38,* 372–375.

Beutler, L. E., Johnson, D. T., Neville, C. W., Jr., & Workman, S. N. (1973a). Some sources of variance in "accurate empathy" ratings. *Journal of Consulting and Clinical Psychology, 40,* 167–169.

Beutler, L. E., Johnson, D. T., Neville, C. W., Jr., Workman, S. N. & Elkins, D. (1973b). The A–B therapy-type distinction, accurate empathy, nonpossessive warmth, and therapist genuineness in psychotherapy. *Journal of Abnormal Psychology, 82,* 273–277.

Beutler, L. E., & McNabb, C. (1981). Self-evaluation for the psychotherapist. In C. E. Walker (Ed.), *Clinical practice of psychology* (pp. 397–440). New York: Pergamon.

Beutler, L. E., & Mitchell, R. (1981). Differential psychotherapy outcome among depressed and impulsive patients as a function of analytic and experiential treatment procedures. *Psychiatry, 44,* 297–306.

Beutler, L. E., Pollack, S., & Jobe, A. M. (1978). "Acceptance," values and therapeutic change. *Journal of Consulting and Clinical Psychology, 46,* 198–199.

Binderman, R. M., Fretz, B. R., Scott, N. A., & Abrams, M. H. (1972). Effects of interpreter credibility and discrepancy level of results on responses to test results. *Journal of Counseling Psychology, 19,* 399–403.

Blackburn, I. M., Bishop, S., Glen, A. I. M., Whalley, L. G., & Christie, J. E. (1981). The efficacy of cognitive therapy in depression: A treatment trial using cognitive therapy and pharmacotherapy, each alone and in combination. *British Journal of Psychiatry, 139,* 181–189.

Blase, J. J. (1979). A study of the effects of sex of the client and sex of the therapist on clients' satisfaction with psychotherapy. *Dissertation Abstracts International, 39,* 6107B–6108B.

Bloom, L. J., Weigel, R. G., & Trautt, G. M. (1977). "Therapeugenic" factors in psychotherapy: Effects of office decor and subject–therapist sex pairing on the perception of credibility. *Journal of Consulting and Clinical Psychology, 45,* 867–873.

Brehm, S. S., & Brehm, J. W. (1981). *Psychological reactance: A theory of freedom and control.* New York: Academic Press.

Brooks, L. (1974). Interactive effects of sex and status on self-disclosure. *Journal of Counseling Psychology, 21,* 469–474.

Brooks, V. R. (1981). Sex and sexual orientation as variables in therapist's biases and therapy outcomes. *Clinical Social Work Journal, 9,* 198–210.

Brown, R. D. (1970). Experienced and inexperienced counselors' first impressions of clients and case outcomes: Are first impressions lasting? *Journal of Counseling Psychology, 17,* 550–558.

Brucato, L. L. (1980). Therapist and client expectancies: Educated guesses or casual agents? *Dissertation Abstracts International, 41,* 1493B–1494B.

Brunink, S. A., & Schroeder, H. E. (1979). Verbal therapeutic behavior of expert psychoanalytically oriented, gestalt, and behavior therapists. *Journal of Consulting and Clinical Psychology, 47,* 567–574.

Bruschi, G. (1982). Qualities of therapists and outcome in weight reduction groups. *Dissertation Abstracts International, 42,* 4764A–4765A.

Bryson, S., & Cody, J. (1973). Relationship of race and level of understanding between counselor and client. *Journal of Counseling Psychology, 20,* 495–498.

Buckley, P., Karasu, T. B., & Charles, E. (1981). Psychotherapists view their personal therapy. *Psychotherapy: Theory, Research and Practice, 18,* 299–305.

Butcher, J. N., Braswell, L., & Raney, D. (1983). A cross-cultural comparison of American Indian, black, and white inpatients on the MMPI and presenting symptoms. *Journal of Consulting and Clinical Psychology, 51,* 587–594.

Caligor, J. A. (1976). Perceptions of the group therapist

and the dropout from group. *Dissertation Abstracts International, 36,* 3591B.

Carkhuff, R. R., & Pierce, R. (1967). Differential effects of therapist race and social class upon patient depth of self-exploration in the initial clinical interview. *Journal of Consulting Psychology, 31,* 632–634.

Carson, R. C. (1967). A and B therapist "types": A possible critical variable in psychotherapy. *Journal of Nervous and Mental Disease, 144,* 47–54.

Carson, R. C., & Heine, R. W. (1962). Similarity and success in therapeutic dyads. *Journal of Consulting Psychology, 26,* 38–43.

Carson, R. C., & Llewellyn, C. E., Jr. (1966). Similarity in therapeutic dyads: A reevaluation. *Journal of Consulting Psychology, 30,* 458.

Cartwright, R. D., & Lerner, B. (1963). Empathy, need to change, and improvement with psychotherapy. *Journal of Consulting Psychology, 27,* 138–144.

Cartwright, R. D., & Vogel, J. L. (1960). A comparison of changes in psychoneurotic patients during matched periods of therapy and no therapy. *Journal of Consulting Psychology, 24,* 121–127.

Cavenar, J. O., Jr., & Werman, D. S. (1983). The sex of the psychotherapist. *American Journal of Psychiatry, 140,* 85–87.

Celotta, B., & Bode, P. (1982). Role of shared experience: A preference study. *Psychological Reports, 51,* 311–315.

Charone, J. K. (1981). Patient and therapist treatment goals related to psychotherapy outcome. *Dissertation Abstracts International, 42,* 365B.

Chartier, G. M., & Weiss, L. (1974). A–B therapists and clinical perception: Support for a "super A" hypothesis. *Journal of Consulting and Clinical Psychology, 42,* 312.

Childress, R., & Gillis, J. S. (1977). A study of pretherapy role induction as an influence process. *Journal of Clinical Psychology, 33,* 540–544.

Chinsky, J. M., & Rappaport, J. (1970). Brief critique of the meaning and reliability of "accurate empathy" ratings. *Psychological Bulletin, 73,* 379–382.

Cicchetti, D. V., & Ryan, E. R. (1976). A reply to Beutler et al.'s study: Some sources of variance in accurate empathy ratings. *Journal of Consulting and Clinical Psychology, 44,* 858–859.

Cimbolic, P. (1972). Counselor race and experience effects on black clients. *Journal of Consulting and Clinical Psychology, 39,* 328–332.

Claiborn, C. D., & Schmidt, L.D. (1977). Effects of presession information on the perception of the counselor in an interview. *Journal of Counseling Psychology, 24,* 259–263.

Cooley, E. J., & Lajoy, R. (1980). Therapeutic relationship and improvement as perceived by clients and therapists. *Journal of Clinical Psychology, 36,* 562–570.

Cornsweet, C. (1983). Nonspecific factors and theoretical choice. *Psychotherapy: Theory, Research and Practice, 20,* 307–313.

Corrigan, J. D. (1978). Salient attributes of two types of helpers: Friends and mental health professionals. *Journal of Counseling Psychology, 25,* 588–590.

Corrigan, J. D., Dell, D. M., Lewis, K. N., & Schmidt, L. D. (1980). Counseling as a social influence process: A review. *Journal of Counseling Psychology Monograph, 27,* 395–441.

Corsini, R. J. (Ed.) (1981). *Handbook of innovative psychotherapies.* New York: Wiley.

Costello, R. M., Baillargeon, J. G., Biever, P., & Bennett, R. (1979). Second-year alcoholism treatment outcome evaluation with a focus on Mexican-American patients. *American Journal of Drug and Alcohol Abuse, 6,* 97–108.

Cox, W. M. (1978). Where are the A and B therapists, 1970–1975? *Psychotherapy: Theory, Research and Practice, 15,* 108–121.

Cross, D. G., & Sheehan, P. W. (1982). Secondary therapist variables operating in short-term insight-oriented and behavior therapy. *British Journal of Medical Psychology, 55,* 275–284.

Curran, T. F. (1976). Anxiety reduction as a preliminary to group treatment. *Psychotherapy: Theory, Research and Practice, 13,* 354–360.

Cutler, R. L. (1958). Countertransference effects in psychotherapy. *Journal of Consulting Psychology, 22,* 349–356.

Davis, J. D., & Skinner, A. E. G. (1974). Reciprocity of self-disclosure in interviews: Modeling or social exchange? *Journal of Personality and Social Psychology, 29,* 779–784.

Davis, J. D., & Sloan, M. L. (1974). The basis of interviewee matching of interviewer self-disclosure. *British Journal of Social and Clinical Psychology, 13,* 359–367.

Deaux, K. (1984). From individual differences to social categories: Analysis of a decade's research on gender. *American Psychologist, 39,* 105–116.

Dell, D. M. (1973). Counselor power base, influence attempt, and behavior change in counseling. *Journal of Counseling Psychology, 20,* 399–405.

Dembo, R., Ikle, D. N., & Ciarlo, J. A. (1983). The influence of client–clinician demographic match on client treatment outcomes. *Journal of Psychiatric Treatment and Evaluation, 5,* 45–53.

Dent, J. K., & Furse, G. A. (1978). *Exploring the psychosocial therapies through the personalities of effective therapists* (DHEW Publication No. ADM 77-527). Washington, DC: U.S. Government Printing Office.

Derlega, V. J., Harris, M. S., & Chaikin, A. L. (1973). Self-disclosure reciprocity, liking and the deviant. *Journal of Experimental Social Psychology, 9,* 277–284.

Dies, R. R. (1977). Group therapist transparency: A critique of theory and research. *International Journal of Group Psychotherapy, 27,* 177–200.

Donnan, H. H., & Mitchell, H. D., Jr. (1979). Preferences for older versus younger counselors among a group of elderly persons. *Journal of Counseling Psychology, 26,* 514–518.

Donner, L., & Schonfield, J. (1975). Affect contagion in beginning psychotherapists. *Journal of Clinical Psychology, 31,* 332–339.

Dougherty, F. E. (1976). Patient–therapist matching for prediction of optimal and minimal therapeutic outcome. *Journal of Consulting and Clinical Psychology, 44,* 889–897.

Duckro, P., Beal, D., & George, C. (1979). Research on the effects of disconfirmed client role expectations in psychotherapy: A critical review. *Psychological Bulletin, 86,* 260–275.

Edinger, J. A., & Patterson, M. L. (1983). Nonverbal involvement and social control. *Psychological Bulletin, 93,* 30–56.

Eells, J. F. (1964). Therapists' views and preferences concerning intake cases. *Journal of Consulting Psychology, 28,* 382.

Ehrlich, R. P., D'Augelli, A. R., & Danish, S. J. (1979). Comparative effectiveness of six counselor verbal responses. *Journal of Counseling Psychology, 26,* 390–398.

Ekman, P. (1964). Body position, facial expression, and verbal behavior during interviews. *Journal of Abnormal and Social Psychology, 68,* 295–301.

Ellis, A. (1962). *Reason and emotion in psychotherapy.* New York: Lyle Stuart.

Epperson, D. L. (1981). Counselor gender and early premature terminations from counseling: A replication and extension. *Journal of Counseling Psychology, 28,* 349–356.

Epperson, D. L., Bushway, D. J., & Warman, R. E. (1983). Client self-terminations after one counseling session: Effects of problem recognition, counselor gender, and counselor experience. *Journal of Counseling Psychology, 30,* 307–315.

Ewing, T. N. (1974). Racial similarity of client and counselor and client satisfaction with counseling. *Journal of Counseling Psychology, 21,* 446–449.

Fairbanks, L. A., McGuire, M. T., & Harris, C. J. (1982). Nonverbal interaction of patients and therapists during psychiatric interviews. *Journal of Abnormal Psychology, 91,* 109–119.

Farber, B. A. (1983). The effects of psychotherapeutic practice upon psychotherapists. *Psychotherapy: Theory, Research and Practice, 20,* 174–182.

Feifel, H., & Eells, J. (1963). Patients and therapists assess the same psychotherapy. *Journal of Consulting Psychology, 27,* 310–318.

Feldstein, J. C. (1979). Effects of counselor sex and sex role and client sex on client's perceptions and self-disclosure in a counseling analogue study. *Journal of Counseling Psychology, 26,* 437–443.

Felipe, N. J., & Sommer, R. (1966). Invasion of personal space. *Social Problems, 14,* 206–214.

Fiedler, F. E. (1950). The concept of an ideal therapeutic relationship. *Journal of Consulting Psychology, 14,* 239–245.

Fiester, A. R., & Rudestam, K. E. (1975). A multivariate analysis of the early dropout process. *Journal of Consulting and Clinical Psychology, 43,* 528–535.

Fisher, E. H., & Howard, K. I. (1984, June). *The process of outcome in psychotherapy as a function of gender-pairing.* Paper presented at the Society for Psychotherapy Research, Lake Louise, Ontario, Canada.

Fiske, D. W., Cartwright, D. S., & Kirtner, W. L. (1964). Are psychotherapeutic changes predictable? *Journal of Abnormal and Social Psychology, 69,* 418–426.

Fiske, D. W., & Goodman, G. (1965). The posttherapy period. *Journal of Abnormal Psychology, 70,* 169–179.

Foreman, S. A., & Marmar, C. R. (1984, June). *Therapist actions which effectively address initial poor therapeutic alliances.* Paper presented at the Society for Psychotherapy Research, Lake Louise, Ontario, Canada.

Forer, B. R. (1969). The taboo against touching in psychotherapy. *Psychotherapy: Theory, Research and Practice, 6,* 229–231.

Forsyth, N. L., & Forsyth, D. R. (1982). Internality, controllability, and the effectiveness of attributional interpretations in counseling. *Journal of Counseling Psychology, 29,* 140–150.

Frances, A., & Clarkin, J. F. (1981a). Differential therapeutics: A guide to treatment selection. *Hospital and Community Psychiatry, 32,* 537–546.

Frances, A., & Clarkin , J. F. (1981b). No treatment as the prescription of choice. *Archives of General Psychiatry, 38,* 542–545.

Frank, J. D. (1973). *Persuasion and healing: A comparative study of psychotherapy* (rev. ed.). Baltimore: Johns Hopkins University Press.

Fretz, B. R. (1966). Postural movements in a counseling dyad. *Journal of Counseling Psychology, 13,* 335–343.

Gallagher, D. E., & Thompson, L. W. (1982). Treatment of major depressive disorder in older adult outpatients with brief psychotherapies. *Psychotherapy: Theory, Research and Practice, 19,* 482–490.

Ganahl, G. F. (1982). Effects of client, treatment, and therapist variables on the outcome of structured marital enrichment. *Dissertation Abstracts International, 42,* 4576B.

Gardner, W. E. (1972). The differential effects of race, education and experience in helping. *Journal of Clinical Psychology, 28,* 87–89.

Garfield, S. L., & Affleck, D. C. (1961). Therapists' judgments concerning patients considered for psychotherapy. *Journal of Consulting Psychology, 25,* 505–509.

Garfield, S. L., Affleck, D. C., & Muffly, R. A. (1963). A study of psychotherapy interaction and continuation of psychotherapy. *Journal of Clinical Psychology, 19,* 473–478.

Garfield, S. L., & Bergin, A. E. (1971). Personal therapy, outcome and some therapist variables. *Psychotherapy: Theory, Research and Practice, 8,* 251–253.

Garfield, S. L., & Kurtz, R. (1976). Personal therapy for the psychotherapist: Some findings and issues. *Psychotherapy: Theory, Research and Practice, 13,* 188–192.

Garfield, S. L., & Kurtz, R. (1977). A study of eclectic views. *Journal of Consulting and Clinical Psychology, 45,* 78–83.

Getz, H. G., & Miles, J. H. (1978). Women and peers as counselors: A look at client preferences. *Journal of College Student Personnel, 19,* 37–41.

Gilbert, L. A. (1981). Toward mental health: The benefits of psychological androgyny. *Professional Psychology, 12,* 29–38.

Goin, M. K., Yamamoto, J., & Silverman, J. (1965). Therapy congruent with class-linked expectations. *Archives of General Psychiatry, 13,* 133–137.

Goldstein, A. P. (1960). Therapist and client expectation of personality change in psychotherapy. *Journal of Counseling Psychology, 7,* 180–184.

Goldstein, A. P. (1971). *Psychotherapeutic attraction.* New York: Pergamon.

Goldstein, A. P., Heller, K., & Sechrest, L. B. (1966). *Psychotherapy and the psychology of behavior change.* New York: Wiley.

Goldstein, A. P., & Simonson, N. R. (1971). Social psychological approaches to psychotherapy research. In A. E. Bergin & S. L. Garfield (Eds.), *Handbook of psychotherapy and behavior change* (pp. 154–195). New York: Wiley.

Goldstone, M. G. (1971). Differences in prognosis for psychotherapy as a function of client race. *Dissertation Abstracts International, 33,* 4992B–4993B.

Gomes-Schwartz, B. (1978). Effective ingredients in psychotherapy: Prediction of outcome from process variables. *Journal of Consulting and Clinical Psychology, 46,* 1023–1035.

Gomes-Schwartz, B., & Schwartz, J. M. (1978). Psychotherapy process variables distinguishing the "inherently helpful" person from the professional psychotherapist. *Journal of Consulting and Clinical Psychology, 46,* 196–197.

Gottschalk, L. A., Mayerson, P., & Gottlieb, A. A. (1967). Prediction and evaluation of outcome in an emergency brief psychotherapy clinic. *Journal of Nervous and Mental Disease, 144,* 77–96.

Grantham, R. J. (1973). Effects of counselor sex, race, and language style on black students in initial interviews. *Journal of Counseling Psychology, 20,* 553–559.

Greenberg, L. S., & Dompierre, L. M. (1981). Specific effects of Gestalt two-chair dialogue on intrapsychic conflict in counseling. *Journal of Counseling Psychology, 28,* 288–294.

Greenberg, R. P. (1969). Effects of presession information on perception of the therapist and receptivity to influence in a psychotherapy analogue. *Journal of Consulting and Clinical Psychology, 33,* 425–429.

Greenberg, R. P., & Staller, J. (1981). Personal therapy for therapists. *American Journal of Psychiatry, 138,* 1467–1471.

Griffith, M. S., & Jones, E. E. (1978). Race and psychotherapy: Changing perspectives. In J. H. Masserman (Ed.), *Current psychiatric therapies* (Vol. 18, pp. 225–235). New York: Grune & Stratton.

Grigg, A. E. (1961). Client response to counselors at different levels of experience. *Journal of Counseling Psychology, 8,* 217–222.

Grigg, A. E., & Goodstein, L. D. (1957). The use of clients as judges of the counselor's performance. *Journal of Counseling Psychology, 4,* 31–36.

Guild, M. (1969). Therapeutic effectiveness of analyzed and non-analyzed therapists. *Dissertation Abstracts International, 30,* 1897B–1898B.

Gunderson, J. G. (1978). Patient–therapist matching: A research evaluation. *American Journal of Psychiatry, 135,* 1193–1197.

Gulas, I. (1974). Client–therapist congruence in prognostic and role expectations as related to clients' improvement in short-term psychotherapy. *Dissertation Abstracts International, 35,* 2430B.

Gurman, A. S. (1973). Instability of therapeutic conditions in psychotherapy. *Journal of Counseling Psychology, 20,* 16–24.

Gurman, A. S. (1977). The patient's perception of the therapeutic relationship. In A. S. Gurman & A. M. Razin (Eds.), *Effective psychotherapy: A handbook of research,* (pp. 503–543). New York: Pergamon.

Guttman, M. A. J., & Haase, R. R. (1972). Effect of experimentally induced sets of high and low "expertness" during brief vocational counseling. *Counselor Education and Supervision, 11,* 171–178.

Gynther, M. D. (1972). White norms and black MMPI's: A prescription for discrimination? *Psychological Bulletin, 78,* 386–402.

Gynther, M. D. (1979). Ethnicity and personality: An update. In J. N. Butcher (Ed.), *New developments in the use of the MMPI* (pp. 113–140). Minneapolis: University of Minnesota Press.

Haase, R. F., & Tepper, D. T., Jr. (1972). Nonverbal components of empathic communication. *Journal of Counseling Psychology, 19,* 417–424.

Haccoun, D. M., & Lavigueur, H. (1979). Effects of clinical experience and client emotion on therapists' responses. *Journal of Consulting and Clinical Psychology, 47,* 416–418.

Hansen, J. C., Moore, G. D., & Carkhuff, R. R. (1968). The differential relationships of objective and client perceptions of counseling. *Journal of Clinical Psychology, 24,* 244–246.

Harper, R. G., Wiens, A. N., & Matarazzo, J. D. (1978). *Nonverbal communication: The state of the art.* New York: Wiley.

Hart, L. E. (1981). An investigation of the effect of male therapists' views of women on the process and outcome of therapy with women. *Dissertation Abstracts International, 42,* 2529B.

Hartley, D. L. (1969). Perceived counselor credibility as a function of the effects of counseling interaction. *Journal of Counseling Psychology, 16,* 63–68.

Hattie, J. A., Sharpley, C. F., & Rogers, H. J. (1984). Comparative effectiveness of professional and paraprofessional helpers. *Psychological Bulletin, 95,* 534–541.

Heffernon, A., & Bruehl, D. (1971). Some effects of race of inexperienced lay counselors on black junior high school students. *Journal of School Psychology, 9,* 35–37.

Heine, R. W., & Trosman, H. (1960). Initial expectations of the doctor–patient interaction as a factor in continuance in psychotherapy. *Psychiatry, 23,* 275–278.

Heitler, J. B. (1976). Preparatory techniques in initiating expressive psychotherapy with lower-class, unsophisticated patients. *Psychological Bulletin, 83,* 339–352.

Heller, K., & Goldstein, A. P. (1961). Client dependency and therapist expectancy as relationship maintaining variables in psychotherapy. *Journal of Consulting Psychology, 25,* 371–375.

Henning, L. H., & Tirrell, F. J. (1982). Counselor resistance to spiritual exploration. *Personnel and Guidance Journal, 61,* 92–95.

Heppner, P. P., & Dixon, D. N. (1978). Effects of client perceived need and counselor role on client's behaviors. *Journal of Counseling Psychology, 25,* 514–519.

Heppner, P. P., & Dixon, D. N. (1981). A review of the interpersonal influence process in counseling. *Personnel and Guidance Journal, 59,* 542–550.

Heppner, P. P., & Heesacker, M. (1982). Interpersonal influence process in real-life counseling: Investigating client perceptions, counselor experience level, and counselor power over time. *Journal of Counseling Psychology, 29,* 215–223.

Heppner, P. P., & Heesacker, M. (1983). Perceived counselor characteristics, client expectations, and client satisfaction with counseling. *Journal of Counseling Psychology, 30,* 31–39.

Heppner, P. P., & Pew, S. (1977). Effects of diplomas, awards, and counselor sex on perceived expertness. *Journal of Counseling Psychology, 24,* 147–149.

Hill, C. E. (1975). Sex of client and sex and experience level of counselor. *Journal of Counseling Psychology, 22,* 6–11.

Hill, C. E., Carter, J. A., & O'Farrell, M. K. (1983). A case study of the process and outcome of time-limited counseling. *Journal of Counseling Psychology, 30,* 3–18.

Hill, J. A., Howard, K. I., & Orlinsky, D. E. (1970). The therapist's experience of psychotherapy: Some dimensions and determinants. *Multivariate Behavioral Research, 5,* 435–451.

Hoehn-Saric, R., Frank, J. D., Imber, S. D., Nash, E. H., Stone, A. R., & Battle, C. C. (1964). Systematic preparation of patients for psychotherapy: I. Effects on therapy behavior and outcome. *Journal of Psychiatric Research, 2,* 267–281.

Hoehn-Saric, R., Liberman, B., Imber, S. D., Stone, A. R., Frank, J. D., & Ribich, F. D. (1974). Attitude change and attribution of arousal in psychotherapy. *Journal of Nervous and Mental Disease, 159,* 234–243.

Hoffman, M. A., & Spencer, G. P. (1977). Effect of interviewer self-disclosure and interviewer-subject sex pairing on perceived and actual subject behavior. *Journal of Counseling Psychology, 24,* 383–390.

Holliday, P. B. (1979). Effects of preparation for therapy on client expectations and participation. *Dissertation Abstracts International, 39,* 3517B.

Holroyd, J. C., & Brodsky, A. M. (1977). Psychologists' attitudes and practices regarding erotic and nonerotic physical contact with patients. *American Psychologist, 32,* 843–849.

Holroyd, J. C., & Brodsky, A. M. (1980). Does touching patients lead to sexual intercourse? *Professional Psychology, 11,* 807–811.

Holzman, M. S. (1962). The significance of the value systems of patient and therapist for the outcome of psychotherapy. *Dissertation Abstracts, 22,* 4073.

Horn-George, J. B., & Anchor, K. N. (1982). Perceptions of the psychotherapy relationship in long- versus short-term therapy. *Professional Psychology, 13,* 483–491.

Horowitz, M. J., Marmar, C., Weiss, D. S., DeWitt, K. N., & Rosenbaum, R. (1984). Brief psychotherapy of bereavement reactions: The relationship of process to outcome. *Archives of General Psychiatry, 41,* 438–448.

Houts, A. C. (1984). Effects of clinician theoretical orientation and patient explanatory bias on initial clinical judgments. *Professional Psychology: Research and Practice, 15,* 284–293.

Howard, K., Rickels, K., Mock, J. E., Lipman, R. S., Covi, L., & Baumm, N. C. (1970). Therapeutic style and attrition rate from psychiatric drug treatment. *Journal of Nervous and Mental Disease, 150,* 102–110.

Hoyt, M. F. (1980). Therapist and patient actions in "good" psychotherapy sessions. *Archives of General Psychiatry, 37,* 159–161.

Hoyt, M. F., Xenakis, S. N., Marmar, C. R., & Horowitz, M. J. (1983). Therapists' actions that influence their perceptions of "good" psychotherapy sessions. *Journal of Nervous and Mental Disease, 171,* 400–404.

Hubble, M. A., Noble, F. C., & Robinson, S. E. (1981). The effect of counselor touch in the initial counseling session. *Journal of Counseling Psychology, 28,* 533–535.

Humphries, R. H. (1982). Therapeutic neutrality reconsidered. *Journal of Religion and Health, 21,* 124–131.

Jacobs, D., Charles, E., Jacobs, T., Weinstein, H., & Mann, D. (1972). Preparation for treatment of the disadvantaged patient: Effects on disposition and outcome. *American Journal of Orthopsychiatry, 42,* 666–674.

Jacobs, M. K., Trick, O. L., & Withersty, D. (1976). Pretraining psychiatric inpatients for participation in group psychotherapy. *Psychotherapy: Theory, Research and Practice, 13,* 361–367.

Jesness, C. F. (1975). Comparative effectiveness of behavior modification and transactional analysis programs for delinquents. *Journal of Consulting and Clinical Psychology, 43,* 758–779.

Johnson, D. T., Workman, S. N., Neville, C. W., Jr., & Beutler, L. E. (1973). MMPI and 16PF correlates of the A–B therapy scale in psychiatric inpatients. *Psychotherapy: Theory, Research and Practice, 10,* 270–272.

Jones, E. E. (1978). Effects of race on psychotherapy process and outcome: An exploratory investigation. *Psychotherapy: Theory, Research and Practice, 15,* 226–236.

Jones, E. E., & Zoppel, C. L. (1982). Impact of client and therapist gender on psychotherapy process and outcome. *Journal of Consulting and Clinical Psychology, 50,* 259–272.

June, L. N., & Smith, E. J. (1983). A comparison of client and counselor expectancies regarding the duration of counseling. *Journal of Counseling Psychology, 30,* 596–599.

Kandel, D. B. (1966). Status homophily, social context, and participation in psychotherapy. *American Journal of Sociology, 71,* 640–650.

Karasu, T., Stein, S. P., & Charles, E. (1979). Age factors in patient–therapist relationship. *Journal of Nervous and Mental Disease, 167,* 100–104.

Kaschak, E. (1978). Therapist and client: Two views of the process and outcome of psychotherapy. *Professional Psychology, 9,* 271–277.

Katz, M. M., Lorr, M., & Rubinstein, E. A. (1958). Remainer patient attributes and their relation to subsequent improvement in psychotherapy. *Journal of Consulting Psychology, 22,* 411–413.

Kaufman, M., & Bluestone, H. (1974). Patient–therapist: Are we free to choose therapy? *Groups: A Journal of Group Dynamics and Psychotherapy, 6,* 1–13.

Kazdin, A. E. (1979). Nonspecific treatment factors in psychotherapy outcome research. *Journal of Consulting and Clinical Psychology, 47,* 846–851.

Kelly, F. D. (1972). Communicational significance of therapist proxemic cues. *Journal of Consulting and Clinical Psychology, 39,* 345.

Kerr, B. A., & Dell, D. M. (1976). Perceived interviewer expertness and attractiveness: Effects of interviewer behavior and attire and interview setting. *Journal of Counseling Psychology, 23,* 553–556.

Kilmann, P. R., & Howell, R. J. (1974). Effects of structure of marathon group therapy and locus of control on therapeutic outcome. *Journal of Consulting and Clinical Psychology, 42,* 912.

King, D. G., & Blaney, P. H. (1977). Effectiveness of A and B therapists with schizophrenics and neurotics: A referral study. *Journal of Consulting and Clinical Psychology, 45,* 407–411.

Kirshner, L. A., Genack, A., & Hauser, S. T. (1978). Effects of gender on short-term psychotherapy. *Psychotherapy: Theory, Research and Practice, 15,* 158–167.

Knapp, P. H., Levin, S., McCarter, R. H., Wermer, H., & Zetzel, E. (1960). Suitability for psychoanalysis: A review of one hundred supervised analytic cases. *Psychoanalytic Quarterly, 29,* 459–477.

Kolb, D. L., Beutler, L. E., Davis, C. S., Crago, M., & Shanfield, S. (In press). Patient personality, locus of control, involvement, therapy relationship, drop-out and change in psychotherapy. *Psychotherapy: Theory, Research and Practice.*

Kopoian, S. S. (1982). The effects of therapists' A–B status, experience and education, and of client variables on psychotherapy outcome. *Dissertation Abstracts International, 42,* 4196B.

Krauskopf, C. J., Baumgardner, A., & Mandracchia, S. (1981). Return rate following intake revisited. *Journal of Counseling Psychology, 28,* 519–521.

Krebs, R. L. (1971). Some effects of a white institution on black psychiatric outpatients. *American Journal of Orthopsychiatry, 41,* 589–596.

Kreisberg, G. J. (1978). The relationship of the congruence of patient–therapist goal expectancies to psychotherapy outcome and duration of treatment. *Dissertation Abstracts International, 38,* 3890B.

Kumar, U., & Pepinsky, H. B. (1965). Counselor expectancies and therapeutic evaluations. *Proceedings of the 73rd Annual Convention of the American Psychological Association, 21,* 357–358.

LaCrosse, M. B. (1980). Perceived counselor social influence and counseling outcomes: Validity of the Counselor Rating Form. *Journal of Counseling Psychology, 27,* 320–327.

Lambert, M. J., & Bergin, A. E. (1983). Therapist characteristics and their contribution to psychotherapy outcome. In C. E. Walker (Ed.), *The handbook of clinical psychology* (Vol. 1, pp. 205–241). Homewood, IL: Dow Jones-Irwin.

Lambert, M. J., & DeJulio, S. S. (1977). Outcome research in Carkhuff's Human Resource Development Training Programs: Where is the donut? *Counseling Psychologist, 6,* 79–86.

Lambert, M. J., & DeJulio, S. S. (1978, March). *The relative importance of client, therapist, and technique variables as predictors of psychotherapy outcome: The place of therapist "nonspecific" factors.* Paper presented at the meeting of the American Psychological Association, Scottsdale, AZ.

Larson, D. G. (1980). Therapeutic schools, styles, and schoolism: A national survey. *Journal of Humanistic Psychology, 20,* 3–20.

Lasky, R. G., & Salomone, P. R. (1977). Attraction to psychotherapy: Influences of therapist status and therapist–patient age similarity. *Journal of Clinical Psychology, 33,* 511–516.

LaTorre, R. A. (1977). Pretherapy role induction procedures. *Canadian Psychological Review, 18,* 308–321.

Lazarus, A. A. (1980). *The practice of multimodal therapy.* New York: McGraw-Hill.

Lee, D. Y., Hallberg, E. T., Jones, L., & Haase, R. F.

(1980). Effects of counselor gender on perceived credibility. *Journal of Counseling Psychology, 27,* 71–75.

Lerner, B. (1972). *Therapy in the ghetto: Political impotence and personal disintegration.* Baltimore: Johns Hopkins University Press.

Lerner, B. (1973). Democratic values and therapeutic efficacy: A construct validity study. *Journal of Abnormal Psychology, 82,* 491–498.

Lesser, W. M. (1961). The relationship between couseling progress and empathic understanding. *Journal of Counseling Psychology, 8,* 330–336.

Levant, R. F., & Shlien, J. M. (1984). *Client-centered therapy and the person-centered approach.* New York: Praeger.

Lewis, J. M., & Johansen, K. H. (1982). Resistances to psychotherapy with the elderly. *American Journal of Psychotherapy, 36,* 497–504.

Lewis, K. N. (1983, August.). *The impact of religious affiliation on therapists' judgments of clients.* Paper presented at American Psychological Association Convention, Anaheim, CA.

Lick, J. R., & Heffler, D. (1977). Relaxation training and attention placebo in the treatment of severe insomnia. *Journal of Consulting and Clinical Psychology, 45,* 153–161.

Lieberman, M. A., Yalom, I. D., & Miles, M. B. (1973). *Encounter groups: First facts.* New York: Basic Books.

Lohmann, J., & Mittag, O. (1979, July). *The assessment of perceived therapist behavior as a contribution to indication research.* Paper presented at the meeting of the Society for Psychotherapy Research, Oxford, England.

Lorion, R. P. (1973). Socioeconomic status and traditional treatment approaches reconsidered. *Psychological Bulletin, 79,* 263–270.

Lorion, R. P. (1974). Patient and therapist variables in the treatment of low-income patients. *Psychological Bulletin, 81,* 344–354.

Lorr, M. (1965). Client perceptions of therapists: A study of the therapeutic relation. *Journal of Consulting Psychology, 29,* 146–149.

Luborsky, L., Chandler, M., Auerbach, A. H., Cohen, J., & Bachrach, H. M. (1971). Factors influencing the outcome of psychotherapy. *Psychological Bulletin, 75,* 145–185.

Luborsky, L., Crits-Christoph, P., Alexander, L., Margolis, M., & Cohen, M. (1983a). Two helping alliance methods for predicting outcomes of psychotherapy: A counting signs vs. a global rating method. *Journal of Nervous and Mental Disease, 171,* 480–491.

Luborsky, L., & McLellan, A. T. (1981). Optimal matching of patients with types of psychotherapy: What is known and some designs for knowing more. In E. Gottheil, A. T. McLellan, & K. A. Druley (Eds.), *Matching patient needs and treatment methods in alcohol and drug abuse* (pp. 51–71). Springfield, IL: Charles C. Thomas.

Luborsky, L., McLellan, A. T., Woody, G. E., & O'Brien, C. P. (1983b, July). *Therapists' success rates and their determinants.* Paper presented at the meeting of the Society for Psychotherapy Research, Sheffield, England.

Luborsky, L., Mintz, J., Auerbach, A., Christoph, P., Bachrach, H., Todd, T., Johnson, M., Cohen, M., & O'Brien, C. P. (1980). Predicting the outcome of psychotherapy: Findings of the Penn Psychotherapy Project. *Archives of General Psychiatry, 37,* 471–481.

Luborsky, L., Singer, B., & Luborsky, L. (1975). Comparative studies of psychotherapies: Is it true that "everyone has won and all must have prizes"? *Archives of General Psychiatry, 32,* 995–1008.

Luborsky, L., Woody, G. E., McLellan, A. T., O'Brien, C. P., & Rosenzweig, J. (1982). Can independent judges recognize different psychotherapies? An experience with manual-guided therapies. *Journal of Consulting and Clinical Psychology, 50,* 49–62.

Malan, D. H. (1976). *Toward the validation of dynamic psychotherapy.* New York: Plenum Press.

Mann, B., & Murphy, K. C. (1975). Timing of self-disclosure, reciprocity of self-disclosure, and reactions to an initial interview. *Journal of Counseling Psychology, 22,* 304–308.

Marshall, K. A. (1977). Empathy, genuineness and regard: Determinants of successful therapy with schizophrenics? A critical review. *Psychotherapy: Theory, Research and Practice, 14,* 57–64.

Martin, D. O., & Thomas, M. B. (1982). Black student preferences for counselors: The influence of age, sex, and type of problem. *Journal of Non-White Concerns in Personnel and Guidance, 10,* 143–153.

Martin, P. J., Moore, J. E., & Sterne, A. L. (1977). Therapists as prophets: Their expectancies and treatment outcome. *Psychotherapy: Theory, Research and Practice, 14,* 188–195.

Martin, P. J., & Sterne, A. L. (1975). Prognostic expectations and treatment outcome. *Journal of Consulting and Clinical Psychology, 43,* 572–576.

Martin, P. J., & Sterne, A. L. (1976). Post-hospital adjustment as related to therapists' in-therapy behavior. *Psychotherapy: Theory, Research and Practice, 13,* 267–273.

Martin, P. J., Sterne, A. L., & Hunter, M. L. (1967). Share and share alike: Mutuality of expectations and satisfaction with therapy. *Journal of Clinical Psychology, 32,* 677–683.

Martin, R. M., & Prosen, H. (1976). Psychotherapy supervision and life tasks: The young therapist and the middle-aged patient. *Bulletin of the Menninger Clinic, 40,* 125–133.

Marx, J. H., & Spray, S. L. (1972). Psychotherapeutic "birds of a feather": Social-class status and religiocultural value homophily in the mental health field. *Journal of Health and Social Behavior, 13,* 413–428.

Marziali, E. A. (1984). Prediction of outcome of brief psychotherapy from therapist interpretive interventions. *Archives of General Psychiatry, 41,* 301–304.

Marziali, E., Marmar, C., & Krupnick, J. (1981). Therapeutic alliance scales: Development and relationship to psychotherapy outcome. *American Journal of Psychiatry, 138,* 361–364.

Marziali, E. A., & Sullivan, J. M. (1980). Methodological issues in the content analysis of brief psychotherapy. *British Journal of Medical Psychology, 53,* 19–27.

Matthews, J. G., & Burkhart, B. R. (1977). A–B therapist status, patient diagnosis, and psychotherapy outcome in a psychiatric outpatient population. *Journal of Consulting and Clinical Psychology, 45,* 475–482.

Maurer, R. E., & Tindall, J. H. (1983). Effect of postural congruence on client's perception of counselor empathy. *Journal of Counseling Psychology, 30,* 158–163.

McCarron, L. T., & Appel, V. H. (1971). Categories of therapist verbalizations and patient–therapist autonomic response. *Journal of Consulting and Clinical Psychology, 37,* 123–134.

McCarthy, P. R., & Betz, N. E. (1978). Differential effects of self-disclosing versus self-involving counselor statements. *Journal of Counseling Psychology, 25,* 251–256.

McKee, K., & Smouse, A. D. (1983). Clients' perceptions of counselor expertness, attractiveness, and trustworthiness: Initial impact of counselor status and weight. *Journal of Counseling Psychology, 30,* 332–338.

McNair, D. M., Callahan, D. M., & Lorr, M. (1962). Therapist "type" and patient response to psychotherapy. *Journal of Consulting Psychology, 26,* 425–429.

McNair, D. M., Lorr, M., & Callahan, D. M. (1963). Patient and therapist influences on quitting psychotherapy. *Journal of Consulting Psychology, 27,* 10–17.

McNeal, B. F., Johnston, R., & Aspromonte, V. A. (1970). Effect of accurate forecasts on length of hospital stay of psychiatric patients. *Journal of Consulting and Clinical Psychology, 35,* 91–94.

Meara, N. M., Pepinsky, H. B., Shannon, J. W., & Murray, W. A. (1981). Semantic communication and expectations for counseling across three theoretical orientations. *Journal of Counseling Psychology, 28,* 110–118.

Mehrabian, A. (1968). Inference of attitudes from the posture, orientation, and distance of a communicator. *Journal of Consulting and Clinical Psychology, 32,* 296–308.

Mehrabian, A. (1970). When are feelings communicated inconsistently? *Journal of Experimental Research in Personality, 4,* 198–212.

Mejia, J. A. (1981). Contributions of therapist relationship and structuring skills to marital therapy outcome variance in a Hispanic clinical couple population. *Dissertation Abstracts International, 42,* 779B.

Mendelsohn, G. A. (1968). *Client–counselor compatibility and the effectiveness of counseling.* Unpublished manuscript, University of California, Berkeley.

Mendelsohn, G. A., & Geller, M. H. (1963). Effects of counselor–client similarity on the outcome of counseling. *Journal of Counseling Psychology, 10,* 71–77.

Mendelsohn, G. A., & Geller, M. H. (1967). Similarity, missed sessions, and early termination. *Journal of Counseling Psychology, 14,* 210–215.

Mendola, J. J. (1982). Therapist interpersonal skills: A model for professional development and therapeutic effectiveness. *Dissertation Abstracts International, 42,* 4201B.

Merluzzi, T. V., Merluzzi, B. H., & Kaul, T. J. (1977). Counselor race and power base: Effects on attitudes and behavior. *Journal of Counseling Psychology, 24,* 430–436.

Messer, S. B., & Meinster, M. O. (1980). Interaction effects of internal vs. external locus of control and directive

vs. nondirective therapy: Fact or fiction? *Journal of Clinical Psychology, 36,* 283–288.

Miles, J. E., McLean, P. D., & Maurice, W. L. (1976). The medical student therapist: Treatment outcome. *Canadian Psychiatric Association Journal, 21,* 467–472.

Miller, R. C., & Berman, J. S. (1983). The efficacy of cognitive behavior therapies: A quantitative review of the research evidence. *Psychological Bulletin, 94,* 39–53.

Mindess, H. (1953). Predicting patients' responses to psychotherapy: A preliminary study designed to investigate the validity of the "Rorschach Prognostic Rating Scale." *Journal of Projective Techniques, 17,* 327–334.

Mintz, E. E. (1969). On the rationale of touch in psychotherapy. *Psychotherapy: Theory, Research and Practice, 6,* 232–234.

Mintz, J., O'Brien, C. P., & Luborsky, L. (1976). Predicting the outcome of psychotherapy for schizophrenics: Relative contributions of patient, therapist, and treatment characteristics. *Archives of General Psychiatry, 33,* 1183–1186.

Mintz, J., & Luborsky, L. (1971). Segments vs. whole sessions: Which is the better unit for psychotherapy research? *Journal of Abnormal Psychology, 78,* 180–191.

Mintz, J., Luborsky, L., & Auerbach, A. H. (1971). Dimensions of psychotherapy: A factor-analytic study of ratings of psychotherapy sessions. *Journal of Consulting and Clinical Psychology, 36,* 106–120.

Mitchell, K. M., & Atkinson, B. (1983). The relationship between therapist and client social class and participation in therapy. *Professional Psychology, 14,* 310–316.

Mitchell, K. M., Bozarth, J. D., & Krauft, C. C. (1977). A reappraisal of the therapeutic effectiveness of accurate empathy, nonpossessive warmth, and genuineness. In A. S. Gurman & A. M. Razin (Eds.), *Effective psychotherapy: A handbook of research* (pp. 482–502). New York: Pergamon.

Mitchell, K. M., & Hall, L. A. (1971). Frequency and type of confrontation over time within the first therapy interview. *Journal of Consulting and Clinical Psychology, 37,* 437–442.

Mitchell, K. M., & Namenek, T. M. (1970). A comparison of therapist and client social class. *Professional Psychology, 1,* 225–230.

Mogul, K. M. (1982). Overview: The sex of the therapist. *American Journal of Psychiatry, 139,* 1–11.

Morey, E. L., & Watkins, J. T. (1974). Locus of control and effectiveness of two rational-emotive therapy styles. *Rational Living, 9,* 22–24.

Morgan, R. W. (1978). The relationships among therapeutic alliance, therapist facilitative behaviors, patient insight, patient resistance and treatment outcome in psychoanalytically oriented psychotherapy. *Dissertation Abstracts International, 38,* 3408B.

Morgan, R., Luborsky, L., Crits-Christoph, P., Curtis, H., & Solomon, J. (1982). Predicting the outcomes of psychotherapy by the Penn Helping Alliance Rating Method. *Archives of General Psychiatry, 39,* 397–402.

Morrow, C. (1980). The effect of matching sex role attitude of client and therapist on therapy outcome. *Dissertation Abstracts International, 41,* 1120B.

Murphy, G. E., Simons, A. D., Wetzel, R. D., & Lustman, P. J. (1984). Cognitive therapy and pharmacotherapy. *Archives of General Psychiatry, 41*, 33–41.

Murphy, K. C., & Strong, S. R. (1972). Some effects of similarity self-disclosure. *Journal of Counseling Psychology, 19*, 121–124.

Myers, J. K., & Auld, F., Jr. (1955). Some variables related to outcome of psychotherapy. *Journal of Clinical Psychology, 11*, 51–54.

Neimeyer, G. J., & Gonzales, M. (1983). Duration, satisfaction, and perceived effectiveness of cross-cultural counseling. *Journal of Counseling Psychology, 30*, 91–95.

Nix, V. C. (1978). A study of the religious values of psychotherapists. *Dissertation Abstracts International, 39*, 1965B.

Norcross, J. C., & Prochaska, J. O. (1983). Clinicians' theoretical orientations: Selection, utilization, and efficacy. *Professional Psychology: Research and Practice, 14*, 197–208.

Norkus, A. G. (1976). Sex of therapist as a variable in short-term therapy with female college students. *Dissertation Abstracts International, 36*, 6361B–6362B.

O'Malley, S. S., Chong, S. S., & Strupp, H. H. (1983). The Vanderbilt Psychotherapy Process Scale: A report on the scale development and a process-outcome study. *Journal of Consulting and Clinical Psychology, 51*, 581–586.

Orlinsky, D. E., & Howard, K. I. (1975). *Varieties of psychotherapeutic experience: Multivariate analyses of patients' and therapists' reports.* New York: Teachers College Press.

Orlinsky, D. E., & Howard, K. I. (1976). The effects of sex of therapist on the therapeutic experiences of women. *Psychotherapy: Theory, Research and Practice, 13*, 82–88.

Parloff, M. B., Waskow, I. E., & Wolfe, B. E. (1978). Research on therapist variables in relation to process and outcome. In S. L. Garfield & A. E. Bergin (Eds.), *Handbook of psychotherapy and behavior change* (2nd ed., pp. 233–282). New York: Wiley.

Patterson, G. R., & Forgatch, M. S. (In press). Therapist behavior as a determiner for client noncooperation: A paradox for the behavior modifier. *Journal of Consulting and Clinical Psychology.*

Patterson, M. L. (1982). A sequential functional model of nonverbal exchange. *Psychological Review, 89*, 231–249.

Patterson, V., & Heilbron, D. (1978). Therapist personality and treatment outcome: A test of the interaction hypothesis using the Campbell A–B scale. *Psychiatric Quarterly, 50*, 320–332.

Pattison, J. E. (1973). Effects of touch on self-exploration and the therapeutic relationship. *Journal of Consulting and Clinical Psychology, 40*, 170–175.

Peebles, M. J. (1980). Personal therapy and ability to display empathy, warmth, and genuineness in psychotherapy. *Psychotherapy: Theory, Research and Practice, 17*, 258–262.

Priddy, D. A., & Stone, G. L. (1983). Reaction to attributional counseling. *Journal of Counseling Psychology, 30*, 455–456.

Prochaska, J. O. (1984). *Systems of psychotherapy: A transtheoretical analysis* (2nd ed.). Homewood, IL: Dorsey Press.

Prochaska, J. O., & Norcross, J. C. (1983). Contemporary psychotherapists: A national survey of characteristics, practices, orientations, and attitudes. *Psychotherapy: Theory, Research and Practice, 20*, 161–173.

Proctor, E. K., & Rosen, A. (1981). Expectations and preferences for counselor race and their relation to intermediate treatment outcomes. *Journal of Counseling Psychology, 28*, 40–46.

Propst, L. R. (1980). The comparative efficacy of religious and nonreligious imagery for the treatment of mild depression in religious individuals. *Cognitive Therapy and Research, 4*, 167–178.

Propst, L. R., Ostrom, R., & Watkins, P. (1984, June). *The efficacy of religious cognitive-behavioral therapy for the treatment of clinical depression in religious individuals.* Paper presented at the Society for Psychotherapy Research, Lake Louise, Ontario, Canada.

Raia, J. R. (1973). Encoded and decoded semantic differentiated meaning of counselor attire, seating and office proxemic variables. *Dissertation Abstracts International, 33*, 3959B.

Razin, A. M. (1977). The A–B variable: Still promising after twenty years? In A. S. Gurman & A. M. Razin (Eds.), *Effective psychotherapy: A handbook of research* (pp. 291–324). New York: Pergamon.

Remer, P., Roffey, B. H., & Buckholtz, A. (1983). Differential effects of positive versus negative self-involving counselor responses. *Journal of Counseling Psychology, 30*, 121–125.

Ricks, D. F. (1974). Supershrink: Methods of a therapist judged successful on the basis of adult outcomes of adolescent patients. In D. F. Ricks, A. Thomas, & M. Roff (Eds.), *Life history research in psychopathology* (Vol. 3, pp. 275–297). Minneapolis: University of Minnesota Press.

Rodolfa, E. R., Rapaport, R., & Lee, V. (1983). Variables related to premature terminations in a university counseling service. *Journal of Counseling Psychology, 30*, 87–90.

Rogers, C. R. (1957). The necessary and sufficient conditions of therapeutic personality change. *Journal of Consulting Psychology, 21*, 95–103.

Rogers, C. R., Gendlin, E. T., Kiesler, D. J., & Truax, C. B. (1967). *The therapeutic relationship and its impact: A study of psychotherapy with schizophrenics.* Madison, WI: University of Wisconsin Press.

Rosenthal, R., Blanck, P. D., & Vannicelli, M. (1984). Speaking to and about patients; Predicting therapists' tone of voice. *Journal of Consulting and Clinical Psychology, 52*, 679–686.

Rozensky, R. H., & Bellack, A. S. (1976). Individual differences in self-reinforcement style and performance in self- and therapist-controlled weight reduction programs. *Behavior Research and Therapy, 14*, 357–364.

Rush, A. J., Beck, A. T., Kovacs, M., & Hollon, S. (1977). Comparative efficacy of cognitive therapy and pharmacotherapy in the treatment of depressed outpatients. *Cognitive Therapy and Research, 1*, 17–37.

Ryan, V. L., & Gizynski, M. N. (1971). Behavior therapy in retrospect: Patients' feelings about their behavior therapists. *Journal of Consulting and Clinical Psychology, 37*, 1–9.

Sachs, J. S. (1983). Negative factors in brief psychotherapy: An empirical assessment. *Journal of Con-*

sulting and Clinical Psychology, 51, 557–564.

Saeger, K. E. (1979). Therapist and client levels of ego development, ego development discrepancy, and affective attitudes and outcome in psychotherapy. *Dissertation Abstracts International, 39,* 5583B.

Sattler, J. M. (1977). The effects of therapist–client racial similarity. In A. S. Gurman & A. M. Razin (Eds.), *Effective psychotherapy: A handbook of research* (pp. 252–290). New York: Pergamon.

Schaffer, N. D. (1982). Multidimensional measures of therapist behavior as predictors of outcome. *Psychological Bulletin, 92,* 670–681.

Scher, D. (1971). Attribution of personality from voice: A cross cultural study on interpersonal perception. *Proceedings of the 79th Annual Convention of the American Psychological Association, 6,* 351–352.

Scher, M. (1975). Verbal activity, sex, counselor experience, and success in counseling. *Journal of Counseling Psychology, 22,* 97–101.

Schindler, F. E., Berren, M. R., & Beigel, A. (1981). A study of the causes of conflict between psychiatrists and psychologists. *Hospital and Community Psychiatry, 32,* 263–266.

Schneiderman, L. (1965). Social class, diagnosis and treatment. *American Journal of Orthopsychiatry, 35,* 99–105.

Seligman, M. R. (1968). The interracial casework relationship. *Smith College Studies in Social Work, 39,* 84.

Shapiro, D. A., & Shapiro, D. (1982). Meta-analysis of comparative therapy outcome studies: A replication and refinement. *Psychological Bulletin, 92,* 581–604.

Shaw, B. F. (1983, July). *Training therapists for the treatment of depression: Collaborative study.* Paper presented at the meeting of the Society for Psychotherapy Research, Sheffield, England.

Silverman, J. (1967). Personality trait and "perceptual style" studies of the psychotherapists of schizophrenic patients. *Journal of Nervous and Mental Disease, 145,* 5–17.

Simon, W. E. (1973). Age, sex, and title of therapist as determinants of patients' preferences. *Journal of Psychology, 83,* 145–149.

Simons, A. D., Garfield, S. L., & Murphy, G. E. (1984). The process of change in cognitive therapy and pharmacotherapy for depression. *Archives of General Psychiatry, 41,* 45–51.

Simons, J. A., & Helms, J. E. (1976). Influence of counselor's marital status, sex, and age on college and noncollege women's counselor preferences. *Journal of Counseling Psychology, 23,* 380–386.

Sloane, R. B., Cristol, A. H., Pepernik, M. C., & Staples, F. R. (1970). Role preparation and expectation of improvement in psychotherapy. *Journal of Nervous and Mental Disease, 150,* 18–26.

Sloane, R. B., Staples, F. R., Cristol, A. H., Yorkston, N. J., & Whipple, K. (1975). *Psychotherapy versus behavior therapy.* Cambridge, MA: Howard University Press.

Smith, E. W. (1972). Postural and gestural communication of A and B "therapist types" during dyad interviews. *Journal of Consulting and Clinical Psychology, 39,* 29–36.

Smith, M. L., Glass, G. V., & Miller, T. I. (1980). *The benefits of psychotherapy.* Baltimore: Johns Hopkins University Press.

Smith-Hanen, S. S. (1977). Effects of nonverbal behaviors on judged levels of counselor warmth and empathy. *Journal of Counseling Psychology, 24,* 87–91.

Snider, J. F. (1979). The experience of successful psychotherapy as reported by "cured" schizophrenic patients and their therapists. *Dissertation Abstracts International, 39,* 3539B–3540B.

Staples, F. R., & Sloane, R. B. (1976). Truax factors, speech characteristics, and therapeutic outcome. *Journal of Nervous and Mental Disease, 163,* 135–140.

Stein, D. M., & Lambert, M. J. (1984). On the relationship between therapist experience and psychotherapy outcome. *Clinical Psychology Review, 4,* 127–142.

Stephens, J. H., Shaffer, J. W., & Zlotowitz, H. I. (1975). An optimum A–B scale of psychotherapist effectiveness. *Journal of Nervous and Mental Disease, 160,* 267–281.

Stoltenberg, C. D., & Dixon, D. N. (1983). Analysis of verbal interactions of A–B type therapists during therapy. *Psychological Reports, 53,* 115–120.

Strassberg, D., Roback, H., D'Antonio, M., & Gabel, H. (1977). Self-disclosure: A critical and selective review of the clinical literature. *Comprehensive Psychiatry, 18,* 31–39.

Strong, S. R. (1968). Counseling: An interpersonal influence process. *Journal of Counseling Psychology, 15,* 215–224.

Strong, S. R., & Schmidt, L. D. (1970). Expertness and influence in counseling. *Journal of Counseling Psychology, 17,* 81–87.

Strupp, H. H. (1977). A reformulation of the dynamics of the therapist's contribution. In A. S. Gurman & A. M. Razin (Eds.), *Effective psychotherapy: A handbook of research* (pp. 1–22). New York: Pergamon.

Strupp, H. H. (1980a). Success and failure in time-limited psychotherapy: A systematic comparison of two cases (Comparison 1). *Archives of General Psychiatry, 37,* 595–603.

Strupp, H. H. (1980b). Success and failure in time-limited psychotherapy: A systematic comparison of two cases (Comparison 2). *Archives of General Psychiatry, 37,* 708–716.

Strupp, H. H. (1981). Toward the refinement of time-limited dynamic psychotherapy. In S. H. Budman (Ed.), *Forms of brief therapy* (pp. 219–242). New York: Guilford.

Strupp, H. H., & Bloxom, A. L. (1973). Preparing lower-class patients for group psychotherapy: Development and evaluation of a role-induction film. *Journal of Consulting and Clinical Psychology, 41,* 373–384.

Strupp, H. H., & Hadley, S. W. (1979). Specific vs. nonspecific factors in psychotherapy. *Archives of General Psychiatry, 36,* 1125–1136.

Sullivan, P. L., Miller, C., & Smelser, W. (1958). Factors in length of stay and progress in psychotherapy. *Journal of Consulting Psychology, 22,* 1–9.

Sunbury, J. F. (1981). Marital therapy outcome: The influence of client, therapist, and treatment variables at follow-up. *Dissertation Abstracts International, 42,* 1195B.

Sweet, A. A. (1984). The therapeutic relationship in behavior therapy. *Clinical Psychology Review, 4,* 253–272.

Taube, C. A., Burns, B. J., & Kessler, L. (1984). Patients

of psychiatrists and psychologists in office-based practice: 1980. *American Psychologist, 39,* 1435–1447.

Taylor, F. G., & Marshall, W. L. (1977). Experimental analysis of a cognitive-behavioral therapy for depression. *Cognitive Therapy and Research, 1,* 59–72.

Taylor, M. C., & Hall, J. A. (1982). Psychological androgyny: Theories, methods, and conclusions. *Psychological Bulletin, 92,* 347–366.

Tennen, H., Rohrbaugh, M., Press, S., & White, L. (1981). Reactance theory and therapeutic paradox: A compliance-defiance model. *Psychotherapy: Theory, Research and Practice, 18,* 14–22.

Terestman, N., Miller, J. D., & Weber, J. J. (1974). Blue-collar patients at a psychoanalytic clinic. *American Journal of Psychiatry, 131,* 261–266.

Terrell, F., & Terrell, S. (1984). Race of counselor, client sex, cultural mistrust level, and premature termination from counseling among black clients. *Journal of Counseling Psychology, 31,* 371–375.

Tessler, R. C. (1975). Clients' reactions to initial interviews: Determinants of relationship-centered and problem-centered satisfaction. *Journal of Counseling Psychology, 22,* 187–191.

Tracey, T. J., & Ray, P. B. (1984). Stages of successful time-limited counseling: An interactional examination. *Journal of Counseling Psychology, 31,* 13–27.

Troll, L. E., & Nowak, C. (1976). "How old are you?"—The question of age bias in the counseling of adults. *Counseling Psychologist, 6,* 41–44.

Truax, C. B., Fine, H., Moravec, J., & Millis, W. (1968). Effects of therapist persuasive potency in individual psychotherapy. *Journal of Clinical Psychology, 24,* 359–362.

Truax, C. B., & Wargo, D. G. (1969). Effects of vicarious therapy pretraining and alternate sessions on outcome in group psychotherapy with outpatients. *Journal of Consulting and Clinical Psychology, 33,* 440–447.

Tuma, A. H., May, P. R. A., Yale, C., & Forsythe, A. B. (1978a). Therapist characteristics and the outcome of treatment in schizophrenia. *Archives of General Psychiatry, 35,* 81–85.

Tuma, A. H., May, P. R. A., Yale, C., & Forsythe, A. B. (1978b). Therapist experience, general clinical ability, and treatment outcome in schizophrenia. *Journal of Consulting and Clinical Psychology, 46,* 1120–1126.

Turner, S., & Armstrong, S. (1981). Cross-racial psychotherapy: What the therapists say. *Psychotherapy: Theory, Research and Practice, 18,* 375–378.

Turner, R. M., & Ascher, L. M. (1982). Therapist factor in the treatment of insomnia. *Behaviour Research and Therapy, 20,* 33–40.

Tyson, C. L. (1979). Physical contact in psychotherapy. *Dissertation Abstracts International, 39,* 4601B.

Vaccaro, V. M. (1981). The effect of the therapist's level of expectation on the outcome of planned short term treatment. *Dissertation Abstracts International, 42,* 1626B.

Vandenbos, G. R., & Karon, B. P. (1971). Pathogenesis: A new therapist personality dimension related to therapeutic effectiveness. *Journal of Personality Assessment, 35,* 252–260

Van der Veen, F. (1965). Effects of the therapist and the patient on each other's therapeutic behavior. *Journal*

of Consulting Psychology, 29, 19–26.

Wadsworth, R. D., & Checketts, K. T. (1980). Influence of religious affiliation on psychodiagnosis. *Journal of Consulting and Clinical Psychology, 48,* 234–240.

Warren, N. C., & Rice, L. N. (1972). Structuring and stabilizing of psychotherapy for low-prognosis clients. *Journal of Consulting and Clinical Psychology, 39,* 173–181.

Watkins, J. (1984). *Comparison of cognitive therapy, pharmacotherapy, and combination treatments.* Unpublished manuscript.

Wenegrat, A. (1976). Linguistic variables of therapist speech and accurate empathy ratings. *Psychotherapy: Theory, Research and Practice, 13,* 30–33.

White, G. D., & Pollard, J. (1982). Assessing therapeutic competence from therapy session attendance. *Professional Psychology, 13,* 628–633.

Whitehorn, J. C., & Betz, B. J. (1960). Further studies of the doctor as a crucial variable in the outcome of treatment with schizophrenic patients. *American Journal of Psychiatry, 117,* 215–223.

Widgery, R., & Stackpole, C. (1972). Desk position, interviewee anxiety, and interviewer credibility: An example of cognitive balance in a dyad. *Journal of Counseling Psychology, 19,* 173–177.

Wilkins, W. (1979). Expectancies in therapy research: Discriminating among heterogeneous nonspecifics. *Journal of Consulting and Clinical Psychology, 47,* 837–845.

Wilkins, W. (1984). Psychotherapy: The powerful placebo. *Journal of Consulting and Clinical Psychology, 52,* 570–573.

Williams, B. M. (1974). Trust and self-disclosure among black college students. *Journal of Counseling Psychology, 21,* 522–525.

Williams, S. L., Dooseman, G., & Kleifield, E. (1984). Comparative effectiveness of guided mastery and exposure treatments for intractable phobias. *Journal of Consulting and Clinical Psychology, 52,* 505–518.

Wilson, P. H., Goldin, J. C., & Charbonneau-Powis, M. (1983). Comparative efficacy of behavioral and cognitive treatments of depression. *Cognitive Therapy and Research, 7,* 111–124.

Wogan, M. (1970). Effect of therapist–patient personality variables on therapeutic outcome. *Journal of Consulting and Clinical Psychology, 35,* 356–361.

Wynne, M. F. (1982). Client and therapist expectations related to the outcome of crisis intervention therapy with black clients. *Dissertation Abstracts International, 42,* 4220B.

Xenakis, S. N., Hoyt, M. F., Marmar, C. R., & Horowitz, M. J. (1983). Reliability of self-reports by therapists using the Therapist Action Scale. *Psychotherapy: Theory, Research and Practice, 20,* 314–320.

Yalom, I. D., Houts, P. S., Newell, G., & Rank, K. H. (1967). Preparation of patients for group therapy. *Archives of General Psychiatry, 17,* 416–427.

Yamamoto, J., James, Q., Bloombaum, M., & Hattem, J. (1967). Racial factors in patient selection. *American Journal of Psychiatry, 124,* 630–636.

Yost, E., Allender, J., Beutler, L. E., & Chaisson-Stewart, G. M. (1983). Developments in the treatment of depression among the elderly. *Arizona Medicine, 40,* 402–407.

Young, A. H. (1973). Race of psychotherapist and client

and perception of variables relevant to therapy outcome. *Dissertation Abstracts International, 33,* 5506A.

Young, R. C., Glick, I. D., Hargreaves. W. A., Braff, D., & Drues, J. (1979). Therapist A–B score and treatment outcome with psychiatric inpatients: A table of random numbers. *British Journal of Medical Psychology, 52,* 119–121.

Zeiss, A. M., Lewinsohn, P. M., & Munoz, R. F. (1979). Nonspecific improvement effects in depression using interpersonal skills training, pleasant activity schedules or cognitive training. *Journal of Consulting and Clinical Psychology, 47,* 427–439.

Zeldow, P. B. (1978). Sex differences in psychiatric evaluation and treatment. *Archives of General Psychiatry, 35,* 89–93.

Zeldow, P. B. (1982). The androgynous vision: A critical examination. *Bulletin of the Menninger Clinic, 46,* 401–413.

8

PROCESS AND OUTCOME IN PSYCHOTHERAPY

DAVID E. ORLINSKY

University of Chicago

KENNETH I. HOWARD

Northwestern University

INTRODUCTION

Most researchers today would probably concede that at least some of the varied forms of psychotherapy have a beneficial impact on patients who remain in treatment for a reasonable period of time. Statistical meta-analyses of outcome data such as that provided by Smith, Glass, and Miller (1980), together with the careful scholarship of Bergin (1971), Bergin and Lambert (1978; in this volume), and others, have done much to quiet the skepticism aroused by Eysenck's (1952) earlier challenge to the field. Yet the question remains, "What is 'effectively therapeutic' about psychotherapy?" Research that focuses on the relation of process to outcome addresses that question. Our assignment is to distill that research into the rudiments of an answer.

The literature that reports quantitative data on the relation of process to outcome is impressive in its

We gratefully acknowledge the assistance of April Howard, Steven Saunders, Diane Wallace, and Marcia Bourland.

extent, if not always in its quality. Beginning to accumulate at an accelerating pace in the early 1950s, that literature now covers a span of more than three decades. It is part of an even larger literature pertaining to virtually every aspect of the clinical therapeutic enterprise. For that reason it is best to begin by stating the boundaries within which we have searched for relevant studies.

For reasons of ecological validity we have limited ourselves to research conducted on "real" patients and therapists in "real" treatment situations. The patients were people receiving psychological help for personal and interpersonal problems, and for disturbances in emotional, cognitive, or behavioral functioning. The therapists were recognized mental health professionals or professionals-in-training. The treatments provided were those conducted in outpatient clinics, university counseling centers, psychiatric hospitals, social agencies, and (less frequently) private practice.

We further limited our review of studies by focusing only on those that analyzed "process" variables in relation to outcome. By "process" we mean everything that can be observed to occur between, and within, the patient and the therapist during their work together. This comprehensive definition points toward the actual events occurring within therapy sessions, as witnessed by the participants themselves or by nonparticipant observers. This has the advantage of identifying a circumscribed, researchable set of interactions between specific persons at specific times and places.

We established this definition of "process" on the basis of a systemic analysis that functionally divided the events constituting, influencing, and influenced by psychotherapy into "input," "process," and "output" variables (Howard & Orlinsky, 1972). By "input" we mean all the functional antecedents and potential determinants of the therapeutic process. Generally speaking, these include (1) the personal and professional characteristics of *patients* (e.g., gender, diagnosis) and their life situation (e.g., socioeconomic status); (2) the personal and professional characteristics of *therapists* (e.g., age, type of training) and their life situation (e.g., parental status); (3) the *organization and community* within which therapy takes place (e.g., an urban community mental health clinic); and (4) the cultural *belief and value orientations* in terms of which psychotherapy is construed as a meaningful activity (e.g., an ethic of self-improvement).

"Output" refers to the consequences of therapeutic process in this same "functional environment": (1) in the life and person of the *patient*; (2) in the life and person of the *therapist*; (3) in the *groups and communities* of which they are part; and (4) with regard to the *systems of belief and value* in which they participate. In relation to output, outcome is a narrower and more clinically practical concept. It refers only to output with respect to the life and person of the patient and must be judged in terms of some particular value standard. Outcome, like marriage, is "for better or worse," as Strupp, Hadley, and Gomes-Schwartz (1977) made clear. The patient's life should be demonstrably better in some way, or the patient's personality improved— from somebody's point of view—before therapy is counted as a success.

We have already said enough to indicate what "the relation of process to outcome in psychotherapy" means to us. We review no studies of input, process, or output per se, no studies of the relation of input to process, nor of input to output. What fol-

lows is a review, analysis, and synthesis of quantitative empirical studies of the relationships between process and outcome variables, as we have defined these terms.

We have tried diligently to search out all published and accessible books, monographs, articles and dissertations on the subject in the English language through December 1984. Although we have no illusion that we have fully succeeded in this, we expect that the reader will find our substantial bibliography a useful base for further research.

The literature on psychotherapeutic process and outcome covers a large number of variables and a diversity of specific measures. The task that confronts us is one of cumulating the findings of many different studies into a coherent body of knowledge. This task requires that a meaningful way be found to group the variables and to categorize the measures.

In an earlier review we presented an atheoretical conceptual scheme for this purpose based upon a methodological analysis of variable domains (Orlinsky & Howard, 1978). This scheme successfully organized the psychotherapy research literature, but was framed at a level of generality that made it applicable to events observable in any type of human relationship. The present review, by contrast, organizes the literature in terms of a model that is specific to psychotherapy. This new *substantive* model subsumes rather than replaces the *methodological* model of 1978; later in this chapter we will discuss the conceptual relationship between them.

The conception of psychotherapy offered below is organized with research interests chiefly in mind. What we are seeking is an empirically based "generic" understanding of psychotherapy, concerned with "active ingredients" rather than "brand names." However, we believe that such an understanding will have considerable clinical value and will effectively accommodate the special virtues of diverse clinical orientations.

In this generic model, five conceptual elements are included as constituents of psychotherapeutic process: (1) The *therapeutic contract* defines the purpose, format, terms, and limits of the enterprise. (2) *Therapeutic interventions* comprise the "business" of helping carried on under the terms of the therapeutic contract. (3) The *therapeutic bond* is an aspect of the relationship that develops between the participants as they perform their respective parts in therapeutic interventions. (4) *Patient self-*

relatedness refers to the patient's ability to absorb the impact of therapeutic interventions and the therapeutic bond. (5) *Therapeutic realizations,* such as insight, catharsis, discriminant learning, and so on, occur within the session and presumably are productive of changes in the patient's life or personality, which become the subject of outcome evaluations.

The *therapeutic contract* is a sine qua non of psychotherapy. We doubt that this contract ever takes the form of a legal document signed by a party of the first part and a party of the second part (the terms used by Menninger, 1958). Yet, as in every relationship, it is essential that those involved have some degree of consensual understanding concerning who they are to one another—and, being such, of what they should, what they may, and what they should not do together. The therapeutic contract is therefore just the plan and not the substance of psychotherapy; it is the blueprint that is to be followed in constructing a therapeutic situation. It becomes eventful as an element of therapeutic process, however, when it is distorted or violated, because significant departures from the plan change the essential nature of the enterprise. If patient and therapist decide to become friends, or business partners, they cease to be patient and therapist (as these roles are defined in most versions of the therapeutic contract). When properly implemented, on the other hand, the therapeutic contract is absorbed into the substance of therapeutic interventions and therapeutic bond. A salient element at the inception and termination of therapy, and at times of crisis, the therapeutic contract otherwise fades into the background.

Therapeutic interventions are acts that include what is generally thought of as the techniques of psychotherapy, that is, the specific tasks and procedures presented by the therapist in response to the manifest problems presented by the patient. The use of different therapeutic techniques, along with the recognition of different forms of patient problems, is perhaps the major point of difference among the diverse theories of psychotherapy. Yet no matter what the theory, therapeutic interventions presumably occupy the greater part of the time that patient and therapist spend together.

The *therapeutic bond* is an aspect of the relationship that forms between patient and therapist as they implement the therapeutic contract by engaging in therapeutic interventions. In our 1978 review,

we distinguished three major aspects of the therapeutic bond: (1) role-investment, that is, the degree to which each participant puts himself (or herself) into therapy; (2) empathic resonance, that is, the extent to which the two participants are on the same wavelength; and (3) mutual affirmation, that is, the measure of care for one another's well-being that develops between the participants. From one point of view, these could be seen as a generalization of Rogers' (1957) concept of "therapist-offered conditions," transforming them from traits of individual therapist behavior into bilateral characteristics of the relationship per se. The therapeutic bond also bears a family resemblance to the psychoanalytically derived concept of the "helping alliance" (Bordin, 1979; Luborsky, 1984), and to the empathic positive transference as formulated in "self-psychology" (Kohut, 1984). The point that probably requires most emphasis about our conception of the therapeutic bond is its reality. It is not an imaginary projection of the patient's past transferred or projected on to the current relationship between patient and therapist; ideally, it is the most realistic apect of that current relationship. Positive and negative unconscious transferences and countertransferences (Freud, 1912) may also be recognized as aspects of the therapeutic relationship, but when they occur their typical effect is to subvert the therapeutic contract and to distort the therapeutic bond. Indeed, it is only the effective role-investment, empathic resonance, and mutual affirmation of patient and therapist that can keep unconscious transferences from disrupting the relationship; and if the therapeutic bond is sufficiently strong, it may permit these transferences to be turned to therapeutic advantage.

Patient self-relatedness refers to such aspects of patients' psychological functioning during therapy as their affective and ideational responsiveness, their self-attunement and self-definition, their self-evaluation, and their self-control. Clinically, various patterns of patient self-relatedness tend to be formulated in terms such as "openness" versus "defensiveness." What is at stake is the patient's ability to absorb the impact generated explicitly by therapeutic interventions, and implicity by the therapeutic bond. The frame of mind that a patient is in during therapy should influence how much of it is (to use Piagetian language) "assimilated" by the patient, and how much the patient can "accommodate" to new conditions experienced in therapy.

Therapeutic realization refers to the effects of therapeutic interventions and of the therapeutic bond within the therapy session—questioning problematic assumptions, gaining insight, feeling better, mastering anxiety, and so on. Realizations of the stipulated goals of therapeutic interventions, of course, may also occur after a therapy session is over. When they do so, however, they still occur to the patient within the frame of refererence defined by the patient role. Therapeutic realizations such as insight, enhanced morale, and the like should be sustained in the patient's personal functioning and applied in the patient's life roles outside of therapy before they are counted as changes to be evaluated as criterion measures of outcome.

We shall use these five elements of our substantive model of therapy to organize the present review of empirical findings relating process to outcome. Within each of the substantive sections of the review, findings will be grouped by observational perspective. Accordingly, process subcategories will include *nonparticipant observations* in the form of (1) observer judgments or objective indices ("Concurrent Activity" in the 1978 model) and *participant observations* in the form of (2) patient reports and (3) therapist reports ("Concurrent Experience" in the 1978 model).

We shall also differentiate among types of outcome measure according to the evaluative perspectives from which they were made. The uneven quality of published reports permits moderately reliable distinctions to be drawn between global outcome evaluations made from (1) the patient's perspective, (2) the therapist's perspective, and (3) the diagnostician's perspective (which includes independent clinical interviewers, trained raters of case materials, and case supervisors). An additional, more heterogeneous category of outcome measurement consists of (4) objective indicators, tests, and scales. This last category includes actuarial data (e.g., number of days of hospitalization) as well as standardized psychometric tests and rating scales from which scores are computed, whether the test responses are generated by patients (e.g., MMPI or Butler-Haigh Q Sort), by therapists, or by independent clinical judges (as with target symptom rating scales).

The three observational perspectives on therapeutic process are cross-referenced with these four

outcome categories in analyzing findings within each of the substantive sections of the review. In many studies several different measures of process and of outcome were used, spanning more than one category in each domain. In such cases we counted the findings within each process-by-outcome subcategory as a finding worthy of separate note, so that a single study may be represented in several subcategories. Where some findings of a particular study within a single process-by-outcome subcategory were statistically significant and others were not, we counted that subcategory as significant. Also, when differential findings within a particular process-by-outcome subcategory were reported for different populations (e.g., neurotics and schizophrenics), we counted them as independent studies of the relation of process to outcome. However, when it was clear that essentially the same findings on a single data base had been reported in more than one publication, those findings were counted only once. Although these inclusion rules somewhat overrepresent the number of significant findings, they have the virtue of showing researchers which of the process-by-outcome subcategories have yielded results and which have not. As we have already noted, the studies reviewed vary considerably in quality. In summarizing results, we have chosen to ignore this issue in favor of a search for replicated findings.

A quantitative summary of findings will be presented in tabular form in each section of the review that covers a sufficient number of studies to warrant such treatment. Detailed lists of specific references will also be given. In the tables we distinguish between positive, negative, and null findings according to the arbitrary but venerable criterion of the .05 level of significance. We do so not because we wish to perpetuate confusion between statistical and clinical "significance," but merely in order to have a reasonably stringent standard for sorting out reported findings. This, of course, is no more than an unhappy compromise between two off-setting "truths." On the one hand, it is often possible to find a few statistically significant changes in scores on outcome measures (particularly if one uses enough of them) that do not correspond to any really meaningful changes in the patients' clinical status. On the other hand, research studies are often conducted with such small samples of patients and therapists, and with measurement instruments of such imperfect reliability, that only the most powerful effects reach even the 95 percent level of the statistical probability.

What follows, therefore, is a rather coarse-grained sorting of empirical findings concerning the relation of various elements of psychotherapeutic process to various categories of outcome. The reader should bear this in mind, together with the consideration that it is the best we can do under present circumstances to marshal the facts that should help to answer our guiding question: "What is 'effectively therapeutic' about psychotherapy?"

THE THERAPEUTIC CONTRACT

As we have noted, the therapeutic contract is a sine qua non of psychotherapy. If a professional therapist is in a room talking with a person who is obviously emotionally distressed, they are not necessarily engaged in psychotherapy. The two persons could be spouses, siblings, friends, neighbors, or the like. In other words, their interactions could be governed by completely different rules and role expectations than those governing therapeutic interaction. Although the two individuals talking in that room had all the qualifications for the roles of patient and therapist, they would not actually *be* patient and therapist unless they agreed jointly to govern their relationship by the terms of a therapeutic contract. A therapeutic contract consists essentially of the understanding (i.e., the rules and role expectations) that governs each party's role performance vis-á-vis the other. In this section we shall review studies bearing, first, on certain provisions of the therapeutic contract, and then on some immediate aspects of its implementation.

Provisions of the Therapeutic Contract

A fair number of studies have investigated the effects on outcome of such provisions of the therapeutic contract as (1) the number of patients to be treated concurrently (e.g., individual vs. group psychotherapy); (2) the timing of therapy sessions; (3) the term of the contract (e.g., time-limited vs. unlimited psychotherapy); and (4) payment of fee.

Collectivity

Collectivity refers to the size and composition of the social unit in which therapy is conducted. Individual psychotherapy refers to the dyadic unit of one pa-

tient and one therapist. Group psychotherapy generally refers to a small group consisting of one or two therapists and anywhere from 2 or 3 to about 10 or 12 unacquainted and unrelated patients. The latter stipulation distinguishes the social unit in group psychotherapy from the unit involved in family therapy, where one or two therapists work with several members of a primary family, usually the married couple and one or more of their children. In multiple therapy, on the other hand, two or more therapists may jointly work in treating a single patient. Numerous variations have been tried in practice, but most process-outcome studies in the literature have concentrated on comparisons of individual versus group psychotherapy (see Gurman, Kniskern, & Pinsof, this volume, for a review of research on family therapy).

Table 8.1 presents 14 findings drawn from 12 studies. Eleven of the findings show no significant difference in outcome between individual and group psychotherapy; the other three favor individual over group therapy. On this evidence one would be tempted to conclude that it makes little difference as to whether therapy is conducted in an individual or group format. This, at least, would be a fair conclusion if applied only to patients who were willing to remain in the format to which they were assigned.

Schedule

The effect of variations in the scheduling of sessions is difficult to test because all aspects of scheduling cannot be simultaneously controlled. Those aspects are frequency of session, length of session, number of sessions, and calendar length of course of treatment. Most of the process-outcome studies in the literature have concentrated on the frequency of sessions—usually once weekly versus more frequent meetings—with greater or lesser control over the other factors. Since there is good evidence to believe that number of sessions is strongly related to outcome (see the section on Treatment Duration below), we have treated studies that confounded frequency with overall number of sessions as though they pertained only to the latter (see Table 8.31).

Table 8.2 presents 18 findings concerning the effect of frequency of therapy sessions on outcome drawn from 11 studies. Thirteen of the 18 findings showed no significant difference in outcome between once weekly and other more or less frequent schedules.

TABLE 8.1 Collectivity: Individual vs. Group

Reference	Outcome Perspective[a]	Finding[b]
Frank et al. (1959)	S	0
Gelder et al. (1967)	S	0
Haimowitz & Haimowitz (1952)	S	0
Hargreaves et al. (1974)	P	+
Hargreaves et al. (1974)	P	0
Herz et al. (1974)	S	+
Herz et al. (1974)	S	0
Hobbs (1978)	S	0
Imber et al. (1957)	R	0
Newcomer & Morrison (1974)	S	0
O'Brien et al. (1972)	S	+
Schmidt (1982)	S	0
Stone et al. (1961)	S	0
Thorley & Craske (1950)	P	0

SUMMARY

	Outcome Perspective				
	Patient −0+	Therapist −0+	Rater −0+	Score −0+	Total −0+
Indiv. > Group	0 2 1	0 0 0	0 1 0	0 8 2	0 11 3

a "Outcome Perspective" refers to the way in which outcome was evaluated. "P" indicates patient ratings, "T" indicates therapist ratings, "R" indicates that outcome was evaluated by an independent clinical rater, and "S" is used to show that some objective score (e.g., MMPI) was used.
b Findings are categorized as "−" (a statistically significant difference favoring group psychotherapy), "0" (no significant difference), and "+" (a statistically significant difference favoring individual psychotherapy).

TABLE 8.2 Schedule: Session Frequency (1 per week +)

Reference	Outcome Perspective[a]	Finding[b]
Bierenbaum et al. (1976)	S	+
Caillier (1981)	S	0
Cappon (1964)	P	+
Cappon (1964)	T	+
Graham (1958)	P	+
Graham (1958)	P	−
Heinicke (1969)	S	0
Kernberg et al. (1972)	S	0
Lorr et al. (1962)	P	0
Lorr et al. (1962)	T	0
Lorr et al. (1962)	S	0
McNair & Lorr (1960)	P	0
McNair & Lorr (1960)	T	0
McNair & Lorr (1960)	R	0
McNair & Lorr (1960)	S	0
Ross et al. (1974)	S	0
Van Slambrouck (1973)	S	0
Zirkle (1961)	S	0

SUMMARY

	Outcome Perspective				
	Patient −0+	Therapist −0+	Rater −0+	Score −0+	Total −0+
1/wk > other	1 2 2	0 2 1	0 1 0	0 8 1	1 13 4

a See Table 8.1, footnote a.
b Findings are categorized as "−" (a statistically significant difference favoring once-a-week psychotherapy), "0" (no significant difference), and "+" (a statistically significant difference favoring another schedule).

Again, as with collectivity, it might be tempting to conclude that this provision of therapeutic contracts has no effect on outcome. The one study of formal psychoanalytic treatment does not contradict this impression (Kernberg et al., 1972). In general it seems that once weekly sessions are as beneficial for patients as more frequent therapy, other things being equal.

Term

The term of a contract specifies the period for which it is to be in force. In psychotherapy, it refers to whether or not there is a prior agreement between patient and therapist as to how long therapy will last. After having a certain vogue in the 1960s, the comparison of time-limited with unlimited therapy seems not to have attracted much attention from psychotherapy researchers.

Table 8.3 summarizes seven findings drawn from five studies, the results of which seem reasonably promising. Three of the findings showed time-limited therapy to be superior to unlimited therapy. Three others showed no significant difference between the two, while only one showed an advantage for unlimited therapy.

One caution in comparing time-limited with unlimited therapy is that patients who receive time-limited treatment may actually attend *more* sessions than patients in unlimited therapy. The median number of sessions that patients receive in ordinary unlimited therapy appears to be about 5 or 6 (Garfield, 1978). Contracts in time-limited therapy often call for 16 to 20 sessions or more, leading these patients to stay in therapy longer than they might have otherwise, even if they do not fully complete the number of sessions specified in the time-limited contract. Perhaps the fairest conclusion to draw on the basis of these studies is that the issue of time-limited psychotherapy has had an unfortunately time-limited fascination for process-outcome researchers.

Fee Payment

A final aspect of the therapeutic contract that has received occasional attention in process-outcome research is payment versus nonpayment of a fee for service. Only two studies met our criteria for inclusion in this review (Pope, Geller, & Wilkinson, 1975; Rosenbaum, Friedlander, & Kaplan, 1956). One showed a positive association of fee payment with outcome and one did not. In both cases the maxi-

TABLE 8.3   Term: Time-limited (+) vs. Unlimited (−)

Reference	Outcome Perspective[a]	Finding[b]
Henry & Shlien (1958)	S	0
Henry & Shlien (1958)	S	−
Muench (1965)	S	0
Munro & Bach (1975)	P	+
Munro & Bach (1975)	S	+
Reid & Shyne (1969)	S	+
Shlien et al. (1962)	S	0

SUMMARY

Outcome Perspective

	Patient − 0 +	Therapist − 0 +	Rater − 0 +	Score − 0 +	Total − 0 +
limit > no limit	0 0 1	0 0 0	0 0 0	1 3 2	1 3 3

[a]See Table 8.1, footnote a.
[b]Findings are categorized as "−" (a statistically significant difference favoring unlimited psychotherapy), "0" (no significant difference), and "+" (a statistically significant difference favoring time-limited psychotherapy).

mum fee charged seems quite low, even taken in the context of the period at which the study was done. Although this is an area in which more research should be done, investigators ought to recognize that fees per se are not a sufficient measure of the actual psychological cost of treatment to the patient; other factors (missed work time, fee in the context of the patient's financial resources, emotional costs, etc.) need to be considered (e.g., see Newman & Howard, 1986).

Implementation of the Therapeutic Contract

A number of studies have reported findings that can be construed as relevant to contract implementation. These concern (1) the timeliness of implementation, (2) preparation of patients to ensure their understanding of role expectations, (3) compliance with expectations to engage in conversational behavior, and (4) manner of implementing the "doctor" and "patient" roles.

Timeliness

Four studies examined the effect on outcome of imposing a delay by placing patients on a waiting list before starting therapy, comparing them with similar patients who began therapy with little or no delay. Three of the studies found a significant negative effect for wait-listed patients (Roth et al., 1964; Uhlenhuth & Duncan, 1968b; Zeiss, Lewinsohn, & Munoz, 1979); the fourth found a near significant negative effect (Gordon & Cartwright, 1954). Another study, with a very small sample, found a near significant negative effect on outcome for those cases in which there was a notable number of therapist cancellations and a turnover of therapists (Kaufman, Frank, Friend, Heims, & Weiss, 1962).

On the patient's side of the issue, a recent study reported that patients who missed one of their first four scheduled sessions were significantly more likely to have poorer outcomes than those who kept all appointments (Peiser, 1982). A convergent finding comes from an earlier study, which showed patient outcome to be significantly negatively correlated with the number of sessions that patients missed (Rosenbaum et al., 1956).

Obviously there is not a large enough body of evidence here to draw a definitive conclusion, but all four categories of outcome measures are represented, and there is an impressive degree of consistency in the findings. Since these studies are predictive of negative outcomes in a field of research where positive or null findings predominate, we are inclined to call attention to their practical implications even as we urge researchers to gather more evidence.

Role Preparation

Therapists are normally given at least two years of academic training and supervisory coaching to make them reasonably competent role performers, and often take further training and years of practice before attaining a level of personal mastery. Patients generally only get on-the-job training for their part in therapy, which may be why many do not remain more than a few sessions, and why those who return for further treatment at a later time seem to work more effectively.

The idea of formal role preparation for patients is still a novelty in practice, even though not entirely new to researchers. For example, the research group of the Phipps Clinic at Johns Hopkins University published a notable series of reports of research on pretreatment preparation of patients beginning in the early 1960s (Hoehn-Saric et al., 1964).

Table 8.4 presents a total of 34 findings drawn from 18 studies. A glance at this table is sufficient to show that the balance strongly favors role preparation procedures. Twenty-one of the 34 findings show significantly better outcomes accruing to patients who received some form of early role preparation, with a number of positive findings for each of the four outcome categories. Only patient-rated global outcome shows less than a majority of significant positive findings, and no study has demonstrated a significant negative effect of therapy pretraining.

Perhaps the most important aspect of this research is the finding that patients who generally have a poor prognosis (e.g., those of a lower socioeconomic status) can in fact benefit from psychotherapy when given some preparation. One study of lower-class patients also showed that benefits for such patients are further increased if therapists, too, are given explicit preparation for dealing with persons whose values and life situations are unfamiliar to them (Jacobs, Charles, Jacobs, Weinstein, & Mann, 1972).

Conversational Behavior

In most of the modern psychotherapies, conversation is the only overt behavior required for implementation of the therapeutic contract, and it is certainly an essential instrument in all of them. If the

TABLE 8.4 Role Preparation

Reference	Outcome[a]	Finding[b]
Eisenberg (1981)	P	+
Eisenberg (1981)	S	+
Friedlander (1981)	P	+
Friedlander (1981)	T	+
Gadaleto (1977)	S	0
Hoehn-Saric et al. (1964)	P	0
Hoehn-Saric et al. (1964)	T	+
Hoehn-Saric et al. (1964)	R	+
Hoehn-Saric et al. (1964)	S	+
Jacobs et al. (1972)	R	+
Liberman et al. (1972)	P	0
Liberman et al. (1972)	R	0
Liberman et al. (1972)	S	0
Piper et al. (1982)	P	0
Piper et al. (1982)	S	0
Rich (1979)	S	+
Sloane et al. (1970)	S	+
Strupp & Bloxom (1973)	P	+
Strupp & Bloxom (1973)	T	0
Strupp & Bloxom (1973)	S	+
Truax & Carkhuff (1967)	S	+
Truax & Wargo (1969)	S	+
Truax et al. (1966)	P	0
Truax et al. (1966)	T	+
Truax et al. (1966)	R	+
Truax et al. (1966)	S	+
Truax et al. (1970)	S	0
Warren & Rice (1972)	P	+
Warren & Rice (1972)	T	+
Warren & Rice (1972)	S	+
Wogan et al. (1977)	P	+
Yalom et al. (1967)	P	0
Zarchan (1978)	P	0
Zarchan (1978)	T	0

SUMMARY

Outcome Perspective

	Patient − 0 +	Therapist − 0 +	Rater − 0 +	Score − 0 +	Total − 0 +
Prep > No Prep	0 6 5	0 2 4	0 1 3	0 4 9	0 13 21

[a]See Table 8.1, footnote a.
[b]Findings are categorized as "−" (a statistically significant difference favoring *no* role preparation), "0" (no significant difference), and "+" (a statistically significant difference favoring role preparation).

patient doesn't talk much of the time, and the therapist doesn't talk some of the time, then it would be hard to claim that psychotherapy is actually taking place.

Table 8.5 summarizes 25 findings drawn from 13 studies on the relation to therapeutic outcome of the sheer amount of talk by patients and therapists. The popularity of speech quantity as a variable may be due less to its theoretical relevance than to the ease and undoubted objectivity with which it can be measured. Presumably, what the patient and therapist have to say is more important than how much they have to say. Yet surprisingly enough, 12 of the 25 measures of patient and therapist speech quantity were positively and significantly related to patient outcome. Table 8.5 shows that a majority (7 of 11) of findings relating the amount of *patient* speech to outcome were significantly positive—positive findings were obtained in all categories of outcome measures, but the category of objective indices and tests showed the greatest proportion.

The studies regarding the amount of *therapist* speech were more equivocal. Only 5 of the 14 findings were significantly positive, while 8 showed no relationship of therapist talkativeness to patient benefit, and 1 showed a significantly negative relationship.

Perhaps it is fair, and not so surprising after all, to conclude that it *is* important that patients talk.

Styles of Role Implementation
In the medical model of the doctor–patient relationship one encounters a significant differentiation between roles on the dimension of authority. The doctor is the expert who prescribes treatment for the patient, and it is a principal obligation of the patient role to comply with the doctor's prescription (Parsons, 1964). In contrast to this, writers on psychotherapy have stressed the patient's initiative as a crucial factor in treatment. Although the therapist may be presumed to have expertise in matters relating to the patient's condition, the relationship between them is often supposed to be one of active collaboration, rather than directive authority. The therapist's special expertise is deemphasized, and the patients' responsibility for contributing to the solution of their own problems is stressed.

Tables 8.6 and 8.7 present the results of process-outcome studies that examine the manner in which therapists and patients, respectively, implement their contractual roles. Table 8.6 summarizes 25 findings comparing the effect on outcome of therapist directiveness and therapist collaborativeness. Twelve of those 25 findings indicate a significantly more positive outcome when therapists perform in a collaborative rather than an authoritarian manner. This association is actually most pronounced when the therapist's role implementation is observed by therapists themselves, although it holds good for all categories of outcome measures. Seven of the 11 findings significantly favor the therapist's "encouraging independence," and none favors therapist directiveness. Patients' perceptions of the therapist's manner in the doctor role show pretty much the same pattern, but observer judgments based on ratings of recorded excerpts of therapy show the reverse. The *participant* observations of patients and therapists together show 11 of 17 findings significantly favor therapist collaborativeness, and none favors therapist directiveness. In contrast, *nonparticipant* observations of therapist manner show that 3 of 8 findings significantly favor therapist directiveness, while only 1 favors therapist collaborativeness. Whatever the explanation of this particular reversal, it would seem that the therapeutic process is in this instance manifested differently to participant observers than it is to nonparticipant observers.

A more consistent pattern emerges with regard to the patient's role implementation. Table 8.7 summarizes the findings of 13 studies comparing the effects on outcome of patient collaboration and patient dependency. Thirteen of the 20 findings significantly favor patient collaboration, and none favors patient dependency. This overall figure includes all observational perspectives and all categories of outcome measures. However, the effects occur most frequently in three subcategories: (1) patient reports of process by patient outcome; (2) therapist reports of process by therapist outcome; and (3) observer judgments of process by objective indices and tests of outcome. Thus, those who perceive the patient as collaborative also tend to perceive the patient as having improved.

The greater part of the evidence reviewed shows rather strong support for the beneficial impact of a collaborative manner of implementation of patient and therapist roles. This need not be construed as implying an extreme equalitarianism, or a denial of ability and expertise on the therapist's part. Careful examination of the studies involved indicates that

TABLE 8.5 Talking

Reference	Variable	Outcome Perspective[a]	Finding[b]
THERAPISTS' SPEECH			
Barrington (1961)	Mean reaction time;	T	0
Barrington (1961)	words/response; number of responses; number of breaks in responses	S	0
DiLoreto (1971)	Percent time speaking	S	0
Friedlander (1981)	Verbal productivity	P	+
Friedlander (1981)	Verbal productivity	T	+
Rogers (1973)	Total number of remarks	S	0
Scher (1975)	Verbal activity	P	0
Scher (1975)	Verbal activity	T	0
Staples & Sloane (1976)	Total speech time; mean reaction time; duration of utterance	S	0
Staples & Sloane (1976)	Number of speech units	S	−
Truax (1970b)	Length of response	P	+
Truax (1970b)	Length of response	T	+
Truax (1970b)	Length of response	S	0
Wogan et al. (1977)	Verbal activity	S	+
PATIENTS' SPEECH			
DiLoreto (1971)	Percent time speaking	S	+
McDaniel et al. (1981)	Number of utterances	P	+
McDaniel et al. (1981)	Number of utterances	T	+
McDaniel et al. (1981)	Number of utterances	R	+
McDaniel et al. (1981)	Number of utterances	S	+
Scher (1975)	Verbal activity	P	0
Scher (1975)	Verbal activity	T	0
Sloane et al. (1975) (also Staples et al., 1976)	Total speech time; mean speech duration; mean reaction time	S	+
Staples & Sloane (1976)	Total speech time; mean reaction time	S	+
Yalom et al. (1967)	Verbal activity	P	0
Yalom et al. (1967)	Verbal activity	R	0

SUMMARY

Outcome Perspective

	Patient − 0 +	Therapist − 0 +	Rater − 0 +	Score − 0 +	Total − 0 +
Therapist	0 1 2	0 2 2	0 0 0	1 5 1	1 8 5
Patient	0 2 1	0 1 1	0 1 1	0 0 4	0 4 7

[a]See Table 8.1, footnote a.
[b]Findings are categorized as "−" (a statistically significant difference favoring less talking), "0" (no statistical difference), and "+" (a statistically significant difference favoring more talking by patient or therapist).

TABLE 8.6   Relating: Therapist Collaboration (+) vs. Authority (−)

Reference	Process Perspective[a]	Outcome Perspective[b]	Finding[c]
Alexander et al. (1976)	O	R	−
Ashby et al. (1957)	O	T	−
Ashby et al. (1957)	O	S	0
Baer et al. (1980)	T	T	0
Baker (1960)	O	S	−
Cooley & Lajoy (1980)	P	P	0
Cooley & Lajoy (1980)	P	T	0
Cooley & Lajoy (1980)	T	P	+
Cooley & Lajoy (1980)	T	T	+
Coons (1972)	O	S	+
Hartley & Strupp (1983)	O	S	0
Heine (1950)	P	P	+
Jacobs & Warner (1981)	T	T	+
Jacobs & Warner (1981)	T	R	+
Lorr (1965)	P	P	+
Lorr (1965)	P	T	+
Martin & Sterne (1976a)	P	S	+
Mintz et al. (1971)	O	T	0
Morrison et al. (1978)	T	S	+
Morrison & Newcomer (1975)	T	S	0
Rudy (1983)	T	P	+
Rudy (1983)	T	T	+
Rudy (1983)	T	S	0
Sloane et al. (1975) (also Staples et al., 1976)	O	S	0
Sloane et al. (1975) (also Staples et al., 1976)	P	S	0

SUMMARY

Outcome Perspective

Process Perspective	Patient − 0 +	Therapist − 0 +	Rater − 0 +	Score − 0 +	Total − 0 +
Observer	0 0 0	1 1 0	1 0 0	1 3 1	3 4 1
Patient	0 1 2	0 1 1	0 0 0	0 0 1	0 2 4
Therapist	0 0 2	0 1 3	0 0 1	0 3 1	0 4 7
Total	0 1 4	1 3 4	1 0 1	1 6 3	3 10 12

[a]"Process Perspective" refers to how the process ratings were made. "Observer" indicates that a nonparticipant made the ratings, "Patient" indicates that the patient (P) made the ratings, and "Therapist" indicates that process was evaluated by the therapist (T).

[b]"Outcome Perspective" refers to the way in which outcome was evaluated. "P" indicates patient ratings, "T" indicates therapist ratings, "R" indicates that outcome was evaluated by an independent clinical rater, and "S" is used to show that some objective score (e.g., MMPI) was used.

[c]"Findings" are reported as "+" (therapist collaboration was found to be significantly related to outcome), "0" (no significant difference was found), or "−" (therapist authority was significantly related to outcome).

TABLE 8.7   Relating: Patient Collaboration (+) vs. Dependency (−)

Reference	Process Perspective[a]	Outcome Perspective[a]	Finding[b]
Conrad (1952)	T	T	+
Crowder (1972)	O	S	+
Grigg & Goodstein (1957)	P	P	+
Hartley & Strupp (1983)	O	S	+
Heine (1950)	P	P	+
Landfield (1971)	T	R	+
Landfield (1971)	T	R	0
Lorr & McNair (1964b)	T	T	0
Lorr & McNair (1964b)	T	P	0
Rosenbaum et al. (1956)	T	T	+
Rudy (1983)	P	P	0
Rudy (1983)	P	T	+
Rudy (1983)	P	S	0
Saltzman et al. (1976)	P	P	+
Saltzman et al. (1976)	P	T	0
Saltzman et al. (1976)	T	P	+
Saltzman et al. (1976)	T	T	+
Schauble & Pierce (1974)	O	S	+
Sloane et al. (1975) (also Staples et al., 1976)	T	S	0
Tovian (1977)	P	R	+

SUMMARY

Process Perspective	Outcome Perspective				
	Patient − 0 +	Therapist − 0 +	Rater − 0 +	Score − 0 +	Total − 0 +
Observer	0 0 0	0 0 0	0 0 0	0 0 3	0 0 3
Patient	0 1 3	0 1 1	0 0 1	0 1 0	0 3 5
Therapist	0 1 1	0 1 3	0 1 1	0 1 0	0 4 5
Total	0 2 4	0 2 4	0 1 2	0 2 3	0 7 13

[a]See Table 8.6, footnotes a and b.
[b]"Findings" are reported as "+" (patient collaboration was found to be significantly related to outcome), "0" (no significant difference was found), or "−" (patient dependency was significantly related to outcome).

the crucial factors are the therapists' encouragement of patient initiative, and the patients' assumption of an active role in resolving their problems.

THERAPEUTIC INTERVENTIONS

Therapeutic interventions comprise the most salient substantive element in psychotherapy. That element is also the most "intentional" aspect of psychotherapy. To the person who thinks of therapy as technique—specific procedures deliberately carried out by the therapist, the patient, or both together—therapeutic interventions are the only, or only important, element in psychotherapy. Other therapists are more inclined to think of therapy as a process of natural healing that occurs within a caring relationship, but even they must think of something to "do" while that spontaneous relationship is developing—something, indeed, that hopefully will facilitate its growth. In this section we shall deal first with therapeutic interventions made by therapists, and then with the patients' part in these procedures.

Therapists' Interventions

The following things that therapists do have been studied in relation to patient outcome: (1) interpretation or giving insight; (2) confrontation or giving feedback; (3) exploration and questioning; (4) giving support and encouragement; (5) giving advice; (6) reflection; and (7) self-disclosure. Of course, any particular mode of intervention can be done adroitly or clumsily, and thus it seems appropriate to include several studies of therapist skillfulness in this section. Researchers have also shown interest in the content-focus or target of therapeutic interventions, especially of interpretation and confrontation, since *what* therapists interpret or confront in their patients may also have an impact on outcome.

Interpretation

An interpretation is essentially an explanatory statement intended to clarify the meaning of an action or experience. When therapists say something like, "I think what you are really telling me is . . . ," or, "When she did that it must have made you feel . . . ," they are giving interpretations.

Do interpretations help? Table 8.8 presents 22 findings evaluating the impact of interpretations on outcome. Eleven of the 22 findings showed interpretations to have a significantly positive effect on outcome, but 8 showed no association and 3 showed a significantly negative impact. [For the record, 2 of the 3 negative findings were reported for borderline and psychotic patients, in a study that also reported positive effects of interpretation with neurotic and personality disordered patients (Jacobs & Warner, 1981).] Although positive findings occurred in all four categories of outcome measures, the proportion of positve findings was comparatively higher for the subcategory of patient process by patient outcome, and also for therapist process by therapist outcome.

Clearly one cannot say that interpretation is a consistently effective, or even necessarily a safe, therapeutic intervention. Nor can one say that interpretation is generally an ineffective (or dangerous) procedure, since half the research findings do indicate that patients benefit when interpretation is used. Given this situation, it seems reasonable to assume

that other important factors act to neutralize or potentiate the impact of interpretation on patient outcome.

Confrontation

Confrontation differs from interpretation as a therapeutic technique in its effort to foster, not just insight into meaning, but rather a directly meaningful experience. It can take the form of feedback from therapist to patient or can occur through procedures (such as the Gestalt "two-chair" technique) that are designed to produce self-confrontation. Confrontation in psychotherapy carries no implication of hostile encounter; whether they are blunt or tactful, it is their direct experiential quality that is emphasized.

Table 8.9 summarizes seven findings on the effects of confrontation. The small number here is offset by their striking consistency in showing that use of confrontation is significantly and positively associated with patient outcome. Those who wish to reserve judgment on confrontation can note that Table 8.9 reveals many process-outcome subcategories for which no studies have yet been done. However, the evidence presently available suggests that confrontation is a potent form of intervention.

Content Focus

By their very nature, interpretations and confrontations are about something in particular. It makes little sense to suppose that all interpretations, or all confrontations, are of equal therapeutic value, no matter what they are about. Several process-outcome studies that have examined the effects of particular content focus shed some light on this issue.

Table 8.10 presents findings on the effects of three content foci: (1) the patient's feelings and affective states; (2) here-and-now events in the therapeutic situation generally; and more specifically (3) the patient's transference reactions to the therapist. All of the studies happen to have been made from the external observer's perspective on therapeutic process.

Five studies are relevant to the issue of focusing on patient affect, and 5 of the 10 findings drawn from these studies show a significantly positive association with patient outcome. These reflect outcome evaluations by independent clinical judges or by objective indices and tests. The other 5 show a null relationship, suggesting that focusing on affect

TABLE 8.8 Therapeutic Intervention: Interpretation

Reference	Process Perspective[a]	Outcome Perspective[a]	Finding[b]
Abramowitz & Abramowitz (1974)	O	S	+
Elliott et al. (1982)	O	P	+
Elliott et al. (1982)	O	T	0
Elliott et al. (1982)	P	P	+
Elliott et al. (1982)	P	T	0
Elliott et al. (1982)	T	P	0
Elliott et al. (1982)	T	T	+
Gomez (1982)	O	S	+
Heine (1950)	P	P	+
Jacobs & Warner (1981)	T	T	+
Jacobs & Warner (1981)	T	R	+
Jacobs & Warner (1981)	T	T	−
Jacobs & Warner (1981)	T	R	−
Kernberg et al. (1972)	O	S	0
Malan (1976)	O	R	+
Mintz et al. (1971)	O	T	0
Reid & Shyne (1969)	T	R	0
Reid & Shyne (1969)	T	S	0
Rosenbaum et al. (1956)	T	T	+
Semon & Goldstein (1957)	O	S	0
Sloane et al. (1975) (also Staples et al., 1976)	O	S	−
Sloane et al. (1975)	P	P	+

SUMMARY

Process Perspective	Outcome Perspective				
	Patient − 0 +	Therapist − 0 +	Rater − 0 +	Score − 0 +	Total − 0 +
Observer	0 0 1	0 2 0	0 0 1	1 2 2	1 4 4
Patient	0 0 3	0 1 0	0 0 0	0 0 0	0 1 3
Therapist	0 1 0	1 0 3	1 1 1	0 1 0	2 3 4
Total	0 1 4	1 3 3	1 1 2	1 3 2	3 8 11

[a]See Table 8.6, footnotes a and b.

[b]"Findings" are reported as "+" (interpretation was found to be significantly positively related to outcome), "0" (no significant association was found), or "−" (interpretation was significantly negatively related to outcome).

is sometimes but not always helpful, although (on the basis of these few studies) it is not likely to be harmful.

The nine findings relevant to a general here-and-now interpretive focus reveal a rather different pattern. Six of the nine showed the here-and-now focus to have no significant association with patient outcome, while three indicated a negative effect.

The three negative findings were all obtained when the here-and-now focus occurred in a context of *low* empathy and genuineness on the therapist's part (Mitchell, 1971).

Concentration on the patient's transference reactions to the therapist overlaps somewhat with a focus on affect and the here-and-now situation, but it explicitly links one aspect of the patient's immedi-

TABLE 8.9   Therapeutic Intervention: Confrontation

Reference	Process Perspective[a]	Outcome Perspective[a]	Finding[b]
Greenberg & Dompierre (1981)	O	P	+
Greenberg & Rice (1981)	O	P	+
Johnson (1971)	O	S	+
Kaschak (1978)	P	P	+
Kaschak (1978)	T	T	+
Mainord et al. (1965)	O	S	+
Truax & Wittmer (1973)	O	S	+

SUMMARY

Outcome Perspective

Process Perspective	Patient − 0 +	Therapist − 0 +	Rater − 0 +	Score − 0 +	Total − 0 +
Observer	0 0 2	0 0 0	0 0 0	0 0 3	0 0 5
Patient	0 0 1	0 0 0	0 0 0	0 0 0	0 0 1
Therapist	0 0 0	0 0 1	0 0 0	0 0 0	0 0 1
Total	0 0 3	0 0 1	0 0 0	0 0 3	0 0 7

[a]See Table 8.6, footnotes a and b.
[b]"Findings" are reported as "+" (confrontation was found to be significantly positively related to outcome), "0" (no significant association was found), or "−" (confrontation was significantly negatively related to outcome).

ate feelings to their origin in earlier relations with parents. As can be seen in Table 8.10, the pattern of findings resembles that found with affect focus: four of the six were significantly and positively related to outcome (again, in the same two outcome subcategories), and two were unrelated. Again, it appears that focusing on the patient's transference reactions can be helpful, but whether it will be or not depends on other factors yet to be determined.

Exploration

Therapists often use questions, not just to gather information, but to help patients explore aspects of their experience. Table 8.11 summarizes 22 findings on the effectiveness of such exploration as a therapeutic technique. The overall pattern of results is familiar: 10 of the 22 showed a significantly positive association of exploration with outcome, and 12 showed no relationship. Positive findings occurred in all categories of outcome measures, but were proportionately more frequent in two subcategories: observer-rated process by therapist evaluation, and therapist-reported process by objec-

tive indices and tests. Here, too, we find a form of intervention that is often but not very consistently helpful, suggesting an interaction effect between therapeutic technique and other circumstances.

Support

Another therapeutic intervention that is commonly made by therapists is the giving of support and encouragement. Table 8.12 summarizes 25 findings on the impact of supportive interventions. Although 6 of the 25 are significantly positive findings and none are negative, more than three-quarters show a null association between specific therapist efforts to give support and patient outcome. Thus, while it may be occasionally helpful, and is not harmful, this mode of intervention does not appear to have much consistent impact.

Advice

Three studies have concerned themselves with the effect on outcome of therapists' giving advice, with mixed results. Elliott, Barker, Caskey, and Pistrang (1982) found that advice, as perceived by therapists and by nonparticipant raters, was positively related

TABLE 8.10   Therapeutic Intervention: Interpretive Focus

Reference	Process Perspective[a]	Outcome Perspective[a]	Finding[b]
AFFECT FOCUS			
Alexander et al. (1976)	O	R	+
Alexander et al. (1976)	O	S	+
Barrington (1961)	O	T	0
Barrington (1961)	O	S	0
Beutler & Mitchell (1981)	O	S	+
Nichols (1974)	O	S	+
Truax & Wittmer (1971a)	O	P	0
Truax & Wittmer (1971a)	O	T	0
Truax & Wittmer (1971a)	O	R	+
Truax & Wittmer (1971a)	O	S	0
HERE-NOW FOCUS			
Abramowitz & Jackson (1974)	O	S	0
Kernberg et al. (1972)	O	S	0
Malan (1976)	O	R	0
Mitchell (1971)	O	P	0
Mitchell (1971)	O	T	0
Mitchell (1971)	O	S	0
Mitchell (1971)	O	P	−
Mitchell (1971)	O	T	−
Mitchell (1971)	O	S	−
TRANSFERENCE FOCUS			
Kernberg (1976)	O	S	+
Malan (1976)	O	R	+
Marziali (1984)	O	P	0
Marziali (1984)	O	T	0
Marziali (1984)	O	S	+
Mintz (1981)	O	R	+

SUMMARY

Interpretive Focus	Patient − 0 +	Therapist − 0 +	Rater − 0 +	Score − 0 +	Total − 0 +
Affect	0 1 0	0 2 0	0 0 2	0 2 3	0 5 5
Here-now	1 1 0	1 1 0	0 1 0	0 2 3	0 5 5
Transference	0 1 0	0 1 0	0 0 2	1 3 0	1 5 4

(Column group header: *Outcome Perspective*)

[a] See Table 8.6, footnotes *a* and *b*.

[b] "Findings" are reported as "+" (focus was found to be significantly positively related to outcome), "0" (no significant association was found), or "−" (focus was significantly negatively related to outcome).

TABLE 8.11   Therapeutic Intervention: Exploration

Reference	Process Perspective[a]	Outcome Perspective[a]	Finding[b]
Elliott et al. (1982)	P	P	0
Elliott et al. (1982)	P	T	0
Elliott et al. (1982)	T	P	0
Elliott et al. (1982)	T	T	0
Elliott et al. (1982)	O	P	0
Elliott et al. (1982)	O	T	0
Gomes-Schwartz (1978)	O	P	0
Gomes-Schwartz (1978)	O	T	+
Gomes-Schwartz (1978)	O	R	0
Gomes-Schwartz (1978)	O	S	0
Heine (1950)	P	P	+
O'Malley et al. (1983)	O	P	0
O'Malley et al. (1983)	O	T	+
O'Malley et al. (1983)	O	R	0
O'Malley et al. (1983)	O	S	+
Rogers (1973)	O	S	+
Rounsaville et al. (1981)	T	S	+
Sloane et al. (1975) (also Staples et al., 1976)	O	S	0
Suh et al. (1986)	O	T	+
Suh et al. (1986)	O	R	+
Suh et al. (1986)	O	S	+
Weiner & Weinstock (1973)	T	S	+

SUMMARY

Process Perspective	Outcome Perspective				
	Patient − 0 +	Therapist − 0 +	Rater − 0 +	Score − 0 +	Total − 0 +
Observer	0 3 0	0 1 3	0 2 1	0 2 3	0 8 7
Patient	0 1 1	0 1 0	0 0 0	0 0 0	0 2 1
Therapist	0 1 0	0 1 0	0 0 0	0 0 2	0 2 2
Total	0 5 1	0 3 3	0 2 1	0 2 5	0 12 10

[a]See Table 8.6, footnotes a and b.
[b]"Findings" are reported as "+" (exploration was found to be significantly positively related to outcome), "0" (no significant association was found), or "−" (exploration was significantly negatively related to outcome).

to outcome evaluations made by therapists, but that other process-outcome subcategories showed null findings. In the Temple study (Sloane, Staples, Cristol, Yorkston, & Whipple, 1975; Staples, Sloane, Whipple, Cristol, & Yorkston, 1976) no association was found between therapist advice, rated by nonparticipant observers, and patient outcome assessed by objective indices and tests. However, Rounsaville, Weissman, & Prusoff (1981) reported a significant negative impact of giving advice, when that

intervention was observed from the therapist's perspective and evaluated by objective indices and tests. There are still too few findings to suggest an interpretable pattern, but giving advice does not appear to be an aid in psychotherapy.

Reflection

Reflection is a technique of restatement that is used by therapists to check the accuracy of their understanding of what patients have said, to clarify the

TABLE 8.12 Therapeutic Intervention: Support

Reference	Process Perspective[a]	Outcome Perspective[a]	Finding[b]
Dreiblatt & Weatherly (1965)	T	S	+
Elliott et al. (1982)	P	P	0
Elliott et al. (1982)	P	T	0
Elliott et al. (1982)	T	P	0
Elliott et al. (1982)	T	T	0
Elliott et al. (1982)	O	P	0
Elliott et al. (1982)	O	T	0
Feifel & Eells (1963)	P	P	0
Feifel & Eells (1963)	T	T	0
Kaschak (1978)	P	P	0
Kaschak (1978)	T	T	0
Reid & Shyne (1969)	T	R	0
Reid & Shyne (1969)	T	S	0
Rogers (1973)	O	S	+
Rosenbaum et al. (1956)	T	T	0
Ryan & Gizynski (1971)	T	P	+
Ryan & Gizynski (1971)	T	R	+
Sloane et al. (1975)	P	P	+
Sloane et al. (1975) (also Staples et al., 1975)	O	S	0
Truax (1970a)	O	P	+
Truax (1970a)	O	T	0
Truax (1970a)	O	R	0
Truax (1970a)	O	S	0
Werman et al. (1976)	P	T	0
Werman et al. (1976)	P	R	0

SUMMARY

Process Perspective	Outcome Perspective				
	Patient − 0 +	Therapist − 0 +	Rater − 0 +	Score − 0 +	Total − 0 +
Observer	0 1 1	0 2 0	0 1 0	0 2 1	0 6 2
Patient	0 3 1	0 2 0	0 1 0	0 0 0	0 6 1
Therapist	0 1 1	0 4 0	0 1 1	0 1 1	0 7 3
Total	0 5 3	0 8 0	0 3 1	0 3 2	0 19 6

[a]See Table 8.6, footnotes a and b.
[b]"Findings" are reported as "+" (support was found to be significantly positively related to outcome), "0" (no significant association was found), or "−" (support was significantly negatively related to outcome).

patient's meaning, and to facilitate further exploration by the patient of certain aspects of experience (e.g., reflection of feeling). Seven studies have reported results on the absolute or comparative effectiveness of reflection as a technique of psychotherapy.

Only a few findings have been based on participant observations of therapeutic process. Thus, Elliott et al. (1982) found no significant associations between reflection, reported by patients or by therapists, with outcome as evaluated either by patients or by therapists. These four findings were replicated by Rounsaville et al. (1981), who found no association between reflection measured from the therapist's viewpoint and outcome evaluated by objective indices and tests.

Two studies have presented data on reflection as measured by nonparticipant observers. Elliott et al. (1982) also found no significant relationships from this perspective between reflection and either patient or therapist evaluations of outcome. Earlier, Rogers (1973) found the same result when outcome was assessed by objective indices and tests.

In four other studies, reflection (rated by nonparticipant observers) was compared with other modes of intervention. Two recent, rather elegant experiments have found "empathic reflection" to be less effective than the Gestalt two-chair technique when outcome was evaluated from the patient's perspective (Greenberg & Dompierre, 1981; Greenberg & Rice, 1981). In an earlier work, Baker (1960) found reflection to be less effective than a "leading" technique when outcome was evaluated by patients. Ashby, Ford, Guerney, and Guerney (1957) also found reflection to be comparatively less effective than more leading interpretive interventions when outcome was assessed by the therapists, but to be of equivalent value when outcome was assessed by objective indices and tests.

Reflection seems to be neither helpful nor harmful in itself, and thus compares poorly with techniques that do have some therapeutic potency.

Therapist Self-disclosure

Therapists can use themselves as "instruments of therapy" (Orlinsky & Howard, 1975) in various ways, one of which is to describe aspects of themselves or of their personal experiences to patients. The utility of such self-disclosure has been examined in five studies. Two studies have measured self-disclosure from the vantage points of both patients and therapists, in relation to outcome as evaluated by both patients and therapists. Elliott et al. (1982) found that none of these four combinations yielded significant results. Hayward (1974) did find a significantly positive association between amount of therapist self-disclosure and two of several outcome measures.

Four studies have reported findings on self-disclosure as rated by nonparticipant observers. Elliott et al. (1982) found a significantly positive association between this process perspective and outcome evaluated by therapists, but only a nonsignificant trend for outcome evaluated by patients. Dickenson (1969) found that therapist self-disclosure had a positive effect on outcome for a sample of juvenile delinquents, but not for hospitalized psychiatric patients, when outcome was assessed by objective indices and tests. On the other hand, Alexander, Barton, Schiavo, and Parsons (1976), working with juvenile delinquents and their families, found no significant association between therapist self-disclosure and patient outcome, assessed either by independent judges or by an objective index. Beutler and Mitchell (1981) also found no relationship between self-disclosure and outcome measured by objective indices and tests.

The net impression is that therapist self-disclosure may occasionally be helpful, but is generally not a powerful mode of therapeutic intervention.

Therapist Skillfulness

Therapist skillfulness is an important, but little studied, variable in process-outcome research. Five studies that report data relevant to this issue underscore the importance of this concern. An early investigation by Shyne and Kogan (1957) found a significant positive correlation between "overall caseworker skill" rated by nonparticipant observers and outcome assessed by independent judges. A few years later, Feifel and Eells (1963) reported that therapist skillfulness was judged by therapists to be the most important factor influencing outcome, although this was less salient from the patient's perspective.

In their report on the lengthy Menninger project, Kernberg et al. (1972) noted a significantly positive association between therapist skillfulness and outcome, especially for patients low in ego-strength, when these variables were rated by nonparticipant judges. Sloane et al. (1975), in their account of the Temple project, reported that therapist skillfulness was retrospectively nominated as contributing importantly to their improvement by more than 70 percent of successful psychotherapy patients. Finally, in a study utilizing the Vanderbilt Negative Indicator Scale, Sachs (1983) found that observer judgments of errors in therapeutic technique were significantly and negatively associated with outcome, evaluated jointly from the perspectives of patient, therapist, and independent clinician.

All in all, these few studies show an impressive

consistency in finding therapist skillfulness to be a significant determinant of patient outcome.

Patient Participation in Therapeutic Interventions

Patients in psychotherapy are not passive recipients of therapeutic interventions. As noted earlier with regard to implementing the therapeutic contract, outcome is optimized when patients actively collaborate in the therapeutic process. Several specific aspects of patient participation have been studied as possible determinants of outcome: (1) patient self-exploration; (2) the quality, exploration, and expression of patient feelings; (3) the discussion of patient problems; and (4) the patient's attention to here-and-now aspects of the therapeutic situation. A somewhat different dimension is the patient's aptitude or suitability for psychotherapy, reflected in such things as prognostic expectations. Patient suitability, as a process measure, resembles therapist skillfulness in being concerned not so much with what the participants do as with how well they do it.

Patient Self-exploration

This mode of patient participation was formulated as a key element in the client-centered theory of psychotherapy and has been extensively studied by students and associates of Carl Rogers. Table 8.13 summarizes 37 findings relating outcome to patient self-exploration. All but one of these findings focused on process as rated from excerpts of recorded therapy by nonparticipant observers (despite the phenomenological emphasis of Rogers' theory). Somewhat surprisingly, the overwhelming majority of findings (26 out of 37) showed no significant process-outcome relationship, across all categories of outcome measurement. The only process-outcome subcategory in which a substantial proportion (over half) of the findings were significantly positive was the one defined by nonparticipant process observations and therapists' outcome evaluations.

One reason for the impressive failure to find a greater proportion of positive results is the use of the Truax scale to measure this variable in so many of the studies. Nineteen of the findings utilized this scale, and only two of these were positive. Thirteen other findings used variedly different measurement procedures, and of these five were positive and one (done with hospitalized schizophrenics in group

psychotherapy) showed a negative effect for patient self-exploration.

Another plausible reason for finding so low a proportion of significant effects is the likelihood that patient self-exploration is a very common occurrence in psychotherapy. If so, it would often be found in unsuccessful as well as successful cases. Whether or not this is so, we are forced to search elsewhere for powerful patient contributions to therapeutic outcome.

Affective Arousal

Process-outcome researchers have concentrated on three aspects of patient affective arousal: (1) the presence of negative affect; (2) the immediacy of affective expression; and (3) the extent of catharsis or affective "discharge."

Patient distress and hostility have been the chief forms of negative affect examined in relation to outcome. Table 8.14 presents 21 findings on the impact of negative patient affect on outcome. The pattern of results is mixed: overall 8 of the 21 show a significant positive association between negative patient affect and outcome, from all outcome perspectives except the patient's; 4 of the 21 show a significant negative association with outcome; 9 of the 21 show no relationship with outcome.

If we consider that patients often come to therapy precisely because they are experiencing high levels of negative affect, then we might construe the large number of findings relating negative affect in therapy to positive outcome as an indication of the importance of bringing those feelings into the therapeutic process. They can be dealt with most directly, and perhaps be resolved most effectively, when treated in vivo. A possible interpretation of the discrepancy between significant positive and negative findings is that patients who continue to experience a great deal of negative affect as therapy proceeds are those who are not being helped. Some support for this conjecture can be drawn from the fact that several of the studies that showed that patient distress and hostility were predictive of better outcomes focused particularly on early treatment sessions.

The manner in which patients bring their feelings into the therapeutic discourse also has been the subject of study, especially by researchers working in the context of client-centered theory. Table 8.15

TABLE 8.13 Therapeutic Intervention: Patient Self-exploration

Reference	Process Perspective[a]	Outcome Perspective[a]	Finding[b]
Braaten (1961)	O	T	+
Braaten (1961)	O	S	+
DiLoreto (1971)	O	S	0
Gomes-Schwartz (1978)	O	P	0
Gomes-Schwartz (1978)	O	T	+
Gomes-Schwartz (1978)	O	R	0
Gomes-Schwartz (1978)	O	S	0
Kirtner & Cartwright (1958)	O	T	+
Kurtz & Grummon (1972)	O	P	0
Kurtz & Grummon (1972)	O	T	0
Kurtz & Grummon (1972)	O	S	0
McDaniel et al. (1981)	O	P	0
McDaniel et al. (1981)	O	T	0
McDaniel et al. (1981)	O	R	0
McDaniel et al. (1981)	O	S	0
Mitchell et al. (1973)	O	P	0
Mitchell et al. (1973)	O	T	0
Mitchell et al. (1973)	O	R	0
Mitchell et al. (1973)	O	S	0
O'Malley et al. (1983)	O	P	0
O'Malley et al. (1983)	O	T	+
O'Malley et al. (1983)	O	R	0
O'Malley et al. (1983)	O	S	+
Prager (1971)	O	P	0
Prager (1971)	O	T	0
Prager (1971)	O	R	0
Prager (1971)	O	S	0
Schauble & Pierce (1974)	O	S	+
Seeman (1954)	O	T	+
Sloane et al. (1975) (also Staples et al., 1976)	O	S	0
Strassberg et al. (1975)	O	S	−
Traux (1968)	O	S	+
Traux & Wargo (1969)	O	S	0
Traux et al. (1970)	O	S	0
van der Veen & Stoler (1965)	O	T	0
van der Veen & Stoler (1965)	O	S	0
Vargas (1954)	O	T	+

SUMMARY

Outcome Perspective

Process Perspective	Patient − 0 +	Therapist − 0 +	Rater − 0 +	Score − 0 +	Total − 0 +
Observer	0 6 0	0 5 6	0 5 0	1 10 4	1 26 10
Patient	0 0 0	0 0 0	0 0 0	0 0 0	0 0 0
Therapist	0 0 0	0 0 0	0 0 0	0 0 0	0 0 0
Total	0 6 0	0 5 6	0 5 0	1 10 4	1 26 10

[a]See Table 8.6, footnotes a and b.
[b]"Findings" are reported as "+" (patient self-exploration was found to be significantly positively related to outcome), "0" (no significant association was found), or "−" (self-exploration was significantly negatively related to outcome).

TABLE 8.14 Patient Negative Affect: Distress and Hostility (+)

Reference	Process Perspective[a]	Outcome Perspective[a]	Finding[b]
Baer et al. (1980)	T	T	+
Bottari & Rappaport (1983)	P	S	+
Brown (1970)	T	T	0
Conrad (1952)	T	T	+
Crowder (1972)[c]	O	S	+
Hartley & Strupp (1983)	O	S	−
Mintz et al. (1971)	O	T	−
Mintz et al. (1971)	O	T	0
Peiser (1982)	T	R	+
Prager (1971)	T	P	0
Prager (1971)	T	T	0
Prager (1971)	T	R	0
Prager (1971)	T	S	0
Roether & Peters (1972)[c]	T	S	+
Rounsaville et al. (1979)[c]	T	S	−
Rounsaville et al. (1979)	T	S	−
Saltzman et al. (1976)	P	P	0
Saltzman et al. (1976)	P	T	0
Saltzman et al. (1976)[c]	P	P	0
Saltzman et al. (1976)[c]	P	T	+
Truax (1971)[c]	O	S	+

SUMMARY

Outcome Perspective

Process Perspective	Patient − 0 +	Therapist − 0 +	Rater − 0 +	Score − 0 +	Total − 0 +
Observer	0 0 0	1 1 0	0 0 0	1 0 2	2 1 2
Patient	0 2 0	0 1 1	0 0 0	0 0 1	0 3 2
Therapist	0 1 0	0 2 2	0 1 1	2 1 1	2 5 4
Total	0 3 0	1 4 3	0 1 1	3 1 4	4 9 8

[a]See Table 8.6, footnotes a and b.
[b]"Findings" are reported as "+" (patient negative affect was found to be significantly positively related to outcome), "0" (no significant association was found), or "−" (patient negative affect was significantly negatively related to outcome).
[c]Hostility.

presents 25 findings on the relation of outcome to the immediacy of affective expression. Fifteen of these findings showed that affective immediacy was significantly related to outcome. Strangely enough, this has not been studied at all from the patient's process perspective, and in only two studies from the patient's perspective on outcome. Almost all of the findings were based on nonparticipant observations of process, and most of the positive findings occur in two of the three process-outcome subcate-gories for which there are studies. Despite these limitations, affective immediacy seems to be significantly implicated in the attainment of therapeutic benefit.

The third aspect of affective arousal that has been studied is that of discharge or catharsis. Modern psychotherapy began at the end of the nineteenth century as a cathartic (i.e., a cleansing or purifying) procedure for the release of aroused but unexpressed emotion. There has been renewed interest in this

TABLE 8.15 Patient Affective Immediacy

Reference	Process Perspective[a]	Outcome Perspective[a]	Finding[b]
Braaten (1961)	O	T	+
Braaten (1961)	O	S	+
Gendlin et al. (1960)	T	T	+
Kiesler (1971)[c]	O	T	+
Kiesler (1971)[c]	O	S	+
Kiesler (1971)[d]	O	T	0
Kiesler (1971)[d]	O	S	0
Kiesler et al. (1967)[c]	O	S	0
Kirtner & Cartwright (1958)	O	T	+
Schauble & Pierce (1974)	O	S	+
Tomlinson (1967)[c]	O	S	0
Tomlinson (1967)[d]	O	S	+
Tomlinson & Hart (1962)[c]	O	P	+
Tomlinson & Hart (1962)[c]	O	T	+
Tomlinson & Hart (1962)[c]	O	S	+
Tomlinson & Hart (1962)[d]	O	P	0
Tomlinson & Hart (1962)[d]	O	T	0
Tomlinson & Hart (1962)[d]	O	S	0
Tomlinson & Stoler (1967)[c]	O	S	0
Tomlinson & Stoler (1967)[d]	O	S	+
van der Veen (1967)[c]	O	S	+
van der Veen (1967)[d]	O	S	0
van der Veen & Stoler (1965)	T	T	+
van der Veen & Stoler (1965)	T	S	0
Walker et al. (1960)[c]	O	T	+

SUMMARY

Process Perspective	Outcome Perspective				
	Patient − 0 +	Therapist − 0 +	Rater − 0 +	Score − 0 +	Total − 0 +
Observer	0 1 1	0 2 5	0 0 0	0 6 7	0 9 13
Patient	0 0 0	0 0 0	0 0 0	0 0 0	0 0 0
Therapist	0 0 0	0 0 2	0 0 0	0 1 0	0 1 2
Total	0 1 1	0 2 7	0 0 0	0 7 7	0 10 15

[a]See Table 8.6, footnotes a and b.
[b]"Findings" are reported as "+" (patient affective immediacy was found to be significantly positively related to outcome), "0" (no significant association was found), or "−" (patient affective immediacy was significantly negatively related to outcome).
[c]Level of "Experiencing" or "Process" scale score.
[d]Increase in "Experiencing" or "Process" scale score.

aspect of therapy in recent years, and a few studies have explored the impact of affective discharge on patient outcome. A partially relevant experiment by Hoehn-Saric et al. (1972) found that suggestions for beneficial change under induced emotional arousal were more effective than in emotionally unaroused states, when outcome was assessed by objective indices and tests; however, no significant effects were noted for outcome measured from either the patient's or the therapist's perspective. Nichols

(1974) found a significant positive association between level of observer-rated emotional discharge
in patients and outcome assessed by objective indices and tests. Bierenbaum, Nichols, and Schwartz
(1976) also reported some evidence of a significantly positive effect of emotional catharsis, as seen
by external observers, upon outcome evaluated by
independent clinicians and by objective indices and
tests. Werman, Agle, McDaniel, and Schoof (1976)
found that patients mentioned "ventilation" as the
most prominent of several sources of improvement
in their condition. On the other hand, Cabral, Best,
and Paton (1975) measured abreaction in group
psychotherapy patients from the nonparticipant
viewpoint and failed to find any relationship with
outcome evaluated from either the patient's perspective or that of the independent clinician. The
number of studies is too small to draw any conclusion except, perhaps, that this seems a promising
area for further investigation.

Problem Focus

There is a common view of psychotherapy that
suggests it is at bottom rather similar to the "personal service" provided by a friendly bartender or
sympathetic hairdresser, that is, an opportunity to
unburden oneself about one's problems. Whatever
patients may talk about with those other professionals, it is certainly true that they talk about problems
in psychotherapy. Yet to what extent is that an
essential part of the therapeutic process? Do patients who focus more intensively on problematic
issues fare better in terms of outcome?

When the patients' perspective on process and
on outcome is considered, the answer seems to be
"yes." For example, Feifel and Eells (1963) reported that "having the opportunity to talk over
problems" was the most frequently mentioned of
several helpful factors. Most of the Temple project
patients regarded as successful in psychotherapy
mentioned "being able to talk to an understanding
person" as having been important to them (Sloane
et al., 1975). Similarly, Kaschak (1978) noted that
"having someone to talk to" was ranked second as
a significant source of change by patients. All of
these were retrospective findings not amenable as
reported to evaluation by our statistical criterion,
and thus should not be viewed as "hard" evidence.

Other studies add a bit more to the picture. Piper,
Doan, Edwards, and Jones (1979) found that the
patient's percentage of total work time, measured
from a nonparticipant process perspective, was
significantly and positively related to outcome evaluated by objective indices and tests. However,
Rounsaville et al. (1981) found that therapists' estimates of the percentage of time patients discussed
their primary problem area was unrelated to outcome measured by objective indices and tests.

The critical factor in all this may have been formulated by Schauble and Pierce (1974), who found
that outcome (assessed by objective indices and
tests) was significantly and positively related to the
way that patients viewed and discussed their problems. Patients who manifested a strong and increasing sense of responsibility for their own feelings and
actions in problem situations received more benefit
than those who viewed their problems "externally,"
as something that simply happened to them.

Here-and-Now Focus

Another focus of patient involvement is the therapy
situation itself, that is, relations with the therapist
and in group therapy with other patients as well.
From the process perspective of the nonparticipant
observer, sometimes the patient's here-and-now
focus seems to matter and sometimes it doesn't.
Braaten (1961) found that patients' increasing exploration of their relationship with their therapists
was significantly and positively associated with outcome evaluated from the therapist's standpoint, but
was unrelated to outcome assessed by objective
indices and tests. Oclatis (1978) also found that
discussion of the therapeutic relationship by the
patient was unrelated to outcome assessed by objective indices and tests. However, Wogan, Getter,
Amder, Nichols, and Okman (1977) found that in
group psychotherapy the patients' discussion of
within-group topics versus topics external to the
group had a significantly positive association with
outcome assessed by objective indices and tests.

When viewed from the therapist's process perspective, the only significant impact of patients' here-
and-now focus was also found in the context of
group psychotherapy. Yalom, Houts, Zimerberg,
and Rand (1967) found that patients' revealing their
feelings about other group members was associated
with better outcomes as evaluated by patients themselves. However, the same authors found no impact
of that variable on outcome assessed by independent clinicians, and also no impact on either patient

or clinician outcome perspective for therapists' estimates of their patients' ability to focus on a here-and-now level. Additionally, both Seeman (1954) and Gendlin, Jenney, and Schlien (1960) failed to find any significant association between therapists' perceptions of their patients' here-and-now focus and outcome evaluated by therapists.

This variable has still not been measured from the patients's perspective, but with the possible exception of group therapy there seems to be no evidence that patients' here-and-now focus contributes to therapeutic outcome.

Patient Suitability

Just as all therapists are not equally skillful at making therapeutic interventions, so all patients do not have an equal aptitude for therapeutic procedures. The patient's adeptness or skill in therapeutic procedures constitutes the basis of prognostic judgments, when these are founded on observations of process rather than on input data such as intelligence or social class. Table 8.16 presents 20 findings on the relation of patient suitability to outcome. All but two of the findings are based on the therapist's process perspective, although they pertain to all four categories of outcome measures. Overall, 13 of the 20 findings showed a significantly positive association between outcome and patient suitability, with no significant negative results. The two studies based on the patient's perspective were consistent in showing that patient's positive expectations of benefit were also fulfilled.

Since prognostic evaluations based on actual process are generally made by therapists themselves, their expectations are likely to have some reactive influence on what they do with their patients. The same chicken-and-egg consideration applies to patients' expectations. How much is accurate prediction, and how much is self-fulfilling prophecy?

THE THERAPEUTIC BOND

Therapeutic interventions are made in the context of a relationship between two (or more) persons. Those persons are linked to one another through their respective roles as patient and therapist. The roles per se are defined and connected by the reciprocal rights and obligations implicit or explicit in the therapeutic contract. But the relationship between the persons who are patient and therapist necessarily transcends the patient and therapist roles. The therapeutic contract does shape, and should govern, the human relationship that in a sense grows up around it; but it is also qualified, conditioned, and vitiated or enhanced by the way the persons in the roles affect each other.

The relationship between the persons who are patient and therapist necessarily transcends the patient and therapist roles, because persons as such are more comprehensive, more varied, more complex than any single role. No matter how basic the role may be to them, no matter how heartfelt their commitment or how much time they devote to it, persons are always something more than their favorite or most familiar role. No one can be just a mother or just a manager or just a therapist. The mother is a woman; has been a daughter; probably a wife; possibly a sister; certainly a student, a friend, a neighbor, a citizen; and so on. The therapist was someone's child, student, neighbor, friend, and so on; and has a life of some sort outside of therapy.

All the other things that two persons are synergistically combine to actualize and humanize the way they take on their roles with one another. It is this total relationship that patient and therapist have with each other—as patient and therapist, and as persons with other involvements, other characteristics—that can grow, or fail to grow, into a therapeutic bond.

Our conception of the therapeutic bond is intended to be analogous to a chemical bond. Some elements form very strong and stable combinations; others react with explosive energy; others do little more than prevent each other from occupying the same space at the same time. Although no doubt too simple an analogy for human relationships, it is not altogether misleading to talk of a personal chemistry between people. People attract and repel each other, spontaneously and intuitively. For example, relationships heat up and cool off; are volatile or inert; crystallize or disintegrate. In terms such as these, we would say that a truly therapeutic bond between patient and therapist feels solid, resonant, and warm to them.

The concept of the therapeutic bond emerged, for us, from the extensive review of process-outcome studies that we did for the 1978 version of this chapter. Our interpretive synthesis of the findings

TABLE 8.16 Therapeutic Intervention: Patient Suitability

Reference	Process Perspective[a]	Outcome Perspective[a]	Finding[b]
Berman (1980)	T	S	+
Brown (1970)	T	T	+
Landfield (1971)	T	R	+
Lerner (1972)	T	P	0
Lerner (1972)	T	T	0
Lerner (1972)	T	S	0
Lindsey et al. (1976)	T	S	+
Lipkin (1954)	P	T	+
Martin et al. (1977)	T	S	+
Martin & Sterne (1975)	T	S	+
Prager (1971)[c]	T	P	0
Prager (1971)[c]	T	T	0
Prager (1971)[c]	T	R	0
Prager (1971)[c]	T	S	0
Ryan & Gizynski (1971)	P	R	+
Saltzman et al. (1976)	T	P	+
Saltzman et al. (1976)	T	T	+
Sloane et al. (1975)	T	S	+
Strupp et al. (1963)	T	T	+
Strupp et al. (1964)	T	T	+

SUMMARY

	Outcome Perspective				
Process Perspective	Patient − 0 +	Therapist − 0 +	Rater − 0 +	Score − 0 +	Total − 0 +
Observer	0 0 0	0 0 0	0 0 0	0 0 0	0 0 0
Patient	0 0 0	0 0 1	0 0 1	0 0 0	0 0 2
Therapist	0 2 1	0 2 4	0 1 1	0 2 5	0 7 11
Total	0 2 1	0 2 5	0 1 2	0 2 5	0 7 13

[a]See Table 8.6, footnotes a and b.
[b]"Findings" are reported as "+" (patient suitability was found to be significantly positively related to outcome), "0" (no significant association was found), or "−" (patient suitability was significantly negatively related to outcome).
[c]Early phase of therapy.

suggested three principal characteristics of the therapeutic bond:

> There is an intense and effective investment of energy in relationship roles, evident both in the patient's self-expressive emotional attachment to the therapist (or to the group), and in the therapist's active collaboration through whichever techniques he or she feels most capable and confident in using. . . .

A second element associated with cohesiveness of the social bond in beneficial psychotherapy is the good personal contact, the solid grounding in one another, that is made by the participants. This personal contact is characterized by mutual comfortableness and trust, a lack of defensiveness on both sides, seen in the patient's spontaneity and the therapist's genuineness; and also by a strong and sensitive rapport, a sense of being on the same wavelength, that arises *through empathic resonance and reciprocal understanding. . . .*

There is, finally, an expansive mutual good will mobilized between participants in beneficial psychotherapy—a strong sense of affirmation that is not merely acceptance but . . . acceptance and encouragement of independence, that can be challenging as well as supportive out of concern and respect for the other person's basic interests and autonomy. (Orlinsky & Howard, 1978, p. 317)

We referred to these three "strands" or dimensions of the therapeutic bond as, respectively, *role-investment*, *empathic resonance*, and *mutual affirmation*. Whereas in 1978 we presented these concepts to summarize the cumulative findings, we have now chosen to use them to organize the initial presentation of findings, and thus to test their power to impose theoretical order on a heterogeneous mass of facts. Each of the three dimensions involves a complex of interrelated empirical variables, and each can be viewed in terms of the patient's contribution, the therapist's contribution, and the interactive product of their joint contributions to the therapeutic bond.

Role-Investment
Goffman (1961) has suggested that persons are variably attached to or invested in the roles they enact, and deliberately or spontaneously communicate their personal orientations to their roles. A person may be highly invested in a role, experiencing behavior in that role as genuinely self-expressive; on the other hand, a person may give subtle or rather broad signals to indicate that "This really isn't me." In the latter case people sometimes burlesque the part to some degree, indicating that they do not take their role, and do not particularly want others to take their role, very seriously; or they convey the impression that the role is something they are "just doing," perhaps for extrinsic reasons, and act somewhat mechanically, or with an air of inner reserve.

Process-outcome researchers have investigated several variables that reflect the degree of role-investment or role-distance expressed by patients and therapists. A quality of therapists' relational behavior that has been much studied under the

influence of Rogerian theory is genuineness or self-congruence. For some reason, evidently, it never occurred to anyone to investigate patient genuineness. A similarly one-sided variable, studied with respect to therapists, is credibility and confidence versus unsureness. On the other hand, patient motivation has been studied, but not therapist motivation. However, one facet of role-investment that has been studied for both patients and therapists is active engagement versus detachment.

Therapist Engagement versus Detachment
Table 8.17 summarizes 24 findings on the impact of therapist engagement versus detachment. Overall, 12 of the 24 findings showed that therapist engagement had a significantly positive effect on patient outcome, while there were none that showed a beneficial effect of therapist detachment. The association between therapist engagement and outcome is most striking when the process perspective involved patients' perceptions; but a majority of the findings based on observer ratings of recorded therapy sessions showed the same significantly positive relationship. Only the therapists' observations of their active engagement showed a predominance of null findings with regard to outcome, perhaps because therapists' own role-expectations require them to see themselves as actively engaged with all patients.

Therapist Credibility versus Unsureness
Table 8.18 presents the findings on the impact of therapist credibility and confidence (i.e., self-credibility) versus unsureness. Again, the overall figures show that therapist credibility was significantly and positively associated with patient outcome in 12 of the 18 findings, whereas therapist unsureness was never positively associated with outcome—across all categories of outcome measures and in this case including the therapist's process perspective. Therapists may perceive themselves as actively engaged with all their patients, but one suspects that they don't feel equally confident or credible with all patients. In any event, the evidence strongly indicates from varied perspectives that the therapist's active engagement and credibility both have a significant influence on patient outcome.

Therapist Genuineness
Table 8.19 summarizes 53 findings concerning the impact of therapist genuiness or self-congruence.

TABLE 8.17 Therapist Role-investment: Engagement (+) vs. Detachment (−)

Reference	Process Perspective[a]	Outcome Perspective[a]	Finding[b]
Bent et al. (1976)	P	P	+
Beutler & Mitchell (1981)	O	S	0
Church (1982)	O	S	+
Crowder (1972)	O	S	+
DiLoreto (1971)	O	S	0
Friedlander (1981)	O	P	+
Friedlander (1981)	O	T	+
Grigg & Goodstein (1957)	P	P	+
Jones & Zoppel (1982)	P	P	0
Kaufman et al. (1962)	T	T	0
Lerner (1972)	T	S	0
Morgan et al. (1982)	O	S	0
Pierce & Schauble (1970)	O	S	+
Rosenbaum et al. (1956)	T	T	+
Saltzman et al. (1976)	P	P	0
Saltzman et al. (1976)	P	T	+
Saltzman et al. (1976)	T	P	0
Saltzman et al. (1976)	T	T	0
Seeman (1978)	T	S	0
Sloane et al. (1975) (also Staples et al., 1976)	O	S	0
Sloane et al. (1975) (also Staples et al., 1976)	T	S	0
Strupp et al. (1964)	P	T	+
Strupp et al. (1964)	P	P	+
Tovian (1977)	P	R	+

SUMMARY

Process Perspective	Outcome Perspective				
	Patient − 0 +	Therapist − 0 +	Rater − 0 +	Score − 0 +	Total − 0 +
Observer	0 0 1	0 0 1	0 0 0	0 4 3	0 4 5
Patient	0 2 3	0 0 2	0 0 1	0 0 0	0 2 6
Therapist	0 1 0	0 2 1	0 0 0	0 3 0	0 6 1
Total	0 3 4	0 2 4	0 0 1	0 7 3	0 12 12

[a]See Table 8.6, footnotes a and b.
[b]"Findings" are reported as "+" (engagement was found to be significantly positively related to outcome), "0" (no significant association was found), or "−" (detachment was significantly negatively related to outcome).

This mass of findings indicates that genuineness had an occasional but not consistent significantly positive association with outcome: 20 of the 53 findings were positive; 1, in group therapy with chronic schizophrenic inpatients, was significantly negative (Truax, Carkhuff, & Kodman, 1965); the other 32 were not significantly related to outcome. Examined more closely, Table 8.19 shows a rather special pattern of findings. Therapist-process by therapist-outcome was the only cell in which therapists' perceptions of their own genuiness showed any relationship to outcome. This apparent solipsism was

TABLE 8.18   Therapist Role-investment: Credibility (+) vs. Unsureness (−)

Reference	Process Perspective[a]	Outcome Perspective[a]	Finding[b]
Alexander et al. (1976)	O	R	+
Alexander et al. (1976)	O	S	+
Beutler et al. (1975)[c]	P	P	+
Beutler et al. (1975)[c]	P	T	+
Beutler et al. (1975)[d]	P	T	0
Melnick & Pierce (1971)	P	S	0
Rudy (1983)	T	P	0
Rudy (1983)	T	T	0
Rudy (1983)	T	S	+
Ryan & Gizynski (1971)	P	P	+
Ryan & Gizynski (1971)	P	R	+
Ryan & Gizynski (1971)	T	P	+
Ryan & Gizynski (1971)	T	R	+
Tovian (1977)	P	R	+
Truax et al. (1968)	O	P	+
Truax et al. (1968)	O	T	+
Truax et al. (1968)	O	S	0
Truax & Lister (1970)	O	S	0

SUMMARY

Outcome Perspective

Process Perspective	Patient − 0 +	Therapist − 0 +	Rater − 0 +	Score − 0 +	Total − 0 +
Observer	0 0 1	0 0 1	0 0 1	0 2 1	0 2 4
Patient	0 0 2	0 1 1	0 0 2	0 1 0	0 2 5
Therapist	0 1 1	0 1 0	0 0 1	0 0 1	0 2 3
Total	0 1 4	0 2 2	0 0 4	0 3 2	0 6 12

[a]See Table 8.6, footnotes a and b.
[b]"Findings" are reported as "+" (credibility was found to be significantly positively related to outcome), "0" (no significant difference was found), or "−" (unsureness was significantly negatively related to outcome).
[c]Attitude—dissimilar dyads.
[d]Attitude—similar dyads.

somewhat mitigated in the case of patients' perceptions of therapist genuineness: a majority of positive findings occurred only for the subcategory of patient-process by patient-outcome, but positive findings were also obtained with therapist outcome assessments and especially for objective indices and tests. Some positive findings for therapist genuineness have also been based on observer ratings of therapeutic process, particularly in relation to outcome measured by objective indices and tests. Comparing the three process perspectives, genuineness was significantly related to outcome about half the time when patients' perceptions of genuineness were used, but only about one-third of the time when nonparticipant observations or therapist perceptions were used. The net impression is that therapist genuineness, as an aspect of therapists' role-investment, is most important when measured from the patient's perspective, but even then therapist genuineness is not as strongly linked to outcome as are therapist engagement and therapist credibility.

Patient Engagement

Table 8.20 summarizes the findings from 10 studies regarding the impact of patients' active engagement. Overall, 13 of the 18 findings showed this

TABLE 8.19   Therapist Role-investment: Genuineness

Reference	Process Perspective[a]	Outcome Perspective[a]	Finding[b]
Abramowitz & Abramowitz (1974)	P	S	0
Barrett-Lennard (1962)	P	T	+
Barrett-Lennard (1962)	P	S	+
Barrett-Lennard (1962)	T	T	+
Barrett-Lennard (1962)	T	S	0
Barrington (1967)	O	S	0
DiLoreto (1971)	O	S	0
Garfield & Bergin (1971)	O	P	0
Garfield & Bergin (1971)	O	T	0
Garfield & Bergin (1971)	O	S	0
Gross & DeRidder (1966)	P	S	+
Halkides (1958)	O	S	+
Hansen et al. (1968)	P	S	0
Hansen et al. (1968)	O	S	+
Jones & Zoppel (1982)	P	P	0
Kiesler et al. (1967a)	P	S	0
McClanahan (1974)	P	P	+
McNally (1973)	P	P	+
McNally (1973)	T	P	0
Melnick & Pierce (1971)	O	S	+
Mendola (1982)	P	S	0
Mitchell et al. (1973)	P	P	0
Mitchell et al. (1973)	P	T	0
Mitchell et al. (1973)	P	R	0
Mitchell et al. (1973)	P	S	+
Mitchell et al. (1973)	T	P	0
Mitchell et al. (1973)	T	T	+
Mitchell et al. (1973)	T	R	0
Mitchell et al. (1973)	T	S	0
Mitchell et al. (1973)	O	P	0
Mitchell et al. (1973)	O	T	0
Mitchell et al. (1973)	O	R	0
Mitchell et al. (1973)	O	S	0
Rucker (1983)	P	S	+
Saltzman et al. (1976)	T	P	0
Saltzman et al. (1976)	T	T	+
Schauble & Pierce (1974)	O	S	+
Sloane et al. (1975)	P	S	0
Sloane et al. (1975) (also Staples et al., 1976)	O	S	0
Staples & Sloane (1976)	O	S	0
Tausch et al. (1970)	P	P	+
Truax (1963)	O	S	+
Truax (1966)	P	S	+
Truax et al. (1965)	O	S	−
Truax et al. (1966)	O	S	+
Truax et al. (1971)	O	S	0
van der Veen (1967)	O	S	0

(continued)

TABLE 8.19   *(Continued)*

Reference	Process Perspective[a]	Outcome Perspective[a]	Finding[b]
van der Veen & Stoler (1965)	P	T	0
van der Veen & Stoler (1965)	P	S	0
van der Veen & Stoler (1965)	T	T	+
van der Veen & Stoler (1965)	T	S	0
van der Veen & Stoler (1965)	O	T	+
van der Veen & Stoler (1965)	O	S	0

SUMMARY

Outcome Perspective

Process Perspective	Patient − 0 +	Therapist − 0 +	Rater − 0 +	Score − 0 +	Total − 0 +
Observer	0 2 0	0 2 1	0 1 0	1 9 6	1 14 7
Patient	0 2 3	0 2 1	0 1 0	0 6 5	0 11 9
Therapist	0 3 0	0 0 4	0 1 0	0 3 0	0 7 4
Total	0 7 3	0 4 6	0 3 0	1 18 11	1 32 20

[a]See Table 8.6, footnotes a and b.
[b]"Findings" are reported as "+" (therapist genuineness was found to be significantly positively related to outcome), "0" (no significant association was found), or "−" (therapist genuineness was significantly negatively related to outcome).

measure of patient role-investment to have a significantly positive association with outcome. Positve findings were obtained for all categories of outcome, but the most dramatic incidence occurred for therapists' outcome assessments. Although not all process-outcome combinations have been studied, the scatter of positive findings across the three process perspectives suggests that patient role-engagement is an important factor in therapy outcome.

Patient Motivation

Six of the seven studies that investigated the impact of patient motivation on outcome did so from the process perspective of therapist observation. When patient evaluations were used as a criterion of outcome, no significant relationship was found (Prager, 1971). On the other hand, when therapist evaluations were used as the standard of outcome, three out of four studies showed a significantly positive association (Baer, Dunbar, Hamilton, & Beutler, 1980; Conrad, 1952; Strupp, Wallach, Wogan, & Jenkins, 1963; but not Prager, 1971). For outcome assessed by independent clinicians, two significantly positive findings were noted (Landfield, 1971; Ma-

lan, 1976) along with one null finding (Prager, 1971). Both of the studies using objective indices or tests as outcome measures—one from the nonparticipant observer's process perspective (Hartley & Strupp, 1983) and one from the therapist's process perspective (Prager, 1971)—showed no association between outcome and patient motivation. This limited amount of evidence suggests that the variable is worthy of further investigation. Curiously, there have been no studies as yet of patient motivation from the patient's process perspective, although degree of patient distress may bear on this issue.

Reciprocal Role-investment

The only two findings we located that reflected directly on the joint involvement of patient and therapist in their reciprocal roles support the impression that role-investment is a consequential aspect of the therapeutic bond. For example, in an early study from Rogers' group at the University of Chicago, Halkides (1958) found that outcome was significantly and positively associated with patient-therapist correspondence in level of affective intensity. Waterhouse (1982), using data from Strupp's Van-

TABLE 8.20 Patient Role-investment: Engagement

Reference	Process Perspective[a]	Outcome Perspective[a]	Finding[b]
Gendlin et al. (1960)	T	T	+
Grigg & Goodstein (1957)	P	P	+
Jones & Zoppel (1982)	P	P	+
Kapp et al. (1964)	P	P	+
Lorr & McNair (1964b)	T	P	+
Lorr & McNair (1964b)	T	T	+
Ryle & Lipshitz (1976)	T	P	0
Ryle & Lipshitz (1976)	T	T	+
Ryle & Lipshitz (1976)	O	P	0
Ryle & Lipshitz (1976)	O	T	+
Ryle & Lipshitz (1976)	O	S	0
Saltzman et al. (1976)	P	P	0
Saltzman et al. (1976)	P	T	+
Seeman (1954)	T	T	+
Seeman (1978)	P	S	0
Suh et al. (1986)[c]	O	T	+
Suh et al. (1986)[c]	O	R	+
Suh et al. (1986)[c]	O	S	+

SUMMARY

Outcome Perspective

Process Perspective	Patient − 0 +	Therapist − 0 +	Rater − 0 +	Score − 0 +	Total − 0 +
Observer	0 1 0	0 0 2	0 0 1	0 1 1	0 2 4
Patient	0 1 3	0 0 1	0 0 0	0 1 0	0 2 4
Therapist	0 1 2	0 0 3	0 0 0	0 0 0	0 1 5
Total	0 3 5	0 0 6	0 0 1	0 2 1	0 5 13

[a]See Table 8.6, footnotes a and b.
[b]"Findings" are reported as "+" (patient engagement was found to be significantly positively related to outcome), "0" (no significant association was found), or "−" (patient engagement was significantly negatively related to outcome).
[c]Increase over first three sessions.

derbilt project, found that outcome was significantly and negatively associated with a pattern of therapist negativism and activity in response to patient passivity. Both findings were based on nonparticipant observers' ratings of therapeutic process and on outcome assessed by objective indices and tests: In one, patient and therapist match involvement for involvement, moving ahead; in the other, patient and therapist withhold and provoke, evoke and punish, getting nowhere. That may be something like the clinical picture—but, of course, two findings

hardly make a strong enough hook on which to hang a picture.

Empathic Resonance

Face-to-face communication is a richly textured, multimodal process. The nonverbal, prerational stream of expression that binds the infant to its parents continues throughout life to be a primary medium of intuitively felt, affective-relational communication between persons. These interpersonal "vibrations" that we more or less consciously feel are overlaid by gestures and words bearing concrete and abstract, explicit and implicit, meanings concerning a variety of present or absent referents. Adding to the complexity is the fact that the whole flow of meanings may be variably consistent or inconsistent in its several parts.

Empathic resonance, or the lack of it, is an emergent property of this complex process of interpersonal communication. Its presence is usually indicated by a sense of being "on the same wavelength," a sense of mutual transparency—of being fully heard by, and fully hearing, the other person. In psychotherapy, of course, there is a quantitative differentiation of this process, with the patient as the person who comes to be heard and most of the hearing being done by the therapist. Yet it is necessarily a two-sided process, depending upon the attunement and the expressiveness of each participant. In reviewing studies on the therapeutic impact of empathic resonance, we shall deal in turn with the therapist's and the patient's states of attunement and expressiveness.

Therapist Attunement

The empathic receptiveness of the therapist has been one of the most intensively researched variables in the process-outcome literature. Table 8.21 presents 86 findings on the impact of therapist empathy, drawn from 40 studies. Overall, a bit under half of the 86 findings showed a significantly positive relationship between outcome and therapist empathy, with no significantly negative findings. A comparison of empathy as measured from the three process perspectives, however, reveals an interesting situation. When therapist empathy was reported by patients, 22 of the 31 findings showed a significant effect across all four outcome categories. By contrast, when therapists rated their own empathy, only 2 of the 17 findings showed a significant effect, and those were all in relation to therapist evaluations of outcome.

A further peculiarity is worth noting with regard to therapist empathy as rated from recordings by nonparticipant observers. Overall, in these process-outcome subcategories, 17 of the 38 findings were significantly positive; but a marked difference can be seen according to the type of outcome criterion employed. Only 4 of the 17 findings were significant when patients', therapists', and independent clinicans' global ratings were used; on the other hand,

13 of the 21 findings were significant when outcome was assessed by objective indices and tests.

In sum, there is very strong evidence indicating that therapist empathy makes an important contribution to patient benefit, *when empathy is measured as perceived by patients* generally, and when nonparticipants' ratings of empathy are related to specifically objective measures of outcome. This situation highlights the importance of differentiating among the several observational and evaluative perspectives in psychotherapy research.

Therapist Expressiveness

The varied aspects of therapist expressiveness have been studied almost exclusively from the perspective of nonparticipant observers. Focusing on the therapist's voice quality and expressive stance, for example, Rice (1965) found that by the end of therapy fresh language and expressive vocalization from the therapist were significantly and positively associated with outcome. Commonplace language and vocalization were unrelated to outcome, whereas a significantly negative association with outcome was noted when a relative absence of fresh language and presence of distorted vocalization were observed in the therapist.

Earlier, regarding therapists' linguistic styles, Barrington (1961) had found that use of more sophisticated polysyllabic language had a significantly positive association with outcome assessed both from the therapist's perspective and by objective indices and tests. Alexander et al. (1976) also observed that therapists' use of short, specific, clear communications in treating juvenile delinquents and their families was significantly related to good outcome. Amira (1982), however, found no relationship between outcome and therapists' use of novel, figurative language.

Three studies of therapists' concreteness of expression as a process variable, and assessments of outcome by objective indices and tests, yielded mixed results. DiLoreto (1971), using a nonparticipant scale of concreteness, and Sloane et al. (1975), using patient ratings of therapist concreteness, both found no relationship with outcome. On the other hand, Schauble and Pierce (1974) reported a significantly positive association between outcome and nonparticipant ratings of therapist concreteness.

The number of findings on therapist expressiveness is too small to permit broad generalization, but

TABLE 8.21   Therapist Empathic Resonance: Attunement

Reference	Process Perspective[a]	Outcome Perspective[a]	Finding[b]
Abramowitz & Abramowitz (1974)	P	S	0
Barrett-Lennard (1962)	P	T	+
Barrett-Lennard (1962)	P	S	+
Barrett-Lennard (1962)	T	T	+
Barrett-Lennard (1962)	T	S	0
Barrington (1967)	O	S	0
Bergin & Jasper (1969)	O	R	0
Beutler et al. (1975)	O	T	0
Cooley & Lajoy (1980)	P	P	+
Cooley & Lajoy (1980)	P	T	+
Cooley & Lajoy (1980)	T	P	0
Cooley & Lajoy (1980)	T	T	+
DiLoreto (1971)	O	S	0
Feitel (1968)	P	R	+
Garfield & Bergin (1971)	O	P	0
Garfield & Bergin (1971)	O	T	0
Garfield & Bergin (1971)	O	S	0
Gross & DeRidder (1966)	P	S	+
Halkides (1958)	O	S	+
Hansen et al. (1968)	P	S	0
Hansen et al. (1968)	O	S	+
Kalfas (1974)	P	S	+
Kiesler et al. (1967b)	O	S	+
Kurtz & Grummon (1972)	P	P	0
Kurtz & Grummon (1972)	P	T	+
Kurtz & Grummon (1972)	P	S	+
Kurtz & Grummon (1972)	T	P	0
Kurtz & Grummon (1972)	T	T	0
Kurtz & Grummon (1972)	T	S	0
Kurtz & Grummon (1972)	O	P	0
Kurtz & Grummon (1972)	O	T	0
Kurtz & Grummon (1972)	O	S	+
Landfield (1971)	T	R	0
Lerner (1972)	T	S	0
Lerner (1972)	O	P	0
Lerner (1972)	O	T	0
Lerner (1972)	O	S	0
Lesser (1961)	P	S	+
Lorr (1965)	P	P	+
Lorr (1965)	P	T	+
Magnelli (1976)	O	P	0
Magnelli (1976)	O	T	0
Martin & Sterne (1976a)	P	S	+
McClanahan (1974)	P	P	+
McNally (1973)	P	P	+
McNally (1973)	T	P	0
Melnick & Pierce (1971)	O	S	+

(continued)

TABLE 8.21 *(Continued)*

Reference	Process Perspective[a]	Outcome Perspective[a]	Finding[b]
Mendola (1982)	P	S	0
Mitchell et al. (1973)	P	P	0
Mitchell et al. (1973)	P	T	+
Mitchell et al. (1973)	P	R	0
Mitchell et al. (1973)	P	S	+
Mitchell et al. (1973)	T	P	0
Mitchell et al. (1973)	T	T	0
Mitchell et al. (1973)	T	R	0
Mitchell et al. (1973)	T	S	0
Mitchell et al. (1973)	O	P	0
Mitchell et al. (1973)	O	T	0
Mitchell et al. (1973)	O	R	0
Mitchell et al. (1973)	O	S	0
Peake (1979)	O	S	+
Sapolsky (1965)	P	R	+
Schauble & Pierce (1974)	O	S	+
Sloane et al. (1975) (also Staples et al., 1976)	P	S	0
Sloane et al. (1975) (also Staples et al., 1976)	O	S	0
Staples & Sloane (1976)	O	S	0
Tausch et al. (1970)	P	P	+
Tovian (1977)	P	R	+
Truax (1963)	O	S	+
Truax (1966)	P	S	+
Truax (1966)	O	S	+
Truax et al. (1965)	O	S	+
Truax et al. (1966)	O	P	+
Truax et al. (1966)	O	T	+
Truax et al. (1966)	O	R	+
Truax et al. (1966) (previous four findings: also Truax & Wittmer, 1971a)	O	S	+
Truax et al. (1971)	O	S	+
van der Veen (1967)	O	S	+
van der Veen & Stoler (1965)	P	T	+
van der Veen & Stoler (1965)	P	R	0
van der Veen & Stoler (1965)	P	S	0
van der Veen & Stoler (1965)	T	T	0
van der Veen & Stoler (1965)	T	S	0
van der Veen & Stoler (1965)	O	T	+
van der Veen & Stoler (1965)	O	S	0
van der Veen & Stoler (1965)	T	R	0

(continued)

TABLE 8.21   *(Continued)*

SUMMARY

Process Perspective	Outcome Perspective				
	Patient − 0 +	Therapist − 0 +	Rater − 0 +	Score − 0 +	Total − 0 +
Observer	0 5 1	0 6 2	0 2 1	0 8 13	0 21 17
Patient	0 2 5	0 0 6	0 2 3	0 5 8	0 9 22
Therapist	0 4 0	0 3 2	0 3 0	0 5 0	0 15 2
Total	0 11 6	0 9 10	0 7 4	0 18 21	0 45 41

[a]See Table 8.6, footnotes *a* and *b*.
[b]"Findings" are reported as "+" (therapist attunement was found to be significantly positively related to outcome), "0" (no significant association was found), or "−" (therapist attunement was significantly negatively related to outcome).

the predominance of positive findings should encourage further study.

Patient Attunement

The marked differentiation of patient and therapist roles in communication, referred to above, has so influenced the thinking of researchers that to our knowledge no one has ever developed a measure of patient empathy and used it in conducting a process-outcome study. Had empathy been viewed as the receptive phase in a reciprocal dimension of the therapeutic bond, rather than as an exclusively therapist-offered condition, the theoretical significance of patients' contributions in this regard might have been better appreciated. Until some work is done, we can take note of only two findings based on patient reports of process that are at least partially relevant to the issue. Jeske (1973) observed that patients in group therapy who reported identifying with the experiences of fellow patients had significantly better outcomes than patients who did not. Earlier, Feitel (1968) found that patients who reported they felt understood (a measure not of patient empathy, but of empathic awareness of therapist empathy) improved significantly more than others. Findings to be reviewed in the section later in this chapter on patient self-relatedness concerning patients' openness versus defensiveness also have some bearing on the issue of patient attunement.

Patient Expressiveness

Just as therapist attunement has been studied far more intensively than therapist expressiveness, so patient expressiveness has been investigated more often than patient attunement. For example, patient voice quality and expressive stance have been the subject of several process-outcome studies conducted from the process perspective of nonparticipant raters. Butler, Rice, and Wagstaff (1962) were the first to find a focused, feeling-oriented quality of vocalization in patients to be significantly and positively related to outcome when evaluated from the therapist's perspective and by objective indices and tests (but not when assessed from the patient's perspective). They also found that when an externalizing, nonfeeling-oriented quality was present in patients' speech, outcome was significantly poorer when assessed by patients and therapists (but not objective measures). Similar findings with the same variables were obtained by Rice and Wagstaff (1967), Rice (1973), and Church (1982), but Lerner (1972) found no relationship between outcome and focused voice quality in clinic patients of the lowest socioeconomic strata.

Turning to patient expressiveness as manifested in linguistic style, Roshal (1953) found that increasing variety of word usage was significantly related to patient improvement measured from a combination of outcome perspectives. Among other studies using nonparticipant ratings of patient expressiveness, Barrington (1961) found that patients who used more sophisticated polysyllabic language had significantly better outcomes, and Truax and Wittmer (1971b) found that patients' use of personal as opposed to nonpersonal references was significantly associated with patient improvement (assessed in both studies by objective indices and tests). In the same process-outcome subcategory, however, Amira (1982) found no relation between outcome and patients' use of novel, figurative language.

A final aspect of patient expressiveness involves ease of communication, especially concerning feelings. From the therapist's process perspective, Conrad (1952), Gendlin et al. (1960), and Brown (1970) all found that patient expressiveness was significantly and positively associated with outcome as evaluated by therapists. Lest those findings seem too solipsistic, note that Wogan (1970) found patients' ratings of their ease in communicating were also significantly and positively related to therapists' assessments of outcome. From the opposite end of the spectrum, Landfield (1971) observed that patients viewed by their therapists as unable or unwilling to talk, and as indefinite, inconsistent, or confused in their communications, had significantly poorer outcomes than others.

The net impression of these studies is that patient expressiveness constitutes an especially significant influence on outcome. Admittedly, some of this influence may be confounded with the patient's educational level, and the corresponding enhancement of fit between patient and therapist. But the variables reviewed here include very personal aspects of patient expressiveness, and these too appear to make a favorable difference in therapeutic outcome.

Reciprocal Resonance

A number of process-outcome studies shed some light on the impact of empathic resonance viewed as a function of the relationship. Table 8.22 summarizes 31 findings drawn from 17 studies. In this table, the process perspective labeled "objective index" consists of findings concerning the effect on outcome of increases in actual similarity between patient and therapist on various dimensions (established indirectly by the researcher). Patient and therapist process perspectives include direct perceptions of similarity between them by the participants, with regard to their mutual understanding and other attributes. We have interpreted actually increasing and perceived similarity to imply a heightened state of empathic resonance in the therapeutic relationship.

The results presented in Table 8.22 indicate that empathic resonance is significantly related to patient outcome when viewed from this angle, too. Nearly two-thirds of the 31 findings showed positive relationships with outcome, particularly as evaluated from the patient's or the therapist's perspective.

Again, in comparing the different process perspectives, one notes that the proportion of positive findings is very great for patient reports and for an objective index of similarity, but is almost negligible for therapist perceived similarity.

Mutual Affirmation

Affirmation implies an interest in and an endorsement of a person's well-being, motivating behavior that is essentially caring in quality. Normally this is experienced as warmth and acceptance, but there are occasions when genuine caring leads to confrontation and challenge. Rogers' conceptions of the ideal therapist's unconditionality and positive regard prompted a great deal of research that is relevant to the impact of interpersonal affirmation on therapeutic outcome. Since this too was originally conceived of as a therapist-offered condition, there are many more studies pertaining to therapist affirmation then to patient affirmation; but some studies of patient affirmation do exist, along with some studies of reciprocal affirmation.

Therapist Affirmation

Table 8.23 presents 94 findings on the impact of therapist affirmation, drawn from 47 studies. More than half of the findings show a significantly positive relationship between outcome and therapist affirmation, across all categories of outcome measures. Only 2 of the 94 findings showed a significantly negative impact of therapist warmth and acceptance (Truax et al., 1966, on one of five criteria in a sample where nonpossessive warmth was negatively correlated with genuineness and accurate empathy; Bottari & Rappaport, 1983, scrutinizing the first session only).

As usual, a more careful examination reveals such interesting detail as the fact that the proportion of positive findings is highest across all outcome categories when therapist warmth and acceptance are observed from the patient's process perspective. Here again, the most decisive aspect of therapeutic process seems to be the patient's experience of it. Also noteworthy is the fact that therapists seem to be almost encapsulated in their own perspective: the startling 11 for 11 positive findings occurring for the subcategory of therapist-process by therapist-outcome is not even closely approached in any other therapist-process subcategory! This means that when therapists feel that they are being espe-

TABLE 8.22 Empathic Resonance: Reciprocal Attunement

Reference	Process Perspective[a]	Outcome Perspective[b]	Finding[c]
Astwood (1977)	OI	T	+
Beutler et al. (1975)[d]	OI	P	+
Beutler et al. (1975)[e]	OI	P	0
Beutler et al. (1975)[d]	OI	T	+
Beutler et al. (1975)[e]	OI	T	0
Beutler et al. (1978)	OI	P	+
Boun (1951)	OI	P	+
Cartwright & Lerner (1963)	OI	T	+
Cooley & Lajoy (1980)	OI	P	+
Cooley & Lajoy (1980)	OI	T	+
Horenstein (1974)	OI	S	0
Hunt et al. (1959)	T	T	0
Jeske (1973)	P	S	+
Kreisberg (1978)	OI	P	0
Kreisberg (1978)	OI	T	0
Kreisberg (1978)	OI	S	0
Lesser (1961)	T	S	0
Lesser (1961)	OI	S	+
Magnelli (1976)	OI	P	+
Magnelli (1976)	OI	T	+
Peiser (1982)	T	R	+
Saltzman et al. (1976)	P	P	+
Saltzman et al. (1976)	P	T	+
Saltzman et al. (1976)	T	P	0
Saltzman et al. (1976)	T	T	+
Sapolsky (1965)	P	R	+
Sapolsky (1965)	T	R	0
Schonfield et al. (1969)	OI	P	+
Schonfield et al. (1969)	OI	T	+
Schonfield et al. (1969)	OI	S	0
Ukeritis (1978)	OI	S	+

SUMMARY

Outcome Perspective

Process Perspective	Patient − 0 +	Therapist − 0 +	Rater − 0 +	Score − 0 +	Total − 0 +
Objective Index	0 2 6	0 2 6	0 0 0	0 3 2	0 7 14
Patient	0 0 1	0 0 1	0 0 1	0 0 1	0 0 4
Therapist	0 1 0	0 1 1	0 1 1	0 1 0	0 4 2
Total	0 3 7	0 3 8	0 1 2	0 4 3	0 11 20

[a]"Process Perspective" refers to how the process ratings were made. "Objective Index" (OI) indicates that similarity scores were used. "Patient" indicates that the patient (P) made the ratings, and "Therapist" indicates that process was rated by the therapist (T).
[b]See Table 8.6, footnote b.
[c]"Findings" are reported as "+" (reciprocal attunement was found to be significantly positively related to outcome), "0" (no significant association was found), or "−" (reciprocal attunement was significantly negatively related to outcome).
[d]Patient−therapist dyads initially dissimilar in value orientation.
[e]Patient−therapist dyads initially similar in value orientation.

TABLE 8.23   Therapist Affirmation: Warmth/Acceptance

Reference	Process Perspective[a]	Outcome Perspective[a]	Finding[b]
Abramowitz & Abramowitz (1974)	P	S	0
Alexander et al. (1976)	O	R	+
Alexander et al. (1976)	O	S	+
Barrett-Lennard (1962)	P	T	+
Barrett-Lennard (1962)	P	S	+
Barrett-Lennard (1962)	T	T	+
Barrett-Lennard (1962)	T	S	0
Barrington (1967)	O	S	0
Bent et al. (1976)	P	P	+
Board (1959)	P	P	+
Board (1959)	P	T	0
Bottari & Rappaport (1983)	P	S	+
Bottari & Rappaport (1983)	T	S	−
Brown (1970)	T	T	+
Cooley & Lajoy (1980)	P	P	+
Cooley & Lajoy (1980)	P	T	+
Cooley & Lajoy (1980)	T	P	0
Cooley & Lajoy (1980)	T	T	+
Crowder (1972)[c]	O	R	0
Crowder (1972)[d]	O	R	+
DiLoreto (1971)	O	S	0
Feitel (1968)	P	R	+
Garfield & Bergin (1971)	O	P	0
Garfield & Bergin (1971)	O	T	0
Garfield & Bergin (1971)	O	S	0
Gomes-Schwartz (1978)	O	P	0
(also: O'Malley et al., 1983; Strupp & Hadley, 1979)			
Gomes-Schwartz (1978)	O	T	+
(also: O'Malley et al., 1983; Strupp & Hadley, 1979; Suh et al., 1986)			
Gomes-Schwartz (1978)	O	R	0
(also: O'Malley et al., 1983; Strupp & Hadley, 1979)			
Gomes-Schwartz (1978)	O	S	+
(also Suh et al., 1986)			
Gottschalk et al. (1967)	T	R	0
Gross & DeRidder (1966)	P	S	+
Halkides (1958)	O	S	+
Hansen et al. (1968)	P	S	0
Hansen et al. (1968)	O	S	+
Kernberg et al. (1972)	O	R	+
Kernberg et al. (1972)	O	S	+
Lerner (1972)	T	S	0
Lorr (1965)	P	P	+
Lorr (1965)	P	T	+
Martin & Sterne (1976a)	P	S	0
Melnick & Pierce (1971)	O	S	+

(continued)

TABLE 8.23 *(Continued)*

Reference	Process Perspective[a]	Outcome Perspective[a]	Finding[b]
Mendola (1982)	P	S	0
Mitchell et al. (1973)	P	P	0
Mitchell et al. (1973)	P	T	+
Mitchell et al. (1973)	P	R	0
Mitchell et al. (1973)	P	S	+
Mitchell et al. (1973)	T	P	0
Mitchell et al. (1973)	T	T	+
Mitchell et al. (1973)	T	R	0
Mitchell et al. (1973)	T	S	0
Mitchell et al. (1973)	O	P	0
Mitchell et al. (1973)	O	T	0
Mitchell et al. (1973)	O	R	0
Mitchell et al. (1973)	O	S	0
Peiser (1982)	T	R	+
Rosenbaum et al. (1956)	T	T	+
Rudy (1983)	T	P	+
Rudy (1983)	T	T	+
Rudy (1983)	T	S	0
Ryan & Gizynski (1971)	T	T	+
Saltzman et al. (1976)	P	P	0
Saltzman et al. (1976)	P	T	+
Saltzman et al. (1976)	T	P	0
Saltzman et al. (1976)	T	T	+
Schauble & Pierce (1974)	O	S	+
Seeman (1954)	T	T	+
Sloane et al. (1975)	O	R	0
Sloane et al. (1975) [Truax measure] (also Staples et al., 1976)	P	S	+
Sloane et al. (1975) [Lorr measure] (also Staples et al., 1976)	P	S	0
Sloane et al. (1975)	T	S	+
Strupp & Hadley (1979) (also O'Malley et al., 1983)	O	S	0
Strupp et al. (1963)	T	T	+
Strupp et al. (1964)	P	P	+
Strupp et al. (1964)	P	T	+
Suh et al. (1986)[e]	O	R	+
Truax (1963)	O	S	+
Truax (1966)	P	S	+
Truax et al. (1965) (also Truax, 1966)	O	S	+
Truax et al. (1966)	O	P	−
Truax et al. (1966)	O	T	0
Truax et al. (1966)	O	R	0
Truax et al. (1966)	O	S	0
Truax et al. (1971)	O	S	+
van der Veen (1967)	O	S	0

(continued)

TABLE 8.23   *(Continued)*

Reference	Process Perspective[a]	Outcome Perspective[a]	Finding[b]
van der Veen & Stoler (1965)	P	T	0
van der Veen & Stoler (1965)	T	P	+
van der Veen & Stoler (1965)	T	T	+
van der Veen & Stoler (1965)	T	R	0
van der Veen & Stoler (1965)	T	S	0
van der Veen & Stoler (1965)	O	T	0
Werman et al.(1976)	P	T	+
Werman et al (1976)	P	R	+
Yalom et al. (1967)	T	P	+
Yalom et al. (1967)	T	R	0

SUMMARY

Outcome Perspective

Process Perspective	Patient − 0 +	Therapist − 0 +	Rater − 0 +	Score − 0 +	Total − 0 +
Observer	1 3 0	0 4 1	0 5 4	0 8 9	1 20 14
Patient	0 2 5	0 2 7	0 1 2	0 5 6	0 10 20
Therapist	0 3 3	0 0 11	0 4 1	1 5 1	1 12 16
Total	1 8 8	0 6 19	0 10 7	1 18 16	2 42 50

[a]See Table 8.6, footnotes a and b.
[b]"Findings" are reported as "+" (therapist warmth/acceptance was found to be significantly positively related to outcome), "0" (no significant association was found), or "−" (therapist warmth/acceptance was significantly negatively related to outcome).
[c]Early and middle phases of therapy.
[d]Late phase of therapy.
[e]Increase over first three sessions.

cially warm, they tend to be more satisified with the outcome of their treatment.

Patient Affirmation

Table 8.24 summarizes findings on the relation of outcome to patient warmth or affirmation, drawn from 16 studies. Overall, nearly two-thirds of the 31 findings show a significantly positive relationship between outcome and patient affirmation. One of the negative findings showed hostile competitive patient behavior in the early and middle (but not the final) stages of therapy to be predictive of favorable outcome, when process was determined by non-participant observation and outcome was evaluated by independent clinicians (Crowder, 1972). In general, though, the evidence of a positive association between outcome and patient warmth is fairly consistent across the three process perspectives,

although the pattern did not extend to objective indices and tests among the outcome categories.

Reciprocal Affirmation

Table 8.25 summarizes 19 findings on the impact of reciprocal affirmation between patient and therapist, or between participants in group psycho-therapy. Of the 19 findings, 15 showed significantly positive associations between reciprocal warmth and patient outcome. Most of the findings were made from the patient's or nonparticipant observer's process perspective, and from the patient's or independent clinician's outcome perspective. Where findings occur in any number, they strongly support the cumulative impression that mutual affir-mation is another dimension of the therapeutic bond that has a beneficial impact on patient outcome.

TABLE 8.24 Patient Affirmation

Reference	Process Perspective[a]	Outcome Perspective[a]	Finding[b]
Baer et al. (1980)	T	T	0
Bent et al. (1976)	P	P	+
Board (1959)	P	P	+
Board (1959)	P	T	0
Conrad (1952)	T	T	+
Crowder (1972)[c]	O	R	+
Crowder (1972)[d]	O	R	−
DeJonge (1981)	P	T	+
DeJonge (1981)	P	S	0
Lipkin (1954)	P	T	+
Lorr & McNair (1964b)	T	P	+
Lorr & McNair (1964b)	T	T	+
Rosenbaum et al. (1956)	T	T	+
Rudy (1983)	P	P	0
Rudy (1983)	P	T	+
Rudy (1983)	P	S	0
Ryan & Gizynski (1971)	P	T	+
Saltzman et al. (1976)	P	P	0
Saltzman et al. (1976)	P	T	−
Seeman (1954)	T	T	+
Sloane et al. (1975)	T	S	0
Strupp et al. (1964)	T	P	+
Strupp et al. (1964)	T	T	+
Tovian (1977)	P	R	+
van der Veen & Stoler (1965)	T	R	+
van der Veen & Stoler (1965)	T	R	0
van der Veen & Stoler (1965)	T	S	0
van der Veen & Stoler (1965)	O	S	+
van der Veen & Stoler (1965)	O	S	0
Werman et al. (1976)	P	T	+
Werman et al. (1976)	P	R	+

SUMMARY

Process Perspective	Patient − 0 +	Therapist − 0 +	Rater − 0 +	Score − 0 +	Total − 0 +
			Outcome Perspective		
Observer	0 0 0	0 0 1	1 0 1	0 1 0	1 1 2
Patient	0 2 2	1 1 5	0 0 2	0 2 0	1 5 9
Therapist	0 0 2	0 1 6	0 1 0	0 2 0	0 4 8
Total	0 2 4	0 2 12	1 1 3	0 5 0	2 10 19

[a]See Table 8.6, footnotes a and b.
[b]"Findings" are reported as "+" (patient affirmation was found to be significantly positively related to outcome), "0" (no significant association was found), or "−" (patient affirmation was significantly negatively related to outcome).
[c]Patient support-seeking, early and middle of therapy.
[d]Patient *not* hostile-competitive, early and middle of therapy.

TABLE 8.25 Mutual Affirmation: Relationship/Group Atmosphere

Reference	Process Perspective[a]	Outcome Perspective[a]	Finding[b]
Braaten (1984)	P	S	+
Cabral et al. (1975)	P	P	+
Cabral et al. (1975)	P	R	+
Cabral et al. (1975)	O	P	+
Cabral et al. (1975)	O	R	+
Dickoff & Lakin (1963)	P	P	+
Dickoff & Lakin (1963)	P	T	0
Heine (1950)	P	P	+
Kapp et al. (1964)	P	P	+
Kernberg et al. (1972)	O	S	0
Roether & Peters (1972)	T	S	0
Tovian (1977)	P	R	+
Waterhouse (1982)	O	S	+
Wogan (1970)	P	T	+
Wogan (1970)	T	T	+
Yalom et al. (1967)	P	P	+
Yalom et al. (1967)	P	R	0
Yalom et al. (1967)	O	P	+
Yalom et al. (1967)	O	R	+

SUMMARY

Outcome Perspective

Process Perspective	Patient − 0 +	Therapist − 0 +	Rater − 0 +	Score − 0 +	Total − 0 +
Observer	0 0 2	0 0 0	0 0 2	0 1 1	0 1 5
Patient	0 0 5	0 1 1	0 1 2	0 0 1	0 2 9
Therapist	0 0 0	0 0 1	0 0 0	0 1 0	0 1 1
Total	0 0 7	0 1 2	0 1 4	0 2 2	0 4 15

[a]See Table 8.6, footnotes a and b.
[b]"Findings" are reported as "+" (mutual affirmation was found to be significantly positively related to outcome), "0" (no significant association was found), or "−" (mutual affirmation was significantly negatively related to outcome).

Global Quality of the Therapeutic Bond

A substantial number of published process-outcome studies have related outcome to the overall quality of the therapist's or the patient's contribution to the therapeutic bond, or to the global quality of the bond itself. Because these studies employed overall evaluations of the relationship, the findings could not be differentiated along the dimensions of role-investment, empathic resonance, and mutual affirmation, and so they are reviewed together in this section.

Global Therapist Quality

Table 8.26 summarizes 54 findings on the overall quality of the therapist's interpersonal involvement with the patient. About three-fifths of the findings show a significantly positive association between outcome and the quality of the therapist's general contribution to the therapeutic bond. Regarding the three significantly negative findings, one study showed that the therapist's "optimal empathic relationship," measured by nonparticipant observation, was judged beneficial from the therapist's outcome

TABLE 8.26 Global Relational Quality: Therapist

Reference	Process Perspective[a]	Outcome Perspective[a]	Finding[b]
Abramowitz & Abramowitz (1974)	P	S	0
Barrett-Lennard (1962)	P	T	+
Barrett-Lennard (1962)	P	S	+
Barrett-Lennard (1962)	T	T	+
Barrett-Lennard (1962)	T	S	0
Cain (1973)	P	P	+
Cain (1973)	P	T	0
Cain (1973)	T	P	0
Cain (1973)	T	T	+
Gomez (1982)	O	S	+
Gross & DeRidder (1966)	P	S	+
Hartley & Strupp (1983)	O	S	0
Hansen et al. (1967)	P	S	+
Jacobs & Warner (1981)[c]	T	T	+
Jacobs & Warner (1981)[d]	T	T	−
Jones & Zoppel (1982)	P	P	+
Marziali et al. (1981)	O	S	0
McClanahan (1974)	P	S	+
McNally (1973)	P	P	+
McNally (1973)	O	P	+
McNally (1973)	O	T	+
Melnick & Pierce (1971)	P	S	0
Mintz et al. (1971)[e]	O	T	+
Mintz et al. (1971)[f]	O	T	−
Morgan et al. (1982)	O	S	+
Mullen & Abeles (1971)	O	S	+
Nagy (1973)	O	S	+
O'Malley et al. (1983)	O	P	0
O'Malley et al. (1983)	O	T	+
O'Malley et al. (1983)	O	R	0
O'Malley et al. (1983)	O	S	0
Parloff (1961)	O	S	+
Roback & Strassberg (1975)	P	S	+
Rucker (1983)	P	S	+
Sachs (1983)	O	P	0
Sachs (1983)	O	T	0
Sachs (1983)	O	R	0
Sloane et al. (1975)	P	P	+
Sloane et al. (1975) (also Staples et al., 1976)	P	S	0
Tausch et al. (1969)	P	P	+
Tausch et al. (1969)	P	T	+
Truax (1963)	O	S	+
Truax (1970c) [days unhospitalized]	O	S	0
Truax (1970c) [rate of discharge]	O	S	+
Truax et al. (1966)	O	P	+

(continued)

TABLE 8.26   *(Continued)*

Reference	Process Perspective[a]	Outcome Perspective[a]	Finding[b]
Truax et al. (1966)	O	T	+
Truax et al. (1966)	O	R	0
Truax et al. (1966)	O	S	0
Truax et al. (1970)	O	S	+
Truax et al. (1971)	O	S	+
Truax et al. (1973)	O	T	+
Truax et al. (1973)	O	R	0
Truax et al. (1973)	O	S	0
van der Veen (1967)	P	S	0

SUMMARY

Outcome Perspective

Process Perspective	Patient − 0 +	Therapist − 0 +	Rater − 0 +	Score − 0 +	Total − 0 +
Observer	0 2 2	1 1 5	0 4 0	0 6 9	1 13 16
Patient	0 0 6	0 1 2	0 0 0	0 4 5	0 5 13
Therapist	0 1 0	1 0 3	0 0 0	0 1 0	1 2 3
Total	0 3 8	2 3 10	0 4 0	0 10 14	2 20 32

[a]See Table 8.6, footnotes *a* and *b*.
[b]"Findings" are reported as "+" (therapist global relational quality was found to be significantly positively related to outcome), "0" (no significant association was found), or "−" (therapist global relational quality was significantly negatively related to outcome).
[c]Neurotics and personality disorders.
[d]Borderline conditions and psychotics.
[e]High "Therapist Optimal Empathic Relationship," *low* "Therapist Directiveness."
[f]High "Therapist Directiveness," *low* "Therapist Optimal Empathic Relationship."

perspective only in the context of low therapist directiveness and was detrimental when therapist directiveness was high (Mintz, Luborsky, & Auerbach, 1971). The other negative finding derives from a study in which therapist perceptions of their own empathic warmth was found to be positively associated with outcome assessments by therapists and independent clinicians for neurotics and personality disorders, but detrimental by these same criteria for borderline and psychotic patients (Jacobs & Warner, 1981). Table 8.26 also shows that the highest proportion of positive findings occurred when therapist global quality was rated from the patient's process perspective.

Patient Global Quality
Table 8.27 presents 17 findings on the overall quality of the patient's interpersonal involvement in the

therapeutic bond. All but 3 of the 17 findings were based on nonparticipant observation of the therapeutic process, and those 3 based on the therapist's process perspective were all significantly positive. Of the remaining 14 findings, 11 showed a significantly positive association between outcome and the quality of the patient's general contribution to the therapeutic bond, across all categories of outcome measures.

Global Quality of Bond
Finally, Table 8.28 summarizes 34 process-outcome findings on the overall quality of the interpersonal bond or alliance in psychotherapy. Of the 34 findings, 19 showed a significantly positive association with outcome. The one negative finding indicated that patient outcome, assessed by objective indices and tests, was significantly better for relationships

TABLE 8.27   Global Relational Quality: Patient

Reference	Process Perspective[a]	Outcome Perspective[a]	Finding[b]
Baer et al. (1980)	T	T	+
Gomes-Schwartz (1978)	O	P	0
Gomes-Schwartz (1978)	O	T	+
Gomes-Schwartz (1978)	O	R	+
Gomes-Schwartz (1978)	O	S	+
Hoehn-Saric et al. (1964)	O	T	+
Hoehn-Saric et al. (1964)	O	S	+
Kolb (1982)	T	P	+
Kolb (1982)	T	T	+
Marziali et al. (1981)	O	S	+
Sachs (1983)	O	P	+
Sachs (1983)	O	T	+
Sachs (1983)	O	R	+
Tomlinson (1967)[c]	O	S	0
Tomlinson (1967)[d]	O	S	+
van der Veen & Stoler (1965)	O	T	+
van der Veen & Stoler (1965)	O	S	0

SUMMARY

Process Perspective	Outcome Perspective				
	Patient − 0 +	Therapist − 0 +	Rater − 0 +	Score − 0 +	Total − 0 +
Observer	0 1 1	0 0 4	0 0 2	0 2 4	0 3 11
Patient	0 0 0	0 0 0	0 0 0	0 0 0	0 0 0
Therapist	0 0 1	0 0 2	0 0 0	0 0 0	0 0 3
Total	0 1 2	0 0 6	0 0 2	0 2 4	0 3 14

[a]See Table 8.6, footnotes a and b.
[b]"Findings" are reported as "+" (patient global relational quality was found to be significantly positively related to outcome), "0" (no significant association was found), or "−" (patient global relational quality was significantly negatively related to outcome).
[c]Level of "Relationship" scale score.
[d]Increase in "Relationship" scale score.

that were lower on a nonparticipant measure of patient−therapist complementarity during the middle (but not the early or late) phase of therapy (Dietzel & Abeles, 1975). Somewhat atypically, the proportion of positive findings was lowest in those subcategories involving the patient's process perspective, and was highest in those that involved nonparticipant ratings of process. Despite this minor anomaly, the consistent cumulative impression of all these findings remains that the quality of the therapeutic bond is an extremely important factor in patient outcome.

PATIENT SELF-RELATEDNESS

If therapeutic interventions and the therapeutic bond develop in accordance with the norms of a good therapeutic contract, then the patient will soon discover (and will have helped create) a rich interpersonal environment in psychotherapy. It will be an environment full of new opportunities for self-expression, for relief of burdens long borne in silence, for exploring new modes of understanding, for acquiring new problem-solving skills, and so on.

TABLE 8.28 Global Relational Quality: Reciprocal

Reference	Process Perspective[a]	Outcome Perspective[a]	Finding[b]
Boun (1951)	P	P	+
Boun (1951)	P	T	+
Boun (1951)	T	P	+
Boun (1951)	T	T	+
Dietzel & Abeles (1975)	O	S	−
DiLoreto (1971)	O	S	0
Gaffin (1981)	T	P	0
Gaffin (1981)	T	T	+
Gaffin (1981)	T	S	0
Gaffin (1981)[c]	O	P	+
Gaffin (1981)	O	T	0
Gaffin (1981)	O	S	0
Gomez (1982)	O	S	+
Hansen et al. (1967)	P	S	+
Jones & Zoppel (1982)	P	P	+
Kernberg et al. (1972)	O	S	+
Kolb (1982)	P	P	0
Kolb (1982)	P	T	+
Kolb (1982)	P	S	0
Luborsky et al. (1980) (also Morgan et al., 1982)	O	S	+
Martin & Sterne (1976b)	T	T	+
Martin & Sterne (1976b)	T	S	0
Sachs (1983)	O	P	+
Sachs (1983)	O	T	+
Sachs (1983)	O	R	+
Sloane et al. (1975) (also Staples et al., 1976)	P	S	0
Strupp et al. (1964)	T	P	+
Strupp et al. (1964)	T	T	+
van der Veen & Stoler (1965)	P	T	0
van der Veen & Stoler (1965)	P	R	0
van der Veen & Stoler (1965)	P	S	0
van der Veen & Stoler (1965)	T	T	+
van der Veen & Stoler (1965)	T	R	0
van der Veen & Stoler (1965)	T	S	0

SUMMARY

Outcome Perspective

Process Perspective	Patient − 0 +	Therapist − 0 +	Rater − 0 +	Score − 0 +	Total − 0 +
Observer	0 0 2	0 1 1	0 0 1	1 2 3	1 3 7
Patient	0 1 2	0 1 2	0 1 0	0 3 1	0 6 5
Therapist	0 1 2	0 0 5	0 1 0	0 3 0	0 5 7
Total	0 2 6	0 2 8	0 2 1	1 8 4	1 14 19

[a]See Table 8.6, footnotes a and b.
[b]"Findings" are reported as "+" (reciprocal global relational quality was found to be significantly positively related to outcome), "0" (no significant association was found), or "−" (reciprocal global relational quality was significantly negatively related to outcome).
[c]Last stage of therapy only.

Yet a question remains as to how much of all this the patient can absorb.

The concept of self-relatedness seems relevant to this question. We sometimes say of people that they are in touch with themselves, that they are open to their feelings, that they know their own minds. People may also be out of touch with themselves, closed to their feelings, and—to judge by the differences between what they say and do—quite unaware of their actual thoughts and wishes. One is inclined to believe that the persons who are closer to the former state are better able to take in, digest, and make an enduring part of themselves that which they experience in therapy. On the other hand, when persons are very close to the opposite end of self-relatedness, nothing that happens is likely to influence them.

This dimension of self-relatedness may be formulated somewhat roughly in terms of openness versus defensiveness. Table 8.29 presents the findings of 12 studies concerning the relationship of outcome to patients' openness and defensiveness in psychotherapy. A positive finding in this table represents either a significant association of openness with better outcomes, or a significant association of defensiveness with poorer outcomes. Curiously, these aspects of patient self-relatedness have not been studied from the patient's process perspective

TABLE 8.29   Patient Self-relatedness: Openness (+) vs. Defensiveness (−)

Reference	Process Perspective[a]	Outcome Perspective[a]	Finding[b]
Crowder (1972)	O	S	+
De Vol (1980)	O	P	0
De Vol (1980)	O	T	+
Gendlin et al. (1960)[c]	T	T	+
Hartley & Strupp (1983)	O	S	+
Landfield (1971)	T	R	+
Lorr & McNair (1964b)	T	P	+
Lorr & McNair (1964b)	T	T	+
Morgan et al. (1982)	O	S	0
Schauble & Pierce (1974)	O	S	+
Seeman (1954)	T	T	+
Strupp et al. (1963)	T	T	+
Tomlinson (1967)	O	S	+
Wargo et al. (1971)	O	P	+
Wargo et al. (1971)	O	T	+
Wargo et al. (1971)	O	S	+

SUMMARY

Process Perspective	Patient − 0 +	Therapist − 0 +	Rater − 0 +	Score − 0 +	Total − 0 +
	Outcome Perspective				
Observer	0 1 1	0 0 2	0 0 0	0 1 5	0 2 8
Patient	0 0 0	0 0 0	0 0 0	0 0 0	0 0 0
Therapist	0 0 1	0 0 4	0 0 1	0 0 0	0 0 6
Total	0 1 2	0 0 6	0 0 1	0 1 5	0 2 14

[a]See Table 8.6, footnotes a and b.
[b]"Findings" are reported as "+" (patient openness was found to be significantly positively related to outcome), "0" (no significant association was found), or "−" (patient defensiveness was significantly negatively related to outcome).
[c]Last session only.

in process-outcome research. However, in the subcategories for which there are data, the results are strikingly consistent. Altogether, 14 of the 16 findings were positive in the sense noted above, giving very strong support to the thesis that patient self-relatedness has an important bearing on therapeutic outcome.

THERAPEUTIC REALIZATION

Perhaps the most familiar example of therapeutic realization for a patient in therapy is the attainment of insight. Other examples that might be cited are conflict resolution, problem solving, relief from distress, and so on. Therapeutic realization refers to all those signs *within the therapeutic process* that indicate that therapy is making a positive impact on the patient. However, these signs in themselves do not guarantee that patients will be able to carry positive changes over into their lives outside of therapy.

Do constructive changes observable during therapy sessions actually predict beneficial outcome in patients? Table 8.30 summarizes 18 findings that are relevant to this issue. Overall, 14 of these 18 show a significantly positive association with out-

TABLE 8.30   Therapeutic Realization

Reference	Process Perspective[a]	Outcome Perspective[a]	Finding[b]
Blau (1950)	O	T	+
Gendlin et al. (1960)	T	T	+
Greenberg & Webster (1982)	O	S	+
Holly (1983)	O	P	+
Holly (1983)	O	T	+
Kernberg et al. (1972)	O	S	+
Morgan et al. (1982)	O	S	+
Rosenman (1955)	O	T	+
Sachs (1983)	O	P	+
Sachs (1983)	O	T	+
Sachs (1983)	O	R	+
Saltzman et al. (1976)	P	P	0
Saltzman et al. (1976)	P	T	+
Saltzman et al. (1976)	T	P	0
Saltzman et al. (1976)	T	T	0
Tovian (1977)	P	R	+
Vargas (1954)	O	T	+
Vargas (1954)	O	S	0

SUMMARY

Outcome Perspective

Process Perspective	Patient − 0 +	Therapist − 0 +	Rater − 0 +	Score − 0 +	Total − 0 +
Observer	0 0 2	0 0 5	0 0 1	0 1 3	0 1 11
Patient	0 1 0	0 0 1	0 0 1	0 0 0	0 1 2
Therapist	0 1 0	0 1 1	0 0 0	0 0 0	0 2 1
Total	0 2 2	0 1 7	0 0 2	0 1 3	0 4 14

[a]See Table 8.6, footnotes a and b.
[b]"Findings" are reported as "+" (therapeutic realization was found to be significantly positively related to outcome), "0" (no significant association was found), or "−" (therapeutic realization was significantly negatively related to outcome).

come, across all categories of outcome measures. The only process perspective for which a sizable number of findings exists is that of nonparticipant observation; here, 11 out of 12 findings are significantly positive. Although the total number of findings is comparatively modest, their direction is reassuringly consistent with our theoretical expectations. Since the environments that patients live in are often hostile to constructive change, it seems worth knowing that the therapeutic realizations patients attain in their sessions may be reasonably robust.

TREATMENT DURATION

The final question we shall address concerning the relation of therapeutic process to outcome is a purely quantitative one: Does the amount of treatment a patient receives, in terms of the number of sessions attended, make a significant difference in the amount of benefit attained? Table 8.31 summarizes 114 findings bearing on this question, drawn from 79 studies. About two-thirds of the 114 findings show a significantly positive association between outcome and length of therapy, across all categories of outcome measures. The proportion of positive findings was lowest for patient outcome evaluations, and highest when outcome was assessed from the therapist's and the independent clinician's perspectives. For objective indices and tests, 23 of the 35 findings were positive. Two apparent anomalies are the negative findings reported by Kaufman et al. (1962) and by Muench (1965). The first was a long-term retrospective analysis of hospitalized childhood schizophrenics, all of whom had had very long courses of treatment; viewed in that context, it seems reasonable that those who failed to improve ultimately received the greatest amount of therapy. The second study compared naturally brief psychotherapy (3−7 sessions) with contractually time-limited therapy of intermediate duration (8−19 sessions) and longer therapy (20+ sessions) among students at a college counseling center and found that students who had briefer therapy did better on two objective measures of outcome. Since the latter was not a controlled experiment with random assignment of patients to treatment groups of different duration, it is plausible to suppose that the students

who required more than brief counseling actually may have been more severely disturbed.

In sum, with the possible exception of patients' global outcome assessments, the evidence rather consistently indicates that patients who have more therapy get more benefit from it. This, of course, is another bit of evidence to support the thesis that therapy is generally beneficial to patients who remain in it for a reasonable period. In fact, in a recent meta-analysis of studies providing detailed data on outcome at different time points, we were able to demonstrate that improvement is a linear function of the logarithm of the number of sessions (Howard, Kopta, Krause, & Orlinsky, 1986). In other words, improvement is proportionately greater in earlier sessions (during which time patients commonly experience considerable relief), and increases more slowly as the number of sessions grows (and the patients' less tractable problems become the focus of treatment). This analysis also suggests a course of diminishing returns with more and more effort required to achieve just noticeable differences in patient improvement.

CONCLUSION

We have reviewed about 1100 research findings concerning the relation of outcome in psychotherapy to various aspects of therapeutic process. The studies from which these findings were drawn cover a 35-year span of scientific research. They reflect the efforts of hundreds of investigators whose contributions, large and small, together make possible the systematic empirical understanding of psychotherapy that we seek. What do all these findings add up to? What is their theoretical yield? What directions ought future research to take in order to further advance our understanding?

A Summary of Findings
The *provisions of the therapeutic contract* that have been studied are the size and composition of the social unit in which therapy takes place (collectivity), the frequency of therapy sessions (schedule), and specification of the length of treatment (term). The findings of the studies we have reviewed indicate comparatively little effect of these provisions on therapeutic outcome. (1) There is no particular difference in outcome for patients treated in group

TABLE 8.31   Treatment Duration

Reference	Outcome Perspective[a]	Finding[b]
Astrachan et al. (1974)	S	0
Astrachan et al. (1974)	S	+
Bailey et al. (1959)	R	+
Bartlett (1950)	R	+
Bottari & Rappaport (1983)	S	+
Brown (1970)	T	+
Brown & Kosterlitz (1964)	R	+
Cabeen & Coleman (1961)	R	+
Cappon (1964)	P	+
Cappon (1964)	T	+
Cartwright (1955)	T	+
Cartwright et al. (1961)	T	+
Cartwright & Lerner (1963)	T	0
Cole et al. (1962)	T	+
Conrad (1952)	T	+
Dana (1954)	R	+
Dorfman (1958)	T	0
Dorfman (1958)	S	0
Dymond et al. (1956)	S	+
Ends & Page (1959)	S	+
Errera et al. (1967)	T	0
Errera et al. (1967)	R	0
Feldman et al. (1958)	T	+
Feldman et al. (1958)	S	+
Fiske et al. (1964)	T	+
Fiske et al. (1964)	S	0
Frank et al. (1959)	S	+
Friedlander (1981)	P	+
Friedlander (1981)	T	+
Garfield & Affleck (1959)	T	+
Garfield & Kurtz (1952)	T	+
Garfield et al. (1971)	P	+
Garfield et al. (1971)	T	+
Garfield et al. (1971)	R	+
Garfield et al. (1971)	S	0
Gelder & Marks (1966)	S	+
Graham (1958)	P	+
Graham (1958)	P	0
Graham (1958)	R	+
Grigg & Goodstein (1957)	P	0
Heilbrunn (1966)	T	0
Herz et al. (1974)	S	0
Hoehn-Saric et al. (1964)	P	0
Hoehn-Saric et al. (1964)	T	+
Hoehn-Saric et al. (1964)	S	+
Holland (1983)	S	+
Jacobs & Warner (1981)	T	+
Jacobs & Warner (1981)	R	+
Johnson (1965)	S	+

(continued)

TABLE 8.31   *(Continued)*

Reference	Outcome Perspective[a]	Finding[b]
Kapp et al. (1964)	P	+
Karle et al. (1981)	S	+
Kaufman et al. (1962)	T	−
Kernberg et al. (1972)	S	0
Kolb (1982)	P	0
Kolb (1982)	T	0
Kolb (1982)	S	+
Lerner (1972)	P	0
Lerner (1972)	T	0
Lerner (1972)	S	+
Lorr & McNair (1964a)	P	0
Lorr & McNair (1964a)	T	0
Lorr et al. (1962)	P	0
Lorr et al. (1962)	T	0
Lorr et al. (1962)	R	+
Lorr et al. (1962)	S	+
Luborsky et al. (1979)	P	+
Luborsky et al. (1979)	T	+
Malan (1976)	R	+
May (1984)	S	+
McNair et al. (1964)	P	0
McNair et al. (1964)	T	0
McNair et al. (1964)	R	0
McNair et al. (1964)	S	+
Mensh & Golden (1951)	R	+
Miles et al. (1951)	S	+
Mitchell et al. (1973)	P	0
Mitchell et al. (1973)	T	0
Mitchell et al. (1973)	R	0
Mitchell et al. (1973)	S	0
Morgan et al. (1982)	S	+
Morrison et al. (1978)	S	+
Muensch (1965)	S	−
Nichols & Beck (1960)	P	0
Nichols & Beck (1960)	T	+
Nichols & Beck (1960)	S	0
O'Connor et al. (1964)	S	+
Patterson et al. (1971)	P	0
Patterson et al. (1971)	T	+
Patterson et al. (1971)	R	0
Reid & Shyne (1969)	R	+
Rosenman (1955)	T	+
Rosenthal & Frank (1958)	T	+
Rosenthal & Levine (1970)	S	+
Rounsaville et al. (1981)	S	0
Rounsaville et al. (1979)	S	+
Ryan & Gizynski (1971)	P	0

(continued)

TABLE 8.31   *(Continued)*

Reference	Outcome Perspective[a]	Finding[b]
Ryan & Gizynski (1971)	T	0
Ryan & Gizynski (1971)	R	0
Schroeder (1960)	T	+
Scully (1983)	S	+
Seeman (1954)	T	+
Shyne & Kogan (1957)	R	+
Standahl & van der Veen (1957)	T	+
Stieper & Weiner (1965)	R	+
Sullivan et al. (1958)	T	+
Taylor (1956)	T	+
Tolman & Meyer (1957)	T	+
Uhlenhuth & Duncan (1968a)	S	+
van der Veen (1967)	S	+
Weitz et al. (1975)	P	+
Werman et al. (1976)	T	0
Werman et al. (1976)	R	0
Yalom et al. (1967)	P	+
Yalom et al. (1967)	R	+

SUMMARY

Outcome Perspective

Process Perspective	Patient − 0 +	Therapist − 0 +	Rater − 0 +	Score − 0 +	Total − 0 +
Objective Index	0 12 8	1 9 28	0 6 15	1 11 23	2 38 74

[a]See Table 8.6, footnote a.
[b]"Findings" are reported as "+" (treatment duration was found to be significantly positively related to outcome), "0" (no significant association was found), or "−" (treatment duration was significantly negatively related to outcome).

or in individual psychotherapy. (2) A once-weekly schedule of sessions is not inferior to, and is sometimes better than, more (or less) frequent sessions. (3) Contracting in advance with a patient for a specific number of sessions (time-limited therapy) is often, but not consistently, a helpful procedure.

The *implementation of the therapeutic contract* has also been studied in several respects: the timeliness of its implementation; the preparation given to patients; the quantitative involvement of participants in the therapeutic conversation; the styles with which they perform their respective roles. The findings indicate that the implementation of the therapeutic contract is more consequential for outcome than the variations in format considered above. (4) Delay in starting treatment on the therapist's part,

and irregularity in attendance on either part, predisposes toward poorer outcomes. (5) Preliminary orientation of patients to their role in therapy makes a definite contribution toward better outcomes, especially for those (e.g., lower socioeconomic status patients) who may have no other models for appropriate patient behavior. (6) The more patients talk during therapy sessions, the better their outcomes are likely to be. (7) The more patients and therapists collaborate in sharing initiative and responsibility, avoiding dependency on the one hand and authoritarian direction on the other, the better is the outcome of their effort likely to be.

Three aspects of *therapeutic interventions made by therapists* were examined: specific techniques; the content focus on interpretation and confrontation; and the therapist's skillfulness. (8) Confrontation, interpretation, and exploration seemed to be frequently but not consistently effective modes of therapeutic intervention, whereas reflection, giving support, giving advice, and therapist self-disclosure showed little differential relation to outcome. (9) Therapists' focusing on patient's affect also was frequently, but not consistently, productive of good outcomes, as was focusing on the patient's transference reactions; however, therapists' focusing on other here-and-now occurrences than patient affect and transference was comparatively ineffective. (10) Therapist skillfulness proved to be a significant factor in patient outcome.

Aspects of *patient participation in therapeutic interventions* were also studied: self-exploration; affective arousal; content focus; adeptness or suitability. (11) The amount of patient self-exploration, as measured by the much used Truax scale, was generally unrelated to patient outcome; but other measures indicated that more extensive self-exploration sometimes was associated with better outcomes. (12) The experience of negative affect, such as distress and hostility, especially early in treatment, was fairly often associated with good outcome. (13) Patients who generally showed greater immediacy of affective expression tended quite consistently to experience better outcomes. (14) Evidence also suggested that the occurrence of affective discharge (i.e., emotional catharsis) in therapy is associated with good outcomes. (15) Patients who talked about problematic issues in therapy had better treatment outcomes, especially if they did so with some sense of responsibility. (16) However, patients' focusing upon the here-and-now occurrences of therapy per se was generally not associated with outcome. (17) Patient suitability or adeptness in therapeutic interventions, like therapist skillfulness, did prove to be a significant factor in therapeutic outcome.

The separate and joint contributions of therapists and patients to various *dimensions of the therapeutic bond* have received intensive study: role-investment; empathic resonance; mutual affirmation; and the overall quality of the relationship. Generally, between 50 and 80 percent of the substantial number of findings in this area were significantly positive, indicating that these dimensions were very consistently related to patient outcome. This was especially true when process measures were based on patients' observations of the therapeutic relationship.

The specific aspects of *therapist role-investment* that have been studied are therapist engagement versus detachment, therapist credibility versus unsureness and therapist genuineness. (18) Therapist engagement, especially as perceived by patients, was consistently associated with better outcomes, and therapist detachment with poorer outcomes. (19) Viewed from all process perspectives, therapist "credibility and confidence" was very consistently related to better outcome; correspondingly, therapist unsureness was related to poorer outcomes. (20) Therapist genuineness or self-congruence, particularly as perceived by patients, was often but not consistently associated with better outcomes.

Parallel aspects of *patient role-investment* that have been studied are patient engagement and patient motivation. (21) Patient engagement was very consistently related to better outcomes, viewed from all process perspectives. (22) Evidence also suggested that patient motivation was frequently, but not consistently, associated with good therapeutic outcome.

Empathic resonance was distinguished into phases of attunement and expressiveness for both patient and therapist, and reciprocal resonance was interpreted in terms of actual and perceived similarity between patient and therapist. (23) Patients' perceptions of therapist empathy were very consistently related to good outcome, but measures of therapists' empathic attunement from other process perspectives were much less consistently associated with good outcome. (24) Patient expressiveness is also very consistently related to good outcome. (25) An empathically resonant relationship between patient and therapist, viewed in terms of objectively measured as well as perceived similarity, was also found to be very consistently associated with good outcome. (Therapists' expressiveness and patients' empathic attunement have been less often studied, but the available evidence suggests that both are also positively associated with outcome.)

The dimension of *mutual affirmation* has been studied with respect to the therapist's warmth or acceptance, the patient's warmth, and the degree of reciprocal affirmation observed in the relationship. (26) Therapists' warmth or acceptance toward their patients, especially but not only as observed by patients, was quite consistently related to good outcome in therapy. (27) Patients' warmth or acceptance toward their therapists was also very consistently and positively related to outcome. (28) Reciprocal affirmation, as reported by patients and by nonparticipant observers, was significantly and positively associated with outcome in a startling 80 percent of the findings surveyed!

The *overall quality of the therapeutic bond* itself, as well as the therapist's and the patient's general contributions to it, has also been the subject of research. (29) The quality of the therapist's general contribution to the relationship was found to be very consistently positively related to outcome. (30) The quality of the patient's general contribution, studied mainly from the perspective of the nonparticipant observer, was found to be positively related to outcome with great consistency. (31) Not surprisingly, the overall quality of the therapeutic bond or alliance also was found to be consistently associated with good outcome, across all process perspectives.

The dimension of openness versus defensiveness was taken to represent the concept of *patient self-relatedness.* (32) Although studied only from the nonparticipant observer's and the therapist's process perspectives, patient openness versus defensiveness was the most consistently positive correlate of therapeutic outcome that we surveyed (88% of the findings statistically significant).

Therapeutic realization—the attainment in therapy sessions of insight, relief, conflict resolution, and so on—has been studied mainly from the perspective of nonparticipant observers. (33) From their viewpoint, therapeutic realization was found to be positively related to good outcome with great consistency.

Finally, no less than 79 studies have examined the relation of *treatment duration* (the sheer amount of therapy, measured in number of sessions attended) to therapeutic outcome. (34) These studies have established that (within limits) treatment duration is consistently associated with outcome.

Theoretical Implications

Having condensed some 1100 findings into slightly less than three dozen summary statements, all that remains is to consider what they mean. To do this requires a generic model of therapeutic process that is capable of accounting for the interrelated workings of (1) the therapeutic contract, (2) therapeutic interventions, (3) the therapeutic bond, (4) the patient's self-relatedness, (5) therapeutic realizations, and, finally, (6) the patient's therapeutic outcome.

The ordering of the components of therapeutic process in their relation to one another, and to the patient's outcome, would have to be compatible with the findings that have just been summarized, and ideally would go beyond the facts to suggest possibilities for new research.

The model we have in mind can be visualized in the form of a flowchart representing both the process and the functional context of psychotherapy (see Figure 8.1). "Process" includes the five elements with which the reader is already familiar: contract, interventions, bond, patient self-relatedness, and therapeutic realization. "Context" includes the specific persons who are directly or indirectly parties to the therapeutic contract (patient, therapist, and ancillary parties if any, such as parents, courts, supervisors, etc.), as well as social structural and cultural aspects of the setting and of the community in which therapy occurs. The various influences of contextual elements on process constitute what we usually have referred to as therapeutic inputs, and the reciprocal influences of therapeutic process on contextual elements constitute what we have called therapeutic outputs (Howard & Orlinsky, 1972). For practical purposes, however, the therapeutic contract and the patient's outcome, respectively, may be construed as the initial and terminal points in the flow of process to outcome. The pathways leading from the initiation of therapy through the formation of a therapeutic contract, to its more or less successful termination in patient outcome, may be most readily discerned by tracing them in reverse order.

The bottom line of our model concerns patient outcome. As rated or measured in most process-outcome studies, "outcome" entails recognition of fairly enduring, relatively large-scale changes made in a patient's life situation or personal functioning. The model we propose here distinguishes between this long-term "macro-outcome," assessed at the end of therapy or at some later time, and relatively short-term "micro-outcomes" that can be assessed in the daily lives of patients between sessions during the course of therapy. Such micro-outcomes constitute subtle but significant steps toward personal transformation: a new way of understanding a familiar situation; a heightened sense of choice in an emotional moment; a willingness to try something one had always avoided before.

Thus, we view macro-outcome as the net result

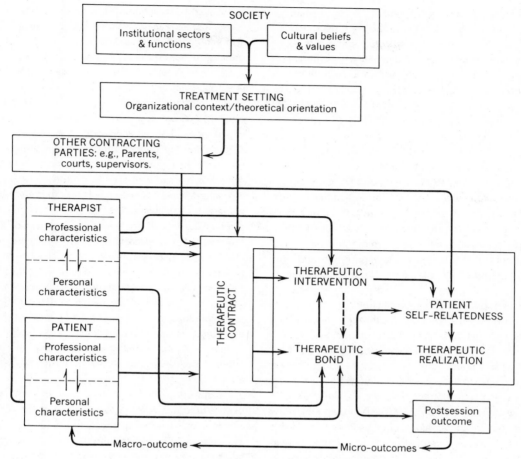

Figure 8.1   A generic model of psychotherapy.

of an extended series of incremental short-term changes. These micro-outcomes reflect the patient's application in everyday situations of the immediate effects produced by particular therapy sessions ("postsession outcome"). Given unfavorable conditions in the patient's life, successful micro-outcomes may dissipate before they can be consolidated into significant macro-outcomes. Under favorable circumstances, however, micro-outcomes should gradually accumulate over the course of therapy and be synthesized by the patient to change the habitual, problematic assumptive systems (schemata, scripts, programs) used in dealing with self and others.

As yet we know comparatively little about how micro-outcomes are produced and synthesized into macro-outcomes. However, we do know that *treatment duration* is positively associated with macro-

outcome. Until studies can provide more detailed information, it seems plausible to assume (1) that the longer patients remain in treatment, the more likely they are to succeed in effecting positive micro-outcomes, and (2) that the greater the number of positive micro-outcomes patients experience, the more likely they are to achieve measurably beneficial macro-outcomes. Moreover, (3) the very consistent positive relation between macro-outcome and therapeutic realizations (the final element of therapeutic process) suggests that these are directly involved in the production of micro-outcomes. Again, it seems plausible to assume that the achievement of *therapeutic realizations* such as insight, resolution of conflicts, or learning of new cognitive and interpersonal skills during therapy sessions should eventually enable patients, in situations outside of therapy, to consistently handle old problematic issues in more effective and more satisfying ways.

Another very consistent association was found between outcome and the quality of *the therapeutic bond*, both as a whole and in its constituent dimensions (reciprocal role-investment, empathic resonance, and mutual affirmation). Figure 8.1 shows two pathways by which the therapeutic bond can influence outcome. A good therapeutic bond should contribute directly to the production of positive micro-outcomes by strengthening the patient's morale (Frank, 1974). Heightened morale changes the patient's manner of self-presentation to others, making self-presentation generally more rewarding to others and tending in turn to elicit more favorable and rewarding responses from them. In addition, it should provide motivation to apply insight and other therapeutic realizations to situations outside of therapy.

A good therapeutic bond should also contribute indirectly to patient outcome through the mediation of therapeutic realization and patient self-relatedness. Elsewhere we have presented data suggesting that the therapeutic bond conveys implicit affective messages to the patient containing information that is highly relevant to the patient's self-evaluation (Orlinsky & Howard, 1986). A therapeutic bond characterized by high role-investment, empathic resonance, and mutual affirmation should powerfully imply, for example, that the patient's personal concerns and feelings are worthy of serious interest. Such a message is all the more believable when it is tacitly demonstrated by another's manner of relating. If the patient is not too self-preoccupied for this message to be received, nor so self-deprecating as to find it unbelievable, then the therapeutic bond will have influenced outcome by a second route.

Patient self-relatedness was conceived as a manifestation, within the therapeutic process, of the patient's personality structure (the state aspect of a trait-state continuum). The concept of self-relatedness follows from a view of the person as being both the subject and object of experience [in the language of Mead (1956), both an "I" and a "me"]. From this perspective, the process of social interaction involves the person in a double dialectic: one between "I" and "you"; the second between "I" and "me." Through the former, persons maintain responsive contact with others in their immediate surroundings; through the latter, they become self-conscious, self-evaluative, self-regulating (and, alas, also self-defeating) actors. Under normal circumstances, the two dialectics intertwine and influence each other. A person who is very self-critical, for example, is likely to respond to others in a defensively "sensitive" manner. By the same token, a person to whom appreciation is shown is likely to experience enhanced self-worth.

Logically, the generic model of psychotherapy presented in Figure 8.1 should include therapist self-relatedness as well as patient self-relatedness as a process element. Our sense is that therapist self-relatedness has its greatest influence on the therapist's ability to contribute to the formation of the therapeutic bond; at least it has been our experience that therapists who approach their sessions in a self-attuned state are better able to be empathically resonant with their patients (Orlinsky & Howard, 1986). Yet the fact of the matter is that therapist self-relatedness has not been made a focus of process-outcome research (with the possible exception of the relational variable "genuineness," if the latter is interpreted in Rogerian terms as "self-congruence.")

Patient self-relatedness, on the other hand, has been studied in relation to outcome in the form of variables such as openness and defensiveness. These presumably control the degree to which patients can accommodate or absorb information that is not readily assimilable to habitual schemata. When patients are open and nondefensive, therapeutic interventions such as interpretation or confrontation can be absorbed that may be constructively inconsistent with, and thereby mutative of, their core working assumptions concerning self and others. When patients are open and nondefensive, similar affective messages implicit in the therapeutic bond can also be received. If this line of reasoning is correct, patient self-relatedness should be consistently associated with outcome, as observed, because it is a major precondition for the production of therapeutic realizations.

This view of the matter also helps to explain the somewhat inconsistent association observed in process-outcome research between patient outcome and *therapeutic interventions*. Interpretation, confrontation, and exploration were often but not generally associated with outcome. The reason why outcome should be less consistently associated with therapeutic interventions than with the therapeutic bond, according to the model shown in Figure 8.1, is that therapeutic interventions do not influence therapeutic realization directly, but require an "open" state of patient self-relatedness for this influence to become effective. The therapeutic bond, on the other hand, does have a direct impact on postsession outcome through the enhancement of patient morale, in addition to its indirect effect on therapeutic realization.

The existence of other important connections between therapeutic interventions, the therapeutic bond, and the patient's self-relatedness is suggested by the generic model of psychotherapy proposed in Figure 8.1. The arrow connecting the therapeutic bond to patient self-relatedness indicates that the former should influence the latter; for example, a strong bond should enhance the patient's openness to therapeutic interventions by providing a safe, supportive but stimulating environment (Orlinsky & Howard, 1986). Again, the arrow connecting the therapeutic bond to therapeutic interventions indicates that a good bond should also enhance the patient's willingness to engage in therapeutic interventions. Although these are process-process connections for which research has not been reviewed in this chapter, they suggest some further reasons why the therapeutic bond is so strategic an aspect of therapeutic process.

What factors, in turn, facilitate the development of the therapeutic bond? Our generic model indicates that one factor should be the accumulation of meaningful therapeutic interventions. Two paths of influence are indicated. One arrow represents a weak but direct influence, suggesting that merely engaging in help-seeking and help-giving activities, without further consideration of their effectiveness, tends (at least in the initial stages of treatment) to build the component of the bond defined as reciprocal role-investment, since therapeutic interventions demonstrate the therapist's capacity and commitment to help the patient. As the therapist gains credibility in the patient's eyes, the patient should become more genuinely trusting.

A surer but less direct path of influence from therapeutic interventions to the therapeutic bond is indicated by arrows connecting (1) interventions to realization, mediated by the patient's self-related-

ness, and (2) therapeutic realization to the therapeutic bond. (A parallel loop connects the implicit emotional message conveyed by the therapeutic bond through patient self-relatedness to therapeutic realization, and then back to the therapeutic bond.) This line of influence corresponds to the familiar principle that nothing succeeds like success. When therapeutic interventions are actually seen and felt to be helpful by the patient, the therapist's credibility, and the patient's investment in and affirmation of the therapeutic bond should be enhanced. By the same token, when therapeutic interventions are experienced as threatening or harmful, the therapeutic bond should be correspondingly impaired.

The generic model proposed in Figure 8.1 indicates that two other factors influence the development of the therapeutic bond. The actual implementation of the *therapeutic contract* by patient and therapist is the first. Our review has shown that if the therapist creates no barriers or delays, if the patient is prepared to come and talk, and if the two establish an actively collaborative style of relating, then a good therapeutic bond should begin to develop. When the opposite of these conditions obtain, development of the therapeutic bond should be impaired.

The final source of influence on the development of the therapeutic bond that our generic model suggests lies beyond the process of therapy itself (and beyond the scope of research reviewed in this chapter). Personal characteristics of the patient and of the therapist, in themselves and in their compatibility, should determine the potentials and the limits of the therapeutic bond created between specific individuals. For example, certain characteristic styles of interpersonal behavior interact in ways that facilitate establishment of a stable bond, whereas others do not (Carson, 1969). It also seems reasonable to suppose that the potential for the emergence of disruptive transference and countertransference reactions in the relationship is determined by the personalities of the individual participants, and by the ways in which their personalities unconsciously mesh.

Most of the paths linking patient outcome to the initial element in our generic model, the *therapeutic contract*, have now been traced. All that remains is to indicate that the range of therapeutic interventions to be used in treatment tends to be stipulated in the therapeutic contract, insofar as the therapist undertakes to perform one or another type of treatment, for example, interpretation in psychoanalysis, or empathic reflection in client-centered therapy. [Other arrows in Figure 8.1 suggest that (1) therapists' professional characteristics, such as technical skillfulness and experience, and (2) the state of the therapeutic bond tend to influence the timing and choice of specific therapeutic interventions from the range stipulated in the therapeutic contract.] For the sake of completeness, we may also note in passing that our generic model indicates a joint determination of the therapeutic contract (1) by the patient and the therapist, who are the principal contracting parties, (2) by other contracting parties who have an interest in the establishment and outcome of the therapeutic relationship, (3) by characteristics of the treatment setting, and (4) by the social institutions and the value orientations of society, which may be viewed as an ever-present silent partner in the therapeutic enterprise.

Suggestions for Future Research

Anyone who has read this far will have received numerous impressions about the needs and possibilities for future research on the relation of process to outcome (and for research on the determinants of, and relations between, process elements themselves). We will belabor only a few of the most obvious points.

Outcome

Perhaps the most urgent need is to bring conceptual order to the domain of outcome measures. Global evaluations of patient improvement and estimates of pre−post change in overall functioning do not provide enough information to support much theoretical interpretation. Four points seem most important.

First, descriptive ratings of a patient's condition and life situation must be separated as much as possible from evaluative judgments, so that we may know what has changed, as well as how much someone liked it. It would also help if the cultural values that are used in these evaluative judgments could be made explicit.

Second, the separate descriptive and evaluative perspectives of patients, therapists, independent clinicians, patients' significant others, and other "objective" sources need to be kept distinct. That the

world looks and feels different from different perspectives is simply a fact of life that we shall have to live with. If outcome findings from diverse sources fail to converge, combining them does nothing except to create further confusion.

Third, attention should be given to changes that patients make in their lives, as well as changes that occur in their personalities. A significant reorganization of one's life situation or a change in one's style of conducting specific involvements may be at least as relevant in evaluating therapy as reorganization of one's self-concept or reduction in symptomatology.

Finally, researchers should shift some of their attention from macro-outcomes, assessed at the end of treatment or even later, to micro-outcomes, assessed systematically over the course of treatment. A greater focus on micro-outcomes should make it possible to trace the specific changes that occur in a patient's life and personality to events and patterns occurring in therapy sessions. The study of micro-outcomes should also lead to a fuller understanding of how these small-scale changes cumulate into macro-outcomes.

Process

There is a greater degree of conceptual order available in the domain of process measures, but there is still not sufficient understanding of the differences between the several process perspectives. Therapy, too, looks different when observed from the points of view of patients, therapists, and nonparticipant observers.

Researchers should try to study process from more than one perspective, and make a conscientious effort to keep them distinct. Mapping the various points of convergence and divergence among perspectives is an important task. Areas of divergence may reflect particularly important aspects of therapeutic process, rather than mere "method" variance.

If the results of research on psychotherapy are ever to become useful to clinicians, there is also a very special need to find reliable means of translating between the different process perspectives. Practicing therapists can observe the events of therapy from only one perspective. Since there is not always a point-for-point correspondence between what therapists can observe and what patients or nonparticipants perceive about therapy, researchers must help discover the correlates of those other viewpoints within the therapist's perspective.

Process and Outcome

Analysis of empirical findings into process-by-outcome subcategories highlights two facts that should be of some interest to researchers. The first is that research effort has been very unevenly distributed across the 12 subcategories. Some combinations of process perspective by outcome category have been intensively studied (e.g., nonparticipant process observations by objective indices and tests, and therapists' process ratings by therapists' outcome assessments); others have been virtually neglected (e.g., patient process by independent clinicians' outcome). Researchers might want to examine the studies they design to assure themselves that their choice of variables is methodologically representative as well as theoretically relevant.

A second fact is that different process-outcome subcategories have been disproportionately productive of significant results. The very highest percentage of significant findings occurs in the subcategory defined by therapists' process reports and therapists' outcome evaluations. A very high proportion of significant findings also occurs in the subcategory defined by patients' process reports and patients' outcome evaluations. If these were the only process-outcome subcategories in which significant findings consistently occurred, one would have to confront some very sticky questions about vested interests and halo effects. At the very least, researchers would be well advised to include at least some crossover in perspectives when matching process and outcome variables.

Theory

The most interesting suggestions for future research always come from theory. In the course of this review, we have developed a conceptual model to organize and interpret a large amount of empirical data. The presentation of our generic theory of psychotherapy has been necessarily sketchy, but we hope that its basic components and their interrelations have been made sufficiently clear to permit others to find it a source of worthwhile ideas. For example, one idea that should repay systematic investigation is our claim that the impact of therapeutic interventions on outcome depends on the patient's state of self-relatedness. Another is our

proposal that the quality of the therapeutic bond affects the patient's self-relatedness, and thus that continued exposure to a good therapeutic bond should enhance a patient's openness to therapeutic interventions. Because it is a generic model, too, we hope that researchers of varying theoretical orientations will find it useful.

Effective Therapeutic Process

We conclude by returning to the question with which we started: "What is 'effectively therapeutic' about psychotherapy?" Based on the review of process-outcome studies now completed, our provisional answer to that question is as follows: (1) The patient's and therapist's therapeutic bond—that is, their reciprocal role-investment, empathic resonance, and mutual affirmation—is effectively therapeutic. (2) Certain therapeutic interventions, when done skillfully with suitable patients, are effectively therapeutic. (3) Patient's and therapist's focusing their interventions on the patient's feelings is effectively therapeutic. (4) Preparing the patient adequately for participation in therapy and collaborative sharing of responsiblity for problem solving are effectively therapeutic. (5) Within certain limits, having more rather than less therapy is effectively therapeutic.

APPENDIX I
THE INTERRELATION OF PROCESS FACET AND PROCESS ELEMENT CONCEPTIONS

Readers familiar with our chapter in the 1978 edition of this *Handbook* may have some interest in comparing the conceptual model used to organize process-outcome research findings in that volume with the one that has been used in the present edition. The 1978 scheme was essentially a methodological formulation of the domains of process and context (i.e., input and output) variables. Four process facets and four context facets were distinguished by constructing a nested series of distinctions based on observational perspectives (participant vs. nonparticipant) and observational frames of reference (synchronic vs. diachronic). The four process facets were (1) *co-oriented activity* (nonparticipant, synchronic), (2) *concurrent experience* (participant, synchronic), (3) *normative organiza-*

tion (nonparticipant, diachronic), and (4) *communicated meaning* (participant, diachronic; called "symbolic dramatization" in 1978).

These process facets were conceived of as complementary analytical constructs, rather than as empirical categories; that is, more like size, color, and weight than like bananas, oranges and basketballs. A complete description of *any* interpersonal event (e.g., a wrestling match, a dinner party, a therapy session) would require reference to all four process facets.

By contrast, the concepts we have used to organize the present chapter are conceived of as empirical elements involved in *one* specific form of interpersonal event: psychotherapeutic process. The 1978 process facet model consists of a formal definition of categories of process variables, based on modes of observation. The 1986 process element conception comprises a substantive model of

therapeutic process, based ultimately on clinical research and practice.

Logically, the two conceptions should be viewed as interdependent structures. The 1986 generic model of process elements does not replace the earlier methodological model of process facets, but rather subsumes it. In the present chapter, process facets have been rendered in terms of the observational perspectives they represent. The patients' and the therapists' perspectives on therapeutic process correspond primarily to individual components of the facet of *concurrent experience*, and secondarily to *communicated meaning*. The objective raters' perspective and the use of objective indices correspond mainly to individual components of *co-oriented activity*, with the major exception being provisions of the therapeutic contract that involve *normative organization*. The reason for indicating observational perspectives alone in the present

TABLE 8.32   The Interrelation of Process Facet and Process Element Conceptions

Process Element	Process Facet			
	Co-oriented Activity	Concurrent Experience	Normative Organization	Communicated Meaning
Therapeutic Contract	Negotiative, instructive, & regulative transactions	Reciprocal understanding of & attitudes to contract	Specification of goals, format, procedures, & terms	Ideational & value schema of helping relationship
Therapeutic Interventions	"Technical" transactions between participants	Participants' perceptions of effectively helpful acts	Skillfulness & conformity to specified procedures	Problem-centered verb/nonverb. discourse
Therapeutic Bond	Investment, rapport, & affirmation transactions	Experience of investment, rapport, & affirmation	Conformity to norms of the helping relationship	Relationship-centered verb/nonverb. discourse
Patient Self-relatedness	Behaviors expressing openness/defensiveness	Self-activation, awareness, evaluation, & regulation	Patient conformity to specified mode of experiencing	Assumptive content of self-instructive messages
Therapeutic realization	Enhance well-being, assurance, orientation	Felt shift, reorganization in cog/emotional perspective	Attainment of specified process goals	Improved assumptions re: self/object-world

chapter, rather than process facets (i.e., observational perspective differentiated by temporal frame of reference), was that process was observed in the synchronic frame of reference in by far the greater part of the research we reviewed.

Because most research to date has been formulated within the synchronic mode of observation—focusing on moment-by-moment actions and experiences of patients and therapists—it does not necessarily follow that future research ought to be similarly constrained. One great advantage of the 1978 process facet model is that it systematically disclosed aspects of therapeutic process that could be, but have not been, observed. The function of theory in science is not just the organization of observational data but also the anticipation of significant phenomena on which observations ought to be made.

In this spirit, we offer in Table 8.32 a summary statement of the interrelations between the process facet and process element conceptions. Each process element is systematically cross-tabulated with each process facet to define an observable aspect of therapeutic process that could be taken as a focus of research. We hope that others will find it suggestive. When sufficient research has been done on these aspects, or on others derived from a still more refined set of conceptions, the eventual result should be a scientifically grounded, empirically substantiated, clinically useful generic theory of psychotherapy.

REFERENCES

Abramowitz, S.I., & Abramowitz, C.V. (1974). Psychological-mindedness and benefit from insight-oriented group therapy. *Archives of General Psychiatry, 30,* 610–615.

Abramowitz, S.I., & Jackson, C. (1974). Comparative effectiveness of there-and-then *vs.* here-and-now therapist interpretations in group psychotherapy. *Journal of Counseling Psychology, 21,* 288–293.

Alexander, J.F., Barton, C., Schiavo, R.S., & Parsons, B.V. (1976). Systems-behavioral intervention with families of delinquents: Therapist characteristics, family behavior, and outcome. *Journal of Consulting and Clinical Psychology, 44,* 656–664.

Amira, S.A. (1982). Figurative language and metaphor in successful and unsuccessful psychotherapy. *Dissertation Abstracts International, 43,* 1244B.

Ashby, J.D., Ford, D.H., Guerney, B.G., & Guerney, L.F. (1957). Effects on clients of a reflective and a leading type of psychotherapy. *Psychological Monographs, 71,* 24.

Astrachan, B.M., Brauer, L., Harrow, M., & Schwartz, C. (1974). Symptomatic outcome in schizophrenia. *Archives of General Psychiatry, 31,* 155–160.

Astwood, W.P. (1977). Congruence of patient and therapist understanding of psychotherapy and its effect on treatment outcome as perceived by the psychotherapist. *Dissertation Abstracts International, 37,* 4662B.

Baer, P.E., Dunbar, P.W., Hamilton, J.E., II, & Beutler, L.E. (1980). Therapists' perceptions of the psychotherapeutic process: Development of a psychotherapy process inventory. *Psychological Reports, 46,* 563–570.

Bailey, M.A., Warshaw, L., & Eichler, R.M. (1959). A study of factors related to length of stay in psychotherapy. *Journal of Clinical Psychology, 15,* 442–444.

Baker, E. (1960). The differential effects of two psychotherapeutic approaches on client perceptions. *Journal of Counseling Psychology, 7,* 46–50.

Barrett-Lennard, G.T. (1962). Dimensions of therapist response as causal factors in therapeutic change. *Psychological Monographs, 76,* 43, (Whole No. 562).

Barrington, B.L. (1961). Prediction from counselor behavior of client perception and of case outcome. *Journal of Counseling Psychology, 8,* 37–42.

Barrington, B.L. (1967). The differential effectiveness of therapy as measured by the Thematic Apperception Test. In C.R. Rogers, E.T. Gendlin, D.J. Kiesler, & C.B. Truax (Eds.), *The therapeutic relationship and its impact: A study of psychotherapy with schizophrenics.* Madison: University of Wisconsin Press.

Bartlett, M.R. (1950). A six-month follow-up of the effects of personal adjustment counseling of veterans. *Journal of Consulting Psychology, 14,* 393–394.

Bent, R.J., Putnam, D.G., Kiesler, D.J., & Nowicki, S., Jr., (1976). Correlates of successful and unsuccessful psychotherapy. *Journal of Consulting and Clinical Psychology, 44,* 149.

Bergin, A.E. (1971). The evaluation of therapeutic outcomes. In A.E. Bergin & S.L. Garfield (Eds.), *Handbook of psychotherapy and behavior change.* New York: Wiley.

Bergin, A.E., & Jasper, L.G. (1969). Correlates of empathy in psychotherapy: A replication. *Journal of Abnormal Psychology, 74,* 477–481.

Bergin, A.E., & Lambert, M.J. (1978). The evaluation of therapeutic outcomes. In S.L. Garfield & A.E. Bergin (Eds.), *Handbook of psychotherapy and behavior change* (2nd edition). New York: Wiley.

Berman, J.S. (1980). Social bases of psychotherapy: Expectancy, attraction and the outcome of treatment. *Dissertation Abstracts International, 40,* 5800–5801B.

Beutler, L.E., Johnson, D.T., Neville, C.W., Jr., Elkins, D., & Jobe, A.M. (1975). Attitude similarity and therapist credibility as predictors of attitude change and improvement in psychotherapy. *Journal of Consulting and Clinical Psychology, 43,* 90–91.

Beutler, L.E., & Mitchell, R. (1981). Differential psychotherapy outcome among depressed and impulsive patients as a function of analytic and experiential treatment procedures, *Psychiatry, 44,* 297–306.

Beutler, L.E., Pollack, S., & Jobe, A.M. (1978). "Acceptance," values, and therapeutic change. *Journal of Consulting and Clinical Psychology, 46,* 198–199.

Bierenbaum, H., Nichols, M.P., & Schwartz, A.J. (1976). Effects of varying session length and frequency in brief emotive psychotherapy. *Journal of Consulting and Clinical Psychology, 44,* 790–798.

Blau, T.H. (1950). Report on a method of predicting success in psychotherapy. *Journal of Clinical Psychology, 6,* 403–406.

Board, F.A. (1959). Patients' and physicians' judgments of outcome of psychotherapy in an outpatient clinic. *Archives of General Psychiatry, 1,* 185–196.

Bordin, E.S. (1979). The generalizability of the psychoanalytic concept of the working alliance. *Psychotherapy: Theory, Research and Practice, 16,* 252–260.

Bottari, M.A., & Rappaport, H. (1983). The relationship of patient and therapist-reported experiences of the initial session to outcome: An initial investigation. *Psychotherapy: Theory, Research and Practice, 20,* 355–358.

Boun, O.H. (1951). *An investigation of therapeutic relationship in client-centered psychotherapy.* Unpublished doctoral dissertation, University of Chicago.

Braaten, L.J. (1961) The movement from non-self to self in client-centered psychotherapy. *Journal of Counseling Psychology, 8,* 20–24.

Braaten, L.J. (1984). Predicting effectiveness of group psychotherapy through measurements of individually perceived group atmosphere. Presentation at the 8th International Congress of Group Psychotherapy, Mexico City.

Brown, J.S., & Kosterlitz, N. (1964). Selection and treatment of psychiatric outpatients. *Archives of General Psychiatry, 11,* 425–440.

Brown, R.D. (1970). Experienced and inexperienced counselors' first impressions of clients and case outcomes: Are first impressions lasting? *Journal of Counseling Psychology, 17,* 550–558.

Butler, J.M., Rice, L.N., & Wagstaff, A.F. (1962). On the naturalistic definition of variables: An analogue of clinical analysis. In H.H. Strupp & L.L. Luborsky (Eds.), *Research in psychotherapy* (Vol. 2). Washington, DC: American Psychological Association.

Cabeen, C.W., & Coleman, J.C. (1961). Group therapy with sex offenders: Description and evaluation of group therapy program in an institutional setting. *Journal of Clinical Psychology, 17,* 122–129.

Cabral, R.J., Best, J., & Paton, A. (1975). Patients' and observers' assessments of process and outcome in group therapy: A follow-up study. *American Journal of Psychiatry, 132,* 1052–1054.

Caillier, P.M. (1981). Effects of session frequency and session duration on process and outcome in short term time-limited psychotherapy. *Dissertation Abstracts International, 42,* 364–365B.

Cain, D.J. (1973). The therapist's and client's perceptions of therapeutic conditions in relation to perceived interview outcome. *Dissertation Abstracts International, 33,* 6071B.

Cappon, D. (1964). Results of psychotherapy. *British Journal of Psychiatry, 110,* 35–45.

Carson, R.C. (1969). *Interaction concepts of personality.* Chicago: Aldine.

Cartwright, D.S. (1955). Success in psychotherapy as a function of certain actuarial variables. *Journal of Consulting Psychology, 19,* 357–363.

Cartwright, D.S., Robertson, R.J., Fiske, D.W., & Kirtner, W.L. (1961). Length of therapy in relation to outcome and change in personal integration. *Journal of Consulting Psychology, 25,* 84–88.

Cartwright, R.D., & Lerner, B. (1963). Empathy, need to change, and improvement with psychotherapy. *Journal of Consulting Psychology, 27,* 138–144.

Church, M.S. (1982). Sequential analysis of moment-by-moment psychotherapy interactions. *Dissertation Abstracts International, 42,* 4185B.

Cole, N.J., Hardin Branch, C.H., & Allison, R.B. (1962). Some relationships between social class and the practice of dynamic psychotherapy. *American Journal of Psychiatry, 118,* 1004–1012.

Conrad, D.C. (1952). An empirical study of the concept of psychotherapeutic success. *Journal of Consulting Psychology, 16,* 92–97.

Cooley, E.J., & Lajoy, R. (1980). Therapeutic relationship and improvement as perceived by clients and therapists. *Journal of Clinical Psychology, 36,* 562–570.

Coons, W.H. (1972). Psychotherapy and verbal conditioning in behaviour modification. *Canadian Psychologist, 13,* 3–29.

Crowder, J.E. (1972). Relationship between therapist and client interpersonal behaviors and psychotherapy outcome. *Journal of Counseling Psychology, 19,* 68–75.

Dana, R.H. (1954). The effects of attitudes towards authority on psychotherapy. *Journal of Clinical Psychology, 10,* 350–353.

DeJonge, V.K. (1981). The effect of liking of the therapist on successful outcome in marriage therapy. *Dissertation Abstracts International, 41,* 3263–3264A.

De Vol, T.I. (1980). Adaptive regression in psychotherapy. *Dissertation Abstracts International, 40,* 4477B.

Dickenson, W.A. (1969). Therapist self-disclosure as a variable in psychotherapeutic process and outcome. *Dissertation Abstracts International, 30,* 2434B.

Dickoff, H., & Lakin, M. (1963). Patients' views of group psychotherapy: Retrospections and interpretations. *International Journal of Group Psychotherapy, 13,* 61–73.

Lietzel, C.S., & Abeles, N. (1975). Client–therapist complementarity and therapeutic outcome. *Journal of Counseling Psychology, 22,* 264–272.

DiLoreto, A.O. (1971). *Comparative psychotherapy: An experimental analysis.* Chicago: Aldine-Atherton.

Dorfman, E. (1958). Personality outcomes of client-centered child therapy. *Psychological Monographs, 72,* Whole No. 456.

Dreiblatt, I.S., & Weatherly, D. (1965). An evaluation of the efficacy of brief-contact therapy with hospitalized psychiatric patients. *Journal of Consulting Psychology, 29,* 513–519.

Dymond, R.F., Grummon, D.L., & Seeman, J. (1956). Patterns of perceived interpersonal relations. *Sociometry, 19,* 166–177.

Eisenberg, G.M. (1981). Midtherapy training: Extending the present system of pretherapy training. *Dissertation Abstracts International, 41,* 2754B.

Elliott, R., Barker, C.B., Caskey, N., & Pistrang, N. (1982). Differential helpfulness of counselor verbal response modes. *Journal of Counseling Psychology, 29,* 354–361.

Ends, E.J., & Page, C.W. (1959). Group psychotherapy and concomitant psychological change. *Psychological Monographs, 73,* Whole No. 480.

Errera, P., McKee, B., Smith, C., & Gruber, R. (1967).

Length of psychotherapy. *Archives of General Psychiatry, 17,* 454–458.

Eysenck, H.J. (1952). The effects of psychotherapy: An evaluation. *Journal of Consulting Psychology, 16,* 319–324.

Feifel, H., & Eells, J. (1963). Patients and therapists assess the same psychotherapy. *Journal of Consulting Psychology, 27,* 310–318.

Feitel, B. (1968). *Feeling understood as a function of a variety of therapist activities.* Unpublished doctoral dissertation, Teachers' College, Columbia University.

Feldman, R., Lorr, M., & Russell, S.B. (1958). A mental hygiene clinic case survey. *Journal of Clinical Psychology, 14,* 245–250.

Fiske, D.W., Cartwright, D.S., & Kirtner, W.L. (1964). Are psychotherapeutic changes predictable? *Journal of Abnormal and Social Psychology, 69,* 418–426.

Frank, J.D. (1974). Psychotherapy: The restoration of morale. *American Journal of Psychiatry, 131,* 271–274.

Frank, J.D., Gliedman, L.H., Imber, S.D., Stone, A.R., & Nash, E.H. (1959). Patients' expectancies and relearning as factors determining improvement in psychotherapy. *American Journal of Psychiatry, 115,* 961–968.

Freud, S. (1912/1963). The dynamics of the transference. In P. Rieff (Ed.), *Therapy and technique.* New York: Macmillan Collier Books.

Friedlander, M.L. (1981). The effects of delayed role induction on counseling process and outcome. *Dissertation Abstracts International, 41,* 3887–3888B.

Gadaleto, A.I.F. (1977). Differential effects of fidelity in client pretraining on client anxiety, self-disclosure, satisfaction and outcome. *Dissertation Abstracts International, 38,* 2503B.

Gaffin, G.L. (1981). Client–therapist complementarity as it relates to the process and outcome of psychotherapy. *Dissertation Abstracts International, 42,* 1603B.

Garfield, S.L. (1978). Research on client variables in psychotherapy. In S.L. Garfield & A.E. Bergin (Eds.), *Handbook of psychotherapy and behavior change* (2nd ed.). New York: Wiley.

Garfield, S.L., & Affleck, D.C. (1959). An appraisal of duration of stay in outpatient psychotherapy. *Journal of Nervous and Mental Disease, 129,* 492–498.

Garfield, S.L., & Bergin, A.E. (1971). Therapeutic conditions and outcome. *Journal of Abnormal Psychology, 77,* 108–114.

Garfield, S.L., & Kurz, M. (1952). Evaluation of treatment and related procedures in 1,216 cases referred to a mental hygiene clinic. *Psychiatric Quarterly, 26,* 414–424.

Garfield, S.L., Prager, R.A., & Bergin, A.E. (1971). Evaluation of outcome in psychotherapy. *Journal of Consulting and Clinical Psychology, 37,* 307–313.

Gelder, M.G., & Marks, I.M. (1966). Severe agoraphobia: A controlled prospective trial of behaviour therapy. *British Journal of Psychiatry, 112,* 309–319.

Gelder, M.G., Marks, I.M., Wolff, H.H., & Clarke, M. (1967). Desensitization and psychotherapy in the treatment of phobic states: A controlled inquiry. *British Journal of Psychiatry, 113,* 53–73.

Gendlin, E.T., Jenney, R.H., & Shlien, J.M. (1960). Counselor ratings of process and outcome in client-centered therapy. *Journal of Clinical Psychology, 16,* 210–213.

Goffmann, E. (1961). *Role distance. Encounters: Two studies in the sociology of interaction.* Indianapolis: Bobbs-Merrill.

Gomes-Schwartz, B.A. (1978). Effective ingredients in psychotherapy: Prediction of outcomes from process variables. *Journal of Consulting and Clinical Psychology, 46,* 1023–1035.

Gomez, E.A. (1982). The evaluation of psychosocial casework services to Chicanos: A study of process and outcome. *Dissertation Abstracts International, 43: 3A,* 925.

Gordon, T., & Cartwright, D.S. (1954). The effect of psychotherapy on certain attitudes toward others. In C. Rogers & R.F. Dymond (Eds.), *Psychotherapy and personality change.* Chicago: University of Chicago Press.

Gottschalk, L.A., Mayerson, P., & Gottlieb, A.A. (1967). Prediction and evaluation of outcome in an emergency brief psychotherapy clinic. *Journal of Nervous and Mental Disease, 144,* 77–96.

Graham, S.R. (1958). Patient evaluation of the effectiveness of limited psychoanalytically-oriented psychotherapy. *Psychological Reports, 4,* 231–234.

Greenberg, L.S., & Dompierre, L.M. (1981). Specific effects of Gestalt two-chair dialogue on intrapsychic conflict in counseling. *Journal of Counseling Psychology, 28,* 288–294.

Greenberg, L.S., & Rice, L.N. (1981). The specific effects of a Gestalt intervention. *Psychotherapy: Theory, Research and Practice, 18,* 31–37.

Greenberg, L.S., & Webster, M.C. (1982). Resolving decisional conflict by Gestalt two-chair dialogue: Relating process to outcome. *Journal of Counseling Psychology, 29,* 468–477.

Grigg, A. E., & Goodstein, L.D. (1957). The use of clients as judges of the counselor's performance. *Journal of Counseling Psychology, 4,* 31–36.

Gross, W.F., & DeRidder, L.M. (1966). Significant movement in comparatively short-term counseling. *Journal of Counseling Psychology, 13,* 98–99.

Haimowitz, N.R., & Haimowitz, M.L. (1952). Personality changes in client centered therapy. In W. Wolff & J.A. Precher (Eds.), *Success in psychotherapy.* New York: Grune & Stratton.

Halkides, G. (1958). *An experimental study of four conditions necessary for therapeutic change.* Unpublished doctoral dissertation, University of Chicago.

Hansen, J.C., Moore, G.D., & Carkhuff, R.R. (1968). The differential relationships of objective and client perceptions of counseling. *Journal of Clinical Psychology, 24,* 244–246.

Hansen, J.C., Zimpfer, D.G., & Easterling, R.E. (1967). A study of the relationships in multiple counseling. *Journal of Educational Research, 60,* 461–463.

Hargreaves, W.A., Showstack, J., Flohr, R., Brady, C., & Harris, S. (1974). Treatment acceptance following intake assignment to individual therapy, group therapy, or contact group. *Archives of General Psychiatry, 31,* 343–349.

Hartley, D.E., & Strupp, H.H. (1983). The therapeutic alliance: Its relationship to outcome in brief psychotherapy. In J. Masling (Ed.), *Empirical studies of psychoanalytical theories* (Vol. 1). Hillsdale, NJ: The Analytic Press.

Hayward, R.H. (1974). Process and outcome consequences of therapist self-disclosure. *Dissertation Abstracts International, 34,* 6210–6211B.

Heilbrunn, G. (1966). Results with psychoanalytic therapy and professional commitment. *American Journal of Psychotherapy, 20,* 89–99.

Heine, R.W. (1950). *An investigation of the relationship between change in personality from psychotherapy as reported in patients and the factors seen by patients as producing change.* Unpublished doctoral dissertation, University of Chicago.

Heinicke, C.M. (1969). Frequency of psychotherapeutic sessions as a factor affecting outcome: Analysis of clinical ratings and test results. *Journal of Abnormal Psychology, 74,* 553–560.

Henry, W.E., & Shlien, J. (1958). Affective complexity and psychotherapy: Some comparisons of time-limited and unlimited treatment. *Journal of Projective Techniques, 22,* 153–162.

Herz, M.I., Spitzer, R.L., Gibbon, M., Greenspan, K., & Reibel, S. (1974). Individual vs. group aftercare treatment. *American Journal of Psychiatry, 131,* 808–812.

Hobbs, G.W. (1978). A program evaluation of individual and group psychotherapy in a unversity counseling center. *Dissertation Abstracts International, 38,* 5572B.

Hoehn-Saric, R., Frank, J.D., Imber, S.D., Nash, E.H., Stone, A.R., & Battle, C.C. (1964). Systematic preparation of patients for psychotherapy: 1. Effects on therapy behavior and outcome. *Journal of Psychiatric Research, 2,* 267–281.

Hoehn-Saric, R., Leiberman, B., Imber, S.D., Stone, A.R., Pande, S.K., & Frank, J.D. (1972). Arousal and attitude change in neurotic patients. *Archives of General Psychiatry, 26,* 51–56.

Holland, S. (1983). Evaluation of community-based treatment programmes: A model for strengthening inferences about effectiveness. *International Journal of Therapeutic Communities, 4,* 285–306.

Holly, D.T. (1983). The relationship of couples' collaborative and adversarial behaviors to outcomes in marital therapy. *Dissertation Abstracts International, 43,* 2339B.

Horenstein, D. (1974). The effects of confirmation or disconfirmation of client expectations upon subsequent psychotherapy. *Dissertation Abstracts International, 34,* 6211B.

Howard, K.I., & Orlinsky, D.E. (1972). Psychotherapeutic processes. *Annual Review of Psychology, 23,* 615–668.

Howard, K.I., Kopta, S.M., Krause, M.S., & Orlinsky, D.E. (1986). The dose-effect relationship in psychotherapy. *American Psychologist, 41,* 159–164.

Hunt, J. McV., Ewing, T.N., LaForge, R., & Gilbert, W.M. (1959). An integrated approach to research on therapeutic counseling, with samples of results. *Journal of Counseling Psychology, 6,* 46–54.

Imber, S.D., Frank, J.D., Nash, E.H., Stone, A.R., & Gliedman, L.H. (1957). Improvement and amount of therapeutic contact: An alternative to the use of no-treatment controls in psychotherapy. *Journal of Consulting Psychology, 21,* 309–315.

Jacobs, D., Charles, E., Jacobs, T., Weinstein, H., & Mann, D. (1972). Preparation for psychotherapy of the disadvantaged patient. *American Journal of Orthopsychiatry, 42,* 666–674.

Jacobs, M.A., & Warner, B.L. (1981). Interaction of therapeutic attitudes with severity of clinical diagnosis. *Journal of Clinical Psychology, 37,* 75–82.

Jeske, J.O. (1973). Identification and therapeutic effectiveness in group therapy. *Journal of Counseling Psychology, 20,* 528–530.

Johnson, D.J. (1971). The effect of confrontation in counseling. *Dissertation Abstracts International, 32,* 180A.

Johnson, R.W. (1965). Number of interviews, diagnosis and success of counseling. *Journal of Counseling Psychology, 12,* 248–251.

Jones, E.E., & Zoppel, C.L. (1982). Impact of client and therapist gender on psychotherapy process and outcome. *Journal of Consulting & Clinical Psychology, 50,* 259–272.

Kalfas, N.S. (1974). Client-perceived therapist empathy as a correlate of outcome. *Dissertation Abstracts International, 34,* 5633A.

Kapp, F.T., Gleser, G., Bessenden, A., Emerson, R., Winget, J., & Kashdan, B. (1964). Group participation and self-perceived personality change. *Journal of Nervous and Mental Disease, 139,* 255–265.

Karle, W., Corriere, R., Hart, J., & Klein, J. (1981). The Personal Orientation Inventory and the Eysenck Personality Inventory as outcome measures in a private outpatient clinic. *Psychotherapy: Theory, Research & Practice, 18,* 117–122.

Kaschak, E. (1978). Therapist and client: Two views of the process and outcome of psychotherapy. *Professional Psychology,* May, 271–277.

Kaufman, I., Frank, T., Friend, J., Heims, L.W., & Weiss, R. (1962). Success and failure in the treatment of childhood schizophrenia. *American Journal of Psychiatry, 118,* 909–913.

Kernberg, O.F. (1976). Some methodological and strategic issues in psychotherapy research: Research implications of the Menninger Foundation's psychotherapy research project. In R.L. Spitzer & D.F. Klien (Eds.), *Evaluation of psychological therapies.* Baltimore: Johns Hopkins University Press.

Kernberg, O.F., Bernstein, C.S., Coyne, R., Appelbaum, D.A., Horwitz, H., & Voth, T.J. (1972). Psychotherapy and psychoanalysis: Final report of the Menninger Foundation's psychotherapy research project. *Bulletin of the Menninger Clinic, 36,* 1–276.

Kiesler, D.J. (1971). Patient experiencing and successful outcome in individual psychotherapy of schizophrenics and psychoneurotics. *Journal of Consulting and Clinical Psychology, 37,* 370–385.

Kiesler, D.J., Klein, M.H., Mathieu, P.L., & Schoeninger, D. (1967a). Constructive personality changes for therapy and control patients. In C.R. Rogers, E.T. Gendlin, D.J. Kiesler, & C.B. Truax (Eds.), *The therapeutic relationship and its impact: A study of psychotherapy with schizophrenics.* Madison: University of Wisconsin Press.

Kiesler, D.J., Mathieu, P., & Klein, M.H. (1967b). Process movement in therapy and sampling interviews. In C.R. Rogers, E.T. Gendlin, D.J. Kiesler, & C.B. Truax (Eds.), *The therapeutic relationship and its impact: A study of psychotherapy with schizophrenics.* Madison: University of Wisconsin Press.

Kirtner, W.L., & Cartwright, D.S. (1958). Success and failure in client-centered therapy as a function of initial in-therapy behavior. *Journal of Consulting Psychology, 22,* 329–333.

Kohut, H. (1984). *How does analysis cure?* Chicago: University of Chicago Press.

Kolb, D.L. (1982). An examination of process and outcome: The roles of patient locus of control, perception of the quality of the therapeutic relationship and involvement in therapy. *Dissertation Abstracts International, 42,* 4581B.

Kreisberg, G.J. (1978). The relationship of the congruence of patient–therapist goal expectancies to psychotherapy outcome and duration of treatment. *Dissertation Abstracts International, 38,* 3890B.

Kurtz, R.R., & Grummon, D.L. (1972). Different approaches to the measurement of therapist empathy and their relationship to therapy outcome. *Journal of Consulting and Clinical Psychology, 39,* 106–115.

Landfield, A.W. (1971). *Personal construct systems in psychotherapy.* Chicago: Rand McNally.

Lerner, B. (1972). *Therapy in the ghetto.* Baltimore: Johns Hopkins University Press.

Lesser, W.M. (1961). The relationship between counseling progress and empathic understanding. *Journal of Counseling Psychology, 8,* 330–336.

Liberman, B.L., Frank, J.D., Hoehn-Saric, R., Stone, A.R., Imber, S.D., & Pande, S.K. (1972). Patterns of change in treated psychoneurotic patients: A five-year follow-up investigation of the systematic preparation of patients for psychotherapy. *Journal of Consulting and Clinical Psychology, 38,* 36–41.

Lindsey, C.J., Martin, P.J., & Moore, J.E. (1976). Therapists' expectancies and treatment outcome: Some overlooked factors. *Psychological Reports, 38,* 1235–1238.

Lipkin, S. (1954). Clients' feelings and attitudes in relation to the outcome of client-centered therapy. *Psychological Monographs, 68,* Whole No. 372.

Lorr, M. (1965). Client perceptions of therapists: A study of the therapeutic relation. *Journal of Consulting Psychology, 29,* 146–149.

Lorr, M., & McNair, D.M. (1964a). Correlates of length of psychotherapy. *Journal of Clinical Psychology, 20,* 497–504.

Lorr, M., & McNair, D.M. (1964b). The interview relationship in therapy. *Journal of Nervous and Mental Disease, 139,* 328–331.

Lorr, M., McNair, D.M., Michaux, W., & Raskin, A. (1962). Frequency of treatment and change in psychotherapy. *Journal of Abnormal and Social Psychology, 64,* 281–292.

Luborsky, L. (1984). *Principles of psychoanalytic psychotherapy.* New York: Basic Books.

Luborsky, L., Mintz, J., Auerbach, A., Christoph, P., Bachrach, H., Todd, T., Johnson, M., Cohen, M., & O'Brien, E.P. (1980). Predicting the outcome of psychotherapy: Findings of the Penn Psychotherapy Project. *Archives of General Psychiatry, 37,* 471–481.

Luborsky, L., Mintz, J., & Christoph, P. (1979). Are psychotherapeutic changes predictable? Comparison of a Chicago counseling center project with a Penn Psychotherapy Project. *Journal of Consulting and Clinical Psychology, 47,* 469–473.

Magnelli, R.G. (1976). An investigation of the role of personal construct systems and empathy in the psycho-

therapeutic relationship. *Dissertation Abstracts International, 37,* 468B.

Mainord, W.A., Burk, H.W., & Collins, L.G. (1965). Confrontation vs. diversion in group therapy with chronic schizophrenics as measured by a "positive incident" criterion. *Journal of Clinical Psychology, 21,* 222–225.

Malan, D.H. (1976). *Toward the validation of dynamic psychotherapy.* London: Plenum.

Martin, P.J., Hunter, M.L., Guhr, K.E., & Acree, N.J. (1977). Therapists' expectancies and patients' improvement in treatment: The slope of the link. *Psychological Reports, 40,* 443–453.

Martin, P.J., & Sterne, A.L. (1975). Prognostic expectations and treatment outcome. *Journal of Consulting and Clinical Psychology, 43,* 572–576.

Martin, P.J., & Sterne, A.L. (1976a). Post-hospital adjustment as related to therapists' in-therapy behavior. *Psychotherapy: Theory, Research and Practice, 13,* 267–273.

Martin, P.J., & Sterne, A.L. (1976b). Subjective objectivity: Therapists' affection and successful psychotherapy. *Psychological Reports, 38,* 1163–1169.

Marziali, E. (1984). Prediction of outcome of brief psychotherapy from therapist interpretive interventions. *Archives of General Psychiatry, 41,* 301–304.

Marziali, E., Marmar, C., & Krupnick, J. (1981). Therapeutic alliance scales: Development and relationship to psychotherapeutic outcome. *American Journal of Psychiatry, 138,* 361–364.

May, J.M. (1984). *Number of sessions and psychotherapy outcome: Impact on community mental health center services.* Unpublished doctoral dissertation. Loyola University of Chicago.

McClanahan, L.D. (1974). Comparison of counseling techniques and attitudes with client evaluation of the counseling relationship. *Dissertation Abstracts International, 34,* 5637A.

McDaniel, S.H., Stiles, W.B., & McGaughey, K.J. (1981). Correlations of male college students' verbal response mode use in psychotherapy with measures of psychological disturbance and psychotherapy outcome. *Journal of Consulting and Clincal Psychology, 49,* 571–582.

McNair, D.M., & Lorr, M. (1960). Therapists' judgments of appropriateness of psychotherapy frequency schedules. *Journals of Consulting Psychology, 24,* 500–506.

McNair, D.M., Lorr, M., Young, H.H., Roth, I.I., & Boyd, R.W. (1964). A three-year follow-up of psychotherapy patients. *Journal of Clinical Psychology, 20,* 258–264.

McNally, H.A. (1973). An investigation of selected counselor and client characteristics as possible predictors of counseling effectiveness. *Dissertation Abstracts International, 33,* 6672–6673A.

Mead, G.H. (1956). Self. In A. Strauss (Ed.), *The social psychology of George Herbert Mead.* Chicago: University of Chicago Press.

Melnick, B., & Pierce, R.M. (1971). Client evaluation of therapist strength and positive–negative evaluation as related to client dymanics, objective ratings of competence and outcome. *Journal of Clinical Psychology, 27,* 408–410.

Mendola, J.J. (1982). Therapist interpersonal skills: A

model for professional development and therapeutic effectiveness. *Dissertation Abstracts International, 42*, 4201B.

Menninger, K. (1958). *Theory of psychoanalytic technique.* New York: Basic Books.

Mensh, I., & Golden, J. (1951). Factors in psychotherapeutic success. *Journal of the Missouri State Medical Association, 48*, 180–184.

Miles, H.W., Barrabee, E.L., & Finesinger, J.E. (1951). Evaluation of psychotherapy, with a follow-up of 62 cases of anxiety neuroses. *Psychosomatic Medicine, 13*, 83–105.

Mintz, J. (1981). Measuring outcome in psychodynamic psychotherapy. *Archives of General Psychiatry, 38*, 503–506.

Mintz, J., Luborsky, L., & Auerbach, A. (1971). Dimensions of psychotherapy: A factor-analytic study of ratings of psychotherapy sessions. *Journal of Consulting and Clinical Psychology, 36*, 106–120.

Mitchell, K., Bozarth, J., Truax, C., & Krauft, C. (1973). *Antecedents to psychotherapeutic outcome.* Arkansas Rehabilitation Research and Training Center, University of Arkansas (NIMH Final Report, MH 12306).

Mitchell, R.M. (1971). Relationship between therapist response to therapist-relevant client expressions and therapy process and client outcome. *Dissertation Abstracts International, 32*, 1853B.

Morgan, R., Luborsky, L., Crits-Christoph, P., Curtis, H., & Solomon, J. (1982). Predicting the outcomes of psychotherapy by the Penn Helping Alliance Rating Method. *Archives of General Psychiatry, 39*, 397–402.

Morrison, J.K., Libow, J.A., Smith, F.J., & Becker, R.R. (1978). Comparative effectiveness of directive *vs.* nondirective group therapist style on client problem resolution. *Journal of Clinical Psychology, 34*, 186–187.

Morrison, T.L., & Newcomer, B.L. (1975). Effects of directive vs. non-directive play therapy with institutionalized mentally retarded children. *American Journal of Mental Deficiency, 79*, 666–669.

Muench, G.A. (1965). An investigation of the efficacy of time-limited psychotherapy. *Journal of Counseling Psychology, 12*, 294–299.

Mullen, J., & Abeles, N. (1971). Relationship of liking, empathy, and therapist's experience to outcome of therapy. *Journal of Counseling Psychology, 18*, 39–43.

Munro, J.N., & Bach, T.R. (1975). Effect of time-limited counseling on client change. *Journal of Counseling Psychology, 22*, 395–398.

Nagy, T.F. (1973). Therapist level of functioning and change in clients' quantifiable anxiety level and verbal behavior. *Dissertation Abstracts International, 34*, 873–879B.

Newcomer, B.L., & Morrison, T.L. (1974). Play therapy with institutionalized mentally retarded children. *American Journal of Mental Deficiency, 78*, 727–733.

Newman, F.L., & Howard, K.I. (1986). Therapeutic effort, treatment outcome and national health policy. *American Psychologist, 41*, 181–187.

Nichols, M.P. (1974). Outcome of brief cathartic psychotherapy. *Journal of Consulting and Clinical Psychology, 42*, 403–410.

Nichols, R.C., & Beck, K.W. (1960). Factors in psycho-

therapy change. *Journal of Consulting Psychology, 24*, 388–399.

O'Brien, C.P., Hamm, K.B., Ray, B.A., Pierce, J.F., Luborsky, L., & Mintz, J. (1972). Group vs. individual psychotherapy with schizophrenics: A controlled outcome study. *Archives of General Psychiatry, 27*, 474–478.

Oclatis, K.A. (1978). The effects of patient feedback on the process and outcome of brief psychotherapy. *Dissertation Abstracts International, U*, 1119B.

O'Connor, J.F., Daniels, G., Flood, C., Karush, A., Moses, L., & Stern, L.G. (1964). An evaluation of the effectiveness of psychotherapy in the treatment of ulcerative colitis. *Annals of Internal Medicine, 60*, 587–602.

O'Malley, S.S. Suh, C.S., & Strupp, H.H. (1983). The Vanderbilt psychotherapy process scale: A report of the scale development and a process-outcome study. *Journal of Consulting and Clinical Psychology, 51*, 581–586.

Orlinsky, D.E., & Howard, K.I. (1975). *Varieties of psychotherapeutic experience.* New York: Teachers' College Press.

Orlinsky, D.E., & Howard, K.I. (1978). The relation of process to outcome in psychotherapy. In S.L. Garfield & A.E. Bergin (Eds.). *Handbook of psychotherapy and behavior change* (2nd ed.). New York: Wiley.

Orlinsky, D.E., & Howard, K.I. (1986). The psychological interior of psychotherapy: Explorations with the Therapy Session Reports. In L.S. Greenberg & W.M. Pinsof (Eds.), *The psychotherapeutic process: A research Handbook.* New York: Guilford Press.

Parloff, M.B. (1961). Therapist–patient relationships and outcome of psychotherapy. *Journal of Consulting Psychology, 25*, 29–38.

Parsons, T., (1964). Definitions of health and illness in the light of American values and social structure. In *Social Structure and Personality.* New York: The Free Press.

Patterson, V., Levene, H., & Breger, L. (1971). Treatment and training outcomes with two time limited therapies. *Archives of General Psychiatry, 25*, 161–167.

Peake, T.H. (1979). Therapist–patient agreement and outcome in group therapy. *Journal of Clinical Psychology, 35*, 637–646.

Peiser, I. (1982). Similarity, liking and missed sessions in relation to psychotherapy outcome. *Dissertation Abstracts International, 42*, 4587B.

Pierce, R.M., & Schauble, P.G. (1970). A note on the role of facilitative responsibility in the therapeutic relationship. *Journal of Clinical Psychology, 26*, 250–252.

Piper, W.E., Debbane, E.G., Bienvenu, J-P., & Garant, J. (1982). A study of group pretraining for group psychotherapy. *International Journal of Group Psychotherapy, 32*, 309–325.

Piper, W.E., Doan, B.D., Edwards, E.M., & Jones, B.D. (1979). Cotherapy behavior, group therapy process, and treatment outcome. *Journal of Consulting and Clinical Psychology, 47*, 1081–1089.

Pope, K.S., Geller, J.D., & Wilkinson, L. (1975). Fee assessment and outpatient psychotherapy. *Journal of Consulting and Clinical Psychology, 43*, 835–841.

Prager, R.A. (1971). The relationship of certain client

characteristics to therapist-offered conditions and therapeutic outcome. *Dissertation Abstracts International, 31,* 5634–5635B.

Reid, W.J., & Shyne, A.W. (1969). *Brief and extended casework.* New York: Columbia University Press.

Rice, L.N. (1965). Therapist's style of participation and case outcome. *Journal of Consulting Psychology, 29,* 155–160.

Rice, L.N. (1973). Client behavior as a function of therapist style and client resources. *Journal of Counseling Psychology, 20,* 306–311.

Rice, L.N., & Wagstaff, A.K. (1967). Client voice quality and expressive styles as indexes of productive psychotherapy. *Journal of Consulting Psychology, 31,* 557–563.

Rich, L.D. (1979). Effects of training clients to be ready for individual psychotherapy upon outcomes of psychotherapy. *Dissertation Abstracts International, 40,* 1382B.

Roback, H.B., & Strassberg, D.S. (1975). Relationship between perceived therapist-offered conditions and therapeutic movement in group psychotherapy. *Small Group Behavior, 6,* 345–352.

Roether, H.A., & Peters, J.J. (1972). Cohesiveness and hostility in group psychotherapy. *American Journal of Psychiatry, 128,* 1014–1017.

Rogers, C.R. (1957). The necessary and sufficient conditions of therapeutic personality change. *Journal of Consulting Psychology, 21,* 95–103.

Rogers, M.B.M. (1973). Therapists' verbalization and outcome in monitored play therapy. *Dissertation Abstracts International, 34,* 424B.

Rosenbaum, M., Friedlander, J., & Kaplan, S.M. (1956). Evaluation of results of psychotherapy. *Psychosomatic Medicine, 18,* 113–132.

Rosenman, S. (1955). Changes in the representation of self, other, and interrelationship in client-centered therapy. *Journal of Counseling Psychology, 2,* 271–278.

Rosenthal, D., & Frank, J.D. (1958). The fate of psychiatric clinic outpatients assigned to psychotherapy. *Journal of Nervous and Mental Disease, 127,* 330–343.

Rosenthal, A.J., & Levine, S.V. (1970). Brief psychotherapy with children: A preliminary report. *American Journal of Psychiatry, 127,* 646–651.

Roshal, J.G. (1953). The type-token ratio as a measure of changes in behavior variability during psychotherapy. In W.U. Snyder (Ed.), *Group report of a program of research in psychology.* State College, PA: Pennsylvania State College Press.

Ross, W.F., McReynolds, W.T., & Berzins, J.I. (1974). Effectiveness of marathon group psychotherapy with hospitalized female narcotic addicts. *Psychological Reports, 34,* 611–616.

Roth, I., Rhudick, P.J., Shaskan, D.A., Slobin, M.S., Wilkinson, A.E., & Young, H. (1964). Long-term effects on psychotherapy of initial treatment conditions. *Journal of Psychiatric Research, 2,* 283–297.

Rounsaville, B.J., Weissman, M.M., & Prusoff, B.A. (1981). Psychotherapy with depressed outpatients: Patient and process variables as predictors of outcome. *British Journal of Psychiatry, 138,* 67–74.

Rounsaville, B.J., Weissman, M.M., Prusoff, B.A., & Herceg-Baron, R. (1979). Process of psychotherapy among depressed women with marital disputes. *American Journal of Orthopsychiatry, 49,* 505–510.

Rucker, I.E.V. (1983). Counseling outcomes and perceived counselor social influence: Validity of the counselor rating form extended. *Dissertation Abstracts International, 43,* 2355–2356B.

Rudy, J.P. (1983). Predicting therapy outcome using Benjamins' structural analysis of social behavior. *Dissertation Abstracts International, 43,* 534B.

Ryan, V.L., & Gizynski, M.N. (1971). Behavior therapy in retrospect: Patients' feelings about their behavior therapies. *Journal of Consulting and Clinical Psychology, 37,* 1–9.

Ryle, A., & Lipshitz, S. (1976). An intensive case-study of a therapeutic group. *British Journal of Psychiatry, 128,* 581–588.

Sachs, J.S. (1983). Negative factors in brief psychotherapy: An empirical assessment. *Journal of Consulting and Clinical Psychology, 51,* 557–564.

Saltzman, C., Luetgert, M.J., Roth, C.H., Creaser, J., & Howard, L. (1976). Formation of a therapeutic relationship: Experiences during the initial phase of psychotherapy as predictors of treatment duration and outcome. *Journal of Consulting and Clinical Psychology, 44,* 546–555.

Sapolsky, A. (1965). Relationship between patient–doctor compatibility, mutual perceptions and outcome of treatment. *Journal of Abnormal Psychology, 70,* 70–76.

Schauble, P.G., & Pierce, R.M. (1974). Client in-therapy behavior: A therapist guide to progress. *Psychotherapy: Theory, Research and Practice, 11,* 229–234.

Scher, M. (1975). Verbal activity, sex, counselor experience, and success in counseling. *Journal of Counseling Psychology, 22,* 97–101.

Schmidt, M.M. (1982). Amount of therapist contact and outcome in a multimodel depression treatment program. *Dissertation Abstracts International, 42,* 3441B.

Schonfield, J., Stone, A.R., Hoehn-Saric, R., Imber, S.D., & Pande, S.K. (1969). Patient–therapist convergence and measures of improvement in short-term psychotherapy. *Psychotherapy: Theory, Research and Practice, 6,* 267–271.

Schroeder, P. (1960). Client acceptance of responsibility and difficulty of therapy. *Journal of Consulting Psychology, 24,* 264–271.

Scully, T.M. (1983). Strategic family therapy with conduct disordered children and adolescents: An outcome study. *Dissertation Abstracts International, 43,* 3042B.

Seeman, J. (1954). Counselor judgments of therapeutic process and outcome. In C. Rogers & R.F. Dymond (Eds.), *Psychotherapy and personality change.* Chicago: University of Chicago Press.

Seeman, L. (1978). Early improvement in family therapy and its relationship to engagement and outcome. *Dissertation Abstracts International, 39,* 398B.

Semon, R.G., & Goldstein, N. (1957). The effectiveness of group psychotherapy with chronic schizophrenic patients and an evaluation of different therapeutic methods. *Journal of Consulting Psychology, 21,* 317–322.

Shlien, J.M., Mosak, H.H., & Dreikurs, R. (1962) Effects of time limits: A comparison of two psychotherapies. *Journal of Counseling Psychology, 9,* 31–34.

Shyne, A.W., & Kogan, L.S. (1957). *A study of compo-*

nents of movement. New York: Institute of Welfare Research, Community Service Society.

Sloane, R.B., Cristol, A.H., Pepernik, M.C., & Staples, F.R. (1970). Role preparation and expectation of improvement in psychotherapy. *Journal of Nervous and Mental Disease, 150,* 18–26.

Sloane, R.B., Staples, F.R., Cristol, A.H., Yorkston, N.J., & Whipple, K. (1975). *Psychotherapy vs. behavior therapy.* Cambridge: Harvard University Press.

Smith, M.L., Glass, G.V., & Miller, T.I. (1980). *The benefits of psychotherapy.* Baltimore: Johns Hopkins University Press.

Standahl, S.W., & van der Veen, F. (1957). Length of therapy in relation to counselor estimates of personal integration and other case variables. *Journal of Consulting Psychology, 21,* 1–9.

Staples, F.R., & Sloane, R.B. (1976). Truax factors, speech characteristics, and therapeutic outcome. *Journal of Nervous and Mental Disease, 163,* 135–140.

Staples, F.R., Sloane, R.B., Whipple, K., Cristol, A.H., & Yorkston, N. (1976). Process and outcome in psychotherapy and behavior therapy. *Journal of Consulting and Clinical Psychology, 44,* 340–350.

Stieper, D.R., & Wiener, D.N. (1965). *Dimensions of psychotherapy.* Chicago: Aldine.

Stone, A.R., Frank, J.D., Nash, E.H., & Imber, S.D. (1961). An intensive five-year follow-up study of treated psychiatric outpatients. *Journal of Nervous and Mental Disease, 133,* 410–422.

Strassberg, D.S., Roback, H.B., Anchor, K.N., & Abramowitz, S. I. (1975). Self-disclosure in group therapy with schizophrenics. *Archives of General Psychiatry, 32,* 1259–1261.

Strupp, H.H., & Bloxom, A.L. (1973). Preparing lower class patients for group psychotherapy: Development and evaluation of a role-induction film. *Journal of Consulting and Clinical Psychology, 41,* 373–384.

Strupp, H.H., & Hadley, S.W. (1979). Specific vs. nonspecific factors in psychotherapy: A controlled study of outcome. *Archives of General Psychiatry, 36,* 1125–1136.

Strupp, H.H., Hadley, S.W., & Gomes-Schwartz, B. (1977). *Psychotherapy for better or worse.* New York: Jason Aronson.

Strupp, H.H., Wallach, M.L., & Wogan, M. (1964). The psychotherapy experience in retrospect: A questionnaire survey of former patients and their therapists. *Psychological Monographs, 78,* Whole number 11.

Strupp, H.H., Wallach, M.S., Wogan, M., & Jenkins, J.W. (1963). Psychotherapists' assessments of former patients. *Journal of Nervous and Mental Disease, 137,* 222–230.

Suh, C.S., O'Mally, S.S., & Strupp, H.H. (1986). The Vanderbilt process scale and the negative indicator scale. In L.S. Greenberg & W.M. Pinsof (Eds.), *The psychotherapeutic process: A research handbook.* New York: Guilford Press.

Sullivan, P.L., Miller, C., & Smelser, W. (1958). Factors in length of stay and progress in psychotherapy. *Journal of Consulting Psychology, 22,* 1–9.

Tausch, R., Eppel, H., Fittkau, B., & Minsel, W. (1969). Variablen und zusamenhange in der gesprachspsychotherapie. *Zeitschrift fur Psychologie, 176,* 93–102.

Tausch, R., Sander, K., Bastine, R., & Friese, H. (1970).

Variablen und ergebnisse bei client-centered psychotherapie mit alternierenden psychotherapeuten. *Sonderdruck aus Psychologische Rundschau, 21,* 29–37.

Taylor, J.W. (1956). Relationships of success and length in psychotherapy. *Journal of Consulting Psychology, 20,* 332.

Thorley, A.S., & Craske, N. (1950). Comparison and estimate of group and individual methods of treatment. *British Medical Journal, 1,* 97–100.

Tolman, R.S., & Meyer, M.M. (1957). Who returns to the clinic for more therapy? *Mental Hygiene, 41,* 497–506.

Tomlinson, T.M. (1967). The therapeutic process as related to outcome. In C.R. Rogers, E.T. Gendlin, D.J. Kiesler, & C.B. Truax (Eds.), *The therapeutic relationship and its impact: A study of psychotherapy with schizophrenics.* Madison: University of Wisconsin Press.

Tomlinson, T.M., & Hart, J.T., Jr. (1962). A validation study of the process scale. *Journal of Consulting Psychology, 26,* 74–78.

Tomlinson, T.M., & Stoler, N. (1967). The relationship between affective evaluation and ratings of therapy process and outcome with schizophrenics. *Psychotherapy: Theory, Research and Practice, 4,* 14–18.

Tovian, S.M. (1977). *Patient experiences and psychotherapy outcome.* Unpublished doctoral dissertation, Northwestern University.

Truax, C.B. (1963). Effective ingredients in psychotherapy: An approach to unraveling the patient–therapist interaction. *Journal of Counseling Psychology, 10,* 256–263.

Truax, C.B. (1966). Therapist empathy, warmth, and genuineness and patient personality change in group psychotherapy: A comparison between interaction unit measures, time sample measures, patient perception measures. *Journal of Clinical Psychology, 22,* 225–229.

Truax, C.B. (1968). Therapist interpersonal reinforcement of client self-explanatory and therapeutic outcome in group psychotherapy. *Journal of Counseling Psychology, 15,* 225–231.

Truax, C.B. (1970a). Therapist's evaluative statements and patient outcome in psychotherapy. *Journal of Clinical Psychology, 26,* 536–538.

Truax, C.B. (1970b). Length of therapist response, accurate empathy and patient improvement. *Journal of Clinical Psychology, 26,* 539–541.

Truax, C.B. (1970c). Effects of client-centered psychotherapy with schizophrenic patients: Nine years pretherapy and nine years post-therapy hospitalization. *Journal of Consulting and Clinical Psychology, 35,* 417–422.

Truax, C.B. (1971). Degree of negative transference occurring in group psychotherapy and client outcome in juvenile delinquents. *Journal of Clinical Psychology, 27,* 132–136.

Truax, C.B., Altman, H., Wright, L., & Mitchell, K.M. (1973). Effects of therapeutic conditions in child therapy. *Journal of Community Psychology, 1,* 313–318.

Truax, C.B., & Carkhuff, R.R. (1967). *Toward effective counseling and psychotherapy,* Chicago: Aldine.

Truax, C.B., Carkhuff, R.R., & Kodman, F., Jr. (1965). Relationships between therapist-offered conditions and patient change in group psychotherapy. *Journal of Clinical Psychology*, 21, 327–329.

Truax, C.B., Fine, H., Morane, J., & Millis, W. (1968). Effects of therapist persuasive potency in individual psychotherapy. *Journal of Clinical Psychology*, 24, 359–362.

Truax, C.B., & Lister, J.L. (1970). Effects of therapist persuasive potency in group psychotherapy. *Journal of Clinical Psychology*, 26, 396–397.

Truax, C.B., & Wargo, D.G. (1969). Effects of vicarious therapy pre-training and alternate sessions on outcome in group psychotherapy with outpatients. *Journal of Consulting and Clinical Psychology*, 33, 440–447.

Truax, C.B., Wargo, D.G., Frank, J.D., Imber, S.D., Battle, C.C., Hoehn-Saric, R., Nash, E.H., & Stone, A.R. (1966). Therapist empathy, genuineness, and warmth and patient therapeutic outcome. *Journal of Consulting Psychology*, 30, 395–401.

Truax, C.B., Wargo, D.G., & Volksdorf, N.R. (1970). Antecedents to outcome in group counseling with institutionalized juvenile deliquents: Effects of therapeutic conditions, patient self-exploration, alternate sessions, and vicarious therapy pretraining. *Journal of Abnormal Psychology*, 76, 235–242.

Truax, C.B., & Wittmer, J. (1971a). Effects of therapist's focus on patient anxiety source and the interaction with the therapist's level of accurate empathy. *Journal of Clinical Psychology*, 27, 297–299.

Truax, C.B., & Wittmer, J. (1971b). Patient non-personal reference during psychotherapy and therapeutic outcome. *Journal of Clinical Psychology*, 27, 300–302.

Truax, C.B., & Wittmer, J. (1973). The degree of the therapist's focus on defense mechanisms and the effect on therapeutic outcome with institutionalized juvenile delinquents. *Journal of Community Psychology*, 1, 201–203.

Truax, C.B., Wittmer, J., & Wargo, D.G. (1971). Effects of the therapeutic conditions of accurate empathy, non-possessive warmth, and genuineness on hospitalized mental patients during group therapy. *Journal of Clinical Psychology*, 27, 137–142.

Uhlenhuth, E.H., & Duncan, D.B. (1968). Subjective change with medical student therapists: I. Course of relief in psychoneurotic outpatients. *Archives of General Psychiatry*, 18, 428–438.

Uhlenhuth, E.H., & Duncan, D.B. (1968b). Subjective change with medical student therapists. II. Some determinants of change in psychoneurotic outpatients. *Archives of General Psychiatry*, 18, 532–540.

Ukeritis, M.D. (1978). A study of value convergence in a group psychotherapy setting. *Dissertation Abstracts International*, 39, 4488B.

van der Veen, F. (1967). Basic elements in the process of psychotherapy: A research study. *Journal of Consulting Psychology*, 31, 295–303.

van der Veen, F., & Stoler, N. (1965). Therapist judgments, interview behavior and case outcome. *Psychotherapy: Theory, Research and Practice*, 2, 158–163.

Van Slambrouck, S. (1973). Relation of structural parameters to treatment outcome. *Dissertation Abstracts International*, 33, 5528B.

Vargas, M.J. (1954). Changes in self-awareness during client-centered therapy. In C.R. Rogers & R. F. Dymond (Eds.), *Psychotherapy and personality change*. Chicago: University of Chicago Press.

Walker, A., Rablen, R.A., & Rogers, C.R. (1960). Development of a scale to measure process change in psychotherapy. *Journal of Clinical Psychology*, 16, 79–85.

Wargo, D.G., Millis, W.E., & Hendricks, N.G. (1971). Patient rational verbal behavior as an antecedent to outcome in psychotherapy. *Psychotherapy: Theory, Research and Practice*, 8, 199–201.

Warren, N.C., & Rice, L.N. (1972). Structuring and stabilizing psychotherapy for low-prognosis clients. *Journal of Consulting and Clinical Psychology*, 39, 173–181.

Waterhouse, G.C.J. (1982). Countertransference in short-term psychotherapy: Interpersonal diagnosis and reciprocal response. *Dissertation Abstracts International*, 42, 4218B.

Weiner, M.B., & Weinstock, C.S. (1973). The effects of a resocialization program on cognitive and physical functioning in an elderly population. Paper presented at the 81st annual meeting of The American Psychological Association, Montreal, Canada.

Weitz, L.J., Abramowitz, S.I., Steger, J.A., Calabria, F.M., Conable, M., & Yorus, G. (1975). Number of sessions and client-judged outcome: The more the better? *Psychotherapy: Theory, Research and Practice*, 12, 337–340.

Werman, D.S., Agle, D., McDaniel, E., & Schoof, K.G. (1976). Survey of psychiatric treatment effectiveness in a medical student clinic. *American Journal of Psychotherapy*, 30, 294–302.

Wogan, M. (1970). Effect of therapist-patient personality variables on therapeutic outcome. *Journal of Consulting and Clinical Psychology*, 35, 356–361.

Wogan, M., Getter, H., Amdur, M.J., Nichols, M.F., & Okman, G. (1977). Influencing interaction and outcomes in group psychotherapy. *Small Group Behavior*, 8, 25–46.

Yalom, I.D., Houts, P.S., Zimerberg, S.M., & Rand, K.H. (1967). Prediction of improvement in group therapy. *Archives of General Psychiatry*, 17, 159–168.

Zarchan, D. (1978). Effects of social class and role-induction on drop out, expectations, and attraction in outpatient psychotherapy. *Dissertation Abstracts International*, 39, 1914B.

Zeiss, A.M., Lewinsohn, P.M., & Munoz, R.F. (1979). Nonspecific improvement effects in depression using interpersonal, cognitive and pleasant events focused treatments. *Journal of Consulting and Clinical Psychology*, 47, 427–439.

Zirkle, G.A. (1961). Five minute psychotherapy. *American Journal of Psychiatry*, 118, 544–546.

PART III

BEHAVIORAL AND COGNITIVE THERAPIES

9

BEHAVIOR THERAPY WITH ADULTS

PAUL M.G. EMMELKAMP

Academic Hospital
Department of Clinical Psychology
Groningen

INTRODUCTION

While in the early days behavior therapy was defined as the application of "established laws of learning," or was viewed to be based on "modern learning theories," more recently behavior therapy has become broader in its conceptualization. The claim that established behavior therapy procedures (e.g., aversion therapies and systematic desensitization) are exclusively based on learning paradigms seems nowadays no longer tenable. The experimental literature does not support such a claim, rather it shows that additional factors such as cognitive processes (e.g., expectancy) play an important role (Emmelkamp, 1982a; Emmelkamp & Walta, 1978). Some behavior therapists now rely heavily on mediational concepts in explaining the effects of the therapeutic procedures (Bandura, 1977). This trend has even led to the development of a new school of behavior therapists; several books on cognitive-behavior therapy have already appeared, and two journals are devoted entirely to the cognitive-behavioral approach—*Journal of Cognitive Psychotherapy* and *Cognitive Therapy and Research*.

At present at least four schools of behavior therapists can be distinguished. There are first, those therapists who still view behavior therapy as the application of "learning theory," second, others who rely heavily on mediational concepts and a third school that comprises technical eclecticists or multimodal behavior therapists, who use whatever technique seems to work. Finally, a category of workers view behavior therapy as an experimental-clinical approach. The latter group does not adhere to one specific theory, but stresses the necessity of testing theories and evaluating treatment with real clinical patients as subjects. Thus, this behavioral approach is characterized by its emphasis on methodology instead of by a specific theoretical orientation. This is not to say that learning theories or cognitive theories have been abandoned by the proponents of the experimental-clinical approach; rather they hold that their status as explanatory principles to explain the development and treatment of disorders must be empirically verified with clinical patients rather than taken for granted.

Behavior therapy would best proceed unencumbered by parochial adherence to one specific theory. In the author's view, behavioral theories and therapies should be based on experimental evidence with real clinical patients rather than on orthodoxy or faith.

In this chapter the emphasis will be on studies using clinical patients as subjects. A number of studies have evaluated treatment procedures with *non*clinical subjects, especially in the area of depression and anxiety disorders. Typically, mildly distressed volunteers, usually students, are invited to participate in a therapy-outcome study. The external validity, that is, the extent to which results of analogue studies can be generalized to clinical populations, is still a matter of dispute (Borkovec & Rachman, 1979; Emmelkamp, 1982a; Kazdin, 1978).

Kazdin (1978) has argued that any psychotherapy-outcome study will be an analogue by the very nature of experimental research. Rather than dichotomizing therapy-outcome studies into analogue or nonanalogue research, Kazdin (1978) pointed out that laboratory analogue research may differ from clinical treatment along several dimensions (e.g., target problems, manner in which clients are recruited, therapists, treatment and assessment procedures).

Subject samples consisting only of slightly distressed individuals are quite susceptible to experimental demand (e.g., Emmelkamp & Boeke, 1977) and decrease the chances that the results of such experiments will generalize to actual clinical populations. In the area of anxiety disorder, a number of researchers (e.g., Borkovec & Rachman, 1979) argue that generalizing from analogue to clinical subjects is more likely to succeed when samples show comparably intense anxiety responses.

While comparable intensity of distress may facilitate generalizing from analogue to clinical studies, there are several other important differences between clinical and analogue populations that may preclude generalization of findings on normal college students to a clinical population. First, patients who apply for treatment in a clinical setting differ from normal controls and phobic or depressed students (the typical subjects of analogue therapy research) on various measures of psychopathology (Branham & Katahn, 1974; Chambless, Hunter & Jackson, 1982; Hall & Goldberg, 1977; Olley & McAllister, 1974). Second, subjects in analogue and clinical studies may differ with respect to motivation (Borkovec & Rachman, 1979). Third, in the area of

anxiety disorders, the type of target problem treated in clinical studies and analogue studies differs widely. While analogue researchers have typically employed students with small animal phobias, dating anxiety, or public speaking anxiety as subjects, agoraphobia forms the greatest category of phobias seen in clinical settings. Generalizing from findings on socially anxious analogue subjects to agoraphobia may be more risky than generalizing to social phobics (Emmelkamp, Mersch, & Vissia, 1985b).

Scope Of The Chapter

This chapter provides an overview of the current status of behavior therapy with adult disorders. Emphasis throughout will be on the application of behavioral procedures on clinical patients. Since separate chapters in this volume are devoted to behavioral medicine and behavior therapy with children, these topics will not be dealt with in this chapter. Cognitive interventions are covered only insofar as these procedures are contrasted with behavioral procedures or form an integral part of cognitive-behavioral procedures. For a more detailed discussion of cognitive therapy, the reader is referred to the chapter by Hollon and Beck.

The research on behavior therapy with adults has proliferated to such an extent that it is impossible to provide a comprehensive review of the whole area in one chapter. Since the last edition of this *Handbook*, significant progress has been made in a number of areas, although the development of effective behavioral treatments has advanced in an uneven fashion. Therefore, the scope of this chapter is limited to those disorders where the behavioral approach has been most influential. This chapter will review the state of the art of current behavioral approaches to anxiety disorders, depression, alcoholism, sexual dysfunctions, paraphilias, and marital distress. Recent comprehensive reviews of other areas can be found in Bellack, Hersen, and Kazdin (1982), Foa and Emmelkamp (1983) and in two review series: *Progress in Behavior Modification* and *Annual Review of Behavior Therapy*.

ANXIETY DISORDERS

During the last 20 years a great number of procedures have been developed that aim at reducing anxiety, such as systematic desensitization, flooding, exposure in vivo, covert reinforcement, (covert) modeling, and anxiety management procedures. It is impossible, however, to deal with all of these within the scope of this chapter. For a critical review the reader is referred to Emmelkamp (1982a).

The element that most of these treatments have in common is exposure to distressing stimuli. Exposure can be carried out in two ways: (1) in imagination, in which patients must imagine themselves to be in a certain anxiety-arousing situation, or (2) in vivo, in which the patient is really exposed to the situation. Exposure in vivo is usually more effective than exposure in imagination (Emmelkamp & Wessels, 1975). Other important variables in exposure treatments are the degree of anxiety and the duration of exposure trials. Exposure can be either self-controlled (as in systematic desensitization in which the patient himself decides when to begin on a more difficult item), or controlled by the therapist, such as in flooding or prolonged exposure in vivo. Sometimes additional components are added to the exposure. In systematic desensitization, relaxation is added to exposure for distressing stimuli. There is no evidence, though, that relaxation is essential to a successful treatment (Emmelkamp, 1982a). Modeling, the showing of approach behavior by the therapist or someone else in anxious situations, also appears to add little to the effect of exposure itself.

The most successful exposure programs are those carried out in vivo, during a longer uninterrupted period of time (prolonged), and in which escape and avoidance of the phobic situation is prevented (Emmelkamp, 1982a). A number of complaints remain in which it is difficult or impossible to realize exposure in vivo, and here methods using imagery may be of help (e.g., thunderstorm phobia).

In this section, research into the effects of treatment with clinical patients will be discussed. A detailed review is provided of the effectiveness of clinical treatments on agoraphobia, social anxiety, simple phobias, generalized anxiety disorder, panic disorder, and obsessive-compulsive disorder.

Agoraphobia

Systematic research programs carried out over the last 15 years have significantly enhanced our knowledge over optimal treatment conditions for agoraphobics. Detailed reviews have been provided elsewhere (Emmelkamp, 1982a, 1982b; Mathews, Gelder, & Johnston, 1982); here only the main findings will be summarized.

1. *Prolonged exposure in vivo is superior to imaginal exposure.* Most studies that investigated this issue found exposure in vivo superior to imaginal exposure (Emmelkamp, 1974; Emmelkamp & Wessels, 1975; Stern & Marks, 1973; Watson, Mullett, & Pilley, 1973). Mathews et al. (1976) found both procedures about equally effective, but their imaginal procedure involved exposure in vivo homework assignments.

2. *Prolonged exposure in vivo is superior to brief exposure.* Stern and Marks (1973) compared short (four half-hour sessions) with long (two-hour) sessions. Prolonged exposure in vivo sessions were clearly superior to shorter ones.

3. *Group exposure is about equally effective as individually conducted exposure programs.* There are now a number of studies attesting to the clinical effectiveness of exposure in vivo programs conducted in groups (e.g., Emmelkamp, Kuipers, & Eggeraat, 1978; Emmelkamp & Mersch, 1982; Emmelkamp, Brilman, Kuipers, & Mersch, 1986). Studies comparing individual and group exposure in vivo found no clear differences in effectiveness (Emmelkamp & Emmelkamp-Benner, 1975; Hafner & Marks, 1976). Besides the aspect of saving therapist time, groups may provide the patient with coping models and may lead to fewer dropouts.

Hand, Lamontagne, and Marks (1974) compared cohesive and uncohesive groups of agoraphobics. At follow-up it was found that cohesive groups improved more than uncohesive groups. However, Teasdale, Walsh, Lancashire, and Mathews (1977) could not replicate this finding.

A related issue was investigated by Sinnott, Jones, Scott-Fordham, and Woodward (1981). They hypothesized that a neighborhood-based exposure in vivo program would be more effective than a clinic-based exposure program since exposure tasks in the natural environment could lead to rewarding social contact, which reinforces the likelihood of successful completion of homework assignments. In their study (1) neighborhood-based treatment, (2) clinic-based treatment, and (3) no-treatment control were compared. All exposure patients received homework assignments, but the subjects in the neighborhood group were encouraged to use each other as "target destinations." There was some evidence that the neighborhood-based group was the most effective.

4. *Anxiety evocation during exposure in vivo is not essential.* Hafner and Marks (1976) investigated this issue and found that deliberate anxiety provocation during exposure in vivo did not enhance treatment effectiveness. The only controlled study that investigated the influence of tranquilizers during exposure in vivo found no significant differences between diazepam and placebo in phobia reduction after exposure in vivo (Hafner & Marks, 1976).

5. *Frequent practice is more effective than spaced practice.* Foa, Jameson, Turner, and Payne (1980a) compared 10 sessions of frequent practice with 10 sessions of spaced practice in a crossover design. In the frequent practice condition, treatment was conducted on consecutive days, whereas in the spaced condition sessions were held once a week only. Results indicated that frequent practice was more effective than spaced practice. Foa et al. (1980a) suggest that the superiority of the frequent condition may be due to the fact that frequent practice provides less opportunity for accidental exposure between treatment sessions and for the reinforcement of avoidance or escape behavior. The latter explanation, however, is less likely, since having the opportunity to escape during exposure in vivo does not have the detrimental effects as once thought (de Silva & Rachman, 1984).

6. *Treatment can be conducted as a self-help program.* The first self-management program was developed by Emmelkamp (1974). Treatment consisted of self-controlled exposure plus feedback (self-observation). After an instructional phase in the presence of the therapist, the patient had to carry on alone. The procedure involves a graduated approach by the patient in the actual feared situation. The client had to walk alone on a route through the city with instructions to turn back on experiencing undue anxiety. The client had to record the duration of each trial and to write this down in a notebook. Then, he had to enter the phobic situation in the same way. This procedure was repeated until the 90-minute session was over. At the end of each

session, the patient had to send the results to the therapist. This treatment was found to be equally effective as therapist-controlled prolonged exposure (Emmelkamp, 1974).

The effectiveness of self-observation as a self-management procedure was further demonstrated in the studies by Emmelkamp (1980), Emmelkamp and Emmelkamp-Benner (1975), and Emmelkamp and Wessels (1975). In contrast with results found with prolonged exposure in vivo, with this self-management program most patients went on to make further gains during follow-up (Emmelkamp, 1974, 1980; Emmelkamp & Kuipers, 1979).

Mathews, Teasdale, Munby, Johnston, and Shaw (1977) developed another self-management program for agoraphobics. Their program differs from our program in that the *patients' spouses* were actively involved in planning and encouraging practice attempts. Furthermore, their patients had to remain in the phobic situation long enough for anxiety to decline, rather than to return on experiencing undue anxiety as is the case with self-observation. Several controlled studies have now been conducted demonstrating to the effectiveness of this program (see Mathews, Gelder, and Johnston, 1982).

7. *Effects of exposure programs are long-lasting.* Follow-up reports ranging from four to nine years after treatment were published by Emmelkamp and Kuipers (1979), McPherson, Brougham, and McLaren (1980), and Munby and Johnston (1980). Generally, improvements brought about by the treatment were maintained. However, results of the behavioral treatment were variable. Some patients were symptom free, some were moderately improved, and a few patients did not benefit at all.

Cognitive Therapy
Cognitive therapy programs for agoraphobia have usually employed one or more of the following two cognitive strategies: (1) self-instructional training and (2) rational-emotive therapy.

With *self-instructional* training, patients are instructed to substitute positive coping self-statements for the anxiety-engendering self-statements. Generally, four stages are differentiated: preparing for a stressor, confronting or handling a stressor, possibly being overwhelmed by a stressor, and, finally, reinforcing oneself for having coped (Meichenbaum,

1975). During treatment sessions, patients cognitively rehearse self-instructional ways of handling anxiety by means of an imagination procedure.

Ellis (1962) uses an A−B−C framework of *rational-emotive therapy*. A refers to an Activating event or experience, B to the person's Belief about the activating (A) event, and C to the emotional or behavioral Consequence, assumed to result from the Beliefs (B). The critical elements of treatment involve determining the (irrational) thoughts that mediate the anxiety and confronting and modifying them so that undue anxiety is no longer experienced. According to Ellis there are certain irrational beliefs quite common. To give two examples: "The idea that if something seems dangerous or fearsome, you must become terribly occupied with and upset about it," and "The idea that your past remains all-important and that, because something once strongly influenced your life, it has to keep determining your feelings and behavior today" (Ellis, 1962).

In rational-emotive therapy the therapist challenges the underlying irrational beliefs in a Socratic-like fashion.

Several studies investigating cognitive therapy of agoraphobia have been reported. Emmelkamp et al. (1978) compared cognitive therapy with prolonged exposure in vivo in a crossover design. Exposure in vivo was found to be far more effective than cognitive therapy both on the behavioral measure and on phobic anxiety and avoidance scales. Treatment was conducted in a relatively short time period (one week), however, which might be too short to result in significant cognitive changes. Moreover, the use of a crossover design precluded conclusions about possibly delayed effects of the cognitive therapy.

In a following study (Emmelkamp & Mersch, 1982) three treatments were compared in a between-group design: (1) cognitive therapy, (2) prolonged exposure in vivo, and (3) a combination of self-instructional training and prolonged exposure in vivo. The combined therapeutic package was included to investigate whether self-instructional training would enhance the effectiveness of exposure in vivo. Treatment consisted of eight two-hour sessions spread over four weeks. In contrast with the Emmelkamp et al. (1978) study, more emphasis was placed on insight into unproductive thinking:

Patients had to analyze their own feelings in terms of Ellis' A−B−C model. At the posttest prolonged exposure in vivo and the combined procedure were clearly superior to cognitive therapy. At one month follow-up, however, the differences between the treatments had partly disappeared due to a continuing improvement in the cognitive therapy condition and a slight relapse in the exposure in vivo condition. Self-instructional training did not enhance the effects of exposure in vivo: The combined procedure was no more effective than the exposure in vivo condition.

A third study that evaluated the effects of cognitive therapy was reported by Williams and Rappoport (1983). Agoraphobics were assigned to two conditions: (1) exposure in vivo and (2) exposure in vivo plus self-instructional training. Treatment was directed to their driving disabilities; other fears were not dealt with. Although both conditions improved on subjective anxiety, only the non-cognitive group gained significant benefit from treatment on the behavioral measure.

Cognitive therapy procedures have differed in the emphasis on insight into irrational beliefs and the training of incompatible positive self-statements. Several analogue studies (e.g., Carmody, 1978; Glogower, Fremouw, & McCroskey, 1978; Thorpe, Amatu, Blakey, & Burns, 1976) investigated which component of cognitive restructuring was the most productive, but these studies have produced conflicting results.

Emmelkamp et al. (1986) investigated the differential effectiveness of self-instructional training, (SIT), rational emotive therapy (RET), and prolonged exposure in vivo with agoraphobics. In addition to the short-term effects after three weeks of treatment, possibly delayed effects of treatments were asessed one month after treatment, during which period patients received no further treatment. This was done to give patients the opportunity to integrate and practice their cognitive strategies in the natural environment. After this treatment-free period all patients received three weeks of prolonged exposure in vivo and were reassessed, to assess possible interactions between cognitive strategies and exposure in vivo.

Results at midtreatment and posttest are depicted in Figure 9.1. At mid-treatment most patients (10 out of 14) in the exposure condition were rated either as much improved (5) or improved (5), whereas in the RET condition 11 out of 15 patients were rated as failure and only one as much improved. The results of the SIT condition were in between those of the exposure and RET condition. After the second block of treatment, the RET-exposure condition still had the most failures. None of the patients in the exposure-exposure condition was rated a failure at the posttest.

The results of that study clearly suggest that exposure in vivo is more effective than the cognitive treatments in reducing anxiety and avoidance of agoraphobics. Although both SIT and RET resulted in statistically significant improvements on most measures, the clinical improvements achieved were generally less impressive, especially with RET, where most patients were rated as failures. The lack of clinical improvement in anxiety and avoidance after RET cannot be accounted for by inadequate application of the cognitive therapy (see Hollon & Beck, this volume). RET was the only treatment that led to significant changes in irrational beliefs at midtreatment, thus demonstrating the construct validity of the cognitive therapy. However, the cognitive changes did not result in substantially clinical improvements in anxiety and avoidance.

During the one-month waiting period after the first treatment block, the SIT condition showed continuing improvement, whereas the RET condition did not. This suggests that the continuing improve-

ment after cognitive therapy in the Emmelkamp and Mersch (1982) study may have been due to the self-instructional component, rather than to insight into irrational beliefs. In contrast to the Emmelkamp and Mersch (1982) study, exposure patients in the Emmelkamp et al. (1986) study continued to improve on anxiety and avoidance scales during the waiting period. This can perhaps best be explained by the fact that exposure patients in the present study did receive homework assignments between treatment sessions, whereas the patients in the Emmelkamp and Mersch (1982) study had not received instructions to practice between sessions.

Although patients in the cognitive conditions were not instructed to practice in phobic situations, some, especially in the SIT condition, spontaneously started to do so on their own initiative. Improvement seemed to be related to whether patients did practice or did not. Thus, it is questionable whether the improvements achieved with the cognitive treatments were due to cognitive restructuring per se or to nonspecific factors (e.g., being in therapy), which motivated patients to practice in the feared situations.

Finally, Mavissakalian, Michelson, Greenwald, Kornblith, and Greenwald (1983) investigated the impact of self-instructional training and paradoxical intention on exposure in vivo. With paradoxical intention, patients were instructed to welcome the

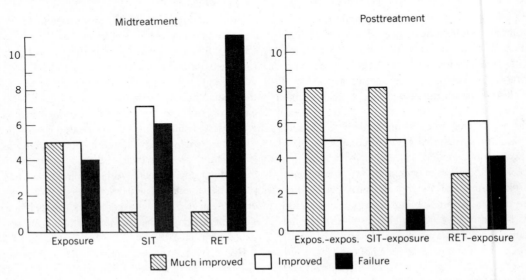

Figure 9.1. Number of patients rated as improved on pooled rating for anxiety and avoidance at mid-treatment and post-treatment. Reprinted with permission (From Emmelkamp et al., 1986), Sage Publications.

fear and to attempt to exaggerate it and to become as panicky as possible. Patients practiced these procedures twice during each group therapy session and were encouraged to practice their newly learned cognitive coping strategies regularly and to apply them in actual anxiety-provoking situations. Treatment consisted of 12 weekly 90-minute group sessions. At the end of the treatment period, paradoxical intention resulted in greater gains than self-instructional training. However, groups that were treated with self-instructional training continued to improve after the posttest, which resulted in equivalent long-term effectiveness of the two treatments. Since an exposure-only group was not included, it is unclear whether the cognitive strategies enhanced the effects of exposure.

To summarize, all studies on agoraphobics found exposure in vivo to be superior to cognitive therapy immediately after treatment. Generally, cognitive therapy led to a slight improvement on anxiety and avoidance. One study (Emmelkamp & Mersch, 1982) found cognitive therapy almost as effective as exposure in vivo, but only in the long run, which was partly due to a relapse of the exposure in vivo group. It should be noted that a relapse after exposure in vivo is uncommon. One of the reasons to account for this partial relapse may be the fact that patients were not instructed to expose themselves in vivo as homework assignments as is usually done.

Why did cognitive therapy produce such poor results in the treatment of agoraphobics while others claim to have achieved such impressive results with similar cognitive modification procedures? First, most other studies were analogue studies: The effects of treatments in analogue studies might be more strongly influenced than in clinical trials by demand characteristics and expectation of therapeutic gain. It seems probable that the intelligence of the patients in clinical trials on the average will have been lower than that of the typical subjects in analogue research (students). Cognitive therapy might well be more effective with intelligent students used to thinking rationally than with less intelligent clinical populations. Further, the degree of physiological arousal in anxiety-engendering situations, too, might differ considerably for agoraphobics and for subjects in analogue studies. It is quite possible that cognitive therapy constitutes an effective form of treatment for low physiological reactors (such as

the subjects of analogue studies), although such treatment is less effective with high physiological reactors (such as agoraphobics). Finally, it might be quite possible that anxiety of agoraphobics is less cognitively mediated than in the case of social anxiety or test anxiety, which have been the common treatment targets of cognitive therapy in analogue research.

Marital Complications

It has been suggested that the intimate relationship of agoraphobic patients with their marital partner may be of critical importance in the development and maintenance of the patient's agoraphobic symptoms. A number of different authors (e.g., Andrews, 1966; Barlow, Mavissakalian, & Hay, 1981; Chambless & Goldstein, 1980; Fry, 1962; Goodstein, 1981; Goodstein & Swift, 1977; Hafner, 1982; Hand & Lamontagne, 1974; Lazarus, 1966; Webster, 1953) have suggested that agoraphobia may more suitably be described in terms of both an interpersonal, particularly marital, conflict and an intrapsychic conflict. For instance, it has been observed clinically that marital satisfaction increases in proportion to improvement of agoraphobic symptoms or that improvement in the phobia is associated with more marital satisfaction in the patient, but with *dissatisfaction* in the spouse (Barlow et al., 1981; Hafner, 1977, 1982; O'Brien, Barlow, & Last, 1982).

In attempts to clarify the relationship between marital difficulties and agoraphobia three avenues have generally been followed.

First, it has been investigated whether partners of agoraphobics are themselves psychiatrically disturbed. In a recent study (Arrindell & Emmelkamp, 1985a) that investigated this particular issue, it was clearly shown that the partners of female agoraphobics were not more defensive or psychologically more disturbed than controls.

Second, a number of investigations have sought to examine the influence of interpersonal difficulties on the outcome of behavior therapy. Hudson (1974), working with agoraphobics who received prolonged exposure in vivo treatment, found that patients from "sick families" showed much less improvement than patients from "well-adjusted" families. Milton and Hafner (1979) treated patients with prolonged exposure in vivo and found that patients whose marriages were rated as unsatisfactory before treatment improved less during treatment and were significantly more likely to relapse during follow-up than those patients with satisfactory marriages. Bland and Hallam (1981) related the level of marital satisfaction with response to exposure in vivo treatment and found a significant difference between "good marriage" and "poor marriage" groups with respect to phobic severity. At a three-month follow-up, the "poor marriage" group showed a significantly greater tendency to relapse compared with the "good marriage" group. Interestingly, improvement was found to be associated with patient's satisfaction with spouse. Spouse's dissatisfaction with the patient was not related to outcome of treatment. Emmelkamp (1980) divided agoraphobics into low and high marital satisfaction groups. All patients were treated with self-controlled exposure in vivo. After four treatment sessions, almost no significant differences between groups were found. Patients with low marital satisfaction improved as much as patients with high marital satisfaction. Neither at the posttest nor at one-month follow-up was self-controlled exposure in vivo influenced by the interpersonal problems of agoraphobics. Similar results were found by Arrindell, Emmelkamp, and Sanderman (1986) and Cobb, Mathews, Childs-Clarke, and Bowers (1984). The findings of the latter studies are in contrast to the findings of Bland and Hallam (1981), Milton and Hafner (1979), and Hudson (1974).

In the studies reviewed so far, marital satisfaction was assessed before the start of treatment. It is conceivable that patients might find it difficult to admit dissatisfaction with their partner before a therapeutic relationship has developed. Therefore, a patient's account of the relationship in the course of treatment might give a more accurate picture of satisfaction with spouse than pretreatment indices of marital satisfaction. In a study by Emmelkamp and Van der Hout (1983), the information with respect to marital satisfaction was gathered retrospectively from the therapists' files. It was hypothesized in advance that patients who complained about their partners during treatment were more likely to become treatment failures with exposure in vivo as compared with patients who did not complain about their partner. Results revealed that complaints about the partner did differentiate failures from successful cases.

Third, a relatively small number of studies have addressed themselves to the issue of whether improvement of phobic patients is associated with negative changes in the partner, either psychologically or in the marital relationship. While clinical anecdotes suggest that phobic removal might lead to an exacerbation of interpersonal problems (e.g., Hafner, 1977; Hand & Lamontagne, 1974), controlled studies did not find such negative effects on the marital relationship (e.g., Arrindell & et al. 1986; Bland & Hallman, 1981; Cobb et al., 1984).

Given the emphasis that has been put on the possible role of marital difficulties in the etiology and maintenance of agoraphobia, it is surprising that hardly any methodologically sound study has been conducted with the aim of scrutinizing whether the marriages of agoraphobics differ from those of controls. Most of the available studies emphasizing the importance of marriage quality in the etiology of agoraphobia (e.g. Fry, 1962; Hafner, 1981; Holmes, 1982; Torpey & Measy, 1973; Webster, 1953) are based on confusing methodologies, which limits the drawing of definite conclusions. Despite these shortcomings, these studies have, at times, provided an abundance of comments concerning the quality of marriage in agoraphobics and their partners.

Buglass and her associates (1977) compared agoraphobic housewives and their spouses with normal control couples in terms of domestic activities (i.e., the execution of specified family tasks), decision making in a number of areas, and manifest interaction ratings (assertion−compliance and affection−dislike). The most striking feature of the comparison between the two groups of couples was their similarity with respect to the above criterion measures. Arrindell and Emmelkamp (1986) investigated the quality of the marital relationship of agoraphobic patients and their partners by comparing their marriages with those of three groups: (1) nonphobic psychiatric patients and their partners, (2) maritally distressed couples, and (3) nondistressed (happily married) couples. The findings of this study indicate that agoraphobics and their spouses tend to be comparable to happily married subjects in terms of marital adjustment, intimacy, and needs, while nonphobic psychiatric patients and their partners are comparable to maritally distressed subjects. It could be argued that agoraphobics are more inclined to repress conflicts than other groups, but a controlled study found little or no evidence that this was indeed the case (Arrindell & Emmelkamp, 1985b).

How to explain the finding that clinical reports with respect to the marital functioning of agoraphobics are not in line with results from empirical studies? Hafner (1982) has noted that one reason for this may be that " . . . a self-perpetuating myth has arisen, with clinicians seeing in their own patients only what has been reported by other clinicians. The more powerful the myth, the wider the clinical consensus, which in turn strengthens the myth" (p. 83).

Couples Treatment

Several studies investigated whether the involvement of the spouse as co-therapist could enhance treatment effectiveness. Cobb et al. (1984) found that the spouse-aided exposure was no more effective than when exposure was conducted with the patient alone. In contrast, Barlow, O'Brien, and Last (1984) found a clear superiority for the spouse-aided exposure condition, when compared to the nonspouse group on measures of agoraphobia. Results are thus inconclusive and further research in this area is needed.

Finally, the effects of treatment focusing on the marital relationship rather than on the phobia was evaluated by Cobb, McDonald, Marks, and Stern (1980). Subjects were both agoraphobics and obsessive-compulsives who also manifested marital discord. Exposure in vivo was contrasted with marital treatment and results indicated that exposure in vivo led to improvements with respect to both the phobic obsessive-compulsive problems and the marital relationship, while marital therapy had effect on only the marital relationship but did not improve phobic obsessive-compulsive problems.

Non-exposure Therapies

There has been some discussion about whether exposure to phobic stimuli is a necessary condition in the treatment for phobic disorders (e.g., Boyd & Levis, 1983; de Silva & Rachman, 1981). In the case of agoraphobics, to date there is little evidence that treatment could be successful when exposure does not form an important component of the treatment package. Results of studies investigating whether treatment focusing on the interpersonal difficulties of agoraphobics resulted in clinical im-

provement of the agoraphobia were negative (Chambless et al., 1982; Cobb et al., 1980). Jannoun, Munby, Catalan, and Gelder (1980) investigated the effectiveness of a "problem-solving" treatment, involving the couple's discussion of life stresses and problems. Exposure in vivo was superior to the problem-solving treatment, but one of the two therapists involved obtained unexpectedly good results with problem solving. In a following study (Cullington, Butler, Hibbert, & Gelder, 1984) the good results of problem solving were not replicated. To quote the authors: " . . . problem solving has not been shown to be an effective treatment for agoraphobia and the hypothesis that exposure is a necessary condition for the treatment of agoraphobia still stands" (p. 286).

It has been argued that agoraphobics are quite unassertive: They are not able to stand up for their rights and have often considerable difficulty in expressing their feelings adequately. Therefore, they are often dominated by significant others in their surroundings, especially by parents and husbands. To study the effectiveness of assertiveness training on agoraphobics, Emmelkamp, Van der Hout, and de Vries (1983) contrasted (1) assertiveness training, (2) prolonged exposure in vivo, and (3) a combination of assertiveness training and prolonged exposure in vivo. Only low-assertive agoraphobics were used as subjects (see Figure 9.2).

As for the main measures (behavioral measurement and ratings for phobic anxiety and avoidance), exposure in vivo was found to be superior. However, this difference was not always found to be statistically significant, due to the small number of patients in each condition. On the other hand, assertiveness training was found to be more effective on assertive measures. The combined procedure was *not* more effective than each of the individual treatments on its own. The results of this study indicate that both forms of behavioral treatment have something to offer for unassertive agoraphobics. Exposure in vivo leads to rapid improvement with respect to anxiety and avoidance. On the other hand, assertiveness training leads to more improvement than exposure in vivo with respect to assertiveness. In another study (Emmelkamp, 1980) we found that assertive and unassertive agoraphobics benefited equally from exposure in vivo. Taken together, these data indicate that the most efficient therapeutic strategy is to start with exposure in

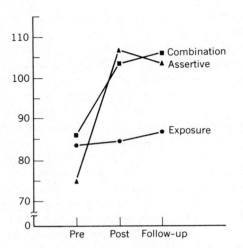

Figure 9.2.   The effects of the treatments on the Adult Self Expression Scale (ASES).

vivo and proceed later to assertiveness training if necessary.

Summary

Over the past 15 years, seemingly effective treatments have been devised for agoraphobia, the most common anxiety disorder presented to health professionals. The value of exposure in vivo programs is now well established. Results of a series of studies conducted by researchers in various countries indicate that cognitive therapy is of little or no avail in the treatment of agoraphobia as far as phobic targets are concerned. Although the "relationship hypothesis" of agoraphobia is still very popular among professionals, there is little experimental evidence to support this conceptualization of agoraphobia. Even if further studies would convincingly demonstrate that unhappily married agoraphobics benefit less from exposure in vivo programs than happily married agoraphobics, it is highly questionable whether this finding would be specific for agoraphobia. The same may hold for almost any disorder; for example, maritally distressed patients—irrespective of type of complaint—may profit less from any treatment that does not directly deal with the marital problems of the patient, than more happy ones. Other approaches (e.g., problem solving, assertiveness training) have been found to be less effective than exposure in vivo programs. It should be noted, however, that these alternative approaches may lead to improvements on other targets than phobic anxiety and avoidance and may prevent relapse.

Social Anxiety

Clinical social anxiety or social phobia consists of disabling fears in social situations that cause patients to avoid such situations. Clinical social anxiety is distinguished from the shyness and social anxiety many individuals experience by the intensity of the fears and the abnormal avoidance of situations involved. A large number of studies have evaluated the effectiveness of various cognitive-behavioral interventions in the treatment of social-evaluative anxiety (including speech anxiety, communication apprehension, interpersonal anxiety, dating anxiety, and unassertiveness) in academic setting with mildly disturbed college students. Here the focus will be on controlled studies in clinical settings.

Generally, three models are distinguished to explain the functioning of social anxiety, each emphasizing different aspects of the disorder. The *skills-deficit model* asserts that social anxiety results from a lack of social skills within the patients' behavioral repertoire. This model suggests that the appropriate goal of treatment should be to assist patients to acquire the skills that they currently lack. Assuming that such lack of social skills provokes anxiety, then anxiety may be overcome through social-skill training. If patients have adequate social skills but are inhibited in social situations by anxiety that has become conditioned to interpersonal settings and avoidance of social situations, the principal goal of treatment should be the direct reduction of social anxiety and avoidance (*conditioned-anxiety model*). Others have stressed that faulty evaluation of one's performance in social situations or "irrational beliefs" mediate social anxiety. Thus, the *cognitive inhibition model* suggests that maladaptive cognitions rather than conditioned anxiety or skills-deficit are responsible for the impairments in social situations. The emphasis on various aspects of social anxiety has led to a number of different treatment strategies.

Systematic Desensitization

Several studies have investigated the effectiveness of systematic desensitization with social-anxious patients (Hall & Goldberg, 1977; Marzillier, Lambert, & Kellett, 1976; Shaw, 1976; Trower, Yardley, Bryant, & Shaw, 1978; Van Son, 1978). In general, limited clinical improvements were achieved. In only three studies was systematic desensitization compared with no-treatment conditions. In neither study was desensitization significantly more effective than controls. In addition, Dormaar and Dijkstra (1975) found no significant between-group differences between psychotherapy and desensitization. Finally, Kanter and Goldfried (1979) found systematic desensitization as self-control more effective than a waiting-list control, using social-anxious community residents as subjects; however, overall improvement was small.

Briefly, systematic desensitization is of limited value with social-anxious patients. Results of studies dealing with real patients contrast with those of studies using analogue populations. In the latter studies desensitization has consistently been found to be effective in the treatment of social anxiety.

Social-skill Training
Social-skill training seems to be of more value in the treatment of social anxiety. However, the evidence in favor of this approach is far from conclusive. Although several studies could not find consistent differences between systematic desensitization and social-skill training (social phobics: Hall & Goldberg, 1977; Shaw, 1976; Trower et al., 1978; social inadequates: Van Son, 1978), results of other studies indicate that social-skill training may be superior (social inadequates: Marzillier et al., 1976; Trower et al., 1978; erythrophobics: Van Son, 1978).

Falloon, Lindley, McDonald, and Marks (1977) investigated whether the addition of modeling and role playing (social-skill training) enhanced the effects of a cohesive goal-directed small group discussion. Their patients had social interaction difficulties, including social phobias. Social-skill training proved to be superior to group discussion alone. The importance of homework assignments was demonstrated by Falloon et al. (1977). Social-skill groups that received daily homework assignments (exposure in vivo exercises) resulted in better outcome than social-skill groups without such homework assignments.

Enhancing Effects of Cognitive Restructuring
Several therapists have developed therapeutic packages that focus on both dysfunctional cognitions and behavioral skills deficits.

Stravinsky, Marks, and Yule (1982) investigated whether cognitive therapy would enhance the effectiveness of social-skill training. Half of the patients received social-skill training, whereas with the other half of the patients social-skill training was combined with cognitive modification. Outcome did not differ significantly between the two treatment conditions at any time on any measure. Both groups reported less anxiety, increased levels of social activities, and improvements with respect to the irrational beliefs they had held.

A second study investigating this issue was reported by Frisch, Elliott, Atsaides, Salva, and Denney (1982). Thirty-four male outpatients who evidenced marked interpersonal impairments or social avoidance were randomly assigned to (1) social-skill training, (2) social-skill training plus "stress management," and (3) a minimal-treatment control condition. Stress management included applied relaxation training and cognitive restructuring. Both active treatment groups resulted in improved social skills at the end of treatment. However, on the anxiety measures no significant improvements were found. The combined approach was about equally effective as social-skill training alone.

Exposure in Vivo
It should be noted that exposure in vivo may account for part of the effects achieved with social-skill training. The role played by modeling in social-skill training is unclear: it is quite possible that modeling is superfluous with most social phobics and that the essential therapeutic ingredients are repeated behavior rehearsal in vivo in the group and the structured homework practice involving real-life rehearsal of feared situations. Falloon, Lloyd, and Harpin (1981) reported a pilot study with 16 socially anxious outpatients who received a treatment program that attempted to maximize rehearsal in real-life settings. Treatment was conducted in small groups. Each patient was grouped with one other patient and a nonprofessional therapist. After behavior rehearsal of problem situations in the clinic, the small group left the clinic and repeatedly rehearsed the same behavior in a real-life setting. Results of this four-week program were similar to that achieved with social-skill training conducted over a 10-week period (Falloon et al., 1977).

Emmelkamp, Mersch, Vissia, and Van der Helm (1985c) compared the effects of (1) exposure in vivo, (2) rational-emotive therapy, and (3) self-instructional training with socially anxious outpatients. Treatment was conducted in small groups. In the exposure in vivo sessions, patients had to confront their feared situations in the group. For example, patients who were afraid of blushing had to sit in front of others with an open-necked blouse until anxiety dissipated. Others who feared that their hands would tremble had to write on the blackboard and to serve tea to the group. All patients had to give speeches in front of the group. An important part of treatment consisted of actual exposure in vivo in real social situations in the town center. Patients had to perform a number of difficult assignments such as making inquiries in shops and offices, speaking to strangers, or visiting bars. Role playing was not applied.

Each of the three therapeutic procedures resulted in significant decrements in anxiety at posttesting, which were either maintained or improved upon at follow-up (see Figure 9.3). In contrast to the results of our studies with agoraphobics (Emmelkamp, et al., 1978; Emmelkamp & Mersch, 1982; Emmelkamp et al., 1986) where exposure in vivo was found to be significantly superior to cognitive interventions, the results with social phobics do not reveal many significant differences. There was a slight superiority for exposure in vivo, but this was significant only on pulse rate.

Interestingly, only the cognitive treatments revealed significant changes in cognitions as measured by the IBT, thus demonstrating the construct validity of the cognitive treatment. The differential effects found after the various treatments make an interpretation of the effects in terms of placebo effects unlikely. Exposure was found to lead to a significant reduction in pulse rate, which is in line with an explanation of the effects of exposure in terms of habituation. On the other hand, exposure did not lead to a change in irrational cognitions, while the irrational beliefs did improve after cognitive treatment. Thus, changes in dependent measures were restricted to those consonant with the treatment approach. This finding is important since other studies failed to show specific effects of behavioral and cognitive strategies (Emmelkamp, 1982a; Hollon & Beck, this volume).

Results of the Emmelkamp et al. (1986) study do not lend support to the skills deficit model of social anxiety. It should be stressed that social-skill training was not part of either treatment, but nevertheless most patients improved—and often clinically significantly—with respect to social anxiety.

Matching of Treatment to Patient
As pointed out by Marzillier and Winter (1983), the most likely single cause of failure in the behavioral treatment of social anxiety is an incomplete or faulty initial analysis of the problem. In clinical practice individual patients' differences needs to be taken into acount in determining the choice of a particular treatment strategy. The time seems to be ripe for investigators to stop subscribing to the myth of patient uniformity and to systematically match treatment to particular clients' characteristics (Emmelkamp & Foa, 1983).

Öst, Jerremalm, and Johansson (1981) investigated the interaction between treatment factors and individual characteristics. Socially anxious outpatients ($n = 32$) were divided into two groups showing different response patterns: behavioral and physiological reactors. Within each group half of the patients were randomly assigned to treatment that focused on the behavioral component (social-skill training) while the other half received treatment that primarily focused on the physiological component (applied relaxation). With applied relaxation, relaxation is taught as a coping response that was applied in vivo in role play situations. Further, patients received homework assignments to apply the relaxation in anxiety-arousing situations. Thus an active

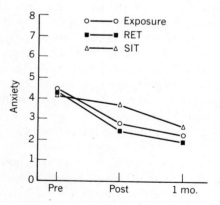

Figure 9.3. The effects of exposure, rational emotive therapy (RET), and self-instructional training (SIT) on the phobic anxiety scale at pre-test, posttest and 1 month follow-up. Reprinted with permission (From Emmelkamp et al., 1985c), Pergamon Press.

ingredient of this procedure involved exposure in vivo. It was hypothesized that patients who were treated with a method that matched their response pattern would achieve better results than the group treated with the other method. The results generally supported the hypothesis.

In a following study (Öst, 1984), socially anxious patients were classified into *cognitive* reactors and *physiological* reactors. Here the hypothesis that matching treatment (cognitive therapy and applied relaxation) to the individual response pattern would increase treatment effectiveness was not corroborated. Cognitive reactors improved to the same extent with both treatment procedures; also for physiological reactors no differential effectiveness of the procedures was shown.

Summary

In sum, there is little evidence that systematic desensitization is of benefit to socially anxious patients. Social-skill training, cognitive therapy, and exposure in vivo have been shown to result in clinical improvements, but no one procedure has been shown to be superior to the other. It is too easy to conceptualize social anxiety in terms of a single theory. Cognitive restructuring, social-skill training, and exposure procedures surely can be critical elements in treatment but no method is so powerful that it can be applied universally across socially anxious patients.

Simple Phobias

The essential feature of simple phobia is a persistent, irrational fear of specific objects and situations others than those involved in agoraphobia and social anxiety. Research in this area was reviewed by Emmelkamp (1979) and Emmelkamp and Kuipers (1985). Generally, exposure in vivo seems to be the most effective and efficient procedure. Here, only more recent developments will be discussed.

Several studies sought to investigate whether teaching behavioral coping skills would enhance the effectiveness of exposure in vivo. Bourque and Ladouceur (1980) investigated whether modeling of approach behavior or physical guidance by the therapist would enhance approach behavior. Subjects were height phobics. Neither modeling nor therapist guidance did enhance the effects of exposure in vivo. Williams, Dooseman, and Kleifield (1984) also addressed this issue. In their study

height phobics and patients with driving phobia were treated by exposure in vivo or a mastery-oriented treatment. All subjects received exposure in vivo, but the treatments differed in the extent to which the therapist provided mastery-induction aids to the subjects. With the mastery-oriented treatment the therapist provided a variety of performance-induction aids and behavioral guidance whenever subjects were having difficulty making progress. These guidance procedures included therapist accompaniment, having the subject focusing on an intermediate goal, eliminating avoidance rituals, and so on. The mastery-oriented treatment proved to be slightly superior to exposure alone.

Cognitive Therapy

Three controlled studies with clinically revelant populations have studied the effectiveness of cognitive strategies in overcoming simple phobias. Biran and Wilson (1981) compared cognitive restructuring and exposure in vivo with phobics with fears of either heights, elevators, or darkness. Exposure in vivo was found to be superior to cognitive restructuring in reducing anxiety and avoidance behavior. When cognitive therapy subjects were offered exposure in vivo after the cognitive therapy, results were comparable to those of the original exposure group.

Girodo and Roehl (1978) contrasted (1) information giving, (2) self-instructional training, and (3) a combined procedure using volunteers with a fear of flying. Anxiety ratings obtained during a normal flight indicated that self-instructional training was no more effective than prior information giving.

Further negative results of self-instructional training were reported by Ladouceur (1983). Phobics with fears of dogs and cats were treated with exposure in vivo with therapist guidance. For a number of individuals, self-instructional training was added to exposure. The treatments were about equally effective at the posttest, but at follow-up the self-instructional training plus exposure condition showed more phobic behavior than the group that had received exposure only.

Individual Differences

Öst, Johansson, and Jerremalm (1982) investigated the interaction between treatment factors and individual characteristics. Claustrophobics were divided into two groups showing different response patterns: behavioral and physiological reactors. Within each group half of the patients received a more psychophysiologically focused method (applied relaxation) or a more behaviorally focused treatment (exposure in vivo). The results showed that for the behavioral reactors exposure in vivo was superior to applied relaxation, whereas the reverse was true for the physiological reactors. The results of this study suggest that it might be important to consider individual differences in response patterns of simple phobics when planning the treatment.

In sum, exposure in vivo has been shown to be effective in the treatment of a variety of simple phobias. There is little or no evidence that cognitive therapy is of any value with this population. With strong physiological reactors it might be wise to teach patients active relaxation coping skills that they can use during the exposure in vivo tasks.

Theoretical Considerations

One of the major challenges to be addressed by research on the treatment of phobias is to advance an adequate theory of the psychological mechanisms through which exposure treatment affects changes. Although it is obvious that almost all behavioral procedures contain elements of exposure to phobic stimuli, this does not elucidate the therapeutic processes involved. Exposure is merely a description of what is going on during treatment and not an explanation of its process (Emmelkamp, 1982a).

In the exposure view emphasis is laid on the duration of the patient's exposure to distressing stimuli, but despite equal amounts of exposure duration, patients show varying degrees of improvements. Usually, exposure is conceptualized as a passive process: subject's initially elevated levels of arousal are generally found to decrease with continued exposure to phobic stimuli over a session (Emmelkamp, 1982a). This process of anxiety reduction as a function of continuous exposure has alternatively been labeled "extinction" or "habituation."

Rather than conceptualizing exposure as a passive process, an alternative conceptual basis for performance-based treatment is provided by cognitive theory. Cognitive theorists (e.g., Bandura, 1977) assume that exposure therapy is effective in that it serves to alter maladaptive cognitive patterns.

Thus, cognitive change is regarded as an important process variable in exposure treatments.

In a study by Emmelkamp and Felten (1985), a first attempt was made to assess the influence of self-statements on subjective anxiety, performance, and psychophysiological responses *during* treatment by exposure in vivo. To assess the influence of cognitive processes, half of the subjects were instructed in adaptive thinking *during* the exposure in vivo task whereas the other half were *not*. Acrophobia was chosen as the target problem in this study, since exposure treatment could be easily standardized, and the exposure task used allowed continuous physiological monitoring. Treatment consisted of climbing the steps of a fire escape. Every third minute patients had to rate their anxiety and heart rate was monitored continuously. Results with respect to performance are presented in Figure 9.4. This figure shows that patients in the course of one treatment session—which lasted 60 minutes—were able to climb gradually higher on this stair. The addition of cognitive self-statements did not influence the performance.

Figure 9.5 shows the heart rate data and subjective anxiety for both treatment conditions. While both groups succeeded in climbing the fire escape, the heart rate decreased over the course of the session, as did the subjective anxiety. After 60 minutes heart rate levels were within normal ranges. The cognitive self-statements did not seem to influence habituation of heart rate but did affect subjec-

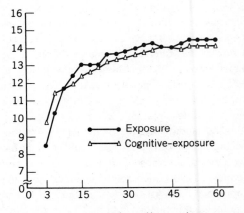

Figure 9.4.   Mean number of hierarchy items performed during the treatment session. Reprinted with permission (From Emmelkamp & Felten, 1985), Pergamon Press.

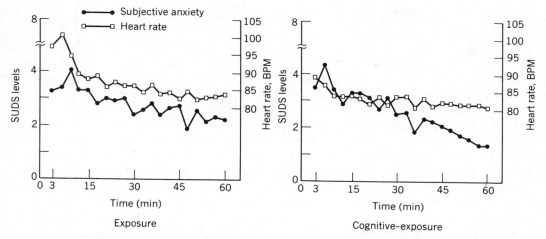

Figure 9.5. Mean heart rate (HR) and mean subjective anxiety level (SUDS) every 3rd min during the treatment session. Reprinted with permission (From Emmelkamp & Felten 1985), Pergamon Press.

tive anxiety at the end of the treatment session. Subjects in both conditions improved significantly on heart rate and on the behavioral measures at the posttest. Significant differences between the exposure and cognitive-exposure condition were found on cognitive measures only. Both on subjective anxiety and cognitions during the behavioral test the cognitive-exposure group was found to be superior to the exposure-alone condition. However, this influenced neither the performance of the subjects nor their psychophysiological arousal.

Within the confines of this study, only a partial attempt could be made to investigate the influence of reduction of subjective anxiety on heart rate and vice versa. Generally, changes in subjective anxiety during treatment did not precede changes in heart rate. This lends some support to the notion that anxiety reduction through exposure is a passive process, leading to more or less synchronous changes in subjective anxiety and psychophysiological arousal.

Anxiety States

Relatively few studies have been conducted that investigated the effectiveness of behavioral and cognitive procedures on patients that suffered from panic disorder or generalized anxiety. Most of the work in this area has focused on relaxation techniques.

Relaxation

Positive results of treatment by progressive muscle relaxation for generalized anxiety have been reported in a series of studies by Lehrer and his colleagues. Live presentation of relaxation appears to be preferred to tape-recorded instruction. When relaxation instruction is tape-recorded, this procedure appears to be ineffective as a method for teaching relaxation as a skill that can be used across situations (Lehrer, 1982). A recent study (Hoelscher, Lichtstein, & Rosenthal, 1984) using an unobtrusive measure of compliance found that only one-fourth of the subjects performed relaxation daily. In several studies progressive relaxation was contrasted with meditation. Two of these studies found both types of relaxation training to be about equally effective (Lehrer, Schoicket, Carrington, & Woolfolk, 1980; Woolfolk, Lehrer, McCann, & Rooney, 1982) while other studies (Heide & Borkovec, 1984; Lehrer, Woolfolk, Rooney, McCann, & Carrington, 1983) found a relatively more powerful effect of progressive relaxation over meditation. The latter studies involved moderately to severely anxious subjects, in contrast to the former studies where the anxiety level of the subject was lower. All studies involved community volunteers rather than clinical patients.

Others have stressed the importance of teaching

relaxation as a coping skill. Clients are trained to recognize the physiological cues of tension and to apply relaxation whenever tension is perceived. A fundamental assumption shared by these various relaxation techniques (e.g., applied relaxation, anxiety management, and cue-controlled relaxation) is that patients learn an active coping skill that they can apply in a variety of anxiety-arousing situations in daily life. Applied relaxation, anxiety management, and cue-controlled relaxation all have been found successful in the treatment of generalized anxiety, but most of these studies are clinically irrelevant since student volunteers were solicited for participation.

Jannoun, Oppenheimer, and Gelder (1982) investigated the effects of anxiety management training on anxious outpatients. Results revealed that anxiety management was effective in reducing anxiety and led to a marked decrease in anxiolytic drug use as compared to a no-treatment condition. Cragan and Deffenbacher (1984) contrasted anxiety management training with relaxation on generally anxious medical outpatients. Both treatments were more effective in reducing anxiety level than a waiting-list control group but both active treatments were found to be about equally effective.

Biofeedback

A number of studies have investigated the influence of various forms of biofeedback (most often EMG) on the anxiety level of anxious patients. Emmelkamp (1982a) and Rice and Blanchard (1982) reviewed the literature in this area and concluded that biofeedback does not have a specific value, since other forms of relaxation training tend to yield comparable clinical effects. More recent studies also found no superior effects of biofeedback training over that achieved with relaxation (Banner & Meadows, 1984; Kappes, 1983; Schilling & Poppen, 1983). Even one of the earlier proponents of EMG biofeedback in anxiety states recently concluded that biofeedback was of little utility in reducing anxiety: "Our experience in EMG feedback training in the treatment of anxiety suggests that the days when biofeedback was claimed to be a panacea for all kinds of disorders are now over, and it is clear that EMG feedback training may not be more effective than other relaxation techniques" (Lamontagne, Lavellee, & Annable, 1983, p. 545).

Cognitive Therapy

Beck, Laude, and Bohnert (1974) and Mathews (1984) have emphasized the maladaptive cognitive responses of individuals with generalized anxiety. Results of their studies suggest that thoughts related to danger are associated with the anxiety of these individuals.

Woodward and Jones (1980) carried out a controlled clinical trial investigating the effectiveness of cognitive restructuring and a modified systematic desensitization procedure on patients with generalized anxiety. In the cognitive restructuring group, the nature of self-defeating statements and irrational beliefs was discussed, and patients also cognitively rehearsed self-instructional ways of handling anxiety by means of an imagination procedure. Clients were asked to imagine an anxiety-provoking situation as vividly as possible and then to replace their negative self-statements with coping self-statements. The desensitization group differed from the cognitive group in the means of coping employed: relaxation was used instead of coping self-statements. In a third treatment group both styles of coping (i.e., relaxation and cognitive self-statements) were trained. The combined procedure improved significantly more than the other two active treatments and control group. Cognitive restructuring failed to result in any improvement.

Ramm, Marks, Yüksel, and Stern (1981) also found meager results from self-instructional training with patients with anxiety states. Positive self-statement training was hardly more effective than negative self-statement training. Thus, at present there is no evidence that cognitive therapy is particularly suited to the treatment of general anxiety, but further research in this area may lead to other conclusions within a few years.

Hyperventilation

Common symptoms of anxiety and panic are dyspnea, palpitations, chest pain, dizziness, sweating, faintness, and fear of dying or going crazy. Many of these symptoms are also associated with hyperventilation. Although anxiety is often connected with hyperventilation, it is unclear whether hyperventilation is a physiological determinant of anxiety or merely a somatic concomitant of the anxiety experienced. The concept of the vicious-circle effect may be helpful to understand the course of the hyperventilation after the first hyperventilation attack. Once initiated, hyperventilation may produce stimuli that lead to reactions that arouse or intensify the hyperventilation. A hyperventilation attack is usually accompanied with severe anxiety that by itself may provoke hyperventilation in the future. A therapeutic package consisting of repeated hyperventilation provocation and breathing exercises has been reported to be effective with patients whose anxiety seemed to be related to hyperventilation (e.g., Clark, 1984; Emmelkamp & Kuipers, 1985), but further controlled studies are needed before firm conclusions can be drawn about the clinical utility of this treatment approach.

Comprehensive Treatment

Barlow et al. (1984) evaluated the effects of a comprehensive treatment consisting of somatically oriented (EMG biofeedback and relaxation) and cognitive treatment. The cognitive component of treatment was based on stress inoculation training and Beck, Emery, and Greenberg's (1985) cognitive therapy for anxiety disorders. The strategies taught included coping self-statements and cognitive restructuring of anxiety-provoking thoughts. The treatment consisted of 18 sessions over a 14-week period. Compared to waiting-list controls, treated patients improved, not only on clinical ratings of improvement, but also on physiological measures, daily self-monitored measures of background anxiety and panic, and questionnaire measures of anxiety. Interestingly, there were no significant differences in outcome across diagnoses, since patients with generalized anxiety disorder and patients with panic disorder responded equally well to treatment. It is unclear which specific component of the treatment package is responsible for the improvement achieved. It should be noted that reductions in muscle tension were not associated with clinical improvement, which suggests that the somatically oriented treatments (that focus on such reductions) did not contribute very much to the overall result of this program.

Concluding Remarks

The state of the art in the treatment of panic disorder and generalized anxiety disorder is preliminary. Although various forms of treatment have shown promise on treatment for anxiety states, there is little evidence that one approach is superior to the other. Although researchers have shown an increased interest in these disorders, the very few clinical studies that have been conducted do not reveal a consistent picture. Different treatments for generalized anxiety and panic disorders vary in terms of how readily they can access and modify different features of anxiety. Where and how a treatment interacts with the anxiety of a patient to produce the most change may be at the level of somatic processes (hyperventilation exercises) or at other levels (e.g., information processing). Change at any level will most likely be associated with change in other features of the anxiety system. As has been noted, some emerging developments are promising, but much more research needs to be done in order to understand these disorders and to be able to devise specific therapeutic approaches.

Obsessive-compulsive Disorders

Obsessive-compulsive disorders are among the most difficult problems to treat, and it is especially in this area that behavioral research has made significant progress over the last 10 years. Research in this area has been extensively reviewed by Emmelkamp (1982a) and here only the main findings will be presented.

There is little evidence that systematic desensitization is of any value with obsessive-compulsive disorders. Beech and Vaughan (1978) reviewed most of the published case studies and found that the reported success rate is slightly over 50 percent. A closer analysis of the successful cases published reveals that the improvement may be due to gradual exposure in vivo plus self-imposed response prevention rather than to systematic desensitization per se (Emmelkamp, 1982a).

The value of prolonged exposure in vivo and response prevention was suggested by uncontrolled studies of Meyer and his colleagues (Meyer, 1966; Meyer & Levy, 1970; Meyer, Levy, & Schnurer, 1974). The essence of their treatment approach, which at the time was called "apotrepic therapy," consists of response prevention, modeling, and exposure in vivo. The treatment involves several stages. After a behavioral analysis, nurses were instructed to prevent the patient from carrying out his rituals. Exposure in vivo was introduced as soon as the total elimination of rituals under supervision was achieved. The therapist increased the stress by confronting the patient with situations that normally triggered obsessive rituals. During this stage of treatment modeling was employed. With modeling the therapist first demonstrated what the patient had to do afterward. For example, the therapist touched contaminated objects such as underwear and he encouraged the patient to imitate. When patients could tolerate the most difficult situations, supervision was gradually diminished. For a more extensive description of exposure in vivo and response prevention, the reader is referred to Emmelkamp (1982a).

Meyer et al. (1974) reported the results of his program with 15 patients. Most patients showed a marked reduction of compulsive behavior. Since then a number of controlled studies have investigated the components of this therapeutic package, the results of which will be briefly summarized.

1. *Gradual exposure in vivo is equally effective as flooding in vivo.* See Boersma, Den Hengst, Dekker, and Emmelkamp (1976); and Marks, Hodgson, and Rachman (1975). Thus, it is unnecessary to elicit high anxiety during in vivo exposure. As gradual exposure evokes less tension and is easier for the patient to carry out by himself, it is to be preferred to flooding.

2. *Modeling does not seem to enhance treatment effectiveness.* Preliminary data (Hodgson, Rachman, & Marks, 1972) suggested that modeling enhanced the effectiveness of exposure in vivo, but subsequent studies found no enhancing effects of modeling (Boersma et al., 1976; Rachman, Marks, & Hodgson, 1973).

3. *Treatment can be administered by the patient in his natural environment.* Emmelkamp and Kraanen (1977) contrasted therapist-controlled exposure and self-controlled exposure. Although no significant differences were found between the two conditions, self-controlled exposure was consistently superior to therapist-controlled exposure at one-month follow-up. Thus, home-based treatment is not only cost-effective but might also result in superior maintenance of treatment-produced change.

4. *Spouse-aided exposure is about equally effective as self-controlled exposure.* This issue was investigated by Emmelkamp and De Lange (1983).

There was a consistent trend for the partner-assisted group to improve more, but this difference failed to reach statistical significance on most measures. The partner-assisted group improved more at the posttest, but at one-month follow-up the difference between the two groups disappeared.

5. *Supplementing in vivo exposure with self-instructional training does not increase therapeutic efficacy.* Emmelkamp, Van der Helm, Van Zanten, and Plochg (1980) compared exposure in vivo and self-instructional training plus exposure in vivo. If anything, exposure in vivo appeared to be superior to the combined approach, although this difference failed to reach statistical significance on most measures. The meager results are in accord with studies on phobics where self-instructional training also did not enhance the effects of exposure in vivo (Emmelkamp & Mersch, 1982; Emmelkamp et al., 1986; Ladouceur, 1983).

6. *Prolonged exposure sessions are superior to shorter ones.* Rabavilas, Boulougouris, and Stefanis, (1976) set out to investigate the optimal duration of exposure sessions. Prolonged exposure in vivo (2 hours) was found to be significantly superior to short exposure segments. Short exposure consisted of 10-minute exposure, followed by 5-minute neutral material followed by 10-minute exposure, and so on, until the 2-hour period elapsed. Short exposure had a deteriorating effect on patient's affective state.

7. *Both exposure to distressing stimuli and response prevention of the ritual are essential components.* Although most behavioral programs include response prevention (either therapist-controlled or self-controlled), few studies investigated the contribution of response prevention directly. The first study to investigate this particular issue was reported by Mills, Agras, Barlow, and Mills (1973). Five obsessive-compulsive patients were studied in single-case designs while treatment conditions were systematically varied. Response prevention was found to be more effective than when patients were simply given instructions to stop the rituals. Other series of single-case studies demonstrated again the value of response prevention (Turner, Hersen, Bellack, Andrasik, & Capparrell, 1980; Turner, Hersen, Bellack, & Wells, 1979). To date, only one controlled between-group study was reported in the literature (Foa, Steketee, & Milby, 1980b). Eight obsessive-compulsive patients served as subjects.

Patients were randomly assigned to two treatment conditions: (1) exposure alone followed by exposure and response prevention and (2) response prevention alone followed by the combined treatment. In total, treatment consisted of 20 sessions. Exposure led to more anxiety reduction but less improvement of rituals, while the reverse was found for response prevention. When the combined treatment was applied at the second period, the differences between the groups on anxiety and ritualistic behavior disappeared.

8. *Attention focusing on the feared stimuli may enhance habituation.* Grayson, Foa, and Steketee (1982) compared distraction (playing video games) with attention focusing during exposure in vivo sessions. Attention focusing did not differ from distraction with regard to within-session habituation, but it did affect the degree of between-session habituation.

9. *Antidepressant drugs (clomipramine) may reduce depressed mood and so enhance compliance.* The only double-blind controlled study comparing the effects of a tricyclic antidepressant (clomipramine) with behavioral treatment (exposure plus response prevention) was conducted at the Maudsley Hospital in London (Marks, Stern, Mawson, Cobb, & McDonald, 1980; Rachman et al., 1979). Results were reported to two-year follow-up. In a 2 × 2 experimental design behavioral treatment (exposure vs. relaxation) and psychopharmacological treatment (clomipramine vs. placebo) were systematically varied. Exposure produced significant lasting improvement in rituals but less change in mood. Clomipramine resulted in significant improvement in rituals and mood, but only in those patients who initially had depressed mood.

10. *The therapist may need to address other targets than the obsessive-compulsive problem.* Clinical observation suggests that obsessive-compulsive patients are often socially anxious and unassertive. In some of these cases the obsessive-compulsive problems might serve the function of avoiding people. Assertiveness training has been applied successfully with a number of cases (e.g., Emmelkamp, 1982c, 1985b; Emmelkamp & Van der Heyden, 1980), but controlled studies in this area are lacking. The positive results of these studies indicate that obsessive-compulsives may benefit from other approaches than exposure in vivo and

emphasize the value of a functional analysis (e.g., Queiroz, Motta, Madi, Sossai, & Boren, 1981).

11. *The effectiveness of behavioral procedures with obsessions is less well-established than with compulsions.* Research into the treatment of obsessions had lagged significantly behind that into the treatment of compulsions, probably due to the small prevalence of patients with obsessional ruminations unaccompanied by rituals.

Although no firm conclusions can be drawn on the basis of the few studies that have been conducted, because of the small number of subjects, it does seem that prolonged exposure in imagination to obsessional material has beneficial effects (e.g., Emmelkamp & Giesselbach, 1981; Emmelkamp & Kwee, 1977), while the results of dismissal training (e.g., thought stopping) are more variable (Emmelkamp & Kwee, 1977; Emmelkamp & Van der Heyden, 1980). Emmelkamp and Giesselbach (1981) investigated whether the effects of prolonged exposure in imagination are due to habituation to the obsessions or, alternatively, could be accounted for by habituation to fear in general. A crossover design was implemented with six patients with obsessional ruminations unaccompanied by compulsive rituals. Half of the patients received six sessions of prolonged exposure to obsessional material followed by six sessions of prolonged exposure to irrelevant cues, and the remaining patients had the treatment in the reverse order. With prolonged exposure to irrelevant cues patients were uninterruptedly exposed to scenes that were made up of situations that anyone would fear. These scenes involved situations such as being burnt to death, being strangled, being devoured by a tiger, dying in an aircrash, and the like. The results of this study indicate that relevant exposure resulted in more improvement than irrelevant exposure. Actually, irrelevant exposure even led to a significant deterioration on the distress rating.

Long-term Effectiveness of Behavioral Treatment
Emmelkamp, Hoekstra, and Visser (1985) evaluated the outcome of behavioral treatment approximately 3.5 years after treatment (range 2–6 years). Obsessive-compulsives who had been treated with exposure in vivo and (self-imposed) response prevention in various treatment outcome studies at our department participated in this study.

Figure 9.6 shows the results on Anxiety (0–8 scales), Depressed Mood (Zung-Self-rating Depression Scale), and Maudsley Obsessional-Compulsive Inventory (MOCI). MOCI scores were available for the last 20 patients only, since the first series of patients had been assessed with the Leyton Obsessional Inventory (Emmelkamp & Rabbie, 1981). The major changes took place within the remarkably short space of one month of intensive behavioral treatment. Generally, results after treatment were maintained throughout the follow-up period. Inspection of Figure 9.6 shows a slight relapse on depressed mood at one-month follow-up. Further improvement occurred between one and six months' follow-ups, however, during which period most patients received additional behavioral treatment. It is important to note that during the period between posttest and one-month follow-up, no treatment was provided. No relapse occurred at 3.5 years' follow-up. This pattern clearly suggests that improvement in depression is related to the behavioral treatment that patients received. At follow-up 24 patients

were rated as "much improved," 10 patients as improved, and 8 patients as failures. To establish whether patients' characteristics could be used as predictors for success of behavioral treatment, regression analyses were conducted on several variables, including age of onset, initial depression, and initial anxiety. Each of these variables was found to correlate with outcome at posttreatment or at one-year follow-up in the Foa et al. (1983) study. We were further interested to know whether perceived parental characteristics could affect treatment outcome. Parental characteristics were assessed by an inventory (EMBU; Arrindell, Emmelkamp, Brilman, & Monsma, 1983b).

Initial anxiety and depression did predict outcome at posttreatment but not at follow-up. Interestingly, age of onset and parental rejection hardly predicted outcome at posttreatment but did so at follow-up. Patients whose symptoms began at an earlier age maintained their gains better at follow-up than did those whose symptoms began later, which corroborates result of Foa et al. (1983). The contri-

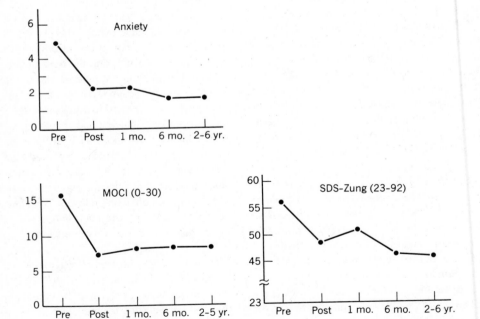

Figure 9.6. Results to 6 years follow-up on anxiety, Maudsley Obsessive-Compulsive Inventory (MOCI) and Self-rating Depression Scale (SDS). Between posttest and 1-month follow-up, no treatment was provided. After 1-month follow-up a number of patients received additional treatment. Reprinted with permission (From Emmelkamp, et al., 1985), Plenum Press.

bution of initial anxiety to posttreatment outcome was only marginally significant. Although initial depression proved to be a better predictor of posttreatment outcome than initial anxiety, there was no relationship with long-term outcome at follow-up. The group that was initially the most depressed improved less on anxiety at the posttest, but this difference disappeared at follow-up, probably because of the continuing treatment these patients received.

DEPRESSION

A number of controlled outcome studies into the effectiveness of cognitive-behavioral interventions for depression have been reported in the last few years. Before embarking on the task of reviewing these studies, I will provide a brief discussion of the major theoretical models of depression that have led to various treatment approaches.

Models

Contemporary cognitive-behavioral formulations of depression fall into three major categories:

1. Cognitive approaches (e.g., Abramson, Seligman, & Teasdale, 1978; Beck, Rush, Shaw, & Emery, 1979).
2. Behavioral approaches (e.g., Lewinsohn & Hoberman, 1982).
3. Self-control theory (e.g., Rehm, 1977).

Cognitive Model

Beck and his colleagues attribute a central role to cognitions in the etiology of depression. Certain cognitive patterns (schemas) become activated and prepotent in depression and structure the kinds of interpretations that are made by the patient. These negative interpretations, consequently, lead to a deterioration of the patient's mood and activation. For a more detailed description of the cognitive theories of depression, the reader is referred to the chapter of Hollon and Beck (this volume). Although the cognitive model of depression has been widely accepted, a few critical remarks need to be made.

Psychiatric patients often demonstrate cognitive dysfunctions, and it is questionable whether thought processes such as making arbitrary interferences, selective abstractions, and overgeneralization are specific for depressed individuals or merely a reflection of psychopathology in general. Further, the fact that depressed mood can be caused by negative thoughts in no way shows that these thoughts are the normal cause of clinical depression (Teasdale & Fennell, 1982). Coyne and Gotlib (1983) recently reviewed the literature on the role of cognition in depression, and their review suggests that neither Beck's nor the learned helplessness model of depression (Abramson et al., 1978) has a strong empirical base. The majority of studies have employed mildly depressed college students who lacked the overt behaviors, somatised anxiety, and physical complaints of clinical depression. As far as clinical depressed patients are concerned, results do not unequivocally support cognitive theories. As Coyne and Gotlib state: " . . . in the absence of further data it is investigators who have been biased in their routine interpretation of depressed-nondepressed differences in term of depressive cognitive biases" (p.479).

Behavioral Model

The behavioral approach is based on the assumption that depressive symptoms result from too low a rate of response-contingent reinforcement and that depression will be ameliorated when the rate of reinforcement for adaptive behavior is increased (Lewinsohn, 1975). Treatment approaches that are suggested by this formulation of depression include (1) reengagement of the depressed individual in constructive and rewarding activities and (2) training in social skills to enhance the individual's capacity to receive social reinforcements resulting from social interactions. It has been suggested (e.g., Lewinsohn & Hoberman, 1982) that lack of social skill could be one of the antecedent conditions producing a low rate of positive reinforcement. Indeed, a number of studies have shown depressed individuals to be less socially skillful than controls (e.g., Coyne, 1976; Jacobson & Anderson, 1984; Lewinsohn, Mischel, Chaplin, & Barton, 1980; Lewinsohn & Shaffer, 1971; Lewinsohn, Weinstein, & Alper, 1970; Libet & Lewinsohn, 1973; Youngren & Lewinsohn, 1980). It should be pointed out, however, that an association between depressed mood and (lack of) social skills does not necessarily imply a causal relationship. It has been suggested (Emmelkamp & Albersnagel, 1979) that depressed individuals have been socially skillful before they became depressed, the depression being responsible for the inadequate social performance. Only prospective studies can answer the question of the direction of causality between depression on the one hand and social skills on the other.

Although it has consistently been found that daily mood ratings correlate with rate of pleasant activities (e.g., Lewinsohn & Hoberman, 1982), this finding does not necessarily imply that increasing pleasant-activity rate will improve mood. Biglan and Craker (1982) studied this issue and found that such increases in pleasant activities did not produce improvements in mood, thus challenging one of the basic assumptions of Lewinsohn's theory of depression.

Self-control Model

Rehm (1977) has proposed a self-control model of depression that provides a framework for integrating the cognitive and behavioral models discussed above. Rehm acknowledges the importance of reinforcement in the development of depression, but he holds that the reinforcement can be self-generated rather than derived from environmental sources. In Rehm's view the depressed mood and the low rate of behavior characteristics for depressed individuals are the result of negative self-evaluations, lack of self-reinforcement, and high rates of self-punishment.

Several studies have been conducted to test Rehm's hypotheses about the role of self-reinforcement in depression, but results are inconclusive (for review see Lewinsohn & Hoberman, 1982). In a more recent series of studies by Heiby (1981, 1983a, 1983b), the interaction between external reinforcement and self-reinforcement was investigated. Results of these studies showed that subjects exhibiting a low frequency of self-reinforcement reported a greater increase in depressed mood following a decrease in environmental reinforcement than individuals exhibiting a high frequency of self-reinforcement. Thus, there is some evidence that reinforcement reduction in the environment may lead to depressed mood for those individuals who engage in a low frequency of self-reinforcement. Interestingly, neither the rate of self-reinforcement alone nor the rate of environmental reinforcement alone was related to depression.

Cognitive-behavioral Interventions

As we have seen, the major approaches differ with respect to the role that they ascribe to the various factors in the etiology and functioning of depression, which leads to different emphases in the various therapeutic procedures based upon these models.

Cognitive therapies focus on changing patients' depressogenic cognitions and hence their depressed affect and behavior. Cognitive therapy aims to help patients identify the assumptions and schemas that support patterns of stereotypical negative thinking and to change specific errors in thinking (Hollon & Beck, this volume). Behavioral approaches attempt to change the unadaptive behavior in order to increase positive reinforcement. Here cognitions are seen as the consequence of depression, and hence it is assumed that these faulty cognitions will change as a result of the behavioral treatment. Self-control therapy aims to change deficits in self-control behavior: self-monitoring, self-evaluation, and self-reinforcement.

Table 9.1 provides an overview of the major outcome studies into depression. Only controlled studies are included, and studies using analogue populations (e.g., volunteering students) have been excluded.

In order to enable cross-study comparisons, criteria for acceptance in the study are provided when available. Both Feigner's criteria and Research Diagnostic Criteria (RDC) indicate that the individual suffers from a depressive disorder.

Behavioral Approaches

Behavioral programs have included two behavioral strategies: (1) increasing pleasant activities and (2) social-skills training either alone or in combination.

Pleasant activities. Increasing pleasant activities by means of homework assignments has been suggested by Lewinsohn (1975) as one way of increasing positive reinforcement to the depressed person. Several studies have investigated whether this approach on its own would be successful in improving depression. Typically, activities that are rated as enjoyable but not engaged in during the last few weeks are given as homework assignments. Activities that appear to be relatively easy are chosen first, while more difficult tasks are assigned in later sessions. While all studies (Gardner & Oei, 1981; Wilson, 1982; Wilson, Goldin, & Charbonneau-Powis, 1983; Zeiss, Lewinsohn, & Munoz, 1979) found this behavioral approach to result in improvement of depression, the question is whether

Table 9.1 Depression: Major Controlled Outcome Studies

Study	Population	Criteria	N	Treatment	Sessions (minutes)	Follow-up	Results
Beck et al. (1985)	Outpatients	Feighner[a] BDI 20[c]	33	(1) Cognitive (2) Cognitive +-amitriptyline	14 × 50 min 16 × 50 min	12 months	Posttest 1 = 2[b] Follow-up 2 > 1[d] (trend)
Blackburn et al. (1981)	Outpatients General practice	RDC[e] BDI ≥ 14	64	(1) Cognitive (2) Drugs (3) Combination	17 × ?	—	Outpatient: 1 = 2 3 > 2 1 > 2 3 > 2 Gen. pract: 1 > 2 3 > 2
Boelens & Debats (1983)	Outpatients	RDC BDI ≥ 16	16	(1) Cognitive-behavioral (2) Behavioral-cognitive	16 × 2 hr	Not yet published	Intermediate test: cognitive = behavioral Posttest: 2 > 1
Comas-Diaz (1981)	Low socioeconomic Puerto Rican women	—	26	(1) Cognitive (2) Behavioral (3) No treatment	5 × 1.5 hr	1 month	Posttest: 1 = 2; 1 & 2 > 3 Follow-up: 1 > 2 (Hamilton)
De Jong et al. (1981)	Inpatients	BDI ≥ 20	20	(1) Cognitive-behavioral (2) Behavioral-cognitive (3) Routine treatment	±14 weeks	Not yet published	1 = 2 1 & 2 > 3
Dunn (1979)	Outpatients	—	20	(1) Cognitive & drugs (2) Support & drugs	16 × 1 hr 8 × 1 hr	6 months	1 > 2
Fleming & Thornton (1980)	Volunteers	BDI ≥ 17	35	(1) Self-control (2) Cognitive (3) Nondirective	8 × 2 hr	1.5 months	Posttest: 1 > 2 & 3 on some measures Follow-up: 1 = 2 = 3
Fuchs & Rehm (1977)	Volunteers	MMPI-D ≥ 70[f]	36	(1) Self-control (2) Nonspecific (3) No treatment	6 × 2 hr	1.5 months	1 > 2 & 3 (posttest)
Gardner & Oei (1981)	Volunteers	BDI ≥ ?	16	(1) Cognitive (2) Task assignments	6 × ?	1 month	1 = 2
Harpin et al. (1982)	Outpatients	Hamilton > 20[g]	12	(1) Cognitive (2) No treatment	20 × ?	3 months	1 > 2 (not statistically significant)
Hersen et al. (1984)	Outpatients & volunteers	Feighner[a] Raskin[h] ≥ 7	120	(1) Social skill + placebo (2) Social skill + amitriptyline (3) Amitriptyline (4) Psychotherapy + placebo	12 × 1 hr ± 6–8 hr Maintenance	6 months	1 = 2 = 3 = 4

(continued)

Table 9.1 (Continued)

Study	Population	Criteria	N	Treatment	Sessions (minutes)	Follow-up	Results
Kornblith et al. (1983)	Volunteers	RDC BDI $\geq$ 20	39	(1) Self-control package (2) Self-monitoring + self-evaluation (3) Didactic principles (4) Psychodynamic group therapy	12 × 1.5 hr	3 months	1 = 2 = 3 = 4
McLean & Hakstian (1979)	?	RDC BDI $\geq$ 23	178	(1) Psychotherapy (2) Relaxation (3) Cognitive (4) Amitriptyline	10 × 1 hr	3 months	3 > all others 2 = 4 1 < all others
McLean et al. (1973)	Outpatients	—	20	(1) Marital therapy (2) Support & drugs	8 × 1 hr	3 months	1 > 2
Murphy et al. (1984)	Outpatients	Feighner[a] BDI $\geq$ 20	70	(1) Cognitive (2) Nortriptyline (3) Cognitive + nortriptyline (4) Cognitive + placebo	20 × 50 min	1 month	1 = 2 = 3 = 4
Rehm et al. (1979)	Volunteers	MMPI-D $\geq$ 70	24	(1) Self-control (2) Assertiveness training	6 × 2 hr	1.5 months	1 > 2 (self-control) 2 > 1 (assertion) 1 > 2 (depression)
Rehm et al. (1981)	Volunteers	RDC MMPI-D $\geq$ 70	49	(1) Self-monitoring (2) Self monitoring + self-evaluation (3) Self-monitoring + self-reinforcement (4) Self-control package (5) No treatment	7 × 1.5 hr		1, 2, 3 & 4 > 5 1 = 2 = 3 = 4
Roth et al. (1982)	Volunteers	RDC BDI $\geq$ 18	26	(1) Self-control (2) Self-control + desimipramine	12 × 2 hr	3 months	1 = 2, more rapid improvement in (2) than in (1)
Rush et al. (1977)	Outpatients	Feighner[a] BDI $\geq$ 20	41	(1) Cognitive (2) Imipramine	15 × 50 min 12 × 20 min	6 months	1 > 2

Study	Population	Criteria	N	Treatments	Sessions	Follow-up	Results
Rush & Watkins (1981)	Outpatients	Feighner[a] BDI ≥ 20	38	(1) Cognitive (group) (2) Cognitive (individual) (3) Individual cognitive + group	20 × 75–90 20 × 50 20 × 50		2 > 1 2 = 3
Sanchez et al. (1980)	Outpatients	MMPI-D ≥ 70	32	(1) Assertiveness training (2) Group psychotherapy	10 × 1.5 hr	1 month	1 = 2 at posttest 1 > 2 at follow-up
Schmidt & Miller (1983)	Volunteers	BDI ≥ 10	54	(1) Individual (2) Small group (3) Large group (4) Bibliotherapy (5) No treatment	8 × 90 min	2 months	1 = 2 = 3 = 4 1 & 2 & 3 & 4 > 5
Shaffer et al. (1981)	Anxious-depressed outpatients	—	34	(1) Cognitive (group) (2) Nondirective (group) (3) Cognitive (individual)	10 × 1.5 hr 10 × 1.5 hr 10 × 1 hr	—	1 = 2 = 3
Teasdale et al. (1984)	General practice	RDC BDI ≥ 20	34	(1) Cognitive (2) Routine treatment	20 × 1 hr	3 months	Posttest 1 > 2 Follow-up 1 = 2
Wilson (1982)	Volunteers	BDI ≥ 20	64	(1) Tasks assignments (2) Relaxation (3) Minimal contact	7 × 1 hr 7 × 1 hr 2 × 1 hr	6 months	1 = 2 = 3 Amitriptyline > placebo
		All conditions with either placebo or amitriptyline					
Wilson et al. (1983)	Volunteers	BDI ≥ 17	25	(1) Cognitive (2) Tasks assignments	8 × 1 hr	5 months	1 = 2 1 & 2 > 3
Zeiss et al. (1979)	Volunteers	MMPI-D ≥ 70	66	(1) Social skill (2) Cognitive (3) Tasks assignments	12 sessions	—	1 = 2 = 3

[a]Feighner = Feighner diagnostic criteria for primary depression.
[b]a = b Treatment a about as effective as treatment b.
[c]BDI = Beck Depression Inventory.
[d]a > b Treatment a is superior to treatment b.
[e]RDC = Research Diagnostic Criteria for major depression.
[f]MMPI = Depression subscale MMPI.
[g]Hamilton = Hamilton Depression Scale.
[h]Raskin = Raskin Depression Scale.

this is due to the increase in pleasant activities per se or due to "nonspecific" variables. In the study of Wilson (1982), improvement of depression was not related to an increase of pleasant activities. Further, Zeiss et al. (1979) found that cognitive therapy and social-skills training led to similar increases in pleasant activites as the condition that had received instructions to increase the rate of pleasant activities. These findings cast doubt on the validity of Lewinsohn's behavioral theory of depression.

Social-skills training. Sanchez, Lewinsohn, and Larson (1980) contrasted group assertion training and group psychotherapy. At posttreatment assertiveness training was slightly more effective than group psychotherapy on measures of assertiveness and depression. The difference in outcome between the treatment formats reached acceptable levels of statistical significance at one-month follow-up. Zeiss et al. (1979) also included a social-skills training condition in their comprehensive study and found this treatment equally effective as cognitive therapy and task assignments. On most measures of social skills, patients were found to have improved at the end of therapy. None of these effects could be directly attributed to the social-skills training, since patients receiving social-skills training did not show more improvement than patients receiving a different treatment modality. It should be noted that a relatively weak mode of assertion training was used—covert modeling—which does not seem to be particularly suited for a clinical population.

Rehm, Fuchs, Roth, Kornblith, and Ramono (1979) compared assertiveness training with training in self-control and found that assertiveness training resulted in more improvement on measures of social skills. However, the self-control therapy resulted in the largest reduction of depressed mood.

The most intensive study to date was conducted by Hersen, Bellack, Himmelhoch, and Thase (1984). Experienced therapists versed in their respective therapies treated 120 depressed outpatients and volunteers. Four treatments were compared: (1) social-skills training plus placebo, (2) social-skills training plus amitriptyline, (3) amitriptyline, and (4) psychotherapy plus placebo. Social skills plus placebo yielded the best clinical results in depression, but this failed to reach acceptable levels of statistical significance. In general, all four treatment formats

were about equally effective. Bellack, Hersen, and Himmelhoch (1983) analyzed behavioral measures of social skills of these patients and found that patients receiving social skills were, after treatment, more similar to normal controls on these measures than patients from the other two groups.

In sum, while a number of studies have shown social-skills training to lead to increased assertiveness and improved social performance, the relationship between improved social performance and reduction in depressed mood remains unclear. The studies conducted so far did not show that social-skills training per se was related to reduction of depression.

Multifaceted programs. Several studies have been reported in which the behavioral treatment involved a combination of graded task assignments and social-skills training. McLean and Hakstian (1979) contrasted this particular behavioral approach with psychotherapy, drug treatment (amitriptyline), and relaxation-control. The results showed unequivocal superiority for the behavioral intervention immediately after treatment. At three-month follow-up, there was still a trend for the behavioral group to be superior to the other approaches, although on most measures the differences were no longer significant.

Comas-Diaz (1981) treated depressed low-income Puerto Rican women living in the United States and contrasted this behavioral approach with cognitive therapy. Patients in treatment groups indicated significantly less depression than those placed in a no-treatment group. No significant differences in success of treatment were found between the behavior and cognitive conditions immediately after treatment. At one-month follow-up, however, the behavior therapy group was superior due to a slight relapse in the cognitive group. A major limitation of this study is that treatment procedures were not strictly separated: The cognitive therapy included assertiveness training, which limits the conclusion to be drawn.

Boelens and Debats (1983) compared this behavioral package with cognitive therapy in a crossover design. Cognitive therapy was along the lines of Beck's model, but behavioral task assignments were excluded. After a waiting period without treatment, half of the patients received cognitive treatment and the other half received the behavioral treatment. After an intermediate test the conditions were crossed. During the waiting period no improvement occurred, but improvement commenced during the active treatment phase. At the intermediate test no differences were found between the two conditions: Cognitive therapy was about equally effective as behavioral treatment. Results at the posttest showed that the cognitive interventions enhanced the effects of the behavioral interventions, while the behavioral interventions did not enhance the effects of the cognitive interventions. Results of this study suggest that both behavioral and cognitive components are important in the treatment of major unipolar depression and that the best combination is to start with behavorial assignments and social-skills training to be followed later on by cognitive restructuring techniques.

De Jong, Henrich, and Ferstl (1981) evaluated a behavioral-cognitive approach that consisted of cognitive therapy and social-skills training with depressed inpatients in a multiple baseline design. While the program was found to result in marked reduction of depression, improved social skills, and changes in faulty thinking patterns, the results of this study suggest that both treatment approaches had a broad effect on depression, skills, and cognitions. Both in the Boelens and Debats and the De Jong et al. studies there was no evidence that each treatment modality selectively influenced the specific target behaviors. Thus both behavioral and cognitive treaments were effective in alleviating depression, yet why this was so remains unclear.

In sum, behavioral programs have shown statistically and clinically significant results in reduction of depression, change of thinking patterns, and improved social performance. Most studies were unable to show, however, that the target behavior directly addressed in the treatment modality was selectively affected. Rather, effects of behavioral programs were "nonspecific"—changing both behavioral and cognitive components—thus precluding conclusions with respect to therapeutic processes responsible for the improvement.

Self-control Therapies

A number of studies by Rehm and his colleagues have evaluated the effectiveness of a self-control therapeutic package and its individual components.

The self-control program developed by Fuchs and Rehm (1977) consists of six weeks of training in self-monitoring, self-evaluation, and self-reinforcement. Subjects were given log forms on which to monitor each day's positive activities (self-monitoring). During the self-evaluation phase of the program, the importance of setting realistic goals in evaluating oneself accurately was stressed. Subjects had to choose subgoals that were concrete and attainable and to rate their accomplished behavior toward those goals. Finally, subjects were instructed to self-administer rewards contingent on accomplishment of a behavioral subgoal (self-reinforcement). Treatment was conducted in a group. This program was found to be slightly more effective than nonspecific group psychotherapy and no-treatment control (Fuchs & Rehm, 1977), cognitive therapy (Fleming & Thornton, 1980), and social-skills training (Rehm et al., 1979) on some measures of depression, but most of these differences were not maintained at follow-up.

Rehm et al. (1981) and Kornblith, Rehm, O'Hara, and Lamparski (1983) evaluated the contribution of the individual components to the overall treatment effect. Results indicated that neither self-evaluation nor self-reinforcement is essential for successful outcome. In the Rehm et al. (1981) study the largest effects were seen in the self-monitoring-only condition. This suggests that the addition of self-evaluation and self-reinforcement may make the treatment unnecessarily complex. Further, nonspecific effects cannot be ruled out. In the Kornblith et al. (1983) study group psychotherapy was found to be about equally effective as the other conditions.

Taking the "self-control" studies together, there is some evidence that this program may be of help in dealing with mild to moderate depression, although the therapeutic processes are not yet well understood. It should be noted that not one study has included clinically depressed patients; all studies treated volunteers who responded to mass-media announcements of the program. In the earlier studies of Rehm and his colleagues, volunteers were less depressed than in the Rehm et al. (1981) and Kornblith et al. (1983) studies. It is important to note that the magnitude of the treatment effect in the later studies was less than that in the previous studies, which suggests that the program was less effective with more severe depression. A final comment concerns the fact that all self-control treatments have been conducted in a group format. It cannot be ruled out that "nonspecific" group processes were more influential in affecting outcome than the self-control procedures. Indeed, 54 percent of patients in the self-control group of Roth, Bielski, Jones, Parker, and Osborn (1982) indicated that the group was the most effective component of the treatment package: "Subjects typically reported that they benefitted from the opportunity to socialize, receive social support, help other members, discover alternative viewpoints, and learn that they were not alone in their depression" (p. 142).

Cognitive Approaches

The studies in this area have been reviewed by Hollon and Beck (this volume), so the discussion here will be brief. While most studies evaluating this approach have found cognitive therapy effective in alleviating depression (see Table 9.1), the question remains whether the improvement comes about through changes in cognitive processes. There is now increasing evidence that cognitive changes are not just the result of cognitive therapy but of a variety of treatment approaches such as behavior therapies and antidepressant drugs. Rush, Beck, Kovacks, Weissenburger, and Hollon (1982) found that compared to an antidepressant drug, cognitive therapy resulted in greater improvements in hopelessness and self-concept. In contrast, Simons, Garfield, and Murphy (1984) found that patients receiving medication did demonstrate significant changes on cognitive measures: Here no superiority for the cognitive group was found on any of these measures. Regardless of treatment modality, failures did not improve on cognitive measures, whereas successfully treated patients did improve. Further evidence that cognitive processes are affected by behavioral approaches was shown by Boelens and Debats (1983), De Jong et al. (1981), and Zeiss et al. (1979). As stated by Simons et al. (1984): "The cognitive distortions that are the focus of cognitive therapy appear to behave more as symptoms of depression than as causes" (p. 49).

One major problem in interpreting the results of cognitive therapy for depression concerns the behavioral components included in the "cognitive" package. Beck's cognitive therapy seeks to uncover dysfunctional depressogenic cognitions and to correct these cognitions by systematic "reality testing."

Actually, this particular treatment approach is an amalgam of cognitive and behavioral interventions, including behavioral tasks assignments and assertiveness training. Very few studies used a "pure" cognitive condition (e.g., Boelens & Debats, 1983); thus it is questionable whether the positive effects of cognitive therapy should be ascribed to the cognitive elements of treatment, to the behavioral elements of treatment, or to nonspecific variables.

Concluding Remarks

There is now increasing evidence that cognitive and behavioral approaches are effective in alleviating depression in mildly to moderately depressed individuals, but no one approach has been found to be consistently superior. The self-control therapy of Rehm and his colleagues has not yet been tested on clinical samples, which precludes conclusions with respect to the clinical effectiveness of this particular approach.

Surpisingly, only one study (McLean, Ogston, & Grauer, 1973) evaluated the effectiveness of behavioral marital therapy with depressed patients. Marital therapy led to improved communication between the couple and amelioration of depression, whereas the control group did not improve. Given the relationship between marital dissatisfaction and depression, future studies in this area are greatly needed.

The principal finding of the present review is that a variety of cognitive-behavioral procedures are successful in improving depression, but one cannot conclude that the specific components of treatment were responsible for improvement. This finding suggests that common elements in these treatments are responsible for the improvements achieved. Such common elements are a clear rationale, highly structured therapy, homework assignments, and the training of skills (either cognitive or behavioral) that the patient can utilize in handling his or her problems.

Unfortunately, long-term follow-up studies are relatively rare. Given the episodic character of depressed mood and the chance of "spontaneous" improvement in the course of time, long-term outcome of behavioral interventions needs to be studied.

Another area where research is highly needed is that of matching patient and treatment. Giving social-skills training to patients who already have adequate social skills or giving cognitive therapy to patients who are not characterized by cognitive dysfunctions seems to be a waste of time. Ideally, instead of the application of standardized treatment procedures, in clinical practice treatment needs to be tailor-made to the needs of the individual patient. Whether such an approach would enhance the effectiveness of cognitive-behavioral treatment remains to be shown, but deserves to be studied.

ALCOHOLISM

The purpose of this section is to provide a selective review of the steadily accumulating literature on the behavioral treatment of alcoholism. Evaluation of work in this area is clouded by the use of poorly defined patient characteristics in most of these studies. Boyd et al. (1983) found at least 10 widely used definitions of alcoholism and at least another 10 that are less widely used. While there is consensus that alcoholism is characterized by excessive drinking, there is no agreement on how much drinking is excessive.

In *DSM-III* "alcohol abuse" is differerentiated from "alcohol dependence," the latter being more or less similar to alcoholism. Alcohol dependence is characterized by either tolerance (need for markedly increased amounts of alcohol to achieve the desired effect) or alcohol withdrawal symptoms after cessation or reduction in drinking. Jellinek (1960) recognized a number of different types of alcoholism. The most serious type was called "gamma" alcoholism. The essential feature of gamma alcoholism is the loss of control, that is, the inability to stop drinking once started. As Jellinek describes it: "Loss of control means that any drinking of alcohol starts a chain reaction which is felt by the drinker as a physical demand for alcohol" (p. 679).

After briefly discussing the current status of "conventional" behavioral procedures such as aversion therapy and covert sensitization, the bulk of the discussion is devoted to recent developments in the behavioral treatment of problem drinking: social-skills training and controlled-drinking approaches.

Aversive Methods
Aversive methods have long been used in the treatment of alcoholism, although interest has waned in the last decade. With aversive conditioning a noxious stimulus (UCS) is paired with actual drinking (CS) or with visual or olfactory cues related to drinking. Aversive conditioning is intended to produce a conditioned aversion to drinking. A variety of aversive stimuli have been used, the most popular of which were electric shock and nausea- or apnea-inducing substances. Covert sensitization is a variant of aversive conditioning wherein images of drinking are paired with imaginal aversive stimuli.

Electrical and Chemical Aversion Therapy
Studies into the effects of electrical aversion therapy have shown this form of treatment generally to be ineffective and there is now a consensus in the field that treatment by electrical aversion therapy should be discontinued, on both clinical (Nathan & Bridell, 1977; Sobell, Sobell, Ersner-Herschfield, & Nirenberg, 1982; Wilson, 1978) and theoretical (Hallam & Rachman, 1976) grounds. The effects of aversion therapy are usually explained in terms of classical conditioning. However, Hallam, Rachman, and Falkowski (1972) failed to find conditioned heart rate or skin-resistance responses following electrical aversion therapy, which seriously questions the theoretical basis of this procedure.

Although taste-aversion conditioning is one of the oldest aversive treatments (Voegtlin & Broz, 1949), interest in emetic aversion therapy declined in favor of electrical-shock aversion therapy. It was argued that shock was a more desirable UCS than drugs in a classical conditioning paradigm to allow for a more exact control of the UCS–CS relationship. Further, there are a number of practical disadvantages associated with chemical aversion therapy that has precluded its widespread use.

More recently, some (e.g., Elkins, 1975) have concluded that nausea rather than electrical stimulation is the preferred noxious basis for the induction of therapeutic aversions to alcohol. In a series of studies by Cannon and his colleagues, it was demonstrated that emetic aversion therapy produced conditioned alcohol aversions (Baker & Cannon, 1979; Cannon & Baker, 1981). In the Cannon and Baker (1981) study psychophysiological, attitudinal, and behavioral responses to alcoholic and nonalcoholic flavors were assessed in alcoholics given either group therapy alone (controls), group therapy plus electrical aversion therapy, or group therapy plus emetic aversion therapy. The emetic therapy subjects showed evidence of a conditioned aversion to alcohol and not to nonalcoholic flavors. Subjects in the other two groups did not show evidence of conditioning.

Cannon, Baker, and Wehl (1981) reported one-year follow-up data for subjects in the Cannon and Baker (1981) study. The results of this follow-up suggest that emetic aversion therapy can enhance posttreatment abstinence rates and that this enhanced outcome is related to the effect of treatment on heart rate response to alcohol. At six months' follow-up emetic subjects were abstinent significantly more days than electrical aversion and control subjects, who did not differ from each other. At one-year follow-up the shock subjects did worst. Now emetic and control subjects were abstinent significantly more days than shock subjects, while there was no difference between emetic and control condition (mean days abstinent = 309, 108, and 305, for emetic, shock, and control Ss, respectively). Further analyses revealed that posttreatment heart-rate response was related to the number of days of abstinence in the year following treatment, irrespective of treatment condition.

In sum, given the poor results, the use of electrical aversion conditioning as a treatment modality with alcoholics should be discontinued. Recent research by Cannon and his colleagues suggests that techniques based on taste aversion conditioning might be more promising. Further controlled studies are necessary to support the clinical efficacy of these techniques. It should be noted that all patients in the Cannon and Baker (1981) study received standard inpatient alcoholism treatment in addition to any aversion therapy, which precludes the drawing of firm conclusions with respect to the clinical efficacy of emetic aversion therapy per se.

Covert Sensitization

Covert sensitization with alcoholics involves the induction of verbally produced nausea following the imagination of a drinking scene. After the patient has imagined himself consuming an alcoholic beverage, disgusting nausea and vomiting scenes are described by the therapist, which end when the patient imagines himself running from the drinking setting. Results of most of the studies into covert sensitization with alcoholics are made uninterpretable by severe methodological limitations (Little & Curran, 1978).

Elkins (1980) provided some evidence that con-

ditioned nausea could be produced in a number of alcoholics receiving covert sensitization treatment. Approximately 90 percent of patients who remained in treatment for at least six covert sensitization sessions reacted with genuine nausea responses as evidenced by swallowing, muscular tremor, and facial grimacing and occasionally by actual vomiting, but only two-thirds of these subjects developed some degree of *conditioned* nausea. Conditioned nausea was defined as "nausea arising as a direct consequence of the subject's focusing on preingestive or ingestive concomitants of typical drinking scenes" (p. 72). Significant degrees of extended abstinence were observed for conditioned-nausea subjects as opposed to other subjects. Since no control groups were used and subjects were inpatients in a traditional alcoholism rehabilitation program, conclusions with respect to covert sensitization as a primary form of treatment are not warranted.

Olson, Ganley, Devine, and Dorsey (1981) compared (1) milieu therapy (control group), (2) covert sensitization, (3) insight-oriented therapy, and (4) a combination of covert sensitization and insight-oriented therapy with 137 alcoholics. All patients participated in a milieu treatment program. At four-year follow-up 36.6 percent of all patients were abstinent, while 73.5 percent were abstinent six months after treatment. The behavioral treatment was significantly superior to the insight-oriented therapy. The insight-oriented group did worse than the routine milieu treatment. The results of this study suggest that adding covert sensitization to a hospital milieu program may be beneficial, whereas adding insight-oriented therapy is not.

Concluding Remarks

Although chemical aversion therapy and covert sensitization appear to have some promise as adjunct techniques in preventing drinking immediately after treatment, their long-term effectiveness is far from proven. On the theoretical side, a simple conditioning interpretation seems inadequate to account for the therapeutic effects achieved. While other theoretical explanations have been proposed, including cognitive expectation factors (Emmelkamp & Walta, 1978) and coping-response information processing (Baker, Cannon, Tiffany, & Gino, 1984), as contributing factors to the outcome of aversive procedures, further experimental work is needed to identify the processes involved.

Social-skill Training

Exposure to a heavy drinking model is likely to increase the risk of relapse and maintenance of heavy drinking. Marlat and Gordon (1980) reported that for alcoholics, 23 percent of relapses involved social pressure situations such as being offered a drink, and in another 29 percent of the cases, drinking behavior was preceded by frustrating situations in which the individual was unable to express anger. There is some evidence that interpersonal anxiety has a strong effect on alcohol consumption (Smail, Stockwell, Canter, & Hodgson, 1984; Stockwell, Smail, Hodgson, & Canter, 1984). Further, some authors have suggested that alcoholics lack general assertiveness skills (O'Leary, O'Leary, & Donovan, 1976; Van Hasselt, Hersen & Milliones, 1978). Taken together, these findings suggest that social-skill training may be a useful treatment procedure.

Oei and Jackson (1980) studied the effects of group and individual social-skill training compared to traditional supportive therapy on alcoholics. Social-skill training subjects improved significantly more than subjects receiving supportive therapy both on alcohol intake, social skills, and social anxiety. Group-skill training was slightly more effective than individual training of social skills. In another study Jackson and Oei (1978) compared (1) social-skill training, (2) cognitive restructuring, and (3) supportive therapy. Immediately after treatment, the social-skill training was the most effective, supportive therapy was the least effective, and the results of cognitive therapy were in between those of the other two treatments. At follow-up three months later the cognitive restructuring patients continued to improve in social skills. Similar results were found in a third study (Oei & Jackson, 1982). Here social-skill training, cognitive restructuring, and a combined treatment—including both skills training and cognitive restructuring—were superior to supportive therapy on all measures. At follow-up 3, 6, and 12 months later, the cognitive restructuring and combined treatment continued to improve, suggesting that the cognitive changes resulted in continued improvement in social behavior.

Chaney, O'Leary, and Marlatt (1978) gave alcoholics social-skill and problem-solving training. With problem-solving training subjects were taught how to define the problem that problematic situations presented by specifying the elements and to generate alternatives and think about the consequences. Forty alcoholics engaged in inpatient treatment were divided into three conditions: (1) a social-skill/problem-solving group, (2) a discussion group, and (3) a control group. In the discussion groups the same problematic situations as were used in the skill-training groups were discussed, and expression of feelings relevant to these situations were encouraged. The skill-training group was significantly superior to both the discussion group and the control group on social skills and decrease in duration and severity of relapse episodes. At one-year follow-up, the skill-training group had an average number of days drunk one-sixth that of the pooled discussion and control conditions.

Jones, Kanfer, and Lanyon (1982) attempted to replicate the study of Chaney ét al. (1978). Contrary to the findings of Chaney et al., Jones et al. (1982) found that both the skills-training and the discussion groups were superior to the control groups and did not differ from each other. To account for the discrepant findings, Jones et al. suggest that the positive results of their discussion group may be due to their patient sample, which was of a higher socioeconomic group than the sample of Cheney et al. They suggest that the coping skills training may be critical for alcoholics of lower socioeconomic status whereas higher functioning alcoholics may require less concrete training procedures to derive clear benefits from an intervention program.

Summary. The controlled studies in this area clearly show beneficial effects of social-skills training with alcoholics. There is some evidence that cognitive restructuring may enhance the effectiveness of the social-skills training program. As to the addition of training in problem-solving skills to social-skills training, results are inconclusive. It does seem that social-skills training may be an important ingredient in multimodal treatment programs for socially anxious alcoholics who lack the necessary social skills.

Controlled Drinking

In the last decade there has been a polemic on the issue of treatment goals for alcoholics. While several years ago there was almost consensus that total abstinence was the only acceptable treatment goal, more recently results of a number of studies have suggested that a substantial number of problem drinkers can learn and maintain a pattern of moderate and nonproblem drinking. This issue has reached the popular press following the publication of the Rand reports (Armor, Polich, & Stambul, 1976; Polich, Armor, & Braiker, 1980). More recently a new dimension to the controversy was added by Pendery, Maltzman, and West's (1982) attack on the data of Sobell and Sobell (1973), who had evaluated controlled-drinking training with diagnosed gamma alcoholics.

Proponents of the abstinence goal for alcoholics hold that alcoholism is more or less an irreversible disease, as illustrated by the Alcoholics Anonymous insistence that its members are but "one drink away from a drunk." There is now considerable evidence (Miller, 1983) that a substantial number of problem drinkers can drink without problems, even when the treatment had focused on total abstinence. Thus, these have been "accidental" moderation outcomes because the patients have been provided with no assistance or encouragement toward moderation (Miller, 1983). It is further often established that very few drinkers who affiliate with Alcoholics Anonymous remain forever sober (e.g., Ogborne & Bornet, 1982). Given the poor outcome of Alcoholics Anonymous groups and of traditional treatment programs focusing on abstinence, there is reason enough to investigate alternative treatment options.

Multimodal Treatments

Sobell and Sobell (1973) investigated the efficacy of a self-control program on male gamma alcoholics: All subjects were evaluated as having a history of physical dependence on alcohol. Since this study has recently been heavily attacked by Pendery et al. (1982), I will discuss it in some detail. Seventy subjects were assigned to either a traditional abstinence-oriented treatment program or to an experimental treatment program. The experimental subjects participated in 17 sessions of intensive broad-spectrum behavioral treatment. Half of the subjects had an objective of controlled drinking, the other half of abstinence. Treatment involved aversion conditioning for inappropriate drinking, problem solving, assertiveness training, education, rehearsal of coping responses, and videotapes of the patient's own drunken behavior. Follow-up measures were taken

at 6 months, 1 year, 1.5 years, and 2 years. Throughout this follow-up period, subjects in the experimental groups either stayed abstinent or controlled their drinking more than individuals in the control condition. Experimental controlled-drinking subjects had fewer drunken days and fewer days in hospitals or jails, and also had more abstinent and controlled drinking days than the experimental abstinent group. Pendery et al. (1982) presented information on long-term treatment outcomes over an approximately 11-year interval for the experimentally treated (controlled-drinking) subjects only, and they reached conclusions that are very different from the conclusions of the Sobells: ". . . our follow-up revealed no evidence that gamma alcoholics had acquired the ability to engage in controlled drinking safely after being treated in the experimental program" (p. 174). Of the 20 experimental subjects treated with a controlled-drinking objective, 4 were found to have died alcohol-related deaths, 8 continued to drink excessively with alcohol-related consequences (job loss, arrest, marital breakup, and related serious physical illness), and 6 were abstaining completely, but only after multiple rehospitalizations. One subject was successful in maintaining his pattern of controlled drinking and one subject was missing.

Two independent commissions (one of the United States House of Representatives and one convened by the Addiction Research Foundation in Canada) have made external inquiries of this study and concluded that there is no reason to doubt the scientific and personal integrity of the Sobells. As noted, Pendery et al. reported only follow-up data of the self-controlled subjects, leaving out follow-up data of the control group. While the results of the 10- to 11-year follow-up data of the controlled-drinking subjects are far from optimistic, these can be evaluated only when compared with the results of the abstinence group. Although the mortality rate reported by Pendery et al. (1982) appears to be high, this appears to be actually lower than the mortality rate of chronic gamma alcoholics in the literature: *"No experimentally-treated Ss died within the first 6 yr following discharge*, a finding that stands in marked contrast to the expected mortality rate for this sample" (Sobell & Sobell, 1984, p. 433). Sobell and Sobell (1984) sought mortality information in the abstinence-oriented group. Six out of 20 of the traditionally treated subjects were found to have died, and the deaths of four of these were clearly alcohol-related; the determinationn of alcohol involvement in the death of the other two cases was less clear. Thus, in terms of mortality rate, the traditionally treated subjects did at least as badly as the controlled-drinking subjects. When placed in this perspective, it does seem that neither a controlled-drinking approach nor more traditional treatment was of lasting benefit to patients diagnosed as gamma alcoholics.

Several investigators have evaluated multifaceted treatment programs for problem drinkers, using controlled drinking as the therapeutic goal. For example Pomerleau, Pertchuk, Adkins, & Bradley (1978) conducted an outpatient program for largely socially intact problem drinkers. Treatment included (1) a functional analysis of the subjects' drinking, using daily drinking records, (2) strengthening of nondrinking activities, (3) training in self-management techniques to control drinking, and (4) the use of a prepaid commitment fee that was refunded for program compliance. At nine-month follow-up, 72 percent of behaviorally treated patients and 50 percent of a traditionally treated control group, which stressed a goal of abstinence, were rated as improved (abstinent or reduced intake), but this difference was not statistically significant. Another finding was that fewer subjects dropped out of the behavioral program (2 of 18) than of the traditional program (6 of 14).

The objective of the Sobell and Sobell (1973) and the Pomerleau et al. (1978) studies was to test the hypothesis that a behavioral program with a controlled-drinking goal would prove superior to a traditional abstinence-oriented program. In these studies the goals of abstinence and controlled drinking were embedded in very different treatment interventions; thus it is unclear whether the difference in outcome should be ascribed to the nature of the interventions or to the drinking goal per se.

To prevent the pitfalls of the studies discussed above, Sanchez-Graig, Annis, Bornet, and MacDonald (1984) investigated the comparative efficacy of abstinence versus controlled drinking when all participants receive the same treatment program. "Early-stage" problem drinkers were randomly assigned to a goal of abstinence or controlled drinking. Treatments in both conditions were identical, ex-

cept for training in controlled drinking that was introduced in the fourth treatment session. Treatment involved self-monitoring of drinking, training in problem-solving, and cognitive coping (self-statements).

The results of this study did not support the hypothesis that assignment to a goal of controlled drinking would produce a better outcome than assignment to a goal of abstinence. Most controlled-drinking clients achieved moderation of alcohol use, and most abstinence-oriented clients failed to abstain but nonetheless moderated their drinking. Six months after treatment, drinking had been reduced from an average of about 51 drinks per week to 13, and this reduction was maintained throughout the second year. Most of the individuals assigned to abstinence rejected this goal from the outset.

Blood Alcohol Discrimination Training
Several studies on the utility of controlled drinking incorporate blood alcohol discrimination training as a component. Alcoholic subjects are given accurate feedback concerning their blood alcohol level under training conditions and have to maintain blood alcohol levels below a specified concentration. It is contended that alcoholics thus learn to monitor level of intoxication (e.g., Caddy & Lovibond, 1976; Vogler, Compton, & Weissbach, 1975). Lansky, Nathan, and Lawson (1978) compared the effects of blood alcohol discrimination training with external cue training (educational instruction on relationship between alcohol doses and blood alcohol level); the latter procedure was found to be the most effective. Thus, blood alcohol discrimination training seems to have limited clinical utility, since just giving alcoholics information and training them to attend to external cues that accompany alcohol intake does achieve even superior results.

Behavioral Self-control Training
Miller and his associates have developed a less intensive controlled-drinking treatment program than the multimodal programs discussed above. This approach, labeled "behavioral self-control training," includes self-monitoring, training in drinking-rate control, self-reinforcement, functional analysis of drinking behavior, and instructions in alternatives to alcohol abuse (Miller & Muñoz, 1982). A series of studies have evaluated this particular approach, and there is some evidence that this program is as effec-

tive as a more extensive multifaceted program (Miller & Hester, 1980). Miller and Baca (1983) reported follow-up data of 69 out of 82 problem drinkers treated by behavioral self-control training. Improvements on drinking were found to be maintained at 2 years' follow-up. Overall success rate was 72 percent at 6 months, 65 percent at 12 months, and 67 percent at 2 years' follow-up.

Although the results of controlled drinking approaches with problem drinkers are impressive, clearly not every alcoholic is suited for such a program. To the extent that controlled drinking succeeds, it appears to succeed with individuals with less severe alcohol problems in terms of duration of illness and physical dependence. Successful controlled drinkers are generally found to be younger, less addicted, with fewer life problems related to alcohol (Miller, 1983). Thus, a controlled drinking program is not the treatment of choice for chronic alcoholics. To quote one of the workers in this field: "The approach has not been the monster let loose upon the world that some from AA predicted nor has it been any panacea" (Pertchuk, 1983, p. 259).

SEXUAL DYSFUNCTIONS[1]

In recent years an increased number of clients have sought treatment for sexual dysfunctions, partly as a result of the development of brief sex therapies, which are now increasingly made accessible to a broad public.

Of most importance has been the publication of Masters and Johnson's (1970) volume in which the brief sex treatment of a large series of males and females was evaluted. Although this study had a number of major methodological shortcomings, at that time it was revolutionary for a number of reasons. First, treatment was highly directive and behaviorially oriented, rather than psychoanalytically oriented, which approach had been most influential up to that time. Second, sexual dysfunctions were conceptualized as relationship dysfunctions rather than as an individually pathological condition; this conceptualization resulted in the emphasis on treating the partners as a couple . Finally, the statistics provided by Masters and Johnson gave the impression of a very high success rate.

Before the publication of Masters and Johnson's (1970) book, behavior therapists had already

[1]Ed. note: See Chapter 1 discussion of values.

treated sexual dysfunctions—most often with systematic desensitization (Wolpe, 1958)—but controlled studies were lacking. Sexual dysfunctions were considered to be the result of phobic-like anxiety and avoidance reactions.

With Masters and Johnson's approach the couple is requested to carry out homework assignments. The assignments start with mutual touching excluding genital areas and intercourse, and gradually develop into full intercourse. When necessary, specific techniques dealing with premature ejaculation, vaginismus, or other specific dysfunctions are added to this program.

Masters and Johnson's program is essentially behavorial in nature and can be conceived of as graded exposure in vivo. Similarly, a number of behavioral procedures currently used in the treatment of sexual dysfunctions can be conceptualized as exposure procedures. Exposure to sexual situations and experiences can be accomplished along several lines: (1) imaginal (e.g., systematic desensitization), (2) in vivo (e.g., graded homework assignments along the lines of Masters and Johnson), and (3) vicarious (e.g., videotapes).

Although there is general agreement that there is a complex relationship between *desire*, *anxiety*, and *performance* in sexual dysfunctions, in most studies dysfunctions are defined as performance problems. Typically, criteria for success of treatment are frequency of orgasm during intercourse, restoration of erectile functioning, and so on. The relationship between desire, anxiety, and performance, however, makes assessment that is primarily based on performance difficult to interpret. Therapy may, for example, improve performance without improving anxiety. Levine and Agle (1978) argued that figures based on performance only may be very misleading: "Most of the men, despite improvement, continued to have profound disturbances in their sexual lives" (p. 246).

The next section involves a review of studies on treatment of sexual dysfunctions; only controlled studies are discussed.

According to Masters and Johnson (1970), orgasmic dysfunctions are usually classified as either primary or secondary. With females primary orgasmic dysfunction is defined as the condition in which a female has never experienced orgasm. Secondary orgasmic dysfunction refers to women who achieve orgasm only in response to restricted types of stimulation, or women who in the past were orgasmic, but who are currently unable to experience orgasm. Other female sexual dysfunctions include vaginismus and dyspareunia.

Male sexual dysfunctions are classified by Masters and Johnson (1970) as primary and secondary impotence, premature ejaculation, and ejaculation impotence.

In recent years attention has been focused on problems of low sexual desire (Friedman, Weiler, LoPiccolo, & Hogan, 1982; Kaplan, 1977, 1979). Patients with an inhibition of sexual desire report a lack of desire in engaging in sexual activities or even aversion of sex. Friedman et al. (1982) report that 69 percent of the cases treated at their Sex Therapy Center included a complaint of low sexual desire. Problems of sexual desire are often not differentiated from other sexual complaints, which inhibits the generalizability of the findings.

Mixed Populations

Systematic Desensitization

A number of controlled studies included males and females with sexual dysfunctions. The first controlled study on the effect of systematic desensitization was conducted by Obler (1973). The subjects were assigned to three conditions: (1) systematic desensitization, (2) group therapy, and (3) no treatment. Systematic desensitization also included assertiveness training. The group therapy was psychoanalytically oriented. Results indicated that the modified systematic desensitization program was more effective than the other two conditions. Systematic desensitization was found to reduce sexual anxiety both on self-report measures and psychophysiologically. A problem in interpreting results of this study is that systematic desensitization and assertiveness training were combined.

Mathews et al. (1976) compared three methods: (1) systematic desensitization plus counseling, (2) Masters and Johnson's program plus counseling, and (3) Masters and Johnson's program with minimal contact. Of 36 couples complaining of sexual difficulties, 18 were classified as primarily male problems and 18 as female. The Masters and Johnson program, consisting of directed practice plus counseling, was found to be more effective than desensitization and the minimal contact treatment. However, conclusions with respect to anxiety reduction are precluded since anxiety was not assessed.

In sum, although systematic desensitization has been found to result in more improvement than psychodynamic group therapy, a modified Masters and Johnson program seems to be more effective.

Masters and Johnson Program

The effectiveness of modified Masters and Johnson programs for couples with mixed dysfunctions was also studied by Clement and Schmidt (1983), Crowe, Gillan, and Golombock (1981), Hartman and Dally (1983), and Heiman and LoPicollo (1983). Masters and Johnson used an intensive treatment format, involving daily therapy sessions by a team of a male and female co-therapist for an intensive two-week period. Crowe et al. (1981), Clement and Schmidt (1983), and Mathews et al. (1976) found that treatment was equally effective when conducted by one therapist as when conducted by two therapists of opposite sex.

As to the intensive treatment format proposed by Masters and Johnson, there is no evidence that daily sessions are superior to two sessions a week (Clement & Schmidt, 1983) or one session a week (Heiman & LoPicollo, 1983). There was even some indication of better results for secondary anorgasmia and erectile failure when treated in the weekly mode (Heiman & LoPicollo, 1983).

In sum, the short-term effectiveness of the Masters and Johnson program has been established in a series of studies, but there is neither evidence that a dual therapist team is essential nor that treatment sessions should be held daily.

Behavioral Marital Therapy

Both Crowe et al. (1981) and Hartman and Dally (1983) evaluated the differential effectiveness of a modified Masters and Johnson program and marital therapy. In the Crowe et al. study (1981) couples who had received marital therapy (n = 16) involving discussion of marital problems, relaxation, and communication training improved as much as couples treated by sex therapy (n = 32) on variables associated with sexual and relationship satisfaction. The results suggest that the Masters and Johnson program is no more effective in the treatment of sexual dysfunctions than marital therapy.

In the Hartman and Dally (1983) study, sexually dysfunctional couples received both sex therapy and marital therapy in a crossover design. Half of the patients received first sex therapy (five sessions) followed by marital therapy (5 sessions), while the order of treatment was reversed with the other couples. Marital therapy consisted of communication-skills and problem-solving training. Sex therapy achieved a superior outcome on the measure of sexual satisfaction, whereas both treatments were equally effective in enhancing marital satisfaction. Contrary to the findings of Crowe et al. (1981), the results of Hartman and Dally suggest that sex therapy helps both sexual and marital problems, whereas marital therapy helps marital problems only. However, given the small number of couples involved (n = 12) and the limited number of treatment sessions in the Hartman and Dally study, more definite conclusions on this issue are precluded.

Male Sexual Dysfunction

Exposure Programs

Based on the notion that erectile failure is associated with (performance) anxiety, two controlled studies have been reported that investigated the effectiveness of systematic desensitization.

Kockott, Dittmar, and Nusselt (1975) attempted to evaluate the effectiveness of systematic desensitization in the treatment of male sexual dysfunctions (impotence). Patients were randomly distributed across three conditions: (1) systematic desensitization, (2) routine therapy, and (3) no treatment. Routine therapy consisted of standardized advice and medication. Results were generally poor as far as performance was concerned. However, systematic desensitization resulted in less subjective anxiety during imagination of sexual intercourse as compared with the other two groups.

Everaerd (1977) compared the effectiveness of systematic desensitization with a Masters and Johnson program in the treatment of erectile impotence and premature ejaculation. Systematic desensitization was found to be less effective than the Masters and Johnson program, corroborating results of Mathews et al. (1976).

Treatment Conducted in Groups

Treatment in the Evereard (1977) and Kockott el al. (1975) studies involved the couple rather than the individual male with the sexual complaint. Recent research indicates that men's group sex therapy offers an alternative for men without steady sexual partners or for men whose partner does not want to be involved in the therapy (e.g., Lobitz & Baker, 1979; Zeiss, Christensen, & Levine, 1978; Zilber-

geld, 1975). Treatment consisted among others of masturbation exercises. Treatment was reported to be successful for a number of males, but these studies were uncontrolled.

Price, Reynolds, Cohen, Anderson, and Schochet (1981) assigned men with secondary erectile failure randomly to either eight sessions of men's group therapy or to a waiting-list control group. Treatment involved sex-education and self-stimulation exercises in which they learned that they could gain, lose, and then regain erections. Sexual intercourse was banned at the beginning of the treatment program. Group sex therapy was superior to the control group in terms of sexual satisfaction. However, the treated group did not differ in the reported frequency of erection difficulties following treatment.

In a following study of the same research group (Reynolds, Cohen, Schochet, Price, & Anderson, 1981), social-skill training was added to the therapy program. Female guest therapists helped men role-play difficult social/sexual situations. Treatment was further identical to that of Reynolds et al. (1981). The men's group met for 10 weekly sessions. Results of treatment were compared with changes during a waiting period before treatment started. In addition to positive attitudinal changes, treatment resulted now also in a significant reduction of erection difficulties. The men reported also a significant reduction in social anxiety, whereas in the previous study, which did not include social-skill training, there was not a reduction in social anxiety.

Biofeedback

There have been some suggestions in the literature that men with erectile failure could profit from biofeedback training (Csillag, 1976; Quinn, Harbinson, & MacAllister, 1970). These studies combined erectile response feedback and exposure to erotic stimuli, however, thus precluding the drawing of conclusions with respect to biofeedback per se.

Reynolds (1980) randomly assigned 30 men with erectile dysfunctions to three groups that received either (1) feedback of erection changes plus segments of erotic film delivered contingent on erection increases, (2) contingent film segments without feedback, or (3) noncontingent film segments. At the end of the training sessions, subjects who had exposure to erotic film segments that were contingent on progressive increases in the erectile response enhanced the voluntary facilitation of erection in the laboratory. Interestingly, the combination of feedback and contingent erotic film resulted in *less* erectile change than the noncontingent film and contingent film alone conditions. Thus, contrary to expectations, the addition of tumescene feedback did not enhance erectile change. It should be noted that clinical improvements were modest. The findings of Reynolds' study seriously question the clinical utility of biofeedback for the treatment of erectile dysfunction.

Summarizing the results of studies into male sexual dysfunctions a few conclusions can be drawn. Gradual exposure in vivo to sexual situations as involved in Masters and Johnson's approach is an important element of treatment for male dysfunctions. Recent innovations, including masturbation exercizes, social-skill training, and cognitive restructuring, may also result in beneficial effects, but whether the addition of these techniques would enhance treatment of a "conventional" Masters and Johnson program has not been investigated. Finally, biofeedback does not seem to be of much value in the treatment of these dysfunctions.

Female Sexual Dysfunctions

Systematic Desensitization

Many articles have reported systematic desensitization in the treatment of female sexual dysfunctions, but we will limit our scope to controlled studies. Munjack et al. (1976) found behavior treatment including systematic desensitization and modeling more effective than no treatment in terms of both orgasmic capacity and decrease in negative feelings. Although their treatment package appeared to be an effective therapy, it is impossible to evaluate the effective ingredients since Munjack et al. included assertiveness training, behavioral rehearsal, masturbation training, and the use of mechanical devices as part of their treatment program.

Sotile and Kilmann (1978) investigated the effects of systematic desensitization with 8 primary and 14 secondary anorgasmic women. The clients served as their own control. In the control period that preceded actual treatment, subjects were asked to read a handout containing general information on female sexual responsivity. Systematic desensitization led to improvements on both sexual anxiety

measures and sexual functioning, including percentage of times that orgasm was achieved during extracoital stimulation. When treatment and control periods were contrasted statistically, systematic desensitization was found to be significantly superior. Sotile and Kilmann (1978) found that secondary subjects reported greater positive changes in orgasmic responsivity to extracoital stimulation than did primary subjects. This finding suggests that anxiety toward sexual functioning may be a more important prohibitive factor in secondary than in primary cases.

Sotile, Kilmann, and Follingstad (1977) investigated the impact of a sexual enhancement workshop with six of the women who had been treated with systematic desensitization in the Sotile and Kilmann study. The workshop included various procedures including masturbation training, fantasy exercises, and sensate focus homework. Results indicated that the workshop facilitated an even greater reduction in reported sexual anxiety than systematic desensitization. However, the workshop did not lead to enhanced orgasmic responsivity for most women. It should be noted that the women who participated in the workshop represented a biased sample, since a number of couples did not wish to participate.

Wincze and Caird (1976) treated 21 women complaining of "essential sexual dysfunction" by either systematic desensitization or video desensitization (modeling). In the modeling condition the hierarchy scenes were presented via videotapes, depicting couples involved in programs on orgasmic dysfunctions. Video desensitization was more effective than systematic desensitization. Both "desensitization" procedures resulted in a reduction of sexual anxiety; however, only 25 percent of the nonorgasmic subjects were able to reach an orgasm at the end of the study. Results of this study suggest that desensitization is less effective when orgasmic dysfunction is the target of the therapy. O'Gorman (1978) compared individual and group desensitization on 40 patients complaining of "frigidity." Group desensitization was found to be superior on patients' self-ratings. However, the group format included group discussion on sexual activities and sex education, which was not part of the individual treatment condition. The outcome of the individual desensitization condition was rather poor: 7 cases were successful, 8 unsuccessful and 5 cases relapsed. The results of this study suggest that sex education rather than (group) desensitization was the important therapeutic ingredient.

Everaerd and Dekker (1982) compared the effect of (1) systematic desensitization, (2) a Masters and Johnson program, and (3) a combination of systematic desensitization and Masters and Johnson. A waiting-list control group was also included in the design. Subjects were 42 women with secondary orgasmic dysfunction. Results showed specific effects for the different treatments. Both treatments were clearly more effective than the control group. The results of the combined group were unimpressive, presumably due to the fact that insufficient time was devoted to each of the particular treatment techniques. Results of this study suggest that systematic desensitization and the Masters and Johnson program reached the same therapeutic goals, although following different courses. Systematic desensitization achieved anxiety reduction first, later on resulting in improved sexual functioning and marital satisfaction. The course of treatment effects in the Masters and Johnson program seems to have been the other way around. Here, sexual functioning and marital satisfaction improved first, ultimately resulting also in a reduction of sexual anxiety. Unfortunately, neither the O'Gorman (1978) nor the Everaerd and Dekker (1982) study provides information with respect to orgasmic functioning at the end of the treatment, thus precluding conclusions with respect to the *orgasmic* functioning.

To date, only one study (Andersen, 1981) compared the relative efficacy of masturbation training and systematic desensitization. Assessment included heterosexual anxiety. Subjects were 30 primary nonorgasmic females. Systematic desensitization included in vivo exercises. Surprisingly, neither treatment led to anxiety reduction. Generally, masturbation training was more effective in increasing sexual arousal and orgasmic capacity than systematic desensitization. Only one out of 10 subjects in the systematic desensitization condition became orgasmic.

Summarizing the results of studies that investigated the effects of systematic desensitization on female sexual dysfunctions, the following conclusions seem warranted. There is considerable evidence that systematic desensitization leads to anxiety reduction, but there is no evidence that systematic desensitization is more effective in reducing anxiety than other approaches such as sex education by means of a videotape, a Masters and Johnson program, or masturbation training. Unfortunately, a number of studies did not provide sufficient information to evaluate whether systematic desensitization leads to improved orgasmic functioning (e.g., Everaerd & Dekker, 1982; O'Gorman, 1978). When orgasmic functioning was evaluated, results of systematic desensitization were generally poor and less than those achieved with masturbation training.

Masters and Johnson Program

Apart from the Everaerd and Dekker (1982) study, just reviewed, a few other controlled studies have been reported investigating the effectiveness of a modified Masters and Johnson program on female sexual dysfunctions.

Everaerd and Dekker (1981) compared a Masters and Johnson program with communication training. Subjects were 42 couples complaining of primary or secondary female orgasmic dysfunction. After 16 therapy sessions, sex therapy was more effective than communication training on sexual functioning. At six months' follow-up sex therapy led to increased marital satisfaction for the females but not for the males, while communication training led to significant increases in marital satisfaction for the males and not for the females.

Mathews and his associates investigated the interaction between drugs and a modified Masters and Johnson program. In the Carney, Bancroft, and Mathews (1978) study, 32 females with sexually "unresponsiveness" received either (1) a Masters and Johnson program plus testosterone or (2) a Masters and Johnson program plus diazepam. It was predicted that women with high anxiety in sexual situations would profit more from diazepam, while women who reported only a lack of sexual desire would do better when sex therapy was combined with testosterone, an androgen. Generally, results favored the testosterone condition, both on measures of the sexual relationship and in the frequency of reported orgasm. The differences in effectiveness of both drug conditions were maintained at six-month follow-up. Interestingly, testosterone was superior to diazepam irrespective of anxiety level of the female.

In a following study of the same research group (Mathews, Whitehead, & Kellett, 1983) 48 sexually "unresponsive" females received either sex therapy plus testosterone or sex therapy plus placebo. The sex therapy was based on the Masters and Johnson program and included guidance in sexual self-stimulation when thought appropriate by the therapist. Contrary to the results of the Carney et al. (1978) study, there was no evidence that testosterone had any effect. There was even some evidence that placebo was more effective on some measures. In retrospect, Mathews et al. (1983) attributed the advantage of testosterone over diazepam in the Carney et al. study to a *negative* influence of diazepam on the effectiveness of the sex therapy. Thus, rather than testosterone being beneficial, diazepam may have seriously interfered with sex therapy, perhaps due to drowsiness as a result of the drug-use prior to the sensate focus exercises. Other treatment variables were also studied in the Carney et al. (1978) and Mathews et al. (1983) studies. In the Carney et al. (1978) study, monthly treatment was equally effective as weekly treatment, but in the Mathews et al. (1983) study, weekly sessions resulted in more improvement than monthly sessions as reported by the females. There was no evidence that a dual therapist team was more successful in enhancing treatment effectiveness than one therapist, corroborating results of Crowe et al. (1981), Clement and Schmidt (1983), and Mathews et al. (1976).

In sum, the Masters and Johnson program has been found to be more effective than communication training. There is no evidence that testosterone enhances improvement. Further, diazepam influences the effects of this sex therapy program negatively.

Masturbation Training

LoPicollo and Lobitz (1972), using a nine-step masturbation program with eight couples, reported that all females were able to reach orgasm at the end of the program. Similar positive effects of self-stimulation exercises were reported by Barbach (1974). In her study 91 percent of 83 women were orgasmic via self-stimulation. In the Barbach program partners were excluded from participation in the treatment because they would interfere with women's self-exploration and communication with

the body. Since then, a number of controlled studies have been conducted investigating the value of self-stimulation exercises in dealing with female orgasmic dysfunctions.

Riley and Riley (1978) compared the effectiveness of a modified Masters and Johnson program with a similar program plus masturbation exercises. Subjects were 40 couples with female primary orgasmic failure. The progress of the patients in the Masters and Johnson program was disappointing. Only 63 percent of the patients became orgasmic by any means and only 47 percent experienced orgasm during coitus at the end of a 12-week period. In contrast, 90 percent of the patients who had received masturbation training were able to attain orgasm, most of them also during sexual intercourse. Results were attained at one-year follow-up.

Ersner-Hershfield and Kopel (1979) studied the effectiveness of a masturbation program both with and without the inclusion of partners with 24 females with primary or secondary orgasmic failure and found this program significantly more effective than no treatment, both with and without the inclusion of partners: 91 percent of 24 primary nonorgasmic women achieved orgasm via self-stimulation.

McMullen and Rosen (1979) investigated the effects of a self-administered masturbation-training program under two different conditions: (1) videotape modeling and (2) written instructions. In addition, a waiting-list control group was included. In the modeling condition subjects viewed an actress portraying a nonorgasmic woman who learns to stimulate herself to orgasm and, finally, reaches orgasm through intercourse. Subjects in the other treatment condition had to read booklets whose content was equivalent to the videotapes. In addition, subjects in both treatment groups were supplied with an electric vibrator to be used at home. Each condition contained 20 women who had never previously experienced orgasm. Both treatment conditions led to orgasmic capacity in about 60 percent of the subjects. None of the subjects in the control group became orgasmic during this time. Modeling did not enhance treatment efficacy.

Cotton-Huston and Wheeler (1983) compared the effects of masturbation training on primary and secondary orgasmic failure with data of patients on a waiting list. Although the treatment group reported having orgasms more frequently through self-stimulation than the control group, this did not generalize to orgasms during intercourse. As noted by the authors, many women listed orgasm during intercourse as their only acceptable goal.

Assertiveness

There is some evidence that sexual dysfunctions are related to unassertiveness (Fahrner, 1983). In the case of assertion in a sexual interaction, assertive behavior might involve a variety of behaviors such as initiating a sexual encounter, requesting specific stimulation, or refusing requests (Delehanty, 1982; Fahrner, 1983). Delehanty (1982) investigated the impact of masturbation training groups on assertiveness of the participants and found a significant increase in assertiveness as measured by questionnaire.

Kuriansky, Sharpe, and O'Connor (1982) reported a two-year follow-up on 19 women who participated in a short-term group therapy using masturbation training and assertiveness training. At the end of treatment 95 percent of the women were able to reach orgasm; at two-year follow-up this was 84 percent. While immediately after treatment 20 percent of the women were able to reach orgasm with a partner, by two years later, nearly half the sample could do so. It should be noted, however, that many of the women who transferred orgasm response to partner-related activities also participated in further marital and/or sex therapy.

In sum, when anxiety reduction is the therapeutic target, both desensitization procedures and a Masters and Johnson program have been shown to be effective. However, anxiety reduction hardly affected orgasmic capacity. Other methods that focus more directly on reaching orgasm (e.g., masturbation training) seem to be more effective in dealing with this target, at least with primary orgasmic failure, but not all clients accept this treatment approach (e.g., Riley & Riley, 1978).

Unfortunately, most studies investigating the effects of masturbation training did not assess sexual anxiety, so that conclusions with respect to anxiety reduction are precluded. The only study that did assess sexual anxiety (Andersen, 1981) found changes in anxiety to be negligible. Finally, there is some evidence that anxiety is more important in secondary cases than primary cases. This suggests that with secondary anorgasmic women, treatment may need to be directed to anxiety reduction, while

this may be less necessary with primary anorgasmic women. It has been suggested that sexual unassertiveness may change as a result of participation in a female group masturbation program (Delehanty, 1982). When sexual assertiveness is the only therapeutic target, however, assertiveness training directed to specific difficulties in social/ sexual encounters seems to be more appropriate (Hammond & Oei, 1982).

Concluding Comment

A number of controlled studies have shown the short-term effectiveness of the behavioral sex therapies, but generally, results are less than originally claimed by Masters and Johnson. For example, Mathews (1983) states that improvements after a modified form of Masters and Johnson are often less than complete. Everaerd (1983) found that with couples complaining of male sexual dysfunction the original complaints showed little improvement. Yet the majority of couples indicated improved satisfaction with their sexual functioning. On the other hand, Arentewicz and Schmidt (1980) found that in half of their patients the improvement of the original symptoms did not lead to improved sexual functioning. In recent years therapeutic goals have changed and orgasm through coition is no longer considered to be the only criterion for success by therapists, although a substantial number of patients still may find this the only acceptable goal (e.g., Cotton-Huston & Wheeler, 1983).

Few studies evaluated the long-term effectiveness of sex therapy. Masters and Johnson (1970) reported a follow-up of their patients up to five years after treatment and found results of treatment maintained. Other recent follow-up studies are less optimistic about the improvements achieved. In a follow-up study 2.5 to 4 years after treatment, Arentewicz and Schmidt (1980) found a slight relapse. Only 50 percent of the patients completed questionnaires. Dekker and Everaerd (1983) reported a follow-up study 5 to 8 years after treatment. Of the original treated patients, 63 percent participated. A substantial number of couples were divorced or had received additional therapy. With the remaining patients ($n = 46$) results of treatment were maintained, although satisfaction with noncoital sex, time spent together, and affection showed a decline at follow-up.

Results of the follow-up studies are difficult to

evaluate because of the limited participations of original treated patients in both the Masters and Johnson (1970), Arentewicz and Schmidt (1980), and Dekker and Everaerd (1983) studies. Assertions concerning the long-term efficacy of sex therapy seems not yet warranted, given the dropouts during treatment, the divorce rate (14% in Arentewicz and Schmidt, and 21% in the Dekker and Everaerd study), the limited participation in the follow-up studies, and the number of patients receiving additional treatment.

PARAPHILIAS

In contrast with the increase in the number of controlled studies into sexual dysfunctions, progress in the area of deviant sexual preferences has been limited. While in the sixties and first half of the seventies a number of controlled studies on behavioral therapies of "sexual deviations" appeared in the literature, only a few such controlled studies were reported more recently. It is now increasingly acknowledged that what once was called sexual perversion or abnormal sexual behavior had been defined by the moral climate of the time. The exclusion of homosexuality per se as a disorder from *DSM-III* shows that considerable changes in attitudes have taken place.

Most of the studies were more or less "controlled" single-case studies, which forms a poor basis to evaluate a particular treatment approach. With a few exceptions the goal of the therapeutic strategies is to change the sexual orientation of the client, as expressed in the following quotation: "For if we cannot afford to control deviant behavior of pedophiliacs by locking them away, we must seek to change it through reorientation" (Kelly, 1982, p. 405).

Homosexuality

Changes in the attitudes toward homosexuality have not been reflected in the research literature on behavior therapy with homosexuality. Russell and Winkler (1977) in reviewing the literature could find no studies, other than a few case studies, that evaluated procedures designed to improve homosexual functioning as (part of a) therapeutic goal. In their own study 27 homosexuals were randomly assigned to either a behaviorally oriented assertive

training group designed to facilitate homosexual functioning or to a nondirective group run by a homosexual guidance service. Assertive training dealt both with assertive behavior in general and with discrimination. Both treatments led to significant improvements in social anxiety and assertiveness, although this was not reflected on the behavioral measure used. Both procedures were about equally effective. Positive effects of assertive training were also reported in case studies by Duehn and Mayadas (1976), Lawrence, Bradlyn and Kelly (1983), McKinley, Kelly, and Patterson (1978), and Phillips, Fischer, Groves, and Singh (1976).

A few studies have been reported on the treatment of homosexuals complaining of sexual dysfunctions. Everaerd et al. (1982) included homosexuals in male-only groups treated for sexual dysfunctions. Treatment consisted of a modified Masters and Johnson program, cognitive restructuring, and social-skill training. Everaerd et al. do not mention whether treatment was as effective for homosexual men as for heterosexual men. Masters and Johnson (1979) applied their sex therapy program to homosexual couples and assert that 90 percent of their patients were improved at the end of treatment. Unfortunately, neither of these studies was controlled.

Given the numerous controlled studies on aversive procedures designed to change a homosexual orientation into a heterosexual one (reviewed by McConaghy, 1982), the relative absence of controlled studies on behavioral procedures to enhance homosexual or bisexual functioning is remarkable.

Exhibitionism

All studies involved treatment procedures directed to reduce deviant interest. Both *aversion therapy* (Evans, 1968, 1970) and *covert sensitization* (Brownell & Barlow, 1976; Brownell, Hayes, & Barlow, 1977; Maletzky, 1974, 1977, 1980a) have been given experimental support as effective in the treatment of exhibitionism. Maletzky (1980a) reported the largest series (n = 155) so far, and follow-up ranged from one to nine years. Treatment was covert sensitization, but for about half of the subjects other procedures were added.

Two studies compared the effects of various treatment procedures. Callahan and Leitenberg (1973) compared aversion therapy and covert sensitization in the treatment of two exhibitionists. Patients were treated with both procedures; generally, treatments were about equally effective.

Rooth and Marks (1974) compared (1) aversion therapy, (2) a self-regulation procedure, and (3) relaxation (control) with 12 exhibitionists. All patients received all three treatments in a counterbalanced order. Relaxation was ineffective, while the aversion therapy was slightly superior to self-regulation. The most effective treatment combination tended to be self-regulation preceded by aversion therapy. At follow-up five months after treatment, 7 out of 12 patients had exposed again. Thus results were meager.

Shame aversion has also been used with exhibitionists. With this procedure the exhibitionist has to undress for an audience, which provokes anxiety and shame. While several authors report successful outcome (e.g., Wickramasekera, 1976), controlled studies are lacking.

Other procedures (e.g., desensitization, assertiveness training, and marital counseling) have also been employed to deal with underlying problems, but controlled studies into the effectiveness of these approaches have not yet been reported.

Pedophilia

Aversive procedures have also been widely applied in the treatment of pedophilia. Results of *electrical aversion therapy* are inconclusive. Quinsey, Bergersen, and Steinman (1976) treated 10 child molesters with aversion therapy and found only slight changes in sexual preference after 20 sessions. The same research group (Quinsey, Chaplin, & Carrigan, 1980) investigated whether biofeedback may enhance the effectiveness of electrial aversion therapy. With the biofeedback procedure the patient was instructed to gain control of his sexual arousal when presented with slides (adult vs. child). Different lights informed the subject whether his penile response to a child or adult slide exceeded a preset criterion. The child criterion was shifted downward and the adult criterion upward over sessions as the patient progressed. Half the patients were treated by biofeedback alone, while the other half received biofeedback plus electrical aversion therapy. The combined procedure was more effective than biofeedback alone on penile responses to slides, the only measure applied. Unfortunately, information over the *clinical* results achieved was not provided; moreover, patients were not randomly

assigned across conditions, thus making it difficult to draw valid conclusions.

Covert sensitization has also been found to be effective in a number of controlled case studies (e.g., Barlow, Leitenberg, & Agras, 1969; Brownwell & Barlow, 1976; Brownell et al., 1977; Levin, Barry, Cambaro, Wolfinsohn, & Smith, 1977), but controlled group studies have not yet been reported.

Orgasmic reconditioning, which implies that clients learn to switch their deviant fantasies during masturbation into fantasies thought to be more appropriate, has also been used, but mostly in combination with aversive procedures directed to reduce deviant interest (e.g., Brownell et al., 1977; Marshall, 1973, 1979; Van Deventer & Laws, 1978). Thus the contribution of the individual components of treatment is difficult to evaluate.

Maletzky (1980b) addressed the issue of whether there is a difference in outcome between self-referred and court-referred pedophiliacs ($n = 38$). Treatment consisted of 24 weekly sessions of covert sensitization and was followed by "booster" session every three months for three years. When assigning 75 percent reduction in covert and overt pedophile behavior as criterion for improvement, 89 percent of the self-referred and 73 percent of the court-referred were rated as improved. Several measures showed a slight superiority of response in the self-referred group. Inspection of the police records over a three-year period revealed that the self-referred group had no charges, while the court-referred group had four charges.

Concluding Remarks

Occasionally, reports have been published on the treatment of voyeurism, transvestism, fetishism, transsexuality, and sadomasochism (reviewed by McConaghy, 1982), but to the best of my knowledge no controlled group studies have been reported.

The major impression obtained from reviewing the literature on sexual deviation is that a number of procedures may be effective in decreasing deviant sexual behavior, although methodological flaws in most of these studies preclude the drawing of firm conclusions. Theoretically, it is often unclear by which processes these procedures work (Barlow, 1982), and the contribution of placebo factors cannot be ruled out (Emmelkamp & Walta, 1978).

Because appropriate arousal patterns do not

usually emerge when deviant arousal is eliminated (Abel & Blanchard, 1976; Brownell et al., 1977), researchers have recently become interested in techniques to increase appropriate arousal such as "orgasmic reconditioning" and "fantasy alternation." Although these methods have been found to be effective in enhancing arousal in a number of case studies, controlled laboratory studies found the improvements achieved variable at best (Conrad & Wincze, 1976; Leonard & Hayes, 1983).

Most of the work in this area is still primarily directed to change the sexual orientation of the individuals rather than providing them help with adjustment to their sexual preferences in a way that is not damaging to society's members. As a result of changing attitudes in the society, an increasing number of therapists in Europe are willing to accept clients in treatment for other therapeutic goals than sexual reorientation per se. The effects of these therapeutic interventions have hardly been investigated.

MARITAL DISTRESS

The topic of this section concerns cognitive and behavioral approaches to the treatment of marital distress. For a more general discussion of marital therapy, the reader is referred to the chapter of Gurman, Kniskern, and Pinsoff (this volume).

Behavior therapy has shown promise in treating marital problems (Jacobson, 1979; Weiss & Wieder, 1982). One treatment approach that has received widespread attention involves teaching distressed couples communication and problem-solving skills followed by behavioral contracting.

It is assumed that reciprocity of reinforcement underlies successful marriages. Behavioral contracting or "reciprocity counseling" is designed to promote marital satisfaction by instigating positive changes in the natural environment. With this approach each partner should provide reinforcement for the reinforcing behavior of his partner according to the "give to get" principle. Several controlled outcome studies have demonstrated the effectiveness of this approach (Baucom, 1982; Hahlweg, Revenstorf, & Schindler, 1982; Jacobson, 1977, 1978). However, some have questioned the external validity of most of the behavioral studies into marital distress (e.g., Gurman & Kniskern, 1978).

Many behavioral studies have to be discounted since they used nonclinical populations. Most of the studies in this area have recruited maritally distressed subjects by means of advertisements in university or local press, but it remains to be shown that the quality of the relationship of distressed couples that jointly decide to improve their marriage is comparable to that of couples seen in clinical settings. The emphasis here will be on studies using clinically distressed couples.

To date, very few controlled studies have been reported that compared behavioral marriage therapy with a nonbehavioral approach, using real clinical patients as subjects. Crowe (1978) compared (1) behavioral marriage therapy, (2) an interpretative approach, and (3) a supportive (control) approach. The behavioral approach was found to be the most effective. However, several methodological confounds limit the conclusions that can be drawn. First, the behavioral therapy consisted of a mixture of reciprocity training and sex therapy along the lines of Masters and Johnson (1970). Which package actually was applied varied from couple to couple. Thus, the relative contribution of the different procedures cannot be determined. Second, most couples were treated by the author, which might have contaminated the results. In the Liberman, Levie, Wheeler, Sanders, and Wallace (1976) study behavioral group therapy was found to be more effective than an interaction-insight oriented group treatment on behavioral measures only. The behavioral group therapy consisted of both communication-skills training and contingency contracting, thus precluding conclusions of each procedure on its own. One major limitation of the Liberman et al. (1976) study is the small number of couples used ($n = 9$); each condition contained one group only.

In a series of studies in the Netherlands, the relative contribution of contingency contracting, communication-skills training, and system-theoretic counseling was evaluated. An important feature is that only severely distressed couples were used as subjects; all couples were referred by a Community Mental Health Center for treatment of their relationship.

In the first study of this series (Boelens, Emmelkamp, MacGillavry, & Markvoort, 1980), contingency contracting and system-theoretic counseling were contrasted. Couples were randomly allocated to three different conditions: (1) reciprocity counseling, (2)system-theoretic counseling, and (3) no-treatment control.

Contingency contracting or reciprocity counseling followed the format used by Azrin, Naster, and Jones (1973) and involved contracting training. Partners established specific behavioral commitments for self and other and compromised with each other. Both treatment groups improved on marital satisfaction (MMQ; Arrindell, Emmelkamp, & Bast, 1983a) and the target problems in contrast to couples from the waiting-list control group. The improvement was maintained six months after the posttest, although a relapse was found for some couples of the system-theoretic counseling group one month after treatment. In contrast, the patients who received contingency contracting continued to improve. The relapse of some system-theoretic counseled couples at one-month follow-up suggests that insight into the interaction pattern alone is insufficient.

Many of the behavioral programs reported in the literature have combined elements from contingency contracting and communication-skills training. As stated by Luber (1978), "These models seem to be largely subjective, random combinations apparently based on the assumption that since each method has accumulated some independent validation they should be effective in unison" (p. 86). Several authors suggest that contingency contracting should be used prior to communication training (e.g., Stuart, 1975; Weiss, Hops, & Patterson, 1973). Others, however, support the use of communication-skills training as a prerequisite to the implementation of contingency contracting (e.g., Rappaport & Harrell, 1975). Some (e.g., Jacobson, 1978; Liberman et al., 1976) have even questioned the utility of contingency contracting as a treatment strategy. Liberman et al. suggest " . . . that contingency contracting is worth just about the paper it's printed on without the family members having adequate interpersonal communication skills" (p. 32). Both Jacobson (1984) and O'Leary and Turkewitz (1978) compared communication training and behavioral exchange directly. No significant differences between the two conditions were found. However, in the Jacobson study there was a trend for the couples who had not received communication training to relapse somewhat at six months' follow-up, while the other couples maintained their treatment gains.

Emmelkamp, Van der Helm, MacGillavry, and Van Zanten (1984) investigated the relative contribution of contingency contracting and communication training on clinically distressed couples. Since the interest was not only in the effects of each procedure on its own but also in the interactional effects when they are joined in a package treatment approach, a crossover design was used. This means that after the pretest, one group of couples received contingency contracting and one communication-skills training; the effect was measured (intermediate test), and then a second period of treatment followed, but now with each group being given the treatment the other group had first received.

Contingency contracting followed the format used in the Boelens et al. (1980) study. Communication-skills training focused on ways to improve communication between spouses. Couples were taught skills that enable them to talk with each other more effectively. Treatment sessions were semistandardized. Approximately half of the time was devoted to structured exercises such as listening and empathy training, spontaneous expressing of feelings, and assertiveness. The second half of each session consisted of discussing marital conflicts (problem-solving training). Modeling, feedback, shaping, and behavior rehearsal were used throughout treatment. The effects of contingency contracting and communication-skills training were broadly comparable. Further, there is no evidence to support the idea that communication-skills training should precede contingency contracting or that contingency contracting should be used prior to communication training.

In a following study (Emmelkamp et al., 1984) an attempt was made to compare communication-skills training and system-theoretic counseling and the interaction between both treatment formats. The relapse of some of the couples after system-theoretic counseling found in the Boelens et al. (1980) study suggested that insight into the interaction pattern alone is insufficient. Therefore, it was investigated whether communication-skills training would enhance the effectiveness of the system-theoretic approach. Couples were treated in a crossover design with seven sessions of communication-skills training and seven sessions of system-theoretic counseling. The order of the treatments was randomly varied.

The most important finding of this study is that

communication-skills training and system-theoretic counseling were about equally effective. The present results corroborate the finding of the Boelens et al. (1980) study in which no difference was found between system-theoretic counseling and another behavioral procedure—contingency contracting.

Summarizing the studies discussed, the following conclusions seem warranted. Both contingency contracting and communication-skills training appear to be at least equally effective as system-theoretic oriented therapy. The effects of both behavioral procedures are broadly comparable. A disadvantage of between-group comparisons as presented here is that it is unclear whether the same couples profit from behavioral and system-theoretic procedures. Rather than continuing comparative studies, there is now a clear need for studies that address the issue of matching individual needs of patients to particular treatments. Who are the failures of behavioral and system-theoretic counseling? Do patients who fail with behavioral approaches also fail with system-theoretic counseling and vice versa? Are specific patients' characteristics related to success or failure with the various approaches? These seem important questions for further research.

Cognitive Interventions

The evolution of behavioral marital therapy has been characterized by a broadened conceptualization of relationship dysfunction and an expanded range of intervention procedures. Of particular significance is the increased attention that behavioral marital therapists have paid to the assessment and modification of cognitive processes that may mediate spouses' behaviors toward one another. A substantial minority of couples have not responded to traditional behavioral marital therapy or have remained distressed after achieving successful behavior change. Based on clinical observations, therapists such as Jacobson and Margolin (1979), O'Leary and Turkewitz (1978), Weiss (1978), and Epstein (1982) have stressed that the impact of behaviors exchanged by spouses is subjective and idiosyncratic and that the planning of behavior change must take into account the individuals' cognitive appraisals of the events in their relationships.

Such clinical observations have led to the inclusion of cognitive restructuring techniques in the repertoires of many behavioral marital therapists. The cognitive strategies generally used in cognitive therapy of marital distress focus on changing irrational beliefs, faulty attributional processes, and negative self-statements. Relatively few studies have investigated the impact of cognitive restructuring techniques in behavioral marital therapy. One of the early attempts to investigate the utility of explicitly focusing upon cognitive factors in behavioral marital therapy was carried out by Margolin and Weiss (1978). In comparing behavioral marital therapy with a treatment including behavioral marital therapy plus cognitive restructuring (teaching the couples that many of their marital problems were due to a lack of relationship skills), they found that behavioral marital therapy plus cognitive restructuring was significantly more effective than behavioral marital therapy on several outcome measures. The highly abbreviated intervention period (four sessions), however, restricts conclusions to be drawn from this study.

Baucom and Lester (1982) reported the results of a study in which 17 maritally distressed couples were randomly assigned to one of three treatment conditions: (1) behavioral marital therapy alone, (2) cognitive restructuring plus behavioral marital therapy, and (3) waiting list. Behavioral marital therapy consisted of communication training, problem solving, and contracting. The combined cognitive-behavioral therapy consisted of six weeks of training in cognitive restructuring followed by six weeks of behavioral therapy. As to the cognitive part of the treatment, through a focus on attribution, the goals of the first three sessions were to help couples see the complexity of problems and the role that each spouse plays in those problems, to view their problems in very clear, specific terms, and to see ways in which the relationship can improve. The remaining sessions focused upon irrational beliefs or unrealistic expectations that distressed couples have.

Results showed that cognitive restructuring plus behavioral marital therapy was equally as effective as behavioral marital therapy alone on most measures, with some indications that cognitive behavioral marital therapy was more effective than behavioral marital therapy on the Irrational Beliefs Test (IBT). Interestingly, cognitive-behavioral marital therapy and behavioral marital therapy did not differ on the Relationship Beliefs Inventory (RBI), the other cognitive variable in the investigation.

The two studies discussed so far investigated the

impact of cognitive restructuring on behavioral marital therapy. Emmelkamp (1985a) compared the efficacy of cognitive restructuring alone versus behavioral marital therapy. Thirty-two clinically distressed couples who applied for treatment in a community mental health center were randomly assigned to two conditions: (1) cognitive restructuring and (2) communication skills training. Treatment consisted of 10 sessions. Cognitive restructuring focused (1) on the causal attributions or explanations that maritally distressed couples give for events that took place in marriage, (2) on individual irrational beliefs that the married individual held for himself or herself or his or her partner (Ellis & Grieger, 1977), and (3) on unrealistic expectations that couples held for the relationship (Eidelson & Epstein, 1982; Epstein, 1982). At the posttest, both groups showed significant improvement on most measures. On the target problems cognitive restructuring proved to be slightly superior to communication-skills training.

Overall, the results of this clinical outcome study indicate that cognitive restructuring might be at least as effective as communication-skills training, but there is little evidence that the effects of both treatments are mediated by changes in either communication patterns or cognitive processes. Rather, the results of this study suggest that changes in communication and irrational relationship beliefs occur irrespective of the particular treatment received, which is in line with previous investigations (Boelens et al., 1980; Emmelkamp et al., 1984).

Concluding Remark

Behavioral marital therapy has been shown to be moderately effective with clinically distressed couples. There is, however, no evidence that it is more effective than system-theoretic approaches. Cognitive therapies have also shown promise in dealing with marital distress. At present, there is, however, no confirming evidence that the treatment procedures achieve their results through the presumed treatment mechanisms.

In none of the studies was an attempt made to match couples to treatment. Thus, at present it is unclear what couple parameters may interact with type of treatment to enhance treatment effectiveness. One of the most important research areas is to investigate which characteristics of couples might interact with type of treatment. It might be reason-able to hold that communication training is indicated when both partners lack the necessary communication skills and, on the other hand, that cognitive restructuring is indicated when both partners hold irrational (relationship) beliefs and expectations. However, the situation becomes more complex when only one of the partners lacks adequate communication skills while the other is highly irrational in his or her (relationship) beliefs, which pattern might be quite common among clinically distressed couples. This indicates that studies are needed that take into account not only differences between couples but also individual differences within couples. Although such studies will be difficult to realize, it is likely that such efforts will produce more new knowledge than studies comparing different treatment procedures irrespective of couples' and individuals' characteristics.

SUMMARY AND CONCLUSIONS

Research on phobias is falling into place. The effects of exposure in vivo are now well established for agoraphobia, simple phobia, and obsessive-compulsive disorders. A gap in our knowledge exists with regard to social anxiety and anxiety states. Although recent developments in this area are promising, there is a great deal to be accomplished by clinical researchers to devise efficient and effective treatments for these disorders.

Studies of the behavioral and cognitive treatment of depression represent one of the more exciting areas of clinical research. The progression of research in this area has advanced our knowledge, but there are still a number of important issues that need to be dealt with. For example, we have no idea why both cognitive and behavioral interventions work with depressed patients, although various researchers provide various theoretical explanations. Unfortunately, to date there is no evidence that either cognitive, behavioral, or self-control theories explain the improvements achieved with these various treatment procedures.

In the area of alcoholism the interest has moved away from aversive procedures into multifaceted self-control programs. Although research indicates that self-control programs are promising with problem drinkers, the results of behavioral methods with chronic alcoholics are disappointing. One of the promising areas for future research is relapse prevention. The results of the few studies that investigated coping skills programs to prevent relapse look promising.

The increased interest in studies of sexual dysfunctions concerns the development and evaluation of time-limited sex therapies. Recently developed behavioral techniques have been extensively investigated and have been found to be effective with a substantial number of clients, but evidence is emerging that casts doubt on the long-term usefulness of these approaches. An area that deserves further study is the treatment of paraphilias. Very few controlled studies have been published in recent years, and progress in this area has been minimal.

Finally, the state of the art in the treatment of marital distress is advanced. One issue deserving a great deal of attention in future research on marital therapy is the integration of behavioral and cognitive interventions.

Although specific therapeutic procedures have been found to be effective in a number of instances, it is important to note that many of the patients are not symptom-free at the end of these programs. Many patients require further therapy, often targeting other problems, including social functioning and marital problems. While clinicians acknowledge that techniques often form only part of a broader therapeutic approach, research in this area is lacking.

There is a gap between clinical practice and behavioral research, which seriously questions the scientific basis of *clinical* behavior therapy. Swan and McDonald (1978) found in a national survey of behavior therapists in the United States significant differences between behavior therapy as it is operationalized in research and behavior therapy as it is applied clinically. They found a minimal relationship between the type of assessment techniques employed in clinical settings and the methods used in research studies. For instance, most clinical behavior therapists who responded to the national survey revealed that relationship enhancement methods were most frequently used by clinicians, whereas research into the effects of these procedures is notoriously lacking.

The predominant type of outcome research in behavior therapy involved between-group studies comparing different procedures or treatment components. In the group designs, within-group variance is perceived as an unfortunate occurrence rather than as a major source of relevant information (Emmelkamp & Foa, 1983). Another strategy, single-case research, focuses on the responsiveness of an individual to a given intervention, but it does not provide information about the generalizability of the results obtained.

A convergence of the generalization and individualization approaches is found in some experimental designs that examine the interaction between treatment factors and individual characteristics. An example of this line of research is provided by the research of Öst and his colleagues discussed in this chapter. Unfortunately, this approach requires a large number of subjects. Inasmuch as the number of patients available for any given study is often limited, the application of this strategy to outcome studies has been rare. An alternative strategy is to calculate group means to obtain information about the generality of the findings and at the same time to examine the responses of the individuals who participated in the study. In this way information is gained on the clinical significance of the results as well as on their generalizability. For example, Jacobson (1977) compared the efficacy of behavioral marriage therapy with a control group; in addition, a single-subject design was employed for each couple who participated in the treatment group. It is regrettable that only a few clinical outcome studies followed this latter strategy (Emmelkamp & Foa, 1983).

While it is often acknowledged that effective clinical behavior therapy is only as good as its initial behavioral analysis, this issue has been totally neglected by researchers. To put it rather simply: Behavior therapy research has been technique rather than problem oriented. Research remains to be done on the reliability and validity of functional analyses. Questions that need to be answered are:

1. Is the functional analysis made by therapist A identical to the functional analysis of the same patient by therapist B?
2. Do identical functional analyses lead to identical treatment decisions?
3. Is treatment based on a functional analysis more effective than a standardized treatment program?

The last question is especially important with respect to the cost-efficiency of treatments.

In light of the growing interest in behavioral assessment procedures, it is somewhat surprising to find that virtually no research has been carried out to develop assessment procedures for daily use in clinical practice. In experimental studies intensive assessment procedures are used that are often omitted in routine clinical practice. For instance, a behavioral assessment procedure currently used in studies with clinically distressed couples is the Marital Interaction Coding System (MICS) of Hops, Wills, Patterson, and Weiss (1971). This assessment procedure and the coding of the videotapes is so time consuming, however, that one can hardly expect that practitioners will use it with their patients. Or, to take another example, behavioral assessment procedures in studies on alcoholism include "operant drinking," "taste test," and "ad lib drinking." While these measures have their value for laboratory studies, their clinical utility seems to be minimal. The limitations of behavioral and psychophysiological assessment as employed in clinical studies of phobic patients have been discussed elsewhere (Emmelkamp, 1982a). There is a clear need for assessment procedures that are less costly and time consuming and that have a more direct bearing on clinical practice. Presumably, a more economical approach is to rely on patients' and relatives' self-reports about their actual behavior in daily life situations rather than to use laboratory behavioral assessment procedures.

Although behavior therapists have been very productive in evaluating the efficacy of various techniques, relatively little attention has been devoted to the therapeutic process. It is astonishing to see how little attention is devoted to the role of the therapeutic relationships among behavior therapists. For example, the authoritative *International Handbook of Behavior Modification* (Bellack et al., 1982) does not even contain a reference to the therapeutic relationship in its index. It is, however, becoming increasingly clear that the quality of the therapeutic relationship may be influential in determining success or failure of behavioral therapies (Emmelkamp & Foa, 1983), although well-controlled studies in this area are rare.

A number of analogue studies have demonstrated that systematic desensitization is influenced by such a therapist condition as the warmth of the voice (Esse & Wilkins, 1978; Morris & Suckerman, 1974a, 1974b). Two studies with clinically phobic and obsessive-compulsive patients found the outcome of exposure in vivo therapy to be related to such "good" therapist characteristics as empathy, positive regard, and congruity (Emmelkamp & Van der Hout, 1983; Rabavilas, Boulougouris, & Perissaki, 1979). Ford (1978) found therapists' qualities to account for more variance in treatment outcome than therapy type.

It is a common misconception that behavior therapists are "unempathic" and apply only techniques. Sloane, Staples, Cristol, Yorkston, and Whipple (1975) studied therapist variables such as genuineness, empathy, and warmth in a group of behavior therapists and psychoanalytically oriented therapists; on some of these dimensions behavior therapists actually exceeded the psychoanalytic therapists. To quote Garfield (1980): "In other words, although adherents of a given orientation may make little or no reference to particular variables in their formal writings, this does not signify that the variables in question are not being utilized by these therapists" (p. 33).

It does seem that studies evaluating the outcome of behavioral techniques whose effects have already been established for the "average" patient are not likely to produce new knowledge. Studies investigating conditions leading to success or failure of these techniques are highly needed. The therapeutic relationship seems to be one area where future research efforts are highly needed. Presumably, results of such research programs may eventually lead to preventing failure in a substantial number of cases.

REFERENCES

Abel, G.G., & Blanchard, E.B. (1976). The measurement and generation of sexual arousal in male sexual deviates. In M. Hersen, R. Eisler, & P. Miller (Eds.), *Progress in behavior modification* (Vol. 2). New York: Academic Press.

Abramson, L.Y., Seligman, M.E.P., & Teasdale, J.D. (1978). Learned helplessness in humans: Critique and reformulation. *Journal of Abnormal Psychology, 87,* 49–74.

Andersen, B.L. (1981). A comparison of systematic desensitization and directed masturbation in the treatment of primary orgasmic dysfunction in females. *Journal of Consulting and Clinical Psychology, 49,* 568–570.

Andrews, J.D.W. (1966). Psychotherapy of phobias. *Psychological Bulletin, 66,* 455–480.

Arentewicz, G., & Schmidt, G. (1980). *Sexuell gestörte Beziehungen*. Berlin: Springer Verlag.

Armor, D.J., Polich, J.M., & Stambul, H.B. (1976). *Alcoholism and treatment*. Santa Monica, CA: The Rand Corporation.

Arrindell, W.A., & Emmelkamp, P.M.G. (1985a). Psychological profile of the spouse of the female agoraphobic patient: Personality and symptoms. *British Journal of Psychiatry, 146,* 405–414.

Arrindell, W.A., & Emmelkamp, P.M.G. (1985b). A test of the repression hypothesis in agoraphobics *Psychological Medicine, 15,* 125–129.

Arrindell, W.A., & Emmelkamp, P.M.G. (1986). Marital adjustment, intimacy and needs in female agoraphobics and their partners: A controlled study. *British Journal of Psychiatry*. (in press)

Arrindell, W.A., Emmelkamp, P.M.G. & Sanderman, R. (1986). The influence of the marital relationship of agoraphobics on the outcome of behavior therapy.

Arrindell, W.A., Emmelkamp, P.M.G., & Bast, S. (1983a). The Maudsley Marital Questionnaire (MMQ). *Personality and Individual Differences, 4,* 457–464.

Arrindell, W.A., Emmelkamp, P.M.G., Brilman, E., & Monsma, A. (1983b). Psychometric evaluation of an inventory for assessment of parental rearing practices: A Dutch form of the EMBU. *Acta Psychiatrica Scandinavica, 67,* 163–177.

Azrin, N.H., Naster, B.J., & Jones, R. (1973). Reciprocity counselling: A rapid learning-based procedure for marital counselling. *Behaviour Research and Therapy, 11,* 365–382.

Baker, T.B., & Cannon, D.S. (1979). Taste aversion therapy with alcoholics: Techniques and evidence of a conditioned response. *Behaviour Research and Therapy, 17,* 229–242.

Baker, T.B., Cannon, D.S., Tiffany, S.T., & Gino, A. (1984). Cardiac response as an index of the effect of aversion therapy. *Behaviour Research and Therapy, 22,* 403–411.

Bandura, A. (1977). A self-efficacy: Toward a unifying theory of behavioral change. *Psychological Review, 84,* 191–215.

Banner, C.N., & Meadows, W.M. (1984). Examination of the effectiveness of various treatment techniques for reducing tension. *British Journal of Clinical Psychology, 22,* 183–194.

Barbach, L.G. (1974). Group treatment of preorgasmic women. *Journal of Sex and Marital Therapy, 1,* 139–145.

Barlow, D. (1982). The context of learning in behaviour therapy. In J.C. Boulougouris (Ed.), *Learning theory approaches to psychiatry*. Chichester: Wiley.

Barlow, D.H., Leitenberg, H., & Agras, W.S. (1969). Experimental control of sexual deviation through manipulation of the noxious scene in covert sensitization. *Journal of Abnormal Psychology, 74,* 596–601.

Barlow, D.H., Mavissakalian, M., & Hay, L.R. (1981). Couples treatment of agoraphobia: Changes in marital satisfaction. *Behavior Research and Therapy, 19,* 245–256.

Barlow, D.H., O'Brien, G.T., & Last, C.G. (1984). Couples treatment of agoraphobia. *Behavior Therapy, 15,* 41–58.

Baucom, D.H. (1982). A comparison of behavioral contracting and problem-solving/communications training in behavioral marital therapy. *Behavior Therapy, 13,* 162–174.

Baucom, D.H., & Lester, G. (1982), November. *The utility of cognitive restructuring as a supplement to behavioral marital therapy*. Paper presented at the annual convention of the Association for the Advancement of Behavior Therapy, Los Angeles.

Beck, A.T., Emery, G., & Greenberg, R.L. (1985). *Anxiety disorders and phobias: A cognitive perspective*. New York: Basic Books.

Beck, A.T., Hollon, S.D., Young, J.E., Bedrosian, R.C., & Budenz, D. (1985). Treatment of depression with cognitive therapy and amitriptyline. *Archives of General Psychiatry, 42,* 142–148.

Beck, A.T., Laude, R., & Bohnert, M.B. (1974). Ideational components of anxiety neurosis. *Archives of General Psychiatry, 31,* 319–325.

Beck, A.T., Rush, A.J., Shaw, B.F., & Emery, G. (1979). *Cognitive therapy of depression*. New York: Guilford.

Beech, H.R., & Vaughan, M. (1978). *Behavioral treatment of obsessional states*. New York: Wiley.

Bellack, A.S., Hersen, M., & Himmelhoch, J.M. (1983). A comparison of social-skills training, pharmacotherapy and psychotherapy for depression. *Behaviour Research and Therapy, 21,* 101–108.

Bellack, A.S., Hersen, M., & Kazdin, A.E. (Eds.). (1982). *International handbook of behavior modification and therapy*. New York: Plenum.

Biglan, A. & Craker, D. (1982). Effects of pleasant-activities manipulation on depression. *Journal of Consulting and Clinical Psychology, 50,* 436–438.

Biran, M., & Wilson, G.T. (1981). Treatment of phobic disorders using cognitive and exposure methods. *Journal of Consulting and Clinical Psychology, 49,* 886–899.

Blackburn, I.M., Bishop, S., Glen, A.I.M., Whaley, L.J., & Christie, J.E. (1981). The efficacy of cognitive therapy in depression: A treatment trial using cognitive therapy and pharmacotherapy, each alone and in combination. *British Journal of Psychiatry, 139,* 181–189.

Bland, K., & Hallam, R.S. (1981). Relationship between response to graded exposure and marital satisfaction in agoraphobics. *Behaviour Research and Therapy, 19,* 335–338.

Boelens, W., & Debats, D. (1983). Vergelijking van een puur gedragsmatige behandeling voor depressieve patienten. In R. Beer & H. Mulders (Eds.), *Psychologische benaderingswijzen van depressie.* Lisse, The Netherlands: Swets and Zeitlinger.

Boelens, W., Emmelkamp, P., MacGillavry, D., & Markvoort, M. (1980). A clinical evaluation of marital treatment: Reciprocity counseling vs. system-theoretic counseling. *Behavioral Analysis and Modification, 4,* 85–96.

Boersma, K., Den Hengst, S., Dekker, J., & Emmelkamp, P.M.G. (1976). Exposure and response prevention in the natural environment: A comparison with obsessive-compulsive patients. *Behaviour Research and Therapy, 14,* 19–24.

Borkovec, T.D., & Rachman, S. (1979). The utility of analogue research. *Behaviour Resarch and Therapy, 17,* 253–261.

Bourque, P., & Ladouceur, R. (1980). An investigation of various performance-based treatments with acrophobics. *Behaviour Research and Therapy*, *18*, 161–170.

Boyd, J.H., Derr, K., Grossman, B., Lee, C., Sturgeon, S., Lacock, D.D., & Bruder, C.I. (1983). Different definitions of alcoholism, *American Journal of Psychiatry*, *140*, 1314–1317.

Boyd, T.L., & Levis, D.J. (1983). Exposure is a necessary condition for fear-reduction: A reply to de Silva and Rachman. *Behaviour Research and Therapy*, *21*, 143–150.

Branham, L., & Katahn, M. (1974). Effectiveness of automated desensitization with normal volunteers and phobic patients. *Canadian Journal of Behavioral Sciences*, *6*, 234–245.

Brownell, K.D., & Barlow, D.H. (1976). Measurement and treatment of two sexual deviations in one person. *Journal of Behavior Therapy and Experimental Psychiatry*, *7*, 349–354.

Brownell, K.D., Hayes, S.C., & Barlow, D.H. (1977). Patterns of appropriate and deviant sexual arousal: The behavioral treatment of multiple sexual deviations. *Journal of Consulting and Clinical Psychology*, *45*, 1144–1155.

Buglass, D., Clarke, J., Henderson, A.S., Kreitman, N., & Presley, A.S. (1977). A study of agoraphobic housewives. *Psychological Medicine*, *7*, 73–86.

Caddy, G.R., & Lovibond, S.H. (1976). Self-regulation and discrimated aversive conditioning in the modification of alcoholics' drinking behavior. *Behavior Therapy*, *7*, 223–230.

Callahan, E.J., & Leitenberg, H. (1973). Aversion therapy for sexual deviation: Contingent shock and covert sensitization. *Journal of Abnormal Psychology*, *81*, 60–73.

Cannon, D.S., & Baker, T.B. (1981). Emetic and electric shock alcohol aversion therapy: Assessment of conditioning. *Journal of Consulting and Clinical Psychology*, *49*, 20–33.

Cannon, D.S., Baker, T.B., & Wehl, C.K. (1981). Emetic and electric shock alcohol aversion therapy: Six and twelve-month follow-up. *Journal of Consulting and Clinical Psychology*, *49*, 360–368.

Carmody, T.P. (1978). Rational-emotive, self-instructional, and behavioral assertion: Facilitating maintenance. *Cognitive Therapy and Research*, *2*, 241–253.

Carney, A., Bancroft, J., & Mathews, A., (1978). Combination of hormonal and psychological treatment for female sexual unresponsiveness: A comparative study. *British Journal of Psychiatry*, *133*, 339–346.

Chambless, D.L., & Goldstein, A. (1980). The treatment of agoraphobia. In A. Goldstein & E.B. Foa (Eds.), *Handbook of behavioral interventions*. Wiley: New York.

Chambless, D.L., Hunter, K., & Jackson, A. (1982). Social anxiety and assertiveness: A comparison of the correlations in phobic and college student samples. *Behaviour Research and Therapy*, *20*, 403–404.

Chaney, E.F., O'Leary, M.R., & Marlatt, G.A. (1978). Skill training with alcoholics. *Journal of Consulting and Clinical Psycholgy*, *46*, 1092–1104.

Clark, D. (1984, Sept.). *A cognitive behavioural approach to the treatment of panic attacks*. Paper presented at the 14th Congress of the European Association for Behavior Therapy, Brussels.

Clement, U., & Schmidt, G. (1983). The outcome of couple therapy for sexual dysfunctions using three different formats. *Journal of Sex and Marital Therapy*, *9*, 67–78.

Cobb, J.P., Mathews, A.A., Childs-Clarke, A., & Blowers, C.M. (1984). The spouse as co-therapist in the treatment of agoraphobia. *British Journal of Psychiatry*, *144*, 282–287.

Cobb, J., McDonald, R., Marks, I., & Stern, R. (1980). Marital versus exposure therapy: Psychological treatments of co-existing marital and phobic-obsessive problems. *Behavioural Analysis and Modification*, *4*, 4–16.

Comas-Diaz, L. (1981). Effects of cognitive and behavioral group treatment on the depressive symptomatology of Puerto Rican women. *Journal of Consulting and Clinical Psychology*, *49*, 627–632.

Conrad, S.R., & Wincze, J.P. (1976). Orgasmic reconditioning: A controlled study of its effects upon the sexual arousal and behavior of adult male homosexuals. *Behavior Therapy*, *7*, 155–166.

Cotton-Huston, A.L., & Wheeler, K.A. (1983). Preorgasmic group treatment: Assertiveness, marital adjustment and sexual function in women. *Journal of Sex and Marital Therapy*, *9*, 296–302.

Coyne, J.C. (1976). Depression and the response of others. *Journal of Abnormal Psychology*, *85*, 186–193.

Coyne, J.C., & Gotlib, I.H. (1983). The role of cognition in depression: A critical appraisal. *Psychological Bulletin.*, *94*, 472–505.

Cragan, M.K., & Deffenbacher, J.L. (1984). Anxiety management training and relaxation as self-control in the treatment of generalized anxiety in medical outpatients. *Journal of Counseling Psychology*, *31*, 123–131.

Crowe, M.J. (1978). Conjoint marital therapy: A controlled outcome study. *Psychological Medicine*, *8*, 623–636.

Crowe, M.J., Gillan, P., & Golombock, S. (1981). Form and content in the conjoint treatment of sexual dysfunction: A controlled study. *Behaviour Research and Therapy*, *19*, 47–54.

Csillag, E.R. (1976). Modification of penile erectile response. *Journal of Behavior Therapy and Experimental Psychiatry*, *7*, 27–29.

Cullington, A., Butler, G., Hibbert, G., & Gelder, M. (1984). Problem-solving: Not a treatment for agoraphobia. *Behavior Therapy*, *15*, 280–286.

De Jong, R., Henrich, G., & Ferstl, R. (1981). A behavioural treatment program for neurotic depression. *Behavioural Analysis and Modification*, *4*, 275–287.

Dekker, J., & Everaerd, W. (1983). A long-term follow-up study of couples treated for sexual dysfunctions. *Journal of Sex and Marital Therapy*, *9*, 99–113.

Delehanty, R. (1982). Changes in assertiveness and changes in orgasmic response occurring with sexual therapy for preorgasmic women. *Journal of Sex and Marital Therapy*, *8*, 198–208.

de Silva, P., & Rachman, S. (1981). Is exposure a necessary condition for fear reduction? *Behaviour Research and Therapy*, *19*, 227–232.

de Silva, P., & Rachman, S. (1984). Does escape behaviour strengthen agoraphobic avoidance? A preliminary study. *Behaviour Research and Therapy*, *22*, 87–91.

Dormaar, M., & Dijkstra, W. (1975). *Systematic desensiti-*

zation in social anxiety. Paper read at the Conference of the European Association of Behaviour Therapy, Madrid.

Duehn, W.D., & Mayadas, N.S. (1976). The use of stimulus-modeling videotapes in assertive training for homosexuals. *Journal of Homosexuality, 1*, 373–381.

Dunn, R.J. (1979). Cognitive modification with depression-prone psychiatric patients. *Cognitive Therapy and Research, 3*, 307–317.

Eidelson, R.J., & Epstein, N. (1982). Cognition and relation maladjustment: Development of a measure of dysfunctional relation beliefs. *Journal of Consulting and Clinical Psychology, 50*, 715–720.

Elkins, R.L. (1975). Aversion therapy for alcoholism: Chemical, electrical or verbal imagery? *The International Journal of the Addictions, 10*, 157–209.

Elkins, R.L. (1980). Covert sensitization treatment of alcoholism: Contributions of successful conditioning to subsequent abstinence maintenance. *Addictive Behaviour, 5*, 67–89.

Ellis, A. (1962). *Reason and emotion in psychotherapy*. New York: Lyle-Stuart.

Ellis, A., & Grieger, R. (1977). *Handbook of rational-emotive therapy*. New York: Springer.

Emmelkamp, P.M.G. (1974). Self-observation versus flooding in the treatment of agoraphobia. *Behaviour Research and Therapy, 12*, 229–237.

Emmelkamp, P.M.G. (1979). The behavioral study of clinical phobias. In M. Hersen, R.M. Eisler, & P.M. Miller (Eds.), *Progress in behavior modification* (Vol. 8). New York: Academic Press.

Emmelkamp, P.M.G. (1980). Agoraphobics' interpersonal problems: Their role in the effects of exposure in vivo therapy. *Archives of General Psychiatry, 37*, 1303–1306.

Emmelkamp, P.M.G. (1982a). *Phobic and obsessive-compulsive disorders: Theory, research and practice*. New York: Plenum.

Emmelkamp, P.M.G. (1982b). Exposure in vivo treatments. In A. Goldstein & D. Chambless (Eds.), *Agoraphobia: Multiple perspectives on theory and treatment*. New York: Wiley.

Emmelkamp, P.M.G. (1982c). Recent developments in the behavioral treatment of obsessive-compulsive disorders. In J. Boulougouris (Ed.), *Learning theories approaches in psychiatry*. New York: Wiley.

Emmelkamp, P.M.G. (1985a). *Cognitive restructuring versus communication training: A comparative outcome study with clinically distressed couples*. Paper presented at 15th Congress of European Association of Behavior Therapy, Munich.

Emmelkamp, P.M.G. (1985b). Compulsive rituals. In C. Last & M. Hersen (Eds.), *Behavior therapy case book* (pp. 57–73). New York: Springer.

Emmelkamp, P., & Albersnagel, F. (1979). Dépression: Une approche clinique et empirique. *Journal de Therapie Comportementale, 1*, 91–106.

Emmelkamp, P.M.G., & Boeke, I. (1977). Demand characteristics in behavioral assessment. *Psychological Reports, 41*, 1030.

Emmelkamp, P.M.G., Brilman, E., Kuiper, H., & Mersch, P.P. (1986). The treatment of agoraphobia: A comparison of self-instructional training, rational emotive therapy and exposure in vivo. *Behavior Modification, 10*, 37–53.

Emmelkamp, P.M.G., & De Lange, I. (1983). Spouse involvement in the treatment of obsessive-compulsive patients. *Behaviour Research and Therapy, 21*, 341–346.

Emmelkamp, P.M.G., & Emmelkamp-Benner, A. (1975). Effects of historically portrayed modeling and group treatment on self-observation: A comparison with agoraphobics. *Behaviour Research and Therapy, 13*, 135–139.

Emmelkamp, P.M.G., & Felten, M. (1985). The process of exposure in vivo: Cognitive and physiological changes during treatment of acrophobia. *Behaviour Research and Therapy, 23*, 219–223.

Emmelkamp, P.M.G., & Foa, E.B. (1983). The study of failures. In E.B. Foa & P.M.G. Emmelkamp (Eds.), *Failures in behavior therapy* (pp. 1–9). New York: Wiley.

Emmelkamp, P.M.G., & Giesselbach, P. (1981). Treatment of obsessions: Relevant vs. irrelevant exposure. *Behavioural Psychotherapy, 9*, 322–329.

Emmelkamp, P.M.G., Hoekstra, R.J., & Visser, S. (1985). The behavioral treatment of obsessive-compulsive disorder: Prediction of outcome at 3.5 years follow-up. In Brenner (Ed.), *Psychiatry: The state of the art*. Vol. 4. New York: Plenum. (pp. 265–270).

Emmelkamp, P.M.G., & Kraanen, J. (1977). Therapist controlled exposure in vivo versus self-controlled exposure in vivo: A comparison with obsessive-compulsive patients. *Behaviour Research and Therapy, 15*, 491–495.

Emmelkamp, P.M.G., & Kuipers, A. (1979). Agoraphobia: A follow-up study four years after treatment. *British Journal of Psychiatry, 134*, 352–355.

Emmelkamp, P.M.G., & Kuipers, A.C.M. (1985). Group therapy of anxiety disorders. In D. Upper & S.M. Ross (Eds.), *Handbook of behavioral group therapy*. New York: Plenum.

Emmelkamp, P.M.G., Kuipers, A., & Eggeraat, J. (1978). Cognitive modification versus prolonged exposure in vivo: A comparison with agoraphobics. *Behaviour Research and Therapy, 16*, 33–41.

Emmelkamp, P.M.G., & Kwee, K.G. (1977). Obsessional ruminations: A comparison between thought-stopping and prolonged exposure in imagination. *Behaviour Research and Therapy, 15*, 441–444.

Emmelkamp, P.M.G., & Mersch, P.P. (1982). Cognition and exposure in vivo in the treatment of agoraphobia: Short-term and delayed effects. *Cognitive Therapy and Research, 6*, 77–90.

Emmelkamp, P.M.G., Mersch, P.P., & Vissia, E. (1985b). The external validity of analogue outcome research: Evaluation of cognitive and behavioral intervention. *Behaviour Research and Therapy, 23*, 83–86.

Emmelkamp, P.M.G., Mersch, P.P., Vissia, E., & Van der Helm, M. (1985c). Social phobia: A comparative evaluation of cognitive and behavioral interventions. *Behaviour Research and Therapy, 23*, 365–369.

Emmelkamp, P.M.G., & Rabbie, D. (1981). Psychological treatment of obsessive-compulsive disorders: A follow-up 4 years after treatment. In B. Jansson, C. Perris, & G. Struwe (Eds.), *Biological psychiatry*. Amsterdam: Elsevier.

Emmelkamp, P.M.G., Van der Helm, M., MacGillavry, D., & Van Zanten, B. (1984). Marital therapy with clinically distressed couples: A comparative evaluation of system-theoretic, contingency contracting and communication skills approaches. In K. Hahlweg & N. Jacobson (Eds.), *Marital therapy and interaction.* New York: Guilford.

Emmelkamp, P.M.G., Van der Helm, M., Van Zanten, B., & Plochg, I. (1980). Contributions of self-instructional training to the effectiveness of exposure in vivo: A comparison with obsessive-compulsive patients. *Behaviour Research and Therapy, 18,* 61−66.

Emmelkamp, P.M.G., & Van der Heyden, H. (1980). The treatment of harming obsessions. *Behavioural Analysis and Modification, 4,* 28−35.

Emmelkamp, P.M.G., & Van der Hout, A. (1983). Failure in treating agoraphobia. In E.B. Foa & P.M.G. Emmelkamp (Eds.), *Failures in behavior therapy.* New York: Wiley.

Emmelkamp, P.M.G., Van der Hout, A., & de Vries, K. (1983). Assertive training for agoraphobics. *Behaviour Research and Therapy, 21,* 63−68.

Emmelkamp, P.M.G., & Walta, C. (1978). The effects of therapy-set on electrical aversion therapy and covert sensitization. *Behaviour Therapy, 9,* 185−188.

Emmelkamp, P.M.G., & Wessels, H. (1975). Flooding in imagination vs. flooding in vivo: A comparison with agoraphobics. *Behaviour Research and Therapy, 13,* 7−16.

Epstein, N. (1982). Cognitive therapy with couples. *American Journal of Family Therapy, 10,* 5−16.

Ersner-Hershfield, R., & Kopel, S. (1979). Group treatment of preorgasmic women: Evaluation of partner involvement and spacing of sessions. *Journal of Consulting and Clinical Psychology, 47,* 750−759.

Esse, J.T., & Wilkins, W. (1978). Empathy and imagery in avoidance behavior reduction. *Journal of Consulting and Clinical Psychology, 46,* 202−203.

Evans, D.R. (1968). Masturbatory fantasy and sexual deviation. *Behaviour Research and Therapy, 6,* 17−19.

Evans, D.R. (1970). Subjective variables and treatment effects in aversion therapy. *Behaviour Research and Therapy, 8,* 147−152.

Everaerd, W. (1977). Comparative studies of short-term treatment methods for sexual inadequacies. In R. Gemme & C.C. Wheeler (Eds.), *Progress in sexology.* Plenum: New York.

Everaerd, W. (1983). Failure in treating sexual dysfunction. In E.B. Foa & P.M.G. Emmelkamp (Eds.), *Failures in behavior therapy* (pp. 392−405) Wiley: New York.

Everaerd, W., & Dekker, J. (1981). A comparison of sex therapy and communication therapy: Couples complaining of orgasmic dysfunction. *Journal of Sex and Marital Therapy, 7,* 278−289.

Everaerd, W., & Dekker, J. (1982). Treatment of secondary orgasmic dysfunction: A comparison of systematic desensitization and sex therapy. *Behaviour Research & Therapy, 20,* 269−274.

Everaerd, W., Dekker, J., Dronkers, J., Van der Ree, K., Staffeleu, J., & Wiselius, G. (1982). Treatment of homosexual and heterosexual dysfunction in male-only groups of mixed sexual orientation. *Archives of Sexual Behaviour, 11,* 1−10.

Fahrner, E.M. (1983). Selbstunsicherheit—ein allgemeines Symptom bei funktionellen Sexualstörungen? *Zeitschrift für Klinische Psychologie, 12,* 1−11.

Falloon, I.R.H., Lindley, P., McDonald, R., & Marks, I.M. (1977). Social skills training of out-patient groups: A controlled study of rehearsal and homework. *British Journal of Psychiatry, 131,* 599−609.

Falloon, I.R.H., Lloyd, G.G., & Harpin, R.E. (1981). The treatment of social phobia: Real-life rehearsal with nonprofessional therapists. *Journal of Nervous and Mental Disease, 169,* 180−184.

Fleming, B.M. & Thornton, F. (1980). Coping skills training as a component in the short-term treatment of depression. *Journal of Consulting and Clinical Psychology, 48,* 652−654.

Foa, E.B., & Emmelkamp, P.M.G. (Eds.). (1983). *Failures in behavior therapy.* New York: Wiley.

Foa, E.B., Jameson, J.S., Turner, R.M., & Payne, L.L. (1980a). Massed vs. spaced exposure sessions in the treatment of agoraphobia. *Behaviour Research and Therapy, 18,* 333−338.

Foa, E.B., Steketee, G., & Milby, J.B. (1980b). Differential effects of exposure and response prevention in obsessive-compulsive washers. *Journal of Consulting and Clinical Psychology, 48,* 71−79.

Foa, E.B., Steketee, G., Grayson, F.B., & Doppelt, H.G. (1983). Success and failure in the behavioral treatment of obsessive-compulsives. *Journal of Consulting and Clinical Psychology, 51,* 287−297.

Ford, J.D. (1978). Therapeutic relationship in behavior therapy: An empirical analysis. *Journal of Consulting and Clinical Psychology, 46,* 1302−1314.

Friedman, J.M., Weiler, S.J., LoPiccolo, J., & Hogan, D.R. (1982). Sexual dysfunctions and their treatment. In A.S. Bellack, M. Hersen, & A.E. Kazdin (Eds.), *International handbook of behavior modification and therapy.* New York: Plenum.

Frisch, M.B., Elliott, C.H., Atsaides, J.P., Salva, D.M., & Denney, D.R. (1982). Social skills and stress management training to enhance patients' interpersonal competencies. *Psychotherapy: Theory, Research and Practice, 19,* 349−358.

Fry, W.F. (1962). The marital context of an anxiety syndrome. *Family Process, 1,* 245−252.

Fuchs, C.Z., & Rehm, L.P. (1977). A self-control behavior therapy program for depression. *Journal of Consulting and Clinical Psychology, 45,* 206−215.

Gardner, P., & Oei, T.S. (1981). Depression and self-esteem: An investigation that used behavioral and cognitive approaches to the treatment of clinically depressed clients. *Journal of Clinical Psychology, 37,* 128−135.

Garfield, S.L. (1980). *Psychotherapy: An eclectic approach.* New York: Wiley.

Girodo, M., & Roehl, J. (1978). Cognitive preparation and coping self-talk: Anxiety management during the stress of flying. *Journal of Consulting and Clinical Psychology, 46,* 978−989.

Glogower, F.D., Fremouw, W.J., & McCroskey, J.C. (1978). A component analysis of cognitive restructuring. *Cognitive Therapy and Research, 2,* 209−223.

Goodstein, R.K. (1981). Agoraphobia: Fear and the family. *Journal of Psychiatric Treatment and Evaluation, 3,* 423−427.

Goodstein, R.K., & Swift, K. (1977). Psychotherapy with phobic patients: The marriage relationship as the source of symptoms and focus of treatment. *American Journal of Psychotherapy, 31,* 284−293.

Grayson, J.B., Foa, E.B., & Steketee, G. (1982). Habituation during exposure treatment: Distraction vs. attention focusing. *Behaviour Research and Therapy, 20,* 323–328.

Gurman, A.S., & Kniskern, D.P. (1978). Behavioral marriage therapy: II. Empirical perspective. *Family Process, 17,* 139–148.

Hafner, R.J. (1977). The husbands of agoraphobic women: Assortative mating or pathogenic interaction? *British Journal of Psychiatry, 130,* 233–239.

Hafner, R.J. (1981). Agoraphobia in men. *Australian and New Zealand Journal of Psychiatry, 15,* 243–249.

Hafner, R.J., (1982). The marital context of the agoraphobic syndrome. In D.L. Chambless & A.J. Goldstein (Eds.), *Agoraphobia: Multiple perspectives on theory and treatment.* New York: Wiley.

Hafner, R.J., & Marks, I.M. (1976). Exposure in vivo in agoraphobics: Contributions of diazepam, group exposure, and anxiety evocation. *Psychological Medicine, 6,* 71–88.

Hahlweg, K., Revenstorf, D., & Schindler, L. (1982). Treatment of marital distress: Comparing formats and modalities. *Advances in Behaviour Research and Therapy, 4,* 57–74.

Hall, R., & Goldberg, D. (1977). The role of social anxiety in social interaction difficulties. *British Journal of Psychiatry, 131,* 610–615.

Hallam, R.S., Rachman, S., & Falkowski, W. (1972). Subjective, attitudinal and physiological effects of electrical aversion therapy. *Behaviour Research and Therapy, 10,* 1–13.

Hammond, P.D., & Oei, T.P.S. (1982). Social skills training and cognitive restructuring with sexual unassertiveness in women. *Journal of Sex and Marital Therapy, 8,* 297–304.

Hand, I., Lamontagne, Y., & Marks, I.M. (1974). Group exposure (flooding) in vivo for agoraphobics. *British Journal of Psychiatry, 124,* 588–602.

Harpin, R.E., Liberman, R.P., Marks, I., Stern, R., & Bohannon, W.E. (1982). Cognitive-behavior therapy for chronically depressed patients: A controlled pilot study. *Journal of Nervous and Mental Disease, 170,* 295–301.

Hartman, L.M., & Dally, E.M. (1983). Relationship factors in the treatment of sexual dysfunction. *Behaviour Research and Therapy, 21,* 153–160.

Heiby, E.M. (1981). Depression and frequency of self-reinforcement. *Behavior Therapy, 12,* 549–555.

Heiby, E.M. (1983a). Toward the prediction of mood change. *Behavior Therapy, 14,* 110–115.

Heiby, E.M. (1983b). Depression as a function of the interaction of self- and environmentally controlled reinforcement. *Behavior Therapy, 14,* 430–433.

Heide, F.J., & Borkovec, T.D. (1984). Relaxation-induced anxiety: Mechanisms and theoretical implications. *Behaviour Research and Therapy, 22,* 1–12.

Heiman, J.R., LoPicollo, J. (1983). Clinical outcome of sex therapy: Effects of daily vs. weekly treatment. *Archives of General Psychiatry, 40,* 443–449.

Hersen, M., Bellack, A.S., Himmelhoch, J.M., & Thase, M.E. (1984). Effects of social skill training, amitriptyline, and psychotherapy in unipolar depressed women. *Behavior Therapy, 15,* 21–40.

Hodgson, R., Rachman, S., & Marks, I. (1972). The treatment of chronic-obsessive-compulsive neurosis: Follow-up and further findings. *Behaviour Research and Therapy, 10,* 181–184.

Hoelscher, T.J., Lichstein, K.L., & Rosenthal, T.L. (1984). Objective vs. subjective assessment of relaxation compliance among anxious individuals. *Behaviour Research and Therapy, 22,* 187–193.

Holmes, J. (1982). Phobia and counterphobia: Family aspects of agoraphobia. *Journal of Family Therapy, 4,* 133–152.

Hops, H., Wills, T.A., Patterson, G.R., & Weiss, R.L. (1971). *The marital interaction coding system (MICS).* Unpublished manuscript, Department of Psychology, University of Oregon.

Hudson, B. (1974). The families of agoraphobics treated by behaviour therapy. *British Journal of Social Work, 4,* 51–59.

Jackson, P., & Oei, T.P.S. (1978). Social skills training and cognitive restructuring with alcoholics. *Drug and Alcohol Dependence, 4,* 369–374.

Jacobson, N.S. (1977). Problem solving and contingency contracting in the treatment of marital discord. *Journal of Consulting and Clinical Psycholgy, 45,* 92–100.

Jacobson, N.S. (1978). Specific and nonspecific factors in the effectivenss of a behavioral approach to the treatment of marital discord. *Journal of Consulting and Clinical Psychology, 46,* 442–452.

Jacobson, N.S. (1979). Behavioral treatment of marital discord: A critical appraisal. In M. Hersen, R.M. Eisler, & P.M. Miller (Eds.), *Progress in behavior modification.* New York: Academic Press.

Jacobson, N.S. (1984). A component analysis of behavioral marital therapy: The relative effectiveness of behavior exchange and communication/problem-solving training. *Journal of Consulting and Clinical Psychology, 52,* 295–305.

Jacobson, N.S., & Anderson, E.A. (Unpublished manuscript, 1984). *Interpersonal skill and depression in college students: A sequential analysis of the timing of self-disclosures.*

Jacobson, N.S., & Margolin, G. (1979). *Marital therapy.* New York: Brunner/Mazel.

Jannoun, L., Munby, M., Catalan, J., & Gelder, M. (1980). A home-based treatment program for agoraphobia: Replication and controlled evaluation. *Behavior Therapy, 11,* 294–305.

Jannoun, L., Oppenheimer, C., & Gelder, M. (1982). A self-help treatment program for anxiety state patients. *Behavior Therapy, 13,* 103–111.

Jellinek, E.M. (1960). *The disease concept of alcoholism.* New Jersey: Hillhouse Press.

Jones, S.L., Kanfer, R., & Lanyon, R.I. (1982). Skill training with alcoholics: A clinical extension. *Addictive Behaviors, 7,* 285–290.

Kanter, N.J., & Goldfried, M.R. (1979). Relative effectiveness of rational restructuring and self-control desensitization in the reduction of interpersonal anxiety. *Behavior Therapy, 10,* 472–490.

Kaplan, H.S. (1977). Hypoactive sexual desire. *Journal of Sex and Marital Therapy, 3,* 3–9.

Kaplin, H.S. (1979). *Disorders of sexual desire.* New York: Brunner/Mazel.

Kappes, B.M. (1983). Sequence effects of relation training, EMG, and temperature biofeedback on anxiety, symptom report, and self-concept. *Journal of Clinical Psychology, 39,* 203–208.

Kazdin, A.E. (1978). Evaluating the generality of findings

in analogue therapy research. *Journal of Consulting and Clinical Psychology*, 46, 673–686.

Kelly, R.J. (1982). Behavioral reorientation of pedophiliacs: Can it be done? *Clinical Psychology Review*, 2, 387–408.

Kockott, G., Dittmar, F., & Nusselt, L. (1975). Systematic desensitization and erectile impotence: A controlled study. *Archives of Sexual Behavior*, 4, 493–500.

Kornblith, S.J., Rehm, L.P., O'Hara, M.W.O., & Lamparski, D.M. (1983). The contribution of self-reinforcement training and behavioral assignments to the efficacy of self-control therapy for depression. *Cognitive Therapy ad Research*, 7, 499–528.

Kuriansky, J.B., Sharpe, L., & O'Connor, D. (1982). The treatment of anorgasmia: Long-term effectiveness of a short-term behavioral group therapy. *Journal of Sex and Marital Therapy*, 8, 29–43.

Ladouceur, R. (1983). Participant modeling with or without cognitive treatment for phobias. *Journal of Consulting and Clinical Psychology*, 51, 942–944.

Lamontagne, Y., Lavellee, Y.J., & Annable, L. (1983). Minor tranquilizers, personality inventory, and EMG feedback with chronic anxious patients. *Comprehensive Psychiatry*, 24, 543–545.

Lansky, D., Nathan, P.E., & Lawson, D.M. (1978). Blood alcohol level discrimination by alcoholics: The role of internal and external cues. *Journal of Consulting and Clinical Psychology*, 46, 953–960.

Lawrence, J.S., Bradlyn, A.S., & Kelly, J.A . (1983). Interpersonal adjustment of a homosexual adult: Enhancement via social skills training. *Behavior Modification*, 7, 41–55.

Lazarus, A.A. (1966). Broad-spectrum behaviour therapy and the treatment of agoraphobia. *Behaviour Research and Therapy*, 4, 95–97.

Lehrer, P.M. (1982). How to relax and how not to relax: A re-evaluation of the work of Edmund Jacobson—I. *Behaviour Research and Therapy*, 20, 417–428.

Lehrer, P.M., Schoicket, S., Carrington, P., & Woolfolk, R.L. (1980). Psychophysiological and cognitive responses to stressful stimuli in subjects practicing progressive relaxation and clinically standardized meditation. *Behaviour Research and Therapy*, 18, 293–303.

Lehrer, P.M., Woolfolk, R.L., Rooney, A.J., McCann, B., & Carrington, P. (1983). Progressive relaxation and meditation. *Behaviour Research and Therapy*, 21, 651–662.

Leonard, S.R., & Hayes, S.C. (1983). Sexual fantasy alternation. *Journal of Behavior Therapy and Experimental Psychiatry*, 14, 241–249.

Levin, S.M., Barry, S.M., Cambaro, S., Wolfinsohn, L., & Smith, A. (1977). Variations of covert sensitization in the treatment of pedophilic behavior: A case study. *Journal of Consulting and Clinical Psychology*, 45, 896–907.

Levine, S.B., & Agle, D. (1978). The effectiveness of sex therapy for chronic secondary psychological impotence. *Journal of Sex and Marital Therapy*, 4, 235–258.

Lewinsohn, P.M. (1975). The behavioral study and treatment of depression. In M. Hersen, R.M. Eisler, & P.M. Miller (Eds.), *Progress in behavior modification* (Vol. 1). New York: Academic Press.

Lewinsohn, P.M., & Hoberman, H.M. (1982). Depres-

sion. In A.S. Bellack, M. Hersen, & A.E. Kazdin (Eds.), *International handbook of behavior modification and therapy*. New York: Plenum.

Lewinsohn, P.M., Mischel, W., Chaplin, W., & Barton, R. (1980). Social competence and depression: The role of illusory self-perception? *Journal of Abnormal Psychology*, 89, 203–212.

Lewinsohn, P.M., & Shaffer, M. (1971). Use of home observations as an integral part of the treatment of depression. *Journal of Consulting and Clinical Psychology*, 37, 87–94.

Lewinsohn, P.M., Weinstein, M., & Alper, T. (1970). A behavioral approach to the group treatment of depressed persons: A methodological contribution. *Journal of Clinical Psychology*, 26, 525–532.

Liberman, R.P., Levie, J., Wheeler, E., Sanders, N., & Wallace, C.J. (1976). Marital therapy in groups: A comparative evaluation of behavioral and interactional formats. *Acta Psychiatrica Scandinavica*, 266, 3–34.

Libet, J., & Lewinsohn, P.M. (1973). The concept of social skill with special reference to the behavior of the depressed persons. *Journal of Consulting and Clinical Psychology*, 40, 304–312.

Little, L.M., & Curran, J.P. (1978). Covert sensitization: A clinical procedure in need of some explanations. *Psychological Bulletin*, 85, 513–531.

Lobitz, W.C., & Baker, E.L. (1979). Group treatment of single males with erectile dysfuntion. *Archives of Sexual Behavior*, 8, 127–138.

LoPiccolo, J., & Lobitz, W. (1972). The role of masturbation in the treatment of orgasmic dysfunction. *Archives of Sexual Behavior*, 2, 163–172.

Luber, R.F. (1978). Teaching models in marital therapy: A review and research issue. *Behavior Modification*, 2, 77–91.

Maletzky, B.M. (1974). "Assisted" covert sensitization in the treatment of exhibitionism. *Journal of Consulting and Clinical Psychology*, 42, 34–40.

Maletzky, B.M. (1977). "Booster" sessions in aversion therapy. The permanency of treatment. *Behavior Therapy*, 8, 460–463.

Maletzky, B.M. (1980a). Assisted covert sensitization. In D.J. Cox & R.J. Daitzman (Eds.), *Exhibitionism: Description, assessment and treatment*. New York: Garland.

Margolin, G., & Weiss, R.L. (1978). Comparative evaluation of therapeutic components associated with behavioral marital therapy. *Journal of Consulting and Clinical Psychology*, 46, 1476–1486.

Marks, I.M., Hodgson, R., & Rachman, S. (1975). Treatment of chronic obsessive-compulsive neurosis by in vivo exposure. *British Journal of Psychiatry*, 127, 349–364.

Marks, I.M., Stern, R.S., Mawson, D., Cobb, J., & McDonald, R. (1980). Clomipramine and exposure for obsessive-compulsive rituals: I. *British Journal of Psychiatry*, 136, 1–25.

Marlat, G.A., & Gordon, J.R. (1980). Determinants of relapse: Implications for the maintenance of behavior change. In P. Davidson (Ed.), *Behavioral medicine, changing health lifestyles*. New York: Brunner/Mazel.

Marshall, W.L. (1973). The modification of sexual fantasies: A combined treatment approach to the reduction of deviant sexual behavior. *Behaviour Research and Therapy, 11*, 557–564.

Marshall, W.L. (1979). Satiation therapy: A procedure for reducing deviant sexual arousal. *Journal of Applied Behavioral Analysis, 12*, 377–389.

Marzillier, J.S., & Winter, K. (1983). Limitations of the treatment for social anxiety. In E.B. Foa & P.M.G. Emmelkamp (Eds.), *Failures in behavior therapy*. New York: Wiley.

Marzillier, J.S., Lambert, C., & Kellett, J. (1976). A controlled evaluation of systematic desensitization and social skills training for socially inadequate psychiatric patients. *Behavior Research and Therapy, 14*, 225–228.

Masters, W.H., & Johnson, V.E. (1970). *Human sexual inadequacy*. Boston: Little, Brown.

Masters, W.H., & Johnson, V.E. (1979). *Homosexuality in perspective*. Boston: Little, Brown.

Mathews, A. (1983). Progress in the treatment of female sexual dysfunctions. *Journal of Psychosomatic Research, 27*, 165–173.

Mathews, A. (1984, Sept.). *Generalized anxiety*. Paper presented at the symposium Anxiety Disorders, 14th Congress of the European Association for Behavior Therapy, Brussels.

Mathews, A., Bancroft, J., Whitehead, A., Hackmann, A., Julier, D., Bancroft, J., Gath, D., & Shaw, P. (1976). The behavioural treatment of sexual inadequacy: A comparative study. *Behaviour Research and Therapy, 14*, 427–436.

Mathews, A., Gelder, M., & Johnston D. (1982). *Agoraphobia*. London: Guilford.

Mathews, A.M., Johnston, D.W., Lancashire, M., Munby, M., Shaw, P.M., & Gelder, M.G. (1976). Imaginal flooding and exposure to real phobic situations: Treatment outcome with agoraphobic patients. *British Journal of Psychiatry, 129*, 362–371.

Mathews, A.M., Teasdale, J.D., Munby, M., Johnston, D.W., & Shaw, P.M. (1977). A home-based treatment program for agoraphobic patients. *Behavior Therapy, 8*, 915–924.

Mathews, A., Whitehead. A., & Kellett, J. (1983). Psychological and hormonal factors in the treatment of female sexual dysfunction. *Psychological Medicine, 13*, 83–92.

Mavissakalian, M., Michelson, L., Greenwald, D., Kornblith, S., & Greenwald, M. (1983). Cognitive-behavioral treatment of agoraphobia: Paradoxical intention vs. self-statement training. *Behaviour Research and Therapy, 21*, 75–86.

McConaghy, N. (1982). Sexual deviation. In A.S. Bellack, M. Hersen, & A.E. Kazdin (Eds.), *International handbook of behavior modification and therapy*. New York: Plenum.

McKinley, T., Kelly, J.A., & Patterson, J. (1978). Teaching assertive skills to a passive homosexual adolescents: An illustrative case study. *Journal of Homosexuality, 3* (2).

McLean, P.D., & Hakstian, A.R. (1979). Clinical depression: Comparative efficacy of out-patient treatment. *Journal of Consulting and Clinical Psychology, 47*, 818–836.

McLean, P.D., Ogston, K., & Grauer, L. (1973). A behavioral approach to the treatment of depression. *Journal of Behavior Therapy and Experimental Psychiatry, 4*, 323–330.

McMullen, S., & Rosen, R.C. (1979). Self-administered masturbation training in the treatment of primary orgasmic dysfunction. *Journal of Consulting and Clinical Psychology, 47*, 912–918.

McPherson, F.M., Brougham, L., & McLaren, S. (1980). Maintenance of improvement in agoraphobic patients treated by behavioural methods—a four-year follow-up. *Behaviour Research and Therapy, 18*, 150–152.

Meichenbaum, D.H. (1975). Self instructional methods. In F.H. Kanfer & A.P. Goldstein (Eds.), *Helping people change*. New York: Pergamon.

Meyer, V. (1966). Modification of expectations in cases with obsessive rituals. *Behaviour Research and Therapy, 4*, 273–280.

Meyer, V., & Levy, R. (1970). Behavioural treatment of a homosexual with compulsive rituals. *British Journal of Medical Psychology, 43*, 63–67.

Meyer, V., Levy, R., & Schnurer, A. (1974). The behavioural treatment of obsessive-compulsive disorder. In H.R. Beech (Ed.), *Obsessional states*. London: Methuen.

Miller, W.R. (1983). Controlled drinking: A history and a critical review. *Journal of Studies on Alcohol, 44*, 68–83.

Miller, W.R., & Baca, L.M. (1983). Two-year follow-up bibliotherapy and therapist-directed controlled drinking training for problem drinkers. *Behavior Therapy, 14*, 441–448.

Miller, W.R., & Hester, R.K. (1980). Treating the problem drinker: Modern approaches. In W.R. Miller (Ed.), *The addictive behaviors*. Oxford: Pergamon.

Miller, W.R., & Muñoz, R.F. (1982). *How to control your drinking* (rev. ed.). Albuquerque: University of New Mexico Press.

Mills, H.L., Agras, W.S., Barlow, D.H., & Mills, J.R. (1973). Compulsive rituals treated by response prevention. *Archives of General Psychiatry, 28*, 524–530.

Milton, F., & Hafner, J. (1979). The outcome of behavior therapy for agoraphobia in relation to marital adjustment. *Archives of General Psychiatry, 361*, 807–811.

Morris, R.J., & Suckerman, K.R. (1974a). The importance of the therapeutic relationship in systematic desensitization. *Journal of Consulting and Clinical Psychology, 42*, 147.

Morris, R.J., & Suckerman, K.R. (1974b). Therapist warmth as a factor in automated systematic desensitization. *Journal of Consulting and Clinical Psychology, 42*, 244–250.

Munby, M., & Johnston, D.W. (1980). Agoraphobia: The long-term follow-up of behavioral treatment. *British Journal of Psychiatry, 137*, 418–427.

Munjack, D., Cristol, A., Goldstein, A., Phillips, D., Goldberg, A., Whipple, K., Staples, F., & Kanno, P. (1976). Behavioral treatment of orgasmic dysfunction: A controlled study. *British Journal of Psychiatry, 129*, 497–502.

Murphy, G.E., Simons, A.D., Wetzel, R.D., & Lustman, P.J. (1984). Cognitive therapy and pharmacotherapy. *Archives of General Psychiatry, 41*, 33–44.

Nathan, P.E., & Bridell, D.W. (1977). Behavioral assessment and treatment of alcoholism. In B. Kissin & H. Begleiter (Eds.), *The biology of alcoholism* (Vol. 5). New York: Plenum.

Obler, M. (1973). Systematic desensitization in sexual disorders. *Journal of Behavior Therapy and Experimental Psychiatry, 4*, 93–101.

O'Brien, G.T., Barlow, D.H., & Last, C.G. (1982). Changing marriage patterns of agoraphobics as a result of treatment. In R.L. Du Pont (Ed.), *Phobia. A comprehensive summary of modern treatment.* New York: Brunner/Mazel.

Oei, T.P.S., & Jackson, P.R. (1980). Long-term effects of group and individual social skills training with alcoholics. *Addictive Behaviors, 5*, 129–136.

Oei, T.P.S., & Jackson, P.R. (1982). Social skills and cognitive behavioral approaches to the treatment of problem drinking. *Journal of Studies on Alcohol, 43*, 532–547.

Ogborne, A.C., & Bornet, A. (1982). Abstinence and abusive drinking among affiliates of Alcoholics Anonymous: Are these the only alternatives? *Addictive Behaviors, 71*, 199–202.

O'Gorman, E.C. (1978). The treatment of frigidity: A comparative study of group and individual desensitization. *British Journal of Psychiatry, 132*, 580–584.

O'Leary, K.D., & Turkewitz, H. (1978). The treatment of marital disorder from a behavioral perspective. In T.J. Paolino & B.S. McCrady (Eds.), *Marriage and marital therapy.* New York: Brunner/Mazel.

O'Leary, D.E., O'Leary, M.E., & Donovan, B.M. (1976). Social skill acquisition and psychosocial development of alcoholics: A review. *Addictive Behavior, 1*, 110–120.

Olley, M., & McAllister, H. (1974). A comment on treatment analogues for phobic anxiety states. *Psychological Medicine, 4*, 463–469.

Olson, R.P., Ganley, R., Devine, V.T., & Dorsey, G.C. (1981). Long-term effects of behavioral versus insight-oriented therapy with inpatient alcoholics. *Journal of Consulting and Clinical Psychology, 49*, 866–877.

Öst, L.G. (1984, Sept.). *Individual response patterns and the effects of different behavioural methods in the treatment of phobias.* Paper presented at the Symposium on Anxiety Disorders, 14th Congress of the European Association for Behavior Therapy, Brussels.

Öst, L.G., Jerremalm, A., & Johansson, J. (1981). Individual response patterns and the effects of different behavioral methods in the treatment of social phobia. *Behaviour Research and Therapy, 19*, 1–16.

Öst, L.G., Johansson, J., & Jerremalm, A. (1982). Individual response patterns and the effects of different behavioral methods in the treatment of claustrophobia. *Behaviour Research and Therapy, 20*, 445–460.

Pendery, M.L., Maltzman, I.M., & West, L.J. (1982). Controlled drinking by alcoholics? New findings and a reevaluation of a major affirmative study. *Science, 217*, 169–175.

Pertchuk, M. (1983). Controlled drinking. In E.B. Foa & P.M.G. Emmelkamp (Eds.), *Failures in behavior therapy,* New York: Wiley.

Phillips, D., Fisher, S.C., Groves, G.A., & Singh, R. (1976). Alternative behavioral approaches to the treatment of homosexuality. *Archives of Sexual Behavior, 5*, 223–228.

Polich, J.M., Armor, D.J., & Braiker, H.B. (1980). Patterns of alcoholism over four years. *Journal of Studies on Alcohol, 41*, 397–415.

Pomerleau, O., Pertchuk, M., Adkins, D., & Bradley, J.P. (1978). A comparison of behavioral and traditional treatment for middle-income problem drinkers. *Journal of Behavioral Medicine, 1*, 187–200.

Price, S., Reynolds, B.S., Cohen, B.D., Anderson, A.J., & Schochet, B.V. (1981). Group treatment of erectile dysfunction for men without partners: A controlled evaluation. *Archives of Sexual Behavior, 10*, 253–268.

Queiroz, L.O., Motta, M.A., Madi, M.B.B.P., Sossai, D.L., & Boren, J.J. (1981). A functional analysis of obsessive-compulsive problems with related therapeutic procedures. *Behaviour Research and Therapy, 19*, 377–388.

Quinn, J.T., Harbinson, J.J.M., & MacAllister, H. (1970). An attempt to shape human penile response. *Behavior Therapy, 8*, 213–216.

Quinsey, V.L., Bergersen, S.G., & Steinman, C.M. (1976). Changes in physiological and verbal responses of child molesters during aversion therapy. *Canadian Journal of Behavioural Science (Montreal), 8*, 202–212.

Quinsey, V.L., Chaplin, T.C., & Carrigan, W.F. (1980). Biofeedback and signaled punishment in the modification of inappropriate sexual age preference. *Behavior Therapy, 11*, 567–576.

Rabavilas, A.D., Boulougouris, J.C., & Perissaki, C. (1979). Therapist qualities related to outcome with exposure in vivo in neurotic patients. *Journal of Behavior Therapy and Experimental Psychiatry, 10*, 293–294.

Rabavilas, A.D., Boulougouris, J.C., & Stefanis, C. (1976). Duration of flooding sessions in the treatment of obsessive-compulsive patients. *Behaviour Research and Therapy, 14*, 349–355.

Rachman, S., Cobb, J., Grey, S., McDonald, B., Mawson, D., Sartory, G., & Stern, R. (1979). The behavioural treatment of obsessional-compulsive disorders with and without clomipramine. *Behaviour Research and Therapy, 17*, 467–478.

Rachman, S., Marks, I., & Hodgson, R. (1973). The treatment of obsessive-compulsive neurotics by modelling and flooding in vivo. *Behaviour Research and Therapy, 11*, 463–471.

Ramm, E., Marks, I.M., Yüksel, S., & Stern, R.S. (1981). Anxiety management training for anxiety states: Positive compared with negative self-statements. *British Journal of Psychiatry. 140*, 367–373.

Rappaport, A.F., & Harrell, J.A. (1975). A behavioral exchange model for marital counseling. In A.S. Gurman & D.G. Rice (Eds.), *Couples in conflict.* New York: Aronson.

Rehm, L.P. (1977). A self-control model of depression. *Behavior Therapy, 8*, 787–804.

Rehm, L.P., Fuchs, C.Z., Roth, D .M., Kornblith, S.J., & Romano, J.M. (1979). A comparison of self-control and assertion skills treatment of depression. *Behavior Therapy, 10*, 429–442.

Rehm, L.P., Kornblith, S.J., O'Hara, M.W., Lamparski, D.J., Romano, J.M. & Volkin, J.I. (1981). An evaluation of major components in a self-control therapy program for depression. *Behavior Modification, 5*, 459–489.

Reynolds, B.S. (1980). Biofeedback and facilitation of erection in men with erectile dysfunction. *Archives of Sexual Behavior, 9*, 101–113.

Reynolds, B.S., Cohen, B.D., Schochet, B.V., Price, S.C., & Anderson, A.J. (1981). Dating skills training in the group treatment of erectile dysfunction for men without partners. *Journal of Sex and Marital Therapy, 7*, 184–194.

Rice, K.M., & Blanchard, E.B. (1982). Biofeedback in the treatment of anxiety disorders. *Clinical Psychology Review, 2*, 557–577.

Riley, A.J., & Riley, E.J. (1978). A controlled study to evaluate directed masturbation in the management of primary orgasmic failure in women. *British Journal of Psychiatry, 133*, 404–409.

Rooth, F.G., & Marks, I.M. (1974). Persistent exhibitionism: Short-term response to aversion, self-regulation, and relaxation treatments. *Archives of Sexual Behavior, 3*, 227–248.

Roth, D., Bielski, R., Jones, M., Parker, W., & Osborn, G. (1982). A comparison of self-control therapy and combined self-control therapy and antidepressant medication in the treatment of depression. *Behavior Therapy, 13*, 133–144.

Rush, A.J., Beck, A.T., Kovacs, M., & Hollon, S. (1977). Comparative efficacy of cognitive therapy and pharmacotherapy in the treatment of depressed outpatients *Cognitive Therapy and Research. 1*, 17–37.

Rush, A.J., Beck, A.T., Kovacs, M., Weissenburger, J., & Hollon, S.D. (1982). Comparison of the effects of cognitive therapy and pharmacotherapy on hopelessness and self-concept. *American Journal of Psychiatry, 139*, 862–866.

Rush, A.J., & Watkins, J.T. (1981). Group versus individual cognitive therapy: A pilot study. *Cognitive Therapy and Research, 5*, 95–103.

Russell, A.R., & Winkler, R. (1977). Evaluation of assertive training and homosexual guidance service groups designed to improve homosexual functioning. *Journal of Consulting and Clinical Psychology, 45*, 1–13.

Sanchez-Graig, M., Annis, H.M., Bornet, A.R., & MacDonald, K.R. (1984). Random assignment to abstinence and controlled drinking: Evaluation of a cognitive-behavioral program for problem drinkers. *Journal of Consulting and Clinical Psychology, 52,.* 390–403.

Sanchez, V.C., Lewinsohn, P.M., & Larson, D.W. (1980). Assertion training: Effectiveness in the treatment of depression. *Journal of Clinical Psychology, 36*, 526–529.

Schilling, D.J., & Poppen, R. (1983). Behavioral relaxation training and assessment. *Journal of Behavioral Therapy and Experimental Psychiatry, 14*, 99–107.

Shaffer, C.S., Shapiro, J., Sank, L.I., & Coghlan, D.J. (1981). Positive changes in depression, anxiety, and assertion following individual and group cognitive behavior therapy intervention. *Cognitive Therapy and Research, 5*, 149–157.

Shaw, P.M. (1976). *A comparison of three behaviour therapies in the treatment of social phobia.* Paper read at the British Association for Behavioral Psychotherapy, Exeter.

Simons, A.D., Garfield, S.L., & Murphy, G.E. (1984). The process of change in cognitive therapy and pharmacotherapy for depression: Changes in mood and cognition. *Archives of General Psychiatry, 41*, 44–51.

Sinnott, A., Jones, R.B., Scott-Fordham, A., & Woodard, R. (1981). Augmentation of in vivo exposure treatment for agoraphobia by the formation of neighbourhood self-help groups. *Behaviour Research and Therapy, 19*, 539–547.

Sloane, R.B., Staples, F.R., Cristol, A.H., Yorkston, N.J., & Whipple, K. (1975). *Psychotherapy versus behavior therapy.* Cambridge, MA: Harvard University Press.

Smail, P., Stockwell, T., Canter, S., & Hodgson, R. (1984). Alcohol dependence and phobic anxiety states: I. A prevalence study. *British Journal of Psychiatry, 144*, 53–57.

Schmidt, M.M., & Miller, W.R. (1983). Amount of therapist contact and outcome in a multidimensional depression treatment program. *Acta Psychiatrica Scandinavica, 67*, 319–332.

Sobell, M.B., & Sobell, L.C. (1973). Alcoholics treated by individualized behavior therapy: One year treatment outcome. *Behaviour Research and Therapy, 11*, 599–618.

Sobell, M.B., & Sobell, L.C. (1984). The aftermath of heresy: A response to Pendery et al.'s (1982) critique of "individualized behavior therapy for alcoholics." *Behaviour Research and Therapy, 22*, 413–440.

Sobell, M.B., Sobell, L.C., Ersner-Hershfield, S., & Nirenberg, T.D. (1982). Alcohol and drug problems. In A.S. Bellack, M. Hersen, & A.E. Kazdin (Eds.), *International handbook of behavior modification and therapy.* New York: Plenum.

Sotile, W.M., & Kilmann, P.R. (1978). Effects of group systematic desensitization on female orgasmic dysfunction. *Archives of Sexual Behavior, 7*, 477–491.

Sotile, W.M., Kilmann, P., & Follingstad, D.R. (1977). A sexual-enhancement workshop: Beyond group systematic desensitization for women's sexual anxiety. *Journal of Sex and Marital Therapy, 3*, 249–255.

Stern, R., & Marks, I.M. (1973). Brief and prolonged flooding: A comparison in agoraphobic patients. *Archives of General Psychiatry, 28*, 270–276.

Stockwell, T., Smail, P., Hodgson, R., & Canter, S. (1984). Alcohol dependence and phobic anxiety states: II. A retrospective study. *British Journal of Psychiatry, 144*, 58–63.

Stravinsky, A., Marks, I., & Yule, W. (1982). Social skills problems in neurotic outpatients: Social skills training with and without cognitive modification. *Archives of General Psychiatry, 39*, 1378–1385.

Stuart, R.B. (1975). Behavioral remedies for marital ills: A guide to the use of operant interpersonal techniques. In A.S. Gurman & D.G. Rice (Eds.), *Couples in conflict.* New York: Aronson.

Swan, G.E., & MacDonald, M.L. (1978). Behavior therapy in practice: A national survey of behavior therapists. *Behavior Therapy, 9*, 799–807.

Teasdale, J.D., & Fennell, M.J.V. (1982). Immediate effects on depression of cognitive therapy interventions. *Cognitive Therapy and Research, 6*, 343–352.

Teasdale, J.D., Fennell, M.J.V., Hibbert, G.A., & Amies, P.L. (1984). Cognitive therapy for major depressive disorder in primary care. *British Journal of Psychiatry, 144*, 400–406.

Teasdale, J.D., Walsh, P.A., Lancashire, M., & Mathews,

A.M. (1977). Group exposure for agoraphobics: A replication study. *British Journal of Psychiatry, 130,* 186–193.

Thorpe, G.L., Amatu, H.I., Blakey, R.S., & Burns, L.E. (1976). Contributions of overt instructional rehearsal and "specific insight" to the effectiveness of self-instructional training: A preliminary study. *Behavior Therapy, 7,* 504–511.

Torpey, D., & Measy, L. (1973). Marital interaction in agoraphobia. *Journal of Clinical Psychology, 30,* 351–354.

Trower, P., Yardley, K., Bryant, B.M., & Shaw, P. (1978). The treatment of social failure: A comparison of anxiety-reduction and skills-acquisition procedures on two social problems. *Behavior Modification, 2,* 41–60.

Turner, S.M., Hersen, M., Bellack, A.S., Andrasik, F., & Capparall, H.V. (1980). Behavioral and pharmacological treatment of obsessive-compulsive disorders. *Journal of Nervous and Mental Disease, 168,* 237–254.

Turner, S.M., Hersen, M., Bellack, A.S., & Wells, K.C. (1979). Behavioral treatment of obsessive-compulsive neurosis. *Behaviour Research and Therapy, 17,* 95–106.

Van Deventer, A.D., & Laws, D.R. (1978). Orgasmic reconditioning to redirect sexual arousal in pedophiles. *Behavior Therapy, 9,* 748–765.

Van Hasselt, V.B., Hersen, M., & Milliones, J. (1978). Social skills training for alcoholics and drug addicts: A review. *Addictive Behaviors, 3,* 221–233.

Van Son, M.J.M. (1978). *Sociale Vaardigheidstherapie.* Amsterdam: Swets und Zeitlinger.

Voegtlin, W., & Broz, W.B. (1949). The conditioned reflex treatment of chronic alcoholism. An analysis of 3125 admissions over a period of ten and a half years. *Annals of Internal Medicine, 30,* 580–597.

Vogler, R.E., Compton, J.V., & Weissback, T.A. (1975). Integrated behavior change techniques for alcoholics. *Journal of Consulting and Clinical Psychology, 43,* 233–243.

Wade, T.C., Baker, T.B., & Hartmann, D.P. (1979). Behavior therapists' self-reported views and practices. *The Behavior Therapist, 2,* 3–6.

Watson, J.P., Mullett, G.E., & Pilley, H. (1973). The effects of prolonged exposure to phobic situations upon agoraphobic patients treated in groups. *Behaviour Research and Therapy, 11,* 531–546.

Webster, A.S. (1953). The development of phobias in married women. *Psychological Monographs, 67,* No. 367.

Weiss, R.L. (1978). The conceptualization of marriage and marriage disorders from a behavioral perspective. In T.J. Paolino & B.S. McCrady (Eds.), *Marriage and marital therapy.* New York: Brunner/Mazel.

Weiss, R.L., & Wieder, G.B. (1982). Marital distress. In A.S. Bellack, M. Hersen, & A.E. Kazdin (Eds.), *International handbook of behavior modification and therapy.* New York: Plenum.

Weiss, R.L., Hops, H., & Patterson, G.R. (1973). A framework for conceptualizing marital conflict, a technology for altering it, some data for evaluating it. In F.W. Clark & L.A. Hamerlynck (Eds.), *Critical issues in research and practice: Proceedings of the Fourth Banff International Conference in Behavior Modification.* Champaign, IL: Research Press.

Wickramasekera, I. (1976). Aversive behavior rehearsal for sexual exhibitionism. *Behavior Therapy, 7,* 167–176.

Williams, S.L., Dooseman, G., & Kleifield, E. (1984). Comparative effectiveness of guided mastery and exposure treatments for intractable phobias. *Journal of Consulting and Clinical Psychology, 52,* 505–518.

Williams, S.L., & Rappoport, J.A. (1983). Cognitive treatment in the natural environment for agoraphobics. *Behavior Therapy, 14,* 299–313.

Wilson, G.T. (1978). Alcoholism and aversion therapy: Issues, ethics and evidence. In G.A. Marlatt & P.E. Nathan (Eds.), *Behavioral approaches to alcoholism.* New Brunswick, NJ: Rutgers Center of Alcohol Studies.

Wilson, P.H. (1982). Combined pharmacological and behavioural treatment of depression. *Behaviour Research and Therapy, 20,* 173–184.

Wilson, P.H., Goldin, J.C., & Charbonneau-Powis, M. (1983). Comparative efficacy of behavioral and cognitive treatments of depression. *Cognitive Therapy and Research, 7,* 111–124.

Wincze, J.P., & Caird, W.K. (1976). The effects of systematic desensitization and video desensitization in the treatment of essential sexual dysfunction in women. *Behavior Therapy, 7,* 387–395.

Wolpe, F. (1958). *Psychotherapy by reciprocal inhibition.* Stanford: Stanford University Press.

Woodward, R., & Jones, R.B. (1980). Cognitive restructuring treatment: A controlled trial with anxious patients. *Behaviour Research and Therapy, 18,* 401–409.

Woolfolk, R.L., Lehrer, P.M., McCann, B.S., & Rooney, A.J. (1982). Effects of progressive relaxation and meditation on cognitive and somatic manifestations of daily stress. *Behaviour Research and Therapy, 20,* 461–468.

Youngren, M.A., & Lewinsohn, P.M. (1980). The functional relationship between depression and problematic interpersonal behavior. *Journal of Abnormal Psychology, 89,* 333–341.

Zeiss, R., Christensen, A., & Levine, A. (1978). Treatment for premature ejaculation through male only groups. *Journal of Sex and Marital Therapy, 4,* 139–143.

Zeiss, A.M., Lewinsohn, P.M., & Muñoz, R.F. (1979). Nonspecific improvement effects in depression using interpersonal skills training, pleasant activity schedules, or cognitive training. *Journal of Consulting and Clinical Psychology, 47,* 427–439.

Zilbergeld, B. (1975). Group treatment of sexual dysfunction in men without partners. *Journal of Sex and Marital Therapy, 3,* 443–452.

10

COGNITIVE AND COGNITIVE-BEHAVIORAL THERAPIES

STEVEN D. HOLLON

Vanderbilt University

AARON T. BECK

University of Pennsylvania

INTRODUCTION

The last two decades have seen a virtual explosion in interest in cognitively focused interventions for a variety of disorders. Centered largely within modern behaviorism, this interest has drawn both from behaviorally trained investigators (e.g., Bandura, Mahoney, Meichenbaum) and from more dynamically trained theorists (e.g., Beck and Ellis). It has sparked the publication of a number of influential treatises and treatment manuals (Beck & Emery, 1985; Beck, Rush, Shaw, & Emery, 1979; Ellis, 1962; Foreyt & Rathjen, 1979; Kendall & Braswell, 1985; Kendall & Hollon, 1979; Mahoney, 1974, 1977; Meichenbaum, 1977; Turk, Meichenbaum, & Genest, 1983), texts on cognitive assessment (Kendall & Hollon, 1981; Merluzzi, Glass, & Genest, 1981), and at least one major journal, *Cognitive Therapy and Research*.

This chapter will examine the empirical support for these cognitively focused interventions. As we shall see, the approaches subsumed within this general heading are diverse, both with regard to the model of change adopted (process) and with regard to the actual therapeutic strategies and techniques utilized to produce change (procedures). In this chapter, we will present an overview of this variation in both presumed process and actual procedure for these various approaches and examine the empirical evidence for each.

Definition of Cognitive Therapy

For the purposes of this chapter, the cognitive and cognitive-behavioral therapies will be defined as those approaches that attempt to modify existing or anticipated disorders by virtue of altering cognitions or cognitive processes. The emphasis in this definition is on the nature of the presumed causal mediators targeted by the therapist for modification. This definition excludes various approaches relying more exclusively on techniques such as systemic desensitization, which, while typically considered behavioral in focus, may use such clearly cognitive processes as imagery in the change process. Since the intended intermediate goal of systematic desensitization is typically not to alter cognition per se, we will not classify it here as a cognitive therapy. Such a definition avoids the problem of reinterpreting all therapies as "cognitive" if they prove to work, as Bandura (1977) and Beck (1971, 1984b) have suggested, by virtue of changing beliefs, so long as that was not the intended intermediate goal of the therapist. Thus, behavioral procedures may prove to work through cognitive mechanisms, but only those therapies explicitly targeted at such processes will be labeled "cognitive."

The specific approaches to therapy that will be reviewed include Ellis's Rational-Emotive Therapy (RET; Ellis, 1962) and its more structured variant, Systematic Rational Restructuring (SRR; Goldfried, DeCanteceo, & Weinberg, 1974), Beck's Cognitive Therapy (CT; Beck, 1964, 1967, 1970; Beck et al., 1979), and Meichenbaum's Self-Instructional Training (SIT; Meichenbaum, 1974, 1977) and Stress Inoculation Training (STI; Meichenbaum, 1975). The emphasis will be on controlled trials in which one or more of the various cognitive or cognitive-behavioral approaches have been contrasted with some alternative approach or control condition.

Variations in Process

Ross (1977) has suggested that there are at least three main avenues for producing change in existing belief systems. The first, *disconfirmation,* involves confronting the individual with evidence that contradicts existing beliefs. The second, *reconceptualization,* involves providing the individual with an alternative construct system for explaining existing observations or experiences. The third, which Ross labels *"insight,"* involves providing the individual with an understanding of the process followed to arrive at a belief. Presumably, the simple recognition of the illogical nature of one's information processing can lead to a revision in one's beliefs.

Other processes may be involved as well. It would appear that self-statement modification approaches (e.g., SIT or STI) may rely heavily on repetition. In these therapies, the emphasis appears to be less on influencing the subjective validity of a given belief or set of beliefs (i.e., the degree to which the client believes something to be true) than on utilizing repetition to increase the likelihood that the individual will think a certain thought in a given situation.

Kendall and Braswell (1985) have distinguished between *distortions,* instances in which the individual holds a belief system that serves him or her poorly, and *deficits,* instances in which the individual simply lacks appropriate mediating cognitions. We would argue that the kinds of processes described by Ross, including empirical disconfirmation, alternative conceptualizations, and process insight, are likely to be the most powerful change processes when distortions or errors are evident in existing belief systems. Conversely, repetition-based approaches may be particularly efficient in the case of deficits, when the goal is to introduce appropriate mediators when none currently exist. We are aware of little empirical support for such speculations at present. We are struck, however, by the fact that most of the clinical work involving Ross's three processes has focused on adult populations, such as depressives, who are believed to exhibit existing pathological belief systems (distortions), while much of the work with preadolescent populations, such as impulsive children, who are presumed to display an absence of appropriate cognitive mediators (deficits), has relied largely on repetition-based strategies.

Variations in Procedure

Just as Kiesler (1966) cautioned against accepting a "uniformity myth" with regard to therapy in general, so too do we need to be careful not to assume that all cognitive therapies are identical. Major variations can be identified, although, to date, there have been few efforts to determine whether these variations differ in terms of the impacts they exert. In addition, the major approaches differ in the degree to which they incorporate behavioral procedures. Further, those interventions utilizing both cognitive and behavioral components can differ with regard to whether those components are simply combined in an additive or sequential fashion (combinations) or integrated with one another in the process of changing beliefs (integrated).

As we shall see, systematic rational restructuring (Goldfried et al., 1974) has typically been implemented as a largely cognitive approach, although it is sometimes combined with various behavioral interventions. Rational-emotive therapy (Ellis, 1962), often considered to be a purely cognitive approach, appears frequently to combine behavioral rehearsal and homework tasks with its efforts at rational reevaluation. Cognitive therapy (Beck, 1970; Beck et al., 1979), despite its name, appears to be a wholly integrative cognitive-behavioral approach, largely by virtue of its reliance on empirical hypothesis testing, although some studies have extracted the more purely cognitive component (e.g., Taylor & Marshall, 1977). Self-instructional training (Meichenbaum, 1974, 1977) and stress inoculation training (Meichenbaum, 1975) are somewhat more difficult to classify. Both are probably best described as cognitive-behavioral combinations, since behavioral procedures are rarely directed explicitly at altering beliefs or cognitive processes directly. Whether cognitive approaches differ from cognitive-behavioral ones, and whether cognitive-behavioral combinations differ from cognitive-behavioral integrations, represents an important set of issues that, unfortunately, can be addressed only indirectly at present. What is apparent is that the different domains of psychopathology have tended to be approached with different cognitive variations. For example, self-instructional training emphasizing repetition has been the primary mode of intervention with impulsive, non-self-controlled children. Systematic rational restructuring and rational-emotive therapy, emphasizing logic and reasoning, have tended to be the predominant mode of intervention for anxiety states, although self-instructional approaches have also been represented. Finally, cognitive therapy, emphasizing empirical hypothesis testing, has tended to be the predominant mode utilized for depression.

The key point for our current purposes is that this confounding of type of cognitive approach with type of disorder will make it difficult to determine whether variable efficacy is a function of the inefficacy of the particular mode, the intransigence of the particular disorder to any cognitive approach, or some specific interaction between the two. Before moving to a consideration of the empirical support for the various approaches with specific disorders, it will first be important to discuss the basic procedures and presumed processes mobilized by each major variant.

Procedures Emphasizing Rationality

Rational-emotive therapy. Rational-emotive therapy (RET; Ellis, 1962) is perhaps the best known and most widely practiced of the cognitive interventions. Developed by Ellis during the 1950s, a cognitive theory of disorder has been advanced and a set of procedures designed to produce change by altering the client's beliefs. As noted by Mahoney and Arnkoff (1978), the newer cognitive and cognitive-behavioral interventions have posed less of a challenge to the basic theory of disorder of RET than to its procedures.

In a series of papers, Ellis (1973, 1980) has attempted to distinguish RET from other cognitive and cognitive-behavioral approaches. In his 1980 treatise, Ellis distinguished between general or nonpreferential RET (which he considers to be synonymous with cognitive-behavior therapy) and preferential RET, in which clients are taught a philosophy of living. This dichotomy overlaps with his earlier distinction between inelegant and elegant cognitive therapy (Ellis, 1973). In each instance, Ellis's preference is clearly for the latter. According to Ellis, general or nonpreferential RET lacks any underlying philosophy, focuses solely on producing symptomatic change, and tends to be grounded in an aphilosophical empiricism, while preferential RET provides a philosophy of living, seeks to reconstruct personality, and posits that the major questions confronting clients are rarely amenable to empirical inquiry (a point with which other cognitive theorists might well disagree). In short, while other cognitive theorists may strive to alter dysfunctional beliefs or attitudes, narrowly defined, Ellis seeks a total alteration in the client's philosophy of life. Whether such a difference in focus actually serves any useful clinical purpose remains an open question.

Procedures in RET have doubtless evolved over the years, but it seems fair to conclude that direct instruction, persuasion, and logical disputation are the major procedural components employed. Patients are trained to recognize their own irrational beliefs and to dispute them actively. The therapist explicitly models more rational beliefs and provides explicit feedback to the client. The course of therapy is largely deductive, with the therapist rapidly identifying the nature of the client's irrational beliefs early in treatment (preferably in the first session), and actively disputing those beliefs. Homework and behavioral assignments are utilized, although typically as practice and rehearsal tasks to solidify cognitive change, rather than as a means of producing such change, as in an empirical hypothesis-testing approach. Although evidence based on prior experience or other sources of factual information may occasionally be used in the disputational process (an example of Ross' first principle) it is rarely sought prospectively. Some effort is also made to examine the process by which conclusions are drawn by reference to the concept of irrational ideas (an example of Ross' third principle), but little formal effort is made to distinguish particular aberrant patterns, as opposed to dysfunctional content. Similarly, little formal attention is paid to systematic repetition. By far the major effort is devoted to providing an alternative philosophical system, that is, an alternative belief system via persuasion (an example of Ross' second principle). In short, RET is applied as a philosophical system, relying largely on persuasion and reason as the means of modifying beliefs.

Systematic rational restructuring. Systematic rational restructuring (Goldfried et al., 1974) was initially conceptualized as a structured set of procedures for operationalizing Ellis' RET. The overall structure of the approach involves the following four major components: (1) presentation of a rationale, typically a version of Ellis' cognitive model, (2) an overview of irrational assumptions, in which the client is exposed to the basic assumptions held by Ellis to underlie all neurotic distress, (3) an analysis of the client's problems in rational-emotive terms, in which specific instances from the client's life are analyzed from a rational-emotive perspective in order to detect which irrational assumptions are operating, and (4) an effort to teach the client to modify his or her internal sentences, during which the client is trained to put into practice what he or she has learned in theory. The primary process mobilized appears to be that of reason or logic. Two processes little appealed to are repetition, a key element in self-instructional training, and empirical hypothesis testing, a key element in Beck's cognitive therapy.

Procedures Involving Empiricism:
Cognitive Therapy
Beck's cognitive therapy (1964, 1967, 1970; Beck et al., 1979) overlaps considerably with Ellis' rational-emotive therapy (Ellis, 1962) and with Goldfried et al.'s (1974) more structured systematic rational restructuring, particularly with regard to its endorsement of a cognitive rationale, but it differs in its emphasis on empirical hypothesis testing as a means of changing existing beliefs. While making extensive use of persuasion and logic, as in those other approaches, cognitive therapists are trained to attempt

to push for an actual prospective test of the client's particular beliefs (Ross' first principle).

Because of this reliance on prospective hypothesis testing, cognitive therapy can be considered a fully integrated cognitive-behavioral intervention. In this approach, behavioral assignments and homeworks are typically presented as experiments designed to allow clients to test formally the validity of their beliefs. Extensive use is also made of the provision of an alternative construct system (Ross' second principle), usually as a prelude to prospective hypothesis testing, along with an explicit focus on various systematic distortions in information processing (Ross' third principle). Little formal use is made of repetition processes as a means of altering belief systems, which may reflect the expectation that repetition alone is a weak process for modifying existing belief systems.

Procedures Emphasizing Repetition
Self-instructional training. The key process in self-instructional training appears to be that of repetition. Drawing on work on children's development of covert speech (Luria, 1961; Vygotsky, 1962), Meichenbaum (1974, 1977) has developed a treatment procedure that combines graduated practice with elements of rational-emotive theory. As practiced by Meichenbaum and Goodman (1971), the procedure involves five steps: (1) first the therapist models the task at hand, verbalizing out loud the steps involved; (2) then the client executes the task at hand while the therapist verbalizes the steps; (3) next the client again executes the task while verbalizing the steps himself or herself out loud; (4) then the client again executes the task while inaudibly moving his or her lips; and (5) finally, the client executes the task while thinking the task through to himself or herself.

The key process in this approach may be the structured sequence provided to facilitate the acquisition of particular cognitions. In effect, the client is led through a sequence in which overt verbalizations are transformed into covert self-verbalizations, or thoughts. As suggested earlier, self-instructional training might well be expected to prove particularly useful in introducing mediating cognitions when appropriate, adaptive mediators do not already exist. SIT does not appear to differ that greatly from either rational-emotive therapy or systematic rational restructuring in terms of how it deals with existing beliefs (distortions). That is, it would appear that SIT therapists rely largely on persuasion and reason to change existing beliefs.

Stress inoculation training. Stress inoculation training (Meichenbaum, 1975) represents a combination of a skills-training acquisition phase with an opportunity for later application practice or rehearsal. The approach involves three main steps. The first goal is to *educate* the client about the nature of stressful or fearful reactions, typically involving the presentation of a cognitive rationale. The second step involves having the client *rehearse* coping behaviors. In particular, those behaviors tend to focus on practicing coping self-statements that can be used when confronted by stress, but also tend to include specific training in behavioral self-control skills like progressive relaxation training. The coping self-statements often are presented in a self-instructional training format. The third and final phase of the training package, the *application* phase, involves testing and practicing these skills in actual arousing or stress-provoking situations. Actual confrontation with real life stressors is preferred, but analogue situations or role-playing are frequently utilized.

The degree to which the cognitive restructuring component of stress inoculation training approximates a more systematic rationality-based restructuring approach (e.g., RET or SRR) as opposed to relying on repetition (as in SIT) tends to vary across studies. In essence, it would appear that this cognitive skills-training component typically involves some combination of restructuring based on reason and persuasion and replacement based on repetition, with little recourse to empirical hypothesis testing.

Other Related Approaches

There are several other approaches to treatment, which, while not solely cognitive in nature, do contain important cognitive aspects. Problem-solving therapy (D'Zurilla & Goldfried, 1971) is a five-step procedure that seeks to train a general cognitive and behavioral set for dealing with various problems encountered in living. Self-control therapies (Kanfer, 1970, 1971; Rehm, 1977) tend to focus on presumed deficits in three core processes, self-monitoring, self-evaluation (the most purely cognitive component), and self-reinforcement. Self-control desensitization (Goldfried, 1971) emphasizes the utilization of desensitization procedures

as an active coping response, training clients to recognize tension and anxiety as cues or signals for the initiation of relaxation. Cognitive factors are involved in covert conditioning (Cautela, 1966, 1967) and covert modeling (Kazdin, 1976), in which imaginal self-presentations are utilized in an effort to alter client processes. Finally, multimodal therapy (Lazarus, 1976) can include explicit cognitive change procedures. While these approaches clearly have cognitive aspects, they typically represent minor aspects of largely behavioral interventions (especially in terms of underlying conceptualization). With the exception of Rehm and colleagues' work with a self-control approach to depression, these approaches will not be systematically reviewed in this chapter.

Implications

As suggested by the preceding discussion, it is insufficient to ask, "Does cognitive therapy work?" Rather, the question should be "Do any of the cognitive or cognitive-behavioral interventions work with any of the specific disorders, and, if so, why?" Although the various approaches all adhere to a cognitive theory of disorder and a cognitive theory of change, those various approaches differ markedly with regard to the processes they emphasize to produce change (e.g., rationality, empiricism, and repetition) and the procedures utilized to mobilize those processes. Further, the various approaches differ with regard to the extent to which behavioral procedures are incorporated and the way in which that incorporation is brought about (e.g., combinations versus integrations). Finally, as we shall see, there has been a tendency for the type of cognitive approach utilized to be confounded with the type of disorder studied.

Addressing the efficacy question is made even more difficult by the frequently spotty descriptions of the actual treatment procedures utilized. Additional complications are introduced by the virtually total absence of any procedural assessments in the literature, that is, treatment manipulation checks designed to ensure that a given approach was adequately implemented. Finally, numerous studies have been conducted utilizing intervention packages that cannot be clearly assigned to any of the specific interventions (rational-emotive therapy, systematic rational restructuring, cognitive therapy, self-instructional training, or stress inoculation training) or the larger process categories (rationality, empiricism, or repetition). Noting these difficulties, we now turn to a review of the controlled trials in the literature evaluating the cognitive and cognitive-behavioral therapies.

SPECIFIC DISORDERS

Depression

Probably no area has received more attention from cognitive and cognitive-behavioral researchers than the area of depression. Beginning with Beck's early theoretical work regarding the role of distorted cognitive content and maladaptive information processing (Beck, 1963, 1967, 1976), depression has been explored from a number of related, but distinct, cognitive perspectives.

With regard to treatment interventions, at least two major cognitive-behavioral approaches, Beck's cognitive therapy (Beck, 1964, 1970; Beck et al., 1979) and Rehm's self-control approach (Rehm, 1977), have been examined in controlled studies. Both major approaches have been tested in a number of trials with relative homogeneity of execution, although some important elements of within-modality variability have occurred. In addition, several variants have appeared in various single studies (cf. Hersen, Bellack, Himmelhoch, & Thase, 1984; McLean & Hakstian, 1979; Zeiss, Lewinsohn, & Munoz, 1979).

Beck's Cognitive Therapy for Depression

Beck's cognitive therapy for depression is, despite its name, a cognitive-behavioral intervention. In essence, clients are trained to use the outcomes of their behaviors to test the accuracy of their beliefs. A detailed therapist's manual is available (Beck et al., 1979), and instruments have been developed for ascertaining the degree of adherence to the basic approach on the part of the practicing therapist, chiefly the Collaborative Study Psychotherapy Rating Scale (CSPRS; Evans et al., 1983; Hollon, Evans, Elkin, & Lowery, 1984) and its forerunner, the Minnesota Therapy Rating Scale (MTRS; DeRubeis, Hollon, Evans, & Bemis, 1982), and Young's Cognitive Therapy Scale (CTS; Young, 1980).

Empirical trials with cognitive therapy.   The efficacy of cognitive therapy has been explored in a number of controlled trials involving both analogue

and fully clinical populations. In the earliest such trial, Shaw (1977) contrasted cognitive therapy with Lewinsohn's behavioral treatment, a nondirective attention control, and a waiting list in the treatment of depressed college students seeking treatment at a university health service. Treatment was conducted by the author in twice-weekly two-hour group sessions over a four-week period. Assessments were made on two self-report measures and by independent judges blind to treatment condition. The results indicated that the cognitive therapy cell evidenced superior improvement on both self-report and clinician-rated measures, with the behavior therapy cell and nondirective controls both superior, in turn, to the wait-list controls. Differences were maintained at a one-month follow-up. Thus, cognitive therapy, executed as an integrated cognitive-behavioral composite, appeared to outperform both behavior therapy, a nondirective control, and a wait-list control.

Taylor and Marshall (1977) provided a parallel comparison to Shaw's report, albeit one relying on college students recruited by newspaper advertisements and an operationalization of cognitive therapy that only partially approximated Beck's approach. Mildly depressed subjects were randomly assigned to either cognitive therapy alone, behavior therapy alone, combined cognitive-behavior therapy, or a wait-list control. The combined cognitive-behavioral therapy most nearly approximated Beck's cognitive therapy, although operationalized as the combination of distinct cognitive and behavioral change procedures, rather than as a true integration. Greater improvement was evident for the combined cognitive-behavioral approach over either single modality alone, each of which, in turn, exceeded the wait-list control. Differences were again maintained at five-week follow-up. Considering the combined cognitive-behavioral treatment to be the closest approximation to Beck's cognitive therapy as executed in Shaw's study, these findings appeared to replicate that earlier study.

Rush, Beck, Kovacs, and Hollon (1977) presented the first major trial contrasting cognitive therapy with tricyclic pharmacotherapy (imipramine) in the treatment of a fully clinical primary, nonpsychotic unipolar depressed outpatient population. Patients receiving cognitive therapy were seen in individual treatment not exceeding 20 one-hour visits over a 12-week period, while patients receiving pharmacotherapy were treated with up to 250 mg per day of imipramine and saw their pharmacotherapists weekly for 12 weeks in half-hour sessions. Medications were tapered beginning in week 10, so that all pharmacotherapy patients were drug-free by week 12. The cognitive therapists were a mixed group of psychiatric residents, psychologists, and psychology graduate students, while the pharmacotherapists were psychiatric residents.

Treatment results indicated superior improvement for the cognitive therapy patients on both a self-report and a clinician-rated measure. Raters were, however, not blind to treatment assignment. Attrition rates were also significantly lower in cognitive therapy than in pharmacotherapy, and there was evidence that treatment gains were maintained over a one-year follow-up (Kovacs, Rush, Beck, & Hollon, 1981).

This study represented the first instance in which a psychosocial treatment, of any type, had even matched, much less exceeded, the efficacy of the tricyclic antidepressants (see Covi, Lipman, Derogatis, Smith, & Pattison, 1974; Daneman, 1961; Friedman, 1975; Klerman, DiMascio, Weissman, Prusoff, & Paykel, 1974, for earlier studies contrasting traditional psychotherapies with pharmacological approaches). As we shall see, subsequent studies have suggested that the initial Rush et al. (1977) trial may have underestimated the efficacy of pharmacotherapy relative to cognitive therapy (an examination of the weekly depression scores by treatment condition suggested that patients in the pharmacotherapy cell actually worsened as a group during the two-week medication withdrawal period *prior* to the posttreatment evaluation), but the basic absolute efficacy of cognitive therapy appears to have been maintained in subsequent trials.

Beck, Hollon, Young, Bedrosian, and Budenz (1985) conducted a comparison between cognitive therapy (again, the cognitive-behavioral integration) and combined cognitive-pharmacotherapy (in this study involving amitriptyline). Patients were selected in a manner analogous to the Rush et al. (1977) trial and randomly assigned to either cognitive therapy, as practiced in Rush et al., or combined cognitive-pharmacotherapy. In the combined modality, each patient saw both a cognitive therapist and, if necessary, a pharmacotherapist (if the treating therapist was a psychiatrist, he or she executed both modalities). Medication levels were not allowed to rise above 200 mg per day. Treatment outcome on both

self-report and clinician-ratings indicated essentially comparable reductions in the two groups, with both evidencing greater change than had been shown by the pharmacotherapy-only cell in Rush et al. This essential comparability between cognitive therapy and combined cognitive-pharmacotherapy held through a one-year follow-up, with fewer relapses than for the drug-only cell in Rush et al. (1977). These findings were interpreted as indicating that the practice of combining cognitive therapy with pharmacotherapy did not undermine any purported prophylactic effect for the psychotherapy.

Blackburn and colleagues (Blackburn, Bishop, Glen, Whalley, & Christie, 1981) provided the first controlled trial in a fully clinical population conducted outside of the Philadelphia center at which Beck's cognitive therapy was developed. Patients drawn from two different settings, a general medical setting and an outpatient psychiatric facility, were randomly assigned to either cognitive therapy alone, tricyclic pharmacotherapy with supportive contact (either desipramine or nortriptyline), or combined cognitive-pharmacotherapy. Cognitive therapy was essentially executed in accordance with the Beck et al. (1979) treatment manual. Results, as indicated by either self-report or clinician rating, indicated an unexplained difference between the two populations. In the general medical setting, the combined approach was not significantly different from the cognitive therapy cell, although both exceeded the medication-only cell. In the psychiatric outpatient setting, the combined approach outperformed both single modalities, which did not differ from one another. Given an extremely poor absolute performance for the pharmacotherapy-only cell in the general medical setting, which evidenced only a 14 percent response rate relative to the more standard 60 to 70 percent response rate typically found in the literature, the possibility that the pharmacological treatment was poorly implemented in that general medical setting cannot be ruled out. While it is never desirable to casually attribute anomalous findings to problems in protocol execution on a post hoc basis, a 14 percent response rate is so inconsistent with the broader literature (cf. Klein & Davis, 1969; Morris & Beck, 1974) that it must be questioned. Unfortunately, no blood plasma medication levels were available to address this concern. Nonetheless, even a questionably adequate pharmacological intervention should have provided a nonspecific comparison for the other approaches. In any event, the combined treatment was either superior to both single modalities or equivalent to cognitive therapy alone (as in Beck et al., 1985), while cognitive therapy alone was either superior to pharmacotherapy alone (as in Rush et al., 1977) or equivalent to it. Given the results of the two studies to be discussed next, it seems likely that cognitive therapy can typically be expected to equal, although not necessarily exceed, tricyclic pharmacotherapy in the treatment of the acute episode. Even more importantly, a two-year posttreatment follow-up indicated that cognitive therapy, whether provided with medications or without, produced a lower relapse rate following treatment cessation than medications alone (Blackburn, Eunson, & Bishop, in press).

Murphy and colleagues (Murphy, Simons, Wetzel, & Lustman, 1984) conducted yet another controlled treatment comparison between cognitive therapy and tricyclic pharmacotherapy. This trial was particularly noteworthy because it was conducted at the Department of Psychiatry at the Washington University in St. Louis, long a stronghold of a biological/pharmacological approach to treatment. Nonpsychotic, nonbipolar primary depressed outpatients of both sexes were randomly assigned to tricyclic pharmacotherapy (desipramine), cognitive therapy (executed as an integration of cognitive and behavioral techniques), cognitive therapy plus pill-placebo, or combined cognitive-pharmacotherapy. Treatment was conducted over a 12-week period, as in the earlier studies. Results, based on self-report and independent clinician ratings, indicated no differences between the four groups, although each of the four evidenced marked improvement, in keeping with the earlier trials. More interestingly, a one-year follow-up indicated that patients receiving cognitive therapy during the acute treatment phase (whether alone, combined with placebo, or combined with medication) evidenced a lower rate of relapse than those not receiving cognitive therapy (Simons, Murphy, Levine, & Wetzel, 1986).

Hollon and colleagues (1985) executed a controlled comparison between cognitive therapy and tricyclic pharmacotherapy. Primary, nonpsychotic, nonbipolar depressed outpatients were randomly assigned to tricyclic pharmacotherapy (imipramine, between 200 and 300 mg per day) plus supportive contact, that same tricyclic treatment with extended (one-year) posttreatment maintenance, cognitive

therapy alone, or combined cognitive-pharmacotherapy. Treatment was executed by experienced professionals within the St. Paul Ramsey Medical Center and the Ramsey County Adult Mental Health Center, guaranteeing a high level of clinical realism. Patients receiving cognitive therapy were seen for a total of 20 one-hour sessions over 12 weeks, while patients in pharmacotherapy were seen weekly in briefer sessions. Patients in the combined approach were seen by separate cognitive therapists and pharmacotherapists. Imipramine/desipramine blood-plasma levels were obtained to identify patients with subtherapeutic tricyclic levels (levels below 180 mg/ml), with treating pharmacotherapists allowed to raise the drug dosage level above 300 mg per day for such patients (or any other patients not evidencing an adequate clinical response).

Patient response was assessed on both self-report and clinician-rated measures, the latter being made from videotaped interviews to ensure that the independent clinical raters remained blind to treatment assignment. At the 12-week posttreatment period, patients in the combined modality were significantly more improved than patients in either pharmacotherapy alone or cognitive therapy alone on one index, the MMPI-D scale (Hathaway & McKinney, 1951), and evidenced nonsignificant trends on the other three measures (including the Beck Depression Inventory: Beck, Ward, Mendelson, Mock, & Erbaugh, 1961; the Hamilton Rating Scale for Depression: Hamilton, 1960; and the Raskin Rating Scale for Depression: Raskin, Schulterbrandt, Reating, & McKeon, 1970). It is noteworthy that only the MMPI-D scale did not exhibit a "floor" effect; that is, scores in the normal range did not approach the minimum scores for the scale, as they did for the other measures. Given that several of the combined treatment group patients exhibited minimum scores on the other three measures, it is possible that those measures failed to reflect the full extent of change.

Posttreatment follow-up over a two-year period provided evidence of a prophylactic effect for both cognitive therapy alone and combined cognitive-pharmacotherapy, each with approximately half the rate evidenced by the drug-treated patients withdrawn from medications at the end of 12 weeks, who evidenced a 70 percent relapse rate. Relapse was also suppressed by medication maintenance, which evidenced a relapse rate over the two-year follow-up period comparable to the cognitive therapy and combined modalities (Evans, Hollon, DeRubeis, Piasecki, Tuason, & Garvey, 1985). While confidence in these findings is undercut by the typical methodological problems inherent in conducting an uncontrolled follow-up (e.g., unscheduled treatment prior to relapse for several patients in each cell, loss of contact with some study subjects, missed reevaluation appointments), it would appear that cognitive therapy, whether provided alone or in combination with pharmacotherapy, may have provided a prophylactic effect against subsequent posttreatment relapse.

In other related studies, Teasdale, Fennel, Hibbert, and Amies (1984) found that the addition of cognitive therapy to "treatment as usual," typically involving antidepressant medications, produced greater change than for that "treatment as usual" condition in an outpatient clinical population. The two conditions did not, however, differ at a three-month follow-up. Covi et al. (1984) found both group cognitive therapy alone and combined group cognitive therapy plus imipramine pharmacotherapy superior to traditional group psychotherapy. Finally, Steuer et al. (1984) found cognitive therapy superior to psychodynamic group psychotherapy on a self-report, but not a clinician-rated, measure of depression in a geriatric population. These last two studies are particularly noteworthy in that cognitive therapy was directly compared with an alternative psychotherapy condition that, presumably, should have controlled for nonspecific expectancy influences.

Predictors of differential response. While it remains unclear precisely who cognitive therapy is differentially indicated for, it does appear that early speculations that it would prove ineffective with endogenous depressives have not been borne out (cf. Blackburn et al., 1981; Hollon et al., 1985). In Hollon et al., for example, endogenous depressives did equally well in cognitive therapy as in pharmacotherapy, while nonendogenous patients tended to be less responsive to drugs alone. The fact that endogenous patients tended to be better responders to either treatment while only the less responsive nonendogenous patients evidenced a differential response (favoring combined cognitive-pharmacotherapy over drugs alone) points up the conceptual

dangers of drawing treatment selection inferences from purely prognostic data. The issue clinically is not which client responds to a given treatment; rather, it is which treatment works best for a given client. Simons and colleagues (Simons, Lustman, Wetzel, & Murphy, 1985) similarly found an apparent indication of differential response based on scores on the Rosenbaum Self-control Scale (Rosenbaum 1980). Patients scoring high on that scale did better in cognitive therapy than in pharmacotherapy, while patients low on measured self-control evidenced a nonsignificant trend favoring pharmacotherapy over cognitive therapy. It may also be the case that patients refractory to other approaches are more likely to prove refractory to cognitive therapy (Fennell & Teasdale, 1982; Harpin, Liberman, Marks, Stern, & Bohannon, 1982), although the existing studies suggesting such a finding have not been conclusive.

Mechanisms of change. There is not, as yet, compelling evidence that cognitive therapy works, when it works, by virtue of changing beliefs and/or information processing, although that remains a very viable possibility. Clearly such changes occur during the course of cognitive therapy, but they also appear to occur during the course of successful pharmacotherapy as well (cf. Hollon et al., 1985; Rush, Beck, Kovacs, Weissenberger, & Hollon, 1982; Simons, Garfield, & Murphy, 1984). In short, while changes in cognitive processes may well mediate reductions in depression in cognitive therapy, the currently available data provide no strong support for that hypothesis over the rival hypothesis that change in cognition is the consequence of change in syndrome depression produced by other, possibly nonspecific, means. Alternately, both Beck (1984a, 1984b) and Simons (1984) have suggested that the existing data are equally compatible with an hypothesis that views cognitive change as a universal mediator of change in depression, that is, causally active in the change process across a variety of therapies including both cognitive therapy and pharmacotherapy. At present, the only statement that can be made with confidence is that change in cognitive processes during treatment is not specific to cognitive therapy. Whether such change causally mediates subsequent change in depression for some or all interventions, or simply reflects state-dependent consequences of reductions in depression produced by other mediational processes, remains to be determined.

Summary. Looking across these various studies, it would appear that cognitive therapy is at least the equal of tricyclic pharmacotherapy in ameliorating the acute treatment episode. The original indication of superiority obtained from Rush et al. (1977) may have been a consequence of the early medication withdrawal, as only a single subgroup in one subsequent study, Blackburn and colleagues' (1981) general medical population, exhibited a similar finding, and that occurred in conjunction with a suspiciously poor pharmacological response. Combined cognitive-pharmacotherapy may prove superior to either modality alone, although the findings in this regard are more equivocal. Although the combined treatment did outperform either single modality in some studies, it never did so by a large margin. In the Hollon et al. (1985) design, for example, the combined treatment cell evidenced an 88 percent response rate relative to a 75 percent response rate evidenced by each single modality. While clearly an increment, it was a modest one, no doubt constrained by the success of each of the single modalities. In three of the four studies that have reported extended follow-ups (Blackburn, et al., in press; Evans, et al., 1985; Simons et al., 1986), cognitive therapy appeared to provide a prophylactic effect relative to pharmacological treatment, while in the fourth (Rush et al., 1977; Kovacs et al., 1981) a similar pattern of findings was evident but was not significant.

On the whole, Beck's cognitive therapy appears to have generated a fairly impressive series of studies supporting its efficacy, particularly in comparison with the tricyclic pharmacotherapies, the current standard of treatment. These studies have typically been executed with fully representative clinical populations, often utilizing experienced therapists, and involving treatment of sufficient frequency and length as to mirror actual clinical practice. Its apparent prophylactic properties are particularly noteworthy in a disorder marked by high rates of relapse and recurrence. Nonetheless, at least two important concerns remain. First, with the exception of the as yet unpublished Covi et al. (1984) and the Steuer et al. (1984) studies, both of which involved group cognitive therapy, the approach has really not been

adequately tested against other psychosocial approaches or even attention-placebo controls. Given the inability to date to establish any specific cognitive mechanisms of change, it still remains possible that the effects of treatment result from nonspecific factors. Second, one remains uncomfortable with what has been, essentially, a series of "tie scores" as a means of establishing a treatment's efficacy. It may still be desirable to execute pharmacotherapy-cognitive therapy trials containing pill-placebo or other minimal treatment controls, simply to establish that when cognitive therapy and pharmacotherapy are equivalent, they are equally effective and not equally ineffective. The currently ongoing NIMH Treatment of Depression Collaborative Research Program (TDCRP; Elkin, Parloff, Hadley, & Autry, 1985) will address both of these issues, but other comparisons would also be helpful in this regard.

Rehm's Self-control Therapy

The other major approach that has been articulated is Rehm's self-control model of depression (Rehm, 1977). Based on Kanfer's self-control theory (Kanfer, 1970, 1971), Rehm's model hypothesizes that the important core behaviors in depression can be described in terms of deficits in the various statges of the self-control sequence. Treatment involves training in systematic self-monitoring, self-evaluation, and self-reinforcement. Treatment has typically been delivered in a structured group format, but individual treatment is also quite feasible. As compared to Beck's cognitive therapy, Rehm's self-control approach spends less time explicitly testing the validity of specific beliefs, but does attend to cognitive processes to some extent, particularly with regard to the self-evaluation phase. Both approaches make explicit use of self-monitoring, although Beck's approach does so more as a means of gathering information, while Rehm's approach is likely to focus on monitoring positive events to increase their salience as a means of combating dysphoria. Finally, Rehm's approach is much more focused on the use of self-reinforcement procedures as a means of enriching the individual's reinforcement schedule even in the face of a nonreinforcing external environment. Thus, while self-control clearly attends, in part, to cognitive processes, its basic model of change is much more nearly related to the self-manipulation of behavioral contingencies than it is to the direct alteration of cognitive processes as in cognitive therapy.

Experimental trials with self-control therapy. Rehm and colleagues have provided a series of controlled trials evaluating the efficacy of self-control therapy. In general, the bulk of the studies have been conducted with female community volunteers treated over a 6- to 12-week period, with treatment typically conducted in a group format. In most cases, treatment has been conducted by graduate students, rather than experienced clinicians.

Fuchs and Rehm (1977) provided the first major trial of a self-control approach in the treatment of depression. Self-control therapy outperformed both a nonspecific attention-placebo and a wait-list control on a variety of measures in a female community volunteer sample. Treatment gains were maintained at a six-week follow-up. In a second project, Rehm, Fuchs, Roth, Kornblith, and Romano (1979) found the self-control approach superior to social skills training on a variety of measures, again in a community volunteer sample. In a pair of dismantling studies, Rehm et al. (1981) found maximum change associated with the self-monitoring component alone, while Kornblith, Rehm, O'Hara, and Lamparski (1983) found that the complete self-control package was again outperformed by its components, as well as by a dynamic group psychotherapy. Finally, Rehm, Lamparski, Romano, and O'Hara (in preparation) found the full self-control package comparable to both a cognitively targeted self-control approach and a behaviorally targeted self-control approach, with all three conditions superior to a wait list. In a companion study, Rehm, Kaslow, Rabin, and Willard (1981) found no differences between the full self-control package and both cognitively and behaviorally targeted self-control packages. Further, no specific differences were evident on cognitive and behavioral variables included as potential mechanism measures.

In one final trial not directly conducted by Rehm's group (although it was conducted by one of his former students), Roth, Bielski, Jones, Parker, and Osborn (1982) contrasted comprehensive self-control therapy versus combined self-control therapy plus antidepressant medication (desipramine). Twenty-six community volunteers were treated over a 12-week interval in individual therapy. No differences were apparent at posttest or at three-month follow-up, although the combined self-control plus pharmacotherapy group appeared to evidence more rapid symptom reduction.

On the whole, this series of studies appeared to provide some support for the efficacy of self-control therapy, although the general reliance on wait-list controls as the primary control procedure did not provide a particularly stringent test to pass. Only in Rehm et al. (1979) and Kornblith et al. (1983) was the approach directly contrasted with an alternative treatment approach, evidencing superior results relative to social-skills training in the first trial and failing to exceed dynamic group psychotherapy in the second. Further, the approach has yet to be directly compared with a tricyclic pharmacotherapy, the current standard of treatment (the Roth et al. [1982] trial evaluated the additive efficacy of tricyclics combined with self-control). Combined with the exclusive reliance on community volunteer samples and inexperienced graduate student therapists (other than Roth et al., 1982), the tests of self-control therapy have, perhaps, lacked in clinical realism. While the findings to date have been generally supportive, it would seem that more powerful comparisons in fully clinical populations would be useful in determining the clinical utility of the approach.

Comparisons of cognitive therapy and self-control therapy. Fleming and Thorton (1980) provided a trial contrasting cognitive therapy (following the unpublished manual developed by Shaw, 1977), behavior therapy (actually the self-control approach presented in an unpublished manual utilized by Fuchs & Rehm, 1977), and a nondirective approach presented as an active treatment condition. Subjects were volunteers recruited from the community. All subjects were seen for treatment in small groups (two each per condition), with two-hour sessions held twice weekly for four weeks. Treatment was provided by minimally trained first-year graduate students who received four hours of training and two hours of supervision per week.

The results indicated essentially comparable changes across each of two self-report and one clinician-rated measure. While all three interventions evidenced significant reductions in depression scores over treatment and reductions were maintained at follow-up, the major finding of note was the relative equivalence of the nondirective condition. Given the essentially tied-score outcome and the minimal clinical representativeness of the therapists and therapy execution, it remains unclear whether gains over time can be attributed to treatment rather than spontaneous remission. Certainly, the findings provide no strong support for either the cognitive therapy or self-control approaches.

Trials Involving Other Approaches

Dunn (1979) reported a trial contrasting an idiosyncratic cognitive-behavioral approach (provided along with medication) versus medication alone in a bona fide clinical sample. Although treatment outcomes on both self-report and clinician ratings favored the cognitive-behavioral (plus medication) cell over drugs alone, the generally marginal execution of the pharmacotherapy condition precluded drawing any strong conclusions. Zeiss et al. (1979) contrasted yet another idiosyncratic "cognitive therapy" with skills-training behavior therapy, a nondirective therapy, and a wait-list control in the treatment of an analogue college student population. All three active treatments proved comparable to one another and superior to the control condition. Curiously, there was no evidence of differential change on various "mechanism" measures (e.g., measures of cognitive content, interpersonal skills, and behavioral activities), leading the authors to conclude that change was produced by nonspecific factors. Finally, McLean and Hakstian (1979) found that a largely behavioral approach with cognitive components outperformed pharmacotherapy, relaxation training, and a control condition in a fully clinical sample.

Summary

Overall, it would appear that there is reasonably good, although far from compelling, evidence supporting the efficacy of cognitive-behavioral approaches to the treatment of depression. Beck's cognitive therapy has clearly shown well in comparisons with tricyclic pharmacotherapy, the current standard of treatment, while Rehm's self-control approach has proven promising, albeit largely in trials that leave something to be desired in terms of their clinical realism. Other, less often studied variants have ranged from promising to disappointing. Particularly noteworthy has been the suggestion of a prophylactic effect (Blackburn et al., in press; Evans et al., 1985; Simons et al., 1986; and perhaps, Kovacs et al., 1981). If confirmed by subsequent, more carefully controlled follow-ups, such prophylaxis could prove the major reason for choosing cognitive therapy or combined cognitive-pharmacotherapy over the less time-consuming pharmacotherapy. Efforts at specifying which patients are most likely to benefit from the approach are just underway, but early indications appear to partially confound clinical lore, which would hold that endogenous depressives would be poor candidates for the approach. The major source of consternation to date has been the failure of simple mechanism models. While cognitive content clearly changes over treatment with cognitive therapy, it also changes in pharmacotherapy. Such a pattern could indicate either the effects of reciprocal causality in a final common pathways model, retaining the specificity of cognitive change as a mediator of syndrome depression change with cognitive therapy, or the noncausal (possibly consequential) status of cognitive processes in depression. This latter possibility is one reason why we believe that proponents of cognitive therapy for depression must still demonstrate that something beyond nonspecific processes are operating to produce the changes noted.

Impulsivity

Impulsivity is typically defined as a behavior pattern of childhood marked by distractibility, attention deficits, and an inability to conform to structure. From a cognitive perspective, impulsivity has typically been conceptualized as a cognitive deficit disorder. That is, impulsive children are seen as lacking cognitive mediators that help control behavior in structured situations. The primary role of cognitive-behavioral interventions in this regard has been to develop mediating cognitions that guide more appropriate behaviors in those situations. While the section to follow will highlight important studies involving cognitive and cognitive-behavioral interventions, the interested reader is directed to a more detailed discussion in Chapter 12 of this volume.

Self-instructional Training

Meichenbaum and Goodman (1971) provided the initial study in the genre when they assigned 15 impulsive children to one of three conditions: (1) *cognitive training,* essentially a combination of modeling and self-instructional training; (2) *attention control,* in which exposure to the materials used in the cognitive training condition was provided without explicit cognitive training; and (3) an *assess-*

ment control group that received no explicit training. Results were measured on three performance tasks, the Porteus Maze, the Matching Familiar Figures Task (MFF; Kagan, 1966), and three performance subtests from the WISC. Children in the cognitive training group generally outperformed children in the other conditions. Efforts to identify generalization to in-class behavior via observational coding and teachers' ratings failed to demonstrate any evidence of generalization. A second study, similar in form to the first but focused on a component analysis of the cognitive training, found that cognitive modeling alone was sufficient to slow response time, but that only the addition of the self-instructional training component reduced actual errors.

Arnold and Forehand (1978) attempted to replicate the earlier Meichenbaum and Goodman (1971) findings. Working with impulsive four- and five-year-olds, children were randomly assigned to one of four conditions: (1) *cognitive training* (CT), modeled after the self-instructional procedures outlined by Meichenbaum and Goodman (1971); (2) *response cost* (RC), applied at posttesting and follow-up assessments, with concurrent exposure to the training materials used in the cognitive training; (3) *cognitive training plus response cost* (CT/RC), the combination of the first two cells; and (4) *placebo training* (PT), consisting of exposure to the stimulus materials used in cognitive training without the cognitive self-instructional training. Training sessions in CT and PT consisted of five sessions over a two-week period. Progress was evaluated on the KRISP, a 10-item matching-to-sample task, and a group-administered 17-item matching-to-sample task administered by the children's teachers in their actual classroom setting. Results indicated significant reductions in error rates for all groups over time on all measures, with no between-group differences on the KRISP, but an apparent main effect for cognitive training on the generalization task. The authors concluded that (1) previous group differences in prior analogue studies that did not control for exposure to the stimulus materials may have been overly generous in attributing reductions in impulsivity to cognitive training and (2) that, nonetheless, cognitive training may well have influenced generalization to the classroom testing situation.

Nelson and Birkimer (1978) contrasted self-instruction plus self-reinforcement with self-instruction alone. Noting that the original Meichenbaum and Goodman (1971) study combined both self-instructional and self-reinforcement components, the authors attempted a partial component analysis. Results indicated that only a combined self-instruction plus self-reinforcement group evidenced changes in performance, suggesting, according to the authors, that self-reinforcement is a necessary component of the complete treatment package.

Parrish and Erickson (1981) evaluated a "scanning strategy" instructional training versus self-instructional training. Contrary to expectations, each individual component of the package (scanning strategy training and self-instructional training) worked as well as the combination, suggesting that either alone was sufficient, at least with regard to academic performance tasks.

Kendall and Finch (1978) presented a major replication and extension of the Meichenbaum and Goodman (1971) work, combining self-instructional training, modeling, and response cost (penalizing subjects via the removal of rewards for "off-task" behavior) into a larger cognitive-behavioral package. Twenty impulsive children, averaging 10 to 11 years of age, all hospitalized for behavior problems, were randomly assigned to one of two conditions. Cognitive treatment consisted of six 20-minute sessions over a four-week period, with stimulus materials for successive sessions consisting of (1) conceptual thinking, (2) attention to detail, (3) recognition of identities, (4) sequential recognition, (5) visual closure, and (6) visual-motor reproduction. Training procedures combined modeling and self-instructional training (as in Meichenbaum & Goodman, 1971) with response-cost behavioral change procedures. The attention-control condition consisted of exposure to the same training materials provided in the cognitive training, but without the self-instructional training or response-cost procedures. Results indicated improved performance on the MFF and improved teachers' ratings of classroom behavior, the latter an indication of treatment generality, with treatment effects remaining stable through a two-month follow-up period. Overall, the study appeared to argue for the effectiveness of the cognitive-behavioral package, both in terms of improved performance on the matching-to-sample task (both increased latency and a reduction in error rates) and generalized in classroom behavior.

The package assembled by Kendall and colleagues includes self-instructional training, modeling, and response-cost contingencies. As described by Kendall and Wilcox (1980), each component is targeted at specific deficits observed in impulsive children. Basic descriptive psychopathology research has indicated that non-self-controlled children exhibit cognitive deficits in problem-solving abilities (Ault, 1973), verbal mediation (Camp, 1977), and information seeking (Finch & Montgomery, 1973), which the self-instructional component is designed to ameliorate. Further, non-self-controlled children have been observed to lack appropriate search-and-scan problem-solving behavior (Drake, 1970; Siegelman, 1969), a deficit that is addressed through the use of modeling procedures. Finally, response-cost procedures (as well as social praise and self-reward) are typically used to suppress off-task behaviors and to maintain attention (Errickson, Wyne, & Routh, 1973; Nelson, Finch, & Hooke, 1975).

Kendall and Wilcox (1980) hypothesized that generalization would be facilitated by providing *conceptual training,* that is, training that applies not only to the specific task at hand but that is also appropriate for other tasks and in other situations, rather than the more standard task-specific training (*concrete training*). However, empirical findings based on teacher ratings failed to support this hypothesis. In yet another effort to enhance generalization of treatment-induced changes, Kendall and Zupan (1981) contrasted a cognitive training package executed in the traditional individual format with a similar package executed in a group format, with both compared to a nonspecific group treatment control. The authors hoped that by providing their cognitive training in a group context, that is, a context more similar to the natural classroom setting, they could enhance generalization. Results indicated comparable improvement on academic performance measures across all groups (a somewhat embarrassing finding, interpreted as a consequence of social-behavior enforcement strategies used by the group leaders to maintain control in the nonspecific group), but specific improvement on teachers' ratings on self-control for children treated in both the individual and the group cognitive training. The hypothesized differences between individual and group cognitive training on the generalization of self-control did not emerge, but only because the individual condition produced

generalization when it had not done so in prior studies. It seems possible that the extended treatment and enriched training materials (earlier studies had relied largely on psychoeducational training tasks only) may have contributed to this finding.

An extended one-year follow-up suggested that some of the treatment gains were maintained, but not all. Children treated in the group cognitive therapy format were found not to differ from a normative control on teachers' self-control ratings, whereas children treated in individual cognitive therapy and nonspecific group therapy did. A different pattern was obtained on teachers' ratings of hyperactivity, on which it was the children treated individually in cognitive therapy who did not differ from a normative control, while the children treated in the other two modalities did. The reason for the variation on these two measures was left unexplained. Further, it is not clear how interpretable treatment group comparisons against a normative standard are in the absence of bona fide group differences between those treatment groups; one is left not comparing treatment groups directly, but rather rejecting the null hypothesis in one comparison (the first treatment group versus the normative sample), failing to reject it in another (the second treatment group versus the normative sample), and comparing that rejection and nonrejection in a way that does violence to conventional notions of hypothesis testing.

Kendall and Braswell (1982) reported a component analysis with impulsive children, isolating the self-instructional component from the modeling and response-cost components. Results indicated that the cognitive-behavioral package was superior to the behavioral treatment on teachers' ratings of self-control, and that both exceeded the attention control on ratings of hyperactivity. Parents' ratings evidenced no differential change as a function of treatment condition, suggesting that behavior changes evident to teachers in a classroom situation did not generalize to ratings of behavior at home. Normative comparisons and a 10-week follow-up supported the superiority of the cognitive-behavioral package, whereas a one-year follow-up failed to evidence the maintenance of any such differences.

Summary

Overall, the treatment of impulsivity via modified self-instructional training, combined with various behavioral components, appears to be one of the more promising areas for cognitive-behavioral interventions. It is probably noteworthy that self-instructional training is the *only* cognitive or cognitive-behavioral intervention that has been utilized with this population. Quite possibly, this reflects the specific appropriateness of a self-instructional approach, based as it is on repetition, that facilitates the acquisition of mediating cognitions for dealing with cognitive deficits. The major issue still unresolved in this area concerns the inconsistent and unpredictable generalizability of treatment-induced changes to other situations (e.g., classroom, home). In short, while internally valid treatment-related changes are frequently evident, questions still remain about the true clinical meaningfulness and generalization outside of the testing situation of those changes.

Anxiety Disorders

We have grouped the various anxiety disorders together as a single unit, although we have retained separate subcategories within this domain. Disorders studied have included a variety of specific fears, including test anxiety, speech anxiety, and social or interpersonal anxiety, typically pursued with subclinical analogue populations, other specific phobias, pursued in both analogue and fully clinical populations, and other anxiety-related disorders, including agoraphobia, generalized anxiety disorder, and obsessive-compulsive disorder, typically sampled from clinical populations. A variety of different cognitive and cognitive-behavioral variations have been utilized in these studies, including RET, systematic rational restructuring, self-instructional training, stress inoculation training, and other, less common variants. Conspicuous by its absence was Beck's cognitive therapy, or any other representative of an empirical hypothesis-testing approach.

Test Anxiety

The treatment of test anxiety provides the prototypic analogue treatment situation. Historically, work in this domain has been motivated as much by theoretical considerations as by any pressing need to meet a clinical demand. While many of the major cognitive and cognitive-behavioral variations are represented, two are not (Ellis's RET has been tested only in unpublished studies and Beck's cognitive therapy is missing). As we shall see, those approaches that have been evaluated have gener-

ally proven effective, with some evidence of greater differential efficacy (*specificity*) when compared to more purely behavioral alternatives.

Systematic rational restructuring. In a project conducted across two different treatment sites, Goldfried, Linehan, and Smith (1978) provided the major controlled evaluation of systematic rational restructuring in the treatment of test anxiety. Volunteer subjects, recruited via newspaper advertisements, were randomly assigned to one of three conditions: (1) systematic rational restructuring, (2) prolonged exposure to an imaginal hierarchy, and (3) a wait-list control. Treatment was conducted in six weekly one-hour sessions by the two senior authors, both experienced clinicians.

Treatment outcome indicated a general superiority for the rational restructuring condition, followed by the prolonged exposure, which was in turn followed by the wait-list control on self-report questionnaire measures of test anxiety. Comparable results were noted on self-report measures of generalized social-evaluative situations. Although only minor differences emerged on preexamination measures of test anxiety, only the rational restructuring group evidenced within-group change over time. Several of the group differences favoring the rational restructuring condition were evident at a six-week follow-up.

Overall, these data supported the efficacy of the systematic rationale restructuring condition. Noting that an earlier Meichenbaum (1972) study (described in a following section) had utilized a complex cognitive-behavioral package consisting of "insight" (an RET approximate), self-instructional training, and modified desensitization, the current authors argued that their project provided the first clear demonstration of the efficacy of a purely cognitive approach in a test-anxious population. Further, the results appeared to point to a greater efficacy (*specificity*) than for a more purely behavior alternative.

Wise and Haynes (1983) attempted to partially replicate and extend the Goldfried et al. (1978) study. Test-anxious college undergraduates, again recruited via advertisements, were assigned to one of three conditions: (1) rational restructuring (executed as in Goldfried et al., 1978), (2) attentional control, in which distraction from task-irrelevant cognitions and refocusing on task-relevant cognitions were presented as coping strategies, and (3) a wait-list control. Treatment was conducted in five weekly one-hour group sessions.

Treatment outcome, as assessed on test-anxiety questionnaires, general-anxiety questionnaires, and a performance task, indicated general superiority for both the rational restructuring and the attentional control conditions over the wait-list control (unfortunately, the analyses were conducted by comparing both "active" treatment groups with the control, rather than with more informative post hoc comparisons). The rational restructuring condition was favored in nonsignificant trends on the generalized anxiety measures over the attentional control, with all other comparisons between the two active treatments nonsignificant. In general, these findings were maintained at an eight-month follow-up. Overall, this study appeared to provide additional support for the superiority of rational restructuring over a no-treatment condition, but little support for the specificity of that efficacy.

Self-instructional training. Meichenbaum (1972) provided the original controlled trial involving a cognitive-behavioral intervention in the test anxiety literature. Starting with the hypothesis that test anxiety consists of two aspects, cognitive worry and autonomically mediated emotionality (Liebert & Morris, 1967), Meichenbaum examined Wine's (1971) contention that traditional systematic desensitization dealt only with the emotionality component. In general, a cognitive modification condition, consisting of a combination of self-statement rehearsal plus behavioral desensitization, typically outperformed both a standard desensitization condition and a wait-list control in a sample of test-anxious college student volunteers. Dependent variables included both self-reports of anxiety and behavioral performance measures, including archival grade-point-average records. Further, treatment gains were generally maintained through a one-month posttreatment follow-up. Overall, this project appeared to be quite supportive of both the efficacy and the differential efficacy (*specificity*) of the combined cognitive-behavioral approach utilized. It should be noted, however, that at least one effort to replicate and extend these findings was able to provide only a partial replication (McCordick, Kaplan, Finn, & Smith, 1979).

In the other major study involving a self-instructional approach, Holroyd (1976) contrasted a cognitive approach combining aspects of RET and SIT with systematic desensitization, a combined cognitive-desensitization condition (most similar to the cognitive-behavioral condition utilized by Meichenbaum, 1972), a psuedo-treatment/meditatation control, and a no-treatment condition. In general, the more purely cognitive approach outperformed the other conditions, which were, in turn, superior to the no-treatment control on most self-report anxiety and behavioral performance measures. In particular, a striking differential improvement was observed in subjects' grade-point averages in the cognitive condition. Treatment gains were typically maintained at a one-month follow-up. The relatively poorer showing of the cognitive-behavioral combination was attributed (on a post hoc basis) to the overall brevity of the intervention package (seven hours total), which allegedly prevented each component from contributing to its full potential.

Stress inoculation training. Two rather modest trials have evaluated stress inoculation training as an intervention for test anxiety. Deffenbacher and Hahnloser (1981) conducted a component analysis of the cognitive versus behavioral components of stress inoculation in an analogue college student sample in which each component outperformed a wait-list control and the full package appeared to outperform each single component. Hussian and Lawrence (1978) contrasted test-specific versus generalized stress inoculation training, again in an analogue college student population. Although the test-specific training exceeded control conditions on measures of test anxiety, the general training condition did not. Overall, these studies provided some support for the efficacy of stress inoculation training, but suffered from being largely analogue in nature and only marginal in their design features.

Summary. There can be little doubt that any of several cognitive and cognitive-behavioral components are effective interventions for test anxiety. This statement most clearly held for the more purely systematic rational restructuring and the combined cognitive and behavioral self-instructional training.

It is also not clear how the different major cognitive and cognitive-behavioral interventions would have compared to one another, or even whether the cognitive-behavioral combination would have proven superior to a purely cognitive approach. What is clear is that, with regard to self-reported anxiety (and, in some cases, actual performance), test anxiety responds to either cognitive or cognitive-behavioral interventions.

Speech Anxiety

Studies on the treatment of speech anxiety have also been uniformly analogue in nature. The literature has ranged from modest studies clearly involving samples of convenience to somewhat more crisply executed designs focused on fine-grained points of theory. As shall be seen, the overall thrust of the literature would have, alone, hardly inspired any great enthusiasm for the cognitive and cognitive-behavioral approaches.

Rational-emotive therapy. RET for speech anxiety has been evaluated in a series of methodologically marginal designs. Karst and Trexler (1970) found both RET and Kelly's fixed-role therapy (Kelly, 1955) superior to a wait-list control in an analogue college student population, with few differences between the two treatment conditions. In an attempted partial replication in a similar population, Trexler and Karst (1972) found RET again superior to a no-treatment control, but only equivocally better on anxiety measures than an attention-placebo despite evidence of greater change for the RET cell on a measure of irrational beliefs. Straatmeyer and Watkins (1974) found little difference between RET (with or without the active disputation component) and either an attention-placebo or a wait-list control. Finally, Thorpe, Amatu, Blakey, and Burns (1976) provided a study that, while primarily a component analysis of self-instructional training, also tested rational-emotive therapy with speech-anxious high school student volunteers. In that design, subjects provided with "insight" into the irrationality of their beliefs (the RET representation) in general responded better than those trained in self-statement rehearsal.

Systematic rational restructuring. Only two rather modest studies have evaluated systematic rational restructuring in the treatment of speech anxiety. In the first, Lent, Russell, and Zamostny (1981) found a rational restructuring condition inferior to cue-controlled desensitization and no better than either an attention-placebo or a wait-list control. Gross and Fremouw (1982) evaluated the interaction between individual differences in the nature of the speech anxiety and type of treatment. In that study, both systematic rational restructuring and progressive relaxation proved superior to a wait-list control. More critically, a subset of the population defined by cluster analysis as evidencing low physiological responsiveness responded significantly better to the cognitive approach than to progressive relaxation. This study may well point to a specific subtype by treatment interaction, one with particular relevance to efforts to account for the failure of treatment effects noted in analogue samples to generalize to clinical populations.

Self-instructional training. In what was the initial study involving a cognitive-behavioral intervention in the treatment of speech anxiety, Meichenbaum, Gilmore, and Fedoravicius (1971) contrasted a cognitive modification (involving a combination of a cognitive rationale with an early version of self-instructional training) versus desensitization, combined cognitive modification plus desensitization, an attention-placebo, and a wait-list control. Again working with an analogue population consisting largely of college student volunteers, the authors found the cognitive modification condition and the desensitization condition comparable to one another, and each superior to the other conditions (including the combined cognitive modification plus desensitization condition) on a variety of self-report anxiety and behavioral performance measures, both at posttreatment and at three-month follow-up. As in Holroyd (1976), the lesser efficacy of the cognitive-behavioral combination was attributed, on a post hoc basis, to the general brevity of each component part.

Weissberg (1977) contrasted a cognitive modification program adapted from Meichenbaum et al. (1971) with various desensitization procedures (some vicarious, some direct) and a wait-list control in an analogue college student population. Although the various active treatments appeared to outperform the wait-list control, no stable pattern of differences was evident between these various active approaches. Fremouw and Zitter (1978) compared skills training versus a combined self-statement rehearsal approach (Meichenbaum et al., 1971) plus relaxation as a coping skill (Goldfried & Trier, 1974) in an analogue college student population. No consistent differences emerged favoring either approach over the other, and neither was more than sporadically superior to either a discussion-placebo or a wait-list control. An effort was made to determine whether Meichenbaum et al.'s (1971) finding of an interaction between treatment type and level of social anxiety (with cognitive restructuring more successful with subjects high in social anxiety) replicated in the present sample. While not significant, a similar treatment by social anxiety level interaction did indicate a trend in the predicted direction. Glogower, Fremouw, and McCroskey (1978) conducted a component analysis of cognitive modification in an analogue college student sample in which they found evidence that they interpreted as suggesting that it was the coping self-statement component that was the primary active ingredient in cognitive modification, with both extinction and the identification of negative self-statements exhibiting lesser degrees of efficacy. Finally, Cradock, Cotler, and Jason (1978) found a self-statement rehearsal procedure, but not systematic desensitization, superior to a wait-list control in working with speech anxiety in female high school students. The two active treatments did not, however, differ from one another.

Summary. A review of the studies in this literature appears to provide a rather modest picture of treatment efficacy. Cognitive and cognitive-behavioral interventions were typically (but not invariably) superior to various attention-placebo and no-treatment controls, but certainly not superior to, and sometimes less effective than, strictly behavioral interventions. No other potentially active treatments besides behavioral interventions (e.g., skills training, systematic desensitization, and relaxation alone) were contrasted with cognitive approaches. Combined cognitive-behavioral approaches clearly did not outperform single modalities, proving less effective than either cognitive or behavioral components in at least one study. RET exhibited a rather lackluster performance in rather lackluster designs,

although systematic rational restructuring and self-instructional training fared little better. In addition, all of the studies reviewed appeared to be largely analogue in nature. The overall adequacy of the various cognitive and cognitive-behavioral approaches in this literature can only be described as modest.

Social Anxiety

A variety of studies have investigated the effect of cognitive and cognitive-behavioral interventions in the treatment of social anxiety. The quality of the studies has ranged from strong (e.g., Glass, Gottman, & Shmurak, 1976; Kanter & Goldfried, 1979) to modest, with RET, systematic rational restructuring, self-control desensitization, and self-instructional training all represented. Only one of the comparisons involved alternate treatment approaches besides either behavioral or attention-control conditions (DiLoreto, 1971). As for test anxiety, no particular rationale appeared to guide the treatment interventions, beyond an adherence to a general cognitive model.

Rational-emotive therapy. In the first of two published trials involving RET for this population, DiLoreto (1971) presented one of the earliest tests of a cognitive approach in the treatment of interpersonal anxiety. Working with undergraduate volunteers, he randomly assigned subjects to either (1) rational-emotive therapy, (2) systematic desensitization, (3) client-centered therapy, (4) attention-placebo discussion, or (4) a waiting-list control. All three active treatments proved superior to the two control groups in terms of anxiety reduction, while the systematic desensitization group was generally superior to the other two active treatment conditions. There appeared to have been an individual differences by treatment interaction, with rational-emotive therapy proving successful only with introverted subjects, and as effective as systematic desensitization for this subpopulation. Further, introversion in this study was correlated with interpersonal anxiety, such that higher levels of interpersonal anxiety also predicted response to rational-emotive therapy. Kanter and Goldfried (1979), among others, have suggested that the various cognitive approaches may prove increasingly more effective as the level of interpersonal anxiety approaches what would be expected in a fully clinical population. Nonetheless, this study provided only partial support for the efficacy of RET. Although RET proved more effective than a wait-list control and an attention-placebo, it was generally less effective than an alternative behavioral intervention, systematic desensitization.

In a second trial, Emmelkamp, Mersch, Vissia, and Van der Helm (1985) found comparable results for rational-emotive therapy, self-instructional training, and in vivo exposure in the treatment of socially anxious outpatients. This trial was particularly interesting in that it involved a bona fide clinical sample. While all three groups did evidence significant reductions in anxiety over treatment, the absence of between-group differences, combined with the absence of minimal treatment controls, makes it difficult to evaluate the absolute efficacy of the interventions sampled.

Systematic rational restructuring. Kanter and Goldfried (1979) provided a comparison of rational restructuring and modified (self-control) desensitization in the treatment of interpersonal anxiety in one of the more competently conducted studies in this literature. Community volunteers recruited by advertisement were randomly assigned to one of four conditions: (1) systematic rational restructuring, executed in accordance with guidelines presented by Goldfried et al. (1974); (2) modified self-control desensitization, operationalized in accordance with Goldfried (1971); (3) combined rational restructuring/self-control desensitization; and (4) a wait-list control.

Treatment outcome was assessed by self-report of interpersonal anxiety (both specific and generalized), observational ratings, and a physiological measure. Significant between-group differences were limited to the self-report measures, on which all three active treatment groups typically outperformed the wait-list control. Nonetheless, the systematic rational restructuring group appeared to outperform the modified desensitization cell on many of the measures. Treatment outcome was essentially maintained or enhanced at a nine-week follow-up. Despite the investigators' initial expectations, pretreatment anxiety levels did not interact with treatment type, as had been suggested in two

earlier studies (DiLoreto, 1971; Meichenbaum et al., 1971).

Shahar and Merbaum (1981) contrasted systematic rational restructuring (Goldfried et al., 1974), self-control desensitization (Goldfried, 1971), and a wait-list control in the treatment of adult volunteers seeking therapy for interpersonal anxiety. Treatment outcomes indicated that both active treatments were superior to the control group on a self-report measure, a difference maintained at a four-month follow-up. The behavioral ratings were more ambiguous, while no changes were evident on the physiological measure. The authors were particularly intent on pursuing client by treatment interactions, reasoning that the more physiologically reactive subjects would be most responsive to the desensitization intervention. While the pattern of within-subgroup changes over time on one behavioral measure was consistent with that hypothesis, the pattern was not robust across the remaining measures.

Self-instructional training. Three studies have evaluated self-statement modification approaches akin to self-instructional training in the treatment of social anxiety. In the first, Glass et al. (1976) found that while male college student volunteers exposed to behavioral skills training (either alone or combined with cognitive modification) generally performed better on role-play vignettes used in training, subjects exposed to cognitive modification (either alone or combined with behavioral skills training) evidenced the greatest improvement on nontraining role-plays. In addition to this greater generality, subjects provided with cognitive modification were also able to initiate more cross-sex telephone calls. Results were generally maintained through a six-month follow-up. In the second study, Elder, Edelstein, and Fremouw (1981) found that a cognitive modification approach (including some elements of rational restructuring but emphasizing self-statement rehearsal) and a behavioral skills training approach were both superior to a wait-list control in an undergraduate analogue population. Of particular interest was an observed treatment by individual difference interaction. Subjects evidencing higher levels of initial social anxiety tended to do better in the cognitive modification, a finding that may parallel earlier, similar indications (DiLoreto,

1971; Meichenbaum et al., 1971). Finally, in the Emmelkamp et al. (1985) trial described in the preceding section on RET in social anxiety, SIT was comparable to both RET and in vivo exposure in the treatment of a bona fide clinical sample.

Summary. In general, systematic rational restructuring, self-control desensitization, and self-statement modification approaches analogous to self-instructional training appeared to fare well in the treatment of social anxiety, with RET somewhat less well supported. Enthusiasm for either systematic rational restructuring or self-control desensitization needs to be tempered by the recognition that while each consistently outperformed wait-list controls, neither was compared to any alternate active treatment other than one another. Further, none of the studies utilized a fully clinical population, although two (Kanter & Goldfried, 1979; Shahar & Merbaum, 1981) did at least utilize community volunteers recruited expressly for a treatment program. Socially phobic patient populations do exist and do constitute an important part of the overall clinical picture. Hence, the near exclusive focus on analogue and community volunteer samples in this literature (only Emmelkamp et al., 1985, utilized a fully clinical population) is somewhat regrettable. Finally, there were several indications of interesting treatment type by subject characteristic interactions (e.g., DiLoreto, 1971; Elder et al., 1981; Shahar & Merbaum, 1981), but little evidence that these potential interactions were particularly robust.

Phobic Disorders

Several studies have investigated the efficacy of various cognitive procedures in the treatment of specific phobias. The bulk of these trials have utilized self-instructional training (or some self-statement modification approach). One study mixed SIT with systematic rational restructuring (Biran & Wilson, 1981) and two (D'Zurilla, Wilson, & Nelson, 1973; Wein, Nelson, & Odom, 1975k) utilized an idiosyncratic approach that essentially involved providing multiple cognitive rationales and an opportunity to discuss prior experiences with the phobic stimulus in the context of those rationales. Only one study utilized an even partially clinically representative population (Biran & Wilson, 1981).

Systematic rational restructuring. A pair of early analogue studies contrasted cognitive restruc-

turing approaches somewhat akin to systematic rational restructuring in the treatment of specific phobias. In the first, D'Zurilla et al. (1973) found little difference between cognitive restructuring, prolonged imaginal exposure, and systematic desensitization in the modification of the fear of dead animals in female undergraduate volunteers. The cognitive restructuring group did exceed a wait-list control on a self-report anxiety measure, while the imaginal exposure group exceeded the wait-list control on a behavioral approach task. In the second study involving snake phobic undergraduate female volunteers, Wein et al. (1975) found a cognitive restructuring condition typically superior to both an attention-placebo and a wait-list control on both self-report and behavioral avoidance measures. Systematic desensitization outperformed these control conditions on the behavioral avoidance task, but not the self-report anxiety measure. In general, despite claims made by the authors for the superiority of the cognitive approach relative to systematic desensitization based on comparisons between each and the control conditions, there were no apparent differences between the two active therapy conditions that were supported by the appropriate direct post hoc comparisons.

In perhaps the most competently conducted trial in this literature, Biran and Wilson (1981) presented a comparison of behavioral and cognitive therapies in a phobic population designed, in part, as a further test of self-efficacy theory (Bandura, 1977). Twenty-two phobic subjects (with phobic fears including heights, darkness, and elevators), responding to advertisements placed in community newsletters, were randomly assigned to one of two conditions: (1) guided exposure or (2) cognitive restructuring. Guided exposure involved the in vivo exposure to a hierarchy of increasingly difficult encounters with the feared situations, with the utilization of performance aids and therapist assistance when necessary. Cognitive restructuring involved three components, modeled after Emmelkamp, Kuiper, and Eggeraat (1978): (1) relabeling, (2) discussing irrational beliefs and rational restructuring, and (3) self-instructional training. The nature of the cognitive modification efforts at the rational restructuring stage was described as follows:

Subjects were presented with phobic situations in imagination and then were requested to ferret out what they were telling themselves about the situation that could be responsible for their anxiety. Emphasis was placed on the specific irrational ideas involved in this type of self-talk. They were then taught how to replace irrational ideas with a more realistic appraisal of the situation (Biran & Wilson, 1981, p. 890).

In a later session, subjects were trained using Meichenbaum's (1977) self-instructional training (SIT) to "replace nonproductive self-statements with more positive and productive ones" (p. 890). Cognitive restructuring homework sheets (Goldfried & Goldfried, 1975) were assigned for use between sessions and reviewed at subsequent meetings. In short, the "cognitive restructuring" modality was both fairly intensive and broad-based, including rationale-giving, training in cognitive restructuring and self-instructional training, and homework assignments. It was, however, purely cognitive in focus, rather than cognitive-behavioral, utilizing neither behavioral combinations (e.g., concurrent exposure) nor integrations (e.g., empirical hypothesis testing).

All therapy in both conditions was conducted by four advanced graduate students in five individual 50-minute treatment sessions over a two- to three-week period. Guided exposure proved superior to cognitive restructuring in enhancing approach behavior, increasing level and strength of self-efficacy, reducing subjective fear, and decreasing physiological reactivity to imagined phobic scenes. High correlations were found between approach behaviors and self-efficacy ratings for both groups, although the cognitive restructuring group tended to overestimate their subsequent performance (that is, anticipatory self-efficacy ratings exceeded subsequent approach behavior). A one-month follow-up indicated essential stability in the findings. Cognitive restructuring subjects subsequently provided with guided exposure evidenced treatment gains comparable to those of the original guided exposure group. Continued stability was noted at a six-month follow-up.

Overall, the findings of this well-executed study appeared to confirm at least one of the two major tenets of Bandura's self-efficacy theory; a largely behavioral procedure outperformed a purely cognitive (symbolic) one in the reduction of avoidance behavior (and the reduction of concurrent phy-

siological arousal and subjective anxiety). The mediational status of cognitive processes, the other component of Bandura's dictum, received only partial support. Although changes in behavior covaried strongly with changes in self-efficacy in the guided exposure condition, it appeared that the cognitive restructuring condition produced greater changes in measured self-efficacy than it did in approach behavior. Had self-efficacy expectations, as measured, been a sufficient mediator of behavior change, this discrepancy should not have occurred.

The findings underscored one aspect emerging as a primary point of this chapter: *cognitive procedures alone are rarely the most effective change procedures.* Whether a cognitive-behavioral combination or integration would have outperformed the behavioral condition alone is unknown, but, in this study, the behavioral procedure was clearly superior to the purely cognitive intervention.

Self-instructional training. Aside from the SRR-SIT amalgamation just described in the Biran and Wilson (1981) study, SIT has been evaluated only in a series of modest analogue trials. Denny, Sullivan, and Thirty (1977) found some evidence that both modeling and the self-verbalization of coping statements reduced spider fears and enhanced approach behavior in college students, but only very brief (two training hours) interventions were utilized. Kanfer, Karoly, and Newman (1975) found that competency-based self-statement rehearsal enhanced behavioral tolerance for the dark relative to situation-redefinition self-statement rehearsal or controls in preschool children. Girodo and Roehl (1978) found evidence that SIT reduced anxiety in flying phobics during a contrived "incident" during in vivo exposure, but the indications were not robust across the measurement battery utilized. Finally, Ladouceur (1983) found SIT plus participant modeling superior to a wait list, albeit no better than participant modeling alone, in the treatment of dog phobias in yet another recruited analogue population. Overall, these rather modest, largely analogue studies can be said to have provided some support for the efficacy of SIT in the treatment of phobic disorders, but only in relation to minimal treatment controls, not alternative behavioral interventions.

Summary. Overall, the various cognitive interventions utilized in these studies generally performed as well as, but not better than, the various behavioral approaches with which they tended to be compared, and better than the various attention-placebo and no-treatment controls. Combined cognitive-behavioral interventions generally performed no better than their constituent single modalities. It should be noted, however, that this rather benign picture derived primarily from the analogue studies. In the only trial with a reasonably clinically representative population (Biran & Wilson, 1981), the cognitive intervention was decidedly inferior to guided exposure behavior therapy. Whether the relative comparability of cognitive versus behavioral approaches does not generalize from analogue to clinical samples or whether the Biran and Wilson outcomes will prove to be anomalous is unclear, but this study does suggest an important constraint to an enthusiastic endorsement of cognitive approaches for specific phobias. Clearly, more work needs to be done with fully clinical specific phobia populations before this discrepancy can be resolved.

Agoraphobia

Clinical agoraphobia has only recently begun to receive concerted attention from cognitive-behavior therapists. In contrast to many of the other disorders we have discussed in this chapter, all of the work reviewed with agoraphobics has involved fully clinical populations. In general, the results to date have not been very encouraging to proponents of cognitive interventions.

In a related pair of studies, Emmelkamp and colleagues (Emmelkamp & Mersch, 1982; Emmelkamp et al., 1978) compared cognitive treatment with in vivo exposure, the current standard of treatment for agoraphobia. In the first study (Emmelkamp et al., 1978), cognitive restructuring consisted of three major components: (1) *relabeling,* or the provision of a cognitive rationale; (2) *discussing irrational beliefs,* in which eight of Ellis' (1962) irrational beliefs were discussed and related to specific examples from the clients' lives; and (3) *self-instructional training,* in which clients were trained to emit more productive self-statements. Clients rehearsed self-instructional methods for handling anxiety by imagining fear-producing situations. Although clients were instructed to do homework assignments between sessions, utilizing Goldfried and Goldfried's (1975) Dysfunctional Thought

Record (DTR) procedures, no effort was made to encourage the clients to hypothesis-test the validity of the more positive replacement beliefs. Thus, the cognitive procedure was a purely cognitive component emphasizing rationality and repetition as its primary change processes.

Twenty-four outpatient agoraphobic clients were randomly assigned to either the cognitive therapy modality or in vivo exposure. Patients in each condition were treated in five two-hour group sessions over a one-week period. Patients were then crossed over to the other treatment during a second week of five two-hour group sessions. Treatment impact was assessed on a battery of outcome measures including an in vivo behavioral approach task, ratings of phobic anxiety and avoidance by an independent observer, and self-reports of anxiety levels.

In vivo exposure was found to be far more effective than cognitive restructuring on both a behavioral measure and on phobic anxiety and avoidance scales. Patients treated first cognitively, then crossed over to in vivo exposure evidenced major improvement only after the crossover.

On the whole, this study was particularly noteworthy for its focus on a fully clinical population. The authors argued that the relative inefficacy of their cognitive intervention derived from its specific unsuitability for their truly clinical sample, perhaps due to the greater arousal engendered for such patient populations than for the presumably less aroused analogue populations utilized in earlier studies that suggested the efficacy of such cognitive approaches (e.g., DiLoreto, 1971; D'Zurilla et al., 1973; Holroyd, 1976; Meichenbaum, 1972; Meichenbaum et al., 1971; Thorpe 1975; Thorpe et al., 1976; Trexler & Karst, 1972; Wein et al., 1975). While such an explanation may indeed hold for the apparent nongenerality of findings from the analogue to the clinical populations, it is important to note that the actual procedures used may not have been the most effective variation of cognitive or cognitive-behavioral components for this population. In addition, the relative brevity of the intervention package may have precluded the effectiveness of the cognitive approach, although, as the authors noted, the total of 10 hours of therapy contact was not inconsiderable. On the whole, this study appeared to provide little support for the use of a purely cognitive approach in a clinically agoraphobic population, although this minimal efficacy may hold for only a specific version of purely cognitive therapy.

Although the authors presented no actual component or mechanism measures, they did note that anecdotal reports by several clients suggested that greater cognitive change was occurring in the in vivo exposure condition than in the cognitive therapy group. For example, clients in the in vivo condition reported that their anxiety diminished over time and that events that they had feared, such as fainting or having a heart attack, did not happen. This may have resulted in an informal hypothesis-testing, altering catastrophic cognitions. Thus, in keeping with Bandura's (1977) dictum, it may well have been that symptom reduction was mediated by changes in cognitive processes that were most powerfully mobilized by behavioral procedures (in vivo exposure). Further experimentation will be required to explore this possibility, but, if true, it may well suggest that an integrated cognitive-behavioral approach, one in which beliefs are subjected to formal, enactive hypothesis-testing procedures (with predictions first articulated, then systematically tested during in vivo exposure, then reevaluated in light of that recent experience), may prove more effective than either purely cognitive or purely behavioral procedures.

In the second study in the sequence, Emmelkamp and Mersch (1982) replicated and extended their earlier study by contrasting cognitive therapy, in vivo exposure therapy, and combined cognitive-exposure therapy in the treatment of clinical agoraphobia. Although not providing a fully integrated cognitive-behavioral approach, the authors did provide a cognitive-behavioral combination. Twenty-seven agoraphobic patients were randomly assigned to the treatment conditions, each conducted in eight two-hour group sessions. At posttest, the in vivo exposure condition and the combined procedure both exceeded the cognitive-only condition on the in vivo behavioral measure and ratings of phobic anxiety and avoidance. By one-month follow-up, however, the cognitive restructuring group had shown continued improvement, with some decrement in the in vivo exposure group on the behavioral measures, and no significant differences were evident. The cognitive restructuring group produced superior improvement

on measures of assertiveness and depression. Thus, although the short-term effects were similar to those found in the earlier Emmelkamp et al. (1978) study, the cognitive modification proved equally effective in the long run. The combination treatment was not significantly superior to the in vivo exposure alone on any measure.

In yet a third study conducted by this research group, Emmelkamp, Brilman, Kuiper, and Mersch (1985) contrasted self-instructional training, rational-emotive therapy, and prolonged in vivo exposure in a clinically agoraphobic population. In general, in vivo exposure clearly outperformed RET, with SIT intermediate in response. In a fourth study, Mavissakalian, Michelson, Greenwald, Kornblith, and Greenwald (1983) found the addition of self-instructional training to in vivo exposure less effective than the addition of paradoxical intent over a 12-week active treatment period. However, no differences were evident over a posttreatment follow-up period.

Finally, Williams and Rappoport (1983) contrasted combined cognitive-behavioral therapy with behavior therapy only in the treatment of driving fears in an agoraphobic population. The cognitive component involved the use of self-distraction, relabeling anxiety and other threatening aspects of the drive, substituting positive expectations for fearful ones, and engagement in task-relevant self-instructions. The behavioral component, common to both groups, involved in vivo exposure to feared driving situations, in six two-hour sessions over a two-week period. Although there was a clear increase in the use of coping cognitions in the cognitive training group, there were no differences in either anxiety reduction or behavior change. The authors argued that their findings indicated that the addition of specific cognitive skills added little over the change produced by in vivo performance.

Overall, these five studies, each with fully clinical populations, provided little support for proponents of cognitive approaches. A purely cognitive intervention proved less effective than a purely behavioral approach in three studies (Emmelkamp & Mersch, 1982; Emmelkamp et al., 1978, 1985); and combined cognitive-behavioral treatment did not improve on behavior therapy alone (Emmelkamp & Mersch, 1982; Williams and Rappoport, 1983). It is not clear that the cognitive approaches utilized were necessarily the optimal selections (we would have preferred a frankly hypothesis-testing approach to the rational-repetition mechanisms mobilized), but the currently available data provide little support for the efficacy of cognitive approaches, either alone or in combination with behavior components, in the treatment of agoraphobia.

Generalized Anxiety Disorder

Virtually no work has yet been attempted with a general anxiety-disordered population. Given the ubiquitousness and historical importance of this diagnostic group, this paucity of experimental work is somewhat surprising. In the one study that has been attempted, a combined cognitive-behavioral approach appeared to be superior to either single modality, although the authors' claims in that regard appeared to be somewhat overstated.

Woodward and Jones (1980) contrasted cognitive restructuring (a self-statement replacement procedure), systematic desensitization, and a combination of the two in the treatment of clinic outpatients suffering from generalized anxiety disorder. A no-treatment control was also included. Twenty-seven clinically representative patients were randomly assigned to two-hour group treatment sessions over an eight-week period.

The combined treatment group proved significantly more effective than either single modality or the control group in reducing scores on a self-reported intensity of anxiety measure (the Fear Survey Schedule, FSS: Wolpe & Lang, 1964). The combined group and the systematic desensitization group were each superior to the other conditions on an anxiety diary assessing anxiety level. No significant differences were noted on several other measures; the severity of anxiety on the FSS, the Zung Self-rating Anxiety Scale (Zung, 1971), a "fear thermometer," or a self-report of anxiety-free behaviors derived from the FSS.

In the absence of any effort to control for experimentwise error rates, this pattern of findings appeared relatively "thin." The authors concluded that ". . . the experiment has shown that a treatment combining both cognitive restructuring and modified SD procedures (cognitive behavior modification) is significantly better than the components of treatment taken separately" (p. 407). This statement held with regard to both components for only

one of the two observed significant differences, and with regard to only the cognitive intervention on the second, and did not hold for the four other variables assessing various aspects of anxiety (all essentially based on self-report). What was clear was that cognitive restructuring alone failed to exceed the no-treatment control on any measure. In this population, cognitive restructuring alone, involving aspects of rational restructuring, self-instructional training, and stress inoculation training, proved relatively ineffectual. While the authors claimed that the addition of a cognitive component to modified systematic desensitization proved advantageous over desensitization alone, that result was obtained on only one of six relevant measures.

The major strength of this design resided in its selection of a fully clinical population, patients with generalized anxiety disorder, and the use of clinically representative treatment strategies, in terms of both length and therapists selected. The results, unfortunately, did not appear as clear-cut as the authors appeared to suggest; evidence for any additive superiority for the cognitive-behavioral combination was limited to a single measure. The cognitive modality alone appeared to be generally ineffective. Clearly, more fully clinical studies of this kind need to be executed with this population before firm conclusions can be drawn. Nonetheless, the apparent lack of generalization of outcomes from the various analogue trials to this and other related fully clinical populations is most troublesome for advocates of cognitive or cognitive-behavioral interventions.

Obsessive-compulsive Disorders

To date, little work has yet been done from a cognitive perspective with this most pernicious of neurotic disorders. Although Beck (1976) and McFall and Wollersheim (1979) have each proposed somewhat distinctive cognitive models of obsessive-compulsive disorders and/or its cognitive-behavioral treatment, no formal investigations have yet been undertaken of these approaches. At this time, the most effective interventions appear to be largely behavioral, particularly the combination of in vivo exposure and response prevention (e.g., Foa, Steketee, & Milby, 1980; Foa & Tillmanns, 1980; Foa et al., 1983; Rachman & Hodgson, 1980). As Wilson (1982) points out, the publication of Rachman and Hodgson's major treatise, *Obsessions and Com-*

pulsions, an exquisitely scholarly review of the natural history of the disorder, current theories of etiology, and current evidence of treatment efficacy, should help galvanize the development of treatments in this area.

In the one study that has evaluated an explicitly cognitive-behavioral composite, Emmelkamp, Van der Helm, van Zanten, and Plochg (1980) compared in vivo exposure with the combination of in vivo exposure plus cognitive restructuring (actually an amalgamation of rational-emotive therapy and self-instructional training). Treatment consisted of two relaxation training sessions and ten 120-minute sessions of either (1) relaxation and exposure or (2) relaxation, self-instructions, and exposure. The portion of time allotted to the cognitive procedures was relatively brief (30 minutes, shared with the relaxation training, of the 120-minute session). Although improvement was noted for both treatment groups, there was no differential gain evident as a consequence of the addition of cognitive procedures to the behavioral exposure.

As Kendall (1982) has noted, the brevity of the cognitive component may have retarded its potential effectiveness, but it also remains possible that explicit cognitive interventions have little to offer in this disorder. Only further research can resolve this issue.

Summary

Overall, it would appear that a major disparity may exist between the utility of the cognitive and cognitive-behavioral approaches for those disorders evaluated in analogue studies versus those efforts conducted with fully clinical populations. Whether this disparity reflects a real limitation to the utility of the cognitive and cognitive-behavior interventions or other factors masking their efficacy with fully clinical populations remains unclear. Two possible factors were the nature of the treatments utilized, which were typically purely cognitive (e.g., Biran & Wilson, 1981; Emmelkamp et al., 1978) or a minimally integrated cognitive and behavioral combination (Woodward & Jones, 1980), and the fact that several of those studies derived from a single research group better known for its work with behavior therapy than its work with cognitive approaches (Emmelkamp & Mersch, 1982; Emmelkamp et al., 1978). In the absence of explicit component measures designed to ensure that the

cognitive and cognitive-behavioral interventions were adequately executed, it remains impossible to determine how fully representative the executions utilized actually were in those studies. This same issue holds, in reverse, for efforts by cognitively oriented theorists to utilize behavioral, pharmacological, or other approaches in systematic comparisons with cognitive approaches.

Assertion Training

There exists a rather large and healthy literature regarding the use of cognitive and cognitive-behavioral interventions in the treatment of assertion problems. In part, the vitality of this literature reflects the important work by Schwartz and Gottman (1976) suggesting that unassertive individuals often suffer from a "dialogue of conflict," in which negative expectations and self-statements block the execution of assertive behaviors in the individual's repertoire. In general, the assessment of change has depended heavily on behavioral role-play tasks (in addition to self-report measures), with generalization being evaluated by distinguishing between situations explicitly utilized during training versus situations not so utilized. An important critique has been raised regarding the specific measurement methodologies utilized. Jacobs and Cochran (1982) have argued that the typical role-play tasks utilized have been too focused on impersonal, relatively trivial interactions that have little generalizability to the real-world relationships of major clinical interest. Jacobs and Cochran have suggested that, in combination with the tendency to rely solely on situations directly sampled during training, this situational triviality has tended to bias comparisons unfairly in favor of explicit behavioral rehearsal formats. If true, this state of affairs would force a reevaluation of some of the major comparisons between behavioral skills-training approaches and the various cognitive and cognitive-behavioral interventions described next.

Rational-Emotive Therapy

Three trials have evaluated rational-emotive therapy in the treatment of assertion problems. In the first, Wolfe and Fodor (1977) found that both behavior therapy (modeling plus behavioral rehearsal) and rational behavior therapy (a cognitive-behavioral combination in which RET was added to the behavioral approach) outperformed consciousness raising and a wait-list control on both training and generalization role-play vignettes in a sample recruited from a community mental health center. With few exceptions, self-report anxiety measures did not differentiate the groups. Although this study provided some support for the efficacy of the cognitive-behavioral combination, it should be noted that that combination evidenced little advantage over behavior therapy alone. Alden, Safran, and Weideman (1978) found a cognitive-behavioral amalgamation of RET and SIT equivalent to behavioral skills training, with both superior to a no-contact control in a mixed community volunteer/college student sample. Finally, Carmody (1978) found little differentation between RET plus behavioral rehearsal, SIT plus behavioral rehearsal, behavioral rehearsal alone, and a wait-list control, again in a mixed community/college student volunteer population. The only differences evident favored all three active treatments over the delayed treatment control on one of several self-report measures and the RET plus behavioral rehearsal combination over the delayed treatment condition on an in vivo refusal task.

In general, these studies typically provided some support for the utility of RET in the treatment of assertion problems, but there was little evidence of any greater efficacy than for more purely behavioral approaches. Further, in every instance, RET was executed in conjunction with some more purely behavioral component, making it difficult to discern whether the cognitive component actually added to the treatment package.

Systematic Rational Restructuring

Linehan, Goldfried, and Goldfried (1979) reported one of the more competently conducted comparisons of cognitive, behavioral, and cognitive-behavioral interventions. Working with an older female population than in many of the other university-based designs (mean age 43.2 years), treatment was provided in eight weekly individual sessions at two geographically distinct centers. Treatment cells consisted of (1) behavioral rehearsal, involving modeling, role-playing, and feedback; (2) systematic rational restructuring, following Goldfried et al. (1974), in which clients were taught to identify and reevaluate negative self-statements in response to the same situational vignettes used for role-playing in the behavioral

rehearsal conditions; (3) combined behavior rehearsal/rational restructuring, which combined the training provided in the first two cells, (4) relationship control, which controlled for therapist contact time in an unstructured discussion, and (5) a wait-list control. Treatment was provided by four male and four female graduate students and postdoctoral fellows. Therapist training appeared particularly rich in this trial, with over 20 hours of prestudy training and ongoing weekly case conferences provided to review treatment procedures.

Treatment outcome was assessed on both self-report and behavior ratings of role-play measures. The combined behavior rehearsal/rational restructuring condition showed superior performance to the wait-list control on each self-report measure. The rational restructuring group proved superior to the wait-list control on most self-report measures, while the behavior rehearsal condition proved superior to the wait-list group on only one. Other than a superior performance by the combined treatment relative to the relationship control on one measure, there were no differences between any of the treatment groups. The combined treatment and the behavioral rehearsal treatment proved superior to the rational restructuring on most of the behavioral ratings based on role-play vignettes, while the rational restructuring alone proved superior to the controls on only a rating of assertion content. Analyses of initial responses in the extended role-play tasks indicated comparable results across the three active treatment conditions, with all superior to controls. Given the lesser efficacy of the rational restructuring group in the extended role-plays, it would appear that the purely cognitive approach provided less persistence in the face of continued interpersonal provocation. An 8- to 10-week follow-up indicated no differences between the four treated groups, although within-group changes were essentially maintained.

Overall, there were some indications of superiority for the combined approach, albeit only in terms of its more frequent superiority to controls than for either the purely cognitive or the purely behavioral interventions. There were no differences between the major treatment groups on the self-report measures or on the facilitation of assertive responses, although the treatments employing behavioral rehearsal were superior in improving the assertion content of those responses. The combined cognitive-behavioral approach clearly did as well as any other approach on any measure and typically proved superior to controls, but it was not typically superior to either the cognitive or behavioral components alone.

Derry and Stone (1979) presented one of the few studies in which a cognitive intervention (actually a cognitive-behavioral combination) proved superior to behavioral rehearsal (in an analogue volunteer population). This superiority emerged, however, after treatments that were provided in only two sessions, making the actual clinical generalizability of the findings suspect.

Hammen, Jacobs, Mayol, and Cochran (1980) provided yet another comparison of social skills training versus a cognitive-behavioral intervention in the treatment of assertion problems. Noting that prior studies had tended to demonstrate equivalence but not differentiation between behavioral, cognitive, and cognitive-behavioral approaches (Alden et al., 1978; Carmody, 1978; Linehan et al., 1979; Wolfe & Fodor, 1977), the authors attempted to explore individual difference by treatment type interactions. In a sample of community volunteers recruited by advertisement, both behavioral skills training and a cognitive-behavioral combination of self-statement rehearsal and behavioral rehearsal outperformed a wait-list control. Although level of dysfunctional thinking (the individual difference variable of interest) was a general prognostic index, it did not predict differential response to the two active therapies. Again, a cognitive-behavioral combination failed to outperform a strictly behavioral intervention.

Self-instructional Training

SIT for assertion problems has been evaluated in six published trials of varying quality. In the earliest such trial, Thorpe (1975) found mixed evidence favoring self-instructional training over systematic desensitization but not behavioral rehearsal on a behavioral role-play measure, with both SIT and behavioral rehearsal superior to a cognitive "rationale-giving" condition on a self-report measure. Safran, Alden, and Davidson (1980), working with a mixed sample of community volunteers and college students, found that high anxious subjects improved more on behavioral measures in a behavioral skills-training approach than they did in SIT, while evidencing the opposite pattern (albeit only as a nonsignificant trend) on a self-report measure. Low anxious subjects showed no evidence of any differential response. Kaplan (1982) found no meaningful differences between a purely cognitive, a purely behavioral, and a cognitive-behavioral combination (the cognitive components involving SIT) in an undergraduate college student sample, although each active treatment outperformed an unstructured contact control. Craighead (1979) attempted to assess whether the degree of discrepancy between existing beliefs and rehearsed self-statements influenced change in a college student sample. In general, both high and moderate self-statement discrepancy conditions outperformed various controls. Differences between the two levels of discrepancy were modest but, if anything, tended to favor the high-discrepancy condition, contrary to predictions.

Kazdin and Mascitelli (1982) provided a particularly competently conducted study evaluating the addition of SIT (with between-session homework) to behavioral rehearsal training. Utilizing nonassertive community volunteers, the combined SIT-behavioral rehearsal condition (with between-session homework) outperformed the other active treatment conditions, including behavioral rehearsal alone, on self-report inventories. Two main effects (adding SIT and adding homework) were evident in the factorial design. Further, subjects in the combined condition were significantly more assertive than normal controls.

These posttest data are clearly at variance with studies suggesting no obvious additive advantage for the cognitive-behavioral combination over a behavioral approach alone (Hammen et al., 1980; Linehan et al., 1979; Wolfe & Fodor, 1977). Whether this discrepancy reflects a crisper execution for the combined approach, a larger sample size, or simply an anomalous outcome remains unclear. The authors did conduct a six-month follow-up involving the two self-report questionnaires. On those measures, the two cells involving homework assignments outperformed the other cells, with no main effect evident for the SIT condition. The authors suggested that the transitoriness of the additive boost provided by the addition of SIT to behavioral rehearsal is quite consistent with the rest of the literature.

Finally, as noted earlier, Jacobs and Cochran (1982) argued that the nature of the "simulated" role-play situations used to access many of the assertion training studies obscured real differences in efficacy between the treatments (Carmody, 1978; Linehan et al., 1979; Wolfe & Fodor, 1977). They noted that most such role-play vignettes involve relatively impersonal encounters with hypothetical persons not particularly important to the subjects—pushy salespeople, uncooperative waiters—in laboratory contexts that are essentially safe. Such "canned," impersonal assertion role-play vignettes may be convenient, but are probably not a truly valid measure of actual changes in assertive behaviors in vivo (Bellack, Hersen, & Turner, 1979).

In order to remedy this alleged deficiency, the authors had unassertive subjects first rate various assertive situations in terms of frequency of occurrence and degree of anxiety generated. Consistent with predictions, they found that the typical impersonal situation utilized in role-play vignettes rarely passed the dual criteria of frequency/anxiety. Instead, predominating situations of concern to the respondents involved handling negative interactions with important figures from the clients' personal lives (e.g., employers, spouses).

These idiosyncratically important assertion situations were then used as the basis for in vivo self-monitoring in conjunction with a treatment outcome study. In a study utilizing community volunteers, the combination of cognitive modification (relying largely on a SIT-like coping self-statement procedure) plus behavioral rehearsal outperformed behavioral rehearsal alone, as assessed by in vivo self-monitoring in real-life situations. Treatment differences on the in vivo self-monitoring had diminished at a six-week follow-up. The authors interpreted these findings as supporting the superiority of the combined cognitive-behavioral approach. While clearly noting that their assessment strategy "sacrificed some rigor for relevance" (p. 74), they argued that the utilization of important in vivo interpersonal situations outweighed the loss of methodological control afforded by the "canned" role-play vignettes. Whether or not their arguments hold up to further empirical scrutiny may have real implications for our understanding of relative treatment efficacy in assertion training.

Summary

Cognitive and cognitive-behavioral procedures generally performed well relative to various controls and equivalently to more purely behavioral interventions. Combined cognitive-behavioral interventions occasionally outperformed purely behavioral interventions (e.g., Jacobs & Cochran, 1982; Derry & Stone, 1979; Kazdin & Mascitelli, 1982), but this finding was not fully robust (e.g., Hammen et al., 1980; Linehan et al., 1979). Given this pattern, it may actually be the case that self-instructional training works better in concert with behavioral components than does systematic rational restructuring (or RET), although the only direct comparison, a fairly modest study, produced no such evidence of differential efficacy. Jacobs and Cochran's critique of standard impersonal role-play assessment vignettes as biased in favor of behavioral rehearsal components appears important and deserving of further empirical evaluation. Again, there was some evidence that pretreatment anxiety level was a mediator of differential response to behavioral versus cognitive components (Safran et al., 1980), although the actual interaction separated different measures within clients. Overall, there is reasonable support for either cognitive or cognitive-behavioral interventions in the treatment of assertion problems and some tantalizing indications of potential superiority for the combined approach.

Anger and Aggression

Self-statement modification programs (self-instructional training variants and stress inoculation training) have been the predominant approaches utilized with aggression and anger control problems. Typically, the studies dealing with aggressiveness have focused on children with behavioral conduct problems (this body of work is reviewed in greater detail in Chapter 12 of this volume), while studies focused on anger have dealt with adults. In the first instance, aggressiveness has been approached as a cognitive deficit, much like impulsivity, while anger has been approached more as a cognitive distortion process in which excessive angry arousal is seen as being mediated by inappropriate or distorted situational appraisals (Novaco, 1979).

Self-instructional Training

Forman (1980) evaluated the relative efficacy of an SIT-based cognitive restructuring approach, response cost, and attention-placebo in a sample of overaggressive elementary school children. In general, while both active treatments typically outperformed the attention-placebo on both teacher and independent observer ratings, there were few differences between them. Camp, Blom, Hebert, and Van Doornick (1977) developed a "Think Aloud" program involving SIT-like procedures to improve self-control in aggressive elementary school children. In comparison to a no-treatment control, with a rather rich schedule of training (daily sessions over six weeks), the active treatment produced improved performance on academic tasks and prosocial behaviors, but no differential reduction in rated aggressiveness. When considered in light of the relatively intensive treatment schedule, the "Think Aloud" program produced surprisingly little change in targeted areas, although it did have a differential impact on academic performance tasks.

Stress Inoculation Training

Novaco (1976) provided the initial trial adapting a self-instructional/stress inoculation procedure to the treatment of anger-control problems. Thirty-four male and female subjects were randomly assigned to one of four conditions: (1) stress inoculation training, (2) relaxation training, (3) combined stress inoculation and relaxation training, and (4) an attention-control. Treatment outcome was assessed on an anger inventory, with self-report and blood pressure measures taken following laboratory provocation tasks. In general, the combined approach produced the greatest change across all measures, typically exceeding the controls and often the relaxation group, with the stress-inoculation-training-alone condition the second most effective cell.

Schlichter and Horan (1981) evaluated the efficacy of a stress inoculation program in the treatment of institutionalized juvenile delinquents between the ages of 13 and 18 with anger-control problems. A full stress inoculation package (including SIT and provocation exposure) proved superior to a partial stress inoculation package (restricting coping skills to relaxation training only) and a no-treatment control on both self-report and role-play tasks. Stress inoculation subjects outperformed control subjects on all measures except institutional behavior ratings, with the latter in vivo observation measure discounted due to poor compliance by the staff observers. Overall, this study provides some support for the efficacy of the stress inoculation package, although the near comparable performance of

the partial stress inoculation condition casts some doubt on the particular contribution of the specific cognitive components, and the absence of adequate in vivo measures (or the absence of differences on them, if adequate) casts some doubts on the external validity of the changes noted.

Summary

Overall, the self-statement modification approaches evidenced some promise in the remediation of aggressive behavior patterns and excessive anger arousal. That is, both self-instructional training and stress inoculation training typically outperformed attention-placebos or no-treatment controls. They did not, however, outperform essentially behavioral alternatives in two of three relevant comparisons (Forman, 1980; Schlichter & Horan, 1981). In a third study (Novaco, 1976), a cognitive-behavioral combination proved superior to either single modality. While more work needs to be done in this area before any firm conclusions can be drawn, clinical utility appears promising with clinical superiority unlikely, with the possible exception of the fully cognitive-behavioral stress inoculation training for anger control.

Schizophrenia

Meichenbaum and Cameron (1973) provided a pair of studies investigating the utility of self-instructional training in the attention, thinking, and language behaviors of hospitalized schizophrenics. In the first study, 15 hospitalized schizophrenics were randomly assigned to one of three conditions: (1) SIT, (2) practice control, and (3) assessment control. Training was executed in a single one-hour session. The self-instructional training utilized modeling and rehearsal to train the patients to self-instruct task-guiding self-statements while working on various performance tasks. Those tasks included a digit symbol substitution task and a digit recall task, with and without distraction. On all measures, the SIT training outperformed the practice control, which, in turn, outperformed the assessment control.

In Study II, 10 inpatient schizophrenics were randomly assigned to either SIT (expanded beyond the training given in Study I) or practice control. Treatment was provided in eight 45-minute training sessions over a three-week period. Treatment outcome was assessed via structured interview (percent of "sick talk"), conceptual behavior on proverbs and inkblot perceptions, and attention on a digit recall task under conditions of distraction and no distraction. The extended SIT produced superior performance on each of the indices (except for the "no distraction" digit recall) at both posttreatment and follow-up. Overall, the results indicated a picture of consistent efficacy for the SIT training in improving and maintaining the schizophrenic subject's performance on attentional, conceptual, and language tasks.

Margolis and Shemberg (1976), however, working with a larger sample, reported a failure to replicate these basic findings (at least Study I). In a well-conducted effort at replication, no significant differences were evident as a function of training type, schizophrenia subtype, or a training by subtype interaction. Although there were several differences between the trials that may have been related to the nonreplication, none appeared to have provided a plausible explanation. Variations in training adequacy may have been a factor, but there is no way of ascertaining that from the published reports. The Margolis and Shemberg sample was restricted to males only, but there was no reason to presume that the efficacy of self-instruction was mediated by subject sex. Finally, practice controls were yoked to self-instructional subjects in terms of exposure to training tasks. This procedure may have influenced outcome, although it is hard to see how. If it did, it should be considered a methodological improvement undermining confidence in the earlier Meichenbaum and Cameron results. Certainly sample size was more adequate in the attempted replication than in the original report. Finally, Margolis and Shemberg reported that subjects found the self-reward component of self-instructional training "silly" or "babyish." Debriefing interviews also suggested that while subjects utilized SIT techniques during training, they had forgotten them by the time of posttesting. If either of these factors operated to suppress training effects, it is not clear why they would not also have operated in the earlier trial.

On the whole, while the findings reported by Meichenbaum and Cameron are somewhat interesting, the failure to replicate by Margolis and Shemberg (of at least Study I) casts some doubts on the robustness of the phenomenon. Further work here is clearly indicated before any strong conclusions can be drawn. More critically, the actual measures utilized have little relevance to phenomena of clinical interest in schizophrenia. At this time, there is little empirical evidence supporting any particular efficacy for the cognitive-behavioral interventions in the treatment of the schizophrenias.

Physical Complaints

Probably no area has received more new attention in the last decade than the role of psychosocial interventions in behavioral medicine. As in any new area, appropriate problems and methodologies are just beginning to be identified, and controlled studies are few. Recent volumes such as Turk et al. (1983) should stimulate additional work in this area. While the section to follow will highlight cognitive and cognitive-behavioral work in this area, the interested reader is directed to the Pomerleau and Rodin chapter in this volume (Chapter 11).

Headache

Three studies have attempted to evaluate the efficacy of various cognitive and cognitive-behavioral interventions in the treatment of headache disorders. In the first, Lake, Rainey, and Papsdorf (1979) found that the addition of RET to biofeedback added little over biofeedback alone in the treatment of migraine headaches. Small cell sizes and relatively brief treatment may have precluded the emergence of any additive impact for the RET component. In the second study, Holroyd and Andrasik (1978) found both a cognitive self-control condition and a combined cognitive self-control plus relaxation condition superior to an assessment-only no-treatment control (at both posttreatment and a six-week follow-up) in the treatment of community volunteers with tension headaches. There was little evidence for the *specificity* of that efficacy, however, as neither active treatment was able to outperform a nonspecific, unstructured "headache discussion" condition. The authors noted that all but one of the subjects in the headache discussion group developed their own ad hoc "cognitive strategies" and suggested that change in that condition may also have been mediated by cognitive mechanisms. Even if cognitive processes mediated change, however, these data provided little evidence to suggest that cognitive procedures were specifically effective in mobilizing those processes.

In a companion study, again involving community volunteers with tension headaches, Holroyd, Andrasik, and Westbrook (1977) found a cognitive self-control condition superior to both a biofeedback condition and a wait-list control. Remarkably, these differences were maintained at both a 15-week and a 2-year follow-up (Holroyd & Andrasik, 1982). While these data did support the *specific* efficacy of the cognitive stress-coping approach, it should be noted that the efficacy of the biofeedback condition in this trial was notably lower than has been observed in other controlled trials. Any claims for the specific efficacy of the cognitive self-control procedure in this design hinge on the adequacy of the execution of the biofeedback condition, which appeared questionable. Overall, the evidence for the efficacy of cognitive-behavioral interventions in the treatment of headache disorders appears, at this time, to be modest at best. These approaches appear to have some efficacy, but it remains unclear how specific that efficacy is or how clinically meaningful is its magnitude.

Pain

Several studies have investigated cognitive interventions in the treatment of pain. In a pair of analogue studies, Horan, Hackett, Buchanan, Stone, and Demchik-Stone (1977) and Klepac, Hauge, Dowling, and McDonald (1981) found evidence that stress inoculation training was superior to exposure alone and various control conditions in dealing with pain induction in analogue populations. In the latter study, each component of the stress inoculation package (relaxation, cognitive coping skills, and exposure) added to the overall efficacy of the package. The lack of generalization from the training situations to additional types of pain-induction situations, however, reduced the potential impact of these studies.

Turner (1982) provided one of the more competently conducted studies in the cognitive intervention literature. In that study, a bona fide clinical sample (all referred by orthopedic surgeons following the inefficacy of conventional medical treatments) were randomly assigned to a cognitive-behavioral treatment package modeled after stress inoculation training, progressive relaxation training, or a wait-list control. Both active interventions proved generally superior to the wait-list control at posttreatment on daily pain ratings, while not differing from one another. It was particularly noteworthy that patients in both active conditions evidenced reduced health care utilization through an 18-month follow-up. This finding, combined with the maintenance of reduced subjective pain ratings, would appear to support the clinical utility of both the cognitive-behavioral and the relaxation interventions. The only suggestion of *specificity* favoring the cognitive-behavioral approach came from reports of greater pain tolerance and capacity to maintain normal activities at posttreatment and one-month follow-up.

Overall, the major conclusion that can be drawn is that, while promising, more work needs to be pursued in this area. The Turner study, in particular, with its fully clinical populations, clinically representative populations, and extended follow-up, represents the kind of work that should be followed up.

Type A Behavior Pattern

Jenni and Wollersheim (1979) attempted to modify Type A behavior patterns. The Type A behavior pattern, involving extreme competitiveness, achievement-orientation, hostility in the face of frustration, sense of time pressure, and fast-moving and emphatic speech (Friedman, 1969), has been linked to coronary heart disease. In their trial, a cognitive therapy based on RET theory and drawing procedurally on SRR was generally no more effective than behavioral stress management training. This is the only controlled trial involving a cognitive-behavioral intervention targeted at this behavior pattern of which we are aware.

Cardiac Catheterization

In a particularly interesting project, Kendall et al. (1979) found a stress inoculation training condition superior to patient education, attention-placebo, and a no-treatment condition in preparing patients for cardiac catheterization. Catheterization is an invasive diagnostic procedure in which a tube is inserted into the heart and dye injected while the patient remains awake and alert. Both the stress inoculation training and the patient education condition reduced anxiety during catheterization, while physicians' ratings of adjustment during surgery favored the cognitive-behavioral condition over all of the others.

Summary

Overall, there appear to be some promising leads to follow regarding the utility of cognitive and cognitive-behavioral interventions for various behavioral medicine problems. In particular, Holroyd and colleagues' work with headache sufferers, Turner's work with low back pain sufferers, and Kendall and colleagues' work with surgical preparation appear to deserve continued exploration. While there appears to be some evidence supporting the efficacy of various cognitive-behavioral interventions for several different problem areas, however, there appears to be little evidence for *specificity*.

Marital Distress

There has been a recent trend to broaden the scope of behavioral marital therapy to incorporate cognitive processes in the treatment package (Berley & Jacobson, 1984; Epstein, 1982; Jacobson, 1984; Jacobson & Margolin, 1979; O'Leary & Turkewitz, 1978; Weiss, 1978). In particular, these authors have stressed the importance of cognitive and perceptual learning processes in mediating the reinforcing and response-inhibiting impact of behavioral marital interventions.

To date, the results of actual intervention trials involving explicit cognitive procedures have been mixed. In an analogue trial, Margolis and Weiss (1978) found the addition of a rational restructuring component to behavioral marital therapy superior to that latter condition alone. Epstein, Pretzer, and Fleming (1982) found a group cognitive approach based on Beck's cognitive therapy superior to communication skills training in a group context. Baucom (1981), however, found little evidence of any additive advantage for cognitive restructuring plus behavioral marital therapy over behavioral marital therapy alone. Emmelkamp et al. (1985) similarly found few differences between cognitive restructuring and communication skills training.

Overall, it would be premature to draw any conclusions based on these several, typically preliminary, studies. It would appear, however, that there is a growing interest in the role of cognitive processes in the marital therapy area. More treatment-related research will doubtless be forthcoming.

Obesity and Eating Disorders

Surprisingly little work has been done to evaluate the utility of cognitive and cognitive-behavioral approaches with regard to obesity and the eating disorders. Only one controlled study exists in the area of obesity, with none currently in the areas of bulimia and anorexia. Efforts to extend cognitively based interventions to such disorders is currently underway (e.g., Clark & Bemis, 1982). The only existent study involving obesity to date has involved the use of self-instructional training.

Dunkel and Glaros (1978) provided the only trial known to us involving the use of a cognitive-behavioral intervention in the treatment of obesity. Forty obese female community volunteers were randomly assigned to one of four treatment conditions: (1) self-instructional training, (2) behavioral stimulus control, (3) combined self-instructional training and stimulus control, and (4) a relaxation control group. Treatment was provided in six weekly 75-minute group sessions delivered by graduate students.

Treatment efficacy was assessed via analysis of weight loss relative to initial pounds overweight. Although analyses of posttreatment differences were, for some reason, not reported, it appeared that the SIT group outperformed all three other conditions. At a seven-week follow-up, only the SIT and combined group evidenced continued weight loss, with both outperforming the stimulus control and relaxation control groups. The authors commented that their findings both supported the efficacy of the SIT and combined interventions, and indicated that stimulus control was "treatment bound," that is, no longer effective after treatment ceases.

As satisfying as such conclusions would be to proponents of cognitive approaches, there are troublesome aspects of the reported study that preclude a wholehearted acceptance of such conclusions. First, the attrition rate was striking (22 of 40 patients dropped out), leaving very small samples for the analyses and real concerns about the possibility of treatment-related attrition and generalizability. Second, it was not clear why the combined group should have done no better than the stimulus control and relaxation groups during active treatment, then "spurted" to equal the SIT-only group by the seven-week follow-up. If, as the authors concluded, it was the SIT component of the combined package that carried the major weight of change, a more comparable pattern of change between the combined and SIT groups would have been expected. These issues, combined with the sketchy nature of the report, undermine confidence in any strong interpretations.

Clearly, considerably more work needs to be done before any clear picture emerges regarding the utility of cognitive interventions in the eating disorders. Given the problems evident in maintaining weight loss in obesity and weight gain in anorexia following initially successful behavior therapy, it would seem to be just a matter of time until such efforts materialize.

Stuttering

Little work has been done utilizing any cognitive intervention in the treatment of stuttering. Presumably, irrational beliefs can be viewed as contributing to speech dysfluencies, either by increasing arousal or by distracting the speaker. To date, only a single study, that involving RET, has been conducted with regard to stuttering.

Moleski and Tosi (1976) provided a trial evaluating the relative efficacy of rational-emotive therapy for stuttering. RET outperformed both systematic desensitization and a no-treatment control on measures of speech fluency, anxiety, and attitudes about speaking in a sample of individuals with clinically relevant speech dysfluencies. This single study, which does not appear to have inspired any subsequent work or greatly influenced the treatment literature in this area, appears to suggest that RET may have a role to play in the treatment of stuttering. Whether the absolute level of efficacy approaches that found for alternative specific interventions (e.g., speech therapy, controlled speaking) remains unknown.

CONCLUSION

Overall, the various cognitive and cognitive-behavioral interventions appear to have fulfilled some, but not all, of their initial promise. With regard to specific areas of disorder, the following conclusions can be drawn:

1. Cognitive therapy for depression, an empirical hypothesis-testing approach, appears to be at least as effective as tricyclic pharmacotherapy in ameliorating the acute episode and, perhaps, provides a prophylactic effect not matched by other approaches. Work to date has largely involved fully clinical outpatient samples, a laudable accomplishment distinguishing this area from most of the remaining areas addressed by cognitive and cognitive-behavioral researchers. Virtually no work, however, has addressed the generalizability of those findings to more severely depressed inpatient populations. Self-control approaches have also shown well, although studies have typically been limited to community volunteers. No other cognitive or cognitive-behavioral variants have been adequately enough tested with depressed populations to allow drawing any conclusions regarding their specific efficacies.

2. Self-instructional procedures appear to be effective in modifying impulsive behavior patterns in children, although the generalizability and full clinical significance of these changes appear to remain open questions. No other approaches have been utilized in this population.

3. A variety of cognitive and cognitive-behavioral interventions have been utilized with various anxiety-based disorders. In general, these approaches (particularly systematic rational restructuring and self-statement modification approaches akin to self-instructional training) tend to be as effective as behavioral interventions and more effective than controls in the treatment of less than fully clinical populations (e.g., test anxiety, speech anxiety, social anxiety, and specific phobias in analogue populations), while more generic cognitive and cognitive-behavioral approaches have not fared well relative to behavioral approaches (especially exposure) with more fully clinical populations. Whether this disparity reflects the true state of nature or other, less meaningful confounds remains unclear, but the resolution of this disparity appears to be particularly important.

4. Cognitive and cognitive-behavioral approaches appear to typically exceed controls and at least to equal purely behavioral interventions in the treatment of assertion problems. While several types of cognitive approaches have been utilized, it remains unclear whether any are superior to the others.

5. Anger and aggression appear to be usefully approached by stress inoculation and/or self-instructional approaches. To date, there is no consistent evidence that those approaches outperform strictly behavioral interventions.

6. Some interesting preliminary work appears to

suggest that various cognitive and cognitive-behavioral approaches may have a role to play in a variety of problems in the areas of behavioral medicine, particularly the areas of pain and preparation for surgery. Again, specificity relative to purely behavioral approaches has not been established.

7. Too little work has been done in the areas of the schizophrenias, marital disorders, obesity and the eating disorders, or speech disorders to draw any meaningful conclusions.

In general, the bulk of the work that has been done involving cognitive approaches has involved nonpsychotic populations. Whether these approaches have any utility with psychotic patient groups remains largely unaddressed. More critically, much of the work that has been reviewed has involved nonclinical populations, clinically unrepresentative treatment durations, and largely inexperienced therapists. The reluctance of researchers skilled in cognitive approaches to undertake clinically representative studies with truly clinical populations remains a distressing feature of this literature. Only the depression literature appears to have dealt with this critique. Finally, the confounding of treatment type by disorder largely precludes specific comparisons between the various cognitive approaches. RET appears to have the least clear empirical support of any of the major variants, although that state of affairs may derive as much from the fact that the bulk of the trials involving that approach were earlier, less rigorously conducted efforts. Finally, while some of the best supported interventions are clearly cognitive-behavioral in nature (e.g., cognitive therapy for depression and self-instructional training packages for impulsivity), it remains unclear whether such combinations or integrations consistently outperform purely cognitive approaches.

More critically, it is not clear that either cognitive or cognitive-behavioral approaches necessarily add anything over and above the purely behavioral approaches. Cognitive approaches have been proposed on the grounds that they would outperform other approaches either in terms of the magnitude of change produced, the generalizability of that change across situations, or the stability of that change over time. In general, there is no clear

support for any of those propositions relative to the more purely behavioral or other alternative interventions, with the possible exception of growing evidence suggesting a prophylactic effect for cognitive therapy for depression. It is also striking to note how few of the empirical trials have compared either cognitive or cognitive-behavioral interventions to anything besides behavioral alternatives or control conditions (the heavy reliance on pharmacological comparisons in the depression literature provides the major counter instance). Given the apparent absence of clear evidence of *specificity* of effect for the cognitive approaches, explicit comparisons with other major psychosocial alternatives (e.g., dynamic or humanistic interventions) would appear informative.

In a related vein, efforts to establish the validity of specific cognitive mechanisms have not typically fared well. In general, change in outcome variables, however produced, has tended to be matched by change in cognitive mechanisms. The bulk of these efforts has involved the utilization of paper-and-pencil self-report measures. It will be interesting to see whether this pattern is maintained as increasingly sophisticated cognitive assessment strategies (e.g., schematic processes: Markus, 1977; Nisbett & Ross, 1980; or cognitive heuristics: Kahneman, Slovic, & Tversky, 1982) are utilized as mechanism measures in such trials.

Finally, future research efforts should attempt to assess the adequacy with which the cognitive and cognitive-behavioral interventions are executed. The development and inclusion of such component measures should permit both an evaluation of the competency with which a given treatment was executed (in essence, a check on the adequacy of the manipulation of the independent variable) and an exploration of which aspects, if any, of the larger treatment packages were actually active in the clinical change process.

In summary, cognitive and cognitive-behavioral procedures appear to have established their efficacy in a variety of disorders. Nonetheless, it is not clear that they are uniformly more effective than other interventions or that cognitive change is specific to those cognitive interventions. It would appear that something of value has been added to the clinical armamentarium, but it remains unclear that these approaches, as a group, work either better than or differently from other alternative interventions. Although much of the earlier promise of cognitive and cognitive-behavioral interventions has been fulfilled, it is clear that important questions remain to be resolved regarding the approaches' ultimate utility and mechanisms of action.

REFERENCES

Alden, L., Safran, J., & Weideman, R. (1978). A comparison of cognitive and skills training strategies in the treatment of unassertive clients. *Behavior Therapy, 9*, 843–846.

Arnold, S. C., & Forehand, R. (1978). A comparison of cognitive training and response cost procedures in modifying cognitive styles of impulsive children. *Cognitive Therapy and Research, 2*, 183–188.

Ault, R. L. (1973). Problem-solving strategies of reflective, impulsive, fast-accurate, and slow-inaccurate children. *Child Development, 44*, 259–266.

Bandura, A. (1977). Self-efficacy: Toward a unifying theory of behavioral change. *Psychological Review, 84*, 191–215.

Baucom, D. H. (1981, Nov.). *Cognitive behavioral strategies in the treatment of marital discord*. Paper presented at the Annual Convention of the Association for the Advancement of Behavior Therapy, Toronto.

Beck, A. T. (1963). Thinking and depression: I. Idiosyncratic content and cognitive distortions. *Archives of General Psychiatry, 9*, 324–333.

Beck, A. T. (1964). Thinking and depression: II. Theory and therapy. *Archives of General Psychiatry, 10*, 561–571.

Beck, A. T. (1967). *Depression: Clinical, experimental, and theoretical aspects*. New York: Hoeber.

Beck, A. T. (1970). Cognitive therapy: Nature and relation to behavior therapy. *Behavior Therapy, 1*, 184–200.

Beck, A. T. (1971), Cognition, affect, and psychopathology. *Archives of General Psychiatry, 24*, 495–500.

Beck, A. T. (1976). *Cognitive therapy and the emotional disorders*. New York: International Universities Press.

Beck, A. T. (1984a). Cognition and therapy. *Archives of General Psychiatry, 41*, 1112–1114.

Beck, A. T. (1984b). Cognitive therapy, behavior therapy, psychoanalysis, and pharmacotherapy: The cognitive continuum. In J. B. W. Williams & R. L. Spitzer (Eds.), *Psychotherapy research: Where are we and where should we go?* New York: Guilford Press.

Beck, A. T., & Emery, G. (1985). *Anxiety disorders and phobias*. New York: Basic Books.

Beck, A. T., Hollon, S. D., Young, J., Bedrosian, R. C., & Budenz, D. (1985). Combined cognitive-pharmacotherapy versus cognitive therapy in the treatment of depressed outpatients. *Archives of General Psychiatry, 42*, 142–148.

Beck, A. T., Rush, A. J., Shaw, B. F., & Emery, G. (1979). *Cognitive therapy of depression: A treatment manual*. New York: Guilford Press.

Beck, A. T., Ward, C. H., Mendelson, M., Mock, J. E., & Erbaugh, J. K. (1961). An inventory for measuring depression. *Archives of General Psychiatry, 4*, 561–571.

Bellack, A. S., Hersen, M., & Turner, S. (1979). Relationship of role playing and knowledge of appropriate behavior to assertion in the natural environment. *Journal of Consulting and Clinical Psychology, 4*, 670–678.

Berley, R. A., & Jacobson, N. S. (1984). Causal attributions in intimate relationships: Toward a model of cognitive-behavioral marital therapy. In P. C. Kendall (Ed.), *Advances in cognitive-behavioral research and therapy* (Vol. 3). New York: Academic Press.

Biran, M., & Wilson, G. T. (1981). Treatment of phobic disorders using cognitive and exposure methods: A self-efficacy analysis. *Journal of Consulting and Clinical Psychology, 49*, 886–899.

Blackburn, I. M., Bishop, S., Glen, A. I. M., Whalley, L. J., & Christie, J. E. (1981). The efficacy of cognitive therapy in depression: A treatment trial using cognitive therapy and pharmacotherapy, each alone and in combination. *British Journal of Psychiatry, 139*, 181–189.

Blackburn, I. M., Eunson, K. M., & Bishop, S. (in press). A two-year naturalistic follow-up of depressed patients treated with cognitve therapy, pharmacotherapy and a combination of both. *British Journal of Psychiatry*.

Camp, B. W. (1977). Verbal mediation in young aggressive boys. *Journal of Abnormal Psychology, 86*, 145–153.

Camp, B. W., Blom, G. E., Hebert, F., & van Doornick, W. J. (1977). "Think aloud": A program for developing self-control in young aggressive boys. *Journal of Abnormal Child Psychology, 5*, 157–169.

Carmody, T. P. (1978). Rational-emotive, self-instructional, and behavioral assertion training: Facilitating maintenance. *Cognitive Therapy and Research, 2*, 241–254.

Cautela, J. R. (1966). Treatment of compulsive behavior by covert sensitization. *Psychological Record, 16*, 33–41.

Cautela, J. R. (1967). Covert sensitization. *Psychological Reports, 20*, 459–468.

Clark, D. M., & Bemis, K. M. (1982). A cognitive-behavioral approach to anorexia nervosa. *Cognitive Therapy and Research, 6*, 123–150.

Covi, L., Lipman, R. S., Derogatis, L. R., Smith, J. E., & Pattison, J. H. (1974). Drugs and group psychotherapy in neurotic depression. *American Journal of Psychiatry, 131*, 191–197.

Covi, L., Lipman, R. S., Roth, D., Pattison, J. H., Smith, J. E., & Lasseter, V. K. (1984, May). *Cognitive group psychotherapy in depression*. Paper presented at the Annual Convention of the American Psychiatry Association, Los Angeles.

Cradock, C., Cotler, S., & Jason, L. A. (1978). Primary prevention: Immunization of children for speech anxiety. *Cognitive Therapy and Research, 2*, 389–396.

Craighead, L. W. (1979). Self-instructional training for assertive-refusal behavior. *Behavior Therapy, 10*, 529–543.

Daneman, E. A. (1961). Imipramine in office management of depressive reactions (a double-blind study). *Diseases of the Nervous System, 22*, 213–217.

Deffenbacher, J. L., & Hahnloser, R. M. (1981). Cognitive and relaxation coping skills in stress inoculation. *Cognitive Therapy and Research, 5,* 211–216.

Denny, D., Sullivan, B., & Thirty, M. (1977). Participant modeling and self-verbalization training in the reduction of spider fears. *Journal of Behavior Therapy and Experimental Psychiatry, 8,* 247–253.

Derry, P. A., & Stone, G. L. (1979). Effects of cognitive-adjunct treatments on assertiveness. *Cognitive Therapy and Research, 3,* 213–222.

DeRubeis, R. J., Hollon, S. D., Evans, M. D., & Bemis, K. M. (1982). Can psychotherapies for depression be discriminated? A systematic investigation of cognitive therapy and interpersonal therapy. *Journal of Consulting and Clinical Psychology, 50,* 744–756.

DiLoreto, A. O. (1971). *Comparative psychotherapy.* Chicago: Aldine-Atherton.

Drake, D. M. (1970). Perceptual correlates of impulsive and reflective behavior. *Developmental Psychology, 2,* 202–214.

Dunkel, L. D., & Glaros, A. G. (1978). Comparison of self-instructional and stimulus control treatments for obesity. *Cognitive Therapy and Research, 2,* 75–78.

Dunn, R. J. (1979). Cognitive modification with depression-prone psychiatric patients. *Cognitive Therapy and Research, 3,* 307–318.

D'Zurilla, T. J., & Goldfried, M. R. (1971). Problem solving and behavior modification. *Journal of Abnormal Psychology, 78,* 107–126.

D'Zurilla, T., Wilson, G. T., & Nelson, R. (1973). A preliminary study of the effectiveness of graduated prolonged exposure in the treatment of irrational fear. *Behavior Therapy, 4,* 672–685.

Elder, J. P., Edelstein, B. A., & Fremouw, W. J. (1981). Client by treatment interactions in response acquisition and cognitive restructuring approaches. *Cognitive Therapy and Research, 5,* 203–210.

Elkin, I., Parloff, M. B., Hadley, S. W., & Autry, J. H. (1985). NIMH Treatment of Depression Collaborative Research Program. *Archives of General Psychiatry, 42,* 305–316.

Ellis, A. (1962). *Reason and emotion in psychotherapy.* New York: Lyle Stuart.

Ellis, A. (1970). *The essence of rational psychotherapy: A comprehensive approach to treatment.* New York: Institute for Rational Living.

Ellis, A. (1973). Are cognitive behavior therapy and rational therapy synonymous? *Rational Living, 8,* 8–11.

Ellis, A. (1980). Rational-emotive therapy and cognitive behavior therapy: Similarities and differences. *Cognitive Therapy and Research, 4,* 325–340.

Emmelkamp, P. M. G., Brilman, E., Kuiper, H., & Mersch, P. P. (1985). The relative contribution of self-instructional training, rational emotive therapy, and exposure in vivo in the treatment of agoraphobia. *Behavior Modification, 2,* 53–59.

Emmelkamp, P. M. G., Kuipers, A. C. M., & Eggeraat, J. B. (1978). Cognitive modification versus prolonged exposure in vivo: A comparison with agoraphobics as subjects. *Behaviour Research and Therapy, 16,* 33–42.

Emmelkamp, P. M. G., & Mersch, P. P. (1982). Cognition and exposure in vivo in the treatment of agoraphobia: Short-term and delayed effects. *Cognitive Therapy and Research, 6,* 77–90.

Emmelkamp, P. M. G., Mersch, P. P., Vissia, E., & Van der Helm, M. (1985). Social phobia: A comparative evaluation of cognitive and behavioral interventions. *Behaviour Research and Therapy, 23,* 365–369.

Emmelkamp, P. M. G., Van der Helm, M., van Zanten, B. L., & Plochg, I. (1980). Treatment of obsessive-compulsive patients: The contribution of self-instructional training to the effectiveness of exposure. *Behaviour Research and Therapy, 18,* 61–66.

Emmelkamp, P. M. G., Van der Helm, M., MacGillavry, D., & Van Zanten, B. (1984). Marital therapy with clinically distressed couples: A comparative evaluation of system-theoretic, contingency contracting, and communication skills approaches. In L. Hahlweg & N. Jacobson (Eds.), *Marital therapy and interaction,* New York: Guilford.

Emmelkamp, P. M. G., Mersch, P. P., Vissia, E., & Van der Helm, M. (1985). Social phobia: A comparative evaluation of cognitive and behavioral interventions. *Behaviour Research and Therapy, 23,* 365–369.

Epstein, N. (1982). Cognitive therapy with couples. *American Journal of Family Therapy, 10,* 5–16.

Epstein, N., Pretzer, S. L., & Fleming, B. (1982). *Cognitive therapy and communication training: Comparisons of effects with distressed couples.* Paper presented at the Annual Meeting of the Association for the Advancement of Behavior Therapy, Los Angeles.

Errickson, E. A., Wyne, M. D., & Routh, D. K. (1973). A response-cost procedure for reduction of impulsive behavior of academically handicapped children. *Journal of Abnormal Child Psychology, 1,* 350–357.

Evans, M. D., Hollon, S. D., DeRubeis, R. J., Auerbach, A., Tuason, V. B., & Wiemer, M. (1983, July). *Development of a system for rating psychotherapies for depression.* Paper presented at the Annual Meeting of the Society for Psychotherapy Research, Sheffield, England.

Evans, M. D., Hollon, S. D., DeRubeis, R. J., Piasecki, J., Tuason, V. B., & Garvey, M. J. (1985). *Relapse/recurrence following cognitive therapy and pharmacotherapy for depression: IV. Two-year follow-up in the CPT project.* Unpublished manuscript, University of Minnesota and the St. Paul-Ramsey Medical Center, Minneapolis - St. Paul, Minnesota.

Fennell, M. J. V., & Teasdale, J. D. (1982). Cognitive therapy with chronic, drug-refractory depressed outpatients: A note of caution. *Cognitive Therapy and Research, 6,* 455–460.

Finch, A. J., Jr., & Montgomery, L. E. (1973). Reflection-impulsivity and information seeking in emotionally disturbed children. *Journal of Abnormal Child Psychology, 1,* 358–362.

Fleming, B. M., & Thorton, D. W. (1980). Coping skills training as a component in the short-term treatment of depression. *Journal of Consulting and Clinical Psychology, 48,* 652–654.

Foa, E. B., Grayson, J. B., Steketee, G. S., Doppelt, H. G., Turner, R. M., & Latimer, P. R. (1983). Success and failure in the behavioral treatment of obsessive-compulsives. *Journal of Consulting and Clinical Psychology, 51,* 287–297.

Foa, E., Steketee, G. S., & Milby, M. B. (1980). Differential effects of exposure and response prevention in obsessive-compulsive washers. *Journal of Consulting and Clinical Psychology, 48,* 71–79.

Foa, E., & Tillmanns, A. (1980). The treatment of obsessive-compulsive neurosis. In A. Goldstein & E. Foa (Eds.), *Handbook of behavioral interventions.* New York: Wiley.

Foreyt, J., & Rathjen, D. (Eds.). (1979). *Cognitive behavior therapy: Research and applications.* New York: Plenum.

Forman, S. A. (1980). A comparison of cognitive training and response cost procedures in modifying aggressive behavior of elementary school children. *Behavior Therapy, 11,* 594–600.

Fremouw, W. J., & Zitter, R. E. (1978). A comparison of skills training and cognitive restructuring-relaxation for the treatment of speech anxiety. *Behavior Therapy, 9,* 248–259.

Friedman, A. S. (1975). Interaction of drug therapy with marital therapy in depressed patients. *Archives of General Psychiatry, 32,* 619–637.

Friedman, M. (1969). *Pathogenesis of coronary artery disease.* New York: McGraw-Hill.

Fuchs, C. Z., & Rehm, L. P. (1977). A self-control behavior therapy program for depression. *Journal of Consulting and Clinical Psychology, 45,* 206–215.

Girodo, M., & Roehl, J. (1978). Cognitive preparation and coping self-talk: Anxiety management during the stress of flying. *Journal of Consulting and Clinical Psychology, 46,* 978–989.

Glass, C. R., Gottman, J. M., & Shmurak, S. H. (1976). Response acquisition and cognitive self-statement modification approaches to dating skills training. *Journal of Counseling Psychology, 23,* 520–526.

Glogower, F. D., Fremouw, W. J., & McCroskey, J. C. (1978). A component analysis of cognitive restructuring. *Cognitive Therapy and Research, 2,* 209–224.

Goldfried, M. R. (1971). Systematic desensitization as training in self-control. *Journal of Consulting and Clinical Psychology, 37,* 228–234.

Goldfried, M. R., DeCanteceo, E. T., & Weinberg, L. (1974). Systematic rational restructuring as a self control technique. *Behavior Therapy, 5,* 247–254.

Goldfried, M. R., & Goldfried, A. P. (1975). Cognitive change methods. In F. H. Kanfer & A. P. Goldstein (Eds.), *Helping people change.* New York: Pergamon Press.

Goldfried, M. R., Linehan, M. M., & Smith, J. L. (1978). Reduction of test anxiety through cognitive restructuring. *Journal of Consulting and Clinical Psychology, 46,* 32–39.

Goldfried, M. R., & Trier, C. (1974). Effectiveness of relaxation as an active coping skill. *Journal of Abnormal Psychology, 83,* 348–355.

Gross, R. T., & Fremouw, W. J. (1982). Cognitive restructuring and progressive relaxation for treatment of empirical subtypes of speech-anxious subjects. *Cognitive Therapy and Research, 6,* 429–436.

Hamilton, M. (1960). A rating scale for depression. *Journal of Neurology, Neurosurgery, and Psychiatry, 23,* 56–61.

Hammen, C. L., Jacobs, M., Mayol, A., & Cochran, S. D. (1980). Dysfunctional cognitions and the effectiveness of skills and cognitive-behavioral assertion training. *Journal of Consulting and Clinical Psychology, 48,* 685–695.

Harpin, R. E., Liberman, R. P., Marks, I., Stern, R., & Bohannon, W. E. (1982). Cognitive behavior therapy for chronically depressed patients. *Journal of Nervous and Mental Disease, 170,* 295–301.

Hathaway, S. R., & McKinley, J. C. (1951). *The Minnesota Multiphasic Personality Inventory Manual.* New York: Psychological Corporation.

Hersen, M., Bellack, A. S., Himmelhoch, J. M., & Thase, M. E. (1984). Effects of social skill training, amitriptyline, and psychotherapy in unipolar depressed women. *Behavior Therapy, 15,* 21–40.

Hollon, S. D., DeRubeis, R. J., Evans, M. D., Tuason, V. B., Wiemer, M. J., & Garvey, M. J. (1985). *Combined cognitive-pharmacotherapy versus cognitive therapy alone and pharmacotherapy alone in the treatment of depressed outpatients: Differential treatment outcome in the CPT project.* Unpublished manuscript, University of Minnesota and the St. Paul-Ramsey Medical Center, Minneapolis-St. Paul, MN.

Hollon, S. D., Evans, M. D., Elkin, I., & Lowery, A. (1984, May). *System for rating therapies for depression.* Paper presented at the Annual Meeting of the American Psychiatric Association, Los Angeles, CA.

Holroyd, K. A. (1976). Cognition and desensitization in the group treatment of test anxiety. *Journal of Consulting and Clinical Psychology, 44,* 991–1001.

Holroyd, K. A., & Andrasik, F. (1978). Coping and the self-control of chronic tension headache. *Journal of Consulting and Clinical Psychology, 46,* 1036–1045.

Holroyd, K. A., & Andrasik, F. (1982). Do the effects of cognitive therapy endure? A two-year follow-up of tension headache sufferers treated with cognitive therapy or biofeedback. *Cognitive Therapy and Research 6,* 325–334.

Holroyd, K. A., Andrasik, F., & Westbrook, T. (1977). Cognitive control of tension headache. *Cognitive Therapy and Research, 1,* 121–134.

Horan, J. J., Hackett, G., Buchanan, J. D., Stone, C. I., & Demchik-Stone, D. (1977). Coping with pain: A component analysis of stress inoculation. *Cognitive Therapy and Research, 1,* 211–222.

Hussian, R. A., & Lawrence, P. S. (1978). The reduction of test, state, and trait anxiety by test-specific and generalized stress inoculation training. *Cognitive Therapy and Research, 2,* 25–38.

Jacobs, M. K., & Cochran, S. D. (1982). The effects of cognitive restructuring on assertive behavior. *Cognitive Therapy and Research, 6,* 63–76.

Jacobson, N. S. (1984). The modification of cognitive processes in behavioral marital therapy: Integrating cognitive and behavioral intervention strategies. In K. Hahlweg & N. S. Jacobson (Eds.), *Marital interaction: Analysis and modification.* New York: Guilford Press.

Jacobson, N. S., & Margolin, G. (1979). *Marital therapy: Strategies based on social learning and behavior exchange principles.* New York: Brunner/Mazel.

Jenni, M. A., & Wollersheim, J. P. (1979). Cognitive therapy, stress management training, and Type A behavior pattern. *Cognitive Therapy and Research, 3,* 61–74.

Kagan, J. (1966). Reflection-impulsivity: The generality and dynamics of conceptual tempo. *Journal of Abnormal Psychology, 71,* 17–24.

Kahneman, D., Slovic, P., & Tversky, A. (1982). *Judgment under uncertainty: Heuristics and biases.* Cambridge, England: Cambridge University Press.

Kanfer, F. H. (1970). Self-regulation: Research, issues and speculations. In C. Neuringer & J. L. Michael (Eds.), *Behavior modification in clinical psychology*. New York: Appleton-Century-Crofts.

Kanfer, F. H. (1971). The maintenance of behavior by self-generated stimuli and reinforcement. In A. Jacobs & L. B. Sachs (Eds.), *The psychology of private events: Perspective on covert response systems.* New York: Academic Press.

Kanfer, F. H., Karoly, P., & Newman, A. (1975). Reduction of children's fear of the dark by competence-related and situational threat-related verbal cues. *Journal of Consulting and Clinical Psychology, 43,* 251–258.

Kanter, N. J., & Goldfried, M. R. (1979). Relative effectiveness of rational restructuring and self-control desensitization in the reduction of interpersonal anxiety. *Behavior Therapy, 10,* 472–490.

Kaplan, D. A. (1982). Behavioral, cognitive, and behavioral-cognitive approaches to group assertion training therapy. *Cognitive Therapy and Research, 6,* 301–314.

Karst, T. O., & Trexler, L. D. (1970). An initial study using fixed role and rational-emotive therapies in treating public speaking anxiety. *Journal of Consulting and Clinical Psychology, 34,* 360–366.

Kazdin, A. E. (1976). Assessment of imagery during covert modeling of assertive behavior. *Journal of Behavior Therapy and Experimental Psychiatry, 7,* 213–219.

Kazdin, A. E., & Mascitelli, S. (1982). Behavioral rehearsal, self-instructions, and homework practiced in developing assertiveness. *Behavior Therapy, 13,* 346–360.

Kelly, G. A. (1955). *The psychology of personal constructs.* New York: Norton.

Kendall, P. C. (1982). Cognitive processes and procedures in behavior therapy. In C. M. Franks, G. T. Wilson, P. C. Kendall, & K. D. Brownell (Eds.), *Annual review of behavior therapy* (Vol. 8). New York: Guilford Press.

Kendall, P. C., & Braswell, L. (1982). Cognitive-behavioral self-control therapy for children: A components analysis. *Journal of Consulting and Clinical Psychology, 50,* 672–689.

Kendall, P. C., & Braswell, L. (1985). *Cognitive-behavioral modification with impulsive children.* New York: Guilford Press.

Kendall, P. C., & Finch, A. J. (1978). A cognitive-behavioral treatment for impulsivity: A group comparison study. *Journal of Consulting and Clinical Psychology, 46,* 110–118.

Kendall, P. C., & Hollon, S. D. (Eds.). (1979). *Cognitive-behavioral interventions: Theory, research, and procedures.* New York: Academic Press.

Kendall, P. C., & Hollon, S. D. (Eds.). (1981). *Assessment strategies for cognitive-behavioral interventions.* New York: Academic Press.

Kendall, P. C., & Wilcox, L. E. (1980). Cognitive-behavioral treatment for impulsivity: Concrete versus conceptual training in non-self-controlled problem children. *Journal of Consulting and Clinical Psychology, 48,* 80–91.

Kendall, P. C., Williams, L., Pechacek, T. F., Graham, L. E., Shisslak, C., & Herzoff, N. (1979). Cognitive-behavioral and patient education interventions in cardiac catheterization procedures. *Journal of Consulting and Clinical Psychology, 47,* 49–58.

Kendall, P. C., & Zupan, B. A. (1981). Individual versus group application of cognitive-behavioral self-control procedure with children. *Behavior Therapy, 12,* 344–359.

Kiesler, D. J. (1966). Some myths of psychotherapy research and the search for a paradigm. *Psychological Bulletin, 65,* 110–136.

Klein, D. F., & Davis, J. M. (1969). *Diagnosis and drug treatment of psychiatric disorders.* Baltimore: Williams & Wilkins.

Klepac, R. K., Hauge, G., Dowling, J., & McDonald, M. (1981). Direct and generalized effects of three components of stress inoculation for increased pain tolerance. *Behavior Therapy, 12,* 417–424.

Klerman, G. L., DiMascio, A., Weissman, M., Prusoff, B., & Paykel, E. (1974). Treatment of depression by drugs and psychotherapy. *American Journal of Psychiatry, 131,* 186–191.

Kornblith, S. J., Rehm, L. P., O'Hara, M. W., & Lamparski, D. M. (1983). The contribution of self-reinforcement training and behavioral assignments to the efficacy of self-control therapy for depression. *Cognitive Therapy and Research, 7,* 499–528.

Kovacs, M., Rush, A. J., Beck, A. T., & Hollon, S. D. (1981). Depressed outpatients treated with cognitive therapy or pharmacotherapy: A one-year follow-up. *Archives of General Psychiatry, 38,* 33–39.

Ladouceur, R. (1983). Participant modeling with or without cognitive treatment for phobias. *Journal of Consulting and Clinical Psychology, 51,* 942–944.

Lake, A., Rainey, J., & Papsdorf, J. D. (1979). Biofeedback and rational-emotive therapy in the management of migraine headache. *Journal of Applied Behavior Analysis, 12,* 127–140.

Lazarus, A. (1976). *Multimodal behavior therapy.* New York: Springer.

Lent, R. W., Russell, R. K., & Zamostny, K. P. (1981). Comparison of cue-controlled desensitization, rational restructuring, and a credible placebo in the treatment of speech anxiety. *Journal of Consulting and Clinical Psychology, 49,* 608–610.

Liebert, R., & Morris, L. (1967). Cognitive and emotional components of test anxiety: A distinction and some initial data. *Psychological Reports, 20,* 975–978.

Linehan, M. M., Goldfried, M. R., & Goldfried, A. P. (1979). Assertion therapy: Skill training or cognitive restructuring. *Behavior Therapy, 10,* 372–388.

Luria, A. (1961). *The role of speech in the regulation of normal and abnormal behaviors.* New York: Liveright.

Mahoney, M. J. (1974). *Cognition and behavior modification.* Cambridge, MA: Ballinger.

Mahoney, M. J. (1977). Reflections on the cognitive learning trend in psychotherapy. *American Psychologist, 32,* 5–13.

Mahoney, M. J., & Arnkoff, D. (1978). Cognitive and self-control therapies. In S. Garfield & A. Bergin (Eds.), *Handbook of psychotherapy and behavior change* (2nd ed.). New York: Wiley.

Margolis, G., & Weiss, R. L. (1978). A comparative evaluation of therapeutic components associated with behavioral marital treatment. *Journal of Consulting and Clinical Psychology, 46,* 1476–1486.

Margolis, R. B., & Shemberg, K. M. (1976). Cognitive self-instruction in process and reactive schizophrenics: A failure to replicate. *Behavior Therapy, 7*, 668–671.

Markus, H. (1977). Self-schemata and processing information about the self. *Journal of Personality and Social Psychology, 35*, 63–78.

Mavissakalian, M., Michelson, L., Greenwald, D., Kornblith, S., & Greenwald, M. (1983). Cognitive-behavioral treatment of agoraphobia: Paradoxical intention vs. self-statement training. *Behaviour Research and Therapy, 21*, 75–86.

McCordick, S. M., Kaplan, R. M., Finn, M. E., & Smith, S. H. (1979). Cognitive behavior modification and modeling for test anxiety. *Journal of Consulting and Clinical Psychology, 47*, 419–420.

McFall, M. E., & Wollersheim, J. P. (1979). Obsessive-compulsive neurosis: A cognitive-behavioral formulation and approach to treatment. *Cognitive Therapy and Research, 3*, 333–348.

McLean, P. D., & Hakstian, A. R. (1979). Clinical depression: Comparative efficacy of outpatient treatments. *Journal of Consulting and Clinical Psychology, 47*, 818–836.

Meichenbaum, D. (1972). Cognitive modification of test-anxious college students. *Journal of Consulting and Clinical Psychology, 39*, 370–380.

Meichenaum, D. (1974). *Cognitive behavior modification.* Morristown, NJ: General Learning Press.

Meichenbaum, D. (1975). A self-instructional approach to stress management: A proposal for stress inoculation training. In I. Sarason & C. D. Spielberger (Eds.), *Stress and anxiety* (Vol. 2). New York: Wiley.

Meichenbaum, D. (1977). *Cognitive-behavior modification.* New York: Plenum.

Meichenbaum, D., & Cameron, R. (1973). Training schizophrenics to talk to themselves: A means of developing attentional controls. *Behavior Therapy, 4*, 515–534.

Meichenbaum, D., Gilmore, J. B., & Fedoravicius, A. (1971). Group insight vs. group desensitization in treating speech anxiety. *Journal of Consulting and Clinical Psychology, 36*, 410–421.

Meichenbaum, D., & Goodman, J. (1971). Training impulsive children to talk to themselves: A means of developing self-control. *Journal of Abnormal Psychology, 77*, 115–126.

Merluzzi, T. V., Glass, C. R., & Genest, M. (Eds.). (1981). *Cognitive assessment.* New York: Guilford Press.

Moleski, R., & Tosi, D. J. (1976). Comparative psychotherapy: Rational-emotive therapy versus systematic desensitization in the treatment of stuttering. *Journal of Consulting and Clinical Psychology, 44*, 309–311.

Morris, J. B., & Beck, A. T. (1974). The efficiency of antidepressant drugs: A review of research (1958–1972). *Archives of General Psychiatry, 30*, 667–674.

Murphy, G. E., Simons, A. D., Wetzel, R. D., & Lustman, P. J. (1984). Cognitive therapy and pharmacotherapy, singly and together, in the treatment of depression. *Archives of General Psychiatry, 41*, 33–41.

Nelson, W. J., Jr., & Birkimer, J. C. (1978). Role of self-instruction and self-reinforcement in the modification of impulsivity. *Journal of Consulting and Clinical Psychology, 46*, 183.

Nelson, W. M., III, Finch, A. J., Jr., & Hooke, J. F. (1975). Effects of reinforcement and response-cost on cognitive style in emotionally disturbed boys. *Journal of Abnormal Psychology, 84*, 426–428.

Nisbett, R. E., & Ross, L. (1980). *Human inference.* Englewood Cliffs, NJ: Prentice-Hall.

Novaco, R. W. (1976). Treatment of chronic anger through cognitive and relaxation controls. *Journal of Consulting and Clinical Psychology, 44*, 681.

Novaco, R. W. (1979). The cognitive regulation of anger and stress. In P. C. Kendall & S. D. Hollon (Eds.), *Cognitive-behavioral interventions: Theory, research, and procedures.* New York: Academic Press.

O'Leary, K. D., & Turkewitz, H. (1978). Marital therapy from a behavioral perspective. In T. J. Paolino, Jr., & B. S. McCrady (Eds.), *Marriage and marital therapy: Psychoanalytic, behavioral, and systems theory perspectives.* New York: Brunner/Mazel.

Parrish, J. M., & Erickson, M. T. (1981). A comparison of cognitive strategies in modifying the cognitive style of impulsive third grade children. *Cognitive Therapy and Research, 5*, 71–84.

Rachman, S., & Hodgson, R. (1980). *Obsessions and compulsions.* Englewood Cliffs, NJ: Prentice-Hall.

Raskin, A., Schulterbrandt, J. C., Reating, N., & McKeon, J. J. (1970). Differential response to chlorpromazine, imipramine, and placebo: A study of hospitalized depressed patients. *Archives of General Psychiatry, 23*, 164–174.

Rehm, L. P. (1977). A self-control model of depression. *Behavior Therapy, 8*, 787–804.

Rehm, L. P., Fuchs, C. Z., Roth, D. M., Kornblith, S. J., & Romano, J. M. (1979). A comparison of self-control and assertion skills treatments of depression. *Behavior Therapy, 10*, 429–442.

Rehm, L. P., Kaslow, N. J., Rabin, A. S., & Willard, R. (1981, Aug.). *Prediction of outcome in a behavior therapy program for depression.* Paper presented at the Annual Meeting of the American Psychological Association, Los Angeles.

Rehm, L. P., Kornblith, S. J., O'Hara, M. W., Lamparski, D. M., Romano, J. M., & Volin, J. (1981). An evaluation of major components in a self-control behavior therapy program for depression. *Behavior Modification, 5*, 459–490.

Rehm, L. P., Lamparski, D. M., Romano, J. M., & O'Hara, M. W. (In preparation). *Cognitive, behavioral and combined versions of a self-control therapy program for depression.* Unpublished manuscript, University of Houston, Houston, TX.

Rosenbaum, M. (1980). A schedule for assessing self control behaviors: Preliminary findings. *Behavior Therapy, 11*, 109–121.

Ross, L. (1977). The intuitive psychologist and his shortcomings. In L. Berkowitz (Ed.), *Advances in experimental social psychology* (Vol. 10). New York: Academic Press, pp. 173–220.

Roth, D., Bielski, R., Jones, M., Parker, W., & Osborn, G. (1982). A comparison of self-control therapy and combined self-control therapy and antidepressant medication in the treatment of depression. *Behavior Therapy, 13*, 133–144.

Rush, A. J., Beck, A. T., Kovacs, M., & Hollon, S. D. (1977). Comparative efficacy of cognitive therapy and pharmacotherapy in the treatment of depressed outpatients. *Cognitive Therapy and Research, 1,* 17–38.

Rush, A. J., Beck, A. T., Kovacs, M., Weissenberger, J., & Hollon, S. D. (1982). Comparison of the effects of cognitive therapy on hopelessness and self-concept. *American Journal of Psychiatry, 139,* 862–866.

Safran, J. D., Alden, L. E., & Davidson, P. O. (1980). Client anxiety level as a moderator variable in assertion training. *Cognitive Therapy and Research, 4,* 189–200.

Schlichter, K. J., & Horan, J. J. (1981). Effects of stress inoculation on the anger and aggression management skills of institutionalized juvenile delinquents. *Cognitive Therapy and Research, 5,* 359–366.

Schwartz, R., & Gottman, J. M. (1976). Toward a task analysis of assertive behavior. *Journal of Consulting and Clinical Psychology, 44,* 910–920.

Shahar, A., & Merbaum, M. (1981). The interaction between subject characteristics and self-control procedures in the treatment of interpersonal anxiety. *Cognitive Therapy and Research, 5,* 221–224.

Shaw, B. F. (1977). Comparison of cognitive therapy and behavior therapy in the treatment of depression. *Journal of Consulting and Clinical Psychology, 45,* 543–551.

Siegelman, E. (1969). Reflective and impulsive observing behavior. *Child Development, 40,* 1213–1222.

Simons, A. D. (1984). In reply. *Archives of General Psychiatry, 41,* 1114–1115.

Simons, A. D., Garfield, S. L., & Murphy, G. E. (1984). The process of change in cognitive therapy and pharmacotherapy for depression. *Archives of General Psychiatry, 41,* 45–51.

Simons, A. D., Lustman, P. J., Wetzel, R. D., & Murphy, G. E. (1985). Predicting response to cognitive therapy of depression: The role of learned resourcefulness. *Cognitive Therapy and Research, 9,* 79–89.

Simons, A. D., Murphy, G. E., Levine, J. E. & Wetzel, R. D. (1986). Cognitive therapy and pharmacotherapy for depression. *Archives of General Psychiatry, 43,* 43–48.

Steuer, J. L., Mintz, J., Hammen, C. L., Hill, M. A., Jarvik, L. F., McCarley, T., Motoike, P., & Rosen, R. (1984). Cognitive-behavioral and psychodynamic group psychotherapy in treatment of geriatric depression. *Journal of Consulting and Clinical Psychology, 52,* 180–189.

Straatmeyer, A. J., & Watkins, J. T. (1974). Rational emotive therapy and the reduction of speech anxiety. *Rational Living, 9,* 33–37.

Taylor, F. G., & Marshall, W. L. (1977). Experimental analysis of a cognitive-behavioral therapy for depression. *Cognitive Therapy and Research, 1,* 59–72.

Teasdale, J. D., Fennell, M. J. V., Hibbert, G. A., & Amies, P. L. (1984). Cognitive therapy for major depressive disorder in primary care. *British Journal of Psychiatry, 144,* 400–406.

Thorpe, G. L. (1975). Desensitization, behavior rehearsal, self-instructional training and placebo effects on assertive-refusal behavior. *European Journal of Behavior Analysis and Modification 1,* 30–44.

Thorpe, G. L., Amatu, H. I., Blakey, R. S., & Burns, L. E. (1976). Contribution of overt instructional rehearsal and specific insight to the effectiveness of self instructional training. *Behavior Therapy, 7,* 504.

Trexler, L. D., & Karst, T. O. (1972). Rational emotive therapy, placebo, and no treatment effects on public speaking anxiety. *Journal of Abnormal Psychology, 79,* 60–67.

Turk, D. C., Meichenbaum, D., & Genest, M. (1983). *Pain and behavioral medicine: A cognitive-behavioral perspective.* New York: Plenum.

Turner, J. A. (1982). Comparison of group progressive-relaxation training and cognitive-behavioral group therapy for chronic low back pain. *Journal of Consulting and Clinical Psychology, 50,* 757–765.

Vygotsky, L. (1962). *Thought and language.* New York: Wiley.

Watson, D., & Friend, R. (1969). Measurement of social-evaluative anxiety. *Journal of Consulting and Clinical Psycholgy, 33,* 448–457.

Wein, K. S., Nelson, R. O., & Odom, J. V. (1975). The relative contributions of reattribution and verbal extinction to the effectiveness of cognitive restructuring. *Behavior Therapy, 6,* 459–474.

Weiss, R. L. (1978). The conceptualization of marriage from a behavioral perspective. In T. J. Paolino & B. S. McCrady (Eds.), *Marriage and marital therapy: Psychoanalytic, behavioral, and systems theory perspectives.* New York: Brunner/Mazel.

Weissberg, M. (1977). A comparison of direct and vicarious treatments of speech anxiety: Desensitization, desensitization with coping imagery, and cognitive modification. *Behavior Therapy, 8,* 606–620.

Williams, S. L., & Rappoport, A. (1983). Cognitive treatment in the natural environment for agoraphobics. *Behavior Therapy, 14,* 299–313.

Wine, J. (1971). Test anxiety and direction of attention. *Psychological Bulletin, 76,* 92–104.

Wise, E. H., & Haynes, S. N. (1983). Cognitive treatment of test anxiety: Rational restructuring versus attentional training. *Cognitive Therapy and Research, 7,* 69–78.

Wolfe, J. L., & Fodor, I. G. (1977). Modifying assertive behavior in women: A comparison of three approaches. *Behavior Therapy, 8,* 567–574.

Wolpe, J., & Lang, P. J. (1964). A fear survey schedule for use in behavior therapy. *Behaviour Research and Therapy, 2,* 27–30.

Woodward, R., & Jones, R. B. (1980). Cognitive restructuring treatment: A controlled trial with anxious patients. *Behaviour Research and Therapy, 18,* 401–407.

Young, J. (1980). *The development of the Cognitive Therapy Scale.* Unpublished manuscript. Center for Cognitive Therapy, Philadelphia, PA.

Zeiss, A. M., Lewinsohn, P. M., Munoz, R. F. (1979). Nonspecific improvement effects in depression using interpersonal skills training, pleasant activity schedules, and cognitive training. *Journal of Consulting and Clinical Psychology, 47,* 427–439.

Zung, W. W. K. (1971). A self-rating scale for anxiety. *Psychosomatics, 12,* 371–384.

11

BEHAVIORAL MEDICINE AND HEALTH PSYCHOLOGY

OVIDE F. POMERLEAU

University of Michigan

JUDITH RODIN

Yale University

INTRODUCTION

Behavioral medicine and health psychology have achieved remarkable visibility in a relatively short time, in psychology and medicine as well as with the general public. Because of the breadth and diversity of the activities subsumed, incorporating to varying degrees the interests of clinical psychology, psychosomatic medicine, medical psychology, behavior modification therapy, and medical epidemiology, behavioral medicine and health psychology are highly evocative terms. They have become "buzzwords" for the 1980s. Some have dismissed the

Acknowlegments: Preparation of this chapter was facilitated by the authors' participation in the MacArthur Foundation Network on Determinants and Consequences of Health-Promoting and Health-Damaging Behavior (Yale Health Psychology Node). Ovide Pomerleau was the principal author of the sections on behavioral medicine; Judith Rodin, of the sections on health psychology.

burgeoning interest in relationships between behavior and physical health as merely a passing fad; others have labeled the movement "old wine in a new bottle." At the other extreme, a few proponents have projected limitless expansion, with behavioral/psychological explanations of disease supplanting traditional biomedical considerations and, by implication, minimizing the need for acute medical care. In light of this, keeping to the middle ground, we have chosen as our task (1) defining behavioral medicine and health psychology in accordance with current usage, (2) reviewing a few representative activities in depth so as to highlight perspectives rather than surveying entire fields, and (3) identifying trends that seem most promising for the future.

History

Both behavioral medicine and health psychology developed and expanded during an era of growing recognition that many of the risk factors for serious illness and premature death involved lifestyle and were behavioral in nature (e.g., Lalonde, 1974; U.S. Department of Health, Education and Welfare, 1978; U.S. Public Health Service, 1976). Indeed, behaviors such as cigarette smoking, excessive drinking, illicit drug use, overeating, nonadherence to medical regimes, and maladaptive responses to social pressure play significant and often critical roles in such conditions as cardiovascular disease, respiratory disorders, cancer, diabetes mellitus, cirrhosis of the liver, and injuries due to accidents or violence. The growth of behavioral medicine and health psychology provided the context for the scientific reexamination of these problems. Moreover, the development of increasingly sophisticated techniques of organic and surgical intervention in scientific medicine had been associated with spectacular success in the treatment of certain conditions, but at the price of ignoring less salient interrelationships between behavior and disease as well as the patient's desire to be perceived as a whole person rather than as an assemblage of organs and tissues (Pomerleau, 1982). Health psychology and behavioral medicine were, in part, reactions to this trend.

To a considerable extent, clinical behavioral medicine was made possible about 10 years ago by the availability and apparent efficacy of new technologies for changing behavior—in particular, biofeedback for psychophysiological disorders (e.g., Birk, 1973) and self-management techniques for the prevention of chronic disease (e.g., Pomerleau, Bass, & Crown, 1975). Clinical behavioral medicine had been anticipated and was influenced by the application of behavior therapy techniques to problems in health care (e.g., Katz & Zlutnick, 1975).

Interest in health psychology began around the time of the inception of behavioral medicine. It was made possible less by specific technological developments than by a growing recognition (e.g., Schofield, 1979) that the study of various diseases presented a neglected opportunity for psychological research. In 1975 an American Psychological Association Task Force on Health Research (APA, 1976) commented that psychology had played a full and active role in the mental health field and should, therefore, also be able to contribute to an understanding of susceptibility to physical illness, adaptation to such illness, and motivation of prophylactic behaviors (Matarazzo, 1980). In 1978 Division 38 (Health Psychology) of the American Psychological Association was established, coalescing a surge of excitement and activity in this area during the late 1970s.

Definitions and Scope of Activities

Behavioral Medicine

With respect to the scope and formal definition of behavioral medicine as a field, several influences are noteworthy. Among them, psychosomatic medicine played a key role. The conceptual origins of psychosomatic medicine were psychoanalytic, with an emphasis on the resolution of unconscious conflicts to relieve specific "psychosomatic" diseases (Alexander, 1950). At the time clinical behavioral medicine was emerging, new formulations had broadened the purview of psychosomatic medicine considerably, redefining the field as the study of the interplay between psychosocial and physiological variables in disease (Weiner, 1977). The influence of the "biopsychosocial" perspective can be seen in the first formal attempt at a definition of behavioral medicine, in which the new field was characterized as one concerned with the development of "behavioral science knowledge and techniques relevant to the understanding of physical health and illness" (Schwartz & Weiss, 1977). Subsequently, this formulation was amended by Schwartz and Weiss (1978) to suggest that behavioral medicine was the integration of behavioral and biomedical knowledge and techniques relevant to health and illness.

In contrast, Pomerleau and Brady (1979) chose to assign a critical role to modern behaviorism, defining behavioral medicine as the application of behavior modification therapies to medical disorders and problems in health care and the conduct of research contributing to the functional analysis and understanding of behavior relevant to physical health. As described in detail elsewhere (Pomerleau, 1979a, 1982), a narrower focus was espoused to give behavioral medicine a clear sense of identity in the critical period during which it had to establish itself within the existing medical-treatment and health-care system. It was argued that behavior modification therapies were well delineated, that they showed continuing promise of being able to offer clinicians useful prescriptions for dealing with health problems, and that they carried with them a strong tradition of empirical research. A willingness to demonstrate efficacy in outcome research and clinical trials (Pomerleau et al., 1975) was seen as crucial for establishing the credibility of behavioral medicine as an adjunct to conventional medical care and for providing an antidote to skepticism concerning the modifiability of health-related habits.

Some recent developments illustrate the continuing evolution of behavioral medicine. Surwit, Williams, and Shapiro (1982) point out that a feature of behavioral approaches is that they work backwards from demonstrated pathophysiology to the identification of relevant behavioral interventions. Furthermore, the behavioral model focuses on operationally definable constructs in which treatment involves modification of physiology or alteration of behaviors related to disease; unlike its psychosomatic predecessor, the demonstration that particular psychosocial variables are causally related to the course of a disease is no longer a precondition for intervention. Thus, by taking pathophysiology as its beginning point, behavioral medicine applies to all medical disorders, not just those defined as psychological or psychophysiological in nature (Surwit, Feinglos, & Scovern, 1983).

Health Psychology

There has been greater consensus regarding a definition of health psychology than of behavioral medicine. The definition overwhelmingly accepted by members of Division 38 conveys the diversity of its endeavors: Health psychology was described as the aggregate of the educational, scientific, and professional contributions of psychology as a discipline to the promotion and maintenance of health, prevention and treatment of illness, and identification of etiologic and diagnostic correlates of health, illness, and related dysfunction; health psychology was also to be concerned with the analysis and improvement of the health care system and with health policy formulations.

Within health psychology a specialized area, behavioral health, has emerged, in which the maintenance of health and prevention of illness and dysfunction are emphasized. As proposed by Matarazzo (1980), behavioral health "stresses individual responsibility in the application of behavioral and biomedical science knowledge and techniques for the maintenance of health and the prevention of illness and dysfunction by a variety of self-initiated individual or shared activities" (p. 813). This area of inquiry rides at the crest of a major social change in America today, as millions of people alter their habits and way of life to promote and maintain good health.

At present, health psychology encompasses the interests of psychologists concerned with physical health in general as well as those concerned with behavioral health and behavioral medicine. As the definition suggests, health psychology also includes the activities of psychologists working in applied health care settings and of those involved in policy formulation. Thus, health psychology is a broad endeavor and is less restricted in its functions than behavioral medicine. Pomerleau and Brady's (1979) definition of behavioral medicine provides a sharper differentiation between behavioral medicine and health psychology than the Schwartz and Weiss (1977, 1978) definitions, in which these distinctions blur.

In keeping with this, we will focus on the contributions of behavioral medicine to the understanding of behavioral factors in normal physiological processes and the pathophysiology of disease; we will characterize health psychology by identifying its contributions to the understanding of the socioenvironmental and individual differences in behavior that influence health and illness. Even in so doing we note, however, that at the level of the individual practitioner/researcher there may be overlapping activity (as is the case for the present authors). Many psychologists work in and are identified with both fields and investigate a broad array of problems, with variables ranging from macrosocial factors to biological processes.

Chapter Content

We will first review recent scientific investigations in behavioral medicine and health psychology to give a sense of their potential. The section on behavioral medicine will examine selected research and treatment to illustrate current activity. One of the objectives of this section is to introduce the behavioral or social scientist to biological observations that are critical to an understanding of biobehavioral phenomena.[1] Over the past few years, there has been a shift from descriptive and correlational studies of situational and behavioral factors in disease and

---

[1] For the reader who is unfamiliar with biomedical terminology, the use of an up-to-date medical dictionary may be helpful: e.g., *Dorland's Illustrated Medical Dictionary*, W. B. Saunders Co., Philadelphia; *Stedman's Medical Dictionary*, Williams & Wilkins Co., Baltimore; *Taber's Cyclopedic Medical Dictionary*, F. A. Davis, Philadelphia.

health to multivariate functional analyses that incorporate behavioral, physiological, biochemical, and hormonal response as well as subjective or social variables. This trend holds much promise for the future, for greater knowledge about the interactions between biobehavioral mechanisms and pathophysiological processes may provide the scientific basis for more effective, rational approaches to prevention and management.

The section on health psychology will discuss two prototypic questions. The first explores the theoretical construct of control as it applies to numerous issues and areas in the health domain, for example, Type A personality, major life stressors, medical procedures, and patient−practitioner relationships. The second focuses on the issues of adherence to medical regimens and examines a few of the different theoretical approaches that have been brought to bear to explain this important problem. Included will be theories on interpersonal dynamics involving differences in power, and on information processing.

This chapter will conclude with a section that briefly explores future directions in both fields. It will also consider how the theoretical integration of topics in each field may lead to exciting new conceptual and empirical developments, with important implications for treatment.

BEHAVIORAL MEDICINE

Stress: Mechanisms and Treatment

There has been much debate as to whether stress should be defined as a stimulus (stressor), or a response (distress), or as an interaction between an organism and its environment. In common parlance, the word *stress* is often used to refer to an environmental event or crisis that is thrust upon the individual, taxing available biological and psychological resources or requiring unusual responses. Stressful situations include psychological and physical loss, absence of stimulation, excessive stimulation, frustration of anticipated reward, and conflict, as well as presentation and anticipation of noxious events (Zegans, 1982). The Life Events Model of Holmes and Rahe (1967), in which the magnitude of critical life changes in a given period is related to the likelihood of subsequent bodily illness, exemplifies an emphasis on the stimulus aspects of stress.

Although useful at the descriptive level, the approach has been criticized for minimizing the importance of intervening reactive variables, such as anticipatory responses and coping skills. For example, in a study of pregnancy and birth complications, 90 percent of the women with high life-change scores but low coping resources experienced one or more complications, while only 33 percent of the women with equally high life-change scores but high coping resources experienced difficulties (Nuckolls, Cassel, & Kaplan, 1972). Approaches that emphasize the stimulus aspects of stress have been of heuristic value, but they seem to be limited in their ability to evaluate and assess the clinical impact of stress.

Within the biological sciences, stress has most commonly been conceptualized as a physiological response (e.g., Cannon, 1932; Selye, 1956). This approach is perhaps best exemplified by the pioneering work of Selye (1956), who popularized the term in his writings on the General Adaptation Syndrome. According to Selye, stress is the nonspecific response of the body to any demand made on it, consisting of an initial "alarm reaction," followed by a state of "resistance" during which initial symptoms diminish or vanish, and, after prolonged exposure to noxious stimulation, by a state of "exhaustion" or inanition. More recently, the role of psychological processes in determining physiological stress states has gained recognition. Numerous studies (e.g., Mason, 1974; Weiss, 1972) have strengthened the argument that many of the stress responses described by Selye are also produced by psychological variables. For these reasons, researchers like Lazarus (1977) have questioned the advisability of describing stress uniquely as either stimulus or response and propose instead to define stress in broader terms, by incorporating stimulus and response components with intervening psychobiological processes. Accordingly, stress is seen as transactional, involving both adaptive and maladaptive adjustments (Holroyd, 1979). In this chapter, stress will be examined largely from this perspective, the discussion of mechanisms emphasizing response considerations and the discussion of treatment focusing on transactional aspects.

Stimuli that are most likely to elicit a stress response are those that are novel, intense, rapidly changing, unexpected, persistent, fatiguing, or noxious (Zegans, 1982). When an individual is exposed to such stimuli, a cascade of subjective, behavioral, autonomic, and neurochemical changes occur, influenced by previous history or perceptual set. The initial behavioral response involves orientation and identification, cessation of other activity, and increased arousal. The physiological concomitants of arousal include potentially reversible increases in sympathetic tone, resulting in increased catecholamine (norepinephrine and epinephrine) release from the adrenal medulla and, if prolonged and intense, the release of glucocorticoids such as cortisol from the adrenal cortex (Kopin, 1980). Sustained, these homeostatic, protective responses are associated with distress and disregulation. In humans, symptoms of acute stress can include headache, labile essential hypertension, bruxism, sleep disorders, anxiety, heart palpitations, irritable colon, and gastric ulcer. Severe or chronic stress has been linked to irreversible disease, including kidney impairment, malignant hypertension, atherosclerosis, duodenal ulcer, and a compromised immune defense that results in increased risk of infections and cancer (Selye, 1956). In this section, stress mechanisms will be reviewed with a special focus on sympathetic adrenomedullary and pituitary adrenocortical responses. The implications of what is known about homeostatic and pathophysiological mechanisms will be considered for stress management as it applies to heart disease and cancer.

The Sympathetic-adrenal and Pituitary-adrenal Response

The anterior pituitary gland (adenohypophysis), the sympathetic branch of the autonomic nervous system, and the adrenal medulla and cortex play a key role in the physiological mediation of the stress response. Stimulation of sympathetic nerves to the adrenal medulla causes large quantities of epinephrine and norepinephrine to be released into the circulating blood, whence they are carried to the tissues of the body. These hormones have about the same effects as those caused by direct sympathetic stimulation, though hormonal action is nearly 10 times longer lasting and can stimulate body metabolism to as much as twice its normal rate. Part of this process includes breakdown of stored sugar in the liver (glycogenolysis), resulting in increased blood sugar to provide energy. Norepinephrine causes constriction of most peripheral blood vessels (e.g., to the skeletal musculature) while increasing cardiac

rate and inhibiting gastrointestinal activity; epinephrine has similar effects on most vascular beds, though it does cause mild vasodilation in both skeletal and cardiac muscle (Guyton, 1981). The net result of these effects is increased arterial pressure and blood flow to skeletal muscles as well as increased cellular metabolism and glucose availability, in preparation for situations that call for fight or flight.

In response to stimulation by corticotropin releasing factor (CRF) from the hypothalamus, the anterior pituitary secretes adrenocorticotropic hormone (ACTH) into the circulation (Krieger, 1983). ACTH in turn triggers the release of glucocorticoids from the cortex of the adrenal gland. The most important of these hormones released into the blood is cortisol, which has wide-ranging effects on metabolism. These effects include increased storage of sugar in the liver (gluconeogenesis) and elevated blood sugar (due to a moderate reduction of cellular glucose utilization) as well as breakdown of proteins and fats outside the liver, in preparation for the synthesis of critical substances and anticipation of increased energy demands (Guyton, 1981). An important additional effect of cortisol is a reduction of the inflammation that often accompanies trauma, bacterial infection, or other tissue damage.

Corticotropin releasing factor from the hypothalamus stimulates the pituitary release not only of ACTH but also of beta-endorphin, an endogenous opioid with potent pain reducing (antinociceptive) and anxiolytic effects (van Ree & de Wied, 1981). Some physiological effects of beta-endorphin include facilitation of the release of the catecholamines from the adrenal medulla and of glucagon (which promotes glycogenolysis) from the pancreas. Recent research has shown that the pituitary thus coordinates two important components of the response to stress: an initial response in which ACTH enhances the perception of pain (Bertolini & Gessa, 1981) and a subsequent response in which beta-endorphin inhibits affective and emotional reactions to pain (Amir, Brown, & Amit, 1980).

Neuroanatomical and neuropsychological research continues to specify the brain structures that transmit the cognitive-affective representations of the cerebral cortex to the regulatory centers that control hormonal and autonomic activity (Zegans, 1982). The evidence indicates that the limbic system, which incorporates the hypothalamus and has connections to the neocortex, serves as a major center for emotional and behavioral change (Gray, 1982; Redmond, 1979). Limbic structures are thus seen as modulators of the hypothalamic releasing factors that control pituitary function; these structures also project to those parts of the reticular formation that determine sympathetic tone and hence arousal level (Guyton, 1981). In particular, the hippocampus is linked to the pituitary adrenocortical system, which has been associated with depression and giving up, whereas the amygdala is linked to the sympathetic adrenomedullary system, associating it with anger and arousal (Henry & Meehan, 1981). From this perspective, the function of the limbic system is to integrate the cognitive aspects of stimulus appraisal with its affective components, thereby coordinating the somatic expression of emotion and related states (Ellendorf & Parvizi, 1980).

Stress and Cardiovascular Disease

The sympathetic adrenomedullary system forms the critical link between stress and cardiovascular disease (Herd, 1981). As described above, sympathetic nervous system stimulation causes the release of the catecholamines, norepinephrine and epinephrine, from the adrenal medulla. Free fatty acids, which provide energy for skeletal muscles and the heart and which can be converted by the liver into other lipid-carrying substances such as cholesterol, are released from adipose tissue by catecholamine activity. In addition, catecholamine enhancement causes peripheral vasoconstriction while elevating cardiac rate and output. Finally, aldosterone is released from the adrenal cortex as part of the stress reponse, thereby decreasing the excretion of sodium and water from the kidney and increasing blood volume. Thus, the overall physiological effect of stress is enhanced lipid mobilization concurrent with elevated blood pressure and cardiac stimulation (Guyton, 1981).

Increased free fatty acid levels promote adherence of blood platelets in regions where slight irregularities occur in the inner surface (intima) of the blood vessels. If cholesterol levels are also elevated (under the influence of stress, diet, or genetic factors), a plaque, or cholesterol deposit, can form. As local degeneration of the blood vessel continues, its inner diameter narrows and the vessel loses its elasticity, resulting in a condition called atherosclerosis or hardening of the arteries. The coronary arteries,

which carry oxygenated blood to the ventricles of the heart, are critically affected by this condition. Moreover, chronic metabolic demands on the heart, such as pumping against elevated resistance to blood flow through the small arteries in hypertension, or acute metabolic demands from stress-induced stimulation by the catecholamines, create special problems because the oxygen requirements of heart muscle are increased at the same time as oxygen availability is diminished due to narrowing of the coronary arteries (ischemia). If the ischemia is severe, part of the cardiac muscle may cease to function (a process known as myocardial infarction), and the heart can no longer pump effectively or maintain a normal rhythm. If the capacity of the coronary vessels to carry oxygen to the heart is compromised through atherosclerosis or if the heart muscle has been weakened through previous ischemic episodes, sudden death from loss of the ability to produce coordinated contractions (ventricular fibrillation) can occur (Guyton, 1981).

Studies in numerous laboratories have suggested that people with enhanced sympathetic reactivity are at increased risk of developing cardiovascular disease. For example, people displaying Type A behavior (competitiveness, sense of time urgency, and aggressiveness) show sharp increases in plasma catecholamines (Friedman, Byers, Diamant, & Rosenman, 1975) and blood pressure (Dembroski, MacDougall, Herd, & Shields, 1979) in response to a social challange, compared with less reactive people, who are classified as Type B. Glass (1977) has proposed that the Type A person has a special need to maintain control over his or her environment and that his or her excessive coping efforts stimulate catecholamine activity. According to this model, chronic overstimulation of the sympathetic adrenomedullary system sets the stage for atherosclerotic disease and its various clinical manifestations (Herd, 1981).

Further refinement of this perspective is illustrated in two recent studies on the Type A behavior pattern: Glass et al. (1980) investigated the effects of harassment and competition on cardiovascular and plasma catecholamine responses. They found that the presence of a hostile opponent during competition elicited significantly greater increases in systolic blood pressure, heart rate, and plasma epinephrine in Type A subjects than in Type B subjects. Compared to Type B, Type A subjects, then, seemed to be selectively predisposed toward enhanced reactivity to hostile interactions and performance challenge. Williams et al. (1982) also observed that during a mental arithmetic task, Type A subjects showed significantly greater muscle vasodilation and norepinephrine, epinephrine, and cortisol secretion than Type B subjects. But, interestingly, when Type A subjects were presented with a reaction-time, sensory-intake task, only those subjects with a family history of cardiovascular disease (myocardial infarction, angina, or hypertension) showed a significant elevation of cortisol levels, although the entire group exhibited increased testosterone secretion (which has been shown to increase atherogenesis). Despite cardiovascular and neuroendocrine hyperresponsivity, Type A subjects performed no better than Type B on either the mental work or the sensory-intake task. Williams et al. interpreted their findings as suggesting that Type A reactivity to environmental challenge is more selective than had been previously assumed, with respect to both the stressful stimuli that cause reactions and the physiological responses to a given stressor. This research is currently being extended from the laboratory to more naturalistic settings, as will be discussed in the section on health psychology.

The clinical significance of the greater reactivity of the Type A person is still under investigation. In a prospective study, Rosenman et al. (1975) reported that Type A men have twice the incidence of coronary heart disease as have Type B men. The components of pattern A (e.g., hostility, a sense of time urgency, competitiveness) that are necessary for the development of clinical heart disease, however, have not been delineated. Though much more work remains to be done, some of the pathophysiological mechanisms have been identified. Cortisol, for example, stimulates catecholamine synthesis and inhibits catecholamine degradation, thus providing potentiation of a given level of sympathetic activation (Kopin, 1980). Evidence for the clinical relevance of the interaction between the hormones of the adrenal medulla and cortex is provided by the observation that elevated cortisol levels correlate with increased severity of coronary atherosclerosis (Troxler, Sprague, Albanese, Fuchs, & Thompson, 1977). Though much more work needs to be done, the prospects for a better understanding of psychological contributions to pathophysiological mechanisms in heart disease seem quite good.

Stress and Immune Function

Over the past few decades, the study of the relationship between stress and the immune system has gone from clinical observation and speculation to the accumulation of an extensive literature documenting the effects of psychosocial and physical factors on host-defense responses along with a new name, "psychoneuroimmunology" (see Ader, 1981).

The immune system is responsible for maintaining the integrity of the organism against external agents such as bacteria and viruses and endogenous substances such as neoplasms (e.g., tumors). Events that facilitate or interfere with immune function are of critical importance for survival. Two main types of immunologic reaction have been distinguished (Golub, 1981; Sell, 1980): humoral, involving B lymphocytes (white blood cells that are formed in bone marrow), or cellular, involving T lymphocytes (white blood cells that mature in the thymus and other lymph organs). Humoral immunity involves synthesis and release of antibodies by the B lymphocytes. The antibodies are proteins (immunoglobulins) that are specific for the attacking agent (antigen). Antibodies act by combining with the antigen to remove it or by neutralizing its poisonous substances. The humoral immune response is a major defense against acute bacterial infections. Cell-mediated immunity does not involve antibodies, but rather is based on the development of specialized T lymphocytes that are sensitized to the antigen. Sensitized lymphocytes can destroy the invader directly by releasing toxins or indirectly by attracting macrophages, specialized white blood cells that ingest foreign bodies. Cell-mediated immune responses protect against viral, fungal, and slow bacterial infections; they also provide surveillance against neoplasms. While the humoral response usually diminishes after the invading agent is destroyed, under some conditions the cellular response can persist for a decade or more, thus providing lasting immunity from various disease-causing agents.

In addition to B and T lymphocytes and macrophages, a number of other cell types and plasma components are involved in the immunologic process, including monocytes, mast cells, polymorphonuclear leukocytes, the complement system, interferon, and natural killer cells (Sell, 1980). Numerous factors, including age, nutrition, genetics, temperature, circadian rhythm, and various drugs, have been shown to affect immune function (Borysenko & Borysenko, 1982). It has been known for some time that stress can influence resistance to various diseases, including tuberculosis, acute respiratory infections, cold sores (Herpes Simplex I), infectious mononucleosis, and acute febrile disorders (Jemmott & Locke, 1984). Using animals, experimental stressors such as physical restraint, unavoidable electric shock, loud noises, isolation, and crowding have also been shown to increase susceptibility or to exacerbate disease (Ciaranello et al., 1982).

The sympathetic-adrenal and pituitary-adrenal systems have been shown to modulate immune activity. Present evidence suggests that stress-induced release of pituitary ACTH results in decreased immune activity due to the deleterious effects of corticosteroids from the adrenal cortex (Fauci, 1978). The corticosteroids, though complex in their actions, are both antiinflammatory and immunosuppressive; increases in cortisol have been associated with decreased lymphocyte response to stimulation by an antigen and decreased ability to destroy foreign cells (Claman, 1972).

With respect to the sympathetic-adrenal hormone responses, epinephrine has been shown to stimulate the maturation of immature lymphocytes, but in mature cells, it depresses metabolic, proliferative, cytotoxic, and secretory immune activity, including the production of antibodies and interferon (which is involved in antiviral host-defense processes; Jemmott & Locke, 1984). Norepinephrine, on the other hand, seems to enhance both B and T lymphocyte response (Hall & Goldstein, 1981). There is also anatomical and physiological evidence for sympathetic innervation of the thymus gland (which serves as source of white blood cells in neonates) and of the spleen (which is involved in the formation and storage of white blood cells), suggesting that the autonomic nervous sytem can play a direct role in immunomodulation (Jemmott & Locke, 1984). The demonstration that immune function can be conditioned (Ader & Cohen, 1981) indicates additional pathways by which psychological stress can modify immune function. The mechanisms by which stress can modulate immune activity are extremely complicated and still not well understood.

As will be described in greater detail in the section on health psychology, a complementary line of behavioral research has focused on the control of stressful events. For example, repeated exposure to intermittent, inescapable foot shock in animals has been shown to produce a condition called "learned helplessness" (Maier & Seligman, 1976). The condition, a kind of passive coping, is characterized by severe deficits in escape or avoidance responding to subsequent aversive stimulation, as well as by central catecholamine depletion and stimulation of the pituitary adrenocortical system (Visintainer, Volpicelli, & Seligman, 1982). The learned helplessness effect can be blocked by opioid antagonists, indicating that inescapable shock stimulates the release of endogenous opioids (e.g., beta-endorphin), which (independently of stressful stimulation) have been shown to impair behavioral performance (Whitehouse, Walker, Margulies, & Bersh, 1983). In contrast to escapable shock (which reinforces active coping), inescapable shock leading to learned helplessness has been shown to cause immunosuppression (Laudenslager, Ryan, Drugan, Hyson, & Maier, 1983) and to enhance tumor growth (Sklar & Anisman, 1979).

Although the above research indicates that endogenous opioids like beta-endorphin might be involved in immunosuppression (Shavit, Lewis, Terman, Gale, & Liebeskind, 1984), it should be noted that beta-endorphin and ACTH are both derived from a common precursor and are often released together (Krieger, 1983). Whether beta-endorphin actually mediates immunosuppression or simply accompanies immunosuppression from ACTH-stimulated cortisol release remains to be determined; nor can the possibility that inescapable shock depresses immune activity through norepinephrine depletion (Anisman, & Zacharko, 1984) be dismissed at this time. While much more work needs to be done, the animal models of loss of control resemble and may be similar to human situations like bereavement and severe depression— psychological states associated with abnormal immune function (Bartrop, Luckhurst, Lazarus, Kiloh, & Penny, 1977) and increased incidence of cancer (Fox, 1981).

The Treatment of Stress

Of several competing formulations, the transactional model has come to exert the greatest influence on psychological treatment of stress (Cameron & Meichenbaum, 1982). A central assumption, supported by numerous experiments (Frankenhauser, 1975a, 1975b; Miller, 1980), is that neuroregulatory and hormonal responses to stress are modulated by interactions between the individual and his or her environment.

Psychosocial (like physical) stressors have been shown to elicit two general endocrine patterns: aggression or competition is associated with increased sympathetic adrenomedullary activity and elevated catecholamine levels, resulting in increases in blood sugar and blood pressure and concomitant behavioral energizing to meet the metabolic and activity demands of situations that call for fight or flight; on the other hand, situations that involve diminished reward or thwarting of active coping are associated with increased pituitary adrenocortical activity and elevated corticosteroid levels, resulting in enhanced storage of sugar and reduced metabolic and physical activity consistent with conservation or restoration of energy balance. Generalizations about the two systems and their interrelationships are complicated by contradictory or incomplete information. As Miller (1982) has observed, some investigators have examined the catecholamine response to stressful stimulation and others the corticosteroid response, but few have studied both simultaneously. Frankenhauser (1976) has advanced the speculative though intriguing hypothesis that catecholamine stimulation varies with arousal, independent of affective tone, whereas corticosteroid release varies with the aversiveness of the situation.

Stoyva and Anderson (1982) have classified stress-management techniques as emphasizing either rest or coping. Examples of "rest" therapies include relaxation training, biofeedback (involving temperature, electrodermal, or electromyographic activity reduction), and systematic desensitization. In Stoyva and Anderson's model, these techniques are seen as particularly useful in situations that produce excessive or chronic stimulation of sympathetic adrenomedullary activity (Hoffman et al., 1982). Examples of "coping" therapies include assertiveness and social-skills training, modified self-statements, behavioral rehearsal, and various imaging techniques. By implication, coping methods should be helpful in situations involving novelty, uncertainty, and suspenseful anticipation in which

the pituitary adrenocortical response is entrained (Mason, 1972). Stoyva and Anderson (1982) hold that alternation between adaptive coping and rest is the key to stress management for most people, and they hypothesize that people who are stress susceptible or who have stress-related disorders are defective in their ability to shift from an active coping to a more passive rest mode.

Various procedures have been developed to prevent or diminish the adverse effects of stress on psychological functioning and well-being. Rather than provide a compilation of stress-management techniques that duplicates readily available overviews (e.g., the *Handbook of Stress,* edited by Goldberger & Breznitz, 1982), this section will review procedures that illustrate the use of behavioral intervention to modify critical stress-induced pathophysiological processes. The disease states represented are heart disease and cancer, the leading causes of illness and premature death in Western industrialized nations (Taylor, Denham, & Ureda, 1982).

Coronary heart disease. The relationship between stress and coronary heart disease has been reviewed in some detail above. The traditional risk factors—elevated serum cholesterol, obesity, hypertension, diabetes, cigarette smoking, and lack of exercise—do not fully explain the development of heart disease, even when age and family history are taken into account (Jenkins, 1971). The inclusion of the Type A, coronary-prone behavioral pattern, however, has repeatedly been shown to improve the prediction of heart disease (e.g., Friedman & Rosenman, 1974). Suinn (1980) has postulated that there is an interaction between stress and the Type A pattern, suggesting that the Type A person's reaction to stress is an overlearned and exaggerated (maladaptive) coping response involving the self-imposition of deadlines, excessive competitiveness, and aggressiveness. Glass (1977) has defined the Type A pattern as one involving "a characteristic style of responding to environmental stressors that threaten an individual's sense of control" (p. 181). This hyperreactivity to psychosocial stress is manifested physiologically by elevated catecholamine levels, heart rate, and blood pressure (Dembroski, MacDougall, Shields, Petito, & Lushene, 1978; Krantz & Durel, 1983). For this reason, stress management has been advocated as a means of reducing the risk of subsequent heart disease for persons exhibiting the Type A pattern of behavior.

Suinn (1974) developed a cardiac stress management program emphasizing short-term interventions to modify an excessive sense of time urgency and impatience, to decrease anxiety, and to enhance self-control. Starting two to four weeks after myocardial infarction, Type A subjects were taught to use deep muscle relaxation exercises in conjunction with gradual exposure to increasingly stressful imagery (a desensitization procedure). Guided imagery techniques involving behavior rehearsal were employed, in which patients were asked to visualize an interaction that usually prompted a Type A reaction. In the context of a relaxed state, the patients were taught to substitute alternative behaviors for their usual Type A response. Compared with a control group that received an identical cardiac rehabilitation program, stress-management patients achieved substantial reductions in daily tension and changes in lifestyle. Serum cholesterol levels decreased 2.6 mg (from 233.7 to 231.1) in controls, much less than the 15-mg drop (from 229.1 to 214.1) found in stress-management patients. The lipid reductions replicated previous findings showing that changing the response to stress affects cholesterol levels in accordance with subjective reports of psychological relief (Suinn, 1980).

Further substantiation of the approach comes from Roskies, Spevack, Surkis, Cohen, and Gilman (1978), who studied healthy Type A persons selected on the basis of scores on the Structured Interview (Rosenman, 1978), a standardized interview designed to measure both the mannerisms and content of the Type A pattern. One group of subjects was treated using psychotherapy organized around the theme that Type A behaviors represented a striving for mother's love and guilt about ambition resulting from identification with the father; a second group was trained in deep muscle relaxation, in daily self-monitoring of tension, and in the use of relaxation techniques to cope with stress. Participants were seen once weekly for 15 weeks. Both groups achieved significant reductions in serum cholesterol and systolic blood pressure without major changes in diet, exercise, or smoking behavior. Though not significantly different, cholesterol levels decreased more in the stress-management group (40.7 mg) than the psychotherapy group (16.1 mg).

Both groups indicated improvements in physical and psychological symptoms; in addition to significant decreases in cholesterol and systolic blood pressure, an increase in satisfaction with life was reported along with decreased time urgency. A subsequent study by Roskies et al. (1979) demonstrated even greater effects for stress management with Type A participants who exhibited clinical signs of coronary heart disease. Roskies et al. concluded that while stress management was superior to psychotherapy, clinical status (contributing to increased perception of vulnerability in the group with signs of heart disease) was also an important factor in determining and sustaining a favorable outcome.

Numerous additional studies have been conducted on the modification of Type A behavior since the initial reports of Suinn (1974) and Roskies et al. (1978). Most have involved small and/or poorly defined samples, and the measures used to evaluate outcome have held a tenuous relationship to the Type A pattern and heart disease (Roskies, 1983). The difficulty of specifying a coronary-prone behavior pattern is evinced by the fact that a majority of the adult male working population in North America could be classified as Type A, to a greater or lesser degree (Rosenman, 1974); furthermore, individuals categorized as extreme Type A's do not exhibit a greater incidence of coronary heart disease than those classified as less extreme (Rosenman et al., 1975). Recent studies demonstrating cardiovascular and neuroendocrine hyperreactivity to standardized behavioral challenges in subpopulations of Type A subjects (see Krantz & Manuck, 1984, for a review) seem promising; they show potential for identifying the critical components of the coronary-prone behavior pattern under specified eliciting conditions and for describing them in terms of unique physiological stress-response mechanisms. A more precise determination of the controlling variables involved should lead to greater efficiency and effectiveness of treatment interventions.

Cancer. As mentioned above, a growing body of evidence has been amassed in support of the belief that stress has an adverse effect on immune function. The relationship between stress and immune function should not be oversimplified, however, as indicated by studies showing that a stressor (e.g., electric shock) administered *prior* to inoculation with a cancer-causing (oncogenic) virus reduces the incidence of tumors and retards their growth, whereas the same stressor administered *after* inoculation with the virus increases tumorogenesis (Riley, 1981). Monjan and Collector (1977) have also shown that chronic stress can cause initial immunosuppression followed by a rebound enhancement of immune activity.

The observation that stress-induced immune suppression promotes tumor activity suggests that blocking the adverse biochemical effects of stress might be beneficial. Reitura, Seifter, and Zisblatt (1973) administered metyrapone (a chemical that inhibits corticosterone production) to stressed mice, blocking the typical stress syndrome and increasing resistance to a cancer-producing virus. Riley (1981) has suggested that other substances such as progesterone or vitamin A might be useful in blocking the destructive effects of corticoid elevation without undesirable depletion of critical hormones below normal physiological levels. The possibility of using pharmacological or behavioral interventions to modify mechanisms that interfere with or suppress immune activity during stress states is still largely untested.

Some investigators have examined adaptive responses and coping strategies in cancer patients: an active, confronting style seems to characterize people who come through this experience more successfully, whereas those who are more passive, avoiding, and capitulating experience more difficulties (Holland & Rowland, 1981). In related research examining differences in emotionality, women who exhibited elevated ratings of hostility and anxiety (indicators of increased sympathetic tone and catecholamine activity) survived longer following treatment for breast cancer than women who did not (Derogatis, Abeloff, & Melisaratos, 1979). Similarly, a correlation between long-term survival and the expression of emotional distress, especially anger, has been observed in breast cancer patients (Gorzynski et al., 1980); but the immunological implications of the slightly elevated cortisol levels observed in the long-term survivors are not clear.

The development of behavioral interventions that take into account the pathophysiological processes by which stress affects illness represents a major challenge for behavioral medicine. A particular deficiency is indicated by the paucity of clinical studies that document the effects of therapy on pathophysiology. Though a promising start has been made in the area of cardiovascular disease and many exciting possibilities have been identified in the area of immune function, success will ultimately depend upon much more systematic exploration of basic psychological, physiological, and endocrinological mechanisms in stress. Moreover, well-controlled clinical trials of stress management will be required, involving careful measurement of behavior, of biochemical response patterns, of relevant pathophysiological processes such as atherosclerosis or immunosuppression, and of treatment outcome.

Smoking: Mechanisms and Treatment

Cigarette smoking is the principal preventable cause of chronic disease and death in the United States (Califano, 1979). Though the health risks of smoking have been extensively documented and widely publicized, one-third of the population still smokes. Smoking cessation programs have compiled a discouraging record (Hunt, Barnett, & Branch, 1971), despite imaginative efforts to identify and manipulate various social, psychological, and biological factors (Hunt & Matarazzo, 1978; Pomerleau, 1980); currently, only one-fourth to one-third of treated smokers achieve long-term abstinence (Lichtenstein & Brown, 1982; Pechacek, 1979). The explanation of how such a behavior can persist in defiance of its well-publicized hazards constitutes an important problem for behavioral medicine.

The prevalence and refractoriness of the smoking habit suggest that reinforcement for the behavior must be very powerful. Yet many of the reported subjective effects are diffuse (Jarvik, 1979) and in some ways paradoxical (Gilbert, 1979). The psychological consequences of smoking vary from smoker to smoker and in different situations. They include temporary improvements in concentration and the ability to tune out irrelevant stimuli, better memory (long-term recall), facilitation of psychomotor performance (especially on boring or fatiguing tasks), increased alertness and arousal, decreased anxiety and tension, pleasurable sensations, and enhancement of pleasurable activities (Pomerleau & Pomerleau, 1984b). The positive effects of smoking are short-lived, lasting less than half an hour, and are subtle, resulting in modest facilitation and minimal disruption of ongoing activity (Wesnes & Warburton, 1983). The consequences of not smoking include not only the absence of the positive effects listed above and the deficits that constitute their antithesis, but also increased hunger, irritability, and craving for cigarettes (Shiffman, 1982).

Resolution of the issue of whether smoking is intrinsically rewarding or simply escape from nicotine withdrawal has been fraught with difficulty. Most explanations characterize smoking as the latter: the smoker smokes in order to avoid or escape an aversive state of nicotine withdrawal (e.g., Schachter, 1978). In addition to the appeal of simplicity, the nicotine addiction model has a certain amount of empirical support (Jarvik, 1979; Pomerleau, Fertig, & Shanahan, 1983). As an exhaustive explanation of smoking, however, it has serious shortcomings. For one thing, the cigarette withdrawal syndrome per se seems insufficient to account for the difficulty most smokers experience in quitting (Karras, 1982). The symptoms are hard to demonstrate and define even at their peak (Shiffman & Jarvik, 1976). Moreover, identification of the circumstances surrounding recidivism (Pomerleau, Adkins, & Pertschuk, 1978), retrospective analysis of situations associated with craving (Myrsten, Elgerot, & Edgren, 1977), and examination of events that trigger smoking (Epstein & Collins, 1977) indicate that stimuli signaling dysphoric states, cognitive demands, or pleasant activities—events extrinsic to the nicotine-addiction cycle—reliably increase the probability of smoking. Such stimuli may set the occasion for either negative reinforcement (escape from pain or anxiety) or positive reinforcement (enhancement or production of pleasurable states). The critical point is that smoking seems to cause changes in the internal milieu that smokers will go to some trouble to achieve and that some of these alterations seem to be independent of negative reinforcement provided by escape or avoidance of nicotine withdrawal (Pomerleau & Pomerleau, 1984b).

Recent demonstrations of nicotine-stimulated changes in central neuroregulator activity suggest physiological mechanisms that might account for some of the psychological effects of smoking, particularly those effects not associated with the nicotine-addiction cycle. This section will review a few of these mechanisms and will consider their implications for the understanding and treatment of smoking.

Biobehavioral Mechanisms in the Reinforcement of Smoking

The acute psychoactive effects of inhaling cigarette smoke are largely attributable to the alkaloyd nicotine (Jarvik, 1979). Within a few seconds, up to one-fourth of inhaled nicotine crosses the blood–brain barrier into the central nervous system. Although the drug elicits a variety of peripheral changes, including the release of norepinephrine from sympathetic postganglionic sites and epinephrine from the adrenal medulla (Jarvik, 1979), the weight of evidence shows that the reinforcing effects of nicotine from smoking are centrally mediated (Carruthers, 1976; Schechter & Jellinek, 1975; Stolerman, Goldfarb, Fink, & Jarvik, 1973).

The ability of nicotine to modify various psychological states has been linked to the stimulation of neurons containing the neurotransmitter, acetylcholine, in the central nervous system (CNS) (Balfour, 1982). Nicotine administration has been shown to produce antinociception in animals, and anxiety reduction has also been inferred (Battig, 1980; Gilbert, 1979; Hutchinson & Emley, 1973). Stimulation of acetylcholine receptors by nicotine has been found to account for these effects (Sahley & Berntson, 1979; Tripathi, Martin, & Aceto, 1982). At the human level, smoking has been shown to elevate the threshold for aversive shock (Silverstein, 1982) and for cold pressor pain (Pomerleau, Turk, & Fertig, 1984) as well as to reduce anxiety (Pomerleau et al., 1984). Over the years, various studies have provided evidence suggesting that nicotine from smoking improves long-term memory (Andersson, 1975; Myrsten & Andersson, 1978). Enhancement of memory by nicotine is congruent with demonstrations that cholinergic agonists (drugs that activate acetylcholine receptors in cholinergic neurons) facilitate serial learning in normal human subjects, while antagonists (blockers) interfere with it (Sitaram, Weingartner, & Gillin, 1978). Smoking has also been shown to increase visual surveillance, reaction time, mental efficiency, and rapid information processing. Wesnes and Warburton (1983) have proposed that stimulation by nicotine of central cholinergic pathways that control electrocortical arousal accounts for these effects.

Stimulation of CNS catecholamine neurons by nicotine also occurs (Balfour, 1982), as indicated by increased release and turnover of norepinephrine and dopamine in the hypothalamus and several other brain locations (Andersson, Fuxe, Eneroth, & Agnati, 1982; Westfall, 1974). Carruthers (1976) attempted to make a case for the role of CNS norepinephrine receptors as the final common pathway in the mediation of pleasure from smoking. His argument was based mainly on observations that norepinephrine is released at "pleasure" centers in the brain, particularly in the hypothalamus, in response to electrical brain self-stimulation (Wise & Stein, 1969) as well as to nicotine (Hall & Turner, 1972). Carruthers also pointed out that norepinephrine release could account for a number of the virtues claimed for smoking, including enhanced powers of concentration, lowering of error rates, and facilitation of sustained performance (see Wesnes & Warburton, 1978, 1983). Subsequent research, although not ruling out the contribution of norepinephrine to the reward of smoking, has indicated that the processes involved may be considerably more complicated and that other neurotransmitters, especially dopamine, may be responsible for the mediation of pleasure in brain—reward pathways (Wise, 1983). Finally, nicotine's amphetaminelike stimulation of central catecholamine activity (Balfour, 1982; McCarty, 1982) is believed to account for the appetite reduction and lower body weight observed in smokers (Grunberg, 1982; Wack & Rodin, 1982).

A number of studies indicate that, in addition to altering neurotransmitter activity, nicotine from smoking stimulates the release of neurohormones (endogenous peptides) from the anterior and posterior pituitary. Nicotine has been found to release arginine vasopressin reliably (Husain, Frantz, Ciarochi, & Robinson, 1975). Several investigators have reported pronounced increases in cortisol levels from smoking also (e.g., Wilkins et al., 1982), leading to the inference that adrenocorticotropic hormone (ACTH) might be released. In a study in which ACTH was measured directly, however, nicotine at moderate doses stimulated cortisol release without appreciable ACTH release (Seyler, Fertig, Pomerleau, Hunt, & Parker, 1984). Naloxone, an opioid antagonist, has been shown to produce a significant reduction in smoking, suggesting that endogenous opioids might be released by nicotine

from smoking (Karras & Kane, 1980). A recent study by Pomerleau, Fertig, Seyler, and Jaffe (1983) has replicated and extended the above observations, demonstrating a significant dose-response relationship between plasma nicotine and plasma beta-endorphin; in the same study, vasopressin also exhibited a linear dose relationship, but ACTH did not.

The significance of these findings is that, independently of smoking or nicotine administration, endogenous peptides have been shown to function as neuromodulators, playing an adaptive role in such psychological processes as memory, anxiety, and perception of pain and pleasure (van Ree & de Wied, 1981). For example, beta-endorphin seems to function as part of the homeostatic response to pain or stressful stimulation (Amir et al., 1980). The antinociceptive and anxiolytic properties of beta-endorphin have been well-documented (Millan & Emrich, 1981), and direct administration of beta-endorphin has been shown to be positively reinforcing in both animals and humans (van Ree & de Wied, 1981). Vasopressin, to take another example, has been shown to promote memory consolidation and retrieval in animals (Bohus, Kovacs, & de Wied, 1978). That it exerts a similar influence on humans is indicated by reports of memory enhancement following intranasal administration of a vasopressin analogue (Weingartner et al., 1981).

Pomerleau and Pomerleau (1984b) have hypothesized that because nicotine serves to alter the bioavailability of neuroregulators (a category that includes both neurotransmitters and neurohormones), the drug is used by smokers to regulate or fine-tune the body's normal adaptive mechanisms. They have promulgated a neuroregulator model of smoking in which external cues in the environment that are unrelated to the nicotine-addiction cycle are believed to control smoking behavior in the following way:

A task such as driving an automobile may prompt smoking because sustained psychomotor performance and alertness were enhanced in the past as a result of increased cholinergic and/or noradrenergic [norepinephrine] activity from smoking. Similarly, cues for dysphoric states such as anxiety or even physical pain may trigger smoking because uncomfortable sensations have *previously been alleviated by the anxiolytic or antinociceptive effects of nicotine-stimulated cholinergic activity and/or beta-endorphin release. By analogy, socializing, coffee drinking, or the completion of a meal may also contribute to the initiation of smoking because nicotine-stimulated dopaminergic activity and/or beta-endorphin release enhance pleasure. These "extra" cigarettes, superimposed upon the negative reinforcement schedule that constitutes escape from nicotine withdrawal, come under stimulus control as a consequence of both positive and negative reinforcement provided by temporary improvements in performance or affect. Thus, affective states or cognitive demands that can be modified in a favorable or adaptive way by nicotine-stimulated neuroregulatory activity may become discriminative stimuli (S^D's) for smoking. The number of affective states or performance demands that could serve as S^D's for smoking is potentially quite large, providing a plausible explanation for the thorough interweaving of the smoking habit into the fabric of daily living. (p. 507)*

Although the neuroregulator model subsumes the nicotine-addiction model in a straightforward way and provides functional links between smoking behavior and its biological substrate, much more systematic exploration will be required to complete the task. What is known about neuroregulators in general and about their functional relationships with nicotine in particular is still sketchy.

It will be necessary to differentiate carefully between the effects of smoking that are independent of the nicotine addiction cycle and those that simply relieve nicotine withdrawal. In a critical experiment, Silverstein (1976, 1982) demonstrated that shock-endurance thresholds were lowest (indicating least tolerance of pain) in smokers who were prevented from smoking, somewhat higher in smokers permitted to smoke low-nicotine cigarettes, and higher still in smokers given high-nicotine cigarettes. The endurance thresholds of smokers in the high-nicotine condition were not significantly different from those of nonsmokers not smoking, leading Schachter (1978) to conclude that the principal consequence of smoking is relief from the painful and anxiety-provoking state of nicotine withdrawal. Schachter believed that the other effects of smoking were insufficient to maintain the habit.

It is noteworthy that both Silverstein (1976, 1982) and, a few years earlier, Nesbitt (1973) had observed significantly higher pain *awareness* thresholds in smokers smoking high-nicotine cigarettes than in nonsmokers not smoking; the importance of this finding was minimized. Given the known impact of demand characteristics and other psychological variables on pain endurance measures (Gelfand, 1964; Wolff & Horland, 1967), pain awareness may constitute a more accurate indicator of the effects of smoking. Thus, by this criterion, the data generated by Schachter's associates, Nesbitt and Silverstein, suggest that smoking does indeed provide more than termination of nicotine withdrawal. The observation of reliable increases in pain-endurance and pain-awareness thresholds as well as decreases in state anxiety after smoking in minimally deprived smokers by Pomerleau et al. (1984) and in (non-pharmacologically dependent) ex-smokers (Fertig, Pomerleau, & Sanders, in press) strengthens the argument. These new findings are entirely consistent with previous demonstrations of antinociception and anxiety reduction from nicotine administration in nondependent animals (Battig, 1980; Gilbert, 1979). The data strongly suggest that both withdrawal-independent and withdrawal-dependent processes need to be taken into account in future research on the reinforcement of smoking.

The Treatment of Smoking

Despite extensive psychological and pharmacological research and the recognition for several decades that smoking is a major public health problem, the treatment of smoking still leaves much to be desired. A few recent attempts to devise comprehensive programs will be presented here to establish a context for the discussion of the practical implications of research on biobehavioral reinforcement mechanisms.

Bernstein (1969) exhaustively reviewed attempts to help people quit smoking in the 1960s and was forced to conclude that very little in the way of useful knowledge had been contributed beyond the rather elementary observations that smoking behavior was widespread and was extremely resistant to long-term modification. Because of an increasing emphasis on carefully controlled clinical trials and of developments in social learning theory and behavior modification (Bandura, 1969), current reviews of smoking treatment are somewhat more encouraging (e.g., Bernstein & Glasgow, 1979; Lichtenstein & Brown, 1982). Among the more promising procedures are aversive smoking and stimulus control/contingency management programs.

Aversive smoking combines the principles of extinction, negative practice, and aversive conditioning, using stimuli from the cigarettes themselves as the aversive component. The procedure assumes that the positive reinforcing aspects of a stimulus are reduced and become aversive if that stimulus is presented at an artificially elevated frequency or intensity. The most successful use of aversive smoking can be found in the work of Lichtenstein (Lichtenstein & Penner, 1977), using a technique called rapid smoking. The procedure calls for smoking cigarettes at a rapid rate (inhaling smoke about six seconds after each exhalation) until no more can be tolerated. Sessions are repeated on a daily basis until the smoker no longer reports a desire to smoke; booster sessions are provided if the desire returns. In a recent review of several studies using the procedure, the abstinence rate was 54 percent in short-term follow-up and 36 percent in long-term follow-up (two to six years after treatment). Though the method is a clear improvement over previous approaches, there are some problems that may make it less than the optimal procedure for the elimination of smoking. In particular, individuals with cardiopulmonary diseases—those who most need to quit—are the least likely to tolerate intense exposure to tobacco smoke without ill effects.

Another social learning approach to the modification of smoking behavior involves stimulus control. The basic assumption is that smoking is associated with or controlled by environmental cues and that the prevalence of these cues (discriminative or conditional stimuli) contribute to the persistence of the habit (Bernstein & Glasgow, 1979). Treatment involves gradual elimination of smoking through programmed restriction of the range of stimuli that lead to smoking. Typically, self-monitoring is used to increase awareness of smoking. Contingency contracting, in which deposited money is reimbursed, also facilitates the attainment of specified goals. Pomerleau (Pomerleau, 1979b; Pomerleau et al., 1978) devised an integrated treatment procedure that employed stimulus control and contingency management techniques, including stimulus analysis and self-monitoring, interference with situational control from environmental stimuli, social and mon-

etary reinforcement of behavior incompatible with smoking, and follow-up sessions scheduled at increasing intervals (Pomerleau & Pomerleau, 1984a). Results were as favorable as those reported for rapid smoking, with 61 of the first 100 participants quitting smoking after eight sessions of treatment and 32 not smoking a year after the onset of treatment (Pomerleau, 1979b). The recidivism rate of 49 percent also compares favorably with the 70 to 75 percent recidivism reported for nonbehavioral clinics by Hunt and Bespalec (1974).

Though social learning theory and behavior modification have contributed to the technology of smoking cessation, relatively little attention has been directed toward the elucidation of the biobehavioral mechanisms underlying smoking. As a result, current behavioral treatment for smoking, while representing an improvement over previous practice, is pragmatic and empirical in its orientation. Although trial-and-error approaches to treatment may eventually yield better outcomes, the experience of scientific medicine suggests that it might be more expeditious to develop therapies based on an understanding of fundamental processes.

The model implicit in social learning theory as it applies to smoking has been described at some length elsewhere (Pomerleau, 1981). To the extent that the smoking habit is based on conditioning, this model suggests that successful termination of the act of smoking requires the extinction of most or all of the reflexes that underlie the stimulus control of the habit. A critical task is the integration of new knowledge about the neurochemical consequences of smoking with behavior modification and social learning theory. Though there are no clear guidelines for how best to proceed, the suggestions that follow are testable and are offered as an attempt to stimulate both basic and applied research on smoking.

As has been noted above, neurochemical changes associated with particular psychological states, such as increased alertness, reduced anxiety, memory facilitation, and pleasure, reliably attend smoking. Events that cause deficits in these states or stimuli that signal performance demands or even pleasure may well serve as discriminative stimuli for smoking, thus setting the occasion for both positive and negative reinforcement (Pomerleau & Pomerleau, 1984b). The data also suggest that some smoking occurs simply to avoid or escape nicotine withdrawal in an addictive cycle, defining an additional negative reinforcement contingency (Jarvik, 1979; Russell, 1978; Schachter, 1978).

Accordingly, in the context of a learning-based treatment program, smoking reduction or termination might be facilitated by short-term administration of an opioid antagonist (see Karras & Kane, 1980) to block the pleasurable/anxiolytic/antinociceptive effects of nicotine-stimulated beta-endorphin release. Such a procedure might hasten the extinction of key smoking behaviors and help disrupt the stimulus control of the habit. In the early abstinence phase of treatment, a number of different techniques might be useful to provide relief in situations in which smoking has been used to bolster affect or improve performance. Hypothetically, vasopressin (which can be administered as a nasal spray; Weingartner et al., 1981) or dietary lecithin/choline (precursors of acetylcholine; Sitaram et al., 1978) could be useful in alleviating the memory deficits caused by the termination of smoking. Likewise, enhancement of catecholaminergic activity by oral administration of tyrosine (a catecholamine precursor) might provide a temporary means of counteracting symptoms resulting from the nonavailability of nicotine (McCarty, 1982), such as weight gain (Grunberg, 1982; Wack & Rodin, 1982), drowsiness, fatigue, or impaired concentration (Jaffe & Jarvik, 1978). Finally, particularly for smokers who are highly nicotine-dependent or who have reported considerable discomfort in previous attempts to quit, temporary administration of replacement nicotine in the form of gum or chewing tobacco might provide a useful adjunct to habit-change techniques (Raw, Jarvis, Feyerabend, & Russell, 1980). Aerobic exercise, sustained long enough to stimulate both central catecholamine activity (Ransford, 1982) and beta-endorphin release (Farrell, Gates, Maksud, & Morgan, 1982), might constitute a healthful behavioral substitute for smoking. Though the above are obvious inferences from the neuroregulator model of smoking, none has been tested systematically in treatment research. The possibility of combining biological and behavioral findings into a unified therapy for smoking has been noted (Ashton & Stepney, 1982), but its potential has yet to be exploited.

Unlike alcohol and many other drugs of abuse that impair performance, nicotine from smoking seems to enhance the capacity of many normal people to work and enjoy themselves. From this perspective, smoking serves as a coping response, with nicotine stimulating neuroregulatory activity to provide the wherewithal to respond to situational demands with improved performance or affect. Most smokers in the post–Surgeon General's Report era are aware that smoking causes a variety of serious health problems, ranging from bronchitis to lung cancer, but the ultimate aversive consequences of smoking, though potentially of great magnitude, are delayed and have less influence on ongoing behavior than the smaller, immediate consequences (Ainslie, 1975). Thus, a critical task for behavioral medicine is to generate greater knowledge about the physiological and psychological effects of smoking in order to provide scientific criteria for selecting substitute coping responses during treatment and for identifying those activities and habits that constitute healthful and sustainable alternative to smoking following cessation. Biobehavioral research using nicotine as a "pharmacological scalpel" may also help elucidate basic biological reinforcement mechanisms as well as provide a useful model of substance abuse in general (Pomerleau & Pomerleau, 1984b). Such clinically-targeted basic research may eventually lead to the generation of treatment interventions that are both rational and effective.

HEALTH PSYCHOLOGY

Control

It has been argued that the desire to make decisions and affect outcomes, that is, to exercise control, is a basic feature of human behavior (Adler, 1929; White, 1959). According to some theoreticians (e.g., Kelley, 1967, 1971), people attempt to understand and explain their behavior and the behavior of others because they are motivated to attain cognitive control. This view proposes that attributional processes are to be understood not only as a means of providing individuals with a view of their world, but as a means of encouraging and maintaining their effective exercise of control in that world. The strong tendency for individuals to overestimate their degree of personal control over events that are objectively random (e.g., Langer, 1975; Wortman, 1975) is consistent with the assumption that they are motivated to believe that they are able to control their environment.

Variations in control have been shown to affect arousal and perceived stress. The perception of having control over aversive stimuli, such as shock, loud noise, or test taking, reduces the stressfulness of that event in the period preceding exposure to the stimulus. On the other hand, diminished feelings of control increase arousal in stressful situations (e.g., Bowers, 1968; Gatchel & Proctor, 1976; Geer, Davison, & Gatchel, 1970; Stotland & Blumenthal, 1964). In addition, perceptions of control lead to greater endurance of aversive stimuli (e.g., Bowers, 1968; Kanfer & Seider, 1973; Staub, Tursky, & Schwartz, 1971). The crucial variable in these studies is the individual's *perception* of control. Holding objective level of control and exposure to the noxious stimulus constant, people who believe they have more control exhibit reduced distress (e.g., Geer et al., 1970). Furthermore, greater feelings of control have been shown to enhance satisfaction and performance in a variety of situations (Glass & Singer, 1972; Liem, 1975; Perlmutter & Monty, 1977; Stotland & Blumenthal, 1964), while uncontrollable situations lead to performance decrements (e.g., Glass & Singer, 1972; Hiroto & Seligman, 1975; Seligman, 1975).

Health and the Control Construct

The relationship between loss of control and the onset of poor health has been the focus of substantial research in the past decade. Stimulated by the early, intriguing work of Schmale and Iker (1966), many studies have pursued the question of how feelings of loss of control might be related to negative health outcomes, and indeed might stand as a central mechanism in the etiology of disease. In the Schmale and Iker (1966) studies, psychiatrists examined a group of patients, all of whom had had suspicious cancerlike symptoms found in routine Pap smear tests. At this point in time, the cancer was only suspect. On the basis of psychiatric evaluation, patients were rated in regard to their feelings of control. Those who were high in feelings of helplessness and hopelessness were more likely actually to develop cancer. Of course, from these data one could not tell whether hopelessness led to cancer or whether cancer, even before it was diagnosed, led to helplessness. But the data were suggestive and striking, and when the theoretical construct of con-

trol became more firmly rooted in psychological inquiry, these investigations gained more momentum with better controlled designs and experimental procedures.

Type A Personality

We have reviewed the data elucidating the Type A construct in general in the behavioral medicine section. Here we focus particularly on the attempt to understand Type A behavior on the basis of control-relevant processes (Glass, 1977). In a variety of experimental tasks used by Glass and his associates, Type A's appeared to work hard to succeed, suppressed subjective states (e.g., fatigue) that might interfere with task performance, exhibited rapid pacing of their activities, and expressed hostility after being harassed in their efforts at task completion. All of these, Glass (1977) asserts, are in the interest of exerting control over environmental demands and requirements, which must be at least minimally stressful for such effects to occur. A coronary-prone behavior pattern may thus be described as a characteristic style of responding to environmental stressors that threaten an individual's sense of control. Type A's are engaged in a struggle for control, whereas Type B's are relatively free of such concerns, and hence free of characteristic pattern A traits.

If Type A behavior is a strategy for coping with uncontrollable stress, enhanced performance reflects an attempt to assert and maintain control after its loss has been threatened. This interpretation receives support from experiments using a variety of techniques for inducing lack of control, including various partial reinforcement procedures that were perceived as differentially uncontrollable (Matthews, 1982). It may be that noncontingency has to be extremely salient, however, to produce these effects. A series of reactance studies also presents evidence supporting the control interpretation of Type A behavior. If Type A's are more easily threatened by a loss of control than are Type B's, they should show more resistance to a coercive communication. Several studies have shown these hypothesized effects (Carver, 1980; Rhodewalt & Comer, 1982).

In conclusion, Type A's are individuals who are more vulnerable than other people to real or imagined threats of loss of control both behaviorally and physiologically. Not only are they more stressed by loss of control than Type B's and try harder to regain it, but their secretion of both epinephrine and norepinephrine appear more responsive to uncontrollability (Glass et al., 1980). Several studies point to the potential pathophysiological consequences of this tendency (Glass, 1977; Rosenman, 1978). Confusion in the literature has characterized Type A individuals as being overly in control. Rather, our reading of the literature supports Matthews' (1982) assertion that Type A behavior is a strategy for coping with, and induced by, uncontrollable stress. In this case the enhanced performance of Type A's in many situations is a result of their attempt to assert and maintain control after its loss has been threatened. Such an interpretation would underscore the importance of perceived control but suggests that excessive attempts to have and keep control, which appears associated with personality characteristics such as Type A, may have maladaptive health consequences.

Life Change

Several investigators have considered whether control mediates the effects of major life changes on health. While some studies have found that uncontrollable events are more strongly associated with psychological disturbance than controllable events, including suicide, depression, and distress symptomatology, other investigators have reported no effects of the controllability of events among psychiatric inpatients including schizophrenics and alcohol abusers (Dohrenwend, 1973; Dohrenwend, 1974; Fontana, Marcus, Noel, & Rakusin, 1972; Husaini & Neff, 1980; Jacobs & Meyers, 1976; Mueller, Edwards, & Yarvis, 1978; Paykel, 1974). These inconsistent results are not attributable to the method of measuring controllability; rather, results seem to vary by the dependent variable measured. Uncontrollable events are consistently more strongly associated than controllable events with depressive outcomes (clinical depression, depressive symptoms, suicide attempts). When the dependent measure is of conditions less clearly linked with depression (schizophrenia, alcohol abuse, psychiatric status), inconsistent findings are obtained.

Using both retrospective and prospective designs, Suls and his colleagues further tried to sort out when life events perceived as beyond one's personal control would be related to psychological and physiological distress and symptomatology

(Mullen & Suls, 1982; Suls, 1982). In both domains, uncontrollable events were related to future distress, but only if they were also undesirable. Uncontrollable positive events had no negative effects, suggesting an important modification of the view (Seligman, 1975) that exposure to all uncontrollable events, either positive or negative in nature, leads to stress and helplessness.

In the section on behavioral medicine, we reviewed the effects of stress per se on endocrine and immune response. Both the endocrine and immune systems also appear responsive to the *uncontrollability* of the stressful event. Lack of control-relevant behaviors will generally activate both the pituitary adrenal system (Sachar, 1975; Visintainer et al., 1982) and the sympathetic-adrenal system (Frankenhaeuser, 1975a; Visintainer et al., 1982). For example, subjects who were able to choose the intensity of aversive noise to which they were exposed secreted significantly less cortisol than no-choice subjects who were exposed to the same intensity of noise for the same amount of time (Lundberg & Frankenhaeuser, 1978). In addition, novice parachute jumpers showed a marked rise in hormone levels at the time of their first jump from a mock training tower, but the amount that these levels decreased in subsequent jumps was correlated with skill at mastering this task (Ursin, Baade, & Levine, 1978). Furthermore, it has been shown that the amount of hydrocortisone produced by women awaiting breast tumor biopsy is negatively correlated with their feelings of having some control in, and coping with, the situation (Katz, Weiner, Gallagher, & Hellman, 1970).

Corticosteroids are implicated in diseases caused by the immune system since elevated levels reduce immune functioning (Gabrielson & Good, 1967; Gisler, 1974). In healthy individuals, there are usually homeostatic regulatory mechanisms effectively counteracting the suppressive properties of corticosteroids (Northey, 1965; Rose & Sabiston, 1971; Solomon, 1969). Although it is difficult to isolate the exact causal sequence, homeostatic regulatory mechanisms may be less effective in individuals who are ill (Timiras, 1972). Since loss of control leads to elevated corticosteroid levels, it may weaken the immune system, thereby affecting relapse and the development of other problem conditions. Our own data from a prospective study of people aged 62 to 91 show alteration in immunocompetence as a function of the effects of a stressful event on one's sense of control (Rodin, 1983a). If the same objective stressor did not affect the person's sense of control, it did not have an immunosuppressive effect. In animals, inescapable shock leading to learned helplessness has been shown to cause immunosuppression (Laudenslager et al., 1983).

Consistent with these findings, feelings of helplessness and an inability to control one's environment are associated with the onset of immune-related diseases such as some cancers (Schmale & Iker, 1966; Sklar & Anisman, 1979; Visintainer et al., 1982). While many of these assertions have been based on correlational findings, experimental manipulations of control, which lead to clear changes in endocrine and immune system responses, give strong support to the suggestions that loss of control figures importantly in the etiology and course of disease.

Medical Procedures

Illness itself often threatens a patient's sense of control. Although people generally see a health care professional only when they are ill, the difficulties and symptoms that lead them to seek professional help may diminish their feelings of control. The sensations and experiences they encounter are unfamiliar and frightening, leading to confusion about how to make sense out of them or cope with them (Janis & Rodin, 1979). When people are confronted with physical illnesses, their ability to regulate their physiological processes is threatened (Brody, 1980). When they are faced with psychological and medical concerns, they feel a lowered sense of efficacy (e.g., Bandura, Adams, Hardy, & Howells, 1980).

There is now a fair amount of empirical work testing the effects of control enhancement in medical settings. Some control interventions in the health domain give patients a great deal of preparatory information, including precise descriptions of expected reactions, medical procedures, and the like, as in Johnson's (1975) work with gastroendoscopy patients. These interventions enable patients to make plans for coping with the predicted stress, which can enhance feelings of control. The consequences of such preparation are to reduce significantly the degree of pain experienced, the need for medication following surgery, and the time needed for postoperative recovery (Johnson, 1975). Focusing attention on the task at hand may also increase

control in other ways. For example, Pranulis, Dabbs, and Johnson (1975) found that patients had better reactions to anesthesia and surgery when their focus of attention was directed away from their own emotional reactions as passive recipients of treatment to specific tasks that made them feel more in control as active collaborators with the staff.

The value of directing the patient's attentional focus was directly tested in a study of the effectiveness of a cognitive reappraisal technique with surgical patients by Langer, Janis, and Wolfer (1975). Without encouraging the denial of realistic threats, their procedure encouraged patients to feel confident about being able to deal effectively with whatever pains, discomforts, and setbacks were subsequently encountered. The increased predictability and greater feelings of self-efficacy led to less distress, according to nurses' blind ratings, and to a decreased use of postoperative medication.

Other studies have shown similar beneficial outcomes by actually providing patients with the opportunity to have some degree of control. Work with breast cancer patients has shown that patients do better, as measured by rate of recovery from surgery, when they have had a two-stage surgical procedure as compared with those who have undergone a one-stage procedure in which biopsy and breast removal are done simultaneously if surgery is necessary (Taylor & Levin, 1976). With a two-stage procedure, the patient is notified about the results of the biopsy and often actively participates in the decision to resort to surgery. The patient's knowledge that she has a malignancy and her psychological preparation in advance for the removal of the breast, as well as her actual participation in the relevant planning and decision making, are likely to enhance her feelings of personal control.

In a field experiment, Langer and Rodin (1976) assessed the effects of an intervention designed to encourage elderly nursing home residents to make a greater number of choices and to feel more in control of their day-to-day lives. The results indicated that residents in the group given more responsibility became more active and reported feeling less unhappy than a comparison group of residents that was encouraged to feel that the staff would care for them and try to satisfy their needs. Eighteen months later, the responsible patients showed a significantly greater improvement in health than patients in the comparison group. Even death rate was marginally different between the two groups, suggesting possible life-promoting effects of enhanced feelings of control (Rodin & Langer, 1977).

In a different type of study of the consequences of variations in control and predictability, subjects in the control-enhanced condition were able to determine both the frequency and duration of a series of visits that they received from college undergraduates (Schulz, 1976). Two additional groups were given different forms of predictability over the visits, although they did not have control over frequency and duration, and the fourth group was a baseline-comparison group. The results of this study, in the short run, were comparable to those of Langer and Rodin (1976), showing significant improvements in activity, happiness, and alertness. In their follow-up, however, Schulz & Hanusa (1978) found that persons who had previously improved in psychological and physical health status when an important positive event was made predictable and controllable for them, exhibited significant decline after the study was terminated.

Schulz and Hanusa (1978) suggested that the interventions used by Rodin and Langer altered subjects' self-attributions regarding their ability to control outcomes in their institutional environment. The communication delivered to the experimental group, which emphasized their responsibility for themselves and their outcomes, probably encouraged subjects to make internal, stable, and global attributions. And as predicted by attribution theory, the gains evidenced by the experimental group persisted over time. On the other hand, in the Schulz (1976) study, increased control could be attributed by subjects only to unstable factors, thus predicting why the impact of the intervention would be just temporary. In addition, subjects' expectations for controlling or predicting important events in their lives may have been raised by the intervention, and then abruptly violated when the study terminated and the experimenters and visitors disappeared. Perhaps the decline would have been avoided if subjects had been provided with substitute predictable or controllable events.

In another study (Rodin, 1983b), elderly nursing home residents were specifically taught coping skills that enhanced their sense of personal control and increased dramatically the number of control-relevant behaviors that they were able to exercise. It was found that these subjects showed a significant reduction in feelings of stress, significant increases in problem-solving ability, and, most strikingly, significant long-term reductions in corticosteroid level correlated with increased feelings of control. Eighteen months following this intervention, the control/coping skills group showed substantial improvements in health.

Patient—Practitioner Relationships

Recently, it has been advocated that patients be encouraged to be more active participants in the practitioner—patient relationship (e.g., Brody, 1980; Coyne & Widiger, 1978; Deeds et al., 1979; Eisenthal, Emery, Lazare, & Udin, 1979). However, these proposals have not been based upon a solid theoretical framework. The literature on the construct of control provides such a foundation (Schorr & Rodin, 1982). This formulation is especially attractive since feelings of control are affected by many aspects of a patient's relationship with a health care practitioner (see Schorr & Rodin, 1982, for a full description).

Efforts to increase patients' perceived control seem especially important since it has been suggested that when feeling powerless, patients will resist therapeutic recommendations in order to balance the power and control in the patient—practitioner relationship. In fact, some see resistance as part of the therapist—patient power struggle that is inevitable in therapy. Nonetheless, questions still remain regarding how much self-care and responsibility are optimal (Linn & Lewis, 1979). Further complicating this issue is the likelihood that some individuals may benefit more than others from being highly involved in their own treatment. Personality-based expectancies and beliefs about health and illness may determine the efficacy of patient-oriented approaches to health care.

In studies that made the patient a more active participant in treatment (Cromwell, Butterfield, Brayfield, & Curry, 1977), that heightened the patient's sense of choice (Mills & Krantz, 1979), or that provided for self-monitoring or self-care (Berg & LoGerfo, 1979), there appear to be substantial individual differences in reaction to these kinds of treatment interventions. Cromwell et al. (1977) found that heart patients showing the best outcomes on several rehabilitation outcome measures were those given treatments congruent with their own control beliefs, and investigators using a health locus of control measure found that subjects in treatment conditions congruent with their control beliefs expressed more satisfaction than reported higher compliance with the medical regimen (Lewis, Morisky, & Flynn, 1978; Wallston, Wallston, Kaplan, & Maides, 1976).

Increased feelings of control when the situation is actually not controllable may also have detrimental physiological and psychological effects in the long run (Janis & Rodin, 1979). We have described such consequences for Type A individuals, for example, who seem to persevere in their efforts to assert and maintain control over events that others have recognized are uncontrollable. Most aspects of the health care situation, however, are actually controllable if practitioners and settings extend to patients the opportunities for control. In the nursing home study by Langer and Rodin (1976), the setting was willing to provide residents with opportunities for greater control. Thus, when feelings of self-efficacy were raised, the environment provided options for a greater exercise of control. In other situations, it may be necessary to change the environment to allow the opportunity for greater control *before* people's feelings of control are bolstered.

Adherence

It is probably safe to say the patients' failure to adhere to prescribed medical and psychotherapeutic regimens is one of the most serious problems in health care today. In medical care or in psychotherapy, resistance can take one of two major forms. In the first form, the patient rejects the provider of care because of the provider's characteristics as a person, because of expectations not met in the therapeutic relationship, or because of the patient's rejection of the provider's position of authority (Baekeland & Lundwall, 1975; Hayes-Bautista, 1976). The second type of resistance involves acceptance of the provider of treatment, but rejection of the specific advice that the provider gives, for example, because it is too costly, painful, or difficult to perform.

While many theories of nonadherence have been proposed (e.g., Becker, 1976; Haynes, Taylor, & Sackett, 1979; Sackett & Haynes, 1976; Stone, 1979), applications aimed at increasing compliance have continued to appear unsuccessful. Recent work in health psychology has provided some new perspectives in this effort. In this section we will

consider information processing during times of stress such as illness and the interpersonal dynamics of dyads in which the members are unequal in power. In the next section we will discuss the relationship between control and adherence.

Information Processing

A cognitive view of noncompliance argues that it may be due to information processing variables that make noncompliance the natural outcome. How a patient processes and comes to understand his or her symptoms and physical sensations appear to affect compliance with medical recommendations. Generally, patients' compliance depends on their understanding of the disorder which, in turn, depends on three things: information provided by the health care system, sensations and symptoms arising from the body that are highly salient, and patients' past experience with illness. Noncompliance can occur because people generate their own representations of danger and their own coping reactions to help them deal with present and potential health threats.

Symptoms and the patients' beliefs about their determinants form the patients' implicit theory of illness. It is argued that these perceptions and beliefs around an experience of symptoms become a schema of the illness experience, which guides the search for, and interpretation of, further information and determines subsequent behavior (Leventhal, Meyer, & Nerenz, 1980). It appears that representing the illness as highly palpable symptoms often allows for the selection of specific coping efforts, and it has been suggested that because symptoms are felt, they may exert very potent control over behavior. The assumption that schemas can have a sensory component and a cognitive component is similar to Zajonc's (1980) distinction between affective and cognitive schemas. Current research efforts attempt to describe their different effects on information processing and retrieval.

Meyer, Leventhal, and Gutman (1985) used both cross-sectional and longitudinal data to provide a picture of symptom evaluation processes underlying compliance or noncompliance to hypertension treatment. Six groups of patients who varied in the length of time that they had been hypertensive, their degree of compliance with recommendations, and their degree of control were interviewed regarding their beliefs about high blood pressure and its treatment. They were also asked what they had been told by medical authorities.

There were three major findings in the Meyer et al. (1985) study: (1) Although medical authority denies that bodily sensations are reliably associated with blood pressure elevations, the great majority of respondents thought otherwise and believed that they could identify clear symptoms. (2) The belief and use of sensation monitoring developed over time and experience with hypertension, so that it was greater with more experienced hypertensives. The symptoms that were monitored changed over time as well. (3) Because patients believed that they could monitor the symptoms of high blood pressure, they expected their treatment to modify those symptoms, and their compliance depended on the extent to which they perceived beneficial effects as a result of the treatment. The Meyer et al. (1985) data revealed that the interpretations developed by patients were organized around specific themes. For example, some patients saw hypertension as a stress disease, others as an ingestive disease. These schematic beliefs or structures were different from person to person because they were based on different concrete experiences, and so they had different effects on compliance behavior and the nature of the coping responses people employed.

Pennebaker (in press) has shown that individuals become aware of internal physical sensations at some times and not others, and this may affect their adherence to medical recommendations. For example, when external demands are low, or when people are feeling ill, especially helpless or out of control, the probability of attending to internal sensations increases. Schemas guide their search for particular sensations, and just as schemas restrict the information that people glean from the environment, so too do schemas also restrict and shape information that people experience from internal sensations. This type of explanation accounts for the enormous rash of illness reported after the publicized nuclear reactor accident at Three Mile Island, Pennsylvania, since there appear to have been few if any effects of the radiation itself (Baum, Fleming, & Singer, 1982).

Information-processing models also suggest that adherence may be influenced by the amount of conflict involved in making a difficult decision because conflict per se affects how and what information is processed (Janis & Mann, 1977). In the health care area, many decisions entail a high degree of decisional conflict. The more severe the anticipated losses for each of the available alternatives, the greater the stress engendered by decisional conflict. Janis and Mann (1977) describe five basic patterns of coping with such conflict, each of which is assumed to be associated with a specific set of antecedent conditions and a characteristic level of stress. These patterns were derived from an analysis of the research literature on how people react to emergency warnings and public health messages that urge protective action. The five coping patterns are (1) unconflicted persistence, (2) unconflicted change, (3) defensive avoidance, (4) hypervigilance, and (5) vigilance. While the first two patterns are occasionally adaptive in saving time and emotional wear and tear, they often lead to defective decision making if the person must make a vital choice. Similarly, defensive avoidance or hypervigilance may occasionally be adaptive, but they generally reduce one's chances of averting serious losses. According to Janis and Mann's empirical analysis, all four are regarded as defective patterns of decision making. The fifth pattern, vigilance, generally leads to decisions of the best quality when the person is in conflict, and thereby increases the likelihood of adherence.

According to Janis and Mann's analysis, the vigilance pattern occurs only when the following three conditions are present: (1) awareness of serious risks for whatever alternative is chosen; (2) hope of finding a better alternative; and (3) belief that there is adequate time to search and deliberate before the decision is reached. These three conditions appear to be essential for the psychological preparation needed to deal with postdecisional stress as well, especially in cases where adherence to a decision entails some degree of suffering.

In contrast to Janis and Mann's conflict model, rationalistic cognitive models of personal decision making have also been applied to health decisions. The most well known is the "subjective expected utility" model, which postulates that whenever people select a course of action, they do so in a fairly rational way by comparing the values and probabilities of the consequences that are expected to follow from each of the available alternatives (Edwards, 1954; Raiffa, 1968). As applied to making a vital, health-relevant decision, this model suggests that people first make the best possible estimate of the probability that each of the expected consequences will occur. Next, they evaluate the relative importance of each of the anticipated favorable and unfavorable consequences, which represent their expected utility value from the point of view of the decision maker. The health belief model is essentially a subjective expected utility model, and correlational evidence from several studies provides partial support for its ability to describe how people decide whether or not to adhere to medical recommendations (Becker, 1976; Becker et al., 1977). The model does not, however, account for lengthy maladaptive delays in decisions to seek medical assistance among patients who experience symptoms relevant to a variety of diseases (Hackett & Cassem, 1975). Ignorance does not account for the majority of instances of procrastination. Rather, these behaviors seem like efforts to ward off anxiety by avoiding thinking about threatening cues. Conflict models seem better able to handle maladaptive patterns of coping with threat than rational decision-making models.

Information-processing theories suggest that adherence may be increased by better assessment and manipulation of the nature of the information constituting patients' beliefs about the determinants of their health and illness. It is also hypothesized that attentional processes and the demands made upon them shift over the course of treatment, which may have striking effects on adherence (Kristeller & Rodin, 1984).

According to Kristeller and Rodin (1984), in the early phases of treatment, patients should be helped to attend to advice in the face of high uncertainty and identify the symptoms of the disorder more clearly. Clinicians must elicit and modify any health schemas that may interfere with the processing of relevant cues. For example, the anxious patient might benefit from some type of relaxation training, in order to increase attention. Systematic desensitization has been used to treat "blood" phobics so that they could tolerate standard medical procedures (Connolly, Hallam, & Marks, 1976). These individuals are incapable of attending even briefly to the medical procedure itself without being flooded by an overwhelming parasympathetic response.

Care must be taken that information be rephrased

in nontechnical vocabulary and should be unambiguous (Blackwell, 1979); the necessary information should be repeated on different occasions, and the patient should be asked to demonstrate, formally or informally, a sufficient level of comprehension. For example, surgeons have tested patients on the information contained in the consent form for intestinal bypass surgery for weight reduction before being willing to perform the surgical procedure (Stellar & Rodin, 1980).

It is not surprising that investigators have found that patients who were able to recall the information about their illness that their physicians had given them had lower error rates in following recommendations (Hulka, Cassel, Kupper, & Burdette, 1976). This may explain their findings that adherence drops off sharply as the complexity of the treatment regimen increases. It is also noteworthy that studies specifically assessing understanding suggest that well over half the patients tested misunderstood their physician's instructions (Svarstad, 1976). Stone (1979) highlights an important point regarding the type of information that is being communicated. While it seems clear that knowledge about the prescribed regimen—what to do—increases adherence, it is less certain that knowledge about the illness per se, or the rationale for the regimen, does so (Kasl, 1975; Haynes, 1976; Matthews & Hingson, 1977). This suggestion and its implications merit further investigation.

Attention to new information may also be improved by highlighting what is important. Restricted environmental stimulation training (REST) is an unusual approach developed by Suedfeld (1980) that successfully increases vigilance and adherence. Self-monitoring, a mainstay of most behavioral therapies, can be thought of as a procedure that increases the client's focus of attention on problem cues and behaviors that interfere wtih adherence. Biofeedback is a type of specialized self-monitoring; normally silent physiological signals are amplified so that the individual can become aware of them. Although biofeedback is usually utilized as a direct treatment technique, this increased awareness may also serve to focus the patient's attention on vague or subliminal symptoms. Baile and Engel (1978) have used heart-rate monitoring for cardiac rehabilitation in this manner.

The work of Beck (1976), Goldfried (1979),

Kanfer and Seidner (1973), Mahoney (1974), and Meichenbaum (1977) all reflect a growing appreciation for the role of information-processing variables in psychotherapeutic procedures. An integration of perspectives of cognitive therapy with the work on information-processing variables in adherence to health-relevant decisions may prove to be quite fruitful.

Power in the Patient–Practitioner Dyad

Theories of social influence have focused on the different types of power available to physicians and therapists to increase the likelihood of adherence to therapeutic regimens. It is hypothesized that describing and explaining bases of power may provide clearer intervention strategies. An individual's power is his or her ability to shape another's behavior, that is, his or her potential influence (French & Raven, 1959). There are several sources of power that allow authority figures such as physicians and therapists to exert social influence over their patients; fewer sources may be available to patients. French and Raven (1959) have identified six sources of power: (1) expert power, (2) coercive power, (3) reward power, (4) legitimate power, (5) informational influence, and (6) referent power.

Expert and legitimate power. The availability of expert and legitimate power in the patient–practitioner relationship is the most obvious. They are based, respectively, on the professional's genuine skill and superior knowledge, and on the legitimacy of the professional role, which carries with it the right to exert influence. These bases of power are dependent upon the influencing agent, but do not rely on direct surveillance for their effectiveness.

Health care often begins when the patient has a problem that is brought to the expert. According to Stone (1979), this is generally reformulated by the expert after examining the symptoms and giving and analyzing tests. Throughout this diagnosis period, the clinician is "in charge" of the problem-solving process by virtue of expertise and legitimacy and concentrates on the aspects of the problem for which his or her legitimacy and expertise are most relevant. But physicians and psychotherapists using expert or legitimate power, by virtue of their training and role, often exclude from consideration other aspects of the patient's life situation such as work commitments or child care that may be critical determinants of the patient's ability to carry out subsequent recommendations (Innes, 1977). As Stone (1979) points out, the expert often does not know and fails to inquire about the meaning to the patient of such consequences as time lost from work, impairment of sexual function, and embarassment from public (or even private) display of therapeutic devices.

Reward and coercive power. The interpersonal context of the patient–practitioner interaction provides considerable opportunity for the professional to use coercive and reward power. Coercive power stems from the ability of the influencing agent to mediate punishment, and reward power from his or her ability to mediate rewards. Coercive and reward power generally require surveillance to be effective. Praise, warmth, time, and availability are but a few of the tokens of the practitioner's esteem that he or she can convey or withhold, contingent on the patient's performance. Some physicians give their favorite patients free drug samples or even reduced rates, so economic incentives also contribute to the bases of their reward power. Patients seeking these tangible or intangible rewards may consciously engage in "good-patient behavior," often at great personal cost to their health and well-being (Lorber, 1975; Taylor, 1979).

Information power. Professionals also have considerable informational power at their disposal. Informational power derives from the intrinsic persuasiveness of the influencing message (Raven, 1965). The influence process here is based on real cognitive changes that emerge from the information per se and therefore, once these changes have taken place, they are independent of the continued power of the influencing agent.

The level of distress provoked by information has been considered an important component of the power of that information. Although a large number of relevant experiments have been reported, we cannot yet formulate any definitive rule about the intensity of emotional arousal that most clearly increased the effectiveness of information (see Janis, 1967, 1971; McGuire, 1968; Rogers & Mewborn, 1976). Some attitude-change experiments show less acceptance of precautionary health recommendations when very strong fear appeals are used in warning messages than when milder ones are used

(Janis & Terwilliger, 1962; Rogers & Thistlethwaite, 1970). Similar experiments, however, show a gain in effectiveness when strong threat appeals are used, and these experiments point to the facilitating effects of fear arousal (for example, Insko, Arkoff, & Insko, 1965; Leventhal, Singer, & Jones, 1965).

Changes in feelings of vulnerability to a threat and subsequent adoption of a recommended course of action apparently depend upon the relative strength of facilitating and interfering reactions, both of which are likely to be evoked whenever a warning by an authority arouses fear. Consequently, we cannot expect to discover any simple generalization applicable to all warnings about health that will tell us whether strong fear-arousing presentations that vividly depict the expected dangers or milder versions that merely allude to the threats will be more effective in general. Rather, we must expect the optimal level of fear arousal to vary for different types of threat, for different types of recommended action, and for different personalities.

Relevant information, at optimal levels of arousal, about the illness and treatments, if it is combined with realistic assurances, can function as stress inoculation to increase patients' adherence to difficult decisions (see Girodo, 1977; Janis, 1958; Janis & Mann, 1977; Meichenbaum, 1977). Preparatory information functions as a form of stress inoculation if it enables a person to increase his or her tolerance for postdecisional stress by developing effective reassurances and coping mechanisms.

Supporting evidence for the effectiveness of stress inoculation comes from a variety of controlled field experiments with people who decided to undergo surgery (Egbert, Battit, Welch, & Bartlett, 1964; Johnson, 1966; Schmidt, 1966; Schmitt & Woolridge, 1973; Vernon & Bigelow, 1974). These studies indicate that when physicians or nurses give preoperative information about the stresses of surgery and ways of coping with those stresses, adult patients show less postoperative distress and sometimes better recovery from surgery. Positive results on the value of stress inoculation have also been found in studies of childbirth (Breen, 1975; Levy & McGee, 1975) and noxious medical examinations requiring patients to swallow tubes (Johnson & Leventhal, 1974). Field experiments by Moran (1963) and Wolfer and Visitainer (1975) with children on pediatric surgery wards yielded similar results.

Informational power, if it is successful, has certain distinct advantages. It leads to independent change on the part of the patient, who can now readily see the basis for compliance, yet does not require surveillance; it is independent of the professional, and perhaps it also builds patients' self-esteem in that they now feel that they have some control through their own knowledge of their fate.

Referent power. Of all the sources of power, referent power is probably the least used in medical health care at the present time, although it is widely used in psychotherapy. Referent power is the social power that is based on the target's identification or desire for identification with the influencing agent. Persons have referent power for those who perceive them as likable, benevolent, admirable, and accepting and their motivating power derives from this source. This source of power is found largely in the socioemotional aspect of the patient–practitioner relationship.

There are several different ways that health care providers foster the type of relationship that results in their becoming significant reference persons for their patients or clients (Berscheid & Walster, 1969; Byrne, 1971; Janis, 1983; Levinger & Breedlove, 1966; Tedeschi, 1974). One way is to make salient the similarities between oneself and the patient, particularly with regard to beliefs, attitudes, and values. A second way is to talk and act in a manner that conveys a benevolent attitude toward the patient, and willingness to provide help out of a genuine sense of caring about the patient's welfare. Still another technique, which may overlap somewhat with the second way, is to be seen as accepting, which conveys to the patient that he or she is held in high regard as a worthwhile person despite whatever weaknesses and shortcomings might be apparent. Quite clearly, some clinicians cannot spend enough time with their patients to become referent individuals. But others, such as oncologists or psychotherapists, do see their patients for a longer period of time and therefore may make effective use of referent power.

It is clear that research needs to be directed to the conditions under which referent power and the other sources of power are effective sources of motivation in the relationship between health care professionals and their patients, and thereby promote adherence. Thus far there has been little systematic investigation of the bases of social power that are best suited for different types of patients, for different settings, and for different types of changes in behavior. It is possible, for example, that referent power is most effective when behavioral options are seen as available and controllable by the patient and when long-term adherence to medical regimens is desirable. Referent power may also be effective when patients are somewhat upset and need to have their anxiety reduced by an open and reassuring person before they can attend to and follow health-relevant measures. On the other hand, when patients are extremely anxious or depressed, their dependency needs may increase, making other sources of social power more effective.

There is certainly evidence that authorities who have expert and reward power can be effective, even when they do not enhance patient self-esteem (Janis, 1983). This can occur especially under conditions where the health care professional continually monitors the patient's behavior. Where constant monitoring is not possible or practical, however, the use of referent power to promote internalization of recommended actions may prove to be more successful. Expert, coercive, or reward power may also be more effective than referent power in situations where feelings of control are stress-inducing for the patient, especially when the individual believes that there are actions that he or she ought to be taking but is not able to initiate (Averill, 1973). Expert power may be especially advantageous in those instances where the patient would suffer from making futile attempts to control health-relevant processes or accept responsibility for health-relevant outcomes that are uncontrollable. But these possible generalizations are speculations that require systematic investigation.

BEHAVIORAL MEDICINE AND HEALTH PSYCHOLOGY: THE FUTURE

The use of psychological procedures in the management of medical problems and the burgeoning interest in understanding health-promoting and health-damaging behaviors are the culmination of various developments in psychology and medicine over several decades (Matarazzo, 1984; Miller, 1981, 1983). Assuming that these trends are sustained, behavioral medicine and health psychology will continue to be characterized by their ability to assimilate different disciplines and perspectives in the service of these objectives. By way of illustration, two such developments will be discussed briefly here: (1) the integration of biological and behavioral research in behavioral medicine, and (2) the adaptation of recent findings in social psychology to clinical problems in health psychology.

Stress and Smoking: Pathophysiological and Biobehavioral Interactions

In the section on behavioral medicine, the discussion on stress emphasized pathophysiological processes in heart disease and cancer, whereas that on smoking focused on biobehavioral reinforcement mechanisms. Here we shall explore the reciprocity between stress and smoking, examining how components of the response to stress may potentiate some of the reinforcing consequences of smoking, which in turn exacerbate the impact of stress. While the ideas that follow are admittedly speculative, inquiries into the nature of interactions between pathophysiological and biobehavioral mechanisms are useful at this time as they are testable with present research techniques and they point the way toward broader conceptualizations in behavioral medicine.

As has been mentioned, the initial response to an acute stressor is a homeostatically protected stimulation of metabolic, neuronal, inflammatory, and immune activity mediated, in part, by increased catecholamine levels. With chronic or severe stress, however, the pituitary adrenocortical system is also activated, and endogenous opioids such as beta-endorphin and glucocorticoids such as cortisol are released. According to recent theory (Munck, Guyre, & Holbrook, 1984), stress-induced increases in glucocorticoid levels function not to protect against the source of stress itself (as was originally hypothesized by Selye), but rather to set homeostatic limits on the primary defense mechanisms for stress. The secondary response to stress is sufficiently delayed in relation to the initial stress response to allow appropriate defense mechanisms to become activated. Once primary catecholamine defense reactions have dealt with a stress-induced disturbance and the glucocorticoids have subsequently suppressed these reactions, activity of the pituitary–adrenocortical axis is reduced through a negative feedback process (Vernikos-Danellis & Heyback, 1980).

These cybernetic mechanisms have important implications for the understanding of stress and coping. For example, severe depression is often accompanied by hypersecretion of cortisol (Mason, 1968), which is usually resistant to feedback suppression from the administration of dexamethasone, a potent synthetic corticosteroid (Sachar, 1981). It is believed that the reason for the lack of feedback suppression by corticosteroid administration is that functional depletion of central norepinephrine in depression results in loss of inhibitory control over corticotropin releasing factor (by norepinephrine), leading to hypersecretion of ACTH and cortisol (Sachar, 1981). Drugs and other treatments that increase the amount of functional norepinephrine available in the brain have been shown to cause behavioral activation and to counteract depression, while those that reduce central norepinephrine produce sedation and depression (Schildkraut & Kety, 1967). The critical link to stress and coping is provided by the demonstration that active coping responses, such as escape from electric shock or even fighting in rats, increase central norepinephrine levels and decrease plasma corticosteroids, whereas inescapable shock (the "learned helplessness" procedure) or even sustained physical exertion has the opposite effect (Barchas & Freedman, 1963; Weiss, 1971; Weiss, Stone, & Harrell, 1970).

In a review of the phenomenon, Miller (1980) observed that these mechanisms may have evolved because of their adaptive value. He proposed that the depressive effects of a lower level of brain norepinephrine induced by failure and helplessness might have the value of saving the individual from wasting energy by continual striving in a hopeless situation. On the obverse side, the elating effects of a higher level of brain norepineprine might have the value of increasing activity in situations where it might lead to success. But, according to Miller, biochemical overactivity of the depletion-depressive mechanism and/or an unusually severe situation in which coping responses are not available may ultimately contribute to a depletion of norepinephrine, producing an emotional depression that reduces the probability of successful coping, leading to failure and further depletion of norepinephrine, and so on in a vicious circle.

The crucial role of brain norepinephrine was demonstrated in a series of experiments with rats. Weiss and Glazer (1975) found that stressors, such as a single series of inescapable shocks or a session that involved extended swimming in cold water, depleted brain norepinephrine and interfered with subsequent shock-avoidance behavior. Administration of a drug that increased central norepinephrine levels (pargyline, a monoamine oxidase inhibitor) was found to counteract the effects of prior stress, and pretreatment with a drug that depleted norepinephrine (tetrabenazine) produced aftereffects that were indistinguishable from those of a single stress pretreatment (Glazer, Weiss, Pohorecky, & Miller, 1975).

Weiss and his colleagues (see Miller, 1980) hypothesized that if the effects of a single stress exposure were achieved via depletion of norepinephrine (and possibly dopamine), repeated daily exposure to stress should increase the activity of tyrosine hydroxylase, an important enzyme in the synthesis of norepinephrine. In several experiments, they demonstrated that rats "toughened" by prior exposure to a daily series of inescapable shocks exhibited a higher level of tyrosine hydroxylase activity, less depletion of brain norepinephrine, less interference with subsequent shock-avoidance learning, and less cortiscosteroid secretion, compared with rats that had received only one day of inescapable shock exposure. Repeated daily exposure to a drug that also decreased central norepinephrine levels produced similar improvements in resistance to stress. While these experiments demonstrated that prior daily exposure to stress could build up physical and behavioral tolerance to stress, the investigators conceded that the mechanisms were not well understood and that the contribution of several important parameters was still largely unexplored: For example, if prior exposures to stress were spaced too closely, their effects might be so pronounced that instead of increasing tolerance to stress, they would have the effect of overwhelming homeostatic defenses. Conversely, if stress exposures came too far apart, their stimulating value might be dissipated by the passage of time, and no increase in tolerance to stress would be derived.

The effects of vigorous physical exercise are similar to those of the stressors mentioned above (Carr & Fishman, 1985). Furthermore, a mechanism for a possible interaction between exercise and smoking has been suggested by observations of increased norepinephrine turnover (and beta-endorphin release) following cigarette smoking. Some of the similarities and differences between the two habits can now be examined more closely. During sustained aerobic exercise and vigorous muscular activity in trained and untrained human subjects, peripheral catecholamine levels have been shown to rise and then subside at termination (Carr & Fishman, 1985). Using animals, recent experiments involving radio-labeled precursors and related techniques have demonstrated that normal levels of central norepinephrine are maintained during exercise because their synthesis as well as turnover is stimulated by physical activity (Ransford, 1982). These findings suggest that regular, daily exercise might provide increased stress tolerance in a manner analogous to the "toughening" (repeated stress) procedure described by Miller (1980). Some corroboration of the stress-protecting effects of regular exercise is provided by the observation that well-trained athletes show *decreased* cortisol output (using pretraining levels as baseline) during moderate exercise (Tharp, 1975).

The initial effects of smoking a cigarette, with respect to catecholamines, seem to be similar to those of exercise. Smoking causes peripheral norepinephrine and epinephrine levels to rise (Jarvik, 1979); nicotine administration stimulates central norepinephrine and dopamine release (Westfall, 1974) and increases the turnover of these neurochemicals in key brain areas, resulting in central depletion when sustained (Andersson et al., 1982). The crucial difference between the two habits seems to be that the smoker keeps stimulating catecholamine activity by lighting up every half hour or so, and as a consequence may elevate peripheral catecholamine levels out of proportion to their homeostatic, protective function. The regular exerciser, on the other hand, maintains normal catecholamine levels after athletic activity but has achieved an improved ability to synthesize and break down catecholamines, thereby enhancing protection against the stressors of daily living. Both habits can be seen as coping responses, but smoking is clearly maladaptive.

Although artificially stimulating central catecholamine activity and neuropeptide release by inhaling nicotine in smoke seems to be highly reinforcing to the smoker—especially under anxiety-provoking or stressful conditions (Pomerleau & Pomerleau, 1984b)—the resulting repeated elevation of peripheral catecholamines seems to be harmful. At special

risk may be smokers classified as Type A, whose catecholamine reactivity to stressors such as performance demands or competitive challenges has been noted; not only do people classified as Type A seem to smoke more than those classified as Type B (Jenkins, Rosenman, & Zyzanski, 1968), but the Type A behavior pattern and smoking constitute independent but multiplicative risk factors for coronary heart disease (Glass, 1977; Jenkins, Zyzanski, & Rosenman, 1976). The mechanisms by which smoking contributes to heart disease are still not well understood. The rate of myocardial infarction in smokers, however, is related to the nicotine content of cigarettes smoked, suggesting that nicotine-stimulated catecholamine enhancement is the pathophysiological agent rather than carbon monoxide or other smoke constituents (Hill & Wynder, 1974). Evidence is accumulating that stimulation of the sympathetic adrenomedullary system by nicotine contributes to atherosclerosis, increased blood clotting, and cardiac arrhythmias (Su, 1982). Thus, for smokers—especially smokers who exhibit the Type A behavior pattern—stress and smoking comprise a positive feedback process with negative health implications. The demonstration of how biobehavioral reinforcement mechanisms in smoking contribute to the pathophysiology of heart disease constitutes a major challenge and opportunity for behavioral medicine in the 1980s.

Control and Adherence: Social Psychology Research on Clinical Problems

An interesting bridge occurring within health psychology (as evidenced by the material in this chapter) is the integration of theories and problems in social and clinical psychology (described at greater length in Chapter 3). The important role of control-relevant processes for understanding the problem of adherence will be described as an example, although many other relationships exist. Cross-fertilization of the theories and domains of the social and clinical fields offers great promise for furthering the understanding of health promotion and disease prevention as well as the determinants of treatment and the course of illness.

Although there has been a recent trend toward increased patient participation in all aspects of health care, including preventive activities, the effort has derived more from a growing interest in consumer advocacy than from any theory of human behavior.

The literature on the construct of control provides a relevant framework and may be especially useful for explaining adherence to health promotion or treatment regimens. Many of the problems of nonadherence arise in different phases of health care because events and behaviors have an impact on patients' sense of control. In the analysis below, we will proceed sequentially along the course of treatment, as a conceptual exercise, to point out the important role of perceived control throughout the health care process.

We have described how the very act of seeking help may diminish patients' sense of control, thus lessening confidence in the ability to regulate responses and to produce desired outcomes. Nonadherence may, in part, derive from patients' sense of helplessness and lack of control produced by the health problem itself. Nonetheless, patients do enter treatment with certain expectations regarding the nature of the care, which if not addressed adequately, appear to jeopardize adherence (Benarde & Mayerson, 1978; Eisenthal et al., 1979; Hayes-Bautista, 1976; Kasl, 1975; Kleinman, Eisenberg, & Good, 1978). The theory of control argues that this occurs because of the effects of such inattention on patients' sense of self-efficacy, resulting in further perceived inability and unwillingness to follow the prescribed regimen.

Expectancies that patients have about what will take place in treatment are likely to provide them with a sense of predictability about the health care interaction. It follows from the literature reviewed earlier that when these expectancies are not met or aspects of the situation arise that were not anticipated, the resultant feelings of unpredictability may have a negative effect on the likelihood of adherence.

The problems of unclear and inaccurate expectancies concerning what will take place and how one is expected to behave are especially prominent in psychotherapy (see Chapter 6). In medical treatment as well, it has been advocated that as a first step, patients should be provided with a clear statement about what they can expect from the practitioner and what is expected of them (Deeds et al., 1979; Schorr & Rodin, 1982). We believe these benefits accrue because clear and confirmed expectancies greatly increase patients' sense of control and self-efficacy.

It has been proposed that adherence also increases when patients are given the opportunity to express their point of view in the health care transaction, for example, regarding goals for the interaction and opinions about the nature of their problem and how it should be handled (e.g., Brody, 1980; Eisenthal et al., 1979; Kasl, 1975; Kleinman et al., 1978). Negotiation in the professional–patient interaction also leads to more satisfaction and better adherence (e.g., Benarde & Mayerson, 1978; Kleinman et al., 1978). Control theorists hypothesize that patients' feelings of control are enhanced under these conditions. If patients leave the health care situation feeling that the treatment is not entirely appropriate because their beliefs and goals have not been included, then they may modify the treatment by combining the professional's recommendations with their own view of how the problem should be handled, for example, using folk remedies (Hayes-Bautista, 1976) to increase their feeling of being in control of the situation. Evidence indicating positive consequences from negotiation has begun to accumulate (e.g., Eisenthal et al., 1979; Hefferin, 1979).

At some point in treatment, the health care process calls for patient involvement in the implementation of the treatment plan. For some health care problems, implementation rests primarily in the hands of the professional, for instance, in performing surgery. But even surgical patients must begin to assume some responsibility for the implementation of health care decisions later on. For many situations, implementation of health care decisions rests primarily with the patient, for example, in the management of chronic illnesses such as diabetes. For control over the implementation of treatment to have beneficial effects, patients must believe that a given course of action will lead to desirable health outcomes, that a response–outcome contingency exists, and that they personally have the skills to carry out the course of action effectively, that is, that they have self-efficacy. In other words, even if patients believe that a given course of action is effective in leading to positive health outcomes, they may still feel out of control because they perceive themselves as not having the ability or skills necessary to carry out the required treatment. Because low feelings of self-efficacy seem to lead to diminished persistence in coping with stressful situations (e.g., Bandura et al., 1980), people who believe that they may not be successful in carrying out a course of therapy will be less likely to adhere. Thus, in order for a person's sense of control to be enhanced, with benefits for health outcomes, it is necessary for practitioners to bolster *both* belief in the effectiveness of the treatment that is decided upon and the feeling that the practitioner has the skills to carry out the treatment.

For adherence to be maintained over a sustained period of time, it is necessary that patients internalize the health care program that the practitioner and patient have worked out (Rodin & Janis, 1979). If internalization occurs, health care behaviors become an integral part of the person's life and the attitudes and beliefs underlying the program are incorporated into the person's belief system. Once internalization occurs, external inducements for adhering to the program are no longer required; as a result, feelings of control may be further enhanced. Internalization is especially important to ensure that health care behaviors continue, if necessary, after the relationship with the health care practitioner is terminated or made less frequent. Feelings of self-efficacy, in turn, may be necessary for maintenance of treatment benefits. In addition, people have been shown to be more likely to internalize attitudes and behaviors when external inducements are not present (e.g., Lepper, Greene, & Nisbett, 1976).

In order to enhance maintenance of the changes brought about in treatment, practitioners should foster two types of cognitions (Cameron, 1978), each of which should promote feelings of control, hypothetically. First, patients should see themselves as having learned new coping skills for dealing with health or psychological concerns, skills that will not disappear when contact with the professional is made less frequent or terminated. Second, patients should give credit to themselves as change agents rather than to external factors (Rodin, 1978). For example, patients who have brought their hypertension under control should be encouraged to attribute the improvement to their own efforts to cope with the disorder, for instance, by making changes in the daily living that include remembering to take medications, exercising, and changing dietary habits.

Through stress inoculation procedures, patients should be prepared to handle difficulties and setbacks that arise once treatment is terminated or made less frequent. For example, patients should be prepared to handle backsliding (Marlatt, 1978). If temporary failure to maintain the health changes

is seen as evidence that all their health care gains are lost, then adherence will be threatened. If patients are taught to see backsliding as a signal to reexert control by reactivating the coping skills they have learned, however, then health care gains are likely to be maintained.

The task of health care delivery will probably be accomplished more effectively if the patient is involved as fully as possible at every stage of the treatment. The extent and the conditions under which the patient's perceived control is beneficial merit further consideration, since different sources of power (as used by both the physician and the patient) may have quite different effects on control as perceived by the patient, affecting health outcomes. Millman (1982) suggests that too extensive a belief in personal control by patients may foster erroneous attributions of responsibility for having caused health-related problems, leading to guilt and, perhaps, poorer self-care. As noted by Brickman et al. (1982), however, one can conceptually separate attributions of blame for having caused one's health problems from those of responsibility for some aspects of the solution. Generalizing from this analysis, it is possible to see how someone entering the health care system could take credit for causing the health problem and for its solution, for only one of these and not the other, or for neither. Considering which of these combinations of patient responsibility and control is beneficial to the patient and under what conditions is an intriguing research question. Our own work has suggested that it may be quite important for patients to feel responsible for at least some aspects of the solution to their health problems, but not for their cause (Rodin, 1982).

CONCLUSION

The foregoing discussion of behavioral medicine and health psychology has emphasized four areas—stress, smoking, control, and adherence. As noted in the introduction, there is considerable overlap between behavioral medicine and health psychology. For example, stress is also a major theme in health psychology, and adherence is a critical problem for behavioral medicine. There are, however, important distinctions. Behavioral medicine, as currently practiced, is an interdisciplinary field concerned with interventions using behavioral and related therapies for medical problems as well as with biobehavioral research on health and disease. Stress and smoking were chosen in order to demonstrate the interplay of biological and behavioral variables. Health psychology, on the other hand, focuses on psychology as a discipline and is concerned with understanding health-promoting and health-damaging behaviors, employing the various psychological methodologies and technologies available. Control and adherence provide excellent examples of psychological problems with important theoretical and practical implications for health.

We expect that the two fields will continue to be shaped by environmental contingencies similar to the ones that led to their development. Behavioral medicine, for instance, has been influenced by the need to modify health-related behaviors in a clinically useful way and by the desirability of developing a research tradition that is compatible with the biomedical model. Insistence on well-defined treatment procedures and on accountability in controlled clinical trials will continue to provide the basis for improved therapeutic efficacy. Behavioral medicine still has a way to go before the processes that underlie the interactions between behavior and health are as well understood as the homeostatic and pathophysiological mechanisms whose clarification has contributed to the successes of modern medicine. A critical task for behavioral medicine is the conduct of research on biobehavioral mechanisms. An emphasis on the elucidation of such processes will make possible a shift from correlational and descriptive studies to a functional analysis of behavioral and biological variables in health and disease.

Behavioral medicine has responded to the challenge of having to establish itself in the health care system. Health psychology, with its more academic orientation and somewhat lower public visibility, enjoys greater freedom to concentrate on projects with long-term benefits. Accordingly, health psychology can address itself to the enterprise of integrating psychological, sociological, epidemiological, and medical information as it applies to health-promoting and health-damaging behaviors. Future growth and development will depend on its ability to exploit this opportunity.

REFERENCES

Ader, R. (Ed.). (1981). *Psychoneuroimmunology.* New York: Academic Press.

Ader, R., & Cohen, N. (1981). Conditional immunopharmacologic responses. In R. Ader (Ed.), *Psychoneuroimmunology* (pp. 281–319). New York: Academic Press.

Adler, A. (1929). *The science of living.* New York: Greenberg.

Ainslie, G. (1975). Specious reward: A behavioral theory of impulsiveness and impulse control. *Psychological Bulletin, 82,* 463–496.

Alexander, F. G. (1950). *Psychosomatic medicine, its principles and applications.* New York: Norton.

Amir, S., Brown, Z. W., & Amit, Z. (1980). The role of endorphins in stress: Evidence and speculations. *Neuroscience and Biobehavioral Reviews, 4,* 77–86.

Andersson, K. (1975). Effects of cigarette smoking on learning and retention. *Psychopharmacologia, 41,* 1–5.

Andersson, K., Fuxe, P., Eneroth, P., & Agnati, L. F. (1982). Effects of acute central and peripheral administration of nicotine on hypothalamic catecholamine nerve terminal systems and on the secretion of adenohypophyseal hormones in the male rat. *Medical Biology, 60,* 90–111.

Anisman, H., & Zacharko, R. M. (1984). Stress and neoplasia: Speculations and caveats. *Behavioral Medicine Update, 5* (2 & 3), 27–35.

APA Task Force on Health Research. (1976). Contributions of psychology to health research: Patterns, problems, potentials. *American Psychologist, 31,* 263–274.

Ashton, N., & Stepney, R. (1982). *Smoking: Psychology and pharmacology.* New York: Tavistock.

Averill, R. (1973). Personal control over aversive stimuli and its relationship to stress. *Psychological Bulletin, 80,* 286–303.

Baekeland, F., & Lundwall, L. (1975). Dropping out of treatment: A critical review. *Psychological Bulletin, 82,* 738–783.

Baile, W. F., & Engel, B. T. (1978). A behavioral strategy for promoting treatment compliance following myocardial infarction. *Psychosomatic Medicine, 40,* 413–419.

Balfour, D. J. K. (1982). The effects of nicotine on brain–neurotransmitter systems. *Pharmaceutical Therapeutics, 16,* 269–282.

Bandura, A. (1969). *Principles of behavior modification.* New York: Holt, Rinehart & Winston.

Bandura, A., Adams, N. E., Hardy, A. B., & Howells, G. N. (1980). Tests of the generality of self-efficacy theory. *Cognitive Therapy and Research, 4,* 39–66.

Barchas, J. D., & Freedman, D. X. (1963). Brain amines: Response to physiological stress. *Biochemistry and Pharmacology, 12,* 1232–1235.

Bartrop, R. W., Luckhurst, E., Lazarus, L., Kiloh, L. G., & Penny, R. (1977). Depressed lymphocyte function after bereavement. *The Lancet,* April 16, 834–836.

Battig, K. (1980). The smoking habit and psychopharmacological effects of nicotine. *Activitas Nervosa Superior, 22,* 274–288.

Baum, A., Fleming, R., & Singer, S. (1982). Stress at Three Mile Island: Applying psychological impact analysis. In L. Bickman (Ed.), *Applied social psychology annual.* Beverly Hills: Sage.

Beck, A. T. (1976). *Cognitive therapy and the emotional disorders.* New York: International Universities Press.

Becker, M. H. (1976). Sociobehavioral determinants of

compliance. In D. L. Sackett & R. B. Haynes (Eds.), *Compliance with therapeutic regimens.* Baltimore, Johns Hopkins Press.

Becker, M. H., Haefner, D.P., Kasl, S. V., Kirscht, J. P., Maiman, L. A., & Rosenstock, I. M. (1977). Selected psychosocial models and correlates of individual health-related behaviors. *Medical Care, 156,* 27–48.

Benarde, M. A. & Mayerson, E. W. (1978). Patient–physician negotiation. *Journal of the American Medical Association, 239,* 1413–1415.

Berg, A. O., & LoGerfo, J. P. (1979). Potential effect of self-care algorithms on the number of physician visits. *New England Journal of Medicine, 300,* 535–537.

Bernstein, D. (1969). Modification of smoking behavior: An evaluation review. *Psychological Bulletin, 71,* 418–440.

Bernstein, D., & Glasgow, R. (1979). Smoking. In O. F. Pomerleau & J. P. Brady (Eds.), *Behavioral medicine: Theory and practice* (pp. 233–253). Baltimore, Williams & Wilkins.

Berscheid, E., & Walster, E. H. (1969). *Interpersonal attraction.* Reading, MA: Addison-Wesley.

Bertolini, A., & Gessa, G. L. (1981). Behavioral effects of ACTH and MSH peptides. *Journal of Endocrinological Investigation, 4,* 241–251.

Birk, L. (Ed.) (1973). *Biofeedback: Behavioral medicine.* New York: Grune & Stratton.

Blackwell, B. (1979). Treatment adherence: A contemporary overview. *Psychosomatics, 20,* 27–35.

Bohus, B., Kovacs, G.L., & de Wied, D. (1978). Oxytocin, vasopressin and memory: Opposite effect on consolidation and retrieval processes. *Brain Research, 157,* 414–417.

Borysenko, M., & Borysenko, J. (1982). Stress, behavior, and immunity: Animal models and mediating mechanisms. *General Hospital Psychiatry, 4,* 59–67.

Bowers, K. S. (1968). Pain, anxiety, and perceived control. *Journal of Consulting and Clinical Psychology, 32,* 596–602.

Breen, D. (1975). *The birth of a first child: Towards an understanding of femininity.* London: Tavistock.

Brickman, P., Rabinowitz, V., Karuza, J., Coates, E., Cohn, E., & Kidder, L. (1982). Models of helping and coping. *American Psychologist, 37,* 368–384.

Brody, D. S. (1980). Psychological distress and hypertension control. *Journal of Human Stress, 6,* 2–6.

Byrne, D. (1971). *The attraction paradigm.* New York: Academic Press.

Califano, J. A. (Ed.), (1979). *Smoking and health: A report of the Surgeon General.* Washington, DC: U.S. Department of Health, Education, and Welfare (DHEW Publication No. PHS 79-50066).

Cameron, R. (1978). The clinical implementation of behavior change techniques: A cognitively oriented conceptualization of therapeutic "compliance" and "resistance." In J. P. Foreyt & D. P. Rathjen (Eds.), *Cognitive behavior therapy: Research and application.* New York: Plenum.

Cameron, R., & Meichenbaum, D. (1982). The nature of effective coping and the treatment of stress related problems: A cognitive-behavioral perspective. In L. Goldberger & S. Breznitz (Eds.), *Handbook of stress: Theoretical and clinical aspects* (pp. 695–710). New York: Free Press.

Cannon, W. B. (1932). *The wisdom of the body.* New York: Norton.

Carr, D. B., & Fishman, S. M. (1985). Exercise and the endogenous opioids. In K. Fotherby & S. Pal (Eds.), *Exercise endocrinology.* New York: Walter De Gruyter.

Carruthers, M. (1976). Modification of the noradrenaline related effects of smoking by beta-blockade. *Psychological Medicine, 6,* 251–256.

Carver, C. S. (1980). Perceived coercion, resistance to persuasion, and the Type A behavior pattern. *Journal of Research in Personality, 19,* 467–481.

Ciaranello, R., Lipton, M., Barchas, J., Barchas, P. R., Bonica, J., Ferrario, C., Levine, S., & Stein, M. (1982). In G. R. Elliott & C. Eisdorfer (Eds.), *Stress and human health* (pp. 189–254), New York: Springer.

Claman, H. N. (1972). Corticosteroids and lymphoid cells. *New England Journal of Medicine, 287,* 388–397.

Connolly, J., Hallam, R. S., & Marks, J. M. (1976). Selective association of fainting with blood-injury-illness fear. *Behavior Therapy, 8,* 8–13.

Coyne, J. C., & Widiger, T. A. (1978). Toward a participatory model of psychotherapy. *Professional Psychology, 9,* 700–710.

Cromwell, R. L., Butterfield, E. C., Brayfield, F. M., & Curry, J. J. (1977). *Acute myocardial infarction: Reaction and recovery.* St. Louis: Mosby.

Deeds, S. G., Bernheimer, E., McCombs, N. H., McKenney, J. M., Richardson, D. W., & Fink, J. W. (1979). Patient behavior for blood pressure control: Guidelines for professionals. *Journal of the American Medical Association, 241,* 2534–2537.

Dembroski, T. M., MacDougall, J. M., Herd, J. A., & Shields, J. L. (1979). Effects of level of challenge on pressor and heart rate response in Type A and B subjects. *Journal of Applied Social Psychology, 9,* 209–228.

Dembroski, T. M., MacDougall, J. M., Shields, J. L., Petito, J., & Lushene, R. (1978). Components of the Type A coronary-prone behavior pattern and cardiovascular responses to psychomotor challenge. *Journal of Behavioral Medicine, 1,* 159–176.

Derogatis, L. R., Abeloff, M. D., & Melisaratos, N. (1979). Psychological coping mechanisms and survival time in metastatic breast cancer. *Journal of the American Medical Association, 242,* 1504–1508.

Dohrenwend, B. P. (1974). Problems in defining and sampling the relevant populations of stressful life events. In B. S. Dohrenwend & B. P. Dohrenwend (Eds.), *Stressful life events: Their nature and effects.* New York: Wiley.

Dohrenwend, B. S. (1973). Life events as stressors: A methodological inquiry. *Journal of Health and Social Behavior, 14,* 167–175.

Edwards, W. (1954). The theory of decision making. *Psychological Bulletin, 51,* 380–417.

Egbert, L. D., Battit, G. E., Welch, C.E., & Bartlett, M. K. (1964). Reduction of postoperative pain by encouragement and instruction of patients. *New England Journal of Medicine, 270,* 825–827.

Eisenthal, S., Emery, R., Lazare, A., & Udin, H. (1979). "Adherence" and the negotiated approach to patienthood. *Archives of General Psychiatry, 36,* 393–398.

Ellendorf, F., & Parvizi, N. (1980). Role of extrahypothalamic centers in neuroendocrine integration. In M. Matta (Ed.), *The endocrine function of the brain* (pp. 297–327). New York: Raven.

Epstein, L., & Collins, F. (1977). The measurement of situational influences of smoking. *Addictive Behaviors, 2,* 47–54.

Farrell, P. A., Gates, W. K., Maksud, M. G., & Morgan, W. P. (1982). Increases in plasma beta-endorphin/beta-lipotropin immunoreactivity after treadmill running in humans. *Journal of Applied Physiology, 52,* 1245–1249.

Fauci, A. S. (1978). Mechanisms of the immunosuppressive and anti-inflammatory effects of glucocorticosteroids. *Journal of Immunopharmacology, 9,* 1–25.

Fertig, J. B., Pomerleau, O. F., & Sanders, B. (in press). Nicotine-produced antinociception in minimally deprived smokers and ex-smokers. *Addictive Behaviors.*

Fontana, A. F., Marcus, J. L., Noel, B., & Rakusin, J. M. (1972). Prehospitalization coping styles of psychiatric patients: The goal directedness of life events. *Journal of Nervous and Mental Disease, 155,* 311–321.

Fox, B. H. (1981). Psychosocial factors and the immune system in human cancer. In R. Ader (Ed.), *Psychoneuroimmunology* (pp. 103–157). New York: Academic Press.

Frankenhauser, M. (1975a). Experimental approaches to the study of catecholamines and emotion. In L. Levi (Ed.), *Emotions: Their parameters and measurement* (pp. 209–234). New York: Raven.

Frankenhauser, M. (1975b). Sympathetic-adrenomedullary activity, behaviour and the psychosocial environment. In P. H. Venables & M. M. Christie (Eds.), *Research in psychophysiology* (pp. 71–94). New York: Wiley.

Frankenhauser, M. (1976). The rate of peripheral catecholamines in adaptation to understimulation and overstimulation. In G. Serban (Ed.), *Psychopathology of human adaptation* (pp. 173–191). New York: Plenum.

French, J. R. P., Jr., & Raven, B. H. (1959). The bases of social power. In D. Cartwright (Ed.), *Studies in social power* (pp. 150–167). Ann Arbor: Institute for Social Research, University of Michigan.

Friedman, M., Byers, S.O., Diamant, J., & Rosenman, R. H. (1975). Plasma catecholamine response of coronary-prone subjects (Type A) to a specific challenge. *Metabolism, 4,* 205–210.

Friedman, M., & Rosenman, R. H. (1974). *Type A behavior and your heart.* New York: Knopf.

Gabrielsen, A. E., & Good, R. A. (1967). Chemical suppression of adaptative immunity. In F. J. Dixon, Jr., & J. H. Humphrey (Eds.), *Advances in immunology* (Vol. 6). New York: Academic Press.

Gatchel, R. J., & Proctor, J. D. (1976). Physiological correlates of learned helplessness in man. *Journal of Abnormal Psychology, 85,* 27–34.

Gelfand, S. (1964). The relationship of experimental pain tolerances to pain threshold. *Canadian Journal of Psychology, 18,* 36–42.

Geer, J. H. Davison, G. C., & Gatchel, R. I. (1970). Reduction of stress in humans through non-vertical perceived control of aversive stimulation. *Journal of Personality and Social Psychology, 16,* 731–738.

Gilbert, D. (1979). Paradoxical tranquilizing and emotional reducing effects of nicotine. *Psychological Bulletin, 86,* 643–661.

Girodo, M. (1977). Self-talk: Mechanisms in anxiety and stress management. In C. Spielberger & I. G. Sarason (Eds.), *Stress and anxiety* (Vol. 4). Washington, DC: Hemisphere.

Gisler, R. H. (1974). Stress and the hormonal regulation of the immune response in mice. *Psychotherapy and Psychosomatics, 23,* 197–208.

Glass, D. C. (1977). *Behavior patterns, stress, and coronary disease.* New York: Erlbaum.

Glass, D. C., Krakoff, L. R., Contrada, R., Hilton, W. E., Kehoe, K., Mannucci, E. G., Collins, C., Snow, B., & Elting, E. (1980). Effect of harassment and competition upon cardiovascular and catecholamine responses in Type A and B individuals. *Psychophysiology, 17,* 453–463.

Glass, D. C., & Singer, J. E. (1972). *Urban stress: Experiments on noise and social stressors.* New York: Academic Press.

Glazer, H. I., Weiss, J. M., Pohorecky, L. A., & Miller, N. E. (1975). Monoamines as mediators of avoidance–escape behavior. *Psychosomatic Medicine, 37,* 535–543.

Goldberger, L., & Breznitz, S. (Eds.). (1982). *Handbook of stress: Theoretical and clinical aspects.* New York: Free Press.

Goldfried, M. R. (1979). Anxiety reduction through cognitive-behavioral intervention. *Personality and Psychopathology,* BK# 10146, 117–152.

Golub, E. S. (1981). *The cellular basis of the immune response: An approach to immunobiology* (2nd ed.). Sunderland, MA: Sinauer Associates.

Gorzynski, J. G., Holland, J., Katz, J. L., Weiner, H., Zumoff, B., Fukushima, O., & Levin, J. (1980). Stability of ego defenses and endocrine responses in women prior to breast biopsy and ten years later. *Psychosomatic Medicine, 42,* 323–328.

Gray, J. A. (1982). *The neuropsychology of anxiety: An inquiry into the functions of the septo-hippocampal system.* New York: Oxford University Press.

Grunberg, N. E. (1982). The effects of nicotine and cigarette smoking on food consumption and taste preferences. *Addictive Behavior, 7,* 317–331.

Guyton, A. C. (1981). *Textbook of medical physiology* (6th ed.). Philadelphia: Saunders.

Hackett, T. P., & Cassem, N. H. (1975). Psychological management of the myocardial infarction patient. *Journal of Human Stress, 1,* 25–38.

Hall, G. H., & Turner, G. H. (1972). Effects of nicotine on the release of ^3H-noradrenaline from the hypothalamus. *Biochemical Pharmacology, 21,* 1829–1838.

Hall, N. R., & Goldstein, A. L. (1981). Neurotransmitters and the immune system. In R. Ader (Ed.), *Psychoneuroimmunology* (pp. 521–543). New York: Academic Press.

Hayes-Bautista, D. E. (1976). Modifying the treatment: Patient compliance, patient control and medical care. *Social Science and Medicine, 10,* 233–238.

Haynes, R. B. (1976). A critical review of the "determinants" of patient compliance with therapeutic regimens. In D. L. Sackett & R. B. Haynes (Eds.), *Compliance with therapeutic regimens.* Baltimore: Johns Hopkins University Press.

Haynes, R. B., Taylor, D. W., & Sackett, D. L. (Eds.).

(1979). *Compliance in health care*. Baltimore: Johns Hopkins University Press.

Hefferin, E. A. (1979). Health goal setting: Patient–nurse collaboration at Veterans Administration facilities. *Military Medicine, 144*, 814–822.

Henry, J., & Meehan, J. (1981). Psychosocial stimuli, physiological specificity and cardiovascular disease. In H. Weiner, M. A. Hofer, & A. J. Stunkard (Eds.), *Brain, behavior, and bodily disease* (pp. 305–335). New York: Raven.

Herd, J. A. (1981). Behavioral factors in the physiological mechanisms of cardiovascular disease. In S. M. Weiss, J. A. Herd, & B. H. Fox (Eds.), *Perspectives on behavioral medicine*. New York: Academic Press.

Hill, P., & Wynder, E. L. (1974). Smoking and cardiovascular disease. *American Heart Journal, 87*, 491–496.

Hiroto, D. S., & Seligman, M. E. P. (1975). Generality of learned helplessness in man. *Journal of Personality and Social Psychology, 31*, 311–327.

Hoffman, J. W., Benson, H., Arns, P. A., Stainbrook, G. L., Landsberg, L., Young, J. B., & Gill, A. (1982). Reduced sympathetic nervous system responsivity associated with the relaxation response. *Science, 215*, 190–192.

Holland, J. C., & Rowland, J. H. (1981). Psychiatric, psychosocial, and behavioral interventions in the treatment of cancer: An historical review. In S. M. Weiss, J. A. Herd, & B. N. Fox (Eds.), *Perspectives in behavioral medicine* (pp. 235–260). New York: Academic Press.

Holmes, T. H., & Rahe, R. H. (1967). The social readjustment rating scale. *Journal of Psychosomatic Research, 11*, 213–218.

Holroyd, K. A. (1979). Stress, coping, and the treatment of stress-related illness. In J. R. McNamara (Ed.), *Behavioral approaches to medicine: Application and analysis* (pp. 191–226). New York: Plenum.

Hulka, B. S., Cassel, J. C., Kupper, L. L., & Burdette, J. A. (1976). Communication, compliance, and concordance between physicians and patients with prescribed medications. *American Journal of Public Health, 66*, 847–853.

Hunt, W. A., Barnett, L. W., & Branch, L. G. (1971). Relapse rates in addiction programs. *Journal of Clinical Psychology, 27*, 455–456.

Hunt, W., & Bespalec, D. (1974). An evaluation of current methods of modifying smoking behavior. *Journal of Clinical Psychology, 30*, 431–438.

Hunt, W. A., & Matarazzo, J. D. (1978). Three years later: Recent developments in the experimental modification of smoking. *Journal of Abnormal and Social Psychology, 81*, 107–114.

Husain, M. K., Frantz, A. C., Ciarochi, F., & Robinson, A. G. (1975). Nicotine stimulated release of neurophysin and vasopressin in humans. *Journal of Clinical Endocrinology and Metabolism, 41*, 1113–1117.

Husaini, B. A., & Neff, J. A. (1980). Characteristics of life events and psychiatric impairment in rural communities. *Journal of Nervous and Mental Disorders, 168*, 159–166.

Hutchinson, R., & Emley, G. (1973). Effects of nicotine on avoidance, conditioned suppression and aggression response measures in animals and man. In W. Dunn (Ed.), *Smoking behavior: Motives and incentives* (pp. 171–196). Washington DC: Winston.

Innes, J. M. (1977). Does the professional know what the client wants? *Social Science and Medicine, 11*, 635–638.

Insko, C. A., Arkoff, A., & Insko, V. M. (1965). Effects of high and low fear arousing communications upon opinions toward smoking. *Journal of Experimental Social Psychology, 1*, 256–266.

Jacobs, S., & Myers, J. (1976). Recent life events and acute schizophrenic psychosis-controlled study. *Journal of Nervous and Mental Disorders, 162*, 75–87.

Jaffe, J., & Jarvik, M. (1978). Tobacco use and the tobacco use disorder. In M. Lipton, A. DiMascio, & K. Killam (Eds.), *Psychopharmacology: A generation of progress* (pp. 1665–1676). New York: Raven.

Janis, I. L. (1958). *Psychological stress: Psychoanalytic and behavioral studies of surgical patients*. New York: Wiley.

Janis, I. L. (1967). Effects of fear arousal on attitude change: Recent developments in theory and experimental research. In L. Berkowitz (Ed.), *Advances in experimental social psychology* (Vol. 3). New York: Academic Press.

Janis, I. L. (1971). *Stress and frustration*. New York: Harcourt, Brace, Jovanovich.

Janis, I. L. (1983). The role of social support in adherence to stressful decisions. *American Psychologist, 38*, 143–160.

Janis, I. L., & Mann, L. (1977). *Decision making: A psychological analysis of conflict, choice, and commitment*. New York: Free Press.

Janis, I. L., & Rodin, J. (1979). Attribution, control and decision making: Social psychology and health care. In G. C. Stone, F. Cohen, & N. E. Adler (Eds.), *Health psychology: A handbook*. San Francisco: Jossey-Bass.

Janis, I. L., & Terwilliger, R. (1962). An experimental study of psychological resistance to fear-arousing communications. *Journal of Abnormal and Social Psychology, 65*, 403–410.

Jarvik, M. (1979). Biological influences on cigarette smoking. In N. Krasnegor (Ed.), *The behavioral aspects of smoking* (NIDA Research Monograph 26) (pp. 7–45). Rockville, MD: National Institute on Drug Abuse.

Jemmott, J. B. & Locke, S. E. (1984). Psychosocial factors, immunologic mediation, and human susceptibility to disease: How much do we know? *Psychological Bulletin, 95*, 78–108.

Jenkins, C. D. (1971). Recent evidence supporting psychologic and social risk factors for coronary disease. *New England Journal of Medicine, 284*, 244–255.

Jenkins, C. D., Rosenman, R. H., & Zyzanski, S. J. (1968). Cigarette smoking: Its relationship to coronary heart disease and related risk factors in the Western collaborative group study. *Circulation, 38*, 1140–1155.

Jenkins, C. D., Zyzanski, S. J., & Rosenman, R. H. (1976). Risk of new myocardial infarction in middle-aged men with manifest coronary heart disease. *Circulation, 53*, 342–347.

Johnson, J. E. (1966). The influence of purposeful nurse–patient interaction on the patient's postoperative course. *A.N.A. Monography Series #2: Exploring Medical-Surgical Nursing Practice*. New York: A.N.A.

Johnson, J. E. (1975). Stress reduction through sensation information. In I. G. Sarason & C. D. Spielberger (Eds.), *Stress and anxiety* (Vol. 2). New York: Wiley.

Johnson, J. E., & Leventhal, H. (1974). Effects of accurate expectations and behavioral instructions on reactions during a noxious medical examination. *Journal of Personality and Social Psychology, 29,* 710–718.

Kanfer, F. H., & Seider, M. L. (1973). Self-control: Factors enhancing tolerance of noxious stimulation. *Journal of Personality and Social Psychology, 25,* 381–389.

Karras, A. (1982). Neurotransmitter and neuropeptide correlates of cigarette smoking. In W. B. Essman & L. Valzelli (Eds.), *Neuropharmacology: Clinical applications* (pp. 41–67). New York: Spectrum.

Karras, A., & Kane, J. (1980). Naloxone reduces cigarette smoking. *Life Sciences, 27,* 1541–1545.

Kasl, S. V. (1975). Issues in patient adherence to health care regimens. *Journal of Human Stress, 1,* 5–17.

Katz, J. L., Weiner, H., Gallagher, T. F., & Hellman, I. (1970). Stress, distress, and ego defenses: Psychoendocrine response to impending breast tumor biopsy. *Archives of General Psychiatry, 23,* 131–142.

Katz, R. C., & Zlutnick, S. (Eds.). (1975). *Behavioral therapy and health care.* Elmford, NY: Pergamon.

Kelley, H. H. (1967). Attribution theory in social psychology. In D. Levine (Ed.), *Nebraska symposium on motivation.* Lincoln: University of Nebraska Press.

Kelley, H. H. (1971). Attribution theory in social interaction. In E. E. Jones, D. E. Kanouse, H. H. Kelley, R. E. Nisbett, S. Valins, & B. Weiner (Eds.), *Attribution: Perceiving the causes of behavior.* New York: General Learning Press.

Kleinman, A., Eisenberg, L., & Good, B. (1978). Culture, illness and care: Clinical lessons from anthropologic and cross-cultural research. *Annals of Internal Medicine, 88,* 251–258.

Kopin, I. (1980). Catecholamines, adrenal hormones, and stress. In D. Krieger & J. Hughes (Eds.), *Neuroendocrinology* (pp. 159–166). Sunderland, MA: Sinauer Associates.

Krantz, D. S., & Durel, L. A. (1983). Psychobiological substrates of the Type A behavior pattern. *Health Psychology, 2,* 393–411.

Krantz, D. S., & Manuck, S. B. (1984). Acute psychophysiologic reactivity and risk of cardiovascular disease: A review and methodologic critique. *Psychological Bulletin, 96,* 435–464.

Krieger, D. T. (1983). The multiple faces of pro-opiomelanocortin, a prototype precursor molecule. *Clinical Research, 31,* 342–353.

Kristeller, J., & Rodin, J. (1984). A three-stage model of treatment continuity: Compliance, adherence and maintenance. In A. Baum, S. Taylor, & J. E. Singer (Eds.), *Handbook of psychology and health.* Hillsdale, NJ: Erlbaum.

LaLonde, M. (1974). *A new perspective on the health of Canadians.* Ottawa, Canada: Ministry of Health and Welfare.

Langer, E. J. (1975). The illusion of control. *Journal of Personality and Social Psychology, 32,* 311–328.

Langer, E. J., Janis, I., & Wolfer, J. (1975). Reduction of psychological stress in surgical patients. *Journal of Experimental Social Psychology, 11,* 155–165.

Langer, E. J., & Rodin, J. (1976). The effects of choice and enhanced personal responsibility for the aged: A field experiment in an institutional setting. *Journal of Personality and Social Psychology, 34,* 191–198.

Laudenslager, M. L., Ryan, S. M., Drugan, R. C., Hyson, R. L., & Maier, S. F. (1983). Coping and immunosuppression: Inescapable but not escapable shock suppresses lymphocyte proliferation. *Science, 221,* 568–570.

Lazarus, R. S. (1977). Psychological stress and coping in adaptation and illness. In Z. J. Lipowski, D. R. Lipsitt, & P. C. Whybrow (Eds.), *Psychosomatic medicine: Current trends and clinical applications* (pp. 14–26). New York: Oxford University Press.

Lepper, M. R., Greene, D., & Nisbett, R. E. (1976). Undermining children's intrinsic interest with extrinsic reward: A test of the over-justification hypothesis. *Journal of Personality and Social Psychology, 28,* 129–137.

Leventhal, H., Meyer, D., & Nerenz, D. (1980). The common sense representation of illness danger. In S. Rachman (Ed.), *Contributions to medical psychology.* Oxford: Pergamon.

Leventhal, H., Singer, R. P., & Jones, S. (1965). Effects of fear and specificity of recommendation upon attitudes and behavior. *Journal of Personality and Social Psychology, 2,* 20–29.

Levinger, G., & Breedlove, J. (1966). Interpersonal attraction and agreement: A study of marriage partners. *Journal of Personality and Social Psychology, 3,* 367–372.

Levy, J. M., & McGee, R. K. (1975). Childbirth as crises: A test of Janis' theory of communication and stress resolution. *Journal of Personality and Social Psychology, 31,* 171–179.

Lewis, F. M., Morisky, D. E., & Flynn, B. S. (1978). A test of the construct validity of health locus of control: Effects of self-reported compliance for hypertensive patients. *Health Education Monographs, 6,* 138–148.

Lichtenstein, E., & Brown, R. A. (1982). Current trends in the modification of cigarette dependence. In A. S. Bellack, M. Herson, & A. E. Kazdin (Ed.), *International handbook of behavior modification and therapy* (pp. 575–604). New York: Plenum.

Lichtenstein, E., & Penner, M. (1977). Long-term effects of rapid smoking treatment. *Addictive Behavior, 2* 109–112.

Liem, G. R. (1975). Performance and satisfaction as affected by personal control over salient decisions. *Journal of Personality and Social Psychology, 31,* 232–240.

Linn, L. S., & Lewis, C. D. (1979). Attitudes towards self-care among practicing physicians. *Medical Care, 17,* 183–190.

Lorber, J. (1975). Good patients and problem patients: Conformity and deviance in a general hospital. *Journal of Health and Social Behavior, 16,* 213–225.

Lundberg, U., & Frankenhauser, M. (1978). Psychophysiological reactions to noise as modified by personal control over noise intensity. *Biological Psychology, 6,* 51–59.

Mahoney, M. J. (1974). *Cognitive behavior modification.* Cambridge, MA: Ballinger.

Maier, S. F., & Seligman, M. E. (1976). Learned helplessness: Theory and evidence. *Journal of Experimental Psychology, 105,* 3–46.

Marlatt, G. A. (1978). Craving for alcohol, loss of control, and relapse: A cognitive-behavioral analysis. In P. F. Nathan, G. A. Marlatt, & T. Loberg (Eds.), *Alcohol-*

ism: New directions in behavioral research and treatment. New York: Plenum.

Mason, J. W. (1968). Organization of psychoendocrine mechanisms. Psychosomatic Medicine, 30, 568–808.

Mason, J. W. (1972). Organization of psychoendocrine mechanims. In N. S. Greenfield & R. A. Sternbach (Eds.), Handbook of psychophysiology (pp. 3–91). New York: Holt.

Mason, J. W. (1974). Specificity in the organization of neuroendocrine response profiles. In P. Seeman & G. Brown (Eds.), Frontier in neurology and neuroscience research (pp. 68–80). Toronto: University of Toronto.

Matarazzo, J. D. (1980). Behavioral health and behavioral medicine: Frontiers for a new health psychology. American Psychologist, 35, 807–817.

Matarazzo, J. D. (1984). Behavioral immunogens and pathogens in health and illness. In C. J. Scheirer & B. L. Hammonds (Eds.), Psychology and health: Master Lecture Series (Vol. 3). Washington, DC: American Psychological Association.

Matthews, D., & Hingson, R. (1977). Improving patient compliance: A guide for physicians. Medical Clinics of North America, 61, 879–889.

Matthews, K. A. (1982). Psychological perspectives on the Type A behavior pattern. Psychological Bulletin, 91, 293–323.

McCarty, M. F. (1982). Nutritional support of central catecholaminergic tone may aid smoking withdrawal. Medical Hypotheses, 8, 95–102.

McGuire, W. J. (1968). Selective exposure: A summing up. In R. P. Abelson, E. Aronson, W. J. McGuire, T. M. Newcomb, M. J. Rosenberg, & P. H. Tannenbaum (Eds.), Theories of cognitive consistency: A sourcebook. Chicago: Rand-McNally.

Meichenbaum, D. (1977). Cognitive behavior modification: An integrative approach. New York: Plenum.

Meyer, D., Leventhal, H., & Gutman, M. (1985). Common sense models of illness: The example of hypertension. Health Psychology, 4, 115–135.

Millan, D. M., & Emrich, H. (1981). Endorphinergic systems and the response to stress. Psychotherapy and Psychosomatics, 36, 43–56.

Miller, N. E. (1980). Effects of learning on physical symptoms produced by psychological stress. In H. Selye (Ed.), Selye's guide to stress research (Vol. 1, pp. 131–167). New York: Van Nostrand Reinhold.

Miller, N. E. (1981). An overview of behavioral medicine: Opportunities and danger. In S. M. Weiss, J. A. Herd, & B. H. Fox (Eds.), Perspectives on behavioral medicine (pp. 3–22). New York: Academic Press.

Miller, N. E. (1982). Motivation and psychological stress. In D. W. Pfaff (Ed.), The physiological mechanisms of motivation (pp. 409–432). New York: Springer-Verlag.

Miller, N. E. (1983). Behavioral medicine: Symbiosis between laboratory and clinic. Annual Review of Psychology, 34, 1–31.

Millman, S. (1982). The ideology of self-care: Blaming the victim of illness. In A. Johnson, O. Grusky, & B. Raven (Eds.), Human services in the 1980s: Social science. Boston, MA: Auburn.

Mills, R. J. & Krantz, D. S. (1979). Information, choice, and reactions to stress: A field experiment in a blood bank with laboratory analogue. Journal of Personality and Social Psychology, 37, 608–620.,

Monjan, A., & Collector, M. (1977). Stress-induced modulation of immune function. Science, 196, 307–308.

Moran, P. A. (1963). An experimental study of pediatric admission. Unpublished master's thesis, Yale University School of Nursing, New Haven, CT.

Mueller, D. P., Edwards, D. W., & Yarvis, R. M. (1978). Stressful life events and community mental-health center patients. Journal of Nervous and Mental Disorders, 166, 16–24.

Mullen, B., & Suls, J. (1982). Know thyself: Stressful life changes and the ameliorative effect of private self consciousness. Journal of Experimental Social Psychology, 18, 43–55.

Munck, A., Guyre, P. M., & Holbrook, N. J. (1984). Physiological functions of glucocorticoids in stress and their relation to pharmacological actions. Endocrine Reviews, 5, 25–44.

Myrsten, A. L., & Andersson, K. (1978). Effects of cigarette smoking on human performance. In R. E. Thornton (Ed.), Smoking behavior (pp. 156–167). London: Churchill Livingstone.

Myrsten, A. L., Elgerot, A., & Edgren, B. (1977). Effects of abstinence from tobacco smoking on physiological and psychological arousal levels in habitual smokers. Psychosomatic Medicine, 39, 25–38.

Nesbitt, P. (1973). Smoking, physiological arousal, and emotional responses. Journal of Personality and Social Psychology, 25, 137–144.

Northey, W. T. (1965). Studies on the interrelationship of cold environment, immunity and resistance to infection. I. Qualitative and quantitative studies on the immune response. Journal of Immunology, 94, 649–657.

Nucholls, C. B., Cassel, J., & Kaplan, B. H. (1972). Psychosocial assets, life crises and the prognosis of pregnancy. American Journal of Epidemiology, 95 431–441.

Paykel, E. S. (1974). Recent life events and clinical depression. E. K. Gunderson & R. H. Rahe (Eds.), Life, stress, and illness. (pp. 134–163). Springfield, IL: Charles C. Thomas.

Pechacek, T. (1979). Modification of smoking behavior. In N. Krasnegor (Ed.), The behavioral aspects of smoking (NIDA Monograph 26) (pp. 127–188). Rockville, MD: National Institute on Drug Abuse.

Pennebaker, J. W. (in press). Social and perceptual factors affecting symptom reporting and hysterical contagion. In M. J. Colligan & J. W. Pennebaker (Eds.), Occupatonal health and social behavior. Hillsdale, NJ: Erlbaum.

Pennebaker, J. W., Burnam, M. A., Schaeffer, M. A., & Harper, D. C. (1977). Lack of control as a determinant of perceived physical symptoms. Journal of Personality and Social Psychology, 35, 167–174.

Perlmutter, L. C., & Monty, R. A. (1977). The importance of perceived control: Fact or fantasy? American Scientist, 65, 759–765.

Pomerleau, O. F. (1979a). Behavioral medicine: The contribution of the experimental analysis of behavior to medical care. American Psychologist, 34, 654–663.

Pomerleau, O. F. (1979b). Commonalities in the treatment and understanding of smoking and other self-management disorders. In N. K. Krasnegor (Ed.), Behavioral analysis and treatment of substance abuse

(NIDA Research Monograph 25) (pp. 140–156). Rockville, MD: National Institute on Drug Abuse.

Pomerleau, O. F. (1980). Why people smoke: Current psychobiological theories. In P. Davidson (Ed.), *Behavioral medicine: Changing health lifestyles* (pp. 94–115). New York: Brunner/Mazel.

Pomerleau, O.F. (1981). Underlying mechanisms in substance abuse: Examples from research on smoking. *Addictive Behaviors, 6,* 187–196.

Pomerleau, O. F. (1982). A discourse on behavioral medicine: Current status and future trends. *Journal of Consulting and Clinical Psychology, 50,* 1030–1039.

Pomerleau, O. F., Adkins, D., & Pertschuk, M. (1978). Predictors of outcome and recidivism in smoking-cessation treatment. *Addictive Behaviors, 3,* 65–70.

Pomerleau, O. F., Bass, F., & Crown, V. (1975). The role of behavior modification in preventive medicine. *New England Journal of Medicine, 292,* 1277–1282.

Pomerleau, O. F., & Brady, J. P. (1979). Introduction: The scope and promise of behavioral medicine. In O. F. Pomerleau & J. P. Brady (Eds.), *Behavioral medicine: Theory and practice.* Baltimore: Williams & Wilkins.

Pomerleau, O. F., Fertig, J. B., Seyler, L. E., & Jaffe, J. (1983). Neuroendocrine reactivity to nicotine in smokers. *Psychopharmacology, 83,* 61–67.

Pomerleau, O. F., Fertig, J. B., & Shanahan, S. O. (1983). Nicotine dependence in cigarette smoking: An empirically-based, multivariate model. *Pharmacology, Biochemistry, and Behavior, 19,* 291–299.

Pomerleau, O. F., & Pomerleau, C. S. (1984a). *Break the smoking habit: A behavioral program for giving up cigarettes.* W. Hartford, CT: Behavioral Medicine Press (first published in 1977 by Research Press, Champaign, IL).

Pomerleau, O. F., & Pomerleau, C. S. (1984b). Neuroregulators and the reinforcement of smoking: Towards a biobehavioral explanation. *Neuroscience and Biobehavioral Reviews, 8.*

Pomerleau, O. F., Turk, D. C., & Fertig, J. B. (1984). The effects of cigarette smoking on pain and anxiety. *Addictive Behavior, 9,* 265–271.

Raiffa, H. (1968). *Decision analysis.* Reading, MA: Addison-Wesley.

Ransford, C. P. (1982). A role for amines in the antidepressant effect of exercise: A review. *Medicine and Science in Sports and Exercise, 14,* 1–10.

Raven, B. (1965). Social influence and power. In I. D. Steiner & M. Fishbein (Eds.), *Current studies in social psychology.* New York: Holt, Rinehart & Winston.

Raw, M., Jarvis, M. J., Feyerabend, C., & Russell, M. A. (1980). Comparison of nicotine chewing-gum and psychological treatments for dependent smokers. *British Medical Journal, 281,* 481–482.

Redmond, D. E. (1979). New and old evidence for the involvement of a brain norepinephrine system in anxiety. In W. E. Fann, I. Karacan, A. D. Porkorney, & R. L. Williams (Eds.), *Phenomenology and treatment of anxiety* (pp. 153–203). New York: S. P. Medical & Scientific Books.

Reitura, G., Seifter, J., & Zisblatt, M. (1973). Metyrapone-inhibited oncogenesis in mice inoculated with a murine sarcoma virus. *Journal of the National Cancer Institute, 51,* 1983–1985.

Rhodewalt, F., & Comer, R. (1982). Coronary-prone behavior and the experience of reactance in the choice elimination paradigm. *Personality and Social Psychology Bulletin, 8,* 152–158.

Riley, V. (1981). Biobehavioral factors in animal work on tumorigenesis. In S. M. Weiss, J. A. Herd, & B. H. Fox (Eds.), *Perspectives on behavioral medicine* (pp. 183–214). New York: Academic Press.

Rodin, J. (1978). Somatopsychics and attribution. *Personality and Social Psychology Bulletin, 4,* 531–540.

Rodin, J. (1982). Patient practitioner relationships: A process of social influence. In A. Johnson, O. Grusky, & B. Raven (Eds.), *Human services in the 1980s: Social science perspectives.* Boston: Auburn House.

Rodin, J. (1983a). *Aging, control and health.* Eastern Psychological Association Presidential Address, Philadelphia.

Rodin, J. (1983b). Behavioral medicine: Beneficial effects of self control training in aging. *Revue Internationale de Psychologie, 32,* 153–181.

Rodin, J., & Janis, I. L. (1979). The social power of health care practitioners as agents of change. *Journal of Social Issues, 35,* 60–81.

Rodin, J., & Langer, E. J. (1977). Long-term effects of a control-relevant intervention with the institutionalized aged. *Journal of Personality and Social Psychology, 35,* 897–902.

Rogers, R. W., & Mewborn, C. R. (1976). Fear appeals and attitude change: Effects of a threat's noxiousness, probability of occurrence, and the efficacy of coping responses. *Journal of Personality and Social Psychology, 34,* 54–61.

Rogers, R. W., & Thistlethwaite, D. L. (1970). Effects of fear arousal and reassurance on attitude change. *Journal of Personality and Social Psychology, 15,* 227.

Rose, J. E. M., & Sabiston, B. H. (1971). Effects of cold exposure on the immunologic response of rabbits to human serum albumin. *Journal of Immunology, 107,* 339.

Rosenman, R. H. (1974). The role of behavior patterns and neurogenic factors in the pathogenesis of coronary heart disease. In R. S. Eliot (Ed.), *Stress and the heart* (pp. 123–141). New York: Futura.

Rosenman, R. H. (1978). The interview method of the assessment of the coronary-prone behavior pattern. In T. M. Dembroski, S. Weiss, J. Shields, S. G. Haynes, & M. Feinleib (Eds.), *Coronary-prone behavior* (pp. 55–69). New York: Springer-Verlag.

Rosenman, R. H., Brand, R. J., Jenkins, C. D., Friedman, M., Straus, R., & Wurm, M. (1975). Coronary heart disease in the Western Collaborative Group Study: Final follow-up experience of 8 1/2 years. *Journal of the American Medical Association, 233,* 872–877.

Roskies, E. (1983). Modification of coronary-risk behavior. In D. Krantz, A. Baum, & J. E. Singer (Eds.), *Handbook of psychology and health* (pp. 231–276). Hillsdale, NJ: Erlbaum.

Roskies, E., Kearney, H., Spevack, M., Surkis, A., Cohen, C., & Gilman, S. (1979). Generalizability and durability of treatment effects in an intervention program for coronary-prone (Type A) managers. *Journal of Behavioral Medicine, 2,* 195–207.

Roskies, E., Spevack, M., Surkis, A., Cohen, C., & Gilman, S. (1978). Changing the coronary-prone (Type A) behavior pattern in a non-clinical population. *Journal of Behavioral Medicine, 1,* 201−216.

Russell, M. (1978). Self-regulation of nicotine intake by smokers. In K. Battig (Ed.), *Behavioral effects of nicotine* (pp. 108−122). Basel: Karger.

Sachar, E. J. (1981). Psychobiology of affective disorders. In E. R. Kandel & J. H. Schwartz (Eds.), *Principles of neural science* (pp. 611−619). New York: Elsevier/ North-Holland.

Sachar, E. J. (1975). Neuroendocrine abnormalities in depressive illness. In E. J. Sachar (Eds.), *Topics in psychoendocrinology.* New York: Grune & Stratton.

Sackett, D. L., & Haynes, R. B. (Eds.) (1976). *Compliance with therapeutic regimens.* Baltimore, MD: Johns Hopkins University Press.

Sahley, T., & Berntson, G. (1979). Antinociceptive effects of central and systemic administration of nicotine in the rat. *Psychopharmacology, 65,* 279−283.

Schachter, S. (1978). Pharmacological and psychological determinants of smoking. *Annals of Internal Medicine, 88,* 104−114.

Schechter, M., & Jellinek, P. (1975). Evidence for a cortical locus for the stimulus effect of nicotine. *European Journal of Pharmacology, 34,* 65−73.

Schildkraut, J. J., & Kety, S. S. (1967). Biogenic amines and emotion. *Science, 156,* 21−30.

Schmale, A., & Iker, H. (1966). The psychological setting of uterine cervical cancer. *Annals of the New York Academy of Sciences, 125,* 807−813.

Schmidt, R. L. (1966). *An exploratory study of nursing and patient readiness for surgery.* Unpublished masters's thesis, Yale University School of Nursing, New Haven, CT.

Schmitt, F. E., & Woolridge, P. J. (1973). Psychological preparation of surgical patients. *Nursing Research, 22,* 108−116.

Schofield, W. (1979). The clinical psychologist as a health professional. In G. C. Stone, F. Cohen, & N. E. Adler (Eds.), *Health psychology.* San Francisco: Jossey-Bass.

Schorr, D., & Rodin, J. (1982). The role of perceived control in practitioner−patient relationships. In T. A. Wills (Ed.), *Basic processes in helping relationships.* New York: Academic Press.

Schulz, R. (1976). Effects of control and predictability on the physical and psychological well being of the institutionalized aged. *Journal of Personality and Social Psychology, 33,* 563−573.

Schulz, R., & Hanusa, B. H. (1978). Long-term effects of control and predictability-enhancing interventions: Findings and ethical issues. *Journal of Personality and Social Psychology, 36,* 1194−1201.

Schwartz, G. E., & Weiss, S. M. (1977). What is behavioral medicine? *Psychosomatic Medicine, 36,* 377−381.

Schwartz, G. E., & Weiss, S. M. (1978). Behavioral medicine revisited: An amended definition. *Journal of Behavioral Medicine, 1,* 249−251.

Seligman, M. E. P. (1975). *Helplessness: On depression, development, and death.* San Francisco: Freeman.

Sell, S. (1980). *Immunology, immunopathology, and immunity* (3rd ed.). New York: Harper & Row.

Selye, H. (1956). *The stress of life.* New York: McGraw-Hill.

Seyler, L. E., Fertig, J. B., Pomerleau, O. F., Hunt, D., & Parker, K. (1984). The effects of smoking on ACTH and cortisol secretion. *Life Sciences, 34,* 37−65.

Shavit, Y., Lewis, J. W., Terman, G. W., Gale, R. P., & Liebeskind, J. D. (1984). Opioid peptides mediate the suppressive effect of stress on natural killer cell cytotoxicity. *Science, 223,* 188−190.

Shiffman, S. (1982). Relapse following smoking cessation: A situational analysis. *Journal of Consulting and Clinical Psychology, 50,* 71−86.

Shiffman, S., & Jarvik, M. (1976). Smoking withdrawal symptoms in two weeks of abstinence. *Psychopharmacologia, 50,* 35−39.

Silverstein, B. (1976). *An addiction explanation of cigarette-induced relaxation.* Unpublished dissertation, Columbia University.

Silverstein, B. (1982). Cigarette smoking, nicotine addiction, and relaxation. *Journal of Personality and Social Psychology, 42,* 946−970.

Sitaram, N., Weingartner, H., & Gillin, J. C. (1978). Human serial learning: Enhancement with arecholine and choline and impairment with scopolamine. *Science, 201,* 274−276.

Sklar, L. S., & Anisman, H. (1979). Stress and coping factors influence tumor growth. *Science, 205,* 513−515.

Solomon, G. F. (1969). Stress and antibody response in rats. *International Archives of Allergy and Applied Immunology, 35,* 97−104.

Staub, E., Tursky, B., & Schwartz, G. E. (1971). Self-control and predictability: Their effects on reactions to aversive stimulation. *Journal of Personality and Social Psychology, 18,* 157−162.

Stellar, E., & Rodin, J. (1980). Workshop III—Research needs. *American Journal of Clinical Nutrition, 33,* 526−527.

Stolerman, I., Goldfarb, T., Fink, R., & Jarvik, M. (1973). Influencing cigarette smoking with nicotine antagonists. *Psychopharmacologia, 28,* 247−259.

Stone, G. C. (1979). Patient compliance and the role of the expert. *Journal of Social Issues, 35,* 34−59.

Stotland, E., & Blumenthal, A. (1964). The reduction of anxiety as a result of the expectation of making a choice. *Canadian Review of Psychology, 18,* 139−145.

Stoyva, J., & Anderson, C. (1982). A coping−rest model of relaxation and stress management. In L. Goldberger & S. Breznitz (Eds.), *Handbook of stress: Theoretical and clinical aspects* (pp. 745−763). New York: Free Press.

Su, C. (1982). Actions of nicotine and smoking on circulation. *Pharmaceutical Therapeutics, 17,* 129−141.

Suedfeld, P. (1980). *Restricted environmental stimulation: Research and clinical application.* New York: Wiley.

Suinn, R. M. (1974). Behavior therapy for cardiac patients. *Behavior Therapy, 5,* 569−571.

Suinn, R. M. (1980). Pattern A behaviors and heart disease: Intervention approaches. In J. M. Ferguson & C. B. Taylor (Eds.), *Comprehensive handbook of behavioral medicine* (Vol. 1, pp. 5−27). New York: S.P. Medical & Scientific Books.

Suls, J. (1982). Social support, interpersonal relations and health: Benefits and liabilities. In G. Sanders & J. Suls (Eds.), *The social psychology of health and illness.* Hillsdale, NJ: Erlbaum.

Surwit, R. S., Feinglos, M. N., & Scovern, A. W. (1983). Diabetes and behavior: A paradigm for health psychology. *American Psychologist, 38,* 255–262.

Surwit, R. S., Williams, R. B., & Shapiro, D. (1982). *Behavioral approaches to cardiovascular disease.* New York: Academic Press.

Svarstad, B. L. (1976). Physician-patient communication and patient conformity with medical advice. In D. Mechanic (Ed.), *The growth of bureaucratic medicine: An inquiry into the dynamics of patient behavior and the organization of medical care.* New York: Wiley.

Taylor, R. B., Denham, J. W., & Ureda, J. R. (1982). Health promotion: A perspective. In R. B. Taylor, J. R. Ureda, & J. W. Denham (Eds.), *Health promotion: Principles and clinical applications* (pp. 1–18). Norwalk, CT: Appleton-Century-Crofts.

Taylor, S. E. (1979). Hospital patient behavior: Reactance, helplessness, or control? *Journal of Social Issues, 35,* 156–184.

Taylor, S. E., & Levin, S. (1976). *The psychological impact of breast cancer: Theory and research.* San Francisco: West Coast Cancer Foundation.

Tedeschi, J. T. (1974). Attributions, liking and power. In T. Huston (Ed.), *Foundations of interpersonal attraction.* New York: Academic Press.

Tharp, G. D. (1975). The role of glucocorticoids in exercise. *Medicine and Science in Sports, 7,* 6–11.

Timiras, P. S. (1972). *Developmental physiology and aging.* New York: Macmillan.

Tripathi, J., Martin, B., & Aceto, M. (1982). Nicotine-induced antinociception in rats and mice: Correlation with nicotine brain levels. *Journal of Pharmacology and Experimental Therapeutics, 221,* 91–96.

Troxler, R. G., Sprague, E. A., Albanese, R. A., Fuchs, R., & Thompson, A. J. (1977). The association of elevated plasma cortisol and early atherosclerosis as demonstrated by coronary angiography. *Atherosclerosis, 26,* 151–162.

Ursin, H., Baade, E., & Levine, S. (1978). *Psychology of stress.* New York: Academic Press.

U.S. Department of Health, Education, and Welfare. (1978). *Healthy people: The Surgeon General's Report on Health Promotion and Disease Prevention* (PHS 79-55071). Washington, DC: Public Health Service.

U.S. Public Health Service. (1976). *The forward plan for health, FY 1978–82.* Washington, DC: U.S. Government Printing Office.

van Ree, J. M., & de Wied, D. (1981). Brain peptides and psychoactive drug effects. In Y. Israel, F. Glaser, H. Kalant, R. Popham, W. Schmidt, & R. Smart (Eds.), *Research advances in alcohol and drug problems* (pp. 67–105). New York: Plenum.

Vernikos-Danellis, J., & Heyback, J. P. (1980). Psychophysiologic mechanisms regulating the hypothalamic-pituitary-adrenal response to stress. In H. Selye (Ed.), *Selye's guide to stress research* (Vol. 1, pp. 206–249). New York: Van Nostrand Reinhold.

Vernon, D. T. A., & Bigelow, D. A. (1974). Effect of information about a potentially stressful situation on responses to stress impact. *Journal of Personality and Social Psychology, 29,* 50–59.

Visintainer, M.A., Volpicelli, J. R., & Seligman, M. E. (1982). Tumor rejection in rats after inescapable or escapable shock. *Science, 216,* 437–439.

Wack, J. T., & Rodin, J. (1982). Smoking and its effect on body weight and the systems of caloric regulation. *American Journal of Clinical Nutrition, 35,* 366–380.

Wallston, B. S., Wallston, K. A., Kaplan, G. D., & Maides, S. A. (1976). Development and validation of the Health Locus of Control (HLC) Scale. *Journal of Consulting and Clinical Psychology, 44,* 580–585.

Weiner, H. (1977). *Psychobiology and human disease.* New York: Elsevier.

Weingartner, H., Gold, P., Ballenger, J., Smallberg, S., Summers, R., Rubinow, D., Post, R., Goodwin, F. (1981). Effects of vasopressin on human memory functions. *Science, 211,* 601–603.

Weiss, J. M. (1971). Effects of coping behavior in different warning signal conditions on stress pathology in rats. *Journal of Comparative and Physiological Psychology, 77,* 1–13.

Weiss, J. M. (1972). Psychological factors in stress and disease. *Scientific American,* June, 104–113.

Weiss, J. M., & Glaser, H. I. (1975). Effects of acute exposure to stressors on subsequent avoidance-escape behavior. *Psychosomatic Medicine, 37,* 499–521.

Weiss, J. M., Stone, E. A., & Harrell, N. (1970). Coping behavior and brain norepinephrine level in rats. *Journal of Comparative and Physiological Psychology, 72,* 153–160.

Wesnes, K., & Warburton, D. M. (1978). The effects of cigarette smoking and nicotine tablets upon human attention. In R. E. Thornton (Ed.), *Smoking behavior* (pp. 131–147). London: Churchill Livingstone.

Wesnes, K., & Warburton, D. M. (1983). Smoking, nicotine, and human performance. *Pharmacology and Therapeutics, 21,* 189–208.

Westfall, T. C. (1974). Effect of nicotine and other drugs on the release of ^{3}H-norepinephrine and ^{3}H-dopamine from rat brain slices. *Psychopharmacology, 13,* 693–700.

White, R. W. (1959). Motivation reconsidered: The concept of competence. *Psychological Review, 66,* 297–323.

Whitehouse, W. G., Walker, J., Margulies, D. L., & Bersh, P. J. (1983). Opiate antagonists overcome the learned helplessness effect but impair competent escape performance. *Physiology and Behavior, 30,* 731–734.

Wilkins, J., Carlson, H., van Vunakis, H., Hill, M., Gritz, E., & Jarvik, M. (1982). Nicotine from cigarette smoking increases circulating levels of cortisol, growth hormone, and prolactin in male chronic smokers. *Psychopharmacology, 78,* 305–308.

Williams, R. B., Lane, J. D., Kuhn, C. M., Melosh, W., White, A. D., & Schanberg, S. M. (1982). Type A behavior and elevated physiological and neuroendocrine responses to cognitive tasks. *Science, 218,* 483–485.

Wise, C. D., & Stein, L. (1969). Facilitation of brain self-stimulation by central administration of norepinephrine. *Science, 163,* 299–301.

Wise, R. A. (1983). Brain neuronal systems mediating reward processes. In J. E. Smith & J. D. Lane (Eds.), *The neurobiology of opiate reward processes* (pp. 405–438). New York: Elsevier Biomedical.

Wolfer, J. A. & Visintainer, M. A. (1975). Effects on pediatric surgical patients of psychological preparation and stress-point nursing care. *Nursing Research, 24,* 244–255.

Wolff, B., & Horland, A. (1967). Effects of suggestion upon experimental pain: A validation study. *Journal of Abnormal Psychology, 72,* 402–407.

Wortman, C. B. (1975). Some determinants of perceived control. *Journal of Personality and Social Psychology, 31,* 282–294.

Zajonc, R. B. (1980). Feeling and thinking: Preferences need no interferences. *American Psychologist, 35,* 151–175.

Zegans, L. S. (1982). Stress and the development of somatic disorders. In L. Goldberger & S. Breznitz (Eds.), *Handbook of stress: Theoretical and clinical aspects* (pp. 134–152). New York: Free Press.

PART IV

CHILD AND FAMILY THERAPIES

12

CHILD AND ADOLESCENT BEHAVIOR THERAPY

THOMAS H. OLLENDICK

Virginia Polytechnic Institute
and State University

INTRODUCTION

The application of behavioral principles to the problems of children and adolescents has a long and rich tradition. It would be inaccurate, however, to portray the development of this tradition as an uninterrupted march of progress. Rather, progress has been cyclical, with advances coming in bursts followed by periods of solidification and, at other times, intellectual stagnation. Following the excitement and enthusiasm generated by Watson and his colleagues for the principles of respondent conditioning during the 1920s, a dormant period ensued. In fact, not until the 1960s did a clear resurgence of interest occur. This renewed interest, firmly grounded in the principles of operant conditioning, remained in the foreground for some years. In the 1970s, perhaps because of disenchantment with endless demonstrations of the application of operant principles to countless behaviors, researchers slowly turned their attention to treatment approaches based on principles of vicarious conditioning and social learning. Presently, in the 1980s, a

new wave of enthusiasm has occurred with the advent of cognitive-based procedures. This evolving trend should not, however, be misconstrued to mean that treatments based on principles of respondent, operant, and vicarious conditioning are no longer useful or viable; in fact, they are very much alive and well, as we shall see. It is, however, evident that specific procedures have waxed and waned in popularity.

Clearly, we are at an exciting time in the field of behavior therapy with children and adolescents. An *exhaustive* review of the literature by Gelfand and Hartmann in 1968 found only 70 studies related to the behavioral treatment of children and adolescents. In a *selective* review 13 years later, Ollendick and Cerny (1981) reported over 1000 studies! In response to this expanding literature and the need to provide a focus for behavioral research applicable to children and youth, a new journal, *Child Behavior Therapy*, was founded in 1979. Recently, the title of this journal was changed to *Child and Family Behavior Therapy* to reflect the importance of family influences on child and adolescent behavior. In addition to this timely journal, four major textbooks have been published (Gelfand & Hartmann, 1975; Graziano & Mooney, 1984; Ollendick & Cerny, 1981; Ross, 1980) and several comprehensive reviews have been completed (e.g., Franks, 1982; Harris, 1983a; O'Leary & Carr, 1982). A flurry of activity has been evident. Clearly, behavior therapists have expended considerable effort on the specific needs of children and adolescents and have researched a variety of techniques for the remediation and prevention of behavior disorders in these populations.

At this point, it may be appropriate to ask, "What is child and adolescent behavior therapy?" What are its distinguishing characteristics? The exact distinctions between behavior therapy—whether with children and adolescents or with adults—and other types of therapy have been difficult to specify. Different authors have emphasized different aspects of the therapeutic process: some define behavior therapy by the techniques employed (e.g., London, 1972); others define behavior therapy by its allegiance to learning principles (e.g., Wolpe, 1976); still others define it by its methodological approach to behavior change (e.g., Yates, 1975). Perhaps the most integrative definition of behavior therapy is that provided by Franks and Wilson (1978), who assert that it is "an approach, a methodological prescription, *a way of ordering data about human beings to bring about therapeutic change*" (p. 14, italics added). This definition makes it clear that behavior therapists bring to the therapy situation a common treatment approach that is characterized by two general features: a methodology that is empirically based and an approach that relies on behavioral models to make sense out of the data gathered in the therapy setting.

Applied to children and adolescents, the essence of behavior therapy is that it represents a conceptual perspective that is derived from learning theory and that is based on empirical methodology and focuses specifically on adjustment problems of children and adolescents (Ollendick & Cerny, 1981). It should be noted, however, that behavior therapy with any population does not represent *one* model of behavior. Rather, it represents a fairly large number of behavioral models (e.g., the classical conditioning model, the operant conditioning model, the vicarious conditioning model, and the cognitive model), all of which have come to be subsumed under a

common rubric because they claim allegiance to the same assumptions and principles of behavioral psychology (Ollendick and Cerny, 1981). Further, in recent years, concerted efforts have been made to examine these principles of behavioral psychology in light of the principles of developmental and social psychology. Importantly, these "other" principles have been invoked to broaden the horizon of the behavioral approach in an attempt to better understand, and account for, the complexities of child and adolescent behavior (Harris & Farrari, 1983; Ollendick & Hersen, 1984; Wahler & Graves, 1983). As noted recently by Franks (1982), interaction and reciprocity of these principles of psychology are among the hallmarks of contemporary behavior therapy.

This evolving picture of just what constitutes behavior therapy is evident in contemporary attempts to delineate specific characteristics of this approach when applied to children and adolescents. For purposes of this chapter, several leading authorities[1] in behavior therapy were requested to respond to the following open-ended statement: "Child and adolescent behavior therapy is. . . ." Responses, though variable, tended to parallel basic elements contained in the definition offered by Ollendick and Cerny (1981). Hans Eysenck states that "like adult behavior therapy, [it] is made up of a number of treatments based on the principles of learning theory." Joseph Wolpe asserted that "child behavior therapy is the use of experimentally (or empirically) established principles of learning or related principles for the purpose of overcoming learned unadaptive habits in children." Cyril Franks noted that it "is the application of the principles and practice of behavior therapy, appropriately defined to children and adolescents. As such it should involve all who interact in any meaningful fashion with the child or children concerned. One final point: Even more so than with adults, child behavior therapists must be sensitive to data generated by developmental psychologists, especially with respect to developmental norms and to pertinent advances in related disciplines." Ben Lahey indicated that it is an "approach to solving the psychological problems of children (and adolescents) that intentionally influences the process of *normal* behavior change (i.e.,

[1]Permission to reproduce these quotes obtained from the cited authors.

learning, cognition, development, etc.) to produce more adaptive functioning." Dan O'Leary offered that it is "the application of principles of psychology, especially learning, developmental, and social psychology, to the change of children's (and adolescents') behavior." Herb Quay indicated that "this appellation *should* refer to the application of empirically demonstrated principles to the modification of children's (and adolescents') deviant behavior. In my view, the techniques may be operant, respondent, or more broadly 'social learning' but the underlying principles must be firmly established under carefully controlled conditions. Thus, I would rule out play therapy, child psychoanalysis, 'dynamic' psychotherapy, counseling, value-clarification, and the like." Finally, Alan Ross stood by the definition offered in his book, *Child Behavior Therapy*: "Like behavior therapy, in general, [it] is best defined as an empirical approach to psychological problems. It entails continuous evaluation of therapeutic interventions and thus calls for objectively defined terms and measurable procedures. It can thus be said that child behavior therapy is the application of psychology to the alleviation of the psychological distress of children. As such, it is an open-minded, self-correcting, and constantly changing field of endeavor."

As is evident from these contemporary definitions, specific emphasis in child and adolescent behavior therapy is placed upon (1) principles of behavioral psychology, most notably principles of learning; (2) use of strategies or procedures that are methodologically sound and empirically validated; and (3) application of such principles and procedures to adjustment problems of children and adolescents. Though not a clear or universal emphasis, increasingly greater attention is being directed toward other principles of psychology, in particular, those associated with developmental and social psychology. Such "expansionism" is likely to result in a more sophisticated and productive approach to problems of children and adolescents, even though this forces the approach outside of the usual definition of "behavioral."

Assessment in Child and Adolescent Behavior Therapy

As noted by Ross (1978) in his review of behavior therapy with children for the second edition of this *Handbook*, the first and essential step in any attempt to intervene in a child's problem must be a careful assessment of the problem and its situational determinants. Broadly speaking, the goals of behavioral assessment are to identify antecedent and consequent events that serve as controlling variables for the problem or target behaviors and to design and evaluate a treatment program for such behaviors based on this "functional" analysis. Importantly, controlling variables include one's subjectively felt cognitions and physiological reponses as well as one's overt behaviors.

Mash and Terdal have synthesized the many viewpoints of child behavioral assessment, describing the process as "a range of deliberate problem-solving strategies for understanding children and childhood disorders" (1981, p. 8). More recently, Ollendick and Hersen have expanded Mash and Terdal's basic notion to indicate that "child behavioral assessment can be described as an exploratory, hypothesis-testing process in which a range of specific procedures are used in order to understand a given child, group, or social ecology and to formulate and evaluate specific intervention strategies" (Ollendick & Hersen, 1984, p. 6). They put forth three distinguishing characteristics that guide the selection of specific assessment procedures: First, multiple assessment strategies should be used in order to obtain as complete and accurate a "picture of the child" as possible; second, only those procedures that are empirically based and validated should be selected; and, third, procedures chosen should be sensitive to, and mindful of, normal developmental processes.

Early child behavioral assessment procedures were directed toward identification of discrete and highly specific target behaviors and their controlling variables. Observable behaviors like pinching, hitting, eye contact, and smiling were isolated for study and modification. While the importance of careful and systematic assessment of target behaviors should not be underestimated (in fact, such practice remains the hallmark of child behavioral assessment), more recent advances have incorporated a broader view of child behavior and its determinants. Assessment strategies in the behaviorist's armamentarium now include the clinical interview, self-monitoring, standardized testing, rating forms from significant others (e.g. peers, parents, and teachers), and self-report measures in addition to the more commonly used behavioral observation procedures Acceptability of this multimethod approach, however, rests firmly on the availability of a set of measures that are psychometrically sound and developmentally sensitive (Ollendick & Hersen, 1984).

Undoubtedly, a variety of factors enters into determining exactly which assessment tools should be used. Mash and Terdal (1981) identify six factors: (1) characteristics of the problem behavior (e.g., heightened physiological arousal, inhibitive self-statements, deficient social skills); (2) characteristics of the child (e.g., age, sex, intellectual level); (3) characteristics of the referral source (e.g., parents, teachers, social workers); (4) characteristics of the assessment and treatment setting (e.g. home, school, institution, clinics); (5) characteristics of the social milieu (e.g., socioeconomic status, religious affiliation, cultural practices); and (6) the specific purposes of assessment (e.g., diagnosis, placement, intervention). As can be seen, it would be naive to suggest that any one assessment method or set of methods would be appropriate for all of these interactive conditions. The selection of assessment methods is a highly idiographic process; in some instances, behavioral observation alone suffices. In others, it may be necessary to supplement these observations with ratings from the child's or adolescent's parents and teachers, as well as the individual's own self-report to specific problematic situations, in order to obtain as "complete a picture" as possible. It should be evident, however, that a "test battery" approach for child and adolescent behavioral assessment is not being recommended. The exact procedures to be used depend upon a variety of factors including those suggested by Mash and Terdal (1981) as well as the personnel, time, and resources available to the assessor (Ollendick & Cerny, 1981).

Just as assessment procedures must be psychometrically sound and empirically validated, they must also be sensitive to developmental processes and changes when used with children and adolescents. Such developmental processes have clear implications for the selection of specific assessment methods, as well as target behaviors for evaluation of therapeutic change. For example, self-monitoring requires the ability to compare one's own behavior against a standard and to accurately judge occurrence or nonoccurrence of targeted events and behaviors. Most children below six years of age lack the requisite ability to *accurately* self-monitor and, consequently, may not benefit from such an

assessment strategy. In fact, the limited research available suggests that this procedure may be counterproductive when used with young children, resulting in confusion and impaired performance (e.g., Higa, Tharp, & Calkins, 1978; Wasserman, 1983). Similarly, age-related variables place limitations on the use of many self-report instruments with children. Frequently, such scales are developed as downward extensions of adult scales (e.g., Kovaac's Childhood Depression Inventory and Scherer and Nakamura's Fear Survey Schedule) and may not be useful for younger children. For example, although many children under eight years of age appear to understand the fear stimulus items on Scherer and Nakamura's (1968) Fear Survey Schedule, they are unable to grasp the notion of rating fear on a 5-point scale. When a 3-point scale is used, however, the children are able to reliably and validly rate their fear (Ollendick, 1983a). Other methods of child and adolescent behavioral assessment, including direct behavioral observation, are not without their age-related constraints. While untested at this time, it certainly seems plausible that reactivity to behavioral observation may increase with age. Young children are known to readily adapt to an adult's presence, while adolescents are equally known to be well aware of an adult's observation and to alter their behavior accordingly, at least while the adult is present! Awareness of these developmental trends should assist in the selection and evaluation of specific assessment strategies.

Developmental changes also have clear implications for the selection of specific target behaviors. In this regard, the use of normative information is invaluable. Normative data provide information about the child's behavior relative to the behavior of other children (or adolescents) in an appropriate reference group (e.g., age, sex, culture). "Normal" age and gender trends have been established for several behaviors, including fears (Bauer, 1980), aggressive behavior (Olweus, 1979), withdrawn behavior (Furman, 1980), and cross-dressing behavior (Rekers, 1978). Similarly, Achenbach and Edelbrock (1981) have carefully delineated the prevalence of various parent-reported behavior problems for clinically referred and nonreferred boys and girls aged 4 to 16. Interestingly, as can be seen in Figure 12.1, some behaviors show a linear decline in prevalence with age (e.g., fear, whining), others show a linear increase in prevalence with age (e.g., alcohol and drug abuse, delinquency), while

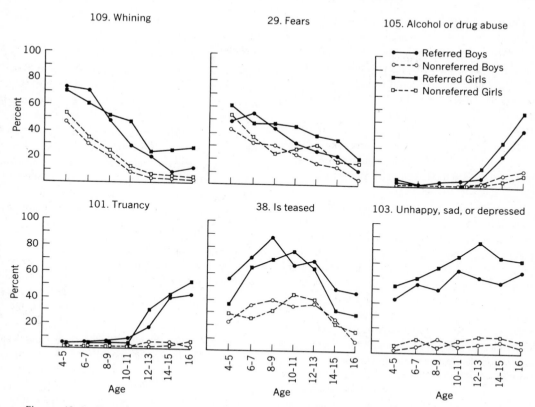

Figure 12.1   Prevalence of various parent-reported behavior problems for referred and nonreferred boys and girls aged 4 to 16. (From C. Edelbrock, "Developmental considerations." in T.H. Ollendick & M. Hersen [Eds.], *Child behavioral assessment: Principles and procedures.* New York: Pergamon Press, 1981. Copyright by Pergamon Press, Inc. Reprinted by permission.)

still others show curvilinear relationships (e.g., worrying, harming self). Thus, normative comparisons can be used not only to identify which behaviors are excessive and which behaviors are deficient but also to evaluate more precisely change in behavior over time. Behavioral assessors must be continually aware of the extent to which behavior change is a function of intervention versus normal developmental change due to maturation.

A Note on Diagnosis in Child and Adolescent Behavior Therapy

Much has been written about the role of psychiatric diagnosis in behavioral assessment and treatment (e.g., Harris, 1983b; Harris & Powers, 1984; Nelson & Barlow, 1981). While most behaviorists eschew the diagnostic process and object strongly to its use, others have acknowledged its potential utility in their behavioral practice. For example, Harris

and Powers (1984) have proposed an integrative model that relies on a functional analysis of both specific target behaviors and those nomothetically related behaviors that are part of specific diagnostic categories. That is, the specific criteria used to establish any one diagnosis in the newly revised *Diagnostic and Statistical Manual* (*DSM-III*, APA, 1980) may prompt inquiry into a wider range of collateral responses, and controlling variables, than might otherwise occur. In effect, the diagnostic process may lead to a more careful examination of behaviors that covary in any one individual (i.e., response-response relationships). Such is necessary if we are to move beyond the simple assessment and modification of "one behavior at a time." As noted by Voeltz and Evans (1982), "an emphasis upon lawful intra- and inter-organism response-response relationships to augment our traditional concern for response-stimulus relationships" (p. 160) is necessary.

Of course, attention to response-response relationships does not require acceptance nor direct use of *DSM-III*. Presently, many questions remain about the empirical foundations for its diagnostic categories, the reliability associated with its use, and the differential validity of its groupings of specific disorders (Achenbach & Edelbrock, 1983; Quay, 1979, 1986). While *DSM-III* may be better than *DSM-II*, interjudge reliability studies have called its reliability into question and multivariate studies have questioned the validity of many of its diagnostic categories.

Consistent with its empirical focus, adherents of child and adolescent behavior therapy have shown greater allegiance to the statistical-based multivariate approach than the intuitive-based *DSM-III* approach. Multivariate statistical research aimed at the discovery of the structure of psychopathological disorders among children and adolescents has been going on for some 40 years (Quay, 1986). Basically, the various multivariate analytic methods first determine the observed correlation between more or less specific characteristics (response covariation) and then elucidate the patterns or groupings (factors) among the observed covariations. Based on a large number of such studies, Achenbach and others have suggested three major broad-band factors of deviant behavior in children and adolescents: externalizing disorders, which include the narrower band conduct disorder and hyperactivity disorders; internalizing disorders, including the narrower band anxiety and withdrawal disorders; and the pervasive developmental disorders, which include mental retardation and the psychotic disorders. Importantly, attention to these broad-band factors of child and adolescent behavior may prompt the examination of a set of collateral behaviors and serve to elucidate potential response-response relationships that might otherwise be missed. For this reason, the child and adolescent behavior therapy literature in this chapter is organized around these major patterns of deviant behavior. In my doing so, many areas that demonstrate the application of behavioral principles to problems of children and adolescents will not be addressed (e.g., behavioral pediatrics, child abuse). Such a shortcoming is inevitable in such a project. The present chapter is intended to illustrate representative efforts and trends in the field of behavior therapy applied to children and adolescents; it is not intended to be exhaustive.

TREATMENT OUTCOME STUDIES

Anxious-withdrawn Behavior
Although *DSM-III* (APA, 1980) distinguishes among the more common phobic disorders and three principle types of anxiety disorders in children (separation anxiety disorder, avoidant disorders, and overanxious disorder), these subgroupings have not received strong empirical support (e.g., Achenbach & Edelbrock, 1983; Ollendick, 1983b; Quay, 1986). Rather, factor analytic studies have consistently identified a broader band of child behavior disorders, usually labeled anxious-withdrawn behaviors. In this section, the behavioral treatment of these "internalizing" behaviors will be examined.

Systematic Desensitization and Its Variants
The behavioral treatment of children and adolescents who evince fear, anxiety, and withdrawn behavior dates back to the early efforts of Mary Cover Jones and her treatment of "Peter" (Jones, 1924). Peter, a three-year-old, was fearful of rabbits, fur coats, and other related objects. As is now well known, Peter was treated by progressively bringing the feared rabbit closer and closer to him while he was engaged in a pleasurable behavior, eating. Gradually, Peter's fear was eliminated not only for the rabbit but also for related stimuli (e.g., fur coats). While this early study is oftentimes cited as an illustration of deconditioning, it is important to note that fearless children and a favored assistant whom Peter called "papa" were also present during the deconditioning process. It is certainly possible that modeling of fearless behavior, as well as reinforcement for approach behavior, was operative in this case study (Ollendick & Cerny, 1981).

Nonetheless, deconditioning is one of the most frequently used treatment strategies with fearful and anxious children. Based on the early efforts of Jones and Watson, as well as Masserman's early research in experimental neuroses, Wolpe (1958) developed systematic desensitization as a graduated deconditioning technique. In this paradigm, anxiety and fear are viewed as classically conditioned responses that can be unlearned through deconditioning or counterconditioning procedures. In this procedure, the anxiety-producing stimuli are presented in the presence of stimuli that elicit responses incompatible with anxiety. In this manner, the anxiety is said to be "counterconditioned" and inhibited by the incompatible response. To be effective, it is necessary to systematically pair, in a graduated fashion, the anxiety-arousing stimuli (either imaginally or in vivo) with the competing stimuli to elicit the incompatible response.

Historically, systematic desensitization involved imaginal representation of the anxiety-arousing stimuli and has employed relaxation as the competing, inhibiting response. While these procedures appear to work well with adolescents and older children, younger children appear to have difficulty in fully acquiring the muscular relaxation response and in being able to adequately image the fear-producing stimuli (Ollendick & Cerny, 1981). As a result, in vivo desensitization (as originally used by Jones) and emotive imagery (in which feelings of self-assertion, pride, mirth, or affection are used as the anxiety-antagonistic response) have become increasingly popular, at least with young children (Hatzenbuehler & Schroeder, 1978; Ollendick, 1979a). These variants have evolved as a result of the acknowledged developmental limitations of young children. However, it must also be noted that not all fears or anxieties of children are amenable to in vivo treatment (e.g., fear of dying) and that it is not always possible to secure therapeutic control over diverse counterconditioning agents (e.g., eating). For these instances, progress must be made in tailoring standard muscular relaxation procedures to young children and in creatively using a variety of stimulus cues (e.g., sights, sounds, smells) to help young children better image the anxiety-arousing agents.

Several studies, including single-case reports, experimental analogue designs, and group treatment reports, have attempted to evaluate the efficacy of systematic desensitization and its variants for anxious and fearful children and adolescents. As noted most succinctly by Wells and Vitulano (1984), although many of these case studies are clinically interesting and examine a variety of childhood fears (e.g., dogs, dark, dentists, school, bees, and loud noises), they possess many of the shortcomings attendant to uncontrolled case studies.

While these uncontrolled case studies are highly suggestive of the efficacy of systematic desensitization and its variants, they are not conclusive. However, a recent study by Van Hasselt, Hersen, Bellack, Rosenbloom, and Lamparski (1979) clearly illustrates the value of controlled single-case methodology. In this study, an 11-year-old multiphobic child

(blood, heights, and test-taking) was treated with standard desensitization procedures in a multiple baseline fashion (Hersen & Barlow, 1976). Fear of heights was treated first, followed by fear of blood, and then fear of taking tests. In addition, consistent with the tripartite assessment of anxiety that characterizes the behavioral approach (e.g., Borkovec, Weerts, & Bernstein, 1977), measures of motoric, cognitive, and physiological aspects of anxiety were obtained for each of these fears. Results indicated that relaxation alone had little or no effect on the three channels of anxiety, whereas desensitization proper led to significant reductions in both motoric and cognitive aspects of anxiety but not physiological ones. As can be seen in Figure 12.2, which depicts results for the cognitive measure, these changes occurred for each fear only when systematic desensitization was applied specifically to that fear. Such results affirm the controlling effects of this procedure. Other controlled single-case studies are reviewed by Ollendick (1983b) and Wells and Vitulano (1984), who conclude that these procedures are generally effective for a wide variety of fears and anxieties.

In addition to these uncontrolled and controlled single-case studies, at least six analogue studies of systematic desensitization have been reported with children and adolescents (Barabasz, 1973, 1975; Kelley, 1976; Kondas, 1967; Mann & Rosenthal, 1969; Ultee, Griffen, & Schellekens, 1982). These studies have been classified as analogue studies because they involved the treatment of mild fears in nonreferred subject populations and/or because they involved only a brief trial of systematic desensitization (e.g., three sessions or less). In all studies, except for that of Kelly (1976), which involved the treatment of very young children under 5 years of age and which did not employ a counterconditioning agent, systematic desensitization was found to be effective. Subject populations ranged from 5 to 16 years in age; fears ranged from specific phobias to interpersonal anxieties. Consistent with our earlier observations, one study (Ultee et al., 1982) found that in vivo desensitization was more effective than imaginal desensitization with 5- to 10-year-olds. At older ages, both imaginal and in vivo procedures appear to be equally effective, although a critical test of this conclusion has not yet been undertaken.

Surprisingly, only one group outcome study has

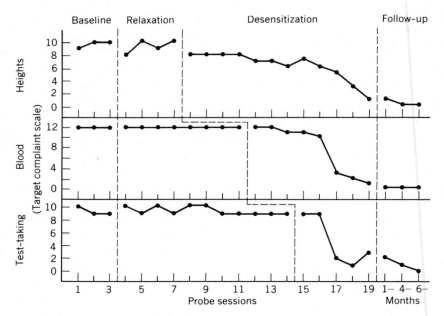

Figure 12.2 Cognitive responses (Target Complaint Scale) in probe sessions during baseline, relaxation training, systematic desensitization, and follow-up. (From V. B. Van Hasselt, M. Hersen, A. S. Bellack, N. D. Rosenbloom, & D. Lamparski, "Tripartite assessment of the effects of systematic desensitization in a multiphobic child: An experimental analysis" [Figure 2]. *Journal of Behavior Therapy and Experimental Psychiatry*, 1979, *10*,, 57–66. Copyright by Pergamon Press, Inc. Reprinted by permission.)

been conducted with clinically phobic children and adolescents. This study (Miller, Barrett, Hampe, & Noble, 1972) compared imaginal desensitization, psychotherapy, and no treatment in 67 children aged 6 to 15 years, most of whom were school phobic. The only major methodological weakness in this otherwise well-controlled study is that parents in both treatment groups received intensive parent counseling based on operant principles. Not only were the effects of the two treatments per se confounded, their differential efficacy was clouded by the similarity in parental intervention. Perhaps these confounds were responsible for the findings. Essentially, Miller et al. (1972) found significant improvement on parental report measures for the two treatment conditions but not for the no-treatment condition. That is, the two treatment groups did not differ with respect to their relative efficacy. Unfortunately, behavioral observation of the children in the setting in which they were fearful and self-report measures of fear were not obtained in this study. Whether differences would have been obtained on these measures is unknown; clearly, this highly intriguing study is in need of systematic replication and

extension before claims to the relative efficacy of systematic desensitization procedures over more traditional psychotherapeutic ones can be claimed.

Although not truly variants of systematic desensitization, flooding and implosion are also based on classical conditioning principles (deconditioning) and require the child to be exposed to anxiety-arousing stimuli for anxiety reduction to occur. In contrast to the graduated approach of systematic desensitization, these procedures entail prolonged exposure, either imaginally or in vivo, to the most anxiety-producing stimuli. During these extinction-based procedures, the conditioned fear stimuli are repeatedly presented in the absence of the original unconditioned stimuli. In this manner the individual learns that there really is nothing to be afraid of, and the anxiety response is weakened. When using this approach, it is critical that the conditioned stimuli be presented in the absence of the unconditioned stimuli. For example, if a child who is fearful of dogs were being treated in vivo, it would be important to ensure that the dog not actually bite or attack the child. Such an occurrence would undoubtedly result in renewed conditioning. The child would continue to avoid dogs and evince even greater fear in their presence. This is an obvious risk that must be considered before the use of such procedures can be endorsed. Perhaps because of these risks, very few clinical studies using these procedures have been reported (Ollendick & Gruen, 1972; Smith & Sharpe, 1970). Nonetheless, Marks (1975) reports that techniques based on flooding and implosion achieve consistently good results with adults; it is time that their systematic use with children be undertaken and carefully evaluated.

In summary, systematic desensitization, emotive imagery, flooding, and implosion all represent reasonably effective procedures for anxiety-based disorders in children. While several questions remain, they represent viable options and are welcome additions to the behaviorally oriented clinician's armamentarium.

Modeling-based Procedures

Treatments based on classical conditioning principles emphasize the role of direct learning experiences in the acquisition, maintenance, and reduction of anxieties and fears. In contrast, treatments based on vicarious conditioning principles focus upon observational learning or modeling. That is, learning and behavior changes are said to occur as a function of observing other people's behavior and its consequences for them (Bandura, 1969).

Modeling involves demonstrating nonfearful behavior in the anxiety-producing situation *and* showing the child an appropriate response to use in the fearful situation. Thus, anxiety is reduced and appropriate skills are learned. After the demonstration, the child is instructed to model or imitate performance of the model. Following repeated rehearsals of the observed behaviors, the child is provided feedback and reinforcement for performance that matches that of the model. Thus, operant principles are used frequently to maintain the desired behaviors once they are acquired via the modeling process.

Three types of modeling have been described: filmed modeling, live or in vivo modeling, and participant modeling. Filmed modeling consists of having a child observe a film in which a model (usually of similar characteristics to the targeted child) displays progressively more intimate interaction with the feared object or setting, whereas live modeling entails having the child observe a *live* model (again,

usually of similar characteristics to the fearful child) engage in graduated interactions with a *live* feared object or actually participate in real-life situations found to be anxiety producing. Participant modeling, on the other hand, consists of live modeling *plus* physical contact with a therapist (or fearless peer) who physically guides the child through the fearful situation. Thus, in addition to observing another interact fearlessly, the child is provided physical and psychological support and direct contact with the therapist *while* performing the appropriate behavior. Ritter (1968) refers to this procedure as "contact desensitization."

Based on a review of modeling studies with fearful children and adolescents, Ollendick (1979a) has noted that filmed modeling is effective in about 25 to 50 percent of cases, live modeling in about 30 to 67 percent, and participant modeling in 80 to 92 percent. A clear ordering of effectiveness is evident in these studies: filmed modeling being least effective, live modeling intermediate, and participant modeling most effective. It should be noted, however, that nearly all of these studies could be classified as analogue studies. That is, they dealt with mild to moderate fears in nonclinical populations.

Nonetheless, these procedures are potentially effective for more highly fearful children and in the prevention of anxieties associated with visits to dentists, hospitalization, and surgery. Illustratively, Ross, Ross, and Evans (1971) used modeling procedures (along with social reinforcement) in the treatment of a six-year-old boy whose fear and avoidance of relationships with peers was so extreme that he actively avoided peers and refused to even watch filmed presentations featuring young children. Prior to treatment, systematic behavioral observations revealed that the child interacted with peers less than once every 5 minutes (the average child interacted approximately 11 times per 5-minute period) and that he engaged in 52 avoidance behaviors during a 2½-hour observation period (e.g., running away from an approaching peer, hiding during group activity). Treatment, while necessarily elaborate and extended, consisted primarily of establishing generalized imitation, participant modeling, and social reinforcement. Following treatment, the child was observed to interact an average of 10 times during each 5-minute period (a rate comparable to his peers) and to display only 4 avoidance behaviors over a 2½-hour period (again, comparable to that of his peers). Upon follow-up, two months after the cessation of treatment, he was observed to "join ongoing play groups, initiate verbal contacts, and sustain effective social interactions, all with children who were complete strangers to him." (Ross et al., 1971, p. 277). Clearly, significant clinical improvement was noted in this uncontrolled case study.

Based on this early study, as well as those of O'Connor (1969, 1972), modeling procedures have been used increasingly with socially withdrawn children who are socially anxious and/or unassertive in social situations (Ollendick, 1981). As originally noted by O'Connor, many of these children are grossly deficient in social skills, which seriously handicaps them in the acquisition of "complex behavioral repertoires necessary for social interaction" (O'Connor, 1969, p. 15). Several well-controlled single-case and group outcome studies affirm the efficacy of modeling-based procedures in the acquisition of these skills (see Van Hasselt, Hersen, Bellack, & Whitehill, 1979, for a comprehensive review).

Illustrative of the single-case approach is a study by Bornstein, Bellack, and Hersen (1977) in which four withdrawn children between 8 and 11 years of age were treated in a multiple baseline across behaviors design. Following careful assessment of specific behavioral deficits (e.g., poor eye contact, inaudible speech, and low rate of verbal requests), each deficit was treated in a sequential fashion. As can be seen in Figure 12.3, specific deficits were remediated when, and only when, they were specifically addressed in the treatment regimen. Such results affirm the controlling effects of the treatment procedures.

Using similar procedures, Ladd (1981) demonstrated the efficacy of modeling strategies (variously labeled coaching or social skills training) in a group outcome study. In this study, socially withdrawn 8- to 10-year-old children were randomly assigned to skill training, attention control, and no-treatment control groups. Children were identified on the basis of behavioral observation and sociometric measures and were trained on very specific behaviors: how to ask questions of peers, how to offer useful suggestions and directions to peers, and how to provide supportive statements to them. Unlike their control group counterparts, trained children spent a greater percentage of time engaging in the trained skills following treatment and at follow-up (four weeks later) and evidenced significant and lasting

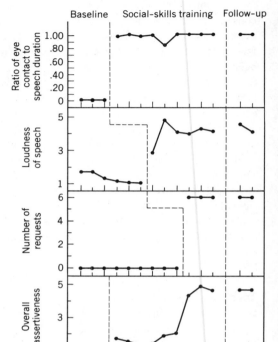

Figure 12.3 Probe sessions during baseline, social skills treatment, and follow-up for training scenes for Jane. A multiple baseline analysis of ratio of eye contact while speaking to speech duration, loudness of speech, number of requests, and overall assertiveness. (From M. R. Bornstein, A. S. Bellack, & M. Hersen, "Social skills training for unassertive children: A multiple baseline analysis." [Figure 3]. *Journal of Applied Behavior Analysis*, 1977, *10*, 183–195. Copyright by the Society of Experimental Analysis of Behavior, Inc. Reprinted by permission.)

gains in peer acceptance. Control group children remained the same or declined on both of these measures. Similar findings have been obtained by Oden and Asher (1977) and LaGrecca and Santogrossi (1981), among others.

In addition to fearful and withdrawn children, modeling procedures have been used most productively in the *prevention* of anxiety and fear in children about to undergo hospitalization or surgical procedures. Based on an early study by Melamed and Siegel (1975) in which children about to have surgery were shown a film depicting a child who gradually comes to cope with his fears of an operation, a host of studies have been conducted (King, Hamilton, & Murphy, 1983; Melamed, Robbins, Smith, & Graves, 1980; Peterson, Schultheis, Ridley-Johnson, Miller, & Tracy, 1984; Peterson & Shigetomi, 1981). In general, these group outcome studies have found that children who were shown films of the preparation and conduct of surgery (in comparison to attention control or no-treatment control group children) were less fearful *and* posed fewer behavior problems post-surgery. Typically, the number of medical complications and the duration of hospitalization were reduced as well.

In sum, modeling procedures have been used frequently and productively in the treatment of anxious, fearful, and withdrawn children and adolescents. In addition, a number of studies have begun to delineate specific parameters of modeling that appear to enhance its efficacy. These include the use of models similar in age and sex, the use of multiple models instead of ony one model, and the use of coping models (e.g., Bandura & Manlove, 1968; Kornhaber & Schroeder, 1975; Meichenbaum, 1971). These characteristics are reviewed in detail by Graziano, DeGiovanni, and Garcia (1979), especially as they apply to treatment of fearful or anxious children. As with systematic desensitization and its variants, modeling-based procedures have received strong empirical support for their utility, at least with mild to moderate fears and anxieties. As noted by Ollendick (1979a) and O'Leary and Carr (1982), however, most of these studies have been analogue in nature and the efficacy of these procedures with clinically referred youngsters is in need of empirical evaluation. Further studies comparing modeling procedures with other behavioral procedures, as well as more traditional procedures, are sorely lacking.

Operant-based Procedures

In contast to systematic desensitization and modeling, both of which assume that anxiety must be reduced or eliminated before approach behavior will occur, procedures based on principles of operant conditioning make no such assumption. Briefly, operant conditioning refers to a type of learning in which behaviors are altered by the consequences that follow them (Kazdin, 1975). For fear reduction, operant-based procedures assert that acquisition of approach responses to the fear-producing situation

is sufficient and that anxiety reduction, per se, is unnecessary. Thus, one child's school phobia may result from excessive positive reinforcement at home in the form of attention or affection, whereas another child's school phobia might result from the negative reinforcement received when he or she avoids unpleasant or aversive situations in school (Ollendick & Mayer, 1984). This model most forcefully calls for a thorough assessment of the positive and negative reinforcing stimuli that produce or maintain anxious, fearful, or withdrawn behaviors (Ayllon, Smith, & Rogers, 1970; Hersen, 1970; Neisworth, Madle, & Goeke, 1975).

Operant-based programs have been most useful in the modification of school phobia behavior (e.g., Ayllon et al., 1970; Doleys & Williams, 1977; Hersen, 1970; Kennedy, 1965; Rines, 1973; Weinberger, Leventhal, & Beckman, 1973). Illustratively, Ayllon et al. (1970) treated an 8-year-old girl through a home-based operant approach. Following collection of extensive baseline information in the home and school, a shaping procedure was implemented. The girl was taken to school toward the end of the school day by an assistant who remained with her until school was dismissed. Each successive day, she was taken to school earlier. By the seventh day of this procedure, she was able to remain in school all day without the presence of the assistant. Contingent upon each step, the young girl was reinforced by the assistant and her mother. Similarly, Rines (1973) presented a case study in which a school-based contingency management program was implemented with a 12-year-old girl who was described as "unmanageable" in the school setting. Although she did not refuse to attend school entirely, she made numerous phone calls from school to her mother, who invariably made arrangements to have her sent home from school. To reverse this trend, school personnel were instructed not to let her call home and her teachers were advised as to how to ignore her crying behavior in the classroom. Additionally, teachers and mother were instructed to reinforce positive behaviors in both school and home settings. Upon follow-up, she was attending school regularly and achieving high grades.

Operant procedures also have been used in the treatment of socially avoidant children (e.g., Allen, Hart, Buell, Harris, & Wolf, 1964; Clement & Milne, 1967) and children who display mild fears such as fear of the dark, riding on school buses, and sitting on the toilet (e.g., Leitenberg & Callahan, 1973; Luiselli, 1977, 1978; Pomerantz, Peterson, Macholin, & Stern, 1977). Only the study by Leitenberg and Callahan (1973), however, used a control group design. In this study, fear of the dark as assessed by parental report and the child's willingness to remain in a dark room for an extended period of time (five minutes) was studied in relatively normal kingergarten children. Children were assigned to either a treatment or no-treatment group. Following eight sessions of treatment (consisting of practice staying in the darkened room, feedback, and reinforcement), children in the treatment group were able to stay longer in the darkened room than control children. Additional analyses revealed that four out of seven children in the treatment group were able to stay in the dark room for the entire five minutes. None of the control children was able to do so. As noted, however, the "treatment" was effective for only four of the children, resulting in a 57 percent treatment success rate.

This rate is somewhat distressing since these children were not clinic-referred and their fears were relatively mild. Thus, evidence for reinforced practice with fearful children is very sparse indeed. Only a few uncontrolled case studies attest to its efficacy. Clearly, studies of greater experimental rigor are needed.

In sum, evidence for the utility of operant-based procedures in the treatment of anxious and withdrawn behaviors in children and adolescents is less convincing than that found for procedures based on principles of classical or vicarious conditioning. Almost all support for use of these procedures is based on uncontrolled clinical case studies or analogue studies in which children were not referred for treatment. Although speculative, it may be the case that these procedures are less effective because they do not directly attempt to reduce or inhibit the subjectively perceived anxiety. Anxiety reduction, as well as response acquisition, may be necessary for behavior change to occur. Clearly, future studies should explore these possibilities systematically and directly compare the efficacy of classical, vicarious, and operant-based procedures.

Cognitive-based Procedures

As noted in the Introduction, cognitive strategies for the treatment of child and adolescent behavior disorders are currently in vogue. According to Ledwidge (1978), a cognitive-based procedure can be defined as a "treatment approach that aims at modifying behavior and emotion by influencing the client's pattern of thought" (p. 356). In these procedures, an attempt is made to alter specific perceptions, images, thoughts, and beliefs through direct manipulation and restructuring of faulty, maladaptive cognitions. A variety of procedures have been described including Beck's (1976) cognitive therapy, Ellis' (1970) rational psychotherapy, Goldfried, Decenteceo, and Weinberg's (1974) systematic rational restructuring, Lazarus' (1974) cognitive restructuring, Meichenbaum's (1977) verbal self-instruction training, and Spivack and Shure's (1974) problem-solving approach. Although there are clear differences among these approaches, they share a common focus: the direct modification of faulty cognitions (as assessed through verbal behavior) in order to effect constructive behavior change.

Briefly, it is necessary to review the underlying principles of these procedures prior to depicting their use with children and adolescents. Basically, it is assumed that maladaptive thinking leads to maladaptive behavior. Thus, "self-statements" or "self-talk," as it is variously labeled, is believed to be perceived by the individual as plausible and logically related to the situation. For example, a child exhibiting intense fear of social interaction might think, "If I tell him I want to play, he might laugh at me" and "I know he won't let me anyway; everyone hates me." These self-statements inhibit the child from emitting an appropriate approach response and, in turn, serve to confirm the child's expectation and reinforce him or her for the avoidant response. The presence of self-statements such as these have been clearly affirmed in the literature. For example, Zatz and Chassin (1983) have recently documented the cognitions of test-anxious children. Anxious children not only endorse more debilitating statements (e.g., "I'm doing poorly . . . I don't do well on tests like this . . . Everyone usually does better than me"), they also ascribe to fewer facilitative, coping statements (e.g., "I am bright enough to do this . . . I am doing the best that I can . . . I do well on tests like this"). Stefanek (1983) has affirmed a similar pattern of self-statements for socially withdrawn children.

Probably the most frequently used cognitive approach with anxious and fearful children is verbal self-instruction training (Graziano & Mooney, 1980, 1982; Graziano, Mooney, Huber, & Ignasiak, 1979; Kanfer, Karoly, & Newman, 1975). In the first application of this approach, Kanfer et al. (1975) treated five- to six-year-old children who were afraid of the dark in an analogue study. Three groups of children were formed. The first group rehearsed active control or competence-mediating statements (e.g., "I am a brave boy (girl) and I can handle the dark"); the second group rehearsed statements aimed at reducing the aversive quality of the stimulus situation itself (e.g., "The dark is not such a bad place to be"); and the third group rehearsed neutral statements (e.g., "Mary had a little lamb"). When later exposed to a darkness-tolerance test, both the competence and stimulus groups surpassed the neutral group in duration. The competence and stimulus groups did not differ from each other, however, suggesting that adaptive statements were acquired under both conditions.

Subsequent to this analogue study, Graziano and his colleagues conducted one of the few relatively well-controlled studies to date with clinically phobic children (Graziano & Mooney, 1980; Graziano et al., 1979), including a 2½- to 3-year follow-up (Graziano & Mooney, 1982). Forty children between 6 and 13½ years of age were treated. The children were severely nighttime fearful, displaying panic behavior (e.g., frequent crying and frightened calling out to the parents) that had disrupted the families nearly every night for a mean of 5 years (range = 1.5 to 10.3 years' duration). Children were randomly assigned to a treatment and a "waiting-list" control group. The treatment rationale, illustrative of the cognitive approach, was as follows: "All of you have told us you are afraid of the dark or of being alone. As you know, some kids are afraid in the dark and others are not. The main difference between you and those other kids who are not afraid is that those other kids know how to *make* themselves not be afraid. In this class, we are going to teach you how to make yourselves less afraid. We are going to teach you how to relax, *think pleasant thoughts*, and *say special words*, all of which will help you become braver" (p. 209, italics added). Results clearly attested to the efficacy of this approach: significant changes were noted only for the treatment group on a host of variables including number of minutes to get in bed and time to fall asleep, self-reported willingness to go to sleep, and proportion of days that delaying tactics (e.g., ask for water, light on) were used. Following treatment, the "waiting-list" group was also treated. In total, 39 of the 40 children showed significant change in behav-

ior as judged against a strict criterion: 10 consecutive nights of fearless nighttime behaviors. Long-term follow-up information was obtained 2½ to 3 years after treatment from 34 of the 40 families using a mail questionnaire and extensive telephone contacts. Maintenance of improvement was noted for 31 of the 34 children.

Unfortunately, this clinically significant study included three technical shortcomings: First, treatment was not solely cognitive in nature, precluding the possibility of evaluating this study as a true test of the cognitive position. Both relaxation training and operant reinforcement were also used. Second, evidence of the long-term maintenance of the gains would have been better had multiple sources of information been obtained (e.g., child and parent self-report, clinical interview, and direct behavioral observation). As is, the authors relied solely upon parental report. Third, an attention-control group was not used, making it difficult to determine whether attention alone might have been efficacious. This latter possibility is unlikely, however, given the long-term nature of these real-life fears. These shortcomings notwithstanding, this study represents more closely the type of clinically relevant studies that must be undertaken in order to substantiate the utility of such procedures.

Cognitive restructuring procedures (Lazarus, 1974) have been used infrequently with children and adolescents. Nonetheless, they would appear to be useful. In a well-controlled single-case study, Ollendick (1979b) demonstrated the use of such procedures with a 16-year-old anorectic male. Initially, in this case study, systematic desensitization was used and was found to be effective in altering excessive fear of eating and gaining weight in this adolescent. Its effects were short-lived, however, and when treatment was withdrawn in systematic phases, substantial weight was lost. In an effort to gain greater control over his behavior, additional assessment was conducted and revealed that he was frequently observed saying, "I can't eat . . . I'll get fat again." It was hypothesized that this self-defeating self-statement (along with several similar ones) served to maintain poor eating habits, heightened anxiety, and low body weight. Accordingly, his cognitions were addressed in greater detail. Specifically, the five categories of weight-relevant thoughts proposed by Mahoney and Mahoney (1975) were examined: (1) thoughts about pounds gained ("I've tried to eat that food but haven't gained a pound"); (2) thoughts about capabilities ("There's no way I can gain weight again"); (3) excuses about not gaining weight ("If those other kids liked me, I could gain weight"); (4) thoughts about inappropriate standard setting ("I threw up this morning, there's no use to try. I may as well give up"); and (5) thoughts about how peers would perceive him ("Nobody will like me if I gain weight"). In between treatment sessions, he was asked to self-monitor and record "self-statements" about these areas. During sessions this "homework" was reviewed and his thoughts were "restructured" to be more realistic and adaptive (e.g., "If I gain weight, it is true that some kids might not like me. Other kids will like me, however. Besides, what difference will it make whether they like it or not. I will feel better"). As can be seen in Figure 12.4, weight gain was realized and maintained over

a two-year period. It should be noted, however, that treatment was extensive and that it followed a successful trial of systematic desensitization. Whether cognitive restructuring alone would have been effective is unknown. Certainly, this procedure warrants additional study with children of other ages and across different anxieties and fears.

Finally, the problem-solving cognitive approach espoused by Spivack and Shure (1974) has been used increasingly with socially withdrawn children and young adolescents (e.g., Allen, Chinsky, Larcen, Lochman, & Salnger, 1976; Elardo & Caldwell, 1979; McClure, Chinsky, & Larcen, 1978; Weissberg et al., 1981; Winett, Stefanek, & Riley, 1983). Basically, children in these programs have been instructed in problem-solving strategies such as generating alternative solutions, means-ends thinking, and consequential thinking. In general,

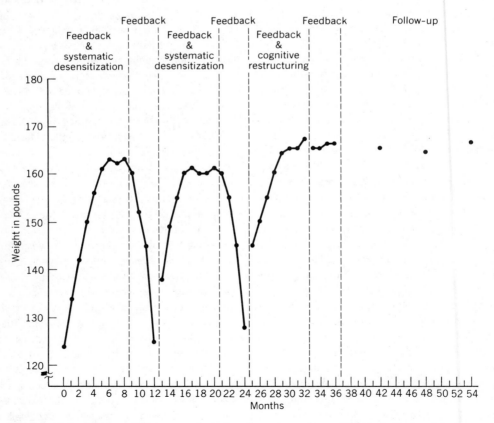

Figure 12.4 Rick's weight in pounds during the various phases of the experimental design. (Adapted from T. H. Ollendick, "Behavioral treatment of anorexia nervosa: A five-year study" [Figure 1]. *Behavior Modification*, 1979, *3*, 124–135. Copyright by Sage Publications, Inc. Reprinted by permission.)

preschoolers and school-age children and adolescents have been shown to improve on self, teacher, and behavioral ratings as a result of such programs. It should be noted that these strategies are most effective for youngsters who are basically withdrawn and who are not able to generate appropriate ways of responding.

In sum, the newer cognitive-based procedures show considerable promise in the treatment of anxious, fearful, and withdrawn children. While initial findings suggest that effects produced in such programs may be long-term and generalizable, a clear and well-controlled demonstration of such maintenance and generalization is not yet available (Meador & Ollendick, 1984; Neilans & Israel, 1981). As with the other procedures reviewed, considerably more investigation is necessary before the utility of these procedures can be said to be firmly established.

Summary

In sum, behavioral procedures for the treatment of anxious and withdrawn behaviors have enjoyed wide popularity. Procedures based on classical conditioning, operant conditioning, vicarious conditioning, and cognitive principles have proven to be generally effective, *at least in the short run*. While studies supporting the use of these procedures were presented separately, it is evident that many studies combined these procedures in an integrative package. Moreover, much research remains to be conducted. First, demonstration of the long-term efficacy of these procedures is needed. Second, comparative studies are needed in order to examine the relative superiority, or lack thereof, of these procedures over more traditional ones. Third, comparative studies among the behavioral procedures themselves are called for. Which behavioral procedures are most effective for which behavioral problems? Finally, greater attention must be paid to both assessment and methodological issues. Not infrequently, only one source of information has been sought in these studies, leaving open the question of just how effective the procedures are across response modalities and within response-response covariations. Further, it is necessary to employ appropriate control groups; all too frequently studies have simply compared a behavioral approach to no treatment. Clearly, we must advance in methodological sophistication before we can place firm confidence in our procedures.

Oppositional and Aggressive Behaviors

In addition to internalized, overcontrolled behaviors such as anxiety, fear, and social withdrawal, factor analytic studies have identified a second subset of children's behavior problems, those labeled externalized and *undercontrolled* (Achenbach, 1966; Achenbach & Edelbrock, 1978; Peterson, 1961). Included in this "symptom cluster" are problem behaviors characterized by noncompliance, restlessness, irresponsibility, lying, tantrums, stealing, and aggression. Further, for younger children this cluster is frequently associated with hyperactivity, and for older children, with delinquent activities (Barkley, 1982; Herbert, 1982).

These "undercontrolled" behaviors cut across several *DSM-III* categories: Conduct Disorder (of which there are four subtypes: undersocialized, aggressive; undersocialized, nonaggressive; socialized, aggressive; and socialized, nonaggressive), Oppositional Disorder, Attention Deficit Disorder (with and without hyperactivity), and Antisocial Personality Disorder. As noted recently by Wells and Forehand (1984), the reliability and validity of these specific *DSM-III* categories remain doubtful. For example, reliability studies show that clinicians agree only about half of the time on these specific diagnoses (e.g., Mattison, Cantwell, Russell, & Will, 1979; Mezzich & Mezzich, 1979), and one of the few validity studies (e.g., Henn, Bardwell, & Jenkins, 1980) fails to substantiate critical predictive relationships. At least at this stage of our knowledge, the more fine-grained distinctions offered by *DSM-III* are not borne out empirically. Nonetheless, it is evident that these problems are frequently observed in clinical settings and that they are particularly refractory to change. Many studies report that between 50 and 75 percent of clinic referrals are for acting-out behaviors (e.g., Bernal, Duryee, Pruett, & Burns, 1968; Kent & O'Leary, 1976; Patterson, 1974; Rutter, Tizard, Yule, Graham, & Whitmore, 1976), and other studies consistently show the relative persistence of such behaviors (e.g., Loeber, 1982; Olweus, 1979; Robins, 1978). As noted most forcefully by Loeber (1982), this continuity appears highest for those youths who start their antisocial behavior at an early age, who evince such behaviors at a high frequency across multiple settings (e.g., home, school), and who exhibit both overt (e.g., aggression, excessive quarreling, disobedience, and fighting) and covert (e.g., lying, stealing, truancy, and vandalism) behaviors. For these youths, it is estimated that roughly one-half to two-thirds will evidence antisocial behaviors as adults (Loeber, 1982).

Prior to examining the efficacy of learning-based treatments for these behaviors, brief comment about the relationship between hyperactivity and aggressive behaviors is called for. Although hyperactivity has been isolated as a narrow-band syndrome by Achenbach and others (e.g., Achenbach & Edelbrock, 1978; Quay, 1979), considerable evidence suggests that the overlap between hyperactive and aggressive behavior is extensive. For example, Safer and Allen (1976) have shown that up to 75 percent of children with Attention Deficit Disorder with Hyperactivity have conduct problems, and factor analytic studies have indicated a high positive correlation between hyperactive behaviors and conduct problems (e.g., Goyette, Connors, & Ulrich, 1978). Further, Sandberg, Rutter, and Taylor (1978) were unable to distinguish between these two groups on such factors as pre- and perinatal complications, neurological abnormalities, social class, psychiatric status of mother, or long-term prognosis, whereas Sandberg, Wisselberg, and Shaffer (1980) were unable to differentiate between these groups on biological or psychosocial background variables. While controversy certainly remains on this diagnostic issue, no one has devised an empirical scheme to enable researchers or clinicians to arrive at a *reliable* differential diagnosis (O'Leary, 1980; O'Leary & Carr, 1982).

In the sections that follow, treatment procedures based on operant and vicarious conditioning, as well as cognitive processes, will be reviewed. Unlike behavioral treatment of internalizing behaviors, treatments derived from classical conditioning principles have been used rarely in the treatment of externalizing conduct problems. This state of affairs is undoubtedly related to prevailing assumptions that such behaviors are not affectively mediated and, accordingly, are not emotionally conditioned. Because of space constraints, focus in this chapter will be placed primarily on treatment of two of the most frequent conduct problems, noncompliance and aggression.

Operant-based Procedures

In recent years, use of operant-based treatment procedures for conduct problems has mushroomed. In clinic, institutional, and home settings, systematic efforts have been directed toward reprogramming the social environment in order to alter the antecedent and consequent events that maintain these undesired behaviors. Such efforts have included parent behavioral training, token economic systems, contingency contracting, and punishment procedures. Not infrequently, each of these approaches has been used as part of an overall treatment program.

Several reviews affirm the feasibility and efficacy of using parents as behavior modifiers, especially for conduct problems (e.g., Berkowitz & Graziano, 1972; Forehand & Atkeson, 1977; Nay, 1979; O'Dell, 1974; Wells & Forehand, 1981). In these programs, parents are trained to apply differential social consequences to specific child behaviors. For example, in the Forehand program for younger children (two to eight years old), parents are taught to increase a set of "attending and following skills" that can be used in general positive interactions with the child and to deliver verbal and nonverbal rewards for specific behaviors (Forehand & McMahon, 1982). Typically, homework assignments are given to the parent to spend a period of time with the child (usually one 15-minute period a day) in order to maximize opportunities to attend to and reward appropriate behaviors. In addition, one or two prosocial behaviors are identified (e.g., following directions, sharing with a sibling), and the parent is instructed to "catch" the child engaging in these behaviors and to appropriately reward him or her. As noted by Wells and Forehand (1984), many children will show decreases in oppositional and minor aggressive behaviors with the use of these reinforcement strategies alone. For other children, especially those who show more frequent and serious aggressive behaviors, it is necessary to use specific punishment procedures (e.g., Budd, Green, & Baer, 1976; Roberts, 1982; Roberts, Hatzenbuehler, & Bean, 1981). First, parents are trained how to give clear, concise commands, no more than one or two at a time, and not to repeat any given command more than once. If the child fails to comply with the command, a verbal warning of impending consequences is delivered. If the child still does not comply (usually within a five-second period), the parent is instructed in use of a time-out procedure (confinement to a chair for a three- to five-minute period). Following release from time-out, the command is reissued. If necessary, this process is repeated until compliance occurs. The Forehand programs appear most effective with younger children (Wells & Forehand, 1984).

For older children and adolescents, Patterson's treatment program seems more appropriate. Treatment is divided into three phases. In the first phase, parents are taught basic social learning concepts (e.g., Patterson, 1977; Patterson & Guillion, 1976) so that a common "language" of intervention exists. Upon mastery of this material, parents are taught to define, track, and record both deviant and prosocial behaviors over a preintervention period. Daily phone calls to the home occur during this time to prompt parents to collect and record their observations. In the third phase, parents are trained to develop a point system whereby the child or adolescent earns or loses points contingent on positive and negative behaviors, respectively. Points, in turn, are exchanged *daily* for backup rewards previously selected by the child or adolescent. In addition, parents are instructed to use positive social reinforcers (smiles, praise, pat on the back) for appropriate behaviors and time-out procedures for inappropriate behaviors. Thus, multiple positive consequences (e.g., social praise and earning of points) and multiple negative consequences (e.g., time-out and loss of points) are available in this program. It differs most clearly from the Forehand program in its specific use of a point procedure and its involvement of the child or adolescent in determination of the exact reinforcers to be earned. While not yet systematically confirmed, these two additions may be critical elements in the efficacy of this program for older children and adolescents (Patterson, 1982).

Partial support for the need to involve the adolescent in such decision making is derived from the early work of Alexander and Parsons (1973), who used a contingency contracting approach with delinquent adolescents and their families. The treatment program centered around the development of negotiation skills. Such skills were developed and consequated by a series of behavioral contracts that were jointly determined by the adolescent and his family. A number of families were randomly assigned to this group as well as no-treatment, family systems, and psychodynamically oriented therapy groups. The behavioral contracting group showed a recidivism rate (6 to 18 months following treatment) of 26 percent compared to 47 percent, 50 percent, and 73 percent, respectively, for the family systems, no-treatment, and psychodynamic family programs. Such findings were confirmed in a subsequent

follow-up study (Alexander, Barton, Schiavo, & Parsons, 1976).

Although not all reports in the literature have found parent and family behavioral training programs to be effective (e.g., Ferber, Keeley, & Shemberg, 1974; Weathers & Liberman, 1975) or to be maintained over time (e.g., Sanders & James, 1983), findings across studies have been generally positive (e.g., Sanders & Glynn, 1981; Wells & Forehand, 1981, 1984). Further, comparative group outcome studies have shown that behavioral parent training is superior to no treatment (Karoly & Rosenthal, 1977; Peed, Roberts, & Forehand, 1977; Wiltz & Patterson, 1974), to attention placebo controls (Walters & Gilmore, 1973), to "client-oriented parent counseling" (Bernal, Klinnert, & Schultz, 1980), and to broad-spectrum community-based treatment approaches (Fleischman, 1981; Patterson, Chamberlain, & Reid, 1982).

Several areas in behavioral parent training remain to be examined systematically, however. Foremost among them are methodological and generalization issues. For example, parents are presumably trained in a set of skills in these studies but are rarely evaluated for their acquisition. More typically, success of such programs is based on parent report of the child's behavior or direct observation of child behavior itself. There is clearly a need to establish that parents actually acquire the parenting skills and *use* them before firm conclusions about their importance for efficacy can be drawn. Further, questions remain as to the most efficacious way to train such skills (e.g., Adesso & Lipson, 1981; O'Dell et al., 1982; Webster-Stratton, 1981). Such studies need to examine specific teaching formats, content, and techniques *and* identify the active therapeutic ingredients in what are often broad-spectrum treatment programs (Ollendick & Cerny, 1981). Other studies need to examine generalization and maintenance issues (Baum & Forehand, 1983). While a few studies suggest that teaching parents self-control skills (e.g., Wells, Greist, & Forehand, 1980) and more generalized social learning concepts (e.g., McMahon, Forehand, & Greist, 1981) are effective in maintaining the trained skills, such reports are scarce and in need of systematic replication. Other trends, including "parent enhancement training" (Greist et al., 1982) and "behavioral family therapy" (Greist & Wells, 1983), seem to hold considerable promise but are also in need of extension and replication. In these latter approaches, emphasis is placed on the fact that parents and families are part of a functional system in which their own psychological adjustment and involvement in the community at large are determinants of noncompliant or aggressive behavior in their children and adolescents (e.g., Wahler, 1980; Wahler & Afton, 1980; Wahler & Graves, 1983). Given these trends, it is probable that we will see a movement away from "parent training" per se and a move toward "behavioral family therapy" in years to come.

It is also possible to treat conduct disorder problems like aggression in the classroom setting, along with home-based intervention. Illustrative of this approach, Kent and O'Leary (1976) implemented an operant program with a group of boys consisting of (1) teacher and parental praise, encouragement, and other forms of positive attention (e.g., pat on the back, smile, wink); (2) decreased use of teacher threats and reprimands; and (3) special privileges at home, such as extra television or special trips when the child evidenced gains on a "daily report card" completed by the teacher. Further, parents were instructed to spend about a half an hour a day with their sons assisting them in homework. When compared to a no-treatment group, behavioral observations and teacher ratings affirmed that the behavioral group had improved more on social and academic behavior than did the no-treatment group. At follow-up nine months later, however, the nontreated group had also improved and differences were no longer significant. These findings were replicated by Kent and O'Leary (1977) with a second group of aggressive boys. As with the earlier study, treated boys improved more than did untreated ones at termination of therapy; however, no differences were evident at follow-up. Results of these two studies suggest that treatments were effective in reduction of aggressive behavior but that similar reduction would occur over an extended period of time in the absence of treatment. As with Miller et al.'s (1972) study of phobic children, however, the benefits associated with more immediate reductions in problematic behaviors should not be readily dismissed.

Other operant-based procedures such as extinction (e.g., Forehand, Roberts, Doleys, Hobbs, & Resick, 1976; Hart, Allen, Buell, Harris, & Wolf, 1964), differential reinforcement (e.g., Allen & Harris, 1966; Madsen, Becker, & Thomas, 1968), re-

sponse cost (e.g., Burchard & Barrera, 1972; Iwata & Bailey, 1974; McLaughlin & Malaby, 1972), time-out (e.g., Hobbs & Forehand, 1975, 1977; Kendall, Nay, & Jeffers, 1975; Porterfield, Herbert-Jackson, & Risley, 1976), and overcorrection (e.g., Azrin & Powers, 1975; Bornstein, Hamilton, & Quevillon, 1977; Matson, Horne, Ollendick, & Ollendick, 1979) have all been successfully used in classroom modification programs. Typically, these studies have been well-controlled single-case studies, all of which have shown marked reductions in noncompliant, oppositional, and aggressive behaviors. Use of these procedures is limited only by the absence of well-controlled group outcome studies to affirm their efficacy. Their utility, however, is illustrated in the Matson et al. (1979) study. In this study, restitutional and positive practice overcorrection procedures were used to reduce "aggressive and disruptive behaviors which interfered with learning" in 20 children who ranged between 3 and 12 years of age. Target behaviors included hitting, kicking, property destruction, taking items from others, shoving, screaming, tantrums, and general noncompliance. Briefly, restitutional overcorrection required the child to return the environment to a better condition than that which existed prior to the occurrence of the inappropriate behavior, while positive practice overcorrection required the child to repeatedly practice appropriate behaviors that were functionally incompatible with the misbehavior. As can be seen in Figure 12.5, both procedures were highly effective. Further, maintenance of the gains was evident throughout the remainder of the summer session in which these "adjustment problem" children were enrolled.

Not infrequently, children and adolescents with conduct disorders are removed from their homes and placed in treatment programs based on behavior management principles. Foremost among these settings is Achievement Place, a community-based, family-style group home for six to eight predelinquent or delinquent youth under the direction of teaching parents (Fixsen, Phillips, & Wolf, 1972, 1973; Wolf, Phillips, & Fixsen, 1975). The model of teaching parents and a family-style environment for such youngsters has proven to be a very popular and productive one (Herbert, 1982). Based on contingency management and token economic procedures, gains have been documented in academic skills, conversation skills, self-management skills,

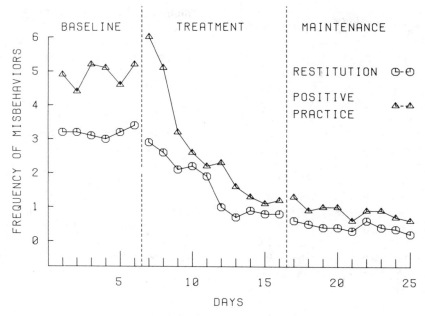

Figure 12.5 Mean number of misbehaviors per child for each of the two groups: Restitution and positive practice. (From J. L. Matson, A.M. Horne, D.G. Ollendick, & T. H. Ollendick, "Overcorrection: A further evaluation of restitution and positive practice" [Figure 1]. *Journal of Behavior Therapy and Experimental Psychiatry*, 1979, 10, 295–298. Copyright by Pergamon Press, Inc. Reprinted by permission.)

conflict negotiation skills as well as cleanliness, punctuality, and other more basic prosocial skills. A point system is the primary treatment procedure in this program. Each adolescent is provided with a card on which is listed a description of specific target behaviors, the performance criteria, and the number of points earned or lost. Points are exchangeable for privileges and other backup reinforcers. Over time, the point system is faded out and the youth is placed on a merit system in which all privileges are free.

Following this, the Homeward Bound phase is implemented in which youths spend more time at home with their parents. Concurrently, the youths and their families are instructed in how to negotiate behavioral contracts—that is, how to determine which behaviors are desirable and what privileges can be earned. In short, youths gradually move from the artificial environment (i.e., points) to a more naturalistic one (home reinforcement). Several evaluative reports of this program are available, not only for the original Achievement Place but also for the many replications in the United States and

elsewhere (Wolf et al., 1975). In general, they show that this program results in short-term as well as long-term success. That is, court contacts and recidivism rates are lower for Achievement Place youth than diverse contrast groups from more traditional institutional settings (Herbert, 1982). For example, in an early study, Trotter (1973) reported that an Achievement Place group of boys had a much lower recidivism rate two years following completion of the program (19%) than did a group of boys from a state institution (53%). This finding was replicated in a later study by Kirigin, Braukmann, Fixsen, Phillips, and Wolf (1975). In this study, recidivism rates two years following treatment were 22 percent for an Achievement Place group and 47 percent for an institutional group. In more recent years, Jones (1979) has completed a comparative evaluation of 27 programs using the Achievement Place model and 25 other home-based programs not using this model. This is an important comparison since earlier studies compared Achievement Place to institutional settings, not other home-based programs. While the

Achievement Place programs were found to be superior in school performance, cost, and community acceptance, they were not superior to these other home-based programs in offense or recidivism rates. Thus, while Achievement Place programs have been found to be superior to institutional programs in reducing recidivism, they have not been found to be superior to other home-based programs. The treatment of youths in the community in which they live appears to be an important element in the success of both Achievement Place and other home-based programs. Additional efforts will be required to ascertain the precise and active ingredients in these community-based programs and their relative efficacy over time.

The relative efficacy of these community-based programs nothwithstanding, many adolescents who do not respond to such programs or to more traditional parole and counseling services are incarcerated in juvenile delinquent training facilities. Typically, youths in these programs have a history of repeated offenses including assault, breaking and entering, and robbery. As noted by O'Leary and Carr (1982), it was in such institutional settings that important early behavioral work was conducted. Representative of these programs are the CASE II project (Contingencies Applied to Special Education—Phase II) in Washington, D.C. (Cohen & Filipczak, 1971), the Youth Center Research Project in California (Jesness, DeRisi, McCormick, & Qedge, 1972), and the ADAPT (A Diagnostic and Prescribed Treatment) program in Indiana (Lynch & Ollendick, 1977). In each of these programs, a token economy was employed to develop programmatic academic and social skills, and contingency contracting, with explicit contingencies, was used to foster individualized target goals. In all cases, recidivism rates one or two years following discharge were substantially lower for these special behavioral programs than for more general institutional programs. When these behavioral programs were compared to other, more active treatment programs such as those based on transactional analysis (e.g., Jesness, 1975), however, differences were not obtained. For example, Jesness (1975) has shown that recidivism rates are equally low for both behavioral and transactional programs at one year (32%) and two years (48%) compared to general institutional programs (recidivism rates of 43% and 70% at one- and two-year follow-up, respectively). Further,

Cohen and Filipczak (1971) have shown that even these differences in recidivism between behavioral and traditional institutional programs disappear at three-year follow-up. Thus, the main effect of these behavioral programs appears to be to improve academic and social behavior *while* the individual is incarcerated and to delay the delinquent's return to the institution. Apparently, the behavioral interventions conducted in these institutions is not sufficient to produce long-term maintenance of gains in the community setting (O'Leary & Carr, 1982).

Perhaps these somewhat discouraging results should not be unexpected. A basic assumption of these programs is that a change in behavior in the institutional setting will accompany the individual upon return to the community—no matter what its "temptations, deprivations, or other disadvantages" (Herbert, 1982, p. 128). In fact, it is somewhat surprising that effects of these programs have persisted for up to two years in the face of nonreinforcing home, neighborhood, and community influences. It is evident that future studies should explore systematic maintenance and generalization strategies to ensure long-term stability of change, as suggested by Stokes and Baer (1977) and Drabman, Hammer, and Rosenbaum (1979), among others. In this regard, person variables such as locus of control should not be disregarded as potential maintenance and generalization agents. Illustratively, Jesness and DeRisi (1973) and Ollendick, Elliott, and Matson (1980) have shown that individuals who are internally controlled respond most favorably to behavioral programs. In the Ollendick et al. (1980) study, for instance, internally oriented youths committed fewer offenses during the institutional program and manifested lower recidivism rates one year after discharge (28%); on the other hand, externally oriented youths committed nearly double the number of institutional offenses and evinced a 58 percent recidivism rate one year after discharge. Such findings affirm the notion that both the person and his or her environment are important determinants of behavior change.

In sum, a variety of operant-based procedures have been used in the treatment of noncompliant, oppositional, and aggressive behavior in children and adolescents. In general, these procedures have been highly successful in producing clear decrements in these conduct disorder problems and in enhancing more positive, social behaviors. Considerable work remains to be achieved, however. Most notable are studies that examine the long-term maintenance of change and its generalization across persons, behaviors, and settings.

Modeling-based Procedures

Just as modeling-based procedures have enjoyed popular use with anxious and withdrawn behaviors, so too have they been used frequently with oppositional and aggressive ones. As we noted earlier, new responses can be acquired and old responses already in a child's behavioral repertoire can be facilitated, inhibited, or disinhibited through modeling. The power of observational learning was shown in an early study by Bandura (1965). Nursery school children observed a film in which a model exhibited both verbal and physical aggression toward a Bobo doll. For one group of children, the model was rewarded for aggressive behavior; for a second group the model was punished; and for a third group, the model received no consequences for aggressive behavior. When given the subsequent opportunity to play with the doll, children who observed the model punished displayed less verbal and physical aggression than those who observed the model under the other two conditions. When the model was punished, aggressive responding was inhibited in the children.

Children and adolescents referred for aggressive and oppositional behavior frequently display a variety of inappropriate behaviors including "poor peer relations" and accompanying social skills deficits. For example, Ollendick (1981) noted that children "at risk" for delinquency were characterized by a variety of social skill deficits, while Loeber and Patterson (1981) reported that 72 percent of children and adolescents referred to the Oregon Social Learning Center had poor peer relationships. Further, McFall and his colleagues have demonstrated poorer social skills of delinquent boys (Freedman, Rosenthal, Donahue, Schlundt, & McFall, 1978) and delinquent girls (Gaffney & McFall, 1981) compared to nondelinquent youngsters. In fact, the Freedman et al. (1978) study showed that specific social skills deficits discriminate subgroups *within* a delinquent population as well. Delinquent boys who displayed more violent behavior and who more frequently violated rules had poorer social skills than the less disruptive boys. As noted by Wells and Forehand (1984), there appears to be a direct relationship between aggressive behavior and social skills deficits.

Based on these findings, modeling-based procedures aimed at teaching appropriate social skills have flourished. In most of these studies, other specific strategies including instruction, feedback, behavior rehearsal, and reinforcement have been used in addition to modeling. Thus, these procedures are highly complex and not pure exemplars of modeling alone. This package of procedures has come to be known as "social skills training" (Bellack & Hersen, 1977).

In one of the first applications of these procedures, McNamara (1968) successfully treated a highly aggressive preschool child. In subsequent studies, older aggressive children (e.g., Bornstein, Bellack, & Hersen, 1980; LaGreca & Santogrossi, 1980) and adolescents (e.g., Elder, Edelstein, & Narick, 1979; Goodwin & Mahoney, 1975; Kaufmann & Wagner, 1972; Ollendick & Hersen, 1979; Sarason, 1978; Sarason & Ganzer, 1973; Spence & Marzillier, 1979, 1981; Thelen, Fry, Dollinger, & Paul, 1976) have been treated successfully. In these studies, however, only short-term changes in social behavior have been evidenced and the superiority of these procedures over more traditional psychotherapeutic practices is sometimes evident (cf. Ollendick & Hersen, 1979; Sarason, 1978; Sarason & Ganzer, 1973) and sometimes illusory (cf. Spence & Marzillier, 1979, 1981; Thelan et al., 1976). Further, while studies with juvenile delinquents have shown that such procedures lead to enhanced institutional functioning (e.g., Ollendick & Hersen, 1979; Spence & Marzillier, 1979), they have not shown reliable decrements in recidivism rates (Spence & Marzillier, 1981)—the ultimate test of treatment efficacy.

Thus, while modeling-based procedures have been shown to be effective in short-term change of socially disruptive and aggressive behaviors, they have not been found to be associated with more long-term changes. Perhaps these somewhat discouraging findings should not be unexpected; after all, 20 years ago Bandura (1965) warned us about the distinction between *learning* a response and the subsequent *performance* of that response. Although observational learning can occur in the absence of response consequences, consequences determine whether the modeled response is actually performed. In many of these modeling-based social skill studies, new responses are indeed evidenced. Their subsequent expression in the natural environment is not. Perhaps such expression depends on appropriate consequences in the natural environment—an occurrence of low probability (Patterson & Cobb, 1971).

Cognitive-based Procedures

As noted previously, cognitive-based procedures are being used with increasing frequency in the treatment of a variety of child and adolescent behavior disorders. The treatment of conduct disorders such as noncompliance, oppositional behavior, and aggression are no exception. Based firmly on the notion that maladaptive thoughts, expectations, and self-statements lead to maladaptive behavior (Kendall, 1977), these strategies have enjoyed initial success, although a number of issues remain, as we shall see.

In most of these studies, procedures consisted of some combination of verbal self-instruction training ("What is my problem?" "What is my plan?" "Am I using my plan?" and "How did I do?"), systematic alteration of faulty self-statements, and social problem-solving strategies. In one of the first systematic applications of these procedures with aggressive and impulsive children, Camp, Blom, Hebert, and von Doornenck (1977) devised the "Think Aloud" program. Content of the program included both cognitive, impersonal problems such as those used by Meichenbaum and Goodmann (1971) and interpersonal problem-solving games as described by Shure and Spivack (1978). A "copycat" format was used in order to engage the young children in the use of these cognitive strategies. In comparison to an untrained no-treatment group, the trained group evidenced greater gains in prosocial behavior in the classroom (although not significantly greater reductions in aggressive behaviors per se) and in performance on a variety of cognitive tests (e.g., WISC-R Mazes, Matching Familiar Figures Test). Thus, while gains were noted,

they tended to be limited to laboratory-like tasks and not to include the primary target behavior of aggression. Similar findings have been reported by Kendall and Finch (1976, 1978) and Lochman, Nelson, and Sims (1981) for impulsive, overly active, and aggressive children. That is, changes have been noted on first-order experimental tasks but have not generalized readily to the natural environment.

Cognitive-based procedures have also been used to modify aggressive behaviors in delinquent adolescents (Snyder & White, 1979) and high school students who are "at risk" for school truancy and dropout (Sarason & Sarason, 1981). For example, Snyder and White (1979) reasoned that their group of delinquent adolescents had failed to develop appropriate use of self-statements for regulation of their own behavior. To test this hypothesis, the adolescents were assigned to one of three groups: self-instructional training, contingency awareness training, and an assessment-only control condition. Prior to treatment, immediately following treatment, and two months after treatment, the adolescents were observed on three dependent measures: absence from scheduled classes, failure to assume and complete social/self-care responsibilities, and frequency of impulsive behaviors. In the self-instructional group, the concept of private speech as a means to regulate behavior was introduced and illustrated through concrete examples (e.g., learning to drive a car, learning a new dance). The effects of self-verbalization on inappropriate behaviors was then examined, focusing on problems that the adolescents exhibited in their day-to-day interactions. This analysis included the situation or setting in which the behavior took place, the exact verbalization that accompanied the behavior, the behavior itself, and its consequences. Snyder and White (p. 230) provide the following example below.

In the second phase of treatment, the self-defeating nature of self-statements like "The hell with that, this feels too good" were examined and more adaptive self-statements like "Time to get up

Situation	Verbalization	Behavior	Consequences
A cottage counselor says, "Time to get up"	"The hell with that, this feels too good"	Staying in bed	Lose token points for failure to get out of bed

already? Damn, it feels good to stay in bed. If I get up, I'll get the points I need for cigarettes. O.K., I need to open my eyes and sit up. Good—I made it" were modeled. Adolescents rehearsed repeatedly these new self-statements while covertly imagining themselves in the situation itself.

In the contingency awareness group, the adolescents also defined problem situations and explored specific behaviors and their consequences, but did not address nor rehearse specific self-statements. The assessment control group was simply assessed prior to treatment, following treatment, and at follow-up. Results showed that the self-instruction group demonstrated marked improvement in performance of daily living requirements (school attendance and completion of social/self-care responsibilities) and a decrease in impulsive behaviors after treatment compared to both the contingency awareness and assessment control groups. These changes were maintained or enhanced at two-month follow-up. Unfortunately, however, information related to whether these adolescents used these skills following discharge from the institution and whether they affected subsequent recidivism rates is not reported. Thus, once again, evidence as to the generalization of these strategies to extratraining settings is not available.

In sum, while the newly developed cognitive-based procedures show considerable promise, a number of questions remain (Hobbs, Moguin, Tyroler, & Lahey, 1980; Meador & Ollendick, 1984). Foremost among these are those related to maintenance and generalization of the trained skills and the relative superiority of these strategies over more traditional behavioral and nonbehavioral approaches. Surprisingly, very little research has been accomplished that addresses these very important issues.

Summary

In sum, behavioral interventions for oppositional and aggressive children and adolescents show considerable promise. Across several studies, such interventions have been shown to be superior to no interventions, at least in terms of short-term results. However, comparisons to other treatment modalities are either sorely lacking or, when present, ambiguous in their findings. Additional comparative research that examines the long-term maintenance and generalization effects of treatment is clearly

called for. Further, the problems in our current state of research noted under discussion of anxious and withdrawn behavior apply equally well to oppositional and aggressive ones. Namely, greater sophistication in both assessment practices and methodological rigor is needed.

Pervasive Developmental Disorders

In addition to the two major categories of internalized, *overcontrolled* (anxious, withdrawn) and externalized, *undercontrolled* (oppositional, aggressive) "symptom clusters" identified in factor analytic studies (see Achenbach & Edelbrock, 1978), other studies have affirmed a third cluster of behaviors, the pervasive developmental disorders. Traditionally, these disorders have been labeled as the "psychotic" or "mentally retarded" disorders (e.g., Harris, 1983b; Harris & Powers, 1984). Within the psychotic group, two primary categories have been described: autism and childhood schizophrenia. While differences between these two groups are relatively well established (e.g., Lovaas, 1979; Schreibman & Mills, 1983; Steffen & Karoly, 1982), behavioral interventions for both have been focused on the elimination of numerous maladaptive behaviors (e.g., self-injurious behavior, self-stimulation, and disruptive, aggressive behavior) and the enhancement of more adaptive patterns of behaviors (e.g., imitation, verbal behavior, and prosocial behavior). Similarly, while retarded children and adolescents do not display the same characteristics of autistic and schizophrenic children, they do evince pervasive delays in motor, intellectual, and social development, like their psychotic counterparts. As noted by O'Leary and Carr (1982), these findings have fostered a trend away from treatment based on diagnostic categories (e.g., autism, childhood schizophrenia, mental retardation), toward treatment focused on specific *behavior problems* common to these three groups of children.

The behavioral treatment of such problems has been limited almost solely to operant-based procedures. While occasional reports of the use of respondent-based procedures in the treatment of fears or anxieties in such children and adolescents have surfaced (e.g., Ollendick & Ollendick, 1982), they have been sparse. Further, use of modeling-based procedures have been infrequent, with a few very notable exceptions (e.g., Varni, Lovaas,

Koegel, & Everett, 1979), and the use of cognitive-based procedures has been nonexistent. The exact reason for this state of affairs is not totally clear, although assumed cognitive limitations and attentional liabilities in these populations are usually pro-offered. However, in that such children and adolescents are capable of acquiring relatively sophisticated self-control strategies (e.g., Shapiro, 1984; Shapiro & Klein, 1980; Shapiro, McGonigle, & Ollendick, 1980), these assumptions need to be examined more critically in the future.

Operant-based Procedures

Many developmentally disabled children display self-injurious (e.g., head banging, face scratching, and self-slapping) and self-stimulatory behaviors (e.g., body rocking, hand flapping, and twirling of objects in front of the eyes). They also display severe forms of aggression and tantrums. These behaviors are not only a problem in their own right; perhaps more important, they preclude effective learning. As a result, most behavioral interventions have concentrated upon the reduction of such behaviors prior to the development of more acceptable ones. One or more of the following procedures have been used toward this end: extinction (e.g., Corte, Wolf, & Locke, 1971; Lovaas & Simmons, 1969; Risley, 1968), differential reinforcement (e.g., Carr, Newsom, & Binkoff, 1980; Lovaas, Freitag, Gold, & Kassorla, 1965; Repp & Deitz, 1974, 1978), time-out (e.g., Calhoun & Lima, 1977; Wolf, Risley, Johnston, Harris, & Allen, 1967; Wolf, Risley, & Mees, 1964), overcorrection (e.g., Foxx & Azrin, 1973; Harris & Romanczyk, 1976; Ollendick, Shapiro, & Barrett, 1981), and physical punishment such as slaps, distasteful solutions, and electric shocks (e.g., Koegel & Covert, 1972; Lovaas, Berberich, Perloff, & Schaeffer, 1966; Romanczyk, 1977). Use of these procedures has been reviewed in considerable detail by Margolies (1977), Harris and Ersner-Hershfield (1978), Ollendick and Cerny (1981), and DiLorenzo and Ollendick (1984). Illustrations of these procedures follow.

One of the earliest and most influential studies in which self-injurious behavior was shown to be maintained by social reinforcement and in which extinction procedures were used is that of Lovaas and Simmons (1969). Two children, both with extended histories of self-injury, were treated. Prior to treatment, both children had been placed in physical restraints to prevent physical injury. When restraints were removed, a flurry of self-injurious behavior occurred: striking the head with fists and hitting the head against the side of the bed. During extinction trials (1½ hours in duration), physical restraints were removed and the adult, who was presumably reinforcing, left the room. During the first extinction trial, 900 self-injurious behaviors were noted for the first child while 2750 were noted for the second child. All within 1½ hours! Affirming the potential utility of extinction procedures, however, these behaviors were reduced to zero in 53 and 10 sessions, respectively. Interestingly, the procedure was more immediately effective with the child with the highest frequency of self-injury. While this study was uncontrolled, it was of clear heuristic value in that it led directly to the notion that self-destructive behaviors may be learned operant responses that may be directly under the influence of antecedent and consequent events. This study served as a springboard for several other studies that utilized more rigorous single-subject designs to illustrate the controlling effects of extinction procedures.

The use of differential reinforcement procedures in the treatment of stereotypic behaviors is illustrated in a study by Repp, Deitz, and Speir (1974). In this study, differential reinforcement procedures were combined with extinction procedures to reduce lip flapping, rocking, and finger flicking in three retarded youngsters. During the differential reinforcement procedure, the children were hugged and verbally praised if they did not emit the stereotypic responses during the prescribed interval of time. Initial time intervals were brief and were increased in duration as subjects demonstrated increasingly greater control over their self-stereotypic behaviors. Over sessions, the self-stereotypic behaviors were reduced for all three individuals. Numerous other studies affirm the utility of differential reinforcement procedures (Margolies, 1977).

Early attempts to employ time-out procedures are exemplified in the uncontrolled case study of "Dickey" reported by Wolf and his colleagues (Wolf et al., 1964, 1967). When first seen at 3½, Dickey exhibited a wide range of behaviors including tantrums, head banging, glasses throwing, and aggressive pinching. Upon emitting these behaviors, he was placed in his room (where presumably positive reinforcement was removed) until the behaviors had ceased. Differential reinforcement procedures were also used to establish more appropriate behaviors. This combined approach was effective in eliminating these problems and, over a period of years, was useful in helping him acquire normal speech and appropriate social and self-help skills. He continued to improve to the point that he was eventually placed in a regular public school classroom, where he was accepted by his peers and viewed as socially appropriate by his teachers (Nedelman & Sulzbacher, 1972). A major strength of this otherwise uncontrolled case study is its close attention to case management and its intensive follow-up of a youngster from preschool age through early adolescent years.

Not all applications of time-out for self-stimulation and self-injurious behaviors have been successful, however (Harris & Ersner-Hershfield, 1978). Perhaps this should not be unexpected. In fact, since these behaviors frequently are self-reinforcing (Carr, 1977) and time-out procedures do not physically prevent their occurrence, these procedures may not always be the treatment of choice (Ollendick & Cerny, 1981). Only in instances where self-injury or self-stimulation is a function of specific reinforcing events (e.g., social attention) would the removal of these reinforcers be expected to be effective.

Overcorrection, a procedure whereby work and effort are required in order to remedy negative consequences of inappropriate behavior, has also been used productively with a wide range of behaviors including self-stimulation, self-injury, and aggressive disruptive behaviors (see reviews by Axelrod, Brantner, & Meddock, 1978; Foxx & Bechtel, 1982; Hobbs, 1976; Ollendick & Matson, 1978). Two types of overcorrection have been described: restitution and positive practice. In restitutional overcorrection, the individual is required to restore the environment to an improved state over that existing prior to the occurrence of the inappropriate behavior. In positive practice overcorrection, the person is required to repeatedly practice appropriate behaviors that are functionally incompatible with the inappropriate behavior. Restitutional and positive practice overcorrection have been used alone or in combination. During the overcorrection procedure, graduated guidance is used to ensure that positive practice or "restitutional" acts are performed (Foxx & Azrin, 1972).

In one of the first studies examining its utility, Foxx and Azrin (1973) described the reduction of self-stereotypic behaviors in four children described as autistic and retarded. For two of the children who exhibited self-stimulatory mouthing, a restitutional procedure was used; for the other two who exhibited self-stereotypic head weaving and hand clapping, positive practice procedures were used. Restitutional overcorrection for mouthing consisted of cleansing the children's gums and teeth with an antiseptic solution for two minutes contingent on each occurrence of mouthing. This procedure was used to cleanse the oral area and to teach more appropriate hygienic care. Graduated guidance was used to ensure compliance. Results indicated rather dramatic reductions in mouthing behaviors that were subsequently maintained by a verbal warning procedure. For the other two children, positive practice overcorrection consisted of five minutes of functional movement training. For example, for head weaving the child was instructed to move her head in one of three positions in order to bring her head movements under functional control. Again, graduated guidance was used to ensure compliance and to "guide" the functional movements. As with restitutional procedures, positive practice overcorrection resulted in immediate reductions in these self-stimulatory behaviors.

The use of positive practice overcorrection procedures is also illustrated in a controlled single-case study by Ollendick et al. (1981). In this study, an 8-year-old girl (Jane) who engaged in repetitive self-sterotypic hand posturing was treated. Jane was described as "severely emotionally disturbed in association with brain damage" and had a long history of self-stereotypic and self-injurious behavior. In particular, her self-stereotypic behavior interfered with the use of her hands; her mental and motor functioning was estimated to be between 18 and 30 months of age (as determined by the Bayley Scales of Infant Development and the Vineland Social Maturity Scale). Throughout treatment, Jane was engaged in a series of visual-motor performance tasks and the number of self-stereotypic responses as well as performance on the academic tasks was recorded. In this particular study, positive practice overcorrection was compared to a simple physical restraint and a no-treatment condition. An alternating treatments design was used. Positive practice overcorrection consisted of appropriate manipulation of the task materials for 30 seconds contingent on each sterotypic response. That is, the experimenter positioned his hands on the wrists of the child and manually guided her hands into the correct placement of the materials. Physical restraint consisted of a manual restraining of the child's hands on the tabletop for 30 seconds, contingent on each occurrence of the sterotypic behavior. No consequences for sterotypic behavior were in effect in the no-treatment condition. As can be seen in Figure. 12.6, positive practice overcorrection was highly effective in reducing the hand posturing and in enhancing

task performance. Physical restraint, while more effective than no treatment, was less effective than the positive practice overcorrection procedure.

Although maintenance of these reductions was evident for several weeks or months in the Foxx and Azrin (1973) and Ollendick et al. (1981) studies, other studies have questioned the durability of over-correction procedures when used alone (cf. Matson, Ollendick, & Martin, 1979). However, long-term stability with these procedures is evident when they are combined with differential reinforcement procedures. For example, Kelly and Drabman (1977)

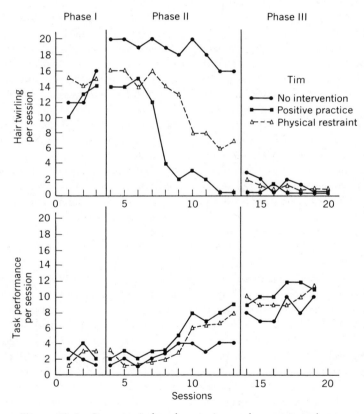

Figure 12.6 Stereotypic hand posturing and accurate task performance for Jane across experimental conditions. The data are plotted across the three alternating time periods according to the schedule that the treatments were in effect. The three treatments, however, were presented only during the alternating-treatments phase. During the last phase, positive practice overcorrection was used during all three time periods. (From T. H. Ollendick, E.S. Shapiro, & R. P. Barrett, "Reducing stereotypic behaviors: An analysis of treatment procedures utilizing an alternating treatments design" [Figure 3]. Behavior Therapy, 1981, 12, 570−577. Copyright by Association for Advancement of Behavior Therapy. Reprinted by permission.)

reported that a combination of positive practice overcorrection and differential reinforcement of other behaviors reduced self-injurious eye poking to zero levels. Further, they demonstrated that these effects generalized to another setting immediately following treatment and that the effects were durable. Similar findings have been reported by DeCatanzaro and Baldwin (1978), who successfully treated head hitting in two profoundly retarded boys. Thus, while overcorrection may be highly effective in reducing inappropriate behaviors, differential reinforcement of appropriate behavior may be required to produce long-term maintenance of these effects.

Finally, physical punishment procedures such as slaps, distasteful solutions, and electric shocks have been used for behaviors that are particularly refractory to change. Although these procedures have been shown to be effective (e.g., Koegel & Covert, 1972; Lovaas & Simmons, 1969; Romanczyk, 1977), they are currently in disfavor because of ethical considerations associated with their use (cf. Matson & DiLorenzo, 1983). Unfortunately, such considerations are oftentimes based on emotional grounds and misunderstandings, rather than well-grounded facts. Lichtenstein and Schreibman (1976) conclude their review of shock procedures by stating,

> Treatment for autistic children, regardless of modality, is usually slow and difficult. We cannot afford to abandon any therapeutic approach with this population without a careful analysis of the costs and benefits. The decision to use electric shock as a therapeutic agent should be evaluated according to objective criteria including the child's needs, the feasibility of using the procedure in the child's environment, and available alternatives. It appears that the correct use of shock in punishment paradigm leads to both positive direct effects and positive side effects (p. 172).

Further, Repp and Deitz (1978) make a cogent argument that shock is defensible on both legal and ethical grounds *when* other reductive procedures are shown to be ineffective. They describe a case in which a child's head banging prevented placement in a less restrictive community setting. The institution in which the child had been placed prohibited the use of electric shock. Subsequently, the child was transferred to a different institution that allowed use of shock under carefully controlled conditions and only for self-abusive behaviors. In this new institution, two applications of electric shock suppressed the self-injurious behavior, and the child was able to be placed in a community setting. Further, control of head banging generalized to the new setting and was maintained. As Repp and Deitz (1978) note, the rights of retarded persons to function in the least restrictive environment must be ensured. Thus, while ethical issues remain with the use of physical punishment procedures and their use cannot be endorsed routinely (Ollendick & Cerny, 1981), it is evident that they are effective procedures and useful, especially when other procedures have been tried and failed.

Just as operant-based procedures have been used to decelerate select aberrant behaviors, so too have they been used to expand the behavioral repertoire of severely impaired individuals. As noted earlier, these children and adolescents frequently demonstrate gross deficits in adaptive behavior. A number of strategies have been used, including shaping, positive reinforcement, and negative reinforcement. Among the behaviors increased have been eye contact, imitation, verbal behavior, language skills, peer interaction, prosocial behavior, and classroom attending behavior (see Margolies, 1977).

In an early study, Brooks, Morrow, and Gray (1968) commented upon the importance of appropriate eye contact for effective social interaction: "As long as gaze aversion is typical in a subject, normal social interaction is not possible. Once visual attention responses are established, the work of training other social skills can begin" (p. 309). Brooks et al. (1968) were able to establish visual attention in a 19-year-old deaf autistic girl; measures taken during baseline, positive reinforcement, and withdrawal phases demonstrated the power of the contingencies. In this case, positive reinforcement consisted of candy. McConnell (1967) demonstrated the effectiveness of social reinforcement made contingent on eye contact in a 5½-year-old autistic boy, while Foxx (1977) illustrated the uses of negative reinforcement (release from a modified overcorrection procedure) to increase eye contact in autistic and retarded children. Clearly, based on these studies as well as others (Margolies, 1977), eye contact is capable of being established through basic operant procedures.

Using similar procedures, establishment of imitative behavior has also been shown. Autistic children, in particular, tend not to imitate actions of those around them. This inability to imitate may contribute to the autistic child's limited behavioral repertoire. Learning to imitate would seem to be a critical factor in development.

Viewing observational learning from an explicit shaping and reinforcement standpoint (in contrast to Bandura's notion that observational learning can occur through mere observation of modeled behavior with the accompanying cognitive activities), several investigators have *produced* imitative behavior in these children (e.g., Craighead, O'Leary, & Allen, 1973; Hingtgen, Coulter, & Churchill, 1967; Lovaas, Koegel, Simmons, & Long, 1973; Metz, 1965). Such behaviors seem to be especially important for speech training. Use of these procedures is presented in detail by Lovaas et al. (1973): (1) the child receives reinforcement for vocalizing any sounds whatsoever; (2) a temporal discrimination is then established by reinforcing the child only for vocalizations that were emitted within a five-second period following vocalization made by the therapist; (3) next, only those vocalizations that approximated in sound those of the therapist were reinforced; (4) the child was reinforced for discriminating between two sounds; and (5) the child was reinforced for increasingly finer discriminations involving three or more sounds. Quite obviously, such a process is a slow and tedious one. Nonetheless, Lovaas and his colleagues have carefully delineated the process from imitative sounds to functional speech. The distinction between speech and meaningful language is an important one, however, and the degree to which meaningful language has been acquired in these studies is questionable. Nonetheless, the initial success of this approach in building functional speech in previously mute or echolalic children should not be underestimated; it is one of the most significant achievements of the behavioral approach (Lovaas, 1977).

In addition to eye contact and functional speech, other behaviors shaped in autistic and retarded children have been peer interaction (e.g., Lovaas et al., 1965; Means & Merrens, 1969), cooperative behavior (e.g., Hingtgen, Saunders, & DeMyer, 1965), and attending classroom skills (e.g., Koegel & Rincover, 1974). Clearly, operant-based procedures have been found to be useful in accelerating appropriate behaviors as well as decelerating inappropriate ones.

Summary

Collectively, the literature supports the notion that a wide range of operant-based reductive procedures are useful in the elimination of behaviors such as self-injury and self-stimulation and that a wide range of operant-based enhancement procedures are effective in building more appropriate behaviors like verbal behavior and prosocial skills. Caution should be taken, however, since proper experimental controls are lacking in much of this body of research. That is, much of the support is based solely on single-case design studies that do not control for nonspecific treatment factors. In these studies there is no assurance that the observed changes were due to specific treatment procedures per se, rather than to extraneous variables. Additionally, well-controlled group studies are badly needed to assess the relative effectiveness of these procedures and to compare them to nonbehavioral strategies. Other studies are needed to determine the maintenance and generalization of change. As has been noted by several reviewers (e.g., Harris & Ersner-Hershfield, 1978; Margolies, 1977), the durability and generalization to new settings of these changes have not been addressed adequately. Although parent training programs and community-based treatment homes for such individuals are just now on the horizon, they appear to be highly promising (Lovaas, 1979). These problems aside, a real beginning in the habilitation of these individuals has been evidenced through the proper application of behavioral treatment strategies.

Persistent Issues in Child and Adolescent Behavior Therapy

The Question of Successful Outcome[2]

In preceding sections, the utility of behavioral procedures with children and adolescents has been

[2]Following the completion of this chapter, the author became aware of a meta-analytic review of psychotherapy outcome research with children conducted by Rita J. Casey and Jeffrey S. Berman and to be published in the *Psychological Bulletin*. In this review, both behavioral and nonbehavioral treatment strategies are addressed. The conclusions drawn from this review are similar to those offered here, namely, that "there is little evidence to support that some forms of treatment are superior to others . . . it is difficult to conclude that behavioral treatments are superior." These conclusions, although stated more forcefully than those in the present review, are important since they were arrived at through meta-analytic procedures, which collapsed behavioral and nonbehavioral studies across age, presenting complaints, and response measures.

documented. In general, this review *suggests* that these procedures are highly effective in the treatment of a host of behavioral problems, ranging from autism and mental retardation to conduct disorders and anxiety disorders. Clearly, the aim and scope of these procedures are extensive.

Yet clear empirical support for their use is not as strong as is often surmised. Much of the "support" resides in either poorly controlled case studies (i.e., A–B designs) or in only marginally controlled group outcome studies (i.e., treatment vs. no-treatment designs). Further, while a substantial amount of support appears to come from well-controlled single-case studies (i.e., reversal, withdrawal, multiple baseline, multi-element, alternating treatment, and random stimulus designs), the external validity of these studies is unknown. That is, we do not know how representative these findings are, nor to which populations they apply. Are only successful applications reported in the literature? Are subjects selected for these single-case studies truly representative of children and adolescents who display similar behavior problems? Or are they selected on the basis of subtle, yet-to-be-determined features that lead them to be more responsive to single-case approaches? While there are no direct nor easy answers to these questions, they demand careful scrutiny and systematic examination.

This state-of-the-art is illustrated in a recent review of the behavioral treatment of school phobia completed by us (Ollendick & Mayer, 1984). This review, like that of other recent reviews (Gelfand, 1978; Jones & Kazdin, 1981; Yule, Hersov, & Treseder, 1980), revealed that nearly all studies in this area were uncontrolled case reports. Of course, threats to internal validity cannot be ruled out in such studies; that is, there is no way of determining whether treatment per se was responsible for observed changes in behavior. It may be the case that improvement would have occurred in the absence of treatment. Because the long-term prognosis for untreated school phobia is unknown, these limitations are particularly unsettling.

Equally unsettling in this particular area of study is the absence of well-controlled single-case studies and only *one* group outcome study (Miller et al., 1972). As will be recalled from our earlier discussion, imaginal desensitization was compared to a more traditional psychotherapeutic approach and to a no-treatment condition. In brief, Miller et al. (1972) found that the two active treatments were superior to a no-treatment condition, but that the two treatments were not significantly different from one another. Further, no differences among the two treatment conditions and the control condition were found on objective evaluations at posttreatment and follow-up two years later (Hampe, Noble, Miller, & Barrett, 1973). Unfortunately, behavioral observations or reports of return to school were not reported. As noted earlier, this study was also flawed methodologically in that treatment procedures were contaminated both across and within treatment conditions. Nonetheless, it represents the only published effort to evaluate such procedures in a reasonably well-controlled group outcome design. Its findings are obviously not overly supportive of the efficacy of one of the most frequently used behavioral procedures—systematic desensitization.

Thus, while behavioral procedures have been widely and productively used with school-phobic youngsters, empirical support for their use is sparse. Rather, their support resides more frequently in uncontrolled case studies. As noted recently by Kazdin (1981), such case studies *can* be useful *if* they base their findings on objective data and *if* they report the progress of more than one subject. In the treatment of school phobia, objective measures are readily available in the form of school attendance; yet many of the uncontrolled case studies and the one group outcome study (Miller et al., 1972) failed to report even these data. Further, only two published reports have included systematic replication of procedures across subjects (e.g., Kennedy, 1965; Ollendick & Mayer, 1984). In these studies, Kennedy (1965) reported the successful use of operant-based procedures for all 50 cases in his study, while Ollendick and Mayer (1984) reported the successful use of respondent-based procedures for 32 of 37 school-phobic children. Although results of these studies are impressive, it should be clearly acknowledged that both were uncontrolled group outcome studies. Nonetheless, consistent with arguments offered by Kazdin (1981), they support the *clinical* use of these procedures.

What seems to be needed at this stage in the evaluation of child and adolescent behavior therapy is an increased attention to more sophisticated outcome designs. In addition to being compared to no-treatment conditions (in which behavioral approaches appear to fare well), behavioral approaches need to be compared to attention-control groups (which control for expectation and demand characteristics) and to other, more traditional procedures (i.e., drug treatment, transactional analysis, play therapy, etc.). In this latter regard, based on our literature review, it is not at all clear that behavioral procedures are, in fact, superior. Finally, it seems time to systematically evaluate the relative efficacy of behavioral procedures within and across diverse child behavior problems. Are cognitive-based procedures more effective than operant-based procedures in the treatment of aggressive behavior? In the treatment of withdrawn behavior? In the final analysis, the question "Does behavior therapy (in its various forms) work with children and adolescents?" will need to be rephrased to something like "What type of behavior therapy is effective with what type of child and adolescent behavior and under what set of conditions?" Clearly, this is a complex question that requires a high level of conceptual sophistication and methodological rigor. The field of child and adolescent behavior therapy, if it is to progress beyond its current rudimentary stage, must address this challenge.

The Question of Maintenance and Generalization

A challenge of equal magnitude resides in the demonstration of maintenance and generalization of behavior change across different settings, behaviors, and individuals and over time. As we have noted, most studies demonstrating the efficacy of behavioral procedures have been limited to a demonstration of short-term efficacy in highly specific situations. What happens when treatment procedures are withdrawn? Are treatment effects durable? Do they transfer to new settings, new behaviors, and other children? Although definitive answers to these questions are not yet available, accumulating evidence suggests that maintenance and generalization do not occur automatically. As noted some time ago by Baer and his colleagues, it is more desirable to program their occurrence than to lament their absence (Baer, Wolf, & Risley, 1968; Stokes & Baer, 1977).

A number of strategies to ensure maintenance and generalization have been proposed (e.g., Baer et al., 1968; Drabman et al., 1979; Marholin & Siegel, 1978). Among them are the following:

1. Teach behaviors that permit the child to enter an environment that naturally reinforces or punishes the targeted behaviors.

2. Teach significant others to provide appropriate contingencies in the natural environment.
3. Incorporate discriminative stimuli in the treatment setting that are likely to occur in the posttreatment environment.
4. Fade contingencies gradually during training to an intermittent schedule that is consistent with that of the posttreatment environment.
5. Teach the child to control the contingencies and antecedent conditions of his or her own behavior.
6. Provide the child a set of cognitive skills to mediate his or her ongoing behavior.

The utility of some of these procedures can be illustrated briefly by the parent training literature. As we have noted, short-term changes in deviant child behavior can be accomplished by training parents as behavior modifiers. However, maintenance of these changes over time has been less evident. For example, several authors have noted that it is necessary to fade therapist contact (Herbert & Baer, 1972), to provide refresher or "booster" courses (Patterson, 1974; Wahler, 1975), and to teach parents self-control procedures (Wells et al., 1980) in order to maintain both parent and child behavior upon cessation of treatment. In the absence of such procedures, treatment effects quickly dissipate and, in at least one study (Johnson & Christensen, 1975), deviant behaviors actually *increased* above baseline levels at follow-up.

Clearly, we must begin to systematically address *and* report the maintenance and generalization of behavior change. The simple and immediate demonstration of behavior change will no longer suffice; rather, we must begin to show that our effects are long-lasting and generalizable. In this pursuit, we should attend to Baer et al.'s eloquent admonition and not just simply expect such efforts to occur. We must actively program their occurrence.

The Question of Multimethod Assessment

In the introduction, it was suggested that child and adolescent behavioral assessment must rest upon a set of strategies that are empirically based, developmentally sensitive, and multimethod in scope. How well has this objective been met in the literature? It can be safely stated that this goal, while admirably stated, has *not* been realized. Seemingly, we have been more content to restrict our focus to highly specific target behaviors and to ignore important response-response covariations as suggested by Wahler and Graves (1983) and Voeltz and Evans (1982), among others.

While a wide variety of assessment procedures are available (e.g., the behavioral interview, other-reports, self-reports, behavioral observations), rarely are they used in combination. Use of a multi-method approach would seem to provide us more information about the "reach" of our procedures. Do they affect subjectively perceived emotional states as well as objectively observed behaviors? Do parents and significant others observe the changes? What about one's peers? Are the changes in behavior socially valid? Answers to these questions require that changes in behavior be developmentally sensitive and that they be useful to the individual in his or her natural environment. Use of multiple procedures allows for an examination of these issues.

The potential necessity of multiple assessment is clearly exemplified in the parent training literature. As is now well known (e.g., Wells & Forehand, 1984), referral of children for conduct disorder problems is as frequently associated with parent distress as it is child misconduct. In this instance, demonstrating both child and parent behavior change, as well as mutual perceptions of change (i.e., self-report and other-report), will be critical.

The Question of Prevention

Although behavioral procedures have been shown to be effective in general, the cost and "reach" of these procedures have been questioned in recent years (e.g., Felner, Jason, Moritsugu, & Farber, 1983; Nietzel, Winett, MacDonald, & Davidson, 1977). As noted nearly 20 years ago by Albee (1967), there will never be a sufficient number of professionals to meet the ever-increasing demand for direct services. Epidemiological studies indicate that about one-fourth of elementary school children evince adjustment problems (Werry, 1979). Further, as new facilities for children open, waiting lists quickly develop (Zax & Cowen, 1976). Moreover, Jason (1983) estimates that if all mental health professionals adopted the traditional one-to-one service delivery mode, they would reach about 2 percent of those in need of services. These projections are quite disconcerting to the behaviorally oriented practitioner when it is realized that only one-third of practicing child and adolescent thera-

pists are behaviorally oriented (Tuma & Pratt, 1982). Clearly, given the relatively small number of behavioral practitioners, our efficacious treatment procedures are reaching a small minority of children in need of services (Ollendick & Winett, 1984). Further, as with all interventions that are directed toward reducing or eliminating behavioral problems once they occur, these procedures are extremely time-consuming and costly.

In contrast to interventions at this habilitative level, we might be better advised to channel our efforts into primary and secondary preventive efforts (Caplan, 1964). In secondary prevention, efforts are directed toward children who show early signs of problematic behavior, and the objective is to shorten the duration or severity of the problem by early and prompt interventions. In primary prevention, emphasis is placed on identifying "high-risk" children who *might* likely display problematic behavior in the future and to determine those environmental conditions that appear to be related to the development of specific behavioral problems. Thus, primary and secondary prevention frequently entails examination of change at societal levels, as well as individual and small-group levels. Further, primary prevention efforts can be directed toward the promotion of competency-related behavior and toward settings that maintain such behaviors in an attempt to inoculate or immunize children to stressful events.

As noted most directly by Jason (1977, 1981), behavioral approaches based on classical, operant, and vicarious learning principles are as useful in primary and secondary preventive efforts as they are in more direct, habilitative ones. Recent efforts have also evidenced the application of cognitive-behavioral procedures and information-processing tactics in the prevention of child behavior disorders (Ollendick & Winett, 1984). These programs range from Poser's (1970) "antecedent systematic desensitization" model for children about to make their first visit to a dentist and Ollendick's (1979c) operant-based immunization model to help children deal more constructively with frustration and failure to Melamed and Siegel's (1975) modeling-based procedures to prevent anxiety associated with hospitalization and surgery and Spivack and Shure's (1974) "cognitive-social problem solving" model to build social competencies. Clearly, a variety of procedures have been attempted in pursuit of the prevention goals. Whether or not approaches based on the prevention model actually *prevent* behavior problems from occurring, however, remains to be seen. To date, claims of prevention have been based more on the intuitive appeal of the model than on actual demonstrable effects. Considerably more research is needed to evaluate both the short- and long-term effects of such interventions. As we have noted elsewhere (Ollendick & Cerny, 1981), until such time, primary and secondary prevention remains an "admirable goal in need of empirical verification."

Nonetheless, prevention strategies derived from learning-based procedures show considerable promise in preventing child behavior problems. The demonstrated efficacy of the learning-based procedures described in this chapter notwithstanding, our future efforts might be productively directed toward development, refinement, and evaluation of prevention strategies.

CONCLUSION

Child and adolescent behavior therapy has a long and rich tradition in the field of clinical psychology. Nearly 65 years have elapsed since Watson's early demonstration of the utility of behavioral procedures in both the conditioning and deconditioning of behavioral problems in children. As we have noted, progress over these years has been sporadic with specific procedures waxing and waning in popularity. Today, we have arrived at a rich amalgam of procedures that benefit not only from respondent, operant, and vicarious models but also from cognitive, information-processing models. In a sense, child and adolescent behavior therapy has matured.

Yet, as we have seen, much remains to be achieved and, in fact, the field of child and adolescent behavior therapy can best be described as being in its own "stage" of adolescence. Its identity, though strongly wedded to learning theory and methodological rigor, is currently in question. While the field is growing up, firm and unambiguous support for its efficacy is currently lacking. Able to effect immediate and short-term change, the field is not unlike an adolescent discerning whether such changes result in more durable and lasting effects.

We should hasten to add, however, that considerable support for the utility of behavioral procedures with children and adolescents exists. While more sophisticated questions from both conceptual and methodological standpoints remain, we can safely conclude that the area of child and adolescent behavior therapy represents an exciting enterprise and has much to offer children and adolescents who evince behavioral problems in living.

REFERENCES

Achenbach, T. M. (1966). The classification of children's psychiatric symptoms: A factor analytic study. *Psychological Monographs, 80*, 1–37.

Achenbach, T. M., & Edelbrock, C. S. (1978). The classification of child psychopathology: A review and analysis of empirical efforts. *Psychological Bulletin, 85*, 1275–1301.

Achenbach, T. M., & Edelbrock, C. S. (1981). Behavioral problems and competencies reported by parents of normal and disturbed children aged 4 through 16. *Monographs of the Society for Research in Child Development, 46* (1, Serial No. 188).

Achenbach, T. M., & Edelbrock, C. S. (1983). Taxonomic issues in child psychopathology. In T. H. Ollendick & M. Hersen (Eds.), *Handbook of child psychopathology.* New York: Plenum.

Adesso, V. J., & Lipson, J. W. (1981). Group training of parents as therapists for their children. *Behavior Therapy, 12*, 625–633.

Albee, G. W. (1967). The relation of conceptual models to manpower needs. In E. L. Cowen, E. A. Gardner, & M. Zax (Eds.), *Emergent approaches to mental health problems.* New York: Appleton-Century-Crofts.

Alexander, J. F., Barton, C., Schiavo, R. S., & Parsons, B. V. (1976). Systems-behavioral intervention with families of delinquents: Therapist characteristics, family behavior, and outcome. *Journal of Consulting and Clinical Psychology, 44*, 656–664.

Alexander, J. F., & Parsons, B. V. (1973). Short-term behavioral intervention with delinquent families. *Journal of Abnormal Psychology, 81*, 219–225.

Allen, G. J., Chinsky, J. M., Larcen, S. W., Lochman, J. E., & Salinger, H. V. (1976). *Community psychology and the schools: A behaviorally-oriented approach.* Hillsdale, NJ: Erlbaum.

Allen, K. E., & Harris, F. R. (1966). Elimination of a child's excessive scratching by training the mother in reinforcement procedures. *Behaviour Research and Therapy, 4*, 79–84.

Allen, K. E., Hart, B. M., Buell, J. S., Harris, F. R., & Wolf, M. M. (1964). Effects of social reinforcement on isolate behavior of a nursery school child. *Child Development, 35*, 511–518.

American Psychiatric Association. (1980). *Diagnostic and statistical manual of mental disorders* (3rd ed.). Washington, DC: Author.

Axelrod, S., Brantner, J. P., & Meddock, T. D. (1978). Overcorrection: A review and critical analysis. *Journal of Special Education, 12*, 367–391.

Ayllon, T., Smith, D., & Rogers, M. (1970). Behavioral

management of school phobia. *Journal of Behavior Therapy and Experimental Psychiatry, 1*, 125–138.

Azrin, N. H., & Powers, M. A. (1975). Eliminating classroom disturbances of emotionally-disturbed children by positive practice procedures. *Behavior Therapy, 6*, 525–534.

Baer, D. M., Wolf, M. M., & Risley, T. R. (1968). Some current dimensions of applied behavior analysis. *Journal of Applied Behavior Analysis, 1*, 91–97.

Bandura, A. (1965). Influence of models' reinforcement contingencies on the acquisition of imitative responses. *Journal of Personality and Social Psychology, 1*, 589–595.

Bandura, A. (1969). *Principles of behavior modification.* New York: Holt, Rinehart & Winston.

Bandura, A., & Menlove, F. L. (1968). Factors determining vicarious extinction of avoidance behavior through symbolic modeling. *Journal of Personality and Social Psychology, 8*, 99–108.

Barabasz, A. F. (1973). Group desensitization of test anxiety in elementary school. *The Journal of Psychology, 83*, 295–301.

Barabasz, A. F. (1975). Classroom teachers as paraprofessional therapists in group systematic desensitization of test anxiety. *Psychiatry, 38*, 388–392.

Barkley, R. A. (1982). Guidelines for defining hyperactivity in children. In A. E. Kazdin & B. B. Lahey (Eds.), *Advances in clinical child psychology* (Vol. 5). New York: Plenum.

Bauer, D. (1980). Childhood fears in developmental perspective. In L. Hersov & I. Berg (Eds.), *Out of school.* New York: Wiley.

Baum, C. G., & Forehand, R. (1983). Long-term follow-up assessment of parent training by use of multiple outcome measures. *Behavior Therapy, 12*, 643–652.

Beck, A. T. (1976). *Cognitive therapy and the emotional disorders.* New York: International Universities Press.

Bellack, A. S., & Hersen, M. (1977). *Research and practice in social skills training.* New York: Plenum.

Berkowitz, B. P., & Graziano, A. M. (1972). Training parents as behavior therapists: A review. *Behaviour Research and Therapy, 10*, 297–317.

Bernal, M. E., Duryee, J. S., Pruett, H. L., & Burns, B. J. (1968). Behavior modification and the brat syndrome. *Journal of Consulting and Clinical Psychology, 32*, 447–455.

Bernal, M. E., Klinnert, M. D., & Schultz, L. A. (1980). Outcome evaluation of behavioral parent training and client-centered parent counseling for children with conduct problems. *Journal of Applied Behavior Analysis, 13*, 677–691.

Borkovec, T. D., Weerts, T. C., & Bernstein, D. A. (1977). Assessment of anxiety. In F. R. Ciminero, K. S. Calhoun, & H. E. Adams (Eds.), *Handbook of behavioral assessment.* New York: Wiley.

Bornstein, M. R., Bellack, A. S., & Hersen, M. (1977). Social skills training for unassertive children: A multiple-baseline analysis. *Journal of Applied Behavior Analysis, 10*, 183–195.

Bornstein, M. R., Bellack, A. S., & Hersen, M. (1980). Social skills training for highly aggressive children. *Behavior Modification, 4*, 173–186.

Bornstein, P. H., Hamilton, S. B., & Quevillon, R. P.

(1977). Behavior modification by long-distance: Demonstration of functional control over disruptive behavior in a rural classroom setting. *Behavior Modification, 1*, 369–380.

Brooks, B. D., Morrow, J. E., & Gray, W. F. (1968). Reduction of autistic gaze aversion by reinforcement of visual attention response. *Journal of Special Education, 2*, 307–309.

Budd, K. S., Green, D. R., & Baer, D. M. (1976). An analysis of multiple misplaced parental social contingencies. *Journal of Applied Behavior Analysis, 9*, 459–470.

Burchard, J. D., & Barrera, F. (1972). An analysis of timeout and response cost in a programmed environment. *Journal of Applied Behavior Analysis, 5*, 271–282.

Calhoun, K. S., & Lima, P. P. (1977). Effects of varying schedules of timeout on high and low rate behaviors. *Journal of Behavior Therapy and Experimental Psychiatry, 8*, 189–194.

Camp, B., Blom, G., Herbert, F., & Van Doornenck, W. (1977). "Think aloud": A program for developing self-control in young aggressive boys. *Journal of Abnormal Child Psychology, 5*, 157–169.

Caplan, G. (1964). *Principles of preventive psychiatry.* New York: Basic Books.

Carr, E. G. (1977). The motivation of self-injurious behavior: A review of some hypotheses. *Psychological Bulletin, 84*, 800–816.

Carr, E. G., Newsom, C. D., & Binkoff, J. A. (1980). Escape as a factor in the aggressive behavior of two retarded children. *Journal of Applied Behavior Analysis, 13*, 113–129.

Clement, P. W., & Milne, D. C. (1967). Group play therapy and tangible reinforcers used to modify the behavior of 8-year-old boys. *Behaviour Research and Therapy, 5*, 301–312.

Cohen, H. L., & Filipczak, J. (1971). *A new learning environment.* San Francisco: Jossey-Bass.

Corte, H. E., Wolf, M. M., & Locke, B. J. (1971). A comparison of procedures for eliminating self-injurious behavior of retarded adolescents. *Journal of Applied Behavior Analysis, 4*, 201–213.

Craighead, W. E., O'Leary, K. D., & Allen, J. S. (1973). Teaching and generalization of instruction following in an autistic child. *Journal of Behavior Therapy and Experimental Psychiatry, 4*, 171–176.

DeCatanzaro, D. A., & Baldwin, G. (1978). Effective treatment of self-injurious behavior through a forced arm exercise. *American Journal of Mental Deficiency, 32*, 433–439.

DiLorenzo, T. M., & Ollendick, T. H. (1984). Punishment. In R. P. Barrett & S. E. Bruening (Eds.), *Treatment of severe behavior disorders: Contemporary approaches with the mentally retarded.* New York: Plenum.

Doleys, D. M., & Williams, S. C. (1977). The use of natural consequences and a make-up period to eliminate school phobic behavior: A case study. *Journal of School Psychiatry, 15*, 44–50.

Drabman, R. S., Hammer, D., & Rosenbaum, M. S. (1979). Assessing generalization in behavior modification with children: The generalization map. *Behavioral Assessment, 1*, 203–219.

Elardo, P. T., & Caldwell, B. M. (1979). The effects of an

experimental social development program on children in the middle childhood period. *Psychology in the Schools, 16,* 93−100.

Elder, J. P., Edelstein, B. A., & Narick, M. M. (1979). Adolescent psychiatric patients: Modifying aggressive behavior with social skills training. *Behavior Modification, 3,* 161−178.

Ellis, A. (1970). *The essence of rational psychotherapy: A comprehensive approach to treatment.* New York: Institute for Rational Living.

Ferber, H., Keeley, S. M., & Shemberg, K. M. (1974). Training parents in behavior modification: Outcomes of and problems encountered in a program after Patterson's work. *Behavior Therapy, 5,* 415−419.

Felner, R. D., Jason, L. A., Moritsugu, J., & Farber, S. S. (Eds.). (1983). *Preventive psychology: Theory, research, and practice.* New York: Pergamon.

Fixsen, D. L., Phillips, E. L., & Wolf, M. M. (1972). Achievement Place: The reliability of self-reporting and peer-reporting and their effects on behavior. *Journal of Applied Behavior Analysis, 5,* 19−30.

Fixsen, D. L., Phillips, E. L., & Wolf, M. M. (1973). Achievement Place: Experiment in self-government with pre-delinquents. *Journal of Applied Behavior Analysis, 6,* 31−47.

Fleischman, M. J. (1981). A replication of Patterson's "Intervention for boys with conduct problems." *Journal of Consulting and Clinical Psychology, 49,* 342−351.

Forehand, R., & Atkeson, B. M. (1977). Generality of treatment effects with parents as therapists: A review of assessment and implementation procedures. *Behavior Therapy, 8,* 575−593.

Forehand, R., & McMahon, R. J. (1982). *Helping the noncompliant child: A clinician's guide to parent training.* New York: Guilford.

Forehand, R., Roberts, M. W., Doleys, D. M., Hobbs, S. A., & Resick, P. A. (1976). An examination of disciplinary procedures with children. *Journal of Experimental Child Psychology, 21,* 109−120.

Foxx, R. M. (1977). Attention training: The use of overcorrection avoidance to increase eye contact of autistic and retarded children. *Journal of Applied Behavior Analysis, 10,* 489−499.

Foxx, R. M., & Azrin, N. H. (1972). Restitution: A method of eliminating aggressive-disruptive behavior of retarded and brain damaged patients. *Behavior Research and Therapy, 10,* 15−27.

Foxx, R. M., & Azrin, N. H. (1973). The elimination of autistic self-stimulatory behavior by overcorrection. *Journal of Applied Behavior Analysis, 6,* 1−14.

Foxx, R. M., & Bechtel, D. R. (1982). Overcorrection. In M. Hersen, R. M. Eisler, & P. M. Miller (Eds.), *Progress in behavior modification* (Vol. 13). New York: Academic Press.

Franks, C. M. (1982). Behavior therapy with children and adolescents. In C. M. Franks, G. T. Wilson, P. C. Kendall, & K. D. Brownell (Eds.), *Annual review of behavior therapy: Theory and practice* (Vol. 8). New York: Guilford.

Franks, C. M., & Wilson, G. T. (1978). *Annual review of behavior therapy theory and practice* (Vol. 6). New York: Brunner/ Mazel.

Freedman, B. J., Rosenthal, L., Donahue, C. P., Schlundt, D. G., & McFall, R. M. (1978). A social-behavioral analysis of skill deficits in delinquent and nondelinquent adolescent boys. *Journal of Consulting and Clinical Psychology, 46,* 1448−1462.

Furman, W. (1980). Promoting social development: Developmental implications for treatment. In B. B. Lahey & A. E. Kazdin (Eds.), *Advances in clinical child psychology* (Vol. 3). New York: Plenum.

Gaffney, L. R., & McFall, R. M. (1981). A comparison of social skills in delinquent and nondelinquent adolescent girls using a behavioral role-playing inventory. *Journal of Consulting and Clinical Psychology, 49,* 959−967.

Gelfand, D. M. (1978). Social withdrawal and negative emotional states: Behavior therapy. In B. B. Wolman, J. Egan, & A. O. Ross (Eds.), *Handbook of treatment of mental disorders in childhood and adolescence.* Englewood Cliffs, NJ: Prentice-Hall.

Gelfand, D. M., & Hartmann, D. P. (1968). Behavior therapy with children: A review and evaluation of research methodology. *Psychological Bulletin, 69,* 204−215.

Gelfand, D. M., & Hartmann, D. P. (1975). *Child behavior analysis and therapy.* New York: Pergamon.

Goldfried, M. R., Decenteceo, E. T., Weinberg, L. (1974). Systematic rational restructuring as a self-control technique. *Behavior Therapy, 5,* 247−254.

Goodwin, S. E., & Mahoney, M. J. (1975). Modification of aggression through modeling: An experimental probe. *Journal of Behavior Therapy and Experimental Psychiatry, 6,* 200−202.

Goyette, C. H., Conners, C. K., & Ulrich, R. F. (1978). Normative data on Revised Conners' Parent and Teacher Rating Scales. *Journal of Abnormal Child Psychology, 6,* 221−236.

Graziano, A. M., DeGiovanni, I. S., & Garcia, K. A. (1979). Behavioral treatment of children's fears: A review. *Psychological Bulletin, 86,* 804−830.

Graziano, A. M., & Mooney, K. C. (1980). Family self-control instruction for children's nighttime fear reduction. *Journal of Consulting and Clinical Psychology, 48,* 206−213.

Graziano, A. M., & Mooney, K. C. (1982). Behavioral treatment of "nightfears" in children: Maintenance of improvement at 2½- to 3-year follow-up. *Journal of Consulting and Clinical Psychology, 50,* 598−599.

Graziano, A. M., & Mooney, K. C. (1984). *Children and behavior therapy.* New York: Aldine.

Graziano, A. M., Mooney, K. C., Huber, C., & Ignasiak, D. (1979). Self-control instruction for children's fear reductions. *Journal of Behavior Therapy and Experimental Psychiatry, 10,* 221−227.

Greist, D. L., Forehand, R., Rogers, T., Breiner, J., Furey, W., & Williams, C. A. (1982). Effects of parent enhancement therapy on the treatment outcome and generalization of a parent training program. *Behavior Research and Therapy, 20,* 429−436.

Greist, D. L., & Wells, K. C. (1983). Behavioral family therapy with conduct disorders in children. *Behavior Therapy, 14,* 37−53.

Hampe, E., Noble, H., Miller, L. C., & Barrett, C. L. (1973). Phobic children one and two years posttreatment. *Journal of Abnormal Psychology, 82,* 446−453.

Harris, S. L. (1983a). Behavior therapy with children. In

M. Hersen, A. E. Kazdin, & A. S. Bellack (Eds.), *The clinical psychology handbook*. Elmsford, NY: Pergamon.

Harris, S. L. (1983b). DSM-III: Its implications for children. *Child Behavior Therapy, 1*, 37–48.

Harris, S. L., & Ersner-Hershfield, R. (1978). Behavioral suppression of seriously disruptive behavior in psychotic and retarded patients: A review of punishment and its alternatives. *Psychological Bulletin, 85*, 1352–1375.

Harris, S. L., & Ferrari, M. (1983). Developmental factors in child behavior therapy. *Behavior Therapy, 14*, 54–72.

Harris, S. L., & Powers, M. D. (1984). Diagnostic issues. In T. H. Ollendick & M. Hersen (Eds.), *Child behavioral assessment: Principles and procedures*. New York: Pergamon.

Harris, S. L., & Romanczyk, R. G. (1976). Treating self-injurious behavior of a retarded child by overcorrection. *Behavior Therapy, 7*, 235–239.

Hart, B. M., Allen, K. E., Buell, J. S., Harris, F. R., & Wolf, M. M. (1964). Effects of social reinforcement on operant crying. *Journal of Experimental Child Psychology, 1*, 145–153.

Hatzenbuehler, L. C., & Schroeder, H. E. (1978). Desensitization procedures in the treatment of childhood disorders. *Psychological Bulletin, 85*, 831–844.

Henn, F. A., Bardwell, R., Jenkins, R. L. (1980). Juvenile delinquents revisited: Adult criminal activity. *Archives of General Psychiatry, 37*, 1160–1163.

Herbert, E. W., & Baer, D. M. (1972). Training parents as behavior modifiers: Self-recording of contingent attention. *Journal of Applied Behavior Analysis, 5*, 139–149.

Herbert, M. (1982). Conduct disorders. In A. E. Kazdin & B. B. Lahey (Eds.), *Advances in clinical child psychology* (Vol. 5). New York: Plenum.

Hersen, M. (1970). Behavior modification approach to a school phobia case. *Journal of Clinical Psychology, 26*, 128–132.

Hersen, M., & Barlow, D. H. (1976). *Single case experimental designs: Strategies for studying behavior change*. New York: Pergamon.

Higa, W. R., Tharp, R. G., & Calkins, R. P. (1978). Developmental verbal control of behavior: Implications for self-instructional training. *Journal of Experimental Child Psychology, 26*, 489–497.

Hingtgen, J. N., Coulter, S. K., & Churchill, D. W. (1967). Intensive reinforcement of imitative behavior in mute autistic children. *Archives of General Psychiatry, 17*, 36–43.

Hingtgen, J. N., Saunders, B. J., & DeMyer, M. K. (1965). Shaping cooperative responses in early childhood schizophrenics. In L. Ullmann & L. Krasner (Eds.), *Case studies in behavior modification*. New York: Holt, Rinehart & Winston.

Hobbs, S. A. (1976). Modifying stereotyped behaviors by overcorrection: A critical review. *Rehabilitation Psychology, 23*, 1–11.

Hobbs, S. A., & Forehand, R. (1975). Effects of differential release from timeout on children's deviant behavior. *Journal of Behavior Therapy and Experimental Psychiatry, 6*, 256–257.

Hobbs, S. A., & Forehand, R. (1977). Important parameters in the use of timeout with children: A re-examination. *Journal of Behavior Therapy and Experimental Psychiatry, 8*, 365–370.

Hobbs, S. A., Moguin, L. E., Tyroler, M., & Lahey, B. B. (1980). Cognitive behavior therapy with children: Has clinical utility been demonstrated? *Psychological Bulletin, 87*, 147–165.

Iwata, B. A., & Bailey, J. S. (1974). Reward versus cost token systems: An analysis of the effects on students and teachers. *Journal of Applied Behavior Analysis, 7*, 567–576.

Jason, L. A. (1977). Behavioral community psychology: Conceptualizations and applications. *Journal of Community Psychology, 5*, 303–312.

Jason, L. A. (1981). Prevention and environmental modification in a behavioral community model. *Behavioral Counseling Quarterly, 1*, 91–107.

Jason, L. A. (1983). Preventive behavioral interventions. In R. D. Feiner, L. A. Jason, J. Moritsugu, & S. S. Farber (Eds.), *Preventive psychology: Theory, research, and practice*. New York: Pergamon.

Jesness, C. F. (1975). Comparative effectiveness of behavior modification and transactional analysis programs for delinquents. *Journal of Consulting and Clinical Psychology, 43*, 758–779.

Jesness, C. F., & DeRisi, W. J. (1973). Some variations in techniques of contingency management in a school for delinquents. In J. S. Stumphauzer (Ed.), *Behavior therapy with delinquents*. Springfield, IL: Charles C. Thomas.

Jesness, C. F., DeRisi, W. J., McCormick, P. M., & Qedge, R. F. (1972). *The Youth Center Research Project*. Sacramento, CA: American Justice Institute.

Johnson, S. M., & Christensen, A. (1975). Multiple criteria follow-up of behavior modification with families. *Journal of Abnormal Child Psychology, 3*, 135–154.

Jones, M. C. (1924). The elimination of children's fears. *Journal of Experimental Psychology, 7*, 382–390.

Jones, R. R. (1979). *Therapeutic effects of the Teaching Family Group Home model*. Paper presented at the meeting of the American Psychological Association, New York.

Jones, R. T., & Kazdin, A. E. (1981). Childhood behavior problems in the school. In S. M. Turner, K. S. Calhoun, & H. E. Adams (Eds.), *Handbook of clinical behavior therapy*. New York: Wiley–Interscience.

Kanfer, F. H., Karoly, P., & Newman, A. (1975). Reduction of children's fear of the dark by competence-related and situational threat-related verbal cues. *Journal of Consulting and Clinical Psychology, 43*, 251–258.

Karoly, P., & Rosenthal, M. (1977). Training parents in behavior modification: Effects on perceptions of family interaction and deviant child behavior. *Behavior Therapy, 8*, 406–410.

Kaufman, L. M., & Wagner, B. R. (1972). Barb: A systematic treatment technology for temper control disorders. *Behavior Therapy, 3*, 84–90.

Kazdin, A. E. (1975). *Behavior modification in applied settings*. Homewood, IL: Dorsey Press.

Kazdin, A. E. (1981). Drawing valid inferences from case studies. *Journal of Consulting and Clinical Psychology, 49*, 183–192.

Kelley, C. K. (1976). Play desensitization of fear of darkness in preschool children. *Behavior Research and Therapy, 14,* 79–81.

Kelly, J. A., & Drabman, R. S. (1977). Generalizing response suppression of self-injurious behavior through an overcorrection punishment procedure: A case study. *Behavior Therapy, 8,* 468–472.

Kendall, P. C. (1977). On the efficacious use of verbal self-instructional procedures with children. *Cognitive Therapy and Research, 1,* 331–341.

Kendall, P. C., & Finch, A. J. (1976). A cognitive-behavioral treatment for impulse control: A case study. *Journal of Consulting and Clinical Psychology, 44,* 852–857.

Kendall, P. C., & Finch, A. J. (1978). A cognitive-behavioral treatment for impulsivity: A group comparison study. *Journal of Consulting and Clinical Psychology, 46,* 110–118.

Kendall, P. C., Nay, W. R., & Jeffers, J. (1975). Timeout duration and contrast effects: A systematic evaluation of a successive treatments design. *Behavior Therapy, 6,* 609–615.

Kennedy, W. A. (1965). School phobia: Rapid treatment of fifty cases. *Journal of Abnormal Psychology, 70,* 285–289.

Kent, R. N., & O'Leary, K. D. (1976). A controlled evaluation of behavior modification with conduct problem children. *Journal of Consulting and Clinical Psychology, 44,* 586–596.

Kent, R. N., & O'Leary, K. D. (1977). Treatment of conduct problem children: B.A. and/or Ph.D. therapists. *Behavior Therapy, 8,* 653–658.

King, N. J., Hamilton, D. I., & Murphy, G. C. (1983). The prevention of children's maladaptive fears. *Child & Family Behavior Therapy, 5,* 43–57.

Kirigin, K. A., Braukmann, C. J., Fixsen, D. L., Phillips, E. L., & Wolf, M. M. (1975). *Are community-based corrections effective: An evaluation of Achievement Place.* Paper presented at the meeting of the American Psychological Association, Chicago.

Koegel, R., & Covert, A. (1972). The relationship of self-stimulation to learning in autistic children. *Journal of Applied Behavior Analysis, 5,* 381–387.

Koegel, R., & Rincover, A. (1974). Treatment of psychotic children in a classroom environment: I. Learning in a large group. *Journal of Applied Behavior Analysis, 7,* 45–59.

Kondas, O. (1967). Reduction of examination anxiety and stagefright by group desensitization and relaxation. *Behaviour Research and Therapy, 5,* 275–281.

Kornhaber, R. C., & Schroeder, H. E. (1975). Importance of model similarity on extinction of avoidance behavior in children. *Journal of Consulting and Clinical Psychology, 5,* 601–607.

Ladd, G. W. (1981). Effectiveness of a social learning method for enhancing children's social interaction and peer acceptance. *Child Development, 52,* 171–178.

LaGreca, A. M., & Santogrossi, D. A. (1980). Social skills training with elementary school students: A behavioral group approach. *Journal of Consulting and Clinical Psychology, 48,* 220–227.

Lazarus, A. A. (1974). Cognitive restructuring. *Psychotherapy: Theory, Research, and Practice, 11,* 98–102.

Ledwidge, B. (1978). Cognitive behavior modification: A step in the wrong direction? *Psychological Bulletin, 85,* 353–375.

Leitenberg, H., & Callahan, E. J. (1973). Reinforced practice and reduction of different kinds of fears in adults and children. *Behaviour Research and Therapy, 11,* 19–30.

Lichtenstein, K. L., & Schreibman, L. (1976). Employing electric shock with autistic children: A review of the side effects. *Journal of Autism and Childhood Schizophrenia, 6,* 163–173.

Loeber, R. (1982). The stability of antisocial and delinquent child behavior: A review. *Child Development, 53,* 1431–1446.

Loeber, R., & Patterson, G. R. (1981). The aggressive child: A concomitant of a coercive system. *Advances in Family Intervention, Assessment, and Theory, 2,* 47–87.

Lochman, J. E., Nelson, W. M., & Sims, J. P. (1981). A congitive behavioral program for use with aggressive children. *Journal of Clinical Child Psychology, 10,* 146–148.

London, P. (1972). The end of ideology in behavior modification. *American Psychologist, 27,* 913–920.

Lovaas, O. I. (1979). Contrasting illness and behavioral models for the treatment of autistic children: A historical perspective. *Journal of Autism and Developmental Disorders, 9,* 315–323.

Lovaas, O. I., Berberich, J. P., Perloff, B. F., & Schaeffer, B. (1966). Acquisition of imitative speech in schizophrenic children. *Science, 151,* 705–707.

Lovaas, O. I., Freitag, G., Gold, U. J., & Kassorla, I. C. (1965). Experimental studies in childhood schizophrenia: Analysis of self-destructive behavior. *Journal of Experimental Child Psychology, 2,* 67–84.

Lovaas, O. I., Koegel, R., Simmons, J. O., & Long, J. S. (1973). Some generalization and follow-up measures on autistic children in behavior therapy. *Journal of Applied Behavior Analysis, 6,* 131–165.

Lovaas, O. I., & Simmons, J. Q. (1969). Manipulation of self-destruction in three retarded children. *Journal of Applied Behavior Analysis, 2,* 143–157.

Luiselli, J. K. (1977). Case report: An attendant-administered contingency management program for the treatment of a toileting phobia. *Journal of Mental Deficiency Research, 21,* 283–288.

Luiselli, J. K. (1978). Treatment of an autistic child's fear of riding a school bus through exposure and reinforcement. *Journal of Behavior Therapy and Experimental Psychiatry, 9,* 169–172.

Lynch, K. R., & Ollendick, T. H. (1977). Juvenile corrections: A model program. *American Journal of Corrections, 39,* 6–7.

Madsen, C. H., Becker, W. C., & Thomas, D. R. (1968). Rules, praise, and ignoring: Elements of elementary classroom control. *Journal of Applied Behavior Analysis, 1,* 139–150.

Mahoney, M. J., & Mahoney, K. (1975). Treatment of obesity: A clinical exploration. In B. J. Williams (Ed.), *Obesity: Behavioral approaches to dietary management.* New York: Brunner/Mazel.

Mann, J., & Rosenthal, T. L. (1969). Vicarious and direct counterconditioning of test anxiety through individual and group desensitization. *Behaviour Research and Therapy, 7,* 359–367.

Margolies, P. J. (1977). Behavioral approaches to the

treatment of early infantile autism: A review. *Psychological Bulletin, 84*, 249–264.

Marholin, D., & Siegel, L. J. (1978). Beyond the law of effect: Programming for the maintenance of behavioral change. In D. Marholin (Ed.), *Child behavior therapy*. New York: Gardner.

Marks, I. M. (1975). Behavioral treatments of phobic and obsessive-compulsive disorders: A critical appraisal. In M. Hersen, R. M. Eisler, & P. M. Miller (Eds.), *Progress in behavior modification* (Vol. 1). New York: Academic Press.

Mash, E. J., & Terdal, L. G. (1982). Behavioral assessment of childhood disturbances. In E. J. Mash & L. G. Terdal (Eds.), *Behavioral assessment of childhood disorders*. New York: Guilford.

Matson, J. L., & DiLorenzo, T. M. (1983). *Punishment and its alternatives: New perspectives for contemporary behavior therapy*. New York: Springer.

Matson, J. L., Horne, A. M., Ollendick, D. G., & Ollendick, T. H. (1979). A further evaluation of restitution and positive practice. *Journal of Behavior Therapy and Experimental Psychiatry, 10*, 295–298.

Matson, J. L., Ollendick, T. H., & Martin, J. E. (1979). Overcorrection revisited: A long-term follow-up. *Journal of Behavior Therapy and Experimental Psychiatry, 10*, 11–13.

Mattison, R., Cantwell, D. P., Russell, A. T., & Will, L. A. (1979). A comparison of DSM-II and DSM-III in the diagnosis of childhood psychiatric disorders: III. Multiaxial features. *Archives of General Psychiatry, 36*, 1217–1222.

McClure, L. F., Chinsky, J. M., & Larsen, S. W. (1978). Enhancing social problem-solving performance in an elementary school setting. *Journal of Educational Psychology, 70*, 504–513.

McConnell, O. L. (1967). Control of eye contact in an autistic child. *Journal of Child Psychology and Psychiatry and Allied Disciplines, 8*, 249–257.

McLaughlin, T., & Malaby, J. (1972). Reducing and measuring inappropriate verbalizations in a token classroom. *Journal of Applied Behavior Analysis, 5*, 329–333.

McMahon, R. J., Forehand, R., & Greist, D. L. (1981). Effects of knowledge of social learning principles on enhancing treatment outcome and generalization on a parent training program. *Journal of Consulting and Clinical Psychology, 49*, 526–532.

McNamara, J. R. (1968). The broad based application of social learning theory to treat aggression in a preschool child. *Journal of Clinical Psychology, 26*, 245–247.

Meador, A. E., & Ollendick, T. H. (1984). Cognitive behavior therapy with children: An evaluation of its efficacy and clinical utility. *Child and Family Behavior Therapy, 6*, 25–44.

Means, J. R., & Merrens, M. R. (1969). Interpersonal training for an autistic child. *Perceptual and Motor Skills, 28*, 972–974.

Meichenbaum, D. (1971). Examination of model characteristics in reducing avoidance behavior. *Journal of Personality and Social Psychology, 17*, 298–307.

Meichenbaum, D. (1977). *Cognitive-behavior modification*. New York: Plenum.

Meichenbaum, D., & Goodman, J. (1971). Training impulsive children to talk to themselves: A means of developing self-control. *Journal of Abnormal Psychology, 77*, 115–126.

Melamed, B., Robbins, R., Smith, S., & Graves, S. (1980). *Coping strategies in children undergoing surgery*. Paper presented at the American Psychological Association, Montreal.

Melamed, B., & Siegel, J. (1975). Reduction of anxiety in children facing hospitalization and surgery by use of filmed modeling. *Journal of Consulting and Clinical Psychology, 43*, 511–521.

Metz, J. R. (1965). Conditioning generalized imitation in autistic children. *Journal of Experimental Child Psychology, 2*, 389–399.

Mezzich, A. C., & Mezzich, J. E. (1979). *Diagnostic reliability of childhood and adolescent behavior disorders*. Paper presented at the American Psychological Association, New York.

Miller, L. C., Barrett, C. L., Hampe, E., & Noble, H. (1972). Comparison of reciprocal inhibition, psychotherapy, and waiting list control of phobic children. *Journal of Abnormal Psychology, 79*, 269–279.

Nay, W. R. (1979). Parents as real life reinforcers: The enhancement of parent training effects across conditions other than training. In A. P. Goldstein & F. H. Kanfer (Eds.), *Maximizing treatment gains: Transfer enhancement in psychotherapy*. New York: Academic Press.

Nedelman, D., & Sulzbacher, S. I. (1972). Dicky at 13 years of age: A long-term success following early application of operant conditioning procedures. In G. Semf (Ed.), *Behavior analysis and education*. Lawrence: University of Kansas Press.

Neilans, T. H., & Israel, A. C. (1981). Towards maintenance and generalization of behavior change: Teaching children self-regulation and self-instructional skills. *Cognitive Therapy and Research, 2*, 189–195.

Neisworth, J. T., Madle, R. A., & Goeke, K. E. (1975). "Errorless" elimination of separation anxiety: A case study. *Behavior Therapy and Experimental Psychiatry, 6*, 79–82.

Nelson, R. O., & Barlow, D. H. (1981). Behavioral assessment: Basic strategies and initial procedures. In D. H. Barlow (Ed.), *Behavioral assessment of adult disorders*. New York: Guilford.

Nietzel, M. T., Winett, R. A., MacDonald, M. L., & Davidson, W. S. (1977). *Behavioral approaches to community psychology*. New York: Pergamon.

O'Connor, R. D. (1969). Modification of social withdrawal through symbolic modeling. *Journal of Applied Behavior Analysis, 2*, 15–22.

O'Connor, R. D. (1972). Relative efficacy of modeling, shaping, and the combined procedures for modification of social withdrawal. *Journal of Abnormal Psychology, 79*, 327–334.

O'Dell, S. (1974). Training parents in behavior modification: A review. *Psychological Bulletin, 81*, 418–433.

O'Dell, S. L., O'Quinn, J. O., Alford, B. A., O'Briant, A. L., Bradlyn, A. S., & Giebenhain, J. E. (1982). Predicting the acquisition of parenting skills via four training methods. *Behavior Therapy, 13*, 194–208.

Oden, S., & Asher, S. R. (1977). Coaching children in social skills for friendship making. *Child Development, 48*, 495–506.

O'Leary, K. D. (1980). Pills or skills for hyperactive children. *Journal of Applied Behavior Analysis, 13*, 191–204.

O'Leary, K. D., & Carr, E. G. (1982). Childhood disorders. In G. T. Wilson & C. Franks (Eds.), *Contemporary behavior therapy*. New York: Guilford.

Ollendick, T. H. (1979a). Fear reduction techniques with children. In M. Hersen, R. M. Eisler, & P. M. Miller (Eds.), *Progress in behavior modification* (Vol. 8). New York: Academic Press.

Ollendick, T. H. (1979b). Behavioral treatment of anorexia nervosa: A five-year study. *Behavior Modification, 3*, 124–135.

Ollendick, T. H. (1979c). Success and failure: Implications for child psychopathology. In A. J. Finch & P. C. Kendall (Eds.), *Clinical treatment and research in child psychopathology*. New York: Spectrum.

Ollendick, T. H. (1981). Assessment of social interaction skills in school children. *Behavioral Counseling Quarterly, 1*, 227–243.

Ollendick, T. H. (1983a). Reliability and validity of Revised Fear Survey Schedule for Children (FSSC-R). *Behaviour Research and Therapy, 21*, 685–692.

Ollendick, T. H. (1983b). Anxiety-based disorders in children. In M. Hersen (Ed.), *Outpatient behavior therapy: A clinical guide*. New York: Grune & Stratton.

Ollendick, T. H., & Cerny, J. A. (1981). *Clinical behavior therapy with children*. New York: Plenum.

Ollendick, T. H., Elliott, W. R., & Matson, J. L. (1980). Locus of control as related to effectiveness in a behavior modification program for juvenile delinquents. *Journal of Behavior Therapy and Experimental Psychiatry, 11*, 259–262.

Ollendick, T. H., & Gruen, G. E. (1972). Treatment of a bodily injury phobia with implosive therapy. *Journal of Consulting and Clinical Psychology, 38*, 389–393.

Ollendick, T. H., & Hersen, M. (1979). Social skills training for juvenile delinquents. *Behaviour Research and Therapy, 17*, 547–554.

Ollendick, T. H., & Hersen, M. (1984). *Child behavioral assessment: Principles and procedures*. New York: Pergamon.

Ollendick, T. H., & Matson, J. L. (1978). Overcorrection: An overview. *Behavior Therapy, 9*, 830–842.

Ollendick, T. H., & Mayer, J. (1984). School phobia. In S. M. Turner (Ed.), *Behavioral treatment of anxiety disorders*. New York: Plenum.

Ollendick, T. H., & Ollendick, D. G. (1982). Anxiety disorders in the mentally retarded. In J. L. Matson & R. P. Barrett (Eds.), *Psychopathology of the mentally retarded*. New York: Grune & Stratton.

Ollendick, T. H., Shapiro, E. S., & Barrett, R. F. (1981). Reducing sterotypic behaviors: An analysis of treatment procedures utilizing an alternating treatments design. *Behavior Therapy, 12*, 570–577.

Ollendick, T. H., & Winett, R. A. (1984). Behavioral preventive interventions with children: Current status, conceptual issues, and future directions. In P. H. Bornstein & A. E. Kazdin (Eds.), *Handbook of clinical behavior therapy with children*. New York: Dorsey Press.

Olweus, D. (1979). Stability of aggressive reaction patterns in males: A review. *Psychological Bulletin, 86*, 852–875.

Patterson, G. R. (1974). Interventions for boys with conduct problems: Multiple settings, treatments, and criteria. *Journal of Consulting and Clinical Psychology, 42*, 471–481.

Patterson, G. R. (1977). *Families: Applications of social learning to family life* (rev. ed.). Champaign, IL: Research Press.

Patterson, G. R. (1982). *Coercive family processes*. Eugene, OR: Castalia.

Patterson, G. R., Chamberlain, P., & Reid, J. B. (1982). A comparative evaluation of a parent-training program. *Behavior Therapy, 13*, 638–650.

Patterson, G. R., & Cobb, J. A. (1971). A dyadic analysis of aggressive behaviors. In J. P. Hill (Ed.), *Minnesota symposium on child psychology* (Vol. 5). Minneapolis: University of Minnesota Press.

Patterson, G. R., & Gullion, M. E. (1976). *Living with children: New methods for parents and teachers* (rev. ed.). Champaign, IL: Research Press.

Peed, S., Roberts, M., & Forehand, R. (1977). Evaluation of the effectiveness of a standard parent training program in altering the interaction of mothers and their noncompliant children. *Behavior Modification, 1*, 323–350.

Peterson, D. R. (1961). Behavior problems of middle childhood. *Journal of Consulting Psychology 25*, 205–209.

Peterson, L., Schultheis, K., Ridley-Johnson, R., Miller, D. J., & Tracy, K. (1984). Comparison of three modeling procedures on the presurgical and postsurgical reactions of children. *Behavior Therapy, 15*, 197–203.

Peterson, L., & Shigetomi, C. (1981). The use of coping techniques to minimize anxiety in hospitalized children. *Behavior Therapy, 12*, 1–12.

Pomerantz, P. B., Peterson, N. T., Macholin, D., & Stern, S. (1977). The in vivo elimination of a childhood phobia by a paraprofessional interventionist at home. *Journal of Behavior Therapy and Experimental Psychiatry, 8*, 417–421.

Porterfield, J. K., Herbert-Jackson, E., & Risley, T. R. (1976). Contingent observation: An effective and acceptable procedure for reducing disruptive behavior of young children in a group setting. *Journal of Applied Behavior Analysis, 9*, 55–64.

Poser, E. G. (1970). Toward a theory of behavioral prophylaxis. *Journal of Behavior Therapy and Experimental Psychiatry, 1*, 39–45.

Quay, H. C. (1979). Classification. In H. C. Quay & J. S. Werry (Eds.), *Psychopathological disorders of childhood* (2nd ed.). New York: Wiley.

Quay, H. C. (1986). A critical analysis of DSM-III as a taxonomy of psychopathology in childhood and adolescence. In T. Millon & G. Klerman (Eds.), *Contemporary issues in psychopathology*. New York: Guilford.

Rekers, G. A. (1978). Sexual problems: Behavior modification. In B. B. Wolman (Ed.), *Handbook of treatment of mental disorders in childhood and adolescence*. Englewood Cliffs, NJ: Prentice-Hall.

Repp, A. C., & Deitz, S. M. (1974). Reducing aggressive and self-injurious behavior of institutionalized retarded children through reinforcement of other behaviors. *Journal of Applied Behavior Analysis, 7*, 313–325.

Repp, A. C., & Deitz, D. (1978). On the selective use of

punishment: Suggested guidelines for administrators. *Mental Retardation, 16,* 250–254.

Rines, W. B. (1973). Behavior therapy before institutionalization. *Psychotherapy: Theory, Research, and Practice, 10,* 281–283.

Risley, T. R. (1968). The effects and side effects of punishing the autistic behaviors of a deviant child. *Journal of Applied Behavior Analysis, 1,* 21–34.

Ritter, B. (1968). The group desensitization of childrens' snake phobias using vicarious and contact desensitization procedures. *Behaviour Research and Therapy, 6,* 1–6.

Roberts, M. W. (1982). The effects of warned versus unwarned timeout procedures on child noncompliance. *Child and Family Behavior Therapy, 4,* 37–53.

Roberts, M. W., Hatzenbuehler, L. C., & Bean, A. W. (1981). The effects of differential attention and timeout on child noncompliance. *Behavior Therapy, 12,* 93–99.

Robins, L. N. (1978). Study of childhood predictors of adult antisocial behavior: Replication from longitudinal studies. *Psychological Medicine, 8,* 611–622.

Romanczyk, R. G. (1977). Intermittent punishment of self-stimulation: Effectiveness during application and extinction. *Journal of Consulting and Clinical Psychology, 45,* 53–60.

Ross, A. O. (1978). Behavior therapy with children. In S. L. Garfield & A. E. Bergin (Eds.), *Handbook of psychotherapy and behavior change* (2nd ed.). New York: Wiley.

Ross, A. O. (1980). *Psychological disorders of children: A behavioral approach to theory, research, and therapy.* New York: McGraw-Hill.

Ross, D., Ross, S., & Evans, T. A. (1971). The modification of extreme social withdrawal by modification with guided practice. *Journal of Behavior Therapy and Experimental Psychiatry, 2,* 273–279.

Rutter, M., Tizard, J., Yule, W., Graham, P., & Whitmore, K. (1976). Research report: Isle of Wight studies, 1964–1974. *Psychological Medicine, 6,* 313–332.

Safer, D. J., & Allen, R. P. (1976). *Hyperactive children: Diagnosis and management.* Baltimore: University Park Press.

Sandberg, S. T., Rutter, M. L., & Taylor, E. (1978). Hyperkinetic disorder in psychiatric clinic attenders. *Developmental Medicine and Child Neurology, 20,* 278–299.

Sandberg, S. T., Wieselberg, M., & Shaffer, D. (1980). Hyperkinetic and conduct problem children in a primary school population: Some epidemiological considerations. *Journal of Child Psychology and Psychiatry, 21,* 293–311.

Sanders, M. R., & Glynn, T. (1981). Training parents in behavioral self-management: An analysis of generalization and maintenance. *Journal of Applied Behavior Analysis, 14,* 223–237.

Sanders, M. R., & James, J. E. (1983). The modification of parent behavior: A review of generalization and maintenance. *Behavior Modification, 7,* 3–27.

Sarason, I. G. (1978). A cognitive social learning approach to juvenile delinquency. In R. Hare & D. Schalling (Eds.), *Psychopathic behavior: Approaches to research.* London: Wiley.

Sarason, I. G., & Ganzer, V. J. (1973). Modeling and group discussion in the rehabilitation of juvenile delinquents. *Journal of Counseling Psychology, 20,* 442–449.

Sarason, I. G., & Sarason, B. R. (1981). Teaching cognitive and social skills to high school students. *Journal of Consulting and Clinical Psychology, 49,* 908–919.

Scherer, M. W., & Nakamura, C. Y. (1968). A fear survey schedule for children. *Behaviour Research and Therapy, 6,* 173–182.

Schreibman, L., & Mills, J. I. (1983). Infantile autism. In T. H. Ollendick & M. Hersen (Eds.), *Handbook of child psychopathology.* New York: Plenum.

Shapiro, E. S. (1984). Self-monitoring procedures. In T. H. Ollendick & M. Hersen (Eds.), *Child behavioral assessment: Principles and procedures.* New York: Pergamon.

Shapiro, E. S., & Klein, R. D. (1980). Self-management of classroom behavior with retarded/disturbed children. *Behavior Modification, 4,* 83–97.

Shapiro, E. S., McGonigle, J. J., & Ollendick T. H. (1980). An analysis of self-assessment and self-reinforcement in a self-managed token economy with mentally retarded children. *Applied Research in Mental Retardation, 1,* 223–240.

Shure, M. B., & Spivack, G. (1978). *Problem-solving techniques in childrearing.* San Francisco: Jossey-Ross.

Smith, R. E., & Sharpe, T. M. (1970). Treatment of a school phobia with implosive therapy. *Journal of Consulting and Clinical Psychology, 35,* 239–243.

Snyder, J. J., & White, M. J. (1979). The use of cognitive self-instruction in the treatment of behaviorally-disturbed adolescents. *Behavior Therapy, 10,* 227–235.

Spence, S. H., & Marzillier, J. S. (1979). Social skills training with adolescent male offenders: I. Short-term effects. *Behaviour Research and Therapy, 17,* 7–16.

Spence, S. H., & Marzillier, J. S. (1981). Social skills training with adolescent male offenders: II. Short-term, long-term, and generalized effects. *Behaviour Research and Therapy, 19,* 349–368.

Spivack, G., & Shure, M. B. (1974). *Social adjustment of young children.* San Francisco: Jossey-Bass.

Stefanek, M. E. (1983). *Self-statements of aggressive, withdrawn, and popular children.* Paper presented at the Southeastern Psychological Association, Atlanta.

Steffen, J. L., & Karoly, P. (Eds.). (1982). *Autism and severe psychopathology: Advances in child behavioral analysis and therapy* (Vol. 2). Lexington, MA: Lexington Books.

Stokes, T. F., & Baer, D. M. (1977). An implicit technology for generalization. *Journal of Applied Behavior Analysis, 10,* 349–367.

Thelen, M. H., Fry, R. A., Dollinger, S. J., & Paul, S. C. (1976). Use of videotaped models to improve the interpersonal adjustment of delinquents. *Journal of Consulting and Clinical Psychology, 44,* 492.

Trotter, R. J. (1973). Behavior modification: Here, there, and everywhere. *Science News, 103,* 260–263.

Tuma, J. M., & Pratt, J. M. (1982). Clinical child psychology practice and training: A survey. *Journal of Clinical Child Psychology, 11,* 27–34.

Ultee, C. A., Griffiaen, D., & Schellekens, J. (1982). The reduction of anxiety in children: A comparison of the effects of systematic desensitization in vitro and systematic desensitization in vivo. *Behaviour Research and Therapy, 20,* 61–67.

Van Hasselt, V. B., Hersen, M., Bellack, A. S., Rosenbloom, N., & Lamparski, D. (1979). Tripartite assessment of the effects of systematic desensitization in a multiphobic child: An experimental analysis. *Journal of Behavior Therapy and Experimental Psychiatry, 10,* 57–66.

Van Hesselt, V. B., Hersen, M., Bellack, A. S., & Whitehill, M. B. (1979). Social skills assessment and training for children: An evaluative review. *Behaviour Research and Therapy, 17,* 413–437.

Varni, J. M., Lovaas, O. I., Koegel, R. L., & Everett, N. L. (1979). An analysis of observational learning in autistic and normal children. *Journal of Abnormal Child Psychology, 7,* 31–43.

Voeltz, L. M., & Evans, I. M. (1982). The assessment of behavioral interrelationships in child behavior therapy. *Behavioral Assessment 4,* 131–165.

Wahler, R. G. (1975). Some structural aspects of deviant child behavior. *Journal of Applied Behavior Analysis, 8,* 27–42.

Wahler, R. G. (1980). The insular mother: Her problems in parent–child treatment. *Journal of Applied Behavior Analysis, 13,* 207–220.

Wahler, R. G., & Afton, A. D. (1980). Attentional processes in insular and noninsular mothers: Some differences in their summary reports about child behavior problems. *Child Behavior Therapy, 2,* 25–41.

Wahler, R. G., & Graves, M. G. (1983). Setting events in social networks: Ally or enemy in child behavior therapy? *Behavior Therapy, 14,* 19–36.

Walter, H. T., & Gilmore, S. K. (1973). Placebo versus social learning effects in parent training procedures designed to alter the behavior of aggressive boys. *Behavior Therapy, 4,* 361–377.

Wasserman, T. H. (1983). The effects of cognitive development on the use of cognitive behavioral techniques with children. *Child & Family Behavior Therapy, 5,* 37–50.

Weathers, L., & Liberman, R. P. (1975). The family contracting exercise. *Journal of Behavior Therapy and Experimental Psychiatry, 6,* 208–214.

Webster-Stratton, C. (1981). Modification of mothers' behaviors and attitudes through a videotape modeling group discussion program. *Behavior Therapy, 12,* 634–642.

Weinberger, G., Leventhal, T., & Beckman, G. (1973). The management of chronic school phobia through the use of consultation with school personnel. *Psychology in the School, 10,* 83–88.

Weissberg, R. P., Gesten, E. L., Rapkin, B. D., Cowen, E. L., Davidson, E., Flores de Apodaca, R., & McKim, B. J. (1981). Evaluation of a social problem-solving training program for suburban and inner-city third-grade children. *Journal of Consulting and Clinical Psychology, 49,* 251–261.

Wells, K. C., & Forehand, R. (1981). Childhood behavior problems in the home. In S. M. Turner, K. S. Calhoun, & H. E. Adams (Eds.), *Handbook of clinical behavior therapy.* New York: Wiley.

Wells, K. C., & Forehand, R. (1984). Conduct and oppositional disorders. In P. H. Bornstein & A. E. Kazdin (Eds.), *Handbook of clinical behavior therapy with children.* New York: Dorsey Press.

Wells, K. C., Greist, D. L., & Forehand, R. (1980). The use of self-control package to enhance temporal generality of a parent training program. *Behaviour Research and Therapy, 18,* 347–353.

Wells, K. C., & Vitulano, L. A. (1984). Anxiety disorders in children. In S. M. Turner (Ed.), *Behavioral treatment of anxiety disorders.* New York: Plenum.

Werry, J. S. (1979). Epidemiology. In H. C. Quay & J. S. Werry (Eds.), *Psychopathological disorders of childhood* (2nd ed.). New York: Wiley.

Wiltz, N. A., & Patterson, G. R. (1974). An evaluation of parent training procedures designed to alter inappropriate aggressive behavior of boys. *Behavior Therapy, 5,* 215–224.

Winett, R. A., Stefanek, M., & Riley, A. W. (1983). Preventive strategies with children and families. In T. H. Ollendick & M. Hersen (Eds.), *Handbook of child psychopathology.* New York: Plenum.

Wolf, M. M., Philips, E. L., & Fixsen, D. L. (1975). *Achievement Place Phase II: Final report.* Lawrence, KS: Department of Human Development.

Wolf, M., Risley, T., Johnston, M., Harris, F., & Allen, E. (1967). Application of operant conditioning procedures to the behavior problems of an autistic child: A follow-up and extension. *Behaviour Research and Therapy, 5,* 103–111.

Wolf, M., Risley, T., & Mees, H. (1964). Application of operant conditioning procedures to the behavior problems of an autistic child. *Behaviour Research and Therapy, 1,* 305–312.

Wolpe, J. (1958). *Psychotherapy by reciprocal inhibition.* Stanford: Stanford University Press.

Wolpe, J. (1976). Behavior therapy and its malcontents: I. Denial of its bases and psychodynamic fusionism. *Journal of Behavior Therapy and Experimental Psychiatry, 7,* 1–6.

Yates, A. J. (1975). *Theory and practice in behavior therapy.* New York: Wiley.

Yule, W., Hersov, L., & Treseder, J. (1980). Behavioral treatments of school refusal. In L. Hersov & I. Berg (Eds.), *Out of school.* New York: Wiley.

Zatz, S., & Chassin, L. (1983). Cognitions of text-anxious children. *Journal of Consulting and Clinical Psychology, 51,* 526–534.

Zax, M., & Cowen, E. L. (1976). *Abnormal psychology: Changing conceptions.* New York: Holt, Rinehart & Winston.

13

RESEARCH ON THE PROCESS AND OUTCOME OF MARITAL AND FAMILY THERAPY

ALAN S. GURMAN

University of Wisconsin

DAVID P. KNISKERN

University of Cincinnati

WILLIAM M. PINSOF

Northwestern University

We shall not cease from exploration and the end of all our exploring will be to arrive where we started and know the place for the first time.

T. S. Eliot

When the first two authors published their chapter (Gurman & Kniskern, 1981b) on the "knowns and unknowns" of family therapy research in the *Handbook of Family Therapy* (Gurman and Kniskern, 1981a), they opened that review with the same quote from T. S. Eliot. As will soon be seen, Eliot's immortal words characterize the state of thinking about family therapy research even more tellingly now than they did five years ago. In order for the reader to appreciate the

salience of Eliot's words for the current scene in family therapy research, we begin this analysis and commentary by briefly reviewing the on-again, off-again history of research in the field.

THE HISTORY OF FAMILY THERAPY RESEARCH

Family therapy may be defined as any psychotherapeutic endeavor that explicitly focuses on altering the interactions between or among family members and seeks to improve the functioning of the family as a unit, or its subsystems, and/or the functioning of individual members of the family. This is the goal regardless of whether or not an individual is identified as "the patient." Family therapy typically involves face-to-face work with more than one family member (albeit possibly in varying combinations over time), although it may involve only a single family member for the entire course of treatment (Bowen, 1978; Fisch, Weakland, & Segal, 1982; Gurman, 1984a).

Although this definition may be less than poetic, it conveys something of the complexity and variety of current thinking about the essence of family therapy (Gurman & Kniskern, 1981a). For example, contrary to the perceptions of many outside the family field, family therapy is not merely another treatment method or modality in the armamentarium of psychotherapists, in that direct contact between a therapist and multiple family members is not required. Thus, as Pinsof (1984) emphasizes, while family therapy focuses on "the natural (in vivo) interpersonal context in which psychiatric or psychological problems occur, individual or intrapsychic change may be an additional goal. The systemic theoretical underpinnings of family therapy are not tied to the number of people directly involved in treatment at any given time, but focus on the goals and conceptual framework of the therapy." While conjoint treatment of more than one family member is probably the mode in practice, the conceptual grounding of family therapy in general systems theory (von Bertalanffy, 1968) and cybernetics (Bateson, 1972, 1974; Keeney, 1983) does not require this treatment format. Bona fide family treatments may variously focus on the symptoms and functioning of the index patient, or on the qualitative aspects of relationships between or among family members (Gurman & Kniskern, 1981a).

The explosive impact of family therapy on the professional mental health scene in the last three decades, but especially in the last decade, has been astounding by almost any criterion. For example, whereas in 1973 there existed only one journal in the field, there now exist about two dozen therapy journals published in English and in several other languages. The rate of appearance of new books in the field is remarkable and probably exceeds even the frequency of new books in the then rapidly expanding field of behavior therapy in the 1970s.

In the United States alone, there exist more than 300 training programs in family therapy (Bloch & Weiss, 1981), approximately half of which offer graduate degrees. Since Bloch and Weiss (1981) have estimated that at least 10,000 people in North America were involved in family therapy training and education in 1978–1979, it may be estimated that as many as 15,000 people are currently annually receiving such training worldwide. In 1975, the membership of the American Association for Marriage and Family Therapy, the oldest professional family therapy association, was just over 7000, and is now almost 13,000. Moreover, training in the field is not limited to mental health clinicians, but is also increasingly apparent in the training of primary care physicians (Doherty & Baird, 1983).

From Turning Points to Consolidation

We mention these indices of the growth of the field to make a particular point. To the novice in the field, and certainly to those outside it, the gamut of training opportunities, the charismatic leadership of the conceptual leaders, and the challenges of systemic thinking to traditional linear cause-and-effect models of psychopathology are usually the most visible and attention-drawing characteristics of the family therapy field. In the face of the current conceptual ferment and fervor in the field, it often goes unnoticed, or is forgotten, that family therapy, like behavior therapy, but unlike most other dominant psychotherapies, had its very beginnings in clinical research (Broderick & Schrader, 1981; Wynne, 1983). The Schizophrenic Communication Research Project (Bateson, Jackson, Haley, & Weakland, 1956) in Palo Alto, and the groups at Yale University (Lidz, Cornelison, Fleck, & Terry, 1957) and the National Institute of Mental Health (Bowen, 1978; Wynne, Ryckoff, Day, & Hirsch, 1958) launched the field by studying various aspects of schizophrenic processes in families. In the 1950s, "it was taken for granted that a therapist and a researcher were of the same species" (Haley, 1978, pp. 73–74); "research and treatment were fundamentally fused" (Wynne, 1983, p. 114). Marital therapy, now viewed by most clinicians as a subspecialty of family therapy, emerged earlier and independently (Broderick & Schrader, 1981; Gurman, 1985). This difference in the origins of "marital" versus "family" therapy may partially account for the difficulties that are sometimes seen in integrating different segments of the field.

In the next two decades, however, "family therapy and family research became different realms" (Wynne, 1983, p. 115). In 1967 it was necessary to convene the now famous "Dialogue Between Family Researchers and Family Therapists" (Framo, 1972), in which eminent leaders in these two domains were to share their knowledge and creativity in an effort to bridge the (seemingly never-ending [cf. Barlow, 1981; Strupp, 1981]) clinical-research gap. For various reasons, such a bridging goal went unrealized.

After a sobering decade of quiescence in the research realm, Gurman and Kniskern (1978a, 1978b) published two works that marked the beginning of an acute awareness of and concern with empirical issues that were emerging in the field that has continued to this date. Although the first "state of the art" reviews of research on family (Wells, Dilkes, & Trivelli, 1972) and marital (Gurman, 1973b) therapy had appeared several years earlier, the data reviewed in those papers were so scant and derived from studies of such poor quality that few conclusions could be drawn that were robust enough to have implications for theory development, clinical practice, or public health policy. Gurman and Kniskern's (1978b) comprehensive review of over 200 outcome studies, combined with Pinsof's (1981) review of family therapy process studies, signaled the fact that research in family therapy had become a permanent contour in the landscape of the field.

In the several years since the appearance of those works, research has taken a noticeably more prominent place at a professional organizational level. In 1978, the American Association for Marriage and Family Therapy (AAMFT) granted its first award for "Outstanding Contribution to Marital and Family Therapy." Four years later the AAMFT, largely a clinical and training-oriented body, continued and broadened its official sanction of the significance of research for the field by granting its first annual cumulative career award for "Distinguished Contribution to Family Therapy Research." One year earlier, the American Family Therapy Association had initiated the annual granting of similar awards for career-long contributions by researchers.

The year 1982 also saw the creation of an annual miniversion of the famous 1967 "Dialogue" conference (Framo, 1972) at the meeting of the National Council on Family Relations, where several dozen prominent family therapy researchers, theoreticians, and clinicians gathered to meet in caucuses on various topical areas of the field. That same year, the Editorial Board of the journal *Family Pro-*

cess, under the leadership of its editor, Donald Bloch, initiated the Family Therapy Research Consortium, a multidisciplinary, geographically and theoretically diverse group of about a dozen prominent family theorists and researchers. In 1984, with the cooperation and sponsorship of the staff of the National Institute on Mental Health, the Consortium and several other leading family researchers met for a three-day "State of the Art in Family Therapy Efficacy Research" conference to develop methodological and conceptual guidelines and recommendations for future empirical study in the field.

Thus, after some rather dramatic false starts early in its 30-year history, by the 1980s research had come to occupy a truly significant, and undoubtedly permanent, place in the field of family and marital therapy. By the middle of this decade, it was clear that while marital and family therapy had demonstrated its general efficacy (Gurman & Kniskern, 1978a, 1981b), research was needed that went beyond merely amassing further evidence of its effectiveness to investigating mechanisms of change in systemically oriented treatment. Also, at about the same time that research had established what seemed to be an unshakable grasp on the attention of the field, and had gained its sanction as well, fundamental challenges to the methods of "normal science" (Kuhn, 1970) and to common assumptions of psychotherapy research abruptly emerged from certain quarters within the family field.

Throwing Down and Taking Up the Epistemological Gauntlet

Epistemology is the branch of philosophy concerned with theories of knowledge, of how we know what we know. In recent years, the field of family therapy has seen a vociferous and even passionate upsurge of interest in what have alternatively come to be called "the new epistemologies" (Allman, 1982; Coyne, Denner, & Ransom, 1982; Keeney & Sprenkle, 1982; Wilder, 1982), cybernetic epistemology (Bateson, 1972), circular epistemology (Hoffman, 1981), systemic epistemology (Colapinto, 1979), ecological epistemology (Auerswald, 1972), or ecosystemic epistemology (Keeney, 1983). All of these alternative but similar ways of knowing are, as Dell (1980) has pointed out, virtually indistinguishable from the essential ideas of Gregory Bateson (1972, 1979). The traditional epistemology of physics has been the guiding epistemological basis for most psychotherapy research, grounded in Newtonian science and logical positivism. The fundamental assumptions of such science are that "there is a world that exists independently of cognizing experience" (Manicas & Secord, 1983), and that that reality is best conceived in a fashion that implies linear causality. The shift to a world view based in reciprocal determinism has led some observers (e.g., Tomm, 1983) to challenge the suitability of a linear investigative model for the study of circular phenomena, such as psychotherapy. The emergent emphasis on the shift from the cybernetics of observed systems to a cybernetics of observing systems has been crisply captured in Bloch's (1982) observation that "The map and the mapmaker are recursively and indissolubly linked."

Merkel (1983) has concisely summarized the essential principles and premises that differentiate the "new" from the "old" science and the "new" from the "old" epistemology.

1. In place of an emphasis on descriptions of force, power, energy, hierarchy, and matter is an emphasis on information, pattern, and relationship (though it certainly is the case that a high proportion of family therapy theorists and clinicians use notions of force, power, hierarchy, and structure effectively).

2. The emphasis on linear causality (A→B) is replaced by an emphasis on circular causality (A⇌B). Neither the drawing of "partial arcs" (Keeney, 1983) nor their pragmatic value is denied. Rather, the emphasis is on the risk of overlooking the fact that they are "approximations of whole patterns of recursion" (Keeney, 1983).

3. The ecological interdependence of the parts of systemic wholes implies that the "whole" cannot be understood adequately or accurately by analyses that break wholes into their component parts or by analyses of the parts in isolation. Klein and Gurman (1980) have detailed the consequences of doing so for psychotherapy analogue research.

4. Since no parts of the whole are "independent," and causality is circular, there is little meaning in thinking of any one part of a system as "controlling" another part.

5. In the absence of such dualisms, there can be no "unbiased" observers making observa-

tions about an "objective" external world. Rather "observation" reflects the punctuation of the observer (Colapinto, 1979). That is, the observer does not respond passively to, but partially creates, the reality that is observed.

Given these premises, critics of "normal science" (e.g., Tomm, 1983) have argued that some of the hallowed hallmarks of psychotherapy research, such as controlled experimental designs, are thrown to the winds. For example, with circular causality, there can be no distinction between "independent" ("cause") and "dependent" ("effect") variables. Importantly, the systemic approach does not afford us merely a different unit for analysis, but requires that we "look at *how* these parts are connected, and this is a commitment to process as well as structure" (Segal & Bavelas, 1983, p. 67). As we shall see, this shift of perspective carries significant implications for family therapy research and for the field of psychotherapy research in general.

Two dominant themes emerging from this systemic critique of traditional psychotherapy research center on the issues of *objectivity* and *causality*. Gurman (1983b) has recently considered these systemically derived arguments. He notes that the notion of objectivity carries two particularly evocative connotations, first, that a measurement is both "real" and "true," that is, that the map one draws is the territory; and second, that "objective" measures are free of investigator (observer) bias and are, hence, value-free.

Colapinto (1979), in his epistemological critique of the value of empirical evidence, argued that operational definitions, especially those based on direct observational methods, are but the researchers' way of "punctuating" reality. Though true to systemic thinking, it is arguable whether this critique reminds traditional researchers of anything they are not already aware of (though it may be true that such awareness often seems to recede significantly). Still, the tradition of social science gives full credence to this systemic position, as noted by Campbell's (1976) statement that "The language of science is subjective, provincial, approximative and metaphoric, never the language of reality itself." Likewise, Gurman and Kniskern (1981b) have indicated, in the context of family therapy outcome research, that so-called "objective changes are no more real than are those based on patient reports, and do not deserve the label of superiority often assigned to them" (p. 769).

The charge by systemic critics that traditional researchers often delude themselves that their measurements are value-free seems to strike at a more common research blind spot. Colapinto (1979) makes the point well in noting that empirical evidence is organized by nonempirical decisions. As we have noted elsewhere, "Even with the least inferential of indices, the choice of content has to have been made by people" (Gurman & Kniskern, 1981b, p. 769). The danger here lies in believing that observational measurement is, ipso facto, value-free, when researchers do not acknowledge the meaning (their meaning) of their choice of content (Foster & Gurman, 1985; Gurman & Klein, 1980; Margolin, Talovic, Fernandez, & Onorato, 1983).

Gurman (1983b) noted that empirically based operational definitions (the meanings ascribed to, not inhering in, behaviors) derive their value by virtue of the fact that "these procedures . . . require us to make our values explicit; for when we remain unaware of the values (ascribed meanings) implicit in our operational definitions and measurement methods, our biases may be revealed all the more readily and certainly" (p. 231).

As for the causality argument, Gurman (1983b) has noted that psychotherapy research is linearly culpable only when it asks naive questions, for instance, "Is therapy A more effective than therapy B?" What is studied in ecologically valid research are interaction effects. Indeed, powerful main effects are so rare that they should be considered highly suspect. Obviously, psychotherapy research can never be genuinely wholistic. Nonetheless, as Gurman (1983b) illustrates, there are numerous ways in which traditional research designs and procedures routinely, though implicitly, acknowledge context, connectedness, and interdependence; for example: (1) the study of the interactive effects of patient, therapist, treatment, and setting variables; (2) the use of multidimensional change measures; (3) the use of multiple vantage points for assessing change; and (4) the use of repeated measures to assess both levels and patterns of change over time.

Despite the fervor of the arguments raised recently about "old" and "new" epistemologies, the chasm between the two may not be as great as

has been perceived. Thus, Keeney (1983) has urged us to remember that "epistemological conversion does not necessarily mean a complete disconnection from historical traditions. Instead, it has more to do with inheriting a new world view within which other traditions are seen in a new light." In a similar spirit of rapprochement, Kniskern (1983) has written that "The realization that the map is not the territory does not require that we throw away all our old maps. We must, however, keep in mind that a map is a map" (p. 61). Still, even with ecumenical acknowledgment of the salient biases of which the "new epistemologists" remind traditional researchers, it is to be noted (Gurman, 1983b; Kniskern, 1983) that established methods and designs have thus far yielded data on the outcomes (Gurman & Kniskern, 1978a, 1978b; Kniskern & Gurman, 1981, 1984) and, to a lesser extent, the process (Pinsof, 1981) of marital and family therapy that carry clear implications for both clinical practice and training. Unfortunately, the passion with which advocates of the "new epistemology" criticize the continuing use of family therapy research methods based on the "old" epistemology has been rarely translated into the development of experimental designs more consistent with ecosystemic views. Steier (1984), for one, has proposed some useful ways in which the shift from observed to observing systems might influence data analytic techniques. To our knowledge, there does not yet exist a single outcome study of family therapy whose design has been perceptibly influenced by such ecosystemic ideas. Thus, as will soon become self-evident, both the outcome studies reviewed in this chapter and the review of family therapy outcome research itself have been, respectively, carried out and written in terms of the more familiar model of linear causality.

Perhaps the major implication of all this recent philosophic ferment in the family field is that there lurks a genuine danger for a field that has always creatively and productively challenged established tradition (Hoffman, 1981) and that uncritical and unreflective yielding up to traditional thinking and practice in the research domain may stifle the emergence of alternative methods of systematically coming to "know" the mechanisms of change in family therapy. Given the relative youth of research in the field, it may be counterproductive for verification-oriented research to eclipse discovery-oriented research (Gurman & Kniskern, 1981b; Schwartz & Breunlin, 1983). Daniel Yankelovich (in Smith, 1972) has warned of this danger:

The first step is to measure whatever can be easily measured. This is okay as far as it goes. The second step is to disregard that which can't be measured or give it an arbitrary quantitative value. This is artificial and misleading. The third step is to presume that what can't be measured easily isn't very important. This is blindness. The fourth step is to say that what can't be measured really doesn't exist. This is suicide (p. 286).

The Plan for this Chapter

Some of these salient epistemological issues will be referred to at various points in this chapter. In what follows, we will consider the existing evidence regarding the efficacy of family and marital therapy for specific clinical disorders and clinical populations; evidence of the efficacy of the major "schools" of family therapy; research on family therapy training; the current state of family therapy process research; issues in the assessment of change in family therapy; and some implications of a systemic perspective for assessing change in individual psychotherapy. We will conclude with a brief consideration of the relationship between research and the practice of family therapy. In contrast to our earlier major reviews (Gurman & Kniskern, 1978a; Pinsof, 1981), we will not exhaustively detail each of the studies in the literature, but will summarize the major trends of findings in the field, with an eye toward their theoretical meaning, clinical implications, and implications for future research, at times describing in detail specific major research projects in order to highlight and illustrate representative work in various domains. The reader wishing to study more closely the evidence for the trends and conclusions we present may refer to Table 13.1 for a guide to and through the massive research literature that has evolved in the last decade and a half.

As can be seen from Table 13.1, the appearance of research reviews has increased at an impressive rate during the last few years. Many of these reviews, as is true of research reviews in general, have been rather prosaic treatises, while a few have touched off some interesting, and at times provocative, commentaries and exchanges of views

(cf. Gurman & Kniskern, 1978a, 1978c, 1978d, 1985; Stanton & Todd, 1980; Todd & Stanton, 1983; Wells, 1980; Wells & Dezen, 1978a, 1978b; Wells & Gianetti, 1985; Williams & Miller, 1981). Moreover, as Liberman (1976) has noted, "reviews tend to become reified and viewed as providing a form of intellectual satisfaction to practitioners and potential researchers that substitutes for the hard work of actually designing and executing (outcome) studies." We hope that what follows will offer a minimal basis for misplaced reification, along with substantial provocation of intellectual curiosity.

Before proceeding further, we think it is important to stress the reason for the shift of emphasis in our original *Handbook* chapter (Gurman & Kniskern, 1978a) from one of detailed analysis of virtually every extant outcome study and examination of broad patterns of findings, to one, in this chapter, of attempting to delineate and forge closer linkages among theory, research, and clinical practice. In 1978, there was a need in the field for a comprehensive consideration of whether, in fact, the family and marital therapies, as a group, had amassed reasonable evidence of efficacy. We believe that our earlier review, and those of others (see Table 13.1), have now established convincingly that, in general, the practice of family and marital therapy leads to positive outcomes. Family therapy no longer needs to justify its existence on empirical grounds. In the last seven years, the field has advanced sufficiently, both conceptually and methodologically, to allow, indeed even require, that data bearing on more fine-grained and specific questions be considered. The family therapy research field, like the field of family therapy generally, is now a good deal more mature developmentally, and is, thus, more open to self-criticism and thoughtful self-reflection. Thus, the reader who is familiar with our earlier review (Gurman & Kniskern, 1978a) should not mistake the apparently somewhat more conservative tone of this chapter, compared to that of its predecessor, with any sense on our part of decreased hopefulness for the field. Indeed, we believe that the progress achieved in the last few years offers the basis for even more confidence about the salience of systemic thinking and practice than did the research we reviewed in 1978.

We also recognize that publication of this third edition of the *Handbook* may swiftly render previous editions quite inaccessible. Therefore, we will

TABLE 13.1 Reviews of Family Therapy Research: A Summary

Author(s)	Date	Area Reviewed
Lebedun	1970	Group marital counseling
Gurman	1971	Group marital therapy
Patterson	1971	Behavioral family therapy
Wells et al.	1972	Family therapy (excluding behavioral)
Gurman	1973b	Marital therapy[a]
Beck	1975	Marital counseling
Greer & D'Zurilla	1975	Behavioral marriage therapy
Gurman	1975	Marital therapy
Kniskern	1975	Family therapy[a]
Patterson et al.	1976	Behavioral marriage therapy
Jacobson & Martin	1976	Behavioral marriage therapy
Steinglass	1976	Family therapy of alcoholism
Gurman & Kniskern	1977	Marital enrichment programs
Janzen	1977	Family therapy of alcoholism
Strelnick	1977	Multiple family group therapy
Benningfeld	1978	Multiple family therapy
DeWitt	1978	Family therapy (excluding behavioral)
Gurman & Kniskern	1978a	Marital and family therapy, divorce therapy
Gurman & Kniskern	1978b	Deterioration in marital and family therapy
Gurman & Kniskern	1978c	Behavioral marriage therapy
Jacobson	1978b	Marital therapy
Luber	1978	Marital commmunication skills training and contingency contracting models
Wells & Dezen	1978a	Family therapy (excluding behavioral)
Reiss & Steinglass	1978	Family therapy
Birchler	1979	Marital communication skills
Gurman & Kniskern	1979a	Marital and family therapy
Jacobson	1979	Behavioral marriage therapy
Linehan & Rosenthal	1979	Behavioral marital and family therapy
Masten	1979	Family therapy for childhood disorders
Patterson & Fleischmann	1979	Behavioral family intervention
Stanton	1979	Family therapy of drug abuse
Williams & Miller	1981	Marital therapy (a review of reviews)
Olson et al.	1980	Marital and family therapy
Aponte & VanDeusen	1981	Structural family therapy
Bagarozzi & Rauen	1981	Premarital counseling
Gurman & Kniskern	1981b	Family and marital therapy
Hof & Miller	1981	Marital enrichment programs
Pinsof	1981	Family therapy process research
Wampler	1982a	Minnesota Couples Communication Program
Wampler	1982b	Minnesota Couples Communication Program (meta-analysis)
Levant	1983	Parent Effectiveness Training
Russell et al.	1983	Family therapy
Sprenkle & Storm	1983	Divorce therapy
Todd & Stanton	1983	Family therapy
Beach & O'Leary	1984	Marital therapy
Jacobson et al.	1984a	Behavioral marital therapy
Baucom & Hoffman	in press	Marital therapy

[a]The appearance of the terms "family therapy" or "marital therapy" without qualifying adjectives (e.g., "behavioral") indicates a wide-ranging review of all family or marital treatment methods, respectively.

succinctly summarize here the major conclusions from our earlier review (Gurman & Kniskern, 1978a), which we believe have not been contravened and do not require modification on the basis of more recent data. Issues addressed by the other major conclusions from that earlier review that, in our view, require updating and revision are considered elsewhere in the rest of this chapter.

1. Nonbehavioral marital and family therapies produce beneficial outcomes in about two-thirds of cases, and their effects are superior to no treatment.
2. When both spouses are involved in therapy conjointly in the face of marital problems, there is a greater chance of positive outcome than when only one spouse is treated.
3. The developmental level of the identified patient (e.g., child/adolescent/adult) does not affect treatment outcomes significantly.
4. Positive results of both nonbehavioral and behavioral marital and family therapies typically occur in treatment of short duration, that is, 1 to 20 sessions.
5. Marital and family therapies at times may be associated with both individual (identified patient) and relationship deterioration.
6. A therapist "style" of providing little structuring of early treatment sessions and confrontation of highly affective material may be reliably associated with observed deterioration effects and is clearly more deterioration promoting, in general, than a style of stimulating interaction and giving support.
7. Family therapy is probably as effective as and possibly more effective than many commonly offered (usually individual) treatments for problems attributed to family conflict.
8. There is no empirical support for the superiority of co-therapy compared with marital or family therapy conducted by a single therapist.
9. A reasonable mastery of technical skills may be sufficient for preventing worsening or for maintaining pretreatment family functioning, but more refined therapist relationship skills seem necessary to yield genuinely positive outcomes.
10. Certain family variables, for example, identified patient diagnosis, quality of family inter-

action, and family constellation, exert unreliable effects on clinical outcomes.

Against this background of the major findings revealed in our original review (Gurman & Kniskern, 1978a), we now turn to more recent developments in family therapy research.

RESEARCH ON THE OUTCOMES OF MARITAL AND FAMILY INTERVENTIONS

Outcomes with Specific Populations and Problems

From a systemic perspective, the issue of how to define a clinical population for research purposes raises a number of important and, in some cases, controversial issues. Of major significance is the matter of which social unit is to be chosen to demonstrate the boundary of "the patient." Goldstein (1984) reminds us that:

> an essential tenet of the family system model is that the diagnosis of the identified patient should be secondary to the diagnosis of the systemic dysfunction. If we follow this to its logical conclusion, then the selection of families for a research study on efficacy should be based on family-level diagnoses and not those of the identified patients.
>
> The notion that a family diagnostic system can be developed is an appealing one. . . . As yet, no accepted system for family diagnosis exists and it is questionable whether families could be selected on the basis of these dimensions alone for a controlled study of the efficacy of family therapy. (p. 1)

There are four major methods for defining and selecting a family population for study. This can be accomplished by identification of family interaction styles or systemic dynamics (Russell, Olson, Sprenkle, & Atilano, 1983), developmental and/or constellational/compositional similarities (e.g., Gartner, Fulmer, Weinshel, & Goldbank, 1978; Goldstein, 1984), presenting complaints or symptoms, or traditional individual psychiatric diagnoses. As we noted elsewhere (Gurman & Kniskern, 1981b), "many, if not most family therapists will be likely to revolt against the latter two options, especially the last option . . . [because of their beliefs about] the conceptual and clinical inadequacy of individual diagnoses" (p. 754). Yet, as Goldstein (1984) continues, "As unpalatable as it may seem to the theorist who organizes his clinical data on a family system level, it is probably not feasible to evaluate a family without considering the nature of the disorder presented by the identified patient. So, it appears that efficacy studies of family therapy will have to select samples initially on the type and severity of the disorder in the identified patient" (p. 2).

Even the most responsible of reviewers cannot review that which does not exist. Since studies of family therapy outcome based on family systemic diagnoses do not exist, we will eschew attempting the impossible. Thus, we will consider what is currently known about the efficacy of various family treatment methods with specific clinical problems that have most often been diagnosed in individual terms. As esthetically displeasing as it may be to some observers, there is no existing empirical evidence that sample selection based on identified patient diagnosis precludes the development of effective, specifically applied family treatment methods. Indeed, quite the opposite is true, as will be seen subsequently. But just as not all problems brought to family therapists involve "psychiatric disorders," there also exists a large body of research on the treatment of explicitly rational and interactional problems (often subsumable, for the conservative reader, under relevant *DSM-III* Axes I and II diagnoses), which will also be considered here. The issue of how to define "the patient" will be explored further in the section of this chapter dealing with process research.

Child and Adolescent Disorders

While family therapy is applied regularly to the widest possible range of disorders of childhood and adolescence, research on family therapy outcomes with these populations has clustered in three areas: psychosomatic disorders, juvenile delinquency and conduct disorders, and mixed emotional/behavioral disorders.

Psychosomatic disorders.   One of the most influential bodies of both clinical/theoretical and research investigations in the family field of the last two decades has emerged in the work on Structural Family Therapy (Minuchin, 1974; Minuchin & Fish-

man, 1981), largely at the Philadelphia Child Guidance Clinic (PCGC). Based on a clearly delineated model of the characteristics of psychosomatic family functioning that emphasizes enmeshed subsystem boundaries, parental overprotectiveness, behavioral rigidity, poor conflict-resolution skills, and children's involvement in marital conflict, structural therapists have evolved a highly teachable method of therapy aimed at unbalancing and restructuring these predictable interaction processes.

In the most comprehensive report of these studies (Minuchin, Rosman, & Baker, 1978), the Philadelphia group reported the outcomes of structural therapy with 53 anorexics and their families. Outcome criteria included both objective measures of weight gain, rehospitalization, and measures of identified patient psychosocial functioning at home, in school, and with peers. Treatment lasted an average of 6 months, and at follow-up periods of from 1 to 84 months, 86 percent of the patients were rated as substantially improved or recovered, with the need for rehospitalization being extremely rare. Although the PCGC psychosomatic studies did not include untreated control groups and did not report any outcome data on system level functioning, their findings must be considered impressive in light of the generally very poor prognosis for anorexia (Hsu, 1980; Swift, 1982).

The PCGC studies also included families with adolescent with diabetes mellitus and chronic asthma (Minuchin et al., 1975). Using both psychosocial measures of patient functioning and unobtrusive physiological measures (blood sugar levels, respiratory functioning), an improvement rate of 90 percent for these combined samples was obtained. Unfortunately, these impressive results have not yet been replicated.

A more recent study in the structural-strategic tradition of family therapy with (female) bulimic patients has buttressed the findings of the PCGC group (Schwartz, Barrett, & Saba, 1983). These authors treated 30 consecutive adolescent and young adult bulimic patients (mean chronicity 6.8 years) and their families for an average of 33 sessions over a 9-month period. Treatment combined family and individual sessions and included a variety of both symptom-specific interventions aimed at eliminating the binge–purge cycle and system level interventions. Schwartz et al. tracked clinical changes in four areas: symptom control, changes in family relationships, changes in life goals or career, and changes in patients' extrafamilial relationships. In a preliminary report of findings on the first criterion, the authors rated patient change on one of four levels: (I) nearly always in control, 1 or fewer episodes per month; (II) usually in control, 2 episodes per month to 2 per week; (III) control somewhat problematic, 2 to 4 episodes per week; or (IV) major control problem, 5 or more episodes per week. Before therapy, the mean frequency of weekly episodes was 19.3 (range 5–63), with every patient at level IV functioning. Based on 29 closed cases, 19 (66%) were at level I, 3 (10%) at level II, 3 (10%) were at level III, and 4 (14%) at level IV. At followup periods of from 1 to 42 months, all patients with level I outcomes maintained their improvements, 2 of the 3 level II patients fell to level III, and all level III or IV patients remained unchanged from post-therapy.

Juvenile delinquency. To date, the most important series of studies of family therapy with juvenile delinquents and their families have been those of Alexander and his colleagues (Alexander & Parsons, 1973; Klein, Alexander, & Parsons, 1977; Parsons & Alexander, 1973). The treatment applied in these studies was Functional Family Therapy (FFT) (Barton & Alexander, 1981), a method drawing upon both behavioral methods such as contingency contracting and modeling and cognitively oriented paradoxical reframing interventions. In their initial report (Alexander & Barton, 1976), 40 families of "soft" status offense (e.g., runaways, curfew violators) delinquents were randomly assigned to FFT, FFT plus individual therapy, individual therapy alone, or no treatment. All families receiving family therapy improved on the central measure of supportiveness/defensiveness, while families not receiving family treatment did not improve, and those in the control condition seemed to deteriorate on this family interaction measure.

Having successfully tested the efficacy of FFT to produce positive effects on the theoretically central (Alexander, 1973) dimension of delinquent family interaction, a follow-up study (Parsons & Alexander, 1973) was undertaken to determine whether modifying these family processes would affect the rates of delinquent recidivism. Families were randomly assigned to FFT, client-centered family therapy, psychodynamic-eclectic family therapy, or no

treatment. FFT families showed the greatest gains on several communication measures, and at from 3 to 15 months' follow-up showed a lower rate of recidivism (26%, vs. 47% for client-centered therapy, 50% for untreated controls, and 73% for dynamic-eclectic therapy).

An additional follow-up focused on the effects of treatment on the referral rates for delinquent behavior on the part of siblings of the original identified patients (Klein et al., 1977). These data, which essentially replicated the earlier findings, showed the following percentages of sibling court contacts at 2½ to 3 years' follow-up: FFT, 20 percent; client-centered therapy, 59 percent; dynamic-eclectic therapy, 63 percent; no treatment, 40 percent. These data, then, suggest apparent preventive effects of FFT with "soft" delinquents, their families, and their siblings, and also suggest that the original FFT (Alexander & Parsons, 1973) may have helped these families deal more adaptively with the predictable adolescent crises of their initially non-index adolescents.

While these findings are impressive, and while they were obtained by rather inexperienced therapists, it must be noted that their sample was not representative of delinquent families, in that 70 percent of these Utah families were Mormon and can be assumed to have had stronger emotional ties and a clearer hierarchical organization than many families in religiously more heterogeneous communities. In addition, as with the impressive results presented in research on the structural therapy of psychosomatic disorders, these findings remain to be replicated.

Conduct disorders of childhood. Other subpopulations of families with children engaged in antisocial behavior have also received attention in the family therapy research literature. Especially well studied has been the treatment of persistent conduct disorders involving both aggressive behavior (e.g., physical violence against persons or property, intrafamilial disobedience) and nonaggressive behavior (e.g., stealing, lying, truancy, fire setting). Without any doubt, the interventions most often studied in the treatment of conduct disorders have been those known generically as "parent management training" (Patterson, 1982), which has been examined in hundreds of studies (e.g., Forehand & Atkeson, 1977; Gordon & Davidson, 1981; Kazdin, 1984; O'Dell, 1974; Tavormina, 1974). Parent management training involves a variety of procedures derived from social learning theory (Patterson, 1982) in which parents are trained to modify their children's behavior in the home. Intervention includes didactic instruction of the parent(s) in social learning principles such as reinforcement, punishment, extinction, and contingency contracting, training parents in behavioral pinpointing of problematic undesired behavior, and the like.

Without peer in this area of family intervention has been the sustained research program of Patterson and his colleagues at the Oregon Social Learning Center. Patterson and colleagues have treated over 200 of these families in research protocols over almost two decades. The "identified patient" is typically a preadolescent child (mostly boys) aged 3 to 12, who demonstrates aggressive behavior and is referred for outpatient treatment. Large numbers (about 50%) of these children have also been involved in nonaggressive acting-out behavior such as stealing, truancy, and fire setting, and many of the children display problematic behavior in their classrooms as well as in their homes. Treatment duration in the various Oregon studies has varied from several sessions to several months. The outcomes of treatment have been based on parent ratings of deviant child behavior, the ratings of teachers, and observational measures of parent–child interaction in the home.

Several major trends in the findings from Patterson's group may be identified. First, parent management training has been found to be superior in its effects to no treatment (Patterson, 1974a; Patterson, Chamberlain, & Reid, 1982; Patterson & Fleischmann, 1979; Walter & Gilmore, 1973; Wiltz & Patterson, 1974), and treatment effects have been maintained at follow-up periods of up to 18 months (Fleischmann, 1981; Fleischmann & Szykula, 1981; Patterson & Fleischmann, 1979). Second, changes in classroom behavior have been documented as a result of these in-home interventions (Patterson, Cobb, & Ray, 1973). Third, nontargeted child deviant behavior has also been shown to change significantly in some reports (Patterson, 1974a, 1974b). Fourth, the deviant behavior of siblings of the identified patient, who are at risk for conduct disorders, has been shown to have reduced as a consequence of parent management training focused on the index child (Arnold, Levine, & Patterson, 1975). This finding parallels that of

Klein et al. (1977) in the Functional Family Therapy treatment of families with adolescent juvenile delinquents described previously. And fifth, reductions in maternal psychopathology, especially depression, have been found along with increases in mothers' self-esteem (Patterson & Fleischmann, 1979; Patterson & Reid, 1973).

The efficacy of parent management training for the treatment of childhood conduct disorders has not always been found to be as effective in other studies as it has been in the Oregon work (Kazdin, 1984). This has raised questions of significant clinical importance regarding the factors beyond intervention per se that influence outcome. As Kazdin (1984) notes, families characterized by father absence, low socioeconomic status, severe marital discord, parental psychopathology, and weak maternal social support systems not infrequently show fewer gains at termination of parent management training and less maintenance of gains at follow-up. Since parent–child interaction does not occur in an ecological vacuum, it is important that the kinds of interpersonal and intrapersonal dimensions noted by Kazdin as affecting the outcomes of parent management training receive attention in future research. Studies that have reported clinically important changes in non-index patients (i.e., siblings, mothers) as a result of behavioral family intervention support this need for a wide-ranging consideration of factors beyond parent–child interaction that may affect treatment outcome, and for systematically sensitive evaluation of the outcomes of treatment. This latter matter will be considered later in this chapter in our discussion of the assessment of change in family therapy.

In conclusion, we agree with Kazdin's (1984) overall assessment of the current status of parent management training: "No other intervention for antisocial children has been investigated so thoroughly . . . and has shown as favorable results" (p. 14).

Studies of mixed childhood and adolescent disorders. Gurman and Kniskern (1978a) and Masten (1979) have reviewed studies of family therapy involving child and adolescent identified patients. Except for studies of the treatment of psychosomatic disorders, juvenile delinquency, and various conduct disorders of the sort just considered, almost all other existing studies of the family treatment of childhood and adolescent disorders have failed to use homogeneous (identified patient) samples. Virtually every other family therapy study has selected patient samples in such a way as to preclude the reaching of meaningful conclusions about the efficacy of specific treatments with specific patient populations. These studies, unfortunately, have almost routinely (1) included both child and adolescent IPs, thereby masking likely developmental differences in response to treatment (e.g., Santa-Barbara et al., 1979); (2) reported on IPs with such diagnostic heterogeneity as to mask an additional source of likely differential treatment responsiveness (e.g., Ro-Trock, Wellisch, & Schooler, 1977; Wellisch & Ro-Trock, 1980; Wellisch, Vincent, & Ro-Trock, 1976); or (3) treated patients described as diagnostically homogeneous but without sufficient diagnostic information as to allow replication of sample selection (e.g., Garrigan & Bambrick, 1975, 1977, 1979).

Thus, although there exist several dozen family therapy outcome studies of patient populations mixed as to developmental level and/or diagnosis (type and severity), little can be gleaned from this aggregate body of research that carries either significant theoretical meaning or clinical implications. Perhaps the most reliable statement that can be made on the basis of all these studies is that, in heterogeneous samples of family therapy with childhood and/or adolescent behavioral problems and psychopathology, approximately two-thirds to three-quarters of cases can be expected to improve when treated by any of several well-defined family methods or eclectic methods (Gurman & Kniskern, 1978a; Masten, 1979).

Adult Disorders

As we noted at the beginning of this chapter, a major formative thrust in the early days of family therapy involved various creative investigations of the role of the family in schizophrenia. For nearly two decades relatively little was heard from family therapists on the matter of schizophrenia. Since these patients are often not the clientele preferred in private practice, perhaps it was that family therapists sought greener pastures, so to speak. It is also possible that family therapy, as it was practiced until recently, was not having a significant impact on these families. In any case, sparked in part by exciting theoretical and clinical developments on

"families in schizophrenic transaction" (Selvini, Boscolo, Cecchin, & Prata, 1978) and in part by widespread deinstitutionalization policies regarding schizophrenic patients (in the United States, at least) and a concomitant emphasis on community-based psychosocial management (e.g., Hogarty, Goldberg, & Schooler, 1974), a rapid upsurge of interest in family treatment of schizophrenia has emerged. Nor have family therapists of recent vintage been shy about testing their mettle with other major psychiatric disorders. In this section, we will spotlight the major programmatic research efforts to date of family therapists' attempts to deal with several such adult disorders: schizophrenia, substance abuse, affective disorders, and anxiety disorders. This organization reflects our belief that future studies of the efficacy of marital and family therapy will be most illuminating if they use homogeneous patient samples.

Schizophrenia. This upsurge of interest in the treatment of schizophrenia among family therapists has hardly been accompanied by consensus as to the nature of schizophrenia, or its treatment. Among systems purists, schizophrenia is not considered a psychopathological condition of an individual, but a signal of interpersonal conflict, usually involving developmental impasses within a family (e.g., Haley, 1980). The "stress/vulnerability" family theorists (e.g., Anderson, Hogarty, & Reiss, 1981; Berkowitz, Kuipers, Eberlein-Frief, & Leff, 1981; Falloon et al., 1985; Goldstein, Rodnick, Evans, May, & Steinberg; 1978; also see Rohrbaugh, 1983), on the other hand, assume that schizophrenia involves a "core, biological deficit which makes the patient vulnerable to stressful stimulation from the environment" (Rohrbaugh, 1983, p. 30), in particular, "stimulation" from critical and intrusive family members. In the last decade, virtually all empirical studies of family intervention and schizophrenia have grown out of the stress/vulnerability model.

In the first of these studies, Goldstein et al. (1978) examined the interaction effects of moderate versus low-dose fluphenazine enanthate with family-oriented crises intervention versus no psychosocial treatment in an aftercare (following hospitalization averaging two weeks) treatment program of 104 acute (mostly first episode), young, predominantly white schizophrenics. Psychosocial intervention consisted of six weekly two-hour meetings with the index patients and their families, with an emphasis on education about the relationship between stress and schizophrenia and the development of stress management procedures. At six-week follow-up, patients who had received family therapy plus moderate dose neuroleptics showed no rehospitalization relapse, while patients who had received low dose neuroleptics without family intervention showed a 24 percent relapse rate. At six-month follow-up, these treatment differences were even larger, with high dose plus family therapy-treated patients again having no relapses, and low dose without family therapy patients having relapsed in 48 percent of the cases. At six-week follow-up, family therapy's strongest therapeutic effect was on "negative" schizophrenic symptoms, for example, withdrawal and blunted affect. This family therapy effect remained at six-month follow-up only in combination with standard dose medication.

More recently, interest has focused on the relationship between a particular family affective interaction style, "expressed emotion" (EE), and its relationship to relapse among schizophrenic patients (Vaughn & Leff, 1976). EE is defined as family members' attitudes of criticalness, overinvolvement, and hostility toward each other. Vaughn and Leff (1976) found that patients living in high EE family environments, in combination with high patient—family rates of contact (35 or more hours per week), had a major negative impact on patients' probabilities of relapse, even when patients were continuing neuroleptic treatment.

The first study to report attempts to modify the schizophrenic's family environment was conducted in London (Berkowitz et al., 1981; Leff, Kuipers, Berkowitz, Eberlein-Vries, & Sturgeon, 1982). The London group randomly assigned 24 high-risk (high rates of family contact in high EE environments), recently discharged patients and their families to one of four conditions: (1) outpatient drug treatment (fluphenazine decanoate); (2) a "package of social interventions" consisting of educational lectures to family members on the etiology, symptoms, course, and management of schizophrenia; (3) relatives' groups (no patients present); or (4) one-hour in-home family therapy sessions (range: 1–25 meetings). The relatives' group intermixed high and low EE relatives "as a means of altering the coping styles of the high EE relatives so as to resem-ble more closely those of low EE relatives" (Leff et al., 1982, p. 123). The in-home sessions included techniques that "varied from dynamic interpretations to behavioral interventions" (p. 123).

Over the nine-month period of the study, the social intervention group showed a relapse rate (based on the Present State Examination [Wing, Cooper, & Sartorius, 1974] of schizophrenic symptoms) of 9 percent versus 50 percent in the medication condition. Family-oriented intervention produced a significant reduction in the "critical comments" dimension of EE, and a near-significant reduction of "overinvolvement," and there were no relapses in families with such reductions. The aim of reducing EE was achieved with 73 percent of the families treated, whereas families in the medication condition did not evidence any reduction in EE. At two-year follow-up (Leff, 1983), 8 of 10 patients in the medication condition had relapsed, while only 1 of 7 experimental patients who were able to be followed up had relapsed.

Falloon et al. (1985) and his colleagues (Falloon et al., 1982) also treated schizophrenic patients at high risk for relapse as determined by their having high EE family environments or the presence of other significant environmental stressors such as poor premorbid adjustment or multiple recent psychiatric hospitalizations. Thirty-six patients were randomly assigned to in-home behavioral family therapy (emphasizing family education, interpersonal problem-solving, and contingency management procedures) or to in-clinic individual supportive psychotherapy. Patients in both conditions received "optimal" maintenance level neuroleptics. Nine-month assessment of treatment effects favored family management in terms of both patient relapse (6% vs. 44%), level of symptomatology (based on blind rating scale assessments), and social functioning. Keith and Matthews (1984) have noted that since this study did not include a no-treatment condition, "the improvement seen with family management is relative only to a deterioration in the individual [treatment] group" (p. 83). We find this criticism to be inappropriate, since Falloon et al. (1982) had a more stringent control group than a no-treatment group. Since family intervention was more effective than standard treatment, it seems reasonable to infer that it would have been more effective than no treatment.

Finally, while data analyses on the outcomes of

"psychoeducational" family therapy (Anderson, Hogarty, & Reiss, 1980, 1981) are not yet completed, they also provide very encouraging preliminary findings. Anderson, Reiss, and Hogarty (1985) randomly assigned 102 consecutively admitted patients meeting Research Diagnostic Critera for schizophrenia or schizoaffective disorder to psychoeducational family therapy (PFT), individual social-skills training (SST), a combination of PFT and SST (COM), or supportive individual therapy (SUP). Whenever possible, patients in all conditions were maintained on a minimal effective dose of fluphenazine decanoate. Preliminary findings (Anderson et al., 1985) based on 88 treatment "takers" showed the following relapse rates in the year following hospital discharge for treatment takers: PFT—19 percent, SST—21 percent, COM—0 percent, SUP—36 percent. When all study patients were considered, a significant effect on lowering relapse occurred only for patients receiving family therapy. An "uncensured estimate" (i.e., patients not sorted as to degree of treatment compliance) of relapse in the second year of treatment showed the following relapse rates: PFT—25 percent, SST—35 percent, COM—22 percent, SUP—57 percent. The somewhat higher one-year relapse rate in the Anderson et al. (1986) study, compared to the studies of Goldstein et al. (1978), Falloon et al. (1982), and Leff et al. (1982), was attributable to the use of a longer follow-up period in the Anderson et al. (1986) study; the comparable nine-month relapse rate found by Anderson et al. (1986) was only 3.6 percent (Anderson, 1985). As Anderson et al. (1986) point out, their two-year follow-up results demonstrate that "these approaches forestall relapse but in no way provide 'prevention' per se" (p. 34). Still, evidence from clinical judgments of patients' "degree of illness" and "change in clinical state" at follow-up make it clear that neither FFT nor SST were "simply maintaining poorly adjusted patients in the community just to make the relapse rates 'look good' " (p. 34).

Though the particular treatment programs whose research has been highlighted here vary in terms of their use of specific intervention components, they generally have several major features in common: an explicit emphasis on educating the relatives of the index patient regarding the nature, course, prognosis, and so on of schizophrenia as an illness; inclusion of neuroleptic medication; modification of relatives' expectations of their affected family member's social and symptomatic functioning; use of multiple family support groups; and the systematic teaching of problem-solving and crisis-management strategies and skills. As Rohrbaugh (1983) has put it, "Whatever the format [of treatment], the emphasis is on reducing stress [on the index patient] by lowering the family's emotional temperature" (p. 30).

By way of contrast to the results of intervention with these psychoeducational family-based management approaches, the more "systemic" family therapies put forth in the field as offering effective treatments for schizophrenia-involved families (e.g., Family Systems Therapy [Bowen, 1978], Strategic Family Therapy [Haley, 1980], and the Milan Model [Selvini et al., 1978]) to date have provided meager (cf. Haley, 1980) evidence of the efficacy of their methods. As Rohrbaugh (1983) has provocatively, yet accurately, summarized the matter, "If one had to choose a [family] treatment paradigm on the basis of solid research findings alone, the stress/vulnerability view (and associated psychoeducational methods) would win by default" (p. 31).

Substance abuse. Despite the widespread problems of both drug and alcohol abuse, as well as family therapists' clinical involvement in treating such problems (Kaufman & Kaufman, 1979; Stanton, 1979; Stanton, Todd & Associates, 1982), very little empirical study of the efficacy of any of several common family-involved treatments (e.g., marital therapy, family therapy, multifamily group therapy) has appeared (Olson, Russell, & Sprenkle, 1980; Stanton, 1979). In the field of marital–family therapy, the majority of the few studies of the treatment of alcoholism that have appeared have been studies of marital therapy, while the majority of the few studies of the treatment of drug abuse that have appeared have been studies of family therapy.

Reviews by Gurman and Kniskern (1978a) and Jacobson (1978b) suggest that conjoint couples therapy in groups for alcohol-involved marriages may be both the preferred marital therapy format and superior to individual treatment of the alcoholic (usually husband) spouse. In one of the most methodologically sound studies to date in this domain, O'Farrell, Cutter, and Floyd (1985) randomly assigned couples with alcoholic husbands to 10 weekly sessions of either a behavioral (BMT) or an interactional couples therapy (ICT) or no-marital-therapy control group (NMT). Patients in all three conditions were involved in a 28-day inpatient rehabilitation program or a 7-day detoxification program, followed by a standard outpatient program of individual alcoholism counseling, including encouragement of the use of Antabuse and participation in Alcoholics Anonymous. BMT included behavior rehearsal and weekly homework assignments, an Antabuse contract, the planning of shared recreational activities, the bilateral initiation of daily caring behavior, and communication and problem-solving training. ICT emphasized mutual support, the sharing of feelings, problem-solving through discussion, and verbal insight. All the specific treatment components of BMT were excluded from ICT. At 12 to 14 weeks after the second pretreatment assessment, BMT showed significant changes on measures of marital adjustment (MA), degree of desired relationship change (RC), marital stability (MS), and positive communication (PC), while ICT showed significant changes on the RC and PC measures. NMT couples showed no significant change on any of these measures. BMT was superior to NMT on the MA, MS, and PC measures, while ICT was superior to NMT on RC and PC. BMT surpassed ICT on MA, with no differences between BMT and ICT on RC, MS, or PC. There was no marital measure on which ICT surpassed BMT. Finally, though the alcoholic husbands in all three treatment conditions showed substantial, but not differential, short-term improvement in their drinking behavior, there was marginal evidence that BMT husbands had fewer alcohol-involved days than ICT or NMT husbands. It is important to note the authors' acknowledgment that "In the final analysis, the prediction that BMT would produce marital relationship changes in alcoholics superior to those produced by a frequently used alternative marital therapy received only partial support . . ." (p. 164). Moreover, the marginal superiority of BMT over ICT was, in large measure, accountable to superior change in BMT on measures of overt marital interaction that are highly reactive to behavioral treatment. Finally, the use of Antabuse is not a "behavioral" treatment technique and was required (vs. encouraged) only in the BMT condition. This short-term chemical blocking of alcohol use may have facilitated marital interaction changes independently of or in interaction with

those attributable to BMT's formal treatment components. Since Antabuse contracts were not included in the ICT condition, it is not possible to disentangle its possible confounding effects.

The family therapy research literature on the treatment of drug abuse has predominantly been the study of Structural-Strategic Family Therapy, and it is this family therapy method that has thus far documented the strongest evidence of success (Scopetta et al., 1977; Stanton, 1979; Stanton, Todd, & Associates, 1982; Stanton et al., 1979). Clearly, the most sophisticated study of the family treatment of drug abuse, and one of the most impressive of all family therapy outcome studies, has been that of Stanton, Todd, and their colleagues at the Philadelphia Child Guidance Clinic in Philadelphia. In addition to several other eligibility criteria, index patients were male opiate addicts under age 36, addicted to heroin for at least two years, who had made two or more previous detoxification efforts and were initially involved in a methadone maintenance program. Patients were randomly assigned to one of four treatment conditions: Paid Family Therapy ($N = 21$; $5 per family member per sesson attended, plus "clean" urine required), Unpaid Family Therapy ($N = 25$), Paid Family Movie Placebo ($N = 19$; consisting of anthropological films about familes in foreign cultures), or (unpaid) treatment-as-usual consisting of Individual Counseling plus methadone ($N = 53$). Family therapy lasted an average of 4.5 to 5 months, or about 10 sessions per case. While Paid Family Therapy (PFT) was no more effective than Unpaid Family Therapy (UFT) on several measures of drug use, it surpassed placebo conditions on six of nine drug use measures, and resulted in more regular attendance at treatment sessions than UFT (Stanton, Stier, & Todd, 1982). In addition to the UFT condition leading to decreases in family conflict and increases in involvement of addicts' fathers in family interaction, PFT was associated with from 1.4 to 2.7 times more positive change on various measures of drug (e.g., opiate, nonopiate, alcohol) use than treatment-as-usual individual counseling at termination of therapy and at follow-up. Patients in the PFT and UFT conditions combined achieved better outcomes on four of five drug categories than did patients in the two nonfamily conditions ($p < .05$). Unfortunately, expected treatment gains in the psychosocial areas of improved patient *employment status or school enrollment were not achieved.*

Affective Disorders and Anxiety Disorders

Although the clinical treatment of affective disorders has become something of a cause célèbre in psychiatric circles the last several years and has inspired such enormous research undertakings as the National Institute of Mental Health Collaborative Study of Depression, family and marital therapists have written little on the subject in either clinical or research reports, and to date, only three such studies have appeared (Friedman, 1975; Glick & Clarkin, 1985; McLean, Ogston, & Grauer, 1973). In similar absent fashion, family therapists have devoted little investigative energy to the treatment of anxiety disorders (Barlow, O'Brien, & Last, 1984; Cobb, McDonald, Marks, & Stern, 1980; Emmelkamp & deLange, 1983).

Affective disorders. Friedman (1975) compared a 12-session conjoint marital therapy program (insufficiently described to allow replication) with a 12-session marital therapy plus chemotherapy procedure in the treatment of 196 depressed (88% "neurotic" or "reactive") patients randomly assigned to one of these conditions or to chemotherapy plus minimal contact or a placebo plus minimal contact condition. At four weeks, the drug plus marital therapy condition showed an effect superior to marital therapy alone on measures of symptom change and patients' perception of their marital relationships, whereas at 12 weeks marital therapy alone was superior on measures of perceptions of the marriage and family role task performance.

McLean et al. (1973), treating 20 depressed patients (16 female, 4 male) referred by primary care physicians and described as being married to "cooperative" spouses, randomly assigned them to either eight sessions of behavioral marital therapy emphasizing contracting and behavioral exchanges or to a mixed "control" condition that included medication, group or individual therapy, or combinations thereof. Patients in the couples treatment improved significantly more than in the alternate treatments on measures of mood, verbal interaction style, and target behaviors, and these differences were maintained at three-month follow-up.

In the best designed and largest scale study to date of family therapy for affective disorders, Glick and Clarkin (1985) randomly assigned 54 consecutively admitted patients with major affective disorder (ages 15 to 35) to either standard multimodal inpatient treatment (ST), consisting of individual, group, milieu, and somatic therapies, or to Inpatient Family Intervention (IFI), consisting of the same multimodal treatment plus a minimum of six family sessions ($\bar{x}$ = 8.9). The goals and methods of the IFI were based, in part, on the psychoeducational family therapy of Anderson et al. (1981) and Goldstein et al. (1978), described earlier. These goals included helping family members accept and understand their depressed family member's current condition; identification of possible precipitating stressors and of potential future stressors; identification of stress-producing aspects of the family's interaction; planning to minimize and/or manage future stressors; and acceptance of the identified patient's need for postdischarge outpatient treatment.

Outcome targets included global patient functioning, symptom severity, work/primary role functioning, social functioning, family functioning, leisure time involvement, and postdischarge treatment compliance. Preliminary six-month follow-up results showed the following major findings: (1) IFI patients as a group had better outcomes at discharge on global functioning measures than ST patients; (2) female IFI patients had better symptomatic and role functioning outcomes at both discharge and follow-up than female ST patients, while male IFI patients showed no such difference; (3) female IFI patients showed better postdischarge treatment compliance at follow-up than female ST patients, with no such difference between IFI and ST male patients; and (4) while there was no treatment effect at either discharge or follow-up on family attitudes toward their symptomatic family member, the families of IFI patients showed greater willingness at both points in time to seek and accept help from mental health professionals.

Anxiety disorders. Marital conflict has been implicated as both an etiological and a maintenance factor in cases of adult anxiety disorders such as agoraphobia and obsessive-compulsive disorders. Two major issues that have been investigated in this regard are (1) the effects on marital relationships of treating such disorders on individual versus "spouse-aided" (Hafner, 1985) therapy, and (2) the effects of marital conflict on the outcomes of treatment for these disorders. The majority of studies in this realm have dealt with agoraphobia in women treated by standard behavioral exposure therapy. Some studies have found that successful individual treatment of married female agoraphobics is associated with deteriorating marital relationships or the emergence of psychiatric symptoms in the initially nonsymptomatic spouse (usually husbands) (e.g., Hafner, 1977; Milton & Hafner, 1979), while others have not confirmed such findings (e.g., Bland & Hallam, 1981). Moreover, several reports suggest both that such negative effects do not occur when the nonsymptomatic spouse is actively included in treatment as a sort of junior therapist (Bland & Hallam, 1981; Emmelkamp, 1980), and that including the nonsymptomatic spouse may even improve the marital relationship (Bland & Hallam, 1981; Emmelkamp, 1980; Mathews, Teasdale, Munby, Johnston, & Shaw, 1977). Including the nonsymptomatic spouse in therapy has occasionally (e.g., Cobb, Mathews, Childs-Clarke, & Blowers, 1984) been found to lead to no better outcome than individual treatment, but the preponderance of evidence suggests that spouse-involved treatment is more effective (Barlow, O'Brien, Last, & Holden, 1983; Barlow et al., 1984; Mathews et al., 1977), though these superior effects often are not maintained at follow-up.

While some investigators (e.g., Cobb et al., 1984; Emmelkamp, 1980) have not found pretreatment level of marital adjustment to predict treatment outcome, others have confirmed such a predicted relationship (Bland & Hallam, 1981; Hafner, 1977, 1979; Mathews et al., 1977; Milton & Hafner, 1979). The most sophisticated test of the marital conflict—agoraphobic outcome hypothesis has come in the recent work of Barlow and colleagues (Barlow et al., 1983). This group compared the patient-alone (PA) exposure treatment of 14 married agoraphobic women to a parallel spouse-included (SI) treatment of 14 patients. Their findings suggested that the SI condition led to greater improvement on agoraphobic measures at posttest and faster improvement in patients' social, work, and family functioning, though these latter differences disappeared at follow-up. While only slight improvement in marital satisfaction was evident for couples in well adjusted pretherapy marriages, there were major increases in marital satisfaction in the SI group for initially poorly adjusted relation-

ships. Most interestingly, Barlow et al. (1984) found that inclusion of husbands from low satisfaction marriages in therapy led to improvement in index patient wives almost at a par with the level of change achieved by agoraphobic wives from well-adjusted marriages, whereas when husbands from low satisfaction marriages were not involved in treatment, their wives improved significantly less.

In an exposure treatment study of 12 married obsessive-compulsive (mostly women) patients randomly assigned to either a PA or SI treatment condition, Emmelkamp and deLange (1983) found significant change in both groups, with SI-treated patients showing greater improvement at posttest on measures of obsessive-compulsive targets, mood, and social adjustment (not maintained at one-month follow-up), but no difference in sexual or general marital adjustment.

In almost all the studies of exposure treatment of agoraphobic and obsessive-compulsive patients, patients have been referred for treatment of their anxiety disorder only. In contrast, Cobb et al. (1980) treated 11 couples who complained of both an obsessive-compulsive disorder or phobia and chronic and severe marital discord, randomly assigning them at first to either SI exposure therapy or conjoint behavioral marital therapy (BMT) not focused on anxiety symptoms. The alternative treatment was provided three months after completing the initially assigned 10-session therapy. Exposure therapy led to significant improvement in both phobic/obsessive-compulsive targets and marital problems, while BMT led to marital improvement only, suggesting that where marital conflict coexists with an anxiety disorder in one spouse, exposure treatment should precede BMT.

Finally, two reports by Hafner and colleagues (Badenoch, Fisher, Hafner, & Swift, 1984; Hafner, Badenoch, Fisher, & Swift, 1984) of "spouse-aided individual therapy" (SAIT) for mixed chronic psychiatric disorders have appeared recently. This conjoint treatment is a nonmaritally oriented, symptom-centered, problem-solving approach. Comparing individual therapy with SAIT, Hafner et al. found the latter superior on measures of both symptoms and marital satisfaction, whereas individual therapy led to decreased marital satisfaction and increased depression in both partners at three-month follow-up.

In summary, then, with the sole exception of

Friedman (1975), every study to date of the effectiveness of conjoint husband—wife therapy for adult affective and anxiety disorders has involved some variant of behavioral therapy, that is, behavioral marital therapy, exposure therapy, or problem-solving therapy. Even more significantly, positive clinical outcomes with regard to both presenting problems and marital satisfaction have been reported in numerous studies in which treatment focuses on the index patient's symptoms and in which nonsymptomatically centered marital interaction was not an explicitly targeted area for change. Such clinical foci, of course, do not imply that these interventions have no impact on the marital system in nonsymptomatic arenas, though probably the majority of marital and family therapists would not construe some, or perhaps even any, of these therapies (e.g., spouse-aided exposure therapy) to be "marital" therapy. These data, as a group, then, are reminiscent of the findings reported earlier on the family treatment and management of schizophrenia (Rohrbaugh, 1983, and see previous text). They suggest that there exist a number of adult (and perhaps child and adolescent) psychiatric disorders that may improve significantly in treatment that explicitly and systematically maintains a focus on the symptomatic person as "the patient," without attempting to defocus the "patient" by redefining that person's problem as a "family" or "marital" problem (cf. Umbarger & White, 1978), all the while remaining sensitive to the contribution of family members' behavior to the persistence and modification of the index patient's symptoms. While these data do not inherently disconfirm hypotheses about the often-assumed (e.g., Haley, 1976; Madanes, 1981) systemic function of certain adult psychiatric symptoms, they do challenge the clinical necessity of routinely reframing such problems in this fashion. In this way, these data are consistent with the views of certain other family therapists (e.g., Fisch et al., 1982) who argue that persistent symptoms reflect the unwitting and recurrent application of misguided "solutions" to problems by both the patient and those people with whom the patient regularly interacts about the problem.

Marital Conflict

The origins of "marital therapy" differ from those of contemporary family therapy, the former evolving in the "marriage counseling" tradition and in the psychoanalytically oriented practices of interpersonally oriented psychiatry in the third and fourth decades of this century (Broderick & Schrader, 1981; Nichols & Everett, 1985), the latter in the content of the treatment of adult psychiatric disorders, most notably schizophrenia (Hoffman, 1981; Rohrbaugh, 1983) and symptomatic children and adolescents. Despite these differences in origin, marital therapy is now almost universally viewed as a subtype of family therapy (Gurman & Kniskern, 1979b), and the clinical practice of "family" therapy usually includes and perhaps is predominated by the treatment of problems involving marital conflict (Gurman, 1985). Although marital therapy is practiced in the treatment of both adult disorders and interpersonal conflict (Jacobson & Gurman, 1986), the overwhelming majority of research on marital therapy has focused on relational difficulties. Marital treatment that focuses on individual adult disorders such as depression, phobias, and alcohol abuse has already been considered earlier in this chapter. Hence, in this section, our attention will be focused on marital therapy for explicitly interactional problems. Additionally, since numerous critical reviews of this literature have already appeared (e.g., Baucom & Hoffman, 1985; Beach & O'Leary, 1984; Beck, 1975; Gurman, 1973a; Gurman & Kniskern, 1978a; Jacobson, 1978b, 1984; Jacobson & Martin, 1976; Williams & Miller, 1981), we will emphasize here the major issues and trends of the findings reported to date.

Given the increasing tendency in the family field toward the development of "integrative" models of marital conflict and methods of marital therapy (e.g., Gurman, 1981; Pinsof, 1983; Stanton, 1981), discussing independent "schools" of marital therapy probably does not correspond well to the practices of most clinicians. Nonetheless, partitioning the research into "behavioral" and "nonbehavioral" domains, as we have done previously (Gurman & Kniskern, 1978a), does reflect the reality that there are two quite distinct marital therapy research literatures, the literature dealing with behavioral marital therapy (BMT; Greer & D'Zurilla, 1975; Jacobson, 1984; Jacobson & Martin, 1976), which contains dozens of outcome studies, and that dealing with all other "brands" of couples therapy (e.g., psychodynamic, strategic, systemic), which is almost a null set.

"Nonbehavioral" marital therapy. Experimental studies of relationally focused marital therapy that are not limited to behavioral treatment or communication skill training are rare (cf. Gurman & Kniskern, 1978a). To make interpretive matters worse, the existing studies (Baucom & Lester, 1982; Boelens, Emmelkamp, MacGillavry, & Markvoort, 1980, Crowe, 1978; Epstein & Jackson, 1978; Johnson & Greenberg, 1985a, 1985b; O'Farrell et al., 1985) have little in common in terms of the treatment methods used.

Two studies were of cognitive therapy (CT) or cognitive behavior therapy (CBT). Epstein and Jackson's (1978) controlled study featured an "insight interaction group" and an assertiveness training group. By providing instruction and feedback on the impact of couples' verbal and nonverbal behavior, the "insight" condition sought to increase spouses' awareness of their behavioral interaction patterns, and directive interventions to promote alternative behavior were held to a minimum. Couples in the "insight" condition improved on only 1 of 11 categories of verbal behavior and showed no differences at posttest on self-reported marital satisfaction. Baucom & Lester's (1982) comparative study of BMT alone versus CT plus BMT showed the two treatments to be about equally effective in terms of spouses' behavior change requests, communication skill, and marital adjustment, with CT plus BMT more effective on indices of marital expectations.

Crowe (1978) randomly assigned 42 couples to BMT, group-analytic couples' therapy (Skynner, 1981), or a control group. He found no significant differences on individual or sexual adjustment or target complaints between the two treatments at posttest and 18-month follow-up, with no maintenance of earlier gains in the "insight" treatment at long-term follow-up.

Boelens et al. (1980) compared ten sessions of group-based behavioral contingency contracting and a strategic therapy modeled after Haley (1976). The latter treatment was designed to "provide partners insight into their overt and covert power-struggles, assuming this insight to lead to a change in interaction and communication patterns" (p. 90). Both groups improved significantly on both self-report measures and assessor ratings of marital adjustment, but not on observational measures of problem-solving skill, with no differences between the two treatments. While both groups maintained improvement from pretest scores on self-report measures at six-month follow-up, only the "strategic" therapy couples showed evidence of relapse at follow-up.

O'Farrell et al.'s (1985) comparative study of behavioral couples' group therapy and "interactional" couples' group therapy has already been described in our discussion of substances abuse, and its limitations noted.

Finally, Johnson and Greenberg (1985a) compared cognitive behavioral marital therapy (CBMT) and Emotionally Focused Couples Therapy (EF) emphasizing the role of affect and intrapsychic experience. Forty-five couples were randomly assigned to one of these two active treatments or to a wait-list control group. After eight treatment sessions, both treated groups showed significant gains over untreated controls on measures of goal attainment, marital adjustment, level of intimacy, and target complaints. EF therapy was superior to CBMT on marital adjustment, intimacy, and reduction of target complaints, and at eight-week follow-up, marital adjustment scores for the experientially treated couples remained higher than for CBMT couples. A recent partial replication of the Johnson and Greenberg (1985b) study, in which waiting-list couples from the initial study received eight sessions of EF therapy, found significant changes on most of the dependent variables examined in the original study (Johnson & Greenberg, 1985b), although the overall effect size was slightly less than half of that fund in the first study. This difference was probably attributable to the use of novice therapists in the replication study.

Unfortunately, the "nonbehavioral" therapies studies by Crowe (1978) and Boelens et al. (1980) bear little resemblance to the marital therapies they purportedly investigated. The therapist's provision of "insight" is almost never an aim of strategic therapy (cf. Boelens et al., 1980; Stanton, 1981), and the disallowing of directive therapist interventions (Crowe, 1978; O'Farrell et al., 1985) is inconsistent with both the specific model (Skynner, 1981) of psychodynamic therapy attempted to be tested in one case (Crowe, 1978) and with all extant psychodynamic marital therapies (cf. Gurman, 1978; 1981; Sager, 1981). Importantly, what the four "insight"-only treatments discussed here (Boelens et al., 1980; Crowe, 1978; Epstein & Jackson,

1978; O'Farrell et al., 1985) tell us is that "insight," whether based on the interpretation of conflicts and defenses (Crowe, 1978), underlying power struggles (Boelens et al., 1980), or the relational impact of observable behavior (Epstein & Jackson, 1978; O'Farrell et al., 1985), when provided in the virtual absence of concrete therapist directives for behavior change, is not an especially effective approach to the treatment of marital problems. By way of contrast, when attention to out-of-awareness experience and feelings is paired with active therapist efforts to reframe and modify overt behavior and to translate the connection between inner experience and overt behavior, as in the Johnson and Greenberg (1985a, 1985b) studies, much more impressive outcomes are achieved.

All this said, it remains the case that there has been very little controlled empirical study of any of the "nonbehavioral" marital therapies, let alone of the salient treatment components in any of these therapies. Nonetheless, there does exist a body of research evidence that bears on the issue of the general efficacy of some variations of such "nonbehavioral" couples' therapies. Gurman and Kniskern (1978a, 1978b, 1981a) reviewed data on the rates of improvement in a mixture of such therapies in which both partners were regularly involved in treatment, and found that 65 percent of 1122 couples treated in 29 studies were rated as improved on a diverse number of patient self-reports, therapist evaluations, and independent assessor's ratings. While the modal study used only a single evaluative perspective and a single change measure, Gurman and Kniskern (1978a) judged these overall results to be consistent with the findings of the numerous studies they also reviewed that included comparison and control conditions; for example, in 22 of 30 (70%) comparisons of conjoint therapy versus therapy for marital problems provided in individual or (stranger) group therapy, conjoint therapy emerged superior, and in 12 controlled studies involving conjoint treatment, therapy was superior to no treatment 75 percent of the time.

Gurman and Kniskern's (1978a, 1978c) analysis has been criticized (Jacobson & Weiss, 1978) because of its use of the more recently outmoded "box-score" approach to integrating the findings of a large body of outcome literature. Such an approach to reviewing a research literature is purported to be inherently limited because of its combi-

nation of studies of unequal design quality and, more basically, because of the intrusion of the reviewer's subjective bias and value-based judgments, which are known at times to lead different reviewers to reach different conclusions about the same body of research (cf. Gurman & Kniskern, 1978a; Jacobson, 1978b; Wells & Giannetti, 1985). More recent alternative analytic techniques, such as meta-analysis (Smith & Glass, 1977; Smith, Glass, & Miller, 1981), standardizes and makes replicable the practices and criteria for reviewing large bodies of data to establish more dependable generalizations and allows for the systematic (vs. "eyeball") investigation of the impact of numerous potentially significant variables (e.g., treatment length, patient diagnosis) on treatment outcome. Moreover, meta-analysis assesses the size or magnitude of a treatment effect rather than simply assessing the probability of whether the effects found in given studies were due to chance.

Though the advent of meta-analytic studies of psychotherapy outcomes has not gone without criticism (e.g., Rachman & Wilson, 1980), two meta-analyses of individual psychotherapy research (Landman & Dawes, 1982; Shapiro & Shapiro, 1983) subsequent to the original meta-analyses (Smith & Glass, 1977; Smith et al., 1981) in this area are of particular and immediate relevance to the criticisms (Jacobson & Weiss, 1978) of Gurman and Kniskern's (1978a, 1978c) box-score analysis. Shapiro and Shapiro (1983) replicated and refined the original Smith and Glass meta-analysis and, contrary to the view that box-score analyses misleadingly aggregate data from studies of varying methodological adequacy, found that several of the design variables they investigated (e.g., random assignment of patients to treatments, random assignment of therapists) were not significantly correlated with treatment effect sizes. Moreover, they concluded that their findings were "broadly in agreement with those of most previous reviews, whether conventional or meta-analytic" (p. 496).

Landman and Dawes (1982) selected from the original Smith and Glass (1977) meta-analysis only those studies of high methodological quality and subjected them to meta-analysis. Cohen (1984) succinctly summarized the Landman and Dawes data by noting that "with all this [refinement] they found no material differences in the conclusions from their sample of good studies drawn from the same batch of researches that Smith, Glass and Miller used" (p. 336), that is, a batch that included methodologically marginal and inadequate studies. Thus, there is indirect, but relevant, evidence to suggest that the box-score—based conclusions reached by Gurman and Kniskern (1978a, 1978b, 1978c) about the efficacy of nonbehavioral marital therapy may not be affected appreciably by more empirically reliable and valid analytic methods, though the acid test of this prediction, of course, will be an empirical rather than a logical one.

Other relevant findings from Gurman and Kniskern's (1978a, 1978b) review demonstrated that deterioration during (due to methodological limitations, one cannot say "because of") conjoint couples' therapy appeared to occur only about half as often as during individual treatment of marital difficulties and that positive outcomes accrued much more often to conjoint than to "individual" marital therapy. These conclusions have recently been critiqued by Wells and Giannetti (1985), who argued that the methodological inadequacy of the studies Gurman and Kniskern (1978a, 1978b) originally reviewed was so great as to preclude *any* conclusion about the efficacy of individual marital therapy (IMT). In their rejoinder, Gurman and Kniskern (1985) acknowledged the accuracy of some of Wells and Gainnetti's criticisms of the inclusion of some of the studies in question, yet found most of their critics' concerns to be largely unwarranted. Stimulated by their critics, Gurman and Kniskern reanalyzed the data from the studies they had reviewed earlier and, on the basis of this reanalysis, tentatively suggested the following hypothesis-generating (not confirmatory) reinterpretation of the meaning of the data in the original studies: "There is suggestive, and consistent, evidence that marital therapy which combines a predominant use of IMT with other (usually conjoint) treatment formats may be less effective than marital therapy which combines a secondary use of IMT with other (usually conjoint) treatment formats." Controlled investigations of this hypothesis are clearly called for in light of its practical and conceptual significance.

Gurman and Kniskern (1985) also updated their position regarding the relative empirical status of IMT and conjoint marital therapy (including behavioral marital therapy) and concluded: (1) There is very little acceptable empirical evidence of the inefficacy of IMT (in agreement with Wells and Gian-

netti); (2) there is no evidence, acceptable or otherwise, of the efficacy of IMT (also in agreement with Wells and Giannetti); and (3) there is a large body of acceptable evidence of the efficacy of conjoint marital therapy (see Gurman & Kniskern, 1978a, and this chapter). Thus, they argued, "The null hypothesis regarding IMT (i.e., no difference between IMT and no therapy) has not yet been disconfirmed, whereas the null hypothesis regarding conjoint marital therapy has been disconfirmed repeatedly." Gurman and Kniskern therefore modified their earlier position that the comparative findings on IMT and conjoint therapy were "persuasive enough to question routinely the value of individual therapy for marital problems" (1978a, p. 835) to one that "there is ample warrant for the position that conjoint therapy can, for now, be considered the treatment of choice for marital problems." Finally, we also concur with Todd and Stanton's (1983) note that "it is important not to overgeneralize . . . it may be premature to claim superiority for marital treatment when the presenting problem is an 'individual' one, e.g., wife's depression" (p. 94). We also acknowledge that, beyond the very broad-stroke implications of these data for clinical decision making, there is little of substance in the research literature of "nonbehavioral" (mostly psychodynamic-eclectic) marital therapy to guide or inform the more refined and specific decisions that therapists must make every day in clinical practice.

Behavioral marital therapy.   As noted earlier, numerous studies of the efficacy of behavioral marital therapy (BMT) have been published, especially in the last decade, and in terms of both the number and quality of this body of research, BMT has no peer in the marital sphere. Thus, it is no surprise that several analytic reviewers (e.g., Baucom & Hoffman, 1985; Beach & O'Leary, 1985; Greer & D'Zurilla, 1975; Gurman & Kniskern, 1978a; Jacobson, 1978b; Jacobson, Follette, & Elwood, 1984; Jacobson & Martin, 1976; Jacobson et al., 1984c) of this literature have already appeared and, given that most of these have been published in very accessible sources, our aim here will be to identify the major questions and issues thus far investigated in BMT and to summarize the evidence bearing on them. For these purposes, we are heavily indebted to the very recent reviews of Beach & O'Leary (1985), Baucom and Hoffman (1985), and Jacobson et al. (1984a), whose critical integrative analyses include numerous studies that did not exist when we (Gurman & Kniskern, 1978a) first examined this literature and upon which we draw here relentlessly and unabashedly.

BMT versus control groups. Seven studies (Baucom, 1982; Baucom & Lester, 1982; Hahlweg, Schnidler, Revenstorf, & Brengelmann, 1984; Jacobson, 1977, 1978a; Mehlman, Baucom, & Anderson, 1983; Turkewitz & O'Leary, 1981) of the treatment of clinically distressed couples have compared BMT to *waiting-list control* couples on observational measures of *communication skill*, and all but one (Turkewitz & O'Leary, 1981) showed significant decreases in negative verbal behavior compared to controls. Among these studies only those of Jacobson (1977, 1978b) and Baucom (1982) have provided evidence of increases in positive verbal behavior. Eight studies (Baucom, 1982; Baucom & Lester, 1982; Boelens et al., 1980; Ewart, 1978b; Girodo, Stein, & Dotzenroth, 1980; Hahlweg et al., 1984; Jacobson, 1985; Mehlman et al., 1983) have assessed the efficacy of BMT relative to wait-list controls in regard to improvement of *presenting problems* and *requests for behavior change*, and all but one (Girodo et al., 1980) showed BMT to yield significant changes. Finally, in 8 of the 11 studies referred to here, couples receiving BMT showed more improvement on self-report measures of *marital satisfaction and adjustment* than did control couples.

Four studies comparing BMT to various *attention control and nonspecific control* groups (Azrin et al., 1980; Crowe, 1978; Jacobson, 1978c; Liberman, Levine, Wheeler, Sanders, & Wallace, 1976), typically involving affective expression without behavioral skill training, have provided only very mixed and inconsistent results on measures of communication skill, target problem resolution, and marital satisfaction.

In summary, then, on measures tapping the three major domains of outcome assessment mentioned before, BMT has shown inconsistent evidence of superiority to attention-placebo control conditions, but much more consistent evidence of superiority to wait-list conditions. As Baucom and Hoffman (1985) emphasize, increases in positive communication behavior (vs. decreases in negative behavior) have not been consistently demonstrated, and this should be a matter of some concern to BMT therapists, given the usual aims of marital therapy based on social learning and social exchange theory (e.g., Jacobson & Margolin, 1979).

BMT versus other marital therapies. Ten studies of clinically distressed couples have compared BMT to other marital therapies, from strategic (Boelens et al., 1980; Emmelkamp, van der Helm, MacGillavry, & van Zanten, 1984) to psychodynamic-experiential (Crowe, 1978; Johnson & Greenberg, 1985a, 1985b; O'Farrell et al., 1985) to communication training (Girodo et al., 1980; Hahlweg, Schindler, & Revenstorf, 1982; Turkewitz & O'Leary, 1981) to cognitive restructuring therapy (Baucom & Lester, 1982). While Boelens et al. (1980) found significant improvement on multiple measures for both treatments and almost no differences between treatments, as noted earlier, serious doubts must be raised about the correspondence of Boelens et al.'s "strategic" therapy to standard descriptions (e.g., Haley, 1976) of that approach. The same question of external validity applies to Emmelkamp et al. (1984), who used the same "strategic" therapy. Crowe's (1978) study has also been commented on earlier with regard to its (lack of) fidelity to psychodynamic couples' therapy. O'Farrell et al.'s (1985) "interactional" couples' group therapy for alcoholism emphasized mutual support, sharing of feelings, problem solving through discussion, and verbal insight. Although behavioral treatment components noted in our earlier discussion of this study were necessarily not present in this "interactional" treatment for design reasons, this limitation seriously compromised the external validity of this treatment condition, in that psychodynamic/insight-oriented marital therapy typically includes such directive techniques (Gurman, 1981). Moreover, as noted in our discussion of the treatment of substance abuse, the comparative effects on outcome of "interactional" couples' therapy and behavioral couples' therapy was confounded by the requirement of Antabuse contracts in the former condition. Thus, in contrast to the conclusion of Baucom and Hoffman (1985) that existing evidence shows BMT to be equally effective to systemic and psychodynamic marital therapies, we believe that the three studies (Baucom & Lester, 1982; Boelens et al., 1980; Emmelkamp et al., 1984) on which they base this conclusion, and the more recent study of O'Farrell et al. (185), do not constitute comparative tests of anything other than poorly defined or inappropriately limited alternatives to BMT. The only study to date that attempted to compare a bona fide psychodynamic-experiential marital therapy with BMT (Johnson & Greenberg, 1985a), found equal effectiveness between treatments on some measures, and superior outcomes for experiential-psychodynamic therapy on several others.

BMT Treatment Components. A small number of studies (Baucom, 1982; Ewart, 1978a; Emmelkamp et al., in press; Jacobson, 1978a, 1984; Turkewitz & O'Leary, 1981) have examined combinations of common BMT treatment components, the comparative effectiveness of these components, and the order effects administration of these components. The components of BMT may include communication training, problem-solving training, and contingency contracting of different types (Jacobson & Margolin, 1979). The findings of these studies have not revealed significant or consistent outcome differences in terms of the relative potency of such treatment components administered alone, of variations of contingency contracting, of combinations of components, or of the order in which the components are applied, though there is suggestive evidence (Ewart, 1978a; Jacobson, 1984; Turkewitz & O'Leary, 1981) that the use of behavior exchange training without contingency contracting may be less effective than exchange training with contingency contracting. Finally, one comparison of one-couple conjoint BMT vs. conjoint group BMT (Hahlweg et al., 1984) found conjoint BMT superior to conjoint group BMT on two of seven outcome measures (though both were superior to the control condition), while another (Bennun, 1984) found no differences between these treatment formats, or in comparison to a BMT approach with only one spouse participating in treatment.

Predictors of BMT outcome. While the research literature on "nonbehavioral" marital therapies include no studies of predictors of treatment response, several such BMT studies do exist and present clinically relevant findings. BMT may be more effective with (1) younger couples (Hahlweg et al., 1984; Turkewitz & O'Leary, 1981); (2) couples who evidence continuing commitment to their

relationship (i.e., have taken fewer private and public steps toward divorce; Beach & Broderick, 1983; Crowe, 1978; Ewart, 1978b, Hahlweg et al., 1984); and (3) couples who, despite relationship problems, maintain some emotional connectedness (e.g., sexual involvement and caring and tenderness). That feelings of continuing commitment and caring should increase the chances of positive therapy outcomes is hardly unexpected and probably obtains in the practice of "nonbehavioral" marital therapies as well.

The magnitude and significance of BMT outcomes. Even in the face of aggregate data demonstrating the efficacy of BMT, questions may be raised about both the magnitude of positive changes reported in between-group comparisons and their clinical significance. Hahlweg and Markman (1983) recently presented a meta-analysis of 81 dependent measures from 17 BMT studies, and found (1) an average "effect size" of 0.92, suggesting that the typical couple receiving BMT improved more than 82 percent of untreated couples or couples receiving "nonspecific" treatment; (2) nearly identical effect sizes for self-report and observational outcome criteria; and (3) stable effect sizes at follow-up.

Baucom and Hoffman (1985) and Jacobson et al. (1984c) have considered data bearing on the clinical significance of outcome findings in BMT. Baucom and Hoffman identified eight studies that used standard versions of either the Marital Adjustment Scale (Locke & Wallace, 1959) or the Dyadic Adjustment Scale (Spanier, 1976), the two most widely used self-report marital satisfaction measures. These studies also presented mean group scores and examined marital samples with pretreatment scores in the "distressed" range (MAS $<$ 100; DAS $<$ 92). Three studies reported posttest means in the nondistressed range, while five reported posttest means in the distressed range. The implication of these analyses, that "a substantial proportion of couples are still distressed at the end of BMT" (Baucom & Hoffman, 1985, p. 14), was independently corroborated in Hahlweg and Markman's (1983) effect size meta-analyses.

Jacobson et al. (1984c) provide still more detailed clarification of some recent BMT outcome findings in terms of their clinical significance. Using a reliable change index based on the standard error of measurement, Jacobson et al. (1984c) classified

BMT couples into categories of improved, unimproved, and deteriorated based on a reanalysis of data from four previously published studies, with a total of 148 couples. Using a posttest score falling outside the range of marital distress as the criterion for clinical significance, they found that 54.7 percent of the couples had improved significantly, and that deterioration at termination was infrequent (weighted $\bar{x} = 4.6\%$). This deterioration rate was very similar to deterioration rates previously reported for "nonbehavioral" couples' therapy (Gurman & Kniskern, 1978b). In slightly less than two-fifths of the improved cases, only one spouse reported a clinically significant increase in marital satisfaction. Slightly more than one-third of the couples had moved from distressed to nondistressed status at the end of therapy, and at six-month follow-up about 60 percent maintained their treatment gains, with 28 percent of the remaining couples showing deterioration and 12 percent showing additional improvement beyond termination. By way of comparison, wait-list couples rarely improved (13.5%), while the majority (69.2%) did not change, and many (17.3%) deteriorated.

Jacobson et al.'s (1984c) criteria for determining the proportion of couples in these four studies who qualified as significantly clinically improved were obviously much more demanding than criteria typically used to estimate treatment "success" rates and are not even comparable to such alternative criteria and approaches (cf. Gurman & Kniskern, 1978a, 1981b). While Jacobson et al.'s (1984c) and Baucom and Hoffman's (1985) analyses make it clear that many BMT couples remain clinically distressed after therapy, these data cannot be used to argue that BMT is less effective than other marital therapies since parallel data analyses of the effects of other marital therapies simply do not exist. Moreover, Jacobson et al.'s improvement data are noticeably less impressive than those offered in other analyses (cf. Gurman & Kniskern, 1978a). As Jacobson et al. (1984c) conclude, ". . . the absence of conventions for designating a couple as improved has led to an inflated estimate of [BMT's] success rate. It is almost inevitable that the same is true of other approaches" (p. 503).

Divorce Therapy

Divorce is a process with profound structural, interactional, and psychological consequences for those who must endure it. The name "divorce therapy" is, in fact, something of a misnomer, in that family therapists of all orientations deal regularly with the dissolution process, and the techniques of divorce-oriented intervention have not evolved conceptually in the context of any single theory of family change or method of treatment (Rice & Rice, 1985). Although the aims of these variegated interventions vary from case to case, they typically include aiding the divorcing partners in dealing with their loss and reestablishing themselves functionally either as nonmarried adults, as single parents, and/or as functional co-parents, minimizing the potential negative psychological effects of divorce on children (Wallerstein, 1984), decreasing adversarial parental interaction over child custody and visitation and, where appropriate, offering a forum in which the possibility of reconciliation is considered. To date, there have appeared 22 empirical studies of the effects of divorce intervention (Sprenkle & Storm, 1983), in only 6 of which was the possibility of reconciliation a clinical issue. These studies were all conducted in the context of conciliation courts, so that the couples involved had already taken many of the steps (Weiss & Cerreto, 1975) toward divorce. In only 2 studies to date (Beck & Jones, 1973; Cookerly, 1973) were clinical outcomes assessed in the context of couples receiving general (non-divorce-oriented) marital therapy. Thus, in 14 of these 22 studies, the decision to divorce already had been reached at the outset of treatment.

As a group, these 22 studies have been of marginal methodological quality: only 6 included a no-treatment control group, 7 included random assignment to treatment conditions, 8 included a follow-up of at least 3 months, and all but one of the outcome measures with demonstrated reliability and validity were based on client self-report, with behavioral measures occurring rarely. On the positive side of the methodological ledger, 13 of the studies have used replicable standardized treatments.

The subgroup of divorce intervention studies ($n = 6$) with the highest design quality, yielding the most consistent and clinically relevant findings, have involved *divorce mediation* (Coogler, 1978). Mediation usually occurs after divorce is an accepted fact, before the court's issuance of its final divorce orders, and is offered as an alternative to the usual adversarial process. It generally emphasizes resolution of child custody and/or visitation disputes. In all mediation studies involving a comparison with alternative interventions, mediation has been associated with (1) a higher rate of pretrial agreements; (2) a higher level of satisfaction with the agreements; (3) major reductions in the amount of litigation after final court orders; (4) an increase in joint custody agreements; and (5) with only one exception, decrease in public expenses such as custody studies and court costs (Sprenkle & Storm, 1983). Moreover, data from these studies as a group have led to a clinically useful description of those couples for whom mediation is likely to achieve its desired effects:

> . . . the ideal candidates are couples mediating around a limited number of issues, for whom the level of conflict is moderate, and in which both spouses feel able to represent themselves in the negotiations. Both accept the divorce and have begun the process of "letting to." The mediation occurs early in the dissolution process and before receiving court orders (either temporary or permanent). There are not third parties significantly involved in the dispute. Both parties sense some ability to communicate and cooperate with the other. Money is no a major issue in the divorce, and there are adequate resources to carry on as a single person. Finally, the attorneys support the mediation process. (Sprenkle & Storm, 1983, p. 250)

Studies carried out under the rubric of *conciliation courts counseling* ($n = 6$), in which reconciliation was an aim of treatment, have demonstrated a significantly greater number of reconciliations in experimental groups than in no-treatment control groups, but the durability of these outcomes is open to question because of the very brief amount of time (3, 4, and 9 weeks) transpiring between the start of treatment and the time of assessing reconciliation status.

Postdivorce group treatments for divorced individuals have been examined in six studies (Sprenkle & Storm, 1983). These group treatments, which usually include both didactic and experiential components, and range from 4 to 10 sessions, have yielded consistently positive outcomes, with the most common dependent change measure being that of self-esteem, one of the major individual psy-

chological dimensions of concern to divorce therapists (Rice & Rice, 1985).

Finally, two studies (Greene, Lee, & Lustig, 1973; Toomim, 1972) of *separation counseling* have appeared, finding 67 percent and 44 percent of the treated couples eventually divorcing. Given the existing lack of data on the base rates of couples in conjoint marital therapy or in structured separation counseling (often a phase of conjoint therapy) who go on to divorce, and the severe methodological problems of these two studies (Sprenkle & Storm, 1983), these findings cannot be interpreted meaningfully.

Conclusion. It is clear, then, that to date, of the major forms of "divorce therapy" that have undergone empirical scrutiny, mediation has received the strongest and most consistent support. But since divorce is a family affair and involves the restructuring of the lives and interactions of many people beyond the marital dyad, it is most unfortunate that, thus far, no study of any of the conjoint methods of divorce therapy has assessed the effects of treatment on the children of divorce. Nor has there been a single study in which children were themselves participants in the therapy experience. Such studies are urgently needed on both clinical and public-policy grounds. Moreover, divorce does not end with a judge's issuance of final divorce orders. Most divorced adults go on to remarry, and many families involved in remarriage also experience family crises (Sager et al., 1983), as do single-parent families (Morawetz & Walker, 1984). Research on clinical intervention with both of these family structures is also called for.

Preventive Interventions

In addition to family therapists' attention to the involvement of the family system in the treatment of both psychiatric disorders and explicitly relational problems with clinical populations of families and married couples, there has also been a long-standing interest in preventive interventions in family, and especially marital, life. Although *premarital counseling* and *enrichment programs* for well-functioning married couples and families have rarely attracted much attention from what may be considered the "mainstream" of the family therapy movement, especially that contingent working in psychiatric settings, considerable interest has been shown in these domains of intervention by clinicians whose professional heritage is more closely linked with the "marriage counseling" (Broderick & Schraeder, 1981) wing of the field.

Premarital Counseling

Though intervention techniques vary widely in premarital counseling, for example, from didactic to experiential methods, the fundamental common aims of such programs are "to help prospective mates evaluate their relationship and acquaint them with the ways by which they might build a more happy and successful marriage" (Bagarozzi & Rauen, 1981, p. 13). The goals of premarital counseling programs are largely preventive, informational, and educational rather than remedial or reparative. The research on premarital programs (as distinct from premarital counseling conducted conjointly with one couple at a time) has been reviewed by Gurman and Kniskern (1977) and Bagarozzi and Rauen (1981). The latter authors' major conclusions about the empirical status of these programs, though based on a larger data base of experimental studies than that of Gurman and Kniskern, are almost identical to those reached earlier by Gurman and Kniskern: (1) the outcomes achieved at posttest cannot be reliably attributed to the interventions used, since only 6 of the existing 13 experimental studies included untreated control groups; (2) internal validity has been severely compromised in general in that only (the same) 6 of the existing studies have randomly assigned couples to treatment conditions: (3) dependent change measures have gone beyond participants' self-report to include observationally based ratings, for instance, of communication skill, in only 4 studies; (4) even though communication and problem-solving skill enhancement are almost always treatment goals, the use of different skill training methods and of nonstandardized dependent measures of skill precludes meaningful assessment of treatment effects on these dimensions; and (5) long-term follow-up of the programs' impact has been almost nonexistent, which is especially noteworthy in light of the fact that one of the commonly desired results of these programs is reduction of the probability of divorce.

Still more recently, Giblin, Sprenkle, and Sheehan (1985), in their meta-analysis of enrichment outcome studies, found an average effect size (Glass, McGaw, & Smith, 1981) of .53 for premari-

tal interventions, based on a limited data pool of 43 effect sizes.

Marital and Family Enrichment

A large number of programs designed to "enrich" marital relationships have emerged in the last two decades (L'Abate, 1981). These programs offer growth-inducing and relationship-skill-enhancement experiences to couples whose interactions are basically sound but who wish to make their relationships even more satisfying. Enrichment programs are modally provided in either single-weekend "retreats" or in six to eight consecutive weekly meetings of about two hours each.

Giblin et al. (1985) have recently offered the most comprehensive analysis of the full range of marital and family enrichment research. Their meta-analysis of premarital, marital, and family enrichment programs was based on studies involving 3886 couples and families (8365 individuals), with 1691 identified effect sizes. Across these three areas of enrichment, which included 23 different enrichment programs, a mean effect size of .44 was found, meaning that the "average person" participating in these programs change for the better more than 67 percent of people who do not participate.

In addition to the effect size of .53 noted before for premarital interventions, Giblin et al. found average effect sizes of .42 and .55 for marital and family programs, respectively. The programs with by far the most positive outcomes were Guerney's (1977) marital Relationship Enhancement (RE) and Parent—Adolescent Relationship Development (PARD), with identical effect sizes of .96.

Giblin et al. found that while the average effect size at post test (.44) decreased somewhat (to .34) at the end of follow-up periods of from 2 to 52 weeks ($\bar{x} = 12$ weeks), positive effects were still maintained. Consistent with other reviews (e.g., Bagarozzi & Rauen, 1981; Gurman & Kniskern, 1977) of enrichment research, the preponderance (76%) of effect sizes were based on participants' self-reports. Also consistent with previous analyses, much larger effect sizes were found for behavioral measures (E.S. = .76) than for self-report measures (E.S. = .35). In similar fashion, based on Gurman and Kniskern's (1977) classification of enrichment outcome criteria, Giblin et al. found effect sizes of .63 on measures of relationship skills enhancement, .34 on measures of overall marital and family satisfaction and adjustment, and .23 on measures of individual functioning and personality (e.g., self-esteem).

Two additional findings from this meta-analysis are also of interest. Contrary to the oft-held clinical belief that clinically relevant change is more likely to occur when larger family units (e.g., entire nuclear family) are treated, Giblin et al. found that programs involving parent–child dyads only yielded more positive outcomes than programs involving whole families. The meaning of this finding is uncertain, however, since the effects of whole family versus parent–child dyad intervention could not be disentangled from the inclusion of qualitatively different treatment goals and intervention methods.

Of a somewhat more controversial nature was Giblin et al.'s finding that appears to contradict the clinical lore that enrichment programs are not likely to be effective with "clinical," that is, highly distressed, samples. These authors found that an analysis of variance comparing studies with from 0 to 34 percent of the sample identified as distressed with studies in which 35 percent or more of the sample was distressed, yielded mean effect sizes of .27 and .51, respectively ($p < .001$). These findings tentatively challenge the common belief of the inapplicability of enrichment programs to "clinical" samples. An alternative interpretation of those results cannot be ruled out, however; that is, that when a significant subsample of subjects in an enrichment study are clinically quite distressed, ceiling effects (to be more expected in nondistressed samples) are less likely to reduce the chances of detecting statistically significant change.

Of the several well-established programs (e.g. Association of Couples for Marital Enrichment [Mace & Mace, 1976]; Minnesota Couples Communication Program [Miller, Nunnally, & Wackman, 1977]; Relationship Enhancement [Guerney, 1977]; and Marriage Encounter [Bosco, 1972]), we have selected the Minnesota Couples Communication Program (MCCP) and Marriage Encounter for more detailed discussion here, because they are the most widely used.

MCCP.   This program, now known as the CCP, involves 3 to 7 couples meeting in groups for three hours weekly for four weeks. CCP aims to increase direct and open communication through enhanced awareness of self, the relationship, and the couple's "conflict rules." Over 50,000 couples have participated in the program (Brock & Joanning, 1983). From its very beginning, CCP has been tied closely to empirical research, and by the time of Wampler's (1982a, 1982b) two comprehensive reviews of CCP research, 26 studies had been completed on 24 independent samples, with 20 of these in published form. Wampler (1982a, 1982b) reviewed these same outcome studies in two separate reports. The first (1982a) used the traditional "voting" or "box-score" method of integrating findings, while the second used the meta-analysis (Glass et al., 1981) approach. We will first summarize the results of Wampler's box-score review and then qualify some of those findings on the basis of her meta-analysis.

The major design characteristics of these studies were that (1) using Gurman and Kniskern's (1978a) criteria for rating the design quality of outcome studies, 50 percent of the studies were "very good," 20 percent "good," and 30 percent "fair"; (2) the majority used a no-treatment control group; (3) random assignment was used in 70 percent of the studies; (4) follow-up data were gathered in over half the studies; (5) intervention was almost always standardized, and group leaders had successfully completed official CCP instructor training; (6) the majority of clients were well educated, middle class, and Caucasian; (7) rather small samples were used; and (8) implementation checks on the fidelity of the interventions were absent.

Wampler's (1982a) major findings showed (1) no measurable effect on self-disclosure; (2) positive effects on spouse's interaction recall; (3) positive effects on self-report measures of communication quality in only 2 of 9 studies; (4) positive effects on general relationship satisfaction in 7 of 13 studies; and (5) no evidence of deterioration. The findings were largely the same at both posttest and follow-up. Despite these mixed self-report results, all of the 5 studies that received "very good" design quality ratings reported positive effects on communication quality and/or overall relationship satisfaction.

On behavioral measures of "communication style" and other communication skills, outcomes were much more consistently positive across a variety of indices, with 9 of the 10 studies using such dependent measures showing a treatment effect. Moreover, in the 6 studies that tested for therapist (leader) effects, none were found, lending support to the idea that the above findings represent genuine treatment effects.

These findings of a strong positive effect on behavioral changes, a moderately positive effect on relationship satisfaction, a weak positive effect on perceived communication quality, and weak evidence for the durability of effects in all domains of self-report were corroborated by Wampler's (1982b) subsequent meta-analytic review of the CCP program. Her meta-analysis, however, found that the large positive changes on behavioral measures persisted at follow-up, that changes in overall relationship satisfaction decreased at follow-up, and that changes in perceived communication quality increased at follow-up. In brief, Wampler's meta-analysis revealed a more impressive pattern of positive change than had her earlier box-score tally. Wampler's meta-analytic findings are consistent with Giblin et al.'s (1985) more recent finding of an average effect size of .44 for CCP studies. Still, it must be considered that behavioral measures may be more subject to the demand characteristics of the evaluation setting than self-report measures. People may learn, particularly being in the experimental setting a second time, to act "right" and give the experimenter what they believe is expected.

Finally, in what is probably the most sophisticated study of CCP's effects to date, Joanning (1982) found that while there were positive effects on measures of behavioral communication skill, perceived communication quality, and overall marital adjustment at posttest, at five-month follow-up a large proportion of couples had virtually returned to pretest levels of marital adjustment. Posttreatment follow-up also revealed that 70 percent of the couples had difficulty incorporating the skills they had learned into everyday life. Moreover, the heightened sense of intimacy reported at posttest by 90 percent of the couples had vanished (statistically speaking) at follow-up.

Marriage encounter. This finding of rather short-lived intimacy "highs" in both Joanning's (1982) study of the CCP and in Wampler's (1982a, 1982b) reviews also has been noted in the few investigations done to date on the Marriage Encounter program (Doherty & Walker, 1982; Lester & Doherty, 1983), and noted earlier (Gurman & Kniskern, 1977) as a common finding in a variety of marital enrichment experiences. Marriage Encounter, a multidenominational, church-sponsored program aimed at "revitalizing marriages and restoring relationships to their original level of intimacy" (Lester & Doherty, 1983, p. 183) has now reached approximately one and a half *million* couples worldwide. The long-term effects of this 44-hour, single-weekend experience have been most thoroughly studied to date by Doherty and his colleagues (Doherty & Walker, 1982; Lester & Doherty, 1983), who conducted an uncontrolled, retrospective mail questionnaire follow-up study of 129 couples (78% return rate).

Eighty-four percent of husbands and 75 percent of wives reported positive global effects on their marriages at from 1 to 10 years post-Encounter. The "dialogue technique" is the central intervention component of the Encounter weekends and involves spouses reflecting on a topic, recording their feelings about it in a notebook, exchanging notebooks, and then discussing their feelings, with *discouragement* at problem solving. This technique was viewed as helpful by 66 percent of the husbands and 60 percent of the wives. Modest positive effects were found on participants' retrospective satisfaction immediately following the Encounter weekend (55% of husbands, 42% of wives). In addition, 40 percent of the respondents reported at least one negative evaluation of the program's impact. Using the more stringent and conservative criterion for assessing negative effects of at least three negative effects noted per couple, Lester and Doherty (1983) found evidence for "potentially serious negative effects" (p. 187) in 9.3 percent of their sample. Doherty and Walker (1982) assess these findings as probably being attributable to the program's intensity of opening up highly charged areas of feeling by the couple without providing a problem-solving structure within which these intense feelings might be handled, and to the dramatic alteration of couples' expectations for marriage in a very brief period of time. Doherty's modestly positive evaluation of the outcomes of Marriage Encounter have recently received more broadly based confirmation from Giblin et al.'s (1985) finding of an average Marriage Encounter effect size of .42, an effect size that was almost exactly the same as the average effect size (.44) of all existing marital and family enrichment programs. Based on their findings of the existence of deterioration from Marriage

Encounter, Doherty and Walker recommended (1) more systematic efforts to screen out distressed couples; (2) encouragement of and referral to follow-up marital therapy, as needed; and (3) training of Encounter group leaders in crisis intervention techniques.

A SUMMARY ANALYSIS OF THE EFFECTIVENESS OF THE MAJOR SCHOOLS OF MARITAL AND FAMILY THERAPY

Given the recent and apparently continuing proliferation of family therapy approaches, the recently resuscitated and increased commitment in the field to empirical validation, and the existence, as noted early in this chapter, of numerous disparate critical reviews of family therapy outcome research, it seems appropriate to us at this time in the evolution of the field to take stock of the existing evidence regarding the efficacy of the major "schools" of family and marital therapy. This summary assessment is not offered with the intention of dissuading adherents to given "schools" from continuing their current practices, for the absence of evidence of efficacy obviously does not confirm inefficacy. Nor is this summary offered with the intention of sanctifying the practices of other "schools," since no method of family or marital therapy has accumulated incontrovertible evidence of universal effectiveness, and many important questions about these latter methods remain to be investigated. It is still too early to accept or dismiss any approach, and in general we have little certainty about what actually occurred in the treatments reflected in this summary analysis, since process data have almost never been gathered in the studies on which this analysis is based. Thus, we may be dealing with what may be called "alleged orientations." Moreover, this presentation should not be taken as support for "school-based" research, since such research, though common in the field of psychotherapy research, is unlikely to shed much light on the mechanisms of change or effects of specific interventions, which need to be examined independent of the alleged orientations of clinicians. Despite these interpretive caveats, we believe that this summary may serve as a potential stimulus for the enormous amount of empirical work that still needs to occur in the field.

The "schools" considered here (see Table 13.2) are those that we believe would be agreed upon by most family therapists and teachers of family therapy as having had enduring impact on the thinking and practices of significant numbers of clinicians and which, in our judgment, are in regular use with genuine clinical help-seeking populations, as distinct from people seeking "enrichment" experiences (cf. Levant, 1983, 1984). Given the trends toward theoretical and technical integration in the field noted earlier, we recognize that examining the evidence of efficacy of given "schools" may have limited meaning to many practitioners, yet research on such integrative models is largely nonexistent. The clinical disorders and problems identified in Table 13.2 obviously do not encompass the full range of difficulties treated by family therapists, but they do accurately reflect the domains of investigative activity reviewed in this chapter and in earlier reviews of family therapy research.

These summary estimates of efficacy are not based on psychometrically reliable change indices such as those of Jacobson et al. (1984b). Rather, they reflect our estimates of the degree of confidence we have of the evidential basis for the efficacy of given approaches, based on the amount of research on a method to date, the typical quality of that research, and the degree of efficacy documented in reports on each method. Naturally, we would like to believe that these estimates are reliable, accurate, and totally unaffected by any personal biases on our part, though other reviewers might "read" the cumulative findings differently (cf. Gurman & Kniskern, 1978a, 1978c, 1985; Wells & Denzen, 1978a, 1978b; Wells & Giannetti, 1985). Olson et al. (1980) have provided a somewhat similar summary of improvement rates by type of theory. In contast to Table 13.2, their summary analysis simply indicated which problem X treatment pairings "yielded some degree of documented effectiveness" (p. 980). While Table 13.2 also indicates such pairings, it provides a more differential assessment of the effectiveness of the therapies listed by virtue of considering the three major "schools" of marital and family therapy, whereas Olson et al. included only 6 of these, plus four non-school-specific modalities of family intervention (e.g., family crisis intervention). Finally, Table 13.2 includes all the "presenting problems" listed by Olson et al. (1980, p. 980) except for "school and work phobias," and also includes three major disorders (schizophrenia, anxiety disorders) and problems (divorce adjustment) not included by Olson et al.

A rating of "3" in Table 13.2 denotes that the efficacy of an approach for a given problem seems firmly established, while a rating of "2" denotes less confidence in the method for the treatment of a given problem, but enough to justify a definitely non-neutral and slightly positive estimate of its efficacy. A "1" is used for those methods that have received at least some (even very) tentative empirical support, but for which the data base is generally too small to warrant greater confidence (e.g., Milan Systemic therapy for childhood and adolescent problems [Tomm, 1982]; Multigenerational Therapy of mixed marital and family problems [Baker, 1982; Williamson, Bray & Malone, 1984]; Bowen Family Systems Therapy for marital conflict [Burden & Gilbert, 1982]; Strategic Family therapy for schizophrenia and other psychoses [Haley, 1980]; McMaster Problem Centered Systems Therapy [Santa-Barbara et al., 1979] and Brief Focal Psychodynamic Family Therapy [Kinston & Bentovim, 1978] for mixed neurotic and psychosomatic child and adolescent problems; and Brief Interactional Therapy of the Mental Research Institute for mixed clinical disorders [Weakland, Fisch, Watzlawick, & Bodin, 1974]). A "0" denoted that the approach in question has simply never been tested with a given population, problem, or disorder. We would like to have added categories of -3, -2, and -1, which would represent the establishment of confidence that a given approach was either of no value or was contraindicated for a particular problem. Unfortunately, to date it is not possible to reach such empirically justifiable conclusions.

We will mention here only briefly those trends in our efficacy estimates that are striking: (1) of the 15 family and marital therapy approaches, 6 have shown at least moderately positive evidence of efficacy with at least one clinical disorder or problem; (2) with the arguable exception (Gurman, 1981) of Psychodynamic Therapy, all the methods with at least moderately positive evidence of efficacy for some problems are highly directive in nature; (3) there are 4 disorders (schizophrenia, substance abuse, juvenile delinquency, marital discord) for which we now have at least moderately positive evidence of the efficacy of more than one method of family treatment; (4) there are 7 disorders for which

at least moderately positive evidence exists that at least one method is effective; and finally (5) outcome research of any sort has been conducted on only 35 of the 150 method × problem combinations (23%), and evidence of at least probable effectiveness (ratings of "2" or "3") has been demonstrated for only 13 (9%) of these combinations. In addition, it must be acknowledged that this summary analysis of the effectiveness of marital and family therapies is essentially of the traditional "boxscore" variety, the weaknesses of which have been considered earlier. Even the repeated documentation of the positive effects of the specific treatment methods discussed in this section of this chapter is not a sufficient substitute for the evaluation of the size of treatment effects. Unfortunately, the size of treatment effects of specific marital and family therapies, or of these therapies as a whole, has not yet been systematically and comprehensively evaluated, though such analyses do exist in the domain of enrichment programs (Giblin et al., 1985; Wampler, 1982b), as discussed earlier.

Although the summary estimates of the efficacy of marital and family therapy shown in Table 13.2 might suggest a greater warrant for pessimism than our preceding substantive discussion of numerous specific studies, such an overall impression would be unduly influenced by our having included in Table 13.2 all of the treatment methods that have not yet been tested empirically. In fact, as a rule, when family therapy treatment methods have been tested rigorously, significantly positive, and at times extremely impressive, outcomes have been documented.

The Outcomes of Family Therapy Training

As the impact of systematic thinking has broadened, the demand for training in marital and family therapy, as noted early in this chapter, has increased enormously. Evidence of the importance attached to the establishment of guidelines and standards for training programs can be seen in many forms, two of which are especially noteworthy. In 1978, the Commission on Accreditation for Marriage and Family Therapy Education was established by the American Association for Marriage and Family Therapy as an autonomous body whose purpose was the development of program training standards and evaluation of centers' applications for accreditation. Second, in 1984, the American Psychiatric Asso-

TABLE 13.2   Overall Estimates of the Effectiveness of Various Marital and Family Therapies for Specific Disorders and Problems

Type of Therapy	Adult Disorders					Child/Adolescent Disorders			Marital Problems	
	Schizophrenia	Substance Abuse	Affective Disorders	Anxiety Disorders	Psychosomatic Disorders	Juvenile Delinquency	Conduct Disorders	Mixed Disorders	Marital Discord	Divorce Adjustment
Behavioral	2[a]	2[b]	1	3[c]	0	3[d]	3[d]	0	3	1[e]
Bowen FST	0	0	0	0	0	0	0	0	0	0
Contextual	0	0	0	0	0	0	0	0	0	0
Functional	0	0	0	0	0	2	0	0	0	0
Humanistic[f]	0	0	0	0	0	0	0	0	0	0
McMaster PCSTF	0	0	0	0	1	1	1	1	0	0
Milan Systemic	0	0	0	0	0	1	1	1	0	0
MRI Interactional	0	0	0	0	0	1	1	1	1	0
Multigenerational: other[g]	0	0	0	0	0	0	0	0	1	0
Psychoeducational	3	0	1	0	0	0	0	0	1	0
Psychodynamic-Eclectic	0	2[h]	0	0	1	0	1	1	2	1
Strategic	1	⎰2[i]	0	0	1	0	0	0	0	0
Structural	0	⎱2[i]	0	0	2	0	0	0	0	0
Symbolic-Experiential	0	0	0	0	0	0	0	0	0	0
Triadic	0	0	0	0	0	0	0	1	0	0

Note. 3 = effectiveness established; 2 = effectiveness probable; 1 = effectiveness uncertain; 0 = effectiveness untested.
[a] = Behavioral Family Management.
[b] = Alcohol Abuse.
[c] = Spouse-assisted exposure therapy.
[d] = Parent Management Training.
[e] = Divorce Mediation.
[f] = Satir (1967).
[g] = Based on Framo (1976) and Williamson (1981, 1982a, 1982b).
[h] = Conjoint Couples Groups for Alcoholism.
[i] = Integrative Structural/Strategic Therapy (Stanton et al., 1982)

ciation issued a major task force report on family therapy and psychiatry, with a major emphasis on training.

The last two decades have witnessed the appearance of hundreds of programmatic descriptions of training and supervisory practices (Liddle & Halpin, 1978) and the clear description of school-specific training methods (Gurman & Kniskern, 1981a; Liddle, Schwartz, & Breunlin, in press; Whiffen & Byng-Hall, 1982). Despite all this, and the emergence of some conceptually very sophisticated models for training and supervision (e.g., Liddle,

Breunlin, Schwartz, & Constantine, 1984; Liddle & Schwartz, 1983), to date little formal evaluation of training practices or programs has been forthcoming (Kniskern & Gurman, 1979). A small number of reports have surveyed the effects on respondents' clinical practices as a result of both general training background and beliefs (e.g., Haldane & McCluskey, 1980, 1981) and participation in specific training programs (e.g., Byles, Bishop, & Horn, 1983).

To our knowledge, there have appeared only five empirical studies of the effects of replicable training experiences on student therapists' acquisition of specific clinical skills (Byles et al., 1983; Kaplan, Rosman, Liebman, & Honig, 1977; Lange & Zeegers, 1978; Mohammed & Piercy, 1983; Tucker & Pinsof, 1984). All five of these studies have examined trainers' acquisition of executive skills (e.g, activity level, variety and specificity of interventions, problem-solving and communication skill, session structuring), two (Byles et al., 1983; Tucker & Pinsof, 1984) have documented enhancement of perceptual-conceptual skills (e.g., use of an inter-personal/systematic perspective), and one (Mohammed & Piercy, 1983) has demonstrated positive changes in trainees' relationship skills (e.g., warmth, empathy, appropriate use of humor).

As Tucker and Pinsof (1984) comment, there are two possible and worthwhile goals in regard to training research. The first is evaluating the extent to which family therapy training programs achieve their goals. The second is to evaluate whether family therapy training programs increase the therapeutic efficacy of their trainees. The first goal is more accessible at this time and has been addressed in the several existing studies cited previously. These empirical studies provide some direct evidence to suggest that some forms of family therapy training accomplish certain training goals.

In regard to the second (efficacy) goal, research addressing that issue is plagued by all of the problems involved in training research as well as all of the problems involved in outcome research. Thus, training research on this issue is enormously difficult to conduct. Although there now exists no *direct* research evidence that training experiences in marital-family therapy in fact increase the effectiveness of trainees, there is some indirect, suggestive evidence relevant to this question. For example, Tucker and Pinsof (1984) provide preliminary evidence that trainees became more active and used a wider range of interventions over the course of training. Pinsof (1979) found that advanced therapists at McMaster also used a wider range of interventions and were also significantly more active than beginners. Shapiro and Budman (1973) found some preliminary evidence that the major factor that families who had dropped out of therapy complained about was their therapists' low activity level early in treatment. These reports suggest that trainees in certain programs become like experts in

other programs, and that the trainees and experts were both less likely to engage in activities (or the lack thereof) that one study found to be linked to premature termination. Thus, while family therapy training research is still in its infancy, some promising developments have emerged recently.

RESEARCH ON THE PROCESS OF MARITAL AND FAMILY THERAPY

Historically, research on the process of family and marital therapy has concerned itself primarily with what occurs within the spatiotemporal confines of the family or marital therapy session. In contrast, outcome research within the family and marital therapy field has concerned itself primarily with what occurs outside of the session limits, particularly after the course of therapy ceases. In terms of these conventional definitions, process-outcome research within the marital-family field attempts to relate what goes on within the sessions to the status of the patients outside of the sessions after therapy is over.

We believe that these traditional definitions are no longer particularly useful for family or marital therapy research, and that a new understanding of process research needs to be nourished. That understanding is not primarily methodological, but conceptual. As discussed briefly in the preceding section of this chapter on the assessment of outcome in family therapy, it involves a new way of thinking about psychotherapy and psychotherapeutic change. That way of thinking might be initially referred to as a process or change perspective. This perspective, in part, has emerged most prominently in regard to individual therapy process research. That area of investigation has experienced a renewed burst of interest within the last several years (Rice & Greenberg, 1984). A critical aspect of the "new process perspective," however, derives from family therapy theory and represents a significant contribution from the family field to the general field of psychotherapy research.

Prior to elaborating this new perspective, we will briefly review the history of process research in the family therapy field and summarize the current state of process research on family therapy. We will then delineate certain new developments within family therapy research that hold great promise for illuminating the process of change in family therapy. We will conclude this section by examining the implications of a family therapy process perspective for the study of all forms of psychotherapy.

Family Therapy Process Research: A Historical Overview

Compared to the field of individual therapy process research, there has been very little family therapy process research. In the only published major review of family therapy process research to date, Pinsof (1981) identified several research groups and individual researchers who had begun to develop instruments to measure aspects of family therapy process. A major portion of that review was a methodological "primer on process research" for family therapy researchers (Sprenkle & Piercy, 1984) and was intended to improve the methodological and conceptual quality of family therapy process research.

In terms of substantive findings, Pinsof (1981) concluded that the small amount of research on the process of family therapy up to 1980 had not yet begun to produce a clear and consistent body of knowledge. Typically, each researcher or research group developed his or her own research instrument, used it in one or two studies, and then abandoned family therapy process research altogether. Researchers had not built on each other's work, and, in general, the methodological quality of most family therapy process research was poor.

However, a few research groups had begun to develop some high-quality process research instruments and were beginning to use them in programmatic process studies to create a solid foundation for future research. Still, no clear process-outcome links had emerged at that time, and the bulk of family therapy theory remained empirically unsubstantiated.

A full consideration of why the rate of development of process research in the family therapy area has been so slow goes well beyond the scope of the present discussion and involves many factors, ranging from the scientific to the economic and political. To some extent, this slow rate of progress and the high rate of family therapy process researcher dropouts must be seen as a reaction to the tremendous complexity of family therapy process research and the early stage of the field's development.

Investigating the process of individual therapy is an extremely complex endeavor. It involves tracking, over time, distinct aspects of the behavior and/or experience of the therapist and the patient. This task presents researchers with difficult and complex methodological and conceptual problems that must be resolved. Over the 40 years that researchers have been investigating the process of individual therapy, a significant number of these problems have been resolved and some clear solutions are emerging (Greenberg & Pinsof, 1985a; Rice & Greenberg, 1984).

In family therapy process research, the researcher has to deal with all of the problems involved in individual therapy process research as well as those unique to the family therapy context. Most obviously, the therapy is more complicated because it usually involves more than one patient. Consequently, the therapist may speak to all members as a group, to different subsystems, or to specific family members. Every intervention, regardless of the explicit target (the person(s) to whom it is specifically directed) has potential impact on all family members present. The therapist may also speak to one subsystem about another (e.g., "Your wife is feeling very threatened by your anger"), which may represent an indirect approach to the primary subject of the intervention.

Family therapy not only represents an additive complication, but actually creates a new interpersonal gestalt that is not adequately addressed by the methods, procedures, and designs of individual therapy process research. The process analysis task in family therapy is more difficult and progress will of necessity be slower, particularly during these early years of its development. The lack of monetary support for such research also retards the rate of progress in the field. Additionally, publish-or-perish pressure for young researchers and dissertation pressure for graduate students diminish the likelihood of engaging in such complex, expensive, and time-consuming research in the early and frequently most productive phases of a researcher's career. Thus, the slow rate of progress in family therapy process research should not be cause for alarm or despair. It is a very difficult domain to research, the field has received minimal financial support, and it is very early in the field's development. Our expectations for achievement must be tailored to the pragmatic and developmental realities of the field.

The Current State of Family Therapy Process Research

Since Pinsof's (1981) review, the status of family therapy process research has not changed dramatically. By and large, most of the researchers and research groups identified in that review have not continued their earliest investigative activities. Benjamin and her colleagues (Benjamin, Foster, Roberto, & Estroff, 1985) have continued developing their very sophisticated model for the Structural Analysis of Social Behavior (SASB) and have applied it to the theoretical analysis of families in treatment. However, they have yet to apply the instruments derived from the model (self-report measures and a coding system) to the specific, quantitative analysis of family therapy process.

Some new researchers have entered the field and produced some interesting instruments and findings. For instance, Piercy, Laird, and Mohammed (1983) reported the development and evaluation of an observer rating scale for the global measurement of the therapeutic skills of family therapists of different theoretical orientations. Russell, Atilano, Anderson, Jurich, and Begin (1984) reported an initial study on a therapist checklist of "intervention strategies" that appeared to be related to outcome. In an intriguing single-session analysis, Stiles (1985) has applied his individual therapist coding system to a transcript of Nathan Ackerman. Like much prior research, these efforts are worthwhile new beginnings.[1]

A major gap that still exists in the field is the lack of attention to the study of nonverbal behavior in the process of family therapy. Certain coding systems, such as Pinsof's (1980) FTCS, identify how often and the way in which the therapist verbally addresses nonverbal family behavior, but no one in the field has developed and implemented an empirical and quantitative methodology for studying paralinguistic (voice quality) and kinesic (posture and facial expression) behaviors. Birdwhistell's (1970) and Scheflen's (1973) initial forays into the

kinesic area have not been developed further and Ekman's (Ekman, Friesen, & Ellsworth, 1972) important work in the area of facial expression of emotion has not been expanded into the area of family therapy process.

Although this deficit is unfortunate, particularly given the amount of attention clinical theorists have devoted to the nonverbal realm, it is understandable. Just studying the verbal behavior of multiperson process is very difficult; examining nonverbal behavior is overwhelmingly complicated and extremely expensive as well. Nevertheless, the dearth of work in this area represents a major shortcoming in the current state of family therapy process research.

Although there have not been dramatic changes within the field, there have been some significant, subtle developments. Several of the research groups identified by Pinsof (1981) have continued their work on family therapy process and have produced some valuable instruments and research strategies. These research groups have a strong likelihood of continuing to produce process-oriented research that will eventually illuminate how family therapy works (or fails). The bulk of this review will focus on these groups and their work. What makes the work of these groups so promising is that it is so closely linked conceptually and methodologically to the new process perspective that is emerging within the general field of psychotherapy research. To set the context, we will briefly discuss certain key elements of this new perspective that are operationalized in the work of these groups.

The New Process Perspective

The problem. The primary task of process research is and must be the identification of significant relationships between process and outcome variables. The new process perspective, which can be formulated as a series of new guidelines for psychotherapy research concerned with the process of treatment, has developed in response to a serious problem. That problem is the failure of most previous psychotherapy research, within any modality, to consistently identify any links between process and outcome variables (Orlinsky & Howard, 1978). Many researchers have lamented the fact that study after study fails to demonstrate that the specific components or ingredients of any particular thera-

---

[1]As part of a major study of the process and outcome of family therapy, Kiesler, Sheridan, Winter, and Kolevzon (1981) developed the highly sophisticated Family Therapist Intervention Coding System, the validity and reliability of which, unfortunately, have not yet been tested.

peutic approach appear to be consistently related to the outcome of that treatment. Typically, this paucity of process-outcome findings leads to assertions about the importance of the "nonspecific" effects of all psychotherapeutic treatments.

Most psychotherapists and many psychotherapy researchers find this conclusion problematic. Our experience and our conviction suggest that what we do in therapy does make a difference to the outcome of treatment. We teach our students day after day to carry out certain types of interventions with certain types of patients because we believe that such interventions will make a difference. Our experience with our own patients suggests that what we do as clinicians is related to our success and failure.

Researchers, coming from this perspective, assert that the lack of consistent process-outcome findings is at least in part due to the fact that the field has yet to find the salient variables, powerful instruments to measure the salient variables, and research strategies that will uncover the links they believe exist in practice. What we are referring to as the new process perspective represents an emerging concensus about the variables, instruments, and designs that are most likely to yield pragmatically and conceptually significant process-outcome findings. A number of the key guidelines of the new perspective are identified below.

Smaller is better. Conventional process-outcome studies have generally used one of two research strategies. The first involves relating some aspect of the therapist's and/or patient's behavior and/or experience at some point in treatment with the outcome of treatment measured at termination. The second strategy is to average measurements of process variables over the course of treatment and then to relate these averaged indices to patient outcome at termination.

These strategies are based on at least three questionable assumptions. The first assumption is that it should be possible to find a linkage between what occurred in therapy at some relatively early or middle point of treatment, for example, the eighth session, and the outcome of therapy after the full course of treatment. The possibility of other intervening events affecting the outcome is too great, unless the event(s) that occurred at the earlier time was so beneficial or traumatic that its effects would overwhelm the impact of subsequent events and

interventions. In other words, the multitude and complexity of events across time will almost always vitiate or negate the long-term effects of time-linked process measures on termination-based outcome variables.

The second assumption pertains to the averaging approach, with which it is hoped that an averaged measure of some process variable over the course of therapy will result in a statistically significant relationship between that variable and some patient outcome variable at the conclusion of treatment. Gurman's (1973b) research on the instability of therapeutic conditions in individual psychotherapy, and research on the Experiencing Scale (Klein, Mathieu-Coughlin, & Kiesler, 1985) suggest that process variables vary significantly both over the course of therapy and even within single treatment sessions, so that mean measures may obscure the variation that may be related to outcome.

The third and most profound assumption underlying conventional process-outcome strategies involves the fundamental process-outcome distinction itself. This distinction was initially criticized by Kiesler (1971) as one of the major "homogeneity myths" of psychotherapy research. A key problem with this distinction is that it treats outcome as a simple, static phenomenon that is best measured in some definitive sense at the conclusion of treatment and/or at some follow-up point after treatment. This view of outcome has been referred to as "The Big O."

Kiesler and others more recently (Greenberg & Pinsof, 1985b; Rice & Greenberg, 1984) have argued for a process approach to outcome that views outcome as a changing, ongoing, and fluid process that is not necessarily best measured at termination or at any other single point. Outcome thus becomes a series, over time, of "little O's." This perspective views outcome as a process. Psychotherapy research then becomes the analysis of the interaction between processes that occur within treatment (conventionally defined as process variables) and outside treatment (conventionally defined as outcome variables). This approach represents a new "process" perspective on psychotherapy research and overcomes many of the conceptual problems embodied in the assumptions enumerated before.

The most critical implication of this new process perspective for contemporary psychotherapy research is that, to borrow from a stance generated by the environmental movement of the late 1960s and 1970s, *smaller is better*. This can also be referred to as the "small chunk" or "episode theory" of psychotherapy research. This approach translates into a research strategy that attempts to elucidate the relationship between process and outcome variables that are more closely linked in time. For instance, the researcher could examine the outcome of specific interventions within a session (e.g., whether the couple stopped fighting after the therapist's interpretation), afer a session (e.g., whether they stopped fighting for the next several days), or within a small set of sessions. This strategy is designed to diminish the likelihood of other events and experiences diluting the link between the process and outcome variables of interest. It involves an emphasis on what Pinsof (1981, p. 735) referred to as "proximal" as opposed to "distal" outcome.

The emphasis on smaller process-outcome units fits the current developmental phase of family therapy research far more appropriately than an emphasis on long-term process-outcome links. Such long-term links may eventually emerge, but they must evolve out of the accumulation of knowledge about the smaller, short-term links. To some extent, this strategy involves the implicit admission that we have been too ambitious (grandiose?) in our research objectives. It is no small achievement within the field of psychotherapy research, however, to be able to demonstrate that certain interventions in certain phases of therapy are consistently related to certain types of patient changes during those phases, independent of the status of the patient at termination. The development of such knowledge would constitute a major advance for the field of family therapy research.

Process as change. Historically, process research has focused on describing the behavior and/ or experience of the therapist(s) and/or patient(s) independent of particular types of events. For instance, sampling within and across psychotherapy sessions has usually been determined by the methodologically based quest for a representative sample of the variable in question. Thus, Accurate Empathy (Truax & Carkhuff, 1967) or Experiencing (Klein et al., 1985) might be sampled during random segments of a session or at regular points over the course of therapy.

This approach recently has been challenged (Greenberg & Pinsof, 1985b; Rice & Greenberg, 1984) as partially responsible for the lack of significant process-outcome findings, and also as partially responsible for the lack of clinical relevance of much psychotherapy research. In contrast to such a methodologically based sampling procedure, the new process perspective argues for a conceptually focused sampling procedure that is directly linked to some type of proximal outcome. Specifically, process research should focus increasingly on "chunks" or "episodes" of therapy in which some kind of theoretically significant change has occurred. As Greenberg and Pinsof (1985b) have argued, this approach also overcomes researchers' disregard for most process research because of its lack of relationship to outcome. Transforming process research into change research establishes a prima facie process-outcome link.

This approach requires the identification of a specific, clinically significant occurrence within a treatment session. Subsequently, the researcher examines what preceded and followed the change in an effort to begin to develop causal, or at least correlational, hypotheses about the events that may be related to the change. The change of interest would usually concern some type of patient variable, but need not be limited to patient variables if other types of variables (therapist or patient–therapist) seem relevant.

The psychotherapeutic alliance. Another major advance within the field of individual therapy process research that is part of the emerging process perspective concerns the alliance between the patient and the therapist. The therapeutic or working alliance was presented in early psychoanalytic literature as a critical component of the therapeutic process (Bibring, 1937; Sterba, 1934). More recently, a number of psychodynamic and psychoanalytic theorists have attempted to refine the concept of the alliance (Bordin, 1979; Greenson, 1965). The most exciting development in this realm has been that within the last decade a number of psychotherapy research groups in North America have developed a loosely linked network studying the alliance in individual therapy. They have developed different instruments to measure the strength of the alliance and have found that the strength of the alliance seems consistently to be related to outcome.

Currently there is tremendous excitement within the psychotherapy research community about the potential of the alliance as (1) a potent predictor of outcome and (2) an organizing and focal construct for subsequent process research. Particularly, there is considerable interest in the possibility of linking specific therapist and patient behaviors to the alliance as an intervening variable that mediates the effects of those behaviors or vice versa. Until very recently, alliance theory and research have not emerged within family therapy theory and/or research.

High-quality, specificity-based instruments. There is a clear consensus within the field of process research that methodological sophistication, particularly in the area of instrument development for tapping process variables, is a necessary requirement for successful process research. Clearly, given all of the foregoing, it is not a sufficient requirement, but it is essential. Simple, unreliable, and poorly conceived instruments developed by researchers who have not familiarized themselves with the methodological and conceptual issues involved in studying social interaction in general and psychotherapy interaction in particular are not likely to produce significant results under any circumstances. This is particularly true in the extremely complicated area of family therapy process research.

Along with methodological sophistication in instrument construction, the field of psychotherapy process research is becoming increasingly committed to the use of process instruments that describe the specific behaviors of the therapy participants sequentially over time. The overriding question in psychotherapy research is still the specificity question (Bergin, 1971), which in its newest incarnation might be rendered as, "What are the specific effects of specific interventions by specified therapists at specific points in time with particular types of patients with particular presenting problems?"

To begin to answer this question, researchers must have ways of identifying specific interventions and the specific effects or reactions to those interventions by patients at specific points in time. Global rating schemes that merely identify whether something occurred in a session, as opposed to where and when it occurred, are of minimal research value in answering the specificity question. They may be useful, however, to identify points in treatment that are likely to be productive targets of a more fine-grained analysis. Similarly, compliance or adherence ratings of manual-based therapies are minimally informative and minimally useful in elucidating specific processes of change in psychotherapy.

A particular shortcoming of such global coding or process analysis systems is that they do not permit sequential analyses of psychotherapy interaction. If we are to study change, we must identify its antecedent conditions and its sequelae. In other words, the scientific investigation of the therapeutic process must be rooted in time. Process analysis systems must permit examination of sequences of behavior and experience that will highlight the mechanisms of change. Global, impressionistic measures that ignore time and do not identify specific behaviors and/or processes may have been appropriate at the earliest developmental stages of the field, and may have limited use as crude indicators of change, but genuine scientific progress will primarily be the product of specificity-oriented measurement systems.

Significant Developments in Family Therapy Process Research
This section examines two research programs in the area of family therapy that we believe hold promise for the future of the field by virtue of their degree of association with the new process perspective delineated previously. A critical aspect of these programs is their programmatic nature.

The Family Institute of Chicago group. Pinsof and his colleagues at the Family Institute of Chicago and the Department of Psychiatry and Behavioral Sciences at the Northwestern University Medical School have developed and evaluated several process predictors of outcome in individual, couple, and family therapy. Additionally, they are attempting to determine the extent to which the same factors predict outcome in those three different therapeutic contexts. A methodological goal of the project has been the development and application of process and outcome measurement packages that can be used across the three clinical contexts to permit comparison without obscuring critical components of each modality. The project is based on a post-hoc extreme-groups design that identifies the most and least successful cases within each context and then compares the "processes" that occurred within the extreme groups.

In regard to the "smaller is better" idea, the project focuses on eight treatment unit blocks. Every eight units all patients undergo a major outcome evaluation. A "treatment unit" consists of a week in which therapy has occurred, which means that the minimum time interval between major evaluation points for any particular case is eight weeks. Since treatment in the project, which is based on Pinsof's Problem Centered model (1983), is not time-limited, a research case may consist of numerous eight-unit blocks.

The extreme-groups design and the use of the eight-unit block are intended to maximize the likelihood of finding process-outcome links. The assumption is that such links are far more likely to emerge within a relatively limited time period, such as every eight weeks, than during an open-ended time period based on the overall course of therapy. The decision to use the eight-unit block was based on the impression that more frequent administration of the complete outcome battery would place too great a research burden on the patients and would jeopardize the therapy as well as the research. Eight units seemed to be the shortest feasible major evaluation interval.

The overall project is designed to proceed in stages. The first and current stage focuses primarily on the first eight-unit block and attempts to relate process measurements within the period to pre-post changes on the outcome measures within that period. The second stage will focus on the second eight-unit block, also taking into consideration the findings from the first block. For instance, a major focus is on what occurs within the second eight sessions in cases that deteriorated within the first eight units but improved after the second eight-unit block. Subsequent stages of the research will focus on subsequent treatment blocks. The overall research strategy resembles what Mishler and Waxler (1975) referred to as the "moving window" that moves progressively over the course of treatment, focusing at any one moment on a particular eight-unit treatment block.

To take an even closer look at the process of outcome, Pinsof (1982) developed the Intersession Report. This instrument is administered to every patient in each context before every therapy session. It takes about two minutes to complete and asks patients to indicate, on a five-point scale, whether their life has improved, stayed the same, or deteriorated since their last therapy session. The patient makes ratings in at least nine areas: physical health, work, attitudes toward self, relations with mates, parents, friends, and so on.

The Intersession Report was designed with three goals: (1) to enable researchers to locate change points in patient's lives in the course of therapy; (2) to identify the direction and locus (life area) of the change at those points; and (3) to begin to provide a profile of when, where, and how change occurs over the course of treatment. The Intersession Report is designed to provide researchers with an outcome "snapshot" before every session. Currently, Pinsof and his colleagues are in the process of analyzing the reliability and validity of the Intersession Report. Initial results are very encouraging.

The primary process measures that will be used in the process predictors of outcome project are the Family Therapist Coding System (Pinsof, 1980) and the Integrative Psychotherapy Alliance Scales (Pinsof & Catherall, 1984). Both of these are new instruments designed to be applicable to family and marital therapy process as well as the process of individual therapy. They permit delineation of the unique as well as common features of the three modalities without obscuring specific components of each modality.

The Family Therapist Coding System (FTCS; Pinsof, 1980) is an observer-rated coding system that uses nine predominantly nominal scales to identify specific verbal behaviors of family, marital, and individual therapists from a variety of orientations (psychodynamic, behavioral, cognitive, etc.). It is one of the first coding systems in process research that incorporates the concept of *reconstructivity*. The FTCS was designed to permit clinically meaningful reconstruction of most therapist interventions from the coded data. The system achieves maximum reconstructivity when all nine scales are used simultaneously. However, to test specific research hypotheses, subsets of the nine scales can be used independently of the other scales in the system. One of the major purposes of reconstructivity is to increase the clinical relevance and meaningfulness of process data.

The validity and reliability of the FTCS has been

tested in several studies conducted by Pinsof and his colleagues and is also being tested at other research centers in North America. In the first study, Tucker and Pinsof (1984) found a number of significant changes in the in-therapy verbal behavior of 19 family therapy trainees over the course of the first year of the two-year therapy training program at the Center for Family Studies/The Family Institute of Chicago. The average interrater reliability of the FTCS, based on Cohen's k, was .63. Specific scale reliabilities ranged from .83 to .41, and all of them differed significantly from chance ($p < .001$).

Analysis of variance on the FTCS data (Tucker & Pinsof, 1984) revealed that after one year of training, trainee therapists, in initial interviews with a family role-played by trained actors, became more active, used a wider range of interventions, focused more on negative affect, and attended more to parental role behavior and the extended nuclear family system. Subsequent log linear analyses of the same data (Pinsof, 1985) revealed a host of significant pre—post differences. Some of them included a greater emphasis on negative behavior, facts, interpretations of family behavior, increased supportiveness, increased specificity about dealing with time, more frequent comments to the parental couple as a unit, and a greater emphasis on the family of origin of the parents.

A subsequent study reported by Pinsof (1985) focused on changes over the entire two-year (pretest, mid-test at the end of one year, and posttest at the end of the second and final year) program for 9 of the 19 subjects in the original study. Unfortunately, due to a machine malfunction, the posttest (end of second year) data for the rest (6) of the trainees was destroyed. Even with such a small N, however, an ANOVA revealed a number of significant findings. Specifically, over the two years the therapist-trainees continued to become more active, more directive, and more focused on the parents as a married couple. They also addressed people more indirectly (talked to one person about another in the session), used more open questions, and focused more on multiple as opposed to isolated events.

The third and major test of the FTCS involved a reanalysis of the raw data used by Pinsof (1979) to establish the methodological characteristics of a precursor of the FTCS, the Family Therapist Behavior Scale. In this reanalysis, Pinsof (1985) used the FTCS to compare eight complete sessons carried out by advanced therapists in a supervisory context with eight complete sessions done by beginning-level therapists in a normal (nonsupervisory) context. All sessions were initial interviews with real patient families conducted at the McMaster University Medical School (Pinsof, 1979).

To thoroughly assess reliability, Pinsof overlapped a third of the two coders' coding assignments in this study. The mean k for all nine scales of the FTCS was .70. Specific scale k's ranged from .93 to .49. All scale reliabilities differed significantly from chance ($p < .001$). Log linear analyses revealed many significant differences between the two groups. Some of the most significant differences ($p < .001$) were that the advanced therapists were more active, used a wider range of interventions, focused more on nonverbal behavior and disagreements within the family, explicitly refocused the discussion more, were more interpretive, focused more on process and communication per se, focused more on the here-and-now, addressed more comments to specific family members, were more personal (more "I" and "You" statements), dealt more with the couple as spouses (versus as coparents), used more open questions, and focused more on the temporal (sequential) relationships between events.

These studies support the reliability and discriminant validity of the FTCS. The FTCS offers the field of family therapy research, as well as the field of individual therapy research, a promising, high-quality, extremely specific instrument for quantitatively describing the verbal behavior of psychotherapists. The instrument is not tied to a particular theory of therapy and can be applied to therapist behavior in different modalities and orientations without obscuring their unique characteristics. The next research step involves testing the predictive validity of the FTCS, that is, its ability to reveal process-outcome links.

The other process instrument developed by the Chicago group is the Integrative Psychotherapy Alliance Scales (IPAS; Pinsof & Catherall, 1984). This instrument derives from an effort to formally expand alliance theory and research into the family therapy field. It also derives from the goal of formally introducing a more interpersonally systemic perspective to the alliance in individual therapy. It consists of three scales: the Individual Therapy Alliance Scale (ITAS), the Couple Therapy Alliance

Scale (CTAS), and the Family Therapy Alliance Scale (FTAS). Each scale consists of approximately 25 to 30 self-report items (each consisting of a statement and an agree–disagree rating) and is designed to be filled out by each patient at the end of a therapy session. In the process predictor's study at the Family Institute of Chicago, the appropriate version of alliance scale (individual, couple, or family) is administered to each patient at the end of every session. It takes approximately three to five minutes to complete.

The instrument is based in part on Bordin's (1979) definition of the alliance as a multidimensional construct consisting of *tasks, goals* and *bonds.* Pinsof and Catherall label these three subdimensions as the *Content* dimension of the alliance. To this dimension they have added the *Interpersonal System* dimension, which consists of *Self–Therapist* (I and the therapist), *Other–Therapist* (my partner, other members of my family, others who are important to me, and the therapist), and *group–therapist* (us and the therapist) subdimensions.

The six subdimensions of the two dimensions form a three by three matrix. Each instrument consists of at least two items drawn from each cell of the matrix. For instance, the item "The therapist is not helping me" comes from the Self-Therapist/Tasks cell for all three instruments, whereas the item "My partner cares about the therapist as a person" comes from the Other–Therapist/Bonds cell of the Couple Therapy Scale matrix. The items from the six cells dealing with the other– and group–therapist dimensions for the different scales are worded slightly differently in order to accommodate the unique interpersonal aspects of individual (no "other" present), couple (one "other" present), and family (multiple "others" present) therapy.

To date, a reliability and a predictive validity study have been conducted to begin evaluating the methodological adequacy of the three Alliance scales. For the reliability study, patients at various points in treatment at the Family and Child Clinic at the Family Institute of Chicago filled out the appropriate alliance scale after two consecutive sessions. The Pearson *r* rate–rerate reliabilities were .71 for the Individual Scale ($N = 18$), .79 for the Couple Scale $N = 17$), and .83 for the Family Scale ($N = 14$) (Pinsof & Catherall, 1984).

The validity study (Catherall, 1984) related one-time alliance measurements of patients in ongoing

therapy with therapist-reported measures of therapeutic progress, based on a measure derived from Storrow (1960). Each of the alliance scales (ITAS, $N = 28$; CTAS, $N = 48$; FTAS, $N = 33$) correlated positively ($p < .05$) with at least one of the five dimensions of the outcome (treatment progress) instrument. High alliance scores for all three instruments were most consistently related to the Stress Management outcome dimension. These preliminary data support the reliability and validity of the IPAS. Further methodological research is currently in process testing the factor structure of the IPAS and evaluating the construct validity of the six alliance subdimensions.

The next step in the predictors study is to attempt to relate outcome changes within the first eight-unit block to the therapeutic processes that occurred within that block. The FTCS and the IPAS will be used as complementary measures to tap the key process variables. A major goal of the research project is to identify the FTCS predictors of the alliance, in other words, to determine the therapist behaviors that are associated with a positive and negative therapeutic alliance in each of the therapeutic contexts.

The Oregon School Learning Center group. As noted earlier in this chapter, Patterson and his colleagues at the Oregon Research Institute have been involved in rigorously investigating the outcome of behavioral family therapy with families with aggressive children for the past 15 years (Patterson, Reid, Jones, & Conger, 1975). Recently, the thrust of their research has taken them into the area of process research. Chamberlain, Patterson, Reid, Kavanaugh, and Forgatch (1984) reported the development of a coding system for characterizing resistant and cooperative behaviors of clients during family therapy sessions—the Client Resistance Code (CRC).

Eschewing global rating scales, Chamberlain et al. (1984) developed the CRC as a seven-category "molecular system to quantify client resistance" (p. 145). Five of the categories pertain to resistant behaviors ("client responses that diverted or impeded the direction set by the therapist"), and two pertain to cooperative behaviors ("responses that followed the direction set by the therapist"). Due to the very low frequency of certain resistant behaviors, their final data analysis collapsed the five resistant codes into one "resistant" category and the two cooperative codes into one "cooperative" category.

In order to test a number of hypotheses about resistant behaviors in the treatment of families with aggressive children, Chamberlain et al. (1984) studied two videotaped therapy sessions from the initial phase of therapy, two sessions from the middle phase of therapy, and two from the termination or final phase of therapy. Using this sampling procedure, they examined 27 cases that included treatment failures and successes as well as self-referred and agency-referred cases. Their basic datum was the *rpm*—the rate per minute of resistant behaviors manifested by the parents (mostly mothers) within the sampled sessions.

As predicted, they found that there was significantly more resistant behavior during the middle phase of therapy when the therapists were actively involved in attempting to teach the parents behavior management skills. Additionally, they found that dropouts manifested significantly higher resistance rates than continuers and that similar differences characterized clearly successful and unsuccessful cases. Agency-referred cases were also more resistant than self-referred cases. The CRC was found to be highly reliable: proportion of agreement was .75 (for all seven codes), and correlations were significant (*p* < .001). The results of this study support both the reliability and the construct validity of the CRC.

Building on this research, Patterson and Forgatch (1985) conducted two studies to test several hypotheses about the behavioral determinants of client resistance. Since the primary determinants that were of interest concerned the verbal behaviors of the therapist, they used a seven-category, nominal scale developed by Forgatch and Chamberlain (1982) to characterize the relevant verbal behaviors of the therapist—the Therapist Behavior Code (TBC), designed to complement the CRC. Reliability data for the TBC were comparable to those for the CRC, .75 for all seven categories.

In the first study, Patterson and Forgatch used the TBC and the CRC (independently) to examine the immediate effects (by means of conditional probabilities) of certain types of therapist behaviors on client's (mother's) resistance within the treatment of six cases presenting with child management problems. As predicted, Teach and/or Confront behaviors on the part of the therapist were associated with

significant increases (beyond base rate) in the rate of the mother's Resistant behaviors. Patterson and Forgatch found moderate support in certain cases for their hypothesis that Support and Facilitate therapist behaviors would be associated with decreased patient resistance. They found no support for their hypothesis that Reframe behaviors were associated with reduced rates of Resistant behaviors.

In the second study, Patterson and Forgatch (1985) examined the causal link between therapist behavior and client resistance. Seven therapist–parent dyads participated in a single-subject, A–B–A–B design. During the B condition, therapists increased their Teach and Confront behaviors; during the A condition they attempted to avoid using these behaviors. The findings provided strong support for the hypothesis that mothers would be significantly more resistant during the B condition.

Patterson and Forgatch (1985) interpret the results of these two studies, along with Chamberlain et al.'s (1984) mid-phase results showing increased client resistance during the middle, teaching phase of therapy, as support for the assumption that therapist behavior is a significant determinant of client resistance. Additionally, they take these findings as support for their notion that effective therapists not only must teach but also must possess intervention skills for overcoming the resistance elicited by their teaching behavior.

Patterson and Forgatch also mention some pilot work that suggests that novice therapists produce more resistant behaviors in their clients over the entire course of treatment than do experienced therapists, which may be due to their lack of skills for dealing with client resistance. Additionally, the report found some evidence that depressed and/or hostile mothers are more likely to increase the level of their resistance as therapy progresses, further complicating the therapeutic task for novice and experienced therapists.

The work of the Patterson group is significant, not only because it is the first programmatic family therapy research that is beginning to illuminate the determinants of client resistance, but also because it is blazing a methodological path for other researchers to follow. In terms of the "smaller the better" issue, Patterson's group is focusing on a specific type of client behavior (resistance) that experimentally and empirically seems to be critically related to the outcome of treatment. They are attempting to examine the antecedent conditions (therapist behaviors) that increase and decrease client resistance in an effort to make their therapy more effective. As such, their process investigations not only focus on smaller, theoretically critical units, but also directly target change.

Their use of specific, nominal coding systems that microanalytically examine the therapeutic process, and their application of those systems with the care and rigor that has characterized all of their previous investigations of family interaction process, makes their work consistent with the new process perspective's concern with specificity and methodological sophistication. Additionally, their development of the CRC offers the field a new instrument for examining client process that seems to hold great promise. An extremely interesting aspect of the CRC, particularly in its collapsed, two-category form, is its similarity to Alexander, Barton, Schiavo, and Parsons' (1976) Supportive/Defensive Coding System, which has revealed a fairly consistent link between family dysfunction and defensive behavior. Alexander et al.'s Supportive and Defensive codes may be tapping the same behaviors targeted by Patterson et al.'s Resist and Cooperate codes.

Currently, Patterson's group is continuing their exploration of therapy process by focusing even more microanalytically on therapist behaviors associated with increasing and decreasing the rate of client resistance. Their focus on a particular type of event and its antecedent and consequent conditions is strikingly similar to Luborsky's Symptom/Context Method (Luborsky & Auerbach, 1969), and to Rice and Greenberg's (Greenberg, 1984) Task Analysis, both of which are central features of the new process paradigm in individual psychotherapy research.

A FAMILY SYSTEMS PERSPECTIVE ON PSYCHOTHERAPY RESEARCH

Recently it has been argued (Reiss, 1984; Ryder, 1984a, 1984b) that while, as the present review suggests, family therapy research has documented the effectiveness of family therapy, it has offered little of scientific value. That is, existing research has taught us little about how families operate and how families change. Ryder (1984a) refers to most family therapy research as "politically motivated" (p. 1), and suggests that "the goal of much outcome

research . . . [has been] justification, not information" (1984b, p. 3). Reiss (1984) argues that what has passed as family therapy "research" has, in fact, been evaluation. We agree with these arguments but would simultaneously emphasize that, in addition to its confirmatory functional success, existing research has also provided at least some limited bases for clinical decision making (Gurman, 1983; Gurman & Kniskern, 1978a, 1978b, 1981b; Todd & Stanton, 1983). The argument advanced by such colleagues rests fundamentally on two much warranted observations and criticisms: First, that insufficient attention has been paid to the study of therapeutic process in family therapy, and second, that, as Schacht and Strupp (1984) have noted in the context of assessing outcome in individual therapy, "researchers continue to employ measures derived from descriptive traditions that are simply unrelated to a theory of change process" (p. 3). In the next section of this chapter, we will examine recent advances and future prospects for the study of change processes in family therapy. Here, we will selectively and briefly address some of the major considerations involved in approaching the perennial issue of outcome criteria in marital and family therapy research.

As a "frame" for what follows here, we enthusiastically endorse Schacht and Strupp's (1984) Principle of Problem-Treatment-Outcome congruence (P-T-O congruence) as a general heuristic guideline for enhancing the conceptual power and vitality of family therapy outcome research. Writing from a systematically informed view of individual therapy outcome measurement, Schacht and Strupp characterize "a researcher's choice among outcome measures as an essentially aesthetic endeavor," which emphasizes "the inevitable role of values and perspective" (p. 4). Their P-T-O congruence principle, proposed as a "conceptual and aesthetic standard for negotiating the complexities of selecting and designing outcome measures" (p. 5), is that:

The intelligibility of an outcome measure (and correspondingly our satisfaction with it) is a function of the similarity, isomorphism or congruence between how we characterize (or measure) the clinical problem, how we conceptualize the process of therapeutic change, and how we characterize the clinical outcome.

[Thus], outcome should be characterized in the same form and units of analysis as the clinical problem . . . the language used to describe both the problem and the outcome should lend itself to formulation of cogent theoretical links between the problem, the intervention process and the therapeutic outcome. This means that simply administering the same instrument pre- and post-treatment does not satisfy the principle of P-T-O congruence, unless the instrument also articulates with the core theoretical and conceptual dimensions of the hypothesized therapeutic process. Frequently used pre- and post-measures such as MMPI elevations or SCL-90 symptom profiles provide only a pseudo-congruence. Such measures have psychometric utility, especially for making comparisons to normative groups, but they lack heuristic value for the task of understanding the nature of psychotherapeutic change and the relationships of process to outcome. (p. 5)

Schacht and Strupp (1984), in adopting their systemic view, note that:

Because psychotherapy doesn't produce just one effect (or even one set of "multidimensional" effects), and because there is no uniform way of measuring effects, there are potentially as many outcomes as there are outcome evaluators. The beauty of a measure truly rests in the eye of the beholder, and choice among outcome measures reduces, in the final analysis, to an aesthetic judgment based on the evaluator's interests, intellectual commitments, social values, clinical theories, and personal visions. (p. 4)

Assessment of Change
Elsewhere in a similar systemic vein, we have written extensively about the need for assessment of change that is sensitive to the irreducibility and nonequivalence of multiple perspectives, and to differentiation between and discrimination among multiple levels of systemic experience (Gurman & Kniskern, 1978a, 1978b, 1981; Kniskern & Gurman, 1981, 1984, 1985). Since our earlier publications on criterion issues in family therapy research are still readily accessible, we will primarily limit our remarks to a brief identification of the main issues involved in the three major domains that must

be considered in assessing the psychotherapeutic change from a systemic stance: perspectives for assessing change, levels and units for assessing change, and the meaning of time in assessing change.

A Perspective on Perspectives
Although others (e.g., Lebow, 1981; Wynne, 1984) in addition to ourselves have written of the need for assessing change from multiple perspectives, only a paucity of research on family intervention has taken on this challenge. The basic rationale for assessing change from mulitple perspectives has been, in our view, best articulated by Fiske (1975), who has argued that a source of data is not a measuring instrument: "instead of seeking to minimize [differences in perception], researchers should seek to identify the unique components of the perceptions and judgments from each source" (p. 23). Such a position is obviously entirely consistent with the self-evident notion that there exists no single "objective" reality, only multiple realities. While discussions of "perspectives," or rather vantage points, usually refer to patient (family), therapist, observer/researcher, and societal views (Gurman & Kniskern, 1978a; Strupp & Hadley, 1977), the major controversies on this matter typically identify patients and therapists as the most problematic parties.

The patient's (family's) perspective.   Patient-generated ratings, like those of therapists, are usually criticized because they are subject to potential (or, some would say, inevitable) "distortion." On the other side, Wynne (1984) writes that researchers "have an ethical responsibility to give high priority to the assessment of desired change as perceived by the family members themselves" (p. 3). Again, following Fiske (1975), we believe that both clinical theory and practice can only be enhanced by further understanding of the complexities and structures of patient (family) phenomenology in regard to both the process and the outcome of treatment.

While pursuing such understanding, there are several important considerations that must not be forgotten. For example, Wynne (1984) notes that, with regard to the family's view of their presenting problem: (1) presenting problems may be described at levels of abstraction and concreteness that vary widely both within and between families; (2) families will vary in how articulate they are in describing their problems, with some being more likely to demonstrate their problems in their behavior than to express it in words; and (3) some families describe their problems in ways they think the therapist will prefer to hear, as a means of testing the therapist, or out of loyalty to the referring person (when that person is not part of the family system).

Lebow (1981) also points to an important methodological issue pertaining to the family's perspective, involving the fact of potentially differing views among family members. Alternative methods for dealing with this problem are to average the ratings of family members, select the report of one family member or of the members of one subsystem, for example, parental, or obtain a consensus report. While the first approach includes data from all family members, it results in a loss of data on differences among members, a potentially important loss of data within conceptual models that emphasizes circular questioning and the evocation of comparative perspectives (e.g., the Milan approach); the second approach by definition precludes certain members' input, but may be quite consonant with other models (e.g., Structural); and the third likewise precludes obtaining individualized ratings, yet may also be consistent with the aims of certain family treatment methods (e.g., the McMaster Problem Centered Model).

Consistent with the urgent need noted earlier for tying research to theory in the family field, the choice among such alternatives to this practical problem involved in patient (family) assessments of outcome should be dictated by attempting to maintain a conceptual congruence between definition of a problem, its treatment, and assessment of its change (cf. Schacht & Strupp, 1984). Who reports on the outcomes of therapy and how the reports are to be understood should "fit" what is being evaluated.

A final illustration of how the conceptual underpinnings of a family therapy method should be tied to the choice of outcome criteria in general, and especially choices of rater perspective, has been noted by Sluzki (1984). He points out that, beyond all the usual criticisms of using patient satisfaction ratings, such ratings may contain an inherent, though rarely acknowledged, bias in favor of the "cozier" family therapies, which emphasize the therapist's affective connectedness with the family, in comparison to family therapies, such as strategic

and brief interactional therapy (Fisch, Weakland, & Segal, 1981), that allegedly downplay the salience of the therapist's personal characteristics. Sluzki argues that, in fact, one might well expect, in such therapies, only a low positive, or even a negative, correlation between patient ratings of general satisfaction with treatment and their observable behavioral outcomes.

The therapist's perspective. The therapist has similarly been questioned as an "accurate" reporter of the outcomes of psychotherapy, even though, like patients (families), therapists offer a unique view of clinical change, which, like the family's view, should be understood rather than impulsively (compulsively?) dismissed. What is truly unique to the therapist's perspective, in comparison to those of the family and observers, external judges, and the like, is that the family therapist (indeed, the individual therapist as well) is simultaneously both an "outsider" to the *family system* per se, and an "insider" to the *treatment system* of family-plus-therapist (cf. Gurman & Kniskern, 1978a; Olson, 1974). As Wynne (1984) emphasizes, "From the standpoint of systemic theories of so-called circular causality, the clinician changes and becomes part of the problem definition as soon as he or she starts to engage with the family"; therefore, ". . . it is desirable to try to specify the presenting problem from the therapist's perspective in terms of the *therapeutic system, not of the family*" (p. 5, emphasis added). Thus, the therapist's judgment of the quality of the family's functioning should not be reviewed as an "external" rating, insofar as the therapist's rating incorporates and necessarily reflects his or her perspective as a member of the therapeutic system.

Levels and Units of Change

Since systems are organized hierarchically, the assessment of change in psychotherapy must tap multiple levels of biopsychosocial experience. On several previous occasions (e.g., Gurman & Kniskern, 1978a, 1978b, 1981b; Kniskern & Gurman, 1984) we have proposed a matrix of assessment priorities that we believe is relevant to the complex decisions involved in choosing the levels of systemic experience to be evaluated in examining the outcomes of any family therapy method. The assessment priorities, in our schema, are a function of various familial units (e.g., identified patient, marriage, family system) and various treatment contexts (e.g., child as identified patient) and family constellations (e.g., one-child family, childless marriage). Thus, if the "patient" improves, but his or her spouse deteriorates in relationship to the therapy, that deterioration must be figured into the outcome equation in order to evaluate accurately the costs and benefits of the therapy. We have also proposed (Gurman & Kniskern, 1981b) a set of guidelines for the selection of assessment instruments at various levels of evaluative inference, along with guidelines for the ideal rating source for making judgments at these various levels. Here, we will emphasize some of the issues involved in selecting appropriate target variables from a systemic vantage point.

As Russell et al. (1983) and Olson (1984) point out, and as the preceding review of the outcomes of family therapy demonstrates, most discussions of the results of marital and family therapy have focused on resolution of or improvement in families' presenting problems or change in identified patients. Yet from a systems perspective, symptoms, presenting problems, and the like cannot be understood adequately without reference to the (usually interpersonal) systems context in which they are embedded. While most, but not all, models of family therapy emphasize that symptoms are both system-maintained and system-maintaining, it is axiomatic among all family therapists that symptoms, presenting problems, and so on are inevitably linked to various dimensions of family interaction. Indeed, it is ironic that it is just such hypothesized links between symptom and system that are rarely discussed in the empirical literature (cf. Russell et al., 1983). And yet, investigations of these very hypothesized links between symptom and system are essential for an adequate empirical appraisal of the conceptual foundations of these treatment methods. In our earlier work (e.g., Gurman & Kniskern, 1978a) we have argued for the routine inclusion in studies of marital and family therapy outcome of measures of change in the identified patient (where one exists), the marriage, and the nuclear family system. Wynne (1984) extends the principle underlying these priorities by emphasizing that "Family variables should be selected because they are indices of family change that are hypothetically *linked to therapeutic change* in a presenting problem or disorder" (p. 8, emphasis added), a position consistent with Schacht and Strupp's P-T-O congruence principle cited earlier, and one with which we agree entirely. On the grounds

of enhancing the bidirectional connection between family theory and family therapy research alone, we believe that routine evaluation of system-level variables is called for in studies of treatment outcome and that these variables should be evaluated in regard to their hypothesized linkage with and relevance to presenting problems.

Despite the aforementioned "axiom" among family therapists that symptoms and symptom variables are inevitably linked, there is a rather broad range of opinion among family therapy researchers as well as family therapists about the degree of centrality to be assigned to resolution of presenting problems. For example, certain family therapists (e.g., Fisch et al., 1981) argue that problem resolution should be the *sole* criterion of therapeutic efficacy, others (e.g., Jacobson, 1985; Todd & Stanton, 1983) argue that resolution of presenting problems should be considered the *most important* or *ultimate* criterion of outcome, while still others (e.g., Gurman & Kniskern, 1981b; Wynne, 1984) believe that while change in presenting problems should always be assessed in outcome studies, it represents but *one among many* important change criteria. These divergent views aside, it appears likely that marital and family therapy researchers will continue to demonstrate a high degree of interest in unraveling the complex, theoretically fascinating, and clinically important strands of the connections between individual symptoms and presenting problems, on the one hand, and system dynamics and the process of therapeutic change, on the other.

Time and the Assessment of Change
Standard therapy outcome designs call for assessment of relevant patient variables pretherapy, posttherapy, and at some point of follow-up. This conventional strategy, however, obscures in significant ways many of the complexities of the meaning of time in assessing change in all forms of psychotherapy. A systemic perspective, on the other hand, allows the researcher to "see" the value of alternative temporal emphases in assessing change. This perspective suggests the need for proximal and distal sensitivity in change assessment.

Proximal sensitivity to outcome assessment refers to the various modifications of treatment goals, hence, of their evaluation, over the course of therapy. Three types of "proximal" goal modifications may be discerned: evolving goals, emerging goals, and reordered goals. *Evolving goals* (Wynne, 1984) refer to the redefinition of "reframing" of presenting problems so commonly observed early in family therapy, in which the therapist attributes a meaning to the family's presenting problem that differs from the family's initial definition or view; for instance, one spouse's "depression" is reframed as secondary to or reflective of a depriving, nonreinforcing, "depressing" marital relationship. Such evolving goals, and the processes by which they are arrived at, have not yet been studied empirically in family therapy (or, it would seem, in any other method of psychotherapy).

Emerging goals are any additional goals deemed worthy of therapeutic attention by any participants in therapy beyond those initially sought. Emerging goals, then, are different from evolving goals in that no new reframing of presenting problem occurs. For example, a couple may enter therapy because of their frequent arguing about their children and, after some significant improvement in that realm has been achieved, may desire help from the therapist in dealing with the couple's ambivalent feelings about how to deal with problems involving their aging parents.

The notion of *reordered goals* refers to the reordering or reprioritizing of multiple initial goals. For example, a couple may enter therapy to stop their fighting about their division of household responsibilities and finances and after a few sessions come to see their mutual sexual inhibitions, identified initially as problematic but not as important as their other concerns, are of greater concern, and may request that the emphasis of therapy be changed.

None of these three types of goal modification, so common in clinical practice, has yet been studied in family therapy research, despite their obvious salience in potentially understanding both the patterning and the process of therapeutic change. Systems theory reminds us that family therapy, like any method of psychotherapy, is not a static process in which fixed goals are defined, and "treatments" are "applied" to them. Rather, therapy is a co-evolutionary process of change, and the assessment of change must increasingly attend to these issues of goal modification and incorporate such changing goals into the profile of outcome measures.

Distal Sensitivity

It is generally recognized that the substantive findings obtained in follow-up of psychotherapy studies are influenced by the timing of the follow-up, for example, that a very brief follow-up may demonstrate treatments effects that vanish, at least statistically, over longer periods of time, or that short-term follow-up may fail to show treatment effects that require longer incubation periods. Therefore, it is often recommended that both short-term and long-term follow-ups be conducted (e.g., Lebow, 1981). The need for such temporal differentiations in assessing treatment outcome was discussed at some length in the section of this chapter on process research in underscoring the requirement for increasing specificity of the links between therapeutic process and outcome.

Lebow (1981) has pointed out that treatment effects at times may be masked or interpreted incorrectly by paying equal (or greater) attention to long-term than to short-term effects in studies of family therapy. Since marital and family therapy not infrequently addresses developmental impasses that resolve without psychotherapy (as is true of individual therapy as well), it is the rate at which resolution of these issues occurs that is central; thus, even in the absence of absolute differences between treatment and matched control groups of such families, "speeding up the rate of change constitutes success" (p. 180), and long-term follow-up may even be unnecessary.

Consistent with our emphasis on the need for improved articulation of theory and research on family therapy, as discussed here in the context of outcome assessment, Lebow (1981) concludes that "In general, outcome is best evaluated at more than one point in time, with intervals between assessments best chosen in relation to the type of problem for which the intervention was conceived" (p. 180). Here, again, we see the relevance of Schacht and Strupp's (1984) P-T-O congruence principle as applied to the selection and understanding of the timing of follow-up of treatment outcome.

Family Systems Theory and Process Research

Similar systemic arguments can also be made in regard to investigating the process of any kind of psychotherapy (Pinsof, 1984). The critical issue is whom the researcher (and, secondarily, the therapist) defines as the patient. If the patient or patients are defined as only the individuals in the office, then process research evaluates only the behavior and/or experience of those individuals, particularly in regard to their responses to the therapist's intervention. If one adopts a family system perspective, however, the patient becomes what Pinsof (1983) has referred to as the *patient system*. The patient system consists of all the human systems that are or may be significantly involved in the maintenance and/or resolution of the presenting problems.

In individual psychotherapy, the identified patient is the only member of the patient system who is ever directly involved in treatment. In conjoint therapies, different members of the patient system may be directly involved at different points in treatment. The concept of the patient system does not dictate who is involved directly in treatment at what point, but rather who must be considered in planning and evaluating the impact of any particular intervention. The patient system concept determines the scope of the therapist's map of the patient terrain, not the roads or pathways that the therapist will use to explore that terrain. Thus, for example, Szapocznik, Kurtines, Foote, Perez-Vidal, and Hervis (1983) found very positive outcomes of one-person brief strategic-structural family therapy with drug abusing (largely Cuban American) adolescents and young adults, who were first treated with a variety of techniques to restructure their internalized representations of their families and were then engaged as "therapeutic allies" (p. 892) to carry out interpersonal restructuring within their families.

A family systems perspective brought to bear on the process of psychotherapy in any modality defines that process as a feedback loop that includes the therapist and the patient system in a circular, mutually influencing, ongoing interaction. To demonstrate how this perspective might apply to individual therapy, consider the situation in which a therapist attempts to help a depressed male patient become more assertive. If the therapist is "successful" in traditional terms, the patient may begin to become more assertive with the member of his patient system (family, close friends, etc.). If the members of these systems react negatively to this change, criticize the therapy and the therapist, and so on, their responses to the therapist's intervention and to the patient's response to that intervention are going to become significant factors that will affect subsequent process. In turn, the therapist's reaction to the patient's reaction to critical patient system members will have a significant impact on the subsequent reactions of the critical patient system members and the patient himself.

Once a family systems perspective becomes a component of the new process perspective, the researcher confronts the not insignificant problem of how to study the reactions of patient system members not directly involved in treatment. Pinsof and Catherall's (1984) Individual Therapy Alliance Scale directly asks patients about the way in which they perceive the people who are important to them reacting to the therapy and the therapist. In essence, they tap the patient's perception of the alliance between the therapist and the patient system members not directly involved in treatment. Other research strategies might involve directly assessing the patient system members' reactions through home visits, phone calls, or the like.

Process research is complicated enough without recognizing the need to consider members of the patient system not directly involved in therapy. The methodological problems involved in studying their contribution to the process of therapy are formidable. At a minimum, however, they need to be put on process researchers' maps of the terrain to be studied. Ideally, process research will go further than this minimum and attempt to actually study what Pinsof (1984) calls the "indirect patient system," a concept about which Haley (1971) had written in different terms. This system critically affects the process and outcome of all forms of treatment and must become part of the process research equation.

FAMILY THERAPY RESEARCH AND THE PRACTICE OF FAMILY THERAPY

Psychotherapy research is done for both political reasons aimed at informing various public-policy decisions and for scientific reasons aimed at improving our conceptual understanding of how people change. While these two sets of aims are sometimes seen as orthogonal, if not downright antagonistic (e.g., Reiss, 1984; Ryder, 1984a, 1984b), it is our view that they are, or should be, synergistic in their common purpose of enhancing the potency of clinical intervention. Politically motivated therapy research is directed toward guiding us in our collective judgments about which existing treatments, on average, are "best" (most helpful) for which clinical problems. Scientifically motivated research is directed toward refining and sharpening our knowledge of human behavior and how it may be changed for the better in order to move beyond our current level of efficacy. Though others will certainly take issue with our position, we believe that the ultimate goal of psychotherapy research is to increase therapy's positive effects, decrease its negative effects, and accomplish both of these aims as efficiently and cost-effectively as possible. The final common pathway that our research efforts must travel, then, is the therapist himself or herself. If psychotherapy research, whatever its multiple motivations, does not have a meaningful impact on practicing clinicians, its continued pursuit must be seriously questioned. In this concluding section, we will consider some of the major reasons why psychotherapy research, including family therapy research, has had so little impact on clinicians and will suggest some partial antidotes to this perennial impasse.

Despite numerous attempts at seduction and mutual courtship, it remains the case that clinicians and therapy researchers have failed to consummate a "meaningful" and lasting relationship, as has been observed, commented on, and lamented repeatedly (e.g., Barlow, 1981; Gurman, 1983a, 1984b; Strupp, 1981). Many reasons for the typical clinician's disregard of, if not disdain for, psychotherapy research have been suggested, for example, identification with charismatic clinical teachers and yielding to the temptations of received wisdom, the existence of training programs that involve de facto education about clinical work and empirical work as independent and nonsynergistic enterprises. There are also several characteristics of the tenor and emphases in psychotherapy research itself, including family therapy research, that we believe severely limit the extent to which therapists take heed of empirical findings and attempt to modify their clinical practices on the basis of such findings. Schwartz and Breunlin (1983) interviewed a number of family therapists and family therapy researchers about "Research: Why Clinicians Should Bother with It." They reported that "Most of the practitioners . . . found most [research papers] to be of little relevance to their work. . . . The picture of research that emerged was of an *inaccessible* domain of knowledge, which might contain something of value, but which usually seemed hopelessly *remote* from the experience of the clinician" (p. 24). This widespread sense among clinicians that therapy research is too removed from day-to-day clinical experience derives from four major aspects of research. These involve clinicians' reactions to comparative outcome studies, the relatively rare appearance of process research, the nature of measures used to gauge the efficacy of treatment, and the conventional manner in which research findings are reported in the literature.

Comparative Outcome Studies

While comparative outcome studies are necessary for "politically motivated" research (Ryder, 1984a, 1984b) to guide public-policy decisions, there are some understandable reasons why they usually fall on deaf ears (and blind eyes) among clinicians. First, as Gurman (1983b) has commented, and every clinician knows intuitively, "What is studied in clinically meaningful . . . research are interaction effects. Indeed, powerful main effects are rare and should be considered highly suspect" (p. 232). Jacobson (1985) echoes the view that "There may be relatively few such efforts in nature, that is, real differences between widely used treatments that would emerge across the entire population of clients and therapists." That is, as all clinicians are aware and systemically oriented therapists emphasize, comparative outcome studies aimed simply at examining the relative efficacy of two or more treatments are usually destined to be ecologically invalid, as their focus is restricted to only a single, decontextualized piece of the therapeutic context called "the treatment." That is, family therapy, like any psychotherapy, involves and is more than "the treatment" in a linearly applied sense. Moreover, few therapists acutally practice the way therapists do in comparative studies. Because of the fact that virtually any widely practiced method of therapy is probably more effective than no treatment, null results, that is, the absence of statistically striking differences on most change measures, are to be expected in comparative studies.

Second, the types of comparative studies of interest to most family clinicians, including those committed to a given method, are not those pitting Family Therapy A against Family Therapy B, but those that are reflective of the kinds of therapist decision making required in clinical practice, for instance, multimodal practice in which medication, individual sessions, conjoint sessions, and the like, may be used in sequence or in combination.

There is a third dimension to comparative outcome studies, or, more accurately, to the interface between such studies and the consumers thereof, that limit their impact on practice. Even if main effects were more common and ecologically valid, and even if findings of "no difference" between treatments were far less common, assuming that clinicians would change their beliefs and behavior based on such studies is, as one of us (ASG) has said, "preposterously naive" (quoted in Schwartz & Breunlin, 1983, p. 25). Simply put, "psychotherapists do not advocate or practice different approaches on the basis of their relative scientific status. . . . As therapists, we are attracted to different approaches on the basis of a large number of both rational and irrational factors. . . The choice of a favorite method of psychotherapy . . . is always very personal" (Gurman, 1983a, pp. 19–20), and, among other things, is likely to reflect an intuitive, and at times consciously arrived at, sense of a "good fit" between the demands of working in a particular way and what we recognize about how we "work" as individuals. This inevitable urge to preserve a strong sense of congruence and integrity between what therapists do and who therapists *are* will always severely limit the impact on practice of discordant research findings.

Yet the clinician who is committed to a given school of therapy is not beyond being influenced by research. The kind of research that large numbers of the committed will listen to is that which created the possibility for enhancing the efficacy, applicability, and disseminability of the therapeutic approach to which, for whatever reasons, the therapist is already deeply and personally committed. Such research will necessarily examine complex interactions among therapist, family, and technique variables as they bear on theoretically and clinically important questions that pertain to given methods of therapy. Elsewhere (Kniskern & Gurman, 1981) we have proposed in detail what we view as some of the crucial within-school questions for many of the most influential approaches to family therapy. As Jacobson (1984) notes, "Conclusions regarding the process of change are possible only with carefully controlled intramodel component studies which creatively combine dismantling, constructive and parametric research strategies" (p. 304).

Process Research

As this chapter makes clear, process research in family therapy is still in its infancy. Yet it is this domain of family research that, when approached

as we have suggested earlier, with direct linkages to outcome assessment, is likely to have the greatest impact on practicing family therapists. While therapists are, of course, concerned with what happens in families outside of treatment sessions, it is what happens within sessions that is most familiar to them. And while, as noted earlier, family therapy process research is more complicated than individual therapy process research by virtue of its involving more than one patient, it is this very complexity, of which clinicians are routinely aware, that may render process research of interest to clinicians.

As we noted earlier in our summary analyses of the current empirical status of the efficacy of the major family therapy approaches, little can be gleaned from most of those outcome studies about what actually occurred in the course of treatment. Gurman has noted that, as a result, "People have to resort to their stereotypic fantasies of what, for example, structural family therapy might have been like in that situation" (quoted in Schwartz & Breunlin, 1983, p. 25).

Our earlier proposal for component analysis studies and process studies within given family therapy methods should not be read mistakenly as encouraging therapeutic isolationism and competitiveness. Quite to the contrary, much of our own work (e.g., Gurman, 1981; Pinsof, 1983) over the last decade demonstrates our personal predilections for and commitment to integrative models of marital and family therapy. In addition to within-school process studies, we believe that the study of common effective elements and mechanisms of change in family therapy, irrespective of their "parent" schools of thought, is essential to further conceptual and clinical development in the field. Just as different families require different therapies and different students require different learning experiences, we believe that different types of therapists will be differentially responsive to different types of therapy research including process research (Gurman, 1983b). Thus, theoretical "purists" may listen more attentively to process research on their chosen methods, while integrative therapists (whose numbers, we suspect, actually exceed those of the purists) may listen more attentively to process research that is aimed at elucidating salient mechanisms of change in marital and family therapy that cut across particular highly preferred and cathected models. Many possibilities could be identified for studying common change mechanisms and processes in diverse family therapies, such as : (1) the induction in family members of a set of perceptions and attributions about their presenting problem that differ from those they initially show; (2) relatedly, the transformation of the family's view of their problem, where clinically appropriate, from individualistic to interactional or systemic; (3) modification of the permeability of channels available for the exchange of information; (4) the creation of alternative modes of problem solving, whether through "direct" or "indirect" intervention; (5) the modification of symptom-related affective arousal; (6) the modification of dysfunctional generational boundaries and other forms of hierarchial incongruities; and (7) the modification of the rates and relative proportions of prosocial and aversive interpersonal behaviors (Gurman, 1984a).

Outcome Measures and Variables

Just as criticism has been directed at recent meta-analytic reviews of individual therapy outcome research on the grounds that the studies included in those analyses were not representative of therapy as it is commonly practiced, the kinds of change criteria used in the typical outcome study have not offered a representative sampling of the kinds of dimensions of change that are of most concern to therapists (if not their patients). We have discussed some of the issues involved in the selection of outcome measures and variables that are systemically relevant earlier in this chapter and elsewhere (e.g., Gurman, 1983b; Gurman & Kniskern, 1978a, 1981b), and we will not belabor our views on this matter here. Suffice it to say, at this juncture, that the kind of research strategy we favor for assessing change in family therapy (and individual therapy as well) requires multiperspective, multilevel, and multidimensional assessment, with the particular change foci of a given investigation derived, in large measure, from a solid conceptual and clinical base, as in Schacht and Strupp's (1984) P-T-O congruence principle. While the interpretive complexity of such a multivariate matrix of outcomes may be substantial, such a matrix, from a systemic vantage point, would be more reflective of "true change," in that multiple realities about change would be represented (Gurman & Kniskern, 1978a). With multiple realities thus represented, the consumer of research would have greater options to allow his or her own values to influence his or her perception of the meaning

of findings from any given study of outcome. In this way, the appearance of such matrices might help to counteract one of the major sources of family therapists' disregard of outcome research findings, as described by Schwartz and Breunlin (1983, p. 27): "Underlying traditional research methods is a belief in an *absolute* reality that can be measured objectively, as opposed to a relativistic belief that the version of reality measured will be a function of one's point of reference and of the degree to which the act of measuring affects the phenomenon being measured."

Reporting Research Findings

The use of such a matrix of change measures would provide a basis for both theoreticians and clinician consumers to construct various multidimensional *profiles* of change that interest them (Frude, 1980). Opportunities for constructing such profiles would be a major step forward in being responsive to clinicians' criticisms of the final researcher-induced obstacle for bridging the clinician–researcher gap under consideration here, namely, the manner in which findings of psychotherapy outcome studies are conventionally reported in the literature. Such matrices point to the inevitable variability of effect of outcomes for given families and family members across response domains and measures.

Likewise, when outcome findings are reported solely in terms of group data based on inferential statistics, the variability of therapeutic response for a given measure is grossly obscured. Group data and conventional tests of statistical significance only tell the reader whether the results obtained are likely to have been due to chance. But the data that matter to clinicians are those that are disguised by group data, for it is not possible to judge from such a presentation the likelihood that a particular client may respond well to the treatment under study. Moreover, such data presentations by themselves do not allow the clinician-reader to judge the magnitude of the differences between two treatments, or between treatment and no-treatment groups.

As partial antidotes to this constraint on the clinical relevance of outcome data for clinicians, several proposals have recently appeared. Possible criteria for clinical significance discussed by Jacobson et al. (1984b) include (1) an index reflecting how far a client/family has moved during therapy relative to control-group families; (2) an index locating the family somewhere in the distribution of change scores achieved by other treated families; (3) an index designating how different a family is from what one would predict by the use of linear regression, based on a pretest score; and (4) an index reflecting the percentage of control group subjects whom the treated family has passed while in therapy. Finally, Gurman and Kniskern (1981b) have suggested the reporting of other descriptive data in addition to conventional group data: (1) the proportion of cases showing clinically significant improvement, clinically insignificant improvement, and clinically significant worsening for each outcome criterion measure; and (2) the breadth of treatment effects, shown as the number and percentage of change criteria on which each case improves, shows no change, or shows deterioration, presented as a series of frequency distributions.

While the approaches noted are obviously not of equal statistical reliability, and while each involves disadvantages and limitations (Jacobson et al., 1984b), we believe that they all deserve serious consideration for use in reporting the outcomes of all studies of psychotherapy, not family therapy alone. Any strategy for the reporting of treatment outcomes that may help to make research findings less mystifying to clinicians, more clinically relevant, and less removed from the language and concerns of everyday clinical practice should at least be entertained thoughtfully.

CODA

As we noted at the beginning of this chapter in tracing the history of family therapy research, the field of family therapy began in contexts in which clinicians and researchers were not only not separated by divergent or contradictory aims, but in many cases were even the very same people. While there is no justification, we believe, for attempting to convert all, or even most, family therapists into clinical researchers, the tension-filled and chronic gap of mistrust between family clinicians and family researchers must be narrowed increasingly if research is to be kept informed of, conversant with, and linked to evolving clinical theory and practice, and if evolving clinical practice is to move beyond received wisdom handed down from one generation

of family therapists to the next. The organization and emphases in this chapter reflect our attempt to review and comment on the current state of family therapy research and on its future prospects in such a way as to underscore the need for continued dialogue and collaboration among family clinicians, theoreticians, and researchers.

In addition, we believe that much of what thinking systemically implies for the study of the process and outcome of marital and family therapy, it implies for the continuing study of individual psychotherapy as well. We have thus taken the liberty of going beyond the artificial boundary of "family therapy research" to note some of the most important ways in which the implications of systemic thinking may also be relevant to individual therapy research.

REFERENCES

Alexander, J. F. (1973). Defensive and supportive communication in normal and deviant families. *Journal of Consulting and Clinical Psychology, 40,* 223–231.

Alexander, J. F., & Barton, C. (1976). Behavioral systems therapy for families. In D.H.L. Olson (Ed.), *Treating relationships.* Lake Mills, IA: Graphic.

Alexander, J., Barton, C., Schiavo, R. S., & Parsons, B. V. (1976). Systems-behavioral intervention with families of delinquents: Therapist characterists, family behavior and outcome. *Journal of Consulting and Clinical Psychology, 44,* 656–664.

Alexander, J., & Parsons, B. (1973). Short-term behavioral intervention with delinquent families: Impact on family process and recidivism. *Journal of Abnormal Psychology, 81,* 219–225.

Allman, L. (1982). The aesthetic preference. Overcoming the pragmatic error. *Family Process, 21,* 43–56.

Anderson, C. M. (1985). Personal communication.

Anderson, C. M., Hogarty, G. E., & Reiss, D. J. (1980). Family treatment of adult schizophrenic patients: A psychoeducational approach. *Schizophrenia Bulletin, 6,* 490–505.

Anderson, C. M., Hogarty, G., & Reiss, D. J. (1981). The psychoeducational family treatment of schizophrenia. In M. J. Goldstein (Ed.), *New developments in interventions with families of schizophrenics.* San Francisco: Jossey-Bass.

Anderson, C. M., Reiss, D. J., & Hogarty, G. E. (1985). *Schizophrenia in the family: A practitioner's guide to psychoeducation and management.* New York: Guilford.

Alexander, J. F., & Parsons, B. (1973). Short-term behavioral intervention with delinquent families: Impact on family process and recidivism. *Journal of Abnormal Psychology, 81,* 219–225.

Aponte, H., & VanDeusen, J. (1981). Structural family therapy. In A. Gurman & D. Kniskern (Eds.), *Handbook of family therapy.* New York: Brunner/Mazel.

Arnold, J., Levine, A., & Patterson, G. R. (1975). Changes

in sibling behavior following family intervention. *Journal of Consulting and Clinical Psychology, 43,* 683–688.

Auerswald, E. (1972). Families, change, and the ecological perspective. In A. Ferber, M. Mendelsohn, & A. Napier (Eds.), *The book of family therapy.* New York: Jason Aronson.

Azrin, N. H., Besalel, V. A., Bechtel, R., Michalicek, A., Mancera, M., Carroll, D., Shuford, D., & Cox, J. (1980). Comparison of reciprocity and discussion-type counseling for marital problems. *American Journal of Family Therapy, 8,* 21–28.

Badenoch, A., Fisher, J., Hafner, J., & Swift, H. (1984). Predicting the outcome of spouse-aided therapy for persisting psychiatric disorders. *American Journal of Family Therapy, 12,* 59–71.

Bagarozzi,D. A., & Rauen, P. (1981). Premarital counseling: Appraisal and status. *American Journal of Family Therapy, 9,* 13–30.

Baker, F. P. (1982). *Framo's method of integration of family of origin with couples therapy: A follow-up study of an intergenerational approach.* Unpublished doctoral dissertation, Temple University.

Barlow, D. H. (1981). On the relation of clinical research to clinical practice: Current issues, new directions. *Journal of Consulting and Clinical Psychology, 49,* 147–155.

Barlow, D. H., O'Brien, G. T., & Last, C. (1984). Couples treatment of agoraphobia. *Behavior Therapy, 15,* 41–58.

Barlow, D. H., O'Brien, G. T., Last, C. G., & Holden, A. E. (1983). Couples treatment of agoraphobia: Initial outcome. In R. Spitzer & J. B. Williams (Eds.), *Psychotherapy research: Where are we and where should we go?* New York: Guilford.

Barton, C., & Alexander, J. F. (1981). Functional family therapy. In A. Gurman & D. Kniskern (Eds.), *Handbook of family therapy.* New York: Brunner/Mazel.

Bateson, G. (1972). *Steps to an ecology of mind.* New York: Ballantine.

Bateson, G. (1979). *Mind and nature.* New York: Dutton.

Bateson, G., Jackson, D. D., Haley, J., & Weakland, J. H. (1956). Toward a theory of schizophrenia. *Behavioral Science, 1,* 251–264.

Baucom, D. H. (1982). A comparison of behavioral contracting and problem-solving/communications training in behavioral marital therapy. *Behavior Therapy, 13,* 162–174.

Baucom. D. H. (1983). Conceptual and psychometric issues in evaluating the effectiveness of behavioral marital therapy. In J. P. Vincent (Ed.), *Advances in family intervention, assessment and theory* (Vol. 3). Greenwich, CT: JAI Press.

Baucom, D. H. The active ingredients of behavioral marital therapy: The effectiveness of problem-solving/ communication training, contingency contracting, and their communication. In K. Hahlweg & N. S. Jacobson (Eds.), *Marital interaction: Analysis and modification.* New York: Guilford.

Baucom, D. H., & Hoffman, J. A. (in press). The effectiveness of marital therapy: Current status and application to the clinical setting. In N. Jacobson & A. Gurman (Eds.), *Clinical handbook of marital therapy.* New York: Guilford.

Baucom, D. H., & Lester, G. W. (1982, Nov.). *The utility of cognitive restructuring as a supplement to behavioral marital therapy.* Paper presented at the annual meeting of the Association for the Advancement of Behavior Therapy, Los Angeles.

Beach, S. R., & Broderick, J. E. (1983). Commitment: A variable in women's response to marital therapy. *American Journal of Family Therapy, 11,* 16–24.

Beach, S. R., & O'Leary, K. D. (1985). The current status of outcome research in marital therapy. In L. L'Abate (Ed.), *Handbook of family psychology and psychotherapy.* Homewood, IL:

Beck, D. F. (1975). Research findings in the outcomes of marital counseling. *Social Casework, 56,* 153–181.

Beck, D. F., & Jones, M. A. (1973). *Progress on family problems: A nationwide study of clients' and counselors' views on family agency services.* New York: Family Service Association of America.

Benjamin, L., Foster, S., Roberto, L., & Estroff, S. (1985). Breaking the family code: Analysis of videotapes of family interactions by structural analysis of social behavior (SASB). In L. Greenberg & W. Pinsof (Eds.), *The psychotherapeutic process: A research handbook.* New York: Guilford.

Benningfeld, A. B. (1978). Multiple family therapy systems. *Journal of Marriage and Family Counseling, 4,* 25–34.

Bennun, I. (1984). Marital therapy with one spouse. In K. Hahlweg & N. S. Jacobson (Eds.), *Marital interaction: Analysis and modification.* New York: Guilford.

Berkowitz, R., Kuipers, L., Eberlain-Frief, R., & Leff, J. (1981). Lowering expressed emotions in relatives. In M. J. Goldstein (Ed.), *New developments in interventions with families of schizophrenics.* San Francisco: Jossey-Bass.

Bergin, A. (1971). The evaluation of therapeutic outcomes. In A. Bergin & S. Garfield (Eds.), *Handbook of psychotherapy and behavior change: An empirical analysis.* New York: Wiley.

Bibring, E. (1937). Therapeutic results of psychoanalysis. *International Journal of Psychoanalysis, 18,* 170–189.

Birchler, G. R. (1979). Communication skills in married couples. In A. Bellack & M. Herzen (Eds.), *Research and practice in social skills training.* New York: Plenum.

Birdwhistell, R. (1970). *Kinesics in context: Essays on body motion communication.* Philadelphia: University of Pennsylvania Press.

Bland, K., & Hallam, R. S. (1981). Relationship between response to graded exposure and marital satisfaction in agoraphorics. *Behaviour Research and Therapy, 19,* 335–338.

Bloch, D. A. (1982, Aug.). Personal communication.

Bloch, D. A., & Weiss, H. M. (1981). Training facilities in marital and family therapy. *Family Process, 20,* 133–146.

Boelens, W., Emmelkamp, P., MacGillavry, D., & Markvoort, M. (1980). A clinical evaluation of marital treatment: Reciprocity counseling vs. system-theoretic counseling. *Behavioural Analysis and Modification, 4,* 85–96.

Bordin, E. S. (1979). The generalizability of the psychoanalytic concept of the working alliance. *Psycho-*

therapy: Theory, Research and Practice, 16, 252–260.

Bosco, A. (1972). *Marriage Encounter: The re-discovery of love.* St. Meinard, IN: Abbey Press.

Bowen, M. (1978). *Family therapy in clinical practice.* New York: Jason Aronson.

Brock, G. W., & Joanning, H. (1983). A comparison of the relationship enhancement program and the Minnesota Couple Communication Program. *Journal of Marital and Family Therapy, 9*, 413–421.

Broderick, C. B., & Schrader, S. (1981). The history of professional marital and family therapy. In A. Gurman & D. Kniskern (Eds.), *Handbook of family therapy.* New York: Brunner/Mazel.

Burden, S., & Gilbert, J. (1982). Stage III marital conflict. *The Family, 10*, 27–39.

Byles, J., Bishop, D. S., & Horn, D. (1983). Evaluation of a family therapy training program. *Journal of Marital and Family Therapy, 9*, 299–304.

Campbell, D. (1976). Quoted in M. Mahoney, *Scientist as subject.* Cambridge, MA: Ballinger.

Catherall, D. R. (1984). *The psychotherapeutic alliance in family, marital and individual psychotherapy.* Unpublished doctoral dissertation, Psychology Program, Department of Psychiatry and Behavioral Sciences, Northwestern University.

Chamberlain, P., Patterson, G., Reid, J., Kavanaugh, K., & Forgatch, M. (1984). Observation of client resistance. *Behavior Therapy, 15*, 144–155.

Cobb, J. P., Mathews, A. M., Childs-Clarke, A., & Blowers, C. M. (1984). The spouse as co-therapist in the treatment of agoraphobia. *British Journal of Psychiatry, 144*, 282–287.

Cobb, J., McDonald, R., Marks, I., & Stern, R. (1980) Marital versus exposure therapy: Psychological treatments of co-existing marital and phobic-obsessive problems. *Behavioral Analysis and Modification, 4*, 3–16.

Cohen, J. (1984). The benefits of meta-analysis. In J. B. Williams & R. L. Spitzer (Eds.), *Psychotherapy research: Where are we and where should we go?* New York: Guilford.

Colapinto, J. (1979). The relative value of empirical evidence. *Family Process, 18*, 427–441.

Coogler, O. J. (1978). *Structured mediation in divorce settlement.* Lexington, MA: Lexington Books.

Cookerly, J. R. (1973). The outcome of the six major forms of marriage counseling: A pilot study. *Journal of Marriage and the Family, 35*, 608–611.

Coyne, J. C., Denner, B., & Ransom, D. C. (1982). Undressing the fashionable mind. *Family Process, 21*, 391–396.

Crowe, M. J. (1978). Conjoint marital therapy: A controlled outcome study. *Psychological Medicine, 8*, 623–636.

Dell, P. F. (1980). Researching the family theories of schizophrenia: An exercise in epistemological confusion. *Family Process, 19*, 321–335.

DeWitt, K. (1978). The effectiveness of family therapy: A review of outcome research. *Archives of General Psychiatry, 35*, 549–561.

Doherty, W. J., & Baird, M. (1983). *Family therapy and family medicine.* New York: Guilford.

Doherty, W. J., & Walker, B. J. (1982). Marriage encounter casualties: A preliminary investigation. *American Journal of Family Therapy, 10*, 15–25.

Erman, P., Friesen, W. V., & Ellsworth, P. (1972). *Emotion on the human face: Guidelines for research and an integration of findings.* New York: Pergamon.

Emmelkamp, P. M. G. (1980). Agoraphobics' interpersonal problems: Their role in the effects of exposure in vivo therapy. *Archives of General Psychiatry, 37*, 1303–1306.

Emmelkamp, P. M. G., & deLange, I. (1983). Spouse involvement in the treatment of obsessive-compulsive patients. *Behaviour Research and Therapy, 21*, 341–346.

Emmelkamp, P., van der Helm, M., MacGillavry, D., & van Zanten, B. (1984). Marital therapy with clinically distressed couples: A comparative evaluation of system-theoretic, contingency contracting and communication skills approaches. In K. Hahlweg & N. S. Jacobson (Eds.), *Marital therapy and interaction.* New York: Guilford.

Epstein, N., & Jackson, E. (1978). An outcome study of short-term communication training with married couples. *Journal of Consulting and Clinical Psychology, 46*, 207–212.

Ewart, C. K. (1978a, Aug.). *Behavior contracts in couple therapy: An experimental evaluation of quid pro quo and good faith models.* Paper presented at the meeting of the American Psychological Association, Toronto.

Ewart, C. K. (1978b, Nov.). *Behavioral therapy with older couples: Effects of training measured by the marital adjustment scale.* Paper presented at the annual meeting of the Association for the Advancement of Behavior Therapy, Chicago.

Falloon, I. R. H., Boyd, J. L., McGill, C. W., Razani, J., Moss, H. B., & Gilderman, A. M. (1982). Family management in the prevention of exacerbations of schizophrenia. *New England Journal of Medicine, 306*, 1437–1440.

Falloon, I., Boyd, J. L. & McGill, C. W. (1985). *Family care of schizophrenia.* New York: Guilford.

Fisch, R., Weakland, J., & Segal, L. (1981). *The tactics of change.* San Francisco: Jossey-Bass.

Fiske, D. W. (1975). A source of data is not a measuring instrument. *Journal of Abnormal Psychology, 84*, 20–23.

Fleischmann, M. J. (1981). A replication of Patterson's "Intervention for boys with conduct problems." *Journal of Consulting and Clinical Psychology, 49*, 343–351.

Fleischman, M. J., & Szykula, S. A. (1981). A community setting replication of a social learning treatment for aggressive children. *Behavior Therapy, 12*, 115–122.

Forehand, R., & Atkeson, B. (1977). Generality of treatment effects with parents as therapists: A review of assessment and implementation procedures. *Behavior Therapy, 8*, 575–593.

Forgatch, M., & Chamberlain, P. (1982). *The therapist behavior code.* Unpublished instrument, Oregon Social Learning Center, Eugene, OR.

Foster, S., & Gurman, A. (1985). Social change and couples therapy. In C. Nadelson & M. Palonsky (Eds.), *Marriage and divorce: Contemporary perspectives.* New York: Guilford.

Framo, J. L. (Ed.). (1972). *Family interaction: A dialogue between family researchers and family therapists.* New York: Springer.

Framo, J. L. (1976). Family of origin as a therapeutic resource for adults in marital and family therapy: You can and should go home again. *Family Process, 15,* 193–210.

Friedman, A. S. (1975). Interaction of drug therapy with marital therapy in depressive patients. *Archives of General Psychiatry, 32,* 619–637.

Frude, N. (1980). Methodological problems in the evaluation of family therapy. *Journal of Family Therapy, 2,* 29–44.

Garrigan, J. J., & Bambrick, A. F. (1975). Short term family therapy with emotionally disturbed children. *Journal of Marriage and Family Counseling, 1,* 379–385.

Garrigan, J. J., & Bambrick, A. (1977). Family therapy for disturbed children: Some experimental results in special education. *Journal of Marriage and Family Counseling, 3,* 83–93.

Garrigan, J. J., & Bambrick, A. F. (1979). New findings in research on go-between process. *International Journal of Family Therapy, 1,* 76–85.

Gartner, R. B., Fulmer, R. H., Weinshel, M., & Goldklank, S. (1978). The family life cycle: Developmental crises and their structural impact on families in a community mental health center. *Family Process, 17,* 47–58.

Giblin, P., Sprenkle, D., & Sheehan, R. (1985). Enrichment outcome research: A meta-analysis of premarital, marital and family findings. *Journal of Marital and Family Therapy, 11,* 257–271.

Glick, I. D., & Clarkin, J. F. (1985). *Inpatient family intervention for affective disorders.* Unpublished manuscript, Cornell University Medical Center.

Girodo, M., Stein, S. J., & Dotzenroth, S. E. (1980). The effects of communication skills training and contracting on marital relations. *Behavioral Engineering, 6,* 61–76.

Glass, G., McGaw, B., & Smith, M. (1981). *Meta-analysis in social research.* Beverly Hills, CA: Sage.

Goldstein, M. J. (1984, Jan.). *Family composition and other structural/contextual co-variates.* Paper presented at the NIMH State of the Art Conference on Family Therapy Research, Bethesda, MD.

Goldstein M. J., Rodnick, E. H., Evans, J. R., May, P. R. A., & Steinberg, M. R. (1978). Drug and family therapy in the aftercare of acute schizophrenia. *Archives of General Psychiatry, 35,* 1169–1177.

Gordon, S., & Davidson, N. (1981). Behavioral parent training. In A. Gurman & D. Kniskern (Eds.), *Handbook of family therapy.* New York: Brunner/Mazel.

Greenberg, L. S. (1984). Task analysis: The general approach. In L. Rice & L. Greenberg (Eds.), *Patterns of change.* New York: Guilford.

Greenberg, L., & Pinsof, W. (Eds.). (1985a). *The psychotherapeutic process: A research handbook.* New York: Guilford.

Greenberg, L., & Pinsof, W. (1985b). Process research: Current trends and future perspectives. In L. Greenberg & W. Pinsof (Eds.), *The psychotherapeutic process: A research handbook.* New York: Guilford.

Greene, B. L., Lee, R. R., & Lustig, N. (1973). Treatment structured distance as a maneuver in marital therapy. *Family Coordinator, 20,* 15–22.

Greenson, R. R. (1965). The working alliance and the transference neurosis. *Psychoanalytic Quarterly, 34,* 155–181.

Greer, S. E., & D'Zurilla, T. J. (1975). Behavioral approaches to marital discord and conflict. *Journal of Marriage and Family Counseling, 1,* 299–315.

Guerney, B. G. (1977). *Relationship enhancement.* San Francisco: Jossey-Bass.

Gurman, A. S. (1971). Group marital therapy: Clinical and empirical implications for outcome research. *International Journal of Group Psychotherapy, 21,* 174–189.

Gurman, A. S. (1973a). The effects and effectiveness of marital therapy: A review of outcome research. *Family Process, 12,* 145–170.

Gurman, A. S. (1973b). Instability of therapeutic conditions in psychotherapy. *Journal of Counseling Psychology, 20,* 16–24.

Gurman, A. S. (1975). Some therapeutic implications of marital therapy research. In A. Gurman & D. Rice (Eds.), *Couples in conflict.* New York: Jason Aronson.

Gurman, A. S. (1978). Contemporary marital therapies: A critique and comparative analysis of psychodynamic, behavioral and systems theory approaches. In T. Paolino & B. McCrady (Eds.), *Marriage and marital therapy.* New York: Brunner/Mazel.

Gurman, A. S. (1981). Integrative marital therapy: Toward the development of an interpersonal approach. In S. Budman (Ed.), *Forms of brief therapy.* New York: Guilford.

Gurman, A. S. (1983a, July). *Psychotherapy research and the practice of psychotherapy.* Presidential Address, Society for Psychotherapy Research, Sheffield, England.

Gurman, A. S. (1983b). Family therapy research and the "new epistemology." *Journal of Marital and Family Therapy, 9,* 227–234.

Gurman, A. S. (1984a, Jan.) *Issues in the specification of family therapy interventions.* Paper presented at the NIMH State of the Art Conference on Family Therapy Research, Bethesda, MD.

Gurman, A. S. (1984b). Analogue research and the family therapist. *Family Process, 24,* 341–345.

Gurman, A. S. (1985). *Casebook of marital therapy.* New York: Guilford.

Gurman, A. S., & Klein, M. H. (1980). The treatment of women in marital and family conflict: Recommendations for outcome evaluation. In A. Brodsky & R. Hare-Mustin (Eds.), *Research on psychotherapy with women.* New York: Guilford.

Gurman, A. S., & Kniskern, D. P. (1977). Enriching research on marital enrichment programs. *Journal of Marriage and Family Counseling, 3,* 3–11.

Gurman, A. S., & Kniskern, D. P. (1978a). Deterioration in marital and family therapy: Empirical, clinical and conceptual issues. *Family Process, 17,* 3–20.

Gurman, A. S., & Kniskern, D. P. (1978b). Research on marital and family therapy: Progress, perspective and prospect. In S. Garfield & A. Bergin (Eds.), *Handbook of psychotherapy and behavior change: An empirical analysis* (2nd ed.). New York: Wiley.

Gurman, A. S., & Kniskern, D. P. (1978c). Behavioral marriage therapy: II. Empirical perspective. *Family Process, 17,* 139–148.

Gurman, A. S., & Kniskern, D. P. (1978d). Technolatry,

methodolatry, and the results of family therapy. *Family Process, 17,* 275–281.

Gurman, A. S., & Kniskern, D. P. (1979a). The outcomes of family therapy: Implications for training and practice. In G. Berenson & H. White (Eds.), *Annual review of family therapy, 1978.* New York: Human Sciences Press.

Gurman, A. S., & Kniskern, D. P. (1979b). Marital therapy and/or family: What's in a name? *AAMFT Newsletter, 10*(3), 1, 5–8.

Gurman, A. S., & Kniskern, D. P. (1981a). *Handbook of family therapy.* New York: Brunner/Mazel.

Gurman, A. S., & Kniskern, D. P. (1981b). Family therapy outcome research: Knowns and unknowns. In A. Gurman & D. Kniskern (Eds.), *Handbook of family therapy.* New York: Brunner/Mazel.

Gurman, A. S., & Kniskern, D. P. (1985). Individual marital therapy: Have reports of your death been somewhat exaggerated? *Family Process.*

Hafner, R. J. (1977). The husbands of agoraphobic women and their influence on treatment outcome. *British Journal of Psychotherapy, 131,* 289–294.

Hafner, R. J. (1979). Agoraphobic women married to abnormally jealous men. *British Journal of Medical Psychology, 52,* 99–104.

Hafner, R. J. (1985). Marital therapy for agoraphobia. In N. S. Jacobson & A. S. Gurman (Eds.), *Clinical handbook of marital therapy.* New York: Guilford.

Hafner, R. J., Badenoch, A., Fisher, J., & Swift, H. (1984). Spouse-aided versus individual therapy in persisting psychiatric disorders: A systematic comparison. *Family Process, 22,* 385–399.

Hahlweg, K., & Markman, H. J. (1983, Dec.). *The effectiveness of behavioral marital therapy: Empirical status of behavior techniques in preventing and alleviating marital distress.* Paper presented at the annual meeting of the Association for the Advancement of Behavior Therapy, Washington, DC.

Hahlweg, K., Schindler, L., Revenstorf, D. (1982). Treatment of marital distress: Comparing formats and modalities. *Advances in Behaviour Research and Therapy, 4,* 57–74.

Hahlweg, K., Schindler, L., Revenstorf, D., & Brengelmann, J. C. (1984). The Munich marital therapy study. In K. Hahlweg & N. S. Jacobson (Eds.), *Marital interaction: Analysis and modification.* New York: Guilford.

Haldane, D., & McCluskey, U. (1980). Working with couples and families: Experience of training, consultation and supervision. *Journal of Family Therapy, 2,* 163–179.

Haldane, D., & McCluskey, U. (1981). Working with couples: Psychiatrists, clinical psychologists and social workers compared. *Journal of Family Therapy, 3,* 363–388.

Haley, J. (1971). A review of the family therapy field. In J. Haley (Ed.), *Changing families.* New York: Grund & Stratton.

Haley, J. (1976). *Problem solving therapy.* San Francisco: Jossey-Bass.

Haley, J. (1978). Ideas which handicap therapists. In M. Berger (Ed.), *Beyond the double bind.* New York: Brunner/Mazel.

Haley, J. (1980). *Leaving Home: The therapy of disturbed young people.* New York: McGraw-Hill.

Hof, L., & Miller, W. R. (1981). *Marriage enrichment: Philosophy, process and program.* Bowie, MD: R. Brady Co.

Hoffman, L. (1981). *Foundations of family therapy.* New York: Basic Books.

Hogarty, G. E., Goldberg, S. C., & Schooler, N. R. (1974). Drug and sociotherapy in the aftercare of schizophrenic patients. *Archives of General Psychiatry, 31,* 609–618.

Hsu, L. K. G. (1980). Outcome of anorexia nervosa: A review of the literature. *Archives of General Psychiatry, 37,* 1041–1046.

Jacobson, N. S. (1977). Problem-solving and contingency contracting in the treatment of marital discord. *Journal of Consulting and Clinical Psychology, 45,* 92–100.

Jacobson, N. S. (1978a). Specific and nonspecific factors in the effectiveness of a behavioral approach to the treatment of marital discord. *Journal of Consulting and Clinical Psychology, 46,* 442–452.

Jacobson, N. S. (1978b). A review of research on the effectiveness of marital therapy. In T. Paolino & B. McCrady (Eds.), *Marriage and marital therapy.* New York: Brunner/Mazel.

Jacobson, N. S. (1979). Behavioral treatments for marital discord: A critical appraisal. In M. Hersen, R. Eisler, & P. Miller (Eds.), *Progress in behavior modification* (Vol. 7). New York: Academic Press.

Jacobson, N. S. (1984). A component analysis of behavioral marital therapy: The relative effectiveness of behavior exchange and communication/problem-solving training. *Journal of Consulting and Clinical Psychology, 52,* 295–305.

Jacobson, N. S. (1985). Family therapy outcome research: Potential pitfalls. *Journal of Marital and Family Therapy, 11,* 149–158.

Jacobson, N. S, & Follette, W. C. (1985). Clinical significance of improvement resulting from two behavioral marital therapy components. *Behavior Therapy.*

Jacobson, N. S., Follette, W. C., & Elwood, R. W. (1984a). Outcome research on behavioral marital therapy: A methodological and conceptual reappraisal. In K. Hahlweg & N. Jacobson (Eds.), *Marital interaction: Analysis and modification.* New York: Guilford.

Jacobson, N. S., Follette, W. C., & Revenstorf, D. (1984b). Psychotherapy outcome research: Methods for reporting variability and evaluating clinical significance. *Behavior Therapy, 15,* 336–352.

Jacobson, N. S., Follette, W. C., Revenstorf, D., Baucom, D. H., Hahlweg, K., & Margolin, G. (1984c). Variability in outcome and clinical significance of behavioral marital therapy: A reanalysis of outcome data. *Journal of Consulting and Clinical Psychology, 52,* 497–504.

Jacobson, N. S., & Gurman, A. S. (Eds.). (1986). *Clinical Handbook of Marital Therapy.* New York: Guilford.

Jacobson, N. S., & Margolin, G. (1979). *Marital therapy: Strategies based on several learning and behavior exchange principles.* New York: Brunner/Mazel.

Jacobson, N. S., & Martin, B. (1976). Behavioral marriage therapy: Current status. *Psychological Bulletin, 83,* 540–556.

Jacobson, N. S., & Weiss, R. L. (1978). Behavioral marriage therapy: III. The contents of Gurman et al. may be hazardous to our health. *Family Process, 17*, 149–164.

Janzen, C. (1977). Families in the treatment of alcoholism. *Journal of Studies on Alcohol, 38*, 114–130.

Joanning, H. (1982). The long-term effects of the couple communication program. *Journal of Marital and Family Therapy, 8*, 463–468.

Johnson, S. M., & Greenberg, L. S. (1985a). Differential effects of experiential and problem-solving interventions in resolving marital conflict. *Journal of Consulting and Clinical Psychology, 53*, 175–184.

Johnson, S. M., & Greenberg, L. S. (1985b). Emotionally focused couples therapy: An outcome study. *Journal of Marital and Family Therapy, 11*.

Kaplan, S., Rosman, B., Liebman, R., & Honig, P. (1977). The log as a behavioral measure in a program to train pediatric residents in child psychiatry. *Speical Interest Group/Health Profession Education Bulletin*.

Kaufman, E., & Kaufman, P. N. (Eds.). (1979). *Family therapy of drug and alcohol abuse*. New York: Gardner.

Kazdin, A. E. (1984). Treatment of conduct disorders. In J. Williams & R. Spitzer (Eds.), *Psychotherapy research: Where are we and where should we go?* New York: Guilford.

Keeney, B. P. (1983). *The aesthetics of change*. New York: Guilford.

Keeney, B. P., & Sprenkle, D. (1982). Ecosystemic epistemology: Critical implications for the aesthetics and pragmatics of family therapy. *Family Process, 21*, 1–19.

Keith, S. J., & Matthews, S. M. (1984). "What works with what?": Schizophrenia. In J. B. Williams & R. Spitzer (Eds.), *Psychotherapy research: Where are we and where should we go?* New York: Guilford.

Kiesler, D. J. (1971). Experimental designs in psychotherapy research. In A. Bergin & S. Garfield (Eds.), *Handbook of psychotherapy and behavior change: An empirical analysis*. New York: Wiley.

Kiesler, D. J., Sheridan, M. J., Winter, J. E., & Kolevzon, M. S. (1981). *Family Therapist Intervention Coding System (FTICS)*. Unpublished manuscript, Family Institute of Virginia.

Kinston, W., & Bentovim, A. (1978). Brief focal family therapy when the child is the referred patient. 2: Methodology and results. *Journal of Child Psychology and Psychiatry, 19*, 119–143.

Klein, M., & Mathieu-Coughlin, P., & Kiesler, D. J. (1985). The experiencing scales. In L. Greenberg & W. Pinsof (Eds.), *The psychotherapeutic process: A research handbook*. New York: Guilford.

Klein, N. C., Alexander, J. F., & Parsons, B. V. (1977). Impact of family systems intervention on recidivism and sibling delinquency: A model of primary prevention and program evaluation. *Journal of Consulting and Clinical Psychology, 45*, 469–474.

Klein, M. H., & Gurman, A. S. (1980). Ritual and reality: Some clinical implications of research designs. In L. Rehm (Ed.), *Behavior therapy for depression*. New York: Academic Press.

Kniskern, D. P. (1975, June). *Research prospects and perspectives in family therapy*. Paper presented at the Annual Meeting of the Society for Psychotherapy Research, Boston.

Kniskern, D. P. (1983). The new wave is all wet. *Family Therapy Networker, 7*, 38, 60–62.

Kniskern, D. P., & Gurman, A. S. (1979). Research on training in marriage and family therapy: Status, issues and trends. *Journal of Marital and Family Therapy, 5*, 83–94.

Kniskern, D. P., & Gurman, A. S. (1981). Advances and prospects for family therapy research. In J. P. Vincent (Ed.), *Advances in family intervention, assessment and theory* (Vol. 2). Greenwich, CT: JAI Press.

Kniskern, D. P., & Gurman, A. S. (1984). Future directions for family therapy research. In A. Jurich & D. Bagarozzi (Eds.), *Marital and family therapy: New directions in theory, practice and research*. New York: Human Sciences Press.

Kniskern, D. P., & Gurman, A. S. (1985). A marital and family therapy perspective on deterioration in psychotherapy. In D. Mays & C. Franks (Eds.), *Negative effects in psychotherapy and what to do about it*. New York: Springer.

Kuhn, T. S. (1970). *The structure of scientific revolutions*. (2nd ed.). Chicago: University of Chicago Press.

L'Abate, L. (1981). Skill training programs for couples and families. In A. Gurman & D. Kniskern (Eds.), *Handbook of family therapy*. New York: Brunner/Mazel.

Landman, J. T., & Davies, R. M. (1982). Psychotherapy outcome: Smith and Glass' conclusions stand up under scrutiny. *American Psychologist, 37*, 504–546.

Lange, A., & Zeegers, W. (1978). Structured training for behavioral therapy: Methods and evaluation. *Behavioral Analysis and Modification, 2*, 211–225.

Lebedun, M. (1970). Measuring movement in group marital counseling. *Social Casework, 51*, 35–43.

Lebow, J. (1981). Issues in the assessment of outcome in family therapy. *Family Process, 20*, 167–188.

Leff, J. (1983, July). *A followup of the London schizophrenia project*. Paper presented at the Society for Psychotherapy Research, Sheffield, England.

Leff, J., Kuipers, L., Berkowitz, R., Eberlein-Vries, R., & Sturgeon, D. (1982). A controlled trial of social intervention in the families of schizophrenic patients. *British Journal of Psychiatry, 141*, 121–134.

Lester, M. E., & Doherty, W. J. (1983). Couples' long-term evaluations of their marriage encounter experience. *Journal of Marital and Family Therapy, 9*, 183–188.

Levant, R. F. (1983). *Client-centered skills training programs for the family: A review of the literature*. Unpublished manuscript, Boston University.

Levant, R. F. (1976, May). *Toward a counseling psychology of the family: Psychological-educational and skills training programs*. Unpublished manuscript, Boston University.

Lieberman, R. P. (1976, May). Personal communication.

Liberman, R., Levine, J., Wheeler, E., Sanders, N., & Wallace, C. J. (1976). Marital therapy in groups: A comparative evaluation of behavioral and interaction formats. *Acta Psychiatrica Scandinavica, 266*, 1–34.

Liddle, H. A., Breunlin, D. C., Schwartz, R. C., & Constantine, J. A. (1984). Training family therapy supervisors: Issues of content, form and context. *Journal of Marital and Family Therapy, 10*, 139–150.

Liddle, H. A., & Halpin, R. (1978). Family therapy training and supervision literature: A comparative review. *Journal of Marriage and Family Counseling, 4*, 77–98.

Liddle, H. A., & Schwartz, R. C. (1983). Live supervision/consultation: Conceptual and pragmatic guidelines for family therapy trainees. *Family Process, 22*, 477–490.

Liddle, H. A., Schwartz, R., & Breunlin, D. (Eds.). (1985). *Family therapy training.* New York: Guilford.

Lidz, T., Cornelison, A. R., Fleck, S., & Terry, D. (1957). The intrafamilial environment of schizophrenic patients: II. Marital schism and marital skew. *American Journal of Psychiatry, 114*, 241–248.

Linehan, K. S., & Rosenthal, T. L. (1979). Current behavioral approaches to marital and family therapy. *Advances in Behaviour Research and Therapy, 2*, 99–143.

Locke, H. J., & Wallace, K. M. (1959). Short marital-adjustment and prediction tests: Their reliability and validity. *Marriage and Family Living, 21*, 251–255.

Luber, R. F. (1978). Teaching models in marital therapy: A review of research issues. *Behavior Modification, 2*, 77–91.

Luborsky, L., & Auerbach, A. H. (1969). The symptom-context method: Quantitative studies of symptom formation in psychotherapy. *Journal of the American Psychoanalytic Association, 17*, 68–99.

Mace, D., & Mace, V. (1976). Marriage enrichment: A preventative group approach in couples. In D. Olson (Ed.), *Treating relationships.* Lake Mills, IA: Graphic.

Madanes, C. (1981). *Strategic family therapy.* San Francisco: Jossey-Bass.

Manicas, P., & Secord, P. (1983). Implications for psychology of the new philosophy of science. *American Psychologist, 38*, 399–413.

Margolin, G., Talovic, S., Fernandez, V., & Onorato, R. (1983). Sex role considerations and behavioral marital therapy: Equal does not mean identical. *Journal of Marital and Family Therapy, 9*, 131–145.

Masten, A. S. (1979). Family therapy as a treatment for children: A critical review of outcome research. *Family Process, 18*, 323–335.

Mathews, A., Teasdale, J., Munby, M., Johnston, D., & Shaw, P. A. (1977). Home-based treatment programme for agoraphobia. *Behavior Therapy, 8*, 915–924.

McLean, P. D., Ogston, K., & Grauer, L. (1973). Behavioral approach to the treatment of depression. *Journal of Behavior Therapy and Experimental Psychiatry, 4*, 323–330.

Mehlman, S. K., Baucom, D. H., & Anderson, D. (1983). Effectiveness of cotherapists versus single therapists and immediate versus delayed treatment in behavioral marital therapy. *Journal of Consulting and Clinical Psychology, 51*, 258–266.

Merkel, H. (Chair). (1983). *Research implications of the new epistemologies: A highly speculative, pragmatically reprehensible, aesthetically noxious leap into the future.* Panel presented at the 41st Annual Conference of the American Association for Marriage and Family Therapy, San Francisco.

Miller, S., Nunnally, E. W., & Wackman, D. B. (1977). *Minnesota Couple Communication Program.* Minneapolis: Interpersonal Communication Programs.

Milton, F., & Hafner, R. J. (1979). The outcome of behavior therapy for agoraphobia in relation to marital adjustment. *Archives of General Psychiatry, 36*, 907–911.

Minuchin, S. (1974). *Families and family therapy.* Cambridge, MA: Harvard University Press.

Minuchin, S., Baker, L., Rosman, B., Liebman, R., Milman, L., & Todd, T. (1975). A conceptual model of psychosomatic illness in children. *Archives of General Psychiatry, 32*, 1031–1038.

Minuchin, S., & Fishman, H. C. (1981). *Techniques of family therapy.* Cambridge, MA: Harvard University Press.

Minuchin, S., Rosman, B., & Baker, L. (1978). *Psychosomatic families.* Cambridge, MA: Harvard University Press.

Mishler, E., & Waxler, N. (1975). The sequential patterning of interaction in normal and schizophrenic families. *Family Process, 14*, 17–50.

Mohammed, Z., & Piercy, F. (1983). The effects of two methods of training and sequencing on structuring and relationship skills of family therapists. *American Journal of Family Therapy, 11*, 64–71.

Morawetz, A., & Walker, G. (1984). *Brief therapy with single-parent families.* New York: Brunner/Mazel.

Nichols, W., & Everett, C. (1985). *Family therapy: An integrative approach.* New York: Guilford.

O'Dell, S. (1974). Training parents in behavior modification. *Psychological Bulletin, 81*, 418–433.

O'Farrell, T. J., Cutter, H. S. G., & Floyd, F. J. (1985). Evaluating behavioral marital therapy for male alcoholics: Effects on marital adjustment and communication from before to after treatment. *Behavior Therapy, 16*, 147–167.

Olson, D. H. (1974). *Insiders' and outsiders' views of relationships: Research strategies.* Paper presented at the Symposium on Close Relationships, University of Massachusetts.

Olson, D. H. (1984, Jan.). *Outcome variables and issues in family therapy research.* Paper presented at the NIMH State of the Art Conference on Family Therapy Research, Bethesda, MD.

Olson, D. H., Russell, C. S., & Sprenkle, D. H. (1980). Marital and family therapy: A decade review. *Journal of Marriage and the Family, 42*, 973–994.

Orlinsky, D. E., & Howard, K. I. (1978). The relation of process to outcome in psychotherapy. In S. Garfield & A. Bergin (Eds.), *Handbook of psychotherapy and behavior change: An empirical analysis* (2nd ed.). New York: Wiley.

Parsons, B. V., & Alexander, J. F. (1973). Short term family intervention: A therapy outcome study. *Journal of Consulting and Clinical Psychology, 41*, 195–201.

Patterson, G. R. (1971). Behavioral intervention in the classroom and in the home. In A. Bergin & S. Garfield (Eds.), *Handbook of psychotherapy and behavior change.* New York: Wiley.

Patterson, G. R. (1974a). Interventions for boys with conduct problems: Multiple settings, treatment and criteria. *Journal of Consulting and Clinical Psychology, 42*, 471–481.

Patterson, G. R. (1974b). Retraining of aggressive boys by their parents. Review of recent literature and follow-up evaluations. *Canadian Psychiatric Association Journal, 19*, 142–161.

Patterson, G. R. (1982). *Coercive family process*. Eugene, OR: Castalia.

Patterson, G. R., Chamberlain, P., & Reid, J. B. (1982). A comparative evaluation of a parent-training program. *Behavior Therapy, 13*, 638–650.

Patterson, G. R., Cobb, J. A., & Ray, R. S. (1973). A social engineering technology for retraining families of aggressive boys. In H. Adams & I. Unikel (Eds.), *Issues and trends in behavior therapy*. Springfield, IL: Charles C. Thomas.

Patterson, G. R., & Fleischmann, M. J. (1979). Maintenance of treatment effects: Some considerations concerning family systems and follow-up data. *Behavior Therapy, 10*, 168–185.

Patterson, G. R., & Forgatch, M. S. (1985). *Therapist behavior as a determinant for client resistance: A paradox for the behavior modifier*. Unpublished manuscript. Oregon Social Learning Center, Eugene, OR.

Patterson, G. R., & Reid, J. B. (1973). Intervention for families of aggressive boys: A replication study. *Behavior Research and Therapy, 11*, 383–394.

Patterson, G. R., Reid, J. B., Jones, R. R., & Conger, R. E. (1975). *A social learning approach to family intervention: Families with aggressive children* (Vol. 1). Eugene, OR: Castalia.

Patterson, G. R., Weiss, R. L., & Hops, H. (1976). Training of marital skills. In H. Leitenberg (Ed.), *Handbook of behavior modification and behavior therapy*. Englewood Cliffs, NJ: Prentice-Hall.

Piercy, F. P., Laird, R. A., & Mohammed, Z. (1983). A family therapist rating scale. *Journal of Marital and Family Therapy, 9*, 49–60.

Pinsof, W. M. (1979). The family therapist behavior scale (FTBS): Development and evaluation of a coding system. *Family Process, 18*, 451–461.

Pinsof, W. M. (1980). *The Family Therapist Coding System (FTCS) coding manual*. Center for Family Studies/The Family Institute of Chicago, Institute of Psychiatry, Northwestern Memorial Hospital.

Pinsof, W. M. (1981). Family therapy process research. In A. S. Gurman & D. Kniskern (Eds.), *The handbook of family therapy*. New York: Brunner/Mazel.

Pinsof, W. M. (1982). *The Intersession Report*. Unpublished instrument. Center for Family Studies/The Family Institute of Chicago, Institute of Psychiatry, Northwestern Memorial Hospital.

Pinsof, W. M. (1983). Integrative problem centered therapy: Toward the synthesis of family and individual psychotherapies. *Journal of Marital and Family Therapy, 9*, 19–36.

Pinsof, W. M. (1984, Jan.). *Process-outcome research in family and marital therapy: Issues and recommendations*. Paper presented at the NIMH Conference on Family Therapy Efficacy Research, Bethesda, MD.

Pinsof, W. M. (1985). The process of family therapy: The development of the Family Therapist Coding System. In L. Greenberg & W. Pinsof (Eds.), *The psychotherapeutic process: A research handbook*. New York: Guilford.

Pinsof, W. M., & Catherall, D. R. (1984). *The integrative psychotherapy alliance: Family, couple and individual therapy scales*. Unpublished paper. Center for Family Studies/The Family Institute of Chicago, Institute of Psychiatry, Northwestern Memorial Hospital.

Rachman, S. J., & Wilson, G. T. (1980). *The effects of psychological therapy*. (2nd enlarged ed.). New York: Pergamon.

Reiss, D. (1984, Jan.). *Theoretical versus tactical inferences, or, how to do family psychotherapy research without dying of boredom*. Paper presented at the NIMH Conference on the State of the Art in Family Therapy Research, Rockville, MD.

Reiss, D., & Steinglass, P. (1978). *Family therapy outcome studies: A report of the state of the art and recommendations for future directions*. Rockville, MD: National Institute of Mental Health.

Rice, J. K., & Rice, D. G. (1985). *Divorce therapy*. New York: Guilford.

Rice, L. N., & Greenberg, L. S. (Eds.). (1984). *Patterns of change*. New York: Guilford.

Rohrbaugh, M. (1983). Schizophrenia research: Swimming against the mainstream. *Family Therapy Networker, 7*, 29–31, 61–52.

Ro-Trock, G. R., Wellisch, D., & Schooler, J. (1977). A family therapy outcome study in an inpatient setting. *American Journal of Orthopsychiatry, 47*, 514–522.

Russell, C. S., Olson, D. H., Sprenkle, D. H., & Atilano, R. B. (1983). From family symptom to family system: Review of family therapy research. *American Journal of Family Therapy, 11*, 3–14.

Russell, C. S., Atilano, R. B., Anderson, S., Jurich, A., & Bergen, L. (1984). Intervention strategies: Predicting family therapy outcome. *Journal of Marital and Family Therapy, 10*, 241–252.

Ryder, R. G. (1984a, Jan.). *The holy grail: Proven efficacy in family therapy*. Paper presented at the NIMH Conference on the State of the Art in Family Therapy Research, Rockville, MD.

Ryder, R. G. (1984b). *Coherent diversity: Views and recommendations following the NIMH/FP workshop on efficacy research in family therapy*. Unpublished manuscript, University of Connecticut.

Sager, C. J. (1981). Couple contracts and marital therapy. In A. Gurman & D. Kniskern (Eds.), *Handbook of family therapy*. New York: Brunner/Mazel.

Sager, C. J., Brown, H. S., Crohn, H., Engel, T., Rodstein, E., & Walker, L. (1983). *Treating the remarried family*. New York: Brunner/Mazel.

Santa-Barbara, J., Woodward, C. A., Levin, S., Goodman, J. T., Streiner, D., & Epstein, N. B. (1979). The McMaster Family Therapy Outcome Study: An overview of methods and results. *International Journal of Family Therapy, 1*, 304–323.

Satir, V. (1967). *Conjoint family therapy*. Palo Alto: Science and Behavior Books.

Schacht, T. E., & Strupp, H. H. (1984, June). *Psychotherapy outcome: Individualized is nice, but intelligible is beautiful*. Paper presented at the Annual Meeting of the Society for Psychotherapy Research, Lake Louise, Canada.

Scheflen, A. E. (1973). *Communicational structure: Analysis of a psychotherapy transaction*. Bloomington, IN: Indiana University Press.

Schwartz, R. C., Barrett, M. J., & Saba, G. (1983, Oct.). *Family therapy for bulimia*. Paper presented at the Annual Conference of the American Association for Marriage and Family Therapy, Washington, DC.

Schwartz, R. C., & Breunlin, D. (1983). Research: Why clinicians should bother with it. *Family Therapy Networker, 7*, 23–27, 57–59.

Scopetta, M., Szapocznik, J., King, O., Ladner, R., Alegre,

C., & Tillman, W.S. (1977). *The Spanish drug rehabilitation research project: A National Institute on Drug Abuse demonstration grant, 1974–1977: A final report.* Miami: University of Miami Family Guidance Center.

Segal, L., & Bavelas, J. B. (1983). Human systems and communication theory. In B. B. Wolman & G. Stricker (Eds.), *Handbook of family and marital therapy.* New York: Plenum.

Selvini, M., Boscolo, L., Cecchin, E., & Prata, G. (1978). *Paradox and counterparadox.* New York: Jason Aronson.

Shapiro, D. A., & Shapiro, D. (1983). Comparative therapy outcome research: Methodological implications of meta-analysis. *Journal of Consulting and Clinical Psychology, 51,* 42–53.

Shapiro, R., & Budman, S. (1979). Defection, termination and continuation in family and individual therapy. *Family Process, 12,* 55–67.

Skynner, A. C. R. (1981). An open-systems, group analytic approach to family therapy. In A. Gurman & D. Kniskern (Eds.), *Handbook of family therapy.* New York: Brunner/Mazel.

Sluzki, C. (1984, Jan.). Personal communication.

Smith, A. (1972). *Supermoney.* New York: Random House.

Smith, M. L., & Glass, G. V. (1977). Meta-analysis of psychotherapy outcome studies. *American Psychologist, 32,* 752–760.

Smith, M. L., Glass, G. V., & Miller, T. I. (1981). *The benefits of psychotherapy.* Baltimore: Johns Hopkins University Press.

Spanier, G. B. (1976). Measuring dyadic adjustment: New scales for assessing the quality of marriage and similar dyads. *Journal of Marriage and the Family, 38,* 15–28.

Sprenkle, D. H., & Piercy, F. P. (1984). Research in family therapy: A graduate level course. *Journal of Marital and Family Therapy, 10,* 225–240.

Sprenkle, D. H., & Storm, C. L. (1983). Divorce therapy outcome research: A substantive and methodological review. *Journal of Marital and Family Therapy, 9,* 239–258.

Stanton, M. D. (1979). Family treatment approaches to drug abuse problems: A review. *Family Process, 18,* 251–280.

Stanton, M. D. (1981). Marital therapy from a structured/strategic viewpoint. In P. Sholevar (Ed.), *Handbook of marriage and marital therapy.* New York: Spectrum.

Stanton, M. D., Steier, F., & Todd, T. C. (1982). Paying families for attending sessions: Counteracting the dropout problem. *Journal of Marital and Family Therapy, 8,* 371–373.

Stanton, M. D., & Todd, T. (1980). A critique of the Wells and Dezen review of the results of nonbehavioral family therapy. *Family Process, 19,* 169–176.

Stanton, M. D., Todd, T. C., and Associates. (1982). *The family therapy of drug abuse and addiction.* New York: Guilford.

Stanton, M. D., Todd, T. C., Steier, F., Van Duesen, J. M., Marder, L., Rosoff, R. J., Seaman, S. F., & Skibinski, E. (1979). *Family characteristics and family therapy of heroin addicts: Final report 1974–1978.* Submitted to the National Institute on Drug Abuse, Grant No. R01DA 00119.

Steier, F. (1984, Jan.). *Family structure and family therapy efficacy research: Toward a coherent methodology.* Paper presented at the NIMH Conference on the State of the Art in Family Therapy Research, Bethesda, MD.

Steinglass, P. (1976). Experimenting with family treatment approaches to alcoholism, 1950–1974. *Family Process, 15,* 97–124.

Sterba, R. (1934). The fate of the ego in analytic therapy. *International Journal of Psychoanalysis, 15,* 117–126.

Storrow, H. A. (1960). The measurement of outcome in psychotherapy. *Archives of General Psychiatry, 2,* 142–146.

Stiles, W. B. (1985). Development of a taxonomy of verbal response modes. In L. Greenberg & W. Pinsof (Eds.), *The psychotherapeutic process: A research handbook.* New York: Guilford.

Strelnick, A. H. (1977). Multiple family group therapy: A review of the literature. *Family Process, 16,* 307–326.

Strupp, H. H. (1981). Clinical research, practice, and the crises of confidence. *Journal of Consulting and Clinical Psychology, 499,* 216–219.

Strupp, H. H., & Hadley, S. W. (1977). A tripartite model of mental health and therapeutic outcomes: With special reference to negative effects in psychotherapy. *American Psychologist, 32,* 187–196.

Swift, W. J. (1982). The long-term outcome of early onset anorexia nervosa: A critical review. *Journal of the American Academy of Child Psychiatry, 21,* 38–46.

Szapocznik, J., Kurtines, W. M., Foote, F. H., Perez-Vidal, A., & Hervis, O. (1983). Conjoint versus one-person family therapy: Some evidence for the effectiveness of conducting family therapy through one person. *Journal of Consulting and Clinical Psychology, 51,* 889–899.

Tavormina, J. B. (1974). Basic models of parent counseling. *Psychological Bulletin, 81,* 827–835.

Todd, T. C., & Stanton, M. D. (1983). Research on marital and family therapy: Answers, issues and recommendations for the future. In B. B. Wolman & G. Stricker (Eds.), *Handbook of family and marital therapy.* New York: Plenum.

Tomm, K. (1982, June). *The Calgary family therapy outcome study.* Paper presented at the Annual Meeting of the American Family Therapy Association, Boston.

Tomm, K. (1983). The old hat doesn't fit. *Family Therapy Networker, 7,* 39–41.

Toomim, M. K. (1972). Structured separation with counseling: A therapeutic approach for couples in conflict. *Family Process, 11,* 299–310.

Truax, C. B., & Carkhuff, R. R. (1967). *Toward effective counseling and psychotherapy: Training and practice.* Chicago: Aldine.

Tucker, S. J., & Pinsof, W. M. (1984). The empirical evaluation of family therapy training. *Family Process, 23,* 437–456.

Turkewitz, H., & O'Leary, K. D. (1981). A comparative outcome study of behavioral marital therapy and communication therapy. *Journal of Marital and Family Therapy, 7,* 159–169.

Umbarger, C., & White, S. L. (1978). Redefining the problem: Individual symptom and family system. *International Journal of Family Counseling, 6,* 19–24.

Vaughn, C., & Leff, J. (1976). The measurement of expressed emotion in the families of psychiatric patients. *British Journal of Psychology, 15,* 157–165.

von Bertalanffy, L. (1968). *General systems theory.* New York: Braziller.

Walter, H. I., & Gilmore, S. K. (1973). Placebo versus social learning effects in parent training procedures designed to alter the behavior of aggressive boys. *Behavior Therapy, 4,* 361–377.

Wallerstein, J. (1984). The impact of divorce on children. In C. C. Nadelson & D. C. Polonsky (Eds.), *Marriage and divorce: A contemporary perspective.* New York: Guilford.

Wampler, R. S. (1982a). The effectiveness of the Minnesota Couple Communication Program: A review of research. *Journal of Marital and Family Therapy, 8,* 345–356.

Wampler, R. S. (1982b). Bringing the review of literature into the age of quantification: Meta-analysis as a strategy for integrating research findings in family studies. *Journal of Marriage and the Family, 44,* 1009–1023.

Weakland, J. H., Fisch, R., Watzlawick, P., & Bodin, A. M. (1974). Brief therapy: Focused problem resolution. *Family Process, 13,* 141–168.

Weiss, R. L., & Cerreto, M. (1975). *Marital status inventory: Steps to divorce.* Unpublished manuscript, University of Oregon.

Wellisch, D. R., & Ro-Trock, G. R. (1980). A three-year follow-up of family therapy. *International Journal of Family Therapy, 2,* 169–175.

Wellisch, D. K., Vincent, J., & Ro-Trock, G. K. (1976). Family therapy versus individual therapy: A study of adolescents and their parents. In D. H. L. Olson (Ed.), *Treating relationships.* Lake Mills, IA: Graphic.

Wells, R. A. (1980). Tempests, teapots (and research design): Rejoinder to Stanton and Todd. *Family Process, 19,* 177–178.

Wells, R. A., & Dezen, A. E. (1978a). The results of family therapy, revisited: The nonbehavioral methods. *Family Process, 17,* 251–274.

Wells, R. A., & Dezen, A. E. (1978b). Ideologies, idols (and graven images?): Rejoinder to Gurman and Kniskern. *Family Process, 17,* 283–286.

Wells, R. A., Dilkes, T., & Trivelli, N. (1972). The results of family therapy: A critical review of the literature. *Family Process, 7,* 189–207.

Wells, R. A., & Giannetti, V. (1985). Individual marital therapy: A critical reappraisal. *Family Process.*

Whiffen, R., & Byng-Hall, J. (Eds.). (1982). *Family therapy supervision.* New York: Grune & Stratton.

Wilder, C. (1982). Muddles and metaphors: A response to Keeney and Sprenkle. *Family Process, 21,* 397–400.

Williams, A. M., & Miller, W. R. (1981). Evaluation and research on marital therapy. In G. P. Sholevar (Ed.), *The handbook of marriage and marital therapy.* Jamaica, NY: Spectrum.

Williamson, D. S. (1981). Personal authority via termination of the intergenerational hierarchial boundary: A "new" stage in the family life cycle. *Journal of Marital and Family Therapy, 7,* 441–452.

Williamson, D. S. (1982). Personal authority via termination of the intergenerational hierarchical boundary: Part II—The consultation process and the therapeutic method. *Journal of Marital and Family Therapy, 8,* 125–137.

Williamson, D. S. (1982b). Personal authority in family experience via termination of the intergenerational hierarchical boundary: Part III—Personal authority defined and the power of play in the change process. *Journal of Marital and Family Therapy, 8,* 309–323.

Williamson, D. S., Bray, J. H., & Malone, P. E. (1984). *Personal authority in the family system via termination of the intergenerational hierarchical boundary: IV—An evaluation of the effects of intergenerational consultation on marital and family behavior.* Houston Family Institute, unpublished manuscript.

Wiltz, N. A., & Patterson, G. R. (1974). An evaluation of parent training procedures designed to alter inappropriate aggressive behavior of boys. *Behavior Therapy, 5,* 215–221.

Wing, J. K., Cooper, J. E., & Sartorius, N. (1974). *Measurement and classification of psychiatric symptoms.* Cambridge, England: Cambridge University Press.

Wynne, L. C. (1983). Family research and family therapy: A reunion? *Journal of Marital and Family Therapy, 9,* 113–118.

Wynne, L. C. (1984, Jan.). *Definable problems in family therapy efficacy research.* Paper presented at the NIMH Conference on the State of the Art in Family Therapy Research, Rockville, MD.

Wynne, L. C., Ryckoff, I. M., Day, J., & Hirsch, S. I. (1958). Pseudo-mutuality in the family relations of schizophrenics. *Psychiatry, 21,* 205–220.

PART V

SPECIAL TOPICS

14

RESEARCH ON BRIEF PSYCHOTHERAPY

MARY P. KOSS

Kent State University

JAMES N. BUTCHER

University of Minnesota

Once viewed as a superficial and expedient treatment to be used only in "emergency" situations until long-term therapy could begin, brief psychotherapy is now considered to be a treatment of choice for most patients. Several factors account for the contemporary emphasis upon brief treatment methods in clinical practice:

1. It is now generally recognized that patients, when they enter psychological treatment, do not anticipate that their program of treatment will be prolonged but believe that their problems will require a few sessions at most (Garfield, 1978). Indeed, patients typically come to psychological treatment seeking specific and focal problem resolution, not for general personality "overhauls" as assumed in the past.
2. Brief therapy methods, once thought to be appropriate only to less severe problems, have actually been shown to be effective with severe and chronic problems if treatment goals are kept reasonable.
3. Brief treatment methods have generally the same success rates as longer term treatment programs.
4. Most insurance companies or prepaid health programs recognize the benefits of brief therapy and now limit the liability of payment for therapy in the case of psychological problems to a number of sessions that would fall within a brief treatment modality. Budman and Gurman (1983) observe that institutional supports (e.g., limits on therapy duration, staff training in brief methods) are important in determining whether *planned* brief psychotherapy becomes a dominant practice in a given setting. "If such supports do not exist, therapy will probably be either unplanned and brief (because so many patients drop out or unilaterally terminate) or, for a smaller number of patients, continuous and open-ended" (p. 282).

627

This chapter will provide an overview of the contemporary practice of brief psychotherapy and will examine the existing research evidence on its effectiveness. In the overview, we will examine the major historical developments that influenced brief psychotherapy methods and survey a variety of brief therapy approaches. Then, the characteristics common to brief as opposed to long-term psychotherapy will be delineated. Later, the process by which brief psychotherapeutic change is brought about will be discussed and the research literature supporting these hypothesized change mechanisms will be reviewed. Finally, we will examine studies of effectiveness of brief treatment methods.

THE CLINICAL PRACTICE OF BRIEF PSYCHOTHERAPY

Some Historical Antecedents

During the early days of psychoanalysis, the treatment period was often quite brief. As analytic treatment became more involved with transference interpretation and less involved with focal symptom relief, however, the course of treatment concomitantly became more prolonged (Malan, 1963). Some early efforts were made by a few psychoanalytic theorists to reverse the trend and shorten psychoanalysis. Ferenczi (1920) attempted to keep analysis short by assigning a more active, directive role to the analyst. Alexander and French (1946) conducted studies in an effort to abbreviate analytic treatment. They believed that neurotic adjustment had become a problem for a larger proportion of the population than could be treated by traditional psychoanalysis. Thus, they adapted techniques from psychoanalysis that would "give rational aid to all those who show early signs of maladjustment" (p. 341). They pointed out that psychodynamic principles could be used for therapeutic effect, regardless of the length of treatment.

Much of the impetus for brief treatment came as a result of psychological emergencies. In periods of great stress in which many individuals experience psychological difficulties and "breakdowns," available treatment resources and traditional therapeutic techniques have not been sufficient to handle the problems. During World War II, when a large number of soldiers developed stress-related symptoms, short-term treatment programs were designed to

provide treatment as soon as possible after the initial breakdown had occurred. This early form of crisis intervention was aimed at stress reduction, symptom relief, and prevention of further breakdown by helping the individual to restore self-esteem and avoid further retreat into maladjustment (Grinker & Spiegel, 1944a, 1944b; Kardiner, 1941).

Another important development in emergency brief psychotherapy was initiated by Lindemann. As a result of his work with families of victims of the Coconut Grove nightclub fire in 1943, Lindemann (1944) published his classic study on crisis intervention. He delineated phases of grief work through which people must go to free themselves from the deceased and readjust to the environment without the deceased person. Lindemann's contribution to understanding bereavement and the grieving process and his demonstration that people can be helped to work through grief established the efficacy of crisis-intervention therapy.

Another, more recent development contributing to the thrust of briefer psychotherapies was the free clinic movement of the 1960s (Glasscote, Raybin, Reifler, & Kane, 1975). During this period, there was a great deal of social upheaval created by the anti–Vietnam War movement and other political "counterculture" activities, widely accessible drugs, and changing moral standards. As a result many individuals experienced both situational and personal turmoil that often led to a need for psychological help. At the same time, there was widespread mistrust of "traditional" institutions; thus, many people in need of psychological help were without acceptable treatment resources.

This isolation from traditional mental health resources resulted in the development of counterculture "rap" centers, drop-in clinics, and other alternative agencies. The free clinics provided a nonestablishment staff who shared the values and spoke the language of the "disenfranchised." Many of these clinics provided limited services such as drug, draft evasion, or abortion counseling by nonprofessional volunteers. There also were numerous clinics that were operated by volunteer professionals who provided more or less "traditional" counseling in a nontraditional setting (Butcher, Stelmachers, & Maudal, 1984).

Another important historical development in brief treatment has been the use of behavioral techniques in the modification of behavior. The brief treatment of behavioral problems using learning-based principles has a long history. The demonstration of "unlearning" by Watson and Rayner (1920) is a classic one. Even though the mainstream of psychological treatment mostly ignored the beneficial effects of behavioral therapy until more recently (Wolpe, 1952), there have been, for some time, working "behaviorists" in the treatment realm (Holmes, 1936; Jones, 1931; Terhune, 1960).

Considering behavioral therapy as a brief therapy may be questioned by some clinicians, since behavioral treatment, in fact, may be fairly long-term and may not fit well in the "psycho-" prefix often preceding the word therapy. However, sufficient numbers of behavioral techniques are integral parts of effective brief therapy as to require their presentation in the historical context. The directive nature of brief psychotherapy that will be discussed later entails the use of some behavioral procedures, language, and "habits" such as checking up on the effectiveness of outside-therapy assignments.

Approaches to Brief Psychotherapy

The clinical literature on brief psychotherapy is quite consistent in considering a 25-session contact as the upper limit of a brief treatment. The theoretical rationale governing the setting of time limits in brief therapy will be discussed more fully later. Approaches to brief psychotherapy can be classified as psychodynamically oriented, crisis-oriented, behavioral, and other verbal psychotherapies. The following discussion includes therapeutic approaches designed for the one-to-one individual outpatient psychotherapy of nonpsychotic adults with any type of behavioral problem. We have excluded from consideration group treatment, family therapy, marital counseling, telephone approaches to psychotherapy, preventive interventions, and inpatient programs. Auerbach and Kilmann (1977) have reviewed many of the approaches to crisis intervention that are not covered in this chapter. Some of the remaining approaches are covered in other chapters of this text. Because the focus of this volume is on empirical research findings, our presentation of clinical methods in this section is brief. We provide this guide to the published clinical literature, however, for the benefit of readers who wish to read further about the available techniques.

Psychodynamically Oriented Techniques

Psychodynamically oriented approaches to brief psychotherapy are most numerous (see Table 14.1). The goals of these systems include developing at least limited psychogenetic understanding of the focal problem. Interpretations are still the major therapeutic technique, but they are usually slightly modified for the brief format. Interpretations are designed to be integrative instead of regressive. They focus on present circumstances, not on childhood experiences (Sarvis, Dewees, & Johnston, 1958). Positive transference is generally thought to be essential to the success of brief therapy. Interpretations of negative transference may be made, but allowing a transference neurosis to develop is considered undesirable. Discussions of psychodynamically oriented techniques include "Psychoanalytic Therapy" (Alexander & French, 1946), "Adlerian Psychotherapy" (Ansbacher, 1972), "Focal Psychotherapy" (Balint, Ornstein, & Balint, 1972), "Emergency and Brief Psychotherapy" (Bellak & Small, 1965), "Brief Psychotherapy" (Burdon, 1963), "Dynamic Psychotherapy" (Davanloo, 1978), "Applied Psychoanalysis" (Deutsch, 1949), "Active Psychoanalytic Technique" (Ferenczi, 1920), "Brief Psychotherapy" (Gillman, 1965), "Psychoanalysis and Brief Psychotherapy" (Gutheil, 1944), "Short-term Psychotherapy" (Hoch, 1965), "Brief Dynamic Psychotherapy" (Horowitz et al., 1984), "Interpersonal Psychotherapy" (Klerman, Weissman, Rounsaville, & Chevron, 1984), "Time-limited Psychotherapy" (Lewin, 1966; Malan, 1963, 1976a, 1976b; Mann, 1973), "Supportive-expressive Therapy" (Luborsky, 1984), "Short-term Insight Psychotherapy" (McGuire, 1965a, 1965b), "Anxiety-provoking Psychotherapy" (Merrill & Cary, 1975; Semrad, Binstock, & White, 1966; Sifneos, 1972), "Time-limited Dynamic Psychotherapy" (Strupp & Binder, 1984), and "Short-term Psychotherapy" (Wolberg, 1980).

Brief Behavior Therapies

Most behavior therapies, though treatment length is not a primary consideration, qualify as brief forms of therapy, since they can be completed within the time limits of brief psychotherapy. For example, Wolpe's (1952) series of 70 cases were seen for 4 to 125 interviews. Reviews of behavioral techniques are available (Bergin & Suinn, 1975; Lazarus,

TABLE 14.1 Approaches to Brief and Crisis-Oriented Psychotherapies

Psychodynamically Oriented	Brief Cognitive/ Behavioral	Crisis-Oriented	Miscellaneous Brief Verbal Therapies
Alexander & French (1946) (psychoanalytic therapy)	Beck (1976, Beck et al, 1984) (cognitive restructuring therapy)	A. General support	A. Eclectic
Ansbacher (1972)		Coleman (1960) (dynamically oriented supportive psychotherapy)	Budman & Gurman (1983) (integrative brief psychotherapy)
Balint et al. (1972) (focal psychotherapy)	Buda (1972) (logotherapy)		
Bellak & Small (1965)		Coleman & Zwerling (1959)	B. Hypnotherapy
Burdon (1963)	Ellis & Grieger (1977) (rational-emotive therapy)	Sifneos (1972) (anxiety suppressive therapy)	Frankel (1973)
Davanloo (1978)			London (1947)
Deutsch (1949) (applied psychoanalysis)	Frankl (1960) (paradoxical intention)	B. Generic crisis intervention	Stein (1972, 1975)
Ferenczi (1920) (active psychoanalytic technique)		Caplan (1964)	Wolberg (1965a, 1965b, 1980)
Gillman (1965)	Gelder et al. (1967)	Lindemann (1965)	C. Cathartic psychotherapy
Heiberg et al. (1975)	Hogan (1966, 1967)	Klein & Lindemann (1961)	Nichols (1974)
Hoch (1965)	Levis & Carrera (1967) (implosive therapy)		Nichols & Reifler (1973)
Horowitz et al. (1984)		C. Individual crisis intervention	D. Confrontation problem-solving
Klerman et al. (1984) (interpersonal psychotherapy)	Meichenbaum (1977) (self-instructional therapy)	Butcher et al. (1976, 1984) (crisis therapy)	Garner (1970)
Lewin (1966)			
Malan (1963, 1976a, 1976b)	Mitchell & Orr (1974) (massed desensitization)	Harris et al. (1963) (precipitating stress approach)	
Mann (1973) (time-limited psychotherapy)		Hoffman & Remmel (1975)	
McGuire (1965a, 1965b) (short-term insight psychotherapy)	Phillips & Weiner (1966)	Jacobson et al. (1965, 1979)	
Merrill & Cary (1975)	Reid (1975) (task-centered casework)	Levy (1966)	

TABLE 14.1 *(Continued)*

Psychodynamically Oriented	Brief Cognitive/ Behavioral	Crisis-Oriented	Miscellaneous Brief Verbal Therapies
Semrad et al. (1966)		Sifneos (1972) (crisis support therapy)	
Sifneos (1972) (anxiety-provoking psychotherapy)	Suinn et al. (1970) (accelerated massed desensitization)		
Strupp & Binder (1984) (time-limited dynamic psychotherapy)			
Wolberg (1965a, 1965b, 1980) (short-term psycho-therapy)			

1971; Wilson, 1981). Especially brief modifications of traditional behavior techniques include "Implosive Therapy" (Hogan, 1966, 1967; Levis & Carrera, 1967), "Massed Desensitization" (Gelder, Marks, & Wolff, 1967; Mitchell & Orr, 1974), and "Accelerated Massed Desensitization" (Suinn, Edie, & Spinelli, 1970). These modified approaches to desensitization include fewer but longer sessions.

Several cognitive behavior therapies, treatment approaches that use verbal or cognitive mediation to bring about behavior change, fit into a brief treatment mode. These approaches, such as "Rational-emotive Therapy" (Ellis & Grieger, 1977), "Self-instructional Therapy" (Meichenbaum, 1977) or "Cognitive Restructuring Therapy" (Beck, 1976; Beck, Rush, Shaw & Emery, 1984) assume an active role on the part of the therapist and employ techniques to encourage cognitive mediation and early therapeutic change.

"Logotherapy" and paradoxical intention (Buda, 1972; Frankl, 1960) have been categorized by Phillips and Weiner (1966) as behavior therapies. Paradoxical intention is a technique for teaching a patient to deal with anticipatory fear situations. Whenever patients feel anticipatory anxiety about a potential terrible outcome, they are asked to visualize that it has already happened.

"Task-centered Casework" (Reid, 1975) includes many behavioral techniques. In this approach, tasks to be worked on in therapy are developed collaboratively. A task (or goal) may state the general direction of action ("become more assertive") or may specify the exact behavior ("ask for a raise"). Specific techniques for accomplishing the tasks include modeling, rehearsal, and guided practice.

Crisis-oriented Therapies

Jacobson, Strickler, and Morley (1968) describe four levels of crisis intervention, all of which are effective with certain types of clients. The first level is environmental manipulation, where the helper serves as a referral source. The second level, general support, involves active listening without threatening or challenging. Approaches to supportive crisis therapy include "Anxiety Suppressive Therapy" (Sifneos, 1972) and "Dynamically Oriented Supportive Psychotherapy" (Coleman, 1960; Coleman & Zwerling, 1959). In the third level, the generic approach, a particular crisis is believed to have a similar meaning to most affected individuals, regardless of their personality dynamics. Generic crisis intervention requires that the therapist have a thorough knowledge of techniques that are particularly helpful in resolving specific crises. This approach is well described by Caplan (1964) and Klein and Lindemann (1961). The fourth level is labeled the individual approach and stresses understanding the personality dynamics of patients and helping them to develop an understanding of why the present situation developed into a "crisis." Characteristic of individual approaches to crisis intervention are "Crisis Therapy" (Butcher et al., 1984), "Precipitating Stress Approach" (Harris, Kalis, & Freeman, 1963), "Early Access Brief Treatment" (Jacobson, 1965, 1979), "Crisis Oriented Psychotherapy" (Levy, 1966), and "Crisis Support Therapy" (Sifneos, 1972).

Miscellaneous Brief Verbal Therapies

A number of brief therapy approaches fail to fit into the categories presented above. For example, Budman and Gurman (1983) describe "Integrative Brief Psychotherapy," which includes various techniques including family and systems approaches.

Several clinicians (Frankel, 1973; London, 1947; Stein, 1972, 1975; Wolberg, 1965b, 1980) have discussed the value of hypnosis, hypnoanalysis, and narcoanalysis as techniques of brief therapy. Hypnosis is usually used as a treatment for a "target symptom" (Wolberg, 1980) in conjunction with other techniques, but occasionally recovery can be effected solely through the use of hypnosis. Wolberg (1965b) states, however, that symptoms that serve an important purpose in the psychological economy may resist influence.

Brief cathartic psychotherapy emphasizes emotional catharsis (Bierenbaum, Nichols, & Schwartz, 1976; Nichols, 1974; Nichols & Reifler, 1973). Techniques include role-playing, repetition of affect-laden phrases, and expressive movements such as striking the couch. These procedures are designed to intensify the emotional tone of the sessions and to promote affective discharge. The confrontation problem-solving technique (Garner, 1970) is a short-session psychotherapy designed for use by nonpsychiatrically trained physicians.

Common Technical Characteristics of Brief Approaches

A survey of brief approaches to psychotherapy reveals a core of technical points considered essential by most practitioners of short-term treatment. We will present a summary of the extensive clinical literature on the following important common technical characteristics: utilization of time, limitation of goals, focus of sessions, activity of the therapist, use of assessment, flexibility of therapeutic roles, timing of the intervention, therapeutic use of catharsis, characteristics of the therapeutic relationship, and criteria for patient selection. No attempt will be

made to summarize in detail all the studies or issues on each of these variables, since entire books have been devoted to the topics. We will provide a general summary of the characteristics at the end of the section.

The factors to be discussed here have received wide attention in the clinical literature. In the section following our condensed summary of clinical techniques, relevant research on some process variables in brief psychotherapy will be discussed.

Limited Time

Time is one of the major variables differentiating brief approaches from other forms of psychotherapy. Consequently, most brief therapists have been careful to define the maximum number of therapeutic interviews they consider "brief" and to discuss the meaning and effect of the short time limit on the progress of therapy. Alexander and French (1946) felt that brief therapy should be limited to 40 sessions, but they often concluded their own cases in as few as three sessions. Today, most practitioners agree that 25 sessions is the upper limit of "brief" therapy, with as many clinicians recommending courses of treatment lasting from 1 to 6 sessions as those who recommend the longer 10- to 25-session treatment. Crisis-oriented therapists follow Lindemann's (1944) conceptualization of crisis as a time-limited phenomenon that is resolved one way or another in 6 weeks. Thus, most crisis-oriented psychotherapy is very brief (see Table 14.2).

Slightly longer therapy durations may occur in focal psychotherapy (Balint et al., 1972; Malan, 1963, 1976a, 1976b), which usually averages 10 to 40 sessions, and anxiety-provoking psychotherapy (Sifneos, 1972), which lasts 2 to 12 months. Leeman and Mulvey (1975) report procedures that require 3 to 7 months of therapy.

Many therapists recommend telling the patient during the first session that the therapy will be brief and time limited (see Table 14.2). The patient may be told of a fixed limit on the number of sessions that are available or may be given a calendar date when therapy will end. Informing patients of the time limits accomplishes three therapeutic goals. It confronts the patient with the reality of work, encourages optimism through the therapist's confidence that improvement is possible in a relatively short time, and provides a set of shared goals of what therapy

TABLE 14.2 Common Technical Characteristics of Crisis-Oriented and Brief Psychotherapy Systems

Time Factors	Selection of Patients	Goals of Therapy	Technical Factors
A. One- to six-session procedures	A. Appropriate to all	A. Removal or amelioration of most disabling symptom	A. Develop positive expectancies/transference
Bellak & Small (1965)	Budman & Gurman (1983)	Bellak & Small (1965)	Aldrich (1968)
Bloom (1981)	Gillman (1965)	Cummings & Follet (1976)	Ansbacher (1972)
Coleman (1960)	Parad & Parad (1966)	Greenblatt et al. (1963)	Baum & Felzer (1964)
Coleman & Zwerling (1959)	Wolberg (1965a, 1965b, 1980)	Grinker & Spiegel (1944a, 1944b)	Bellak & Small (1965)
Frankel (1973)		Hoch (1965)	Bonstedt (1970)
Greenblatt et al. (1963)		Lester (1968)	Butcher et al. (1983)
Harris et al. (1963)		Malan (1963, 1976a, 1976b)	Frank (1974)
Howard (1965)		Norman et al. (1963)	Lick & Bootzin (1975)
Jacobson (1965, 1979)		Parad (1967)	Malan (1963, 1976a, 1976b)
Jacobson et al. (1965)		Waltzer et al. (1963)	Sifneos (1968, 1972)
Koegler & Cannon (1966)		Wolberg (1965a, 1965b)	Small (1972)
Levy (1966)			
Miller (1968)			
Rosenthal (1965)			

(continued)

TABLE 14.2 *(Continued)*

Time Factors	Selection of Patients	Goals of Therapy	Technical Factors
Saul (1951)			Strupp & Binder (1984)
Socarides (1954)			Wolberg (1965a, 1965b, 1980)
Spoerl (1975)			
Stein et al. (1967)			
B. Up to 25-session procedures	B. Behavioral problems of acute onset	B. Prompt reestablishment of equilibrium	B. Focus on primary problem
Ansbacher (1972)	Alexander & French (1946)	Coleman (1960)	Ansbacher (1972)
Barten (1965)	Bellak & Small (1965)	Coleman & Zwerling (1959)	Balint et al. (1972)
Bonime (1953)	Berliner (1941)	Harris et al. (1963)	
Burdon (1963)	Gottschalk et al. (1967)	Jacobson (1965)	Bellak & Small (1965)
Davanloo (1978)	Hoch (1965)	Kris (1960)	
Horowitz et al. (1984)	McGuire (1965a, 1965b)	Normand et al. (1963)	Binder et al. (1983)
Jacobs et al. (1968)	Straker (1966)		
Klerman et al. (1984)	Visher (1959)	Waltzer et al. (1963)	Bonstedt (1970)
Lindemann (1944)	Wolberg (1965a, 1965b)	Wolberg (1965a, 1965b)	Budman & Gurman (1983)
Mann (1973)			

McGuire (1965a, 1965b)

Meyer et al. (1967)

Schoenberg & Carr (1963)

Seitz (1953)

Shlein et al. (1962)

Sifneos (1972)

Stewart (1972)

Stone (1951)

Straker (1966)

Strupp & Binder (1984)

Terhune (1960)

C. Up to 40 sessions

Balint et al. (1972)

Leeman & Mulvey (1975)

C. Previously good adjustment

Gillman (1965)

Harris & Christiansen (1946)

McGuire (1965a, 1965b)

C. Develop understanding of current disturbance

Bellak (1960)

Burdon (1963)

Gillman (1964)

Harris et al. (1963)

Haskell et al. (1969)

Horowitz et al. (1984)

Koegler (1966)

Malan (1963, 1976a, 1976b)

Mann (1973)

Phillips & Weiner (1966)

Semrad et al. (1966)

Small (1972)

Stekel (1950)

Wolberg (1965b)

C. Use of active techniques

Avnet (1965a, 1965b)

Barten (1971)

(continued)

TABLE 14.2 (Continued)

Time Factors	Selection of Patients	Goals of Therapy	Technical Factors
Malan (1963, 1976a, 1976b)	Pumpian-Mindlin (1953)	Davanloo (1978)	Baum & Felzer (1964)
Sifneos (1972)	Sifneos (1972)	Frank (1966)	Bellak & Small (1965)
	Straker (1966)	Harris et al. (1963)	Bonstedt (1970)
	Visher (1959)	Horowitz et al. (1984)	Budman & Gurman (1983)
		Klerman et al. (1984)	Burdon (1963)
		Malan (1963, 1976a, 1976b)	Butcher et al. (1983)
		Sifneos (1972)	Davanloo (1978)
		Strupp & Binder (1984)	Ferenczi (1920)
		Wolberg (1965a, 1965b)	Gillman (1965)
			Gross (1968)
			Hoch (1965)
			Lester (1968)
			Malan (1963, 1976a, 1976b)
			Mann (1973)

D. Recommend specific communication of time limits

Ansbacher (1972)

Budman & Gurman (1983)

Ferenczi (1920)

Haskel et al. (1969)

Levy (1966)

Malan (1963)

Mann (1973)

Meunch (1965)

Phillips & Johnston (1954)

D. Good ability to relate

Berliner (1941)

Davanloo (1978)

Gottschalk et al. (1967)

Malan (1963)

McGuire (1965a, 1965b)

Pumpian-Mindlin (1953)

Sifneos (1972)
Visher (1959)

D. Patient should choose goals

Bellak & Small (1965)

Rosenbaum (1964)

Wolberg (1965b, 1980)

McGuire (1965a, 1965b)

Merrill & Cary (1975)

Perlman (1975)

Sarvis et al. (1958)

D. Use of persuasion, suggestion, formulation of plans of action, factual information

Baker (1947)

Barten (1965)

Bellak & Small (1965)

Budman & Gurman (1983)

Butcher et al. (1983)

Gelb & Ullman (1967)

(continued)

637

TABLE 14.2 (Continued)

Time Factors	Selection of Patients	Goals of Therapy	Technical Factors
Sarvis et al. (1958)			Mann (1973)
Seitz (1953)			Saul (1951)
Shlein et al. (1962)			Sifneos (1972)
Small (1971)			Small (1971)
Stekel (1950)			Stein et al. (1967)
Straker (1966)			Visher (1959)
			Wolberg (1965b)
E. Variable session length/spacing	E. Lower-class membership		E. Early assessment
Barten (1965)	Hunt (1966)		Barten (1969)
Bloom (1981)	Imber et al. (1956)		Bellak & Small (1965)
Budman & Gurman (1983)	Jacobson (1965)		Butcher et al. (1983)
Cattell et al. (1963)	Lief et al. (1961)		Fenichel (1954)
Cummings & Vandenbos (1979)	Lorion (1973, 1974)		Grinker & Spiegel (1944a & 1944b)
Garner (1970)	Normand et al. (1963)		Klein & Lindemann (1959)
Koegler (1966)	Rosenthal & Frank (1958)		
	Strassi & Messer (1976)		

Koegler & Cannon (1966)

Levy (1966)

Rabkin (1977)

Wolberg (1980)

F. Marginally adjusted or severely limited

Barten (1971)

Parad (1967)

Wolberg (1965b, 1980)

Morley (1965)

Sifneos (1972)

Small (1972)

F. Flexible choice of specific techniques

Alexander & French (1946)

Budman & Gurman (1983)

Errera et al. (1967)

Hoch (1965)

Malan (1963)

Mann (1973)

Small (1972)

Stein et al. (1967)

Wayne (1966)

Wolberg (1965b)

(continued)

TABLE 14.2 (Continued)

Time Factors	Selection of Patients	Goals of Therapy	Technical Factors
			G. Prompt inter-vention
			Bellak & Small (1965)
			Harris et al. (1963)
			Jacobson et al. (1965)
			Rosenthal (1965)
			Small (1972)
			H. Allow for ventilation
			Alexander & French (1946)
			Baker (1947)
			Butcher et al. (1983)
			Erlich & Phillips (1963)

Frank (1974)

Lindemann (1944)

Mann (1973)

Semrad et al. (1966)

Small (1972)

Wolberg (1965b)

Wolpe & Lazarus (1966)

can and cannot do. Additionally, definite time limits give the therapy the added structure of having a definite beginning, middle, and end. Budman and Gurman (1983) observe, "Whatever else is focused on during treatment, the brief therapist must maintain a constant ancillary focus on the time issue" (p. 284).

While most practitioners adhere to the standard 45- to 60-minute hour and the 1-week interval, there is variability in both length and spacing of sessions. Sessions of 10 to 20 minutes have been advocated by Barten (1965), Cattell, MacKinnon, and Forster (1963), Garner (1970), Koegler (1966), and Koegler and Cannon (1966). Short sessions are used most frequently where service demands are great, such as in the military, or where supportive goals are the object of the therapy. Crisis-oriented approaches, particularly, may use variable session lengths (Levy, 1966). The initial session may be long in order to obtain all necessary information and allow for the emotional ventilation that may occur at this stage of crisis. Later sessions might then be shorter.

Close spacing of initial sessions with gradually increasing intersession intervals and a planned follow-up or booster session has also been advocated by some clinicians (e.g., Budman & Gurman, 1983; Wolberg, 1980). Thus, while brief psychotherapy always involves a relatively small number of sessions, they may be spaced out over a number of months. The use of multiple courses of brief therapy over many years as opposed to a single course of unlimited long-term therapy has been recommended by a number of writers (e.g., Bloom, 1981; Budman & Gurman, 1983; Cummings & Vandenbos, 1979; Rabkin, 1977).

After noting the range of options in the length, spacing, and session duration of brief therapies, Budman and Gurman (1983) conclude, "(to paraphrase Thurber) 'There is no length in number.' What is, in fact, being examined in any discussion of brief treatment is therapy in which the time allotted to treatment is rationed" (p. 277). Wolberg (1980) noted that integrating changed self-concepts into behavior is often a lengthy process. The long-term therapist observes these changes during the "working through" period. The brief therapist, who must discharge a patient before the changes are complete, may consequently be vulnerable to occasional feelings of dissatisfaction with the results of

therapy. Due to the amount of energy required to terminate patients and the high activity level required, brief therapy has been considered more emotionally demanding of the therapist than longer term therapy (Budman & Gurman, 1983).

Limited Goals

The time limitations of brief psychotherapy make many of the goals of traditional psychotherapy such as extensive personality reconstruction or dynamic insight into psychogenetic origins of behavior impossible. Brief psychotherapy requires that "therapeutic perfectionism" (Malan, 1963) and "prejudices of depth" (Wolberg, 1965b) be abandoned. Ursano and Dressler (1974) found that the focal nature of brief psychotherapy was actually the essential difference between brief and long-term psychotherapy rather than the traditional idea that brief therapy was more supportive and long-term therapy was more exploratory.

Most brief psychotherapists strive to accomplish one or more of the following goals: removal or amelioration of the patient's most disabling symptoms as rapidly as possible (see Table 14.2); prompt reestablishment of the patient's previous emotional equilibrium; and development of the patient's understanding of the current disturbance and increased coping ability in the future. The patient frequently brings to therapy an idea of the symptoms he or she would most like to alleviate. Most clinicians suggest that the patient have major input in choosing the goals of limited therapy.

Sarvis et al. (1958) suggest that many psychotherapists have adopted the infectious disease model of psychotherapy. In this view, disturbing behaviors are seen as diseases and psychotherapeutic techniques are seen as a specific and permanent cure (like antibiotics) that will transform the patient into a healthy individual for the rest of his or her life. They emphasize that adaptive coping is a lifelong process and psychotherapy can only hope to increase a patient's coping skills. An alternative to the infectious disease model of psychotherapy is the "general practice model" (Cummings & Vandenbos, 1979), where treatment is focused on the immediate problem but the patient is allowed to return as needed.

There is today a broader acceptance of limited goals in therapy. Pardes and Pincus (1981) concluded, "There are people who want relief from a specific symptom, help with a particular area of their personality functioning, improvements of their relationships with a certain person, and so forth, and there has been an increasing acceptance within the mental health provider community that such restriction of goals is consistent with a legitimate and important therapeutic enterprise" (p. 12–13).

Development of a Working Alliance

Goldfried (1980) noted that the therapeutic relationship is considered a primary change strategy across any school of psychotherapy. Freud originally described the therapeutic alliance as the shared value and implicit understanding between the patient and therapist that they work toward the same goal—the patient's improvement. A number of writers (e.g., Bordin, 1976; Gomes-Schwartz, 1978; Hartley & Strupp, 1983; Marziali, Marmar, & Krupnick, 1981) have chosen the term "working alliance" to emphasize the interactional nature of a therapeutic relationship.

The time constraints of brief therapy require that a working alliance be developed quickly. Psychoanalytically oriented therapists often discuss the importance of positive transference to the success of brief psychotherapy (see Table 14.2). While strong feelings of warmth, liking for the therapist, trust, admiration, and confidence are often considered unrealistic in long-term therapy and are interpreted as such, they are considered necessary for success in the time-limited situation. Most brief therapists recommend developing a confident attitude and communicating this hope and expectation of change to the patient. Malan (1963, 1976b) feels that the therapist's enthusiasm has a critical effect on therapeutic outcome. He notes that many young therapists experience several brief, dramatic "cures" early in their careers that they are unable to duplicate in later years. Waning enthusiasm for one's therapeutic techniques may account for this phenomenon.

Maintenance of Focus

The goals of brief therapy can be accomplished most effectively if therapeutic attention is carefully focused on thorough exploration of a primary problem area (see Table 14.2). Small (1971) believes, "Achievement and maintenance of a focus can be regarded as the single most important technical aspect of brief psychotherapy. . ." (p. 121). Budman and Gurman (1983) conclude that the major technical error related to negative outcomes in brief therapy is the failure of the therapist to structure or focus the sessions.

The focus should be determined as early in the course of therapy as possible. Most often the focus is a current problem in the patient's life. Wolberg (1965b) and Malan (1963) suggest that the focus be determined in the first interview and communicated to the patient as part of the description of the terms and structure of the therapy. After the first session the patient's verbalizations are kept centered on the problem area that is the focus through skillful use of "selected attention" (Malan, 1963) and "benign neglect" (Pumpian-Mindlin, 1953). Childhood memories, dreams, or transference interpretations may all have a place in brief therapy, but only if they are directly related to the focus (Wolberg, 1965b). Malan (1976b) further noted in the recent follow-up study of brief and analytic therapy: "Those cases will tend to be successful who present a focus early and have the motivation to work through it. This will tend to lead to short, successful therapy" (p. 203).

High Therapist Activity

Maintaining a focus requires that the therapist participate more actively in the therapeutic process than is characteristic of many long-term approaches. Generally, being "active" means talking more, directing the conversation when necessary, actively exploring areas of interest, offering support and guidance, formulating plans of action for the patient to follow, assigning homework, teaching problem solving, and encouraging a constructive life philosophy. Wolberg (1980) notes that passivity is "anathema" in brief therapy. A more active therapeutic style is reported to be especially helpful with lower-class patients. Gelb and Ullman (1967) conclude that a well-trained therapist can guide clients toward behavior and interaction different from their customary modes, and lead them to more satisfactory and productive lives.

Budman and Gurman (1983) emphasize the importance of a patient's real-life, outside-therapy behavior over the importance of behavior in the consulting room. Brief therapists often actively foster behavior change through the use of homework assignments, involvement of significant others in treatment, and the use of adjunctive aids to therapy such as self-help organizations.

Rapid, Early Assessment

There is virtually no disagreement in the literature that brief psychotherapy requires exploration and information gathering during the first session (see Table 14.2). Small (1971) noted that "Intervention cannot be made a matter of chance, hence more likely to lengthen rather than shorten the process" (p. 73). A comprehensive review of the issues involved in assessing clients for crisis intervention and a survey of assessment methods are provided by Butcher and Herzog (1982).

The focus of assessment differs among therapists. Many crisis-oriented therapists strive for an understanding of the precipitating event of the crisis and the dynamic meaning of the crisis situation in the history of the patient (Harris et al., 1963; Jacobson, 1965; Sifneos, 1972). Small (1972) provided a guide for a psychodynamic formulation for brief therapy assessment. He suggests exploring the complaint, the precipitating cause of the symptoms, antecedent analogues of present behavior, the meanings of the symptoms, and the strengths and weaknesses of the ego system. Sifneos (1972) focuses on understanding unresolved emotional conflicts. Wolberg (1980) attempts to develop a "working understanding of the patient's psychodynamics and an understanding of his neurotic patterns." In addition, he attempts to gauge the degree of homostatic imbalance as indicated by anxiety and its equivalents, the mechanisms of defense that are being used, the amount of self-esteem, dependence—independence, the character of interpersonal relationships, and the disintegrative potential.

Therapeutic Flexibility

Brief and crisis-oriented psychotherapies serve a wide range of patients: anxious, depressed, suicidal, excited, panicky, delirious, assaultive, or antisocial. Meeting the needs of these diverse problems requires a variety of therapeutic techniques. While school identifications exist in brief psychotherapy, most approaches are considerably more eclectic in the choice of interventions than is true of long-term therapy (e.g., Horowitz et al., 1984). Alexander and French (1946) conclude that flexibility of the therapist in adapting interventions to meet the requirements of the individual is the primary technical principle in shortening psychotherapy. Wolberg (1980) suggests that the techniques used in brief psycho-

therapy may come from psychiatry, psychoanalysis, psychology, or sociology.

Promptness of Intervention

Brief therapists strive to provide treatment to a patient as early as possible after the initial request, and they discourage the use of intake interviewers different from the future therapist or lengthy psychometric assessment before therapy has been started.

Most formulations of crisis situations (Caplan, 1964; Lindemann, 1944) stress the time-limited nature of these disequilibriums and the heightened susceptibility to intervention during the crisis period. Crisis intervention centers try to offer an appointment within 24 hours, and many are open 24 hours a day. Bellak and Small (1965) report attempts to reach out immediately to people in disaster through the use of mobile counseling units. Wolkon (1972) found that better outcome occurred in a group of patients who were given immediate crisis therapy than in a group asked to wait several days for an appointment.

Much of the impetus for providing brief forms of therapy stems from the desire to be responsive to a greater range of patients and to cut down the waiting list at clinics. In addition, the emphasis in brief therapy on current life problems suggests the necessity of offering the therapy when a patient has problems and is motivated to work on them.

Encouragement of Ventilation

All major approaches to brief psychotherapy recognize the value of allowing the patient to ventilate emotional tension (see Table 14.2). Most therapists seek to create a therapeutic environment in which the patient feels accepted and safe and in which he or she can express feelings and experience catharsis spontaneously and naturally. A small number of therapists (Nichols, 1974; Nichols & Reifler, 1973; Stampfl & Levis, 1967) deliberately attempt to elicit strong emotions to facilitate tension release.

Selection of Patients

Brief psychotherapy has been attempted with virtually every diagnostic group of patients (Small, 1971). As a result of this diversity, a range of views exists regarding the most suitable types of patients. Wolberg (1965b) advises that any patient thought suitable for psychotherapy should first be tried in brief treatment. Budman and Gurman (1983) also recommend a trial of brief psychotherapy for every patient. If no gains are made, transfer to a different therapist is recommended. This second trial should also involve brief therapy but may include different techniques than the first trial. Gillman (1965) considers regressive long-term therapy to be a disservice to any patient who views his or her functioning prior to the current problem as satisfactory. Parad (1966) suggested that crisis intervention may be most valid for both the very strong and the very weak.

Brief therapy is thought to be more appropriate than long-term therapy for lower socioeconomic class patients (Hoehn-Saric et al., 1964; Jacobson, 1965; Lorion, 1973, 1974). Since the cost of long-term treatment is generally prohibitive for many patients, and brief treatment methods are effective for many types of patients and problems, brief treatment is a highly desirable treatment option for lower socioeconomic class patients. The tactics followed by brief therapists (directiveness, concrete goal orientation, etc.) are both acceptable to lower socioeconomic class patients and are, in many instances, an expected helping mode.

In opposition to these views are most psychodynamically oriented therapists (e.g., Mann, 1973; Sifneos, 1979) who have delineated stringent patient selection criteria. In the opinions of many dynamic psychotherapists, the following types of patients are best suited for brief dynamic techniques (see Table 14.2 for references).

1. *Those in whom the behavioral problem is of acute onset.* A number of therapists have pointed to recent onset as an important selection criterion for brief therapy (see Table 14.2). However, some therapists consider recency of onset irrelevant (e.g., Davanloo, 1979; Strupp & Binder, 1984). Correlated with recent onset is an expressed preference for focal as opposed to diffuse problems.
2. *Those whose previous adjustment has been good.* Many brief psychotherapies are recommended primarily for patients with a history of relatively good psychological and social functioning. However, some clinicians support the use of brief therapy with fairly disturbed patients when the goals are concrete and kept within reach of the patient (Butcher & Maudal, 1976). Malan (1976b) concluded that

the type of psychopathology and the duration of symptoms did not influence outcome. He suggested that even severe and chronic conditions are potentially amenable to brief therapy.

Recently, several brief therapists (e.g., Strupp, Davanloo, & Marziali) have turned their attention to work with "difficult" patients who present severe symptoms often in the context of characterological disturbances.

3. *Those with good ability to relate.* The ability to relate is one of the most important aspects of patient selection for brief psychotherapy. Davanloo (1979) considers the quality of the patient's human relationships (e.g., the presence of at least one meaningful relationship in the past) to be an element of prime importance in determining a patient's suitability to treatment. Marmor (1979) suggests that the outcome of brief therapy can be maximized by selection of patients who relate well with the therapist during the first session and demonstrate the capacity to experience feelings and develop insight. Davanloo (1979) evaluates the patient's ability to respond to trial interpretations.
4. *Those with high initial motivation.* Many therapists have recorded the importance of high initial motivation for successful therapy. Malan (1976b) believes that initial motivation was a more important patient characteristic than any other included in his studies. Sifneos (1979) considers motivation to be of such prognostic significance that he has developed seven criteria to operationalize what he views as its components, including the ability to recognize problems as psychological; the tendency to be introspective and to be given an honest account of emotional difficulties; willingness to participate actively in treatment; curiosity and willingness to understand oneself; willingness to change, explore, and experiment; and willingness to make reasonable sacrifices.

Patients who have been mentioned as being definitely unsuitable for brief therapy are those who desire personality reconstruction, are deeply dependent. act out persistently, or are unrestrainably anxious (Wolberg, 1965b). Castelnuovo-Tedesco (1966) noted that brief treatment does not work if the patient is outspokenly self-centered, passive-dependent, masochistic, or self-destructive. Frank (1974) excluded patients with less than fifth-grade education, organic-toxic illness, mental deficiency, or psychosis. More recently, Strupp and Hadley (1979) and Gomes-Schwartz (1978) found several additional contraindications: pervasive charactero-logical disturbances, profound negativism, and rigidity.

Summary of Common Characteristics of Brief Therapies

An extensive array of opinions on what constitutes brief psychotherapy has been presented in this section. This material provided a glimpse of these views and a guide to the published literature. Can a unitary view of the basic elements or main theme of what constitutes brief psychotherapy be gleaned from the material? It is clear from examining this literature that there are many brief therapies with different foci, structures, goals, tactics, and probably outcomes. However, certain elements characterize most brief therapy approaches:

- Most therapists inform the patient of the time limitations in advance and expect that the focused and limited goals will be achieved in that period.
- Most therapists limit therapeutic goals within attainable reach. Goals such as amelioration of the most disabling symptoms, reestablishment of a previous level of functioning, and development of some understanding of current disturbance and increased coping ability are adopted.
- Most therapists view the development of a therapeutic relationship as an important element in brief therapy, as it is in any form of psychotherapy. With the constraints imposed by the time limitation, the brief therapist is often caught between sometimes mutually antagonistic roles: "relating-understanding" (developing a relationship) and "directive confronting." The success of directive intervention generally depends on the patient's acceptance of the competence, authority, and benevolence of the therapist. This receptive attitude in patients is highly related to the strength and quality of the therapeutic relationship.

- Most brief therapy sessions are centered around concrete content and are focused on the "here and now" instead of early life events.
- Most therapists tend to be both active and directive in relating to the patient in order to maintain direction and organization of the sessions.
- Most therapists believe that effective brief therapy requires an experienced therapist who can keep therapeutic goals in sight and not get bogged down in content that is irrelevant to the agreed-on goals. The necessity of early, rapid assessment in brief therapy underscores the importance of having an experienced therapist. It is important for the therapist to be able to gather relevant information and develop a working formulation during the early sessions. This assessment must provide an understanding of the extent of the patient's problem, the critical nature of the present situation, and the personal resources the patient might have that could be called into play to increase his or her coping skills.
- Most brief therapeutic approaches consider flexibility in the therapist's role an essential element in abbreviating therapy.
- Most brief therapeutic approaches are aimed at prompt early intervention at the onset of symptoms or during an experienced crisis. Certainly one of the attractive features of brief therapy programs is the potential of providing therapeutic contact to more patients. Reaching patients with prompt assistance at an early point in their crisis can aid in resolving immediate problems and prevent more serious or chronic pathology that may require more lengthy treatment at a later date.
- While many therapists consider that selecting the appropriate patients for brief treatment is important, brief therapy is the treatment the great majority of patients receive. Regardless of symptom severity, patients who have a good ability to relate are considered to be better candidates for brief therapy than those who have difficulty forming relationships.

EMPIRICAL STUDIES OF BRIEF PSYCHOTHERAPY

Brief psychotherapy has been described as ". . . a unique proving ground for testing the efficacy and utility of techniques, something that is difficult to accomplish in open-ended approaches" (Strupp, 1981, p. 227). There are a number of reasons researchers choose brief psychotherapy for evaluation of therapy process and outcome:

1. Most of the variables and processes are similar or identical to those in long-term therapy. Consequently, variables important to long-term psychotherapeutic change are studied more easily in the context of a brief therapy contact.
2. Brief therapy provides a greater possibility of control of extraneous influences in a research design.
3. The logistics of arranging and monitoring numbers of patients, therapists, assistants, and significant others is more manageable over a short period of time than over longer periods.
4. The operational criteria for improvement required for sound outcome and process research are easier to define since brief treatment is generally focused and goal-oriented.
5. Important questions that can be answered only by adequate follow-up can be accomplished more readily in the context of a brief therapeutic contact.

Given these practical advantages, it is not surprising that brief methods have been widely used in psychotherapy research.

Research on Brief Psychotherapy Process

What are the factors in brief psychotherapy that contribute to change in the patient? Much of the existing research on psychotherapy relates to this question, since many common elements operate in all forms of psychotherapy, brief or long term (e.g., Goldfried, 1980). Consequently, it is not possible to review here all of the factors that are important to brief psychotherapy. There are relevant reviews elsewhere in this volume that summarize more extensively and focally these broader process variables. This review is limited to variables that have been subjected to empirical investigation within a brief-therapy context. Included are several factors thought to be particularly salient in brief therapy.

Although we have chosen to divide the empirical literature into "process" and "outcome" sections, process data are most valuable in advancing knowledge of the dynamics of change when they are linked to data on the overall outcome of therapy.

Therapeutic Alliance

Many early studies of brief dynamic psychotherapy examined transference, which by definition limited consideration to the patient's relationship to the therapist. Recently there has been a "resurgence of interest in the 'therapeutic alliance' or 'working alliance' . . . (i.e., the interactive patient–therapist relationship)" (Strupp, 1981, p. 228).

A Therapeutic Alliance scale has been developed for use in brief therapy research by Marziali, Marmar, and Krupnick (1981). Items are evenly divided between therapist's contributions and patient's contributions and were designed for use by an expert clinical rater. A later revision (Marziali, 1984) is designed for patient and therapist self-report. Marziali et al. (1981) used raters to determine a therapeutic alliance score for audiotaped psychotherapy sessions for which standardized tests and ratings of global improvements were available. They found that the patient's total contribution to the alliance scale, but not the therapist's total contribution, was highly correlated with outcome. Patients who were rated as making a strong positive contribution to the alliance had good outcomes. In the poor-outcome cases, therapists were not rated badly. "Instead, it appeared that the patients with poor outcome brought a negative disposition to the treatment situation that persisted across the hours of the brief psychotherapy and was relatively intransigent to the therapist's efforts to shore up the alliance" (Marziali et al., 1981, p. 363). Although this study is an important contribution to understanding the therapeutic alliance in brief psychotherapy, it involved a relatively small number of patients and is unreplicated. Further empirical study of the therapeutic alliance is needed.

On the basis of a series of case studies in which successful and unsuccessful patients were compared, Strupp (1980d) observed, ". . . we failed to encounter a single instance in which a difficult patient's hostility and negativism were successfully confronted or resolved" (p. 954). Typically, even experienced professional therapists responded to such patients with counterhostility in the form of coldness, distancing, and other types of rejection. "Thus, major deterrents to the formation of a good working alliance are not only the patient's characterological distortions and maladaptive defenses but—at least equally important—the therapist's personal reaction" (Strupp, 1980d, p. 953).

Frank (1974) summarized research conducted over 25 years and concluded, "The quality of the therapeutic interaction, to which patient, therapist, and therapeutic method contribute, is probably the major determinant of short-term therapeutic response" (p. 338). While studies of the therapeutic alliance have concluded that the patient's contributions are relatively more powerful predictors of outcome than the therapist's contributions, the empirical literature on the therapeutic alliance in brief therapy is too sparse to justify firm conclusions.

Therapist Actions

A therapist action is a "specific meaningful act that the therapist might do" (Hoyt, Marmar, Horowitz, & Alvarez, 1981). Recently, several scales to measure therapist's actions have been developed and/ or used specifically in brief psychotherapy research (e.g., Elliott, 1985; Gomes-Schwartz, 1978; Hill, 1978; Hoyt et al., 1981; Neu, Prusoff, & Klerman, 1978; Stiles, 1980). The various scales differ in the level of analysis at which process variables are studied. Most of the scales are pantheoretical and can be used to explore technical differences between the alternate treatments in comparative studies.

Exemplars of process scales that adopt microanalysis of the therapist's actions are the verbal response mode rating scales. Stiles (1980) defines a verbal response mode as a "category of language that implies a particular *interpersonal* intention. For example, a 'self-disclosure' expresses attitudes, feelings, or opinions to another person" (p. 49). Typical of this level of process analysis is the Counselor Verbal Response Category System (Hill, 1978; Hill et al., 1981), which consists of 14 nominal, mutually exclusive categories of verbal response modes such as minimal encourager, approval reassurance, direct guidance, open question, reflection, and interpretation. A list of 15 counseling intentions supplements the system. Counseling intentions include actions such as fact finding, focus, support, reframing, and analysis of relationship (Hill et al., 1981).

Another group of scales addresses process more globally and results in ratings of entire segments of a session. Representative of these scales is the Vanderbilt Psychotherapy Process Scale (e.g., Gomes-Schwartz, 1978), which is composed of seven factor scales (four represent therapist actions and three represent patient actions). The therapist scales include Therapist Exploration (taps the degree to which the therapist attempted to examine the psychodynamics underlying the patient's problems), Therapist Warmth and Friendliness (reflects the therapist's warmth, caring, and emotional involvement with the patient), Negative Therapist Attitude (gauges attitudes that might threaten or intimidate the patient), and Therapist Advice and Modeling Behavior.

Therapist action scales have been used to investigate whether therapists from different schools of psychotherapy actually talk and behave differently and, if so, whether these differences translate into differential outcome. Gomes-Schwartz (1978) compared ratings of analytic therapists, experiential therapists, and nonprofessional "alternate" therapists on the Vanderbilt Psychotherapy Process Scale. Alternate and experiential therapists exhibited greater Therapist Warmth and Friendliness than analytic therapists. Analytic therapists received higher scores than the other therapists on the Therapist Exploration and Patient Exploration scales. Alternate therapists demonstrated higher scores than analytic but not experiential therapists on the Therapist Advice and Modeling Behavior scale. No differences related to school or training were found on the Therapist Hostility scale. Nevertheless, no differences in therapeutic outcome were found among the three groups of therapists.

Staples, Sloane, Whipple, Cristol, and Yorkston (1976) found that behavior therapists when compared to psychodynamic therapists were more directive, open, genuine, and disclosing. On the basis of their study they concluded, "Differences between behavior therapy and analytically-oriented psychotherapy . . . involved the basic patterns of interactions between patient and therapist and the type of relationship formed. Behavior therapy is not psychotherapy with special 'specific techniques' superimposed on the traditional therapeutic paradigm; rather, the two appear to represent quite different styles of treatment although they share common elements" (p. 1521). However, they reported no major differences in the outcomes achieved through the diverse techniques.

Several studies have explored alterations in therapist behavior both within a single session of psychotherapy and across an entire treatment course (e.g., Hawton, Reibstein, Fieldsend, & Whalley, 1982; Hill, Carter, & O'Farrell, 1983). For example, in a single-case study design, Hill et al. (1983) describe the changes in counselor behavior that occurred over the course of a 12-session brief therapy. Statistical comparison of the first third to the final two-thirds of the treatment course suggested increases in activity level, silence, and interpretations, and decreases in minimal encouragers. Comparison of counselor intentions during the first third to the last two-thirds of the sessions demonstrated increases in direct change attempts and analysis of the relationship, and decreases in clarification. While these comparisons are a necessary starting point, this line of process research will be most valuable when it is extended to differences between successful and unsuccessful therapy. A step in this direction is demonstrated by the study of the therapist actions characteristic of "good" and "bad" hours of psychotherapy (e.g., O'Farrell, Hill, & Patton, in press; Hoyt, Xenakis, Marmar, & Horowitz, 1983). For example, Hoyt et al. (1983) compared the therapist actions in 46 brief dynamic psychotherapy sessions rated for goodness of quality by expert raters. Good sessions were positively correlated with therapist emphasis on patient expression and discussion of patient–therapist relationship, the meaning of the patient's reactions, and the links or patterns between the patient's past and present life.

Negative Therapist Actions

Deterioration or negative effects from psychotherapy have been receiving attention recently (e.g., Bergin, 1963, 1971; Hadley & Strupp, 1976; Strupp, Hadley, & Gomes-Schwartz, 1977). There are a number of reasons why brief psychotherapy might be vulnerable to negative change: the important area of patient and situational assessment may not receive adequate attention under the imposed time pressures; more direct involvement on the part of the therapist might allow greater opportunity for negative impact; the relatively fast pace and the need for prompt therapist intervention may result in premature or incorrect therapeutic action; and finally, the brevity of the intervention and the difficulty or lack of follow-up may not provide the therapist with sufficient time to observe the effects (either positive or negative) of the interventions and take

corrective action. However, no evidence exists to suggest that brief psychotherapy produces any greater negative effects than long-term psychotherapy.

Sachs (1983) has studied negative factors in brief psychotherapy, which she defines as variables that "impede therapeutic progress or are believed to result in negative outcomes (i.e., ineffective therapy and harmful therapy)" (p. 557). She employed the Vanderbilt Negative Indicators Scale (Strupp et al., 1981), which consists of five subscales that reflect patient negative attitudes, therapist exploitative tendencies, errors in technique, problems in the therapeutic relationship, and ineffectiveness. Trained clinical raters listened to audiotaped segments from the first three therapy sessions of 18 male participants in the Vanderbilt Psychotherapy Project (Strupp & Hadley, 1979). In none of the cases were patients judged to have deteriorated in therapy, but in several instances therapy was felt to have been ineffective in inducing change. A statistically significant partial correlation was obtained between errors in technique and outcome. The association was stronger for psychodynamic therapy than for experiential therapy. Thus, while type of technique was not related to outcome, quality of technique was.

Activity Level

The actual activity levels of brief therapists have been explored in a small number of studies. However, few studies have related the therapist's activity level to the outcome of therapy. For example, the therapist was found to speak 40 to 50 percent of the words in two case studies of brief psychotherapy, one of which was successful and one unsuccessful (Hill et al., 1983; O'Farrell, Hill, & Patton, in press). Rusk and Gerner (1972) found that the therapists of successful patients talked for significantly less time in the first third and significantly more in the last third of the interview than therapists of unsuccessful cases. Staples and Sloane (1970; Sloane, Staples, Cristol, Yorkston, & Whipple, 1975) found that the more the patient talked relative to the therapist, the greater the improvement. Also, the longer the duration of the patient's average utterance, the greater the improvement. However, the differential improvement rate between patients who talked more and those who talked less was not as marked in behavior therapy as in psychotherapy.

These studies are an inadequate base on which to form an opinion regarding the optimal range of therapist activity in brief psychotherapy. Analogue studies might be utilized advantageously here since patient's talk time may be related to individual differences, not differences in therapeutic procedures.

Maintenance of Focus

If topics are to be explored in any depth in the context of a brief treatment process, some limits must be exerted on the number of different topics that are considered. Dynamic brief therapists often discuss a "dynamic focus" for a patient. The interpretations the therapist makes are then directed specifically at this focus. Virtually no research exists on the technique of focusing. Malan (1976b) has reported that undirected interpretations are negatively correlated with outcome. However, his work is subject to a number of criticisms (i.e., no control group, ratings made from case notes, ratings not blind.) Lambert (1983) attributed the lack of positive outcome subsequent to brief psychotherapy in a recent case study (Hill et al., 1983) to lack of focus.

Further research on the focus in brief psychotherapy awaits the development of a reliable procedure for formulating an individualized treatment focus for each patient. Recently, two procedures for describing the focus for interventions have appeared (Binder, Strupp, & Schacht, 1983; Horowitz et al., 1984; Strupp & Binder, 1984); and several others are in development.

Interpretation

Most brief psychotherapists consider interpretation to be the therapist's key change-producing behavior. A number of different foci for interpretations have been advocated: Malan (1976a) emphasizes interpretations that link conflicts in the patient—therapist relationship to parental figures; Mann (1973) interprets separation issues; and Davanloo (1979) focuses on obsessional defenses. Inconsistent results have been obtained in studies that have attempted to correlate the number of times a specific type of interpretation is made to therapy outcome.

For example, Malan (1976b) reported that the number of interpretations linking parents and therapist was positively related to outcome. While this finding has been replicated (Marziali & Sullivan, 1980), it has also been challenged (Piper, Debbane, Bienvenu, DeCarofel, & Garant, in press). Piper et al. reported virtually no significant correlations between outcome and any one of several specific types of interpretations.

Depth of exploration in therapy would seem to dictate the kinds of interpretations that are made in a session. Although dynamic therapists have been rated higher in therapist exploration (Gomes-Schwartz, 1978), interpretations offered by behavior therapists have been found to be just as related to past history and dynamics (Sloane et al., 1975). A negative relationship between the total number of interpretations and outcome has been reported (Malan, 1976b; Sloane et al., 1975). This finding suggests that the more the therapists attempted to interpret or clarify problems by giving the patient information related to his or her problem, the less successful the treatment was. It may be that "difficult" patients call forth more heroic therapeutic efforts that find the therapists becoming more and more "interpretive" when therapy is not progressing well.

After consideration of successful versus unsuccessful patients both treated by the same therapists in brief psychotherapy, Strupp (1980a) concluded, "One thing seems incontrovertibly clear: Whatever may bring about therapeutic change, it is not a class of communications, such as interpretations per se, but rather the conjunction of a particular communication by the therapist . . . with a state of 'readiness' existing in that patient that hits the latter 'between the eyes' and leaves a lasting impression. The effectiveness of interpretations depends on their context not their content" (p. 601). Research into "critical events" in psychotherapy (e.g., Rice & Greenberg, 1984) may eventually lead to better understanding of the components of the interpretation process (i.e., markers of patient readiness to apprehend new information, characteristics of therapist's response associated with positive resolution of a critical event).

Some form of interpretation is present in all forms of brief psychotherapy. Although a few studies have examined the ways in which interpretive remarks by the therapist are received and processed, the complete anatomy of the interpretation process has not been well defined.

Patient Actions

Patient action scales have been constructed to parallel the therapist action scales (e.g., Gomes-

Schwartz, 1978; Hill et al., 1981; Hoyt et al., 1981). For example, the Vanderbilt Psychotherapy Process Scale (Gomes-Schwartz, 1978) contains three patient scales that gauge the patient's level of self-examination, the degree to which the patient is actively engaged in the therapy interaction, and the level of negativism, hostility, or distrust displayed by the patient. These scales have been used to examine the impact of various patient behaviors on the process and outcome of therapy. A summary of these studies is presented below.

Involvement

Gomes-Schwartz (1978) considered the relationships between patient actions, therapist actions, and therapy outcome. She found that "patient involvement" was consistently the best predictor of outcome. It accounted for 30 percent of the variance as opposed to 18 percent for "exploratory processes" and 38 percent of the variance as opposed to 24 percent for "therapist offered relationship." She concluded, "Patients who were not hostile or mistrustful and who actively contributed to the therapy interactions achieved greater changes than those who were withdrawn, defensive, or otherwise unwilling to engage in the therapy process. . . . The variables that best predicted change were not related to therapeutic techniques but to the positiveness of the patient's attitude toward his therapist and his commitment to work at changing" (Gomes-Schwartz, 1978, p. 1032).

In an analysis of the verbal response modes used by the patients in the Vanderbilt Psychotherapy Project (McDaniel, Stiles, & McGaughey, 1981), those patients who improved more were those who participated more as measured by their total number of utterances. Stiles and Sultan (1979) coded the therapist and client verbal response modes in 10 psychotherapy transcripts (including a transcript of brief psychotherapy by Wolberg). They found that across the therapies, the profile of therapist response modes varied while the profile of patient response modes was similar. They concluded, ". . . if there is a common core to the verbal psychotherapies, it is more likely to be found in the client's verbal behavior than in the therapist's (Stiles & Sultan, 1979, p. 613).

Pretherapy interpersonal relationships and patients' subsequent degree of involvement in psychotherapy were investigated by Moras and Strupp (1982). The quality of patient's pretherapy interpersonal relationships (i.e., presence of meaningful relationships and absence of mistrust or hostility) was rated from a pretherapy assessment interview conducted by an independent clinician. "The results . . . suggest that an appreciable portion of the variance (up to 25%) in a patient's collaborative participation in therapy can be linked to . . . assessments of interpersonal relations . . . (Moras & Strupp, 1982, p. 408). In a second study (Keithly, Samples, & Strupp, 1980), patient's motivation was rated on the attributes that have been viewed as components of motivation (Sifneos, 1968, 1972, 1979). Motivation was found to be a good predictor of patient involvement in therapy during the first three-quarters of the treatment course but the effect disappeared by the end of therapy. In neither study, however, did the process ratings correlate with therapy outcome.

Strupp (1980b) concludes, "Given the 'average expectable' atmosphere created by a person functioning in the therapeutic role, that is, a person who is basically empathic and benign, the key determinants of a particular therapeutic outcome are traceable to characteristics of the patient . . . if the patient is a person who by virtue of his past life experience is capable of human relatedness and therefore is amenable to learning mediated within that context, the outcome, even though the individual may have suffered traumas, reverses, and other vicissitudes, is likely to be positive" (p. 716). Compared to other areas of process research, several studies support the importance of patient involvement in successful psychotherapy. However, these studies have all utilized data collected at Vanderbilt on a small group of male patients selected to be diagnostically homogeneous. These studies need to be extended to larger and broader patient samples.

Expectation of Receiving Help

An examination of psychotherapy processes is not complete without discussing the importance of hope and expectation (Frank, 1974). The influence of patient expectation on positive therapeutic outcome has become recognized as an important factor to control for in any psychotherapy-outcome study. Patients who believe they are receiving therapy even though contact is minimal generally show greater improvement than control patients who receive no contact (e.g., Cross, Sheehan, & Khan, 1982; Frank, 1974; Sloane et al., 1975). Frank (1974) believes that early psychotherapeutic gains and placebo effects are both due to mobilization of hope. Symptomatic changes due to relearning appear later in therapy.

Not all patient expectations improve the likelihood of therapeutic success, however. Hornstra, Lubin, Lewis, and Willis (1972) surveyed 611 consecutive applicants (and 443 relatives) to a community mental health center. They found that there were unrealistic expectations of services in this predominantly lower socioeconomic class population. The patients studied indicated a desire for *quick commitment on their part*. Only 16.7 percent of the sample felt that regularly scheduled appointments to talk about their problems would be helpful.

Several studies have been reported in which patients were prepared for psychotherapy by films or special interviews in order to reduce unrealistic ideas and enhance positive expectations (e.g., Hoehn-Saric et al., 1964; Sloane, Cristol, Pepernik, & Staples, 1970; Warren & Rice, 1972). Patients who received preparations showed more appropriate behavior, remained in therapy longer, and had better outcomes than patients who failed to receive preparation. Heitler (1976) summarizes, "While further research is needed, it is clear that a variety of preparatory techniques hold promise for facilitating a therapeutic alliance in expressive psychotherapy with unsophisticated patients from any social class, and that these techniques may be particularly useful with lower class patient populations, in which unsophisticated and potentially counterproductive role expectations seem to be more prevalent" (p. 350).

Expectation of receiving help is an important consideration for any type of psychotherapy, but perhaps especially so for brief therapy, since the time constraints require that treatment sessions be fast moving and goal-oriented. Negative expectations may induce fatalistic attitudes that are difficult to overcome in the limited sessions available. Most of the research literature supports the view that expectancy of receiving help is associated with improvement in therapy. However, the exact conditions that account for this improvement have not been fully determined.

Cognitive and Behavioral Change

In patient rankings of the factors critical to improvement in brief psychotherapy, consistently placed near the top of the list is the therapist helping the patient to understand his or her problems (e.g.,

Cross et al., 1982; Sloane et al., 1975). In the Sloane et al. (1975) study it was expected that patients would view the behavioral therapist as directive, and encouraging the patient to try out new behaviors. A somewhat unexpected result was found with regard to patients' views of the analytic therapists' behaviors. Psychotherapy patients also considered the therapist "encouraging him to practice facing the things that bother him" to be one of the most helpful aspects of therapy. Wilson (1981) notes, however, that this type of comparison tends to blur the distinctions between behavioral and dynamic psychotherapy. He observes that the "behavioral practice" in behavior therapy is much more structured and systematic than in psychotherapy. Whether such differences "make a difference" or represent different roads to Rome is the subject of comparative outcome studies that will be considered later in the chapter.

White, Fichtenbaum, and Dollard (1969) studied the messages communicated to patients in brief psychotherapy and related them to rated improvement in adjustment. Patients who learned verbally what the therapist taught were likely to have improved in adjustment. Likewise, patients who learned behaviorally what the therapist taught were improved. While behavioral learning was frequently associated with improved adjustment, insight alone was not found to be sufficient to produce improved adjustment in some areas (e.g., sexual adjustment). A study by Liberman, Imber, Stone, Hoehn-Saric, and Frank (reported in Frank, 1974) showed that patients whose behavioral changes resulted from their own efforts at mastery maintained their progress longer than patients who believed that their changes in treatment were due to a placebo medication.

Actively encouraging a patient to try out new roles and to seek alternative behaviors is an important part of brief therapy, regardless of the therapeutic orientation. Behavior change not only enables patients to modify their present stress-producing environment but, more importantly, helps them develop confidence that they can master the problems that surround them.

The Process of Change in Brief Psychotherapy

In addition to therapist and client actions, the structural features of brief psychotherapy (i.e., time limitations, heightened emotional arousal) may affect the process of change that occurs in treatment. The impact of these features on the process of treatment will now be considered.

Impact of Time Limitations

Is there a unique contribution to therapeutic outcome that lies in the time constraints inherent in brief psychotherapy? Does the time limitation itself result in a process that differs from long-term therapy and produces relatively greater patient improvement in a telescoped time span? Many clinicians believe that the therapeutic process is speeded up by a patient's awareness that therapeutic time is limited. Frank (1959) found some evidence that patients respond more promptly to treatment when they know in advance that the therapy will be limited. Shlien, Mosak, and Dreikurs (1962) compared time-limited (18 sessions) to unlimited (averaging 37 sessions) client-centered therapy. For both groups the improvement that took place occurred early in treatment and then reached a plateau. Smith, Glass, and Miller (1980) concluded that the major impact of psychological treatment occurs in the first 6 to 8 sessions. After this, there is a reduction in impact that lasts for the next 10 sessions.

Piper et al. (1984) interviewed therapists and patients who had participated in a comparative study of psychodynamic therapy that examined individual therapy (brief and long-term) and group therapy (brief and long-term). Brief treatments averaged 22 sessions while long treatments averaged 76 sessions. Statistical analysis suggested the presence of an interaction between the form of therapy and the duration of therapy. Thus, the impact of time limitation was modified by the format of therapy. Therapist and patient comments on the therapy process highlight this finding. Regarding brief individual psychotherapy, both therapists and patients noted a "facilitative atmosphere of time pressure." While the range of problems that was explored was narrow, those problems that were explored were treated in depth. Satisfaction was also expressed with long-term individual therapy by patients but not by therapists. Therapists felt that one session a week for 76 weeks seemed to favor increased resistance and decreased working through. The therapists encountered a number of problems with long-term treatment: Patients tended to defend against affective involvement, to control regression, and to restrict expression of transfer-

ence, which made these processes more difficult to clarify and interpret. In general, patients acted as if there was always plenty of time to work later.

Time limitation was not viewed favorably by therapists and patients assigned to group therapy, however. Both patients and therapists perceived an atmosphere of deprivation. Initial anxiety about working on sensitive issues with others was followed immediately by anxiety over ending. Therapists felt burdened and believed their psychoanalytic approach had proved inappropriate to a brief group format, a setting that seemed to call for structured techniques. The long-term group, on the other hand, was viewed quite favorably. Both patients and therapists felt a high degree of involvement and attentiveness. The presence of a group provided continual stimulation and there was ample time to deal with important issues. However, compared to individual therapy, group therapy resulted in more resistance and less regression and transference.

There is some indication that regular sessions of at least one hour in duration are important for enhancing intense emotional experience. Bierenbaum et al. (1976) studied the relationship of length and frequency of brief psychotherapy sessions and emotional catharsis. They found that patients seen for weekly one-hour sessions experienced more catharsis than patients seen for half-hour sessions twice weekly or patients seen for two hours every two weeks. However, patients who received the most frequent sessions (half an hour twice weekly) improved most on personality tests, regardless of the amount of emotional catharsis produced.

There is some evidence to suggest that behaviorally oriented therapy may be better received as a brief therapeutic contact than more dynamic approaches. Sloane et al.'s (1975) follow-up study of patients who had been treated in either brief analytic or behavior therapy found that none of the behavior therapy patients complained of the brevity of treatment. However, four out of the nine patients who failed to improve in psychotherapy complained about the length of treatment. They concluded that behavioral methods are probably better suited to the very brief durations of therapy; even if treatment does not succeed, patients feel as if they have received a fair trial.

These few studies begin to build empirical support for clinical observations of the impact of time constraints on patient attitudes and the pace of the sessions. Regardless of stated time limitations, however, a major portion of the change attributable to psychotherapy appears to occur early in psychotherapy.

Change Under Heightened Arousal

Brief psychotherapy, especially crisis therapy, is often conducted while the patient is experiencing intense emotions. In addition, the general level of emotional arousal in brief psychotherapy may be higher than that of long-term psychotherapy for the following reasons:

1. The directive (sometimes confrontive) nature of brief therapy often provokes strong feelings in patients.
2. The time limitation on therapy keeps the sessions at a higher pitch.
3. The type of patients selected for brief therapy are often individuals with problems of acute onset who are seeking help in the midst of a life crisis.

Thus, an area of research important to the understanding of brief psychotherapy process is the study of attitude change under heightened emotional arousal. Frank (1974) and his colleagues (Hoehn-Saric et al., 1972) report studies of the effects of emotional arousal on patient susceptibility to focal attitude change in therapy. In one study ether was used to produce emotional arousal, then patients were interviewed about their emotionally charged experiences and were given suggestions concerning a preselected focal concept. Patient's subsequent beliefs shifted in the direction of the therapist's suggestions.

Based on their review of the relationship between affect and change in psychotherapy, Luborsky, Chandler, Auerbach, Cohen, and Bachrach (1971) concluded, ". . . almost any affect is better than no affect." Patients who are anxious or depressed at the beginning of therapy are the ones most likely to benefit from therapy. In fact, some degree of arousal may facilitate change. Saltzman, Luetgert, Roth, Creaser, and Howard (1976) found that individuals who drop out of therapy in the early sessions are those who experience relatively lower levels of anxiety. These studies suggest that attitude change can occur under heightened arousal.

Phases of Brief Psychotherapy

Mann (1973) suggests that there is a predictable pattern to a patient's feelings about treatment over the course of brief psychotherapy. He asserts that initially patients have positive feelings about treatment. In this phase the problem-assessment and contract-formulation goals of therapists mesh with the help-seeking goals of patients. The middle phase of therapy is characterized by sessions that can fluctuate between the following types: frustrating, anxiety provoking, gratifying, freeing, and affirming. Therapists by virtue of their experience expect such fluctuations, but patients do not. In the terminal phase of treatment, patients consolidate the gains of treatment, become aware of its limitations, and resolve their ambivalent feelings about the therapeutic relationship. Thus, they return to a way of experiencing therapy that corresponds to that of therapists. Correlations between patients' and therapists' ratings of session quality generally support these postulated stages (Schwartz & Bernard, 1981).

The stages of brief psychotherapy have also been addressed from a systems perspective (Tracey, 1985; Tracey & Ray, 1984). Here the change process is seen as a movement out of an initial stage of homeostasis, into a state of flux and terminating in a new point of homeostasis. These stages have been explored by comparing the sequence of patient–therapist topic initiation and topic continuation among successful and unsuccessful therapy dyads. Results reveal a pattern of high–low–high complementarity in topic initiation/topic following among successful therapy cases. Therapists in successful dyads were found to initiate more topics during the middle or "conflict" stage of therapy. This finding suggests that in cases with successful outcomes, the middle phase of therapy consisted of the therapist directing attention to issues the patient did not necessarily want to address. Agreement as to the focus then gradually emerged in the final stage of therapy. Where outcome was unsuccessful, clear-cut changes are not seen in complementarity.

Summary: Brief Therapy Process

In this section we have reviewed research studies that focus on processes common to most brief psychotherapy approaches. It has been pointed out that many processes in brief therapy are so similar to those in long-term therapy (e.g., therapeutic alliance, interpretation, and expectancy effects) that they might be studied more easily in the brief context. Nevertheless, there is a paucity of clear findings in many areas of process research in brief therapy, despite the fact that this treatment modality lends itself particularly well to empirical research.

From the studies reviewed in this section, we arrived at several tentative conclusions that might serve as guides to further empirical research. The major importance of the therapeutic alliance was highlighted. Preliminary findings suggest that while the therapeutic alliance is a cooperative relationship, given a therapist with average human qualities and training, the strength of the alliance is most strongly influenced by patient characteristics. Even highly trained professional therapists appear unable to establish relationships with certain types of patients. While a strong therapeutic alliance characterizes cases with good outcomes, studies have not addressed the proportion of outcome variance that is predicted by ratings of alliance made early in therapy. More study of this issue is indicated. In addition, future research might address ways of working with poor prognosis patients, techniques to heighten patient involvement in the therapeutic process, and procedures for strengthening initially negative therapeutic alliances.

A number of process scales have been developed in recent years including therapeutic alliance scales, therapist action scales, patient action scales, conflict scales, and negative factor scales. These scales have made a wide range of new investigations possible. We found process studies, particularly those that analyze psychotherapy at the level of verbal response modes, difficult to evaluate, however, because of the absence of a descriptive data base that defines the parameters of brief psychotherapy. Future research might include application of a set of process scales to a group of exemplary practitioners of brief psychotherapy. Such a study would result in a set of normative values regarding activities such as activity level, percentage of the total conversation contributed by the therapist, number of topics considered, number and kinds of interpretations, handling of critical events, and the like. Such data would amplify clinical writings on brief psychotherapy and would be valuable for purposes of evaluating the technical qualities of future samples of brief psycho-

therapy process—whether in research or in teaching.

We also noted the variety of scales for rating psychotherapy process that have appeared. Although the use of a standard battery of rating scales can be overemphasized at the expense of creativity, rampant individualism in the development of scales makes the process of generalization between studies difficult. Several process rating scales were described earlier that are backed up by appropriate reliability and validity studies. The cumulation of knowledge would be furthered by greater use of a set of common instruments in process studies. The use of author-developed process scales that lack appropriate evidence of a theoretical foundation, internal consistency, reliability, interrater reliability, and content validity should be strongly discouraged.

In the next section, we will turn our attention to the requirements for good-quality outcome studies. At that point, the reader will notice that process studies are often characterized by lack of sufficient attention to the reliable and valid measurement of therapy outcome. Yet the measurement of therapy outcome is quite important in a process study. Process findings derive their major import from their link with the overall outcome of the therapy process. When process differences do not relate to outcome, they lack practical significance, although they do increase our basic knowledge of the therapeutic process. Thus, while studies of the technical actions of therapists have suggested that their behavior differs depending on their training and orientation, these technical differences are not highly predictive of outcome. Several exploratory studies were reviewed that have linked process to outcome through comparison of cases with successful and unsuccessful outcomes. The application of this methodology to a larger series of cases and empirical analysis would be profitable.

A final concern about published studies is whether sufficient attention was paid to ensuring that the therapy process subjected to analysis represented exemplary or even prototypic brief psychotherapy. In the majority of clinics, therapy is of short duration, although the brief duration is often unintentional and represents unilateral terminations on the part of patients. Even though most therapists have had exposure to the practice of short-duration therapy, one cannot assume that they received specific instruction in brief therapy techniques such as formulating a focus, implementing time limitations, limiting goals, and so on. Budman (1981) has gone so far as to suggest that therapists well trained in the practice of long-term psychotherapy lack the specific skills to practice brief psychotherapy and possess skills that interfere in time-limited therapy. Yet it is noted repeatedly in process studies that therapists who participated—while they were experienced—had no training in the use of brief therapy. In these instances, it is possible that the therapy offered under time-limited conditions does not reflect well-conceptualized, planned brief psychotherapy but consists of truncated techniques borrowed from long-term psychotherapy. Future research might consider inclusion of procedures for evaluating the quality of the therapy process that is under study.

The number of process studies of brief psychotherapy is not great. Due to paucity of research, inappropriate reliance must be placed on findings that are actually based on small and unrepresentative populations of patients. Perhaps the blame for the paucity of research stems from the lack of a clearly formulated agenda to stimulate research and from a lack of encouragement of research in the form of release time and incentives in today's cost-conscious medical institutions. Regardless of these considerations, there were major areas of brief psychotherapy process in which no firm conclusions could be reached because of the small number of published studies. We noted that further work was needed to expand our understanding of the basic processes underlying psychotherapy including studies addressing the therapeutic alliance; the choice and maintenance of a focus for therapy; formulation, communication, and timing of interpretations; handling of critical events in psychotherapy; patient–therapist matching; and patient–treatment matching.

RESEARCH ON BRIEF PSYCHOTHERAPY OUTCOME

The outcome research literature on brief psychotherapy addresses three main questions: How does the improvement produced by time-limited methods compare to that produced by time-unlimited methods? Is one brief therapy approach superior to another? What client characteristics are related to maximal outcome with brief methods? Unfortunately, much of the published research does not unequivocally answer these questions because many studies fail to meet the qualifications for good outcome research (e.g., Fiske et al., 1970; Luborsky et al., 1971; Malan, 1973; Meltzoff & Kornreich, 1970). Nevertheless, a small but solid core of studies on brief psychotherapy outcome exists, to which we now turn our attention.

Overall Effectiveness of Brief Psychotherapy

Patient and therapist ratings of therapy outcome are noted to be biased sources of information on the outcome of psychotherapy. Therapists often report more positive change in patients than any other source (e.g., Frank, Gliedman, Imber, Stone, & Nash, 1959; Levene, Breger, & Patterson, 1972). It would be unusual for outcome studies based on patient and therapist ratings to report negative findings, and positive reports are not particularly instructive. In spite of the obvious shortcomings of such a design, numerous studies attesting to the efficacy of brief methods are of this type.

Most of these studies (e.g., Baxter & Beaulieu, 1976; Sifneos, 1972, 1975; Stewart, 1972) report improvement in approximately 70 percent of the cases. For example, Avnet (1965a, 1965b) followed up a large group of patients enrolled in a group health medical plan who had received brief psychotherapy. She found that 81 percent of the patients and 76 percent of the therapists felt that there had been some degree of improvement.

Studies that employ more diverse measures of outcome (i.e., standardized interview procedures, target symptom ratings, clinical observer ratings of improvement, evaluation of social functioning, objective tests, etc.) and untreated control groups for comparison are much more useful but also much more scarce. In general these studies produce evidence suggestive of a high degree of improvement in treated as well as in minimal-contact groups. The largest differential in status is seen upon termination of therapy, when the treated groups are found to be significantly more improved than the untreated groups. These differences disappear on follow-up.

To illustrate, Frank et al. (1959) studied patients treated for six months by psychiatric residents with brief individual therapy, brief group therapy, or minimal-contact therapy. Data gathered immediately after therapy ended indicated that individual-therapy patients improved significantly in social effectiveness from their pretherapy baseline but the minimal-contact and group-therapy patients did not. All treated patients showed lowering of self-rated discomfort, and all improved more than patients who dropped out of therapy during the first month.

Continued negatively accelerated improvement was seen in all groups at the five-year follow-up (Stone, Frank, Nash, & Imber, 1961). At this point, 97 percent of the patients were rated improved in social effectiveness, and there were no significant differences among any groups. The follow-up data, as is often the case, were complicated by the patients' behavior after the period of formal treatment had ended. Many remained in therapy during the follow-up period. A number of studies have demonstrated that as many as 60 percent of brief-treatment patients return for additional therapy (e.g., Budman, Demby, & Randall, 1982; Patterson, Levene, & Breger, 1977).

These findings suggest that the main effect of psychotherapy is to accelerate change, not to produce change that would fail to occur without therapy (Bergin & Suinn, 1975). Nevertheless, psychotherapy may spare patients months of considerable pain and suffering. Many researchers now feel that the question, "Is psychotherapy effective?" has been addressed adequately by existing research (e.g., Smith & Glass, 1977; Smith et al., 1980). Further advances in understanding the effects of psychotherapy now require studies designed with more specificity according to Paul's (1966) famous dictim, "What treatment, by whom, is most effective for which client? . . ." We now turn our consideration to studies that have specifically compared brief treatment to other therapeutic methods.

Comparative Studies of Brief Psychotherapy

A good place to begin consideration of comparative research on brief therapy methods is to examine studies that have compared brief and long-term psychotherapy. For it is much less compelling to consider the relative effectiveness of alternative brief therapy methods if all are inferior to long-term psychotherapy.

Time-limited versus Unlimited Psychotherapy

When the patient is informed during the initial phase of therapy that treatment will be brief and is told the approximate or exact number of sessions that the therapist proposes, the treatment is referred to as time-limited. Time-limited treatment is contrasted to unlimited treatment, where no set limits on the length of treatment are expressed by the therapist, although the patient may be informed that the therapy course is expected to be a long one.

A group of studies that purports to relate to the efficacy of brief therapy methods consists of investigations where the relationship between the amount of change seen in a patient and the number of sessions of therapy he or she had received is analyzed. Luborsky et al. (1971) summarize these findings: "In 20 of 22 studies of essentially time unlimited treatment, the length of treatment was positively related to outcome; the longer the duration of treatment or the more sessions, the better the outcome! It is tempting to conclude . . . that if psychotherapy is a good thing, the more the better. Other interpretations, however, may also fit" (p. 154).

Johnson and Gelso (1980) discuss several important considerations in the interpretation of this group of studies. Among them are source of measurement, time of measurement, and criteria for improvement. When all studies of therapy duration are considered together, 67 percent suggest that more treatment yielded greater improvement. Limiting consideration to the studies that employed therapist-rated outcome, however, raises the figure to 89 percent of the studies in favor of longer duration therapy. Including only studies that utilized behavioral measures or psychological tests lowers the number to 25 percent. These figures suggest bias on the part of therapist-raters, who may tend to feel more invested in long-term therapy and may be more likely to observe changes in patients who have remained for a long duration in therapy (Johnson & Gelso, 1980). Likewise, bias can exist in the criteria for improvement and the outcome measures chosen for use. Studies that employ rating scales that purport to reflect dynamic change such as personality reorganization or structural changes as opposed to overt behavioral change are more likely to favor long-term psychotherapy than studies where outcome measures focus on concrete behavior change.

Time of measurement can also have impact on the results of therapy-duration studies. Studies of therapy duration often confound time per se with time in therapy. For example, Lorr, McNair, Michaux, and Raskin (1964) designed a study that allowed examination of both time and number of sessions. They randomly assigned patients to therapy twice weekly, weekly, or biweekly. Improvement was related to length of treatment but not to the number of treatment sessions. Comparisons should be made at equivalent points (i.e., termination) as well as after equal periods of follow-up. Comparison of time-limited to time-unlimited therapy at follow-up allows consideration of whether time per se fostered further behavior change as well as extended time in unlimited treatment. For example, Shlien et al. (1962) compared time-limited (18 sessions) to time-unlimited therapy (averaging 39 sessions). Comparison of outcome data at the 39-week point demonstrated no group differences. Thus, "Time per se is of great importance in client change. The curative powers of time may be set in motion by counseling but apparently need not be prodded constantly by continuous therapy" (Johnson & Gelso, 1980, p. 79). Frank (1959) hypothesized that improvement in treatment is produced by "nonspecific expectancy of relief," which alleviates discomfort early in therapy independent of the duration of treatment, and by relearning, which is related to time but not necessarily to time spent in treatment.

Many of the studies of therapy relating improvement to therapy duration did not employ planned brief psychotherapy. The subjects in the short-therapy group are often those who unilaterally terminated what was intended by the therapist to be long-term therapy. It is inappropriate to conclude that a patient has received brief psychotherapy when actually he or she received three history-taking sessions preliminary to long-term psychotherapy and then dropped out. Parad and Parad (1968) describe the differences between planned and unplanned brief psychotherapy. Brief psychotherapy techniques differ in crucial aspects (e.g., activity, focus, goals) from time-unlimited psychotherapeutic techniques. The most relevant comparison is between unlimited therapy and planned brief therapy practiced by a therapist experienced in brief techniques.

A small group of comparative studies have attempted a direct comparison of time-limited versus unlimited approaches. Luborsky, Singer, and Luborsky (1975) reviewed these studies and concluded, "Since Otto Rank, treatments that are structured at the outset as time-limited have been thought by some practitioners to be as good as the more usual time-unlimited treatment. The eight available controlled comparative studies are mostly (five out of eight) consistent with this view in that there is no significant difference between the two" (p. 1001).

Recently, it has been suggested that the length and type of therapy significantly interact. Piper et al. (1984) studied 106 outpatients with mild neurotic and characterological problems. Therapists were psychodynamically oriented, experienced male psychiatrists. Each offered four forms of therapy: individual (short and long) and group (short and long). All treatment was psychodynamically oriented, that is, techniques of clarification, interpretation, and exploration were central features. Conflicts were interpreted and traced through current relationships, the therapeutic relationship, and the past. The short treatments averaged 22 sessions while the long treatments averaged 76 sessions. Outcome measures included target symptoms, Structured and Scaled Interview to Assess Maladjustment, among others. Minimal evidence was found for main effects for type of therapy or duration of therapy but ". . . considerable evidence for a type X duration interaction. . . . What was found to be important was the particular form of therapy received, not the general type (individual, group) or the general duration (short-term, long-term). . . " (Piper et al., 1984, p. 275). The best outcomes were observed in the short-term individual and long-term group therapies, whereas the results of short-term group therapy were significantly less positive.

In conclusion, many studies that purport to correlate therapy duration to outcome have methodological problems (e.g., confounding of time with time in treatment, biased raters or criteria, failure to utilize planned brief-therapy techniques) that render them irrelevant to the efficacy of brief methods. Those studies that have directly compared brief and long-term methods have found equal effectiveness. Since brief therapy requires less time (both therapist and patient) and therefore less social cost, it has been suggested that brief methods are equally effective and more cost efficient than long-term psychotherapy (e.g., Piper et al., 1984).

Effectiveness of Alternative Brief Psychotherapy Approaches

Recent studies have examined the comparative outcome of different approaches to brief psychotherapy including behavior therapy, cathartic therapy, client-centered therapy, cognitive therapy, dynamic psychotherapy, Gestalt therapy, rational therapy, and "alternate" psychotherapy as practiced by humane but untrained college professors (e.g., Bolz & Meyer, 1981; Cross et al., 1982; Levene et al., 1972; Nichols, 1974; Nichols & Reifler, 1973; Patterson, Levene, & Breger, 1971; Paul, 1966, 1967; Sloane et al., 1975; Sloane, Staples, Cristol, Yorkston, & Whipple, 1976; Strupp & Hadley, 1979). Overall, there is little support for a statement of significant superiority for any of the diverse approaches to brief psychotherapy examined to date. Several of the larger-scale studies will be examined in more detail to communicate a sense of their design and specific findings.

The effectiveness of brief behavioral versus brief psychodynamic approaches to psychotherapy has been compared in several studies. For example, Sloane et al. (1975) report on the results of four months of psychotherapy or behavior therapy conducted by highly experienced therapists. Patients were typical "complex neurotics" who were matched on demographic variables and severity of symptoms but who were otherwise randomly assigned to the treatment groups and to a minimal-contact wait list. Outcome measures included the Structured and Scaled Interview to Assess Maladjustment; target symptoms; patient, therapist, and clinical rater ratings of improvement; and objective inventories. At posttherapy, all three groups had improved, as reflected in a decrease of rated target symptom severity, but the two treated groups had improved significantly more than the wait-list group. Few significant differences were found between the approaches. All of the significant results favored behavior therapy. For example, at four months, patients treated by behavior therapy were rated improved in work adjustment, social adequacy, and target symptoms while patients treated by psychotherapy were improved on target symptoms and work adjustment only. At the one-year follow-up, behavior therapy patients were rated significantly lower in target symptom severity than psychotherapy patients. However, these data are weakened

because a number of patients sought further therapy subsequent to the four-month experimental treatment period. Sloane et al. (1975) concluded that behavior therapy seemed to produce change slightly sooner and produced more focused change.

Cross et al. (1982) replicated the major design features of the Sloane et al. (1975) study. Therapists were experienced clinicians who specialized in either behavioral therapy or Gestalt/transactional analysis therapy. There were 15 subjects assigned randomly from a preselected pool to one of the treatments or to a wait list. Therapy was conducted in community mental health centers (in Australia). Outcome measures included target symptoms, Structured and Scaled Interview to Assess Maladjustment, an overall adjustment rating, and an objective inventory. The authors' focus was on the maintenance of change during a one-year follow-up period rather than on changes apparent at termination. They observed that positive change occurred on target symptoms during treatment, and these effects continued for a full year. Thus, subjects maintained the progress they had made in therapy without any evidence of deterioration. The authors concluded that the results "showed no appreciable differences between treatment orientations in the level of maintenance of outcome effects, nor were there any marked changes in treatment effects with time" (Cross et al., 1982, p. 108).

Strupp and Hadley (1979) compared five highly experienced therapists who practiced dynamic psychotherapy to five "alternate" therapists (i.e., college professors selected on the basis of a survey to identify the kind of people one would go to for help with a problem). Patients were 64 college males selected on the basis of MMPI configuration; all were depressed, anxious, and socially introverted (2-7-0 syndrome). They were randomly assigned to one of the two treatment groups, to a minimal-treatment control group, or to a silent control group. Outcome measures included patients', therapists', and clinicians' ratings of target symptoms, self-rated overall change, and clinicians' ratings of clinical disturbance. Treatment was offered twice weekly for a total of 25 hours. Results suggested that both treated groups were more improved than the control groups. The greatest amount of change occurred during the treatment period and was maintained at the one-year follow-up. The authors noted, however, that in their study the professors had been carefully selected for caring qualities and worked under close supervision of professionals for consultation and emergencies. Even so, professors experienced difficulty in discharging their assignment (i.e., ran out of relevant material to discuss, were unable to work toward specific goals, were unwilling to treat patients over an extended time period). Thus, their performance, obtained in a closely controlled research context, including some professional consultation and support, is unlikely to represent the spontaneous behavior of the untrained natural healer. Nevertheless, the outcomes were comparable.

Patterson et al. (1971) compared behavior therapy with brief psychotherapy using inexperienced therapists. Patients in behavior therapy rated themselves more improved immediately following therapy than patients treated in brief psychotherapy. The ratings were confirmed by the therapists' and independent judges' ratings. The authors concluded that brief behavior therapy may be learned more readily by inexperienced therapists than brief psychotherapy.

The NIMH funded Collaborative Study of Depression, which is still in progress, promises to be a comparative study of brief psychotherapy methods that offers several advances over former outcome studies. This study is a multicenter clinical trial comparison of the effectiveness of three brief treatment approaches to depression: interpersonal therapy, cognitive therapy, and pharmacological treatment. Therapists practice only one therapeutic modality and were specially selected after successfully mastering an extended training course conducted by an expert clinician. Each therapy modality is supported by a treatment manual that outlines the theoretical foundation of the treatment approach, the specific treatment techniques that are recommended, and the handling of various critical incidents consistent with the philosophy of the approach. Patients were selected for rigid adherence to *DSM-III* diagnostic characteristics of depressive disorders. Data will include a standard battery of outcome and process measures.

Summary: Comparative Studies of Outcome

In summary, comparative studies of brief psychotherapy offer little empirical evidence of differences in overall effectiveness between time-limited and -unlimited therapy or between alternate approaches to brief therapy. In many respects the comparative studies reviewed in this section are representative of well-designed omnibus psychotherapy studies characterized by experienced therapists, clinically representative patients, treatment based on a manual description, multiple outcome measures, several vantage points of change, measurement of change at several points in time, appropriate controls, and follow-up.

Future outcome research must address the issue more prescriptively. The impact of various brief psychotherapies on homogeneous patient populations (including good as well as poor prognosis groups) should be explored. Factorial designs are needed so that the interactions of therapist, patient, and technique can be examined. The theoretical foundation exists for prescriptive assignment of psychotherapy approaches (e.g., Beutler, 1979), but empirical studies are needed.

Research efforts could also be toward further exploration of the relationship between time, time in therapy, and outcome. While it was suggested that behavior change takes time (which need not be spent in continuous psychotherapy), the downward limits on the duration of psychotherapy needed to initiate behavior change have not been investigated empirically. On the other hand, some researchers have turned to slightly longer durations of brief psychotherapy in recent years over former studies. Yet the incremental gains obtained by increasing the number of sessions beyond the average of 12 to 16 typical in outcome studies of brief psychotherapy have not been investigated.

Beyond effectiveness, other considerations in the choice of technical approach are cost-effectiveness, teachability, and acceptability to patients and therapists. While brief psychotherapy has been demonstrated to be equally effective and more cost-effective than unlimited psychotherapy, Hoyt (1985) has described a number of resistances among therapists toward the use of planned, brief psychotherapy. When mandatory limits on psychotherapy are established in an agency, therapists' job satisfaction declines somewhat (Gelso & Johnson, 1983). Strupp (1981) noted little evidence of technical flexibility among established practitioners. Consequently, future research might address retraining formats to improve the image and teach the techniques of brief psychotherapy to experienced clinicians.

Patient Characteristics and Outcome

In this section we focus on the relationship of various patient characteristics to outcome. As we detailed earlier, much of the clinical writing on brief psychotherapy emphasizes the importance of selection of appropriate patients. The recommended criteria include characteristics such as a behavior problem of acute onset; good previous adjustment; good ability to relate; high motivation; and the absence of profound dependency, acting out, self-centeredness, masochism, or self-destructiveness. Empirical studies of these characteristics will now be considered.

Behavior Problem of Acute Onset

Little research attention has been devoted to the relationship of duration of the problem to therapy outcome. Malan (1976b) followed up a group of young patients with recent onset of phobic symptoms who were part of a larger sample of persons treated with brief analytic therapy. These patients did not respond favorably to therapy, but we conjecture that these same patients might have responded better to behavioral treatment. Consequently, we do not think this is necessarily a failure in the "recent onset" hypothesis of patient selection.

Good Previous Adjustment

The review of factors influencing therapeutic outcome by Luborsky et al. (1971) concluded that virtually all of the studies to that date showed that the healthier the patient is to begin with, the better the outcome is. For example, Sloane et al. (1975) found that psychotherapy was more effective with patients whose MMPI-measured psychopathology was lower. A conclusion that better adjustment is related to better outcome is methodologically questionable, however, since global ratings made at the end of treatment tend to be influenced by the patient's actual condition at the time of measurement, regardless of his or her initial level of adjustment (Mintz, 1972). A more detailed discussion of this body of research is available in Chapter 6.

Ability to Relate

Studies have explored the relationship of therapy outcome and the patient's ability to relate to the therapist as well as the quality of patients'

pretherapy interpersonal relationships. Staples and Sloane (1970) studied the relationship between speech patterns, empathic ability, and patient responsiveness to approval and disapproval. They concluded that "individual differences in the capacity to respond to cues provided by a therapist may be an important source of variation in patients' therapeutic potential" (p. 103). Moras and Strupp (1982) reported that the quality of a patient's pretherapy interpersonal relationships—while a potent predictor of the therapeutic alliance—generally had very low correlation with outcome measures.

Motivation

Many therapists have recorded the importance of high initial motivation for successful therapy. Malan (1963) considered that either high initial motivation or a marked increase in motivation during the first sessions was more important than any other patient characteristic included in his study. In his study, 85 percent of the patients who scored highest on the outcome criteria were rated high in motivation. In contrast, 40 percent of the patients who were rated lowest on motivation showed no improvement. Likewise, Keithly et al. (1980) found that rated motivation was predictive of both process and outcome measures. Both the therapists' and independent clinicians' ratings of global change were significantly predicted by pretherapy-rated motivation. They concluded that their results confirm the claims of Malan and Sifneos, who view motivation as a critical factor both in selecting patients for therapy and for predicting the extent of benefit from therapy.

In a study of characteristics of patients referred for brief versus long-term psychotherapy, Ursano and Dressler (1974) found no differences in age, sex, race, marital status, education, or source of referral between patients referred for the two types of psychotherapy. They found a number of factors, however, that were associated with referral to brief therapy: patients with a recent onset of illness (six months) tended to be referred for brief therapy; clinicians who had treated a number of cases with brief methods also tended to refer more patients for brief treatment; patients in brief therapy were more often diagnosed "situational"; patients tended to have less severe problems; and patients tended not to require medication.

Several studies have attempted to determine the

percentage of patients who meet the various selection criteria for brief psychotherapy. Silver (1982) concluded that 20 percent of outpatients would meet Malan's (1976a) criteria. Heiberg (1975) found that 6 percent of an inpatient population met Sifneos' (1975) criteria for motivation for therapy while 20 percent of outpatients meet these criteria (Budman & Stone, 1983).

Lambert (1979) has observed, "Unfortunately, the tendency is for clinicians to specify, on the basis of intuition and theoretical bias, the clients that are most suitable for particular brief therapy interventions, without evaluating these assumptions in a formal research design. Thus, there has been a failure to test the suitability of these treatments with some patients who are presumed unsuitable, but who may very well profit from the approach" (p. 121). It does not appear that acute onset, good previous adjustment, good ability to relate, a focal problem, high initial motivation, lower socioeconomic class, current crises, or a host of other determining variables related to the patient have been shown to be any more highly related to outcome in brief therapy than in longer term therapies.

It has been suggested that selection criteria function to exclude those "deemed least desirable by clinicians practicing in any modality" (Budman & Stone, 1983, p. 941). Strupp (1981) concludes that less than optimally suitable clients ". . . make up a sizable proportion of the patient pool. They represent a largely understudied and underresearched population, and in my view, this is where future clinical and research efforts should be concentrated" (p. 235).

CONCLUSION

Most psychotherapeutic contacts, whether by plan or by premature termination, are brief, lasting less than eight sessions. In recent years, partly because of design, brief psychotherapy has become a treatment of choice. Comparative studies of brief and unlimited therapies show essentially no differences in results. Consequently, brief therapy results in a great saving of available clinical time and can reach more people in need of treatment. It is quite likely that brief therapies will be more widely utilized in the future if government health plans and private insurance companies cover the costs of psychotherapy. Such insurance coverage would likely be limited to relatively few sessions.

We examined a number of brief therapeutic approaches and noted that they could be classified into five broad orientations: psychoanalytic, behavioral, cognitive/behavioral, crisis intervention therapy, and other verbal psychotherapies. A great deal has been written about these brief treatment approaches. In this review, we noted that despite somewhat different theoretical assumptions and treatment strategies, there are several technical characteristics that most brief treatments have in common. Among these are:

1. Promptness of intervention.
2. Rapid, early assessment.
3. A quickly established interpersonal relationship from which to obtain therapeutic leverage.
4. Management of temporal limitation by therapists.
5. Limitation of therapeutic goals.
6. Directive management of the sessions by the therapist.
7. Centering the therapeutic content around a focus.
8. Ventilation or catharsis, an important part of most approaches.
9. Flexibility in choice of technique.

The process variables that are important to brief therapy were reviewed. In that section more attention was paid to the empirical research literature than to the clinical domain in order to ascertain what scientific basis has been established for the processes that we "know" clinically are important to bringing about behavioral change in patients. The published literature is sparse, and many studies suffer from methodological flaws. We found, like so many others before us, that hard facts are scarce, largely because such processes are exceedingly difficult to carve up into objectively measurable quantities.

The importance of the therapeutic alliance in brief treatment was reviewed. Even in behaviorally oriented approaches, where the relationship has been minimized, some focus on the patient—therapist relationship has been shown to be an important variable. Although the quality of the therapeutic relationship is considered by many to be the major determinant in therapeutic change, the operations through which change is brought about are only beginning to be understood. Assuming adequate human qualities and training in the therapist, the quality of the therapeutic alliance appears to be most influenced by patient characteristics, including the quality of past interpersonal relationships and motivation for therapy. The extent to which ratings of therapeutic alliance predict the outcome of brief therapy has not been studied.

Most brief therapies place great emphasis on interpretation, directiveness, and a high therapist activity level. Brief psychotherapies depend on these therapeutic techniques to keep the sessions moving at a productive pace. Research is needed to provide clearer delineation of the effective range of these techniques, as well as guidelines for handling patients who are failing to respond.

The role of time limitation and the uses to which temporal awareness is put is thought to be important in brief psychotherapy. Research studies have pointed to the importance of time limitation in brief therapy for keeping the patient tuned in to the need for rapid goal attainment. While the effectiveness of time-limited approaches has been established, behavior change does require time. The evidence suggests, however, that the time does not have to be spent in continuous psychotherapy.

The instrumentation in brief psychotherapy process research has grown dramatically. Yet studies that utilize these new instruments are hard to interpret because of the lack of a descriptive data base on brief psychotherapy. More attention in future studies needs to be paid to increasing the generalizability of results by use of standardized as opposed to author-constructed process scales. Insufficient attention has been paid to the choice of outcome measures for process studies. Without a link to therapy outcome, process studies lack practical impact. Also, studies of brief psychotherapy process must consider whether the therapists under examination are trained to carry out and actually execute a well-conceptualized, planned brief psychotherapy. Descriptive studies of exemplary practitioners were suggested to establish a clearer understanding of how brief therapy is practiced. Areas of process research that urgently demand study are the difficult

patient, a weak alliance, the uninvolved patient, the interpretation process, and the handling of critical events in psychotherapy.

The outcome research literature on brief therapies suggests that these techniques produce positive change. Behavioral techniques seem to produce change fastest, but are not superior to other brief approaches in overall results. Patients followed up over very long time periods tend to show gradual improvement for several years after treatment. The chief value of brief psychotherapy may be that it helps to accelerate positive change in the patient.

The major outcome studies in brief psychotherapy completed in recent years are well designed and have adequately addressed the overall and comparative effectiveness of brief techniques for heterogeneous groups of complex neurotics. Increased specificity is called for in future outcome research so that issues of patient−therapist and patient−treatment interactions can be described.

In addition, research needs to be directed toward a greater understanding of the relationship between time, time in therapy, and outcome. It was noted that in spite of evidence of cost-effectiveness, brief psychotherapy has a negative image among many clinicians. If the general trend toward cost containment in health care continues, long-term psychotherapy is likely to become less prevalent in the future. Yet some writers have suggested that the ability to carry out brief psychotherapy does not flow directly from the experience of working in settings where the average length of stay in psychotherapy is short. Greater emphasis needs to be placed on training in brief psychotherapy techniques.

In addition to being a clearly viable clinical treatment option, brief psychotherapy has been shown to have value as a long-term therapy analogue and as a format for studying, with some precision, the effectiveness of specific intervention techniques on specific problems. The similarity of many psychotherapeutic processes and some encouraging outcome studies suggest that research on brief psychotherapy may throw light on psychotherapy generally. We are impressed with the need for more sophisticated research designs and more attention to rigor through clearer specification of patients, therapists, and techniques in future studies. We believe that research on brief treatments holds an important key to the study of process and outcome in psychotherapy.

REFERENCES

Aldrich, C. K. (1968). Brief psychotherapy: A reappraisal of theoretical assumptions. *American Journal of Psychiatry, 125*, 585–592.

Alexander, F., & French, T. M. (1946). *Psychoanalytic therapy: Principles and applications.* New York: Ronald Press.

Ansbacher, H. L. (1972). Adlerian psychology: The tradition of brief psychotherapy. *Journal of Individual Psychology, 28*, 137–151.

Auerbach, S. M., & Kilmann, P. R. (1977). Crisis intervention: A review of outcome research. *Psychological Bulletin, 84*, 1189–1217.

Avnet, H. H. (1965a). How effective is short-term therapy? In L. R. Wolberg (Ed.), *Short-term psychotherapy.* New York: Grune & Stratton.

Avnet, H. H. (1965b). Short-term treatment under auspices of a medical insurance plan. *American Journal of Psychiatry, 122*, 147–151.

Baker, E. (1947). Brief psychotherapy. *Journal of the Medical Society of New Jersey, 44*, 260–261.

Balint, M., Orstein, P., & Balint, E. (1972). *Focal psychotherapy.* London: Tavistock.

Barten, H. H. (1965). The 15-minute hour: Brief therapy in a military setting. *American Journal of Psychiatry, 122*, 565–567.

Barten, H. H. (1969). The coming of age of the brief psychotherapies. In L. Bellack & H. H. Barten (Eds.), *Progress in community mental health.* (Vol. 1). New York: Grune & Stratton.

Barten, H. H. (1971). *Brief therapies.* New York: Behavioral Publications.

Baum, O. E., & Felzer, S. B. (1964). Activity in initial interviews with lower-class patients. *Archives of General Psychiatry, 10*, 345–353.

Baxter, J. W., & Beaulieu, D. E. (1976). Impact of short-term, individual psychotherapy: Looking for change. Unpublished manuscript.

Beck, A. T. (1976). *Cognitive therapy and the emotional disorders.* New York: International Universities Press.

Beck, A. T., Rush, A. J., Shaw, B. F., & Emery, G. (1984). *Cognitive therapy of depression.* New York: Guilford.

Bellak, L. (1960). A general hospital as a focus of community psychiatry. A trouble shooting clinic combines important functions as part of hospital's service. *Journal of the American Medical Association, 174*, 2214–2217.

Bellak, L., & Small, L. (1965). *Emergency psychotherapy and brief psychotherapy.* New York: Grune & Stratton.

Bergin, A. E. (1963). The effects of psychotherapy: Negative results revisited. *Journal of Counseling Psychology, 10*, 244–250.

Bergin, A. E. (1971). The evaluation of therapeutic outcomes. In A. E. Bergin & S. L. Garfield (Eds.), *Handbook of psychotherapy and behavior change* (pp. 217–270). New York: Wiley.

Bergin, A. E., & Suinn, R. M. (1975). Individual psychotherapy and behavior therapy. *Annual Review of Psychology, 26*, 509–555.

Berliner, B. (1941). Short psychoanalytic psychotherapy: Its possibilities and its limitations. *Bulletin of the Menninger Clinic, 5*, 204.

Beutler, L. E. (1979). Toward specific psychological therapies for specific conditions. *Journal of Consulting and Clinical Psychology, 47*, 882–892.

Bierenbaum, H., Nichols, M. P., & Schwartz, A. J. (1976). Effects of varying session length and frequency in brief emotive psychotherapy. *Journal of Consulting and Clinical Psychology, 44*, 790–798.

Binder, J. L., Strupp, H. H., & Schacht, T. E. (1983). Countertransference in time-limited dynamic psychotherapy. *Contemporary Psychoanalysis, 19*, 605–623.

Bloom, B. L. (1981). Focused single session therapy: Initial development and evaluation. In S. L. Budman (Ed.), *Forms of brief therapy* (pp. 167–218). New York: Guilford.

Bolz, W., & Meyer, A. E. (1981). The general setting (of the Hamburg Short Psychotherapy Comparison Project). *Psychotherapy and Psychosomatics, 35*, 85–95.

Bonime, W. (1953). Some principles of brief psychotherapy. *Psychiatric Quarterly, 27*, 1–18.

Bonstedt, T. (1970). Crisis intervention or early access brief therapy? *Diseases of the Nervous System, 31*, 783–787.

Bordin, E. S. (1976). The working alliance: Basis for a general theory of psychotherapy. Paper presented at the American Psychological Association, Washington, DC.

Buda, B. (1972). Utilization of resistance and paradox communication in short-term psychotherapy. *Psychotherapy and Psychosomatics, 20*, 200–211.

Budman, S. H. (1981). Introduction. In S. H. Budman (Ed.), *Forms of brief therapy* (pp. 1–5). New York: Guilford.

Budman, S. H., & Gurman, A. (1983). The practice of brief therapy. *Professional Psychology: Research and Practice, 14*, 277–292.

Budman, S. H., & Stone, J. (1983). Advances in brief psychotherapy: A review of recent literature. *Hospital and Community Psychiatry, 34*, 939–946.

Budman, S. H., Demby, A., & Randall, J. (1982). Psychotherapeutic outcome and reduction in medical utilization: A cautionary tale. *Professional Psychology, 13*, 200–207.

Burdon, A. P. (1963). Principles of brief psychotherapy. *Journal of the Louisiana Medical Society, 115*, 374–378.

Butcher, J. N., & Maudal, G. R. (1976). Crisis intervention. In I. B. Weiner (Ed.), *Clinical methods in psychology* (pp. 591–648). New York: Wiley.

Butcher, J. N., & Herzog, J. (1982). Individual assessment in crisis intervention: Observation, life history, and personality. In C. Spielberger & J. N. Butcher (Eds.), *Advances in personality assessment* (Vol. 1, pp. 115–168). Hillsdale, NJ: Laurence Erlbaum.

Butcher, J. N., Stelmachers, Z., & Maudal, G. R. (1984). Crisis intervention. In E. B. Weiner (Ed.) *Clinical methods in psychology* (2nd ed., pp. 572–633). New York: Wiley.

Caplan, G. (1964). *Principles of preventive psychiatry.* New York: Basic Books.

Castelnuovo-Tedesco, P. (1966). Brief psychotherapeutic treatment of depressive reactions. In G. J. Wayne and R. R. Koegler (Eds.), *Emergency psychiatry and brief therapy*. Boston: Little, Brown.

Cattell, J. P., MacKinnon, R. A., & Forster, E. (1963). Limited goal therapy in a psychiatric clinic. *American Journal of Psychiatry, 120,* 255–260.

Coleman, M. D., (1960). Methods of psychotherapy: Emergency psychotherapy. In J. H. Masserman & J. L. Moreno (Eds.), *Progress in psychotherapy*. New York: Grune & Stratton.

Coleman, M. D., & Zwerling, I. (1959). The psychiatric emergency clinic: A flexible way of meeting community mental health needs. *American Journal of Psychiatry, 115,* 980–984.

Cross, D. G., Sheehan, P. W., & Khan, J. A. (1982). Short and long term follow-up of clients receiving insight-oriented therapy and behavior therapy. *Journal of Consulting and Clinical Psychology, 50,* 103–112.

Cummings, N., & Follette, W. T. (1976). Brief psychotherapy and medical utilization. In H. Dorken & Associates (Eds.), *The psychologist today: New developments in law, health insurance, and health practice* (pp. 165–174). San Francisco: Jossey-Bass.

Cummings, N. A., & Vandenbos, G. (1979). The general practice of psychology. *Professional Psychology, 10,* 430–440.

Davanloo, H. (1978). *Basic principles and techniques in short-term dynamic psychotherapy*. New York: Spectrum.

Davanloo, H. (1979). Techniques of short-term dynamic psychotherapy. *Psychiatric Clinics of North America, 2,* 11–22.

Deutsch, F. (1949). *Applied psychoanalysis: Selected lectures on psychotherapy*. New York: Grune & Stratton.

Elliott, R. (1985). Helpful and nonhelpful events in brief counseling interviews: An empirical taxonomy. *Journal of Consulting and Clinical Psychology, 32,* 307–321.

Ellis, A., & Grieger, R. (1977). *Handbook of rational-emotive therapy*. New York: Springer.

Erlich, R. E., & Phillips, P. B. (1963). Short-term psychotherapy of the aviator. *Aerospace Medicine, 43,* 1046–1047.

Errera, P., Braxton, M., Smith, D. C., & Gruber, R. (1967). Length of psychotherapy. *Archives of General Psychiatry, 17,* 454–458.

Fenichel, O. (1954). Brief psychotherapy. In H. Fenichel & D. Rapaport (Eds.), *The collected papers of Otto Fenichel*. New York: Norton.

Ferenczi, S. (1920). The further development of an active therapy in psychoanalysis. In J. Richman (Ed.) (1960) *Further contributions to the theory and techniques of psychoanalysis* (pp. 198–216). London: Hogarth.

Fiske, D. W., Hunt, H. F., Luborsky. L., Orne, M.T., Parloff, M. B., Reiser, M. F., & Tuma, A. H. (1970). The planning of research on effectiveness of psychotherapy. *Archives of General Psychiatry, 22,* 22–32.

Frank, J. D. (1959). The dynamics of the psychotherapeutic relationship. *Psychiatry, 22,* 17–39.

Frank, J. D. (1966). Treatment of the focal symptom: An adaptional approach. *American Journal of Psychotherapy, 20,* 564–575.

Frank, J. D. (1974). Therapeutic components of psychotherapy: A 25-year progress report of research. *Journal of Nervous and Mental Disease, 159,* 325–342.

Frank, J. D., Gliedman, L. H., Imber, S. D., Stone, A. R., & Nash, E. H., (1959). Patients' expectancies and relearning as factors determining improvement in psychotherapy. *American Journal of Psychiatry, 115,* 961–968.

Frankl, V. E. (1960). Paradoxical intention: A logotherapeutic technique. *American Journal of Psychotherapy, 14,* 520–535.

Frankel, F. H. (1973). The effects of brief hypnotherapy in a series of psychosomatic problems. *Psychotherapy and Psychosomatics, 22,* 269–275.

Garfield, S. L. (1978). Research on client variables in psychotherapy. In S. L. Garfield & A. E. Bergin (Eds.), *Handbook of psychotherapy* (rev. ed., pp. 191–232). New York: Wiley.

Garner, H. H. (1970). *Psychotherapy: Confrontation problem solving techniques*. St. Louis: W. H. Green.

Gelb, L. A., & Ullman, A. (1967). As reported anon., in "Instant psychotherapy offered at an outpatient psychiatric clinic." *Frontiers of Hospital Psychiatry, 4,* 14.

Gelder, M. G., Marks, I. M., & Wolff, H. H. (1967). Desensitization and psychotherapy in the treatment of phobic states: A controlled inquiry. *British Journal of Psychiatry, 13,* 53–73.

Gelso, C. J., & Johnson, D. H. (1983). *Explorations in time-limited counseling and psychotherapy*. New York: Teachers College Press.

Gillman, R. D. (1965). Brief psychotherapy: A psychoanalytic view. *American Journal of Psychiatry, 122,* 601–611.

Glasscote, R. M., Raybin, J.B., Reifler, C. B., & Kane, A. W. (1975). *The alternate services: Their role in mental health*. Washington, D.C.: American Psychiatric Service.

Goldfried, M. R. (1980). Toward the delineation of therapeutic change principles. *American Psychologist, 35,* 991–999.

Gomes-Schwartz, B. (1978). Effective ingredients in psychotherapy: Prediction of outcome from process variables. *Journal of Consulting and Clinical Psychology, 46,* 1023–1035.

Gottschalk, L. A., Mayerson, P., & Gottlieb, A. A. (1967). Prediction and evaluation of outcome in an emergency brief psychotherapy clinic. *Journal of Nervous and Mental Disease, 144,* 77–96.

Greenblatt, M., Moore, R., & Albert, R. (1963). *The prevention of hospitalization: Report on the Community Extension Service of the Massachusetts Mental Health Center, Boston, Massachusetts*. New York: Grune & Stratton.

Grinker, R. R., & Spiegel, J. P. (1944a). Brief psychotherapy in war neuroses. *Psychosomatic Medicine, 6,* 123–131.

Grinker, R. R., & Spiegel, J. P. (1944b). *Management of neuropsychiatric casualties in the zone of combat. Manual of military neuropsychiatry*. Philadelphia: W. B. Saunders.

Gross, R. B. (1968). Supportive therapy for the depressed college student. *Psychotherapy: Theory, Research and Practice, 5,* 262–267.

Gutheil, E. A. (1944). Psychoanalysis and brief psychotherapy. *Journal of Clinical Psychopathology, 6,* 207–230.

Hadley, S. W., & Strupp, H. H. (1976). Contemporary views of negative effects in psychotherapy. *Archives of General Psychiatry, 33,* 1291–1302.

Harris, M. R., Kalis, B. L., & Freeman, E. H. (1963). Precipitating stress: An approach to brief therapy. *American Journal of Psychotherapy, 17,* 465–471.

Harris, R. E., & Christiansen, C. (1946). Predictions of response to brief psychotherapy. *Journal of Psychology, 21,* 269–284.

Hartley, D. E., & Strupp, H. H. (1983). The therapeutic alliance: Its relationship to outcome in brief psychotherapy. In J. Masling (Ed.) *Empirical studies of psychoanalytical theories* (Vol. 1, pp. 1–38). Hillsdale, NJ: Analytical Press.

Haskell, D., Pugatch, D., & McNair, D. M. (1969). Time-limited psychotherapy for whom? *Archives of General Psychiatry. 21,* 546–552.

Hawton, K., Reibstein, J., Fieldsend, R., & Whalley, M. (1982). Content analysis of brief psychotherapy sessions. *British Journal of Medical Psychology, 55,* 167–176.

Heiberg, A. (1975). Indications for psychotherapy in a psychiatric clinic population: A survey. *Psychotherapy & Psychosomatics, 26,* 156–166.

Heiberg, A., Sorensen, T., & Olafsen, O. (1975). Short-term dynamic psychotherapy: Three models of treatment. *Psychotherapy and Psychosomatics, 26,* 229–236.

Heitler, J. B. (1976). Preparatory techniques in initiating expressive psychotherapy in lower-class unsophisticated patients. *Psychological Bulletin, 83,* 339–352.

Hill, C. E. (1978). Development of a counselor verbal system. *Journal of Counseling Psychology, 25,* 461–468.

Hill, C. E., Greenwald, C., Reed, K. R., Charles, D., O'Farrell, M. K., & Carter, J. (1981). *Manual for counselor and client verbal response category systems.* Columbus, OH: Marathon Consulting and Press.

Hill, C. E., Carter, J. A., & O'Farrell, M. K., (1983). A case study of the process and outcome of time-limited counseling. *Journal of Counseling Psychology, 30,* 3–18.

Hill, C. E., O'Farrell, M. K., & Carter, J. A. (1983). Reply to Howard and Lambert: Case study methodology. *Journal of Counseling Psychology, 30,* 26–30.

Hill, C. E., & O'Grady, K. (1985). Therapist intentions for describing interventions within psychotherapy sessions. *Journal of Counseling Psychology, 32,* 3–22.

Hoch, P. H. (1965). Short-term versus long-term therapy. In L. R. Wolberg, (Ed.), *Short-term psychotherapy* (pp. 51–66). New York: Grune & Stratton.

Hoehn-Saric, R., Frank, J. D., Imber, S. D., Nash, E. H., Stone, A. R., & Battle, C. C. (1964). Systematic preparation of patients for psychotherapy. Effects of therapy behavior and outcome. *Journal of Psychiatric Research, 2,* 267–281.

Hoehn-Saric, R., Liberman, R., Imber, S. D., Stone, A. R., Pande, S. K., & Frank, J. D. (1972). Arousal and attitude change in neurotic patients. *Archives of General Psychiatry, 26,* 51–56.

Hoffman, D. L., & Remmel, M. L. (1975). Uncovering the precipitant in crisis intervention. *Social Casework, 56,* 259–267.

Hogan, R. A. (1966). Implosive therapy in the short-term treatment of psychotics. *Psychotherapy: Theory, Research and Practice, 3,* 25–32.

Hogan, R. A. (1967). Preliminary report of the extinction of learned fears via short-term implosive therapy. *Journal of Abnormal Psychology, 72,* 106–109.

Holmes, F. B. (1936). An experimental investigation of a method of overcoming children's fears. *Child Development, 7,* 6–30.

Hornstra, R., Lubin, B., Lewis, R., & Willis, B. (1972). Worlds apart: Patients and professionals. *Archives of General Psychiatry, 27,* 553–557.

Horowitz, M. J., Marmar, C., Krupnick, J., Wilner, J., Kaltreider, N., & Wallerstein, R. (1984). *Personality styles and brief psychotherapy.* New York: Guilford.

Howard, H. S. (1965). Of "gimmicks and gadgets" in brief psychotherapy. *Delaware Medical Journal, 37,* 265–267.

Hoyt, M. (1985). Therapist resistances to short-term dynamic psychotherapy. *Journal of the American Academy of Psychoanalysis, 13,* 93–112.

Hoyt, M. F., Marmar, C. R., Horowitz, M. J., & Alvarez, W. F. (1981). The therapist action scale and the patient action scale: Instruments of the assessment of activities during dynamic psychotherapy. *Psychotherapy: Theory, Research and Practice, 18,* 109–116.

Hoyt, M. F., Xenakis, S. N., Marmar, C. R., & Horowitz, M. J. (1983). Therapists' actions that influence their perceptions of "good" psychotherapy sessions. *The Journal of Nervous and Mental Disease, 171,* 400–404.

Hunt, R. G. (1960). Social class and mental illness: Some implications for clinical theory and practice. *American Journal of Psychiatry, 116,* 1065–1069.

Imber, S. D., Frank, J. D., Gliedman, L. H., Nash, E. H., & Stone, A. R. (1956). Suggestibility, social class and the acceptance of psychotherapy. *Journal of Clinical Psychology, 12,* 341–344.

Jacobs, M. A., Muller, J. J., Eisman, H. D., Knitzer, J., & Spilkan, A. (1968). The assessment of change in distress level and styles of adaptation as a function of psychotherapy. *Journal of Nervous and Mental Disease, 145,* 392–404.

Jacobson, G.F. (1965). Crisis theory and treatment strategy: Some sociocultural and psychodynamic considerations. *Journal of Nervous and Mental Disease, 141,* 209–218.

Jacobson, G. F. (1979). Crisis-oriented therapy. *Psychiatric Clinics of North America, 2,* 39–54.

Jacobson, G. F., Strickler, M., & Morley, W. E. (1968). Generic and individual approaches to crisis intervention. *American Journal of Public Health, 58,* 339–343.

Jacobson, G. F., Wilner, D. M., Morley, W., Schneider, S., Strickler, M., & Sommer, G. (1965). The scope and practice of an early-access brief treatment psychiatric center. *American Journal of Psychiatry, 121,* 1176–1182.

Johnson, D. H., & Gelso, C. J. (1980). The effectiveness of time limits in counseling and psychotherapy: A critical review. *The Counseling Psychologist, 9,* 70–83.

Jones, H. E. (1931). The conditioning of overemotional responses. *Journal of Educational Psychology, 22,* 127–130.

Kardiner. A. (1941). *The traumatic neurosis of war.* New York: Hoeber.

Keithly, L. J., Samples, S. J., & Strupp, H. H. (1980). Patient motivation as a predictor of process and outcome in psychotherapy. *Psychotherapy & Psychosomatics, 33,* 87–97.

Klein, D., & Lindemann, E. (1961). Preventive intervention in individual and family crisis situations. In G. Caplan (Ed.), *Prevention of mental disorders in children. Initial exploration* (pp. 283–306). New York: Basic Books.

Klerman, G. L., Weissman, M. M., Rounsaville, B. J., & Chevron, E. S. (1984). *Interpersonal psychotherapy of depression.* New York: Basic Books.

Koegler, R. R. (1966). Brief-contact therapy and drugs in outpatient treatment. In G. J. Wayne & R. R. Koegler (Eds.), *Emergency psychiatry and brief therapy.* Boston: Little, Brown.

Koegler, R. R., & Cannon, J. A. (1966). Treatment for the many. In G. J. Wayne & R. R. Koegler (Eds.), *Emergency psychiatry and brief therapy.* Boston: Little, Brown.

Kris, E. B. (1960). Intensive short-term treatment in a day care facility for the prevention of rehospitalization of patients in the community showing recurrence of psychotic symptoms. *Psychiatric Quarterly, 34,* 83–88.

Lambert, M. J. (1979). Characteristics of patients and their relationship to outcome in brief psychotherapy. *Psychiatric Clinics of North America, 2,* 111–124.

Lambert, M. J. (1983). Comments on "A case study of the process and outcome of time-limited counseling." *Journal of Counseling Psychology, 30,* 22–25.

Lazarus, A. A. (1971). *Behavior therapy and beyond.* New York: McGraw-Hill.

Leeman, C. P., & Mulvey, C. H. (1975). Brief psychotherapy of the dependent personality: Specific techniques. *Psychotherapy and Psychosomatics, 25,* 36–42.

Lester, E. P. (1968). Brief psychotherapies in child psychiatry. *Canadian Psychiatric Association Journal, 13,* 301–309.

Levene, H., Breger, L., & Patterson, V. (1972). A training and research program in brief psychotherapy. *American Journal of Psychotherapy, 26,* 90–100.

Levis, D. J., & Carrera, R. N. (1967). Effects of ten hours of implosive therapy in the treatment of outpatients: A preliminary report. *Journal of Abnormal Psychology, 72,* 504–508.

Levy, R. A. (1966). How to conduct 6 session crisis oriented psychotherapy. *Hospital and Community Psychiatry, 17,* 340–343.

Lewin, K. A. (1966). A method of brief psychotherapy. *Psychiatric Quarterly, 40,* 482–489.

Liberman, B. L., Imber, S. D., Stone, A. R., Hoehn-Saric, R., & Frank, J. D. (1974). Mastery: Prescriptive treatment and maintenance of change in psychotherapy. Cited in J. D. Frank, Therapeutic components of psychotherapy. *Journal of Nervous and Mental Disease, 159,* 325–342.

Lick, J. R., & Bootzin, R. R. (1975). Expectancy factors in the treatment of fear: Methodological and theoretical issues. *Psychological Bulletin, 82,* 917–931.

Lief, H. I., Lief, U. F., Warren, C. O., & Heath, R. C. (1961). Low dropout rate in a psychiatric clinic. *Archives of General Psychiatry, 5,* 200–211.

Lindemann, E. (1944). Symptomatology and management of acute grief. *American Journal of Psychiatry, 101,* 141–148.

Lindemann, E. (1965). Symptomatology and management of acute grief. In H. J. Parad (Ed.), *Crisis intervention: Selected readings* (pp. 7–21). New York: Family Service Association of America.

London, L. S. (1947). Hypnosis, hypno-analysis and narco-analysis. *American Journal of Psychotherapy, 1,* 443–447.

Lorion, R. P. (1973). Socioeconomic status and traditional treatment approaches reconsidered. *Psychological Bulletin, 79,* 263–270.

Lorion, R. P. (1974). Patient and therapist variables in the treatment of low income patients. *Psychological Bulletin, 81,* 344–354.

Lorr, M., McNair, D. M., Michaux, W. W., & Raskin, A. (1964). Frequency of treatment and change in psychotherapy. *Journal of Abnormal and Social Psychology, 64,* 281–292.

Luborsky, L. (1984). *Principles of psychoanalytic psychotherapy: A manual for supportive-expressive treatment.* New York: Basic Books.

Luborsky, L., Chandler, M., Auerbach, A. H., Cohen, J., & Bachrach, H. M. (1971). Factors influencing the outcome of psychotherapy: A review of quantitative research. *Psychological Bulletin, 75,* 145–185.

Luborsky, L., Singer, B., & Luborsky, L. (1975). Comparative studies of psychotherapies. *Archives of General Psychiatry, 32,* 995–1008.

Malan, D. H. (1963). *A study of brief psychotherapy.* London: Tavistock.

Malan, D. H. (1973). The outcome problem in psychotherapy research. *Archives of General Psychiatry, 29,* 719–729.

Malan, D. H. (1976a). *The frontier of brief psychotherapy.* New York: Plenum.

Malan, D. H. (1976b). *Toward the validation of dynamic psychotherapy: A replication.* New York: Plenum.

Mann, J. (1973). *Time-limited psychotherapy.* Cambridge: Harvard University Press.

Marmor, J. (1979). Short-term dynamic psychotherapy. *The American Journal of Psychiatry, 136,* 149–155.

Marziali, E. (1984). Three viewpoints on the therapeutic alliance: Similarities, differences, and association with psychotherapy outcome. *Journal of Nervous and Mental Disease, 7,* 417–423.

Marziali, E., Marmar, C., & Krupnick, J. (1981). Therapeutic alliance scales: Development and relationship to psychotherapy outcome. *American Journal of Psychiatry, 138,* 361–364.

Marziali, E. A., & Sullivan, J. M. (1980). Methodological issues in the content analysis of brief psychotherapy. *British Journal of Medical Psychology, 53,* 19–27.

McDaniel, S. H., Stiles, W. B., & McGaughey, K. J. (1981). Correlations of male college students' verbal response mode use in psychotherapy with measures of psychological disturbance and psychotherapy outcome. *Journal of Consulting and Clinical Psychology, 49,* 571–482.

McGuire, M. (1965a). The process of short-term insight psychotherapy, I. *Journal of Nervous and Mental Disease, 141,* 89–94.

McGuire, M. T. (1965b). The process of short-term insight psychotherapy, II: Content, expectations, and structure. *Journal of Nervous and Mental Disease, 141,* 219–230.

Meichenbaum, D. (1977). *Cognitive behavioral modification.* New York: Plenum.

Meltzoff, J., & Kornreich, M. (1970). *Research in psychotherapy.* New York: Atherton.

Merrill, S., & Cary, G. L. (1975). Dream analysis in brief psychotherapy. *American Journal of Psychotherapy, 29,* 185–193.

Meyer, E., Spiro, H. R., Slaughter, R., Pollack, I. W., Weingartner, H., & Novey, S. (1967). Contractually time-limited psychotherapy in an outpatient psychosomatic clinic. *American Journal of Psychiatry, 124,* 57–68.

Miller, W. B. (1968). A psychiatric emergency service and some treatment concepts. *American Journal of Psychiatry, 124,* 924–933.

Mintz, J. (1972). What is "success" in psychotherapy? *Journal of Abnormal Psychology, 80,* 11–19.

Mitchell, K. R., & Orr, F. E. (1974). Note on treatment of heterosexual anxiety using short-term massed desensitization. *Psychological Reports, 35,* 1093–1094.

Moras, K., & Strupp, H. H. (1982). Pretherapy interpersonal relations, patients' alliance and outcome in brief therapy. *Archives of General Psychiatry, 39,* 405–409.

Morley, W. E. (1965). Treatment of the patient in crisis. *Western Medicine, 3,* 77.

Muench, G. A. (1965). An investigation of the efficacy of time-limited psychotherapy. *Journal of Counseling Psychology, 12,* 294–299.

Neu, C., Prusoff, B. A., & Klerman, G. L. (1978). Measuring the interventions used in the short-term interpersonal psychotherapy of depression. *American Journal of Orthopsychiatry, 48,* 629–636.

Nichols, M. P. (1974). Outcome of brief cathartic psychotherapy. *Journal of Consulting and Clinical Psychology, 42,* 403–410.

Nichols, M. P., & Reifler, C. B. (1973). The study of brief psychotherapy in a college health setting. *Journal of the American College Health Association, 22,* 128–133.

Normand, W. C., Fensterheim, H., Tannenbaum, G., & Sager, C. J. (1963). The acceptance of the psychiatric walk-in clinic in a highly deprived community. *American Journal of Psychiatry, 120,* 533–539.

O'Farrell, M.K., Hill, C. E., & Patton, S. A case study of the process and outcome of time-limited psychotherapy: A methodological replication. Manuscript submitted for publication.

Parad, H. J. (1966). The use of time limited crisis intervention on community mental health programming. *Social Service Review, 40,* 275–282.

Parad, H. J. (1967). *Crisis intervention: Selected readings.* New York: Family Service Association of America.

Parad, H. J., & Parad, L. J. (1968). A study of crisis-oriented planned short-term treatment: Parts I and II. *Social Casework, 49,* 418–426.

Pardes, H., & Pincus, A. (1981). Brief therapy in the context of national mental health issues. In S. H. Budman (Ed.), *Forms of brief therapy* (pp. 7–21). New York: Guilford.

Patterson, V., Levene, H., & Breger, L. (1977). A one year follow-up of two forms of brief psychotherapy. *American Journal of Psychotherapy, 31,* 76–82.

Patterson, V., Levene, H., & Breger, L. (1971). Treatment and training outcomes with two time-limited therapies. *Archives of General Psychiatry, 25,* 161–167.

Paul, G. L. (1966). *Insight versus desensitization in psychotherapy.* Sanford: Stanford University Press.

Paul, G. L. (1967). Insight versus desensitization in psychotherapy two years after termination. *Journal of Consulting Psychology, 31,* 333–348.

Perlman, H. H. (1975). In quest of coping. *Social Casework, 56,* 213–225.

Phillips, E. L., & Johnston, M. H. S. (1954). Theoretical and clinical aspects of short-term, parent–child psychotherapy. *Psychiatry, 7,* 267–275.

Phillips, E. L., & Weiner, D. N. (1966). *Short-term psychotherapy and structural behavior change.* New York: McGraw-Hill.

Piper, W. E., Debbane, E. G., Bienvenu, J. P. & Garant, J. (1984). A comparative study of four forms of psychotherapy. *Journal of Consulting and Clinical Psychology, 52,* 268–279.

Piper, W. E., Debbane, E. G., Bienvenu, J. P., DeCarufel, F. L., and Garant, J. (in press). Relationships between the object focus of therapist interpretations and outcome in short-term, individual psychotherapy. *British Journal of Medical Psychology.*

Pumpian-Mindlin, E. (1953). Consideration in the selection of patients for short-term therapy. *American Journal of Psychotherapy, 7,* 641–652.

Rabkin, R. (1977). *Strategic psychotherapy: Brief and symptomatic treatment.* New York: Basic Books.

Reid, W. J. (1975). A test of a task-centered approach. *Social Work, 20,* 3–9.

Rice, L. N., & Greenberg, L. S. (1984). *Patterns of change: Intensive analysis of psychotherapy process.* New York: Guilford.

Rosenbaum, C. P. (1964). Events of early therapy and brief therapy. *Archives of General Psychiatry, 10,* 506–512.

Rosenthal, D., & Frank, J. (1958). The fate of psychiatric clinic outpatients assigned to psychotherapy. *Journal of Nervous and Mental Disease, 127,* 330–343.

Rosenthal, H. R. (1965). Emergency psychotherapy: A crucial need. *Psychoanalytic Review, 52,* 446.

Roth, R. M., Berenbaum, H. L., & Garfield, S. J. (1969). Massed time-limit therapy. *Psychotherapy: Theory, Research and Practice, 6,* 54–56.

Rusk, T. N., & Gerner, R. H. (1972). A study of the process of emergency psychotherapy. *American Journal of Psychiatry, 128,* 882–885.

Sachs, J. S. (1983). Negative factors in brief psychotherapy: An empirical assessment. *Journal of Consulting and Clinical Psychology, 51,* 557–564.

Saltzman, C., Luetgert, M. J., Roth, C. H., Creaser, J., & Howard, L. (1976). Formation of a therapeutic relationship: Experiences during the initial phase of psychotherapy as predictors of treatment duration and outcome. *Journal of Consulting and Clinical Psychology, 44,* 546–555.

Sarvis, M. A., Dewees, M. S., & Johnston, R. F. (1958). A concept of ego-oriented psychotherapy. *Psychiatry, 22,* 277–287.

Saul, L. J. (1951). On the value of one or two interviews. *Psychoanalytic Quarterly, 20,* 613–615.

Schoenberg, B., & Carr, A. C. (1963). An investigation of criteria for brief psychotherapy of neurodermatitis. *Psychosomatic Medicine, 25,* 253–263.

Schonfield, J., Stone, A. R., Hoehn-Saric, R., Imber, S. D., & Pande, S. K. (1969). Patient–therapist convergence and measures of improvement in short-term psychotherapy. *Psychotherapy: Theory, Research and Practice, 6,* 267–272.

Schwartz, A. J., & Bernard, H. S. (1981). Comparison of patient and therapist evaluations of time-limited psychotherapy. *Psychotherapy: Theory, Research and Practice, 18,* 101–108.

Seitz, P. F. D. (1953). Dyamically oriented brief psychotherapy: Psychocutaneous excoriation syndromes. *Psychosomatic Medicine, 15,* 200–242.

Semrad, E. V., Binstock, W. A., & White, B. (1966). Brief psychotherapy. *American Journal of Psychotherapy, 20,* 576–596.

Shlien, J. M., Mosak, H. H., & Dreikurs, R., (1962). Effects of time limits: A comparison of two psychotherapies. *Journal of Counseling Psychology, 9,* 31–34.

Sifneos, P. E. (1968). Learning to solve emotional problems: A controlled study of short-term anxiety-provoking psychotherapy. In R. Porter (Ed.), *Ciba Foundation* symposium on the role of learning in psychotherapy. London: J. & A. Churchill.

Sifneos, P. E. (1972). *Short-term psychotherapy and emotional crisis.* Cambridge, MA: Harvard University Press.

Sifneos, P. E. (1975). Evaluating the results of short-term anxiety provoking psychotherapy. *Psychotherapy and Psychosomatics, 25,* 217–220.

Sifneos, P. E. (1979). *Short-term dynamic psychology therapy: Evaluation and technique.* New York: Plenum Press.

Silver, R. J. (1982). Brief dynamic psychotherapy: A critical look at the state of the art. *Psychiatric Quarterly, 53,* 275–282.

Sloane, R. B., Cristol, A. H., Pepernik, M. C., & Staples, F. R. (1970). Role preparation and expectation of improvement in psychotherapy. *Journal of Nervous and Mental Disease, 150,* 18–26.

Sloane, R. B., Staples, F. R., Cristol, A. H., Yorkston, N. J., & Whipple, K. (1975). Short-term analytically oriented psychotherapy versus behavior therapy. *American Journal of Psychiatry, 132,* 373–377.

Sloane, R. B., Staples, F. R., Cristol, A. H., Yorkston, N. J., & Whipple, K. (1976). Patient characteristics and outcome in psychotherapy and behavior therapy. *Journal of Consulting and Clinical Psychology, 44,* 330–339.

Small, L. (1971). *The briefer psychotherapies.* New York: Brunner/Mazel.

Small, L. (1972). Crisis therapy: Theory and method. In G. D. Goldman & D. S. Milman (Eds.), *Innovations in psychotherapy.* Springfield, IL: Charles C. Thomas.

Smith, M. L., & Glass, G. V. (1977). Meta-analysis of psychotherapy outcome studies. *American Psychologist, 32,* 752–760.

Smith, M. L., Glass, G. V., & Miller, T. I. (1980). *The benefits of psychotherapy.* Baltimore: The Johns Hopkins University Press.

Socarides, C. W. (1954). On the usefulness of extremely brief psychoanalytic contacts. *Psychoanalytic Review, 41,* 340–346.

Spoerl, R. H. (1975). Single session psychotherapy. *Diseases of the Nervous System, 36,* 283–285.

Stampfl, T. G., & Levis, D. J. (1967). Essentials of implosive therapy: A learning theory based psychodynamic behavioral therapy. *Journal of Abnormal Psychology, 72,* 496–503.

Staples, F. R., & Sloane, R. B. (1970). The relation of speech patterns in psychotherapy to empathic ability, responsiveness to approval and disapproval. *Diseases of the Nervous System, 31,* 100–104.

Staples, F. R., Sloane, R. D., Whipple, K., Cristol, A. H., & Yorkston, N. (1976). Process and outcome in psychotherapy and behavior therapy. *Journal of Consulting and Clinical Psychology, 44,* 340–350.

Stein, C. (1972). Hypnotic projection in brief psychotherapy. *American Journal of Clinical Hypnosis, 14,* 143–155.

Stein, C. (1975). Brief hypnotherapy for conversion cephalgia (repression headache). *American Journal of Clinical Hypnosis, 17,* 198–201.

Stein, H., Murdaugh, J. M., & MacLeod, J. A. (1967). As reported anon., in "Emotional reaction to illness responds to brief psychotherapy." *Frontiers of Hospital Psychiatry, 4,* 15.

Stekel, W. (1950). *Technique of analytical psychotherapy.* London: Bodley Head.

Stewart, H. (1972). Six-months, fixed-term, once weekly psychotherapy: A report on 20 cases with follow-ups. *British Journal of Psychiatry, 121,* 425–435.

Stiles, W. B. (1980). Measurement of the impact of psychotherapy sessions. *Journal of Consulting and Clinical Psychology, 48,* 176–185.

Stiles, W. B., & Sultan, F. E. (1979). Verbal response mode use by clients in psychotherapy. *Journal of Consulting and Clinical Psychology, 47,* 611–613.

Stone, L. (1951). Psychoanalysis and brief psychotherapy. *Psychoanalytic Quarterly, 20,* 215–236.

Stone, A. R., Frank, J. D., Nash, E., & Imber, S. D. (1961). An intensive five-year follow-up study of treated psychiatric patients. *Journal of Nervous and Mental Disease, 133,* 410–422.

Straker, M. (1966). Brief psychotherapy in an outpatient clinic: Evolution and evaluation. *American Journal of Psychiatry, 124,* 39–45.

Strassi, I., & Messer, S. B. (1976). Psychotherapy with patients from lower socioeconomic groups. *American Journal of Psychotherapy, 30,* 29–40.

Strupp, H. H. (1980a). Success and failure in time-limited psychotherapy: A systematic comparison of two cases. Comparison I. *Archives of General Psychiatry, 37,* 595–603.

Strupp, H. H. (1980b). Success and failure in time-limited psychotherapy: A systematic comparison of two cases. Comparison II. *Archives of General Psychiatry, 37,* 708–717.

Strupp, H. H. (1980c). Success and failure in time-limited psychotherapy: With special reference to the performance of a lay counselor. *Archives of General Psychiatry, 37,* 831–841.

Strupp, H. H. (1980d). Success and failure in time-limited psychotherapy: Further evidence. Comparison IV. *Archives of General Psychiatry, 37,* 947–954.

Strupp, H. H. (1981). Toward the refinement of time-limited dynamic psychotherapy. In S. L. Budman (Ed.), *Forms of brief therapy.* (pp. 219–240). New York: Guilford.

Strupp, H. H., & Binder, J. L. (1984). *Psychotherapy in a new key: A guide to time-limited dynamic psychotherapy.* New York: Basic Books.

Strupp, H. H., & Hadley, S. W. (1979). Specific versus nonspecific factors in psychotherapy: A controlled study of outcome. *Archives of General Psychiatry, 36,* 1125–1136.

Strupp, H. H., Hadley, S. W., & Gomes-Schwartz, B. (1977). *Psychotherapy for better or worse: An analysis of the problem of negative effects.* New York: Jason Aronson.

Strupp, H. H., Moras, K., Sandell, J., Waterhouse, G., O'Malley, S., Keithly, L., & Gomes-Schwartz, B. (1981). *Vanderbilt negative indicators scale: An instrument for the identification of deterrents to progress in time-limited dynamic psychotherapy.* Unpublished manuscript, Vanderbilt University.

Suinn, R. M., Edie, C. A., & Spinelli, P. R. (1970). Accelerated massed desensitization: Innovation in short-term treatment. *Behavior Therapy, 1,* 303–311.

Terhune, W. B. (1960). Brief psychotherapy with executives in industry. *Progess in Psychotherapy, 5,* 132–139.

Tracey, T. J. (1985). Dominance and outcome: A sequential examination. *Journal of Counseling Psychology, 32,* 119–122.

Tracey, T. J., & Ray. P. B. (1984). Stages of successful time-limited counseling: An interactional examination. *Journal of Counseling Psychology, 31,* 13–27.

Ursano, R. J., & Dressler, D. M. (1974). Brief vs. long term psychotherapy: A treatment decision. *Journal of Nervous and Mental Disease, 159,* 164–171.

Visher, J. S. (1959). Brief psychotherapy in a mental hygiene clinic. *American Journal of Psychotherapy, 13,* 331–342.

Waltzer, H., Hankoff, L. D., Englehardt, D. M., & Kaufman, I. C. (1963). Emergency psychiatric treatment in a receiving hospital. *Mental Hospitals, 14,* 595–600.

Warren, N. C., & Rice, L. N. (1972). Structuring and stabilizing of psychotherapy for low prognosis clients. *Journal of Consulting and Clinical Psychology, 39,* 173–181.

Watson, J. B., & Rayner, P. (1920). Conditioned emotional reactions. *Journal of Experimental Psychology, 3,* 1–14.

Wayne, G. J. (1966). How long? An approach to reducing the duration of inpatient treatment. In G. J. Wayne & R. R. Koegler (Eds.), *Emergency psychiatry and brief therapy.* Boston: Little, Brown.

White, A. M., Fichtenbaum, L., & Dollard, J. (1969). Measurement of what the patient learns from psychotherapy. *Journal of Nervous and Mental Disease, 149,* 281–293.

Wilson, G. T. (1981). Behavior therapy as a short-term therapeutic approach. In S. H. Budman (Ed.), *Forms of brief therapy* (pp. 131–166). New York: Guilford.

Wolberg, L. R. (1965a). Methodology in short term therapy. *American Journal of Psychiatry, 122,* 135–140.

Wolberg, L. R. (Ed.) (1965b). *Short-term psychotherapy.* New York: Grune & Stratton.

Wolberg, L. R. (1980). *Handbook of short-term psychotherapy.* New York: Thieme-Stratton.

Wolkon, G. H. (1972). Crisis theory, the application for treatment, and dependency. *Comprehensive Psychiatry, 13,* 459–464.

Wolpe, J. (1952). Experimental neurosis as learned behavior. *British Journal of Psychology, 43,* 243–268.

Wolpe,. J., & Lazarus, A. A. (1966). *Behavior therapy techniques.* Oxford: Pergamon.

15

EXPERIENTIAL GROUP RESEARCH: RESULTS, QUESTIONS, AND SUGGESTIONS

THEODORE J. KAUL

Ohio State University

RICHARD L. BEDNAR

Brigham Young University

INTRODUCTION

Once again we find ourselves reviewing and analyzing research developments in the area of small-group treatments. But this time the task feels different, probably because we have completed two major reviews that span four decades of research. Having read so many research reports on the same topic, pondered the scientific merit and meaning of each report, and distilled the essence of these reports for professional publication has left us with a sense of balance and perspective about the scientific well-being of the group disciplines. This sense of perspective does not feel as presumptuous as it may sound. It seems more like what an experienced therapist might feel beginning psychotherapy with the sixty-eighth client with a diagnosis of character disorder. There is a nomothetic predictability about it that may make the idiographic uniquenesses stand out more clearly.

We believe it important to share the perspectives we have acquired about the scientific health of the group disciplines for three reasons. First, we suspect that we may represent an uncommon point of view, one that could be as provocative to some as it would be annoying to others. If our assumption is true, we can provide the reader with a new set of conceptual lenses that may bring new research issues into focus that have not received the consideration we think they deserve. Also, and far more important, the logical implications of our views call for changes in the form, substance, and criteria for evaluating and developing group research.

Second, we will propose additional evaluative criteria for discussing group research. We will attempt to accommodate the frequently conflicted requirements for methodological rigor and conceptual relevance. Group research must be evaluated from both conceptual and methodological perspectives. Anything less is a denial of the complexity of

671

group processes and the step-by-step developments required if research is to clarify the principles that regulate these processes. Future research will have to embrace conceptually poignant variables in studies that build upon themselves developmentally within a carefully considered framework; it must have systematic relevance as well as empirical relevance.

The execution of conceptually salient group research may require methodological modifications. The design issues often are so complex and costly that they may resist solution in any single experiment, even by the most sophisticated researcher. But methodological perfection is only an ideal goal, not yet an achievable one for our field. Gratuitous and self-serving criticisms of important experiments should be avoided. It is equally important that we not encourage the replication of experiments focusing on less important questions, or employ methods that will not allow better questions to be answered. We will evaluate the developmental potential of research reports in this review as well as their methodological rigor.

Third, interpreting group research on a study-by-study basis involves intellectual processes, inferences, and conclusions quite different from those involved in evaluating the group research collectively. The former involves more deductive thought, precision of measurement, and rigor of design and analysis. The latter tends to demand inductive inference about the relevance of research trends, patterns, directions, and the identification of premier issues and concepts. We submit that the pattern and directions of contemporary group research should be subject to as much review and analysis as the individual research reports.

Prior to beginning our literature review, we will discuss some of the methodological and conceptual considerations that we consider central to understanding, interpreting, and improving contemporary group research. We hope to demonstrate that the issues we discuss represent some of the essential guidelines for evaluating the significance of existing research and shaping new directions for future research.

Conceptual and Methodological Concerns

We have discussed some of the conceptual and methodological issues in more detail in earlier publications (Bednar & Kaul, 1978, 1979; Bednar &

Moeschl, 1981; Kaul & Bednar, 1978). We will briefly review some of the more important points of these discussions to provide a context within which to discuss current developments in this field.

Perhaps the best place to begin this discussion is with a summary of the conclusions drawn from other reviews. Several comprehensive reviews suggest quite unequivocally that group treatments have been associated with client improvement in a variety of settings. The data supporting this conclusion have come from a substantial number of independent investigations, with reasonably rigorous and varied experimental procedures (Bednar & Kaul, 1978; Bednar & Lawlis, 1971; Campbell & Dunnette, 1968; Gibb, 1971; Parloff & Dies, 1977; Smith, 1975; Stock, 1964). It is becoming less and less reasonable to assume that all of these affirmative findings are Type I errors. If, indeed, the conjecture of a difference has escaped refutation repeatedly, there may be warrant to induce its truthfulness (Popper, 1979). The accumulated evidence suggests that group treatments have been shown to be effective, at least to some degree under some conditions which are, unfortunately, basically unknown.

Though this single finding is both encouraging and important, we dare not lose track of another equally important observation. After nearly four decades of research, there are no fundamental improvements in our knowledge about the more specific and basic elements of effective group treatments. The situation is similar to that in considering individual psychotherapy (Bergin & Lambert, 1978, 1979; Frank, 1979; Garfield, 1981; Kiesler, 1979), except that in the group domain we may know less about the primary sources of change. Our knowledge is embarrassingly limited on such crucial matters as: (1) how client improvement is mediated by group processes, (2) how the individual can affect group processes, (3) how varied group processes affect the individual, and (4) what dimensions of psychological functioning are most amenable to change via group processes.

Though we may have begun to make progress on these more basic questions, we must ask ourselves why the bulk of published group research continues to be either (1) general outcome studies that do not attempt to isolate specific elements of group treatment process, or (2) process studies that do not attempt to relate group processes to specific dimensions of client outcome. Such studies can shed light only on questions that are less important or have already been "answered;" namely, that group treatments have been associated with client improvement, but the conditions (leadership, group composition, clientele, theoretical orientation, curative factors, etc.) that foster this improvement are basically unknown. We seem to continue engaging in research problems and procedures that will allow us to conclude only that which we already "know." It is time we ask ourselves what it is about our research models that perpetuates these problems.

Conceptual Concerns

We suggest that the most fundamental problem of group research is that its conceptual foundations are inappropriate to many of the essential ingredients of group treatments. This problem may have its origins in the early development of group psychotherapy theories. These theories seem to have their genesis in theories of individual psychotherapy, psychopathology, and personality development (Bednar, 1980). With a few noteworthy exceptions, group theorists have ignored the issue of developing an even partially separate conceptual identity for the group discipline. The result is that the group discipline has borrowed, and failed to modify, major portions of its conceptual identity. The result is more theoretical impoverishment than one might desire. Insofar as there are theories of group work, they have been incorporated and assimilated, but rarely do we find basic concepts and propositions evolving out of prolonged and careful observations of small-group processes. The result is something of a conceptual malaise regarding the primary, unique, and defining characteristics of group treatments (Bednar & Kaul, forthcoming).

The full impact of this problem becomes clearer as we consider the intimate relationship between theory and research. One of the primary functions of theory is to guide the observations of the researcher. Theory can advise the researcher about what to look for and how to look, as well as where it might be found. This is a process of delimiting, focusing, and narrowing the conceptual vision of the researcher to those variables thought to be the most relevant and potent to understanding the problem at hand. If theory does guide research in the manner we are suggesting, it should be apparent why group theories must evolve directly from careful and astute observations of group processes, at

least in part. Unless you assume no differences between the two, the primary conceptual ingredients that guide group research cannot be borrowed from other disciplines and applied to the issues of small-group treatments with the expectation of a clean fit. Such a procedure would stretch any set of concepts beyond their intended range of convenience.

No amount of sophisticated statistical analyses or complex research designs can delineate important relationships between irrelevant or poorly defined conceptual variables, though it may help indirectly. The quality of the experimental output cannot be expected to exceed the quality of the original conceptual input; though serendipitous results may occur, it does not seem good science to expect them. Concept formation and theory development are inextricable from one another. For this reason, the value of many small-group experiments can reasonably and appropriately be judged by their theoretical introduction alone. Within the space limitations of this chapter we will comment on the conceptual adequacy and relevance of the group research.

Operational definitions. We have already mentioned some of the major conceptual problems that burden the group disciplines. It should not be surprising to find some chronic problems in the methods of measurement and procedures used to operationalize these variables as well. Without assuming radical reductionism, the essential problem is one of selecting methods of measurement and operational procedures that accurately capture and preserve the fundamental ingredients of original concepts. An example may provide the best means to illustrate this problem.

Several decades ago, the research literature was filled with studies on the relationship between therapist levels of accurate empathy and client outcome. Much of this evidence was suggestive of an important relationship between empathy and client improvement. Perusal of this literature reveals a problem that was seldom acknowledged, that is, a lack of correspondence between the essential ingredients in the concept of empathy and the way it was measured or experimentally varied.

Conceptually, empathy has at least two fundamental elements. The first is the therapist's ability to comprehend the phenomenological significance of the client's experiences. The second is the therapist's ability to convey to the client this accurate understanding. Measurement of the concept of empathy would require raters with demonstrated ability to function at high levels of accurate empathy. One could not expect raters to recognize and rate accurately a variable they were not expert at themselves. Yet the literature is filled with instances of relatively unselected judges hastily being trained to rate this important and complex variable. It is unknown whether, but most unlikely that, these raters accurately captured the essential elements of accurate empathy no matter what levels of interrater reliability were obtained.

Subsequent analyses of the empathy literature and the various methods used for its measurement suggested that a global rating of a "good guy" was more central to high ratings on accurate empathy than the therapists' perceptual sensitivity and communication skills. In other words, accurate empathy probably was not isolated for study as often as many in our profession assume because of the lack of correspondence between the conceptual meaning of the term and the way in which it was measured in experimental studies.

The process of conceptually defining relevant treatment variables and then operationalizing them in a way that preserves the essential properties of the original concept may well prove to be the most creative and demanding task in group research.

Conceptual parochialism.   Finally, we would like to comment on what appears to be a procedural problem affecting the conceptual development of the group disciplines. Most theoreticians and practitioners of group psychotherapy are behavioral scientists, despite what other adjectives they may use to further define themselves. As behavioral scientists, they have a common background in science as a means for organizing and accounting for their observations. They know that theories are never ultimately correct, that there is always some improvement to be made. Improvements are made by discovering flaws in our theories, perhaps more than by finding confirmation of them (Popper, 1968). In short, behavioral scientists know that understanding increases as we destroy old theories and replace them with new ones that serve our needs more fully.

In spite of this basic philosophical orientation of the behavioral sciences, group work is characterized by a lack of tentativeness. In few cases do we see theoretical differences carefully described and re-

searched as a means of rigorous resolution. Instead, we find ideological schools of thought isolating themselves from other intellectually "contaminating" influences and thereby perpetuating uncontested assumptions and world views. It is extremely rare in the group disciplines to observe advocates of one theoretical position even talking with those of another. It is almost unheard of to notice or acknowledge the limitations of one's position or the potential utility of another's.

One must wonder why the group disciplines persist in such intellectually insulated methods of inquiry. Some of this intellectual isolationism seems to be an attempt to preserve the ideological purity of theoretical systems in the absense of a sound data base. Far more basic to this problem, however, seems to be an apparent inability to understand that different systems of group treatment can be, and should be, based on different units and levels of psychological analysis. Some group models emphasize interpersonal relationships, others focus on group dynamics, and still others are viewed as experiential laboratories in which participants' reality-test new behavior patterns. Each approach can be considered an attempt to understand group psychotherapy from slightly different perspectives. As research is completed that identifies the specific points of benefit in these different theoretical models, it may be possible to integrate these empirical findings into more comprehensive and valid theoretical models of group treatments.

Philosophers of science have long acknowledged the processes of observation, conceptualization, and empirical data collection as basic to theory development. Having theoretical systems representing different units and levels of analysis is important to this process because it can lead to multidimensional approaches to difficult problems. We need to be encouraging our colleagues with different views, not arguing with them. The group disciplines might profit from an understanding that conceptual differences often are useful in the development of a conceptually sound science. We need to understand that meaningful advances in group theory and research must await new research results that provide more precise descriptions of psychological events that represent different levels of personal, interpersonal, and group behavior. For a more complete discussion of this problem, see Bednar and Kaul (forthcoming).

Methodological Issues

The logistical and methodological problems involved in useful group research are no less troublesome than the conceptual problems we have already discussed. In fact, the design and control problems in group research seem to escalate at a factorial rate as germane treatment conditions are represented in multiple group designs. In most cases it is neither feasible nor reasonable to expect any single research project to accommodate all of the design considerations that already have been shown to be experimentally beneficial. For the time being, at least, group researchers need to understand that some of these methodological problems must be patiently accepted, others can be partially avoided, and some experimental error can be minimized by carefully orchestrated trade-offs between experimental methods and variables. The alternative is to persist in asking less important questions.

For those who have not had the dubious distinction of trying to accommodate the staggering multitude of design problems involved in group research, let us briefly illustrate the problem. Suppose a researcher is interested in a question that involves two levels of a treatment condition and its effects on three levels of a personality variable. The most natural result of this basic form of a question is a randomized design with a 2×3 factorial arrangement of treatments. By the time our researcher accommodates the need for (1) multiple group design (8 to 10 groups per call) to control for the ecological effects of different groups within the same treatment conditions, (2) plausible placebo control conditions, (3) replications involving different leadership styles and leader personality variables, (4) controls for test sensitization effects, (5) a large enough subject pool to allow for prescreening and selection with the personality inventory, and (6) one replication of the entire experimental process, we are talking about a research project that could involve 180 psychotherapy groups, 25 to 50 group leaders, and approximately 9000 to 12,000 experimental subjects. Need we say more? One such experiment would exhaust the entire subject pool of several universities, the trained leaders of the same, as well as the funds from several granting agencies.

Because of this logistical complexity, we will discuss some of the more important problems involved in the design and analysis of group research. Our purpose is to provide the reader with sufficient per- spective to judge the merits of group research in a multidimensional framework. Such a framework will more accurately reveal both the assets and the limitations of group research projects. We can discuss these issues at only an introductory level, but we will provide references for those interested in additional reading.

Design complexity. We have discussed the complexity of the group disciplines as well as the questionable conceptual origins of much of the group research. Independently, each of these areas poses formidable obstacles to meaningful advances in the group disciplines. When the problems of these two areas are combined, as they eventually must be in any research project, several methods for evaluating and improving the quality of group research start to come into focus.

One is to use research designs that attempt to capture, rather than minimize, the complexity of small-group processes. The most frequent design of published reports allows the researcher to determine only the effects of a treatment process (independent variable) on client improvement or group processes (dependent variables). Such an approach ignores the multiple sources of influence operating within small-group treatments as well as the interactions among the numerous variables that influence group processes and outcomes. The complexity of the group situation has been suggested by Dies (1977) and by Lieberman, Yalom, and Miles (1973), a complexity that calls for research employing mediating or intervening variables between the independent and dependent variables. For example, instead of studying the effects of pregroup training on client improvement, they argue that it would be more enlightening to know how specific elements of pregroup training affect early group development patterns and styles of group communication, and then how each variable initially affected by pregroup training eventually may influence client outcome. At present, we do not know what chain of events occurs between treatment input and client output, nor are we in much of a position to speculate about it. Attention focused more closely on those intervening and process variables that seem most likely to account for differential client outcomes could bring us to the point where speculation would be warranted. The time is past when it is acceptable for researchers to ignore the relationships between treatment variables, intervening group processes, and differential client outcome in their research designs.

Experimental confounding. The goal in experimental research is to isolate and vary one or more variables, while keeping the *cetaris paribus*'s (all other things being equal) to a minimum. This permits the researcher to estimate the specific effects of isolated treatment variables. A major obstacle is experimental confounding, having experimental results influenced by variables other than those specifically isolated for study. Experimental confounding is a particularly bothersome problem in two areas of group research. They are leadership effects and placebo effects. In both cases, it is virtually impossible to separate and isolate the effects of these two variables from the experimental treatments.

Group leadership variables are almost always confounded with the personality characteristics of the group leader. As with most forms of psychological intervention, leadership is as much an expression of the therapist's personality as it is specific technical procedures. The same is true of placebo effects. The high levels of emotional arousal, attention, and psychological stimulation inherent in most forms of group treatment usually cannot be completely separated from the specific treatment variables isolated for study.

Dies (1977) has outlined five strategies that help control leadership effects. They include (1) matching leaders across experimental conditions, (2) counterbalancing leadership across experimental conditions, (3) specific training for leaders as a means of standardizing treatments across experimental conditions, (4) standardizing leadership effects by the use of structured group treatments (tapes, etc.), and (5) assessment and objective description of leaders across different experimental groups. Each of these methods has major assets and limitations, which are discussed more fully by Dies.

It has been demonstrated empirically and argued rationally that placebo effects do exert important effects on group processes and outcomes (McCardel & Murry, 1974). In view of this evidence, it seems reasonable to expect that researchers plan for appropriate placebo control conditions in all group research. The essence of this control condition would call for experimental and control subjects being exposed to comparable experiences with regard to at least some of the following: (1) the amount

of time at the same treatment facility, (2) interpersonal activities with group members and professional staff that are not specified by the treatment (i.e., are nonspecific to it), (3) expectations for personal involvement and improvement as a result of interpersonal activities, and (4) interpersonal exploration of nonspecific issues in small-group discussions. Such procedures might help ensure that the benefits assumed to be a function of small-group treatments actually exceed the benefits of general and nonspecific interpersonal activity and attention.

The pervasive and limiting influence of these two confounding variables (leadership and placebo) on the accumulated body of group research clearly indicates the need for their more systematic control. Certainly other confounding variables are equally important in specific research projects, but no other variables have so systematically compromised the vitality of the group literature as the uncontrolled effects of leadership and placebo reactivity.

Statistical confounding. In our chapter in the previous edition of this handbook (Bednar & Kaul, 1978), we introduced the idea that experiments in group processes contain two sources of conceptually significant error variance, rather than one. Most investigators have traditionally defined statistical error variance in terms of individual deviations from the grand mean. A second source of statistical error may be operative in groups, however. This error variance may arise when interaction patterns unique to specific groups are confounded with the primary treatment variables and presumed to represent pure treatment effects. In short, error variance in group research may be a function of differences within treatment groups and between them as well. Failure to recognize those two sources of error could lead to systematic overestimates of the statistical significance of treatment effects. The solution to this problem calls for more appropriate partitioning of experimental variance into sources associated with (1) individuals within groups and treatments, (2) individuals between groups and treatments, (3) between treatments, and (4) error.

Since we first raised the possibility of this systematic statistical error, one research project has been completed that provides preliminary evidence on the potential importance of this effect. Woods (1980) employed a randomized design with a $2 \times 2 \times 2$ factorial arrangement of treatments to investigate the effects of several treatment factors on group processes and outcomes. In this study the treatment groups were conceived as being nested within the experimental treatment conditions. This allowed the analysis of variance model to partition the experimental variance into components associated with treatments, individuals, groups, and error. Approaching the data analysis in this manner had a rather profound effect on the nature of the results obtained and the conclusions that could be drawn from the experiment.

Woods reported significant variability among groups within treatment conditions. This finding indicates that groups did respond differentially to the same treatment procedures. Presumably these differences were due to the ecological factors (e.g., group composition, interaction styles, leadership characteristics) unique to each group. Such a finding was not surprising inasmuch as each group as a collective entity can be expected to be as different as individuals within the group. What was surprising was the fact that these unique group factors rivaled the power of the independent variables in accounting for variability on the dependent measures.

A second major finding was that the variability attributable to groups within treatments was significantly greater than that attributable to individuals within groups. The between-group variability accounted for a substantial portion of total experimental variability. Failure to partition the treatment and error variance as Woods did in this study could have resulted in a substantial overestimation of significant treatment effects attributable to the original experimental treatment variables. Different groups responded to the same treatment manipulations in dramatically different ways. Further, the magnitude of these differences was greater within the same treatment conditions than between different treatment conditions. In brief, the unique ecological characteristics of each experimental group had more influence on group outcome than the experimental variables being studied.

This single study, though preliminary in nature, is most sobering. Though there are several competing hypotheses, it is the first evidence to suggest that the group literature may be filled with an epidemic of statistical errors that systematically overestimate the significance of treatment effects associated with group treatments. This study also suggests the wisdom, if not the necessity, of employing designs that

include several groups within each treatment condition whenever possible. Certainly, researchers need to be aware of the degree to which their conclusions from group data can be restricted until findings have been replicated with experiments using several groups in each condition.

This is not as simple as it might seem, however. Given the conceptual difficulties the field faces, designs such as the ones we have been suggesting can be problematic until we have ample reason to believe our research variables represent theoretically potent treatment dimensions. Many of these variables will be suggested by small, one-group-per-cell experiments in which exploratory variables are more clearly defined, measured, and related to other important dimensions of group processes and outcomes. Simple replications of these studies may control many of the unwanted sources of error variance that will be inherent in these projects. The smaller studies, for example, could contribute to enhanced clarity with regard to the variables of group treatment, while those with several groups per cell could suggest their limitations and point the way to further research. Each design has potential benefits and opportunity costs, and each can contribute to answering important group questions.

Descriptive and Evaluative Framework

We have discussed only what we consider to be some of the more fundamental obstacles to developing a significant body of group research. We have reviewed the conceptual foundations of the group disciplines and found them lacking in relevance and precision. Regrettably, but not surprisingly, many of the conceptual variables represented in the group research are plagued by the same difficulties; they seem to have been named before their observation has been completed. We also have noted the multiple sources of complex interpersonal influence available in the small group setting and lamented the fact that most of these intriguing and potent elements of the group treatment process seldom are preserved in even the most sophisticated contemporary research designs. Finally, we have discussed the desirability of the group literature being based on different units and levels of analysis. By doing this the discipline enhances its ability to develop more comprehensive theoretical models.

We pointed out the possibility that the contemporary group literature may be saturated with overestimates of group treatment effects because of systematic errors in the statistical analysis of group data. We also alerted the reader to the distracting effects of placebo reactivity, leadership variability, and a lack of correspondence between conceptual variables and the methods of measurement employed to isolate them for study.

Some of these considerations (design complexity units of analysis and conceptual variables) are particularly suitable for the development of a descriptive matrix that would allow us more accurately to describe, classify, and evaluate group research. This descriptive and evaluative matrix is portrayed in Figure 15.1. Each dimension of this matrix warrants a few explanatory comments.

Units and Levels of Analysis

Basic epistemological considerations suggest the importance of group theory and research that is based on concepts representing different units and levels of analysis. Four common levels of analysis for group treatments are (1) intrapsychic, (2) personal, (3) interpersonal, and (4) group. We can discuss these dimensions only briefly, but the interested reader can find a more complete discussion of

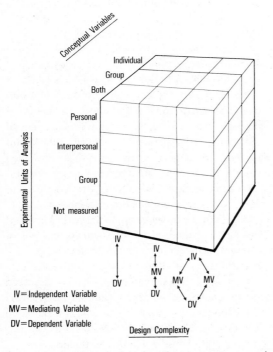

IV = Independent Variable
MV = Mediating Variable
DV = Dependent Variable

Design Complexity

Figure 15.1   Criteria for classifying group research.

the history and relevance of these domains of psychological functioning to group theory and practice in Bednar and Kaul (forthcoming).

The notion of intrapsychic events has held a central role in many theories of psychology. By definition, intrapsychic events take place in the mind and are not available for direct observation. But everyone experiences intrapsychic events as part of everyday life. They are known to us introspectively. Such events, problematic as they are from a theoretical and research point of view, represent one level of analysis central to group research. We mention this class, but have not included it in Figure 15.1 because there is as yet no satisfactory technology by which to bring it into the experimental laboratory (but see Meehl, 1983 for an interesting preliminary approach).

Personal events, though similar to intrapsychic events, are different in one important way: they are relatively observable by others. They refer to individual behavior patterns, response styles, and behavioral dispositions. There may be confusion at times about how one clearly differentiates observable behavior from the intrapsychic events that often are presumed to precede or accompany observable behavior. In difficult assessment situations one must remember that intrapsychic events are accessible only by personal introspection and sometimes reportable by the individual, whereas personal events are also public events with the individual as the primary referent.

In contrast to those approaches that focus on intrapsychic and personal events are those that stress interpersonal phenomena. For some of the newer models of group work, interpersonal events are the most fundamental elements of theory and practice. These models focus on the processes that are related to the initiation and development of interpersonal relationships of all kinds. In each case, however, the focus of observation and analysis is on those factors that succinctly describe major psychological processes that influence the development of relationships. They are observable by self and others, though often requiring greater inference than the personal events mentioned above.

Finally, some models of group treatments focus on the small group as a social system in which the group as a collective entity is the focus of observation and analysis. Proponents of this focal emphasis suggest that each small group acquires a distinct working style and atmosphere that exerts substantial influence on the psychological experience of group members. In experimental terms, the group ethos is the primary independent variable of group psychotherapy. Accordingly, group levels of analysis are essential to an accurate understanding of the field forces that effect all behavior within the small group. Though based on observable behaviors, the inferential demands often are substantial.

Conceptual Variables

In our earlier discussion of the conceptual origins of much of the group research, we expressed the view that there are few studies in which the primary research variables are derived from group treatment models. Instead, we find many of the key concepts investigated being derived from systems of individual psychotherapy, psychopathology, and personality development. Each of these disciplines provides concepts that are fundamental to group theory and practice. But it seems unwise that group research be based on these disciplines alone. Group research efforts based on concepts more indigenous to group processes would offer greater import for the development of group theory.

The reason for this should be clear. Specifically, the way to prove that a phenomenon does not make a difference is to presume that it does, and then proceed to test it rigorously. If no difference can be determined following such tests, then one can assume that the phenomenon is of no importance, at least for the moment. If a treatment theory supposes that the presence of a group is of no importance, or attempts to understand group therapy without giving the presence of the group a central position in group theory, it seems to us that this theory is not the most salubrious environment in which to begin the search for group effects. The search would be better initiated from a theoretical base that presumes that the group does make a difference.

The second dimension of our descriptive matrix will help illustrate the degree to which the group literature is studying essential elements of group psychotherapy or ancillary concepts that are closely associated with group treatments such as psychopathology, psychotherapy, and personality.

Design Complexity

Design adequacy is generally assumed to refer to the traditional requirements of methodological rigor and control as represented in the general experimental literature. These concerns, though certainly central in any research effort, are not necessarily the only important considerations in group research. Many of these requirements can be assumed in the studies we have included in this review. But more to the point, other considerations are of equal importance in the group research. The most basic is the degree to which the design characteristics of group projects recognize and clarify the interrelationships among the numerous sources of influence in the small-group setting. One way of judging design adequacy is by the degree to which studies include intervening and mediating variables.

For our purposes, we will identify three levels of design complexity. They are (1) simply establishing the statistical relationship between an independent variable (group-treatment variable) and a dependent variable (client improvement); (2) establishing the relationship between the independent treatment variable, one mediating variable, and a dependent variable; and (3) establishing the relationship between an independent treatment variable, several mediating and intervening variables, and the effects of each of these mediating variables on different types and levels of client outcome. Each of these three designs differs in its ability to accommodate and clarify the multiple sources of influence in small groups as well as the interrelationships between these important treatment dimensions.

We hope we have persuaded the reader that the conceptual and methodological considerations we have discussed, though relatively few in number, represent some of the more basic concerns in planning for and evaluating significant research in the group disciplines. We recognize that carefully groomed researchers must inevitably despair over the prospects of accepting or tolerating unwelcomed sources of error in their research products. We must also recognize that ignoring some of our more fundamental conceptual, theoretical, and research limitations can lead to unfortunate consequences in our research literature. As we review the existing group literature in this chapter, we invite the reader to judge the relative improvements that could be obtained in both theory development and clinical practice by systematically accommodating some of the principles we have discussed. These relative improvements could pay immediate and handsome dividends in our research products. We are in a position to be much more deliberate in selecting the types of error variance our developing discipline can most comfortably tolerate and, at the very same time, be more prudent when dealing with research questions that reflect crucial issues in our developing science.

OUTCOME RESEARCH

The outcome literature in this section was located by (1) a computer-assisted search using the "psychinfo Database," (2) searching for journal articles published between 1977 and May of 1983 in over 900 periodicals and 1500 books and monographs, and (3) personal correspondence with colleagues, friends, and major research contributors regarding promising, but as yet unpublished research findings. The search resulted in the identification of 477 articles. After eliminating most reports that (1) failed to use appropriate control groups, (2) consisted of case studies, (3) failed to randomly assign subjects to experimental conditions or used inappropriate statistical methods, or (4) did not represent treatment processes closely related to group psychotherapy, we were left with 17 outcome studies. The results of these studies are summarized in Table 15.1. These studies are grouped in the following categories: (1) general outcome studies, (2) outcome studies with specific treatment variables, (3) comparative outcome studies, (4) treatment × personality interaction outcome studies, and (5) premature termination and casualty studies.

We will comment on the research summarized in Table 15.1 briefly. Collectively, this body of literature differs from that which we reviewed in our previous chapter in at least two important ways.

First the good news. More researchers are using multivariate statistical procedures, more studies used experienced therapists and/or real clinical populations, and the use of multiple outcome measures seems far more common. There also is a conspicuous increase in the number of comparative studies reported. All of these observations reflect desirable changes in group research.

Now the bad news. There has been a dramatic decrease in the number of outcome studies reported in all categories other than comparative studies. This decline in published reports is most obvious in the areas of premature terminations, casualties, and person × treatment interaction studies. There continues to be an abundance of general outcome studies; we continue to ask, "Does psychotherapy work?" 20-odd years after Kiesler (1966) suggested more informative questions. It appears that the more vital research issues are suffering the greatest declines as research funds diminish and tenure requirements become more stringent. This is a paradoxical and unwelcome effect the group disciplines cannot accept.

Perusal of the studies contained in Table 15.1 reveals a number of studies that suggest that group treatments have been associated with client improvement in a variety of settings and situations. Additionally, a number of studies include client evaluations several months after treatment was concluded. The eight studies that included posttreatment follow-up are summarized in Table 15.2. Inspection of these findings reveals that (1) four studies reported that client improvement was maintained on all follow-up measures, (2) two studies showed discrepant findings in which client outcome varied with treatment groups or outcome measures, (3) one study reported that the differences between experimental and treatment groups evaporated four weeks after treatment was completed, and (4) one reported increased improvement at the follow-up.

Unfortunately, favorable outcome results are not uniform across investigations; some studies fail to corroborate favorable outcome findings. In some comparisons we find group treatments to be more effective than individual psychotherapy or drug treatments. In other studies these results disappear. These differences are not unexpected, given the history and complexity of psychotherapy research, and the current state of our epistemology. What is peculiar and distressing about group research is the absence of investigations that could help increase our knowledge as to why and how these differences occur. We know virtually nothing about the causal factors associated with the discrepant findings in our literature. We have little evidence by which to suggest, even tentatively, the nature of group clients, leadership practices, communication patterns, stages of group development, and so forth, that are assumed to be causal links in differential client outcome.

Earlier we discussed some of the conceptual limitations of the group disciplines. We indicated that these conceptual problems impose most limiting conditions on the quality of the group research. Evidence to support this assertion is contained in the research published during the last six years. We still can conclude only that group treatments can be associated with client improvement, at least some of the time. We still have virtually no idea why this may, or may not, be the case in a particular situation or setting. Our research procedures, from a technical point of view, are far more impressive than our research products. In spite of our increasing methodological sophistication, our research efforts are not teaching us anything about group psychotherapy that has not been known for at least a decade. In none of the studies we have summarized do we find a *specific* treatment variable isolated for study that is a logical extension of a major conceptual model of group treatment. Even those variables that are indirectly relevant to group treatments tend to be inadequately defined, measured, and operationalized if measured at all. Neither is there a coherent theme that tends to identify and bind these research efforts together. What we have is a collection of highly individualized studies that are not bound together by guiding conceptual principles regarding the fundamental problems that plague the group disciplines. The quality of the conceptual input in our research efforts simply must be improved and better coordinated if we hope to increase our understanding of group dynamics beyond that which we already know. Some promising beginnings may be noted in the Process Studies section to follow, but they have not yet had effect in the outcome research. Before we attend to process, however, there are additional comments to be made about the outcome literature.

Additional Evaluative Criteria

If the problems of the group disciplines persist in the face of research that is methodologically sound when evaluated against traditional criteria, then what is needed is an additional set of criteria for evaluating and developing group research. We will attempt to make a contribution to the solution of this problem by reviewing the existing group literature in the framework we suggested earlier in the chapter.

Our hope is that our analysis not only will clarify the origins of the problem we have identified, but suggest solutions as well. Table 15.3 summarizes the results of rating each outcome study with regard to (1) design complexity, (2) theoretical variables, and (3) experimental variables and their units of analysis.

Inspection of Table 15.3 portrays our arbitrary ratings of the independent and dependent variables from each outcome study listed in Table 15.2. This approach allows us to clarify the theoretical origins of most of the research, the units and levels of analysis represented in the experiments, and design complexity, or the degree to which the experiment attempted to capture rather than minimize the complexity of the group situation. The results of this analysis seem revealing. We find that most of the theoretical variables discussed have little to do with group treatments. Rather, the ideas seem to be drawn from theories of psychopathology, individual psychotherapy, and personality development. Virtually none of the concepts are from group theory per se. The same is true with regard to units and levels of analysis in the experiments. The focus is primarily on the individual. Interpersonal behaviors are the next most common, but quite infrequent, and group phenomena are not represented at all. Most alarming is the absence of specific treatment variables, that is, the absence of clearly defined and measured specific components of the experimental treatments. Group treatment seems implicitly defined as whatever happens in the group, a hardly enlightening definition of the independent variable. Finally, almost all of the research studied only the relationship between an independent and dependent variable. Other research designs that could capture more of the complex interrelationships between independent, intervening, and dependent variables are rarely used. We submit that the deficiencies in the group research as reflected by our ratings are a primary cause for our inability to generate research in the last decade that would allow us to advance our knowledge base, theory development, and clinical practice.

Alternatives Do Exist

Our thesis throughout this section has been that the group psychotherapy research has been perpetuating several peculiar and fatal flaws, perhaps unwittingly. The result has been an absence of funda-

Table 15.1   Outcome Studies

Author	Purpose	Experimental Comparisons
GENERAL STUDIES		
Piper et al. (1977)	Evaluation of ongoing group therapy, implementing a number of group research recommendations.	Dynamic, interactional group therapy. Delayed treatment control.
Elder-Jucker (1979)	Determine whether structured or focused group therapy experience is an important determinant in changes in behavior and attitudes of the aged.	Focused discussion group. Nonfocused (placebo) group. No-treatment control.
SPECIFIC TREATMENTS		
Antonuccio et al. (1982)	Examine leader characteristics related to treatment outcome.	Differential leader characteristics (e.g., locus of control, neuroticism), differential process (e.g., cohesiveness), and client outcome (depression, diagnosis, and social adjustment).
Scott (1976)	Evaluate the effects of leadership training on individuals involved in group exercises.	Professionally led group. Paraprofessionally led group. Control group.
Lundgren & Knight (1977)	Examine relationship between interpersonal needs for control and affection of members and leaders, and member attitudes toward leader and group.	Leaders and trainers in each of the following classifications: low-control, low-affection; low-control, high-affection; high-control, low-affection; high-control, high-affection.
Comparative Studies		
Rush & Watkins (1981)	Assess outcome in group versus individual cognitive therapy.	Group cognitive therapy. Individual cognitive therapy w/ antidepressant medication. Individual cognitive therapy wo/ antidepressant medication.
Fuchs & Rehm (1977)	Compare a behavior therapy program based on a self-control model of depression with a nonspecific group therapy condition.	Self-control group therapy. Nonspecific group therapy. Waiting-list control.

Dependent Variable	Participants/ Leaders	Results
General psychiatric symptomatology (self and observer ratings), interpersonal functioning, patient-rating of improvement.	P: Psychiatric outpatients. L: Psychiatric residents received training in group methods prior to the experiment.	Therapy group improved significantly more than control on all outcome criteria except patient rating of improvement.
Self-esteem, social interaction, depression.	P: Female residents in a home for the aged. L: Graduate students in health education/counseling.	No significant results.
Patient depression, diagnosis, and social adjustment.	P: College students L: Experienced graduate students.	Leaders differed significantly on behavioral and group process measures, but no significant differences in outcome between leaders.
Self-concept, deviant signs.	P: University students and counseling center patients.	No significant change in deviant signs for experimental groups. Professional leaders who were assuring, as opposed to reassuring, had group members who showed a reduction in deviant signs.
Members' attitudes toward group and group leaders.	P: T-group participants. L: T-group leaders.	Low-control, low-affection leaders elicited favorable reactions early in group, but negative reactions later.
Participant and observer ratings of depression.	P: Moderate to severely depressed. L: Experienced therapists—psychiatrists, psychologists, social workers.	Group therapy resulted in significantly poorer results compared to both individual treatments.
Participant and observer ratings of depression, self-control behavior, and attitudes.	P: Depressed women. L: Female master's level psychologists.	Self-control therapy showed significant reduction in depression compared to the other two groups. Also some improvement in self-control for self-control therapy.

(continued)

Table 15.1 *(Continued)*

Author	Purpose	Experimental Comparisons
Anderson (1978)	Compare Rogerian, Gestalt, and self-directed encounter approaches.	Rogerian encounter group. Gestalt sensory-awareness group. Leaderless group. No-treatment control.
Shaffer et al. (1981)	Compare group and individual cognitive behavior therapy for treating anxiety and depression; compare these with an interpersonal group approach.	Cognitive-behavior group therapy. Cognitive-behavior individual therapy. Interpersonal group therapy.
LaPointe & Rimm (1980)	Compare the efficacy of insight, cognitive, and assertiveness group therapies in treating depressed women.	Insight-oriented group. Cognitive group. Assertiveness training program.
Hodgson (1981)	Compare cognitive and behavioral-interpersonal group approaches in treating depression.	Interpersonal skills training program—massed and distributed. Cognitive treatment program—massed and distributed. Hold group.
Comas-Diaz (1981)	Compare cognitive and behavioral group treatment for depression.	Cognitive therapy group. Behavioral treatment group. Waiting-list control.

Person × Treatment Interaction Studies

Steinmetz et al. (1983)	Identify client characteristics associated with outcome in a psychoeducational treatment for depression.	Client characteristics (e.g., adjustment, locus of control, life-stress events) compared with client outcome.

PREMATURE TERMINATION AND CASUALTY STUDIES

Premature Terminations

Lothstein (1978)	To study the effects of careful screening and preparation of clients on group therapy dropout rate.	Group dropouts' versus remainers' questionnaire responses.

Dependent Variable	Participants/ Leaders	Results
Subject alienation, sense of autonomy, empathy within group, attraction toward group.	P: College student volunteers. L: One leader trained in Rogerian and Gestalt approaches.	All groups decreased depression and anxiety over controls. No significant differences between the three treatment conditions.
Depression, anxiety, assertiveness.	P: Referred medical patients. L: Experienced psychologists.	All groups decreased depression and anxiety. No significant differences between groups.
Depression, irrational thinking, and assertiveness.	P: Depressed women volunteers. L: Information not provided.	All three groups made significant improvement in the three measured areas. Assertiveness and insight groups improved more in rationality regarding acceptance, made more gains, and were more assertive than cognitive groups.
Self-ratings of depression, group interpersonal behaviors.	P: Depressed college student volunteers. L: One male/female co-therapy team—predoctoral, experienced.	Both groups more effective than no treatment. Some evidence of superiority of behavioral-interpersonal approach.
Participant, observer, and significant other ratings of depression.	P: Depressed, low SES, unemployed Puerto Rican women. L: One Puerto Rican female therapist.	Significant reduction in depression for both groups. No significant differences between treatments.
Participant rating of depression.	P: Depressed volunteers. L: Graduate students received training prior to experiment.	Participants at all depression levels improved. Those improving most expected change, had perceptions of mastery, were better readers, were younger, and perceived their families as more supportive.
Leaving the group after treatment started, but before it ended.	P: Individuals from urban Cleveland. L: Psychiatric residents, psychology interns, social workers, staff psychologists.	In spite of careful screening and preparation, a dropout rate of 29% occurred. Based on patient report, no significant differences between dropouts and remainers. However, therapists

(continued)

Table 15.1   *(Continued)*

Author	Purpose	Experimental Comparisons
Lothstein (1978) *(continued)*		
Casualties		
Bramlette & Tucker (1981)	Identify positive and negative client change while holding constructed the stated purpose, leadership, and process variables in an encounter group.	Survey of an encounter group experience to identify those who were hurt (made worse) and who had gained (became better) in the group.
Kaplan (1982)	Replicates the Lieberman et al. (1973) study to further test the hazardousness of encounter groups.	Survey of individuals who dropped out; were nominated by group members as casualties; had low questionnaire scores or low leader ratings; entered into psychotherapy or used emergency psychiatric aid.

mentally new research findings to enhance theory development and clinical practice during the last decade. This unhappy state of affairs has persisted, even in the face of heroic efforts on the part of some researchers to improve the design qualities of their research.

Several recent studies meet the traditional design requirements for outstanding research in the behavioral sciences; yet these projects have also failed to contribute fundamentally new findings to our research literature. One way of clarifying why this problem persists would be to take one of the better pieces of contemporary group research, critique it from the methodological and conceptual perspectives we have stressed, and then redesign the project with the changes that would accompany our critique. We then could see whether this would start to improve the data base for future theory development and clinical practice. One caution should be expressed regarding this approach, however. It is important to recognize that our purpose is to help extend our research capabilities by building on those achievements of others. The quality of these

prior contributions clearly needs to be acknowledged and recognized, even as we say it is time to move on to new and more fertile research practices.

One of the better outcome studies in the current literature was completed by Piper, Debbane, and Garant (1977). The purpose of their study was to evaluate an ongoing group treatment program with a wide range of outpatients. These researchers carefully noted virtually all of the group design recommendations provided by past reviewers and incorporated as many of these features into their project as was feasible. The design recommendations included (1) using real clinical populations as experimental subjects, (2) not relying too heavily on inpatients when sampling clinical populations, (3) describing and measuring more carefully the specific group treatment procedures employed in the experimental conditions, (4) specifying more carefully the patient, therapist, and setting variables, (5) integrating process and outcome variables into the research designs, (6) giving more conceptual attention to the primary and unique elements of group treatments, and (7) using multiple outcome measures to

Table 15.1   *(Continued)*

Dependent Variable	Participants/ Leaders	Results
		reported disliking dropouts, and they were perceived as hostile toward therapists.
Questionnaire completed by participants to identify positive and negative change.	P: College students. L: None.	10% were classified as having a negative experience. Yet, of these, 70% were also classified as having had a positive experience, so only 3% had solely negative experience.
Telephone and personal interviews with subjects identified as possible casualities.	P: Undergraduate students. L: One faculty member, six advanced graduate students.	2.3% casualty rate.

assess both individual behavior changes and average change within the group. Piper et al. also suggested that implementing all of these recommendations into a single project represented a herculean task, but that project quality still could be substantially improved by selectively adopting some of these recommendations.

The subjects for their experiment were 48 psychiatric outpatients, referred from neighboring outpatient agencies. These subjects were matched on the basis of sex and selection criteria scores, and then randomly assigned to one of eight groups in a pretest-posttest, control group design (Cook & Campbell, 1979). There were four treatment groups and four control groups. The therapy sessions took place weekly for three months. Multiple outcome measures that included client self-reports, therapist evaluations, and independent ratings and psychometric tests were used to assess the effects of group treatment. Each therapy group was led by a cotherapy team that received specific training for participation in this study. Sophisticated multivariate data analyses were used to test the effects of the

group treatments. The total data-collection period involved several years and included a posttreatment follow-up.

The analysis of the five pooled outcome criteria indicated significantly greater client improvement over a three-month period for the 24 treated patients. This finding was consistent with the general conclusion that group treatments have been associated with client improvement.

Any thoughtful critique of the Piper et al. (1977) study must recognize its many fine assets. These include specific training for the group leaders prior to the experiment, sampling from a clinical population, random assignment of patients to treatments, reasonable control conditions, multiple outcome measures, posttreatment follow-up, and rigorous statistical analyses. Evaluated from the traditional methodological criteria of internal and external validity, the investigation is remarkable in the group literature. This single study may offer more corroboration to the assertion that group treatments may be effective than a hundred poorly designed inquiries.

Even so, another hundred similar studies, as well

TABLE 15.2 Summary of Outcome Studies with Posttreatment Follow-up

Study	Follow-up Measure?	How Long Following Treatment End?	Outcome
Antonuccio et al. (1982)	Yes	4 weeks	Changes on BDI maintained.
Scott (1976)	Yes	6 weeks	Differences between treatments maintained.
Rush & Watkins (1981)	Yes	8 weeks	Differences between treatments maintained.
Fuchs & Rehm (1977)	Yes	6 weeks	Changes maintained on MMPI, but not on self-evaluation questionnaire.
LaPointe & Rimm (1980)	Yes	8 weeks	Changes continued even more.
Hodgson (1981)	Yes	4 weeks	Differences between groups disappeared.
Comas-Diaz (1981)	Yes	5 weeks	Changes maintained for the behavioral group, but not for the cognitive group.
Steinmetz et al. (1983)	Yes	1, 6 months	Improvement maintained.

designed as that of Piper et al., would hold little promise for advancing the group disciplines. If we apply the criteria that we have stressed in this section, the study does not compare favorably on any dimensions. Their data have implications for the question, "Does group psychotherapy work?" but conceptual substance is lacking. The data may have utility in program evaluation, but the positive results could be a function of innumerable factors tangentially related, or unrelated, to group psychotherapy. And the results could represent an accurate estimate of group-therapy effects for this specific situation, but there was no attempt to isolate and clarify the mediating group processes that may help account for client improvement. In sum, the data offer little to advance conceptual or theory development, or clinical practice. In spite of the technical rigor of the investigation, it clearly illustrates the need for group

researchers to consider carefully the implications of their work for conceptual and theoretical development.

Two considerations must guide the redevelopment of the Piper et al. (1977) outcome study. The first is to be clear about the central questions under investigation, a decision that will determine much of the research design. While this must always be decided by the individual investigators, we will modify the Piper et al. question and proceed with the assumption that the two most important questions in group research are *why* and *how*. Why are group treatments effective some of the time, but not all of the time? How do the effects of group treatments come to be? Clearly, these questions are as fundamental as they are broad. They encompass the entire spectrum of activities involved in group treatments such as group composition, leadership char-

TABLE 15.3   Classification of Outcome Studies on Treatment and Outcome Variable Dimensions

Study	Design Complexity	Treatment Variable		Outcome Variable	
		Variable	Experimental Variables	Theoretical Variable	Units of Analysis
Piper et al. (1977)	IV-DV	Individual psychotherapy	Not specified	Psychopathology	Individual
		Group theory	Not specified	Personality	Individual
Elder-Jucker (1979)	IV-DV	Individual psychotherapy	Group	Psychopathology	Individual
Scott (1976)	IV-DV	Individual psychotherapy	Individual	Psychopathology	Individual
Autonuccio et al. (1982)	MV IV-MV-DV MV	Personality Psychopathology	Individual Individual	Psychopathology Group theory	Individual Group
Lundgren & Knight (1977)	IV-DV	Personality	Individual	Personality	Individual
Rush & Watkins (1981)	IV-DV	Individual psychotherapy	Not specified	Psychopathology	Individual
Fuchs & Rehm (1977)	IV-DV	Individual psychotherapy	Not specified	Psychopathology	Individual
		Group theory	Not specified	Personality	Individual
Anderson (1978)	IV-DV	Individual psychotherapy	Not specified	Personality	Individual
		Group theory	Not specified	Group theory	Group
Shaffer et al. (1981)	IV-DV	Individual psychotherapy	Not specified	Psychopathology	Individual
		Group theory	Not specified		
LaPointe & Rimm (1980)	IV-DV	Individual psychotherapy	Not specified	Psychopathology	Individual
Hodgson (1981)	IV-DV	Individual psychotherapy	Not specified	Psychopathology	Individual
Comas-Diaz (1981)	IV-DV	Individual psychotherapy	Not specified	Psychopathology	Individual
Steinmetz et al. (1983)	IV-DV	Personality	Individual	Psychopathology	Individual
Lothstein (1978)	IV-DV	NA	Not specified	NA	Individual
Bramlette & Tucker (1981)	IV-DV	NA	NA	Psychopathology Personality	Individual Individual
Kaplan (1982)		NA	NA	Psychopathology Personality	Individual Individual

acteristics, theoretical orientation, role expectations, communication skills, methods of conflict resolution, communication patterns, group interaction patterns, length of treatment, appropriate matching of clients and treatment modalities, and types of client pathology, to name but a few of the more important considerations. But the breadth of these considerations need not deter us from starting to investigate selected elements of this complex array of variables.

Being clear about the questions we wish to approach is only the first step. The more important and difficult task is to allocate our research resources so as to (1) be sure we are addressing the questions we consider most important and (2) maximize the productivity of our research effort by carefully orchestrating the balance between conceptual relevance and methodological rigor.

With our primary research questions clearly in mind, it is time to reconsider some elements of the Piper et al. study. The most time-consuming part of group research is identifying a client pool, randomly assigning subjects to group treatments, and then running the actual group psychotherapy sessions. There is little room for improvement in the way this task was accomplished by the original researchers. They used a broad spectrum of outpatient clientele, who were randomly assigned to the various experimental and control conditions. This core data organization and collection period was outstanding.

When asking our research questions, however, the shortcomings of this study are most obvious in the following three areas: (1) There were no specific treatment elements isolated and varied, nor was there any discussion of the conceptual antecedents of their study; (2) there were no process measures employed to describe the psychological attributes of the experimental groups, nor was there any attempt to relate group process measures to outcome; and (3) there was no attempt to relate different types of client improvement (or lack of it) to either group process or treatment variables. Each of these considerations represents some important issues involved in group research and could be incorporated into most studies. With the current study almost all of these questions could be addressed by (1) increasing the number of variables measured and (2) altering the data analysis. These are relatively minor changes, particularly in view of the additional information this study could have yielded. Let us illus-

trate these considerations below:

1. The use of multiple outcome measures is becoming more accepted as standard research practice. The specific measures used must be a considered judgment by each investigator. We will only suggest that multiple outcome measures need to be used and ideally would reflect different assessment perspectives (e.g., self-report, psychometric, independent raters, unobtrusive observation). Once the data have been collected, statistical analyses could suggest the different dimensions of change in the sample. If one does not assume that all group treatments affect all clients in the same way, it is important for the outcome measures to reflect the different types, levels, and dimensions of client change. Client change almost certainly is a multidimensional phenomenon, and it is essential that we begin constructing our outcome measures to fit a multidimensional perspective.

2. Increasingly precise description and classification is a characteristic of the more developed sciences and a goal for the developing ones. Because of that, it is imperative that we carefully describe and classify group processes. The most reliable form of description available to us is quantitative measurement, and perhaps the most penetrating is the careful observation of experienced, trained judges. With group treatments, there are more process variables potentially operative than we could expect to describe in any single experiment. Therefore, we must carefully select those dimensions of group treatment for description that most closely fit our theoretical models—theoretical models, we suggest, that have their genesis in group work. Only for purposes of discussion, we suggest the following variables for measurement in the reconsiderations of Piper et al: (1) leader personality characteristics, using the Sixteen Personality Factor Questionnaire (Cattell & Eber, 1956), apparently available to Piper et al.; (2) leader verbal behavior in group sessions, using the Hill Interaction Matrix (HIM; Hill, 1965); (3) both individual and group-level verbal interaction, using the HIM; (4) a measure of group cohesion, such as the Group Atmosphere Scale (Silbergeld, Koenig, Manderscheid, Meeker, & Hornung, 1975); and (5) a measure of the immediacy and intensity of affect expressed in group discussions, using trained raters blind to the hypotheses under consideration. Many other group process measures could be used, of course, but these have been chosen for mention

because they do not appear inconsistent with the treatments employed by Piper et al., and the measures should be relevant to the issues involved in the study.

3.   Thus far, we have discussed measurement as it pertains to the leader, client outcome, and group process. Another important dimension of our modified experiment is the selection of a theoretically important treatment consideration and experimentally varying this across treatment conditions. Since Piper et al. were concerned with client readiness for group treatment, we will suggest the addition of pregroup induction experiences in which some participants receive practice in giving and receiving interpersonal feedback. Other participants will observe videotaped models demonstrating feedback in actual group sessions. This would allow us to compare the effects of two methods of preparing clients for participation in group therapy.

4.   A major shortcoming in the Piper et al. report is that the nature of the treatment itself was not specified. The several therapists were given training, but we are given no indication of its composition or criteria. In addition, it is impossible to determine anything specific about what transpired in the groups. What all of this means is that the group therapy is undefined. We choose to apply the HIM data mentioned before to this question since that appears to fit Piper et al.'s implicit theory. The leaders could be trained to a criterion on the HIM and then their in-group performance on that measure could be related to client-outcome indices.

5.   We now have an experiment that can measure client outcome and group processes in a multidimensional perspective and compare two different methods of preparing clients for group participation.

The next problem is developing a method for data analysis that allows us to maximize the use of these data to determine what variables are associated with more effective and ineffective group treatments. A number of approaches could be used. We will describe only one, not to suggest that this is the preferred method of data analysis, but to illustrate that the problems of the group disciplines can be approached empirically on a step-by-step basis.

A first step could be to rank-order the treatment groups on each of the outcome dimensions revealed by the earlier analysis. This would provide us with descriptive information about the uniformity of change across groups and across dimensions of

client change. Because the research is basically exploratory in nature, we could then use a discriminant function analysis to identify all of the process variables that can significantly discriminate between the most successful and least successful groups on each dimension of client improvement. This would reduce the rather massive amounts of process data to those variables that describe the essential differences between the most successful and least successful treatment groups. We could then take those statistically selected process variables and see whether they are significantly related to the pretreatment induction interviews using analysis of variance procedures.

If all of the suggested changes in the Piper et al. study were made, it could add substantially to the experiment's cost, but there is warrant to believe that the *proportional* increase would be small. No noticeable increase in time would be required from the clients, and any new demands on the therapists seem modest. The great increases would accrue to the experimenters in terms of their time, equipment, and perhaps money. In most cases, less expensive alternatives (than, e.g., the HIM) could be located. If that were possible, we could choose to drop some of the more costly or intrusive dimensions from the investigation. The point is not that any single study should include *every* possible consideration; it is that modest additions might lead to geometrically greater returns from the experimental investment.

The changes in the data collection and data analysis we have suggested would dramatically alter the empirical output of this experiment. Some of the more obvious benefits would be (1) tentative information on how induction methods of preparing clients for group participation are related to group process and outcome measures, (2) tentative information on what processes measured (e.g., leadership characteristics, group and individual verbal behavior patterns, intensity of affect) differentiate the most successful treatment groups from the least successful treatment groups, and (3) tentative suggestions as to how the pretreatment induction interviews and the process measures might be related to different types and levels of client change. All of these findings might make useful contributions that have yet to be made and that provide basic information upon which alterations in theory development and clinical practice could be considered.

Certainly, there are limitations with these procedures. No causal statements are warranted; there is a lack of independence between some of the events that are statistically related, and all of these results would have to be replicated. But there is one important advantage. We can start guessing about the conceptual relationships between the events that have been statisticallly related. More important, we have started to set the stage for a much more sophisticated study next time. If our results were sufficiently important, they would provide the empirical foundations for theoretical speculations, and these theoretical explanations could be tested empirically, using path analysis or structural equations, for example, further improving our knowledge of the causal links between group variables, group process variables, and different types and levels of client improvement.

PROCESS RESEARCH

Because process and outcome research are so intimately related, it should come as no surprise that the problems affecting one also affect the other. Many of those that we have mentioned in the previous sections apply here as well. We will not repeat them except where their reiteration seems necessary. There are, however, two preliminary points that require attention in introducing this review of the process research.

The first point has to do with the relationship of process and outcome, expecially in group research. At the most general level, outcome research is concerned with the effects of group treatment. Much of that work has been of the "Does group therapy work?" kind, and the results, in the main, have suggested that it can. Without the contribution of well-conceptualized and -designed process research, that is about all that can be said about group treatment. It is a scientifically awkward position for the discipline to maintain that there are regularities in effects without being able to specify the causes (or correlates and relationships) of those effects. It is awkward because it is so similar to the circumstances in which superstition may arise. If we define superstition as the misattribution of cause-and-effect relationships, the current state of group research differs only in that we cannot be certain that we have not made the fatal misattribution. We have no way

of telling whether we are prescribing bear fat for baldness or hawk blood for myopia because they have worked sometimes in the past. We have claimed an effect, but in any sense of intellectual honesty cannot claim to know the causal relationships leading to it without solid process research. Scientific and professional ethics make such a position untenable. The necessity of seeking better answers to better questions suggests the importance of process research in group treatment.

The second introductory point has to do with the conceptualization of causal (used in the broad sense) variables. Hempel (1966) suggested that scientific concepts go through several stages of development. They begin as implicit ideas and become more explicit as the terms used to label them gain wider use. This seems to describe the present status of many of the concepts employed in group process research; they have become explicit in the sense that they have gained wide use among investigators. Concepts gain their greatest scientific utility, however, when they are given precise definition verbally, heuristically, and operationally. With regard to the last characteristic of conceptual precision, operational definition, Hempel (and most contemporary philosophers of science) rejected strict reductionism. Instead, Hempel (1966) argued for ". . . a set of bridge principles that do not interpret the theoretical terms individually, but provide an indefinite variety of criteria of application by determining an equally indefinite variety of test implications . . ." (p. 100) for the concepts.

This notion has importance in evaluating group process research. A strictly reductionistic view of group cohesion, for example, would define it by the experimental operations employed in an investigation. That is, group cohesion could be defined as a concept as the regularity of attendance by group members. There is nothing inherently wrong with such a method of operationalizing group cohesion, but it is definitely a limited definition of the concept implied by the wider usage of the term *cohesion*. The normal use of the term implies much more than regularity of attendance, such as attitudes and cognitions of group members toward one another and the group as a whole, verbal and nonverbal behavior of group members, and the affective regard in which the group is held. Each of these others can be more clearly specified than they have been, and each has somewhat different test implications than does attendance. Attendance is one way of assessing cohesion, then, but clearly is not the only legitimate definition of it.

The substitution of bridge principles for strict operationalism is not an invitation to conceptual anarchy, nor is it license for slipshod research. Granted, the concept of group cohesion is poorly defined, implicit, and ambiguous in the therapy literature. That does not mean that the researcher can define it capriciously or haphazardly—there are some criteria of application and some test implications that demand less cognitive gymnastics than others. It may mean just the reverse. The onus is on the investigator to show how the experimental operations are related to the concept, and to show it in a public, intersubjectively testable fashion.

In terms of the group process research, these two preliminary points suggest some evaluation criteria in addition to experimental internal and external validity. Again, this is not to derogate the traditional experimental criteria. They seem necessary for scientific progress. But contrary to what appears to be a common misconception, they are not sufficient to it. Rigorously designed research in the absence of equally rigorous thought about its meanings can lead us to precise estimates of something that has no meaning beyond the immediate experiment. And it can lead us to believe that we know more about the phenomena under investigation than we do. Consequently, we will consider the group process research in terms of several questions in addition to its methodological cleanliness. We will ask whether the research results help to define important group concepts. Furthermore, we will consider whether the results have structural importance or theoretical relevance, and whether that relevance is to theories of the individual or of the group. Finally, and relatedly, we will consider whether the research relates process to outcome, process to process, or process to individual status variables. Each of these, it seems, is an important consideration in determining the present status and future directions of group therapy research.

We considered several different methods of organizing the literature to be summarized below. The first choice was to organize the studies around central issues of concern in the field, but the number of investigations available that would fit this format was too limited. The second was to group them according to design similarity and methodological rigor so that we could consider the results in terms of their experimental validity, but that failed for the same reason. Finally, we hoped to organize the review around variables that represent the presumed curative factors in group therapy, but settled for an approximation of that dictated by the availability of published literature. The topics include: (1) pretherapy training, role induction, and group structure, (2) self-disclosure and feedback, and (3) cohesion. The presentation of these topics will be followed with some evaluative comments and suggestions.

Pregroup Training and Structure

Despite the popularity of self-help books and the media attention given to the different forms of psychological treatment, or perhaps because of them, few clients come to treatment knowing what to expect. Few know how they are expected to behave, and few know what to expect from their therapist. Given the almost limitless variety among therapists, theories and models of psychotherapy, and techniques for approaching the helping process, clients cannot be blamed for their doubt and confusion. Consequently, it is common for therapists to invest differing amounts of time and effort indoctrinating their clients in the demands of the particular treatment approach. Though not without potential benefit to both therapist and client, it can be a time-consuming, expensive, and often tedious task.

The need for client indoctrination apparently is increased as the treatment options are decreased. That is, therapists who for reasons of training, belief, or pragmatic constraints, for example, have one treatment approach available probably have a greater need to socialize their clients to that approach. There may be less urgency as the opportunity increases to match different strategies with different client characteristics or problems. But even the most technically eclectic therapist often is called upon to teach the client how to be a client.

In group treatments, there have been two general approaches to the problem of client indoctrination into the client role: pregroup training and the incorporation of varying amounts of structure into, especially, the earlier sessions. They differ in several ways. Pregroup training has been given orally, through written information, and by videotaped instructions or modeling, while structuring activities almost always involve direct client participation in specific activities appropriate to the group treatment. In addition, pregroup training has been offered by assistants, secretarial staff, and machines, while group structure considerations have been the province of the group therapist. It has been argued that the strategies differ in that one is the preparation for treatment while the other is an integral part of the treatment itself. Such a distinction may have utility for therapists and researchers, but it is an empirical question as to whether it has meaning to clients.

The two approaches to client education are similar in that each has the purpose of inducing treatment-appropriate expectations, attitudes, and behavior in the client. They are similar in that each typically is based upon evidence or beliefs about clients in general; rarely are they specifically tailored to the individual. Each has been studied and can point to research results corroborating its beneficial effects. They are similar, as well, in some of the problems involved in their study.

Some of the methodological issues involved in pretraining role induction and structuring have been discussed by LaTorre (1977) and Friedlander and Kaul (1983). The latter mentioned three considerations that could lead to more accurate understanding of client socialization procedures. First, prognostic and role expectations need to be viewed separately. There is a rather substantial body of research corroborating the effectiveness of introducing prognostic, or outcome, expectations prior to treatment or early in the process (Shapiro & Morris, 1978). The same cannot be said for role expectations, that is, for introducing expectations about how one should behave as a client. Consequently, the two should be studied separately through the use of appropriate control groups. Second, it needs to be shown how the type of client indoctrination (pretraining or structure, role or prognostic) affects important process and outcome dimensions of the group treatments. This would call for multiple, theoretically important but unbiased, indicators of both process and outcome. And, third, investigators need to demonstrate the unique effects of their client socialization procedures beyond what naturally occurs in the group. This would demand an appropriate control group, and pertinent process and outcome indicators, and

perhaps some variant of a time-series design.

The recent investigations selected for this review are summarized in Table 15.4. Three general observations about the summarized research seem warranted. In the first place, there has been a noticeable shift in emphasis since our previous review (Bednar & Kaul, 1978). In that review, there was a preponderance of structure studies, with little attention given to pretraining. That is not the case now, with a 7:3 ratio favoring pretraining. We cannot say why this shift has occurred. There may have been some selection bias in one or the other, but that does not seem tenable. The two approaches to client socialization may be conceptually inseparable, but again that does not seem to be the case in light of the previous discussion. Or it may be that researchers have determined that pretraining is a more promising "fruit fly" by which to approach the salient issues, given the available role-induction literature.

If this last is the case, then our second general observation suggests that researchers may have put their money on a relatively untested horse. We mentioned earlier that prognostic expectations repeatedly have been found to have effects in therapy studies (Shapiro & Morris, 1978), but that role expectations have not. From the information given in Table 15.4, and from a careful reading of the manuscripts from which it was taken, there is not a single study for which we can say with confidence that the two were not confounded. Disregarding Lundgren's (1977) study, for which the distinction may not be appropriate, there is not sufficient information upon which to determine whether role or prognostic expectations, or both, were influenced by the experimental treatments. Most *appear* to have been emphasizing role concerns, and two (Piper, Debbane, Garant, & Bienvenu, 1979; Wogan, Getter, Admur, Nichols, & Okman, 1977) appear to have confounded the two. There is no way of knowing whether the rather mixed results summarized in Table 15.4 are due to this particular ambiguity, other experimental problems, or the nature of the phenomena.

All of this leads to the third general observation. None of the studies summarized, and none that were reviewed, met the three conditions mentioned before. Separation of role and prognostic expectations already has been mentioned. Some employed multiple process indicators, some multiple outcome indicators, and a few had both. Considering all of the research, where there are multiple process measures there seems to be a tendency for the investigators to find process effects, but that tendency does not appear to hold with regard to multiple outcome assessments. Why this might be the case, if indeed it is, is open to question, but it might be that the experimental treatments actually have stressed role induction. Finally, the design of the research makes it impossible to identify any of the effects unique to pretraining and beyond comparable contact with the therapist.

Self-disclosure and Feedback

Self-disclosure is an inherent component of just about all forms of psychological treatment. It is attributed more potency in some approaches and less in others. The causes, correlates, and consequences of self-disclosure are ascribed differently by various writers and practitioners, and there is the predictable variability in how the process is named. But even though it may be labeled differently, and sometimes left implicit, there seems to be a universal notion that clients can profit from disclosing information about themselves, at least under the proper circumstances.

The same is true of feedback. Its centrality to various approaches and the attributions made about the processes involved may differ in degree, but the notion of feedback is not hard to uncover. And, of course, there is considerable variation in the terms employed to denote or connote the concept. Here again, however, there appears to be unanimity of opinion that clients' interests will be served by the appropriate kinds of feedback given under the correct conditions.

If we consider only the extant forms of group treatment, there seems to be less variability on each of these dimensions. More specifically, self-disclosure and feedback generally are posited to possess rather high levels of therapeutic potency. There seems to be less disagreement about the relevant components of the processes. And there is much less ambiguity in how self-disclosure and feedback will be labeled—they almost always are labeled self-disclosure and feedback.

There must be some underlying assumptions about these two processes that might account for their popularity. One seems to be that, in general, people do not communicate openly enough. That

is, as a consequence of human nature, socialization, or other factors, people develop ineffective modes of exchanging information about themselves and others. It is an interesting assumption, and one with ample inductive validity in the experience of many, but it does not seem capable of scientific testing as stated. Another assumption appears to be that people would be better off if they did communicate openly and honestly to one another. This, too, is an engaging assumption, but one that seems to have probabilistic rather than universal implications and to be loaded with ethnocentrism. There is no difficulty in imagining situations in which completely open and honest communication seems to suit no one's purposes, at least the way the world is presently constituted. And there are readily available examples of societies in which such communication is not valued. Finally, this assumption seems incapable of scientific testing in its present form.

It appears that we need to consider self-disclosure and feedback at a different level if we hope to understand them coherently and with increased precision. One way would be to change the assumptions into questions and then change the questions into better questions. As stated above, the questions would be something like, "Do feedback and self-disclosure work?" Changed into better questions, they might take the form, "Under what conditions, and with whom, do self-disclosure and feedback produce what effects?" Each of these components is amenable to operationalization, though this is not to say that it always would be easily accomplished. Specific hypotheses could be developed and subjected to empirical test. Results have the potential to enable us to approach two equally better questions: "What is self-disclosure, and what is it not?" and "What is feedback, and what is it not?"

The recent research in self-disclosure and feedback that passed our screening process is summarized in Table 15.5. Considering self-disclosure first, two investigations provide some interesting suggestions about what kinds of self-disclosures, with whom, produce what kinds of effects. Kirschner, Dies, and Brown (1978) categorized self-disclosures in terms of their intimacy level. High intimacy was defined as "self-revelations that were moderately to highly personal . . ." and low intimacy as "nonpersonal to mildly personal" (p. 1172). Undergraduate

Table 15.4 Pretraining and Structure Studies

Author	Purpose	Experimental Comparisons
PRETRAINING STUDIES LaTorre (1977)	Review of pretherapy role induction studies up to 1977.	
Wogan et al. (1977)	To see if cognitive-experiential pretraining in a clinical situation would affect process variables.	Taped pretraining using cognitive-experiential instruction (3 groups). Structured T-group experience as pretaining (2 groups). No pretraining control. Placebo control.
Garrison (1978)	Compare the impact of a verbal preparation, written preparation, and attention placebo for group therapy.	Preparatory interview. Written introduction. Attention placebo interview.
Piper et al. (1979)	Implement a pretraining procedure combining cognitive and experiential approaches to pretraining.	Three pretraining groups. Two control groups.
Piper & Marrache (1981)	Investigate the potential of using pretraining group behavior to predict therapy group behavior.	Pretraining group behavior.
Piper et al. (1982)	To determine the relative importance of material highly relevant versus minimally relevant to the orientation of ther-	Primary pretraining—emphasizing here-and-now, interpersonal processes, group processes, leader's role.

Dependent Variable	Participants/ Leaders	Results

Conclusions: Pretherapy disclosure of appropriate client and therapist roles enhances process *and* outcome, particularly with minimally or moderately disturbed psychiatric outpatients with little education and therapy experience (possessing inappropriate role expectations). However, these results are confounded by the additional manipulation of outcome and/or time expectancies.

Dependent Variable	Participants/ Leaders	Results
Patient-identified problems. Group interaction.	P: Undergraduate students referred by mental health clinic for group therapy. L: Three Ph.D. psychologists. Three M.S.W.s. Two Clinical Psychology graduate students. Two graduate Social Work students. One graduate student in Educational Psychology.	No significant effects of pretreatments on group interactions or outcomes. However, groups in tape pretreatment had highest overall outcome ratings and placebo condition had lowest. Significant effects appear due to therapist and group composition differences.
Patient expectations toward group. Patient behavior. Dropout rate.	P: Applicants for services at an oupatient clinic. L: Master's level Social Work students. Experienced clinical social worker.	Prepared patients had better attendance records and were judged as manifesting better patient role behavior. No difference between the two treatment groups.
Attendance and dropout rates.	P: Patients referred for group therapy. L: Co-therapist teams composed of a psychiatric resident and a nonmedical professional (psychologist, social worker, or nurse).	Fewer dropouts and higher attendance with a cognitive-experiential pretraining program.
Therapy group behavior.	P: Patients referred for group therapy. L: Co-therapist teams composed of a psychiatrist resident and a nonmedical professional (psychologist, social worker, or nurse).	Significant, positive relationships between a number of pretraining behaviors and therapy behavior. However, psychiatric interview variables were poor predictors of pretherapy and therapy behavior variables.
Attendance and remaining in therapy, therapy process (HIM content and work categories) and outcome	P: Patients referred for group therapy. L: Co-therapist teams composed of a psychiatric	No significant differences among treatments on outcome measures or work levels, although content (percentage

(continued)

Table 15.4 *(Continued)*

Author	Purpose	Experimental Comparisons
Piper et al. (1982) *(continued)*	apy groups in a pretraining procedure.	Secondary pretraining—emphasizing individual patient, past history. Control condition—no pretraining.
Hilkey et al. (1982)	To measure the effects of videotape pretraining on selected process and outcome variables.	Videotape presentation and guided performance experience prior to group. Control groups.
STRUCTURE STUDIES Roach (1976)	Compare the effects of cognitive vs. behavioral presentation of structure, high vs. low level of specificity, and interpersonal vs. intrapersonal content on early group development.	Eight separate treatments reflecting the two levels of the three dimensions of structure compared ($2 \times 2 \times 2$).
Ware & Barr (1977)	The effects of leader structure on self-concept and self-actualization.	Structured experience. Unstructured experience. Control.
Lundgren (1977)	Analyze developmental trends in sensitivity training groups by exploring the sequence of interpersonal issues or problem areas emerging at different points in the group life span.	A record of communication patterns and content themes occurring in five T-groups.

Dependent Variable	Participants/ Leaders	Results
(interpersonal functioning and general psychiatric symptoms).	resident and a nonmedical professional (psychologist, social worker, or nurse).	of personal and relationship statements) was influenced: 9:1, primary; 3.5.1, secondary; 2:1, control.
Anxiety prior to group, self-report of readiness for group, group interaction, movement toward behavioral goals.	P: Inmates at a medium-security penitentiary. L: Counseling psychology, doctoral students, and Ph.D.s.	Pretrained clients had clearer expectations of group treatment, demonstrated more desirable behaviors in the early stages of therapy, and made more progress toward individual goals.
Change in attitudes concerning interpersonal feedback and honesty, group discussion of feelings; the group, awareness of feelings, openness, self-exploration; subject anxiety level; group interaction and cohesion; member satisfaction and level of discomfort.	P: Undergraduate student volunteers. L: Not specified.	Superiority of behavioral structure over cognitive. The effects of varied content or specificity of structure differed according to the method of presentation.
Self-concept, self-actualization, social desirability, and locus of control.	P: Undergraduate student volunteers. L: Not specified.	Both experimental groups scored higher on self-actualization and self-worth than controls. Subjects in structured groups showed more openness, less defensiveness, a higher degree of social desirability, and reported higher feelings of personal worth than the other two conditions.
Categorization of content themes.	P: NTL participants. L: NTL leaders.	Average trends for the five groups suggest a temporal sequence of concerns with involvement, control, openness, conflict, and solidarity problems, respectively.

Table 15.5   Self-disclosure and Feedback Studies

Author	Purpose	Experimental Comparisons
SELF-DISCLOSURE STUDIES		
Kirshner et al. (1978)	Experimentally investigate the link between self-disclosure and cohesiveness.	High intimacy condition containing moderately to highly personal or private self-revelations.
Anchor (1979)	Examine the extent to which it would be appropriate and feasible to differentiate between high- and low-risk self-disclosure in therapy session.	Twelve group-therapy groups.
Berberich et al. (1979)	Explore temporal patterns of self-disclosure in groups—is it different from that in dyadic settings?	Three types of parent groups: behavioral, reflective, and discussion.
Friedlander et al. (1985)	Explore the effects of self-disclosing and nondisclosing leaders on semantic cohesion, client's perceptions, and outcome.	Self-disclosing vs. nondisclosing leadership styles.
FEEDBACK STUDIES		
Jacobs (1977)	To investigate whether past results on the acceptance of feedback (positive vs. negative; behavioral vs. emotional) are the same if the identity of the feedback deliverer is unknown.	Positive vs. negative feedback. Behavioral vs. emotional feedback. Public vs. anonymous feedback.

Dependent Variable	Participants/Leaders	Results
Subjects' willingness to disclose; intimacy level; interpersonal closeness; attitudes toward the group; cohesiveness.	P: Undergraduate student volunteers. L: Audiotapes.	Higher levels of disclosure produced greater group cohesiveness.
Group interaction focusing on types of self-disclosing verbalizations.	P: Clients at a community mental health center. L:	Consistency across groups in relative avoidance of personal group-related self-disclosure (high risk) in comparison to personal group-unrelated self-disclosure (low risk).
Group interaction focusing on types of self-disclosure.	P: 44 mothers, 1 father responding to ads. L: Advanced graduate students in psychology and special education.	The discussion group most resembled dyadic psychotherapy—rises in self-disclosure as a function of time. Self-disclosure in the reflective group was evenly distributed across time. The behavioral group showed a drop in self-disclosure during the middle.
Semantic cohesion; clients' evaluations of leader and group cohesion; specific and global outcome measures.	P: Clients of a college counseling center. L: Advanced doctoral students.	Greater semantic cohesion in groups with nondisclosing leaders. Greater personal satisfaction and behavioral target gains with nondisclosing leaders. No significant differences on ratings of leader or group cohesion attributable to leader's style.
Group cohesion, participant rating of change.	P: Undergraduate student volunteers. L: Co-led by an experienced clinical psychologist and a graduate student.	Positive feedback (public or anonymous) was more credible and led to greater cohesiveness than negative feedback. Positive behavioral feedback is most credible if delivered publicly with emotional feedback or anonymously without. Negative feedback is best delivered publicly without negative emotional feedback. Emotional feedback, if positive, is most credible when delivered publicly—if negative, when delivered anonymously. Pure behavioral or pure emotional feedback

(continued)

Table 15.5 *(Continued)*

Author	Purpose	Experimental Comparisons
Jacobs (1977) *(continued)*		
Lockwood et al. (1978)	Determine the effects of videotape feedback on group behavior.	Videotape feedback. Videotape feedback plus with guided discussion. Verbal feedback from participants. Control—no feedback.
Weber (1980)	To determine if videotape playback influences the therapeutic climate during adolescent group psychotherapy.	A−B−A−B reversal single-subject design consisting of four stages: baseline, videotaping and playback, baseline, videotaping and playback.
Morran & Stockton (1980)	Examine the effects of selected factors that may influence the reception and utilization of feedback.	Positive feedback−negative feedback sequence. Negative feedback−positive feedback sequence.
Stockton & Morran (1981)	Examine the effects of balance, session of delivery, and order of delivery on feedback credibility, impact, and helpfulness.	Positive vs. negative feedback. Feedback in second, fourth, or sixth session. Positive−negative or negative−positive sequence.
Corder et al. (1981)	Study the behavioral and verbal effect of structured videotape feedback in an adolescent therapy group.	Videotape feedback group. Control sessions without videotape feedback.

Dependent Variable	Participants/ Leaders	Results
		groups are more cohesive than mixed feedback groups. Pure behavioral groups report greatest amount of change.
Q-sort on self-evaluation of growth group's role-playing ability.	P: Undergraduate volunteers. L: Leaderless.	No significant results.
Interpersonal verbal interactions of warmth, hostility, and flight.	P: Adolescent inpatients. L: Social worker, clinical psychologist.	During videotape playback, warmth responses increased significantly, flight responses decreased significantly.
Credibility, desirability, and impact of feedback; self-concept.	P: Adult volunteers. L: Advanced doctoral students.	Positive feedback more desirable and impactful than negative feedback; no credibility differences. High self-concept subjects rated negative feedback as more desirable than medium or low self-concept subjects—no differences for credibility or self-concept impact of feedback.
Credibility, desirability, and impact of feedback; self-concept.	P: Adult volunteers. L: Advanced doctoral students.	Rating of positive feedback not influenced by session of delivery. Negative feedback was more credible, impactful, and helpful in later sessions. Negative feedback was most accepted when preceded by positive.
Group process; meeting of group goals.	P: Adolescent inpatients. L: Not given.	Significant differences between sessions preceded by short videotaped feedback sessions and control group sessions on content intimacy levels and frequency of verbal feedback. Differences became less pronounced with time.

(continued)

Table 15.5   *(Continued)*

Author	Purpose	Experimental Comparisons
Soeken et al. (1981)	Investigate the usefulness of between-sessions, written feedback for individuals in short-term married-couples' group therapy.	Therapy group with computer feedback. Therapy group without computer feedback.
Morran et al. (1985)	Determine the effects of leader vs. member delivery of feedback, session of delivery, and feedback valence.	Leader vs. member feedback. Feedback during the second, fourth, or sixth sessions. Positive–negative or negative–positive feedback sequence.
Robison et al. (1982)	Determine the effects of feedback valence and receiver defensiveness on receiver ratings of feedback credibility, desirability, and impact.	Positive–negative and negative–positive feedback sequence. High, moderate, and low levels of subject defensiveness.
Epperson (1979)	Test cognitive dissonance theory account of perceived greater accuracy and desirability of positive feedback.	Positive vs. negative feedback; observational, reactive, inferential feedback; feedback vs. no feedback.
Martin & Jacobs (1980)	Determine the effects of experience with feedback on selection of positive, negative, behavioral, or emotional feedback in free-choice situation.	Positive vs. negative feedback; behavioral, emotional, behavioral and emotional feedback; experience in giving and receiving one combination.
Rose & Bednar (1980)	Determine the effects of valence of self-disclosure and feedback sequencing on group development.	Positive vs. negative feedback; positive vs. negative self-disclosure.

Dependent Variable	Participants/ Leaders	Results
Behavioral and affect parameters.	P: Married couples volunteering because of marital difficulties. L: Psychiatric social worker, psychiatric nurse.	Therapy with feedback produced greater behavioral change and significantly increased the degree of congruence between self and peer ratings, and between self and therapist ratings.
Feedback recipient ratings for degree of accuracy and helpfulness. Observer ratings of feedback message content.	P: Adult volunteers. L: Advanced doctoral students.	Leader feedback of higher quality, but not more readily accepted than member feedback. Feedback of higher quality and more accepted in later sessions. Positive feedback more accepted and of higher quality than negative feedback.
Receiver ratings of feedback credibility, desirability, and impact.	P: Adult volunteers. L: Graduate students in counseling.	Positive feedback was rated as more credible, desirable, and impactful than negative feedback. No difference in feedback ratings among high, moderate, and low defensive subjects.
Recipient ratings of accuracy, usefulness of feedback, interpersonal learning, attraction to group. Rated credibility of leaders and group members.	P: Undergraduate student volunteers. L: Advanced doctoral students.	Positive feedback rated more accurate, useful by recipients; positive feedback groups and their leaders rated more attractive, credible.
Deliverer ratings of accuracy, difficulty. Recipient ratings of credibility, desirability, impact. Type given in free-choice feedback situation.	P: Undergraduate student volunteers. L: Experienced trainers/ clinical psychologists.	Positive feedback rated more accurate, easier to deliver by deliverer; more credible, desirable, impactful by recipient. No experience differences; positive feedback chosen by participants in free choice.
Quality of group interaction, group cohesion, psychological risk.	P: Female undergraduates. L: None.	Feedback facilitated higher quality of group interaction than self-disclosure and cohesion. Negative valence was rated as more risky. Positive-to-negative valence sequence most highly valued by participants.

volunteers instructed in one of these levels of intimacy participated in audiotape-led groups. The results suggest that the participants' levels of intimacy
in self-disclosure were associated with their perceptions of group cohesion. This indicates one way in
which a group process (self-disclosure) may affect
another group process (cohesion). The second
study (Friedlander, Thibodeau, Nichols, Tucker, &
Snyder, 1985) inquired into the effects of the leader's self-disclosing style on group process and outcome variables. Using clients and trainee leaders,
they found no reliable differences across disclosing
styles in how participants rated the leaders' likability,
helpfulness, and stability, nor in their group's cohesiveness. They did report, however, positive associations between the low-self-disclosing leadership
style and process and outcome variables.

With regard to the process variables, Friedlander
et al. (1985) found greater semantic cohesion (essentially, conversational involvement or sticking to
the topic under discussion) in the low-disclosing
leaders' groups. At outcome, participants in those
groups indicated greater overall life satisfaction and
more improvement on an ideographic measure of
specific behavioral goals. These results suggest how
leadership styles may affect group processes (semantic cohesion) and outcome (satisfaction and
goal attainment). Parenthetically, each of these
reports offers a good short course in the considerations and problems of researching the self-disclosures of group participants and leaders. Each attends to the question of "Under what conditions,
and with whom, does self-disclosure produce what
effects?" However, neither offers much guidance
with respect to the other question; neither says very
much about what self-disclosure is and is not.

Feedback seems to have engaged more attention
from group researchers than has self-disclosure,
with the proportion of citations in Table 15.5
roughly approximating that in the published literature. That is satisfying in a sense because feedback
has been attributed curative power in group treatment (cf. Kaul & Bednar, 1978; Yalom, 1975). The
satisfaction is mitigated somewhat by the fact that
the concept itself seems to have developed little as a
result of this attention, a point to which we will
return later.

Operationally, feedback has been considered according to its valence (positive or negative), content
(behavioral, emotional, inferential), source (public,

anonymous; member, leader), delivery format (written, recorded, spoken), and temporal reference
(here-and-now, then-and-there). Researchers have
involved a variety of participants and leaders in the
investigations, studied ongoing therapy groups and
groups created especially for the project, and have
used a variety of designs by which to uncover the
phenomena of interest.

Several generalizations suggest themselves from
a review of the feedback studies summarized in
Table 15.5. First, recipients appear to prefer positive
feedback to negative feedback (cf. Epperson, 1979;
Jacobs, 1977; Martin & Jacobs, 1980; Morran &
Stockton, 1980; Robison, Morran, & Stockton,
1982; Rose & Bednar, 1980). Second, negative
feedback seems to be more likely to be accepted if it
is preceded by positive (Rose & Bednar, 1980;
Stockton & Morran, 1981) or delivered to persons
with high self-concepts (Morran & Stockton, 1980).
And, third, group members find it easier to give
positive than negative feedback (Martin & Jacobs,
1980; Rose & Bednar, 1980). There are others, of
course, but these will serve to provide the flavor.

In terms of relating feedback to outcome or other
process variables, the balance is tipped heavily toward other process dimensions (e.g., cohesiveness).
The ecological validity of many of these studies is so
open to question, however, that even cautious speculations seem premature. For their own legitimate
purposes, for example, several investigators have
members select feedback from prepared lists, hand
them in written form to one another, and wait until
the recipient has made several evaluative decisions
about each one before presenting another. Others
have brought groups together only for an hour or
two. Only two studies summarized looked specifically at outcome indicators (Jacobs, 1977; Soeken,
Manderscheid, Flatter, & Silbergeld, 1981), and
that in a general fashion. Most employed college
students as clients and graduate students as leaders
in an analogue setting. In general, then, the research
contributes but modestly to answering the question
"Under what conditions, and with whom, does
feedback produce what effects?"

The concept of feedback probably came to group
treatment from cybernetics. There, it has a more
specific meaning. Assuming goal-seeking functioning, it is desirable that a system be able to adjust its
future performance on the basis of its past performance. To accomplish that, the system needs infor-

mation about its performance. The information fed back to the system is information about its errors. For example, in an automated air-traffic-control system, the computerized radar establishes a "goal" for an approaching aircraft. That goal includes consideration of altitude, air speed, separation from other traffic, and angle of descent. As long as the approaching plane meets each component of the goal, within established tolerances, the system detects no errors and has nothing to say to it. Once an error is detected, however, the air-traffic-control system is designed to send corrective information to the approaching plane.

The metaphor from cybernetics to group treatment is not perfect, but it does have an attractive quality about it. Even so, that is not the way in which we wish to use it now. Instead let us consider whether the information that we get from our feedback research gets fed back into the system so that we can understand more about people, groups, or feedback. We have discussed the first "better" question, but what about the second? Does the research tell us more about what feedback is and is not? Unfortunately, the answer seems to be, not very much.

One exception may be Epperson's (1979) study. He noted that the common account given for the greater credibility attributed to positive feedback by its recipients was cognitive dissonance reduction (cf. Festinger, 1957). He noted, as well, that this explanation had not yet been tested. He began the process by designing a study similar to those from which the assertion arose, but included measures of opinion change and derogation as well. In general, the pattern of results suggested that cognitive dissonance theory may have relevance to feedback in experiential groups. The study had its share of flaws, and its ecological validity is questionable. Nevertheless, Epperson's research represents the beginnings of a bridge between what happens in group treatment and the large body of cognitive dissonance research. It suggests something of the psychological processes that may be operating, at least some of the time,when feedback is being exchanged. If that line of enquiry holds up, we would know something more about the structure of the concept of feedback.

Cohesion

The terms *cohesion* and *cohesiveness* have wide use in group treatment, so much so that without them group leaders probably would be severely handicapped in describing what happens in their groups. There is near unanimity of opinion that group cohesion is a fundamental dependent variable in the creation of a therapeutic group. That is, much of what is written about how to create, populate, structure, and lead groups has as an important end the development of group cohesion. (If you do such-and-such, it will have thus-and-so effects on cohesion.) Similarly, its presence, cohesiveness, is an equally fundamental independent variable in considering group process and outcome. Much of what is written about group treatment suggests that cohesiveness will have important implications for the course and consequences of treatment. (Different levels of cohesiveness are reliably associated with the following things that happen in groups, and with these therapeutic results.) It would seem that the terms, and the concepts that they connote, present no serious problems to group leaders.

Despite their apparent utility in the practice of group work, however, cohesion and cohesiveness have been a spectacular embarrassment to group theory and research. Over 30 years of effort has not enabled us to achieve an accepted definition of the terms. Literally hundreds of research attempts have made no demonstrable impact on our understanding of the concepts. There is an intractability somewhere in the concepts or in our approaches to their comprehension.

Given their apparent utility for group leaders, it seems unlikely that the intractability is in the concepts themselves. It could be the case, of course, because massive delusions and collective errors of the magnitude required are not unknown. At present, however, the more probable cause seems to lie in our attempts at their scientific comprehension.

A large part of the problem may arise in the way in which we talk about group cohesiveness. Much of the group language suggests that it is a thing or a stable state, while almost everyone recognizes that it is a multidimensional process that varies as a function of an indefinite number of factors. In the measurement of a thing, variability typically is viewed as error and is called unreliability. For example, differences among five measurements of Tom's height, taken within a few minutes of one another, would be considered to represent error. The same thing is true at any given point in the measurement of a process. But the differences in measurement of Tom's height, taken annually for five years, would be considered to represent the process of growth. The variability in those measurements could be compared with the variabilities of others in the estimation of his relative growth rate.

There is no insuperable problem in measuring a state (Tom's height today) and a process (Tom's growth pattern) with the same scale as long as it is a realiable one. And there is no problem in using two different scales as long as the measuring units can be converted. Confusion arises, however, when unreliable or nonreflexive scales (i.e., where the scale values change) are employed. This is particularly true when the unreliable and nonreflexive scales are given the same name, especially so when the scales may be measuring different things, and utterly so

when we have no way of discovering our mistakes.

A few studies that included cohesion as an independent or dependent variable, and in one instance included it as a construct to be measured, are summarized in Table 15.6. The three experiments used different conceptual and operational definitions of cohesiveness, sampled from different populations, and employed different dependent variables. In addition, none of them replicated any other cohesiveness research of which we are aware. Each stands in isolation. There is little reason to expect any cumulative contribution to our understanding of cohesion.

The factor analytic study of cohesion (Piper, Marrache, Lacroix, Richardson, & Jones, 1983) represents an interesting attempt at determining the

Table 15.6   Cohesion Studies

Author	Purpose	Experimental Comparisons
Hurst et al. (1978)	To determine how the leader's style affects group cohesiveness.	Leadership styles (4 dimensions: caring, controlling, meaning attribution, self-expressive).
Flowers et al. (1981)	To determine the effect of cohesiveness on client improvement on high- or low-intensity problems.	Higher vs. lower intensity problems.
Piper et al. (1983)	To determine the factor structure of group cohesion.	Principle component factor analyses, orthogonal rotations.
Piper et al. (1984)	Investigate the effects on measures of cohesion of pre-group interactions.	Interaction with leader, other participants, research associate prior to group.

components of cohesion, though it is crippled by an insufficient N. A principle components factor analysis with orthogonal rotations on nine variables resulted in nine factors—three each for the group, other participants, and the leader. Rather than take these results to indicate a multidimensional composition of cohesion, the authors chose to define cohesion as one of the group factors (commitment to the group), a view consistent with the suggestion of Evans and Jarvis (1980). The other factors, they argued, should be considered as separate group concepts.

Whether Piper et al. (1983) are correct in their definitions is, at the moment, a matter of preference. That is unfortunate but true given the lack of cohe-

sion in the cohesion research. We find ourselves in total agreement with them in their decision to explicate the definition of cohesion. Even if group leaders can manage to process the many components that go into the concept of cohesion as commonly used, it is clear that experimenters cannot.

In concluding the discussion of cohesion in our previous review (Bednar & Kaul, 1978), we suggested "... that editors refuse any research that fails to specify the meaning of cohesion, assesses it in vague and obscure ways, and does not indicate the equivalence between their conceptual and operational definitions" (p. 803). We would add to that an admonition to demand specific information about the group members and leaders, the nature of

Author	Purpose	Experimental Comparisons
Group cohesiveness.	P: High school students. L: Advanced graduate students.	Greater cohesiveness associated with higher caring and self-expressive styles, with caring more necessary.
Observers' judgments of attending-to-the-speaker frequency and content of program disclosures. Outside raters' evaluation of problem resolution.	P: Graduate students. L: Clinical psychology faculty members.	More problems were disclosed in more cohesive sessions; greater improvement on problems disclosed in more cohesive sessions than in less cohesive sessions.
Questionnaire ratings of other participants, leader group as a whole; self-rating of learning. Attendance, promptness, distance from leaders and other members.	P: Adults interested in learning about small groups. L: Experienced professionals.	Three factors named for each of other participants, leader, group as a whole, questionnaire items. For the group as a whole, the mutual stimulation factor was significantly related to perceptions of learning; the commitment factor was related to remaining in the group and distance from the leader.
Questionnaire ratings of other participants, leaders, group as a whole; self-rating of learning. Attendance, promptness, distance from leader and other members.	P: Adults interested in learning about small groups. L: Experienced professionals.	Interaction with other participants was associated with greater attendance, perceived compatibility. Interaction with leader associated with greater perceived compatibility with the leader.

the treatment, and the stage in the group at which cohesion was assessed, and to demand that *at least* a part of the assessment of cohesion include some publicly available (not just raters) assessment format. The literature would not suffer from it.

CONCLUSION

Not too long ago, a cartoon was published in *The American Scientist*. In it, there are two bewhiskered men wearing lab coats. They are standing in front of a blackboard, one of them holding a piece of chalk. On the board, literally covering it, is a truly monumental equation. It contains a few Arabic numerals, but consists mostly of exponents, logs, radicals, and nearly the entire Greek alphabet. In the middle of this amazing composition there are three dots, a box, and another three dots. In the box are written the words, "Then a miracle occurs." One man is saying to the other, who is holding the piece of chalk, "I think you need to be more specific in step two."

In our opinion, only one thing needs to be changed if this cartoon is to describe the current state of affairs in experiential group research. The caption would need to read, "I think you need to be more specific in step *one*." Step one in science is careful observation and description.

We suggest that, as an example, if you plan to do an investigation into the outcomes of group treatment, your needs would be better served if you knew at least two things in advance, and probably three. First, you ought to know what an outcome is. That has been comparatively easy for group researchers. They have commandeered the literature from research in individual treatments and applied it directly to group work. There is nothing intrinsically wrong with that, since a primary goal of much of group treatment is the rehabilitation or enhancement of individuals. It lacks something, however, if the researcher's interest is in discovering something about *group* outcome.

The second thing that would be helpful to know is what a group is. After decades of research and hundreds of investigations, there is nothing approaching consensus about what a therapeutic group is. Skeptics are invited to run a retrospective or current awareness search through their library, using key words such as "group psychotherapy,

group treatment, and group therapy." We did, and received citations ranging from the treatment of couples (that is, *two* clients), through things that we are unable to distinguish from school classes, to entire communities consisting of thousands of people. Each of these could fit the dictionary definition of a group, but they do not seem to be accommodated by any definition that we have found in the group treatment literature.

The third thing that might prove useful in a study of the outcomes of group treatment is what a group treatment is. Even if we could ignore the difficulty of determining what a treatment is, the ambiguity about the definition of a group makes this an issue of some concern. Two examples should help the explication of this point. Systematic desensitization has been offered simultaneously to a number of clients. Similarly, vocational and personal counseling have been offered to numbers of clients through the use of video recordings. Personal observation and the reading of published reports suggest that the presence of the "group" is an economic strategy for the therapist or researcher. The clients may not even speak with one another. The therapist may ignore such typical group considerations as participation in a developing social microcosm, feedback among group members, consensual validation, and reciprocal functioning as helpers and helpees among group members (Kaul & Bednar, 1978). At most, the "group" is ancillary; most commonly, it is incidental. We have no argument with theapeutic or experimental economies. We do have serious reservations, however, about calling procedures such as these group treatments. To do so seems to confound an already cloudy issue. We have chosen to title this chapter "Experiential Group Research" in an attempt to differentiate approaches such as these from approaches in which group participation and group processes are posited to play important roles in the treatment. The distinction seems important in considering the future directions of group research.

The situation is even more critical in group process research. Having some guidance about a group and a group treatment is no less important. It probably is more so. In addition, we cannot be sanguine about the conceptual state of group process. It requires differing amounts of charity, but charity nonetheless, to call group structure, self-disclosure, feedback, and cohesion concepts instead of notions, speculations, or guesses.

More than any other, the thing that prevents our becoming terminally pessimistic about experiential group research is the belief that the notions, or concepts, appear to have such utility for group practices. There is no insurmountable paradox in this. The postures of group therapists and group researchers differ in one important respect. Our understanding of therapist expectations and placebo effects argues persuasively for the therapist's "suspending disbelief" (Schutz, 1962–1966). This is not to say that gullibility is an admirable quality in a therapist, of course. Instead, it recognizes the intrusiveness of an overriding skepticism in the therapeutic situation. Pervasive doubts of the therapist about the procedures or efficacy of a treatment seem inimical to the process; thus, the wisdom of suspending disbelief. Conversely, the canons of science, and especially our understanding of the fallibilty of the human observer, argue convincingly for the scientist's "suspending belief" (Schutz, 1962–1966). Of course, the scientist exhibits a belief in the methods of science in designing and executing investigations. But there is a ubiquitous element of questioning, doubt, and skepticism in science. The scientist, when told that bulls charge red flags will wonder if that is indeed true, whether it is the red or the flag, what the conditions are under which it will occur, and so forth nearly ad infinitum. The suspension of belief motivates scientific inquiry and, parenthetically, motivates alterations in the methods of inquiry.

In his philosophy of science classes at the University of Minnesota, Herbert Feigl used to say that there are only two questions worth asking a scientist: "What do you mean? and How do you know?" The former refers to definitions and descriptions, the latter to the methods employed in searching for knowledge. Our judgment is that group research demands less suspension of disbelief and greater suspension of belief, expecially with regard to the first question. (The second question warrants concern, as well, but the need does not seem as urgent at present.) More specifically, we argue that group researchers should take a consistently skeptical attitude toward the concepts that seem to serve the therapist so well; they need to ask, "What do these terms mean?" Our guess is that if group research is to progress beyond a nearly futile repitition of noncumulative efforts, we will be best served by beginning with a much more rigorous attention to the nature of its fundamental concepts.

Pepinsky (1979) eloquently summarized the situation as we are describing it:

> . . . [T]here remains a danger of reifying events, however natural they appear to the observer. A more basic question, it seems to me, is what are the structural properties of phenomena, where ever they are inferred to occur . . . Progress toward the structural analysis of phenomena will be slow; for those in a greater hurry to get on with the task of making their research scientifically and socially useful, there remains the option of careful observation and inference prior to naming anything. (p. 48)

There seems to have been a reification of events in group research. Group cohesion is a glaring example. It has withstood repeated attempts at its experimental comprehension by social and industrial psychologists—and group researchers—to the point where we earlier described it as intractable. Evans and Jarvis (1980) and Piper et al. (1983) are correct, we believe, in calling for its fragmentation. But the same criticism is warranted with regard to other basic group concepts, too. Group, group treatment, group structure, self-disclosure, and feedback, to name but a few, demand dismemberment.

To return to the cartoon that began this section, we suggested that we need to be more specific in step one. Step one in science is careful observation and description. Ironically, those processes seem more valued in the more well-developed sciences that in what Meehl (1978) has called the soft sciences, a relationship that may be more causal than casual. The meetings and publications of the hard sciences accommodate the reports of careful observations and descriptions with as much respect as the results of experiments. They understand, it appears, that while explanation is the crown of science, description is its base. Group research could profit from the same understanding.

REFERENCES

Anchor, K. N. (1979). High- and low-risk self-disclosure in group psychotherapy. *Small Group Behavior, 10,* 279–283.

Anderson, J. D. (1978). Growth groups and alienation: A comparative study of Rogerian encounter, self-directed encounter, and Gestalt. *Group & Organization Studies, 3,* 85–107.

REFERENCES

Anchor, K. N. (1979). High- and low-risk self-disclosure in group psychotherapy. *Small Group Behavior, 10,* 279–283.

Anderson, J. D. (1978). Growth groups and alienation: A comparative study of Rogerian encounter, self-directed encounter, and Gestalt. *Group & Organization Studies, 3,* 85–107.

Antonuccio, D. O., Lewinsohn, P. M., & Steinmetz, J. L. (1982). Identification of therapist differences in a group treatment for depression. *Journal of Consulting and Clinical Psychology, 50,* 433–435.

Bednar, R. L. (1980). The psychological development of group theory: Early fixation. *Contemporary Psychology, 25,* 167–168.

Bednar, R. L., & Kaul, T. J. (1978). Experiential group research: Current perspectives. In S. L. Garfield & A. E. Bergin (Eds.), *Handbook of psychotherapy and behavior change: An empirical analysis* (2nd ed.). New York: Wiley.

Bednar, R. L., & Kaul, T. J. (1979). Experiential group research: What never happened. *The Journal of Applied Behavioral Science, 11,* 311–319.

Bednar, R. L., & Kaul, T. J. (Forthcoming). *Group theory and practice: A comparative review and analysis.* Columbus, OH: Merrill.

Bednar, R. L., & Lawlis, F. (1971). Empirical research in group psychotherapy. In A. E. Bergin & S. L. Garfield (Eds.), *Handbook for psychotherapy and behavior change.* New York: Wiley.

Bednar, R. L., & Moeschl, M. J. (1981). Conceptual and methodological considerations in the evaluation of group psychotherapies. In P. McReynolds (Ed.), *Advances in psychological assessment* (Vol. 5). San Francisco: Jossey-Bass.

Berberich, R. R., Gabel, H., & Anchor, K. N. (1979). Self-disclosure in reflective, behavioral, and discussion parent-counseling groups. *Journal of Community Psychology, 7,* 259–263.

Bergin, A. E., & Lambert, M. J. (1978). The evaluation of therapeutic outcomes. In S. L. Garfield & A. E. Bergin (Eds.), *Handbook of psychotherapy and behavior change: An empirical analysis* (2nd ed.). New York: Wiley.

Bergin, A. E., & Lambert, M. J. (1979). Counseling the researcher. *The Counseling Psychologist, 8,* 53–56.

Bramlette, C. A., & Tucker, J. H. (1981). Encounter groups: Positive change or deterioration? More data and a partial replication. *Human Relations, 34,* 303–314.

Campbell, J. P., & Dunnette, M. D. (1968). Effectiveness of t-group experiences in managerial training and development. *Psychological Bulletin, 70,* 73–104.

Cattell, R. B., & Eber, H. W. (1956). *Sixteen Personality Factor Questionnaire.* Champaign, IL: Institute for Personality and Ability Testing.

Comas-Diaz, L. (1981). Effects of cognitive and behavioral group treatment on the depressive symptomatology of Puerto Rican women. *Journal of Consulting and Clinical Psychology, 49,* 627–632.

Cook, T. D., & Campbell, D. T. (1979). *Quasi-experimentation: Design and analysis for field settings.* Chicago: Rand-McNally.

Corder, B. F., Whiteside, R., McNeill, M., Brown, T., & Corder, R. F. (1981). An experimental study of the effect of structured videotape feedback on adolescent group psychotherapy process. *Journal of Youth and Adolescence, 10,* 255–261.

Dies, R. R. (1977). Pragmatics of leadership in psychotherapy and encounter group research. *Small Group Behavior, 8,* 229–248.

Elder-Jucker, P. L. (1979). *Effects of group therapy on self-esteem, social interaction, and depression of female residents in a home for the aged.* Unpublished doctoral dissertation, Temple University, Philadelphia, PA.

Epperson, D. L. (1979). *Investigation of positive and negative, observational, reactive, and inferential feedback in experiential groups.* Unpublished doctoral dissertation, Ohio State University, Columbus, OH.

Evans, N. J., & Jarvis, P. A. (1980). Group cohesion: A review and reevaluation. *Small Group Behavior, 11,* 359–370.

Festinger, L. (1957). *A theory of cognitive dissonance.* Evanston, IL: Row-Peterson.

Flowers, J. V., Booraem, C. D., & Hartman, K. A. (1981). Client improvement on higher and lower intensity problems as a function of group cohesiveness. *Psychotherapy: Theory, Research and Practice, 18,* 246–251.

Frank, J. D. (1979). The present status of outcome studies. *Journal of Consulting and Clinical Psychology, 47,* 310–316.

Friedlander, M. L., & Kaul, T. J. (1983). Preparing clients for counseling: Effects of role induction on counseling process and outcome. *Journal of College Student Personnel, 24,* 207–214.

Friedlander, M. L., Thibodeau, J. R., Nichols, M. P., Tucker, C., & Snyder, J. (1985). Introducing semantic cohesion analysis: A study of group talk. *Small Group Behavior.*

Fuchs, C. Z., & Rehm, L. P. (1977). A self-control behavior therapy program for depression. *Journal of Consulting and Clinical Psychology, 45,* 206–215.

Garfield, S. L. (1981). Psychotherapy: A 40-year appraisal. *American Psychologist, 36,* 174–183.

Garrison, J. E. (1978). Written vs. verbal preparation of patients for group psychotherapy. *Psychotherapy: Theory, Research, and Practice, 15,* 130–134.

Gibb, J. R. (1971). The effects of human relations training. In A. E. Bergin & S. L. Garfield (Eds.), *Handbook of psychotherapy and behavior change.* New York: Wiley.

Hempel, C. G. (1966). *Philosophy of natural science.* Englewood Cliffs, NJ: Prentice-Hall.

Hilkey, J. H., Wilhelm, C. L., & Horne, A. M. (1982). Comparative effectiveness of videotape pretraining versus no pretraining on selected process and outcome variables in group therapy. *Psychological Reports, 50,* 1151–1159.

Hill, W. F. (1965). *Hill interaction matrix.* Los Angeles: University of Southern California Youth Study Center.

Hodgson, J. W. (1981). Cognitive versus behavioral-interpersonal approaches to the group treatment of depressed college students. *Journal of Counseling Psychology, 28,* 243–249.

Hurst, A. G., Stein, K. B., Korchin, S. J., & Soskin, W. F. (1978). Leadership style determinants of cohesiveness in adolescent groups. *International Journal of Group Psychotherapy, 28,* 263–277.

Jacobs, M. (1977). A comparison of publicly delivered and anonymously delivered verbal feedback in brief personal growth groups. *Journal of Consulting and Clinical Psychology, 45,* 385–390.

Kaplan, R. E. (1982). The dynamics of injury in encounter groups: Power, splitting, and the mismanagement of resistance. *International Journal of Group Psychotherapy, 32,* 163–187.

Kaul, T. J., & Bednar, R. L. (1978). Conceptualizing group research: A preliminary analysis. *Small Group Behavior, 9,* 173–191.

Kiesler, D. J. (1966). Some myths of psychotherapy research and the search for a paradigm. *Psychological Bulletin, 65,* 110–136.

Kiesler, D. J. (1979). Commentary on Gelso's "Research in counseling: Methodological and professional issues." *The Counseling Psychologist, 8,* 44–46.

Kirshner, B. J., Dies, R. R., & Brown, R. A. (1978). Effects of experimental manipulation of self-disclosure on group cohesiveness. *Journal of Consulting and Clinical Psychology, 46,* 1171–1177.

LaPointe, K. A., & Rimm, D. C. (1980). Cognitive, assertive, and insight-oriented group therapies in the treatment of reactive depression in women. *Psychotherapy: Theory, Research, and Practice, 17,* 312–321.

LaTorre, R. A. (1977). Pretherapy role induction procedures. *Canadian Psychological Review, 18,* 308–321.

Lieberman, M. A., Yalom, I. D., & Miles, M. B. (1973). *Encounter groups: First Facts.* New York: Basic Books.

Lockwood, G., Salzberg, H. C., & Heckel, R. V. (1978). The effects of videotape feedback on self-concept, role-playing ability, and growth in a leaderless therapy group. *Journal of Clinical Psychology, 34,* 718–720.

Lothstein, L. M. (1978). The group psychotherapy dropout phenomenon revisited. *American Journal of Psychiatry, 135,* 1492–1495.

Lundgren, D. C. (1977). Developmental trends in the emergence of interpersonal issues in T groups. *Small Group Behavior, 8,* 179–200.

Lundgren, D. C., & Knight, D. J. (1977). Trainer style and member attitudes toward trainer and group in t-groups. *Small Group Behavior, 8,* 47–63.

Martin, L., & Jacobs, M. (1980). Structured feedback delivered in small groups. *Small Group Behavior, 11,* 88–107.

McCardel, J., & Murray, E. J. (1974). Nonspecific factors in weekend encounter groups. *Journal of Consulting and Clinical Psychology, 42,* 337–345.

Meehl, P. E. (1978). Theoretical risks and tabular asterisks: Sir Karl, Sir Ronald, and the slow progress of soft psychology. *Journal of Consulting and Clinical Psychology, 46,* 806–834.

Meehl, P. E. (1983). Subjectivity in psychoanalytic inference: The nagging persistence of Wilhelm Fliess's Achensee question. In J. Earman (Ed.), *Minnesota studies in the philosophy of science: Vol. X. Testing scientific theories* (pp. 349–411). Minneapolis: University of Minnesota Press.

Morran, D. K., Robison, F. F., & Stockton, R. (1985). Feedback exchange in counseling groups: An analysis of message content and receiver acceptance as a function of leader versus member delivery, session,

and valence. *Journal of Counseling Psychology, 32,* 57–67.

Morran, D. K., & Stockton, R. A. (1980). Effect of self-concept on group member reception of positive and negative feedback. *Journal of Counseling Psychology, 27,* 260–267.

Parloff, M. B., & Dies, R. R. (1977). Group psychotherapy outcome research 1966–1975. *International Journal of Group Psychotherapy, 27,* 281–320.

Pepinsky, H. B. (1979). Second thoughts about research in counseling. *The Counseling Psychologist, 8,* 47–50.

Piper, W. E., Debbane, E. G., Bienvenu, J., & Garant, J. (1982). A study of group pretraining for group psychotherapy. *International Journal of Group Psychotherapy, 32,* 309–325.

Piper, W. E., Debbane, E. G., & Garant, J. (1977). An outcome study of group therapy. *Archives of General Psychiatry, 34,* 1027–1032.

Piper, W. E., Debbane, E. G., Garant, J., & Bienvenu, J. (1979). Pretraining for group psychotherapy. *Archives of General Psychiatry, 36,* 1250–1256.

Piper, W. E., Jones, B. D., Lacroix, R., Marrache, M., & Richardson, A. M. (1984). Pregroup interactions and bonding in small groups. *Small Group Behavior, 15,* 51–62.

Piper, W. E., & Marrache, M. (1981). Selecting suitable patients: Pretraining for group therapy as a method of patient selection. *Small Group Behavior, 12,* 459–475.

Piper, W. E., Marrache, M., Lacroix, R., Richardson, A. M., & Jones, B. D. (1983). Cohesion as a basic bond in groups. *Human Relations, 36,* 93–108.

Popper, K. R. (1968). *Conjectures and refutations.* New York: Basic Books.

Popper, K. R. (1979). *Objective knowledge: An evolutionary approach.* Oxford: Oxford University Press.

Roach, A. M. (1976). *The comparative effects of behavioral vs. cognitive presentation, high vs. low levels of specificity, and interpersonal vs. intrapersonal content of structure on early group development.* Unpublished doctoral dissertation, University of Kentucky, Lexington, KY.

Robison, F. F., Morran, D. K., & Stockton, R. (1982). Effects of valence and receiver defensiveness on acceptance of feedback in counseling groups. Unpublished manuscript, Ball State University, Muncie, IN.

Rose, G. S., & Bednar, R. L. (1980). Effects of positive and negative self-disclosure and feedback on early group development. *Journal of Counseling Psychology, 27,* 63–70.

Rush, A. J., & Watkins, J. T. (1981). Group versus individual cognitive therapy: A pilot study. *Cognitive Therapy and Research, 5,* 95–103.

Schutz, A. (1962–1966). *Collected papers,* 3 volumes. The Hague: Martinus Nijhoff.

Scott, H. (1976). *The effects of leadership training and style on individuals involved in group therapy.* Unpublished doctoral dissertation, United States International University, San Diego, CA.

Shaffer, C. S., Shapiro, J., Sank, L. I., & Coghlan, D. J. (1981). Positive changes in depression, anxiety, and assertion following individual and group cognitive behavior therapy intervention. *Cognitive Therapy and Research, 5,* 149–157.

Shapiro, A., & Morris, L. (1978). Placebo effects in medical and psychological therapies. In S. Garfield & A. Bergin (Eds.), *Handbook of psychotherapy and behavior change: An empirical analysis* (2nd ed.). New York: Wiley.

Silbergeld, S., Koenig, G., Manderscheid, R., Meeker, B., & Hornung, C. (1975). Assessment of environment-therapy systems: The group atmosphere scale. *Journal of Consulting and Clinical Psychology, 43*, 460–469.

Smith, P. B. (1975). Are there adverse afffects of sensitivity training? *Journal of Humanistic Psychology, 15*, 29–47.

Soeken, D. R., Manderscheid, R. W., Flatter, C. H., & Silbergeld, S. (1981). A controlled study of quantitative feedback in married-couples brief group psychotherapy. *Psychotherapy: Therapy, Research, and Practice, 18*, 204–216.

Steinmetz, J. L., Lewinsohn, P. M., & Antonuccio, D. O. (1983). Prediction of individual outcome in a group intervention for depression. *Journal of Consulting and Clinical Psychology, 51*, 331–337.

Stock, D. (1964). A survey of research on t-groups. In L. P. Bradford, J. R. Gibb, & K. D. Benne (Eds.), *T-group theory and laboratory method: Innovation in reeducation*. New York: Wiley.

Stockton, R., & Morran, D. K. (1981). Feedback exchange in personal growth groups: Receiver acceptance as a function of valence, session, and order of delivery. *Journal of Counseling Psychology, 28*, 490–497.

Ware, J. R., & Barr, J. E. (1977). Effects of a nine-week structured and unstructured group experience on measures of self-concept and self-actualization. *Small Group Behavior, 8*, 93–99.

Weber, L. A. (1980). The effect of videotape and playback on an in-patient adolescent group. *International Journal of Group Psychotherapy, 30*, 213–227.

Wogan, M., Getter, H., Amdur, M. J., Nichols, M. F., & Okman, G. (1977). Influencing interaction and outcomes in group psychotherapy. *Small Group Behavior, 8*, 25–45.

Woods, M. (1980). *Relevance, activity, and intermember familiarity as parameters of group structure: Effects on early group development*. Unpublished doctoral dissertation, University of Kentucky, Lexington, KY.

Yalom, I. D. (1975). *The theory and practice of group psychotherapy* (2nd ed.). New York: Basic Books.

16

RESEARCH ON EDUCATIONAL AND VOCATIONAL COUNSELING

ROGER A. MYERS

Teachers College, Columbia University

The conduct and study of educational and vocational counseling are characterized by a persistent focus on patent social roles, especially those of student and worker, and by an equally persistent lack of concern for the unconscious motives of the role-player. To the educational and the vocational counselor, society has assigned the task of assisting people—mostly young people—as they seek to define themselves by choosing, preparing for, entering, progressing in, changing, and reflecting upon productive activity. For obvious reasons, paid employment is the type of productive activity that receives the most attention.

Because delivering such services and inquiring about the conditions and consequences of that delivery fall within the domain of counseling psychology, it is not surprising to find that the guiding principles of the specialty exert a deep-seated influence. The principles prescribe that the efforts of counseling psychologists be devoted to remediation and rehabilitation, to prevention, and to education and development (American Psychological Association [APA], 1981b; Fretz, 1982; Jordaan, Myers, Layton, & Morgan, 1968). Morrill, Oetting, and Hurst (1974) characterized remediation, preven-

tion, and development as the various *purposes* of intervention and described, in a cubic model, various *targets*: individual, primary group, associational group, institution; and various *methods*: direct service, consultation and training, and media. Their work aided the specialty in defining itself and in conceptualizing its helping activities. Though clinical psychology described its functions as "alleviating intellectual, emotional, psychological, and behavioral disability and discomfort" (APA, 1981a, p. 642), the functions of counseling psychology clearly include other matters.

All of this has meaning for defining the zones of inquiry included in this chapter. Although, in an earlier edition (Myers, 1971), it was reasonable to concentrate on studies of counseling activities that were highly similar to what is usually understood as psychotherapy, such an approach no longer seems helpful. Events of the recent past seem to have produced a body of research that is significantly less attentive to helping activities that Morrill et al. (1974) would characterize as direct service for the purpose of remediation. Today studies of educational and vocational counseling are much more frequently focused on programmatic approaches to

715

developmental issues, with training as the main method of intervention and with considerable attention devoted to media and to curricula. The strength of this trend is evident in the approaches that guided two recent influential reviews (Holland, Magoon, & Spokane, 1981; Spokane & Oliver, 1983). Both sets of authors chose the word *interventions* (modified by *career* in one case, by *vocational* in the other) for their titles because, one suspects, *counseling* was too limited a concept to encompass a sphere of activity that had grown and changed.

REVIEWS, CRITIQUES, ADVICE

Since the appearance of the first edition of the *Handbook* (Bergin & Garfield, 1971), reviews of counseling research have appeared with considerable frequency. Six relevant chapters in the *Annual Review of Psychology* have focused on issues pertaining to educational and vocational counseling (Borgen, 1984; Holland et al., 1981; Krumboltz, Becker-Haven, & Burnett, 1979; Pepinsky and Meara, 1973; Super & Hall, 1978; Whiteley, Buckhart, Harway-Herman, & Whiteley, 1975). In addition, the editors of the *Journal of Vocational Behavior* have published a series of review articles on vocational behavior and career development (Bartol, 1981; Betz, 1977; Fretz & Leong, 1982b; Garbin & Stover, 1980; Holcomb & Anderson, 1977; Muchinsky, 1983; Osipow, 1976; Walsh, 1979; Zytowski, 1978). As a consequence, the research on these topics has been more frequently and more carefully scrutinized than in any previous era.

Furthermore, a number of useful analyses and criticisms of counseling research have appeared, each providing a set of prescriptions intended to guide researchers toward better research products.

Goldman: Radical Reform

The most radical of these criticisms was that provided by Goldman (1976). He began his treatise with an alarming challenge.

My thesis is that the overwhelming majority of published research in our field has little or nothing to offer to practitioners. Only a tiny portion of all the research in all the journals and monographs and books has anything meaningful to say to

counselors in schools, colleges, and agencies; indeed, much of it has no discernible value for anyone. (p.543)

This sorry state, as Goldman perceived it, resulted from a variety of inadequacies of the investigations and the investigators that focused on counseling practice. Among the most important shortcomings, he identified the following:

1. The use of opportunistic samples and the failure to examine and describe the subjects or the sites from which they came.
2. The lack of replication and the institutional deterrents to replicating.
3. Low response rates in survey and follow-up studies.
4. The failure to specify the nature of the intervenor as an independent variable.
5. The use of criteria that, in service of statistical analysis, are often trivial and unrelated to the dependent variables of "real-life importance." (p. 545)
6. An excess of precision in data analysis attributable to the availability of computers.
7. An overvaluing of statistically significant findings with no practical meaning.

The source of the difficulties, as Goldman saw it, was the pervasive need for counseling researchers to pursue the practical and relatively intangible problems of the practitioner by focusing too narrowly on the investigative traditions of the physical sciences. Those traditions, in Goldman's view, swing the balance toward rigor and away from meaning in the well-recognized rigor versus meaning epistemological dilemma. To redress the balance, Goldman argued that some promising research trends deserved more attention. He prescribed that investigators forsake their tendencies to understand humans at microscopic levels and concentrate instead on more macroscopic views of the "whole functioning human being" (p. 546). He argued that more would be learned and the ability to generalize would be enhanced if the phenomena of interest were studied in the natural setting rather than in simplifications designed for the laboratory. He further maintained that aggregating observations about research subjects obscured important insights about intraindividual characteristics, and he advocated the use of intensive designs (Thoreson & Anton, 1974). Most important of all, Goldman suggested new frames with which investigators should view themselves and their relationships with the persons being studied. By being aware of the possibilities of investigator bias and of the relative nature of the investigator–subject interaction, researchers could build in simple corrective mechanisms that would (1) guard against the tendency to distort observations and (2) engage the subjects as informed collaborators. Finally, he suggested that studies be designed with early and careful consideration devoted to the dissemination of the results and their meaning to potential consumers.

Gelso: Methodological Pluralism

Though Goldman's call for "A Revolution in Counseling Research" did not incite a revolution of visible proportions, his bothersome criticisms and bold prescriptions did not pass unnoticed. When Gelso (1979) undertook his major review of research in counseling, he responded to several of the criticisms Goldman (1976, 1978) had raised.

Gelso's review was an attempt to describe the state of the art in counseling research by focusing on research strategies, criterion issues, and considerations in the use of samples and control groups. Published in the usual format of The Counseling Psychologist, it was followed by an interesting series of evaluative responses (see The Counseling Psychologist, 1979, Vol. 8, No. 3).

Gelso cited Goldman and others in his treatment of "the polarization of investigative styles along a rigor-relevance dimension" (p. 8). In his view, one of the most prominent trends in the field was the emerging polemic about what constituted acceptable methodology. Recognizing Goldman's (1978) call for a return to the subjective and qualitative methods, Gelso went on to argue that a wide variety of investigative styles was appropriate and helpful. He proposed a classification scheme to characterize research strategies along two dimensions—manipulative versus nonmanipulative and laboratory versus field—and carefully analyzed the strengths and weakness of each of the four types. In the concluding remarks of his section on the state of the art, he labeled the demand for "relevance" as "an albatross that impedes our quest for knowledge and sound practice" (p. 24). He asserted that (1) pleas

for relevance usually meant that methods should be looser and that such an influence would be dysfunctional; (2) relevance to the activity of counseling was too narrow a window for viewing all varieties of inquiry related to the field of counseling; and (3) the concept of relevance needed to be expanded to allow for the many possibilities of indirect relevance.

In pointing to future directions, Gelso lamented the paucity of critical, integrative reviews of research and advocated the utility of programmatic research and, in agreement with Goldman, more replication.

In contrast to Goldman's attack on the adequacy and efficacy of counseling research, Gelso's review provided a basis for considerable optimism about the current state of that research and offered useful suggestions for the future. Gelso sought to enable progress along the lines of inquiry that were already visible by encouraging more variety in investigative strategies, research methods, and goals for inquiry. While Goldman seemed to strive for a drastic revision in the nature of counseling research, Gelso pressed for improvements in the nature of what was already in progress, for a more pluralistic approach to valuing various ways of knowing, and for better preparation of the inquiring practitioners of tomorrow.

It is likely that both reviews served useful purposes: Goldman's to remind investigators that inquiry about practice should be more concerned with the needs of the practitioner and less inhibited by the constraints of psychological science; Gelso's to reaffirm the values of rigor and to encourage investigators to build on the various strengths that several decades of research have yielded. There is little doubt that counseling research will be enriched by the presence of both points of view.

Specific Prescriptions

Three important analyses that followed provided very specific advice about how the state of the art, at least in vocational counseling, could be improved. Oliver (1979) focused her attention on the outcome measures used in career counseling research and identified several departures from what she considered an ideal state. Her advice included recommendations about criteria, instruments, and design. She urged that investigators use multiple criteria, use specific and global measures, emphasize short-term outcomes, and define constructs carefully (see Pepinsky, 1979, p. 48). Her suggestions for instruments included using instruments from previous research, reporting psychometric properties of the instruments used, staying with objective measures whenever possible, and using nonreactive measures. Design recommendations included the use of control groups, random assignment, and estimating the sample size needed.

Fretz (1981) reviewed the studies evaluating career interventions and concluded that despite many differences in method, personnel, and costs, "the evidence suggests that myriad, diverse interventions result in small yet consistently detectable gains" (p. 77). His search for a fuller understanding of the process in order to increase the impact of such treatments led him to erect dimensions of client attributes, treatment parameters, and outcomes. Each of these dimensions was further subdivided to create a comprehensive list as follows:

Client attributes: Demographic, psychological, career related
Treatment parameters: Content domain, interpersonal context, degree of structure
Outcomes: Career knowledge and skills, career behavior, sentiments, effective role functioning

His advice to investigators echoed that of Oliver with regard to the careful definition of the concepts employed, the use of multiple criteria, and the use of measures that had been used in prior research. His strongest arguments, however, were for studies in which different treatments are compared and in which attribute-treatment interactions are observed. In addition, he recommended that the costs of various treatments be analyzed and reported.

Spokane and Oliver (1983) identified 52 studies of vocational interventions published between 1950 and 1980 in which a control group had been used. They integrated these studies with a meta-analysis procedure proposed by Smith and Glass (1977) and Smith, Glass, and Miller (1980). They concluded that for clients receiving any type of vocational intervention, the outcome status exceeded that of 80 percent of the untreated controls. Of the 20 studies in which the effect of an individual counselor interacting with an individual client had been evaluated, the outcome status of the clients exceeded that of 81 percent of the controls. In the studies ($N = 28$) in which the treatment was deliv-

ered by means of supportive groups, structured groups, or classes, the effect size was calculated to be .87. Applying Rosenthal's (1980) formulas for calculating how many unpublished studies with null results would be required to nullify the results of the 52 published studies, they concluded that 670 such studies would be required.

Spokane and Oliver suggested that these overall treatment effects represent a considerable magnitude, despite the tendency of some reviewers (Fretz, 1981, p. 77; Goldman, 1976, p. 545) to regard them as small.

The authors concluded with a section on recommendations for the conduct of future research that seemed to grow from, among other sources, their frustrations while doing their review. They advised that real clients—not subjects earning course credit in Psychology 101—be used, that no-treatment controls be included, that individual differences in pretreatment states be given more attention, and that outcome measures be more carefully selected. They also prescribed more specific, more complete, and more accurate reporting of data and argued that data on effect sizes should be reported routinely. Their review includes a "methodological checklist" of 43 separate items of advice that should be helpful to researchers and reviewers.

Common Themes

The accumulation of advice to investigators available from these reviews and analyses should be enormously helpful for the future of inquiry on educational and vocational counseling. Some common themes emerge, despite the varying opinions and the differing purposes of the authors. For example, it now seems to be taken for granted that what was once thought of as counseling—that is, a process mediated by a counselor and delivered to an applicant-client—must now be viewed as a variety of methods intended to be helpful in a variety of ways for many different kinds of clients who may or may not apply for help with a circumscribed problem.

There is no complacency among the many reviewers about the adequacy of research designs, but most (save Goldman) agree that things are improving in that category. Criterion issues continue to attract the attention of most reviewers (see also Osipow, 1982b), and preferences for multiple criteria, for standardized instruments, and for nonreactive data are identifiable. Most reviewers see the need for improving the quality of reports of research, especially with regard to clarity of definitions, specificity about variables and instruments, and comprehensiveness in presenting results.

Perhaps most important of all, there seems to be a shared optimism—sometimes modified—that the various treatments under investigation do indeed produce desirable effects (see also Campbell, Connell, Kimmel Boyle, & Bhaerman, 1983; Herr, 1982b). According to Holland et al. (1981):

> the beneficial effects are due to the common elements in these divergent treatments: (a) exposure to occupational information; (b) cognitive rehearsal of vocational aspirations; (c) acquisition of some cognitive structure for organizing information about self, occupations, and their relations; and (d) social support or reinforcement from counselors or workshop members. (p. 285)

They also suggested that the consistently positive outcomes can be attributed to the fact that the usual client knows little about appropriate career behavior; hence a small amount of information and support is likely to have an impact.

But more insight is needed, and Holland et al. (1981) offered some deviant advice about how to pursue it. In their opinion, future progress would likely result from "perseverance, reading, and thinking, rather than worrying about methodological perspectives" (p. 300). No doubt, a number of dedicated researchers and scholars skipped quickly over that sentence.

STUDIES OF DECISION MAKING

The making of educational and vocational decisions has always been viewed as the beginning, or at least an early stage, of a developmental process of considerable import. Given our diversified educational system, young people are called upon to make, or avoid, a variety of choices in order to find their way through a complicated educational system. This system provides preparation for and access to a highly differentiated set of work roles and an increasingly varied array of lifestyles. Furthermore, increased concentration on adult development beyond the stages of occupational preparation and

entry (e.g., Gould, 1978; Levinson, Darrow, Klein, Levinson, & McKee, 1978; Vaillant, 1977) has led to a heightened awareness of the need for concern about decision making throughout the life span (Schlossberg, 1976).

No work has been more influential in focusing attention on the importance of decision making in a developmental context than that of Super and his associates (Jordaan & Heyde, 1979; Super, 1953, 1980, 1983b, 1984). Beginning with the notion that people make choices about school and work in order to implement their self-concepts in a world of productive activity, Super noted that preferences and competencies, life situations, and self-concepts change with experience, necessitating a lifelong sequence of choices and adjustments. This sequence has discernible stages with differing tasks at each stage. Movement through these stages is a product of maturation and of the results of reality testing mediated by choices. The consequences of one's choices are synthesizing and compromising— among personal characteristics, the roles one plays, and the evaluations of such role-playing—toward the ongoing development and enactment of the self-concept. Satisfaction, as Super sees it, is proportional to the extent one finds and chooses appropriate outlets for the constantly emerging self-picture.

Tiedeman and his many collaborators have also been influential in helping counselors and researchers to consider decision making in developmental terms. Concerned that Super's (1953) formulations were "focused on external factors (others, society) rather than the internal characteristics of the individual" (Tiedeman & Miller-Tiedeman, 1984, p. 285), Tiedeman and O'Hara (1963) attempted to conceptualize the decision-making process in a way that gave more attention to the concepts of personality and individual responsibility. They described a complex series of decision elements that separated anticipation of a decision from its implementation and further divided these aspects into steps, each of which represented a change in the decider's psychological state as a decision was being resolved. Development, as they conceived it, occurs as a result of multiple decisions, each of which might incorporate awareness of the process, memory of past decisions, and imagination about future experiences. Objecting to Super's use of the word roles— a concept that emphasizes expectations of others—

Tiedeman and O'Hara chose instead to speak of "position choices," which, for them, better represented the personal basis of the action in process. More recent work has emphasized the personal reality of the decider (Miller-Tiedeman & Tiedeman, 1982) and the process of increasing one's sense of power by progressively enhancing one's ability to understand oneself as a decider (Tiedeman, 1983).

Other prominent theorists deemphasize or reject the importance of viewing decision making within developmental frames (Holland, 1973; Krumboltz, 1979) but strongly emphasize the importance of the decision event itself, its antecedents, and its consequences.

Instrumental Behavior

With relatively few important exceptions (Baumgardner, 1977; Harren, 1979; Phillips & Strohmer, 1982), those who theorize and inquire about educational and vocational decision making regard it, following Parsons' (1909) prescriptions, as a rational process of learning about oneself, learning about the opportunities available, and reasoning in a logical fashion about the relationships between these two sets of learnings. Therefore, attempts to help people make such decisions better are often directed toward increasing the probability that the deciders will engage in certain instrumental acts presumed to lead to better understanding of themselves and/or their opportunities.

Probably because of the impressive lead provided in the 1960s by Krumboltz and his collaborators (Krumboltz & Schroeder, 1965; Krumboltz & Thoresen, 1964; Ryan & Krumboltz, 1964; Thoresen & Krumboltz, 1967; Thoresen, Krumboltz, & Varenhorst, 1967), a number of investigators in recent years have focused on interventions that were designed to promote more and better information-seeking behavior.

Fisher, Reardon, and Burck (1976) randomly assigned 42 college students to three treatment groups designed to test the efficacy of a self-help career guidance program. One group was subjected to a module that taught ways of seeking information and included a viodeotape presentation of a typical student being reinforced by a counselor for following the program effectively. A second group got the module without the videotape, and a third group was deprived of the module altogether. The group subjected to the reinforcement videotape subsequently engaged in more frequent and more varied information seeking, leading the investigators to conclude that the videotape of the reinforced model accomplished what was intended. Krivatsky and Magoon (1976) compared two programmatic treatments—Holland's Self-Directed Search (1970) and a modification of it—to traditional counseling for 113 college student volunteers. They found that self-reported information-seeking behavior increased in all three groups and that the three treatments were about equally effective, but that the treatment costs per subject varied from $2.23 for the Self-Directed Search to $13.15 for traditional counseling. Hoffman, Spokane, and Magoon (1981) studied three methods for providing 32 undergraduate volunteers with feedback about their inventoried interests. They used a variety of outcome measures that seemed to indicate the superiority of the interpretation method employing a live counselor, though the groups did not differ in the amount of self-reported information seeking they engaged in after treatment. When the investigators compared the groups on an unobtrusive measure of information seeking, however, the differences in favor of the counselor-mediated method were robust.

Aiken and Johnston (1973) concentrated their effects on how differing client characteristics moderated the effects of a counseling treatment intended to promote information-seeking behavior from undecided college students. The client characteristics of interest were (1) the degree to which a subject's vocational interest patterns were compatible with one another, called consistency; and (2) the degree to which a student displayed attitudes indicative of vocational maturity. After two or three small-group counseling sessions in which counselors used procedures to reinforce indications of seeking information or intending to seek it, a self-report measure of information seeking was administered and readministered three weeks later. Their analyses revealed that, contrary to their hypothesis, the subjects with consistent vocational interest patterns increased the information-seeking behavior more and that differences in vocational maturity did not influence the outcome.

Borman (1972) compared individual counseling plus reinforcement to vocational guidance advice delivered by audiotape by assigning equal portions of motivated and unmotivated vocational school students to both treatments and to an inactive control group. His results suggested that the reinforcement counseling method worked best for unmotivated students but the audiotaped method was more effective for the students motivated to pursue educational and vocational planning. Further concern about differential treatment effects for clients with differing characteristics was exhibited by Young (1979), who sought to compare a treatment designed to confront how much the client valued the concepts "logical" and "responsible" with a treatment that consisted of counseling plus reinforcement. Using male students from rural high schools, he distributed subjects who were high and low on internal locus of control among the treatments. His results provided some support for the conclusion that the value confrontation treatment had a substantial effect on the information-seeking behavior of subjects with high internal control. Though the measure of information seeking was derived from the self-reports of the subjects, Young was able to verify 94 percent of the reported behaviors for a random subsample.

Perhaps the most carefully done attribute-treatment interaction study of promoting information-seeking behavior was that done by Kivlighan, Hageseth, Tipton, and McGovern (1981). They used a vocational interest inventory to identify college undergraduates who were task-oriented and those who were people-oriented. The treatments consisted of structured group counseling methods designed for learning through interaction and learning through individual problem solving. After controlling for pretreatment levels of vocational maturity, they found that congruence between personality type and treatment condition—that is, learning through interaction treatment for people-oriented subjects and learning through individual problem solving for task-oriented subjects—produced the most impressive results. Subjects who experienced treatments congruent with their personality types evaluated the treatments more favorably, gained more in vocational maturity, and engaged in more frequent and more varied information-seeking than their mismatched counterparts. The authors suggested that the failure to pursue the interactions between client characteristics and treatment types might well have masked important differences in the effectiveness of various treatment methods in previous studies.

As these studies illustrate, interest in encouraging young people to learn more about the opportunities available to them continues. Furthermore, there is reason for continued optimism about the efficacy of a variety of structured treatment approaches for increasing this class of instrumental activity. An additional encouraging sign is the appearance of research designs that signal an increasing awareness that all clients are not alike and that all treatment methods are not equally effective for everyone.

Readiness for Decision Making

A noticeable trend in recent investigations of interventions intended to enhance educational and vocational decision making is the concentration on the clients' readiness to make decisions. Herr (1982a) has described the context in which this trend has developed:

> Initially concerned about assessing the traits and factors making up the content of individual choices—e.g., aptitudes, interests, job requirements—recent approaches to assessment in career behavior have been concerned as well about the process of choice: the individual's readiness to choose, knowledge of the choice process, and ability to collect information and weigh its personal value. Rather than considering the latter to be "fixed effects," many counselors have seen them as reflecting various levels of education and experience and therefore modifiable. This view has in turn suggested "teaching the test" in individual and group activities designed to educate the individual to choose. (p. xiii)

The emergence of a variety of assessment tools designed to measure readiness has contributed to this trend. Such instruments as the Career Maturity Inventory (Crites, 1978), the Career Development Inventory (Super, Thompson, Lindeman, Jordaan, & Myers, 1979), the Career Skills Assessment Program (College Entrance Examination Board [CEEB], 1978), and the Career Decision Scale (Osipow, 1980) have made possible psychometric representations of indicators of readiness such as planfulness, self-appraisal, career awareness, decision-making skills, knowledge of occupations, problem solving, and implementation skills. Clients and subjects can be compared in normative fashion, and changes in status can serve as outcome criteria for studies of interventions.

Super (1983a) has argued for the salience of the readiness concept by suggesting that one needs to know whether a client is mature enough for measures of interest and values to have meaning, planful enough to make use of personal data in making educational and vocational decisions, or too remote from a vocational objective to make planning seem worthwhile. Many researchers have endorsed this point of view—though Holland surely has not (Weinrach, 1980)—and have devoted their attention to studying the various ways in which readiness can be promoted.

Smith and Evans (1973) compared a structured learning group guidance treatment with individual vocational counseling for college students who applied for career counseling or responded to the announcements of the experimental program. They found that both treatments were effective in increasing the degree of readiness to make decisions, but the structured treatment was more effective than counseling. Their measure of readiness assessed the stages of vocational development of the subjects according to a scheme based on the theory of Tiedeman and O'Hara (1963). Flake, Roach, and Stenning (1975) identified tenth-grade students who were low on Crites's (1978) measure of vocational maturity and randomly assigned them to a group that received three sessions of individual career counseling and to a control group. The counseled group significantly exceeded the control group on the posttest measure of career maturity and showed significant within-group gains. Mendonca and Siess (1976) focused on such readiness issues as amount and variety of vocational exploratory behavior, specificity of occupational preference, anxiety about vocational issues, self-estimated difficulty with vocational decisions, and problem solving. They randomly assigned undergraduate volunteers to treatments of anxiety management, problem solving, a combination of the two, placebo, and no treatment. There were no treatment effects for the anxiety measures or for difficulty with decisions. The problem-solving treatment worked best for promoting one of several problem-solving outcomes. The anxiety management and the combination treatments were most effective for promoting frequent and varied voca-

tional exploration. Egner and Jackson (1978) evaluated their career decision making structured-learning package by administering it to 161 eleventh-grade student volunteers and comparing them to 173 similar, unmotivated controls. They found that the program led to higher scores for the treated group on their career-maturity measure, but no difference from the controls on decision-making skill. There were indications that the posttest performances on both variables were influenced by IQ and by whether the subjects were from academic or nonacademic curricular tracks.

Rubinton (1980) identified 120 undergraduates who were undecided about their vocational preferences, classified them according to their decision-making styles—rational, intuitive, or dependent (Harren, 1978)—and assigned them randomly to treatments that taught decision making in rational or in intuitive ways. The subjects in the treatment groups became substantially more certain about their vocational preferences, but the treatments did not significantly enhance attitudes indicative of career maturity. For those whose career maturity did increase, the most effective subject-treatment combinations were rational style-rational treatment and intuitive style-intuitive treatment. Overall the largest gains were achieved by the rational decision makers, regardless of treatment type.

Another aspect of readiness that has interested investigators in recent years is that of cognitive complexity. In general, researchers argue that the more differentiated clients are in thinking about impending career decisions, the better equipped they are to engage in effective decision making. For example, Sarnoff and Remer (1982) classified college student subjects as rational, intuitive, and dependent decision makers and assigned them randomly to a guided-imagery treatment and a placebo control group. The criterion of interest was the number of career alternatives the subjects could generate, presumed to be a measure of ideational fluency. Their results indicated that the imagery treatment did produce more ideational fluency, regardless of decision-making style; and that rational deciders produced more career alternatives, though there were no significant style-treatment interactions.

Warner and Jepsen (1979) set out deliberately to assess the efficacy of a matching model to coordinate psychological conceptions of the subjects and the counseling methods. They divided a group of eleventh-grade volunteers into high and low levels of conceptual complexity and randomly assigned them to two group counseling treatments. The treatments consisted of identical curricula for promoting career decision making but varied in degree of structure. Their results produced a significant interaction between subject complexity and treatment structure on a measure of the cognitive complexity of post-high school plans, such that the more structured treatment worked better for the more cognitively complex subjects. There were no effects for two other criteria, career maturity and information seeking.

Bodden and James (1976) designed an experiment to assess the effects of giving occupational information on the cognitive complexity subjects used in thinking about occupations. Their findings indicated that those subjects who were given occupational information became significantly lower in cognitive differentiation when thinking about occupations. Cesari, Winer, Zychlinski, and Laird (1982) hypothesized that Bodden and James had neglected an important subject variable, decidedness-undecidedness, and so they designed a similar study to observe the influence of this moderator. They found that the decidedness variable had no influence, and furthermore the subjects given occupational information did not respond to occupations with less cognitive differentiation.

Appropriateness of Vocational Preference
It remains reasonable to assume that professional assistance with educational and vocational decision-making tasks should lead to the clients' selecting better goals. This assumption is implicit in the attempts to promote appropriate instrumental behaviors and to increase readiness for decision making already reviewed. Unfortunately, the complexities involved in creating indices of better goals have been enormous (see Myers, 1971, pp. 867–871). As a result, researchers in recent years have tended to abandon appropriateness of vocational preference as a desired outcome and concentrate instead on the more manageable and less value-laden behavioral events, such as information-seeking behavior, career maturity, or cognitive complexity. Despite this trend, a small number of investigators have concerned themselves with the question: Do treatments result in better decisions?

Hanson and Sander (1973) identified 60 rural high school boys who were judged to be unrealistic in their vocational plans. Judges classified the subjects on a five-point scale ranging from Overshooting (aspiring to an occupation beyond his capabilities) to Undershooting (could probably succeed at an occupational level higher than his aspiration), and the subjects were randomly assigned to individual career counseling of about three sessions and to group counseling that ranged from four to six sessions. After the treatments, vocational preferences were elicited and rated by three judges, whose ratings were averaged. Their analysis revealed that "overshooters" in the group treatment and "undershooters" in the individual treatment showed marked improvement toward more realistic choices, while others did not. Unfortunately, the decision rules used by the judges were not available in the report.

Mencke and Cochran (1974) conducted life-planning workshops for 64 undergraduate volunteers and anticipated that the treated groups would experience more favorable attitudes, engage in more information seeking, generate more career alternatives, and express more appropriate preferences. No gains were realized in the attitudinal criteria or in the number of alternatives generated, but the treated groups did seek more information and express vocational preferences that were more appropriate. The measure of appropriateness was an index of congruence between preferences and vocational interest on the Self-Directed Search (Holland, 1970), but the authors did not specify their rules for quantifying congruence. Zener and Schnuelle (1976), who investigated the differential effects of the Self-Directed Search and the Vocational Preference Inventory (Holland, 1965), however, did provide the rationale for arriving at measures of congruence. The scheme (Holland, 1972, p. 7) involves comparing the three highest interest scores of the subject to the three-letter codes that characterize each occupation, yielding an ordinal scale of congruence that has a range of seven points. Zener and Schnuelle found that administering the Self-Directed Search did indeed lead to more appropriate preferences, among other things, for a large sample of high school students. Fretz and Leong (1982a) also used Holland's scheme for judging congruence in their attempt to predict outcomes of administering the Self-Directed Search to undergraduate volunteers. They found that, among an array consisting of career maturity, career status, and personality measures, only one career-maturity subscale—a measure of competence at goal selection—predicted congruence for men and none predicted it for women.

Prediger and Noeth (1979) evaluated an intervention consisting of administering an interest inventory and conducting one-session group treatments focused on career planning. Their subjects were high school girls of average academic ability and above, and their purpose was to encourage the girls to reject sex-role stereotypes and consider the full range of occupations. The treated group reported more exploratory activity at four weeks after the treatment, but the differences between them and the controls disappeared at the three-month follow-up. For appropriateness of vocational preference, the treated group exceeded the controls at four weeks, but not at three months, despite the fact that a subset of the treated group was given a second intervention. Their measure of appropriateness was a seven-point scale indicating degree of congruence between measured interests and vocational preferences. They also observed that, treated or not, girls with nontraditional vocational interests tended to have less congruent vocational preferences than girls with traditional interests.

Malett, Spokane, and Vance (1978) evaluated a brief intervention consisting mostly of the Self-Directed Search and found it to be generally ineffective for improving appropriateness of vocational preference. Like most other investigators of this topic, their appropriateness index was a measure of congruence between interests and preference. Unlike the others, however, their congruence measure was based on the 1966 version of the Strong Vocational Interest Blank. A secondary analysis revealed that those subjects whose initial preferences were least appropriate gained most from pre- to posttest whether they received the treatment or not. Surprisingly, these gains were attributable not to changes in vocational preferences but rather to a tendency for measured interest to change in the direction of greater congruence with initial preferences.

SUMMARY OBSERVATIONS: STUDIES OF DECISION MAKING

A review of the outcome studies of this domain indicates clearly that investigators are not studying the sequels of individual, insight-oriented, psychotherapy-based counseling treatments with much frequency. In the 52 studies identified by Spokane and Oliver (1983), only 16 included some form of individual treatment and a far smaller number of those involved attempts to increase client insight. What is clearly evident in the current era is a strong preference to study the effects of structured learning experiences provided in groups or classes. Such learning experiences—for which the word *treatments* increasingly seems like an inappropriate descriptor—usually involve a specific curriculum, a fixed time schedule, and an opportunity for the learners to gain information about their personal characteristics. Frequently they include the teaching of developmental concepts and the opportunity to learn and practice coping skills. Relatively little attention is devoted to the impediments the learner brings to the encounter, and when they are the objects of attention it is more likely that they will be attended to with curricular modifications than with individualized attempts to help.

As others have pointed out, this is a major shift in orientation in educational and vocational counseling, or at least in the research about it. The shift may well be due to the emphasis the counseling specialty places on developmental goals, on increasing everyone's capacity to deal with the decision tasks that life in school and at work imposes. It may also stem from a relatively rapid growth of theory—no matter how imperfect—about what kinds of attitudes, competencies, and orientations are likely to lead to the successful accomplishment of those decision tasks. Certainly the shift gains momentum from the growing technology of vocational guidance, a technology that flows naturally from a historical commitment to differential psychology and to psychometric means of understanding human differences. Of course, it is also possible that outcome research on structured, programmatic interventions is easier to do than is research on the less manageable one-to-one human encounter; hence viewing educational and vocational counseling through the lens of outcome research provides some measure of distortion.

Regardless of its validity as an indicator of activity of a field, it cannot be denied that research on interventions intended to improve decision making is growing rapidly in quantity (see Spokane & Oliver, 1983, pp. 104–105). And despite the rather disapproving views of some scholars (e.g., Crites,

1983; Fretz, 1981; Goldman, 1976), a case can be made for the increasing technical adequacy of that research. The studies of the recent era give evidence of their authors' attention to issues of power by including samples of useful size. Control groups appear in almost all the recent studies, and randomized assignment to conditions is the norm. In the few cases where randomization has not been possible, appropriate precautions have been applied and appropriate cautions prescribed.

Volunteer subjects, rather than self-motivated help seekers, predominate, which may be for some a cause for concern. Yet given the nature of the interventions and the developmental intent of the intervenors, this may well be a tolerable shortcoming. When an intervention is designed and its availability is advertized, those who volunteer are likely to be the best available subjects on which to run the tests of efficacy. The fact that they are not racked with self-doubt or suffering from such psychic discomfort that they must seek professional assistance probably makes them better representatives of the potential client pool when decision making is the target behavior. Since most important career decisions can be postponed for a while without serious penalty, the potential client pool is not as likely to be characterized by strong feelings of deficit or urgency.

Almost without exception, authors of the recent studies have employed multiple outcome criteria, as Oliver (1979) advised. A number of the studies have been executed with appropriate concern for client variables that might have influenced their responses to the treatments, and there is an impressive array of attribute-treatment interaction studies for which Fretz (1981) was such a convincing advocate. Without exception treatment conditions are thoroughly described in the reports and, with few exceptions, results are comprehensively presented.

The case for the conceptual adequacy of the studies is not as easy to make. Though the design of the interventions is generally well done, the choice of outcome criteria leaves a great deal to hope for in future research. For example, it is difficult to understand why information-seeking behavior continues to intrigue so many investigators. As an indicator of exploratory behavior, the criterion has some merit, but hardly enough merit to justify its strong popularity. The usual measure is the client's own report of how many instances and how many kinds of information seeking he or she has engaged in since treatment. Simple counts of frequency and variety become the data, and the psychological meaning of such numbers is difficult to fathom. Is more always better? Are there scalar properties worth considering? (Everyone treats the counts as if they were interval scales.) Are some examples of information seeking more meaningful than others? Only Prediger and Noeth (1979) gave this question any consideration. Are the self-reports accurate? Only Hoffman et al. (1981) and Young (1979) concerned themselves with this trifle.

Perhaps it is time to put this outcome criterion to rest with the recognition that success in helping clients to increase it has been reasonably well demonstrated. After it has been retired for a while, someone may become sufficiently interested in it to make it into a more sophisticated variable by devoting attention to its psychometric properties, its conceptual place in the scheme of things, and its contribution to decision-making events that follow it.

The focus on readiness for decision making as a pretreatment variable and as an outcome criterion seems to indicate a promising direction in this research sector. In a relatively short time, investigators have recognized that clients and potential clients do indeed differ in developmental status when they make themselves available for help and that these differences have meaning for the kind of help they need and for their responses to that help. The widespread use of the omnibus measures of career maturity or career development suggests that this minor technological advance has made an important contribution to the increase in understanding how best to help young people negotiate the decision tasks that face them. What is needed now is a set of more convincing links between the readiness indicators, measures of decision-making attitudes and competencies, and subsequent deciding behavior. While these omnibus measures of readiness have been demonstrated to have impressive content validity, and reasonable concurrent validity, evidence of predictive validity ranges from scarce to nonexistent (see Hilton, 1982; Katz, 1982). Hence, though the state of the art has been advanced by the availability of tools that measure readiness, there is work to be done before achieving complacency about whether the readiness we measure is indeed an orderly precursor of the behavior we intend to promote.

Other indicators of readiness for decision making such as cognitive complexity, decisiveness, and decision-making style also suffer when one considers the degree to which they serve as criteria that adequately represent, or predict, the actual performance of interest. Though each is derived from some segment of some theoretical construction of the decision process, the empirical links have yet to be forged. Jepsen (1983), in his thoughtful treatment of career decision making, suggests that there is reason for optimism about the increasing convergence of research findings and model building. Yet he recognizes that the varieties of interventions designed to promote decision making "are offered as heuristic techniques of an art form rather than algorithms with high certainty of 'solving' personal problems" (p. 16). The need for more and better models is apparent; until that need is met, investigators could render a service if they would devote more attention to the logical argument that connects the readiness criterion they employ to the model of decision making from which it is extracted.

The intense concentration on appropriateness of vocational preference of the past has lessened noticeably in recent years. Today, most investigators are content with a simple index of congruence between measured interests and expressed vocational preference. No doubt this is due in part to the availability of the Holland scheme (1972), which vastly simplifies the decision rules for estimating appropriateness. Because people and occupations are so easily characterized by Holland's method, degrees of appropriateness are arrived at with a simple clerical operation.

It is also probable that investigators in the current era are a good bit more sophisticated about what the expression of a vocational preference stands for in the process of career decision making. No longer is the naming of an occupation one prefers considered to be an important end goal in that process. Increasingly the expression of a preference is seen as a declaration of an intention, or an expectation, to choose. Developmental views of the choice process place the expression of a preference— *specification* for Super, *clarification* for Tiedeman and O'Hara—much nearer the beginning of the process than the end of it. Whereas earlier conceptions of career counseling permitted the belief that the need for assistance ended when a preference was specified (clarified), contemporary thinking places much more emphasis on the importance of the implementing behaviors that follow. As a result, it seems, investigators have assigned a much lower priority number to the expression of an appropriate preference.

It is possible that the diminishing interest in appropriateness of vocational preference is a sign of the decreasing importance of occupations per se in vocational psychology. While occupational entry and persistence have previously served as pillars of vocational psychology, we may be witnessing the effects of a change in focus from occupational status to the process of living a life at work. Such a change would place more emphasis on the ongoing nature of decision-making tasks and, it is to be hoped, on the consequences of having made a decision and a commitment to it. The rare longitudinal studies of career development, now quite old, and a few of the newer retrospective studies (e.g., Levinson et al., 1978; Vaillant, 1977) illustrate such an emphasis. It remains absent, however, from the efforts to assess what follows from treatments intended to improve decision making.

Recent reviewers have concluded that nearly all such treatments lead to gains of one kind or another for the clients or subjects. Whether those gains are small, as Fretz (1981) maintains, or substantial, as Spokane and Oliver (1983) suggest, it is clear that more attention is needed to the theoretical and empirical meaning of the increases the clients demonstrate.

STUDIES OF ROLE FUNCTIONING

Whether educational-vocational decisions are made actively by students or imposed upon them by the structure of an educational system, they inevitably lead to a subsequent period of role enactment. Having entered a school, a university, a major field, or an occupation, one proceeds to play the required role more or less well. Counseling interventions in educational settings have frequently been directed toward a goal of increasing the effectiveness of such role functioning.

Implementing Behaviors

Role enactment necessarily requires the kinds of behaviors that permit access to the role chosen. Once one has decided on a role to be played and made a commitment to that decision, it becomes necessary to engage in acts that increase the probability of getting what one wants. Adkins (1984) has focused on promoting such endeavors among populations that need them most, out-of-school and out-of-work youth and economically disadvantaged adults. His Life Skills/Employability Program is a highly developed treatment curriculum using opportunity information, videotaped practice, and a strong component of group counseling. The target behaviors are choosing, finding, and securing a job. A number of unpublished studies, reviewed by Adkins (1984, pp. 60–64), have indicated that the program has considerable efficacy, especially for clients who have traditionally been the most difficult to influence.

Mature women preparing for entry to school and work are another group that has attracted the attention of those who seek to provide counseling services intended to help clients gain access to a chosen role. The so-called reentry woman is usually characterized as middle-aged, experiencing crisis in identity and integrity, in midlife transition characterized by self-anger, role conflict, feelings of isolation, low self-esteem, and depression (McGraw, 1982). Sandmeyer (1980) reported positive results from a three-day workshop designed to help reentry women to clarify their values, set goals, learn about their abilities and interests, and acquire job-seeking skills. Marris and Mochuzuki (1972) also achieved their goals in helping women feel supported and less isolated and improve their interpersonal relations. At follow-up, the subjects reported more goal clarity, improved self-esteem, and greater decisiveness. Brandenburg (1974), Buckey, Freeark, and O'Barr (1976), and Elshof and Kovek (1977) also reported positive effects of similar interventions, but neglected to provide the data to support the assertions of favorable outcomes. The most rigorous studies of this kind of intervention were those conducted by Berman, Gelso, Greenfeig, Hirsch (1977). In one study the clients gained significantly in decision-making maturity; in the other study self-esteem was enhanced.

Promoting the behaviors that are likely to help in securing a job has attracted the attention of a number of investigators. Speas (1979) randomly assigned 56 prisoners in a prerelease program to four treatment conditions and a control group. The treatments included a videotaped model of desirable interview behaviors, role-playing interviews, the model plus role-playing, and model plus role-playing with videotaped feedback. In general, the model plus role-play treatments, with or without feedback, produced the best interview behavior at posttest and follow-up, though all treated groups surpassed the controls. The subjects were subsequently interviewed by real personnel interviewers and rated according to the probability that they would be hired. Only the model-role-play-feedback group did better than the controls. Austin and Grant (1981) used similar treatment conditions with 60 disadvantaged college students and found that all treated groups improved and surpassed the controls on posttest interviews rated by counselors and by actual college recruiters. The treatments did not differ among themselves in effectiveness, though they did differ in cost.

Hollandsworth, Dressel, and Stevens (1977) subjected 45 college seniors to a treatment that included modeling, response rehearsal, and directed feedback, and another that consisted of didactic presentations and discussion. At the posttest interview the treated groups did better than the controls on four of the nine outcome measures, with the modeling group influencing eye contact and the discussion group influencing length of talk time, ability to explain one's skills, and openness and honesty. On the basis of these findings, Hollandsworth and Sandifer (1979) revised the treatment design and tested the revision on 4100 students in 320 workshops. Unfortunately, the only data they collected were about counselors' and students' satisfaction with the program, both of which were quite high. Stone and Geppert (1979) tested an instructional package, role-play, and a combination of the two on 40 rehabilitation clients and found that role-playing best promoted ratings of hiring probability and that all treatments produced gains over the controls. Harrison et al. (1983) tested a standard modeling treatment, alone and enhanced by giving the subjects a cognitive map and by giving them an acronym for remembering salient elements. For 55 undergraduate volunteers, both enhancements were effective in producing better job interviews three weeks after treatment.

As these recent studies illustrate, there is little doubt that willing learners can be taught to improve the social skills appropriate to a simulated job interview if they are shown what the desirable skills are and given an opportunity to practice them (see also

Sarason & Sarason, 1981). Given the variety of inventive methods for providing such service, this class of implementing behaviors should be improving noticeably in the population.

Commitment and Performance

High-risk Students

A small number of recent studies have been conducted to enhance commitment to a given role and persistence in it. Grala and McCauley (1976) tried a variety of methods to induce 32 chronic truants to return to school. They found that those who had been counseled returned to school with greater frequency than those who had been threatened or encouraged without being counseled. The effect was relatively robust at the outset, but by the fourth week only 4 of the 16 counseled students persisted. Block (1978) demonstrated that a rational-emotive group treatment had remarkably positive effects on the grades, the disruptive behavior, and the class attendance of "high-risk and failure- and misconduct-prone black and Hispanic high school students" (p. 61). A comparison treatment based on psychodynamic principles had none. Serednesky, Cahill, and Engelhart (1974) demonstrated that they could reduce a troubling dropout rate from vocational training by using an aptitude battery and vocational counseling prior to selection. Whyte (1978) was able to enhance the grades of high-risk college freshmen with study skills instruction, group counseling, and individual counseling about locus of control issues.

Study Skills

The notion that academic performance can be improved by teaching more efficient study skills remains popular. Jackson and Van Zoost (1972) were able to increase study skills with varying reinforcement conditions but observed no subsequent gains in grades. Ruppel (1979) successfully increased reading rates by incorporating principles of self-management into a reading-improvement program. Greiner and Karoly (1976) conducted study-skills training by adding to the usual content training in self-monitoring plus self-recording plus planning strategies. Subjects in the last group did best on quizzes and improved their study habits more, but grade-point averages (GPA) were not influenced. Richards (1975) added stimulus control and self-monitoring instruction to study-skills advice and

found that, for final examination scores in a psychology course, self-monitoring was helpful but stimulus control was not. Working with poor readers in junior high school, Harris and Trujillo (1975) found that self-management training worked no better than unstructured group discussions for improving grades six weeks later and not as well by the end of the semester. Finally, Richards and Perri (1978) taught study skills in combination with self-control and problem-solving skills and demonstrated the effectiveness of the problem-solving training as a treatment-maintenance strategy. Gains in GPA were maintained for a year after treatment.

There seems to be no reason to doubt that, like interviewing skills, effective study skills can be learned, even by students in introductory psychology courses who are working for participation credit. A current preference for delivering study-skills treatments accompanied by principles derived from behavior modification is obvious and seems to be increasing the effectiveness of the training (see also Lent & Russell, 1978; Mann, 1972; Mitchell & Ng, 1972). The relationship of improved study skills to overall academic performance is less certainly established, but there are some hopeful indications that one leads to the other.

Test Anxiety

In the minds of many investigators, the most virulent impediment to effective role functioning in an educational setting is being anxious about taking tests. In the last decade, enormous amounts of investigative energy have been devoted to this problem. A variety of treatment strategies have been designed, tested, and compared. A few investigators have even attempted to observe the effects of decreased test anxiety on more meaningful indicators of academic performance. For example, McMillan and Osterhouse (1972) used desensitization training with students high on test anxiety and high and low on generalized anxiety. They found that the treatment was followed by significantly higher examination grades for those students whose generalized anxiety was low. McMahon (1973) hypothesized that students who had the most detailed knowledge about their academic aptitude would experience less test anxiety and achieve higher GPAs. In fact, those students given the most detailed feedback about their aptitude had the most test anxiety and GPA was not influenced at all. Denney and Rupert

(1977) compared desensitization treatments that varied on the dimensions of active coping versus passive reciprocal inhibition and standard desensitization procedures versus self-control procedures. Subjects who got the active coping plus self-control treatment reduced their self-reported test anxiety most, and those in active coping treatments improved their GPAs subsequently. Harris and Johnson (1980) compared two types of desensitization, covert modeling and self-control, for students with high test anxiety. Both methods reduced the test anxiety, but the covert modeling treatment was the only one that was followed by improvement in GPA, which was substantial.

Those investigators who have studied the various means of reducing test anxiety without relating such reduction to academic performance have compared systematic desensitization to cognitive treatments (Kaplan, McCordick, & Twitchell, 1979; Leal, Baxter, Martin, & Marx, 1981; Reister, Stockton, & Maultsby, 1977), covert reinforcement (Kostka & Galassi, 1972), relaxation training (Chang-Liang & Denney, 1976; Russell & Wise, 1976), implosive therapy (Cornish & Dilley, 1973), hypnosis (Melnick & Russell, 1976), biofeedback (Romano & Cabianca, 1978), and psychodrama (Kipper & Giladi, 1978). Nothing beats systematic desensitization, but there are frequent ties. Some investigators have studied the effects of enriching systematic desensitization by adding self-control procedures (Deffenbacher, Mathis, & Michaels, 1979; Deffenbacher & Michaels, 1980; Deffenbacher & Parks, 1979; Spiegler et al., 1976) and anxiety management training (Deffenbacher & Michaels, 1981a, 1981b; Deffenbacher, Michaels, Daley, & Michaels, 1980; Deffenbacher, Michaels, Michaels, & Daley, 1980; Deffenbacher & Shelton, 1978; Richardson & Suinn, 1974). Adding something to the standard desensitization procedures clearly helps, especially to increase the duration of the treatment effects. Vicarious desensitization seems possible (Altmaier & Woodward, 1981), people can be desensitized in large groups (Daley, Bloom, Deffenbacher, & Steward, 1983), paraprofessionals probably can desensitize as well as professional counselors (Russell & Wise, 1976), and some counselor characteristics seem to influence outcomes (Geer & Hurst, 1976; Hudesman & Weisner, 1979).

Kirkland and Hollandsworth (1979), after viewing correlational data that suggested that examination behavior skills were the best predictor of academic performance, were moved to ask "whether anxiety interferes with effective test-taking behavior or whether the lack of effective skills results in test anxiety" (p. 435). They later designed a study to compare a skills-acquisition treatment to cue-controlled relaxation and meditation (Kirkland & Hollandsworth, 1980). In the skills treatment they taught about test anxiety as a skill deficit, emphasizing test-taking strategies, adaptive self-instructional statements, and attention-control skills. Cue-controlled relaxation was described as being designed for the control of excessive somatic reactions and meditation was described as a technique for calming the mind. The skill acquisition treatment surpassed the relaxation methods on a variety of criteria, including subsequent GPA. They concluded their report with the suggestion that it might be "time to give the phrase *test anxiety* a respectful burial and talk about inadequate test performance in terms that more accurately describe what it is, namely, ineffective test taking" (p. 438).

Overview

An enormous contribution to clarity about understanding attempts to improve role functioning in the student role is the review provided by Kirschenbaum and Perri (1982). They began by noting that an examination of previous reviews might lead to the conclusion that "the quoted percentage of studies reporting improvements in grades decreases with time" (p. 77), and that the more detailed the analysis, the less favorable the results. In their analysis they tabulated the percentage of studies resulting in improvement in four criterion categories—GPA, course grades, anxiety, and study-skill attitudes. The studies using each criterion category were divided according to intervention type—behavioral, counseling, self-control, and so on. Their tabulation shows that interventions led to improvements in about one-third of the studies using GPA and grades and about one-half of the studies using measures of anxiety and study-skills attitudes. Multiple-component interventions were generally more successful than single-component ones, behavioral interventions were best for reducing anxiety, and self-control study-skills interventions influenced attitudes most. For duration of effects, multiple-component treatments fared best.

From all the studies available, they identified 20 that they considered better controlled. The analysis of these studies suggested, again, that multicomponent treatments, especially those that included training in study skills and self-control, were the most effective. They concluded with advice about how such studies might be improved and proposed three components that describe the process of improving academic competence. These include motivators of the subjects, study-skills development, and self-regulatory skills development.

Performance at Work

Role functioning on the job and the contributions that counseling interventions can make to it are relatively recent foci for investigative concern. Osipow (1982a) has argued that the opportunities for influencing role functioning at work are rich and that counseling psychologists ought to consider those opportunities more seriously, despite a variety of existing barriers. In fact, the extent to which organizations other than schools use the techniques and procedures of counseling interventions remains something of a mystery. Attempts to solve the mystery have led to frustrating results.

Griffith (1980) attempted to find out how many of the Fortune 500 companies offered career development services and achieved a disappointing 23 percent return rate. The highly suspect numbers he was able to extract suggested that just over half the respondents provided preretirement counseling and fewer than that provided help with career planning and relocating separated employees. Estimates of how many alcohol treatment programs exist range from 1200 (Follman, 1978) to 2400 (Gibson, 1978). Estimates of fairly widespread use of preretirement counseling, at least in larger organizations, are also available (Siegel & Rives, 1978).

Regardless of how much service is available, attempts to evaluate the outcomes of rendering such service are exceedingly rare. This is probably because, as Cairo (1983) has pointed out, helping programs are accepted on the basis of the good intentions they represent, and companies have little interest in publishing the results of evaluations that do take place. (Corporate officers are not retained or promoted on the basis of their publication records.)

Alcohol treatment programs have been studied more than any other type of counseling programs for employees. Most evaluations use the same criterion for evaluating outcomes, number of counseled employees who return to work and do not relapse. Evaluations of large groups of such programs have resulted in success rates of from 50 to 90 percent (Carson, 1976; Lavino, 1978; Ralston, 1977). Though the various studies used different periods for judging "no relapse," it seems safe to assume that in general these programs have been surprisingly effective in dealing with a relatively intractable problem.

Weiner, Akabas, and Sommer (1973) studied the outcomes of counseling services provided for a variety of personal problems to 442 employees. The investigators compared these workers to a matched sample of untroubled workers and found no differences in their piece-work earnings. They concluded that job effectiveness was not diminished by being in treatment. Skidmore, Balsam, and Jones (1974) found dramatic improvement in the attendance records of troubled employees treated in their program. Weissman (1975) got high degrees of posttreatment satisfaction from treated employees. Marshall (1976) got excellent results on reducing turnover and absenteeism with a peer counselor program. Hanson (1981) reported the results of an extensive career development program including workshops, workbooks, and career counseling. Participants' self-reports indicated a variety of gains in career awareness and acceptance of personal responsibility. Six-month follow-up data revealed that participants had initiated a variety of career-enhancing developmental activities and were rated by their supervisors as improved in work quality and quantity, morale, and communication skills.

Effective role functioning while preparing to leave a role is the object of preretirement counseling programs. Boyack and Tiberi (1975) compared a number of approaches and found group counseling and lecture-discussion treatments to be most effective in improving attitudes toward retirement and lecture-discussion most effective for helping participants acquire relevant information. Glamser and DeJong (1975) found that participants in preretirement groups engaged in more preparatory activities than those who were briefed individually about retirement. O'Rourke and Friedman (1972) found no differences between participants and controls on either acquisition of retirement information or attitudes toward retirement.

As Cairo (1983) has made clear, studies of the use of counseling interventions in the workplace have serious conceptual and methodological shortcomings. As was true of the earlier outcome studies of counseling in educational settings, treatments are frequently not described in detail, criterion problems abound, and random assignment to conditions is rare. Be that as it may, it is encouraging to see the beginnings of inquiry on this important topic and the subsequent emergence of research criticisms (Cairo, 1983; Kasschau, 1974).

SUMMARY OBSERVATIONS: STUDIES OF ROLE FUNCTIONING

The studies cited in the section on role functioning illustrate attempts to assess the effectiveness of counseling interventions designed to enhance job-seeking skills and attitudes, increase commitment to a role that has been chosen or assigned, improve the skills necessary to play the role effectively, reduce debilitating anxiety that the role evokes, cope with serious problems that interfere with adequate functioning, and prepare for a satisfying departure. This array suggests that counseling interventions are considered to be potentially useful in many areas of role enactment, even when psychotherapeutic counseling to alleviate psychic discomfort or disability—not covered in this chapter—is excluded. The evidence that the interventions actually are useful seems to be generally in the positive direction, though the rigor with which the evidence was collected and interpreted varies from excellent to poor.

It is encouraging to view the successes that have been demonstrated in helping the disabled and disadvantaged learn the skills and attitudes that increase the probability of their gaining access to productive social roles. For too long investigators considered them high-risk clients and worst-case research subjects. Recently, a handful of researchers have courted the risk, assumed the worst case, and set about to test their interventions anyway. It is to be hoped that studies of this type will emerge with increasing frequency and that some of the more courageous researchers will become curious about

whether enhanced job-seeking skills and attitudes actually contribute to success in securing jobs. It is a fair assumption that they do, but only an assumption.

Similarly encouraging are the few reported successes in helping people committed to a role strengthen that commitment. Interventions that work to keep students who are likely to drop out or be thrown out of school or college in their student roles are worth replicating. And continued successes might well become the foundations of student personnel policies.

Concerning students who are at risk, it is curious to note the conspicuous absence of inquiry in recent years on academic underachievers, those students whose academic performance is significantly below the performance predicted from scholastic aptitude measures. Mitchell and Piatkowska (1974) were able to identify 29 such studies from 1962 to 1972, but attention to the problem has waned visibly since then. Perhaps Mitchell and Piatkowska diverted the trend when their analysis convinced them that the success rates for those studies and a few earlier ones were 18 percent for underachievers, 15 percent for failing achievers, and probably even lower when spontaneous recovery for controls is taken into account.

Though interest in underachievers as such has disappeared from the literature, there has been an enormous increase of interest in improving academic competence in general. Kirschenbaum and Perri (1982) were able to identify 35 intervention studies published from 1974 to 1978 and the popularity has continued unabated since then. In general, success rates for structured attempts to improve academic competence are not high, except when self-reported test anxiety is the criterion, though skillful investigators have been able to demonstrate that the gains that do occur can be maintained.

It is unfortunate that so few of the recent studies use course grades or GPA as criteria along with test anxiety and study-skills attitudes. For those who do not, the argument is that many other things go to make up a course grade or a grade composite. One can agree with that argument and empathize with researchers who want to avoid building certain failure into their experiments. Nevertheless, the essential test of an intervention designed to improve academic performance is subsequent academic performance, and it is a rare educational institution that would index academic performance with the State-Trait Anxiety Inventory, the Achievement Anxiety Test, or the Survey of Study Habits and Attitudes. A word must also be included about the overwhelming number of test anxiety studies in which Psychology 101 students under compulsion to participate are used as subjects. Of course they have the opportunity to volunteer if they have anxiety about taking tests and want to do something about it. Of course this source of subjects is honored in time. Nevertheless, a more liberal sprinkling of spontaneous (vs. reactive) help seekers would enrich the generalizations that flow from such studies.

From the point of view of design, the many studies of improving academic competence are exceedingly well done. Various treatments and various levels of given treatments are compared, subjects are randomly assigned to conditions, data analyses are appropriate, and numbers of subjects are sufficient.

In the realm of studies of interventions for improving performance at work, it is perhaps too early to expect great scientific rigor and sophisticated experimental design. For the time being, such studies will probably continue to be of the program evaluation type, relying on client satisfaction measures, usually without control groups, eschewing random assignment and the withholding of treatment, and employing opportunistic samples. There is time to wait. The introduction of counseling interventions is a recent phenomenon, and the willingness to test their efficacy is still more recent. The history of research in educational and vocational counseling would support the prediction that as investigation of counseling in business and industry increases in volume, critics will view it with alarm, investigators will be guided, and research will improve. For now we can be content with the signs of the increasing acceptance of counseling in the workplace, the early positive signs about the success of the interventions studied so far, and a literature on the topic that is growing, if only slowly.

CONCLUSION

It is always tempting to conclude a chapter such as this one with evaluative judgments about the quality of the research cited and with advice about how future research can be improved. That temptation is lessened in the present case by the fact that so many recent reviewers, cited earlier, have accomplished that task so proficiently. Though all of the available advice on how to improve the state of the art has not been heeded by every investigator, in general the recent research has been thoughtfully and rigorously designed, executed, and reported. Though one can quibble about the overrepresentation of the beleaguered introductory psychology student in the subject pool and the consequent lack of properly motivated help seekers, it must be recognized that most of the interventions evaluated were designed for helping with the normal problems of normal people. Though there is reason for disappointment in the relatively trivial nature of many of the outcome criteria chosen for such studies, it is important to remember that many of the interventions studied are short-term, weak interventions designed to bring about rather specific new learnings that are preparatory to decision making and role enactment.

It does, however, seem reasonable to ask in general and in specific terms what the recent outcome studies provide in the way of guidance to the practitioner. It is probably not intellectually honest to pretend that practitioners wait patiently while researchers explore the mysteries of the helping professions, and then approach their clients with the confidence that their practice is based on scientifically sound principles and thoroughly tested procedures. In fact, counseling as a professional activity has never advanced behind a well-established body of scientific evidence that permits its practitioners to select from methods and procedures whose differences in efficacy had been previously demonstrated. In general, the flow of influence has been in the other direction, with the research following where the practice has led.

Nevertheless, there are lessons to be learned from the rapidly growing literature on educational and vocational counseling, and informed practitioners might well find their practices improved and their sense of well-being increased if they attended to those lessons. Perhaps the most important lesson for practicing counselors is the unavoidable conclusion that what they are doing works. The number of reviewers who arrive at this conclusion continues to mount. So-called box-score tabulations of outcome studies cite success rates that are truly impressive, such as Kirschenbaum and Perri's (1982) 50 percent and 52 percent success rates for studies of test anxiety and study attitudes, and Pickering and Vacc's (1984) 79 percent success rate for short-term career development interventions and 93 percent for long-term interventions. Spokane and Oliver's (1983) meta-analysis, with an average effect size of .85, provides an even more sophisticated basis for optimism. No matter how one accumulates the evidence, there is little doubt that the various methods employed in educational and vocational counseling do indeed lead to their intended consequences. Counselors should know this fact and use it in their own behalf. Best of all, they should take comfort in the fact that the principles and procedures of their art have been tested in a rigorous fashion and have not been found wanting.

A second lesson from the recent outcome research is that educational and vocational counseling has become strongly influenced by the tenets and procedures of behavior modification. Whatever the various reasons for this development might be, its effects are clearly visible and undeniable. Citations of Meichenbaum (1977) and of D'Zurilla and Goldfried (1971) are so frequent in the counseling research literature that one must strongly suspect that they have played important roles in mediating this influence. Hershenson (1983) has explained the popularity of behavior modification within counseling by calling on the theory of history of an Italian philosopher-historian of the eighteenth centry named Giambattista Vico. According to Hershenson, Vico's notion was that history is characterized by progressive cycles of three phases: faith, logic, and power. For these phases the underlying thought patterns are acceptance, understanding, and control, respectively. In counseling, Hershenson said, we have moved from the phase of faith, during which psychoanalysis was the favored approach to counseling, through logic, when trait-and-factory theory dominated, to an era of power, with behavior modification in full sway. Hershenson fully expected that another cycle would come and speculated on what its nature would be. Unless and until the new cycle arrives, counselors would be well advised to sharpen their cognitive-behavioral tools and see that their training programs are preparing counselors with the currently popular ones.

The more specific lessons for practice are enumerated below. They represent assurance to practitioners that when their goals are to influence the various target behaviors, they need not start at the beginning. Many interventions have already been designed and evaluated, and many of them have produced desirable effects.

1. A variety of interventions has been established that enhances the probability that a client will engage in the act of seeking information about opportunities. Such interventions include test interpretations, counselor reinforcing anticipatory statements, viewing an example of someone else being reinforced, value confrontation, and training in problem solving. Client characteristics, such as motivated versus unmotivated, internal locus of control versus external, and people-oriented versus task-oriented, have been shown to influence the response to such interventions. There is some indication that clients' reports about their own information-seeking behavior are reasonably accurate. Counselors who intend to encourage this class of instrumental behavior can choose from among a considerable array of treatments and find some guidance in matching clients with varying characteristics to appropriate treatment types.

2. Certain indicators of readiness for decision making can be influenced by individual counseling, group counseling, workshop participation, and training in anxiety management and problem solving. Attempts to match treatment types to varying decision-making styles of clients have not yielded much insight.

3. Clients can be helped to express more appropriate vocational preferences by a variety of means including counseling, workshops, and interest inventories. Those who aspire too high respond best to group counseling; those who aspire too low do better in individual counseling. Simple measures of appropriateness of preference are available.

4. Effective self-presentation skills for job-seeking interviews have been taught by providing models, by role-playing, in discussion groups, and with cognitive schemes that serve as advanced organizers. The skills are easily learned, especially if the learning includes an opportunity to practice.

5. Attitudes about studying can be improved and anxiety about taking academic tests can be reduced by a variety of treatment methods, the most useful of which include training in study skills and in self-control procedures. Improvement in course grades and in GPA can also be accomplished, though it is not as likely.

Although this is a relatively modest list, it should serve to provide some measure of comfort and assistance for counselors. Furthermore, one can rest assured that this list will grow and that those methods and procedures will continue to be tested with a wider array of clients confronted with the tasks of learning.

REFERENCES

Adkins, W. R. (1984). Life skills education: A video-based counseling/learning delivery system. In D. Larson (Ed.), *Teaching psychological skills* (pp. 44–68). Monterey, CA: Brooks/Cole.

Aiken, J., & Johnston, J. A. (1973). Promoting career information seeking behaviors in college students. *Journal of Vocational Behavior, 3,* 81–87.

Altmaier, E. M., & Woodward, M. (1981). Group vicarious desensitization of test anxiety. *Journal of Counseling Psychology, 28,* 467–469.

American Psychological Association, Committee on Professional Standards. (1981a). Specialty guidelines for the delivery of services by clinical psychologists. *American Psychologist, 36,* 640–651.

American Psychological Association, Committee on Professional Standards. (1981b). Specialty guidelines for the delivery of services by counseling psychologists. *American Psychologist, 36,* 652–663.

Austin, M. F., & Grant, T. N. (1981). Interview training for college students disadvantaged in the labor market: Comparison of five instructional techniques. *Journal of Counseling Psychology, 28,* 72–75.

Bartol, K. M. (1981). Vocational behavior and career development, 1980: A review. *Journal of Vocational Behavior, 19,* 123–162.

Baumgardner, S. R. (1977). Vocational planning:The great swindle. *Personnel and Guidance Journal, 56,* 17–22.

Bergin, A. E., & Garfield, S. L. (Eds.). (1971). *Handbook of psychotherapy and behavior change: An empirical analysis.* New York: Wiley.

Berman, M. R., Gelso, C. J., Greenfeig, B. R., & Hirsch, R. (1977). The efficacy of supportive learning environments for returning women: An empirical evaluation. *Journal of Counseling Psychology, 24,* 324–331.

Betz, E. L. (1977). Vocational behavior and career development, 1976: A review. *Journal of Vocational Behavior, 11,* 129–152.

Block, J. (1978). Effects of a rational-emotive mental health program on poorly achieving, disruptive high school students. *Journal of Counseling Psychology, 25,* 61–65.

Bodden, J. L., & James, L. E. (1976). Influence of occupational information giving on cognitive complexity. *Journal of Counseling Psychology, 23,* 280–282.

Borgen, F. H. (1984). Counseling psychology. *Annual Review of Psychology, 35,* 579–604.

Borman, C. (1972). Effects of a reinforcement style of counseling on information-seeking behavior. *Journal of Vocational Behavior, 2,* 255–259.

Boyack, V. L., & Tiberi, M. A. (1975, Oct.). *A study of pre-retirement education.* Paper presented at a meeting of the Gerontological Society, Louisville, KY.

Brandenburg, J. B. (1974). The needs of women returning to school. *Personnel and Guidance Journal, 53,* 11–18.

Buckey, A., Freeark, K., & O'Barr, J. (1976). Support for returning students. *Adult Leadership, 25,* 21–23.

Cairo, P. C. (1983). Counseling in industry: A selected review of the literature. *Personnel Psychology, 36,* 1–18.

Campbell, R. E., Connell, J. B., Kimmel Boyle, K., & Bhaerman, R. D. (1983). *Enhancing career development: Recommendations for action.* Columbus, OH: National Center for Research in Vocational Education.

Carson, J. H. (1976). Helping industry get rid of its hangover. *Industry Week, 190,* 44–49.

Chang-Liang, R., & Denney, D. R. (1976). Applied relaxation as training in self-control. *Journal of Counseling Psychology, 23,* 183–189.

Cesari, J. P., Winer, J. L., Zychlinski, F., & Laird, I. O. (1982). Influence of occupational information giving on cognitive complexity in decided versus undecided students. *Journal of Vocational Behavior, 21,* 224–230.

College Entrance Examination Board. (1978). *Handbook for Career Skills Assessment Program.* New York: Author.

Cornish, R. D., & Dilley, J. S. (1973). Comparison of three methods of reducing test anxiety: Systematic desensitization, implosive therapy, and study counseling. *Journal of Counseling Psychology, 20,* 499–503.

Crites, J. O. (1978). *Career maturity inventory.* Monterey, CA: CTB/McGraw-Hill.

Crites, J. O. (1983). Research methods in vocational psychology. In W. B. Walsh & S. H. Osipow (Eds.), *Handbook of vocational psychology, Vol. 1, Foundations* (pp. 303–353). Hillsdale, NJ: Erlbaum.

Daley, P. C., Bloom, L. J., Deffenbacher, J. L., & Stewart, R. (1983). Treatment effectiveness of anxiety management training in small and large group formats. *Journal of Counseling Psychology, 30,* 104–107.

Deffenbacher, J. L., Mathis, H., & Michaels, A. C. (1979). Two self-control procedures in the reduction of targeted and nontargeted anxieties. *Journal of Counseling Psychology, 26,* 120–127.

Deffenbacher, J. L., & Michaels, A. C. (1980). Two self-control procedures in the reduction of targeted and nontargeted anxieties—A year later. *Journal of Counseling Psychology, 27,* 9–15.

Deffenbacher, J. L., & Michaels, A. C. (1981a). Anxiety management training and self-control desensitization—15 months later. *Journal of Counseling Psychology, 28,* 459–462.

Deffenbacher, J. L., & Michaels, A. C. (1981b). A 12-month follow-up of homogeneous and heterogeneous anxiety management training. *Journal of Counseling Psychology, 28,* 463–466.

Deffenbacher, J. L., Michaels, A. C., Daley, P. C., & Michaels, T. (1980). A comparison of homogeneous and heterogeneous anxiety management training. *Journal of Counseling Psychology, 27,* 630–634.

Deffenbacher, J. L., Michaels, A. C., Michaels, T., & Daley, P. C. (1980). Comparison of anxiety management training and self-control desensitization.

Journal of Counseling Psychology, 27, 232–239.

Deffenbacher, J. L., & Parks, D. H. (1979). A comparison of traditional and self-control desensitization. *Journal of Counseling Psychology, 26,* 93–97.

Deffenbacher, J. L., & Shelton, J. L. (1978). Comparison of anxiety management training and desensitization in reducing test and other anxieties. *Journal of Counseling Psychology, 25,* 277–282.

Denney, D. R., & Rupert, P. A. (1977). Desensitization and self-control in the treatment of test anxiety. *Journal of Counseling Psychology, 24,* 272–280.

D'Zurilla, T. J., & Goldfried, M. R. (1971). Problem solving and behavior modification. *Journal of Abnormal Psychology, 78,* 107–126.

Egner, J. R., & Jackson, D. J. (1978). Effectiveness of a counseling intervention program for teaching career decision-making skills. *Journal of Counseling Psychology, 25,* 45–52.

Elshof, A. T., & Kovek, C. (1977). Providing a reentry bridge for women: A need-centered continuing education program. *Adult Leadership, 25,* 239–241.

Fisher, T. J., Reardon, R. C., & Burck, H. D. (1976). Increasing information-seeking behavior with a model-reinforced videotape. *Journal of Counseling Psychology, 23,* 234–238.

Flake, M. H., Roach, A. J., Jr., & Stenning, W. F. (1975). Effects of short-term counseling on career maturity of tenth-grade students. *Journal of Vocational Behavior, 6,* 73–80.

Follman, J. F., Jr. (1978). *Helping the troubled employee.* New York: AMACOM.

Fretz, B. R. (1981). Evaluating the effectiveness of career interventions [Monograph]. *Journal of Counseling Psychology, 28,* 77–89.

Fretz, B. R. (1982). Perspective and definitions. *The Counseling Psychologist, 10,* 15–19.

Fretz, B. R., & Leong, F. T. (1982a). Career development states as a predictor of career interventions. *Journal of Counseling Psychology, 29,* 388–393.

Fretz, B. R., & Leong, F. T. L. (1982b). Vocational behavior and career development, 1981: A review. *Journal of Vocational Behavior, 21,* 123–163.

Garbin, A. P., & Stover, R. G. (1980). Vocational behavior and career development, 1979: A review. *Journal of Vocational Behavior, 17,* 125–170.

Gelso, C. J. (1979). Research in counseling: Methodological and professional issues. *The Counseling Psychologist, 8*(3), 7–35.

Geer, C. A., & Hurst, J. C. (1976). Counselor-subject sex variables in systematic desensitization. *Journal of Counseling Psychology, 23,* 296–301.

Gibson, W. D. (1978). They're bringing problem drinkers out of the closet. *Chemical Week, 123,* 85–91.

Glamser, F. D., & DeJong, G. F. (1975). The efficacy of pre-retirement preparation programs for industrial workers. *Journal of Gerontology, 39,* 595–600.

Goldman, L. (1976). A revolution in counseling research. *Journal of Counseling Psychology, 23,* 543–552.

Goldman, L. (Ed.). (1978). *Research methods for counselors.* New York: Wiley.

Gould, R. L. (1978). *Transformations: Growth and change in adult life.* New York: Simon & Schuster.

Grala, C., & McCauley, C. (1976). Counseling truants back to school: Motivation combined with a program for action. *Journal of Counseling Psychology, 23,* 166–169.

Greiner, J. M., & Karoly, P. (1976). Effects of self-control training on study activity and adademic performance: An analysis of self-monitoring, self-reward, and systematic planning components. *Journal of Counseling Psychology, 23,* 495–502.

Griffith, A. R. (1980). A survey of career development in corporations. *Personnel and Guidance Journal, 58,* 537–542.

Hanson, J. T., & Sander, D. L. (1973). Differential effects of individual and group counseling on realism of vocational choice. *Journal of Counseling Psychology, 20,* 541–544.

Hanson, M. C. (1981). Career counseling in organizations. In D. H. Montross & C. J. Shinkman (Eds.), *Career development in the 80's* (pp. 379–392). Springfield, IL: Charles C. Thomas.

Harren, V. A. (1978). *Assessment of career decision-making (ACDM): Counselor/instructor guide.* Unpublished manuscript, Southern Illinois University, Carbondale, IL.

Harren, V. A. (1979). A model of career decision making for college students. *Journal of Vocational Behavior, 14,* 119–133.

Harris, G., & Johnson, S. B. (1980). Comparison of individualized covert modeling, self-control, desensitization, and study skills training for alleviation of test anxiety. *Journal of Consulting and Clinical Psychology, 48,* 186–194.

Harris, M. B., & Trujillo, A. E. (1975). Improving study habits of junior high school students through self-management versus group discussion. *Journal of Counseling Psychology, 22,* 513–517.

Harrison, R. P., Horan, J. J., Torretti, W., Gamble, K., Terzella, J., & Weir, E. (1983). Separate and combined effects of a cognitive map and a symbolic code in the learning of a modeled social skill (job interviewing). *Journal of Counseling Psychology, 30,* 499–505.

Herr, E. L. (1982a). Foreword. In J. T. Kapes & M. M. Mastie (Eds.), *A counselor's guide to vocational guidance instruments* (pp. xiii–xiv). Falls Church, VA: National Vocational Guidance Association.

Herr, E. L. (1982b). The effects of guidance and counseling: Three domains. In E. L. Herr & N. M. Pinson (Eds.), *Foundations for policy in guidance and counseling.* Falls Church, VA: American Personnel and Guidance Association.

Hershenson, D. B. (1983). A Viconian interpretation of psychological counseling. *Personnel and Guidance Journal, 62,* 3–9.

Hilton, T. L. (1982). Career Development Inventory. In J. T. Kapes & M. M. Mastie (Eds.), *A counselor's guide to vocational guidance instruments* (pp. 118–121). Falls Church, VA: National Vocational Guidance Association.

Hoffman, M. A., Spokane, A. R., & Magoon, T. M. (1981). Effects of feedback mode on counseling outcomes using the Strong-Campbell Interest Inventory: Does the counselor really matter? *Journal of Counseling Psychology, 28,* 119–125.

Holcomb, W. R., & Anderson, W. P. (1977). Vocational guidance research: A five-year overview. *Journal of Vocational Behavior, 10,* 341–346.

Holland, J. L. (1965). *Manual for the Vocational Preference Inventory* (6th ed.). Palo Alto, CA: Consulting Psychologists Press.

Holland, J. L. (1970). *The Self-directed Search: A guide to educational and vocational planning.* Palo Alto, CA: Consulting Psychologists Press.

Holland, J. L. (1972). *Professional manual for the Self-directed Search.* Palo Alto, CA: Consulting Psychologists Press.

Holland, J. L. (1973). *Making vocational choices: A theory of careers.* Englewood Cliffs, NJ: Prentice-Hall.

Holland, J. R., Magoon, T. M., & Spokane, A. R. (1981). Counseling psychology: Career interventions, research, and theory. *Annual Review of Psychology, 32,* 279–305.

Hollandsworth, J. G., Jr., Dressel, M. E., & Stevens, T. (1977). Use of behavioral versus traditional procedures for increasing job interview skills. *Journal of Counseling Psychology, 24,* 503–510.

Hollandsworth, J. G., Jr., & Sandifer, B. A. (1979). Behavioral training for increasing effective job interview skills: Follow-up and evaluation. *Journal of Counseling Psychology, 26,* 448–450.

Hudesman, J., & Wiesner, E. (1979). The effect of counselor anxiety on the systematic desensitization of test-anxious college students. *Journal of College Student Personnel, 20,* 415–418.

Jackson, B., & Van Zoost, B. (1972). Changing study behaviors through reinforcement contingencies. *Journal of Counseling Psychology, 19,* 192–195.

Jepsen, D. A. (1983). Career decision making. In L. W. Harmon (Ed.), *Using information in career development: From cognitions to computers* (pp. 13–22). Columbus, OH: National Center for Research in Vocational Education.

Jordaan, J. P., & Heyde, M. G. (1979). *Vocational maturity during the high school years.* New York: Teachers College Press.

Jordaan, J. P., Myers, R. A., Layton, W. C., & Morgan, H. H. (1968). *The counseling psychologist.* Washington, DC: American Psychological Association.

Kaplan, R. M., McCordick, S. M., & Twitchell, M. (1979). Is it the cognitive or the behavioral component which makes cognitive-behavior modification effective in test anxiety? *Journal of Counseling Psychology, 26,* 371–377.

Kasschau, P. (1974). Re-evaluating the need for retirement preparation programs. *Industrial Gerontology, 1,* 42–59.

Katz, M. R. (1982). Career Maturity Inventory. In J. T. Kapes & M. M. Mastie (Eds.), *A counselor's guide to vocational guidance instruments* (pp. 122–125). Falls Church, VA: National Vocational Guidance Association.

Kipper, D. A., & Giladi, D. (1978). Effectiveness of structured psychodrama and systematic desensitization in reducing test anxiety. *Journal of Counseling Psychology, 25,* 499–505.

Kirkland, K., & Hollandsworth, J. G., Jr. (1979). Test anxiety, study skills, and academic performance. *Journal of College Student Personnel, 20,* 431–436.

Kirkland, K., & Hollandsworth, J. G., Jr. (1980). Effective test taking: Skills-acquisition versus anxiety-reduction techniques. *Journal of Consulting and Clinical Psychology, 48,* 431–439.

Kirschenbaum, D. S., & Perri, M. G. (1982). Improving academic competence in adults: A review of recent research. *Journal of Counseling Psychology, 29,* 76–94.

Kivlighan, D. M., Jr., Hageseth, J. A., Tipton, R. M., & McGovern, T. V. (1981). Effects of matching treatment approaches and personality types in group vocational counseling. *Journal of Counseling Psychology, 28,* 315–320.

Kostka, M. P., & Galassi, J. P. (1972). Group systematic desensitization versus covert positive reinforcement in the reduction of test anxiety. *Journal of Counseling Psychology, 21,* 464–468.

Krivatsky, S. E., & Magoon, T. M. (1976). Differential effects of three vocational counseling treatments. *Journal of Counseling Psychology, 23,* 112–118.

Krumboltz, J. D. (1979). A social learning theory of career decision making. In A. M. Mitchell, G. B. Jones, & J. D. Krumboltz (Eds.), *Social learning and career decision making* (pp. 19–49). Cranston, RI: Carroll Press.

Krumboltz, J D., Becker-Haven, J. F., & Burnett, K. F. (1979). Counseling psychology. *Annual Review of Psychology, 30,* 555–602.

Krumboltz, J. D., & Schroeder, W. W. (1965). Promoting career planning through reinforcement. *Personnel and Guidance Journal, 44,* 19–25.

Krumboltz, J. D., & Thoresen, C. E. (1964). The effect of behavioral counseling in group and individual settings on information-seeking behavior. *Journal of Counseling Psychology, 11,* 324–333.

Lavino, J. J. (1978). Personal assistance program. *The Personnel Administrator, 23,* 35–36.

Leal, L. L., Baxter, E. G., Martin, J., & Marx, R. W. (1981). Cognitive modification and systematic desensitization with test anxious high school students. *Journal of Counseling Psychology, 25,* 525–528.

Lent, R. W., & Russell, R. K. (1978). Treatment of test-anxiety by cue-controlled desensitization and study-skills training. *Journal of Counseling Psychology, 25,* 217–224.

Levinson, D. J., Darrow, C. N., Klein, E. B., Levinson, M. H., & McKee, B. (1978). *The seasons of a man's life.* New York: Knopf.

Malett, S. D., Spokane, A. R., & Vance, F. L. (1978). Effects of vocational relevant information on the expressed and measured interest of freshmen males. *Journal of Counseling Psychology, 25,* 292–298.

Mann, J. (1972). Vicarious desensitization of test anxiety through observation of videotaped treatment. *Journal of Counseling Psychology, 19,* 1–7.

Marris, L. G., & Mochuzuki, J. (1972). Search for fulfillment: A program for adult women. *Personnel and Guidance Journal, 50,* 594–599.

Marshall, P. B. (1976). Employee counselors: Opening new lines of communication. *The Personnel Administrator, 21,* 44–48.

McGraw, L. K. (1982). A selected review of programs and counseling interventions for the reentry woman. *Personnel and Guidance Journal, 60,* 469–472.

McMahon, M. P. (1973). Effects of knowledge of ability test results on academic performance and test anxiety. *Journal of Counseling Psychology, 20,* 247–249.

McMillan, J. R., & Osterhouse, R. A. (1972). Specific and generalized anxiety as determinants of outcomes with desensitization of test anxiety. *Journal of Counseling Psychology, 19,* 518–521.

Meichenbaum, D. (1977). *Cognitive-behavior modification: An integrated approach.* New York: Plenum.

Melnick, J., & Russell, R. W. (1976). Hypnosis versus

systematic desensitization in the treatment of test anxiety. *Journal of Counseling Psychology, 23,* 291–295.

Mencke, R. A., & Cochran, D. J. (1974). Impact of a counseling outreach workshop on vocational development. *Journal of Counseling Psychology, 21,* 185–190.

Mendonca, J. D., & Siess, T. F. (1976). Counseling for indecisiveness: Problem-solving and anxiety-management training. *Journal of Counseling Psychology, 23,* 339–347.

Miller-Tiedeman, A. L., & Tiedeman, D. V. (1982). *Career development: Journey into personal power.* Schenectady, NY:Character Research Press.

Mitchell, K. R., & Ng, K. T. (1972). Effects of group counseling and behavior therapy on the academic achievement of test-anxious students. *Journal of Counseling Psychology, 19,* 491–497.

Mitchell, K. R., & Piatkowska, O. E. (1974). Effects of group treatment for college underachievers and bright failing underachievers. *Journal of Counseling Psychology, 21,* 494–501.

Morrill, W. H., Oetting, E. R., & Hurst, J. C. (1974). Dimensions of counselor functioning. *The Personnel and Guidance Journal, 56,* 354–359.

Muchinsky, P. M. (1983). Vocational behavior and career development, 1982: A review. *Journal of Vocational Behavior, 23,* 123–178.

Myers, R. A. (1971). Research on educational and vocational counseling. In A. E. Bergin & S. L. Garfield (Eds.), *Handbook of psychotherapy and behavior change: An empirical analysis* (pp. 863–891). New York: Wiley.

Oliver, L. (1979). Outcome measurement in career counseling research. *Journal of Counseling Psychology, 26,* 217–226.

O'Rourke, J. F., & Friedman, H. L. (1972). An inter-union preretirement training program. *Industrial Gerontology,* Spring, 49–64.

Osipow, S. H. (1976). Vocational behavior and career development, 1975: A review. *Journal of Vocational Behavior, 9,* 129–145.

Osipow, S. H. (1980). *Manual for the Career Decision Scale* (2nd ed.). Columbus, OH: Marathon Consulting & Press.

Osipow, S. H. (1982a). Counseling psychology: Applications in the world of work. *The Counseling Psychologist, 10*(3), 19–25.

Osipow, S. H. (1982b). Research in career counseling: An analysis of issues and problems. *The Counseling Psychologist, 10*(4), 27–34.

Parsons, F. (1909). *Choosing a vocation.* Boston: Houghton-Mifflin.

Pepinsky, H. B. (1979). Second thoughts about research in counseling. *The Counseling Psychologist, 8*(3), 47–49.

Pepinsky, H. B., & Meara, N. M. (1973). Student development and counseling. *Annual Review of Psychology, 24,* 117–150.

Phillips, S. D., & Strohmer, D. C. (1982). Decision-making style and vocational maturity. *Journal of Vocational Behavior, 20,* 215–222.

Pickering, J. W., & Vacc, N. A. (1984). Effectiveness of career interventions for college students: A review of published research. *Vocational Guidance Quarterly, 32,* 149–159.

Prediger, D. J., & Noeth, R. J. (1979). Effectiveness of a

brief counseling intervention in stimulating vocational exploration. *Journal of Vocational Behavior, 14,* 352–368.

Ralston, A. (1977). Employee alcoholism: Response of the largest industrials. *The Personnel Administrator, 22,* 50–56.

Reister, B. W., Stockton, R. A., & Maultsby, M. C. (1977). Counseling the test anxious: An alternative. *Journal of College Student Personnel, 18,* 506–510.

Richards, C. S. (1975). Behavior modification of studying through study skills advice and self-control procedures. *Journal of Counseling Psychology, 22,* 431–436.

Richards, C. S., & Perri, M. G. (1978). Do self-control treatments last? An evaluation of behavioral problem solving and faded counselor contact as treatment maintenance strategies. *Journal of Counseling Psychology, 25,* 376–383.

Richardson, F. C., & Suinn, R. M. (1974). Effects of two short-term desensitization methods in the treatment of test anxiety. *Journal of Counseling Psychology, 21,* 457–458.

Romano, J. L., & Cabianca, W. A. (1978). EMG biofeedback training versus systematic desensitization for test anxiety reduction. *Journal of Counseling Psychology, 25,* 8–13.

Rosenthal, R. (1980). Summarizing significance levels. In R. Rosenthal (Ed.), *Quantitative assessment of research domains* (pp. 33–46). San Francisco: Jossey-Bass.

Rubinton, N. (1980). Instruction in career decision making and decision-making styles. *Journal of Counseling Psychology, 27,* 581–588.

Ruppel, G. (1979). Self-management and reading rate improvement. *Journal of Counseling Psychology, 26,* 451–454.

Russell, R. K., & Wise, F. (1976). Treatment of speech anxiety by cue-controlled relaxation and desensitization with professional and paraprofessional counselors. *Journal of Counseling Psychology, 23,* 583–586.

Ryan, T. A., & Krumboltz, J. D. (1964). Effect of planned reinforcement counseling on client decision-making behavior. *Journal of Counseling Psychology, 11,* 315–323.

Sandmeyer, L. E. (1980). "Choices and changes": A workshop for women. *Vocational Guidance Quarterly, 28,* 352–359.

Sarason, I. G., & Sarason, B. R. (1981). Teaching cognitive and social skills to high school students. *Journal of Consulting and Clinical Psychology, 49,* 908–918.

Sarnoff, D., & Remer, P. (1982). The effects of guided imagery on the generation of career alternatives. *Journal of Vocational Behavior, 21,* 299–308.

Schlossberg, N. K. (1976). The case for counseling adults. *The Counseling Psychologist, 6*(1), 33–36.

Serednesky, G., Cahill, L., & Engelhart, C. I. (1974). Effectiveness of the GATB and counseling combined: Reducing vocational training dropout rates. *Journal of Employment Counseling, 11,* 10–12.

Siegel, S. R., & Rives, J. M. (1978). Characteristics of existing and planned pre-retirement programs. *Aging and Work, 2,* 93–99.

Skidmore, R. A., Balsam, D., & Jones, O. F. (1974). Social work practices in industry. *Social Work, 3,*

280–286.

Smith, M. L., & Glass, G. V. (1977). Meta-analysis of psychotherapy outcome studies. *American Psychologist, 32,* 752–760.

Smith, M. L., Glass, G. V., & Miller, T. I. (1980). *The benefits of psychotherapy.* Baltimore, MD: Johns Hopkins University Press.

Smith, R. D., & Evans, J. R. (1973). Comparison of experimental group guidance and individual counseling as facilitators of vocational development. *Journal of Counseling Psychology, 20,* 202–208.

Speas, C. M. (1979). Job-seeking interview skills training: A comparison of four instructional techniques. *Journal of Counseling Psychology, 26,* 405–412.

Spiegler, M. D., Cooley, E. J., Marshall, G. J., Prince II, H. T., Puckett, S. P., & Skenazy, J. A. (1976). A self-control versus a countercondition paradigm for systematic desensitization: An experimental comparison. *Journal of Counseling Psychology, 23,* 83–86.

Spokane, A. R., & Oliver, L. W. (1983). The outcomes of vocational interventions. In S. H. Osipow & W. B. Walsh (Eds.), *Handbook of vocational psychology* (pp. 99–136). Hillsdale, NJ: Erlbaum.

Stone, C. I., & Geppert, C. C. (1979). Job-interviewing skills training: An empirical investigation of two methods. *Rehabilitation Counseling Bulletin, 22,* 396–401.

Super, D. E. (1953). A theory of vocational development. *American Psychologist, 8,* 185–190.

Super, D. E. (1980). A life-span, life-space approach to career development. *Journal of Vocational Behavior, 16,* 282–298.

Super, D. E. (1983a). Assessment in career guidance: Toward a truly developmental counseling. *Personnel and Guidance Journal, 61,* 555–562.

Super, D. E. (1983b). History and development of vocational psychology: A personal perspective. In S. H. Osipow & W. B. Walsh (Eds.), *Handbook of vocational psychology* (pp. 5–37). Hillsdale, NJ: Erlbaum.

Super, D. E. (1984). Career and life development. In D. Brown & L. Brooks (Eds.), *Career choice and development* (pp. 192–234). San Francisco: Jossey-Bass.

Super, D. E., & Hall, D. T. (1978). Career development: Exploration and planning. *Annual Review of Psychology, 29,* 333–372.

Super, D. E., Thompson, A. S., Lindeman, R. H., Jordaan, J. P., & Myers, R. A. (1979). *Career Development Inventory.* Palo Alto, CA: Consulting Psychologists Press.

Thoresen, C. E., & Anton, J. L. (1974). Intensive experimental research in counseling. *Journal of Counseling Psychology, 21,* 553–559.

Thoresen, C. E., & Krumboltz, J. D. (1967). Relationship of counselor reinforcement of selected responses to external behavior. *Journal of Counseling Psychology, 14,* 140–144.

Thoresen, C. E., Krumboltz, J. D., & Varenhorst, B. (1967). Sex of counselors and models: Effect on client career exploration. *Journal of Counseling Psychology, 14,* 503–508.

Tiedeman, D. V. (1983). Flexible filing, computers, and growing. *The Counseling Psychologist, 11*(4), 33–47.

Tiedeman, D. V., & Miller-Tiedeman, A. (1984). Career decision making: An individualistic perspective. In D. Brown & L. Brooks (Eds.), *Career choice and development* (pp. 281–310). San Francisco: Jossey-Bass.

Tiedeman, D. V., & O'Hara, R. P. (1963). *Career development: Choice and adjustment.* New York: College Entrance Examination Board.

Vaillant, G. E. (1977). *Adaptation to life.* Boston: Little, Brown.

Walsh, W. B. (1979). Vocational behavior and career development, 1978: A review. *Journal of Vocational Behavior, 15,* 119–154.

Warner, S G., & Jepsen, D. A. (1979). Differential effects of conceptual level and group counseling on adolescent career decision-making procedures. *Journal of Counseling Psychology, 26,* 497–503.

Weinter, H. J., Akabas, S. H., & Sommer, J. J. (1973). *Mental health care in the world of work.* New York: Associated Press.

Weinrach, S. G. (1980). Have hexagon will travel: An interview with John Holland. *Personnel and Guidance Journal, 58,* 406–414.

Weissman, A. (1975). A social service strategy in industry. *Social Work, 5,* 401–403.

Whiteley, J. M., Burkhart, M. Q., Harway-Herman, M., & Whiteley, R. M. (1975). Counseling and student development. *Annual Review of Psychology, 26,* 337–366.

Whyte, C. B. (1978). Effective counseling methods for high-risk college freshmen. *Measurement and Evaluation in Guidance, 10,* 198–200.

Young, R. A. (1979). The effects of value confrontation and reinforcement counseling on the career planning attitudes and behavior of adolescent males. *Journal of Vocational Behavior, 15,* 1–11.

Zener, T. B., & Schnuelle, L. (1976). Effects of the Self-directed Search on high school students. *Journal of Counseling Psychology, 23,* 353–359.

Zytowski, D. G. (1978). Vocational behavior and career development, 1977: A review. *Journal of Vocational Behavior, 13,* 141–162.

17

RESEARCH ON MENTAL HEALTH INTERVENTIONS WITH THE DISADVANTAGED

RAYMOND P. LORION

University of Maryland

ROBERT D. FELNER

University of Illinois

OVERVIEW

Nearly a decade has passed since the original version of this chapter was written (Lorion, 1978). Research findings presented at that time nourished the hope that during the coming decade significant increments would occur in our understanding of the nature and resolution of the emotional and behavioral problems of the disadvantaged. That chapter's conclusion reflected that optimism:

> It is appropriate to end this chapter with a reassertion of the cautious optimism with which I began. I believe that we have made significant progress during the past decade in our attempts to provide for the mental health needs of the disadvantaged. Viewed from a historical perspective, it is apparent that we have identified the existence of a problem, delineated some of its most salient pa-

rameters, and begun to design and, to a limited degree, assess a variety of alternative solutions. Our efforts thus far have been unsystematic and inefficient, but is that not the typical pattern of the early stages of scientific pursuits? As we attempt to provide simple solutions to complex problems, the inadequacy of our knowledge has become evident and the limitations of our findings [have] become apparent. Nevertheless, recognition of the parameters involved in the delivery of services to the disadvantaged has increased significantly during the past two decades, and further progress in the area is inevitable. The relative unpopularity of research on the needs and services of the disadvantaged during recent years may reflect the acceptance of earlier pessimism about their appropriateness for, and responsive-

739

ness to, the mental health system. Hopefully, the material in this chapter will contribute to a renewal of interest in the design and conduct of systematic clinical, observational and empirical efforts focusing on the mental health of the disadvantaged. *(Lorion, 1978, p. 932, italics added).*

Unfortunately, the predictions emphasized in the quotation remain unfulfilled. As will be evident in the sections that follow, the identification of effective treatment approaches for the disadvantaged has been, to say the least, neither a popular nor a coordinated activity for mental health researchers. Over the past decade, only limited additions have been made to our scientific understanding of the nature and treatment of mental disorders and behavioral dysfunctions among the disadvantaged. Objectively, it is difficult to remain even guardedly optimistic about eventual achievement of the aforementioned goals. Yet we continue to hope that mental health services can become truly prescriptive (Goldstein & Stein, 1976), pluralistic (Acosta, Yamamoto, & Evans, 1982; Giordano, 1973, 1976), and cost-effective (Lerner, 1972).

In reviewing what has been accomplished thus far and in proposing a research agenda for the coming decade, we thought it appropriate to examine the conceptual basis of work to date. Upon reflection, it became quickly apparent that the earlier predictions and much of their empirical and clinical foundation reflected three major unstated assumptions. Foremost among these was the focus on *direct* (i.e., psychotherapeutic) as opposed to indirect (e.g., consultation) services as the solution of choice for responding to the mental health needs of the disadvantaged. Thus, the "problem" was defined as an incorrect match between psychotherapy strategy and patient. Presumably, therefore, the proper "solution" would correct this mismatch. A second assumption related to the focus on established disorder. To date, emphasis has been placed on *how* to intervene with the disadvantaged rather than *when.* Finally, poverty *qua* poverty was assumed to be a significant obstacle to seeking, obtaining, and remaining in treatment. Yet poverty's contribution to the development and maintenance of psychopathology was not examined. As a result, prior efforts have identified strategies for increasing access, acceptance, and the relevance of services but have not

sought to alter potentially important underlying causes of low-income needs.

Garfield's (1971; Chapter 6 this volume) review of client factors that influence therapeutic outcome provides direct evidence of the fact that the "problem" remains. His report documents that low-income status continues to relate negatively and significantly to obtaining and remaining in treatment. Other investigators provide further data on the extent of the problem. For example, middle-class and majority therapists continue to report negative expectations regarding the likely outcome of their treatment with low-income and minority clients (Turner & Armstrong, 1981). Moreover, some therapists-in-training express very directly their preference for middle- and upper-income patients and for working in private rather than public settings (Kahn, McWilliams, Balch, Chang, & Ireland, 1976). Finally, analogue studies continue to reveal the salience of a patient's economic status to the therapist's diagnostic and prognostic decisions (Benefee, Abramowitz, Weitz, & Armstrong, 1976; Lewis, Balla, & Shanok, 1979; Settin & Bramel, 1981). In combination, these findings argue for both renewed effort and a new perspective on the link between emotional health and economic status. Toward these goals, this chapter examines the assumptions mentioned in terms of their salience to work done thus far and their heuristic potential for subsequent research efforts.

SOCIAL STRATIFICATION PROCEDURES

Preliminary to our discussion, it is important to point out the absence in the mental health literature of a shared operational definition for socioeconomic status (SES) generally and low SES (LSES) specifically. Sociologists speak at length about the conceptual and methodological complexities associated with social stratification (e.g., Bergel, 1962; Bottomore, 1966; Matras, 1984). Yet little of this discussion has been incorporated into mental health research traditions. As a consequence, the rationale for selecting one stratification procedure rather than another is rarely, if ever, provided. Frequently, the primary criterion appears to be expediency, justified perhaps by the perceived self-evident quality of the concept. As a consequence, the mental health literature includes SES distinctions among individuals based only on eligibility for public assistance without, for example, simultaneous consideration of the individual's prior educational or occupational history, only on census characteristics of a neighborhood or school without consideration of the heterogeneity of its residents or students, or only on self-report data without consideration that an unemployed college student's family background is highly relevant to SES determination. Other studies differentiate subjects on the basis of the reported income of the "head of the household" without consideration of the spouses's earnings or based on levels of public assistance support without consideration of other (often informal) sources of income. Additionally, a number of researchers differentiate SES based on ratings of "occupational status" along continua designed specifically for a particular study or on the basis of self-reported assignment to global occupational categories such as "blue collar," "clerical," or "skilled labor." The consequence of this heterogeneity is that the generalizability of much research in this area is unnecessarily limited and apparent (dis-) confirmation of findings unreplicable because of overlap across seemingly distinct social strata.

The solution to this morass requires an appreciation of the inherent complexity of SES differentiation. The concept is multidimensional and involves the simultaneous consideration of economic resources, social prestige, and social influence (Bottomore, 1966). Tumin (1966) defines the process of social stratification as follows: "the arrangement of any social group or society into a hierarchy of positions that are unequal with regard to power, property, social evaluation, and/or psychic gratification" (p. 12). For the most part, the components of this definition are self-explanatory. The exception is "psychic gratification," which as Tumin explains it relates to "all sources of pleasure and contentment that are not classifiable as property, power or evaluation" (p. 12). In essence, Tumin proposes that social strata can be differentiated according to their degree of associated pleasure and self-esteem. Tumin also explains that strata are typically defined in terms of personal characteristics (e.g., education, area of residence), trained skills and abilities (e.g., occupational activity and prestige), and consequences, effects, or degree of influence on others.

In combination, these factors discriminate among social strata by differentiating individuals according to lifestyle, economic resources, and both perceived and actual life options and choices. The concept of "options" is central to SES. Independent of economic resources, belonging to a given SES level includes the perception that one is unable personally or socially to participate in certain activities. Thus, an assembly-line worker may feel too "out-of-place" to dine at an exclusive restaurant or a university president may feel it is inappropriate to attend a demolition derby. Overall, a sensitive stratification procedure must differentiate individuals in terms of the complex of objective and subjective characteristics by which their lifestyles differ from one another.

The mental health literature reports two examples of well-designed stratification procedures. In their classic New Haven study, Hollingshead and Redlich (1958) used the Index of Social Position (ISP) to assign individuals to five SES levels. The ISP originally represented a weighted combination of educational background, occupational status, and area of residence. A subsequent revision omitted residence as a factor and thus allowed for use of the procedure in other settings (Hollingshead, 1957). Either approach identifies five SES levels ranging from highest (level I) to lowest (level V). The range of ISP scores used to define each level was empirically derived so as to maximize heterogeneity across groups. As a consequence the proportion of individuals assigned to the five SES levels is unequal, ranging from 2.7 percent for level I to 9.8, 18.9, 48.4, and 20.2 percent, respectively, for levels II through V. It should be noted that ISP scores are based solely on characteristics of the "head of the household" and do not thereby consider spouse's education or occupation. To our knowledge, there has been no systematic effort to assess the ISP's accuracy in differentiating contemporary lifestyles.

A second major stratification approach is that used by Srole, Langner, Michael, Opler, and Rennie (1962) in the Midtown Manhattan study. They include four factors in assessing an individual's SES background, these being father's education and occupation, total family income, and rent. To maximize precision, respondents were asked three specific questions regarding father's occupation: (1) What kind of work did he do? (2) Did he work for himself or others? (3) About how many people did he have working for (under) him? Six levels of educational and occupational levels were identified and all four variables were combined in a weighted manner to form a composite source. In contrast to the ISP, Srole et al.'s system created six *equally populated* SES levels. They based this decision on the statistical and conceptual advantages of rating scales with equally spaced intervals. A major disadvantage, however, is the noncomparability of these two stratification approaches. For example, Srole et al.'s highest SES group includes 16 percent of the population; an equivalent sample based on ISP scores would include all of levels I and II and a portion of level III. Thus, any attempt to compare SES-related findings across these two procedures at other than a global level (i.e., high vs. low) is immediately problematic.

As noted, a variety of other procedures has been used to assign individuals to SES levels. Frequently, reported occupations are categorized according to the International Standard Classification of Occupations or to an index of occupational prestige (Tumin, 1976). In his recent book on community mental health, Bloom (1984) discusses in detail the methodological utility of social area indicators and census tract data for assessing a community's (as opposed to an individual's) SES characteristics. Finally, numerous researchers assign individuals to SES levels on the basis of relative income or relative total family income. Typically, such procedures create broad income ranges (e.g., below $10,000, $35–50,000, above $50,000) to define SES levels.

The intent of this discussion is primarily to clarify the methodological problems that currently arise in any attempt to integrate SES-relevant research. This is particularly true of research that focuses on examining psychologically relevant variables across SES levels. The field's development has, in our opinion, been curtailed, in part, because of the incomparability of SES levels across stratification procedures. A further obstacle is the lack of a consensus on how to incorporate characteristics of contemporary lifestyle (e.g., two-income families) into traditional procedures such as the ISP. Obviously, any new system creates problems for existing knowledge bases. Nevertheless, the absence of agreement on how to operationalize SES levels has been and will continue to be an impediment to the accumulation of a solid knowledge base on the mental health needs of the disadvantaged.

Poverty and Psychopathology
Poverty and Prevalence

To respond effectively to a problem, it is important that one understand its parameters. The first of these relates to its scope. Nearly three decades ago, Hollingshead and Redlich (1958) reported that "demand," that is, service utilization, was highest among LSES individuals. This finding was neither surprising nor controversial. It merely confirmed the general perception among professionals at that time, that mental health services, especially those involving long-term custodial care for chronic disorders, were used disproportionately by the poor. Presumably, the poor used more services because their needs exceeded those of members of other SES levels. The validity of that assumption has been widely examined and consistently confirmed. For more than a century, epidemiologists have reported that the "true" prevalence (i.e., the number of cases in the community as opposed to the number of treated cases) of mental disorders is highest in the most socioeconomically disadvantaged segments of society (Dohrenwend, 1984; Dohrenwend & Dohrenwend, 1969, 1981a; Dohrenwend et al., 1980). Summarizing these results, Dohrenwend et al. (1980) report that low socioeconomic status (LSES) relates to high rates of schizophrenia, personality disorders, unipolar affective disorders, and severe nonspecific psychological distress. This pattern has been repeatedly observed in studies conducted in the United States and throughout the world. Rates of psychopathology among the poor are consistently highest in urban settings.

The data reviewed by the Dohrenwends argue convincingly for viewing the economically disadvantaged as that segment of the population most at risk for *some* form of mental disorder. Emphasis is placed on the qualifier "some" to highlight for the reader the number of diagnostic conditions whose prevalence relates to LSES. Moreover, it should be noted that whereas the "poor" include disproportionate numbers of women, minorities, and the elderly, observed differences in the prevalence of disorders cannot be explained as a function of sex, race, or age.

Evidence for the latter conclusion is provided in preliminary reports from the Epidemiological Catchment Area (ECA) project currently being conducted by the National Institute of Mental Health collaboratively with four groups of researchers (Regier et al.,

1984). This project represents the largest, most rigorous and comprehensive epidemiological analysis of the nation's mental health. To date, direct interviews of approximately 17,000 scientifically selected respondents (Eaton et al., 1984) have been completed using the Diagnostic Interview Schedule (Robins, Helzer, Croughan, Williams, & Spitzer, 1981). Although ongoing, the ECA project has already reported important information about demographic correlates of the lifetime prevalence of 15 diagnostic categories (using the *DSM-III;* American Psychiatric Association, 1980) including schizophrenia, affective disorders, anxiety disorders, substance use disorders, personality disorders, and eating disorders (Robins et al., 1984). Of specific relevance to this chapter are the following findings reported by Robins et al. (1984):

- At none of the survey sites included in the report were women found to exceed the total rate of disorder for men.
- Based on reported history, the oldest age-group (i.e., above 65 years of age) tended to have the lowest total rate of disorder; the next lowest rate was observed in the 45 to 64 age-group; and the highest rate was found in the 25 to 44 age-group
- Observed differences in rates of total disorders between blacks and others are generally nonsignificant.
- Rates of disorders are lower for college graduates than non-college graduates and for suburban and rural residents than for inner-city residents.

Thus, age, gender, and race do not independently relate to levels of disorder in the population. The two factors that do relate—educational level and residence—were included among Hollingshead and Redlich's (1958) original definition of SES. The direction of noted difference suggests the salience of SES to disorder rates.

Unfortunately, thus far ECA researchers have not reported specific SES-related comparisons. Planned are examinations of the differential rates of total disorder of respondents who are or are not receiving Medicaid and of respondents at varying income levels. Preliminary review of these analyses suggests that the conclusion that the highest rates of disorder occur in the lowest income group will again be supported.[1]

Poverty as an Etiological Factor

It is important, however, to recognize that epidemiological data reflect merely the *level* of disorder in the LSES groups but do not explain its causes. Whereas such data may inform one about levels of service needs, they do not instruct providers about the nature or timing of those services or how they should be delivered. In our view, such decisions should be based on an understanding of *why* rates of disorder are highest in the LSES groups. Unfortunately, that question has received far less attention to date than consideration of LSES levels of disorder and treatment utilization and outcome patterns. Important though the latter may be, their implication for the design of specific intervention strategies would seem to depend on understanding how LSES relates to onset and continuance of emotional and behavioral disorders. Data linking the economically disadvantaged to disproportionately high levels of mental health problems may reflect the operation of quite distinct processes. For example, the trend may reflect the effects of mental disorder on one's economic status. In other words, emotional disorder may reflect inherited cognitive and emotional predispositions that interfere with one's ability to take advantage of opportunities for educational, occupational, and financial success. If disadvantaged at birth, the vulnerable individual would be unable to achieve upward mobility. By contrast, those who initially had access to economic resources would experience difficulty in their attempts to retain that status. Gradually, their inadequacies would result in downward social mobility.

Myerson (1940) and others (e.g., Gruenberg, 1961) refer to this explanation as the "social selection" hypothesis. Selection in this case is used in a Darwinian sense to refer to individual inadequacies that impair functioning and limit one's capacity to respond adaptively to the demands associated with one's cultural and social situation. By contrast, one's mental health status may be a consequence rather than a cause of one's economic status. Thus, the stress of living under continuous economic disadvantage, of moving from one crisis to the next, and of having limited access to educational and occupational opportunities ultimately increases one's vulnerability to emotional disorder and behavioral dysfunction. Faris and Dunham (1939) were early

[1]D. Regier, personal communication, October 1984.

proponents of such a "social causation" explanation linking LSES and rates of mental disorder. According to this view the link is environmentally rather than individually determined. Presumably, any individual is susceptible to disorder if the amount and duration of stress are sufficient. In contrast to the "social selection" hypothesis, the "social causation" view assumes that external/environmental factors are equal if not greater determinants of disorder than individual factors.

Not unlike other "nature versus nurture" debates, the opposition of social selection and social causation has continued without resolution for decades. Several caveats should be mentioned at this point. First, these alternative hypotheses are presented as mutually exclusive for purposes of discussion only. As noted later, it is entirely possible, indeed likely, that both processes operate simultaneously, albeit to different degrees in different situations. Second, there is no intent to suggest that either process, alone or in combination with the other, applies uniformly to all forms of mental disorder. For example, "social selection" factors may contribute significantly to substance abuse rates, whereas "social causation" may explain rates of unipolar affective disorder. Finally, it should be made clear that what is known empirically about the validity of either hypothesis is extremely limited. Yet, in our opinion, the importance of conducting systematic research to clarify the mechanisms linking poverty and mental health status cannot be overstated. We believe that the limited progress that has occurred to date in responding to the needs of the disadvantaged represents the consequence of attempts to find solutions to problems that are not yet clearly understood.

Albeit incomplete, some information is available that relates to the social-selection versus social-causation debate. An early variant of the social-selection position was referred to as the "social-drift" hypothesis. Proponents explained the high rates of emotional disorder in the LSES groups in terms of downward social mobility. Such "social drift" was viewed as the inevitable result of the disruptive consequences of emotional disorder or behavioral dysfunction (e.g., substance abuse). To date, the social drift hypothesis has received some indirect empirical support. For example, Hollingshead and Redlich (1958) reported that the majority of their LSES-treated cases were disadvantaged at birth. Hence, their disorder could not account for their economic dis-

advantage. One could, however, argue that their disorder inhibited their upward mobility. Additional indirect support of the "social drift" explanation is provided by Gibbs (1984). In her recent analysis, Gibbs reviews evidence of the disproportionately high rates of suicide, substance abuse, antisocial behavior, adolescent pregnancy, and unemployment in black youth. She argues that the seriousness and frequency of the existence of these problems literally endanger the survival of these adolescents. Yet their problems do not explain their disadvantaged status since they too were born under severe economic conditions. Again, however, it is possible that their inability to escape from economic disadvantage reflected innate vulnerabilities and limitations. Finally, although the disadvantaged were not categorically identified as a "special population" by the most recent President's Commission on Mental Health,[2] the Task Panel on the "Nature and Scope of the Problem" underlined the link between level of disorders in children and inner-city status (President's Commission on Mental Health, Vol. II, 1978). As reported by Gibbs (1984), the Commission report notes that disadvantaged children (especially those from minority groups) are at serious risk for multiple emotional and behavioral problems. Although their initial disadvantage cannot be blamed on their emotional or behavioral functioning, that functioning may limit their future options.

A corollary of the social-drift hypothesis would predict upward mobility for nondisordered members of the LSES groups. That such movement occurs is established both in national folklore (i.e., the "American dream") and in sociological research (e.g., Lipset & Bendix, 1959). Further evidence of this phenomenon is available in the mental health literature. For example, three longitudinal studies have been reported that followed disadvantaged children for periods ranging from 15 to 30-plus years. The first of these (McCord, 1978) reviewed the status of experimental and control subjects 30 years after a systematic effort to reduce their risk for

---

[2]The omission of the disadvantaged from the Commission's list of special populations (e.g., women, children, minorities) is noteworthy if only to underlie this group's limited political voice in recent years. In view of the Commission's focal interest on the past accomplishments and future directions of the community mental health movement, the absence of a task force on mental health and the disadvantaged is equally noteworthy.

delinquency, that is, the classic Cambridge-Somerville study reported by Glueck and Glueck (1950) and Powers and Witmer (1951). In her report, McCord (1978) observed that a majority of those who had begun life under conditions of economic disadvantage had achieved blue- or white-collar occupational status.

Reporting on a follow-up of children from low-income minority families who participated in early childhood education programs conducted in the 1960s and 1970s, Royce, Lazar, and Darlington (1983) identified a number of positive direct and indirect effects related to educational and occupational attainment. Compared to children not involved in such preschool efforts, experimental children were less likely to require special education placements and more likely to achieve academically. At the same time, however, the investigators acknowledge that a majority of the control children completed high school and subsequently enjoyed occupational success at rates comparable to those of the experimental children. Similar to McCord's (1978) findings, Royce et al.'s (1983) data document upward mobility within originally LSES populations.

Finally, Long and Vaillant (1984) report on a longitudinal study designed specifically to examine the hypothesis that extreme poverty and a chaotic family life produce a self-perpetuating underclass. Their sample included 456 men who were inner-city junior high school youth in 1940. This sample was, in fact, the nondelinquent control for the Cambridge-Somerville study evaluated by McCord (1978). Long and Vaillant interviewed the men when they were approximately 47 years old. Based on ratings of their families made when the men were children, the interview sample was assigned to the following categories: (1) *chronically dependent,* meaning that welfare was the family's primary income source; (2) *multiproblem,* meaning that families reported a minimum of 10 out of a possible 25 problems in functioning (e.g., dependence on welfare, loss of a parent, parental abuse, frequent moves, etc.); (3) *nondependent, nonproblem;* and (4) Class V *nondependent, nonproblem,* meaning that families were LSES but did not report the difficulties of groups 1 and 2. Directly relevant to the issue of social mobility is the finding that:

by age 47, the children of chronically dependent and multiproblem families were, by the measures

used, almost indistinguishable from those without such initial disadvantages. This was true for income, employment and global mental health (Long & Vaillant, 1984, p. 342).

The investigators interpreted their findings as inconsistent with Lewis' (1964) concept of a "culture of poverty." As explained by Long and Vaillant:

for the men in this study, the transmission of their parent's chaotic or dependent life styles was not inevitable or even likely. If their backgrounds are accepted as having the characteristics of an underclass, then the study refutes the hypothesis that the chances of escape from such a class are minimal (p. 344).

At the same time, the investigators emphasize that nearly 30 years of effort were required by those who did escape. Finally, Long and Vaillant's data provide some direct support for the social selection position. They note that 41 of the 42 men who were LSES as adults were alcoholic or mentally ill. For the most part, these men had remained in (a few reportedly "drifted down" to) that social class throughout their lifetime. Adherents of the social selection position would interpret this fact as evidence of an inherited predisposition or vulnerability linking emotional status and SES. In addition, one might speculate that by midlife, individuals so affected would suffer from a combination of economic and emotional/behavorial burdens that, in all likelihood, would limit significantly their potential responsiveness to therapeutic interventions of any kind.

The "Politics" of Poverty Research

Data reviewed thus far make evident the heterogeneity of LSES members with respect to potential upward mobility, psychological health, and perhaps responsiveness to interventions. These data also raise an important question related to the social selection–social causation controversy. If, as suggested by Long and Vaillant (1984), the presence of or potential for disorder (e.g., alcoholism or mental illness) can inhibit "escape" from the LSES groups, to what extent is the outcome inevitable? In effect, can we identify and subsequently influence in a positive way the unique and combined contributions of individual and situational factors that link poverty and emotional disorders?

As noted, those who emphasize individual factors argue that the observed link reflects "selectivity" in an evolutionary sense, that is, the presence of a genetic or constitutional vulnerability or inadequacy that limits the individual's capacity to cope with daily pressures and stressful events and to take advantage of positive opportunities. For example, Gruenberg (1961) suggests that LSES individuals who are not upwardly mobile represent a "residue" of individuals who are highly vulnerable to emotional and behavioral disorder. Such individuals may, for example, be born into families with a history of genetically linked disorders such as schizophrenia, depression, or alcoholism. An example of such a constitutional factor is provided by Long and Vaillant (1984), who report that intelligence and childhood coping skills were highly correlated with subsequent escape from the LSES group. By contrast, "escape" was relatively more difficult for individuals with fewer personal resources than their peers. Because of such forms of "selectivity," the LSES groups would be expected to include disproportionate numbers of such vulnerable individuals and thus disproportionate levels of emotional disorder. This segment of the population, however, would also include individuals whose social status fell as a result of educational/occupational failure and emotional or behavioral disorders. Finally, the LSES groups would also include those born into disadvantage yet whose resources and actions could potentially lead to increased advantage.

It is important to note that if selectivity were operative, then members of these disadvantaged subgroups would differ quite significantly in their appropriateness for and responsiveness to existing forms of mental health intervention. For example, in treating the disadvantaged with genetic and constitutional vulnerabilities, the therapist may be confronted with limited potential for either individual or situational change. Such a patient would likely report a family and personal history of repeated failures and present few personal and social resources with which to resist current pressures and overcome presenting symptoms. Interventions that aimed for significant personal growth and identified improved social status as an indicant of such growth may offer praiseworthy but unrealistic goals. For these disadvantaged individuals, participation in such an intervention would be self-defeating and ultimately reinforce their existing sense of failure and inade-

quacy. Ironically, refusal (manifested perhaps as avoidance or early termination) of such treatment may be the "healthiest" response for such an individual. By contrast, involvement in a supportive intervention in which dependency was both allowed and encouraged may most directly respond to their needs. Such an intervention may seek "merely" to increase the patient's ability to identify and use social and community resources. It may also attempt "merely" to increase the patient's job acquisition and retention skills such that regular employment, even if low-paying and unskilled, becomes possible. Such an intervention may pursue minor but sustainable increases in self-esteem and adaptation as its goals. From the onset, planned outcomes may be limited to observable increments in the ability to cope with predictable stressors in the individual's environment.

Yet therapists who would offer such interventions may be criticized as holding stereotypic and discriminating views of the poor and as unwilling to offer "real treatment" (Lorion 1974a, 1978). Others might even argue that such a therapist holds defeatist, self-fulfilling prognostic views of the poor and is committed to maintaining existing social inequities and the status quo. If such clients are members of minority groups, then the therapist may be labeled as prejudiced and racist (e.g., Thomas & Sillen, 1972). Apart from one's views about the politics of mental health delivery, it should be apparent to the reader that a therapist confronted with an LSES patient faces a dilemma in attempting to provide "appropriate" treatment.

Resolution of that dilemma would be aided significantly by empirically based data that inform the therapist of the differential contribution of social causation and social selection factors to observed prevalence rates. That few research data on this issue currently exist is hardly surprising! Environmental and constitutional factors are rarely orthogonal in real life. Were it possible to assess reliably and validly the constitutional predispositions of individuals to specific mental disorders (or even categories of disorder), one would still be confronted by the inequitable distribution of such predispositions across social environments. Moreover, the critical experiment on this issue would require the longitudinal monitoring of identified individuals over lengthy, if not lifetime, periods. Were such research carried out and its findings replicated, the differential contributions of constitutional and environmental factors could be identified. Data from such studies might then be used to design diagnostic and treatment models necessary for prescriptively responding to LSES mental health needs. At present, however, no such critical experiments have been conducted. Moreover, given current and anticipated federal policies regarding support for research on "social issues," they are unlikely to be supported in the foreseeable future.

Additionally, the politics of such research must be appreciated and debated a priori. Readers should recall the heated response to Jensen's (1969) proposal that research examine the genetic basis of observed racial differences in IQ scores. Doubtless, proposals to study genetic predispositions or constitutional vulnerabilities that contribute to LSES emotional status and related treatment needs will be highly controversial. Proponents of such research may be characterized as "prejudiced" and "blaming the victim" (Ryan 1971). Yet ethics of both conducting and not conducting such research merit careful attention (Sarason, 1984). Included in the discussion should be an appreciation of the mental health service delivery system's consistent inability to respond effectively to LSES needs. The intransigence of that problem as reflected in persistently high rates of mental disorder among LSES individuals and similarly high rates of treatment attrition and avoidance (see Chapter 6 for a detailed discussion of this issue) requires consideration of a wide range of explanatory possibilities, however unpopular some of the alternatives may be.

Independent of political values, research funding priorities, and identified methodological obstacles, however, LSES mental health needs cannot wait for the convergence of necessary factors that would support an "ideal" experiment. Consequently, approximations must be developed whose results clarify LSES' potential etiological contribution to mental disorder and inform the design of viable intervention strategies.

A Quasi-experimental Approach to Poverty Research

Based on more than a decade of work, the Dohrenwends' research may offer such an approximation. In a recent report, they (Dohrenwend & Dohrenwend, 1981a) describe a quasi-experimental strategy for differentiating the contributions of social causation and social selection factors to LSES rates of disorder. Central to their approach is the inclusion of ethnic status in analyzing rates of mental disorder across SES groups. This decision reflects the assumption that "unlike social class, an individual's ethnicity cannot even in a small part be a function of the person's prior psychopathology"[3] (Dohrenwend & Dohrenwend 1981a, p. 134). Yet because of factors such as prejudice and discrimination, some ethnic groups experience considerably more social/environmental stress than others. Thus, according to the social-causation position, certain ethnic groups (i.e., nonwhite) would be expected to have higher levels of psychopathology than others (i.e., white). Ethnicity, however, would differentially affect the relationship between SES and rates of emotional disorder depending on whether social-causation or social-selection factors were primary. Specifically, the Dohrenwends (1981a) propose that the social-causation hypothesis predicts that the level of social/environmental pressure experienced by nonwhites would increase their rates of mental disorder relative to whites *regardless of SES*. In effect, therefore, nonwhites would experience more psychopathology than whites at all SES levels. The Dohrenwends (1981a) argue that such an outcome would support the social-causation position.

By contrast, the social-selection hypothesis assumes that psychopathology is most likely to occur in individuals who are genetically predisposed and thereby physiologically vulnerable to emotional disorder. Independent of ethnicity, upward mobility would be expected in individuals who are economically disadvantaged but constitutionally "strong." Reciprocally, downward mobility would be expected in individuals who are economically advantaged but constitutionally vulnerable. Consequently, were ethnicity *not* included in the analysis, social selection would predict higher rates of emotional disorder in LSES groups. The addition of ethnicity results in a set of predictions for selectivity that contrasts directly with that presented for causation (i.e., that nonwhites would exceed whites in rates of disorder at all SES levels). In effect, since nonwhite status

[3]It should be noted that the Dohrenwends (1981a, b) do not consider the possibility that the distribution of inherited vulnerability and predisposition may differ across ethnic groups. If such were the case, the interpretation of the results of their "quasi-experiment" would be questionable to some and confirmatory of selectivity to others.

represents an obstacle to upward mobility, one would expect a greater proportion of constitutionally strong individuals among LSES nonwhites than LSES whites. Those nonwhites who do reach upper SES levels would presumably represent that ethnic group's constitutionally strongest and healthiest. In combination these two tendencies should decrease rates of disorders among nonwhites at all SES levels. By comparison, the operation of selectivity should result in a disproportionately high level of constitutional vulnerability among LSES whites. This social group would include both those born into and unable to escape economic disadvantage and those whose emotional and behavioral problems resulted in social drift. In combination, these two sets of individuals would constitute a "residue" of vulnerable individuals among LSES whites (Gruenberg, 1961). The Dohrenwends (1981a) predict further that upper-SES white groups (given the pool of resources available to them) would support more dysfunctional individuals in their midst than upper-SES nonwhites. In contrast to what one would expect for nonwhites, the convergence of these factors would produce higher levels of emotional disorder in whites relative to nonwhites *regardless of SES*. Such a finding would support the social-selection position.

In brief, the Dohrenwends (1981a) propose that the social-causation hypothesis would predict *higher* levels of emotional disorder among nonwhites relative to whites at all SES levels. The social-selection hypothesis, by contrast, would predict *lower* levels of emotional disorder among nonwhites relative to whites at all SES levels.

To test these competing predictions, the Dohrenwends (1981a) analyzed findings from research that met two criteria: (1) SES and ethnicity were not confounded, and (2) the mental disorders studied were acceptably operationalized. Admittedly limited in number, studies meeting these criteria were identified and examined in relation to four major diagnostic categories: (1) schizophrenia, (2) personality disorders, (3) "demoralization" (i.e., generalized emotional distress), and (4) affective disorders. With respect to these disorders,[4] the Dohrenwends (1981a) concluded the following:

1. "The weight of the evidence . . . suggests that social causation is more important than social selection in producing the inverse relation-

ships between schizophrenia and social class in multiethnic urban settings in our society" (p. 140).

2. "Even when evidence from twin and adoption studies indicate that there may be a genetic-factor in antisocial personality, the results suggest that environment factors are important as well" (p. 142).

3. "When we compare rates of antisocial behavior and substance abuse in blacks and whites from the same social class we expect, therefore, to get clear-cut social causation outcomes. This is indeed what we find" (p. 142).

Admittedly, these conclusions must be interpreted with caution until replicated. At the same time, however, they should not be ignored. The quasi-experimental strategy used represents a scientifically acceptable approach to the study of a challenging and important question (Campbell & Stanley, 1966). Reasonable predictions are made about the interaction of ethnicity with SES and rates of psychopathology. Carefully selected from rigorously designed research, the data presented allow for their preliminary examination. In interpreting the results of their quasi-experiment, the Dohrenwends (1981a) do not intend to imply that environmental and constitutional factors are orthogonal. Rather, their position is consistent with a diathesis–stress model of disorder, not unlike that proposed for schizophrenia by Meehl (1962) more than two decades ago. In effect, such a model presumes that many disorders reflect the influence of environmental stressors on those who are constitutionally predisposed to react to stress in particular (i.e., dysfunctional) ways. Within such a perspective, the salient question is not whether constitution *or* environment causes disorder but to what degree each influences its evolution. Of the four categories of disorder examined by the Dohrenwends (1981a) in their quasi-experiment, available data suggest that environmental factors are especially important to a cluster involving schizophrenia and personality disorders and to a cluster related to antisocial behavior and problem drinking. The issue is less clear for the affective disorders and demoralization. At present, one can simply conclude for the latter disorders that the contribution

---

[4]Readers are strongly encouraged to review very carefully Dohrenwend and Dohrenwend (1981a) for a detailed presentation of the findings summarized here.

of "genetic and environmental origins vary with time, place and persons" (Dohrenwend & Dohrenwend, 1981a, p. 145).

The Dohrenwends' conclusions have important heuristic and clinical implications for those concerned with the mental health needs of the poor. Clearly, one important next step (beyond replication) is the design of research that elucidates the etiological mechanisms through which the environment alone or in interaction with constitutional factors contributes to pathogenesis.

Pathogenic Mechanisms

Although limited, data are available that provide some insights into pathogenic characteristics of LSES life experiences. Based on the results of their quasi-experimental analyses, the Dohrenwends (1981b) identified the following four alternative hypotheses that would result from a social-causation explanation of psychopathology:

1. The *victimization* hypothesis would explain high levels of psychopathology in LSES individuals as a function of the *number* of stressful life events experienced.

2. The *vulnerability* hypothesis assumes that the individual's ability to cope with stress is mediated by personal resources and social support. Thus, the observed link is a function of inadequate resources.

3. The *additive burden* hypothesis explains the higher prevalence of psychopathology in terms of the independent and additive influence of stressful events, personal dispositions, and available social support.

4. The *chronic burden* hypothesis discounts the importance of stressful events and assumes instead that levels of psychopathology among LSES individuals reflect the effects of long-term personal and situational factors. Thus, it is the combination of individual vulnerability and ongoing situational demands that over time result in the development of pathology.

The readers should note that although they are corollaries of the social-causation position, the hypotheses relating to vulnerability and additive and chronic burdens consider the influence of personal resources or dispositions in their explanation. These resources include factors such as ability to tolerate stress and anxiety, cognitive problem-solving skills,

and potential, genetically linked factors such as affective lability. As such, these hypotheses actually represent statements of the interaction between social causation and social selection. In their review of reported data that might be used post hoc to support or refute these four hypotheses, the Dohrenwends (1981b) underline the fact that attention must be paid *both* to what happens in the LSES individual's life and to what individual and social resources are available to cope with and resolve the demands associated with those events.

Analyses of data reviewed suggest that priority be given to the additive burden corollary. From this perspective, the observed link between levels of psychopathology and LSES represents the result of a cumulative process in which an individual with limited personal resources to deal with adverse and stressful conditions exists in a very demanding environment and is confronted with a series of stressful experiences that exacerbate the intensity of those demands. The occurrence of stressful experiences on a frequent, if not daily, basis has been shown to relate to a sense of limited control over one's environment (i.e., external locus of control; Eron & Peterson, 1982), a fatalistic view of the future (Ross, Mirowsky, & Cockerham, 1983), and a state comparable to Seligman's "learned helplessness" (Strauss, 1979).

LSES individuals confronted with such pressures are also apparently ineffective in acquiring and utilizing available sources of social support in times of difficulty. Evidence for this is reported by Caplan and Killilea (1976), Dohrenwend (1984), and Eron and Peterson (1982). In a most important study of depression in LSES women, Brown, Nibhrolchain, and Harris (1975; Brown & Harris, 1978) examined the influence of inadequate social support on the pathogenesis of depression. For some women, individual vulnerability to pathology (defined as a family history of depression) in the face of stressful events was mediated by a close supportive relationship. Those without such a relationship were found to be at much higher risk for the onset of disorder. Wahler's (1980) research with low-income rural mothers supports the relevance of the availability of a social network to problem resolution. In addition to its effect on the mother's emotional status, an inadequate social network increases the risk of psychopathology in the offspring of such women (Dumas & Wahler, 1983; Wahler, 1980).

In combination, these research findings provide important insights into factors that might contribute to LSES risk for psychopathology. Such insights are not, however, without their historical antecedents. Nearly four decades ago, Arsenian and Arsenian (1948) proposed that mental health practitioners appreciate the emotional and behavioral implications of "tough and easy cultures." Although not empirically validated at the time, their conceptualization of the potential emotional consequences of LSES life is consistent with data just reviewed and provides a useful framework for subsequent clinical service and research with the poor. For that reason, the principal elements of their synthesis of anthropological and psychiatric findings are presented as a bridge between the foregoing review of LSES and psychopathology and the review of therapeutic interventions that follows.

"Tough and Easy Cultures"

Consistent with drive reduction theories of behavior current at the time, the Arsenians proposed that behavior should be understood in terms of biologically and socially determined needs. Such needs are characterized by variable states of tension whose intensity motivates action to satisfy the related need. Within this perspective, behavior can be understood in terms of identifiable goals, that is, states of need satisfaction and tension reduction. In turn, cultures can be differentiated in terms of the "paths" or mechanisms available to individuals to reach their goals, as well as in terms of the properties that characterize available goals. Paths can be compared along the following dimensions:

- *Effectiveness*—the likelihood that the action undertaken will actually lead to the desired goal.
- *Efficiency*—the relative ease of goal attainment via one action versus another.
- *Number*—the multiplicity of options available to reach a given goal.
- *Accessibility*—the availability to an individual of a particular mechanism for reaching a desired goal.
- *Clarity*—the extent to which a particular action is perceived as relevant to attainment of a particular goal.
- *Approval*—the differential value attached to various goal attainment mechanisms.

- *Substitutivity*—the capacity to replace one mechanism for another or to alter a mechanism once initiated.
- *Congruence*—the complementarity or opposition of mechanisms to goal achievement.
- *Cognizance*—the degree to which an individual is aware of the properties of paths and their relevance to goal attainment.

The Arsenians propose that the culture's contribution to psychopathology can be understood, in part, by the difficulty level of its available paths for tension reduction. In effect, a "tough" culture would have few mechanisms available for tension reduction, would limit the effectiveness, efficiency, and acceptability of those that are available, and would maximize the oppositional nature of its goals, that is, the pursuit of one interferes with or obviates pursuit of others. Within such a culture, individuals would exert considerable effort for minimal gain, find many paths to goal attainment inaccessible, and experience considerable frustration. Moreover, the Arsenians note, a tough culture would also limit the range of goals available. Consequently, tough cultures would be tension-producing and -sustaining and thereby elicit in their members self-defeating and pathological behaviors.

The Arsenians predicted that tough cultures would have disproportionately high levels of "nervousness," suicide, diagnosed mental disorders, crime, and substance abuse. One need only review the findings recently reported by Gibbs (1984) and the ECA researchers (Eaton et al., 1984; Regier et al., 1984; Robins et al., 1981, 1984) to appreciate the similarity between this prediction and the current facts of LSES life. The Arsenians' analysis provides yet another impetus for considering extrapersonal factors as contributory if not causal in the development of emotional disorder and behavior dysfunction.

In our opinion, such views merit increased attention from those responsible for the design and delivery of mental health services. As stated initially, the assumption that poverty's influence on mental health needs is limited to interfering with, seeking, obtaining, remaining in, or responding to psychotherapy must be questioned. Evidence has been reviewed that links the onset of some forms of emotional disorder with constitutional vulnerabilities and inherited predispositions. Although possible in members of all SES levels, a disproportionate number of such vulnerable individuals are found in the LSES groups. Inclusion of a comprehensive family and developmental history within the diagnostic interview may provide important information about the patient's individual contributions to the presenting symptoms. In our own clinical work with LSES patients, we have found that academic records often include information highly relevant to problem chronicity.

We do not, however, intend to suggest that "selectivity" is the relevant causal process. As noted by the Dohrenwends and the Arsenians, individual factors are most likely to become pathogenic when combined with a very demanding environment, a series of stressful life events, or both. The implication of these findings is that the presenting disorder(s) may in fact represent an ineffective attempt to respond to external factors. For the clinician, this necessitates that the diagnostic interview include consideration of the patient's lifestyle. Included in such an interview should be consideration of the patient's economic resources and demands, sources of disappointment and frustration, and significant life events (e.g., divorce, separation, illness, job loss, etc.). Particularly salient for many inner-city residents are such stressors as changing residence, the frustration of bureaucratic delays or demands, and encounters with the law.

Without knowledge of such aspects of the patient's life, the clinician's efforts may be doomed from the onset if the salient stressors continue to make demands that exceed the patient's coping skills. At the very least, the Dohrenwends' (1981b) additive burden hypothesis argues for the clinician to focus initially on assisting the patient to resist environmental demands and cope with life events that have had or will have emotional/behavior consequences. To do so, the clinician may apply crisis-intervention or time-limited strategies described subsequently and in detail in Chapter 14 by Koss and Butcher in this volume. It appears that treatment prognosis may be significantly improved if the patient is also assisted in identifying and utilizing sources of support in the natural environment. By facilitating the patient's link into available social networks, the clinician may encounter increased patient commitment to treatment and increased generalization of desired behavior change across settings.[5]

At yet another level, the additive burden hypothesis highlights the importance of examining the two other assumptions discussed at the beginning of this chapter. If, as is suggested by the Dohrenwends' (1981a, b) and Arsenians' analyses and by the supporting data, the conditions of poverty per se are significant pathogens, then the efficiency of direct versus indirect services must be examined. Specifically, one must question whether LSES conditions might be moderated somehow by systematic efforts to minimize the emotional demands associated with LSES life (e.g., public assistance regulations, public housing conditions). Additionally, it might be possible to alter educational curricula to increase LSES skills in such areas as social-skills development, social network utilization, and stress management. In effect, such proposals would represent attempts to intervene *prior to* the onset of disorder or, at least, sufficiently early to avoid many of the secondary complications that arise when symptoms go untreated. Later in this chapter, we shall discuss examples of preventive interventions that have been applied to LSES populations. First, however, consideration will be given to psychotherapeutic approaches for the poor.

THERAPEUTIC INTERVENTIONS WITH THE POOR

As noted repeatedly, the identification of interventions for the mental health needs of the poor has received minimal research attention during the past decade. Little systematic research has been conducted that examines the differential applicability of treatment alternatives for low- versus middle- and upper-SES clients. As reflected in Table 17.1 (p. 765) nearly 10,000 articles were reviewed for relevance to LSES treatment needs. Of these, 138 (approximately 1.5%) met the following minimal criteria for further consideration: subjects were LSES (articles focused on ethnic/minority groups without information relevant to SES were *not* included), some form of outcome was reported, and some attempt was made to assess treatment impact. Review of Table 17.1 makes evident that any attempt

[5]Robert Wahler, Ph.D., of the University of Tennessee is about to initiate a multiyear study of this very phenomenon with LSES families.

to set more rigorous criteria (e.g., use of a control group) would result in a very significant reduction of applicable articles. In fact, the majority (84%) of "research" articles were correlational in nature. Because of the dearth of new information during the past decade, the following section reviews earlier work and adds new data whenever possible. In light of our discussion of the implication of social-selection and social-causation factors to levels of LSES psychopathology and, we believe, treatment responsiveness, the first therapeutic modalities to be discussed will be crisis intervention and time-limited strategies.

Therapists' Assumptions About the Poor

Prior to consideration of specific psychotherapeutic strategies, however, it is appropriate to underline the importance of participant attitudes and expectations to treatment outcome. As noted elsewhere (Lorion, 1974a, 1974b; Lorion & Parron, 1985), what the patient and therapist think, feel, and assume about each other may be at least as important to outcome as the intervention techniques per se. These factors are discussed elsewhere in this volume (i.e., Chapters 6 and 7) and readers are urged to review this material in conjunction with the foregoing review of therapeutic strategies for the poor.

Some emphasis must, however, be placed on the therapist's assumptions and expectations about LSES patients. Intentionally or not, therapists communicate through their words and behavior their views about a patient's appropriateness for treatment. If already uncertain about involvement in mental health treatment, the LSES patient's awareness of such messages may constitute a preliminary step in a negative self-fulfilling prophecy. Fortunately, evidence has been reported that indicates that supervisory consideration of the therapist's views of the poor can have long-term positive consequences (e.g., Bernard, 1965; Jacobs, Charles, Jacobs, Weinstein, & Mann, 1972). Briefly providing the therapist with accurate information about LSES patients' needs, lifestyles, and therapeutic concerns produces increased empathy and expressed interest on the therapist's part and, reciprocally, decreased attrition on the patient's. Thus, it appears that careful preparation of the therapist is an important prerequisite for the delivery of mental health services to LSES patients since such therapists actively assist their patients to understand and take advantage of psychotherapeutic goals and procedures.

As explained elsewhere (Lorion & Parron, 1985), several stereotypes/misconceptions seem especially noteworthy. First among these is the common misperception that "they" are a homogeneous group. Such is hardly the case! The poor include individuals from all racial and ethnic subgroups. Demographically, women are disproportionately represented in this segment of the population, as are children and the elderly. The poor include the chronically unemployed but also significant numbers of unskilled and semiskilled workers. Some have little formal education; others have completed high school yet possess few academic skills; and yet others have been unable to make use of an adequate education due to prejudice or circumstance. Equal variability can be found in LSES individuals' sensitivity to emotional and interpersonal issues, "psychological mindedness," and ambitions for the future.

A related misconception about LSES life is its presumed unending bleakness. Unquestionably, LSES life is demanding and stressful. Few resources, economic and other, are available and frequently the disadvantaged move from one crisis to another. As Gladwin (1967) notes: "being poor means eating poor food and living in unsanitary housing which means missing a lot of work or school, or perhaps being handicapped or not strong enough to handle the heavy manual work which is often the only kind available, and thus being unemployed much of the time and so being poor" (p. 77).

Nevertheless, the poor also experience warmth, humor, and enjoyment in their lives. Disregard of these aspects of LSES life "can limit the therapist's perspective, replace empathy with pity, and inhibit the therapist from recognizing and mobilizing resources which can assist the client to respond to emotional difficulties" (Lorion & Parron, 1985, p. 82). To expand the therapist's perspective on LSES life, it is simply necessary to inquire during the initial interview about how time is spent, how problems are solved, and how joy, however fleeting, occurs.

A third category of misconceptions about the poor involves their presumed unreliability and impulsivity. Such attributions were reported by Hollingshead and Redlich (1958) nearly three decades ago and appear to continue (e.g., Turner & Armstrong, 1981). Careful examination of their validity, however, is important. For example, is a *person* "unreliable" if dependent on inadequate public transportation or private vehicles that are in serious disrepair? Similarly, is a *person* "unreliable" who assumes that an appointment at a public mental health facility is similar to one at a public health facility? In the latter case, the likelihood of being seen "on time" or even within the hour is quite limited. Yet even tardy patients are eventually treated at public health facilities. Such is not always the case in mental health facilities. Rather than sensing appreciation for their efforts to arrive, LSES patients may encounter interpretation of their "resistance." Hardly an experience that encourages a second visit!

Finally, LSES patients have been frequently described as "impulsive," "unable to delay gratification," and insistent that treatment resolve their problem. To appreciate the positive aspects of this attribution, the therapist should recognize that:

> *providing for the needs of oneself and one's family on the resources available from food stamps, welfare, unemployment insurance or even minimum wage (if one is able to negotiate that "much" for the unskilled job available) represents accomplishment of a difficult but critical economic task. Poverty, if nothing else, is characterized by an endless series of unpredictable crises which demand constantly reallocating meager resources from one necessity to another. Everything one owns is already at risk for needing repair, credit, when available, is expensive and short-term, and savings must always be diverted from what is desired to what is needed. The therapist who understands the daily decision-making necessary to survive economic hardship is likely to appreciate both the client's resourcefulness and insistence that treatment be quick and symptoms be addressed immediately. (Lorion & Parron, 1985, p. 83–84).*

The treatment approaches discussed subsequently represent viable strategies for addressing LSES emotional needs. The application of these procedures, however, depends in significant ways on the preconceptions of those who use them. That the poor should have access to mental health services is unquestioned. That the poor will receive appropriate and sensitive mental health services pro-

vided by therapists willing to serve them remains controversial at this time.

Crisis and Time-limited Therapies

As noted, a detailed discussion of crisis intervention and time-limited modalities is provided in Chapter 14. Although no other set of treatment approaches has developed as rapidly during the past decade, it should be noted that little systematic research has been conducted on its applicability to the disadvantaged. Perhaps the match between patient needs and treatment characteristics seems so close that assessment of its empirical validity is seen as unnecessary. More likely, the lack of research on this issue reflects simply the overall disregard of SES-relevant treatment research. Nevertheless, clinical developments in crisis and time-limited modalities argue strongly for their inclusion in the armamentarium of those responsible for serving LSES mental health needs. The reasons for this conclusion are simple. First, the lives of LSES patients are often characterized by significant life crises whose repercussions can be moderated by the early application of crisis-intervention techniques. Second, time-limited approaches offer patients rapid relief from presenting symptoms. They provide both viable solutions to immediate problems and, in many cases, skills for independently resolving future difficulties. Third, LSES patients are less likely to terminate prematurely from time-limited therapies than from more extended treatments (Bloom, 1984). Undoubtedly, therapeutic goals are somewhat easier to achieve if the patient remains in treatment. Finally, such approaches provide excellent opportunities for the clinician to gather valuable diagnostic data relevant to assessing the patient's appropriateness for lengthier insight-oriented modalities. In the process, the patient gains important skills that increase the prognosis for expressive psychotherapy if initiated (Lorion, 1978, provides an extended discussion of LSES patient preparation).

Crisis Intervention

A most valuable resource for understanding crisis-intervention rationale and procedures is provided by Slaikeu's (1984) recently published handbook on this topic. Given the extended discussion of the topic that appears in Chapter 14 of this volume, only two aspects of the topic are presented here: its underlying theoretical assumptions and principal components. Slaikeu explains the rationale for crisis intervention as follows:

All humans can be expected at various times in their lives to experience crises characterized by great emotional disorganization, upset and a breakdown of previously adequate coping strategies. The crisis state is limited (equilibrium is regained in four to six weeks), is usually touched-off by some precipitating event, can be expected to follow sequential patterns of development through various stages, and has the potential for resolution toward higher or lower levels of functioning. Ultimate crisis resolution depends upon a number of factors, including severity of the precipitating event, the individual's personal resources (ego strength experience with previous crises), and the individual's social resources (assistance available from "significant others"). (1984, p. 14).

Thus crises are normal events that can occur to anyone. Some of these events can be anticipated (e.g., the birth of a child, the departure of children from the home, retirement); others cannot (e.g., a natural disaster, an accidental death). Some are precipitous (e.g., an automobile fatality); some evolve slowly (e.g., the dissolution of a marriage). Regardless of their unique characteristics, crises are assumed to share the potential for emotional and cognitive disruption and for catalyzing subsequent emotional disorder. For those reasons, interventions have been designed to assist individuals prepare for or respond to the demands associated with a crisis. Thus, the crisis victim is assisted in understanding the developmental stages through which the crisis has passed or will pass, in recognizing the specific problems resulting from that crisis, and particularly in identifying and applying viable problem-resolution strategies. Slaikeu (1984) describes this process as "working through the crisis."

If the working through is effective, the individual can resume "normal" functioning quickly with minimal sequelae. Moreover, that same individual should have gained an increase in the ability to resolve subsequent crises. Thus crisis intervention, applied *before* the need for traditional mental health services, can reduce or prevent entirely the need for such services. These strategies can be effectively applied by nonprofessional personnel in a multitude of settings including schools, community agencies,

churches, and private homes. Importantly for LSES individuals (Lorion, 1974b), these strategies can be obtained without the stigma often associated with mental health services.

As noted, crisis-intervention strategies represent seemingly very important interventions for LSES individuals. The qualifier "seemingly" is necessary because little systematic research of this potential has occurred. Slaikeu (1984) does not even mention poverty or economic disadvantage in his index! Unquestionably, therefore, a priority issue for the next decade must be assessment of this potential.

Time-limited Approaches

Somewhat more research has been reported on the use of time-limited procedures with LSES patients. Early on, the complementarity of time-limited procedures and the economic, occupational, and attitudinal characteristics of LSES patients was recognized (Frank, 1961; Garfield, 1963; McMahon, 1964; Storrow, 1962). Most importantly, such procedures appear to "fit" the treatment practices of these patients. (Avnet, 1962). It has long been known that most patients participate in fewer than six treatment sessions (Rubenstein & Lorr, 1956). Fewer than half of over 11,000 patients from 53 clinics remained in treatment beyond eight sessions (Rogers, 1960). For 1964, the National Center for Health Statistics (1966) reports an average of fewer than five contacts for almost one million patients seen in psychiatric treatment during that year. Thus, median treatment durations range from 3 to 12 sessions, and if only those patients who actually begin treatment are considered, median durations are between five and six sessions (Garfield, 1971). In actual practice, it appears that instead of dropping out in the middle, LSES patients leave treatment at phenomenologically defined end points (Lorion, 1974a, 1978).

In earlier analyses of mental health services, Strupp and Bergin (1969) and Urban and Ford (1971) emphasized the importance of developing individualized treatment prescriptions that are realistic and problem oriented. In varying degrees, these goals can be reached using brief psychotherapy approaches. The rationale behind these strategies is clearly described by Barton (1971):

Brief therapists share a commitment to provide something meaningful to all those who seek or should be seeking help, in terms that are accept-able and relevant to the patients. These therapists recognize that they must answer some of the patient's needs quickly, and that at times simple, perhaps superficial solutions are more cogent than profound but unduly delayed ones. Simple solutions often have profound preventive conse-quences. Although the objectives are pragmatic, the therapist needs to eschew a dynamic, multi-faceted scrutiny of whatever material emerges, selectively sharing with the patient what is ger-mane and useable. (p. 21).

A variety of time-limited approaches have been described that can be applied to the disadvantaged (Bellak & Small, 1965; Sifneos, 1972; Small, 1971). McMahon (1964), Reiff and Scribner (1964), Riess-man (1964), and Schlesinger and James (1969) specifically recommend that time-limited contacts be established that respond quickly and directly to presenting symptoms. Impressionistic reports of the efficacy of short-term approaches have appeared in the literature for nearly two decades (Avnet, 1962, 1965; Levy, 1966; Wolberg 1967). A more rigorous assessment of brief therapy with the disadvantaged is provided by Koegler and Brill (1967). These in-vestigators compared brief contact therapy with or without medication (where indicated), and tradi-tional long-term, insight-oriented psychotherapy. Patients were randomly assigned to treatment con-ditions, and double-blind procedures controlled for therapist bias in evaluating the drug treatment. Patients having minimal contact met with their ther-apist for a limited number of sessions to discuss practical aspects of their problems and to receive medication (or placebos). Koegler and Brill report no differences in symptom reduction between the brief and traditional treatments lasting beyond six months.

Additional support is provided by Goin, Yama-moto, and Silverman (1965) and Yamamoto and Goin (1966). They report that a sizeable number of their disadvantaged patients showed noticeable reductions in symptoms following participation in brief, problem-oriented treatment. Stone and Crowthers (1972) also found significant decreases in dropout rates following the introduction of crisis-oriented, time-limited psychotherapy. Reportedly, blue-collar families utilized psychiatric services much more comfortably and frequently when they

were available on a prepaid instead of "fee for service" basis and when they provided direct, im-mediate problem focusing.

Unfortunately, there presently exist few system-atic evaluations of short-term treatment approaches with the disadvantaged. Those that do are seriously limited in a number of ways. Assessments of out-come are based either on self-report or on global, psychometrically unsophisticated measures. Never-theless, these procedures are extensively used in community centers.

Bloom (1984) recently proposed a most interest-ing time-limited alternative—single-session psycho-therapy. Based on the often-reported finding that significant symptom reduction occurs during the first session *and* that the modal number of sessions attended is one, Bloom describes "focused single-session therapy" as having the following rules for the therapist.

- Identify a focal problem.
- Do not underestimate client's strengths.
- Be prudently active.
- Explore then present interpretations tentatively.
- Use the interview to start a problem-solving process.
- Keep track of the interview.
- Do not be overambitious.
- Keep factual questions to a minimum.
- Do not be overly concerned about the precipi-tating event.
- Avoid detours.
- Do not overestimate a client's self-awareness.

Although most reports of this intervention are anec-dotal, Getz, Fujita, and Allen (1975) did evaluate the effect of a single-session intervention provided by a paraprofessional for 104 crisis-intervention service patients. Only 40 percent of eligible sub-jects were located. Of those contacted, the majority reported feeling positive about the encounter and found it generally helpful. Additional support for the effectiveness of single-session treatment is reported by Malan, Heath, Bacal, and Balfour (1975). Al-though its empirical basis is quite limited, it does seem that single-session therapy is a viable option for the therapist encountering LSES patients. Obvi-ously, considerably more research is needed to de-termine the limits of applicability of this therapeutic modality and to assess the conditions under which treatment should be extended beyond one sesson.

Behavioral Approaches

Crisis and time-limited interventions emphasize understanding and resolving focal problems. This same emphasis characterizes behavioral therapy. It should be recognized that "behavior therapy" is a generic term referring to an assortment of therapeutic procedures (e.g., modeling, desensitization, aversive psychotherapy, implosion). Behavioral approaches do, however, share certain characteristics that make them relevant for the disadvantaged. Their underlying concept of psychopathology allows for a direct, problem-oriented focus. The behavior therapist does not assume that intrapsychic conflicts must be resolved in order to achieve permanent symptom removal. Thus a basic match exists between the LSES patient's interest in obtaining symptom resolution and the behaviorist's interest in symptom removal (Graziano, 1969).

Although behavioral approaches initially emphasized the resolution of circumscribed problems such as phobias, tics, and sexual perversions, they are also appropriate for generalized dysfunctions such as alcoholism, addictions, depression, and anxiety reactions (Eysenck, 1972; Krasner, 1971; Lazarus, 1972, 1976; Rimm & Masters, 1979). The limited attention given to assessing the effectiveness of behavioral approaches with the working class and poor is most disconcerting. Whereas there are relatively few well-designed outcome studies of insight-oriented therapy outcome with any population, the relative lack of behavioral research targeted to the disadvantaged is conspicuous if only because of the plethora of such studies available for most other populations. Several studies do, however, demonstrate the potential importance of behavioral treatment approaches for disadvantaged individuals. Sloane, Staples, Cristol, Yorkston, and Whipple (1975) conducted a well-designed, carefully controlled comparison of traditional expressive and behavior therapies. In this study, 94 patients suffering from moderately severe neuroses and personality disorders were randomly assigned to traditional, behavioral, or waiting-list control conditions. To maximize their involvement, control patients were promised therapy within four months, were provided with a staff member to call in case of crisis, and were contacted by telephone periodically during the

four-month waiting period. At the end of the experimental period, Sloane et al. (1975) observed that all three groups had improved significantly. However, the behavioral and traditional therapy groups had improved significantly more than their waiting-list controls. No differences, however, in amount of improvement were found between the therapy groups. Nor was there evidence of symptom substitution in any group. In fact, improvement in target symptoms was accompanied by improvement in other symptoms as well.

The results of the Sloane et al. (1975) study are relevant to this chapter for several reasons. First, these results demonstrate that behavior therapy can be at least as effective as expressive psychotherapy with LSES patients. Second, and perhaps most important, Sloane et al. demonstrate that behavior therapy can effectively serve more heterogeneous patient populations than traditional psychotherapies. In their study, the behavior therapists were equally effective with patients from all SES backgrounds. This was not true for the insight-oriented treatment. Finally, this study exemplifies the level of design sophistication appropriate to the complex issues involved in prescriptive analyses. As will become evident later, the Sloane et al. study closely approximates the "ideal" design.

Behavioral approaches have also been shown to have promise for intervention with disadvantaged youngsters. Rogers, Forehand, Griest, Wells, and McMahon (1981) conducted parent training sessions with mothers from low-, medium-, and high-SES groups. Participating mothers had children referred for noncompliant behavior difficulties. Significant improvement in child behavior was obtained at a comparable level for all three groups. Although these findings are encouraging, a study by Dumas and Wahler (1983) was unable to replicate them. Dumas and Wahler (1983) also evaluated the efficacy of a behaviorally oriented parent training program for mothers who were seeking help because of their child's oppositional or noncompliant behavior. Outcome data were collected both at the end of training and at a one-year follow-up. Findings revealed a steady increase in the probability of unsatisfactory outcomes or treatment failure as a function of increasing economic disadvantage. Hence, although behavioral approaches appear promising for reducing mother—child interaction deficits for LSES populations, it also seems clear that there may be factors, yet to be identified, that interfere with the efficacy of such approaches with these groups.

Unfortunately, the dearth of systematic research provides little basis for the clinician to assess and compare insight and behavioral treatment approaches for LSES patients. Indeed, given the broad applicability of behavioral approaches to addressing emotional and behavioral disorders with so many diverse groups, it is both troubling and puzzling that so little is known about their utility with LSES patients. Undeniably, research to fill this void must be conducted at the earliest possible time.

Traditional Insight-oriented Psychotherapy

Since the publication of the original version of this chapter, little has changed with respect to insight-oriented approaches to LSES needs. Research on the effectiveness of such approaches with the disadvantaged and on refinements of treatment procedures and discussion of maximizing their applicability for this target group continue to be lacking. Perhaps this limited research attention mirrors the actual frequency of utilization of insight-oriented approaches with LSES populations. Clinicians may be unwilling to select a treatment with which the disadvantaged patient is least satisfied and typically is unwilling to pursue (Lorion, 1978). Yet the dearth of research on this topic should not be misinterpreted as evidence that insight-oriented approaches are neither used nor effective with the disadvantaged.

Based on what is currently known, one cannot conclude that insight-oriented approaches have not been and cannot be effective with LSES populations (Lorion, 1973). Yet the preceding comment is not intended to suggest that insight-oriented psychotherapy as traditionally provided to middle- and upper-class patients should be made readily available to the disadvantaged. Indeed, Freud (1950) anticipated that dynamically oriented treatments would have to change to respond to the realities of low-income styles:

One may reasonably expect that at some time or other the conscience of the community will awake and admonish it that the poor man has just as much right to help for his mind as he now has for the surgeon's means for saving his life; . . . the task will then arise for us to adapt our techniques to the new conditions. I have no doubt

that the validity of our psychological assumptions will impress the uneducated too, that we shall need to find the simplest and most natural expressions for our theoretical doctrines. (p. 400)

Bernard (1971) provides a more contemporary view of this argument:

In the midst of the current whirlwind of innovative and often controversial effort, it seems especially useful to maintain some historical perspective. Otherwise, in reaction against past failures, one risks throwing out the good with the bad, or needlessly wasting the legacy of valid achievement on which one can build, by trying instead to start from scratch. (p. 62)

Thus, in assessing LSES treatment approaches, mental health researchers must not ignore the potential utility of traditional approaches. Instead of rejecting a priori insight-oriented approaches for the disadvantaged, researchers should attempt to identify their effective components. In this way, the "trappings" can be modified to fit more comfortably into LSES lifestyles without altering their primary therapeutic strategies.

Limited evidence is available demonstrating the positive treatment effect for LSES patients of receiving modified versions of dynamically oriented therapy. For example, Gould (1967) reports that assembly-line workers responded quite well to informal analytic treatment. Early sessions focused on the patient's misconceptions about the nature and goal of mental health treatment (i.e., patient preparation). Whenever possible, psychological jargon was avoided and everyday language was used to communicate salient concepts to the patient. Gould focused on the patient's concern with specific issues as a means of encouraging subsequent discussion of dynamic issues. Occasionally, sessions were held while walking in a nearby park. Gould also reports that session length varied in relation to productivity. At times, treatment lasted only 20 to 30 minutes; at other times, it lasted the full 50 minutes. Where appropriate, problems were accepted at face value and direct advice was offered to the patient.

Unfortunately, Gould did not systematically evaluate his efforts and reports only his impressions of the results of this therapy. Support for Gould's conclusions, however, is provided by Hacker, Illing, and Bergreen (1965), who report similar improvement in working-class patients participating in analytically oriented therapy. These investigators observed a 50 percent reduction in attrition rates once the therapists responded to patients in an increasingly flexible manner. However, since they failed to operationally define their therapeutic procedures and outcome measures, these data can be interpreted only suggestively. Ultimate confirmation of these impressionistic reports depends on their replication under carefully controlled conditions.

There still exists only one reported systematic evaluation of insight-oriented psychotherapy with LSES minority patients. In her excellent book *Therapy in the Ghetto,* Lerner (1972) reports the results of five years of research on outpatient insight-oriented psychotherapy. This project was described at length in our previous chapter (Lorion, 1978). For that reason, it will be only briefly reviewed here. Forty-five LSES patients were seen by 15 different psychotherapists (psychologists and social workers). The 45 patients included 23 black and 22 white outpatients ranging in age from 16 to 57. No specific subject-selection procedures were used for the study. Outcome measures included a variety of patient and therapist self-description and symptom-reduction measures.

Of the 30 patients who completed treatment prior to the end of the study (12 of the remaining 15 dropped out of treatment and 3 were involved in ongoing therapy), 23 showed significant gains in psychological functioning. No significant racial differences in outcome were observed, nor did same-race and cross-racial patient−therapist dyads differ on any measure. These results were supported in the majority of patient and therapist outcome measures used. Lerner emphasizes the extremely significant ($p \leq .005$) relationship found between assessed democratic attitude of the therapist and patient improvement. She interprets this finding as evidence of the fact that democratic or nonauthoritarian attitudes on the part of the therapist "create an ambience which helps clients avail themselves of their own resources, but it may also be that such values make it easier for the very confused and needy people to avail themselves of other good things the therapist has to offer, such as warmth, support, acceptance, protection, understanding, and clarification" (p. 141).

Finally, it should be noted that Lerner's positive results were achieved in less than 9 months and required fewer than 30 sessions. The actual cost per client was somewhere between $200 and $300 for the entire treatment process. Thus, she argues that insight-oriented therapeutic approaches, with understanding and open therapists, are both potentially effective and economically feasible for the disadvantaged. The fact that nearly one-third of her sample (12/45) terminated prematurely underlines, however, the continued importance of developing sensitive procedures for prescriptively matching treatments and patients.

In addition to the few reports of the efficacy of insight-oriented psychotherapy with the disadvantaged noted previously, several recent studies have explored specific factors that may enhance or impede the effectiveness of such approaches for LSES groups. For example, Vail (1978) examined correlates of early termination among lower class black patients in an inner-city mental health clinic. Variables of concern included the race and sex of both patient and therapist, patients' attitudes toward whites, patient's perceptions of therapist's understanding and acceptingness, and, finally, patient−therapist discrepancies in perception of therapy. The only significant intervention characteristic found was sex of the therapist and sex of the patient. Surprisingly, however, same-sex patient−therapist pairs tended to have higher premature termination rates than cross-sex pairs. Further research is needed to determine whether there is something in the nature of the dynamics between cross-race patient−therapist pairs that, in interaction with the sex of each, may act to increase or moderate the degree of threat or comfort a patient experiences.

The match between therapist and patient expectations about the therapy experience has been shown to be one factor that may influence the outcomes achieved by insight-oriented therapists when working with LSES patients. Evans, Acosta, Yamamoto, and Skilbeck (1984) developed an orientation program for therapists to increase the therapist's knowledge about minority and low-income patients and their sensitivity to the requests and problems of this population. Using 29 therapists, generally as their own controls, Evans et al. (1984) evaluated their efficacy with low-income and minority patients before and after they participated in the orientation program. A total of 98 patients were seen by therapists before orientation and 73 after its completion. Four to six weeks after the termination of therapy, patients were sent a questionnaire to assess current problem status, satisfaction with services received, and reasons for discontinuing therapy. At follow-up, patients who were seen by "oriented" therapists responded more positively to the question, "The therapist responded well to me when I tried to tell it like it is" (Evans et al., 1984, p. 95). Further, analysis of audiotapes of initial sessions supported this finding by revealing that oriented therapists provided more explanation and discussion of patient problems and treatment plans than did those who had not been through the orientation. Patients of oriented therapists also reported themselves to be more satisfied, better able to handle their problems effectively, and more likely to return to a therapist should they have a serious emotional problem.

A study by Day and Reznikoff (1980) indicates that the appropriateness of patient expectations and the match between those of the therapists and the patient may be an equally important determinant of therapy outcome with LSES minority children. Children aged 7 through 13 and their parents were asked to complete a survey assessing expectations about treatment at a children's psychiatric clinic one week prior to their first therapy and counseling sessions and again at the end of six sessions. Social class was not related to premature termination nor to appropriateness of expectations. For both low- and middle- or high-income families, however, inappropriateness of parental expectations about treatment was significantly related to dropping out of treatment.

Group Approaches

As questions have been raised about the efficacy of traditional individual approaches for LSES patients, increasing attention has been placed on the development of alternative strategies. One oft-noted shortcoming of the latter strategies is the cultural dissimilarity between patient and therapist and the shortage of LSES bilingual or bicultural therapists available to alleviate this problem (Herrera & Sanchez, 1980; Smith & Glass, 1977). For this reason, group treatment strategies have received attention as one means for reducing the gap between available service providers and LSES individuals in need of service. Moreover, since group approaches involve other individuals with similar backgrounds and problems, these approaches may help LSES minority group members to understand their problems and cope with their difficulties in culturally relevant ways.

Although systematic, well-controlled and evaluated research on the utility of group procedures with the disadvantaged is, as yet, seriously lacking, several promising starts have been made. For example, Herrera and Sanchez (1980) employed a behavioral, problem-focused approach with Spanish-speaking, Mexican-American patients. Based on behavioral ratings of change on target problems, group members were determined to be generally effective in implementing strategies for addressing behavioral deficiencies. Moreover, the investigators report that unlike studies of similar clients in more traditional individual treatment programs, attendance was not a problem. Whereas attendance in 10 randomly selected, similarly sized English-speaking groups at the same clinic averaged only 51 percent, attendance for the Mexican-American patients averaged 76 percent.

Herrera and Sanchez (1980) also report that as a function of the group format, group members were able to establish a more extensive support system than would have been the case if individual therapy were used. Reportedly, new group members more easily accepted some of the concepts and themes central to the treatment program than did the initial group members. The group format seemed to facilitate the development and modification of patient expectations that were congruent with those of the therapist and the clinic than was the case for patients seen individually.

Comas-Diaz (1981) explored the differential efficacy of cognitive and behavior therapy groups for the reduction of depression in low-income Puerto Rican women. The cognitive intervention procedures were based on the work of Beck (1974) and Seligman (1975); the behavioral treatment emphasized the training of social skills and self-reinforcers (Lewinsohn, Weinstein, & Alper, 1970). The study included a waiting-list control group. Overall results at posttreatment revealed that patients in both therapy groups showed significantly less depression than those in the control groups. No significant differences, however, were found between the two treatment conditions in the posttesting. At five-week follow-up, the findings remain unchanged with one exception—individuals in the behavioral treatment group showed significantly fewer clinical symptoms of depression.

In discussing her results, Comas-Diaz (1981) agreed with Herrera and Sanchez (1980) on the increased likelihood that general, nonspecific factors would enhance therapy outcome when group therapy is employed with LSES minority populations. For example, these researchers speculate that group therapy may reduce some of the feelings of isolation of immigrant Puerto Rican women following separation from their extended families, a most significant issue in Puerto Rican culture (Hynes & Werblin, 1977; Maldonado-Sierra & Trent, 1960).

The foregoing discussion of group strategies with the disadvantaged suggests that such approaches can usefully address some of the treatment-delivery difficulties associated with attempting to provide services for LSES and minority patients. Group strategies may be at least as effective as individual strategies, particularly those that are problem-focused. As suggested in our reviews of LSES experiences and in our discussion of time-limited approaches, direct attention to resolving immediate problems may be more consistent with the treatment expectations of disadvantaged patients (Lorion, 1974b). When combined with group approaches in which there is an improved cultural and/or linguistic match between the client and treatment setting, the result may be increased patient comfort and commitment. It must be noted, however, that while these may be plausible assumptions, studies that systematically examine these hypotheses are still lacking. Hence, definitive data on these issues are not yet available.

Marital and Family Approaches

Throughout this chapter we have emphasized the importance of identifying treatment approaches that are salient to LSES lifestyles. Frequently, discussions of the working class stress the importance of family to the attainment and maintenance of their mental health (Gans, 1962; Giordano, 1973; Miller & Mishler, 1959; Miller & Riessman, 1969; Riessman, 1964). Although its composition may differ somewhat, the family is an equally important para-

meter of emotional functioning among the poor and minority groups (Miller & Riessman, 1968; Rainwater, 1966).

Family Approaches

Increasingly, therefore, the disadvantaged family is being perceived as a viable target for mental health services (Chaiklin & Frank, 1973; LaVietes, 1974). Mannino and Shore (1972), for example, described a program to assist low-income families in their interaction with other social systems. The goals of this "ecologically oriented family intervention" included increases in the family's effectiveness as a unit and in its capacity to relate to and effectively deal with relevant social systems (e.g., schools, welfare, medical facilities).

Yet low-income families seem hesitant to use and respond to family services. Rosenblatt and Mayer (1972) and Speer, Fossum, Lippman, Schwartz, and Slocum (1968) report that the major variable on which middle- and low-income families differ in their use of family services was in the number of appointments missed. Although LSES individuals had significantly more difficulty regularly attending sessions than did middle-class patients, they did not differ in rates of treatment continuation. In a well-designed comparative analysis of child psychotherapy, parent counseling, and "information feedback," Love, Kaswan, and Bugental (1972) demonstrated that family-oriented approaches can be effective in serving the needs of the disadvantaged. In this study, 91 families referred because of having a child experiencing serious school-related difficulties were assigned to one of three treatment conditions. Additionally, a "nonreferred" control group was used as a "normal" comparison group to provide baseline data on family and school measures. Dependent measures included school grades, behavioral ratings by objective observers, and ratings of family interactions and communication patterns based on videotape recordings. The results clearly indicated that interventions by parents were significantly more effective in improving their children's performance than child psychotherapy. Post hoc analyses revealed that LSES participants were most responsive to procedures that provided direct information and advice. Heinicke (1975) also evaluated the effects of family treatment on the parents of 112 LSES children identified as displaying developmental lags. Consistent with other studies, she found a positive response to family approaches on measured ratings of effectiveness and on specific measures of adjustment.

The general findings reviewed thus far suggest that family-oriented approaches can be appropriate for the disadvantaged. However, objective evidence of their effectiveness is not readily available (Wells, Dilkes, & Burckhardt, 1976). Case reports of effectiveness are provided by Framo (1969) and Sager, Brayboy, and Waxenberg (1970). A somewhat less subjective evaluation of family therapy with the disadvantaged is provided by Minuchin, Montalvo, Guerney, Rosman, and Schumer (1967). These investigators used a variety of objective-type family interaction tasks to compare 12 ghetto families having a delinquent child with 10 matched "control" families not having a delinquent child. The investigators report that 7 out of 12 experimental families were judged to be clinically improved after treatment on all of the interactional measures. Although suggestive, these results must be verified in a systematic, methodologically sophisticated way. Unfortunately, posttesting was limited to the experimental families. Readers are urged to read Chapter 13 by Gurman, Kniskern, and Pinsof for an extended discusssion of family procedures.

Marital Approaches

If, as Rainwater (1966) suggests, low-income family life is characterized by unstructured marital roles, strategies focusing specifically on improving the marital relationship may be quite relevant to disadvantaged lifestyles. Considerable evidence exists that demonstrates the efficacy of these procedures. Gurman (1973) and Gurman and Kniskern (1978), for example, report that across a variety of marital-therapy approaches and outcome criteria, improvement is found in the majority of treated patients. Most studies used clinic populations primarily made up of disadvantaged families. Moreover, the average treatment duration was fewer than 20 sessions. The reviewers note that marital therapy, like other therapies (Bergin, 1971), can have deleterious effects on some clients. In roughly 2 percent of the cases treated, the referral problem was worse after treatment.

Among the important findings reported by Beck (1976) is the relatively stronger impact of struc-

tured, communication-oriented treatments. A variety of approaches with this emphasis are reported by Olson (1976). Some have been developed specifically with disadvantaged clients. Others, although apparently generalizable, have yet to be proven effective specifically with the disadvantaged.

For example, Stuart (1976) describes a behaviorally oriented program to improve communication skills between marital partners. Interim findings on 200 couples revealed that in 87 percent of the couples treated, at least one spouse met the initial behavioral objectives; in 81 percent of the cases, those objectives were met by both partners. One year after treatment there were only 5 divorces; 5 years later, 174 of the 200 couples remained married and reported reasonable satisfaction with the relationship. In view of these preliminary findings, Stuart's operant approach at improving communication skills merits further consideration.

Cline, Mejia, Coles, Klein, and Cline (1984) have recently attempted to clarify the relationship among a number of different therapist behaviors in marital therapy and behavioral and affective changes in 77 middle- and lower-class couples. Among the more salient findings was a consistent negative relationship between therapist directiveness and behavioral and marital satisfaction outcomes for middle-class couples. By contrast, neither relationship existed between outcome and directiveness for lower-class couples. In fact, for LSES couples the relationships tended to be in the opposite direction. In addition, therapist reflectiveness was related to decreases in positive social behavior for LSES wives and husbands. The opposite was true for middle-class husbands. Finally, there was a strong positive association between therapist relationship orientation and outcome as assessed by marital satisfaction ratings for LSES husbands. These findings are consistent with the previously noted LSES expectations and with the LSES preference for focused, problem-oriented interventions.

Considerably more research will be necessary before the relative costs and benefits of marital and family approaches for disadvantaged clients are identified. At present, we remain dependent on clinical/anecdotal reports and on poorly evaluated results to assess the efficacy of these procedures for the disadvantaged or other segments of society with any degree of certainty. The trend of available findings, however, is consistently positive and suggests that these procedures are worthwhile.

ALTERNATIVE MANPOWER RESOURCES

Any discussion of mental health interventions with the disadvantaged must consider the contributions of paraprofessional personnel (Reiff & Riessman, 1965). These individuals were a key manpower resource during the community mental health center movement's growth period (Bloom, 1984; President's Commission on Mental Health, 1978). Their utilization was initially justified on three pragmatic grounds. First, as discussed at some length earlier in this chapter, the prevalence of mental disorder among the disadvantaged is disproportionate to their numbers in the population. Second, it was known that this segment of society was least likely to perceive the mental health system as relevant to their emotional/ behavioral needs (Gurin, Veroff, & Feld, 1960; Kadushin, 1969). Finally estimates of available and foreseeable mental health professional resources made evident that the nation would face major manpower shortages in the decades ahead (Albee, 1959, 1967; Arnhoff, Rubenstein, & Speisman, 1969; Gartner, 1971). Two decades ago, the convergence of these factors made it timely to question *who* should deliver mental health services (Cowen, 1973; Gartner & Riessman, 1974). Experimentation with this issue evolved from small pilot studies to assume the proportion of a "nonprofessional revolution" (Sobey, 1970).

Preliminary analyses of the effectiveness of paraprofessionals in the mental health system were consistently positive and at times quite enthusiastic (Gartner & Riessman, 1974; Rioch, 1967; Truax, 1967). For the most part, however, these early evaluations were highly subjective and rarely met even basic criteria of scientific rigor (Cowen, 1973; Karlsruher, 1974).

The pragmatic bases that justified the need for paraprofessional personnel during the 1960s and 1970s remain viable even now. As documented by the most recent President's Commission on Mental Health (1978), excess level of service need, unwillingness to accept traditional services, and the absence of sufficient numbers of qualified personnel to provide needed services continue to plague the dis-

advantaged. Fortunately, however, since 1970 the quality and quantity of objective assessments of paraprofessional services have increased substantially. Moreover, in recent years the scientific merits of these assessments have been carefully examined and debated (Durlak, 1979, 1981; Hattie, Sharpley, & Rogers, 1984; Lorion & Cahill, 1980; Nietzel & Fisher, 1981). Interested readers are urged to examine these critical reviews in careful detail. Not only can they provide the basis for determining *at this time* whether the evidence supports use of paraprofessionals in mental health, they can also serve as blueprints for designing scientifically valid assessments of this question in the future.

Applying the 13 methodological criteria used by Luborsky, Singer, and Luborsky (1975) in their assessment of research on professional treatment effectiveness, Durlak categorized 42 studies of paraprofessional effectiveness into five levels of scientific rigor. He concludes that across all levels of research sophistication, the results are directionally consistent, that is that, "the clinical outcomes paraprofessionals achieve are equal to or significantly better than those obtained by professionals" (Durlak, 1979, p. 89). Durlak notes further that "professional mental health education, training and experience are not necessary prerequisites for an effective helping person" (p. 89). In presenting these conclusions, Durlak (1979, 1981) emphasizes the need to accept their tenuousness given the methodological limitations of the reviewed studies.

Durlak's analysis of these 42 studies was examined shortly after its publication with the following conclusion: "As Durlak notes, the consistency of the observed results across a variety of methodological designs and outcome criteria, in spite of identifiable biases against paraprofessionals in some studies, suggests that the conclusion that paraprofessionals are effective psychotherapeutic agents is valid" (Lorion & Cahill, 1980, p. 26).

In this review Lorion and Cahill (1980) also pointed out that any attempt to assess paraprofessional effectiveness must reflect the multiplicity of goals associated with the original rationale for the paraprofessional movement. Included among these goals were: (1) reducing the mental health manpower shortage; (2) providing employment opportunities through federal antipoverty programs; (3) increasing the effectiveness and accessibility of services to the disadvantaged; (4) increasing the efficiency of mental health services by relieving professionals of less skilled tasks; and (5) providing a therapeutic work experience for some paraprofessional caregivers. Appreciation of the heterogeneity of paraprofessionals (e.g., students, B.A. level human service workers, indigenous mental health aides) makes evident the unequal relevance of these goals to diverse subgroups of paraprofessionals. Thus, the need to operationalize "effectiveness" differently for each of these groups becomes apparent, as does the diversity of the mental health problems that each subgroup effectively confronts. Lorion and Cahill (1980) concluded that some data, albeit of highly varied scientific quality, has been reported in support of each of the aforementioned goals. During the next decade, the relevance of those goals distinct from the issue of therapeutic effectiveness is, at this point, highly questionable. Nevertheless, such positive results should not be summarily dismissed. Consideration of the diversity of impacts is important in evaluating the total consequence of any innovative service-delivery strategy.

Durlak's conclusions were not endorsed universally. In a highly critical article, Nietzel and Fisher (1981) argue that Durlak significantly underestimated the methodological limitations of the studies he reviewed. In fact, Nietzel and Fisher suggest that all but 5 of the 42 studies be eliminated from consideration in attempting to answer the paraprofessional versus professional question. Yet the balance of evidence from these 5 studies actually supports the conclusion that under certain conditions, paraprofessionals can be at least as therapeutically effective as professionals. Moreover, in reviewing the 4 additional studies presented as supporting professional effectiveness, legitimate questions can be raised about which side of the argument receives support from their findings. Yet, however questionable their conclusion about the weight of the evidence, Nietzel and Fisher's comments do provide important clarifications about the methodological complexities associated with such research.

The most recent and, in our view, sophisticated analysis of this issue is provided by Hattie et al. (1984), who applied meta-analytic techniques to the studies reviewed by both Durlak (1979) and Nietzel and Fisher (1981). These procedures were applied carefully and without apparent bias. Among the major conclusions resulting from the meta-analysis are the following:

1. Paraprofessionals are at least as effective as professionals.
2. Methodologically sophisticated studies favor paraprofessionals.
3. Levels of experience and training relate to paraprofessional effectiveness.
4. Subsequent research would need to report nearly 900 effects favoring professionals for one to conclude justifiably that the data favor professionals; merely 34 additional effects favoring paraprofessional are needed to effectively finalize the issue in that direction.

The 42 studies in question have been examined with a degree of intensity rarely found in the behavioral sciences. In spite of repeated analyses of their methodological soundness, the reported findings and resulting conclusions are unlikely to be accepted without further debate and question. The issue of concern is too central to be considered closed at this point. If the thrust of this set of reviews is indeed justified, one must, at the very least, consider paraprofessional resources as a legitimate factor in planning mental health services for the disadvantaged. That they can contribute cannot be discounted. What remains unclear, however, are the conditions under which their contributions can be maximized—the types of interventions and patients for which this resource is most appropriate. Additionally, it must be noted that evidence that paraprofessionals *can* do psychotherapy should not be misinterpreted as evidence that they *should* do psychotherapy. In this section and the one that follows, a range of interventions from crisis work to prevention and promotion strategies is discussed. If, as suggested, these alternatives have distinct advantages in responding to the mental health needs of the disadvantaged, then their applicability by paraprofessionals must also be examined.

PSYCHOTHERAPY AND THE DISADVANTAGED: FUTURE DIRECTIONS

The Research Agenda

To inform readers of the low priority attached to research on the mental health needs of the disadvantaged, a table was included in the original version of this chapter (Lorion, 1978). The intent of that table was twofold. First, it made evident that poverty, as a topical area for research, was relatively low on the mental health agenda, as reflected in publication emphases. Nine journals were reviewed to determine the relative emphasis each placed on the mental health needs of the disadvantaged. Relative to all of the articles published in these journals (selected because of their stated interest in the topic) during the period from 1970 to 1975, between 2 and 16 percent of their articles focused on the disadvantaged. Most distressing at that time was that only half of these met even minimal empirical criteria (i.e., they reported a number), only 15 percent used a control group, fewer than 6 percent involved both pre- and postintervention measures, and a mere 2 percent included a follow-up measurement in their design. In discussing the figures reported in that table, emphasis was placed on the importance of using observed trends as a stimulant to increase significantly mental health researchers' investment in work with the disadvantaged (Lorion, 1978).

To assess progress made during the period 1976–1984, we repeated the earlier journal review. Our findings are reported in Table 17.1. The trends reflected in this table are most alarming. In all but one case (i.e., the *Community Mental Health Journal*), previously observed percentages of articles focused on the disadvantaged *decreased*. For the majority of the journals, these decreases are very significant! The range of articles focused on the disadvantaged decreased to between 0.3 and 6 percent. Even more distressing, the percent of the 1976–1984 articles that met even minimal criteria as research reports ranged from 0 to under 5 percent. Thus, not only has attention to the needs of the poor decreased, but the decrease is especially noteworthy with respect to research on understanding and responding to the needs of the disadvantaged.

The reasons for this dramatic reduction are, we assume, multiple. Unquestionably, federal funding of research addressing "social issues" (e.g., poverty, unemployment, inner-city environments) has been significantly reduced since 1980. In conjunction with the near total repeal of the Mental Health System Act of 1980 (P.L. 96-398) and the potentially devastating consequences of this decision for the community mental health center movement

(Bloom, 1984), support for the study or even delivery of mental health services for the poor has become scarce. In effect, prevailing federal policies have communicated directly the low priority attached to examining the links between poverty and psychopathology and to designing, implementing, evaluating, and disseminating strategies for responding to the needs of the poor. The trends represented in Table 17.1 may reveal the clarity with which that message has been received.

We believe, however, that it would be a mistake to explain these trends solely in terms of federal policy. The mental health professions have historically been at best ambivalent in their commitment to working with LSES patients (Lorion, 1974a; Lorion & Parron, 1985). That such ambivalence continues is reflected in the research findings discussed in Chapters 6 and 7 of this volume. Before any signficant gains are likely to be made in our knowledge about the mental health needs of the poor, it is perhaps necessary that we in the professions review our own resistances and countertransferences toward this segment of society. Repeated charges that our therapeutic strategies are irrelevant to the poor (Riessman, Cohen, & Pearl, 1964), absurd (Dumont, 1968), victim-blaming (Ryan, 1971), racist (Thomas & Sillen, 1972), and designed to reinforce the status quo (Rappoport, 1977) simply should not be dismissed. The fact is that for nearly two decades we have focused increasingly less of our conceptual, clinical, and empirical resources on those factors that limit the mental health delivery system's capacity to understand, anticipate, and respond to the needs of its *potential* LSES consumers.

The emphasis placed on the qualifier "potential" is intentional. Our retreat from the poor is matched by their abandonment of the mental health system as a potential resource for resolving emotional problems (President's Commission on Mental Health, 1978). The rapid growth of the self-help movement in combination with the significant contributions to individual problem-solving provided by "natural caregivers" (e.g., neighbors, bartenders, beauticians) suggests that we may soon be (if we are not already!) perceived as superfluous. Although unresearched as a generalizable pattern, it is possible that LSES patients who continue to approach the mental health system for assistance represent that subset without alternative resources or for

TABLE 17.1 Relative Frequency of Appearance of Published Reports on the Disadvantaged in Selected Mental Health Journals, 1976–1984

Journal	Current Period	Total Articles (TA)	Total Articles Disadvantaged (DA)	Percent DA/TA[b]	Disadvantaged Articles[a] by Subgroup				Research Articles by Subgroup			
					Clinical Articles	Theoretical Articles	Total Research	Percent DA Research/ TA	Other Research Reports[d]	Control Group	Pre–Post Measure	Follow-up
Journal of Consulting and Clinical Psychology	1976–1984	1556	13	0.8 (3)	0	2	11	.73(2.5)	6	2	1	2
American Journal of Community Psychology	1976–1984	428	25	5.8 (14)	4	2	19	4.4 (11.7)	16	2	0	1
Community Mental Health Journal	1976–1984	268	17	6.3 (5)	2	3	12	4.5 (2.0)	10	0	1	1
Journal of Community Psychology	1976–1984	436	19	4.4 (6)	4	1	14	3.2 (5.5)	12	0	1	1
Journal of Social Issue	1976–1984	393	1	0.3 (16)	0	1	0	0 (6.6)	0	0	0	0
Archives of General Psychiatry	1976–1984	1299	14	1.1 (2)	0	0	14	1.1 (1.0)	12	1	0	1
American Journal of Orthopsychiatry	1976–1984	565	16	2.8 (15)	7	4	5	.9 (5.2)	3	1	0	1
American Journal of Psychiatry	1976–1984	2832	19	0.7 (3)	2	1	16	.6 (1.3)	14	1	0	1
Journal of Clinical Psychology	1976–1984	1691	14	0.8 (NR)[c]	0	0	14	.8 (NR)	10	3	0	1
Total		9468	138		19	14	105		83	10	3	9

[a] To be included in this category an article had to state that its subjects were LSES. Articles focused on ethnic/minorities were *not* included unless subjects were defined or described as LSES.

[b] Numbers in parentheses refer to similar percentage computed from 1970–1975 review reported in Lorion (1978).

[c] NR = not included in 1978 report.

[d] Includes surveys, correlational studies, and reviews of research findings.

whom those alternatives have not been effective. As a consequence, the mental health system may represent a last resort for LSES individuals. If so, the disappointing treatment attrition and outcome findings associated with LSES patients may reflect the seriousness of their needs *in combination with* a series of prior unsuccessful attempts to obtain assistance from local sources. If such sources are approached unsystematically but sequentially (e.g., family, friends, clergy, primary care physician) and one assumes that some number of problems are solved at each level, then it is possible that the mental health system is approached primarily by those repeatedly frustrated or unsuccessful in prior attempts to obtain help. With a history of such failure, limited faith in the mental health system's ability or desire to help, and an ambivalent service provider, the LSES patient's unwillingness to invest much time, energy, or financial resources in mental health services is understandable.

If the foregoing analysis even approximates the reality of the interface between a frustrated and pessimistic LSES patient and an ambivalent service provider, the situation has all of the components of an inescapable negative self-fulfilling prophecy. Thus, the patient's early departure reinforces the service provider's ambivalence toward LSES patients at the same time that perception of that ambivalence contributed to the LSES patient's doubts about the likelihood that the mental health system could respond to sensed needs. To attempt to conduct research within such a system is difficult at best! It is impossible to estimate from Table 17.1 the number of research efforts abandoned prior to completion or the many articles reviewed and rejected that might have been SES relevant. Our personal experience with such research, however, suggests to us that studies reported may reflect at most one-tenth of those undertaken. If this is the case, the tragedy is doubled. These incomplete studies not only contributed nothing to our knowledge base about LSES mental health needs but may also represent the final attempt by these researchers to undertake investigations on this issue. As a result, past generations of researchers committed to this topic have not been and are not being replenished. Reversing this trend represents, in our view, the mental health disciplines' major challenge for the coming decade.

PREVENTIVE APPROACHES FOR THE DISADVANTAGED

Conceptual Issues

Thus far, we have discussed in some detail the assumption that poverty's impact on psychopathology relates primarily to its interference with the effective utilization of available services. We suggest instead that its contribution to the development and maintenance of pathology be appreciated and examined. In this way, we believe, an important etiological factor may become understood and knowledge translated into responsive treatment modalities.

Interventions described thus far have been consistent with the remaining two assumptions noted earlier—that the needs of the poor should be served through direct rather than indirect services and should focus on established rather than incipient disorder. In the final section of this chapter we will examine briefly preventive interventions that focus instead on potential or developing disorder. In the chapter's title, the term "psychotherapy" was intentionally replaced by the term "mental health interventions" to reflect this intervention option. The seriousness, pervasiveness, and tenacity of emotional and behavioral disorders among LSES subgroups demand that the mental health disciplines seriously consider researching and implementing strategies that avoid or quickly interrupt pathogenic processes. If effective, such interventions can enable LSES individuals to cope more effectively with the stressors characteristic of their lifestyles and to identify and utilize social-support mechanisms. Most importantly, preventive strategies may reduce significantly negative sequences in which stressful events lead to maladaptive behaviors, which, in turn, precipitate other stressful events, and so on.

Discussions of the timeliness of preventive interventions for addressing emotional disorders have appeared with increasing frequency during the past decade (Cowen, 1973; Goldston, 1977; Kessler & Albee, 1975; Lorion, 1983a, 1983b; Lorion & Lounsbury, 1982; Sameroff, 1977). Additionally, a number of volumes have been published that focus specifically on preventive interventions in mental health (e.g., Albee & Joffe, 1977; Bowker, 1983; Felner, Jason, Moritsugu, & Farber, 1983; Miller, O'Neal, & Scott, 1982; Nobel, 1981; Perlmutter,

1982; Price, Ketterer, Bader, & Monahan, 1980). Evidence of the amount of activity associated with this topic is reflected in the almost constant appearance of new professional journals reporting prevention research and programs, in levels of state and local funds attached to preventive/early intervention programs (National Association of State Alcohol and Drug Abuse Directors, 1984), and increasing federal resources to fund research on the prevention of alcohol, drug, and mental disorders (Department of Health and Human Services, 1984, 1985). As the emphasis shifts from justifying the concept of prevention to designing and implementing such programs and to evaluating their results systematically, we expect that the applicability of this category of interventions will become apparent.

A comprehensive analysis of the state-of-the-art in conceptualizing and investigating prevention efforts in mental health is clearly beyond the scope of this section. Interested readers are urged to review the references cited before for such information. Our goal is more modest. Following a brief overview of basic concepts in prevention, we will describe selected examples of preventive interventions targeted to the disadvantaged *for which outcome data are available*. The latter part is emphasized because to this point the number of *implemented* prevention programs far exceeds the number of *researched* prevention programs (Cowen, 1973; Lorion, 1983a).

Although some may argue that the demands for evidence of effectiveness are unfairly stringent for prevention efforts in comparison with those for treatment (Albee, 1981), we would respond that evidence presented in Chapter 5 of this volume argues convincingly for the advantages of rigor in outcome criteria. Additionally, we believe that since the recipients of preventive interventions are not, by definition, experiencing symptomatic distress and often are not even aware of their participation in such an intervention, we have a responsibility for ensuring that iatrogenic effects are nonexistent or at least minimal. Gordon (1983) emphasizes the latter point in his recent editorial on ethical and practical aspects of behaviorally focused prevention efforts. As much as we oppose its "either—or" treatment versus prevention implications, it is a fact that prevention dollars are part of the total pool of human services monies. Consequently, we must be cau-

tious lest scarce funds be allocated to ineffective preventive services that might otherwise be targeted to treatment. At the same time, opponents of preventive efforts cannot deny that preventive interventions potentially represent a major vehicle for positive impact on what has, to date, been an unsolved problem: responding to the mental health needs of the disadvantaged. Caution in disseminating prevention programs should not be used as an excuse to delay the development, implementation, and design of preventive interventions. As Bloom (1984) so accurately states, it is a long-held public health maxim that no condition has ever been controlled by treatment but only through prevention.

In its simplest sense, prevention refers to efforts designed intentionally to reduce the prevalence of disorder or dysfunction in the population. If designed to avoid the onset of disorder, such efforts are termed "primary prevention." Onset may be avoided by altering the conditions or events causally related to the disorder (e.g., to alter the childrearing techniques of abusive or alcoholic parents) or by increasing the individual's capacity to cope with and overcome the consequences of significant life events. Catalano and Dooley (1980) suggest that the former efforts be termed "proactive" whereas the latter be thought of as "reactive." Procedures in the categories of prevention efforts discussed thus far are focused on a disorder or class of disorders. In addition, many (Albee, 1982; Cowen, 1980; Danish, Smyer, & Nowak, 1980) have argued convincingly for the importance of developing "promotion" or "enhancement" strategies that produce generalized increases in an individual's ability to tolerate stress and to function effectively. The consequential link between skill increases and reductions in mental disorders may be indirect at best. Yet proponents argue that they result in meaningful increments in the public health. Indeed, Iscoe (1974) has suggested that we should begin to work toward the development of "competent communities."

Preventive efforts also include activities designed to abort or reverse an incipient pathogenic process. Thus, although onset has not been avoided and early signs of disorder/dysfunction are detectable, an important intervention goal can be to prevent the process from reaching completion. Efforts so intended are termed "secondary prevention" and, typically, involve a combination of early detection and intervention strategies. In general, secondary preventive efforts in mental health occur before a condition meets diagnostic criteria, and these interventions are qualitatively different from those associated with psychotherapy. The advantage of such efforts is that they allow for intervention early in a problem's genesis (e.g., crisis intervention) and prior to the onset of complicating secondary effects (Lorion, 1983a). As such, these efforts ideally assume a higher probability of successful outcome at a reduced cost.

In selecting programs to present, we establish two criteria: that they be targeted to the disadvantaged and that they be adequately researched. The approaches described later are illustrative rather than exhaustive. Hopefully, they will provide the reader with an appreciation of what a preventive orientation can contribute to the resolution of the mental health needs of the disadvantaged.

Preventive Approaches

Preschool programs and their influence on the lives of the youngsters in them have been the focus of much of the prevention-promotion work with the disadvantaged. Although some heated debate continues over the efficacy of such efforts, there is increasing evidence that such programs can have both short- and long-term positive effects on the academic and emotional adaptation of participants (Royce et al., 1983). Perhaps the best known of these programs is Project Head Start (Zigler & Valentine, 1979). Often under fire from critics, this program has nonetheless endured and developed an impressive amount of data to attest to its value. Given this set of circumstances, it may be prudent to pause briefly and consider the sources of the continuing criticism in light of its success. A primary reason for this criticism may be the failure of critics to understand the goals of Head Start. The primary goal was *not* to raise the IQs of children nor to demonstrate the maintenance of these gains over prolonged periods, although this goal has frequently been "assigned" to Head Start programs by their critics. Rather, as Zigler (1979) states: "the creators of Head Start hoped to bring out greater social competence in disadvantaged children" (p. 496). He goes on to note that this goal was sought by "providing services to improve [the child's] health, intellectual ability, and social-emotional development, all of which are components of social competence" (p.

496). It is beyond the scope of this chapter to discuss comprehensively the full set of Head Start evaluation efforts (interested readers are referred to Zigler & Valentine, 1979). Zigler (1979), however, summarizes the findings as follows. He notes that 75 percent of the children in the program who suffered from physical illness or handicaps received treatment through Head Start. Moreover, program children were repeatedly found to do better on preschool achievement tests than poor children who had not participated in Head Start. Admittedly these gains may dissipate if additional support is not provided after the child leaves the program. Zigler (1979) points out that the gains in IQ and achievement test scores may be maintained if parents extend the remedial programs to the home themselves and/or if further special education experiences are provided for the children once they enter elementary school.

Head Start is not alone in its efforts to develop effective intervention programs for economically disadvantaged youngsters. Building on its example, Jason, DeAmicus, and Carter (1978) report on a six-year effort to develop educational interventions for disadvantaged toddlers. During the initial phase of the program, undergraduates were trained to develop helping relationships with inner-city toddlers (ages 10−24 months) who were identified by physicians in a neighborhood health center as evidencing appreciable social or behavioral difficulties. Following the development of the relationship, behavioral procedures were employed to encourage youngsters to rely on verbal rather than nonverbal means of social interaction, to engage in social interaction with adults as well as other youngsters, and to expose youngsters to an assortment of educational materials. Program evaluations revealed the children to be more talkative, active, and interested in their environment following program participation. Furthermore, the program resulted in parents becoming increasingly involved in educational activities with the children. The combination of parent involvement and a structured behavioral curriculum to teach language skills significantly enhanced the children's academic and motor abilities. Overall the authors conclude that such programs may be highly effective and, in agreement with Zigler (1979), argue that "inclusion of parents in the training programs better enables children to maintain whatever gains they have achieved after the termination of the formal program" (Jason et al., 1978, p. 275).

Additional support for the efficacy and utility of early childhood programs with disadvantaged populations comes from Royce et al. (1983). They report on the pooled findings of demonstration studies carried out by a consortium of early childhood investigators. These programs varied considerably in terms of personnel (i.e., paraprofessionals, teachers, and/or mental health professionals) as well as delivery settings and curriculum. Overall, the children in the original samples were 94 percent black and predominantly from LSES families. After the consortium was formed in 1975, a shared set of research questions and measures was applied in follow-up studies carried out in 1976 and 1980. For the 1976 follow-up, 1600 children ages 9 to 19 from the original samples of approximately 3000 participants were included. At the end of the program's first year, significant differences were found between control and program groups on both IQ and achievement tests. The latter differences continued into the early school years. Thus, at immediate posttests, the median program—control achievement test differences had been 7.42 points. At first grade entry, the average difference was still 5.8 points. These effects were, however, not permanent. By the 1976 follow-up (5 to 15 years after the initial intervention), no IQ differences between program and control children were found. Nevertheless, the results of the follow-up assessment revealed that progressively higher percentages of control children experienced grade retentions and/or special education placement. Additionally, among the four samples from the consortium with high-school-aged subjects, program participants were more likely to complete high school than controls. Controlling for sex, ethnicity, and other background factors, the investigators concluded that 15 percent more program participants completed high school than controls.

One of the most striking results to date on the efficacy of early educational intervention comes from the High-Scope Educational Research Foundation Project in Michigan (Clements, Schwenhart, Barnett, Epstein, & Weikart, 1984). The project focused on 123 LSES children with IQs between 60 and 90. These children were randomly divided into experimental and control groups. Experimental subjects participated in a preschool education project. Follow-ups were conducted when the children were 8, 15, and 19 years of age. Of the preschool

group, 67 percent graduated from high school in contrast to 49 percent of the control groups. Furthermore, nearly twice as many of the program children as controls participated in college or vocational training after high school. Finally, the rate of teenage pregnancy among program children was slightly more than half that of the controls. Additionally, program participants were involved in 20 percent fewer arrests than controls.

In addition to preschool intervention programs, other prevention-promotion efforts have been used with the disadvantaged. For example, Kirschenbaum (1979) reported on a social-skills development program in seven inner-city elementary schools. Services were provided by paraprofessionals under professional supervision. Fifteen to 25 percent of children identified as being at high risk because of problem behaviors in school received social-skills oriented services. Of the referred children, 63 percent received both the direct intervention and teacher and parent consultation. The remaining 37 percent received only teacher and parent consultation. The group intervention focused on the improvement of social skills. The primary outcome measure involved teachers' behavioral ratings of the children's interpersonal competence and problems. Results showed that children in both intervention groups were significantly more socially skilled than the untreated controls. No differences, however, were found on problem ratings.

Programs aimed at reducing LSES stress levels by facilitating the mastery of anticipatable life transitions have also been developed. For example, Felner, Ginter, and Primavera (1982) reported on a primary prevention program for children entering high school. This project sought to enhance the coping efforts of participating adolescents by reducing the complexity in the school environment as well as by increasing available social support. These goals were obtained through two major program activities. First, the social system into which the student was entering was partially reorganized to facilitate the student's developing a stable support systems. This was accomplished by creating relatively stable student groups that remained intact from one class to the next. Consequently, the entering freshman experienced consistency in the available social network throughout the day. In addition, this change served to increase the adolescents' perception of the school as a stable, organized, understandable, and cohesive environment. In addition, guidance functions were assigned to homeroom teachers. This step was taken to increase the amount of both instrumental and affective social support available to facilitate access to information concerning school expectations, rules, and regulations.

Overall, the project's major goals were achieved. By the end of ninth grade, the adolescents who participated in the program showed significantly better attendance and academic achievement, as well as more stable self-concepts than children who experienced the transition without participating in the programs. Project participants perceived the school environment as having greater clarity of expectations and organizational structure and higher levels of teacher support than did their nonproject peers.

CONCLUSION

The decreased level of attention and effort that has been focused on LSES mental health needs during the past decade is most distressing. As a consequence of this inactivity, the behavioral sciences have learned little in the past decade. That is unfortunate not only for LSES individuals but for all segments of the population who experience emotional and behavioral problems. Had we learned more about how poverty per se contributes to psychopathology, we would also understand more completely how environmental factors in general contribute positively and negatively to behavioral functioning. Had we developed efficient direct and indirect services for those unable, for a variety of reasons, to remain in or profit from long-term expressive psychotherapies, we might now have available a variety of proven therapeutic modalities that could be applied prescriptively to anyone in need. Most importantly, progress in understanding the factors contributing to the development, maintenance, and remediation of mental disorders in LSES populations might have altered positively the unfortunately unchanged epidemiological fact that the disadvantaged are most affected by emotional disorder. Unquestionably, LSES lifestyles are demanding and would challenge the adaptive potential of even the most effective coping skills. Were we able to improve the LSES individual's capacity to respond to those demands, it is certain that the consequences of that capacity would extend beyond the mental health sphere and have impact also on the nation's educational, economic, and social needs.

Yet for a multitude of reasons, the behavioral sciences have avoided the challenges of the disadvantaged for nearly a decade. As a consequence, a new generation of researchers committed to working on unraveling the complex links between economic disadvantage and emotional status has not been nurtured. That lack of expertise will impede progress in the future and immediate priority should be given to renewing the interests of young investigators in the challenges of the disadvantaged. Achievement of that goal is not likely to be easily accomplished. Federal support for services and research focused on the poor is unlikely to increase in the foreseeable future. Indeed, the very facilities that provide services may themselves be in some jeopardy. The responsibility is therefore on the mental health disciplines to establish the disadvantaged as a priority and to undertake the clinical and empirical efforts necessary to understand and respond to their needs. We believe that a major key to future progress involves the continuation and expansion of efforts to clarify poverty's etiological contribution to emotional and behavioral disorder. Further, we believe that the scope and seriousness of their needs not only argue for but may be best served by preventive interventions. Hopefully, the generation of prevention researchers currently being trained will appreciate the complementarity of their interests and the needs of the disadvantaged. More importantly, we look forward to renewed interest in the poor by all the mental health disciplines. Social issues have a history of waxing and waning; the issue of the disadvantaged merits renewed attention.

REFERENCES

Acosta, F. X., Yamamoto, J., & Evans, L. A. (1982). *Effective psychotherapy for low-income and minority patients.* New York: Plenum.

Albee, G. W. (1959). *Mental health manpower trends.* New York: Basic Books.

Albee, G. W. (1967). The relation of conceptual models to manpower needs. In E. L. Cowen, E. A. Gardner, & M. Zax (Eds.), *Emergent approaches to mental health* (pp. 63–73). New York: Appleton-Century-Crofts.

Albee, G. W. (1981). Politics, power, prevention, and social change. In J. M. Joffe & G. W. Albee (Eds.), *Prevention through political action and social change: Primary prevention of psychopathology* (Vol. 5; pp. 5–25). Hanover, NH: University Press of New England.

Albee, G. W. (1982). Preventing psychopathology and promoting human potential. *American Psychologist, 37*(9), 1043–1050.

Albee, G. W. & Joffe, J. M. (Eds.). (1977). *The issues: An overview of primary prevention*. Hanover, NH: University Press of New England.

American Psychiatric Association (1980). *Diagnostic and statistical manual of mental disorders* (3rd ed.). Washington, DC.

Arnhoff, F. N., Rubenstein, E. A., & Speisman, J. C. (Eds.). (1969). *Manpower for mental health.* Chicago: Aldine.

Arsenian, J., & Arsenian, J. M. (1948). Tough and easy cultures: A conceptual analysis. *Psychiatry, 11*(4), 377–385.

Avnet, H. H. (1962). *Psychiatric insurance: Financing short-term ambulatory treatment.* New York: Group Health Insurance Co., Inc.

Avnet, H. H. (1965). How effective is short-term therapy? In L. R. Wolberg (Ed.), *Short-term psychotherapy.* New York: Grune & Stratton.

Barton, H. D. (Ed.) (1971). *Brief therapies.* New York: Behavioral Publications.

Beck, A. T. (1974). The development of depression: A cognitive model. In P. Friedman & M. Katz (Eds.), *The psychology of depression: Contemporary theory and research.* New York: Wiley.

Beck, D. F. (1976). Research findings on the outcomes of marital counseling. In D. H. L. Olson (Ed.), *Treating relationships* (pp. 431–473). Lake Mills, IA: Graphic.

Beck, D. F., & Jones, M. A. (1973). *Progress on family problems: A nationwide study of clients' and counselors' views on family agency services.* New York: Family Service Association of America.

Bellack, L., & Small, L. (1965). *Emergency psychotherapy and brief psychotherapy.* New York: Grune & Stratton.

Benefee, L. M., Abramowitz, S. I., Weitz, L. J., & Armstrong, S. H. (1976). *American Journal of Community Psychology, 4*(3), 263–273.

Bergel, E. E. (1962). *Social stratification.* New York: McGraw-Hill.

Bergin, A. E. (1971). The evaluation of therapeutic outcomes. In A. E. Bergin & S. L. Garfield (Eds.), *Handbook of psychotherapy and behavior change: An empirical analysis* (pp. 217–270). New York: Wiley.

Bernard, V. W. (1965). Some principles of dynamic psychiatry in relation to poverty. *American Journal of Psychiatry, 122*, 254–267

Bernard, V. W. (1971). Composite remedies for psychosocial problems. *International Psychiatry Clinics, 8*, 61–85.

Bloom, B. L. (1984). *Community mental health* (2nd ed.). Monterey, CA: Brooks/Cole.

Bottomore, T. B. (1966). *Classes in modern society.* New York: Pantheon.

Bowker, J. P. (1983). *Education for primary prevention in social work.* New York: Council on Social Work Education.

Brown, G. W., Nibhrolchain, M., & Harris, T. O. (1975). Social class and psychiatric disturbance among women in an urban population. *Sociology 9*, 225–254.

Brown, G. W., & Harris, T. (1978). *Social origins of depression.* New York: Free Press.

Campbell, D. T., & Stanley, J. C. (1966). *Experimental and quasi-experimental designs for research.* Chicago: Rand-McNally.

Caplan, G., & Killilea, M. (Eds.), (1976). *Support systems and mutual help: Multidisciplinary explorations.* New York: Grune & Stratton.

Catalano, R., & Dooley, D. (1980). Economic change in primary prevention. In R. H. Price, R. F. Ketterer, B. C. Bader, & J. Monahan (Eds.), *Prevention in mental health: Research, policy and practice* (pp. 21–40). Beverly Hills: Sage.

Chaiklin, H., & Frank., C. L. (1973). Separation, service delivery and family functioning. *Public Welfare,* Winter, 2–7.

Clement, J. R., Schwenhart, L. J., Barnett, W. S., Epstein, A. S., & Weikart, D. P. (1984). *Changed lives.* Ypsilanti, MI: High Scope Foundation Press.

Cline, V. B., Mejia, J., Coles, J., Klein, N., & Cline, R. A. (1984). The relationships between therapist behavior and outcome for middle- and lower-class couples in marital therapy. *Journal of Clinical Psychology, 40*, 691–704.

Comas-Diaz, L. (1981). Effects of cognitive and behavioral group treatment on the depressive symptomatology of Puerto Rican women. *Journal of Consulting and Clinical Psychology, 49*, 627–632.

Cowen, E. L. (1973). Social and community interventions. *Annual Review of Psychology, 24*, 423–472.

Cowen, E. L. (1980). The wooing of primary prevention. *American Journal of Community Psychology, 8*(3), 258–284.

Danish, S. J., Smyer, M. A., & Nowak, C. A. (1980). Developmental intervention: Enhancing life-event processes. In P. B. Baltes & O. G. Brim, Jr. (Eds.), *Life-span development and behavior* (Vol. 3). New York: Academic Press.

Day, L., & Reznikoff, M. (1980). Social class, the treatment process, and parents' and children's expectations about child psychotherapy. *Journal of Clinical Child Psychology, 9*, 195–198.

Department of Health and Human Services. (1984). *Prevention activities of the Alcohol, Drug Abuse and Mental Health Administration.* Fiscal Year 1983 Report to Congress. Washington, DC: Author.

Department of Health and Human Services. (1985). *Prevention activities of the Alcohol, Drug Abuse and Mental Health Administration.* Fiscal year 1984 Report to Congress. Washington, DC: Author.

Dohrenwend, B. P. (1984, June). *Social stress and psychopathology.* Paper presented at the meeting of the Vermont Conference on the Primary Prevention of Psychopathology, Burlington, VT.

Dohrenwend, B. P., & Dohrenwend, B. S. (1969). *Social status and psychological disorder: A causal inquiry.* New York: Wiley.

Dohrenwend, B. P., & Dohrenwend, B. S. (1981a). Quasi-experimental evidence on the social-causation–social-selection issue posed by class differences. *American Journal of Community Psychology, 9*(2), 128–146.

Dohrenwend, B. S., & Dohrenwend, B. P. (1981b)

Hypotheses about stress processes linking social class to various types of psychopathology. *American Journal of Community Psychology, 9*(2), 146–159.

Dohrenwend, B. P., Dohrenwend, B. S., Gould, M. S., Link, B., Neugebauer, R., & Wunsch-Hitzig, R. (1980). *Mental illness in the United States: Epidemiologic estimates.* New York: Praeger.

Dumas, J. E., & Wahler, R. G. (1983). Predictors of treatment outcome in parent training: Mother insularity and socioeconomic disadvantage. *Behavioral Assessment, 5,* 301–313.

Dumont, M. (1968). *The absurd healer: Perspectives of a community psychiatrist.* New York: Science House.

Durlak, J. A. (1979). Comparative effectiveness of paraprofessional and professional helpers. *Psychological Bulletin, 86*(1), 80–92.

Durlak, J. A. (1981). Evaluating comparative studies of paraprofessional and professional helpers: A reply to Nietzel and Fisher. *Psychological Bulletin, 89*(3), 566–569.

Eaton, W. W., Holzer, C. E., VonKorff, M., Anthony, J. C., Helzer, J. E., George, L., Burnam, A., Boyd, J. H., Kessler, L. G., Locke, B. Z. (1984). The design of the Epidemiologic Catchment Area Surveys: The control and measurement of error. *Archives of General Psychiatry, 41,* 942–948.

Eron, L. D., & Peterson, R. A. (1982). Abnormal behavior: Social approaches. *Annual Review, 33,* 231–264.

Evans, L. A., Acosta, F. X., Yamamoto, J., & Skilbeck, W. M. (1984). Orienting psychotherapists to better serve low income and minority patients. *Journal of Clinical Psychology, 40,* 90–96.

Eysenck, H. J. (1972). New approaches to mental illness: The failure of a tradition. In H. Gottesfeld (Ed.), *The critical issues of community mental health* (pp. 95–125). New York: Behavioral Publications.

Faris, R. E. L., & Dunham, H. W. (1939). *Mental disorders in urban areas: An ecological study of schizophrenia and other psychoses.* Chicago: Chicago University Press.

Felner, R. D., Ginter, M. & Primavera, J. (1982). Primary prevention during school transitions: Social support and environmental structure. *American Journal of Community Psychology, 10*(3), 277–290.

Felner, R. D., Jason, L. A., Moritsugu, J. N., & Farber, S. S. (Eds.) (1983). *Preventive psychology: Theory, research and practice.* New York: Pergamon.

Framo, J. L. (1969). *In-depth family therapy with a black ghetto, intact family.* Unpublished manuscript, Temple University, Philadelphia.

Frank, J. D. (1961). *Persuasion and healing: A comparative study of psychotherapy.* New York: Schocken Books.

Freud, S. (1950). *Collected papers* (Vol. II). London: Hogarth Press and the Institute of Psychoanalysis.

Gans, H. J. (1962). *The urban villagers.* New York: Free Press.

Garfield, S. L. (1963). A note on patients' reasons for terminating therapy. *Psychological Reports, 13,* 38.

Garfield, S. L. (1971). Research on client variables in psychotherapy. In A. E. Bergin & S. L. Garfield (Eds.), *Handbook of psychotherapy and behavior change: An empirical analysis* (pp. 271–298). New York: Wiley.

Gartner, A. (1971). *Paraprofessionals and their performance.* New York: Praeger.

Gartner, A., & Riessman, F. (1974). The performance of paraprofessionals in the mental health field. In G. Caplan (Ed.), *The American handbook of psychiatry* (Vol. II). New York: Basic Books.

Getz, W. L., Fujita, B. N., & Allen, D. (1975). The use of paraprofessionals in crisis intervention: Evaluation of an innovative program. *American Journal of Community Psychology, 3*(2), 135–144.

Gibbs, J. T. (1984). Black adolescents and youth: An endangered species. *American Journal of Orthopsychiatry, 54*(1), 6–21.

Giordano, J. (1973). *Ethnicity and mental health.* New York: American Jewish Committee.

Giordano, J. (1976). Community mental health in a pluralistic society. *International Journal of Mental Health, 5*(2), 5–15.

Gladwin, T. (1967). *Poverty U.S.A.* Boston: Little, Brown.

Glueck, S., & Glueck, E. (1950). *Unraveling juvenile delinquency.* New York: The Commonwealth Fund.

Goin, M. K., Yamamoto, J., & Silverman, J. (1965). Therapy congruent with class linked expectations. *Archives of General Psychiatry, 13,* 133–137.

Goldstein, A. P., & Stein, N. (1976). *Prescriptive psychotherapies.* New York: Pergamon.

Goldston, S. E. (1977). An overview of primary prevention programming. In D. C. Klein & S. E. Goldston (Eds.), *Primary prevention: An idea whose time has come.* Washington, DC: U.S. Government Printing Office.

Gordon, R. S. (1983). An operational classification of disease prevention. *Public Health Reports, 98*(2), 107–109.

Gould, R. E. (1967). Dr. Strangeclass: Or how I stopped worrying about the theory and began treating the blue-collar worker. *American Journal of Orthopsychiatry, 37,* 78–86.

Graziano, A. N. (1969). Clinical innovation and the mental health power structure: A social case history. *American Psychologist, 24,* 10–18.

Gruenberg, E. M. (1961). Comments on "Social structures and mental disorders. Competing hypotheses of explanation," by H. W. Dunham. In *Causes of mental disorders: A review of epidemiological knowledge, 1959.* New York: Milbank Memorial Fund.

Gurin, G., Veroff, J., & Feld, S. (1960). *Americans view their mental health: A nationwide survey.* New York: Basic Books.

Gurman, A. S. (1973). The effects and effectiveness of marital therapy: A review of outcome research. *Family Process, 12,* 145–170.

Gurman, A. S., & Kniskern, D. P. (1978). Research on marital and family therapy: Progress, perspective, and prospect. In S. L. Garfield & A. E. Bergin (Eds.), *Handbook of psychotherapy and behavior change* (pp. 817–902). New York: Wiley.

Hacker, F. J., Illing, H., & Bergreen, S. W. (1955). Impact of different social settings on type and effectiveness of psychotherapy. *Psychoanalytic Review, 52*(3), 38–49.

Hattie, J. A., Sharpley, C. F., & Rogers, H. J. (1984). Comparative effectiveness of professional and paraprofessional helpers. *Psychological Bulletin, 95*(3), 534–541.

Heinicke, C. M. (1975). Change in child and parent: A social work approach to family intervention. *Ameri-*

can *Journal of Orthopsychiatry, 45*(2), 296–297.

Herrera, A. E., & Sanchez, V. C. (1980). Prescriptive group psychotherapy: A successful application in the treatment of low-income Spanish-speaking clients. *Psychotherapy: Theory, Research and Practice, 17,* 169–174.

Hollingshead, A. B. (1957). *Two-factor index of social position.* Unpublished, New Haven, CT.

Hollingshead, A. B., & Redlich, F. C. (1958). *Social class and mental illness.* New York: Wiley.

Hynes, K., & Werblin, J. (1977). Group psychotherapy for Spanish-speaking women. *Psychiatric Annals, 7,* 52–63.

Iscoe, I. (1974). Community psychology and the competent community. *American Psychologist, 29*(8), 607–614.

Jacobs, D., Charles, E., Jacobs, T., Weinstein, H., & Mann, D. (1972). Preparation for treatment of the disadvantaged patient: Effects on disposition and outcome. *American Journal of Orthopsychiatry, 42,* 666–674.

Jason, L. A., DeAmicus, L., & Carter, B. (1978). Prevention intervention programs for disadvantaged children. *Community Mental Health Journal, 14,* 272–278.

Jensen, A. R. (1969). How much can we boost I.Q. and scholastic achievement? *Harvard Educational Review, 39,* 1–123.

Kadushin, C. (1969). *Why people go to psychiatrists.* New York: Atherton.

Kahn, M. K., McWilliams, S. A., Balch, P., Chang, A. F., & Ireland, J. (1976). Developing a rural mental health service from a base in an academic clinical psychology program. *American Journal of Community Psychology, 4*(2), 113–127.

Karlsruher, A. E. (1974). The nonprofessional as a therapeutic agent. *American Journal of Community Psychology, 2*(1), 61–78.

Kessler, M., & Albee, G. W. (1975). Primary prevention. *Annual Review of Psychology, 26,* 557–591.

Kirchenbaum, D. S. (1979). Social competence intervention and evaluation in the inner city: Cincinnati's Social Skills Development Program. *Journal of Consulting and Clinical Psychology, 47*(4), 778–780.

Koegler, R. R., & Brill, N. Q. (1967). *Treatment of psychiatric outpatients.* New York: Appleton-Century-Crofts.

Krasner, L. (1971). Behavior therapy. *Annual Review of Psychology, 22,* 483–532.

LaVietes, R. L. (1974). Crisis intervention for ghetto children: Contraindications and alternative considerations. *American Journal of Orthopsychiatry, 40,* 795–805.

Lazarus, A. A. (1972). *Clinical behavior therapy.* New York: Brunner/Mazel.

Lazarus, A. A. (1976). *Multimodal behavior therapy.* New York: Springer.

Lerner, B. (1972). *Therapy in the ghetto.* Baltimore, MD: Johns Hopkins University Press.

Levy, R. A. (1966). Six-session outpatient therapy. *Hospital and Community Psychiatry, 17,* 340–343.

Lewinsohn, P., Weinstein, M., & Alper, T. (1970). A behavioral approach to the group treatment of depressed persons: A methodological contribution. *Journal of Clinical Psychology, 4,* 525–532.

Lewis, D. O., Balla, D. A., & Shanok, S. S. (1979). Some evidence of race bias in the diagnosis and treatment of the juvenile offender. *American Journal of Orthopsychiatry, 49*(1), 53–63.

Lewis, O. (1964). The culture of poverty. In J. De Paske & S. N. Fisher (Eds.), *Explosive forces in Latin America.* Columbus, OH: Ohio State University Press.

Lipset, S. M., & Bendix, R. (1959). *Social mobility in industrial society.* Berkeley & Los Angeles: University of California Press.

Long, J. V. F., & Vaillant, G. E. (1984). Natural history of male psychological health, XI: Escape from the underclass. *American Journal of Psychiatry, 141*(3), 341–346.

Lorion, R. P. (1973). Socioeconomic status and traditional treatment approaches reconsidered. *Psychological Bulletin, 79,* 263–270.

Lorion, R. P. (1974a). Patient and therapist variables in the treatment of low-income patients. *Psychological Bulletin, 81,* 344–354.

Lorion, R. P. (1974b). Social class, treatment attitudes, and expectations. *Journal of Consulting and Clinical Psychology, 42,* 520.

Lorion, R. P. (1978). Research on psychotherapy and behavior change with the disadvantaged: Past, present and future directions. In S. L. Garfield & A. E. Bergin (Eds.), *Handbook of psychotherapy and behavior change* (pp. 903–908). New York: Wiley.

Lorion, R. P. (1983a). Evaluating preventive interventions: Guidelines for serious social change agents. In R. D. Felner, L. A. Jason, J. N. Moritsugu, & S. S. Farber (Eds.), *Preventive psychology: Theory, research and practice* (pp. 251–272). New York: Pergamon.

Lorion, P. R. (1983b). Research issues in the design and evaluation of preventive interventions. In J. P. Bowker (Ed.), *Education for primary prevention in social work* (pp. 7–23). New York: Council on Social Work Education.

Lorion, P. R., & Cahill, J. (1980). Paraprofessional effectiveness in mental health: Issues and outcomes. *The Paraprofessional Journal, 1*(1), 12–38.

Lorion, R. P., & Lounsbury, J. W. (1982). Conceptual and methodological considerations in evaluating preventive interventions. In G. J. Stahler & W. R. Tash (Eds.), *Innovative approaches to mental health evaluation* (pp. 23–57). New York: Academic Press.

Lorion, R. P., & Parron, D. L. (1985). Countering the countertransference: A strategy for treating the untreatable. In P. Pederson (Ed.), *Handbook on cross-cultural counseling and therapy* (pp. 79–86). New York: Greenwood Press.

Love, L. R., Kaswan, J., & Bugental, D. E. (1972). Differential effectiveness of three clinical interventions for different socioeconomic groupings. *Journal of Consulting and Clinical Psychology, 39,* 347–360.

Luborsky, L., Singer, B., & Luborsky, L. (1975). Comparative studies of psychotherapies. *Archives of General Psychiatry, 32,* 995–1008.

Malan, D. H., Heath, E. S., Bacal, H. A., & Balfour, F. H. G. (1975). Psychodynamic changes in untreated neurotic patients: II. Apparently genuine improvements. *Archives of General Psychiatry, 32,* 110–126.

Maldonado-Sierra, E., & Trent, R. (1960). The sibling

relationships in group psychotherapy with Puerto Rican schizophrenics. *American Journal of Psychiatry, 117,* 239–244.

Mannino, F. V., & Shore, M. F. (1972). Ecological oriented family intervention. *Family Process, 11,* 499–505.

Matras, J. (1984). *Social inequality, stratification and mobility.* Englewood Cliffs, NJ: Prentice-Hall.

McCord, J. (1978). A thirty-year follow-up of treatment effects. *American Psychologist, 33,* 284–289.

McMahon, J. T. (1964). The working-class psychiatric patient: A clinical view. In F. Riessman, J. Cohen, & A. Pearl (Eds.), *Mental health of the poor* (pp. 283–302). New York: Free Press.

Meehl, P. (1962). Schizotaxia, schizotypy, schizophrenia. *American Psychologist, 17,* 827–838.

Miller, S. M., & Mishler, E. G. (1959). Social class, mental illness, and American psychiatry: An expository review. *Millbank Memorial Fund Quarterly, 37,* 174–199.

Miller, S. M., & Riessman, F. (1968) *Social class and social policy.* New York: Basic Books.

Miller, S. M., & Riessman, F. (1969). The working-class subculture: A new view. In A. L. Grey (Ed.), *Class and personality in society.* New York: Atherton.

Miller, S. O., O'Neal, G. S., & Scott, C. A. (Eds.). (1982). *Primary prevention approaches to the development of mental health services for ethnic minorities.* New York: Council on Social Work Education.

Minuchin, S., Montalvo, B., Guerney, B. G., Rosman, B. L., & Schumer, F. (1967). *Families of the slums: An exploration of their structure and treatment.* New York: Basic Books.

Myerson, A. (1940). Review of "Mental disorder in urban areas: An ecological study of schizophrenia and other psychoses." *American Journal of Psychiatry, 96,* 995–997.

National Association of State Alcohol and Drug Abuse Directors. (1984). *State resources and services related to alcohol and drug abuse problems: An analysis of state alcoholism and drug abuse profile data.* Washington, DC: National Institute on Drug Abuse.

National Center for Health Statistics. (1966). *Characteristics of Patients of Selected Types of Medical Specialists and Practitioners: United States July 1963–June 1964.* Washington, DC: *Public Health Service Publication,* No. 1000, Series 10, #28.

Nietzel, M. T., & Fisher, S. G. (1981). Effectiveness of professional and paraprofessional helpers: A comment on Durlak. *Psychological Bulletin, 89*(3), 555–565.

Nobel, M. (Ed.). (1981). *Primary prevention in mental health and social work.* New York: Council on Social Work Education.

Olson, D. H. L. (1976). *Treating relationships.* Lake Mills, IA: Graphic.

Perlmutter, F. D. (Ed.). (1982). *Mental health promotion and primary prevention.* San Francisco: Jossey-Bass.

Powers, E., & Witmer, H. (1951). *An experiment in the prevention of delinquency: The Cambridge-Somerville Youth Study.* New York: Columbia University Press.

President's Commission on Mental Health. (1978). *Report to the President* (Vol. II). Washington, DC: U. S. Government Printing Office.

Price, R. H., Ketterer, R. F., Bader, B. C., & Monahan, J. (Eds.). (1980). *Prevention in community mental health: Research, policy and practice.* Beverly Hills: Sage.

Rainwater, L. (1966). Crucible of identity: The negro lower-class family. *Deadalus, Journal of the American Academy of Arts and Sciences, 95,* 172–216.

Rappoport, J. (1977). *Community psychology: Values, research and action.* New York: Holt, Rinehart & Winston.

Regier, D. A., Myers, J. K., Kramer, M., Robin, L. N., Blazer, D. G., Haugh, R. L., Eaton, W. W., & Locke, B. Z. (1984). The NIMH Epidemiologic Catchment Area Program. *Archives of General Psychiatry, 41,* 934–941.

Reiff, R., & Scribner, S. (1964). Issues in the new national mental health program relating to labor and low-income groups. In F. Riessman, J. Cohen & A. Preal (Eds.), *Mental health of the poor* (pp. 443–458). New York: Free Press.

Reiff, R., & Riessman, F. (1965). The indigenous paraprofessional. *Community Mental Health Journal,* monograph No. 1.

Riessman, F. (1964). *New approaches to mental health treatment for labor and low-income groups: A survey.* New York: National Institute of Labor Education.

Riessman, F., Cohen, J., & Pearl, A. (Eds.). (1964). *Mental health of the poor.* New York: Free Press.

Rimm, D. C., & Masters, J. C. (1979). *Behavior therapy: Techniques and empirical findings* (2nd ed.). New York: Academic Press.

Rioch, M. J. (1967). Pilot projects in training mental health counselors. In E. L. Cowen, E. A. Gardner, & M. Zax (Eds.), *Emergent approaches to mental health problems* (pp. 110–127). New York: Appleton-Century-Crofts.

Robin, L. N., Helzer, J. E., Craughan, J., Williams, J. B. W., & Spitzer, R. L. (1981). The NIMH Diagnostic Interview Schedule: Version III. Public Health Service (HSS) publication ADM-T-42-3 (5/81, 8/81).

Robin, L. N., Helzer, J. E., Wiessman, M. M., Orvaschel, H., Gruenberg, E., Burke, J. D., & Regier, D. A. (1984). Lifetime prevalence of specific psychiatric disorders in three sites. *Archives of General Psychiatry, 41,* 949–958.

Rogers, L. S. (1960). Drop-out rates and results of psychotherapy in government aided mental hygiene clinics. *Journal of Clinical Psychology, 16,* 89–92.

Rogers, T. R., Forehand, R., Griest, D. L., Wells, K. C., & McMahon, R. J. (1981). Socioeconomic status: Effects on parent and child behavior and treatment outcome of parent training. *Journal of Clinical Child Psychology, 10,* 98–101.

Rosenblatt, A., & Mayer, J. E. (1972). Help-seeking for family problems: A survey of utilization and satisfaction. *American Journal of Psychiatry, 128,* 1136–1140.

Ross, C. E., Mirowsky, J., & Cockerham, W. C. (1983). Social class, Mexican culture, and fatalism: Their effects on psychological distress. *American Journal of Community Psychology, 11*(4), 383–400.

Royce, J. M., Lazar, I., & Darlington, R. B. (1983). Minority families, early education, and later life changes. *American Journal of Orthopsychiatry, 53*(4), 706–720.

Rubenstein, E. A., & Lorr, M. (1956). A comparison of terminators and remainers in out-patient psychotherapy. *Journal of Clinical Psychology, 12*, 345–349.

Ryan, W. (1971). *Blaming the victim.* New York: Random House.

Sager, C. J., Brayboy, T. L., & Waxenberg, B. R. (1970). *Black ghetto family in therapy: A laboratory experience.* New York: Grove Press.

Sameroff, A. J. (1977). Concepts of humanity in primary prevention. In G. W. Albee & J. M. Joffe (Eds.), *The issues: An overview of primary prevention* (pp. 42–64). Hanover, NH: University Press of New England.

Sarason, S. B. (1984). If it can be studied or developed, should it be? *American Psychologist, 39*(5), 477–485.

Schlesinger, B., & James, G. (1969). Psychiatry and poverty—A selected review. *Canadian Medical Association Journal, 101*, 470–477.

Seligman, M. (1975). *Helplessness: On depression, development and death.* San Francisco: Freeman.

Settin, J. M., & Bramel, D. (1981). Interaction of client class and gender in biasing clinical judgment. *American Journal of Orthopsychiatry, 51*(3), 510–520.

Sifneos, P. E. (1972). *Short-term psychotherapy and emotional crisis..* Cambridge, MA: Harvard University Press.

Slaikeu, K. A. (1984). Crisis intervention: *A handbook for practice and research.* Boston: Allyn & Bacon.

Sloane, R. B., Staples, F. R., Cristol, A. Y., Yorkston, N. J., & Whipple, K. (1975). *Psychotherapy versus behavior therapy.* Cambridge, MA: Harvard University Press.

Small, L. (1971). *The briefer psychotherapies.* New York: Brunner/Mazel.

Smith, M. E., & Glass, G. (1977). Meta-analysis of psychotherapy outcome studies. *American Psychologist, 32*, 752–760.

Sobey, F. (1970). *The nonprofessional revolution in mental health.* New York: Columbia University Press.

Speer, D. C., Fossum, J., Lippman, H. S., Schwartz, R., & Slocum, B. (1968). A comparison of middle- and lower-class families in treatment at a child guidance clinic. *American Journal of Orthopsychiatry, 38*, 814–822.

Srole, L., Langer, T. S., Michael, S. T., Opler, M. K., & Rennie, T. A. C. (1962). *Mental health in the metropolis: The midtown Manhattan study.* New York: McGraw-Hill.

Stone, J. L., & Crowthers, V. (1972). Innovations in program and funding of mental health services for blue-collar families. *American Journal of Psychiatry, 128*, 1375–1380.

Storrow, H. A. (1962). Psychiatric treatment and the lower-class neurotic patient. *Archives of General Psychiatry, 6*, 469–473.

Strauss, J. S. (1979). Social and cultural influences on psychopathology. *Annual Review, 30*, 397–415.

Strupp, H. H., & Bergin, A. E. (1969). Some empirical and conceptual bases for coordinated research in psychotherapy. *International Journal of Psychiatry, 7*, 17–90.

Stuart, R. B. (1976). An operant interpersonal program for couples. In D. H. L. Olson (Ed.), *Treating relationships.* Lake Mills, IA: Graphic.

Thomas, A., & Sillen, S. (1972). *Racism and psychiatry.* New York: Brunner/Mazel.

Truax, C. B. (1967). The training of non-professional personnel in therapeutic interpersonal relationships. *American Journal of Public Health, 57*, 1778–1791.

Tumin, M. M. (1966). *Social stratification: The forms and functions of inequality.* Englewood Cliffs, NJ: Prentice-Hall.

Turner, S., & Armstrong, S. (1981). Cross-racial psychotherapy: What the therapists say. *Psychotherapy: Theory, Research and Practice, 18*(3), 375–378.

Urban, H. B., & Ford, D. H. (1971). Some historical and conceptual perspectives on psychotherapy and behavior change. In A. E. Bergin & S. L. Garfield (Eds.), *Handbook of psychotherapy and behavior change: An empirical analysis* (pp. 3–55). New York: Wiley.

Vail, A. (1978). Factors influencing lower-class black patients remaining in treatment. *Journal of Consulting and Clinical Psychology, 46*, 341.

Wahler, R. G. (1980). The insular mother: Her problem in parent–child treatment. *Journal of Applied Behavior Analysis, 13*, 207–219.

Wells, R. A., Dilkes, T. C., & Burckhardt, N. T. (1976). The results of family therapy: A critical review of the literature. In D. H. L. Olson (Ed.), *Treating relationships* (pp. 499–516). Lake Mills, IA: Graphic.

Wolberg, L. R. (1967). *The techniques of psychotherapy, part II.* New York: Grune & Stratton.

Yamamoto, J., & Goin, M. K. (1966). Social class factors relevant for psychiatric treatment. *Journal of Nervous and Mental Disease, 142*, 332–339.

Zigler, E. (1979): Project Head Start: Success or failure? In E. Zigler & J. Valentine (Eds.), *Project Head Start: A legacy of the War on Poverty* (pp. 495–508). New York: Free Press.

Zigler, E., & Valentine, J. (Eds.). (1979). *Project Head Start: A legacy of the War on Poverty.* New York: Free Press.

18

DRUGS AND PSYCHOTHERAPY

GERALD L. KLERMAN
Cornell University Medical Center

INTRODUCTION

Purpose

This chapter reviews the state of knowledge regarding drugs and psychotherapy pertinent to mental health concerns in general, and to the treatment of mental disorders, in particular. It expands on Hollon and Beck's chapter, "Psychotherapy and Drug Therapy: Comparisons and Combinations," in the second edition of this *Handbook* (Hollon & Beck, 1978) and discusses new developments in this active field.

Timeliness

The topic of drugs and psychotherapy is timely. A number of recent publications have reviewed selected aspects of this topic (Beitman & Klerman, 1984; Greenhill & Gralnich, 1983; GAP, 1975).

For a number of reasons it is important that psychologists, psychiatrists, and others in the mental health field be familiar with advances in psychopharmacology and the relationship between drugs and psychotherapy.

1. *For mental health professionals.* All mental health professionals should be aware that large numbers of individuals are using psychoactive drugs. In some instances, this use may be for recreational (nontherapeutic) purposes, as with the use of cocaine or marijuana. In most other instances, these drugs are taken for treatment purposes. Use of drugs for the relief of emotional symptoms and distress is increasingly part of modern culture. Surveys in the United States and other urban, industrial societies find that about 10 percent of the population receive a psychoactive drug in any one year (Balter, Levine, & Manheimer, 1974).

2. *For psychotherapists and other clinicians.* In treatment planning for individual patients, decisions are made based on knowledge of the possible value of drugs in comparison, or in combination, with psychotherapy. Patients often come into treatment with specific expectations, either requesting psychoactive drugs or being opposed to them. A significant proportion of patients in mental health treatment receive a combination of drugs and psychotherapy. This may be the result of an intentional decision by their therapists, or it may be inadvertent, since many patients are taking tranquilizers, sleeping pills, or other medications without their therapist's knowledge.

3. *For researchers and theorists.*
   a. The actions of drugs on mental processes and behavior have generated new knowledge about the long-standing problems of the relationship of brain and behavior and of mind and biology. The fact that defined chemical substances can influence aggression, anxiety, guilt, performance, and so on creates opportunities for research around the neurobiological substrate of mental functioning and behavior.
   b. The comparative and interactive effects of drugs and psychotherapy have implications for theories of treatment.
   c. Understanding the nature of the comparative and interactive effects of drugs and psychotherapy in the treatment of individual disorders, such as schizophrenia, panic disorder, and phobias, can elucidate aspects of the disorder.
4. *For research methodologists interested in design and assessment.* The problems attendant to the design and conduct of experiments, statistical analysis, and the interpretation of results of research provide challenges.

General Approach

It would be useful to make explicit the approach taken to this topic in this chapter. This is the only chapter in the *Handbook* written from the point of view of a biological treatment, in this case psychopharmacology. Most readers of this *Handbook* will have only limited awareness of psychopharmacologic research and practice.

A number of premises are usually implicit in most psychopharmacologic research.

1. There is no one mental health condition, but rather multiple mental disorders and symptom states that require diagnostic assessments for their differentiation and application of specific treatments, including drugs and psychotherapies.
2. Drugs and psychotherapy are best regarded as treatment modalities in the health context; claims for the efficacy and safety of any individual treatment, such as a psychotropic drug or a form of psychotherapy, are to be evaluated as are other treatment modalities, such as

drugs for hypertension or surgery for cancer of the breast.
3. The findings from outcome studies take precedence over those from process studies. Process studies have professional utility and scientific value only to the extent that there is demonstration of the efficacy of the particular therapy.
4. Efficacy is best established by some form of controlled clinical trial design, preferably using randomization. Use of naturalistic designs or comparisons without a control group can provide only limited information regarding the efficacy of a treatment.

This approach embodies what is commonly, but vaguely, referred to as the "medical model." Perhaps these premises would better be regarded as constituting a "health model" rather than a "medical model." Aspects of the medical model are often controversial, and resolution of these controversies is made more difficult by interprofessional rivalries, particularly between psychiatrists and psychologists.

Discussion of the relative efficacy of drugs and psychotherapy in comparison with each other, and in combination, often generates feelings and convictions related to ideology and to interprofessional tensions in the mental health field. Numerous observers of the mental health field have documented the important splits within psychiatry, psychology, and other mental health disciplines (Hollingshead & Redlich, 1958). Mental health professionals are identified with biological, psychodynamic, behavioral, interpersonal, social, and existential schools. Many times the intensity of their feelings and group commitments have the quality of ideology (Armor & Klerman, 1968; Klerman, 1984; Strauss, Schatzman, Bucher, Ehrlich, & Sabshin, 1964).

These ideological and theoretical differences operate within professional groups and contribute to interprofessional tensions. The various mental health professions involved in psychotherapy and treatment of patients are currently involved in competition and rivalry within the "marketplace" for patients, as well as in the intellectual and scientific marketplace. Evaluation of the data on efficacy and safety of drugs alone as well as in comparison and in combination with psychotherapy is made difficult by the fact that psychiatrists, as physicians, are the only mental health professional group legally authorized to prescribe medication, and usually the only mental health professionals whose training has involved exposure to neuroscience and pharmacology. Thus, there may be a tendency for some psychiatrists, as physicians, to overvalue the evidence with regard to psychopharmacology. Nevertheless, psychiatry is not of a single mind on these matters and there are splits within psychiatry, often related to psychodynamic versus biological approaches. On the other hand, many nonpsychiatric mental health professionals, including psychologists and social workers, are skeptical about the value of drugs and emphasize their adverse affects rather than their possible therapeutic value. These attitudes are evident in interpreting the research literature. For example, reviews of psychopharmacologic treatment often ignore the demonstrated efficacy of behavioral techniques for the treatment of phobias or of short-term psychotherapies for depressed patients. Similarly, reviews of psychotherapy often ignore the demonstrated value of drugs for psychoses, certain forms of depression, or panic states.

Furthermore, these tensions are manifested in clinical practice where many patients seek consultation with expectations and preferences regarding the mode of their treatment. Similarly, clinicians approach decision making with regard to individual patients heavily influenced by their professional loyalties and ideological positions. Hopefully, as greater scientific evidence from controlled trials emerges, a more balanced approach to the relative value of drugs and psychotherapy alone, and in combination, for specific disorders will become available.

Organization of This Chapter

This chapter will review several aspects of drugs and psychotherapy. First, the status of psychopharmacology as a scientific discipline will be reviewed. This will include a brief review of the various classes of drugs used in the treatment of emotional symptoms and mental disorders.

Following this, selected issues of research design and methodology will be discussed. Particular attention will be given to the value of factorial designs for the elucidation of interactions as well as of main effects. The possible outcomes of comparative and constructive designs will be defined.

Finally, the status of research and clinical practice for schizophrenia, affective disorders, agoraphobia, panic disorder, and opiate addiction will be reviewed.

SCOPE OF PSYCHOPHARMACOLOGY

Historical Background: The Emergence of Psychopharmacology in the Early 1950s

Psychopharmacology, the study of the relationships between drugs and mental functioning and behavior, emerged as a scientific field in the mid-1950s. This was due to the development of new classes of drugs and the impressive response of psychiatric patients to the new drugs, particularly of hospitalized psychiatric patients to the "tranquilizers" reserpine and the phenothiazines. In the late 1950s and early 1960s, there was rapid development of other new classes of drugs.

Anthropologists report that almost every known society has some ferment, brew, or potion intended to influence behavior for health purposes, recreational use, or often religious rituals.

In Western civilization, interest in drugs that influence behavior and psychological functioning is as old as recorded history. In the mid-nineteenth century, there was high interest in drugs that today would be called psychopharmacologic agents—for example, the attention given to nitrous oxide inhalation in New England, and the fascination with opiates and marijuana among poets and writers in France and England. The introduction of cocaine into clinical ophthalmology in Vienna in the late nineteenth century was attended by the drama around Freud's role and the impact upon his personal and professional life (Byck, 1974). Aldous Huxley (1954) wrote of his personal experiences with the hallucinogenic properties of mescaline in the 1920s. These experiences remained isolated, but seemed to influence writers and philosophers more than physicians and scientists.

It is conventional to date the onset of modern psychopharmacology to the 1950s with the introduction of reserpine and the phenothiazines. It is of note, however, that Cade reported on the value of lithium for manic states in 1949 (Cade, 1949). As so often happens in the history of science, Cade's observations were ignored and did not become the subject of clinical or research interest until the 1960s.

The field of psychopharmacology rapidly developed through the late 1950s. A large number of new compounds were synthesized and introduced into clinical practice. Initially, these compounds were called "tranquilizers." The tranquilizers included reserpine, the phenothiazines, and meprobamate. The terminology changed in the late 1950s and the larger group of tranquilizers was divided into "major tranquilizers" and "minor tranquilizers."

The "major tranquilizers," later called antipsychotics and/or neuroleptics, initially included rauwolfia derivatives and the phenothiazines, which were shown to have efficacy against psychotic states, including mania and schizophrenia. Subsequently, a number of other classes of drugs were shown to have efficacy against psychiatric symptoms and behavior. These classes of drugs include the thioxanthenes, butyrophenones, and the benzodiazepines.

Meprobamate was introduced at about the same time as reserpine and chlorpromazine. Grouping these drugs together as tranquilizers followed theories that ascribed the central role in psychopathology to anxiety. Particularly influenced by psychoanalytic theory, most psychopathological manifestations of neurosis and psychoses were understood as defenses against underlying anxiety. It became apparent, however, that not only were the tranquilizers different on quantitative dimensions, but rather there were also important differences in qualitative patterns. For example, the major tranquilizers were shown to be effective against psychotic states, but produced extrapyramidal side-effects, presumably due to their action on dopamine.

In contrast, meprobamate and the other minor tranquilizers were not demonstrated effective in treatment of psychotic states and had no neuropharmacologic action on dopamine or other catecholamines. Meprobamate showed pharmacologic and therapeutic similarities to the sedative-hypnotic drugs, particularly the barbiturates. Consequently, meprobamate was grouped as one of the minor tranquilizers.

The "minor tranquilizers" have grown rapidly in number and in prescription use. The introduction of the benzodiazepines, particularly diazepan (Valium) and chlordiazepoxide (Librium), led to a rapid expansion in the number of such compounds and in their prescription use.

Two classes of antidepressant drugs became available in the late 1950s, the tricyclic antidepressants, of which imipramine is the prototype, and the MAO inhibitors.

Subsequently, drugs have been introduced that have been effective against manic states (antimanic drugs), against panic states and phobia (antipanic agents), and against obsessive-compulsive symptoms and behaviors.

The combination of scientific controversy and the legal requirements subsequent to the 1962 Kefauver-Harris amendments to the Federal Food and Drug statutes resulted in the development of large numbers of controlled clinical trials for the evaluation of claims for efficacy and safety of various classes of psychotropic drugs. The combination of these historical forces resulted in intense interest among researchers of different professions (psychiatry, neurology, clinical psychology) and scientific disciplines (neurosciences, experimental psychology, pharmacology, medicinal chemistry, biostatistics) in the new field of psychopharmacology.

A number of national and international organizations have developed, notably the American College of Neuropsychopharmacology (ACNP) and the Collegium Internationale Neuropsychopharmacologie (CINP). National organizations for psychopharmacology exist in Canada, the United Kingdom, and many Western European and South American countries. In addition, there are a number of journals, notably *Psychopharmacologie* and the *Journal of Clinical Psychopharmacology*.

A number of textbooks and reviews have appeared; notable are the volume by Klein and associates (Klein, Gittleman, Quitkin, & Rifkin, 1980) and the Generation of Progress series published by the American College of Neuropsychopharmacology (Efron, Cole, Levine, & Wittenborn, 1968; Lipton, DiMascio & Killam, 1978).

Terminology

At this point, it would be useful to review the various terms used regarding drugs relevant to mental processes, psychotherapy, and behavior change. A number of definitions are in order.

First, definitions as to the substances. Among the terms used are *drugs* and *medications*:

Drugs usually refer to any substance, natural or synthetic, that alters bodily functions, including mental processes and behavior. By this definition, tobacco, coffee, tea, alcoholic beverages, marijuana and cocaine are drugs.

Medications usually refers to drugs that are intentionally used for health purposes (i.e., for the treatment of symptoms and illnesses, including emotional and psychological disorders).

Substances and compounds refers to both naturally occurring compounds, such as coffee, tea, or opium, as well as synthetic compounds. A compound is a drug whose chemical structure is known.

An *agent* could be nonchemical, as with radiation or electrical stimulation. Agent is usually used interchangeably with drug, compound, and substance.

The relevant scientific fields include the following:

Psychopharmacology refers to the scientific discipline concerned with the relationship between drugs and behavior and psychological processes.

Behavioral pharmacology refers to a subbranch of the science of pharmacology concerned with drugs that influence behavior. Most members of this subdiscipline come from a background in learning theory, most often Skinnerian theory.

Neuropharmacology is the branch of pharmacology that concerns the action of drugs on the nervous system, particularly the brain. Neuropharmacologic research focuses on the ways in which drugs affect electrophysiologic or neurochemical practices within the brain and the nervous system.

A number of terms are used interchangeably to refer to drugs that influence brain and behavior. The terms include "psychotropic," "psychoactive," and "psychopharmacologic." When used for treatment purposes, the substances are often called "psychopharmacotherapeutic" agents, compounds, drugs, or medication.

Not all of these drugs are intended for therapeutic use. There is no agreement as to which term to use for nontherapeutic uses. Sometimes these drugs are called "recreational drugs," as in the case of marijuana and alcohol. When drugs induce altered mental states, they have been called *psychedelic drugs,* a term popular in the 1960s. The larger class of psychedelic drugs also includes hallucinogenic compounds as a subclass. Hallucinogenic drugs have the capacity to induce hallucinations, usually visual. Included in the group of hallucinogenics are mescaline, LSD, and psilocybin. There is controversy as to whether the tetrahydrocannabinals, the active component of marijuana and other substances derived from cannabis plants, have hallucinogenic properties, particularly when given a purified form at high dose.

Classes of Drugs Used for Treatment of Mental Disorders

There is no single way to classify these drugs. Sometimes they are classified according to their chemical structure (i.e., phenothiazines, tricyclics, benzodiazepines). At other times they are classified according to their mode of neurochemical actions (i.e., monoamine oxidase inhibitors, neuroleptics). In other instances, they may be classified according to their mode of psychological action (i.e., psychomotor stimulants, hallucinogens).

Because our main interest in this chapter is in the use of drugs alone or in combination with methods of psychotherapy or behavior change, for the treatment of mental disorders, we will classify the drugs in this chapter according to their clinical use. Thus, the main classes of drugs include antipsychotics, antidepressants, antianxiety agents, and antimanic drugs.

This usage does not necessarily imply any specific causation for the disorder or even a common mode of mechanism for the therapeutic effects in a given disorder. For example, the etiology of hypertension is not known. Furthermore, it is likely that there is more than one form of hypertension. Nevertheless, there are a number of different classes of compounds that have demonstrated efficacy in reducing blood pressure and contributing to a decrease in mortality and improvement of social and personal functioning. They are conventionally called "antihypertensives." Not only do these drugs have different chemical structures, but they likely act via different pharmacologic mechanisms. Thus, diuretics induce the excretion of fluid, particularly reducing sodium in the body. Other antihypertensive drugs act via blocking autonomic neurotransmitters.

There is a parallel between hypertension and the treatments for depression. Thus, it is possible to treat depression by various classes of drugs and also by various forms of psychotherapy—some of which influence cognitive mechanisms, other interpersonal processes, and behavioral reinforcement.

In the ideal of scientific medicine, knowledge of etiology and pathogenesis provides the most powerful explanation of illness and the rational guide to design of treatments. This is seldom the case, and many of the most effective treatments in modern medicine are not etiologic (i.e., the use of steroids for the treatment of allergic reactions, anticonvulsants, antihypertensives); these drugs are demonstrated effective without knowledge of the etiology of cardiovascular disease or epilepsy.

The therapeutic efficacy of most of these compounds was discovered initially by clinical observation and serendipity, rather than by rational knowledge of pathophysiology or neuropharmacologic mode of drug actions. Efforts to understand the neuropharmacologic and behavioral basis of a therapeutic mode of action have usually followed the demonstration of therapeutic efficacy.

The major classes of drugs are shown in Table 18.1.

Patterns of Prescriptions and Use

There has been a rapid increase in the use of these drugs throughout all industrialized and urbanized countries. Extensive research has been conducted in the United States (Uhlenhuth, Balter, Mellinger, Cisin, & Clinthorne, 1983) as to the patterns of psychotropic drug prescription and the social and psychological factors attendant to their use. In general, approximately 10 to 12 percent of the adult population uses a psychoactive drug at least once during a calendar year. The largest number of drugs used are the antianxiety (or anxiolytic) group, which are used by about 10 percent of the population, antidepressants by perhaps 3 percent, and antipsychotics by 1 percent.

In the majority of instances, these drugs are not prescribed by psychiatrists, but rather by general practitioners, family doctors, and internists. About 50 percent of the patients receiving antianxiety drugs (Uhlenhuth et al., 1983) have concurrent medical illness, and for these patients, the drugs are prescribed with the intent of reducing the emotional concomitance of their physical illness.

Within the mental health field, neuroleptic drugs are widely prescribed in institutional settings, particularly psychiatric units in general hospitals and public mental hospitals, such as VAs and state mental hospitals, where large numbers of psychotic patients are treated. In ambulatory practice, the rate of prescription varies considerably, in part, because of the diagnostic mix, but also because of the professional background and ideological commitments of the practitioners.

Scientific Issues: Establishing Safety and Efficacy

The introduction of these new compounds in the 1950s generated intense controversy as to whether the claims made for their efficacy in states of psychosis, depression, and anxiety were "real," or whether they were due to bias, therapeutic zeal, and placebo effect. In response to this criticism, the quality of scientific research on the safety and efficacy of drugs improved rapidly with the acceptance of the randomized placebo-control trial as the standard design for the assessment of the psychopharmacologic agents. A large number of psychologists, biostatisticians, and methodologists were drawn into the field, particularly because of the influential role played by the National Institute of Mental Health (NIMH) Psychopharmacology Service Center under the leadership of Jonathan O. Cole. The National Institute of Mental Health (NIMH) and the Veteran's Administration (VA) in the United States and the Medical Research Council (MRC) in the United Kingdom sponsored a number of multicenter collaborative trials that demonstrated the feasibility of assessing drugs in a systematic way, and also the efficacy of the new antipsychotic and antidepressant compounds.

A large number of rating scales have been developed in order to assess the changes induced by these compounds. The Hamilton Depression Scale (Hamilton, 1967), the Hopkins Symptom Checklist (Derogatis, Lipman, & Rickels, 1976), the Lorr Scale (Lorr & Klett, 1966), and the Brief Psychiatric Rating Scale (BPRS), developed by Overall and Gorham (1962), are among the best known scales.

Research design issues for the evaluation of treatment, including psychopharmacologic agents, have become major areas of scientific activities. The Society for Clinical Trials publishes a journal, *Controlled Clinical Trials,* in which issues of research design,

TABLE 18.1 Major Psychotherapeutic Drugs

Therapeutic Use	Chemical Structure or Psychopharmacologic Action	Generic Name	Trade Name
Antipsychotics (also called "major tranquilizers" or "neuroleptics")	Phenothiazines		
	Aliphatic	Chlorpromazine	Thorazine
	Piperidine	Thioridazine	Mellaril
	Piperazine	Trifluoperazine	Stelazine
	Thioxanthenes		
	Aliphatic	Chlorprothixene	Taractan
	Piperazine	Thioxthixene	Navane
	Butyrophenones	Haloperidol	Haldol
	Dibenzoxazepines	Loxapine	Loxitane
	Dihydroindolines	Molindone	Moban
	Rauwolfia alkaloids	Reserpine	Sandril
	Benzoquinolines	Tetrabenazine	
Antidepressants	Tricyclic antidepressants (TCAs) Tertiary amines	Amitriptyline	Elavil
		Imipramine	Tofranil
		Doxepin	Sinequan
	Secondary amines	Desipramine	Norpramin
		Nortriptyline	Pamelor
		Protriptyline	Vivactil
	Monoamine Oxidase Inhibitors (MAOIs)	Phenelzine	Nardil
		Tranylcypromine	Parnate
		Pargyline	Eutonyl
		Isocarboxazid	Marplan
Psychomotor Stimulants	Amphetamines	Amphetamine	Benzedrine
		Dextroamphetamine	Dexedrine
	Other	Methylphenidate	Ritalin
Antimanic		Lithium	Eskalith
		Carbamazapine	Tegretol
Antianxiety (also called "anxiolytic" or "minor tranquilizers")	Benzodiazepines	Chlordiazepoxide	Librium
		Diazepam	Valium
		Chlorazepate	Tranxene
		Oxazepam	Serax
		Lorazepam	Activan
	Triazolobenzodiazepine Triazolam	Alprazolam Halcion	Xanax
	Propanediol carbamates	Meprobamate	Miltown
	Barbiturates	Phenobarbital	Luminal

statistical analysis, patient compliance, and related topics are discussed. Although the primary focus of this Society and its journal is upon drug research, many, if not all, of the methological and statistical issues are applicable to the conduct of trials for the evaluation of psychotherapy.

Scientific Issues: Establishing the Mode of Action

The emergence of psychopharmacology occurred simultaneously in the 1950s with the development of modern neurobiology. The neurosciences are currently among the most exciting areas of scientific investigation, and developments in neuropharmacology have been powerful stimuli to clarifying the role of neurotransmitters and neuropeptides in brain functioning.

Concern about mode of action is not limited to anatomical, chemical, or physiologic functioning of the brain. There is active concern for behavioral modes of action, particularly as these compounds influence perception and sensation, motor and affective regulation, and patterns of reward and performance.

Public Policy Issues

A major impetus to these scientific endeavors followed the 1962 Kefauver-Harris Amendments to the Pure Food, Drug and Cosmetic Acts. Prior to 1962, it was not necessary for a pharmaceutical firm to demonstrate efficacy before being permitted to market a new drug. The legislative history behind the federal statutes and the growing power and role of the Food and Drug Administration (FDA) is long and complex. The initial legislation was the 1906 Pure Food and Drug Act, which established the FDA, but gave it power only to regulate the purity of drugs and the labeling as to content. Substances marketed as drugs, as well as foods and cosmetics, had to label their contents and to identify their ingredients so as to ensure purity. There was no requirement for safety or efficacy until 1938, when the safety requirement was mandated following the deaths attendant to the introduction of the new sulfur compounds for treatment of bacterial infections. The development of criteria for safety led to extensive research on toxicity and contributed greatly to the growth of pharmacology and toxicology as scientific and academic disciplines.

The 1962 Kefauver-Harris Amendments were instituted after public reactions over the tragic birth malformations of thalidomide. The thalidomide tragedy was a safety issue rather than an efficacy issue, and the public concern over this episode prompted the Federal statutory extension of FDA authorities to include the requirement of safety.

For the first time, evidence for efficacy was required prior to the approval of a new drug. Today, we take the criteria of safety and efficacy for granted in the health field. These criteria were mandated, however, only after a hard-fought Congressional battle. It took the FDA 10 years to translate its legislative mandate into regulations that provided operational criteria for the definition of efficacy and a set of procedures for the review of claims. The pharmaceutical industry has responded with an increase in recruitment of professional staff skilled in the design and conduct of these experiments and statistical analyses of the data.

Interestingly, safety and efficacy criteria are not included in Federal statutes for all health programs. For example, safety and efficacy of treatments are not required for reimbursement under Medicare or Medicaid. The statute stipulates that reimbursement procedures be "necessary and reasonable." In the United States during the Carter Administration, there was a vigorous debate in Washington over proposals that would have extended the criteria of efficacy to mental health treatment, such as psychotherapy (Klerman, 1983a; London & Klerman, 1982). Similar issues have been raised in the United Kingdom (Aveline, 1984; Editorial, 1984; Shepherd, 1984; Wilkinson, 1984).

RESEARCH DESIGNS AND METHODOLOGY

This section of the chapter will discuss selected issues of designs and methodologies in comparing drugs with psychotherapy, and evaluating the combination of drugs and psychotherapy. Other chapters in this *Handbook* discuss general issues of research design and assessment. In particular, the interested reader is referred to Chapter 2 (by Kazdin).

In the ideal of rational medicine, the flow of information derives from knowledge of etiology and pathogenesis and proceeds through pathophysiology, diagnosis, and ultimately pharmacology and therapeutics. In this ideal, specific treatments for a disorder are arrived at deductively from knowledge of etiology and pathogenesis and result in specific and rational therapeutic interventions. In actual practice, this ideal has seldom been realized. In psychopharmacology, one noticeable exception was the development of L-dopa treatment for Parkinsonism based upon autopsy evidence of a deficiency in dopamine neurons in the basal ganglia of patients with Parkinsonism, combined with knowledge about the neuropharmacology of dopamine in relationship to neuroleptics and other drugs.

Most treatments in medicine and in psychopharmacology have been discovered by serendipity, usually by clinical observation. Scientific strategies for evaluating *that* a treatment works are different from those involved in determining *how* a treatment works. The therapeutic value of many treatments has often been established even though the etiology or pathophysiology of the disorder is uncertain or the mechanism of the underlying action has not been identified (GAP, 1975). For example, the efficacy of vaccination for the prevention of smallpox was established long before the invention of the electron microscope or knowledge of viruses.

Research Designs—Controlled Clinical Trials
There are important parallels in the development of thinking about the nature of evidence for demonstrating the efficacy of drugs and all psychotherapy.

It is agreed that the most powerful evidence for the efficacy and safety of any health intervention, including pharmacologic, surgical, radiation, or psychological treatments, comes from the randomized controlled trial (RCT). This design has been most widely used for evaluating drugs, but it is increasingly being used with other forms of treatment, including psychotherapies.

Although the theoretical basis for the controlled trial goes back to seventeenth-century writings on scientific investigation, the first applications in medical therapeutics did not appear until the twentieth century with the application of placebo-controlled trials in evaluating drugs for angina.

In the new field of psychopharmacology, in the late 1950s, there was considerable debate about the feasibility, desirability, and necessity of clinical trials. This debate centered around the necessity for double-blind design and of the magnitude and significance of the placebo effect. Scientific consensus emerged in the early 1960s through a series of conferences and publications sponsored by the NIMH Psychopharmacology Service Center (Levine, 1978, 1979; Levine, Schiele, & Bouthilet, 1971). The passage of the Kefauver-Harris Amendment ultimately resulted in the FDA formulating regulations that operationalized these criteria. As part of this process, the FDA contracted with the ACNP for scientific guidance in the development of guidelines for the evaluation of antipsychotic, antidepressant, and antianxiety classes of drugs (Wittenborn et al., 1977).

In parallel, controversies about demonstrating the efficacy of psychotherapy were initiated by Eysenck's (1952) now famous article and were followed by intense discussions that culminated in the

guidelines developed by the NIMH Psychotherapy Research Review Committee, published by Fiske et al. (1970). By the mid-1970s, most of these controversies subsided, and currently there is widespread agreement on the necessity for controlled clinical trials for both drugs and psychotherapy (Eysenck, 1966; Fiske et al., 1970; Luborsky, Singer, & Luborsky, 1975).

As Kazdin discusses in Chapter 2, the controlled clinical trial is the major research design for establishing efficacy of psychotherapy. The research strategies employed, following Kazdin's schema, include comparative or constructive strategies.

Comparative and constructive strategies should be employed only if there is evidence that the respective drug and psychotherapy treatments have demonstrated safety and efficacy. In discussing these designs, the assumption will be that there has been prior demonstration of the efficacy of the drug treatment and of the psychotherapy.

Comparative Strategies for Assessing Drugs and Psychotherapies
A number of different designs are employed for comparing drugs and psychotherapy.

Some researchers have advocated a *two-group design,* in which a psychotherapy is compared against a drug. For example, Rush, Beck, Kovacs, and Hollon (1977) compared cognitive therapy against amitriptyline. Scientifically, this is an inadequate design, since in the absence of a control group one cannot conclude that differences between the two treatments are greater than might be expected by time alone. Even though the drug treatments or the psychotherapy have been demonstrated effective by prior studies, the question remains whether the research group has the capacity to detect change. There may be insufficient training of the researchers, or problems in the assessment methods used, or the patient group may be unresponsive to either of the treatments. There may be ethical reasons for not including a nontreatment control group; but scientifically a control group is always necessary.

Another comparative design is the *three-group design,* in which the psychotherapy is compared against a drug, and against a control group. This is the minimum optimal design for comparative assessment.

An interesting and important extension of this three-group design is the four-group design employed in the NIMH Collaborative Study of the Psychotherapy of Depression (Elkin, Parloff, Hadley, & Autry, 1985). Two brief psychotherapies, cognitive behavioral therapy (Beck, Rush, Shaw, & Emery, 1979) and interpersonal psychotherapy (Klerman, Weissman, Rounsaville, & Chevron, 1984b) are being evaluated for efficacy in depressions and compared against a standard drug treatment, imipramine, and a control group that receives psychological management plus placebo. As shown in Figure 18.1, this four-group design represents an extension of the three-group comparative design. Since it does not employ a combined treatment group, however, it is not a factorial design, and it will not be possible to study the interaction of drugs and psychotherapy. Although the data from the study will allow evaluation of the comparative efficacy of the two psychological treatments against each other and in comparison to a pharmacologic standard, it will not be possible to assess the value of combined treatment.

Constructive Strategies

Constructive strategies, employing a number of designs, are useful for studying combination treatment and for elucidating possible interactions. Combined treatments are represented clinically in alternate packages. For establishing the value of combined treatments, some form of constructive strategy is needed.

The four-group factorial design. To evaluate a combined treatment, such as the combination of two drugs (a tricyclic plus a benzodiazepine) or the combination of a drug plus psychotherapy (amitriptyline plus interpersonal therapy), the minimum optimal design is the four-group factorial design. In the factorial design, both treatments are evaluated against each other, against the control group, and against the combination. The factorial allows for statistical tests of interactions (see Figure 18.2).

The placebo effect, selection of control group, and the need for complex design. Until recently, the nature of the control group has been unspecified. In most psychopharmacologic research, the standard control is a placebo treatment group. There is, however, no agreement in psychotherapy research as to what would constitute a standard control group. In psychopharmacologic research, the placebo group provides a control for a "package" of factors: the tendency toward improvement inherent in many disorders; the attention given subjects as part of a research project; and the possible benefit of repeated assessment. In the psychopharmacologic literature, these factors are often called "nonspecific effects." In addition, there is the possible effect of placebo, the social psychological expectation attendant to prescription of a drug by a physician, and the act of pill taking. Often, the placebo effect is used in a general sense to refer to the combination of these nonpharmacologic effects, including expectations, time, and interpersonal transactions.

Discussions of the placebo effect may have distorted the selection of research designs for establishing the efficacy of psychotherapy (Wilkins, 1984). In psychopharmacologic research, the placebo-

Experimental Treatment #1	Experimental Treatment #2	Standard Treatment	Control Group
Cognitive/ Behavioral Therapy	Interpersonal Therapy	Imipramine Plus Psychological Management	Placebo Plus Psychological Management

Figure 18.1 Comparative strategies—the expanded three-group design. (From Elkin, I., Parloff, M. B., Hadley, S. W., and Autry, J. H. NIMH Treatment of Depression Collaborative Research Program. *Archives of General Psychiatry, 42,* 305–316, 1985.)

Drug Treatment

		Psychotherapy	
		Experimental Treatment	Control Treatment
Pharmacotherapy	Experimental Treatment	Combined Treatment Group	Psychotherapy Treatment Group
	Control Treatment	Drug Treatment Group	Control Group

Figure 18.2 Constructive strategies—four-group factorial design for evaluating combined treatment.

control group attempts to simultaneously control a number of nonspecific "specific" pharmacologic features. In psychotherapy research, however, it is exactly these "nonspecific" social psychological processes (patient expectation, personal features of the treatment relationships) that are believed to be among the components of effective psychotherapy.

Supplementing these general problems regarding the selection of controls, there is a specific problem with regard to the possible limitations of placebo-controls in studies of drugs and psychotherapy. The usual setting for the conduct of psychotherapy does not involve the use of a placebo. Use of a placebo group may alter the sociopsychological context of the psychotherapy, especially by generating changes in the expectations of the therapist and of the patient. Therefore, a more powerful design for evaluating combined treatment would be a six-group design, employing a no-pill control group. This design was used in a trial of drugs and psychotherapy in the maintenance of treatment of acute depressions reported by Klerman, DiMascio, Weissman, Prusoff, and Paykel (1974).

By employing a no-pill group, the *six-group design* tests whether the placebo effect produces increment over and above the nonspecific conditions of numerous rating scales and of the illness itself (see Figure 18.3). There seems to be an assumption implicit in much of the placebo literature that the placebo effect is positive in all conditions and in all circumstances. Most of the literature on placebo deals with the expectations around pill taking—its

"magical" quality, dependency expectations—being given the "sick role," and the additional attention of being in a research project. The Boston–New Haven study did not find any placebo effect over the "no-pill" condition in a long-term (eight-month) treatment study of depressives. A drug versus "no-pill" and drug versus placebo difference was found, but no placebo effect was detected over and above the "no-pill" condition in the study. Moreover, no negative interactions between drugs and psychotherapy were observed (Rounsaville, Klerman, & Weissman, 1981). However, others have reanalyzed these data and interpreted them as showing an interaction between pill ingestion via placebo and psychotherapy (Hollon & DeRubeis, 1981).

Hollon and DeRubeis (1981) have proposed an ideal design for studying the interaction of drugs and psychotherapy involving a nine-group design to control for the nonspecific or placebo aspects of psychotherapy. No researcher has yet attempted a nine-group design. A number of four-group design projects have been reported, and they provide some basis for the assessment of combined treatment. There is only one report of a six-group design.

Constructive strategies—standard therapy as the control with psychotherapy or drugs as additional treatment. Although the factorial design is the scientific ideal, there may be valid reasons why it cannot be executed. In the presence of overwhelming evidence for the efficacy of a standard

Drug Treatment

		Psychotherapy	
		Present	Absent
Pharmacotherapy	Drug	Psychotherapy and Amitriptyline	Amitriptyline
	Placebo	Psychotherapy and placebo	Placebo
	No pill	Psychotherapy and no pill	No pill No psychotherapy

Figure 18.3. Constructive strategies—six-group design for evaluating placebo effect in combined treatment. (From Klerman, G. L., DiMascio, A., Weissman, M. M., Prusoff, B., and Paykel, E. Treatment of depression by drugs and psychotherapy. *American Journal of Psychiatry, 131,* 186–191, 1974.)

treatment, it may be considered unethical to withhold standard treatment from patients and assign them to a "no-treatment" control group. This seems to be the case for studies of hospital treatment of acutely psychotic schizophrenic patients, where some form of antipsychotic drug treatment is now considered the standard.

An alternative justification for not employing a no-treatment control derives from the desire to simulate clinical practice. Where a standard treatment exists, the clinician wants to know how much improvement may be gained by adding another treatment as a supplement to the standard treatment. For example, in the maintenance treatment of bipolar patients, "what is the value of adding group or family therapy to the lithium treatment?"

In these designs, which are variations of the constructive strategy, the standard treatment is given to all patients, and certain patients are assigned to the experimental treatment. Of course, the assignment to standard or experimental treatment should be by randomized matching or some similar nonbiased method.

The standard treatment may be a pharmacologic treatment, as in the studies of family therapy of schizophrenics in which all patients receive fluphenazine, an antipsychotic (Goldstein, 1984). The standard treatment may be a psychological treatment, as in the use of exposure treatment in

anxiety disorders (Mavissakalian, 1984). The standard treatment could be a combination of drug and psychotherapy, as in the Philadelphia studies of opiate addicts in which all patients received methadone maintenance drug treatment plus peer counseling as the standard treatment (Woody et al., 1983).

The simple version of this design would be a two-group design, in which one group got the standard treatment alone and the other group got the standard treatment plus an experimental treatment. This design has been employed by Jamison (unpublished) in a comparison of lithium alone versus lithium plus group treatment for outpatients with bipolar affective disorder.

A more complex design is the three-group design employed in the Philadelphia studies of drug addiction (see Figure 18.4). In this design, the standard treatment was methadone maintenance plus peer counseling by ex-addicts. Two experimental forms of psychotherapy were evaluated, cognitive behavioral therapy, as developed by Beck et al. (1979), and supportive-expressive psychodynamic psychotherapy, developed by Luborsky (1984).

A similar design has been employed by Schooler and Keith in the NIMH Treatment Strategies in Schizophrenia Study (unpublished). In this study, the psychopharmacologic dosage is varied, and a form of family management developed by Falloon

Group 1	Group 2	Group 3
No supplemental treatment	Cognitive-behavioral psychotherapy	Supportive-expressive psychotherapy
Standard treatment: Methadone plus peer counseling		

Figure 18.4 Constructive strategies—standard treatment as control and experimental treatments as supplements. (From Woody, G. E., Lurborsky, L., McLellan, T., O'Brien, C. P., Beck, A. T., Blaine, J., Herman, I., and Hole, A. Psychotherapy for opiate addicts: Does it help? *Archives of General Psychiatry, 40,* 639–645, 1983.)

and associates is being evaluated for possible interaction with two levels of drug dosage.

Where a standard treatment exists, the research design may vary the timing and sequence of additional experimental treatments. For example, it is quite common for patients to first receive the standard treatment, and then only those patients who have stabilized in their response are assigned by matching or randomization to experimental conditions involving the standard treatment alone or the standard treatment plus the experimental treatment. This sequencing is closer to clinical practice in which the timing of "packages" is often determined by the clinician based on the degree of response to the standard treatment.

Other Research Designs

A number of other research designs have been employed in drug–psychotherapy use. Retrospective analyses of naturalistic clinical data are often used to support the value of the various treatment programs. For example, Feinsilver and Yates (1984) report a retrospective study documenting a particular sequence for the combined use of psychotherapy and drugs in chronic, treatment-resistant schizophrenic patients. They used naturalistic observation to test the hypothesis that treatment-resistant schizophrenic patients when withdrawn from medications will experience a prolonged aggressive phase and when subsequently remedicated and treated psychotherapeutically, will do better than patients treated by medication alone with the regressive experience.

Kazdin (see Chapter 2) also lists dismantling designs as alternative modes of evaluating psychotherapy. These designs have not been used in psychopharmacology.

Single-case designs have only occasionally been used in psychopharmacologic research (Chassan, 1979; Uhlenhuth, Turner, Purchatzke, Gift, & Chassan, 1977).

The Selection of Subjects and the Role of DSM-III Diagnosis

The criteria for the selection of subjects has been one of the areas of differences between psychopharmacologic and psychotherapeutic research. Most psychopharmacologic research selects patients on the basis of some level of diagnosis. Three levels of diagnosis have been used: symptom, syndrome, or disorder. The diagnostic criteria could be an individual symptom, such as insomnia, anxiety, or weight gain. In other studies, syndromal diagnoses have been used, as in the evaluation of drugs for psychotic states, panic attacks, or endogenous depression. In the ideal of rational medicine, drugs would be tested for treatment of a disorder or disease for which etiology and/or pathogenesis would have been established. Such instances are rare in psychopharmacology. Most psychopharmacologic agents are used for symptomatic and/or syndromal indications. This reality has prompted Klein to emphasize the value of such research in psychopharmacology, not only as a mode of evaluating treatment, but as contributing evidence for validating diagnostic concepts (Klein, 1980).

Early in the history of psychopharmacology, the concept of "target symptom" was widely employed in guiding selection of subjects. Patients were selected on the basis of salient symptoms for which the drug was "targeted." This concept contributed to the terminology of drug classes in psychopharmacology such as "major tranquilizers" or "psychomotor stimulants."

In recent years, there has been a trend toward standardization of selection criteria and procedures with the increasing use of structured interviews for assessment of symptom patterns and of diagnostic algorithms for assigning patients to appropriate groups, usually defined by Research Diagnostic Criteria (RDC; Spitzer, Endicott, & Robins, 1978) or *DSM-III* (Klerman, 1983b).

Since many psychotherapies are not oriented toward the reduction of symptoms or the treatment of a disorder, there often have been disputes over selection criteria when research designs have attempted to combine drugs and psychotherapy. One of the major characteristics of the "new wave" of psychotherapy research is the growing acceptance of the concept of mental disorders as the basis for psychotherapy effect and the increasing attention to diagnosis in patient selection. This trend is evident in the development of psychotherapies for specific disorders, for example, cognitive-behavioral and interpersonal psychotherapies for depression, desensitization and exposure-in-vivo for agoraphobia, and family therapy directed at reducing expressed emotion (EE) in families of discharged schizophrenics. Research on these psychotherapies that are "targeted" for a disorder now employ structured interviews for obtaining information about history and symptoms and research criteria for making diagnoses.

These trends represent a departure from previous periods when classification and diagnosis were deemphasized, and patients were selected for psychotherapy on the basis of personality characteristics, such as ego strength, defensive structure, or MMPI profile.

The use of diagnosis in the design and conduct of research on psychotherapy places psychotherapy research increasingly in the health context. Viewing psychotherapy as a treatment modality legitimizes reimbursement by health insurance companies and other third-party payers, independent of whether the psychotherapy is delivered by a medical practi-

tioner or whether biological factors are considered etiologic for the disorder. For example, biofeedback, relaxation, exercise, and control of diet are behavioral and psychotherapeutic interventions of value for treatment of hypertension.

There are possible adverse consequences attendant upon regarding psychotherapy as a health procedure. In the short term, the "sick role" may enhance the patient's dependency and passivity, promoting compliance and facilitating symptom reduction. In psychodynamic theory, the sick patient's option of the role is often regarded as the patient's attempt to manipulate the transference, particularly to enhance the therapist being seen as authoritarian and paternalistic. In behavioral terms, the concern is that sick-role behavior will be reinforced, particularly those aspects of the sick role that excuse the individual from social responsibility and reinforce avoidant behavior.

These considerations, however, only increase the need for research to assess the efficacy and safety of all aspects of the therapeutic interventions, including the clinical context and sick-role expectation.

Integrity of the Treatments

In psychopharmacologic research, there is usually assurance that the chemical composition of the compound is uniform. Standards of medicinal chemistry ensure clinical purity. Methods of quality control in the pharmaceutical industry are almost always of high standards.

Even with known chemical interplay, in psychopharmacologic research there is concern over whether the drug prescribed does in fact reach the parts of the CNS presumed to produce change. One concern relates to differences in compliance and patient adherence. Another concern follows from the biological variation in the pharmacokinetics and metabolism of the drugs. For these reasons, blood level determinations are increasingly employed in psychopharmacologic research as measures of patient compliance and to control for patient differences in drug absorption and metabolism.

There are parallel problems in psychotherapy research. Ensuring the comparability, purity, and integrity of the psychotherapy between therapists has been one of the serious problems in psychotherapy research, but it is not necessarily an insurmountable problem. There have been a number of methodological advances within this area in the past five years; these include treatment manuals, specialized training of psychotherapists and pharmacotherapists for research, and monitoring the quality of the conduct and process of the therapy.

Treatment manuals serve to identify characteristics of the psychotherapy, including the goals, the tasks, and the recommended sequence from the stages of initiation through termination. Manuals specify methods for assessment of these tasks and operationalize the therapy through definitions and case examples. Manuals include "scripts," which give precise statements of therapist interventions. The first manuals were developed by the behavior therapists (Beck, unpublished). Subsequent manuals have been developed for interpersonal psychotherapy (IPT; Klerman et al., 1984b) and for variations of psychodynamic psychotherapy (Luborsky, 1984; Strupp & Binder, 1984). The IPT manual has been used in comparative and constructive evaluations of drugs and psychotherapy of depression. The Luborsky manual and the Beck manual have been used in studies of psychotherapy and methadone treatment for opiate drug addicts.

Treatment manuals also have been developed for the psychological management associated with pharmacotherapy. Fawcett and Epstein in Chicago were commissioned to develop a comparable manual for the psychological management of drug therapy (Fawcett & Epstein, 1980), as used in the NIMH Collaborative Study for the Treatment of Depression (Elkin et al, 1985).

Training of Psychotherapists and Psychopharmacologists for Research

Another important development in psychotherapy and psychopharmacology research has been the use of standardized training programs based on protocols and manual-specified procedures. Most of these training programs have not been developed to teach inexperienced students to become psychoanalysts and psychotherapists; rather, they have been designed to help experienced therapists learn the particular methods and skills required for the research treatments. Certification criteria for psychotherapists have been developed for research participation, and videotape review has allowed independent assessment (Chevron & Rounsaville, 1983; Chevron, Rounsaville, Rothblum & Weissman, 1983; Weissman, Rounsaville, & Chevron, 1982).

Monitoring the Quality of the Conduct and Process of the Therapy

The availability of manuals and training in their use will not guarantee that the treatment actually delivered in the research project is the psychotherapy specified in the protocol. In order to ascertain this, some method of quality control is needed. In psychopharmacology research, drug plasma levels are useful to evaluate compliance. A number of techniques for monitoring psychotherapy through videotapes and supervision of the therapist based on the tapes have been developed by Luborsky, Woody, McLellan, and O'Brien (1982) in Philadelphia and by Hollon and associates in Minnesota (DeRubeis, Hollon, Evans, and Bemis, 1982; Hollon, Evans, Elkin, & Lowery, 1984) and in the NIMH Collaborative Study of the Treatment of Depression.

Assessment of Outcome and Process

In the design of research on drugs and psychotherapy, a number of decisions are required as to the assessment of change. Among these decisions are: Which variables should be assessed? Who should be the source of information about improvement— the therapist, an indifferent evaluater, the relative, or patient self-report? What is the expected timing of assessments?

Almost all investigators accept that outcome is multidimensional, and almost all research projects use a battery of assessment measures, including therapist global assessment, patient global assessment, symptom assessment by clinical interview and self-report, measures of social adjustment, and measures of personality functioning.

Psychopharmacologic research tends to emphasize assessment of symptomatic variables, usually by means of standardized rating scales. There has been a recent trend toward assessment of social functioning and "quality of life." Comparisons of clinician ratings with patient ratings indicate greater sensitivity to drug effects with clinicians' assessment. In part, this may be due to cognitive effects of affect states, particularly anxiety and depression (Lambert, 1983).

A major issue in drug and psychotherapy research has to do with interaction between the timing of effects and the differential effects of these treatments. Drug effects are often evident within the first weeks, particularly upon psychobiological functions such as sleep, appetite, and psychomotor activity. Psychotherapy effects often take longer to become apparent and alter different variables, such as social functioning, interpersonal relations, or self-esteem. Therefore, it is essential that studies including pharmacotherapies and psychotherapy include measures of sensitivity for both types of treatment and at appropriate time intervals.

Assuming safety and efficacy have been demonstrated for a particular treatment, whether psychopharmacologic or psychotherapeutic, the question then arises, "How does this treatment work?" The investigation of modes of treatment action is a standard approach in pharmacology and in psychotherapy. For example, in the pharmacotherapy of depression, there are hypotheses that the efficacy of antidepressant drugs is mediated through their effects on catecholamine or serotonin neurotransmitters. In the psychotherapy of depression, it is hypothesized that greater improvement occurs via changes in dysfunctional attitudes. If so, the change in dysfunctional attitude should precede the reduction in depressive mood symptoms. Similarly, interpersonal psychotherapy of depression presumes a decrease in role conflict as a mediating influence on the reduction of depressive symptoms. Therefore, analyses of process, particularly the sequence of change, can be an indirect mode of testing the rationale for the psychotherapy. Thus, process research in psychotherapy is the equivalent of research on mode of actions in pharmacology.

Findings from process research may also identify subgroups within the clinical population who are most responsive to the treatment. Thus, findings from process research on cognitive-behavioral therapy may lead to techniques to identify subgroups of depressed patients who are having significant impairments in cognitive style, and would, therefore, be presumably most responsive to this form of therapy. Similarly, it would be hypothesized that patients with agoraphobia without panic disorder would be most responsive to behavior therapy—if there are significant degrees of avoidance behavior—while drug therapy is most effective for patients with panic disorder without avoidance. The interplay between pharmacotherapy and behavioral therapy for agoraphobia involves a debate as to the relative frequency and importance and sequencing of panic attacks and avoidant behavior. The pharmacologic theories presume that the panic attack

precedes the onset of avoidant behavior, and that the avoidant behavior is driven by the aversive distress associated with panic attacks. Process research on the sequence of change in response to drugs and behavior therapy could contribute to resolving these issues.

Even were such data available, caution is needed in generalizing from the sequence of change during treatment to presumed etiology and pathogenesis (Barlow, in press).

Follow-up
Follow-up studies test whether these are enduring effects of the psychotherapy or the drug therapy. Although many psychotherapies claim to have enduring effects based on social learning and the undoing of maladaptive patterns of cognition and interpersonal relations, only a few attempts have been made to test these hypotheses. Notable are the one-year follow-up studies of cognitive therapy (Kovacs, Rush, Beck, & Hallon, 1981) and the one-year, four-year follow-up of depressed patients treated with drugs and IPT (Klerman, 1980; Weissman, Klerman, Prusoff, Sholomskas, & Padian, 1981).

In the treatment of panic disorder and agoraphobia, there is a major controversy as to possible enduring effects of drug and psychotherapeutic treatments. Marks (1976) asserts that patients treated with behavior therapy have enduring effects and points out that patients treated with drug treatment often have a high relapse rate when the drug is discontinued. Marks interprets this as a form of state-dependent learning and uses this as evidence for the superiority of behavior therapy in comparison to pharmacotherapies. Nevertheless, this area is one of continuing dispute and a factorial design study comparing alprazolam with exposure therapy, including a follow-up, is now being developed by Marks (1985b).

Long-term Treatments
Many psychotherapies, particularly those based on psychoanalysis and psychodynamic theory, make claims for the value of long-term treatment. However, empirical support of these claims is very limited. For certain disorders, long-term treatment with psychopharmacologic agents has been demonstrated to have some efficacy. For schizophrenia the neuroleptics are used, particularly long-acting injectable compounds such as fluphenazine deca-

noate; for bipolar disorder, both lithium and tricyclic antidepressants are used to prevent recurrence and relapse. There is significant diagnosis by drug interactions; for bipolar patients, tricyclics may be deleterious because of the induction of excited and manic states. Therefore, for bipolar patients, lithium is the preferred treatment. For nonbipolar (often called unipolar) depressions, both lithium and tricyclics have been shown to be effective (NIH Consensus Development Panel, 1985). For opiate addiction, methadone maintenance treatment is now a standard. A group of research projects using constructive designs have attempted to assess the value of psychotherapy in the context of patients being treated with long-term maintenance therapies. These will be discussed later in the specific diagnostic sections. It is of note that most of the designs based on constructive strategies used in this research are often presumed to be the facilitative interaction described above, namely, that the psychotherapy is unlikely to be effective by itself, but becomes effective in the presence of ongoing medication. This seems to be accepted for the most part in long-term studies of outpatient schizophrenics, opiate addicts, and bipolar patients.

Cost−Benefit and Cost-Effectiveness Assessments

The conventional focus of treatment research in psychopharmacology and psychotherapy has been on measures of safety, efficacy, and related outcomes. In recent years, with the increasing concern about the economic costs of health care, cost−benefit analysis (CBA) and cost-effectiveness analysis (CEA) have been advocated for psychotherapy research (Fein, 1980). It is expected that in future studies, these methods will be applied, particularly to assess whether treatments with equal level of clinical efficacy differ in their cost-effectiveness.

Meta-analysis and Other Techniques Used for Assessing Findings Across Studies

Until recently, most of the discussion about research methodology has focused upon the design, execution, and data analysis of individual studies. Only recently have the fields of psychopharmacology and psychotherapy dealt with the problem of how to compare findings across studies. Early attempts in this area relied heavily on scholarly reviews (Eysenck, 1965; May, 1968a) and the "box score" technique (Luborsky, 1984). Statistical problems

attendant to pooling data across studies are complex. Davis, in an attempt to deal with this problem, has reported on secondary statistical analyses of data from studies evaluating long-term treatment with tricyclic antidepressant drugs and lithium. Davis (1976) used the statistical techniques of Fleiss' (1973) modification of Cochran's (1954) method.

More recently, meta-analysis applied by Smith, Glass, and Miller (1980) has been used for this purpose (see also Kazdin, Chapter 2). Extensions of this technique into psychopharmacology and to combined psychotherapy and pharmacology have also been reported. For example, in the 1980 Smith, Glass, and Miller volume, meta-analysis was applied to drug treatments.

The Royal Canadian and Australian Colleges of Psychiatrists have reported an ambitious quality assurance project in which meta-analysis has been used to assess treatments for agoraphobia and for depressive disorders (Andrews, 1982, 1983).

POSSIBLE OUTCOMES OF RESEARCH ON COMPARATIVE AND COMBINED DRUG PSYCHOTHERAPY TREATMENTS

Having reviewed some of the possible research designs, let us now analyze the possible outcomes for studies of drugs and psychotherapy. The outcomes discussed will focus on comparative and constructive strategies for evaluating combination therapy. Most of the discussion will use results from the four-group design in Figure 18.2.

The advantage of a factorial design is that it is simultaneously a comparison of drugs against psychotherapy and against a control group, as well as a constructive strategy to assess the possible advantage of combining drugs and psychotherapy.

In Figures 18.5 through 18.7, the height of the bars representing treatment outcome is equal for both the psychotherapy and the drug groups. This reflects an attempt to equalize the efficacy of the two forms of treatment. For example, in studies of depression, Rush and Beck (1980) have published evidence from a two-group design that cognitive therapy is equal to efficacy of treatment with a tricyclic antidepressant. Similar findings are reported with interpersonal therapy (Prusoff, Weissman, Klerman, & Rounsaville, 1980). The findings have

challenged the conventional wisdom within the depression field, which has assumed that drugs would
have more impact than any behavioral or psychotherapeutic intervention.

*Outcomes of Constructive Designs for Assess-
ing Combined Drugs and Psychotherapy*
Figure 18.5 catalogues the possible outcomes of the
combined treatment groups in relationship to the
two individual treatments. In Figures 18.6 through
18.9, the left bar refers to the control group, the
middle bar refers to the two active therapies of
pharmacotherapy, and the bar on the right refers to
the combined treatment.

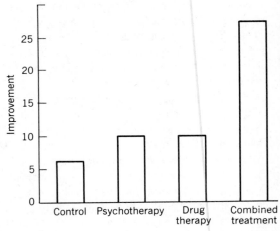

Figure 18.7.   Combined treatment outcome:
Positive effect—synergistic.

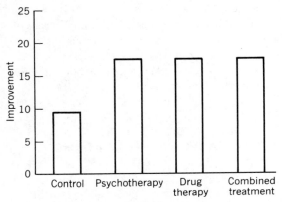

Figure 18.5.   Combined treatment outcome:
No therapeutic effect.

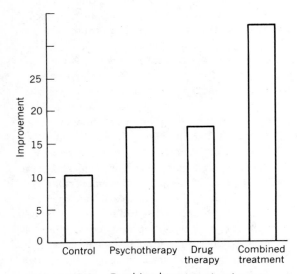

Figure 18.6.   Combined treatment outcome:
Positive effects—additive.

At least three groups of outcomes are reported in
the literature:

1. *No therapeutic effect* (Fig. 18.5): Combined
    treatment provides the same improvement as
    the individual treatments.
2. *Positive effects* (Figs. 18.6–18.9): Combined
    treatment provides improvement over the in-
    dividual treatments.
3. *Negative effects:* Combined treatment shows
    less improvement than the effect of either
    treatment alone.

No Therapeutic Effect of Combined Therapy
No therapeutic effect of combination is depicted in
Figure 18.5. The effects of combined treatment offer no greater benefit than the single treatments,
both of which are better than outcomes for the
control group. This outcome has been reported for
the combination of drugs and cognitive therapy for
depression, in which combined treatment did not
offer any advantage over either amitriptyline or cognitive therapy (Rush & Watkins, 1981; Klerman,
1984a).

Positive Effects of Combined Therapies
In constructed combination treatments, the therapist hopes for some additive effects (Fig. 18.6) in
which the sum is greater than its parts—that the
combined treatment will produce a magnitude of
effect greater than the two individual treatments.

Additive and Synergistic Effects

The ideal effects would be synergistic, the effect of combined treatment being greater than the sum of the two component treatments. This has been reported from some outcomes in the Boston–New Haven project on the treatment of acute outpatient depressives. In this study, the Hamilton Depression Scale showed synergistic effect (Hamilton, 1967). This can also be called a cocktail or martini effect. The assumption in a cocktail is that the combination of gin plus vermouth will produce greater psychopharmacologic "punch" than if equal amounts of gin and vermouth were taken separately.

Facilitative Interaction

A more complex effect is called "facilitation" interaction in which one treatment is effective only when combined with the other. For example, as shown in Figure 18.8, one of the treatments (psychotherapy) is ineffective alone, but the combination is most effective. This is the outcome reported in most studies of hospitalized schizophrenics. Individual psychotherapy alone is ineffective, but when combined with pharmacotherapy, some additive effect occurs. This complex facilitative effect is implicit in current clinical practice with bipolar patients, psychotic depressed patients, and melancholic (or endogenous) depressed patients. Psychotherapy alone is ineffective. Patients with this diagnosis require medication, and the combined treatment offers an advantage.

The converse situation is possible, that is, where the facilitative interaction of the drug therapy alone is ineffective, the psychotherapy alone is effective, and the drug therapy becomes effective in combination only with psychotherapy. This outcome has not been documented, but it is possible. For example, via facilitation of compliance and patient adherence, psychotherapy facilitates the action of drug therapy, which in the absence of some form of psychotherapy would be ineffective.

Drugs Facilitate Psychotherapeutic Accessibility

This hypothesis is embodied in the most commonly stated rationales for the use of combined therapies, and it supports prevailing clinical practice in psychiatry. Advertisements and other promotional materials of many pharmaceutical firms propose that the introduction of their drug facilitates psychotherapy by making the patient "more accessible." The proposed mechanism for this effect is readily specified—the pharmacological action of the drug

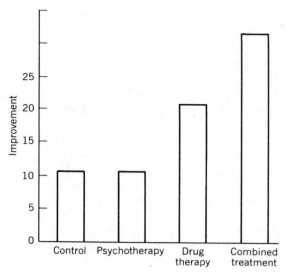

Figure 18.8. Combined treatment outcome: Positive effect—facilitative.

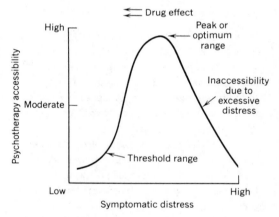

Figure 18.9. Drugs facilitate accessibility to psychotherapy.

ameliorates the presumed CNS dysfunction underlying symptom formation, resulting in reduction of the patient's symptomatology, psychopathology, and/or affective discomfort. Drug-induced reduction in discomfort renders the patient better able to communicate and benefit from psychotherapy. Although some level of anxiety, dysphoria, or symptomatology is believed necessary to provide the "drive" or "motivation" for participation in psychotherapy, this hypothesis presumes that excessive levels of tension, anxiety, or symptom intensity will result in a decrease in the patient's capacity to participate effectively in psychotherapy.

*Drugs Influence the Ego Psychological
Functions Required for Participation in
Psychotherapy*

Another hypothesis predicts that drugs may positively influence the psychotherapeutic process through their pharmacologic action on neurophysiologic substrates for the ego functions necessary for psychotherapeutic participation. Some drugs may influence verbal skills, improve cognitive functioning, improve memory, reduce distraction, and promote attention and concentration. Since it is widely accepted that adequate ego functioning is a prerequisite for psychotherapeutic participation, these psychological functions and abilities are components of the large domain of ego function and enhance the patient's benefit from participation in psychotherapy.

Although the majority of psychoanalysts are skeptical, if not hostile, toward drug therapy, a small group has integrated psychoanalytic thinking with drug therapy (Ostow, 1962).

Drugs Promote Psychotherapeutic Abreaction

Abreaction is one of the basic psychotherapeutic techniques. A number of drugs, especially intravenous barbiturates and amphetamines, have been used to promote this effect. Wikler (1957) referred to such methods as "psychoexploratory" techniques. These drugs help to uncover memory, break down defenses, and bring into consciousness material against which the person otherwise defends. A variant of this practice is the use of LSD, mescaline, and psilocybin to promote "peak experiences" in which the heightened sense of self-awareness and emotional, affective, and bodily experiences that occur under these psychedelic drugs are advocated as facilitating the psychotherapeutic process.

There is a long history of the use of drugs to assist interviewing, mostly with amytal (Kwentus, 1984). In the 1940s, use of intravenous amytal was extended to the development of abreactive treatment, sometimes called narcoanalysis. During World War II, this was widely used in military psychiatry (Grinker & Spiegel, 1945).

During the 1950s, psychedelic drugs were also used to facilitate abreaction (Abramson, 1967). However, controlled studies failed to sustain the early claims for this action of drugs. Currently abreactive therapies are not popular, either in clinical practice or in research.

*Positive Effects of Drug Therapy on Expectation
and Stigma*

In addition to the short-term symptomatic relief of drug therapy, a positive placebo effect may often contribute to a patient's optimism and confidence. The advocates of biological methods, such as the megavitamin treatment of schizophrenia, are often successful in removing some of the stigma from psychiatric illness and making it easier for the patients and their families to accept the definition of themselves as mentally ill. Thus, the request for drug therapy may itself be an indirect attempt of the patient to seek psychotherapeutic counseling. In this context, the skillful psychopharmacologist often uses the patient's initial request for drug therapy as a starting point for initiating psychotherapy.

The previous paragraphs have discussed mechanisms by which drugs may have positive effects on psychotherapy. We now turn to discussions of mechanisms in which psychotherapy may produce positive effects on drug therapy.

*Psychotherapy Facilitates Drug Compliance and
Adherence*

Psychotherapeutic input in psychopharmacology employing techniques of reassurance, psychoeducation methods, and clear instructions will enhance the patient's positive attitude and cooperation.

May (1968b) and others have distinguished between psychological management and psychotherapy. Psychological management refers to extension of general aspects of doctor–patient relationships to enhance drug compliance and patient cooperation and general therapeutic alliance. Psychotherapy, in this view, refers to efforts to influence the patient's symptoms and psychological functions by verbal and behavioral techniques.

Psychotherapy as Rehabilitation Effort

Many drug therapists hypothesize value for psychotherapy as a secondary and ameliorative treatment. They propose that psychotherapy operates not upon etiologic mechanisms or upon the core of the psychological process, per se, but to correct secondary difficulties in interpersonal relations, self-esteem, and psychological functions that follow upon the impact of affective symptoms. In this view, psychotherapy is seen as rehabilitative, rather than as therapeutic, that is, the psychotherapy is an elective rather than a necessary treatment.

Many advocates of this approach employ a sequence in which the drug therapy is initiated first and the psychotherapy is introduced after there has been symptom reduction and stabilization of affective states and early improvement in social adjustment.

Negative Effects of Combined Drugs and Psychotherapy

Much attention has been given to the possible negative effects of introducing drug therapy into psychotherapy. Although relatively little empirical research has been done to test these hypotheses, it is possible to identify a number of proposed interactions.

Negative Placebo Effect of Medication in the Presence of Psychotherapy

Much of the criticism of drug therapy enunciated by psychotherapists in the 1950s implied a negative placebo effect—that pill taking had harmful effects in the presence of psychotherapy. It was hypothesized that the prescription of any drug had deleterious effects upon the psychotherapeutic relationship and upon the attitudes and behavior of both patients and therapist—effects independent of the specific pharmacologic actions of a drug. Moreover, the prescribing of medication promoted an authoritarian attitude on the part of the psychiatrist and enhanced his belief in his biological-medical heritage. At the same time, the patient would become more dependent, place greater reliance on magical thinking, and assume a more passive, compliant role, as is expected in the conventional doctor−patient relationship in fields of medicine other than psychiatry.

Drug-induced Reduction of Symptoms as Patient's Motives for Discontinuing Psychotherapy

The negative-placebo-effect hypothesis assumes only a symbolic and psychological meaning to drug administration. If we assume pharmacologic activity and therapeutic efficacy of the drug, however, then a resultant decrease of the patient's symptoms, anxiety, and tension might reduce the patient's motivation for psychotherapy. The hypothesis predicts that too effective a drug will initiate patient attitudes and behaviors counter to psychotherapy. Thus, if a psychoactive drug, such as a phenothiazine or MAO inhibitor, is highly effective in reducing psychotic turmoil, depression, anxiety, or other symptoms,

the patient's motivation for reflection, insight, and psychotherapeutic work will be lessened. According to this hypothesis, it is predicted that if drug therapy is too effective, patients will no longer seek psychotherapy because they will be satisfied with mere symptom reduction.

Pharmacotherapy Undermines Defense, Providing Symptom-Substitutes

This hypothesis predicts that if the pharmacologic effect of a drug prematurely undercuts some important defenses, symptom substitution or other compensatory mechanisms of symptom formation will ensue. For example, in psychotherapeutic practice, Seitz (1953) reported instances of new symptom formation following hypnosis, and Weiss (1965) cautioned against an overly rapid relief of the anxiety of the agoraphobic—if such anxiety is reduced too rapidly before new defenses are developed, other symptoms may occur. This hypothesis assumes that symptoms maintain a psychic balance between conflict and defenses, and that the precipitous reduction of anxiety, depression, or tension may upset this equilibrium and release deeper conflicts. If so, this disequilibrium would obviously generate new symptoms for the depressive patient; but systematic research data and replications germane to this specific hypothesis are few and inconclusive.

Possible Negative Effects of Psychotherapy on Drug Therapy

Most of the discussion in the literature has focused on possible effects of drug therapy upon psychotherapy. Relatively little attention has been paid to the other part of the process, namely, the impact of psychotherapy upon the patient receiving pharmacotherapy. It is interesting to note how seldom this problem is discussed or even mentioned.

Perhaps, considering the efficacy of drugs in the treatment of affective disorders, and the less extensive body of evidence for the efficacy of psychotherapy, the question should be stated: What negative effects or benefits accrue to the patient, if psychotherapy is added to drug therapy? During the discussions in the 1950s and 1960s, the psychotherapists were the assertive members of the dialogue, and the drug therapists were on the defensive. Now, one can discern a shift with the impact of evidence as to drug efficacy from controlled studies.

Drug Treatments Alone Are Necessary and Sufficient

Some pharmacotherapists make simplistic comparisons of psychotropic drug treatment, especially with endocrine agents such as insulin for diabetes. For those who hold this view, the rectification of the presumed neurophysiologic dysfunction or deficiency is the critical factor, and psychotherapy is considered unnecessary and irrelevant or, at best, neutral. Based on TV and news reports, the concept of "chemical imbalance" has widely diffused into the public as an explanation for depression and bipolar disease. Thus, patients may regard drug treatment as a simple correction of their chemical imbalance. A variation of this view is expressed by some proponents of the lithium treatment of mania. The most extreme version of this view is proposed by those who advocate megavitamin therapy for schizophrenia. Proponents of this view feel that drugs alone are both necessary and sufficient for treatment.

Psychotherapy May Be Symptomatically Disruptive

Furthermore, some pharmacotherapists hypothesize that psychotherapy may be deleterious to the pharmacologic treatment, since symptoms may be aggravated by excessive probing and uncovering defenses. Some psychiatrists who work with depressives and schizophrenics feel that harm is done to the patient by psychotherapeutic intervention, particularly during the acute state, and that during the early recovery process the patient is best left alone to "heal over" and to reconstitute his defenses. There is a dispute between psychotherapists who advocate "working through underlying conflicts" even if it involves "sealing over" by promoting denial, repression, and other defenses, and others who support symptom-reduction. Many pharmacotherapists are concerned that psychotherapy, by focusing on areas of patient conflicts, will increase the levels of emotional tension.

Psychotherapy May Undercut Compliance

The psychotherapists may be overtly or indirectly negative in attitude toward drug therapy and may communicate to the patient in psychotherapy these attitudes, and thus may promote poor compliance on the part of the patient, thus obviating any possible value of drug therapy.

STATUS OF KNOWLEDGE FOR INDIVIDUAL CONDITIONS

Up to this point, this chapter has considered general issues regarding drugs and psychotherapy. We now turn to a selected number of clinical conditions and examine the state of knowledge concerning drugs and psychotherapy in the treatment of these conditions.

Four disorders have been chosen: schizophrenia, affective disorders, agoraphobia and panic disorder, and opiate dependence.

Evaluation of treatments by individual conditions is the standard mode of evaluating pharmacologic treatment. Selection of subjects according to clinical disorders on the basis of standardized diagnostic criteria has contributed to increasing consensus about the relative value of drugs and psychotherapy in selected conditions based on evidence from studies employing moderate-sized samples of carefully assessed and relatively homogeneous patient groups.

SCHIZOPHRENIA

The introduction of the "tranquilizers" in the mid-1950s had greatest impact on hospitalized schizophrenics. The claims for the efficacy of these new drugs on psychotic symptoms and behavior came at a time when there was controversy about the nature of schizophrenia as a disorder and about the efficacy and safety of the interventions advocated for its treatment.

Numerous biological treatments for schizophrenia had been utilized through the first half of the twentieth century. These treatments included dental extraction, colonic resections, tonsilectomy, and adrenalectomy. Their use was based on unsubstantiated presumptions as to the causation of schizophrenia. Therapeutic claims were seldom accompanied by any evidence for efficacy from systematic evaluations and follow-up, let alone controlled trials. By the 1930s, biological treatments of schizophrenia were regarded as unscientific and inhuman (Klerman, 1981).

The situation improved in the late 1930s when three new biological treatments were introduced: electroconvulsive therapy, insulin coma treatment, and prefrontal lobotomy. Because of the drastic nature of these interventions and the strong claims made for their efficacy, considerable debate attended their introduction. These controversies set the stage for reactions to the phenothiazines and reserpine derivatives introduced in the 1950s.

By the 1950s, however, randomized controlled trials were being increasingly adopted in medicine, particularly in studies on treatment of tuberculosis and of angina. Pressure from scientific quarters and from Congress led to the rapid utilization of the controlled trial designs in the new field of psychopharmacology. U.S. governmental agencies, especially the Veterans Administration (VA), and the National Institute of Mental Health (NIMH), and Psychopharmacology Service Center (Cole, Goldberg, & Klerman, 1964), as well as the Medical Research Council (MRC) in the United Kingdom mounted large multicenter studies. These studies demonstrated the feasibility of conducting randomized trials in assessing treatments for mental illness and the importance of multicenter collaborative trials to generate sufficient sample size to ensure generalizability of findings beyond a single setting. By the mid-1960s, the value of drug treatment for symptom reduction of hospitalized schizophrenic patients was conclusively established.

In comparison with the biological treatments of schizophrenia, the psychotherapeutic treatments of schizophrenia developed more slowly. The early efforts arose from psychoanalytic sources. Psychoanalysis had its beginning in central Europe in the last decade of the nineteenth century at the same time as Kraepelin formulated the concept of dementia praecox, later adapted by Bleuler to schizophrenia. Of the various European psychoanalytic schools, the Freudians have had the greatest influence on America. The earliest signs of this influence followed the 1908 visit by Freud and a number of his associates to Clark University in Worcester, Massachusetts (Hale, 1971). More significant, however, was the migration of significant numbers of German, Austrian, and other central European psychoanalysts to America during the 1930s as a result of the Nazi persecution. This group had a profound influence on American psychotherapy.

Interest in the psychopathology of the psychoses, particularly schizophrenia and paranoia, characterized early psychoanalytic writings. Freud's papers established the general principles for the separation of psychotic and neurotic disorders; this psychoanalytic separation is based on the criterion of failure of reality testing by the ego. This psychoanalytic criteria is almost identical to the descriptive psychopathological criteria of impairment of higher mental functions, memory, orientation, language, and cognition derived from nineteenth-century psychology.

It is noteworthy that at the time Bleuler (1959) was developing his concept of schizophrenia, a number of young psychoanalytic psychiatrists were on his staff at the Burgholzli Hospital in Zurich, notably Jung (1956), Brill (1955), and Abraham (1927). The influence of psychoanalytic ideas is evident in Bleuler's *Monograph,* particularly in the theory of association. While Bleuler later minimized the role of psychogenic influences, in his early years he was receptive to the hypothesis that psychogenic influences were operative in the pathogenesis and etiology of schizophrenia.

After World War I, psychoanalytic interest in the psychoses diminished greatly because of Freud's doctrine that the narcissistic neuroses (i.e., psychoses) were not amenable to psychoanalysis, but that psychoanalysis was most suitable for patients with transference neuroses, particularly symptom neuroses. In spite of these theoretical constraints, a number of psychoanalytic writers, particularly Simmel (1929), Federn (1952), and Nunberg (1955), maintained interest in the psychoses. These efforts culminated in the theories of the neo-Freudians and of the emerging interpersonal school, particularly in the writing of Frieda Fromm-Reichmann (1960) and Harry Stack Sullivan (1953). The modification of classic psychoanalytic techniques by Fromm-Reichmann and her associates at Chestnut Lodge led to the widespread application of intensive individual psychotherapeutic efforts to hospitalized schizophrenics. Although the efficacy of this treatment was never supported by systematic studies, the writings of this group had profound influence on a generation of American psychotherapists and contributed greatly to theories of the developmental and intrafamily origin of schizophrenia, (Bowen, 1960; Lidz, Fleck, & Cornelison, 1965; Wynne & Singer, 1963) and to new forms of family therapy.

Efficacy of Drugs and Psychotherapy for Hospitalized Acute Schizophrenics

General issues in evaluating treatments of hospitalized schizophrenics have been discussed in a number of scholarly reviews (Hollon & Beck, 1978; May, 1968b, 1974, 1975).

A large number of studies have documented the efficacy of neuroleptic drugs for the symptomatic treatment of hospitalized schizophrenics. These have been reviewed extensively (Cole, Klerman, & Jones, 1960; Davis, 1965; Gilligan, 1965; Klein et al., 1980).

More recently, the Quality Assurance Project of the Royal Austrialian and New Zealand College of Psychiatrists applied meta-analysis to data from 600 controlled trials of schizophrenia (Andrews et al., in press). They calculated effect size for 200 studies of drugs and 26 studies of psychotherapy or social intervention and found no effect for psychotherapy, but very strong effect for drug therapies.

The most controversial issues are those relating to efficacy of psychotherapy, milieu therapy, and other psychosocial interventions (Mosher & Keith, 1980). Among the studies on psychosocial treatments, five studies have attempted to assess the efficacy of individual psychotherapy for hospitalized acute schizophrenics. These have been reviewed extensively by Hollon and Beck (1978). With the exception of the study in Michigan reported by Karon and VandenBos (1981), the results are negative. Individual psychotherapy without comcomitant medication based on the intensive psychodynamic model has relatively little to offer hospitalized schizophrenics (Klein, 1976; Schooler, 1978).

Comparative studies of the relative efficacy of drugs and psychotherapy are few in number, but generally indicate the greater value of a drug therapy over psychotherapy for symptom reduction and the improvement of social functioning within the hospital setting. Major studies were conducted at Massachusetts Mental Health Center (Grinspoon, Ewalt, & Shader, 1972) and by May (1968a) at Camarillo State Hospital in California. Both studies reported little or no therapeutic efficacy for individual psychotherapy alone. The May study provides evidence for a modest additive effect of psychotherapy when combined with drug therapy. The Grinspoon, Ewalt, and Shader study indicates that the psychotherapy was effective only in the presence of drug treatment. This pattern of results follows the type of outcome called "facilitative interaction" in the previous section on combined treatments.

An important research effort to evaluate intense psychodynamically oriented individual psychotherapy of schizophrenia was undertaken by Stanton et al. (1984) in Boston, and the results were recently reported in a special issue of the Schizophrenia Bulletin (1984). Their study emphasized a constructive design and evaluated two forms of psychotherapy, one based on psychodynamic exploration and the other based on a practical approach. These therapies differed in theoretical focus and in the intensity of contact between the therapist and the patient. The investigators designed the study with the expectation of demonstrating the efficacy of psychotherapy based on psychodynamic theory. This study attempted to assess whether or not psychotherapy offers anything above standard antipsychotic neuroleptic medication. All patients in both psychotherapy treatment groups received antipsychotic medication. The study's design precludes the evaluation of efficacy of psychotherapy against placebo or psychotherapy control condition.

Another feature of the Stanton study was the assessment of a wide range of outcome variables. Treatment studies in psychopharmacology of schizophrenia have been criticized by psychotherapists as relying exclusively on measures of symptom reduction. The Stanton project investigators developed a comprehensive battery of assessments of cognitive functioning, ego activity, social adjustment, and interpersonal relations.

The duration of treatment was two years, and the study employed experienced therapists in both treatment groups. Nevertheless, they had a very high attrition rate, such that only about one-third of the patients initially allocated to the two treatment groups completed the projected two years of treatment. In evaluating this study, one must conclude that the assessment of intensive individual psychotherapy failed to produce evidence for its claims of efficacy. Even in the presence of medication, this treatment failed to achieve any of the goals of the proponents who designed the experiment.

The Nature of the Hospital Milieu

At about the same time that interest in psychotherapy and psychopharmacology of schizophrenia was emerging after World War II, a strong interest in social psychiatry also developed with the main agenda being the mental hospital and the creation of community treatment programs.

Much of this reform centered around countering the adverse effects of the social structure of large mental hospitals upon the clinical course of mental disorders, particularly schizophrenia. A number of significant innovations were introduced, notably open-door policies, restrictions on the use of restraints and seclusion, lessening of the authoritarian social structure, upgrading of status and of training of nurses and other ward personnel, and most notably, the "therapeutic community" concept. Unfortunately for historical analyses, these innovations occurred at about the same time as the introduction of chlorpromazine and reserpine. It is very difficult, in retrospect, to disentangle the relative contributions of these two innovations in the resultant decrease in length of stay of hospitalized schizophrenics and dramatic decrease in the number of patients in mental hospitals. In the United Kingdom, reduction of length of stay and reduction in hospital census had occurred prior to the introduction of the drugs, and social psychiatry advocates offer this as evidence for the power of institutional change. It is likely that the two innovations had an additive effect, and the introduction of the drugs served to accelerate trends already evident before 1950.

A number of attempts have been made to assess the efficacy of milieu therapy alone, without concomitant drug treatment (May & Simpson, 1980a, 1980b). They conclude that active inpatient milieu programs have defined but circumscribed effects, mostly on social adjustment and duration stay.

An interesting controversy around complex drug–milieu interactions occurred during this period. Social psychiatric observers pointed out that the most enthusiastic reports of the efficacy of the new tranquilizers came from public mental hospitals, particularly state, county, and VA hospitals, which were overcrowded, understaffed, and had limited milieu programs. In contrast, better staffed programs, such as those at university hospitals and small institutions, did not report dramatic drug effects. Thus, it was postulated that the degree of success of the new drug therapies was related to the intensity of preexisting treatment programs. A partial attempt to test this hypothesis was reported by Goldberg, Cole, and Klerman (1966). They did find significant differences among institutions participating in a nine-hospital study, such that the drug–placebo differences were less striking in small intensive treatment centers, such as Payne Whitney Clinic at Cornell Medical Center, than at the large public hospitals. However, when adjustment was made for the social background and clinical prognostic characteristics of patients admitted, much of

these milieu differences disappeared, suggesting that the differences in outcome across institutions was contributed to mainly by the better prognosis of patients admitted to smaller institutions than to the milieu influence per se.

A number of controlled studies have documented the value of brief hospitalization using medication (Burhan, 1967; Caton, 1982; Glick, Hargreaves, Raskin, & Kutner, 1975). Whereas prior to 1950, the average length of stay for schizophrenics was over six months, by the 1970s, the length of stay had dropped dramatically to less than two weeks. In controlled studies, there was no advantage to lengths of hospitalization beyond 60 days, compared to shorter duration of hospital stay with more intensive treatment (Caffey, Galbrecht, & Klett, 1971; Herz, Endicott, & Spitzer, 1977). Patients treated with brief periods of hospitalization did not have higher rates of subsequent readmission. Therefore, there does not seem to be an enduring effect of prolonged hospitalization, and the main function of hospitalization seems to be reduction of symptoms, promotion of social adjustment, and transition into aftercare treatment. Brief hospitalization has become part of routine policy, and this clinical practice is reinforced by the fiscal restraints of reimbursement policies.

Still unresolved, however, is the optimal nature of the hospital milieu. The therapeutic community concept developed in the United Kingdom for the treatment of patients with personality disorder, when applied in the United States has been widely advocated for hospitalized acute schizophrenics. These programs emphasize intensive social interaction, verbal expression of feelings and attitudes on the part of the patient, and the blurring of social status boundaries between staff and patients. Recently, these practices have been challenged. Critics suggest that the therapeutic community is a conceptually unsound and clinically ineffective treatment for psychotic schizophrenics. Relying on psychophysiologic studies of arousal level in schizophrenics, they advocate decrease in social interaction, increase in structure, standardization of patient–staff relations, and clear expectation as to role performance and use of medications (Herz et al., 1977; May & Simpson, 1980a; VanPutten, 1973). No controlled studies, however, have been reported to test the differential effects of alternative types of milieu (VanPutten, 1973).

Community Alternatives to Hospital Treatment of Acute Schizophrenics

Because of dissatisfaction with the adverse effects of hospitalization, a number of community alternatives to hospitalization have been proposed. These include day hospital, home treatment with family involvement, and community residences. An impressive body of controlled studies have demonstrated the value of these community treatment alternatives to hospitalization for acutely psychotic individuals.

Day hospitals, first developed in Moscow and modified in London by Bierer (1951), were extended into the United States at the Massachusetts Mental Health Center and at the Yale Psychiatric Institute. A number of controlled studies, notably the study reported by Zwerling and Wilder (1964), demonstrated that approximately 80 percent of acutely ill patients who might otherwise require hospitalization could be treated effectively by a day treatment program. Almost all of these patients were treated with medication.

Another important innovation was the home treatment of schizophrenic states by public health nurses. Pasamanick, Scarpitti, and Dinitz (1967) conducted a well-controlled study in Louisville, Kentucky, that demonstrated the value of home treatment using medication and social psychotherapeutic techniques.

More recently, Mosher has reported on the utility of community residence to promote social rehabilitation of schizophrenics (Mosher & Menn, 1978). Using as a control group patients routinely hospitalized at a nearby county hospital, Mosher claims the superiority of an innovative program based on community residential treatment over standard hospitalization and medication.

Drugs and Psychotherapy for Formerly Hospitalized Patients in Aftercare

There is a small, but growing, sophisticated body of research on the value of drugs and psychotherapy alone, and in combination, in the aftercare of schizophrenics discharged as outpatients. Inpatient findings have been reported by the collaboration among Schooler et al. (1980), Goldberg, Schooler, Hogarty, and Roper (1977) at NIMH, and Hogarty, Schooler, and Ulrich (1979) at Pittsburgh. They have reported research from two sets of studies, one using oral medication, the other emphasizing injectable long-activity medication combined with a ver-

sion of psychotherapy that they call major role training (MRT). The results of this complex study indicate a high efficacy of maintenance drug therapy in reducing the relapse rate, particularly in the first year following discharge. For example, in the placebo-treated group, over 70 percent of the patients experienced relapse and rehospitalization within one year. This rate was considerably reduced by the maintenance treatment with fluphenazine. Relatively little difference has been noted whether the fluphenazine is administered by mouth or by injection. By itself, the social treatment of major role therapy (MRT) was relatively ineffective in influencing the relapse rate. In fact, there is some evidence that for certain patients this had a deleterious effect. However, the combination did offer some added benefits.

Complementing these studies (Goldberg et al., 1977; Hogarty et al., 1979; Schooler et al., 1980) are the important findings from England on expressed emotions (EE). Early studies by Brown, Birley, and Wing (1972) have indicated that families of schizophrenic patients who are high in EE, characterized by critical comments, hostility, censure, and overinvolvement, were associated with higher relapse rate. The adverse impact of the high EE environment could be reduced either through the reduction of the amount of time the patient spent with the family or through the use of medication. The inference was that medication increased the patient's ability to cope with the stressful impact of interfamilial tension. Based upon these findings, a number of family intervention strategies have been developed, most notably by Falloon et al. (1982) in southern California. Four controlled trials report the value of family therapy over individual therapy for newly discharged patients (Goldstein, 1984).

These findings as to the efficacy of family therapy among patients in aftercare have been of sufficient interest for NIMH to design and initiate a multicenter collaborative project on treatment strategies in schizophrenia (Schooler & Keith, unpublished manuscript).

Chronic Hospitalized Patients

There has been a marked decrease in studies on chronically hospitalized schizophrenics in the past decade. In large part, this reflects the impact of the public policy of deinstitutionalization, which has resulted in a dramatic decrease in the resident population in large mental hospitals. In comparison, in 1955, almost 600,000 patients were hospitalized in public mental hospitals, half of whom carried a diagnosis of schizophrenia. By 1980, the number was less than 100,000. The focus of clinical care and public-policy debate has shifted to the needs of patients in the community, particularly the emergence of large numbers of patients who are homeless.

Many of the early studies on drugs and psychotherapy in schizophrenics focused on this population. Almost all of the studies support the value of long-term drug treatment and involve comparative strategies to assess the value of group psychotherapy and social rehabilitative efforts (Schooler, 1978).

A notable exception to this trend are the reports by Paul, Tobias, and Holly (1972). Paul and associates have studied inpatient populations with the hospital diagnosis of schizophrenia and have found many functioning at low social levels. Some of the patients were maintained on medication, whereas others were withdrawn to placebo conditions. Contrary to expectations, there was no difference between the group that was continued on drugs and those transferred to placebo. There were no interactions with social therapy. Schooler interprets the Paul study to support the possibility that withdrawal of drugs from very chronic unresponsive patients will not necessarily lead to an increase in psychopathology. Schooler calls for an attempt to test these hypotheses again. Recent studies of schizophrenia psychopathology have highlighted the value of separating patients with positive versus negative symptoms and correlation of negative symptoms with enlarged brain ventricles on CAT scan and reported unresponsiveness to neuroleptic drugs. Positive symptoms refer to delusions, hallucinations, and overactivity, whereas negative symptoms refer to apathy, withdrawal, absence of affect, and social inactivity. Thus, it is possible that Paul's sample included such patients. However, systematic studies using the positive–negative symptom separation are required to test these hypotheses fully.

Prospects for the Future

Although it is widely accepted that antipsychotic drugs have high degrees of efficacy, particularly in the short term, and over time will prevent relapse, there are a number of troubling aspects of drug treatment of schizophrenia that prompt continued research on combination. A number of investigators have attempted to identify acutely psychotic patients for whom drug treatment is not necessary or even disadvantageous. It is believed that these may be patients responsive to psychotherapy without medication; however, attempts to identify such subgroups have not been successful.

Even with the demonstrated efficacy of medication, particularly the aftercare programs, a substantial percentage of patients still relapse and, over time, a moderate percentage of patients slowly become more chronic and socially disabled. It is hoped that the combination of drugs and various psychosocial interventions such as community residences, day programs, and family involvement will augment the efficacy of treatment programs. The drugs have contributed to patients becoming "better but not well" (Klerman, 1977), and the deinstitutionalization population does exhibit high degrees of social deviance and social dependence. In this context, it is apparent that findings from research studies, particularly about the value of day programs and family programs and the limited value of individual psychotherapy, have not fully diffused into clinical practice. There is a wide gap between current practice and knowledge from research.

The most serious problem, however, has to do with the adverse effects of neuroleptic antipsychotic medication. The most serious effect is the tardive dyskinesia syndrome, which is a result of the cumulative dose and duration of treatment. This serious and at times disabling side effect has prompted various experimental regimens, such as drug holidays, intermittent medication, low-dose strategies, often combined with psychosocial interventions. The hope is that the combination of altering drug dosage and psychosocial interventions will delay or hopefully even prevent the occurrence of tardive dyskinesia as well as promote high levels of social and personal functioning.

AFFECTIVE DISORDERS

The term *affective disorders* refers to a group of clinical conditions that have as their dominant mode of patient presentation disturbances in mood or elation. Sometimes the term *mood disorder* is used for these conditions.

Although affect and mood usually refer to a range of emotions, including anger, guilt and shame, and anxiety, the current convention is to restrict the term *affective disorders* (or *mood disorders*) to disorders in which depression and elation are the major features. Most elations occur as states of hypomania and mania.

The *DSM-III* was the first official diagnostic system to include a separate category of affective disorders. In the past, depressions and manic states were distributed between psychotic and neurotic categories. The decision to group these conditions together in the *DSM-III* is a response to the findings of clinical and epidemiologic research in this area, as well as the evidence for the efficacy of treatments.

Within the affective disorders, it is widely accepted that the major subclassification is between bipolar disorder and depressive disorders. In some terminologies, the depressive disorders are referred to as "unipolar affective disorders" or "nonbipolar affective disorders" in contrast to "bipolar." In this chapter we shall follow the *DSM-III* convention.

Bipolar Affective Disorder

The essential criteria for the diagnosis of bipolar affective disorder is the occurrence of an episode of mania or hypomania during the course of the patient's illness. Almost all patients with mania and hypomania have episodes of depression over the course of their lives.

Treatment of the Acute Manic Episodes

The value of pharmacotherapy for treatment of acute manic espisodes has been well established by numerous controlled trials (Klerman, 1978a). For acute manic episodes, lithium and neuroleptics have demonstrated efficacy. The two neuroleptics best studied are chlorpromazine and haloperidol, although it is likely that all neuroleptics would have similar efficacy.

Psychotherapy alone has seldom been advocated for acute manic episodes. There are descriptions of the psychodynamics, but few psychotherapists advocate the use of psychotherapy alone in the treatment of the acute manic episode. In clinical practice, most patients with acute manic episodes receive drug treatment plus various kinds of psychological management directed at containing the disruptive behavior and laying the groundwork for a treatment alliance for possible psychotherapeutic efforts in the posthospital phase.

Observation about the interpersonal behavior of manic patients, particularly from the work of Janowsky, El-Yousef, and Davis (1974), have contributed to structuring of the milieu considered desirable for the hospital treatment of manic patients. The practical recommendations are that milieu should reduce stimuli, be structured, and set limits, particularly as to the expression of anger and hostility and other aspects of interpersonal behavior. The therapeutic approach, with frequent staff and group meetings and a high level of social participation, is usually considered countertherapeutic for the psychological management of hospitalized acute manic patients.

Treatment of Acute Depressive Episodes with Bipolar Affective Disorder Patients

Although the clinical picture of depression in bipolar patients is similar in most respects to those with nonbipolar depressive disorders, and the treatment program is generally the same, there are some important modifications. The pharmacologic treatment of depressions that occur in the course of bipolar affective illness should not consist of tricyclics alone for prolonged periods of time. For the treatment of depressions that occur in the course of bipolar affective disorder, there is now strong evidence that tricyclics alone often precipitate manic symptoms. Often tricyclics are combined with lithium. Since bipolar illness has a high tendency for recurrence, treatment planning involves long-term management, including psychotherapeutic planning as well as treatment of the acute episode. No systematic studies have been reported.

Long-Term Treatment

For long-term therapy, lithium has been demonstrated as efficacious in preventing recurrences of both the depressive and manic episodes (Davis, 1976; Klerman, 1978b).

Several recent reports (not from controlled clinical trials) have assessed the efforts of combining psychotherapy with lithium treatment for long-term treatment of patients with bipolar affective disorder. Three types of psychotherapeutic treatment have been described: individual psychotherapy based on the psychodynamic model, group therapy, and family and marriage therapy.

As regards individual psychotherapy, a few reports have appeared on the feasibility of conducting psychoanalytically oriented treatment in the presence of lithium (Cooper, 1985; Ostow, 1962). No controlled trials have been reported.

Traditionally, patients with bipolar affective illness have been considered poor candidates for group psychotherapy; however, Shakir, Volkmar, Bacon, and Pfefferbaum (1979) reported a positive experience with a long-term ongoing psychotherapy group composed exclusively of patients with bipolar affective disorders who were receiving maintenance lithium therapy. They found enhanced lithium compliance, although it was difficult to determine whether the relatively high rate of adherence to the drug regimen reflected the effects of group therapy per se or the close supervision received each week. Similar findings from uncontrolled trials have been reported by Powell, Othmer, and Sinkhorn (1977).

Davenport, Ebert, Adland, and Goodwin (1976) reported on the use of couples' therapy groups in conjunction with lithium. Among married bipolar patients on lithium, those in couples' group therapy were reported to have more stable posthospital courses than those given only minimal support beyond medication. Jamison and Goodwin (1983) have described psychotherapeutic techniques for bipolar patients on lithium and their families. Jamison (unpublished) has reported preliminary results of a trial comparing bipolar patients on lithium alone with those receiving family group therapy. Patients receiving group therapy had better compliance, better social adjustment, and less frequent hospitalization.

Depressive Disorders

The diagnostic category of major depression was first delineated in the Feighner criteria (Feighner et al., 1972) and in the Research Diagnostic Criteria (Spitzer, Endicott, & Robins, 1978), and was embodied in the *DSM-III* (APA, 1980). This is a disorder with high prevalence, particularly in outpatient settings, and has been the focus of considerable research on the relationship of drugs and psychotherapy.

Treatment of Acute Depressive Episodes

There is little doubt that the clinical treatment of depressive disorders was revolutionized in the late 1950s by the introduction of the antidepressant

drugs—tricyclics and monoamine oxidase inhibitors (MAOIs). Their effectiveness has been documented in a large number of well-controlled clinical trials (Klein, 1980).

The Royal Australian and New Zealand College of Psychiatrists has applied meta-analysis to the controlled trials of drugs used in depression as part of their Quality Assurance Program. They found psychotherapy effective with neurotic depression and drugs effective for endogenous depression (Andrews et al., 1983).

A number of brief psychotherapies for depression have been developed and evaluated (Rush, 1982). Weissman identified 25 controlled studies in the period of 1974–1984, and over half of these studies involve some study of drug–psychotherapy comparison or combination. Among these therapies, the most widely studied is cognitive behavior therapy developed by Beck et al. (1979). In addition, interpersonal psychotherapy (Klerman et al., 1984) has been developed and evaluated in studies of acute treatment and maintenance treatment. A group of behavioral techniques are widely used, including relaxation techniques, social-skill techniques, and techniques aimed at promoting behavioral mastery (Bellack, Hersen, & Himmelhoch, 1980; Kovacs, 1980; Lewinsohn, Sullivan, & Grosscup, 1982; Rehm & Kornblith, 1979; Thase, 1983). A number of reviews have summarized the efficacy of these treatments for acute depression (Thase, 1983; Weissman, 1984).

Drug–psychotherapy comparison

Data have been reported for comparisons of cognitive behavioral therapy and interpersonal psychotherapy with drugs. The majority of the studies find equivalence or superiority of the psychotherapy compared to antidepressant medication, usually a tricyclic (Bellack, Hersen, & Himmelhoch, 1981; Blackburn, Bishop, Glen, Whalley, & Christie, 1981; McLean & Hakstian, 1979). In the Blackburn study, cognitive therapy was superior to tricyclics among depressed patients in general practice, but not in patients attending psychiatric specialty clinics (Rush, 1982). The data comparing social-skills therapy and drug therapy reports no significant difference (Hersen, 1983). Interpersonal therapy was evaluated in comparison to drugs and also found to be relatively equal in effectiveness (Weissman et al., 1981).

Combination of Drugs and Psychotherapy

The data on the possible additive or synergistic effects of combined drugs and psychotherapy are inconsistent. Interpersonal therapy is reported to be more effective in combination than either drugs or IPT alone for endogenous depression (Klerman et al., 1984b). Blackburn et al. (1981) found that cognitive therapy in combination with tricyclics was superior to either treatment alone, but only among psychiatric outpatients, not among patients attending a general practice. However, this finding was not replicated with social-skills therapy (Bellack et al., 1980).

Possible Interactions with Subtypes of Depression

There is a long-standing controversy as to the desirability and validity of subtypes of depressive disorders. Many diagnostic proposals have been debated, including endogenous versus reactive, psychotic versus neurotic, agitated versus retarded, and so on. In the drug—psychotherapy area, major attention has focused on endogenous subtypes of depression because of the widely held conviction among psychopharmacotherapists that this type of depression responds specifically to tricyclics and ECT. The reports of efficacy of psychotherapy for endogenous patients has challenged conventional wisdom and strongly held theoretical positions. A small number of studies have reported drug—psychotherapy effects on endogenous depression, usually diagnosed by RDC (Spitzer et al., 1978) or by *DSM-III*—Melancholia. Prusoff et al. (1980) reported that endogenous depression responded best to the combination of drugs and psychotherapy and poorly to IPT alone. Patients with situational, also called neurotic or reactive, depressions did equally well with drugs, IPT, or the combination; all active treatments were better than the control. In contrast, Blackburn et al. (1981) did not find a difference in response between endogenous and nonendogenous patients treated with cognitive behavior therapy. Kovacs (1980) did not find a correlation between endogenous depression and poor response to cognitive psychotherapy.

The endogenous—neurotic distinction is still widely used in treatment research, and the Australian Quality Assurance Project endorsed the selective value of psychotherapy, both dynamic psychotherapy and behavioral therapy, for "neurotic" depressions and emphasized the value of drugs and ECT for "endogenous depressions." They endorsed the value of combined treatment.

Specificity and Duration of Effects

The specificity of the psychotherapies has been investigated by studies of content (DeRubeis et al., 1982; Luborksy et al., 1982). Both studies found that independent judges were able to distinguish the forms of psychotherapy being used. Although the treatment procedures can be differentiated, they appear to have a comparable efficacy (DeRubeis et al., 1982; Zeiss, Lewinsohn, & Munoz, 1979). Attempts have been made to study differential outcome with only limited success (Jarvik, Mintz, Steuer, & Gerner, 1982; Zeiss et al., 1979). Kovacs (1983) has attempted to integrate the findings across studies to identify common features of brief psychotherapy for depression that may account for their apparent equivalent efficacy. She identified features such as the clinical diagnosis, time-limited contract, therapeutic activity, and focused nature of the psychotherapy.

Two studies, by Weissman et al. (1981) and by Kovacs et al. (1981), report that acutely depressed patients who had received psychotherapy without drugs were doing better at one-year follow-up.

Many of these issues will hopefully be resolved with the publication of the results from the NIMH Collaborative Study, in which two different psychotherapies, cognitive-behavioral and IPT, are being compared against a tricyclic antidepressant and placebo—psychological management control. Among the important features of this study is the fact that it is being conducted in three clinical sites, which are not the centers where the treatments were initially developed. Thus, it will be possible to disentangle the role of loyalty and commitment to the initiation of the therapy from systematic training in clinical settings. All the therapists selected have experience and training, and their treatment programs are monitored by video- and audiotape. A large-scale prospective study of the interactions between drugs and psychotherapy for recurrent nonbipolar depressions is underway at Western Psychiatric Institute—University of Pittsburgh. Under the leadership of Kupfer and Frank (personal communication, 1984), a large series of patients with recurrent depressions who have been stabilized on medication are then evaluated for medication alone, IPT alone, psychotherapy plus placebo, IPT plus no pill, and combination therapy. This five-cell design is an attempt to respond to some of the issues raised by Hollon concerning the use of placebos and no pills in psychotherapy research. No findings have yet been reported by Frank and Kupfer.

Long-Term Continuation and Maintenance Treatment

While most depressive episodes are self-limited, a substantial percentage of patients experience recurrent or chronic episodes. Both lithium and tricyclic drugs have been demonstrated effective in prevention of relapse (Davis, 1976; Klerman, 1978a). For the long-term treatment of depression, there have been four controlled studies evaluating drugs and psychotherapy.

The maintenance studies were similar in several respects. All employed a factorial design to test psychotherapy in comparison to and in combination with drugs in ambulatory settings. Patients consisted primarily of neurotic depressives, who were followed regularly and received multiple types of outcome assessments of symptoms and social functioning gathered from patient self-reports and clinician evaluations. These studies differed primarily in the type of psychotherapy and length of treatment they offered.

Klerman et al. (1974) examined eight months of maintenance treatment on amitriptyline, placebo, and no-pill, with and without individual interpersonal psychotherapy, in 150 partially recovered depressed women. Covi, Lipman, Derogatis, Smith, and Patterson (1974), in the Baltimore study, compared 16 months of treatment on imipramine, diazepam, and placebo, with or without four months of group therapy, in 149 partially recovered depressed women. Friedman (1975) in the Philadelphia study compared three months of amitriptyline or placebo, with or without marital therapy, in 196 married depressed men and women.

The findings from these three studies were remarkably similar. They indicated that antidepressants, as compared with placebo or psychotherapy, were most efficacious in symptom reduction and in preventing relapse. Although some recovery of social performance occurred as a result of reduction of symptoms, medications themselves had only a limited impact on problems in living. All three studies also showed a positive effect for psychotherapy, as compared with low contact, or to drugs, which was strongest in areas related to problems in living, social functioning, and interpersonal relationships, but less strong for symptoms per se.

These studies allow us to answer, partially, some of the hypotheses about the interactive effects of combined treatments. The Boston–New Haven Study (Klerman et al., 1974), which found a psychotherapeutic effect only in patients who remained symptom free, best supported the hypothesis that drugs have a positive effect on psychotherapy in that the symptom relief, produced more readily by drugs, rendered the patient more accessible to psychotherapy. There was no evidence in any of the studies for a negative interaction between drugs and psychotherapy. Therefore, there was no evidence for the hypothesis that drugs have a negative effect on psychotherapy patients who had experienced early symptom relief. Drugs did not make patients less interested in psychotherapy and did not lead to early termination or poor response to psychotherapy, nor was there any evidence for a negative effect of psychotherapy on drug response. Patients receiving psychotherapy were not symptomatically disrupted.

Other Types of Depression

A number of other depressive types have been identified, most notably dysthymia. The dysthymic criteria in the *DSM-III* identify a group of patients with chronic depressive symptoms, almost always ambulatory, who fluctuate in the levels of distress and in impairment of social functioning. Many of these patients are often diagnosed as having associated personality disorders. Epidemiologic studies indicate that it is a disorder with relatively high prevalence, about 4 percent of the adult population per year. It is likely that many of these patients have been represented in previous studies of outpatient psychotherapy. A number of newly designed studies are underway, but results are not yet available. A large number of patients with depressed mood seek and are treated with either drugs or psychotherapy. The intensity and duration of their treatments may not meet criteria for specific disorders, but controlled studies are not available.

Prospects for the Future

Drug–psychotherapy interactions in the area of affective disorders are among the most intensively investigated. The clinical implications are significant in view of the high prevalence of these disorders. The theoretical implications are also significant in view of similarities among the different psychotherapies, whether interpersonal, cognitive, behavioral, or family–group therapy. It is likely that research now underway will resolve some of the issues, particularly for nonbipolar depressed patients.

ANXIETY STATES, AGORAPHOBIA, AND PANIC DISORDER

Through the 1960s and 1970s, anxiety symptom states were treated predominantly with psychotherapy. The minor tranquilizers, particularly the benzodiazepines, were also extensively prescribed. This use of antianxiety drugs became the subject of social concern and policy debate (Klerman, 1972). When Hollon and Beck (1978) reviewed this area in the previous edition of this *Handbook,* they described a number of studies in which drugs and psychotherapy for anxious patients were evaluated, but few conclusions were possible. Few studies focused on diagnostic subdivisions within the broad category of anxiety states.

In the late 1970s, proposals for subdivisions of anxiety disorders stimulated intense theoretical debate about the psychopathology and diagnosis in anxiety disorders and a growing number of sophisticated research studies. The area of most intense controversy has to do with agoraphobia and panic disorders; however, extensive research is also underway in obsessive-compulsive disorders. These efforts are stimulated in part by the surprising finding that drugs usually regarded as antidepressants, the tricyclics and MAO inhibitors, have demonstrated efficacy in the treatment of agoraphobia through the controversial mechanism of reduction of panic attacks. In parallel with psychopharmacologic investigations and strongly influenced by the efficacy studies with these drugs, there has been a major revision of the nosology and classification of anxiety disorders.

Psychopathologic and Diagnostic Issues—The Proposal to Group Agoraphobia and Panic Together and Separate ·Them from Other Anxiety Disorders
The most far-reaching debates have followed the

proposal to separate panic states and agoraphobia from other anxiety disorders and group them together (Barlow, in press; Klein, 1980b). This proposal, parts of which are embodied in the *Diagnostic and Statistical Manual (DSM-III;* APA, 1980) classification of anxiety disorders, represents a departure from the consensus about anxiety and anxiety disorders that characterized the field since the end of World War I. That consensus viewed anxiety, phobias, and anxiety states on a continuum, with normal anxiety and fear at one end, and anxiety symptoms, anxiety neuroses, and phobic states at the other end. In this model, the clinical states were aligned on the severe end of the continuum and the gradations between them were seen as ones of intensity of distress and degree of social impairment.

In 1960, a number of factors led to questions about the continuity model. (1) The terms used failed to convey precise meaning. David Sheehan has identified 37 different nosologic terms that overlap with anxiety (Sheehan & Sheehan, 1982). (2) Two classes of drugs—the MAO inhibitors and the tricyclics, which by conventional psychopharmacologic logic are called "antidepressants"— were shown to be effective for anxiety disorders. On phenomenologic grounds, these disorders were different from depression. (3) Certain forms of anxiety disorder, particularly agoraphobia, did not respond to neuroleptics or benzodiazepines, the prototypic antianxiety drugs. This was paradoxical. Why should the subjective intensive anxiety states not respond to drugs that were effective against psychiatric forms of anxiety?

In response to these observations, a new diagnostic model emerged in the early 1970s, which proposed a new category, panic disorder, be established and, further, that panic disorder and agoraphobia be grouped together, and that this complex of conditions be separated from the other anxiety states. This model emphasized the discontinuity between panic attacks from other anxiety states.

A central feature of this model holds that the panic attack is a unique psychic experience, not a more intense form of normal fear and generalized anxiety (Barlow, 1984a). Panic attack occurs with the sudden onset of intense fear and anxiety associated with dread and foreboding and fear of being trapped. These cognitive elements were combined with awareness of bodily changes, particularly autonomic arousal manifested by sweating, palpitations, feeling of lightheadedness, and the like.

The initial panic attack and the onset of the episode occur spontaneously without apparent environmental precipitant. The panic attack is regarded as the initiator and reinforcer of the avoidant behavior.

This discontinuity model was partially incorporated in the *DSM-III* classification of anxiety disorders, a decision that has led to considerable controversy within the United States and between American investigators and those in Europe, particularly those who follow the International Classification of Disease (ICD-9; 1980). The validity of separating agoraphobia from other forms of phobia, social phobia and simple phobias, has been widely accepted. The agoraphobic cluster constitutes a separate psychopathological condition. Factor-analytic studies support the grouping together of fears such as fear of public transportation, of driving alone, and so on (Marks, 1985).

Recent clinical (Barlow, 1984a), therapeutic (Klein, 1980), and psychophysiologic studies provide evidence to support the separation of panic attacks from other forms of anxiety (Leckman, Weissman, Merikangas, Pauls, & Prusoff, 1983). Noteworthy in this effort are the recent studies of experimental induction of panic attack via lactate infusion, carbon dioxide inhalation, and yohimbine and other substances (Gorman, 1984). Controversy still continues as to the relationship of panic attacks to agoraphobia. Epidemiologic evidence suggests that in the community, there are a moderate number of patients who have panic attacks without significant phobic avoidance. There also appear to be patients with agoraphobia for whom a history of panic attack is not readily obtainable (Weissman, in press).

Psychological Treatment of Panic and Agoraphobia
Although there are no controlled trials, the consensus among practitioners and researchers is that psychoanalysis and psychoanalytically oriented psychotherapy are of relatively little value for agoraphobia. Weiss (1965) and Weinstock (1959) reported on a mixed group of 46 phobics who completed psychoanalysis and found only 13 percent symptom free. Nemiah (1984) also concluded that psychodynamic psychotherapy, including psychoanalysis, has not

been successful with patients suffering from panic and a variety of phobic disorders.

Freud (1957) initially suggested that to overcome anxiety the patient must expose himself to it. Currently, exposure of patients to the stimuli that induced the anxiety is a standard psychotherapy treatment. Various techniques used include (1) systematic desensitization, (2) flooding in imagination, and (3) exposure in vivo. Studies show that of the three treatments, in vivo exposure treatments have the most immediate effect, but no longer term effect than flooding. Recent research on self-directed exposure shows the effectiveness of exposure instructions. Numerous studies have reported the effectiveness of behavior therapy (Barabasz, 1977; Hand, Lamontagne, & Marks, 1974; Marks, Bird, & Lindley, 1978).

Drug Treatment of Panic and Agoraphobia
Minor tranquilizers, such as diazepam, are generally considered to be ineffective in blocking the acute panic attacks frequently associated with agoraphobia (Hall, Weekes, Harvey, & Andrews, 1982). However, there are very few controlled trials supporting this widely held conclusion (Noyes et al., 1984). One study on chlordiaxepoxide shows it to be incompletely effective in blocking panic attacks. Alprazolam, a triazolobenzodiazepine, has been effective in rapidly blocking panic attacks and reducing the disability, anticipatory anxiety, and phobic avoidance behavior of agoraphobia (Carr & Sheehan, 1984).

Ballenger (1985) has recently reported preliminary results from a large placebo controlled double-blind multicenter trial establishing the efficacy of alprazolam in panic disorder and agoraphobia (see also Klerman, 1985b).

Sheehan, Ballenger, and Jacobsen (1980) compared the efficacy of imipramine, phenelzine, and placebo in a double-blind study in the treatment of endogenous anxiety with phobic symptoms. There was a persistent trend for phenelzine to be superior in efficacy to imipramine; this effect achieved significance on the behavioral outcome measures. Both drug treatments were significantly superior to supportive group psychotherapy and placebo on all outcome measures.

It now appears that there are at least three classes of compounds with demonstrated efficacy for the treatment of panic attack and agoraphobia. These are the tricyclic antidepressants (Liebowitz, 1984), the MAO inhibitors, and the triazolobenzodiazepine alprazolam.

Studies Comparing Drugs and Psychotherapy

A number of studies have attempted to compare drug treatment, usually a tricyclic or an MAO inhibitor, with behavior therapy (Solyom, Solyom, LaPierre, Pecknold, & Morton, 1981; Zitrin, Klein, & Woerner, 1978).

In 1978, Zitrin, Klein, and Woerner reported on a double-blind controlled study of adult phobic patients that compared imipramine with placebo therapy and imaginal desensitization with supportive psychotherapy over a 26-week period. In agoraphobics and mixed phobics, results were significantly better with imipramine than placebo therapy, whereas in simple phobics, there was no difference. There was no significant difference between the results of desensitization and supportive psychotherapy. In 1980, Zitrin, Klein, and Woerner reported data from the same study on the treatment of agoraphobia with combined group exposure in vivo and imipramine or placebo in a randomized double-blind study. Imipramine therapy was significantly superior to placebo therapy. A comparison of these patients with agoraphobia previously treated with imipramine and imaginal desensitization showed superiority of exposure in vivo midway in treatment, but no significant differences between the two groups at the completion of therapy.

Mavissakalian (1984) recently reported on a well-designed study on the comparative aspects of drugs and psychotherapy using imipramine and behavior therapy. He used a constructive design in which patients received self-instruction as the basic treatment. There was a slight advantage to imipramine over therapist-directed exposure therapy. Program practice enhanced the efficacy of imipramine and supported previous findings that imipramine enhanced the effectiveness of program practice. Mavissakalian concludes that there is "mutual potentiation" of the effects of imipramine and exposure.

Combined Treatment

The Zitrin, Klein, and Woerner studies and the recent Mavissakalian study provide partial support for the value of combined treatment. Unresolved is the issue of sequencing. Mavissakalian points out that a substantial proportion of patients will improve by self-instructed exposure.

Issues of Specificity and Duration

Current research focuses on resolving some of the issues on the relative merits of drugs and psychotherapy with respect to specificity and duration.

Behavior and biological therapists differ in the importance they attribute to the panic attack and to avoidant behavior in the pathogenesis of agoraphobia. Biological psychiatrists emphasize the role of the panic attack as the driving force in the phobic avoidance behavior and point to the efficacy of drugs in reducing panic attacks. In contrast, behavior therapists have paid little attention to the panic attack and have focused on assessment of avoidant behavior as an outcome measure. Only recently have systematic techniques become available for the assessment of anxiety disorders (Spitzer & Williams, 1984). Moreover, specific methods for the assessment of panic attacks as distinct from other forms of anxiety have been developed and are now being used in psychophysiologic and therapeutic trials. It now appears that pharmacotherapy will reduce panic attacks. This effect is not mediated through reduction of depression or dysphoria, an issue raised by the fact that MAO inhibitors and tricyclics have predominantly been used for treatment of depression and that a significant percentage of patients with agoraphobia have associated depressive symptoms. However, as Mavissakalian (1984) points out, there are no systematic studies on the effect of drugs on avoidant behavior in the absence of panic attacks.

Conversely, the behavior therapists (Marks, 1985a) have focused their attention on the avoidant behavior. The extent to which behavior therapy techniques will have an effect on panic attacks independent of their established effect on avoidant behavior remains unclear.

Similarly, unresolved controversies attend the issue of duration of effect. Follow-up studies of patients treated with drugs indicate a moderately high relapse rate within one year after discontinuation of drug treatment. In contrast, behavior therapists claim enduring effects of drug therapy (Marks, 1985a). Barlow, O'Brien, and Last (1984) point out that although the majority of patients treated with behavior therapy report sustained benefit, only a very few (5%) report themselves as completely symptom free. Munby and Johnston (1980) report relapse rates of as high as 50 percent in clients treated with behavior therapy. Marks and other behavior therapists have asserted that the benefits of drug therapy are due to state-independent learning and that the disadvantage of drug therapy is the need for continued treatment and the lack of enduring effect. This issue will be resolved in the future with new studies.

Prospects for the Future

Recent efforts have focused on panic and agoraphobia, but there is increasing interest in other forms of anxiety disorders. For obsessive-compulsive disorder, both drugs and psychotherapies have been reported effective, but there are only a small number of comparative studies (Liebowitz, 1984; Marks, 1979, 1981; Marks, Stern, & Mawson, 1980; Solyom & Sookman, 1977).

Interest has also been focused on social phobias. No comparative or combined studies have yet been reported for posttraumatic stress disorder or adjustment disorder with anxious mood.

The recent diagnostic revisions will require reexamination of therapeutic studies on anxiety states prior to 1980. A large number of studies were conducted, particularly with benzodiazepines and other antianxiety drugs, on samples of patients whose diagnostic mix is difficult to determine. Many of these samples probably contain mixtures of obsessive-compulsive and agoraphobic patients, such that conclusions that seemed valid in the 1960s and 1970s are difficult to interpret in the light of current concepts of psychopathology and diagnosis.

OPIATE DEPENDENCE

Of the various groups of patients, opiate-addicted individuals would appear to be the most unlikely candidates for psychotherapy. The literature on the psychopathology, psychodynamics, and personality of these individuals identify them as infantile, dependent, and prone to missing appointments. In view of these prior clinical experiences, recent findings on the value of structured brief psychotherapies are surprising.

Two studies are of particular interest: the studies reported by Rounsaville, Weissman, Crits-Christoph, Wilber, and Kleber (1981), attempting to assess the efficacy of interpersonal psychotherapy (IPT), and the Philadelphia studies reported by Woody and O'Brien (1981) to assess supportive-expressive and cognitive-behavioral treatments. These two studies both used a similar constructive design. All patients were treated with a pharmacologic agent, methadone. All subjects also received the standard counseling given at drug-dependent clinics, namely, peer counseling administered by ex-addicts who come from the same socioeconomic background as the patients. The specific value of the psychotherapeutic techniques are assessed in terms of whether or not the addition of the specific psychotherapy offers anything over and above the standard treatment (i.e., the combination of maintenance treatment with methadone and peer counseling by ex-addicts).

The Yale studies (Rounsaville, Glazer, Williams et al., 1983) had negative outcomes. No additional benefit from interpersonal psychotherapy was found. The authors concluded, however, that the trial of the psychotherapies was not adequate, since they did not have sufficient administrative control over the patient's appointments and other activities, and there was a high degree of noncompliance with the psychotherapy as manifested by missed and lateness for appointments.

The Philadelphia study, however, was conducted in the VA hospital. There was a careful control of attendance, monitoring of urines, and indications of compliance. There were three treatment groups similar to the standard design described earlier in this chapter. The two forms of psychotherapy, cognitive-behavioral therapy and supportive-expressive therapy, were compared to a standard, the standard treatment being methadone treatment plus peer counseling. There was no nontreated control group in the Philadelphia study.

The results indicate the value of the professionally delivered psychotherapy with some slight advantage to supportive-expressive therapy. Contrary to conventional wisdom, professional therapy offers statistically significant improvement over standard treatment (i.e., the combination of methadone plus peer counseling by ex-addicts). Moreover, the indices of improvement were on "hard measures," such as urinary determinations of narcotics, encounters with the law enforcement system, and employment and income.

Another finding from this study is that the degree of efficacy afforded by the professional therapists was greatest in those patients rated independently as having severe degrees of associated psychopathology.

Also of note in this study was the careful attention given to training the therapists in manual-directed therapy and the monitoring of the purity of therapy by independent assessments of the content of tape-recorded therapy sessions. The suggested finding in these studies was that the greatest degree of efficacy was found in those professional psychotherapists who adhered most closely to the manual. As of now, there are no follow-up studies of these data.

CONCLUSIONS

The past decade has seen increased rapprochement between researchers primarily involved in psychopharmacology and psychotherapy. Although significant interprofessional and theoretical tensions exist in clinical practice, researchers have increasingly used comparative and constructive designs to assess the relative value of drugs and psychotherapy. Improved methods of diagnostic assessment, selection of patients, and use of multiple assessment domains for the evaluation of change are now accepted as standard methods. Increasingly sophisticated designs allow direct comparisons and also assess interactions of combined treatment.

Increasing specification of the patient population with associated sample homogeneity is producing progress in selected disorders and increasing consensus in areas of schizophrenia and affective disorders. Controversies continue in the anxiety disorders and in opiate dependence. These conditions do not exhaust the list of clinical states for which research is needed. Hopefully, when the next edition of this *Handbook* is published, it will be possible not only to extend the knowledge in the four conditions described in detail, but to report on progress in other clinical areas such as borderline personality disorders, alcoholism, eating disorders, and chronic pain syndromes, to name a few, where drugs and psychotherapy play important roles in theory and clinical practice.

REFERENCES

Abraham, K. (1927). Notes on the psychoanalytic investigation and treatment of manic-depressive insanity and allied conditions. In *Selected papers on psychoanalysis*. London: Hogarth Press.

Abramson, H.A. (Ed). (1967). *The use of LSD in psychotherapy and alcoholism*. New York: Bobbs-Merrill.

American Psychiatric Association. (1980). *Diagnostic and statistical manual of mental disorders (DSM-III)* (3rd ed.). Washington, DC: American Psychiatric Association.

Andrews, G., Andrews, G., Brodaty, H., Hadzi-Pavlovic, D., Harvey, P.R., Holt, P., Tennant, C., & Vaughan, K. (in press). Treatment outlines for the management of schizophrenia. The Quality Assurance Project. *Australian and New Zealand Journal of Psychiatry*.

Andrews, G., Armstrong, M.S., Brodaty, H., Hadzi-Pavlovic, D., Hall, W., Harvey, P. R., Sansom, D.J., Tennant, C.C., Weeks, P., Grigor, J., Hughson, B.J., Johnson, G., & Kiloh, L.G. (1983). A treatment outline for depressive disorder: The Quality Assurance Project. *Australian and New Zealand Journal of Psychiatry, 17,* 129–146.

Armor, D., & Klerman, G.L. (1968). Psychiatric treatment orientations and professional ideology. *Journal of Health and Social Behavior, 9,* 243–255.

Armstrong, M.S., Brodaty, H., Hall, W., Harvey, P.R., Tennant, C.C., Weeks, P., Cramond, W.A., Barnes, L.H., Macfie, C., & Gormly, J. (1982). A treatment outline for agoraphobia: The Quality Assurance Project. *Australian and New Zealand Journal of Psychiatry, 16,* 25–33.

Aveline, M. (1984). What price psychiatry without psychotherapy? *Lancet,* 856–859.

Ballenger, J.C. (1985, May). *Preliminary findings as to the efficacy of alprazolam and panic disorders.* Presented at NCDEU 25th Anniversary Meeting, Key Biscayne, FL. Unpublished.

Balter, M.B., Levine, J., & Manheimer, D.I. (1974). Cross-national study of the extent of anti-anxiety/sedative drug use. *New England Journal of Medicine, 290,* 769–774.

Barabasz, A.F. (1977). *New technologies in behavior therapy and hypnosis.* South Orange, NJ: Power Publishing.

Barlow, D.H. (in press-a). A psychological model of panic. In B.F. Shaw, F. Cashman, Z.V., Segal, & T.M. Vallis (Eds.), *Anxiety disorder: Theory, diagnosis, and treatment.* New York: Plenum.

Barlow, D.H. (in press-b). The dimensions of anxiety disorders. In A.H. Tuma, & J.D. Maser (Eds.), *Anxiety and the anxiety disorders.* Hillsdale, NJ: Erlbaum.

Barlow, D.H., Cohen, A.S., Waddell, M.T., Vermilyea, B.B., Klosko, J.S., Blanchard, E.B., & DeNardo, P.A. (1984a). Panic and generalized anxiety disorders: Nature and treatment. *Behavior Therapy, 15,* 431–449.

Barlow, D.H., O'Brien, G.T., & Last, C.G. (1984b). Couples treatment of agoraphobia. *Behavior Therapy, 15,* 41–58.

Barlow, D.H., Vermilyea, J., Blanchard, E.B., Vermilyea, B.B., DiNardo, P.A., & Cerny, J.A. (in press). The phenomenon of panic. *Journal of Abnormal Psychology.*

Beck, A.T. (1977). *Cognitive Behaviorial Psychotherapy Manual.* Unpublished.

Beck, A.T., Rush, J., Shaw, B., & Emery, G. (1979). *Cognitive therapy of depression: A treatment manual.* New York: Guilford.

Beitman, B.D., & Klerman, G.L. (Ed). (1984). *Combining pharmacotherapy and psychotherapy in clinical practice.* New York: Spectrum.

Bellack, A.S., Hersen, M., & Himmelhock, J.M. (1980). Social skills training for depression: A treatment manual. *JSAS Cat Select Doc Psychology, 10,* 2156.

Bellack, A.S., Hersen, M., & Himmelhock, J.M. (1981). Social skills training compared with pharmacotherapy in the treatment of unipolar depression. *American Journal of Psychiatry, 138,* 1562–1567.

Bierer, J. (1951). *The day hospital: An experiment in social psychiatry and syntoanalytic psychotherapy.* London: H.K. Lewis.

Blackburn, I.M., Bishop, S., Glen, A.I.M., Whalley, L.J., & Christie, J.E. (1981). The efficacy of cognitive therapy in depression: A treatment trial using cognitive therapy and pharmacotherapy, each alone and in combination. *British Journal of Psychiatry, 139,* 181–189.

Bleuler, E. (1959). *Dementia praecox or the group of schizophrenias, 1911* (trans. J. Zinkin). New York: International Universities Press.

Bowen, J. (1960). A family concept of schizophrenia. In D.D. Jackson (Ed.), *The etiology of schizophrenia.* New York: Basic Books.

Brill, A.A. (1955). *Lectures on psychoanalytic psychiatry.* New York: Vintage.

Brown, G.W., Birley, J.L.T., & Wing, J.K. (1972). Influence of family life on the course of schizophrenic disorders: A replication. *British Journal of Psychiatry, 121,* 241–258.

Burhan, A.S. (1967). Short-term hospital treatment: A study. *Hospital and Community Psychiatry, 20,* 369–370.

Byck, R. (Ed.). (1974). *Cocaine papers by Sigmund Freud.* New York: Stonehill.

Cade, J.F.J. (1949). Lithium salts in the treatment of psychiatric excitement. *Medical Journal of Australia, 36,* 349–357.

Caffey, E.M., Galbrecht, C.R., & Klett, C.J. (1971). Brief hospitalization and aftercare in the treatment of schizophrenia. *Archives of General Psychiatry, 24,* 81–86.

Carr, D.B., & Sheehan, D.V. (1984). Panic anxiety: A new biological model. *Journal of Clinical Psychiatry, 45,* 323–330.

Caton, C.L.M. (1982). Effect of length of inpatient treatment for chronic schizophrenia. *American Journal of Psychiatry, 139,* 856–861.

Chassan, J.B. (1979). *Research design in clinical psychology and psychiatry.* New York: Irvington.

Chevron, E.S., & Rounsaville, B.J. (1983). Evaluating the clinical skill of psychotherapists. *Archives of General Psychiatry, 40,* 1129–1132.

Chevron, E.S., Rounsaville, B.J., Rothblum, E.D., & Weissman, M.M. (1983). Selecting psychotherapists to participate in psychotherapy outcome studies. *Journal of Nervous and Mental Disease, 171,* 348–353.

Cochran, W.G. (1954). Some methods of strengthening the common chi-square tests. *Biometrics, 10,* 417–451.

Cole, J.O., Goldberg, S., & Klerman, G.L. (1964). Phenothiazine treatment in acute schizophrenia. *Archives of General Psychiatry, 10,* 246–261.

Cole, J.O., Klerman, G.L., & Jones, R.T. (1960). Drug therapy. In E.J. Spiegel (Ed.), *Progress in neurology and psychiatry* (Vol. 15, pp. 540–576). New York: Grune & Stratton.

Cooper, A. (1985). Psychiatry update—Combined therapies in psychiatry. Symposium presented at the American College of Psychiatrists, Medical Informa-

tion Systems, Inc., New York.

Covi, L., Lipman, R.S., Derogatis, L.R., Smith, J.E., & Pattison, J.H. (1974). Drugs and group psychotherapy in neurotic depression. *American Journal of Psychiatry, 131,* 191–198.

Davenport, Y.B., Ebert, M.H., Adland, M.L., & Goodwin, F.K. (1976). Couples group therapy as an adjunct to lithium maintenance of the manic patient. *American Journal of Orthopsychiatry, 47,* 496–502.

Davis, J.J. (1965). Efficacy of tranquilizing and antidepressant drugs. *Archives of General Psychiatry, 13,* 552–572.

Davis, J.M. (1976). Overview: Maintenance therapy in psychiatry: II. Affective disorders. *American Journal of Psychiatry, 133,* 1–13.

Derogatis, L.R. Lipman, R.S., & Rickels, K. (1976). The Hopkins Symptom Checklist (HSCL): A self-report symptom inventory. *Behavioral Sciences, 19,* 1–15.
——— (1978). Unpublished instrument. *Hopkins Psychiatric Rating Scale* (HPRS).

DeRubeis, R.J., Hollon, S.D., Evans, M.D., & Bemis, K.M. (1982). Can psychotherapies for depression be discriminated? A systematic investigation of cognitive therapy and interpersonal therapy. *Journal of Consulting and Clinical Psychology, 5,* 744–756.

Editorial. (1984). Psychotherapy: Effective treatment or expensive placebo? *Lancet,* 83–84.

Efron, D.H., Cole, J.O., Levine, J., & Wittenborn, J.R. (1968). *Psychopharmacology: A review of progress, 1957–1967.* Washington, DC: NIMH, Public Health Service.

Elkin, I., Parloff, M.B., Hadley, S.W., & Autry, J.H. (1985). NIMH Treatment of Depression Collaborative Research Program. *Archives of General Psychiatry, 42,* 305–316.

Eysenck, H.J. (1952). The effects of psychotherapy. *Journal of Consulting Psychology, 16,* 319–324.

Eysenck, H.J. (1965). The effects of psychotherapy. *International Journal of Psychiatry 1,* 99–178.

Falloon, I.R.H., Boyd, J.L., McGill, C.W., Razani, J., Moss, H.B., & Gilderman, A.M. (1982). Family management in the prevention of exacerbations of schizophrenia. *New England Journal of Medicine, 306,* 1437–1440.

Fawcett, J., & Epstein, P. (1980). *Clinical management—imipramine–placebo administration manual.* Pharmacotherapy Training Center, Department of Psychiatry, Rush-Presbyterian-St. Luke's Medical Center, Chicago.

Federn, P (1952). *Ego psychology and the psychoses.* New York: Basic Books.

Feighner, J.P., Robins, E., Guze, S.B., Woodruff, R.A., Winokur, G., & Munoz, R. (1972). Diagnostic criteria for use in psychiatric research. *Archives of General Psychiatry, 26,* 57.

Fein, L. (1980). *The efficacy and cost-effectiveness of psychotherapy. Background paper No. 3: The implications of cost-effectiveness analysis of medical technology.* Office of Technology Assessment. Washington, DC: U.S. Government Printing Office.

Feinsilver, D.B., & Yates, B.T. (1984). Combined use of psychotherapy and drugs in chronic, treatment-resistant schizophrenic patients: A retrospective study. *Journal of Nervous and Mental Disease, 172,* 133–139.

Fiske, D.W., Hunt, H.F., Luborsky, L., Orne, M.T.,

Parloff, M.B., Reiser, M.F., & Tuma, A.H. (1970). Planning of research on effectiveness of psychotherapy. *Archives of General Psychiatry, 22,* 22–32.

Fleiss, J.L. (1973). *Statistical methods for rates and proportions.* New York: Wiley.

Freud, S. (1957). On the grounds for detaching a particular syndrome from neurasthenia under the description "anxiety neurosis" (1894). In *The complete psychological works of Sigmund Freud* (standard ed., Vol. II, pp. 26–39), London: Hogarth.

Friedman, A.S. (1975). Interaction of drug therapy with marital therapy in depressed patients. *Archives of General Psychiatry, 32,* 619–637.

Fromm-Reichmann, F. (1960). *Principles of intensive psychotherapy.* Chicago: Phoenix Books.

Garfield, S.L., & Bergin, A.E. (Eds.). (1978). *Handbook of psychotherapy and behavior change* (2nd ed.). New York: Wiley.

Gilligan, J. (1965). Review of literature. In M. Greenblatt, M.H. Solomon, A.S. Evans, & G.W. Brooks (Eds.), *Drug and social therapy in chronic schizophrenia* (pp. 24–76). Springfield, IL: Charles C. Thomas.

Glass, G.V., Smith, M.L., & Miller, T.I. (1980). *The benefits of psychotherapy.* Baltimore: Johns Hopkins Press.

Glick, I.D., Hargreaves, W.A., Raskin, M., & Kutner, J. (1975). Short versus long hospitalization: A prospective controlled study, II: Results for schizophrenic inpatients. *American Journal of Psychiatry, 132,* 385–390.

Goldberg, S.C., Cole, J.O., & Klerman, G.L. (1966). Differential prediction of improvement under three phenothiazines. In J.R. Wittenborn (Ed.), *Prediction of response to pharmacotherapy* (pp. 69–84). Springfield, IL: Charles C. Thomas.

Goldberg, S., Schooler, N.R., Hogarty, G.E., & Roper, M. (1977). Prediction of relapse in schizophrenic outpatients treated by drug and sociotherapy. *Archives of General Psychiatry, 34,* 171–184.

Goldstein, M.J. (1984). Schizophrenia: the interaction of family and neuroleptic therapy. In B.D. Beitman & G.L. Klerman (Eds.), *Combining pharmacotherapy and psychotherapy in clinical practice* (pp. 167–186). New York: Spectrum.

Gorman, J.M. (1984). The biology of anxiety. In L. Grinspoon (Ed.), *Psychiatry update* (Vol. 3, pp. 467–481). Washington, DC: American Psychiatric Press.

Greenhill, M.H., & Gralnich, A. (Eds.). (1983). *Psychopharmacology and psychotherapy.* New York: Free Press.

Grinker, R., & Spiegel, J.B. (1945). *War neurosis.* Philadelphia: Blakiston.

Grinspoon, L., Ewalt, J.R., & Shader, R.I. (1972). *Schizophrenia: Pharmacotherapy and psychotherapy.* Baltimore: Williams & Wilkins.

Group for the Advancement of Psychiatry. (1975). *Pharmacotherapy and psychotherapy: Paradoxes and progress* (Vol. 9), Report #93. New York: Mental Health Materials Center.

Hale, N. (1971). *Freud and the Americans.* New York: Oxford University Press.

Hall, W., Weekes, P., Harvey, R., & Andrews, G. (1982). a survey of practising psychiatrists' views on the treatment of agoraphobia. *Australian and New Zealand Journal of Psychiatry, 16,* 225–233.

Hamilton, M. (1967). *The Hamilton Rating Scale for Depression.* Unpublished manuscript.

Hand, I., Lamontagne, Y., Marks, I.M. (1974). Group exposure (flooding) *in vivo* for agoraphobics. *British Journal of Psychiatry, 134,* 502–507.

Hersen, M. (1983, March 1). Personal communication.

Herz, M.I., Endicott, J., & Spitzer, R.L. (1977). Brief hospitalization: A two-year follow-up. *American Journal of Psychiatry, 134,* 502–507.

Hogarty, G.E., Schooler, N.R., & Ulrich, R. (1979). Fluphenazine and social therapy in the aftercare of schizophrenic patients. *Archives of General Psychiatry, 36,* 1283–1294.

Hollingshead, A., & Redlich, F. (1958). *Social class and mental illness.* New York: Wiley.

Hollon, S.D., & Beck, A.T. (1978). Psychotherapy and drug therapy: Comparison and combinations. In S.L. Garfield & A.E. Bergin (Eds.), *Handbook of psychotherapy and behavior change: An empirical analysis* (pp. 437–485). New York: Wiley.

Hollon, S.D., & DeRubeis, R.J. (1981). Placebo-psychotherapy combinations: Inappropriate representations of psychotherapy in drug–psychotherapy comparative trials. *Psychological Bulletin, 90,* 467–477.

Hollon, S.D., Evans, M., Elkin, I., & Lowery, H.A. (1984, May 9). *System for rating therapies for depression.* Presented at the Annual Meeting of the American Psychiatric Association. Los Angeles, CA. Unpublished.

Huxley, A. (1954). *The doors of perception.* New York: Harper & Row.

Jamison, K. (1984, May). Presented at National Institute of Health Consensus Conference on Maintenance Long-term Treatment of Affective Disorder.

Jamison, K.R., & Goodwin, F.K. (1983). Psychotherapeutic treatment of manic-depressive patients on lithium. In M.H. Greenhil & A. Gralnick (Eds.), *Psychopharmacology and psychotherapy.* New York: Free Press.

Janowsky, D.S., El-Yousef, M.K., & Davis, J.M. (1974). Interpersonal maneuvers of manic patients. *American Journal of Psychiatry, 131*(3), 250–255.

Jarvik, L.F., Mintz, J., Steuer, J., & Gerner, R. (1982). Treating geriatric depression: A 26-week interim analysis. *Journal of the American Geriatrics Society, 30,* 713–717.

Jung, C.G. (1956). *Collected works.* New York: Pantheon Books.

Karon, B.P., & VandenBos, G.R. (1981). *Psychotherapy of schizophrenia: The treatment of choice.* New York: Jason Aronson.

Kazdin, A.E. (1986). Research design and methodology. In S.L. Garfield & A.E. Bergin (Eds.), *Handbook of psychotherapy and behavior change.* New York: Wiley.

Klein, D.F. (1980). Anxiety reconceptualized. *Comprehensive Psychiatry, 21,* 411–427.

Klein, D.F. (1976). Psychosocial treatment of schizophrenia, or psychosocial help for people with schizophrenia. *Schizophrenia Bulletin, 6,* 122–130.

Klein, D.F., Gittleman, R., Quitkin, F., & Rifkin, A. (1980). *A diagnosis on drug treatment of psychiatric disorders.* Baltimore: Williams & Wilkins.

Klerman, G.L. (1972). Psychotropic hedonism vs. pharmacological calvinism. *Hastings Center Report, 2,* 1–3.

Klerman, G.L. (1977). Better but not well: Social and

ethical issues in the deinstitutionalization of the mentally ill. *Schizophrenia Bulletin, 3,* 617–631.

Klerman, G.L. (1978a). Combining drugs and psychotherapy in the treatment of depression. In J.O. Cole, A.F. Schatzberg, & S.H. Frazier (Eds.), *Depression: Biology, psychodynamics, and treatment* (pp. 213–227). New York: Plenum.

Klerman, G.L. (1978b). Long-term treatment of affective disorders. In M.A. Lipton, A. DiMascio, & K.F. Killam (Eds.), *Psychopharmacology: A generation of progress* (pp. 1303–1311). New York: Raven.

Klerman, G.L. (1980). Long-term outcomes of neurotic depressions. In S.B. Sells, R. Crandall, M. Roff, J. Strauss, & W. Pollin (Eds.), *Human functioning in longitudinal perspective: Studies of normal and psychopathic populations* (pp. 58–73). Baltimore: Williams & Wilkins.

Klerman, G.L. (1981). Biological psychiatry research: A paradigm for the relationship between basic investigations and clinical applications. In S. Matthysse (Ed.), *Psychiatry and the biology of the human brain: A symposium dedicated to Seymour S. Kety* (pp. 287–296). North Holland: Elsevier.

Klerman, G.L. (1983a). The efficacy of psychotherapy as the basis for public policy. *American Psychologist, 38,* 929–934.

Klerman, G.L. (1983b). The significance of DSM-III in American psychiatry. In R.L. Spitzer, J.B.W. Williams, & A.E. Skodal (Eds.), *In International perspectives on DSM-III* (pp. 3–25). Washington, DC: American Psychiatric Press.

Klerman, G.L. (1984a). Ideologic conflicts in combined treatments. In B. Beitman & G.L. Klerman (Eds.), *Combining pharmacotherapy and psychotherapy in clinical practice* (pp. 17–34). New York: Guilford.

Klerman, G.L. (1985a, June). *The use of somatic treatments for psychiatric illnesses.* Presented at NIH Consensus Development Conference on ECT. Bethesda, MD.

Klerman, G.L. (1985b, May). *Efficacy of alprazolam in panic disorders: Evidence from the Upjohn multinational trial.* Presented at NCDEU 25th Anniversary Meeting, Key Biscayne, FL. Unpublished.

Klerman, G.L. (1985c). Trends in utilization of mental health services: Perspectives for health services research. *Medical Care. 23,* 584–597.

Klerman, G.L., DiMascio, A., Weissman, M.M., Prusoff, B., & Paykel, E. (1974). Treatment of depression by drugs and psychotherapy. *American Journal of Psychiatry, 131,* 186–191.

Klerman, G.L., Vaillant, G., Spitzer, R.L., & Michels, R. (1984a). The advantages of DSM-III. *American Journal of Psychiatry, 141,* 539–553.

Klerman, G.L., Weissman, M.M., Rounsaville, B., & Chevron, E. (1984b). *Interpersonal Psychotherapy of Depression (IPT).* New York: Basic Books.

Kovacs, M. (1980). The efficacy of cognitive and behavior therapies for depression. *American Journal of Psychiatry, 137,* 1495–1501.

Kovacs, M. (1983). Psychotherapies for depression. In L. Grinspoon (Ed.), *Psychiatry update* (Vol. 2, pp. 511–528). Washington, DC: American Psychiatric Press.

Kovacs, M., Rush, J., Beck, A.T., & Hollon, S.D. (1981). Depressed outpatients treated with cognitive therapy or pharmacotherapy. *Archives of General Psychiatry, 38,* 33–39.

Kupfer, D., & Frank, J. (1984). Personal communication.

Kwentus, J.A. (1984). The drug-assisted interview. In F.G. Guggenheim & M.F. Weiner (Eds.), *The manual of psychiatric consultation and emergency care* (pp. 329–338). New York: Jason Aronson.

Lambert, M.J. (1983). Introduction to assessment of psychotherapy outcome: Historical perspective and current issues. In M.J. Lambert, E.R. Christensen, & S. S. DeJulio (Eds.) *The assessment of psychotherapy outcome* (pp. 3–22). New York: Wiley.

Leckman, J.F., Weissman, M.M., Merikangas, K.R., Pauls, D., & Prusoff, B.A. (1983). Panic disorder and major depression: Increased risk of depression, alcoholism, panic, and phobic disorders in families of depressed probands with panic disorder. *Archives of General Psychiatry, 40,* 1055–1060.

Levine, J. (Ed.). (1978). *Contemporary standards for the pharmacotherapy of mental disease.* New York: Futura Publishing.

Levine, J. (1979). *Coordinating clinical trials in psychopharmacology: Planning, documentation, and analysis.* Washington, DC: U.S. Government Printing Office.

Levine, J., Schiele, B.C., & Bouthilet, L. (Eds.). (1971). *Principles and problems in establishing the efficacy of psychotropic agents.* Washington, DC: U.S. Government Printing Office.

Lewinsohn, P.M., Sullivan, J.M., & Grosscup, S.J. (1982). Behavioral therapy: Clinical applications. In A.J. Rush (Ed.), *Short-term psychotherapies for depression.* New York: Guilford.

Lidz, T., Fleck, S., & Cornelison, A. (1965). *Schizophrenia and the family.* New York: International Universities Press.

Liebowitz, M.R. (1984). The efficacy of antidepressants in anxiety disorders. In L. Grinspoon (Ed.), *Psychiatry update,* (Vol. 3, pp. 503–519). Washington, DC: American Psychiatric Press.

Lipton, M.A., DiMascio, A., & Killam, K.F. (Eds.). (1978). *Psychopharmacology: A generation of progress.* New York: Raven.

London, P., & Klerman, G.L. (1982). Evaluating psychotherapy. *American Journal of Psychiatry, 139,* 709–717.

Lorr, H., & Klett, C.J. (1966). *Inpatient Multidimensional Psychiatric Scale (IMPS).* Palo Alto, CA: Consulting Psychologists Press.

Luborsky, L. (1984). *Principles of psychoanalytic psychotherapy: A manual for Supportive-Expressive Treatment.* New York: Basic Books.

Luborsky, L., Singer, B., and Luborsky, L. (1975). Comparative studies of psychotherapies. Is it true that "everyone has won and all must have prizes"? *Archives of General Psychiatry, 32,* 995–1008.

Luborsky, L., Woody, G., McLellan, A.T., & O'Brien, C.P. (1982). Can independent judges recognize different psychotherapies? An experience with manual-guided therapies. *Journal of Consulting and Clinical Psychology, 50,* 49–62.

Marks, I. (1976). The current status of behavioral psychotherapy: Theory and practice. *American Journal of Psychiatry, 133,* 253–261.

Marks, I. (1979). Cure and care of neurosis, I: Cure. *Psychological Medicine, 9,* 629–660.

Marks, I. (1981). Review of behavioral psychotherapy, I: Obsessive-compulsive disorders. *American Journal of Psychiatry, 138,* 584–592.

Marks, I. (1985a). *Fears, phobias, rituals.* New York: Oxford University Press.

Marks, I. (1985b, Apr. 24–26). *The agoraphobic syndrome.* Presented at International Symposium at the Academy of Medicine, Paris. Unpublished.

Marks, I., Bird, J., & Lindley, P. (1978). Psychiatric behavior therapy—developments and implications. *Behavior Psychotherapy, 6,* 25–36.

Marks, I., Stern, R.S., & Mawson, D. (1980). Clomipramine and exposure for OC rituals: I & II. *British Journal of Psychiatry, 136,* 1–25, 161–166.

Mavissakalian, M.R. (1984). Agoraphobia: Behavioral therapy and pharmacotherapy. In B.D. Beitman & G.L. Klerman (Eds.), *Combining pharmacotherapy and psychotherapy in clinical practice* (pp. 187–212). New York: Spectrum.

May, P.R.A. (1968a). *Treatment of schizophrenia: A comparative study of five treatments.* New York: Science House.

May, P.R.A. (1968b). Anti-psychotic drugs and other forms of therapy. In D.H. Efron, J.O. Cole, J. Levine, & J.R. Wittenborn (Eds.), *Psychopharmacology: A review of progress, 1957–1967* (pp. 1155–1176). Washington, DC: NIMH, Public Health Service.

May, P.R.A. (1974). Treatment of schizophrenia: A critique of reviews of the literature. *Comprehensive Psychiatry, 15,* 179–185.

May, P.R.A. (1975). Schizophrenia: Overview of treatment methods. In A.M. Friedman, H.I. Kaplan, & B.J. Sadock (Eds.), *Comprehensive textbook of psychiatry* (Vol. 2, pp. 1192–1217). Baltimore: Williams & Wilkins.

May, P.R.A., & Simpson, G.M. (1980a). Schizophrenia: Overview of treatment methods. In H.I. Kaplan, A.M. Freedman, & B.J. Sadock (Eds.), *Comprehensive textbook of psychiatry* (Vol. 3, pp. 1192–1240). Baltimore: Williams & Wilkins.

May, P.R.A., & Simpson, G.M. (1980b). Schizophrenia: Evaluation of treatment methods. In H.I. Kaplan, A.M. Freedman, & B.J. Sadock (Eds.), *Comprehensive textbook of psychiatry* (Vol. 3, pp. 1240–1275). Baltimore: Williams & Wilkins.

McLean, P.D., & Hakstian, A.R. (1979). Clinical depression: Comparative efficacy of outpatient treatments. *Journal of Consulting and Clinical Psychology, 47,* 818–836.

Mosher, L.R., & Keith, S.J. (1980). Psychosocial treatment: Individual, group, family, and community support approaches. *Schizophrenia Bulletin, 6,* 10–41.

Mosher, L.R., & Menn, A.Z. (1978). Community residential treatment for schizophrenia: Two-year follow-up. *Hospital and Community Psychiatry, 29,* 715–723.

Munby, J., & Johnston, D.W. (1980). Agoraphobia: The long term follow-up of behavioral treatment. *British Journal of Psychiatry, 137,* 418–427.

Nemiah, J. (1984). Anxiety and psychodynamic theory. In L. Grinspoon (Ed.), *Psychiatry update* (Vol. 3, pp. 426–440). Washington, DC: American Psychiatric Press.

NIH Consensus Development Panel. (1985). Mood disorders: Pharmacologic prevention of recurrences. *American Journal of Psychiatry, 142,* 469–476.

Noyes, R., Jr., Anderson, D.J., Clancy, J., Crowe, R., Slymen, D.J., Ghoneim, M.M., & Hinrichs, J. (1984). Diazepam and propranolol in panic disorder and agoraphobia. *Archives of General Psychiatry, 41,* 287–292.

Nunberg, H. (1955). *Principles of psychoanalysis: Their application to the neuroses.* New York: International Universities Press.

Ostow, M. (1962). *Drugs in psychoanalysis and psychotherapy.* New York: Basic Books.

Overall, J., & Gorham, D. (1962). Brief psychiatric rating scale. *Psychological Reports, 10,* 799–804.

Pasamanick, B., Scarpitti, F.R., & Dinitz, S.L. (1967). *Schizophrenia in the community: An experimental study in the prevention of hospitalization.* New York: Appleton-Century-Crofts.

Paul, G.L., Tobias, L.L., & Holly, B.L. (1972). Maintenance psychotropic drugs in the presence of active treatment programs. *Archives of General Psychiatry, 27,* 106–115.

Powell, B.J., Othmer, E., & Sinkhorn, C. (1977). Pharmacological aftercare for homogeneous groups of patients. *Hospital and Community Psychiatry, 28,* 125–127.

Prusoff, B.A., Weissman, M.M., Klerman, G.L., & Rounsaville, B.J. (1980). Research diagnostic criteria subtypes of depression: Their role as predictors of differential response to psychotherapy and drug treatment. *Archives of General Psychiatry, 37,* 796–801.

Prusoff, B.A., Williams, D.H., Weissman, M.M., & Astrachan, B.M. (1979). Treatment of secondary depression in schizophrenia: A double-blind, placebo, placebo-controlled trial of amitriptyline added to perphenazine. *Archives of General Psychiatry, 36,* 569–575.

Rehm, L.P., & Kornblith, S.J. (1979). Behavior therapy for depression: A review of recent developments. *Progressive Behavior Modification, 7,* 277–318.

Rounsaville, B.J., Glazer, W., Wilber, C.H., Weissman, M.M., & Kleber, D. (1983). Short-term interpersonal psychotherapy in methadone-maintained opiate addicts. *Archives of General Psychiatry, 40,* 629–636.

Rounsaville, B.J., Klerman, G.L., & Weissman, M.M. (1981). Do psychotherapy and pharmacotherapy for depression conflict? Empirical evidence from a clinical trial. *Archives of General Psychiatry, 38,* 24–29.

Rounsaville, B.J., Weissman, M.M., Crits-Christoph, K., Wilber, C., & Kleber, H. (1982). Diagnosis and symptoms of depression in opiate addicts. *Archives of General Psychiatry, 39,* 151–156.

Rush, A.J. (1982). Cognitive therapy of depression. In H. Akiskal (Ed.), *Psychiatric clinics of North America* (pp. 105–128). Philadelphia: Saunders.

Rush, A.J. (1984). Cognitive therapy in combination with antidepressant medication. In B.D. Beitman & G.L. Klerman (Eds.), *Combining psychotherapy and drug therapy in clinical practice* (pp. 121–147). New York: Spectrum.

Rush, A.J., & Beck, A.T. (1980). Behavior therapy in adults with affective disorders. In M. Hersen & A.S. Bellack (Eds.), *Behavior therapy in the psychiatric setting* (pp. 69–93). Baltimore: Williams & Wilkins.

Rush, A.J., Beck, A.T., Kovacs, M., & Hollon, S. (1977). Comparative efficacy of cognitive therapy and pharmacotherapy in the treatment of depressed outpatients. *Cognitive Therapy and Research, 1,* 17–37.

Rush, A.J., & Watkins, J.T. (1981). Group versus individual cognitive therapy: A pilot study. *Cognitive Therapy and Research, 5,* 95–103.

Schooler, N.R. (1978). Antipsychotic drugs and psychological treatment in schizophrenia. In M.A. Lipton, A. DiMascio, & K.F. Killam (Eds.), *Psychopharmacology: A generation of progress* (pp. 1155–1168). New York: Raven.

Schooler, N.R., & Keith, S.J. (unpublished manuscript, 1984). NIMH Protocol for Treatment Strategies in Schizophrenia Study.

Schooler, N.R., Levine, J., Severe, J.B., Brauzer, B., DiMascio, A., Klerman, G.L., & Tuason, V.B. (1980). Prevention of relapse in schizophrenia: An evaluation of fluphenazine decanoate. *Archives of General Psychiatry, 37,* 16–24.

Seitz, P.F. (1953). Experiments in the substitution of symptoms by hypnosis. *Psychosomatics Medicine, 15,* 405–411.

Shakir, S.A., Volkmar, F.R., Bacon, S., & Pfefferbaum, H. (1979). Group psychotherapy as an adjunct to lithium maintenance. *American Journal of Psychiatry, 136,* 455–456.

Shaw, B. (1977). A comparison of cognitive therapy and behavior therapy in the treatment of depression. *Journal of Consultation and Clinics of Psychology, 45,* 543–551.

Sheehan, D.V., & Sheehan, K.H. (1982). The classification of anxiety and hysterical states. Part I. Historical review and empirical delineation. *Journal of Clinical Psychopharmacology, 2,* 235–243.

Sheehan, D.V., Ballenger, J., & Jacobsen, G. (1980). Treatment of endogenous anxiety with phobic, hysterical and hypochondriacal symptoms. *Archives of General Psychiatry, 37,* 51–59.

Shepherd, M. (1984). What price psychotherapy? *British Medical Journal, 288,* 809–810.

Simmel, E. (1929). Psychoanalytic treatment in a sanitorium. *International Journal of Psychoanalysis, 10,* 70–85.

Smith, M.L., Glass, G.V., & Miller, T.I. (1980). *The benefits of psychotherapy.* Baltimore: The Johns Hopkins University Press.

Solyom, C., Solyom, L., LaPierre, Y., Pecknold, J., & Morton, L. (1981). Phenelzine and exposure in the treatment of phobias. *Biological Psychiatry, 16,* 239–247.

Solyom, L., & Sookman, D. (1977). A comparison of clomipramine hydrochloride (Anafranil) and behavior therapy in the treatment of obsessive neurosis. *Journal of International Medical Research, 5,* 49–61.

Spitzer, R.L., Endicott, J., & Robins, E. (1978). Research diagnostic criteria: Rationale and reliability. *Archives of General Psychiatry, 35,* 773–782.

Spitzer, R.L., & Williams, J.B. (1984). Structured Clinical Interview for DSM-III (SCID-10/1/84). Unpublished.

Stanton, A.H., Gunderson, J.G., Knapp, P.H., Frank, A.F., Vannicelli, M.L., Schnitzer, R., & Rosenthal, R. (1984). Effects of psychotherapy in schizophrenia: I. Design and implementation of a controlled study. *Schizophrenia Bulletin, 10,* 520–551.

Strauss, A., Schatzman, L., Bucher, R., Ehrlich, D., & Sabshin, M. (Eds.). (1964). *Psychiatric ideologies and institutions.* New York: Free Press.

Sullivan, H.S. (1953). *The interpersonal theory of psychiatry.* New York: W.W. Norton.

Strupp, H., & Binder, J.L. (1984). *Psychotherapy in a new key.* New York: Basic Books.

Tanna, V.T., Penningroth, P.R., & Wollson, R.F. (1977). Propranolol in the treatment of anxiety neurosis.

Comprehensive Psychiatry, 18, 319–327.

Thase, M.E. (1983). Cognitive and behavioral treatments for depression: A review of recent developments. In F.J. Ayd, I.J. Taylor, & B.T. Taylor (Eds.), *Affective disorders reassessed: 1983* (pp. 234–243). Baltimore: Ayd Medical Communications.

Uhlenhuth, E.H., Balter, M.B., Mellinger, G.D., Cisin, I.H., & Clinthorne, J. (1983). Symptom checklist syndromes in the general population. *Archives of General Psychiatry, 40,* 1167–1173.

Uhlenhuth, E.H., Turner, D.A., Purchatzke, G., Gift, T., & Chassan, J.B. (1977). Intensive design in evaluating anxiolytic agents. *Psychopharmacology, 52,* 79–85.

VanPutten, T. (1973). Milieu therapy: Contraindications? *Archives of General Psychiatry, 29,* 640–651.

Weinstock, H. (1959). Phobias and their vicissitudes. *Journal of American Psychoanalytic Association, 7,* 187–188.

Weiss, E. (1965). *Agoraphobia in the light of ego psychology.* New York: Grune & Stratton.

Weissman, M.M. (1984). The psychological treatment of depression: An update of clinical trials. In R.L. Spitzer & J. Williams (Eds.), *Psychotherapy research: Where are we and where should we go?* (pp. 89–105). New York: Guilford.

Weissman, M.M., Klerman, G.L., Prusoff, B.A., Sholomskas, D., & Padian, N. (1981). Depressed outpatients one year after treatment with drugs and/or interpersonal psychotherapy (IPT). *Archives of General Psychiatry, 38,* 51–55.

Weissman, M.M., Leaf, P.J., Holzer, C.D., & Merikangas, K.R. (in press). The epidemiology of anxiety disorders: A highlight of recent evidence. *Psychopharmacology Bulletin.*

Weissman, M.M., Rounsaville, B.J., & Chevron, E. (1982). Training psychotherapists to participate in psychotherapy outcome studies: Identifying and dealing with the research requirements. *American Journal of Psychiatry, 139,* 1442–1446.

Wikler, A. (1957). *The relation of psychiatry to pharmacology.* Baltimore: Williams and Wilkins.

Wilkins, W. (1984). Psychotherapy: The powerful placebo. *Journal of Consulting and Clinical Psychology, 52,* 570–573.

Wilkinson, G. (1984). Psychotherapy in the market-place. *Psychological Medicine, 14,* 23–26.

Wittenborn, J.R., Klerman, G.L., Uhlenhuth, E.H., Scoville, B., Gardner, E.A., & Graft, S.C. (1977). Testing drugs in anxiety and depression. ACNP-FDA guideline material for the clinical investigation of anxiolytic and antidepressant substances. (FDA/BD-77-167). Washington, DC: Food and Drug Administration, Bureau of Drugs.

Woody, G.E., Luborsky, L., McLellan, T., O'Brien, C.P., Beck, A.T., Blaine, J., Herman, I., & Hole, A. (1983). Psychotherapy for opiate addicts: Does it help? *Archives of General Psychiatry, 40,* 639–645.

Woody, G.E., & O'Brien, C.P. (1981). Psychotherapy for opiate addiction: Some preliminary results. *Annals of the New York Academy of Sciences, 362,* 91–100.

World Health Organization. (1980). *International classification of diseases* (9th ed.). Washington, DC: World Health Organization.

Wynne, L., & Singer, H. (1963). Thought disorder and family relations of schizophrenics. *Archives of General Psychiatry, 9,* 191–197.

Zeiss, A.M., Lewinsohn, P.M., & Munoz, R.F. (1979).

Nonspecific improvement effects in depression using interpersonal skills training, pleasant activity schedules, or cognitive training. *Journal of Consulting and Clinical Psychology, 47,* 427–439.

Zitrin, C.M., Klein, D.F., & Woerner, M.G. (1978). Behavior therapy, supportive psychotherapy, imipramine, and phobias. *Archives of General Psychiatry, 35,* 307–316.

Zitrin, C.M., Klein, D.F., & Woerner, M.G. (1980). Treatment of agoraphobia with group exposure in vivo and imipramine. *Archives of General Psychiatry, 37,* 63–72.

Zwerling, I., & Wilder, J.F. (1964). An evaluation of the applicability of the day hospital in treatment of acutely disturbed patients. *Israel Annual Psychiatry, 2,* 162–166.

PART VI

RESEARCH ON THE TEACHING AND LEARNING OF THERAPEUTIC SKILLS

19

METHODS OF TEACHING THERAPEUTIC SKILL

RUTH G. MATARAZZO

Oregon Health Sciences University

DAVID R. PATTERSON

Univ. of Washington School of Medicine

INTRODUCTION

As psychology increasingly has moved into the arena of professional service, and health professionals increasingly are being required to demonstrate the appropriateness and efficacy of their ministrations to patients or clients, it is appropriate that we show additional concern about the effectiveness with which we are teaching professional skills and the appropriateness of those skills to client benefit. There are increasing numbers of research studies devoted to the task of training therapists, critical reviews of that work, and recommendations (see especially Ford, 1979) for avoiding past research flaws, thus hopefully increasing the value of future research. Knowledge about the value of training is limited by our knowledge about the effectiveness of the particular form of psychotherapy that is likely to be most helpful for a particular type of client. We seem justified in assuming, however, that certain basic therapeutic behaviors are fairly universal

building blocks and that the therapist must become thoroughly grounded in them, later learning to use them with increasing flexibility.

Even in our understanding of the process of teaching the building blocks of therapeutic skill, progress remains slow for a multitude of reasons. Among them are the complex, independent variables (teaching method and trainee) that often cannot be teased apart, difficulty in selecting and measuring dependent (outcome) variables, and probably even greater uncertainties in measuring patient improvement. Training populations that are most available for study are those at the *earliest* stage of learning, so that we know less about teaching intermediate and advanced skills. The important goal of these studies presumably should be to attempt to answer the pragmatic questions of what and how we can train students, with reasonable efficiency of time and resources, to be at least adequately helpful to clients. A number of teaching techniques such as microcounseling, the didactic-experiential program, interpersonal process recall, and others were initiated for this purpose. However, many research studies have focused upon relatively small alterations of teaching method in programs already known to be effective in producing change in trainee behavior, while few have tackled the "proof of the pudding"—that is, client benefit. We still seem to lack concensus on the basic issues of what and how, in a professional-level program, we should teach graduate students, or how well we are doing it. Ivey, whose work has stimulated a large number of studies, has specified a number of discrete, measurable skills that seem to underlie most successful interviews regardless of interviewer orientation or purpose. For the most part, however, his ideas seem to have been pursued at a remarkably superficial level outside of his own group of collaborators. Ivey and Authier (1978) have cautioned that their "role skills" must be used flexibly and meaningfully as the trainee develops skill over time and with supervision. It is the integration of these basic skills that is likely to differentiate the effective therapist from his or her less effective counterpart.

All professions share a concern that their practitioners be competent. Most probably find that minimally adequate standards of performance can be assessed through paper-and-pencil tests or other reasonably objective means that do not require the development of new methods of teaching (beyond didactic or programmed-learning materials) and measurement of competence. Unfortunately, psychologists who are concerned with researching the effectiveness of training in psychotherapeutic skills must grapple with the necessity of evaluating new, integrated (didactic plus experiential) teaching programs and with the need to define and develop new measures of complex outcome variables (for both trainees and clients). It is clear that until we deal more satisfactorily with the latter (delineation, definition, and measurement of student skills and client benefit), we have inadequate means to evaluate the former. This is a complicating factor throughout the studies described below. A few studies have used more than one criterion measure of student interviewer skill or have measured therapist skills in more than one situation, for example, written exercises, videotaped standard client, and actual interview behavior. It is clear that multiple measures of change

are needed because different measures of the same variable may not be highly intercorrelated (e.g., patient and therapist ratings of therapist skill or patient improvement), and we should not assume that one measure is adequate for our purposes.

It appears, too, that our profession has an unusually difficult task in defining pretraining differences among students' skills or aptitudes that may relate to their ability to profit from a specific training program. While the Graduate Record Exam and college grade-point average provide some predictive factors for graduate student academic performance, we have no established measures to predict differential student response to clinical skills training. Although it has long been suspected that there are important differences, as Garfield (1977) concluded, "the criteria used to designate psychotherapeutic requisites are global, non-operationally defined, unsystematically appraised in most instances, and lacking in research designed to appraise their importance". Ivey and Authier (1978) have stated, "Some individuals master the competencies easily and quickly; others need several recycles of training before minimum competencies can be demonstrated" (pp. 306–307). In view of the above, it seems that the typical research procedure, that of measuring average student performance, may well be masking important treatment (training) effects. In addition, the method of measuring *average* student performance tends to turn our attention away from any cues there may be regarding improved selection of *individual* students for psychotherapy training.

HISTORY

It is hard to imagine now that originally the psychotherapeutic hour was considered so mysterious and sacrosanct that a supervisor could not observe it nor could it be recorded for later discussion. This left the relatively slow-moving case-conference method of supervision as the only access to what went on between helper and helpee. It meant that interviewing or intervention skill could be taught only didactically or in simulated situations. Lack of access to the actual interview left us with ineffectual methods of teaching. Long ago, Covner (1944) showed that the student-therapist's verbal recapitulation of the interview contained significant omissions and distortions, and other studies have indicated that it is a relatively ineffective method of teaching interviewing skills (Matarazzo, Phillips, Wiens, & Saslow, 1965; Matarazzo, Wiens, & Saslow, 1966). Muslin, Thurnblad, and Meschel (1981) reported that 54 percent of the themes in videotaped interviews were not reported by medical students in supervision, and some degree of distortion was present in 54 percent of the reported themes.

Psychologists were the first psychotherapists to question the "sanctity" of the therapy hour, at a time when they were restricted from seeing therapy patients in many medical and mental health settings. Thus, it was left to Carl Rogers, working in a university counseling center, to make the first audiotape recordings and use the one-way mirror (Rogers, 1957). He was also the first to define, behaviorally, what to him were the essential, effective ingredients in the therapist's attitude and behavior ("facilitative conditions") that could be measured and evaluated and to specify graded experiences for the training of therapists. The behaviors and attitudes that he deemed to be "necessary and sufficient" conditions for patient improvement were empathic understanding, unconditional positive regard, and congruence or genuineness. He introduced modeling by the supervisor with a real client, role-playing, recording of interviews, and replaying them with the supervisor. He emphasized the importance of the character of the relationship between supervisor and student, which also should involve facilitative conditions.

Rogers was an important stimulus to a relatively large group of researchers who developed rating scales to assess the extent to which the therapist used "facilitative conditions," especially empathic understanding. For a more detailed review of the history of this area of study, see Matarazzo et al. (1966) and Matarazzo (1971, 1978). Truax and Carkhuff (1967) and their collaborators carried out programmatic research on a didactic-experiential training program designed to teach, among other skills, these facilitative conditions.

A number of studies had suggested that high therapist "conditions" were associated with patient depth of self-exploration and benefit generally (Truax & Carkhuff, 1967) and that lack of it was associated with patient deterioration (Bergin, 1963). These facilitative conditions are held by the client-centered group to be universally important in human interaction. Carkhuff (1967) effectively described this orientation. Both counselors and clients are seen as varying on the same dimensions of interpersonal functioning, with high "therapeutic conditions" being the ingredients of effective living: "Facilitators communicate an accurately empathic understanding of deeper as well as the surface feelings of the second person(s); they are freely and deeply themselves in a nonexploitative relationship; they communicate a very deep respect . . . ; and they are helpful in guiding the discussion of personally relevant feelings and experiences in specific and concrete terms". This is the *reverse* of the client in need of help whose words are unrelated to his feelings and whose responses to another, when genuine, are inclined to be *negative*. Such a client has little positive regard for others, and feelings are discussed on an abstract plane. These behaviors are typical of the ineffective person, be he counselor or counselee, and improvement in functioning would take place along the same dimensions. The client-centered programs thus are designed to produce facilitator-therapists who are high on these dimensions.

The client-centered group has published a number of studies suggesting that high therapist conditions in individual psychotherapy, as described above, are associated with constructive patient change, and that the absence of these conditions can lead to deterioration in patient functioning. The research plan in the studies was to have briefly trained judges rate level of therapist "conditions" as reflected in several two- or three-minute taped excerpts of each interview. Truax and Carkhuff (1967) reviewed much of this early work.

RESEARCH ON THE DIDACTIC-EXPERIENTIAL THERAPIST TRAINING PROGRAMS

Truax, Carkhuff, and Douds (1964), Truax and Carkhuff (1967), and Carkhuff (1972) developed programs designed to teach therapists to use the facilitative conditions. They added significant refinements to the earlier training procedures of Rogers and carried out ambitious research programs to measure the effectiveness of their training. They charged that most psychotherapy training programs had taught theory and patient psychodynamics rather than how to relate to a patient and conduct psychotherapy.

They were reinforced in the development of their training theory by research findings of others such as Barrett-Lennard (1962), Feifel and Eells (1963), Gardner (1964), Strupp, Wallach, and Wogen (1964), Lorr (1965), Rice (1965), and Truax et al. (1966), who found that patients valued the warmth, helpfulness, and human characteristics of the therapist (later demonstrated also by Waterhouse, 1979). They also pointed out that therapist warmth and accurate empathy, in turn, had been related to such research-based variables as "depth of patient exploration" and to patient outcome in their own research.

The three central elements of Truax and Carkhuff's (1967) didactic-experiential training program were described as: "(1) a therapeutic context in which the supervisor himself provides high levels of therapeutic conditions; (2) highly specific didactic training in the implementation of the therapeutic conditions; and (3) a quasi-group therapy experience where the trainee can explore his own existence, and his individual therapeutic self can emerge" (p. 242).

More specifically, the steps of the program were described as follows: Students were given extensive reading to do, followed by listening to taped individual psychotherapy sessions to increase their response repertoire. They rated excerpts from these tapes on the scales of "Accurate Empathy," "Nonpossessive Warmth," and "Genuineness." Subsequently, they practiced making responses to tape-recorded patient statements (especially empathic responses). Outside of class, pairs of students alternated playing "therapist" and "patient" roles in sessions that were recorded, brought to supervisory sessions, and rated on the therapeutic conditions scales. After achieving minimal levels of therapeutic conditions, the students had single interviews with real patients. The interviews were tape-recorded and samples were played back for rating by the student, his other peers, and the supervisor. In the sixth week of the program, quasi-group therapy was initiated with the students, who met for two-hour sessions once a week. Truax and Carkhuff (1967) state: "Although the experiential content served as background for the classroom interactions, the experiential qualities came to the foreground in the quasi-group therapy experience, which provided a more concentrated therapeutic encounter" (p. 271). The quasi-group therapy consisted of group discussion centered around the trainees' personal or emotional difficulties experienced in their role as therapists, and thus was not intended to provide personal psychotherapy for them.

The Rogerian-derived Truax and Carkhuff program, then, (1) began with a partial theory of the conditions essential to patient behavioral change; (2) included the development and some testing of instruments for measuring those conditions; (3) cited some research to indicate that these conditions do foster constructive patient change while their absence is a deterrent to constructive change; and (4) reflected, in its particular training steps, specific attempts to foster the appropriate attitudes and behaviors among the students. The authors also made use of ideas from social learning theory, behavior modification theory, and programmed instruction—for example, from social learning and behavior modification theories:

The major implication of the present tentative analysis is that the therapists or counselors who are high in empathy, warmth, and genuineness are more effective in psychotherapy because they themselves are personally more potent positive reinforcers; and also because they elicit through reciprocal affect a high degree of positive affect in the patient, which increases the level of the patient's positive self-reinforcement, decreases anxiety, and increases the level of positive affect communicated to others, thereby reciprocally increasing the positive affect and positive reinforcement received from others. By contrast, counselors or therapists who are low in communicated accurate empathy, nonpossessive warmth and genuineness are ineffective and produce negative or deteriorative change in the patient because they are noxious stimuli who serve primarily as aversive reinforcers and also because they elicit negative affect in the patient (which increases the level of the patient's negative self-reinforcement, increases the level of negative affect and negative reinforcement received from others)" (Truax & Carkuff, 1967, p. 161–162).

Some ideas from programmed instruction can be seen in Truax and Carkhuff's attempt, as carefully as possible in this complex learning situation, to teach a few relatively simple behaviors at one time, provide immediate feedback, and gradually refine discriminations until a defined level of performance is reached and the student is considered ready for the next learning task. Numbers of investigators were stimulated to test the effectiveness of this and similar programs. Ratings of therapist skill on some of the empathy scales were found, however, to be unrelated to patients' ratings of feeling understood or to ratings of patient outcome (Bergin & Jasper 1969; Burstein & Carkhuff, 1968; Caracena & Vicory, 1969; Hansen, Moore, & Carkhuff, 1968; McWhirter, 1963; Truax et al., 1966).

As questions were raised about this program's measurement of empathy, further research indicated that the AE (accurate empathy) scale did not appear to be measuring empathy alone, but probably a more generalized "good–bad" evaluative dimension (Chinsky & Rappaport, 1970; Rappaport & Chinsky, 1972) that was unrelated to the client statement to which it was a response. Furthermore, Mintz and Luborsky (1971) presented evidence suggesting that brief interview segments provide an inadequate picture of therapeutic interaction, and Wenegrat (1974) showed that empathy ratings were related simply to the proportion of therapist statements relating to emotion. Matarazzo and Wiens (1977) found empathy ratings to be related to therapist longer reaction time, fewer interruptions, less use of silence, and longer individual utterances. Matarazzo et al. (1966) had found the same temporal variables in therapy interviews to be related to an independent measure of therapist skill. These efforts coincided with a broader trend toward using more behavioral, objectively measured variables.

The research paradigm of using single subjective ratings of empathy or similar constructs as a therapeutic condition was tarnished, and measurement of these relatively subjective constructs has tended to give way to more easily measured therapist behaviors. Nevertheless, the training methods developed by this didactic-experiential group provided the impetus to further research and development of teaching and training programs. This earlier research had shown the advantages of an organized, step-wise program, the need for measurement of specific, in vivo therapist behaviors, and the need for follow-up measurement of both student-therapist skill maintenance and client change. Indeed, Truax and Carkhuff called attention to the

fact that "supervision" has often involved looking at patient behavior and dynamics, while overlooking the role of the therapist. They challenged the idea that therapeutic failure was usually the result of patient "resistance."

These breakthroughs were indeed important for the effective teaching of psychotherapeutic skill, both because the skills were clearly specified and because a multimodal method of teaching had been developed. Despite the flaws in the above research program, there have been many positive sequelae. One fortunate sequel was the finding that apparently those therapist behaviors that are judged to be "good" or "effective" are intercorrelated (some measurements of empathy have been related to decreased talk-time, decreased number of interruptions, decreased number of therapist "errors," assertiveness in dealing with patient emotions, etc.). Some of the latter concepts are more behavioral and more easily measured than "empathy," and thus we have moved a step ahead.

At this time, there is considerable research interest in brief, integrated programs for the development of basic interviewing skills—programs such as microcounseling, interpersonal process recall, and derivatives of the didactic-experiential program, all of which are appropriate primarily to neophyte therapists. Another continued trend is toward the use of more easily measured therapist variables.

At this point we shall look at some studies of these brief "packaged programs" and note the components of training that seem to determine their effectiveness. We shall then move to some of the relatively sparse research on the teaching of more advanced students through supervision.

RESEARCH ON MICROTRAINING

Ivey et al.'s (1968) "microcounseling" technique established the innovative procedure of teaching one skill at a time—for example, attending, reflection of feeling, summarization, self-disclosure. Each of these skills was broken down into its behavioral components—for example, "attending" includes eye contact, appropriate body language, verbal encouragement to continue, and paraphrasing to indicate that close attention is being paid to content and feeling. The original microtraining program involved five separate steps, including didactic material, modeling of positive and negative examples of the skill, videotaped practice followed by self-confrontation and feedback from an empathic supervisor, and further practice.

A large number of studies have been published on the use of microcounseling and other related training programs as brief, efficient methods to train relatively inexperienced counselors. It would be useful to examine some of these studies, both to assess the effectiveness of the programs and to give at least a sample of the large number of related reports that have appeared in the psychological and educational literature. A number of studies have compared various components of the microcounseling program, attempting to examine their relative effectiveness.

It is important to review briefly the original studies by Ivey (Ivey, Normington, Miller, Morrill, & Haase, 1968; Moreland, Ivey & Phillips, 1973) and his colleagues that stimulated subsequent research in this area. Ivey et al.'s (1968) standard microcounseling technique involved a series of steps in which trainees (1) conducted a five-minute initial interview with a counselee, (2) read a manual on the specific counseling skill for which they were being trained (e.g., attentiveness, accurate reflection, or summarization of feelings), (3) viewed videotaped modeling of specific skills by effective and less effective counselors, (4) viewed their initial interview and identified their own target behavior, and (5) recounseled the same counselee in a second videotaped interview. Using essentially this technique for teaching three different counselor behaviors, Ivey et al. found in their initial studies that counselor skills improved significantly on a pre–posttest basis, as rated by judges. Further, the treatment group showed a significantly greater increase than the control group in the *client's* rating on the Semantic Differential Form and the Counselor Effectiveness Scale (Haase & DiMattia, 1970).

Using an almost identical training procedure, Moreland et al. (1973) found that medical students given six weeks of microcounseling training improved significantly more on overall interviewing skill than a control group of medical students who received "equivalent" interviewing training, which included observation of interviews and verbal feedback from their supervisors. The microcounseling supervisors were rated more highly by the students than were the more "traditional" supervisors. This

was hypothesized to be due to the greater effectiveness of the microcounseling method and to its *specificity* of behavioral feedback rather than to the quality of the teachers, who were either advanced psychiatric residents or faculty. Toukmanian and Rennie (1975) also examined the effectiveness of the microcounseling procedure described above. Their study compared this procedure with a method of human relations training based on a Truax and Carkhuff model. On posttest, both training groups had significantly higher accurate empathy (AE) scores than the controls, and the microtraining group was found to have interviewing skills superior to those of the group undergoing human relations training. Thus, in these two carefully controlled studies, microtraining was found to be more effective than other procedures in improving both the target skills and more general ratings of therapist skill.

The vast majority of research studies on microcounseling training like those discussed above have reported a significant treatment effect both when the treatment group has been compared to controls, and when it has been compared with less well-specified programs. Separate training components of microcounseling have been isolated for evaluation of comparative effect in a number of studies reviewed in the following sections. We found only two studies in which the microcounseling technique did not produce significant improvement in skills. One of the exceptions was a study by Authier and Gustafson (1975) in which the effects of microcounseling, with and without supervision, were examined. They hypothesized that their negative results could be attributed to relatively poor motivation in their subjects, who were paraprofessional counselors working in a drug-treatment unit and who were likely to anticipate no reinforcement for acquisition of microtraining skills. They also questioned whether microcounseling skills are as appropriate for a drug patient population as for a psychiatric patient population. The matter of using different techniques with varying patient populations is one that has come to be addressed by other groups, described later in this chapter.

In the second exception, Pape and Bervan (1983) failed to find significant behavior change when they attempted to teach intake interviewing skills to rehabilitation counselors. The investigators failed to find that their training technique, which included didactic instruction, modeling, and practice with feedback, produced results superior to those of didactic instruction alone or to a delayed-training control group. Some of their training targets were different, however, and some of their ratings were based on two-minute interview segments, a time sample that probably was too brief for valid ratings. The method of rating brief time samples has been brought into serious question in the measurement of other therapeutic skills (e.g., empathy).

Thus the negative findings from the foregoing studies do not seem to pose a serious challenge to the demonstrated effectiveness of microcounseling training in producing immediate training effects at the level for which it was intended: that is, relatively inexperienced undergraduate and graduate students. A number of studies have attempted to examine whether there are crucial and/or less effective ingredients within such a skills training program. Researchers have studied the relative effectiveness of the separate components of microcounseling training, omitting or altering one or more components. Often the results have not approached conclusiveness because of methodological problems. The next sections will describe a few of the aforementioned studies. To date, the variables that have been examined most frequently include the value, individually and in varying combinations, of didactic material (written and oral), modeling, videotaping and self-confrontations, supervisor and peer feedback, and in vivo and simulated practice (including mental rehearsal).

The Effectiveness Of Training Components

Supervision

Supervison is an important variable to be examined with respect to effecting skills acquisition at both the preprofessional and professional levels (discussed later). Supervisory effectiveness appears to depend upon several variables.

Kelley (1971) used supervision per se as a variable within the microcounseling approach (described earlier) in teaching basic counseling skills to master's degree students in counseling and guidance. In one experimental condition the students read an instructional program, conducted a 20-minute interview, reread the instructional booklet, and then listened to their own audiotape (self-reinforced group). The procedure was repeated three times. The results

were compared both to a control group and to a condition in which the students reviewed the tape with a supervisor. On a fourth posttest interview, both experimental groups made significantly greater improvement on the dependent variables than did the control group. The dependent variables included making fewer utterances, using longer latencies, speaking less, and making fewer interruptions. The supervisor-reinforced group performed significantly better than the self-reinforced group on the last two variables (amount of interviewer speech and number of interruptions), suggesting that some interviewer behaviors may be more available to self-awareness than others and that, as a consequence, supervision may be especially important for teaching certain skills although self-confrontation appears to have teaching value.

Quality of the Supervisory Relationship

Quality of the supervisor—student relationship appears to be important. Truax and Carkhuff (1967) described, as one of the three central elements of their training program, "a therapeutic context in which the supervisor himself provides high levels of therapeutic conditions" (p. 242). Rogers (1957) stated that the student-therapist's learning should take place in a facilitative environment such as the effective therapist provides for his patient. The facilitative conditions were seen as growth promoting, as was the role modeling of the supervisor in the provision of empathy, acceptance, and warmth. Conversely, the cold and nonfacilitative supervisor could have a negative effect on the student's growth, would provide a negative role model, and would (due to negative emotional impact) perhaps lead to deterioration in the student's functioning. Truax and Carkhuff (1967) state: "If the trainees could not experience high levels of warmth and regard, understanding and genuineness from the supervisor, then they could not be expected to function at high therapeutic levels, themselves" (p. 262). Ivey (1983) cautions that personal involvement between supervisor and trainee is necessary in order for the trainee to learn to apply the separate skills meaningfully and to help the student through emotional issues. Several studies have suggested that these hypotheses have merit.

Pagell, Carkhuff, and Berenson (1967) found that trainees who were given facilitative conditions by their supervisors offered higher levels of empathy to their own clients. Pierce, Carkhuff, and Berenson (1967) found that volunteer counselors learned little and were inclined to drop out (over 50%) when assigned to a supervisor who provided low facilitative conditions. Dodenhoff (1981) found that trainees who are strongly attracted to their supervisors are more effective at the end of the practicum than those who are less strongly attracted. He hypothesized that this was because of greater acceptance of the supervisors' influence.

Specificity and Immediacy of Supervision

For effective learning, the supervisor must provide specific information and feedback (Payne, Winter, & Perry, 1975). It is clear that the supervisor must have highly specific knowledge and skills that can be imparted to the trainee. Understandably, *immediate* postinterview supervision is more effective than supervision that is delayed by several days (Doyle, Foreman, & Wales, 1977). This is likely to be a factor, as well, for self-reinforcement via video- or audiotape, even though the interview is in part reconstructed and relived by the interviewer during its replay.

Co-counseling

Co-counseling is a teaching technique not infrequently touted. In it, presumably the supervisor models skills for the trainee and encourages participation (practice) followed by subsequent supervisory discussion of the interview. However, "co-counseling" has referred to quite different procedures in various reports and needs to be clearly defined. At the present time, we know little about its effectiveness.

Modeling

Modeling has been used extensively in studies of training psychotherapists and counselors, although the conditions of its use and measurement of its effectiveness have varied enough to produce occasionally conflicting results. In an exceptionally well-designed study, Stone and Vance (1976) compared the independent effects of instructions, modeling, and rehearsal in training 48 volunteer college students in empathic communication. They used eight training groups, representing all factorial combinations, and eliminated trainer differences by having the entire training segment videotaped. They found that all treatment groups experienced significant pre−post effects on the *written* Communication

Index (Carkhuff, 1969) and that the use of *specific* instructions was particularly influential on this measure. Empathy ratings of a critical-incident interview indicated that the combined training effects were greater than the effects of the single training variables, and that *modeling* (five examples of alternating low and high levels of empathy) produced greater effects on empathic communication when the outcome measure was a critical incident *interview*, rather than a written test. Stone and Vance (1976) point to the lack of evidence of a strong relationship between written and interview response ratings. They concluded that modeling seemed to facilitate performance in fairly ambiguous circumstances (interviews), while instructions are more effective when the task is highly structured (written tests).

Eisenberg and Delaney (1970) compared the use of a videotaped model, systematic in vivo reinforcement, and a combination of both in an effort to teach counselor "tacting" response leads (i.e., a response by the therapist leading the client to specify, clarify, or exemplify his or her previous statement) to graduate students in counseling. They found that the videotaped model significantly influenced the counselors' responses to *standard* clients seen on the videotape but did *not* generalize to live interviews. It is noteworthy that this phenomenon has been demonstrated time and again, yet researchers have not been dissuaded from using written, filmed, and other noninterview measures of therapist skill.

Perry (1975) studied the acquisition of empathic skills via verbal instruction followed by either a high- or low-empathy modeled interview, as compared with verbal instruction and no modeling. She found verbal instruction alone to be relatively ineffective. The high-empathy modeling resulted in increasingly empathic communication from baseline to the last section of a taped, simulated interview, while the negative modeling resulted in decreasingly empathic communication, indicating the importance of the supervisor's skills. There was no carryover, however, from trainees' responses in the taped interviews to their behavior in a 15-minute live interview, underscoring again the weakness of noninterview outcome responses as predictors of change in level of behavioral skill. Uhleman, Lea, and Stone (1976) found that the most effective learning took place when didactic instruction preceded modeling, possibly thus directing the learner's attention to the most significant aspects of the model's behavior. The second most effective treatment was modeling followed by instruction, while either condition alone was relatively ineffective. Possibly relating to the foregoing effects of cognitive structuring are studies that have used models to exhibit *both* high and low skills (Eskedal, 1975; Saltmarsh, 1973) and have found that this comparative procedure aids the student's learning of both cognitive and behavioral skill.

Several studies have combined modeling with other skill-enhancing techniques. Kuna (1975) attempted to teach the counseling skill of "restatement" (i.e., essentially reflecting the client's statement) to undergraduate and graduate women. He compared the experimental conditions of (1) an eight-minute lecture component; (2) a lecture and a two-page reading component; (3) a lecture, reading, and modeling (two five-minute interactions) component; and (4) a control group. He found that all three treatments resulted in a significant learning effect, and that the addition of a videotaped model of enhancement techniques did not significantly add to the production rate of target behavior produced by lecture and reading alone. The criteria, however, were ratings of student responses to 10 *videotaped, unrelated counselor statements*, and could be considered more of an intellectual (such as a written exercise) measure than an opportunity for live demonstration of behavioral skill.

Wallace, Horan, Baker, and Hudson (1975) attempted to teach decision-making skills to 54 randomly assigned counseling students and compared the effectiveness of a 20-minute videotaped model, lecture, and written handout with a treatment condition including a lecture and written handout only, and a condition incorporating features of microcounseling (role-playing, videotaping, and supervisor feedback). Performance outcome was based on behavioral ratings from two audiotaped, 15- to 20-minute student-counselor interviews. The investigators found that the microcounseling technique was superior to the other teaching approaches and that the modeling procedure, as used here, produced no gains over the other microcounseling elements.

The general trend of these studies suggests that modeling enhances the acquisition of counseling skills in trainees who have had little or no counseling experience. Modeling includes many factors, how-ever, that can determine its effectiveness, including amount of modeling, preinstructions, and whether contrasting types of modeling are shown. Also, the *measure* of outcome (interview versus simulation) determines whether skill enhancement can be demonstrated.

A number of additional studies have been reported in the literature, but often the meaning of the results is not clear due to extremely brief training (e.g., 5 or 10 minutes' exposure to didactic material describing a specific procedure), highly artificial training (e.g., modeling of responses to brief, unrelated videotaped statements), and the use of artificial outcome measures (written reponses only, responses to brief, unrelated videotaped statements, etc.). Ivey and Authier's (1978) caution appears justified: "Any procedure which is as clearly defined as microtraining has the danger of becoming stereotyped and losing touch with its original goals" (p. 316). Research in this area is most meaningful if it remains relatively close to the conditions of actual training, that is, graduate student population, clear descriptions of the skills to be learned and a rationale for their use, modeling with actual clients of a full (though perhaps abbreviated) interview, the conduct of actual client interviews, feedback from well-trained counselors, and so on. Failure to adhere to these methodological conditions has resulted in a paucity of definitive answers in this area of clinical training.

Practice

The influence of the practice component in psychotherapy training is the subject of a recent comprehensive review by Fuqua and Gade (1982). The authors note that "practice" has referred to written interviewer responses, responses to videotaped clients, student role-play, coached clients, and real clients, and has not escaped conceptual confusion. A few studies have investigated systematically its effects relative to other training variables (e.g., Bailey, Deardorff, & Nay, 1977; O'Toole, 1979; Peters, Cormier, & Cormier, 1978; Stone, 1975; Stone & Vance, 1976). However, methodological problems frequently have made it difficult to interpret the results. For example, Fuqua and Gade argued that Bailey et al. (1977), who found that a combination of treatments (modeling, practice and videotaped feedback, or modeling plus videotape feedback) had a considerably greater effect than practice alone, had failed to include a "modeling only" treatment group. As Fuqua and Gade point out, attending to the appropriate behaviors, practicing them, and then receiving cognitive clarification should indeed have a greater effect on learning than either practice or modeling alone. They point out the need for control of the amount of time devoted to teaching in the various experimental conditions.

In addition, Fuqua and Gade (1982) contend that the failure of Peters et al. (1978) and Stone (1975) to find a stronger practice effect could be attributed to too low a ceiling of measurement and other methodological variables. "Too low a ceiling" refers to the very simple elements of counseling skill that typically have been used (e.g., number of empathic responses) rather than the frequency, appropriateness, and quality of varied responses in a complex situation such as the interview. They point out that, in fact, we all assume practice to be a sine qua non for the development of clinical skill in the psychotherapeutic situation and that we must be using inappropriate design features and methods of measurement if we cannot demonstrate its effects. Unguided practice is relatively ineffective, but the extent and nature of its effect in combination with cognitive input has not been studied adequately. The written exercises that have been used are so simple as to set too low a ceiling for *measurement* of training effects.

Fuqua and Gade (1982) point out, "Even if a trainee has effectively acquired an adequate repertoire of discrete skills, the task remains to modulate or orchestrate the various skills in a therapeutic manner" (p. 288). This complex skill we have not yet learned to measure, but it may prove to be a better ground for studying the effects of practice. They conclude that future studies should (1) minimize the bias due to a low measurement ceiling, (2) use dependent measures that address more effectively the structural correctness and appropriateness of the trainee's response, and (3) address the relative effect of practice variations.

The effect of *mental* practice (as distinguished from in vivo practice) on the acquisition of counselor skill has been a recent focus of Baker and his colleagues (Baker, Scofield, Clayton, & Munson, 1984; Baker, Scofield, Munson, & Clayton, 1983). In the mental practice condition, subjects are instructed to imagine themselves rehearsing specific skills. This relates to the "covert modeling" of Scott,

Cormier, and Cormier (1980). Like "covert modeling," mental practice appears to have some beneficial effect that produces performance superior to that of control groups on relatively simple skills such as "attending."

One must assume that practice contributes to therapy-skill acquisition, but there is little evidence regarding the variables involved and its effectiveness relative to other factors in training. The effectiveness of each of the training variables has been found to be strongest in combination with other techniques, including practice.

In the last section we focused on the effective ingredients within the microcounseling and didactic-experiential skills training programs. Most of the studies used training procedures based on Ivey et al.'s (1968) microcounseling model or Carkhuff's (1967) systematic human relations training. Some other skills training packages do not fit into either of these categories, and are also aimed at basic skills.

STRUCTURED LEARNING THERAPY

Goldstein (1973) developed Structured Learning Therapy (SLT) as a program having many similarities to microtraining. It was intended primarily to teach improved interpersonal skills to *patients*, but has also been applied to counselor training. Goldstein's approach includes systematic teaching of single skills via modeling, role-playing, social reinforcement, and transfer of training. Modeling is by audiotape and includes a rationale for the single skill presented. Role-playing is followed by verbal feedback from other group members. Social reinforcement is given by the group according to specific rules. After all have role-played, the modeling tape is replayed to reinforce the learning. The transfer-of-training aspect of the program is considered to be of primary importance inasmuch as the patients presumably will be using the new skills in a wide variety of social circumstances. Therefore, homework practice is assigned and patients are urged to report back on this outside practice of skills.

Research by Goldstein and his collaborators have shown their program to be effective in increasing psychiatric inpatients' mealtime social behavior (Gutride, Goldstein, & Hunter, 1972) and in training paraprofessional counselors (Goldstein, 1973). In the former study, SLT was more effective than social companionship therapy, and the transfer of training aspect was noted to be a significant portion of the training. Transfer of training was also found to be a potent aspect of training in the latter study.

Two studies have applied an SLT format to counselor training. Rosenthal (1977) made use of Goldstein's (1973) Structured Learning Training to teach confrontation skills to graduate students who were high or low in conceptual level (CL). Rosenthal compared a standard implementation of SLT with a self-instructional variation of the method. "Conceptual level" refers to the trainee's level of conceptual complexity, which takes into consideration such variables as self-responsibility, independence, and ability to generate concepts (Harvey, Hunt, & Schroeder, 1961; Hunt & Sullivan, 1974). On pencil-and-paper measures (two forms of the Counselor Training Questionnaire) and on behavioral ratings, both training techniques resulted in a significant learning effect beyond that of a group that received brief instruction. As predicted, students high in conceptual development benefited more from a self-instructional approach and those low in CL did better with the standard, more externally controlled training program. Differences in the CL groups were found *only* on the pencil-and-paper measures, however, leading again to the question whether such a difference will generalize to practice.

In one of the more thorough, methodologically sound studies of therapist training to date, Bouchard and his colleagues (1980) compared a structured learning format (SLF) with a seminar format in teaching social-skills training to therapists. The therapist population, consisting of graduate students and accredited professionals, was older and more experienced than those included in most studies on therapist-skills training. The authors found that the structured learning format produced greater enhancement of social skills than did the seminar format when outcome was measured by pre−posttest changes on the Rating Scale for Therapist Behavior in Social Skill Training (Wright, Horlich, Bouchard, Mathieu, & Zeichner, 1977), a behavioral scale for assessing a therapist's interview behavior. Unfortunately, Bouchard et al. did not find that these results were associated with significant differences in therapy outcome when the therapists were paired with high-anxious, low-skilled clients. Nevertheless, the effort of Bouchard et al. is an important one in psychotherapy training research because it was done on a population of somewhat experienced therapists; it involves the training of more advanced skills than is typically seen in such studies; and it makes an attempt to assess the impact of the training on actual psychotherapeutic outcome.

TEACHING THE TECHNIQUES OF BEHAVIOR MODIFICATION

Operant conditioning is a widely accepted form of treatment for populations that have been found to be relatively nonamenable to the more traditional forms of psychotherapy (e.g., autistic and retarded children and chronic psychotic adults), as well as for removal of specific disturbing behaviors and symptoms, teaching parents and other environmental agents to modify the nonconforming or other disturbing behaviors of children, etc. There is considerable evidence for concluding that operant conditioning, appropriately conceived and applied, is an effective means of shaping behavior, increasing the number of desired responses, and decreasing or eliminating those behaviors targeted for extinction (see Chapter 12). In this orientation, a therapist is anyone who uses systematic methods to modify the behavior of the targeted individual, and it is relatively feasible to measure both how well he or she has learned to perform as the supervisor recommends, and how effective that performance is in increasing or decreasing the targeted behaviors.

Partly because many of the therapists or trainers have been lay individuals, and because of the relative ease of describing and measuring variables, there has been more complete specification of training programs, measurement of the student-trainer's acquired skill, and of the efficacy of the latter's performance in producing the desired changes in the behavior of the patient-trainee. The psychologist's role often is that of consultant, programming the environment and teaching the principles of behavior modification to the lay therapist-trainer.

PARENT−CHILD BEHAVIOR MODIFICATION

One of the most important areas of application is that of training parents to use operant conditioning with their own children who exhibit problem behaviors. Reisinger, Ora, and Frangia (1976) present a review of behavior therapy research with parents having a child-trainee under age 12. Forehand et al. (1979) and Sanders and James (1983) have reviewed problems of maintenance and generalization of skills. Salzinger, Feldman, and Portnoy (1970) found that behavior modification training is considerably less effective with less educated parents, Wahler (1980) found that the training effects were less well maintained in low SES groups, and Rinn, Vernon, and Wise (1975) found that middle-income parents attended more sessions and were more successful in the training program. Other family problems also appear to be related to poor maintenance. Altering the training approach may be necessary in order to effect changes in lower-class mothers' child-rearing strategies (Jacobson, Bushnell, & Risley, 1969). Didactic presentation alone (Kazdin & Moyer, 1976; Ray, 1965; Sepler & Myers, 1978) has been found to be less effective than more active strategies. Didactic presentation of background principles, demonstration or modeling, observed practice, and feedback all appear to be important components of an effective training package. Training manuals for parents and other nonprofessionals have been written by Patterson (1975), Sulzer-Azaroff and Reese (1982), and others, but these are best used in conjunction with additional methods.

Glogower and Sloop (1976) compared the performance of mothers who were taught the principles of behavior modification, followed by training to change specific target behaviors, with the performance of mothers who were trained only to change target behaviors. They found that the broadly trained mothers dealt better with a wide range of behavior problems and showed better maintenance of skill, while the specifically trained group showed a decrement in score for home behavior change projects at five months' follow-up. However, O'Dell, Flynn, and Benlolo (1977) failed to find a beneficial effect from adding didactic training in behavioral principles to the rest of their program, which included modeling and role-playing. Similarly, Gardner (1972) found that understanding of principles did not affect behavior as much as role-playing. Flanagan, Adams and Forehand (1979) also found video modeling and role-playing to be more potent in teaching time-out procedures to parents than was didactic material. It is puzzling that O'Dell, Krug, Patterson, and Faustman in a later study (1980) failed to find that modeling and role-playing were more effective than didactic presentation. This is not in accord with most other studies.

Salzinger et al. (1970) taught the mothers of brain-injured children to carry out behavior modification programs. Their program included didactic material, record keeping, and review over an extended eight-month period. Degree of success was associated with extent of the parent's conformity to the program. The authors concluded that "we would undoubtedly do better to apply to the parents' behavior the same kind of analysis that we applied to their children's behavior. Parents' no less than their children's behavior is subject to reinforcement contingencies . . ." (p. 23). [A number of studies have pointed to the importance of feedback and reinforcement for the learning and maintenance of skills for psychiatric aides, teachers, and all manner of trainees (Seys & Duker, 1978; Sloat, Tharp, & Gallimore, 1977)]. Rinn, Vernon, and Wise (1975) presented evaluation data on 1100 parents who took a course in Positive Parent Training, in which a partial fee refund was made to the contingent group if they satisfied all requirements for attendance and performance. The contingent (money refund) group attended more sessions and completed more projects than the noncontingent group, indicating the importance of external contingencies. Nay (1979) has suggested several strategies for providing continuing reinforcement to parents.

Eyberg and Matarazzo (1980) compared the effectiveness of five didactic, individual, behavior-modification training sessions for mothers with five mother–child group training sessions that used a semiprogrammed text (Becker, 1971) and home assignments. Modeling, role-playing, observation, and immediate feedback were used for the individual training. The individually trained mothers showed significantly greater improvement and greater satisfaction with the program, which may well have been due to the more active intervention in the individual treatment group, rather than to the individual versus group aspect of the intervention. Walter and Gilmore (1973) used group treatment with 12 families who had a child with severely out of control behavior. In addition to a programmed text, recording of child behavior, and daily telephone contact, their weekly parent group sessions utilized role-playing, modeling, and didactic instruction. Family observations by trained observers disclosed a 61 percent decrease in targeted behavior for the treatment group.

Ferber, Keeley, and Shemberg (1974), also using the Patterson procedure, were unable to duplicate these highly positive results. They noted that the families felt restrained by the presence of the experimenters; that the "coded" behaviors did not adequately reflect the nature and severity of the total family difficulties; and that the treatment effects tended to dissipate by the time of follow-up. As Patterson, Cobb, and Ray (1973) have indicated, some families may require that treatment be extended over a long period of time. Also, *severity* of the problem behavior is likely to be an important factor.

Nay (1975) taught time-out procedures to 77 mothers by means of written and oral didactic instruction, videotaped modeling, and modeling coupled with role-playing each aspect of time-out. As measured by questionnaire, all training techniques were equally useful, but assessment via response in a simulated situation suggested that the modeling and modeling plus role-playing were most effective. Thus, again, method of measurement is all-important. Eyberg and Johnson (1974) found that measurements taken via direct observation of parent-child behavior yielded less evidence of treatment effect than did parent-collected data and reported parent attitude change. They recommended using multiple methods of assessment.

Parents have been trained to treat their own autistic children. Kozloff (1973) describes training parents to interrupt the destructive cycle of negative parent-child interaction and begin a cycle of increased positive reinforcement. He reports great increments in parental skill and improvement in child behavior. Leitenberg, Burchard, Burchard, Fuller, and Lysaght (1977) have shown a beneficial effect upon family relationships when noncompliant behavior is weakened and compliant behavior reinforced.

BEHAVIOR MODIFICATION PROGRAMS IN THE CLASSROOM AND HOSPITAL

Token economies and other behavior modification programs have been established in the classroom,

on hospital wards, and in penal institutions, and other settings. Cotler, Applegate, King, and Kristal (1972), however, found that both teachers and students tended to return to their old behaviors when the specific program was not in effect. Again it is apparent that one needs to continue to reinforce the trainer as well as the trainee. Similar difficulty in getting hospital aides to maintain their "therapeutic" behaviors has been reported (Katz, Johnson, & Gelfand, 1972), although contingent monetary bonuses increased the frequency of their reinforcing behaviors. Gross and Ekstrand (1983) found that public posting of teachers' use of reinforcement resulted in a large increase in teacher praise. This behavior was maintained, however, only after a fading-out, intermittent feedback procedure was used.

Johnson, Katz, and Gelfand (1972) report training undergraduate practicum and work-study students to do behavior modification training with hospitalized psychiatric patients. They point to the importance of the supervisor's providing direct, unambiguous feedback to the trainee and suggestions for alternative ways to handle specific issues.

Bond (1974) notes that *diagnosis* is a more important aspect of treatment in this approach than it is in either the client-centered or psychoanalytic models. He says, "behavior therapists, in using the S−O−R model, focus on the specific organism-environment interactions which are problematic for the client in everyday life" (p. 124). Thus one of the most important goals of (professional) training is that of "behavioral analysis, which involves a careful description of the target behaviors that the client wishes to modify, along with the relevant aspects of environments where these occur." Bond goes on to say, "Behavior therapy's greater specificity encourages a more active strategy of attempting to influence behavior, which permits a relatively immediate check on the success or failure of the strategy."

The programs planned for trainers in behavior modification have dealt with various aspects of therapeutic intervention training: defining the goal-behaviors of the trainer and those of the trainee; manipulating the sources of motivation for both; comparing training methods; and using observational measurement of both trainer and patient. This approach to therapy and therapist training is made possible by the ordinarily observable and delimited nature of the chief complaint (e.g., non-compliance) and the environmental variables that are maintaining it. Also important is the program's well-formulated theoretical base, which determines the choice of specific intervention procedures. Other kinds of therapeutic training, skill acquisition, and patient outcome do not lend themselves as easily to objective measurement. Nonetheless, Loeber and Weisman (1975) note: "Behavior modification programs usually put heavy emphasis on environmental variables, but, remarkably enough, little attention has been paid to the analysis and control of that class of environmental variables comprising the responses emitted by (professional) therapists and trainers . . ." (p. 660).

The supervisor–therapist relationship has an aspect of similarity to the therapist–patient relationship in that guided behavior change is the task of the teacher in both instances. The similarity can be seen more easily in the behavioral approaches where the "patient" is not considered emotionally "ill" but as a "normal" individual who has behavioral excesses or deficits, or maladaptive behaviors that need reshaping.

TREATMENT MANUALS

A particularly interesting development is the appearance of psychotherapy treatment manuals that can be used for, among other things, the training of more advanced therapists in a particular form of treatment for a specific group of clients (depressed, drug dependent, etc.). Training typically has been done through workshops. Learning can be measured by ratings of the therapist's conformity to a specific, written therapy program. These manuals were developed primarily for the purpose of relating comparative patient benefit to several specified, relatively standardized, treatment modalities. The manuals provide criteria for rating the extent to which the therapist does what he or she presumably has been trained to do. A large-scale NIMH (Waskow, Parloff, Hadley, & Autry, 1985) project is comparing three standardized approaches for the treatment of depression.

Manuals have been written for supportive-expressive, psychoanalytically oriented psychotherapy (Luborsky, 1984); the cognitive therapy of depression (CT) (Beck, Rush, Shaw, & Emery, 1979);

the interpersonal psychotherapy of depression (IPT) (Klerman & Neu, 1976; Klerman, Rounsaville, Chevron, Neu, & Weissman, 1979; Klerman, Weissman, Rounsaville, & Chevron, in press); and short-term dynamic psychotherapy (Strupp & Binder, 1983), as well as others. More are in preparation.

The IPT approach to the treatment of depression (Klerman et al., 1979) specifies four areas of therapeutic focus: pathological grief, role disputes, role transitions, and interpersonal deficits. Treatment techniques include reassurance, a nonjudgmental attitude, social manipulation, role-playing, rehearsal, and teaching problem-solving techniques. Neu, Prusoff, and Klerman (1978) found that therapists trained in this orientation used nonjudgmental exploration 45 percent of the time, elicitation 21 percent, clarification 14 percent, and direct advice giving 7 percent of the time. These findings were in accordance with expectations, suggesting that the use of the manuals was effective in teaching a specific therapeutic technique.

Luborsky, Woody, McLellan, O'Brien, and Rosenzweig (1982) conducted research to determine whether three different types of therapists in fact followed their manual-based program and whether judges could differentiate among them and designate reliably which therapeutic orientation was being followed. They found that supportive-expressive therapists were more inclined to focus on "the understanding of the relationship with the patient, including transference," than were therapists of the other orientations. On the other hand, cognitive-behavioral therapists were more directive, monitored current problems more, and more frequently gave advice. Similarly, cognitive-behavioral therapists consumed a significantly larger percent of talk-time (36%) than did the drug counselors (22%), who spoke significantly more than the supportive-expressive therapists (14%). Interestingly, there is no specific directive in the manual as to percent talk-time, but such differences were consistent with the overall, described approach.

With the use of such manuals and ratings of therapist behavior, it has been possible to contrast the techniques associated with each. At this more advanced level of therapy, we see planned differences in the proportions of basic techniques and in the manner of integrating them. Thus, although most therapies use the same basic, "building-block" therapeutic behaviors, advanced levels of performance skill apparently become differentiated according to theoretical orientation. DeReubis, Hollon, Evans, and Bemis (1982) compared ratings of therapist one-hour interviews (two interviews of two therapists), and found both common and differentiating factors between the CT and IPT approaches. In addition to differences in specified technique, the two therapies differed in regard to directiveness.

MISCELLANEOUS TRAINING PROCEDURES

A number of publications describe other training procedures that may be subjected to future research. Some of the procedures are not new. Almost all of the reports of this nature have not yet assessed the impact of their respective approaches through the use of an experimental design. Some of the suggested procedures include the use of brief transcripts of psychotherapy sessions (Kepecs, 1977), tracking errors (Kepecs, 1979), in vivo modeling via observation of experienced therapists from behind one-way mirrors (Goin, Burgoyne, Kline, Woods, & Peck, 1976), presenting process notes from a terminated case to a supervisor and other trainees (Vasile & Shapiro, 1982), experiential training for effectiveness in power-and-sex-salient situations (Gallessich, Gilbert, & Holahan, 1980), the use of a computer (Phillips, 1983), "hospitalizing" students in a state hospital (Ringuette, 1983), and demonstration videotapes (e.g., A. Lazarus' *Multimodal Therapy Training Series*, available from Research Press).

Some interesting approaches to training have been described but not tested empirically. Moreover, even with studies of basic mircocounseling skills and human relations skills, most of the work has not been replicated without alteration of significant variables. There is need for replicated research that uses highly veridical training and outcome variables, for example, real patients, interns or residents, and full training procedures in contradistinction to a few hours of training under simulated conditions. We need to identify the training requirements of more advanced graduate students, develop means to address those needs, and evaluate the impact that the training has on client attitude and outcome. An additional need is to examine the generalization of skills and their permanence. It appears likely that, subsequent to training without

follow-through, trained therapists tend to revert to previous idiosyncratic behaviors. An additional direction for future research could be to distinguish from each other the performance of both trainees and professional psychotherapists who work better with specific client populations (e.g., suicidal, character disorders) and troublesome presenting problems (e.g., terminal illness, grief, client violence). This could be a further step in our understanding of psychotherapy outcome variables.

RESEARCH IN RELATED AREAS

A number of studies in the medical literature have made use of paraprofessionals to help teach interviewing skills to medical students (Helfer, Black, & Teitelbaum, 1975; Stillman, 1978; Stillman & Ruggill, 1978; Stillman, Sabers, & Redfield, 1976, 1977). Mothers also have been a teaching source in these studies. Stillman et al. (1976) trained mothers to give a consistent and authentic history of a child's common medical problem. Medical students in the experimental group interviewed the *trained* mothers and then watched a 30- to 40-minute replay of the interview, during which the mother gave feedback to the student. After several weeks the students interviewed a second mother who was unaware as to whether the student had been involved in the training. Compared to a control group, the trained medical students were given significantly higher process ratings (quality of interviewing) and content scores (amount of information obtained) by the trained mothers.

It appears that more advanced medical training programs, including psychiatric residencies, seldom use integrated teaching programs in psychotherapy or evaluate their students' therapeutic skills. This they have in common with advanced clinical training in psychology.

ISSUES RELATED TO MORE ADVANCED SUPERVISION

There has been little empirical study of the actual *process* of supervision. As the remainder of this chapter will suggest, most of the research on the teaching of psychotherapy has focused on identifying basic training variables and improving highly specific therapist skills. The actual process of continued supervision, the most frequent medium through which the more advanced trainee is taught such skills, has been largely neglected. McColley and Baker (1982) report that their review of the literature which was published between 1950 and 1975 revealed that only nine articles on psychotherapy supervision had been published in psychology journals. On the other hand, they noticed that an increase in publications and professional attention had occurred in this area between 1975 and 1980. Hansen, Pound, and Petro (1976) have pointed out in their review that the published studies on supervision have provided little information as to *what mechanisms* bring about changes in trainee behavior through this process.

One possible reason is that supervision is undefined and amorphous in nature (Miars et al., 1983). Miars and his colleagues have pointed out that the literature on supervision is characterized by diverse theoretical orientations and has tended to focus on "isolated and seemingly unrelated studies of various aspects of supervision" (p. 403). In his review of research on the supervision process, Lambert (1980) points out that supervision is actually a heterogeneous set of conditions tht elude the theoretician's grasp when defined as a unitary variable. Lambert has defined supervision as those "training activities, either group or individual, wherein the supervisor arranges experiences that are aimed at helping the student therapist to modify specific behaviors with particular clients" (p. 425). Lambert's definition remains broad and excludes primarily didactic training (e.g., classroom lectures) and personal experiences (e.g., trainee psychotherapy).

Hess and Hess (1983) conducted a survey of supervision practices among APA-approved predoctoral internships. As they point out, "Although the internship is central to professional training in psychology, little information is available on the extent and nature of psychotherapy supervision provided to interns" (p. 504). They obtained usable responses from 92 programs (61%). On the average, interns were reported to receive one hour of supervision per three hours of psychotherapy, and most commonly this consisted of one-on-one discussion with the supervisor. Next most frequently used was a seminar form of supervision, followed by discussion of audiotaped recordings. Used considerably less frequently were direct observation and

videotaping, although about half of the programs used them "sometimes." Most supervisors had not, themselves, had training in supervision, nor did they see it as an appropriate or feasible part of their internship programs. Yet often interns were being given the role of supervising others. Ongoing training of the supervisors, themselves, was minimal or absent, as was evaluation of their performance. Hess and Hess favor increased emphasis on training for the supervisory role and the development of sound rating scales for continuing assessment of supervisory performance.

Some attempts have been made to identify those supervisor characteristics that facilitate the trainee's appreciation and effective utilization of supervision (Goin & Kline, 1974; Holloway & Wolleat, 1981; Nelson, 1978). Goin and Kline studied videotapes of supervisors who had consistently been rated as "outstanding" by second-year psychiatric residents and compared them with those of supervisors who were rated as "moderately good." The authors concluded, based on a content analysis of the tapes, that the outstanding supervisors made more *didactic* comments (over 50%) about patients and techniques than did their lower rated colleagues. In addition, they were described as falling in the middle of a continuum between extremely passive and authoritatively directive in their style of interaction. The residents reported that the outstanding supervisors made more helpful, information-giving comments about psychotherapy.

Goin and Kline found that the residents' attraction to a more didactic approach challenges a traditional assumption that supervision is an opportunity to foster the trainee's own emotional growth (see Salvendy, 1977, for a discussion of these differing schools of thought). In the above study, the authors did not perform a statistical analysis of the differences they observed between supervisors, and their analysis of distinctions was made on a post hoc basis. However, in a subsequent study they again challenged the oft-stated assumption that it is necessary to deal with the supervisee's personal issues in the supervisory process (Goin et al., 1976). The authors found that in a content analysis of videotapes of 24 psychoanalytic supervisors, 12 made no comments to their supervisees about countertransference, 8 approached it directly, and 4 approached it indirectly.

Nelson (1978) attempted to define those supervisor characteristics that were preferred by trainees. His study involved a survey of 48 trainees, 12 from each of four professional disciplines (clinical psychology, counseling psychology, psychiatry, and social work). *Interest in supervision* was the supervisory characteristic rated as the most valued by the trainees. The highest ranked personality descriptors for a supervisor included flexibility, permissiveness, easy accessibility (self-revealing), and warmth. With regard to *preferred methods* of teaching, the trainees rated the opportunity for *observation of the supervisor* doing therapy the highest, followed by the supervisor's functioning as a co-therapist with the trainee. The trainees ranked videotaping of sessions as the preferred method for the supervisor to acquire information about the trainee's session, followed by direct observation of therapy.

One study examined the impact of trainee personality variables on the supervisory process. Ronnestad (1976) studied the effect of supportive and nonsupportive analogues of supervision on 17 introverted and extroverted student counselors' ratings of their own counseling performance in a beginning "methods" class. The author found that all counselors rated their performance more favorably after supportive supervision and less favorably after nonsupportive supervision. He also found that after undergoing a nonsupportive counseling session, introverts changed their rating into a more negative rating than did extroverts. Ronnestad (1982, 1983) argues for a "developmental" view of supervision, in which the supervisor's mode of teaching is dictated by the trainee's developmental needs. He notes that at the earliest stage of learning, didactic presentation and information-giving assume primacy, whereas, later, clarification, integration, and feedback are appropriate. Inasmuch as most studies of training have been conducted on relative neophytes, the didactic stage has been emphasized in the literature.

The majority of published studies on supervision have framed the process in a unidirectional paradigm. A paper by Steinhelber, Patterson, Cliffe, and Le Goullon (1984) implies a reciprocal process between supervisor and supervisee. They studied amount of supervision, patient change (unfortunately rated by therapist only) as measured by ratings on the Global Assessment Scale (GAS), and *congruence* of theoretical orientation between therapist and supervisor. Supervisor hours were more likely to be devoted to patients with specific diagnoses such as neurosis, personality disorder, and transient situational reaction. Significantly less time was given to supervision involving patients with psychotic disorders and borderline personalities.

The 51 therapists checked their own and their supervisors' orientations (from 17 alternatives), rated their 237 patients on the GAS, and indicated the amount or frequency of supervision with their patients. Overall, when the supervisor–supervisee pair was congruent in orientation, patients were likely to show more improvement on the GAS and the supervisees were more likely to receive high levels of supervision. When amount of supervision was statistically controlled, patient improvement in the low supervision, congruent group remained greater than improvement in the comparable noncongruent group. The mean length of therapy was eight months. *Amount* of supervision regarding a specific patient was not related significantly to GAS change. The authors suggest that perhaps *total* amount of trainee supervisory contact (greater with congruent supervisors) was a significant factor and that *quality* of supervisory relationship is most important. If quality and congruence are interrelated, it is clear that quality and quantity of supervision also are related. Mix of supervisor and supervisee, then, appears to be related to patient benefit, although replication of this result is needed.

Holloway and her colleagues (Holloway, 1982; Holloway & Wampold, 1983; Holloway & Wolleat, 1981; also see Dodenhoff, 1981) have studied supervision from the perspective of the *reciprocal* influence that occurs between supervisor and trainee. In support of this methodological approach, Holloway (1982) cites Leddick and Bernard's (1980) conclusion that conceptualizations of supervision have relied heavily on models of the counseling relationship and that the supervision process has been characterized in global rather than in molecular terms. She reports that the influence of the trainee on the supervisor's behavior has been largely neglected.

In devising a methodology to study the interactional nature of the supervision process, Holloway and Wolleat (1981) adapted Blumberg's System for Analyzing Supervisor-Teacher Interaction (Blumberg, 1970). A series of categories was developed to code both supervisory (e.g., praises, asks for information) and trainee (e.g., gives information) behavior. In their first study using this method, Holloway and Wolleat (1981) concluded that beginning supervisors have response characteristics that remain stable across interviews with different trainees. They believe that the recognition of such predilections or "styles" of behavior are an important first step in developing individualized programs for training supervisors. In a second study using this methodology, Holloway (1982) examined the sequential patterns of verbal behavior that occurred between supervisors (advanced doctoral students) and trainees in a supervisory interview. She found evidence for relatively typical patterns of verbal behavior between supervisors and trainees. For example, when supervisors used supportive communication (reflection of feelings, direct praise, and development of trainees' ideas), the trainees tended to respond with positive social behavior. She also found that when supervisors directly questioned opinions and suggestions from the trainees, they were usually faced with a delayed reaction time from the trainees.

In their most recently published use of this paradigm, Holloway and Wampold (1983) investigated the relationship between such repetitive patterns of supervisor–trainee behavior and trainee satisfaction in supervision. Three conclusions emerged from this study: (1) Negative social behavior (e.g., defensiveness or criticism) shown by either supervisor or trainee enhances the discomfort experienced in the interview and lowers the supervisor's evaluation of the trainee. (2) If the supervisor responds to a trainee's expression of ideas with a request for more ideas, both will evaluate themselves more positively. (3) There is no clear benefit from the supervisor's use of supportive communication when the trainee is already showing positive social/emotional behavior.

Holloway and Wampold (1983) acknowledged several methodological limitations to their study and pointed out that their findings should be considered exploratory. Nevertheless, they found that some of the most frequent supervisor behaviors (supportive communication, or defensive/critical behavior to similar behavior shown by the supervisee) were devalued by the trainee, the supervisor, or both, while reacting to a trainee request by asking for information resulted in positive feelings and behaviors. Thus, some probably typical supervisor behav-

iors are devalued by both trainee and supervisor, while others have positive sequelae.

CONCLUSIONS

It seems clear that we now have some effective teaching programs for the development of basic interviewing skills, although research results are not consistent in indicating which exact sequences of training are best for trainees at a given level of experience. Several authors have reported that there are significant trainee differences in the ease with which they can be trained, and that pre- and postassessment of skills is essential before considering a training sequence to have been completed. It seems clear that one needs to start with well-defined behavioral variables that are didactically presented (written and oral) to the trainee. Programmed texts appear to be effective. Subsequent to this kind of specific cueing, either live or videotaped modeling in actual interviews is desirable and may be most effective if it includes both positive and negative models to enhance cognitive differentiation. Role-played practice interviews ideally should be videotaped and followed by both self-confrontation and feedback from an empathic, warm, skilled, and behaviorally specific supervisor. Self-monitoring alone is not necessarily effective in modifying some kinds of idiosyncratic behaviors (e.g., interviewer percent talk-time and interruptions). Especially if videotape is not available, feedback should be as immediate as possible. Giving specific information and having a supportive attitude are especially important supervisor behaviors. It appears important for supervisor and supervisee to have a similar theoretical orientation. Continued practice and reinforcement are necessary in order to maintain skills. One can assume that increased practice is necessary also to generalize, refine, and learn to use the skills flexibly under varying circumstances. Manuals and videotapes are available for the more advanced therapist to learn specific modes of intervention. The answers are not yet in regarding the relationship of training to client benefit.

Some recurrent problems in the literature involve the use of varied trainee populations that are not similar to the graduate student populations in clinical or counseling psychology programs; moreover, the trainees generally appear to have less psychological sophistication than graduate student populations. Thus it is uncertain that the research results will generalize to the population in which we are most interested. Sometimes training conditions have been greatly different from live clinical interviews, and student skill has been measured by instruments or situations unlike actual interviews. For example, modeling tapes may be truncated or consist of brief, disconnected interchanges that afford little opportunity for the trainee to observe helpee response or counselor success. The trainee needs to hear what the therapist can elicit through skillful interviewing behavior, and how he or she would make use of the material that followed. The measurement of achieved skill soley through written or simulated interview responses has limited the significance of a number of studies. Written or simulated responses appear to measure cognitive awareness but do not predict level of actual behavioral or interviewing skill. For training, the use of didactic material alone, modeling alone, or other isolated techniques are clearly not effective. Trainees apparently respond enthusiastically to some kinds of co-counseling experience, but like a number of related procedures, it suffers from lack of definition and demonstrated effectiveness. When one investigator finds it to be effective and another ineffective, it is very likely because they are referring to different training procedures.

Supervision is the training procedure most likely to be used with advanced clinical students; yet we are only beginning to label the aspects that may be effective or responded to most favorably by students (warmth, specificity, similarity of orientation, interest, etc.). The overwhelming majority of counselors who supervise report that they were never trained in how to do it and are unlikely to be specifically training their own students to become supervisors. (Hopefully, however, they are being good therapist models!) Supervision appears to be done in a fairly traditional way for the most part, (e.g., via seminar or individual case conference), although the majority of supervisors occasionally use videotape, in vivo observation, or a bug-in-the-ear for one-way, in vivo communication from supervisor to supervisee (Gordon, 1975). For the most part, trainee knowledge and skill are not objectively assessed after completing the program except as the trainees take licensure and specialty board examinations. Indeed, the problem of measuring skill even by such credentialing bodies is a major hurdle still to be overcome. While many inventories and behavior rating methods have been used, none has been studied adequately, and some are clearly not sufficiently valid and reliable to be useful.

The isolated skills taught by many of the basic skills-training packaged programs need to be integrated and refined as the trainee moves into a professional counseling role. We know relatively little about how this should be accomplished. Ivey and Authier (1978), however, present an interesting rationale. They describe the need first to learn the basic skills of attending and listening. Subsequently, the trainee moves into the "influencing" skills and, as he or she becomes comfortable with using the separate skills, they presumably begin to be used with confidence and more flexibility. Ivey has differentiated between "basic attending" skills, "influencing" skills, "confrontation," "skill sequencing and structuring," and "skill integration." He also differentiates the use of these skill levels according to "developmental level" of the client. Ivey and Authier (1978) state, "Microtraining procedures are not concerned with producing effective counselors in one session. The primary concern is helping trainees to grow with time" (p. 302). Part of this professional growth process is through the supervisor, who is advised to maintain close personal involvement with the trainee. Without this, the "role skills" are unlikely to be used flexibly and meaningfully. Ivey and Authier also add, "Maintenance and generalization of microcounseling skills should be programmed rather than expected or lamented" (p. 306). This is a maxim with which it is easy to agree.

Programmed manuals open new possibilities for the study of advanced therapist skill acquisition and patient benefit from prescribed programs that can be compared with other prescribed programs in the treatment of specified syndromes. Ongoing extensive research programs should provide a look at new aspects of training in psychotherapeutic skill.

REFERENCES

Authier, J., & Gustafson, K. (1975). Application of supervised and nonsupervised microcounseling paradigms in the training of paraprofessionals. *Journal of Counseling Psychology, 22*, 74–78.

Bailey, K. G., Deardorff, P., & Nay, W. R. (1977). Students play therapist: Relative effects of role playing, videotape feedback, and modeling in a simulated interview. *Journal of Counsulting and Clinical Psychology, 45,* 257–266.

Baker, S. B., Scofield, M. E., Clayton, L. T., & Munson, W. W. (1984). Microskills practice versus mental practice training for competence in decision-making counseling. *Journal of Counseling Psychology, 31,* 104–107.

Baker, S. B., Scofield, M. E., Munson, W. W., & Clayton, L. T. (1983). Comparative effects of teaching basic counseling competencies through brief microskills practice versus mental practice. *Counselor Education and Supervision, 23,* 71–82.

Barrett-Lennard, G. T. (1962). Dimensions of therapist response as causal factors in therapeutic change. *Psychological Monographs: General and Applied, 76,* No. 43 (Whole No. 562).

Becker, W. L. (1971). *Parents are teachers.* Champaign, IL: Research Press.

Beck, A. T., Rush, A. J., Shaw, B. F., & Emery, G. D. (1979). *Cognitive therapy of depression: A treatment manual.* New York: Guilford.

Bergin, A. E. (1963). The effects of psychotherapy: Negative results revisited. *Journal of Counseling Psychology, 10,* 244–250.

Bergin, A. E., & Jasper, L. G. (1969). Correlates of empathy in psychotherapy: A replication. *Journal of Abnormal Psychology, 74,* 477–481.

Blumberg, A. (1970). A system for analyzing supervisor-teacher interaction. In A. Simon & G. Boyer, (Eds.), *Mirrors for behavior* (Vol. 3). Philadelphia: Research for Better Schools.

Bond, J. A. (1974). Behavior therapy, learning theory, and scientific method. *Psychotherapy: Theory, Research and Practice, 11,* 118–132.

Bouchard, M., Wright, J., Mathieu, M., Lalonde, F., Bergeron, G., & Toupin, J. (1980). Structured learning in teaching therapists social skills training. Acquisition, maintenance, and impact on client outcome. *Journal of Consulting and Clinical Psychology, 48,* 491–502.

Burstein, J., & Carkhuff, R. R. (1968). Objective therapist and client ratings of therapist offered facilitative conditions of moderate to low functioning therapists. *Journal of Clinical Psychology, 24,* 240–249.

Caracena, P., & Vicory, J. (1969). Correlates of phenomenological and judged empathy. *Journal of Consulting Psychology, 16,* 510–515.

Carkhuff, R. R. (1967). Toward a comprehensive model of facilitative inter-personal processes. *Journal of Counseling Psychology, 14,* 67–72.

Carkhuff, R. (1969). *Helping and human relations: A primer for lay and professional helpers* (Vols. 1 & 2). New York: Holt, Rinehart, & Winston.

Carkhuff, R. R. (1972). *The art of helping.* Amherst MA: Human Resource Development Press.

Chinsky, J. M. & Rappaport, J. (1970). Brief critique of the meaning and reliability of "accurate empathy" ratings. *Psychological Bulletin, 73,* 379–382.

Cotler, S. B., Applegate, G., King, L. W., & Kristal, S. (1972). Establishing a token economy program in a state hospital classroom: A lesson in training student and teacher behavior. *Behavior Therapy, 3,* 209–222.

Covner, B. J. (1944). Studies in phonographic recordings of verbal material: III. The completeness and accuracy of counseling interview reports. *Journal of General Psychology, 30,* 181–203.

DeReubis, R. J., Hollon, S. D., Evans, M. D., & Bemis, K. M. (1982). Can psychotherapies for depression be discriminated? A systematic investigation of cognitive therapy and interpersonal therapy. *Journal of Consulting & Clinical Psychology, 50,* 744–756.

Dodenhoff, J. T. (1981). Interpersonal attraction and direct-indirect supervisor influence as predictors of counselor trainee effectiveness. *Journal of Counseling Psychology, 28,* 47–52.

Doyle, W. E., Foreman, M. E., & Wales, E. (1977). Efforts of supervision in the training of nonprofessional crisis-intervention counselors. *Journal of Counseling Psychology, 24,* 72–78.

Eisenberg, S. & Delaney, D. J. (1970). Using video simulation of counseling for training counselors. *Journal of Counseling Psychology, 17,* 15–19.

Eskedal, G. A. (1975). Symbolic role modeling and cognitive learning in the training of counselors. *Journal of Counseling Psychology, 22,* 152–155.

Eyberg, S. M., & Johnson, S. M. (1974). Multiple assessment of behavior modification with families: Effects of contingency contracting and order of treatment problems. *Journal of Consulting and Clinical Psychology, 42,* 594–606.

Eyberg, S. M., & Matarazzo, R. G. (1980). Comparison of individual and group instruction in mother–child interaction training. *Journal of Clinical Psychology, 36,* 492–499.

Feifel, H. & Eells, J. (1963). Patients and therapist assess the same psychotherapy. *Journal of Consulting Psychology, 27,* 310–318.

Ferber, H., Keeley, S. M., & Shemberg, K. M. (1974). Training parents in behavior modification: Outcome of and problems encountered in a program after Patterson's work. *Behavior Therapy, 5,* 415–419.

Flanagan, S., Adams, H. E., & Forehand, R. (1979). A comparison of four instructional techniques for teaching parents to use time-out. *Behavior Therapy, 10,* 94–102.

Ford, J. D. (1979). Research in training counselors and clinicians. *Review of Educational Research, 49,* 87–130.

Forehand, R., Sturgis, E. T., McMahon, R. J., Aguar, D., Green, K., Wells, K. C., & Breiner, J. (1979). Parent behavioral training to modify child noncompliance: Treatment generalization across time and from home to school. *Behavior Modification, 3,* 3–25.

Fuqua, D. R., & Gade, E. M. (1982). A critical reexamination of the practice component in counselor training. *Counselor Education and Supervision, 21,* 284–294.

Gardner, G. G. (1964). The psychotherapeutic relationship. *Psychological Bulletin, 61,* 426–437.

Gardner, J. M. (1972). Teaching behavior modification to nonprofessionals. *Journal of Applied Behavior Analysis, 10,* 75–84.

Gallessich, J., Gilbert, L. A. & Holahan, C. K. (1980). A training model to facilitate professional effectiveness in power-and-sex-salient situations. *Professional Psychology, 1,* 15–23.

Garfield, S. L. (1977). Research on the training of professional psychotherapists. In A. S. Gurman & A. Razin

(Eds.), *The therapist's contribution to effective psychotherapy: Empirical assessment.* New York: Pergamon.

Glogower, F., & Sloop, E. W. (1976). Two strategies of group training of parents as effective behavior modifiers. *Behavior Therapy, 7,* 177–184.

Goin, M. K., & Kline, F. M. (1974). Supervision observed. *The Journal of Nervous and Mental Disease, 58,* 208–213.

Goin, M. K., Burgoyne, R. W., Kline, F., Woods, S. M., & Peck, J. S. (1976). Teaching dynamic psychotherapy by observation. *American Journal of Psychotherapy, 30,* 112–120.

Goldstein, A. P. (1973). *Structured learning therapy: Toward a psychotherapy for the poor.* New York: Academic Press.

Gordon, D. A. (1975). A mobile, wireless "bug-in-the-ear" communication system for training and therapy. *Behavior Therapy, 6,* 130–132.

Gross, A. M., & Ekstrand, M. (1983). Increasing and maintaining rates of teacher praise: A study using public posting and feedback training. *Behavior Modification, 7,* 126–135.

Gutride, M., Goldstein, A., & Hunter, G. (1972). *The use of modeling and role playing to increase social interaction among schizophrenic patients.* Unpublished manuscript, Syracuse University.

Haase, R., & DiMattia, D. (1970). The application of the microcounseling paradigm to the training of support personnel in counseling. *Counseling Education and Supervision, 10,* 16–22.

Hansen, J., Moore, G., & Carkhuff, R. (1968). The differential relationship of objective and client perceptions of counseling. *Journal of Clinical Psychology, 24,* 244–246.

Hansen, J. C., Pound, R., & Petro, C. (1976). Review of research on practicum supervision. *Counselor Education and Supervision, 16,* 107–116.

Harvey, O. J., Hunt, D. F., & Schroeder, H. M. (1961). *Conceptual systems and personality organization.* New York: Wiley.

Helfer, R. E., Black, M. A., & Teitelbaum, H. (1975). A comparison of pediatric interviewing skills using real and simulated mothers. *Pediatrics, 55,* 397.

Hess, A. K., & Hess, K. A. (1983). Psychotherapy supervision: A survey of internship training practices. *Professional Psychology: Research and Practice, 14,* 504–513.

Holloway, E. L. (1982). Interactional structure of the supervision interview. *Journal of Counseling Psychology, 29,* 309–317.

Holloway, E. L., & Wampold, B. E. (1983). Patterns of verbal behavior and judgments of satisfaction in the supervision interview. *Journal of Counseling Psychology, 30,* 227–234.

Holloway, E. L., & Wolleat, P. L. (1981). Style differences of beginning supervisors: An interactional analysis. *Journal of Counseling Psychology, 28,* 373–376.

Hunt, D. E., & Sullivan, E. V. (1974). *Between psychology and education.* Hinsdale, IL: Dryden.

Ivey, A. E. (1983). *Intentional interviewing and counseling.* Monterey, CA: Brooks/Cole.

Ivey, A. E., & Authier, J. (1978). *Microcounseling. Innovations in interviewing, counseling, psychotherapy and psychoeducation.* (2nd ed.). Springfield, IL: Charles C. Thomas.

Ivey, A. E., Normington, C. J., Miller, D. C., Morrill, W. H., & Haase, R. F. (1968). Microcounseling and attending behavior: An approach to prepracticum counselor training. *Journal of Counseling Psychology,* Monograph Supplement, 15, No. 5.

Jacobson, J., Bushnell, D., & Risley, T. (1969). Switching requirements in a headstart classroom. *Journal of Applied Behavior Analysis, 2,* 43–47.

Johnson, C. A., Katz, R. C., & Gelfand, S. (1972). Undergraduates as behavioral technicians on an adult token economy ward. *Behavior Therapy, 3,* 589–592.

Katz, R. C., Johnson, C. A., & Gelfand, S. (1972). Modifying the dispensing of reinforcers: Some implications for behavior modification with hospitalized patients. *Behavior Therapy, 3,* 579–583.

Kazdin, A. E., & Moyer, W. (1976). Training teachers to use behavior modification. In S. Yen & R. McIntire (Eds.), *Teaching behavior modification.* Kalamazoo, MI: Behaviordelia.

Kelley, M. D. (1971). Reinforcement in microcounseling. *Journal of Counseling Psychology, 13,* 268–272.

Kepecs, J. G. (1977). Teaching psychotherapy by use of brief transcripts. *American Journal of Psychotherapy, 31,* 383–393.

Kepecs, J. G. (1979). Tracking errors in psychotherapy. *American Journal of Psychotherapy, 33,* 365–377.

Klerman, G., & Neu, C. (1976). *A manual for interpersonal treatment of depression.* Unpublished manuscript, Yale University.

Klerman, G., Rounsaville, B., Chevron, E., Neu, C., & Weissman, M. (1979). *Manual for short-term interpersonal psychotherapy (IPT) for depression.* Unpublished manuscript, Yale University.

Klerman, G. L., Weissman, M. M., Rounsaville, B. J., & Chevron, E. (In press). *The theory and practice of interpersonal psychotherapy for depression.* New York: Basic Books.

Kozloff, M. A. (1973). *Reaching the autistic child: A parent training program.* Champaign, IL: Research Press.

Kuna, D. J. (1975). Lecturing, reading and modeling in counselor restatement training. *Journal of Counseling Psychology, 22,* 542–546.

Lambert, M. J. (1980). Research and the supervisory process. In A. K. Hess (Ed.), *Psychotherapy supervision: Theory, research and practice.* New York: Wiley.

Leddick, G. R., & Bernard, J. M. (1980). The history of supervision: A critical review. *Counselor Education and Supervision,* March, 186–196.

Leitenberg, H., Burchard, J. D., Burchard, S. N., Fuller, E. J., & Lysaght, T. V. (1977). Using positive reinforcement to suppress behavior: Some experimental comparisons with sibling conflict. *Behavior Therapy, 8,* 168–182.

Loeber, R., & Weisman, R. G. (1975). Contingencies of therapist and trainer performance: A review. *Psychological Bulletin, 82,* 660–688.

Lorr, M. (1965). Client perception of therapists: A study of the therapeutic relation. *Journal of Counsulting Psychology, 29,* 146–149.

Luborsky, L. (1984). *Principles of psychoanalytic psychotherapy—A manual for supportive-expressive treatment (SE).* New York: Basic Books.

Luborsky, L., & DeRubeis, R. J. (1984). The use of psychotherapy treatment manuals: A small revolution in psychotherapy research style. *Clinical Psychology Review, 4,* 5–14.

Luborsky, L., Woody, G., McLellan, A. T., O'Brien, C. P., & Rosenzweig, J. (1982). Can independent judges recognize different psychotherapies? An experience with manual-guided therapies. *Journal of Consulting and Clinical Psychology, 5,* 49–62.

Matarazzo, J. D. & Wiens, A. N. (1977). Speech behavior as an objective correlate of empathy and outcome in interview and psychotherapy research. *Behavior Modification, 1,* 453–480.

Matarazzo, R. G. (1971). Research in the teaching and learning of psychotherapeutic skills. In A. Bergin & S. Garfield (Eds.), *A handbook of psychotherapy and behavior change* (pp. 859–924). New York: Wiley.

Matarazzo, R. G. (1978). Research in the teaching and learning of psychotherapeutic skills. In S. Garfield & A. Bergin (Eds.), *A handbook of psychotherapy and behavior change* (2nd ed., pp. 941–966). New York: Wiley.

Matarazzo, R. G., Phillips, J. S., Wiens, A. N., & Saslow, G. (1965). Learning the art of interviewing: A study of what beginning students do and their pattern of change. *Psychotherapy: Theory, Research and Practice, 2,* 49–60.

Matarazzo, R. G., Wiens, A. N., & Saslow, G. (1966). Experimentation in the teaching and learning of psychotherapy skills. In L. A. Gottschalk & A. Auerbach (Eds.), *Methods of research in psychotherapy* (pp. 597–635). New York: Appleton-Century-Crofts.

McColley, S. H., & Baker, E. L. (1982). Training activities and styles of beginning supervisors: A survey. *Professional Psychology, 13,* 283–292.

McWhirter, J. J. (1973). Two measures of the facilitative conditions: A correlational study. *Journal of Counseling Psychology, 20,* 317–320.

Miars, R. D., Tracey, T. J., Ray, P. B., Cornfeld, J. L., O'Farrell, M. O., & Gelso, C. J. (1983). Variation in supervision process across trainee experience levels. *Journal of Counseling Psychology, 30,* 403–412.

Mintz, J., & Luborsky, L. (1971). Segments versus whole sessions: Which is the better unit for psychotherapy process research? *Journal of Abnormal Psychology, 78,* 180–191.

Moreland, J. R., Ivey, A. E., & Phillips, J. S. (1973). An evaluation of microcounseling as an interviewer training tool. *Journal of Consulting and Clinical Psychology, 41,* 294–300.

Muslin, H. L., Thurnblad, R. J., & Meschel, G. (1981). The fate of the clinical interview: An observational study. *American Journal of Psychiatry, 138*(6), 825–833.

Nay, W. R. (1975). A systematic comparison of instructional techniques for parents. *Behavior Therapy, 6,* 14–21.

Nay, W. R. (1979). Parents as real life reinforcers: The enhancement of parent training effects across conditions other than training. In A. P. Goldstein & F. H. Kanfer (Eds.), *Maximizing treatment gains: Transfer enhancement in psychotherapy.* New York: Academic Press.

Nelson, G. L. (1978). Psychotherapy supervision from the trainee's point of view: A survey of preferences. *Professional Psychology, 9,* 539–550.

Neu, C., Prusoff, B., & Klerman, G. (1978). Measuring the interventions used in the short-term interpersonal psychotherapy of depression. *American Journal of Orthopsychiatry, 48,* 629–636.

O'Dell, S., Flynn, J., & Benlolo, L. A. (1977). A comparison of parent training techniques in child behavior modification. *Journal of Behavior Therapy and Environmental Psychiatry, 8,* 261–268.

O'Dell, S., Krug, W., Patterson, J., & Faustman, W. (1980). An assessment of methods for training parents in the use of time-out. *Journal of Behavior Therapy and Experimental Psychiatry, 11,* 21–25.

O'Toole, W. M. (1979). Effects of practice and some methodological considerations in training counseling interviewing skills. *Journal of Counseling Psychology, 26,* 419–426.

Pagell, W. A., Carkhuff, R. R., & Berenson, B. G. (1967). The predicted differential effects of the level of counselor functioning upon the level of functioning of outpatients. *Journal of Clinical Psychology, 23,* 510–512.

Patterson, G. R. (1975). *Families.* Champaign, IL: Research Press.

Patterson, G. R., Cobb, J. A., & Ray, R. S. (1973). A social engineering technology for retraining the families of aggressive boys. In H. E. Adams & I. P. Unikel (Eds.), *Issues and trends in behavior therapy* (pp. 193–210). Springfield, IL: Charles C. Thomas.

Pape, D. A. & Bervan, N. (1983). Effects of training on interviewing skills in rehabilitation counseling. *Rehabilitation Counseling Bulletin, 26,* 164–173.

Payne, P., Winter, D., & Perry, M. A. (1975). Modeling and instructions in training for counselor empathy. *Journal of Counseling Psychology, 22,* 173–179.

Perry, M. A. (1975). Modeling and instructions in training for counselor empathy. *Journal of Counseling Psychology, 22,* 173–179.

Peters, G. A., Cormier, L. S., & Cormier, W. H. (1978). Effects of modeling, rehearsal, feedback and remediation on acquisition of a counseling strategy. *Journal of Counseling Psychology, 25,* 231–237.

Phillips, S. D. (1983). Counselor training via computer. *Counselor Education and Supervision, 23,* 20–23.

Pierce, R., Carkhuff, R. R., & Berenson, B. G. (1967). The differential effects of high and low functioning counselors upon counselors-in-training. *Journal of Clinical Psychology, 23,* 212–215.

Rappaport, J., & Chinsky, J. M. (1972). Accurate empathy: Confusion of a construct. *Psychological Bulletin, 77,* 400–404.

Ray, R. S. (1965). *The training of mothers of a typical child in the use of behavior modification techniques.* Unpublished master's thesis, University of Oregon.

Reisinger, J. J., Ora, J. P., & Frangia, G. W. (1976). Parents as change agents for their children: A review. *Journal of Community Psychology, 4,* 103–123.

Rice, L. N. (1965). Therapists' style of participation and case outcome. *Journal of Consulting Psychology, 29,* 155–160.

Rinn, R., Vernon, J., & Wise, M. (1975). Training parents of behaviorally disordered children in groups. A three-year program evaluation. *Behavior Therapy, 6,* 378–387.

Ringuette, E. L. (1983). A note on experiential learning in professional training. *Journal of Clinical Psychology, 39,* 302–304.

Rogers, C. R. (1957). The necessary and sufficient conditions of therapeutic personality change. *Journal of Consulting Psychology, 21,* 95–103.

Ronnestad, H. (1976). Counselor personality and supervisory styles. *Scandinavian Journal of Psychology,*

17, 56–60.

Ronnestad, M. H. (1982). On the objectives of supervision. *Journal of the Norwegian Psychological Association, 19*, 542–546.

Ronnestad, M. H. (1983). Supervision of psychotherapy: A discussion. *Journal of the Norwegian Psychological Association, 20*, 19–23.

Rosenthal, N. R. (1977). A prescriptive approach for counselor training. *Journal of Counseling Psychology, 24*, 231–237.

Saltmarsh, R. E. (1973). Development of empathic interview skills through programmed instruction. *Journal of Counseling Psychology, 20*, 375–377.

Salvendy, J. T. (1977). Education in psychotherapy: Challenges and pitfalls. *Canadian Psychiatric Association Journal, 22*, 435–440.

Salzinger, K., Feldman, R. S., & Portnoy, S. (1970). Training parents of brain injured children in the use of operant conditioning procedures. *Behavior Therapy, 1*, 4–32.

Sanders, M. R., & James, J. E. (1983). The modification of parent behavior: A review of generalization and maintenance. *Behavior Modification, 7*, 3–27.

Sepler, J. J., & Myers, S. L. (1978). The effectiveness of verbal instruction on teaching behavior modification skills to nonprofessionals. *Journal of Applied Behavior Analysis, 11*, 198.

Seys, D. M., & Duker, P. C. (1978). Improving residential care for the retarded by differential reinforcement of high rates of ward-staff behavior. *Behavior Analysis and Modification, 2*, 203–210.

Scott, A. J., Cormier, W. L. & Cormier, S. L. (1980). Effects of covert modeling and written material on the acquisition of a counseling strategy. *Counselor Education and Supervision, 19*, 259–269.

Sloat, J., Tharp, R., & Gallimore, R. (1977). The incremental effectiveness of classroom based teacher training techniques. *Behavior Therapy, 8*, 810–818.

Steinhelber, J., Patterson, V., Cliffe, K., & Le Goullon, M. (1984). An investigation of some relationships between psychotherapy supervision and patient change. *Journal of Clinical Psychology, 40*, 1346–1353.

Stillman, P. L. (1978). Arizona clinical interview rating scale. In P. L. Stillman, J. S. Ruggill, & J. E. Laguna (Eds.), *The non-physician in medical education* (pp. 35–38). Tucson, AR: University of Arizona Press.

Stillman, P. L., & Ruggill, J. S. (1978). The use of patient instructors (P.I.'s) to teach and evaluate medical interviewing. In P. L. Stillman, J. S. Ruggill, & J. E. Laguna (Eds.), *The non-physician in medical education* (pp. 13–15). Tucson, AR: University of Arizona Press.

Stillman, P. L., Sabers, D. L., & Redfield, D. L. (1976). The use of paraprofessionals to teach interviewing skills. *Pediatrics, 57*, 769–774.

Stillman, P. L., Sabers, D. L., & Redfield, D. L. (1977). Use of trained mothers to teach interview skills to first-year medical students: A follow-up study. *Pediatrics, 60*, 165–169.

Stone, G. L. (1975). Effect of simulation on counselor training. *Counselor Education and Supervision, 14*, 199–203.

Stone, G. L., & Vance, A. (1976). Instructions, modeling and rehearsal: Implications for training. *Journal of Counseling Psychology, 23*, 272–279.

Strupp, H. H., & Binder, J. L. (1983). *Time-limited dynamic psychotherapy: A treatment manual.* Unpublished manuscript. (Available from H. H Strupp, Ph.D., Dept. of Psychology, Vanderbilt University, 134 Wesley Hall, Nashville, TN 37240.)

Strupp, H. H., Wallach, M. S., & Wogan, M. (1964). Psychotherapy experience in retrospect: Questionnaire survey for former patients and their therapists. *Psychological Monographs: General and Applied, 78*, No. 11 (Whole No. 588).

Sulzer-Azaroff, B., & Reese, E. (1982). *Applying behavioral analysis: A program for developing professional competence.* New York: Holt, Rinehart, & Winston.

Toukmanian, S. G., & Rennie, D. L. (1975). Microcounseling versus human relations training: Relative effectiveness with undergraduate trainees. *Journal of Counseling Psychology, 22*, 345–352.

Truax, C. B., & Carkhuff, R. (1967). *Toward effective counseling and psychotherapy: Training and practice.* Chicago: Aldine.

Truax, C. B., Carkhuff, R. R., & Douds, J. (1964). Toward an integration of the didactic and experiential approaches to training in counseling and psychotherapy. *Journal of Counseling Psychology, 11*, 240–247.

Truax, C. B., Wargo, D. G., Frank J. D., Imber, S. D. Battle, C. C., Hoehn-Saric, R., Nash, E. H., & Stone, A. R. (1966). Therapist empathy, genuineness, and warmth and patient therapeutic outcome. *Journal of Consulting Psychology, 30*, 395–401.

Uhleman, M. R., Lea, G. W., & Stone, G. L. (1976). Effects of instructions and modeling on trainees low in interpersonal-communication skills. *Journal of Counseling Psychology, 23*, 509–513.

Vasile, R. G., & Shapiro, L. W. (1982). Open supervision: Modeling psychotherapy supervision as a teaching method for first year psychiatric residents. *Psychiatric Quarterly, 54*, 254–259.

Wahler, R. G. (1980). The insular mother: Her problems in parent–child treatment. *Journal of Applied Behavior Analysis, 13*, 207–220.

Wallace, W. G., Horan, J. J., Baker, S. B., & Hudson, G. R. (1975). Incremental effects of modeling and performance feedback in teaching decision making counseling. *Journal of Counseling Psychology, 22*, 570–572.

Walter, H. I., & Gilmore, J. K. (1973). Placebo versus social learning effects in parent training procedures designed to alter the behavior of aggressive boys. *Behavior Therapy, 4*, 361–377.

Waskow, I. E., Parloff, M. B., Hadley, J. W., & Autry, J. H. (1985). The NIMH Treatment of Depression Collaborative Research Program: Background and research plan. *Archives of General Psychiatry, 42*, 305–310.

Waterhouse, G. J. (1979). *Perceptions of facilitative therapeutic conditions as predictors of outcome in brief therapy.* Paper presented at the European Conference of the Society for Psychotherapy Research, Oxford, England.

Wenegrat, A. (1974). A factor analytic study of the Truax accurate empathy scale. *Psychotherapy: Theory, Research and Practice, 11*, 48–51.

Wright, J. C., Horlick, S., Bouchard, C., Mathieu, M., & Zeichner, A. (1977). The development of instruments to assess behavior therapy training. *Journal of Behavior Therapy and Experimental Psychiatry, 8*, 281–286.

NAME INDEX

SUBJECT INDEX

712178 6/5